W9-AQM-732

American History through Literature
1870–1920

American History through Literature
1870–1920

VOLUME 2 HARPER & BROTHERS
to
POVERTY

TOM QUIRK & GARY SCHARNHORST
Editors in Chief

CHARLES SCRIBNER'S SONS
An imprint of Thomson Gale, a part of The Thomson Corporation

THOMSON
GALE

Detroit • New York • San Francisco • San Diego • New Haven, Conn. • Waterville, Maine • London • Munich

American History through Literature, 1870–1920

Tom Quirk and Gary Scharnhorst, Editors in Chief

LIBRARY OF CONGRESS CATALOGING-IN-PUBLICATION DATA

American History through Literature, 1870–1920 / Tom Quirk and Gary Scharnhorst, editors-in-chief.
  p. cm.
  Includes bibliographical references and index.
  ISBN 0-684-31464-9 (set hardcover : alk. paper) — ISBN 0-684-31465-7 (v. 1 : alk. paper) — ISBN 0-684-31466-5 (v. 2 : alk. paper) — ISBN 0-684-31467-3 (v. 3 : alk. paper) — ISBN 0-684-31493-2 (e-book)
  1. American literature—19th century—Encyclopedias. 2. Literature and history—United States—History—19th century—Encyclopedias. 3. Literature and history—United States—History—20th century—Encyclopedias. 4. United States—History—19th century—Historiography—Encyclopedias. 5. United States—History—20th century—Historiography—Encyclopedias. 6. American literature—20th century—Encyclopedias. 7. History in literature—Encyclopedias. I. Quirk, Tom, 1946– II. Scharnhorst, Gary.

PS217.H57A843 2005
810.9'358'09034—dc22   2005023736

This title is also available as an e-book
ISBN 0-684-31493-2
And may be purchased with its companion set, *American History through Literature, 1820–1870*
ISBN 0-684-31468-1 (6-vol. print set)
Contact your Thomson Gale sales representative for ordering information

Printed in the United States of America
10 9 8 7 6 5 4 3 2 1

Editorial and Production Staff

Senior Editor: Stephen Wasserstein

Project Editor: Alja Kooistra Collar

Assisting Editors: Joann Cerrito, Jennifer Wisinski

Editorial Assistant: Angela Doolin

Manuscript Editors: Susan Carol Barnett, Lisa Dixon, Gretchen Gordon, Jeffrey J. Hill, Teresa Jesionowski, Robert E. Jones, Jean Fortune Kaplan, Eric Lagergren, Maggie Paley, Janet Patterson, Linda Sanders, Jane Marie Todd, Julie Van Pelt

Proofreader: Carol Holmes

Indexer: Katharyn Dunham

Senior Art Director: Pamela Galbreath

Image Acquisitions: Kelly Quin, Jillean McCommons

Imaging: Lezlie Light, Michael Logusz

Cartographer: XNR Productions

Manufacturing Buyer: Wendy Blurton

Assistant Composition Manager: Evi Seoud

Publisher: Frank Menchaca

Contents

CONTENTS

Volume 2

M

N

O

Volume 3

HARPER & BROTHERS

The firm that became Harper & Brothers was established in New York in March 1817, first called J. & J. Harper until the founding brothers James (1795–1869) and John (1797–1875) were joined by their younger brothers Wesley (1801–1870) and Fletcher (1806–1877) and the name was changed on 29 October 1833. The firm led the early industrialization of book publishing and shaped American mass culture with the creation and widespread distribution of *Harper's New Monthly Magazine* and *Harper's Weekly* in the 1850s. The company had its greatest influence in the three decades after the Civil War, when Harper textbooks instructed students, Harper trade books lined family shelves, and Harper periodicals illustrated current affairs and guided national thought. By century's end, however, Harper was considered an old-fashioned "family" publisher, and the evolving literary marketplace compelled its corporate reorganization. Not until nearly 130 years later was the name again changed, this time to Harper & Row, upon the merger of Harper & Brothers with Row, Peterson & Company of Evanston, Illinois, on 30 April 1962. Following other mergers and reorganizations, the firm continues in the early twenty-first century as HarperCollins, one of the largest publishing houses in the world.

HARPER'S BOOK BUSINESS

Harper & Brothers was the leading book publisher in the United States for most of the nineteenth century. By 1859, despite a fire that destroyed its facilities in December 1853, the firm was selling two million volumes annually from its splendid new Franklin Square complex, whose "buildings were the first large commercial buildings to make skeletal use of wrought-iron columns and supporting trusses" (Exman, p. 42). Harper, which had started as a print shop for others' books, soon became one of only three major firms before 1900 that printed and manufactured its own books, and it quickly exploited such technological innovations as stereotyping, electrotyping, and steam presses. Joseph W. Harper Jr., the firm's literary head from 1875 to 1894, believed the company of the 1880s was "inconveniently large" (Tebbel 2:192). It then had about eight hundred employees—mostly in printing and manufacturing—and four thousand books in print. *Bookman's* first list of the ten best-sellers in fiction, issued in 1895, included four Harper titles.

However, in the competitive and unpredictable publishing business no firm, including Harper, ever came close to monopolizing the industry. Of the 111 titles between 1865 and 1914 whose sales equaled 1 percent of the U.S. population in the decade when they were published, Harper had the most of any single firm—nine. And although still one of the largest publishers in 1914, Harper's gross sales were less than 2 percent of the industry total. The power wielded by the House of Harper derived more from cultural influence than from economic dominance.

Before international copyright law was passed in 1891, American publishers operated on a mixture of piracy and principles. The Harpers built their business on legal pirating of popular British works, and British reprints continued to be their major stock-in-trade in

The Harper brothers. From left: Fletcher, James, John, and J. Wesley Harper. Photograph by Mathew Brady, c. 1860. THE LIBRARY OF CONGRESS

the Gilded Age. By then, however, larger publishers had established trade courtesies to limit competition among themselves, and Harper generally paid English authors, often handsomely, in order to foster goodwill, establish quasi-contractual relationships, or secure early access to manuscripts. Against cheap competitors, however, Harper used harsh business tactics, selling books such as the Franklin Square Library at a loss to make piracy of their backlist unprofitable.

Harper & Brothers thus played a prominent but contradictory role in the international copyright debate. The four Harper brothers of the founding generation explicitly opposed international copyright, but in 1875 Joseph W. (known as "Brooklyn Joe" to distinguish him from cousins with the same name) changed the official company stance. He calculated that Harper had already paid about $250,000 to English authors and would be better served if such investment secured legal protection. He cowrote a

draft called the "Harper treaty" that temporarily stimulated international negotiations in 1880, and he participated in copyright discussions throughout the decade. Privately, however, some competitors suggested that Brooklyn Joe wasn't as fully committed to international copyright as he publicly declared.

English reprints were not Harper's only book business. College textbooks and reference works were profitable from the beginning, and the growth of public education made elementary schoolbooks lucrative as well. American works were also increasingly popular, despite being priced higher than English reprints. Civil War accounts and centennial themes provided fertile ground for American writers. Biographies, histories, religious treatises, and exotic travel narratives such as Henry M. Stanley's *Through the Dark Continent* (1878) sold well. In all these genres Harper used its advanced printing abilities and stellar art department to produce distinctively illustrated books.

HARPER'S PERIODICALS

Harper's industrial methods changed book publishing, but its periodicals changed the literary marketplace. Harper was first to integrate book and magazine publishing with the creation of *Harper's New Monthly Magazine* in 1850. The magazine's new form and national reach soon produced unprecedented circulations of 140,000 per month. *Harper's Weekly,* launched in 1857, targeted an even larger—but still scrupulously respectable—audience as a self-proclaimed "family newspaper" (Mott 2:470) subtitled *A Journal of Civilization.* Americans found the weekly's Civil War coverage indispensable, and thereafter its powerful combination of politics, current events, copious illustration, serial fiction, travel writing, and national advertising brought a weekly circulation of 160,000. A second weekly, *Harper's Bazar,* was launched in 1867 and within a few weeks had gained a circulation of 100,000. Envisioned as a *Harper's Weekly* aimed at women, with fashion and home economics replacing politics, its subtitle was *A Repository of Fashion, Pleasure, and Instruction.* By 1880 the *Bazar* had a circulation of 150,000.

Fletcher Harper, the youngest of the four founding brothers, guided these periodicals—and particularly *Harper's Weekly*—until shortly before his death on 29 May 1877. The brothers originally envisioned *Harper's Magazine* as a means to utilize manuscripts, employ their technologically increased printing capacity, and advertise their books. But Fletcher soon perceived the magazines as a fundamentally new enterprise with new editorial challenges and commercial opportunities. He insisted on founding the *Bazar* when his brothers objected. After Fletcher died, his nephew Brooklyn Joe (1830–1896) and his grandson J. Henry Harper (1850–1938) guided the periodicals.

Harper & Brothers further subdivided the "family newspaper" in 1879 by adding *Harper's Young People,* another illustrated weekly. The journal's prospectus cautioned that "in this age of the press, half of the influences which mould mind and character must be drawn from what [young people] read in hours of recreation," and it promised "the best and fittest literature which genius and enterprise can furnish" (Harper, p. 457). The magazine had considerable initial success, but by the early 1890s it was losing money and was discontinued in 1899.

The Harper magazines had considerable cultural influence in postbellum America. Thomas Nast (1840–1902) became a celebrity on *Harper's Weekly's* national stage for his political cartoons attacking New York City's corrupt Tammany Hall. Nast also invented and popularized enduring cultural symbols such as the Republican elephant, the Democratic donkey, and—drawing on his German immigrant heritage—the modern Santa Claus. Nast's cartoons and the editor George William Curtis's editorials demonstrated how powerfully new national media could influence the country's politics. *Harper's Weekly's* abundance of timely illustrations and its early use of visually appealing display ads also influenced the shift toward image-based mass culture.

BUSINESS TRANSITIONS

Harper & Brothers became a legal partnership in May 1860, so when the founding generation died in the 1870s, its sons were in position to continue the business successfully. By the 1890s, however, the company had serious financial problems stemming from the economic depression of 1893, the need to liquidate equities of second-generation partners who had died or retired, and the numerous third-generation Harpers drawing large salaries. Forced to borrow money, Harper & Brothers was reorganized in 1896 as a stock company heavily indebted to J. P. Morgan. In 1899 they failed to make their interest payments and went into receivership, and the Harper family no longer controlled the business.

The new president, George Brinton McClellan Harvey (1864–1928), had been the managing editor and then the editor in chief of Joseph Pulitzer's *New York World,* and he owned the *North American Review,* which he brought with him to Harper. He instituted fiscal reforms, such as replacing hand compositors with linotype machines and inducing most of the Harpers to resign. He also publicized aggressively, most famously by throwing gala birthday dinners for the star house authors Mark Twain (1835–1910) and William Dean Howells (1837–1920). In 1913 Harvey sold *Harper's Weekly* to S. S. McClure and *Harper's Bazar* to William Randolph Hearst, where the spelling of the name was changed to *Harper's Bazaar* in 1929. But even such comparatively modern management did not bring profitability; in 1908, for example, Harper had book sales of over $900,000 but still lost more than $100,000. In 1915 the company's treasurer, C. T. Brainard, replaced Harvey as president. The ensuing cutbacks cost Harper some of its authors, most notably Theodore Dreiser and Sinclair Lewis.

HARPER'S AUTHORS

Not surprisingly Harper published numerous prominent writers of the period, especially in the periodicals. Charles Dudley Warner, Twain's collaborator on *The Gilded Age* (1873), was a prolific Harper contributor, as were Constance Fenimore Woolson, Margaret Deland, Mary E. Wilkins Freeman, and John Kendrick Bangs.

Lew Wallace's *Ben-Hur* (1880) was a blockbuster for Harper, but the $100,000 they agreed to pay for his next novel, *The Prince of India* (1893), hastened their impending bankruptcy. Works confronting social issues included Helen Hunt Jackson's *A Century of Dishonor* (1881), John Hay's *The Bread-Winners* (1884), and Henry Demarest Lloyd's *Wealth against Commonwealth* (1894). In the early twentieth century Harper published Woodrow Wilson's *A History of the American People* (1902), Theodore Dreiser's *Jennie Gerhardt* (1911) and *The Financier* (1912), and Zane Grey's *Riders of the Purple Sage* (1912) as well as books by Mrs. Humphry Ward, O. Henry, Booth Tarkington, Hamlin Garland, and H. G. Wells. An interesting measure of Harper's literary reach was *The Whole Family* (1908), a composite novel by twelve authors including Howells, Freeman, and Henry James. James's *Washington Square* (1881) and *The Ambassadors* (1903) were Harper books, and despite privately disdaining magazines, he contributed often to Harper's periodicals. However, Harper also offended James by ignoring his synopsis of *The Ambassadors* for two years and later by making major mistakes in *The American Scene* (1907).

After his own publishing ventures led to bankruptcy in 1894, Twain became Harper's most famous author. Harper began its uniform New Library edition of Twain's works in 1897; by 1914, Harvey claimed, Twain and his heirs had been paid over $300,000. Twain's friend Howells had the most extensive connections to Harper. In 1885, in the prime of his career, he signed a contract that made him a virtual literary trademark for the house. The contract paid Howells $10,000 a year for the serial rights to his new works, a royalty on book sales, and $3,000 a year to write the "Editor's Study" column for *Harper's Magazine*. After Howells left this contract in 1891 and concluded the "Editor's Study" in March 1892, Harper continued publishing most of his serials and all of his books. In 1901 he returned as a literary adviser and began to write the "Editor's Easy Chair," which he continued until his death in 1920.

HARPER'S ARTISTS

Artists also played a major role in Harper's success. Winslow Homer was a war correspondent for Harper and frequently contributed illustrations thereafter. Charles Parsons (1821–1910), who directed the art department from 1863 until 1889—the great age of American magazine illustration—personally mentored young artists such as Nast, Edwin A. Abbey, Edward Windsor Kemble (Twain's illustrator for *Huckleberry Finn* and other works), Frederic Remington, Howard Pyle, and William Allen Rogers. Charles Stanley

Reinhart was another prolific and respected Harper artist. In *Picture and Text* (1893) Henry James considered illustrators on their artistic merits; he particularly admired Abbey and Reinhart. Remington and Pyle were Harper writers as well as artists, as was George Du Maurier, whose novel *Trilby* (1894) was credited with increasing the circulation of *Harper's New Monthly Magazine* by 100,000, and who was James's illustrator for *Washington Square*.

The development of halftone photoengraving in the 1880s ended the competitive advantage of this fine art department. Halftones enabled photographs to be printed, bypassing the need for expensive illustration by fine-line wood engraving. The *Bazar* began using halftones in 1891, and soon thereafter the new ten-cent monthlies—notably *McClure's, Cosmopolitan, Munsey's,* and *Ladies' Home Journal*—exploited halftones and other innovations to revolutionize the magazine industry again.

HARPER'S INFLUENCE

The Gilded Age House of Harper is often associated with genteel culture and Victorian mores. Certainly its founders were pious, they valued character and industriousness, and they respected business unquestioningly. Their sons inherited from them the conviction that publishers were cultural guardians. In comparison to the robber barons of other industries or the publishing entrepreneurs of the Progressive Era, leaders of the House of Harper prided themselves on maintaining traditions. This self-image was later institutionalized by George Harvey's promotion of the reorganized firm's literary prestige and by subsequent memoirs and house histories. From the beginning, ironically, Harper used modern mass advertising to emphasize the house's traditional values. However, Harper also constructed new class relationships for readers and writers, developed mixed-gender literary spaces, pioneered the use of mass images, and emphasized the churning, urban, commercial "civilization" of its New York milieu. This combination of intellectual tradition and innovative literary commerce constitutes Harper's real historical influence.

See also Book Publishing; Houghton Mifflin; Literary Marketplace

BIBLIOGRAPHY
Primary Works
Abbott, Jacob. *The Harper Establishment: How Books Are Made.* New Castle, Del.: Oak Knoll Press, 2001. A visitor's guide first published by Harper & Brothers in 1855 after the firm moved into new quarters on Franklin

Square; originally subtitled *How the Story Books Are Made.*

Harper, J. Henry. *The House of Harper: A Century of Publishing in Franklin Square.* New York: Harper & Brothers, 1912.

Secondary Works

Exman, Eugene. *The House of Harper: One Hundred and Fifty Years of Publishing.* New York: Harper & Row, 1967.

Hewitt, Rosalie. "Henry James, the Harpers, and *The American Scene.*" *American Literature* 55, no. 1 (1983): 41–47.

Howard, June. *Publishing the Family.* Durham, N.C.: Duke University Press, 2001.

Madison, Charles Allan. *Book Publishing in America.* New York: McGraw-Hill, 1966.

Mott, Frank Luther. *Golden Multitudes: The Story of Best Sellers in the United States.* New York: Bowker, 1947.

Mott, Frank Luther. *A History of American Magazines.* 5 vols. Cambridge, Mass.: Harvard University Press, 1938–1968.

Sheehan, Donald. *This Was Publishing: A Chronicle of the Book Trade in the Gilded Age.* Bloomington: Indiana University Press, 1952.

Tebbel, John. *A History of Book Publishing in the United States.* 4 vols. New York: Bowker, 1972–1981. Vol. 1, *The Creation of an Industry, 1630–1865,* and vol. 2, *The Expansion of an Industry, 1865–1919,* are especially pertinent to the present essay.

Wilson, Christopher P. *The Labor of Words: Literary Professionalism in the Progressive Era.* Athens: University of Georgia Press, 1985.

Gib Prettyman

HARPER'S NEW MONTHLY MAGAZINE

What began as a monthly enterprise for the New York book publishing firm of Harper & Brothers to keep its expensive presses busy and make easy money reprinting popular English fiction evolved into *Harper's New Monthly Magazine,* a periodical that changed in response to the country's developing sense of itself.

AN AUDIENCE OF PLAIN PEOPLE

Early efforts to publish for a mass audience had resulted in publications like the *Police Gazette.* Newspapers, too, were being sensationalized for mass appeal, so when Harper's publisher Fletcher Harper (1806–1877) created a periodical for the "plain people," he clearly had a different idea. The tone was decidedly elevated and the

magazine's contents were primarily republished—writers would say "pirated"—from English periodicals. The editorial content of what began in June 1850 as *Harper's New Monthly Magazine* seemed to be for a quite literate, even somewhat wealthy, audience. At the same time, Harper placed an emphasis on the magazine having plenty of illustrations, presumably to make it more appealing to those "plain people" whose readership he wished to attract.

Harper's New Monthly Magazine's interest and emphasis on illustrations and pure reproductions of art was one quality that made the magazine seem "new," as its title claimed. And as the century progressed, it was in the art department that competition between the general monthlies was most noticeable. In fact, by the end of the century, writers for *Harper's New Monthly Magazine* were complaining about the attention (and commissions) paid to the illustrators of the magazine's articles.

By the early 1900s a good balance of art and editorial substance was achieved. One typical issue from 1902 includes stories by Edith Wharton, Booth Tarkington, Mark Twain, Mrs. Humphry Ward, William Dean Howells, and Mary E. Wilkins Freeman. The art had equally fine representation from Edwin A. Abbey, Howard Pyle, W. A. Rogers, and E. M. Ashe. This issue also includes an article about Aztecs of yesterday and today, written authoritatively by the American anthrolopologist Aleš Hrdlička and illustrated with sketches and a map.

EDITORIAL DIRECTION

As a youth, Henry Mills Alden (1869–1919) had worked as a bobbin boy in the cotton mills and had attended preparatory school and college by earning his keep building fires and cleaning. Like a true Horatio Alger hero, he gave the valedictory address at Ball Seminary and was to make a great success of his college experiences, as well. At Andover Theological Seminary, he met the writer Harriet Beecher Stowe (whose husband was on the faculty at Andover), and she secretly forwarded one of his articles to James Russell Lowell, the editor of the *Atlantic Monthly.* Lowell's encouragement led Alden into more freelance work and gave him his first exposure to professional editors.

Alden began his long career at Harper & Brothers by reading manuscripts and was given increasingly important and demanding positions until, in 1869, he was named managing editor of *Harper's New Monthly Magazine* and could work on ways to put into practice his belief that realistic fiction was the most reliable portrait of life. During Alden's tenure, from 1869 to 1919,

Advertisement for *Harper's New Monthly Magazine*, January 1894. Although the magazine's content was at its editorial peak during the 1890s, circulation was low and competition was keen. THE LIBRARY OF CONGRESS

his helpfulness and courtesy to known and unknown writers alike established a singular relationship between *Harper's New Monthly Magazine* and new American writers. In his book on Alden, Robert Underwood Johnson describes how many American literary figures respected and were grateful to Alden. Alden was equipped with a rare sense of proportion, with sane literary standards, and with a poise unaffected by fads or eccentricities, Johnson continues, adding that Alden once described *Harper's New Monthly Magazine* as the solidest magazine in the world. As an editor, Alden respected and honored that solidity with his own best efforts. In 1874 Fletcher Harper officially turned over all authority of the magazine to Alden, whose quiet yet wise guidance as editor in chief continued until his death in 1919.

George William Curtis, an aristocrat, became the editorial essayist for the Harper periodical in 1853. He was responsible for one of the monthly's earliest regular editorial departments, "The Easy Chair," a column that discussed politics, society, and literature. Despite his elevated social status—as a man of letters with a private fortune—Curtis never condescended to his readers; instead he embodied Fletcher Harper's intent to serve the popular in a "high and generous" sense and in that capacity he continued until his death in 1892.

Meanwhile, Fletcher Harper's retirement in 1875 (two years before his death), resulted in his being replaced as publisher by his grandson, J. Henry Harper. During this period, one sees changes in the choices of articles, no doubt related to the choices of Alden, not the latest Harper. More and more topics about America and fewer items and travelogues about Europe and the holy lands appear. Under J. Henry Harper's watch, a better paper was adopted and a larger type improved the overall appearance of the periodical. This kind of change is subtle but substantial and continued to be introduced throughout the 1880s. Indeed, as the magazine entered its third and fourth decades, *Harper's New Monthly Magazine* introduced other changes that came as new ideas in publishing. The 1870s and 1880s saw a move away from the sentimentality and sweetness that had characterized the magazine's fiction from the 1850s. In addition, fresher tales of travel that were exploratory and descriptive of the American West, Canada, and Mexico began to appear.

The improvements in the magazine were in large part a response to the introduction of competition from other periodicals. As Henry Mills Alden put it, "If you are driving a mettlesome horse, and another spirited steed comes alongside, your horse . . . naturally leaps forward, rejoicing in a good race." A part of the "spirited competition" from *Atlantic Monthly* and *Lippincott's* appears to have been an increasing interest in promoting the work of American authors. Several other popular but less important publications were also appealing to the general reader, but by the 1890s the center of *Harper's New Monthly Magazine*'s competition was—and continued to be for some time—the monthly *Scribner's Magazine,* a periodical with backing from a publishing house as successful as Harper & Brothers.

Another presence driving the editorial changes at the magazine was the arrival of William Dean Howells in 1886. In his own writing and in his columns for *Harper's New Monthly Magazine*—beginning with a department of commentary, chiefly literary, called "The Editor's Study"—Howells waged a battle for the new realistic fiction. Like Alden (whom Howells described as the best editor of the age, "or of any age"), he became known as a friend to new writers, particularly those innovating in realistic fiction. Among those helped by the two men are James Lane Allen, Alice Brown, Rose Terry Cooke, "Charles Egbert Craddock" (the pseudomyn of Mary Noailles Murfree), Stephen Crane, Rebecca Harding Davis, Richard Harding Davis, Margaret Deland, Hamlin Garland, Lafcadio Hearn, Henry James, Amelie Rives, Ruth McEnery Stewart, "Octave Thanet" (Alice French), Maurice Thompson, Mary E. Wilkins Freeman, Owen Wister, and Constance Fenimore Woolson.

EDITORIAL ZENITH AND FINANCIAL DISASTER

Others who played formative editorial roles at the magazine before the end of the century include the humorist John Kendrick Bangs, Charles Dudley Warner, and Thomas Nelson Page. With its impressive editorial leadership, its increasingly popular fictional serials, and its art, *Harper's New Monthly Magazine* was perhaps the most successful of the general periodicals of the 1890s. Mott declares that at the end of the nineteenth century, the magazine had "attained the very zenith of success among the world's periodicals of that class; at any rate, no other magazine can be shown to have been markedly superior to it in literary quality, variety, illustration, and physical appearance."

The magazine's greatest success during its peak decade was George Du Maurier's *Trilby*, serialized in 1894. The story created a national sensation, and as Mott puts it, the craze did not subside until "Trilby's perfect feet and Svengali's perfect villainy were forgotten in the interests aroused in the Spanish-American War." Other major successes of the decade were Mark Twain's *Personal Recollections of Joan of Arc* (published anonymously in 1895) and historical articles by Woodrow Wilson, Theodore Roosevelt, and Albert Bushness Hart. The Spanish-American War was accompanied by much sword-brandishing, as swashbuckling stories were the fashion of the moment. The war was scarcely over before a history of it by Henry Cabot Lodge was begun serially. Although the magazine was at its zenith in the 1890s in terms of editorial content, it was facing much new competition from numerous publications willing to sell at lower cost. *McClure's Magazine,* for example, was considered an upstart by some, but the probing muckraking articles of Lincoln Steffens and Ida Tarbell made the new periodical appealing to writers ready to show realism in life rather than fiction. The serious competition in the magazine world, and a falling-off of the company's book sales, forced Harper & Brothers into bankruptcy. In 1896 appeals were made to J. P. Morgan, who responded by saying that "the downfall of the House of Harper would be a national calamity" (Lapham, p. 10)

and infused the company with several million dollars over the next seven years. What had been a family partnership became a public corporation, but the editorial departments remained essentially the same.

The magazine lost Howells in 1892, although his earlier fight for the respect of writers of realistic fiction had given *Harper's New Monthly Magazine* a significant spot in the history of American fiction. In 1900 Howells, the acknowledged dean of American letters, was welcomed back to the magazine to occupy the "Editor's Easy Chair," a position that had been vacant since Curtis died. Howells and Alden continued their companionable stewardship, and the magazine continued to publish outstanding fiction, including the works of Jack London, Joseph Conrad, and Edith Wharton.

In 1904 Alden invited Henry James to return to the United States and write an essay for the magazine laying out his impressions about current New York City and how it compared to London and Paris. Not surprisingly, James's essay was full of discouraging descriptions about the "terrible town."

Lewis Lapham has suggested that the *Harper's Monthly Magazine* of the early twentieth century (the "new" was dropped in 1900) was no match for the out-of-control tides of events pushing floating pavilions of genteel discourse onto an open sea of violence. In fact, he notes, Harper's refrained from publishing anything—not so much as a paragraph—about the "unpleasantness on the Western Front" (p. 64). So the beginnings of the First World War, "the Great War," was handled much the way that the popular magazine *Godey's Lady's Book* handled the first year of the Civil War—by ignoring it. Soon after the war's end, the closely timed deaths of Alden and Howells in 1919 and 1920, respectively, figured in radical changes that led to a completely redesigned magazine in the early 1920s.

See also Copyright; Harper & Brothers; Periodicals; *Scribner's Magazine*

BIBLIOGRAPHY

Primary Works

Alden, Henry Mills. *Magazine Writing and the New Literature.* New York: Harper & Brothers, 1908.

Allen, Frederick L. *Harper's Magazine, 1850–1950: A Centenary Address.* New York: Newcomen Society in North America, 1950.

Harper, Joseph Henry. *The House of Harper: A Century of Publishing in Franklin Square.* New York: Harper & Brothers, 1912.

Johnson, Robert Underwood. *Commemorative Tribute to Henry Mills Alden.* New York: American Academy of Arts and Letters, 1922.

Lapham, Lewis H. "Hazards of New Fortune: *Harper's Magazine,* Then and Now." *Harper's Magazine,* June 2000.

Secondary Works
Allen, Frederick Lewis. *The Big Change, 1900–1950.* New York: Harper and Row, 1952.

Exman, Eugene. *The House of Harper: One Hundred and Fifty Years of Publishing.* New York: Harper and Row, 1967.

Fischer, John, ed. *Six in the Easy Chair.* Urbana: University of Illinois Press, 1973.

Milne, Gordon. *George William Curtis and the Genteel Tradition.* Bloomington: Indiana University Press, 1956.

Mott, Frank Luther. *A History of American Magazines.* 5 vols. Cambridge, Mass.: Harvard University Press, 1938–1968.

Tebbel, John, and Mary Ellen Zuckerman. *The Magazine in America, 1741–1990.* New York: Oxford University Press, 1991.

Ann Mauger Colbert

HAYMARKET SQUARE

On 4 May 1886 a bomb exploded in Chicago's Haymarket Square. The sudden explosion ended a workers' rally and set off a riot that resulted in the death of seven police officers. No one knows for certain who was responsible for the bomb. All accounts suggest that the rally involving two to three thousand people was peaceful and in the process of ending when the bomb was detonated. What is known is that except for one officer, who died from injuries caused by the bomb, all of the slain policemen were killed by other police officers. Nonetheless, on the morning after the riot, arrest warrants were issued for eight men who were well known in Chicago as anarchist advocates for labor reform. Nine days earlier, on 25 April, four of these eight men had addressed 25,000 people at a rally promoting the eight-hour workday. On 1 May, 300,000 workers across the United States had staged a symbolic strike for the eight-hour movement by staying away from work that day. Two days later in Chicago a battle erupted at the McCormick Reaper Works between union and scab workers. When the police arrived they fired their rifles indiscriminately into the crowd, killing at least two people and wounding several others. The gathering at Haymarket Square on the following evening therefore occurred in a context of high social tension and escalating violence. In fact, after the 1 May strike, the *Chicago Mail* had identified August Spies (1855–1887) and Albert Parsons (1848–1887) as two men to "mark." "Keep them in view," the editorial read. "Hold them personally responsible for any trouble that occurs. Make an example of them if trouble does occur!" On the day after the Haymarket riot, Spies and Parsons, along with other well-known anarchist leaders Samuel Fielden, Louis Lingg, Michael Schwab, Oscar Neebe, George Engel, and Adolph Fischer, were marked as the men who would pay not only for the Haymarket bombing but also for the fears that the labor movement had inspired both in well-to-do Chicago society and across the country. The *Chicago Times* urged the police to be called in and to "fire low and to fire quick." The *Louisville Courier-Journal* struck a tone no different from the *New York Times* when it called the accused men "blatant cattle" who should be "immediately strung up." One would like to say that the arrest of the men polarized the nation, but most of the country agreed with Theodore Roosevelt who boasted that his cowboys needed only plenty of rifles to handle the situation for "my men would shoot well and fear very little." On 11 November 1887, "Black Friday" as the anarchists called it, the future president of the United States and the majority of the nation's newspapers got their wish: Spies, Parsons, Fisher, and Engel were legally executed. Fielden's and Schwab's death sentences were commuted to life in prison. Neebe was sentenced to fifteen years, and Lingg killed himself in his jail cell. The novelist William Dean Howells gave them a fitting epitaph: "They died, in the prime of the first republic the world has ever known, for their opinions' sake" (Avrich, p. 404).

BACKGROUND TO HAYMARKET

The Haymarket tragedy was the culmination of more than a decade of national civic unrest brought on by a series of strikes and economic depressions. More than ten years earlier the *Chicago Tribune* was already spoiling for a fight with the growing labor movement. Addressing "communists" and any other labor organization intent on improving conditions for working people, in 1875 the *Tribune* captured the mood of civic tension and impending violence that characterized the time: "Every lamp-post in Chicago will be decorated with a communistic carcass if necessary to prevent wholesale incendiarism or prevent any attempt at it." The 1877 Railroad Strike, one of the longest worker uprisings in American history,

The riot in Haymarket Square. Illustration from *Harper's Weekly,* 15 May 1886. THE LIBRARY OF CONGRESS

predicted the tragedy at Haymarket Square. This strike entrenched the post–Civil War divide between capital and labor and demonstrated the violent lengths to which organized society would go to repress the labor movement. Lasting two weeks and involving seventeen states, the July 1877 strike began when the Baltimore and Ohio Railroad announced it was cutting wages. All over the country a battle played out between strikers and scabs backed by police and local militia paid for by the employers. In Baltimore, Pittsburgh, and Chicago strikers were shot down by such troops. The fierce battle between strikers and industry excited such a national panic that President Rutherford B. Hayes eventually responded to requests from industry leaders to settle the conflict with federal troops.

If the Civil War had been fought to put an end to slavery, then the post–Civil War period ushered in a fight between capital and labor interests for what constituted a fair wage and fair number of working hours for industrial laborers. The conflict over chattel slavery had given way to a conflict over what many believed to be "wage slavery." As the Haymarket anarchist Albert Parsons argued, "The capitalist in the former system owned the laborer, and hence his product, while under the latter he owns his labor product, and hence the person of the wage-laborer." As the conflict between the Union and the Confederacy transformed into a battle between capital and labor, figures associated with the former conflict became players in the new one. Colonel Frederick Dent Grant, the son of Ulysses S. Grant, was transferred by Hayes from killing American Indians in the Dakota territory to killing workers in the Chicago streets. Twelve people would be killed in the July 1877 strike, five more than at Haymarket, and within a day of Grant's action the strike would be ended. The Civil War hero General William Tecumseh Sherman sounded this ominous warning: "There will soon come an armed contest between capital and labor. They will oppose each other not with words and arguments and ballots, but with shot and shell, gunpowder and cannon. The better classes are tired of the insane howlings of the lower strata and mean to stop them" (Avrich, p. 176).

In retrospect, the Haymarket tragedy was probably inevitable. It was an outgrowth not only of the fight between capital and labor but also a consequence of the larger anxiety the United States felt as it shifted from an agrarian society to an industrial one. In America the anarchist movement emerged out of a variety of other labor groups that began to spring up after the Civil War. The Social Democratic Party, the Workingmen's Party, and, ultimately, the International Working People's Association, itself a federation of many smaller groups, provided the fertile soil for the growth of the anarchist movement. Generally speaking, American anarchists affirmed the complete autonomy of the individual against the coercive impulses of the state. In practice, this meant opposing the ways in which the state sanctioned oppressive forms of private ownership. Anarchists agreed that the state was essentially an instrument of economic injustice dedicated to upholding the anti-egalitarian aims of capitalism. Few anarchists advocated violent overthrow of the state and most were willing to imagine that they could work with and through the state to improve the nation's distribution of its wealth and resources. Parsons, for instance, was typical in arguing that in an anarchist society, reason and common sense should take precedence over laws designed to protect the interests of labor-exploiting manufacturers. Parsons believed that once the artificial human institutions were stripped of their power, a basically good human nature would be allowed to express itelf in the form of individuals pursuing and protecting their own personal interests but not to the disadvantage or harm of others.

While such a position is actually of a piece with mainstrean American thought from Thomas Jefferson to Ralph Waldo Emerson, many of the specific anarchist ideas came from abroad. During this period there was a massive influx of immigrants—in part to supply the burgeoning factories with cheap labor—who brought with them not only their desire for a better life but also new ideas from Europe for how to make a better life possible. Of the eight men convicted for the Haymarket riot, only Albert Parsons had been born and raised in the United States. Most of the others emigrated from Germany, a country associated with radical utopian social ideas. Anarchism, while not specifically a European import, did take on force after the European revolutions of 1848. Indeed, one reason that the Haymarket anarchists could be so quickly and so unfairly punished was because the movement they represented could be easily perceived as an isolated and foreign threat. Even when they advocated a reform that would eventually be accepted as standard practice, such as the eight-hour workday, they were nonetheless tagged by newspapers and most politicians as foreigners and madmen intent on destroying society.

Of course the anarchists did not understand themselves to be destroying society so much as breaking it down in order to rebuild it into something that benefited more of its members. Their arguments about abolishing the existing capital-labor structure drew on the ideas of the anarchists Pierre-Joseph Proudhon and Mikhail Bakunin, who both favored an equal distribution of profits between owners and workers. The best-known anarchist was Johann Most (1846–1906), a German immigrant exiled from Germany after his role in the Paris Commune uprising of 1871. Upon arriving in the United States in 1882, Most became a lightning rod for both supporters and detractors of the anarchist movement. In newspaper articles and speeches, he urged workers to arm themselves and argued that the inequity between rich and poor could be solved only by violence. He even wrote newspaper articles that described how to put together explosives and use them against the rich. With his revolutionary rhetoric and uncompromising stance, Most attracted many admirers, Emma Goldman among them. However, he also excited an extraordinary amount of fear and hatred. At his death in 1906, after serving three different prison terms in the United States, the *New York Times* eulogized him as "an enemy of the human race."

Most's emergence on the American scene made many believe that General Sherman's warning of 1877 was likely to come true. By the time of Haymarket the anarchists also had basically disavowed conventional means of protest such as the ballot box. To them, this was not only a radical stance but a practical one as well. All of them had experienced tainted elections when trying to elect their candidates and witnessed the brutality of the police and the U.S. troops when called in to break up strikes. From the anarchists' perspective, it was the barons of capital, backed up with the force of state and federal troops, who were truly intent on attacking the ideals of equality for which the United States supposedly stood. Short of being silent and continuing to exist under the rules made by the industrialists and manufacturers, their only choice was to do as their enemies did and try to take the law into their own hands. As Samuel Fielden said the night of the Haymarket rally, "A million men hold all the property in this country. The law has no use for the other fifty-four million" (Avrich, p. 205). This does not mean that the Haymarket anarchists took Most's advice and exploded a bomb in Haymarket Square. Even though some of them, August Spies in particular, called on workers to exact a violent revenge for the strikers murdered the night before the Haymarket Massacre, nothing indicates that the condemned men ever did anything more than advance the view that there might come a day where arms would be necessary—hardly an extremist position given arms were being used against them. Ironically, Louis Lingg committed the only known successful bombing when he blew himself up in his cell rather than be executed by the state of Illinois.

THE HAYMARKET TRIAL

By the time the Haymarket anarchists were arrested the atmosphere was charged with such an air of impending revolution that they never really stood a chance of receiving justice. In their eyes, dying as martyrs would likely spur on the societal transformation they hoped was near. In the eyes of their accusers, the issue was to stamp out once and for all the threat posed by the expression of political points of view that suggested capitalism, or the free market, was anything but free. Because the state could not convict the anarchists for throwing the bomb, it tried them for conspiracy—for creating the atmosphere that would encourage a bomb to be thrown. This line of reasoning obligated the state to prove that the anarchists' opinions were inimical to the interests of the state. Insofar as they advocated reorganizing the distribution between capital and labor they were rightly perceived to be dangerous to the interests of the wealthy who controlled the state, if not necessarily the state itself. Albert Parsons pointed out that while the state could not prove he had thrown the bomb, it did prove that "we were, all of us, anarchists, socialists, communists, Knights of Labor, unionists" (Avrich, p. 283). Once the judge in the case ruled that the prosecution need not identify the actual bombthrower or prove that the bombthrower had any connection to the accused, the men's fates were sealed. As Julius S. Grinnell, the prosecuting attorney, told the "gentlemen of the jury," the doctrine of "anarchy is on trial" and these men "were no more guilty than the thousands who follow them." To "convict these men, make examples of them, hang them," was to "save our institutions, our society" (Avrich, p. 284). Grinnell's argument was lost on the jurors because saving society was precisely what their verdict was supposed to accomplish. Given the opportunity to respond to the verdict, the anarchists themselves were left to put what had happened to them in its appropriate social and moral context: "You may pronounce the sentence upon me, honorable judge," said August Spies, "but let the world know that in A.D. 1886, in the State of Illinois, eight men were sentenced to death because they believed in a better future, because they had not lost their faith in the ultimate victory of liberty and justice!" (Avrich, p. 286).

The Haymarket decision was met with something close to national celebration. The *Chicago Tribune* announced that "law has triumphed" and even suggested that a fund of $100,000 be raised to thank the jury "whose honesty and fearlessness made a conviction possible." One prominent dissenter was William Dean Howells, the only significant American literary figure to speak out against the verdict. Although the Haymarket decision inspired many supporters who fought to save the anarchists' lives until every appeal had been tried, Howells's example is telling because it suggests how dangerous it was to stand up for free speech during this time. Internationally, the Haymarket decision drew wide and immediate criticism. Karl Marx's daughter visited the men in prison. Labor organizations sent contributions from Brussels, Madrid, Paris, Rome, and Zurich. In Australia protest rallies were held. And well-known English literary figures such as William Morris, George Bernard Shaw, and Oscar Wilde all spoke out against the verdict. Noting "the spirit of cold cruelty, heartless and careless at once, which is one of the most noticeable characteristics of American commercialism," Morris charged that America was "a society corrupt to the core, and at this moment engaged in suppressing freedom with just the same reckless brutality and blind ignorance as the Czar of all the Russias uses" (pp. 42–43). Howells's criticism was never so pointed. Howells wrote George William Curtis, the editor of *Harper's Weekly*, to declare the case "hysterical and unjust" (Howells, *Selected Letters* 3:193). He could not, however, convince Curtis to reverse the magazine's endorsement of the decision. Nor could Howells convince a single significant American author to side with him. When Howells made his stance against the verdict public by writing the Illinois governor and asking him to stay the men's execution, he found that the nation's newspapers, as well as much of his audience, "abused me as heartily as if I had proclaimed myself a dynamiter" (*Selected Letters* 3:223). Howells was careful in his public pronouncements not to endorse the opinions of the anarchists but only their right to express them. Still, it was a dangerous position for Howells to take and it affected how he was viewed by his readers and admirers. Thus this great proponent of literary realism was made to suffer the irony of being publicly eviscerated for not recognizing the "reality" of American justice.

HAYMARKET IN AMERICAN LITERATURE

Howells was deeply affected by not only the Haymarket tragedy but also the reaction his involvement in it prompted in his readers. His 1890 novel *A Hazard of New Fortunes* draws on the Haymarket episode but without the same sense of focused moral outrage that Howells had expressed in his public stance. In *Hazard* Howells compresses the eight anarchists into one, Lindau. In the novel's key episode, Lindau is present during a strike when a riot occurs. As the police club the strikers, Lindau mockingly shouts, "Ah yes! Glup the strikerss—gif it to them. Why don't you co and glup the bresidents that insoalt your lawss?" (p. 422). As with the Haymarket anarchists, Lindau is responsible neither for the strike nor its attendant violence. His offense is his opinion. Although Lindau is cruelly beaten by the police for expressing his opinion, he is also implicitly blamed for the death of another character who dies as a result of the police violence. Howells presents Lindau sympathetically but is also careful to distance the reader from him. Howells allows Lindau to criticize capitalism (in ways not dissimilar from Howells's own point of view), yet portrays how the expression of those views inevitably leads to violence in American society. In the end, the reader is likely to sympathize with Basil March, the novel's middle-class hero who edits Lindau's best intentions and makes them more palatable to his audience. He tells his son that "men like Lindau" are guilty of letting "their love of justice hurry them into sympathy with violence" and for this "they are wrong" and "die in a bad cause" (pp. 451–452). Howells, however, was never happy with the novel. Writing nearly ten years after its publication, Howells acknowledged that he felt "a tenderness for this character which I feel for no other in the book" (*A Hazard of New Fortunes*, p. 505). He wistfully identified Lindau as "almost" the hero of the novel and admitted that with the "heroic" Lindau's death "I suffered more things than I commonly allow myself to suffer for the adverse fates of my characters" (pp. 508–509). In the end, it seems that Howells, who so bravely spoke out against the Haymarket verdicts, could not master in his art the terrible conflict in American society that the Haymarket tragedy revealed. Nonetheless, *A Hazard of New Fortunes* remains an enduring portrait of that period in American history.

A more scathing attack on the Haymarket injustice is Robert Herrick's *Memoirs of an American Citizen*. Published in 1905, Herrick's novel tells how Harrington rises from relative poverty to become a wealthy titan of industry and eventually a United States senator. Harrington is a ruthless, unscrupulous businessman who justifies his acts through a kind of Social Darwinism that is also an inverted version of the biblical Golden Rule. The pivotal point to his career occurs when he is chosen to serve on the jury for the trial of the Haymarket anarchists. He is told that if he convicts the anarchists he can expect to be promoted. What moral qualms he suffers are suppressed in his recognition that the trial is fixed. He observes: "That was the point of it all—a struggle between sensible folks who went about their business and tried to get all there was in it—like myself—and some scum from Europe, who didn't like the way things are handed out in this world" (p. 74). Although he later experiences some regret for involvement in a trial that "was all a parcel of lies," he accepts that his role as a successful member of society required him to make certain that these "dreamers of wild dreams" were made to "suffer for their foolish opinions, which were dead against the majority," and "thus I performed my duty to society" (p. 74). His role in suppressing the labor movement gives him the push he needs to begin his successful career as a business tycoon. By the end of the novel, when he is elected senator by the very business elements with whom he used to compete for capital, Harrington becomes the embodiment of the alliance between government and big business that sentenced the Haymarket anarchists to death.

One other important novel about Haymarket is Frank Harris's *The Bomb* (1908). What distinguishes this work is Harris's suggestion that the unknown bomber was the well-known anarchist Rudolph Schnaubelt. Subsequent research has shown that Harris's theory is highly unlikely. In the 1980s, the historian Paul Avrich uncovered letters from 1933 that seemed to identify the bombthrower as one George Schwab. Whether Schnaubelt, Schwab, or someone else threw the bomb is not ultimately important because the point of the Haymarket tragedy is that who threw the bomb never mattered in the public's opinion. John Peter Altgeld, governor of Illinois, made this point when in 1893 he pardoned the three living anarchists. Remarking on Judge Joseph E. Gary's decision that the state need not prove who threw the bomb or that the bombthrower acted on the instructions of the accused, Altgeld stated: "In all the centuries during which government has been maintained among men, and crime has been punished, no judge in a civilized country has ever laid down such a rule" (Avrich, p. 423). Altgeld's statement acquitted not only the living anarchists but the ones hanged as well. The governor in effect indicted the judge, the jury, the prosecution, the police, and the newspapers of the time for the men's death. History has agreed with Altgeld: the Haymarket tragedy represents perhaps the greatest miscarriage of justice in American history. Yet if the anarchists' brave stand and sad end remain unknown to most Americans it may also be because the structure of corporate power they battled remains, for the most part, intact.

See also Anarchism; *A Hazard of New Fortunes;* Labor; Socialism

BIBLIOGRAPHY

Primary Works

Altgeld, John Peter. *Reasons for Pardoning the Haymarket Anarchists*. Chicago: n.p., 1893.

Herrick, Robert. *The Memoirs of an American Citizen*. 1905. Edited by Daniel Aaron. Cambridge, Mass.: Harvard University Press, 1963.

Howells, William Dean. *A Hazard of New Fortunes*. 1890. New York: Modern Library, 2002.

Howells, William Dean. *Novels 1886–1888: The Minister's Charge; April Hopes; Annie Kilburn*. New York: Library of America, 1989.

Howells, William Dean. *Selected Letters of W. D. Howells*. Vol. 3, *1882–1891*. Edited by Robert C. Leitz et al. Boston: Twayne, 1980.

Morris, William. "Whigs, Democrats, and Socialists." In his *Signs of Change*. London: Reeves and Turner, 1888.

Secondary Works

Adelman, William J. *Haymarket Revisited: A Tour Guide of Labor History Sites and Ethnic Neighborhoods Connected with the Haymarket Affair*. Chicago: Illinois Labor History Society, 1976.

Avrich, Paul. *The Haymarket Tragedy*. Princeton, N.J.: Princeton University Press, 1984.

Cady, Edwin. *The Realist at War: The Mature Years, 1885–1920, of William Dean Howells*. Syracuse, N.Y.: Syracuse University Press, 1958.

Cady, Edwin. *The Road to Realism: The Early Years, 1837–1885, of William Dean Howells*. Syracuse, N.Y.: Syracuse University Press, 1956.

Carter, Everett. Introduction to *A Hazard of New Fortunes*, by William Dean Howells. Bloomington: Indiana University Press, 1976.

David, Henry. *The History of the Haymarket Affair: A Study in the American Social-Revolutionary and Labor Movements*. 1936. New York: Russell and Russell, 1958.

Foner, Philip S., ed. *The Autobiographies of the Haymarket Martyrs*. New York: Humanities Press, 1969.

Glenn, Robert. W. *The Haymarket Affair: An Annotated Bibliography*. Westport, Conn.: Greenwood Press, 1993.

Kazin, Alfred. *On Native Grounds: An Interpretation of Modern American Prose Literature*. New York: Harcourt, Brace and World, 1942.

Lynn, Kenneth S. *William Dean Howells: An American Life*. New York: Harcourt Brace Jovanovich, 1971.

Nelson, Bruce C. *Beyond the Martyrs: A Social History of Chicago's Anarchists, 1870–1900*. New Brunswick, N. J.: Rutgers University Press, 1988.

Parrish, Timothy. "Haymarket and Hazard: The Lonely Politics of William Dean Howells." *Journal of American Culture* 17, no. 4 (1994): 23–32.

Timothy Parrish

A HAZARD OF NEW FORTUNES

William Dean Howells's (1837–1920) novel *A Hazard of New Fortunes* (1889) takes its title from William Shakespeare's play *King John*, in which English invaders of France are described as "rash, inconsiderate, fiery voluntaries" and are reported to

> have sold their fortunes at their native homes,
> Bearing their birthrights proudly on their backs,
> To make a hazard of new fortunes here.
> *(2.1.70, 72–74)*

The phrase thus alludes to abrupt relocation, disputed territory, and imminent violence. It also conveys dramatic uncertainty through the double meanings of "hazard" and "fortune." To liquidate safe fortunes—"native homes" and "birthrights"—is to hazard (wager) with fortune, a hazardous state of affairs in which the only constant is endless change. This pervasive note of uncertainty was echoed by the illustration on the cover of the now rare paperback first edition: an image of fortune's wheel.

Despite its literary title, the novel's subjects are rooted in the vital political and economic tumult of the late 1880s and intensified by Howells's increasingly pained perceptions of American society and life in general. As a result the novel is a kind of historical crossroads in which a wide range of Gilded Age subjects intersect. When Basil March, the novel's central character, moves from Boston to New York to edit a new literary magazine, he encounters a foreign urban landscape, a starkly commercial literary marketplace, a host of disturbing political ideas, and a percolating socioeconomic unrest that culminates in a labor strike and random violence. More or less directly, then, the plot confronts the literary marketplace, the socioeconomic upheavals of industrialization, the "labor question" and middle-class reactions to it, socialist and anarchist ideas, and perceptions of the modern city. Indirectly the novel touches on the Haymarket affair, immigration and demographic changes, the formulation of literary realism, and even the contemporaneous fervor for utopian thought. Because Howells came to be considered "the Dean of American Letters" and *A Hazard of New Fortunes* is generally regarded as his best work, the novel is read as representative of various social perspectives such as elite culture, the literary establishment, bourgeois culture, feminized culture, middle-class liberalism, Christian socialism, and so on. As this list indicates, exactly what Howells represents and what his novel signifies are very much questions for interpretation.

HOWELLS IN THE 1880s

The author who generally signed his works W. D. Howells—the more formal William Dean was imposed

The cover of the first paperback edition of *A Hazard of New Fortunes*, 1890. SPECIAL COLLECTIONS LIBRARY, UNIVERSITY OF MICHIGAN

upon him later—became a successful novelist and America's leading literary critic in the 1880s. At the same time, it was a period of increasing personal and intellectual uncertainty for him. In February 1881, Howells resigned as editor of the prestigious *Atlantic Monthly* to pursue his own writing. He was always a diligent writer, and freedom from editorial work allowed his literary craft to develop. He began to explore more modern subjects: *A Modern Instance* (1882) examined divorce; *The Rise of Silas Lapham* (1885) probed business ethics; *The Minister's Charge* (1886) took readers on an odyssey through Boston's urban underclass; and *Annie Kilburn* (1889) confronted class inequality and personal political responsibility. These novels were commercially and critically successful, first as serials in leading magazines and then as books. When his Boston publisher, James R. Osgood & Company, went bankrupt in 1885, Howells was free

to sign a lucrative contract with the New York firm of Harper & Brothers, the largest publisher in the United States, paying him ten thousand dollars a year for his basic literary contributions and more for book royalties. The contract also paid him three thousand dollars to write a literary column, and in January 1886 he began writing the influential "Editor's Study" column for *Harper's New Monthly Magazine*. By all measures Howells was a conspicuous literary success.

Not coincidentally he was also controversial. His novels generated controversy as explicit examples of "the new literature" of realism, which was accused of focusing attention on indecent subjects and rejecting higher moral and literary ideals. In addition he touched off a transatlantic feud with the British press in November 1882 for suggesting, in a *Century* magazine article, that Henry James was a better, because more modern, writer than such British luminaries as Charles Dickens and William Makepeace Thackeray. Howells used the prominent "Editor's Study" forum to engage these literary controversies and to fight what the biographer Edwin H. Cady calls the "war" over realism. At first the tone and subjects of these skirmishes were somewhat jocular, and Howells felt confident of his position—which valued realism for its opposition to the impossible simplifications of romance. In early 1886 he joked that his columns were "banging the babes of Romance about" and that his new novel, *April Hopes* (1887), would aim "for the covert discouragement of love-marriages, and the promotion of broken engagements" (*Selected Letters* 3:152, 154). However in the second half of the decade Howells experienced several significant upheavals that transformed him as an artist and a public figure.

"GRIEFS AND HOPES"

The first upheaval was a sort of literary conversion experience: his discovery of Leo Tolstoy (1828–1910). In Tolstoy's works Howells found a powerful model for the social function of literature, a comparatively radical critique of modern industrial society, and a moral outlook that stressed the complicity of the privileged classes in the economic ills of the age. In his "Editor's Study" for July 1887, Howells said of Tolstoy's *What Then Must We Do?* (1886), which he read in the French translation, *Que Faire?*, "After reading it you cannot be quite the same person you were before; you will be better by taking its truth to heart, or worse by hardening your heart against it" (*Editor's Study*, p. 87). Tolstoy's ethics and art slowly precipitated a certain political clarity and social purpose in Howells's thinking, and one hears the echo of Tolstoy's title in the refrain "What is the next thing?" that dominates the doomed dinner celebration in *A Hazard of New Fortunes* (p. 338).

> The central plot device of A Hazard of New Fortunes *is the literary magazine* Every Other Week. *The magazine brings together an unlikely collection of people including the man of letters Basil March, the Southern apologist Colonel Woodburn, the socialist immigrant Lindau, the nouveau riche capitalist Dryfoos, and his Christ-like son Conrad. But at the gaudy dinner intended to advertise their collective success, grave differences among the contributors—and within industrialized America—foreshadow inevitable violence to come.*

The hobby was out, [and] the Colonel was in the saddle with so firm a seat that no effort sufficed to dislodge him. The dinner went on from course to course with barbaric profusion, and from time to time Fulkerson tried to bring the talk back to *Every Other Week*. But perhaps because that was only the ostensible and not the real object of the dinner, which was to bring a number of men together under Dryfoos's roof, and make them the witnesses of his splendor, make them feel the power of his wealth, Fulkerson's attempts failed. The Colonel showed how commercialism was the poison at the heart of our national life; how we began as a simple, agricultural people, who had fled to these shores with the instinct, divinely implanted, of building a state such as the sun never shone upon before; how we had conquered the wilderness and the savage; how we had flung off, in our struggle with the mother country, the trammels of tradition and precedent, and had settled down, a free nation, to the practice of the arts of peace; how the spirit of commercialism had stolen insidiously upon us, and the infernal impulse of competition had embroiled us in a perpetual warfare of interests, developing the worst passions of our nature, and teaching us to trick and betray and destroy one another in the strife for money, till now that impulse had exhausted itself, and we found competition gone and the whole economic problem in the hands of the monopolies—the Standard Oil Company, the Sugar Trust, the Rubber Trust, and what not. And now what was the next thing? Affairs could not remain as they were; it was impossible; and what was the next thing? . . .

All the rest listened silently, except Lindau; at every point the Colonel made against the present condition of things he said more and more fiercely, "You are righdt, you are righdt." His eyes glowed, his hand played with his knife hilt. When the Colonel demanded, "And what is the next thing?" he threw himself forward, and repeated: "Yes, sir! What is the next thing?"

Howells, *A Hazard of New Fortunes*, pp. 337–338.

The second upheaval resulted from the trial, conviction, and execution of the "anarchists" charged in the Haymarket Square bombing. Despite his discovery of Tolstoy, Howells was slow to perceive the severity of corporate capitalism's impact on the United States. In the September 1886 "Editor's Study," Howells wrote that Fyodor Dostoevsky's "formidable and disquieting" and "profoundly tragic" literary style would not apply to American subjects because "there were so few shadows and inequalities in our broad level of prosperity" (*Editor's Study*, pp. 40–41). "We invite our novelists, therefore," Howells wrote, "to concern themselves with the more smiling aspects of life, which are the more American, and to seek the universal in the individual rather than the social interests" (p. 41). These comments were likely written about four months before the column was published—shortly after the events at Haymarket Square in May. At least at first, then, Howells failed to see a connection between the Haymarket bombing and literary concerns. By the summer of 1887, however, he was actively soliciting professional colleagues to join him in protesting the murder conviction of the seven men, whom he now believed had been tried "for socialism and not for murder" and were "doomed to suffer for their opinion's sake" (*Selected Letters* 3:193). He spent several months trying to secure a pardon for the convicted anarchists, and he was the only prominent American to criticize publicly their conviction and execution. The experience turned Howells's thinking explicitly toward the manifest social and political injustices that these men decried.

These experiences led Howells, like so many other intellectuals of the period, to explicit contemplation of social solutions. Edward Bellamy's novel *Looking Backward, 2000–1887* (1888) sparked a national craze for utopian texts, and Howells not only reviewed it favorably but also participated in the organization of the first Nationalist Club in Boston. Such clubs, dedicated to studying and promoting the ideas set forth in the book, were soon established nationwide. Howells also read socialist texts, heard Christian Socialist sermons, and attended socialist meetings. In January 1888 he told his father that "I incline greatly to think our safety and happiness are in that direction; though as yet the Socialists offer us nothing definite or practical to take hold of" (*Selected Letters* 3:216). In a preface for *A Hazard of New Fortunes* written in 1909, Howells recalls it as a period when

> the solution of the riddle of the painful earth through the dreams of Henry George, through the dreams of Edward Bellamy, through the dreams of all the generous visionaries of the past, seemed not impossibly far off. That shedding of blood which is for the remission of sins had been symbolized by the bombs and scaffolds of Chicago, and the hearts of those who felt the wrongs bound up with our rights, the slavery implicated in our liberty, were thrilling with griefs and hopes hitherto strange to the average American breast. (P. 4)

Howells's political and social ruminations were heightened by his move to New York City in February 1888. The Howells family was always moving; he once wrote to his sister, "I suppose you wouldn't be much surprised at getting a letter from me in the moon" (*Selected Letters* 3:207). Still, the Boston area—his wife's native ground and the nation's historic intellectual center—had been home base since Howells arrived as a young "westerner" from Ohio. When they moved to New York, Howells thought Boston "of another planet" compared to New York's "foreign touches of all kinds" and "abounding Americanism" (*Selected Letters* 3:223). The intracultural shock sparked Howells's imagination. He found himself keeping notes and writing sketches in the familiar role of a traveler, and he called the beginning of *Hazard* simply "my N.Y. story" (*Selected Letters* 3:246).

The last major upheaval of this period was an intense personal shock: the death of his eldest daughter Winifred on 2 March 1889 from "a sudden failure of the heart" (*Selected Letters* 3:246). From a modern medical perspective it seems likely that Winny suffered some form of anorexia nervosa, a disease virtually unknown to doctors at the time. A few months before her death at age twenty-six, her weight had fallen to fifty-eight pounds. After years of moving from place to place seeking treatments, Howells ultimately insisted that she be sent to Philadelphia for treatment by S. Weir Mitchell, the prominent doctor whose "rest cure" for "hysterical" women inspired Charlotte Perkins Gilman's psychological horror story "The Yellow Wall-Paper" (1892). Winny was thus away from home when she died, leaving Howells with a crushing sense of guilt. His grief profoundly changed his perception of life and cast a long shadow over the ending of the novel.

COMPOSITION

While the major building blocks of *A Hazard of New Fortunes* were already gathering in his mind, the Harper publishing house initiated the project. In September 1888, Henry Mills Alden, editor of *Harper's Monthly Magazine* and longtime house literary advisor, wrote a letter suggesting that Howells undertake a "feuilleton," a series of literary stories or sketches, for *Harper's Weekly*. Alden and the Harpers envisioned "something very strong and striking" that would "be a powerful presentation of the life of our great metropolis" (Kirk, pp. 18, 19). Such sketches were common in the timely and highly illustrated *Weekly*, and Howells's publishers felt that his controversial status as literary realist and defender of anarchists would help the project to "command the interest of all classes" (Kirk, p. 19). Howells declined to do the sketches and instead wrote a novel for serialization. Interestingly, when the Howells-like Basil March attempts a similar series of "picturesque" sketches within the novel, their social value becomes an explicit subject of discussion. The magazine business also inspired the novel's central organizing device: the fictional magazine *Every Other Week*. As Howells explained to his father, "Basil March simply comes to New York in charge of a literary enterprise, and the fortunes of this periodical form the plot, such as there is" (*Selected Letters* 3:241). *Hazard* is thus both a commercial narrative of urban exploration and a commentary upon such literary forms.

Howells began the novel in October 1888 while he and his wife were, like the fictional Marches, apartment hunting. Just before Christmas of that year Howells reported: "I've written 500 pp., and hope to have 800 done before I begin printing" (*Selected Letters* 3:241). By the time of Winny's death in March of the next year, the first installment was about to appear. His despair "took away everything but work," which he pursued "through the leaden hours and days" (*Hazard*, p. 509). In May 1889 Howells retreated to the Boston area, where the novel seemed to unfold "nearly without my conscious agency" (*Hazard*, p. 4). Howells recalled writing "with the printer at my heels" (p. 3), and William A. Rogers, the prominent Harpers artist and cartoonist who illustrated the serial, reported that "I never saw more than three installments ahead, and that only at the beginning. Later on I had often to read hastily the galley proofs on Thursday afternoon and turn in my drawing Friday morning" (p. 40).

The Marches first appeared in *Their Wedding Journey* (1872) and reappear in several other stories. Despite being familiar and semiautobiographical characters, Howells reports that "when I began speaking of them as Basil and Isabel, in the fashion of *Their Wedding Journey,* they would not respond with the effect of early middle age which I desired in them. . . . It was not till I tried addressing them as March and Mrs. March that they stirred under my hand with fresh impulse" (*Hazard*, p. 3). Howells also subjected the Marches to considerable irony, reflecting the author's pained perceptions of socioeconomic injustice and the restrictions imposed by his own social class. In his long letter of congratulations to Howells after the novel's publication, Henry James teased Howells for this self-flagellation, saying, "Poor March, my dear Howells—what tricks you play him," and signing the letter to "my dear Basil" (Anesko, pp. 277, 278).

Many of *Hazard*'s other elements also derived from identifiable sources. Howells intended the name Dryfoos to signify Pennsylvania Dutch origins similar to those of his own ancestors (*Hazard*, p. 506). The mechanism of the Dryfooses' transformation from hardworking Ohio farmers to nouveau riche New Yorkers who underwrite the publication of *Every Other Week* was inspired by a May 1887 trip to Ohio where Howells observed "a town in full boom from the discovery of natural gas" (*Selected Letters* 3:188). Howells based Lindau, the German immigrant and socialist who works as a translator at *Every Other Week*, on "an old German revolutionist" whom he knew as a young man in Ohio, and the author confessed "a tenderness for the character which I feel for no other in the book, and a reverence for an inherent nobleness in it" (*Hazard*, p. 505). Howells ascribes inspiration for the genial syndicate man and literary entrepreneur Fulkerson to a deceased friend, Ralph Keeler (p. 505). Some readers have seen echoes of Samuel Clemens in Fulkerson's character, and others thought he must be based on S. S. McClure, the publishing entrepreneur who furnished syndicated stories to magazines before founding *McClure's Magazine*. Although Howells denied this, he conceded that if someone were to see in Fulkerson "the circumstances of another friend of mine, still potently and usefully alive, it could not be to the disadvantage of the mainly imaginary Fulkerson" (p. 505). Certainly Howells's ample experience of the magazine business contributed vitality to his portrayals of Fulkerson and the self-indulgent artist Beaton. Into the deaths of the Christ-like Conrad Dryfoos and the fervently moral Lindau, meanwhile, Howells channeled his personal and political pain, admitting that in their cases "I suffered more things than I commonly allow myself to suffer in the adverse fate of my characters" (pp. 508–509).

Immediate events also influenced the composition. "I had the general design well in mind when I began to write it," Howells says in his 1909 preface to *Hazard*, "but as it advanced it compelled into its course incidents, interests, [and] individualities, which I had not known lay near, and it specialized and amplified at points which I had not always meant to touch" (pp. 3–4). For example, Howells's encounter with a street person became the basis for Basil's similar encounter in the novel. More dramatically, a New York streetcar strike in February 1889—a few weeks before the serialization of *Hazard* began—inspired the story "to find its way to issues nobler and larger than those of the love-affairs common to fiction" (p. 4). Coverage of the strike, including vivid illustrations, appeared in the 9 February 1889 issue of *Harper's Weekly*. The serial itself appeared from 23 March to 16 November 1889. It consisted of thirty-four installments and included sixteen illustrations. A cheap paperback edition was published simultaneously with the clothbound edition—a strategy Howells suggested to his friend Henry James as a way to get copies "into the hands of the people" (*Life in Letters* 2:7). The strategy seems to have worked for *Hazard*. In June 1890 Howells wrote that his book "is keeping along in a sort of incredible prosperity with the public" (*Life in Letters* 2:5).

RECEPTION AND CRITICAL HISTORY

Critics generally consider *A Hazard of New Fortunes* to be the high-water mark of Howells's literary achievement, and Howells judged it "the most vital of my fictions, through my quickened interest in the life about me, at a moment of great psychological import" (*Hazard*, p. 4). Despite the excitement the Harpers had envisioned from the project, though, Howells claimed that he heard no talk of his story during the long serialization. Perhaps his literary confidants were less likely to follow a weekly serial, or perhaps Winny's death discouraged casual literary correspondence. Certainly the serial was massively upstaged by the story of the Johnstown Flood disaster of 31 May 1889, which dominated national media, including the *Weekly*, all summer.

Once the book was published, however, private and public reactions were strongly positive. Henry James gently criticized the title and the apartment-hunting section but praised the novel's window on characters and culture. "The life, the truth, the light, the heat, the breadth & depth & thickness," he told Howells, "are absolutely admirable" (Anesko, p. 275). Henry's brother William James, the eminent Harvard psychologist, praised the book as "damned humane" (Alexander, p. 138), and many others added private and public praise. Howells accepted the compliments with a mixture of hope and self-chastisement that matched his grimly resilient sense of the political, literary, and emotional portent of the moment. In response to praise from reformist author and clergyman Edward Everett Hale, Howells wrote "Praise *is* sweet, and I feel as if I might have been the man to deserve it, though I know I'm not. I am all the time stumbling to my feet from the dirt of such falls through vanity and evil will, and hate, that I can hardly believe in that self that seems to write books which help people" (*Life in Letters* 2:4).

Since then critical evaluations of *A Hazard of New Fortunes* have varied considerably, based largely on readers' desires to situate Howells's fictional subjects, literary theories, economic beliefs, and political effects. Given his prominence, critics often treat Howells as a metonym of some definite intellectual or political position. In the decade following *Hazard*'s publication, it became commonplace to consider Howells a socialist. The "fact" of Howells's socialism, together with his utopian *A Traveler from Altruria* (1894) and other overtly political writings of the early 1890s, colored *Hazard* as a bold text representative of the author's heroic political principles. Similarly, younger authors such as Stephen Crane and Theodore Dreiser credited Howells in a general way with enabling their art. By the time of Howells's death on 11 May 1920, he had been lionized as the "Dean of American Letters," and *Hazard* was used as prime evidence of his venerable literary ability and progressive legacy.

But for modern-minded authors in the early twentieth century Howells made a prominent target as a representative of the genteel literary establishment and the Victorian past. H. L. Mencken ridiculed Howells's work as "elegant and shallow," and Frank Norris labeled it "the drama of a broken teacup" (Crowley, *Dean,* pp. 103, 93). From this perspective Howells's writing was considered to be effeminate, dry, and (in terms of the new Freudian analysis) repressed. This overzealous attack culminated in Sinclair Lewis's 1930 acceptance speech for the Nobel Prize in literature in which he ridiculed Howells as like "a pious old maid whose greatest delight was to have tea at the vicarage" (Crowley, *Dean,* p. 108). Such criticisms seldom mentioned *Hazard* or examined any specific works, preferring instead to slur Howells in general terms as a writer of courtship stories and lifeless domestic fictions.

Both lionization and vilification were exaggerations. Howells has since assumed a significant but secondary place among postbellum American authors, overshadowed by his friends Henry James and Samuel Clemens. Since the middle of the twentieth century, critics of *Hazard* have typically been literary scholars or historians who return for specific evidence of the author's political principles and literary methods—whether to defend them or to criticize them. Defenders have praised the novel's liberal intentions and political observations, and regard it as more or less effective social critique. Detractors have viewed it as representative of self-serving middle class ideals and ideologies. These interpretations question Howells's apparently socialist ideals for failing to confront hard political realities. Often literary interpretations turn on the relationship between characters' perspectives and those of the author. As John Crowley shows, Howells did indeed rely on the "mask of fiction" in complex ways to explore his personal milieu. Sophisticated versions of this criticism examine the largely unintentional psychic and social energies in Howells's texts as revealed through such critical lenses as psychoanalytic theory. Weaker readings simply conflate Howells and his characters, taking a given character's statements as representative of the author's fixed perspective.

Controversies over the function of literary realism still bring readers back to *Hazard* as well, although the terms of the debate are constantly changing. Realism, as Howells conceived it, should be honest, enlightening, and transformative. As Conrad Dryfoos says to Basil March, "If you can make the comfortable people understand how the uncomfortable people live, it will be a very good thing" (p. 147). This view of realism stresses its use as a tool, its moral superiority to romance illusions, and its potential for creating documentary knowledge and political insight. It is also rooted in the individualistic assumption that the author's and reader's individual perceptions are the logical basis for essentially individual political action. By contrast theoretical shifts in literary studies away from authorial intention as the primary focus and toward textual and historical contexts have made *Hazard* important for a later generation of critics interested in systematic ideologies and epistemologies rather than in individual perceptions and beliefs. Amy Kaplan explains that, from the perspective of late-twentieth-century literary theory, realism has changed "from a progressive force exposing the conditions of industrial society" into "a conservative force whose very act of exposure reveals its complicity with structures of power" (Kaplan, p. 1). Kaplan and others thus read *Hazard* for the things that Howells's literary and political paradigms circumscribe or actively exclude. Similarly, scholarly concerns with social class and socioeconomic issues make *Hazard* important for modern scholars. Alan Trachtenberg, for example, reads *Hazard* as the reaction of middle-class "nervous intellectuals" in the face of the social and economic changes of the age of incorporation (p. 185), and Daniel Borus notes that "entering the homes and lives of the poor is a task that the narrator does not attempt" (p. 177). Here again, the essential critical questions concern relationships between literary representations and broader historical and political processes.

A Hazard of New Fortunes, then, has come to be more of a historical artifact than a literary classic. Nonetheless, the fact that the novel can be interpreted in so many and conflicting ways is a sign of its continued intellectual relevance—and of its essential fidelity to the complexities of its originating historical situation.

See also Anarchism; Assimilation; *Harper's New Monthly Magazine;* Haymarket Square; Literary Marketplace; New York; Realism; Socialism; Violence; Wealth

BIBLIOGRAPHY
Primary Works
Howells, William Dean. *Editor's Study.* Edited by James W. Simpson. Troy, N.Y.: Whitston, 1983. In facsimile reproductions all of Howells's "Editor's Study" articles are available online at the William Dean Howells Society website, http://guweb2.gonzaga.edu/faculty/campbell/howells/edstudy.htm.

Howells, William Dean. *A Hazard of New Fortunes.* Edinburgh: David Douglas, 1889. Harper & Brothers, 1890. Reprint with an introduction by Everett Carter. Bloomington: Indiana University Press, 1976. The reprint edition is used for quotations and page references in the current article.

Howells, William Dean. *Life in Letters of William Dean Howells.* 2 vols. Edited by Mildred Howells. Garden City, N.Y.: Doubleday, Doran, 1928. Reprint, New York: Russell & Russell, 1968.

Howells, William Dean. *Selected Letters.* 6 vols. Edited by George Arms et al. Boston: Twayne, 1979–1983.

Secondary Works
Alexander, William. *William Dean Howells: The Realist as Humanist.* New York: Burt Franklin, 1981.

Anesko, Michael. *Letters, Fictions, Lives: Henry James and William Dean Howells.* New York: Oxford University Press, 1997.

Borus, Daniel H. *Howells, James, and Norris in the Mass Market.* Chapel Hill: University of North Carolina Press, 1989.

Cady, Edwin H. *The Realist at War: The Mature Years, 1885–1920, of William Dean Howells.* Syracuse, N.Y.: Syracuse University Press, 1958.

Crowley, John W. *The Dean of American Letters: The Late Career of William Dean Howells.* Amherst: University of Massachusetts Press, 1999.

Crowley, John W. *The Mask of Fiction: Essays on W. D. Howells.* Amherst: University of Massachusetts Press, 1989.

Crowley, John W. "The Unsmiling Aspects of Life: *A Hazard of New Fortunes.*" In *Biographies of Books: The Compositional Histories of Notable American Writings,* edited by James Barbour and Tom Quirk. Columbia: University of Missouri Press, 1996.

Kaplan, Amy. *The Social Construction of American Realism.* Chicago: University of Chicago Press, 1988.

Kirk, Clara Marburg. *W. D. Howells, Traveler from Altruria 1889–1894.* New Brunswick, N.J.: Rutgers University Press, 1962.

Lynn, Kenneth S. *William Dean Howells: An American Life.* New York: Harcourt Brace Jovanovich, 1971.

Rogers, William Allen. *A World Worth While: A Record of "Auld Acquaintance."* New York: Harper & Brothers, 1922. Details Rogers's experience of illustrating the serialization of *A Hazard of New Fortunes* for *Harper's Weekly.*

Trachtenberg, Alan. *The Incorporation of America: Culture and Society in the Gilded Age.* New York: Hill and Wang, 1982.

Gib Prettyman

HEALTH AND MEDICINE

The years 1870–1920 saw profound changes in both cultural perceptions and scientific theories of health and disease as well as in the nature and status of health care practitioners, and these changes were intertwined with larger cultural issues of the time. Americans used literary forms not only to reflect upon but also to negotiate and to intervene in questions of health and medicine and the compelling cultural questions of the day.

PERCEPTIONS OF HEALTH AND ILLNESS
Cultural views of illness underwent a gradual shift during this period. In the nineteenth century, disease etiologies were sometimes uncertain and illness was often romanticized. Ailments were seen to come about when the balance among mind, body, and environment went awry. In many cases, sickliness was considered to be the result of a delicate constitution and good breeding, and it was fashionable to have a frail and nervous nature. With the advent of the germ theory of disease and general improvements in scientific knowledge about human physiology and disease causation, illness lost this mystique. "Tuberculosis," writes Diane Price Herndl, "lost much of its exotic appeal when it was proven to be the result of a bacillus, not an artistic or spiritual temperament" (p. 157). Whereas invalids had previously elicited sympathy and even admiration, they came instead to inspire pity and contempt.

PATENT MEDICINES

The rise of the medical profession was threatened by the makers of patent medicines—drugs sold through advertisements in the popular press, often accompanied by health advice and medical guides, whose secret formulas were dubious at best. Marketers of patent medicines capitalized on popular resistance to medical professionalization; for example, Lydia Pinkham's Vegetable Compound, launched in 1876, advocated self-cure with the nostrum as an alternative to the risks of surgery and the perceived impropriety, for women, of revealing medical details to a male stranger. Such drugs were part of the new consumer culture of the period, in which people were bombarded with advertisements. Patent medicines appeared in fiction of the day to indicate the unreliable, profligate, or unwise character of their vendors and consumers. Examples include Selah Tarrant in Henry James's *The Bostonians* (1886), a psychic medium who formerly sold patent medicines, and Edith Wharton's Zeena (*Ethan Frome* [1911]), the self-centered invalid whose consumption of such nostrums does nothing to cure her weakness, poverty, and isolation. Patent medicines achieved their greatest success in the last decades of the nineteenth century; yet by 1910, due largely to the muckraking efforts of progressive journalists and allopaths' increased power to regulate and disperse drugs, patent medicines were on the decline. Central to this effort was Samuel Hopkins Adams's tract *The Great American Fraud* (1906), which exposed the fraudulent nature of most patent medicines and their manufacturers. This successful campaign represents some of the best elements of Progressive Era journalism and activism, yet it also went hand in hand with the "retreat of private judgment" (Starr, p. 127) that solidified the allopaths' dominant position in health care, which would only increase throughout the twentieth century.

In addition to scientific causes, this shift has also been attributed to the rise of consumer society and a concomitant transformation of economic metaphors. Nineteenth-century theories of illness posited that the body was a closed system with a limited amount of life-giving nerve force fueling its functions; thus, medical theories stressed the need to conserve one's resources, advice that was often articulated in the terms of capitalist accumulation of capital. With the growth of consumer culture in the Progressive Era, however, came a shift in ways of thinking about the economies of both money and the body. New theories of mental and physical health posited that saved energy would simply be wasted, and that the way to generate energy was precisely to spend it. T. J. Jackson Lears calls this new faith in abundance, which replaced the model of scarcity, America's "therapeutic worldview": people were encouraged to achieve health and success by spending their resources and thereby generating more. "Advertisers of 'cures'—from electric massagers to soaps, patent medicines, and toothpaste—told Americans that they could buy their way to health"; thus, good health became a "consumer product" (Price Herndl, p. 156). Predictably, then, illness came to be associated with failure, poverty, and profligacy.

Ethereal, romanticized invalid heroines such as Beth in Louisa May Alcott's *Little Women* (1868) and Carol in Kate Douglas Wiggin's "The Birds' Christmas Carol" (1887) therefore gave way after the turn of the century to sufferers whose illnesses were more problematic. The excessively artful death of Edith Wharton's Lily Bart (*The House of Mirth* [1905]), for example, is more an indictment than a celebration of idealized invalidism; and in her 1911 novel *Ethan Frome*, Wharton associates illness with poverty, laziness, and decay. Henry James approaches the shift in cultural perceptions of illness differently, refusing to identify the specific cause of Milly Theale's malady in *The Wings of the Dove* (1902). While some have read this as indicative of James's resistance to the new, more somatic view of illness, others have argued that the gesture allows James to preserve his invalid's romanticism and attractiveness to readers at a time when such a role would otherwise have lost its cachet.

THE RISE OF THE MEDICAL PROFESSION

The advances in bacteriology, therapeutic innovations, and new scientific technologies that so changed cultural perceptions of illness at the century's turn also contributed to a shift in physicians' status. The increasing complexity of scientific information led to specialization, making medical knowledge less accessible to the layperson. In the last three decades of the nineteenth century, "the social distance between doctor and patient increased, while the distance among colleagues diminished as the profession became more cohesive and uniform" (Starr, p. 81). Medical education and certification became increasingly elite and institutionalized, causing a "strengthening of professional status and a consolidation of professional authority" among physicians (Starr, p. 81). A rising empiricism among physicians (paralleled by the style and subject matter of literary realism) helped to solidify their advantage as the keepers of specialized knowledge. These developments in medicine were but one aspect of a general trend toward professionalization in the second half of the nineteenth century, fueled in part by the rise of the middle class, increased access to education, and social tensions around class, gender, and race issues. The professionalization of medicine was shaped by such tensions, for it aimed to solidify the dominance of orthodox practitioners over lay healers, women, nonwhites, and non-Protestants seeking medical careers and the accompanying privileges, status, and legitimacy.

Throughout the late nineteenth century, therefore, those seeking to professionalize medicine struggled not only to command deference from patients but also to fend off competition from various rivals. Many patients still preferred the familiar model of the family doctor, whose appeal derived not from his or her specialized medical knowledge but from his or her perceived strength of character and his or her social equality with those he or she treated; patients tended to distrust the new model of physician and accepted it only gradually. A case in point is *Margaret Fleming,* James A. Herne's play from 1890, which presents an idealized physician of the old school who is the social equal of his patients and treats them in a familiar, holistic manner. In contrast, Dr. Caldwell Sawyer in Charles Hoyt's play *A Temperance Town* (1892) is unconcerned with his patients' welfare, venal and corrupt, and interested only in financial gain. Both works express resistance to and anxiety about the new model of physician as professional authority that came to the fore in the late nineteenth century.

The rise of the medical profession was similarly complicated by conflict within the field over therapeutic philosophy, which was anything but homogeneous. Allopathy (which became the dominant treatment approach, endorsed by the American Medical Association and populated largely by white men of the middle and upper classes) had competed throughout the nineteenth century with other practices, which allopaths dubbed "irregular," such as hydropathy, eclecticism, mind cure, and especially homeopathy. Homeopathy is based on the principle that a condition can be cured by inducing identical symptoms in the body through prescribing minuscule amounts of substances, while allopathy treats a disease by combating its symptoms, using stronger remedies to induce the opposite condition in the body. As allopathy became institutionalized through education and certification systems and therefore came to be recognized as "legitimate" by governmental enti-

ties, non-allopaths were increasingly pushed to the margins of medical practice. Yet allopaths' struggle for popular legitimacy and economic success was certainly ongoing through the turn of the century, and resistance to their ascendancy was often dramatized in literary works such as Herne's play *Shore Acres* (1892), which presents a heroic homeopathic physician, Dr. Warren, in contrast to the moneygrubbing allopath Dr. Leonard. Elizabeth Stuart Phelps, too, chose to make her title character in *Doctor Zay* (1882) an idealized homeopath.

While writers dramatized many issues related to medical professionalization, however, none received more attention than the struggles of women physicians. Having made a brief appearance in works such as Harriet Beecher Stowe's *My Wife and I* (1871), Phelps's "Our Little Woman" (1872), and Mark Twain and Charles Dudley Warner's *The Gilded Age* (1873), the figure of the woman physician rose to the stature of protagonist in three novels of the 1880s: *Doctor Breen's Practice* (1881) by William Dean Howells, *Doctor Zay* (1882) by Phelps, and *A Country Doctor* (1884) by Sarah Orne Jewett; she also made a significant appearance in James's *The Bostonians* (1886). Not surprisingly, this dramatic increase in literary representations of women physicians occurred precisely at a time when women were demanding, and achieving, entry into medical education and practice, as well as into higher education and the professions more generally. The fictional woman physician provided a vehicle for exploring and negotiating the challenges that professional women posed to traditional notions of gender; the most popular issue in such texts, the conflict between marriage and career, was a metaphor for changes in gender relations. Writers would continue to articulate their hopes and anxieties about professional women through the fictional woman physician in the decades to come, in works such as S. Weir Mitchell's *Characteristics* (1892), Annie Nathan Meyer's *Helen Brent, M.D.* (1892), Hamlin Garland's *Rose of Dutcher's Cooly* (1895), the 1897 collection *Daughters of Aesculapius* (whose authors were associated with the Woman's Medical College of Pennsylvania), and Charlotte Perkins Gilman's 1911 novel *The Crux.* Although the proportion of women physicians peaked at 6 percent nationally in 1910, the backlash by the male-dominated medical establishment, which curtailed opportunities for women and other non-elite practitioners, was already under way. Commissioned by the American Medical Association, the Flexner Report of 1910 called for a series of "reforms" that had the effect of closing the profession to most women, nonwhites, the lower classes, and Jews.

S. Weir Mitchell. A prominent nerve specialist in his time, Mitchell is best remembered as a practitioner of the now controversial rest cure for nervous diseases. © CORBIS

AMERICAN NERVOUSNESS

Of all the health issues receiving attention between 1870 and 1920, perhaps none was so prevalent as the increase in nervous diseases—ailments thought to result from weakness or failure of the nervous system, identified generally as "nervousness" or "nervous prostration" and labeled with technical terms such as "neurasthenia," "neuralgia," and "hysteria." So common were these ailments that they made their way into the American lexicon as a way to conceive and negotiate the cultural issues of the day, particularly those having to do with gender, class, race, and national identity. When the neurologist George Miller Beard (1839–1883) coined the term "neurasthenia" for the medical community in 1869, he meant it literally as "nervelessness," a depletion of the nervous energy or "nerve force" thought to fuel the bodily functions. Beard's *American Nervousness: Its Causes and Consequences* (1881) attributed this "epidemic" to the advances and new demands of modern civilization. The predominant perception was that nervousness marked its sufferers as sensitive and refined, possessing superior, more highly evolved constitutions;

Beard therefore claimed that the disease mainly struck the urban elite and professional classes. In fact, the diagnosis of nervousness would be made across divisions of class, race, and region, yet it was often articulated, understood, and treated differently according to the social position of the patient.

Americans used the language of nervousness to articulate late-nineteenth-century anxieties about gender roles, class status, race relations, and many other issues, all of which found expression in imaginative literature. Of particular interest to scholars were the ways that diagnoses and treatments for nervousness were bound up with changing notions of gender. For example, the physician Edward H. Clarke's (1820–1877) *Sex in Education; or, A Fair Chance for the Girls* (1873) cautioned that women's pursuit of education and intellectual stimulation was unhealthy and urged them to embrace childbearing as their biological destiny. While he represented the orthodox view, Clarke was answered in 1874 by Julia Ward Howe, whose edited volume *Sex and Education: A Reply to Dr. E. H. Clarke's "Sex in Education"* included the work of many physicians, writers, and other public figures who contradicted his claims. The medical establishment did, however, hold that nervous women fell ill because of excessive mental exertion or the pursuit of activities beyond their prescribed sphere. One of the best-known treatments proposed for such women was the "rest cure" popularized by the neurologist S. Weir Mitchell (1829–1914). While the cure had its proponents among women, many saw its encouragement of passivity and submissiveness to male authority, and its discouragement of intellectual stimulation, as punitive and retrograde.

Theories of, treatments for, and invocations of nervousness among women frequently appeared in literature of the day, serving as a means to explore these changing notions of feminine roles. Certainly, authors addressed the rest cure itself and the rest cure doctor—in positive portrayals, such as Emma Wolf's 1892 novel *Other Things Being Equal,* and in biting indictments, the most famous being Charlotte Perkins Gilman's tale from the same year, "The Yellow Wall-Paper," in which a woman is driven mad by the treatment and its underlying ideology. Cultural anxieties about women's resistance to the cure and its vision of proper womanhood often manifested themselves in domineering and self-indulgent rest cure patients, as, for example, with Ruth McEnery Stuart's *The Cocoon: A Rest-Cure Comedy* (1915), Gertrude E. Jennings's one-act play *A Rest Cure* (1914), and William B. Maxwell's *The Rest Cure, a Novel* (1910). More generally, Mary E. Wilkins Freeman had women's dissatisfaction with their roles in mind when she also incorporated the topic of nervousness into *Six Trees* (1903), and Gilman's critique of Victorian gender relations has become a classic portrayal of the woman invalid. For their part, doctors often viewed nervous women—particularly hysterical women—with hostility, suspecting that they were using illness to avoid role expectations or that they were malingerers. Thus, one has works such as William Dean Howells's *Letters Home* (1903) and S. Weir Mitchell's *Roland Blake* (1886). Beyond the general antipathy toward women invalids, however, the late nineteenth century saw writers use illness and nervousness specifically to criticize so-called new women; examples include James's *Daisy Miller* (1878) and Mitchell's *Characteristics* (1891) and *A Comedy of Conscience* (1901). Yet Kate Chopin (1851–1904) famously argued against the "new woman" being pathologized in *The Awakening* (1899), in which it is the heroine's old-fashioned husband who sees her behavior as sick and the family physician, Dr. Mandelet, who is sympathetic toward the heroine and understands her plight.

Just as American womanhood was negotiated through the language of nervousness, however, so, too, was American manhood. Physicians such as Mitchell lamented the rising incidence of nervousness among middle-class white men in works such as *Wear and Tear; or, Hints for the Overworked* (first published in 1871). Worried that this nervousness and the idle, feminized existence that it necessitated was a sign of excessive civilization, Mitchell and others turned to working-class men and men of color as models of more vigorous, "primitive" masculinity and prescribed activities associated with the strenuous life as a treatment for male nervousness.

This concern with the physical and psychic rejuvenation of American manhood was dramatized frequently in the literature of the day, which featured the rise of the western and the increased popularity of martial themes and historical romance—"not the romance of encrusted convention and pale idealism, but the romance of fierce emotions and manly actions" found in stories of knighthood and heroic militarism (Lears, p. 104). A notable example is Owen Wister's seminal western *The Virginian* (1902), in which he fictionalized his own medical treatment for nervousness. Prescribed a visit to a Wyoming cattle ranch by Dr. Mitchell, Wister regained his masculine vitality by emulating the hunting and cow-punching prowess of western men; this then became the basis for his western plot, which transplanted the medieval knight onto the western plains. Others, such as Hamlin Garland, wrote accounts of this "West cure" in works such as *Hesper* (1903) and populated the West with nervous male protagonists (as in Garland's 1891

collection *Main-Travelled Roads*). (It is worth noting that such stories had feminine counterparts: for example, Charlotte Perkins Gilman appropriated the West cure for women both in her novel *The Crux* and in her 1915 short story "Dr. Clair's Place.") Beyond the West specifically, Theodore Dreiser dramatized his own "exercise cure" (Lutz, p. 45) in *An Amateur Laborer* (published posthumously in 1983), and even Frank Norris's *The Pit* (1903) uses the medical paradigm to explore competing models of manliness.

RACE SCIENCE AND RACE RELATIONS

Complementing such explorations of gender between 1870 and 1920 were medical theories of race science and miscegenation—theories that were both articulated and criticized by literary writers. Giving voice to the post-Reconstruction backlash against African Americans' claims to freedom, citizenship, and full participation in American society, such theories labeled blackness bestial and inferior and mulatta and mulatto identity "tainted," racially degenerate and impure. In such a climate, fears among white supremacists about the increasing pluralism in American society found expression in paranoia about racial mixing, or miscegenation, and warned against its purportedly negative health effects. For example, William Benjamin Smith's *The Color Line: A Brief in Behalf of the Unborn* (1905) used popular pseudoscience to decry racial mixing as a danger to the health of the white race. Similarly, the physician Josiah Clark Nott propounded his theory of hybrid degeneration, which argued that racial mixing was deleterious for both blacks and whites. Nott's theories found expression in popular racist books, such as Thomas Dixon's *The Leopard's Spots* (1902) and *The Clansman* (1905) and Robert Lee Durham's *Call of the South* (1908).

Many African American writers from this period, however, sought to undermine such racism and its medico-scientific bases precisely by invoking health and medicine themselves, infusing their work with the explicitly political aim of recognizing African Americans as valuable and worthy citizens in a multiracial society. While in her novel *Of One Blood* (1903) Pauline Elizabeth Hopkins invokes the medical angle in order to suggest the sickly, tragic state of mulattoes in America, using the issue of "blood" in multiple ways to indict American race relations at the turn of the century, others critiqued racial inequalities with more optimistic visions of black and mulatta and mulatto characters. Hence, for example, Frances Ellen Watkins Harper's *Iola Leroy; or, Shadows Uplifted* (1892) subverts racist medico-scientific portrayals of black women as lascivious and degraded; Harper also puts the pernicious antimiscegenation and white supremacist arguments in the mouth of a racist southern doctor whose theories of racial degeneracy are debunked by a mulatto physician. In his *Marrow of Tradition* (1901), Charles Waddell Chesnutt in fact turns antimiscegenation theory on its head by locating sickliness, corruption, and degeneracy not in his mulatto characters but in those with "pure" blood.

More specifically, some authors undermined such medico-scientific arguments through portrayals of African American healers. A common convention in literature of the day, for example, was the pairing of a beautiful mulatta heroine with a mulatto physician. In *Iola Leroy*, the successful courtship functions as a healing force in the book and is imbued with "a scientific aura of legitimacy" in opposition to "medical horror stories about hybridization and its consequences" (Davis, p. 164). Such a pairing similarly appears in works such as Amelia Johnson's (b. 1859) *Clarence and Corrine* (1890) and Chesnutt's *Marrow of Tradition*. For Chesnutt, the mulatto physician is a healing influence for both blacks and whites. Additionally, the mixed-blood physician himself undermines the objectification of the black body that was so common during this period: usually the "object of 'scientific' study," he is now himself the scientist (Davis, p. 164). Similarly subversive were narratives that offered positive portrayals of African American women nurses. Whether in fiction, as in *Iola Leroy*, or nonfiction, such as Susie King Taylor's *Reminiscences of My Life in Camp with the 33rd U.S. Colored Troops* (a 1902 memoir of her nursing service during the Civil War), such texts posited the black woman nurse as a positive force for healing and for social and racial regeneration.

PUBLIC HEALTH AND THE AMERICAN BODY POLITIC

While scientists, writers, and others concerned themselves with the vagaries of disease on individual bodies, of equal concern was the well-being of American society as a whole. New scientific discoveries about disease causation dovetailed with anxieties about race, gender, and class issues more generally to influence the ways people thought about the vulnerabilities of both the individual body and the "body politic" and often were negotiated in public health policy as well as in literary venues. One discovery that had a great influence on social policy was the germ theory of disease, first propounded in 1882 by the German bacteriologist Robert Koch. While it would take several decades for this theory completely to supplant earlier notions of disease causation, it did have a growing effect upon the ways that both scientists and laypersons conceived

of health and illness. "As pathologists focused on the cell as the locus of disease and on the microbe as its cause, the blame for diseases shifted from physical environments to the people who inhabited them," and the resulting theories and social policies reflected "both scientific fears of infection and nationalistic fears of infiltration" (Otis, pp. 8, 6–7). Thus developed a growing fear and contempt of the poor, the sickly, and the unclean, and increased anxiety over immigration, the rates of which rose sharply in the last decades of the nineteenth century. Like poverty, immigration therefore became linked with the threat of illness and disability to both the individual and social bodies, and public health policies were developed to combat the perceived problem.

While this anxiety about disease applied to immigrants and the poor generally, immigrants from China were especially reviled. Envisioned as the "yellow peril"—as sick and sickening trespassers who would imperil not only the health of Americans' individual bodies but also the well-being of the body politic—they were characterized as having "putrid flesh, poisoned blood, leprous bodies and leprous souls" (Kraut, p. 83). Such disease imagery inspired an explosion of "yellow peril" narratives ranging from fiction to pseudo-journalism to public health and immigration policies. Complementing the restrictive Chinese Exclusion Act of 1882 and the intrusive medical examinations of Chinese immigrants at points of entry were dystopic works, such as Pierton W. Dooner's 1880 novel *Last Days of the Republic*, in which the United States is vanquished by an insidious, secret Chinese invasion. The rhetoric of the novel echoes new theories of disease causation in which invisible microbes infect the body unseen. Similarly, Jack London invokes the "yellow peril" in "The Unparalleled Invasion" of 1910—but in this case, a burgeoning Chinese population is prevented from taking over the world by an American scientist who uses China's own tactics against it, exterminating the Chinese through germs he has developed in secret. Countering the common perception that the Chinese were invisible invaders who threatened Americans' health and their exclusion from American territory and identity was the work of writers such as Sui Sin Far (also known as Edith Maude Eaton). A champion of the Chinese, she reversed the narrative of illness transmission common in anti-immigration literature. In her story "Its Wavering Image" (1912), for example, it is the white journalist who infiltrates Chinatown and, through stealth and duplicity, betrays it, bringing illness and disease.

Just as Americans' anxieties about immigration found expression in both public health policy and literary venues, so, too, did their concerns about sexually transmitted disease and healthy "breeding," which were similarly understood to have implications for both the individual and social bodies. Sexually transmitted disease was considered a growing public health problem at the turn of the century, particularly because scientists were slow to develop tests and treatments for it. It was not only doctors and common folk who worried over this health issue; eugenicists (those who advocated controlling heredity through selective human breeding) also held that such diseases contributed to a decline in the quality of human "stock." Public health policies, such as mandatory reporting of cases of sexually transmitted disease and disease screening as a prerequisite for marriage, thus often undergirded elitist notions of American identity and of the social body advanced under the guise of social reform. One such reformer was Prince A. Morrow, a eugenicist and a leading figure in the struggle to eradicate sexually transmitted disease as well as the author of *Social Diseases and Marriage* (1904). While some authors were reluctant to address such diseases explicitly in their work (see, for example, William Dean Howells's *The Son of Royal Langbrith* of 1904, which uses neurasthenia as a euphemism for syphilis), many joined public figures such as Morrow in dealing with the issue directly. An early example is Dio Lewis, whose *Chastity; or, Our Secret Sins* (1874) traced the tragic effects of a man's refusal to tell his wife of his infection. Later works would include James Oppenheim's 1910 novel *Wild Oats*, Charlotte Perkins Gilman's 1911 novel *The Crux*, and Eugène Brieux's play *Les Avariés* (1901), which was novelized for American audiences by Upton Sinclair as *Damaged Goods* (1913). Gilman also treated various aspects of the issue in her short fiction, including "Wild Oats and Tame Wheat" (1913) and "The Vintage" (1916). A common issue raised by writers was the damaging effects, particularly on women, of the silence and ignorance about such disease; yet such fictions also served as part of a larger argument about the need to regulate sexuality and marriage among the "unfit" to ensure a healthy body politic.

Health and medicine were thus rich areas of inquiry in the late-nineteenth and early-twentieth-century United States, for they provided a language with which writers could explore the nature and boundaries of American identity and negotiate the dynamic relationships among groups and individuals.

See also Diseases and Epidemics; Pseudoscience; Science and Technology; Sex Education

BIBLIOGRAPHY

Secondary Works

Brandt, Alan M. *No Magic Bullet: A Social History of Venereal Disease in the United States since 1880.* New York: Oxford University Press, 1985.

Browner, Stephanie. *Profound Science and Elegant Literature: Imagining Doctors in Nineteenth Century America.* Philadelphia: University of Pennsylvania Press, 2005.

Davis, Cynthia J. *Bodily and Narrative Forms: The Influence of Medicine on American Literature, 1845–1915.* Stanford, Calif.: Stanford University Press, 2000.

Kahane, Claire. *Passions of the Voice: Hysteria, Narrative, and the Figure of the Speaking Woman, 1850–1915.* Baltimore: Johns Hopkins University Press, 1995.

Kevles, Daniel J. *In the Name of Eugenics: Genetics and the Uses of Human Heredity.* New York: Knopf, 1984.

Kraut, Alan. *Silent Travelers: Germs, Genes, and the "Immigrant Menace."* New York: Basic Books, 1994.

Lears, T. J. Jackson. *No Place of Grace: Antimodernism and the Transformation of American Culture, 1880–1920.* Chicago: University of Chicago Press, 1994.

Lutz, Tom. *American Nervousness, 1903: An Anecdotal History.* Ithaca, N.Y.: Cornell University Press, 1991.

Morantz-Sanchez, Regina Markell. *Sympathy and Science: Women Physicians in American Medicine.* New York: Oxford University Press, 1985.

Otis, Laura. *Membranes: Metaphors of Invasion in Nineteenth-Century Literature, Science, and Politics.* Baltimore: Johns Hopkins University Press, 1999.

Price Herndl, Diane. *Invalid Women: Figuring Feminine Illness in American Fiction and Culture, 1840–1940.* Chapel Hill: University of North Carolina Press, 1993.

Rothfield, Lawrence. *Vital Signs: Medical Realism in Nineteenth-Century Fiction.* Princeton, N.J.: Princeton University Press, 1992.

Sicherman, Barbara. "The Uses of a Diagnosis: Doctors, Patients, and Neurasthenia." In *Sickness and Health in America: Readings in the History of Medicine and Public Health,* edited by Judith Walzer Leavitt and Ronald L. Numbers, pp. 25–38. Madison: University of Wisconsin Press, 1978.

Smith-Rosenberg, Carroll. *Disorderly Conduct: Visions of Gender in Victorian America.* New York: Oxford University Press, 1986.

Stage, Sarah. *Female Complaints: Lydia Pinkham and the Business of Women's Medicine.* New York: Norton, 1979.

Starr, Paul. *The Social Transformation of American Medicine: The Rise of a Sovereign Profession and the Making of a Vast Industry.* New York: Basic Books, 1982.

Jennifer S. Tuttle

HISTORICAL ROMANCE

The finest historical romances seamlessly blend history and novelistic fiction, satisfying both one's educated interest in reconstructions of past events and ways of life and one's fascination with fictional adventures in regions of place and mind rarely represented in the historical record. In *The Scarlet Letter: A Romance* (1850) by Nathaniel Hawthorne (1804–1864) the Puritan New England context is registered accurately and vividly and shown to be a shaping force that—after one child- and story-engendering act of passion—largely determines how the fictional characters think, feel, and behave even when most alienated and rebellious. Hawthorne's masterpiece also exhibits the characteristics that Richard Chase finds in the romance novels that, so he argues, form America's great novel tradition: narrow but deep moral and metaphysical vision, complex narrative artistry, focus on the individual's rather than society's problems, moments of gothic melodrama, and the obliquities of irony, myth, symbol, and allegory.

Chase contrasts the American novel tradition with its parent, the British novel tradition, which is more centrally concerned with the problems of society, approaches them more directly and prosaically, and achieves more harmonious resolutions. Debatable though this sharp contrast between the two novel traditions is, the broad distinction that Chase draws between two kinds of novel—the one sometimes called a "romance," the other nearly always a "novel"— is one that had many distinguished earlier adherents. Hawthorne insisted on this sometimes confusing terminological distinction because he sought to achieve something different generically in *The Scarlet Letter* than would, say, Leo Tolstoy in *War and Peace* (1865–1872), arguably the greatest nineteenth-century historical novel. Both works are profoundly historical, but Tolstoy's masses realistic detail and portrays the life of society with a plenitude that characterizes the novel at its most novelistic.

CLASSICS AND BEST-SELLERS

The generic profile traced in Chase's still-controversial *The American Novel and Its Tradition* (1957) only begins to comprehend the richness and variety of voices that constitute much of the greatness of the American novel tradition. His canonical texts include none by a woman or ethnic minority author. Neither is his résumé of the romance elements in American fiction at all adequate. Still, the works he chooses would appear on most critics' touchstone list of classic American novels. Some, like William Faulkner's *The Sound and the Fury* (1929), are "historical" only in the important sense that they register how the past goes on shaping or misshaping the

---

BEST-SELLING AMERICAN HISTORICAL ROMANCES, 1870–1920: A SELECT LIST

Mark Twain, *The Adventures of Tom Sawyer* (1876)

Lew Wallace, *Ben-Hur* (1880)

Helen Hunt Jackson, *Ramona* (1884)

Mark Twain, *Adventures of Huckleberry Finn* (1885)

Amelia Barr, *The Bow of Orange Ribbon* (1886)

Mark Twain, *A Connecticut Yankee in King Arthur's Court* (1889)

Lew Wallace, *The Prince of India* (1893)

Stephen Crane, *The Red Badge of Courage* (1895)

James Lane Allen, *The Choir Invisible* (1897)

F. Marion Crawford, *Via Crucis* (1898)

Charles Major, *When Knighthood Was in Flower* (1898)

S. Weir Mitchell, *Hugh Wynne, Free Quaker* (1897)

Winston Churchill, *Richard Carvel* (1899)

Paul Leicester Ford, *Janice Meredith* (1899)

Irving Bacheller, *Eben Holden: A Tale of the North Country* (1900)

Winston Churchill, *The Crisis* (1900)

F. Marion Crawford, *In the Palace of the King* (1900)

Mary Johnston, *To Have and to Hold* (1900)

Maurice Thompson, *Alice of Old Vincennes* (1900)

Gertrude Atherton, *The Conqueror* (1902)

Charles Major, *Dorothy Vernon of Haddon Hall* (1902)

Owen Wister, *The Virginian* (1902)

John Fox Jr., *The Little Shepherd of Kingdom Come* (1903)

Winston Churchill, *The Crossing* (1904)

John Fox Jr., *The Trail of the Lonesome Pine* (1908)

---

present. But others have main actions firmly placed in periods before the time of writing: James Fenimore Cooper's *The Prairie* (1828), Mark Twain's *Adventures of Huckleberry Finn* (1885), Herman Melville's *Billy Budd, Sailor* (1891), Stephen Crane's *The Red Badge of Courage* (1895), and Faulkner's *The Bear* (1942). Edith Wharton's *Ethan Frome* (1911) and Willa Cather's *My Ántonia* (1918) are examples of other historical romances that, although ignored by Chase, are assured classics of American literature. More recent contenders would be Maxine Hong Kingston's *China Men* (1980) and Toni Morrison's *Beloved* (1987), which promise to be read long after most other best-sellers are forgotten.

The combination of critical esteem and popularity that greeted *China Men* and *Beloved* might seem unusual. But most works mentioned above sold well when first published. For the American reading public has never been able to get enough of historical romances—long or short, crudely or finely wrought, imported or domestic. In the early 1800s it was wild about Sir Walter Scott's romances. At century's end, a high point in the popularity of historical romances, Polish Henryk Sienkiewicz's *Quo Vadis* (1896) outsold its American competitors. But so huge was the market that many American historical romancers also shared the wealth. While some were literary artists with an elevated sense of vocation and achievement, others saw themselves as primarily "public amusers." In *The Novel: What It Is* (1893), the historical romancer F. Marion Crawford speaks for many of his fellows when he says that novels are "commodities and subject to the same laws . . . as other articles of manufacture" (p. 12). He likewise speaks prophetically for the Hollywood producers whose movie versions have engineered a second coming, even more lucrative than the first, of such spellbinders as Cooper's *The Last of the Mohicans: A Tale of 1757* (1826), Lew Wallace's *Ben-Hur* (1880), and Margaret Mitchell's *Gone with the Wind* (1936).

If these all-time best-sellers answer more closely to Crawford's than to Chase's idea of the American romance novel, they are still impressively crafted narratives. And both Wallace and Mitchell made good-faith efforts to create historically accurate pictures of, respectively, Judea under Roman rule around the time of the Crucifixion and Atlanta, Georgia, shortly before, during, and after the Civil War. The specificity of Cooper's subtitle suggests equal care about such basics as the identity of the Native American tribes allied with the British or with their French antagonists in 1757. But his account of them is as inaccurate as his stark oppositions between "bad" and "good" Indians, "light" and "dark" heroines, are stereotypical. Apparently the romancer got the better of the historian.

In America, then, historical romances have yielded a prolific harvest both of best-sellers and classics. To begin to understand why, one needs to know more about the romance form and the circumstances and events in the story of America that have favored this hybrid narrative genre.

ROMANCE

To say that the romancer got the better of the historian in *The Last of the Mohicans* is to recognize that history and romance sometimes tug in different directions. Regarded solely as a romance, Cooper's novel is brilliantly successful, blending features that Chase mentions—especially gothic melodrama—with others that are the stock-in-trade of prenovelistic forms of

romance ranging from first- to third-century A.D. Greek tales of love and adventure to medieval chivalric romances and Shakespeare's romantic comedies. Deriving miscellaneously from yet earlier oral and written sources such as ancient epic and drama, these well-proven devices include disguises, mysterious origins, secret crimes, hidden marks of identity, abductions and captivities, flight-and-pursuit actions, demonic villains and noble heroes, incredible courage and strength and prowess, brotherly bonding, journeys of initiation, love at first sight, faithful and resourceful heroines, true prophecies, supernatural interventions, combat between men or between men and wild beasts, and occasionally interludes of self-mocking farce.

Although no narrative could combine all of these romance modules in a coherent whole, some incorporate remarkably many. When they do, or depend heavily on a few of these ploys, they may fairly be called romances. The arsenal of options available enables romances to vary widely in tone and texture, form and style. But whether they employ features associated at one end of the romance spectrum with epic (as in many American frontier and war novels) or, at the other end, with tales of courtly love (as in Harlequin romances), their common denominator is this: some of the incidents and personalities they represent are regularly, even ritualistically, met in fiction but rarely—and almost never in clusters—in everyday life.

The old romances' formulaic and probability defying features made them a target of ridicule by eighteenth-century English novelists, whose own fiction portrayed contemporary society in accordance with Enlightenment criteria of probability and "nature." These novelists' close representation of motivation and thought processes was a major advance, but many readers felt that something valuable ("wonder," "nobility," "fine fabling") had been lost. Writing in reaction, the Englishman Horace Walpole fashioned an ersatz chivalric romance, *The Castle of Otranto, a Gothic Story* (1764), set in medieval Italy and chock-full of incredible events. Aiming to combine the romance's emphasis on situations and events remote from contemporary life with the novel's psychological realism, Walpole created the first gothic novel—which was also the first romance novel. Although his "period" trappings were mainly atmospheric, Walpole demonstrated a modern awareness of cultural difference by contending that events his own contemporaries regarded as incredible would have been believed in "an age of superstition."

Sir Walter Scott (1771–1832) took the process of novelistic innovation to the next stage. His historical romances are organized around interchanges between cultures that have radically different worldviews. In

Waverley (1814) and *Rob Roy* (1817), an imaginative young Englishman—who resembles Scott's readers—journeys into the untamed early eighteenth-century Scottish Highlands, where the inhabitants still speak Gaelic and belong to a feudal warrior culture. Opportunities for misunderstanding, conflict, and adventure are almost limitless. Although the costumes differ, the protagonist's encounters with "wild" Highland people and nature reenact—as will so many similar ones in American frontier romances—the encounters between the heroes and dragons or "savages" of ancient romance. But Scott maintains realism by grounding his characters' thoughts and actions in a carefully constructed context of historical events, social practices, and beliefs. The subjective dimension contributes as much to the romance as do the disguises, captivities, and battles: for what seems routine to a Highlander often appears extraordinary or even magical to the uninitiated protagonist—and of course to Scott's readers.

James Fenimore Cooper's (1789–1851) *The Spy* (1821), based on an incident in the War of Independence, is the first American novel to follow Scott's example, but in *The Pioneers* (1823), Cooper breaks truly new, distinctively American ground by depicting an agricultural frontier community and introducing the aged hunter Leatherstocking, former Indian scout and spokesman for a way of life and land use opposed to that of the settlers. Based on childhood memories and family records of early Cooperstown, New York, Cooper's reconstruction of the historical context is even richer than Scott's. His romance plot includes disguises, mysterious origins, brotherly bonding, love triumphant, and moments of farce. Sometimes the romance components integrate well with the dominant story of cultural conflict, as when Leatherstocking rescues the heroine from a panther or demonstrates his astonishing skill with a rifle. Often, however, they seem to be present mainly because readers expected a novel to include mystery and a love story.

Later in his career Cooper moved the Leatherstocking novels to the wilderness, where social-historical detail counted for less and the contest between the retreating natives and the advance guard of white "civilization" more plausibly fit the templates of chivalric romance. But the Leatherstocking romances were not to everybody's taste. Hawthorne loathed physical violence and explicitly rejected the model of epic conflict that underwrote the "Indian romances" of Cooper and the South Carolinian William Gilmore Simms, author of *The Yemassee* (1835). In *The Scarlet Letter* moral rather than physical strength, psychological rather than bodily torture, dominate the action. Yet the shift inward allows for traditional romance elements:

Chillingworth's demonism and disguise, the hidden "identifying" mark on Dimmesdale's breast, the mystery of Pearl's origin, the monstrous parody of brotherly bonding between Chillingworth and Dimmesdale, the appearance in the sky that the guilt-ridden beholders construe as the letter "A" and a supernatural sign.

Heirs of a long sequence of innovation in fictional representation, Cooper and Hawthorne between them anticipated most features of style and form in the historical romances written since. Moreover, by the time of their maturity, national development itself had proceeded sufficiently for them to recognize and suggest ways of dealing with its main issues, trends, and "matters."

THE MATTERS OF AMERICAN HISTORICAL ROMANCE

In an 1822 review of *The Spy*, W. H. Gardiner, a lawyer and frequent contributor to the *North American Review*, identified "three great epochs in American history" especially suitable for historical romances: the colonies' early settlement days, the ongoing era of the "Indian wars," and the Revolutionary War period. These approximated the ancient "matters" of epic poetry, such as the story of Troy, whose cultural significance and interest were so inexhaustible that writers could return to them repeatedly. Bearing in mind future developments, Gardiner's "three epochs" can be reformulated as the matters of (1) the frontier, (2) imperial conquest, (3) black chattel slavery and its aftermath, and (4) fratricidal war. Although these categories ignore American-authored romances such as *Ben-Hur* and Twain's *The Prince and the Pauper* (1881) that have nothing directly to do with American history, most important American historical romances fall into one or two of them. And they accommodate works like Melville's "Benito Cereno" (1855) and Twain's *A Connecticut Yankee in King Arthur's Court* (1889) that deal analogically with American regional conflict and slavery.

From *The Pioneers* onward the frontier has attracted fictionalists with epic aspirations and regional loyalties. The Boston of *The Scarlet Letter* is "a little town, on the edge of the Western wilderness," and despite Hawthorne's reservations about Simms's and Cooper's practice, he too occasionally sounds the epic note—as when he says that the Puritan founders "had fortitude and self-reliance, and, in time of difficulty or peril, stood up for the welfare of the state like a line of cliffs against a tempestuous tide" (p. 238). Hawthorne was only the best writer and historian among many who described life in early New England. Indeed, love of *patria*, a profitable market for "local color," and readily adaptable fictional models ensured that each main region would handsomely memorialize its pioneers and certain charismatic individuals—historical or invented—whose stories are associated with them.

Perhaps the most "storied" of these archetypal frontier figures is Daniel Boone, forever associated with the Wilderness Road and the dangerous early phase of Kentucky's settlement. Historical figures of this stature usually make only cameo appearances in the fictional action, as is the case with Boone in *The Prairie;* in James Lane Allen's lyrical pageant of Kentucky's transition from settlement to civilization, *The Choir Invisible* (1897); and in Elizabeth Madox Roberts's powerful narrative of the earlier Revolutionary War era of "the Dark and Bloody Ground," *The Great Meadow* (1930).

Not every state or region was blessed with a founding figure bearing such a mythic aura. Mississippi's Faulkner invented his own in Thomas Sutpen, the flawed hero of *Absalom, Absalom!* (1936), who is driven by the Old South myth of the dynasty-building patriarch. Other mythic figures invoked in Faulkner's historical romance of the rise, decline, and fall of empire include the biblical Absalom and the fabulous gunslinger of the American "western"—himself an ambiguous regional hero who reluctantly employs violence to bring peace to a frontier community. The western's archetypal hero and plot, first crystallized in Owen Wister's *The Virginian* (1902), themselves owed much to the Leatherstocking Tales and (as Cooper's saga itself did) to the Boone legend. More firmly anchored in social history but likewise indebted to earlier romance treatments of frontier experience is Cather's *My Ántonia,* whose heroine epitomizes the immigrants who, overcoming both social prejudice and wild nature, made a garden of Nebraska and reconstituted "the American People."

But one person's hero of the westward movement was another's rapacious invader, and some frontier romances, while conceding that the spread of "civilization" was paid for in Native American blood, contributed to the process by portraying "bad Indians" as satanic and, bad or good, all of them doomed—the "lastness" of the Mohicans extended to the entire race. But others have been better historians as well as better friends of the victims of Manifest Destiny. Based on a Michigan family's actual letters and journals, Janet Lewis's *The Invasion* (1930) is a moving narrative of racial intermarriage, broken treaties, and gradual extinction of the Algonquin people. Helen Hunt Jackson's best-seller, *Ramona* (1884), likewise a novel of interracial love and marriage, is concerned nearly as much with Anglo-American dispossession of Mexican landholders in post–Civil War California as with the plight of the native Californians. Author as well of *A Century of Dishonor* (1881), a history

of the U.S. government's bad faith in its dealings with Native Americans, Jackson hoped that *Ramona* would do for them what Harriet Beecher Stowe (1811–1896) had done for black slaves in the nineteenth century's best-selling novel.

Stowe's moral and political message in *Uncle Tom's Cabin* (1851–1852) would have been lost if slavery's evils had been presented as other than virulently active and contemporaneous; likewise the African American William Wells Brown's *Clotel; or, The President's Daughter* (1853). But whether they wrote about slavery before or after emancipation, novelists could draw incidents and situations from a group of fugitive slave narratives in which history often seemed to imitate romance. With little stretching of fact, Stowe and Brown and later Twain in *Huckleberry Finn* and *The Tragedy of Pudd'nhead Wilson* (1894) could fashion riveting narratives out of captivity, flight and pursuit, improbable rescues, mysterious origins, and especially disguise. Inevitably these features reappear in portrayals of slavery and its consequences by later African American writers such as Morrison in *Beloved* and Alex Haley in *Roots* (1976). Their perspective and prevailingly somber tone naturally differ from those of Twain who, as a late-nineteenth-century white ironist, was less interested in the sufferings of slaves than in the psychology of social prejudice. How important it has been to expose its mechanisms is shown by Thomas Dixon's racist *The Clansman* (1905), a eulogy of the Ku Klux Klan that was further popularized in D. W. Griffith's film adaptation, *The Birth of a Nation* (1915).

Some searching readings of the effects of slavery on southern society, such as *Absalom, Absalom!* and Allen Tate's *The Fathers* (1938), depict these in relation to the Civil War. Their central theme is fratricidal conflict: between soldiers in gray and blue but also between "white" and unacknowledged "black" half brothers. The violence latent in a society rife with miscegenation and denied blood relationships is likewise revealed in George Washington Cable's novel of early-nineteenth-century New Orleans, *The Grandissimes* (1880), but the later, crisis-period settings of Tate's and Faulkner's books give the family conflicts an extra dimension.

Although most Civil War romances written from a southern perspective pay some attention to the master-slave relationship, they often sentimentalize it and perpetuate stereotypes not only of African Americans but also of southern belles and gallant cavaliers. Ellen Glasgow's *The Battle-Ground* (1902), among the most accomplished of many popular Civil War romances written by southern women, challenges these stereotypes, but its treatment of racial and family divisions lacks the depth achieved by Tate and Faulkner.

In Civil War romances written by northerners, race and slavery are usually justifying abstractions that do not figure seriously in the physical or psychological action. Neither do they in *The Red Badge of Courage*, which adheres so closely to the point of view of Crane's self-preoccupied young protagonist that only here and now exist; there is no historical context. Yet veterans of the war testified that it was the first novel to capture the ordinary soldier's experience of battle, and in that special sense it is a truly historical romance. Ernest Hemingway praised Crane's art and surpassed his model in *A Farewell to Arms* (1929), the only historical romance of World War I written by an American that has achieved classic status.

A great struggle of causes and cultures that was continental in scope and touched nearly every American in some way, the Civil War has probably offered more to the historical romancer's imagination than the American Revolution—itself a civil war with fratricidal consequences that were recognized at the outset in *The Spy*. Following Scott's practice, Cooper also set an irresistible precedent for his successors by introducing a major historical figure, George Washington, briefly but tellingly in the fictional action. The public loved this intrusion of history into fiction, fiction into history, which is why Benjamin Franklin and other Revolutionary War notables are (ironically) portrayed in Melville's *Israel Potter* (1854–1855), Washington and John Paul Jones figure in the American novelist Winston Churchill's *Richard Carvel* (1899), George Rogers Clark appears in Maurice Thompson's Revolutionary War romance of the Indiana frontier *Alice of Old Vincennes* (1900), and Boone makes the fleeting bows mentioned earlier.

According to Mark Twain, historical romances have not just been borne on the tide of history but have sometimes altered its course. Referring in *Life on the Mississippi* (1883) to the Civil War and Scott's popular "sham" representations of chivalry in *Ivanhoe* (1819) and *The Talisman* (1825), Twain ventured that "Sir Walter had so large a hand in making Southern character, as it existed before the war, that he is in great measure responsible for the war" (p. 266). Twain provocatively overstates how much life imitated art, but his "wild proposition" points to the important cultural work that historical romancers—great writers and public amusers alike—have performed by awakening an interest in the past, by memorializing or even inventing heroes, by bringing to book the villains (who might have been heroes in earlier treatments), and by exposing and sometimes helping to reconcile the lingering differences of a heterogeneous nation.

See also Best-Sellers; Frontier; History; New South

BIBLIOGRAPHY

Primary Works

Hawthorne, Nathaniel. *The Scarlet Letter.* 1850. Edited by William Charvat et al. Columbus: Ohio State University Press, 1962.

Twain, Mark [Samuel Clemens]. *Life on the Mississippi.* 1883. New York: New American Library, 1961.

Secondary Works

Bell, Michael Davitt. *Hawthorne and the Historical Romance of New England.* Princeton, N.J.: Princeton University Press, 1971.

Budick, Emily Miller. *Engendering Romance: Women Writers and the Hawthorne Tradition 1850–1990.* New Haven, Conn.: Yale University Press, 1994.

Chase, Richard. *The American Novel and Its Tradition.* Garden City, N.Y.: Doubleday, 1957.

Crawford, F. Marion. *The Novel: What It Is.* 1893. Freeport, N.Y.: Books for Libraries Press, 1969.

Dekker, George. *The American Historical Romance.* Cambridge, U.K., and New York: Cambridge University Press, 1987.

Leisy, Ernest. *The American Historical Novel.* Norman: Oklahoma University Press, 1950.

Miller, Perry. "The Romance and the Novel." In *Nature's Nation,* pp. 241–278. Cambridge, Mass.: Harvard University Press, 1967.

Mott, Frank Luther. *Golden Multitudes: The Story of Best Sellers in the United States.* New York: R. R. Bowker, 1947.

Porte, Joel. *The Romance in America: Studies in Cooper, Poe, Hawthorne, Melville, and James.* Middletown, Conn.: Wesleyan University Press, 1969.

Thompson, G. R., and Eric Carl Link. *Neutral Ground: New Traditionalism and the American Romance Controversy.* Baton Rouge: Louisiana State University Press, 1999.

George Dekker

HISTORY

The *Oxford English Dictionary* describes "history" as "a narrative of past events, [an] account, tale, story." Ever since its founding in 1789, the American republic has placed great emphasis on sharing its story with the world. Although historians have never agreed on a single approach to the study of the past, the years from 1870 to 1920 nevertheless witnessed a revolution in how the majority of historians conveyed their message to the American people.

At the onset of the Gilded Age, wealthy New England gentlemen forged multivolume "grand narratives" that had great appeal to the reading public.

"Popular history" lecturers reached equally wide audiences. By the end of the Great War, however, historians had begun to professionalize. An increasing number held advanced degrees and were somehow linked to American colleges and universities. Simultaneously, historians tried to ground their discipline on science, basing their accounts on indisputable, archival facts. Consciously borrowing from the emerging social sciences, advocates of the New History produced scores of specialized monographs in the hope of improving national life. Yet the tradition of the all-encompassing grand narrative did not die. Rather, it slipped from the hands of professional historians to playwrights, historical novelists, and, especially, filmmakers. Thus, the approach and content of "history," as well as the goals of historians, shifted considerably from the 1870s to 1920s.

LITERARY HISTORIANS

By the time of the Philadelphia Centennial celebration of 1876, history ranked as a respected mode of thought, but it barely existed as a separate discipline. Although about seventy local historical societies had cropped up across the land, as late as 1880 there were only eleven full-time history teachers on a university level. The German seminar system of training scholars had just been introduced to Johns Hopkins University in Baltimore, which produced its first history doctorate in 1882. When people spoke of "history" they usually referred to ancient Greece or Rome, the Renaissance, or the Middle Ages, rather than the relatively brief time period of the American Republic.

The four dominant American history writers of the day—George Bancroft, William H. Prescott, John Motley, and Francis Parkman—have been termed "Romantic men of letters." All had forged literary reputations *before* they began to write history, and all were New England gentlemen of independent wealth who considered writing history their "duty" rather than a way to earn a living. Each produced multivolume accounts that seized on overarching narrative themes, usually involving "progress." In their eyes, "history" was a story filled with intense drama. Moreover, they wrote not merely to entertain, even fascinate, their readers; rather, they wrote to convey moral instruction about the nature of politics, war, and human behavior. Like literature, history remained an essential component of an educated person's moral discourse about the world.

For William H. Prescott (1796–1859) and John Motley (1814–1877), the drama of history lay with Europe and Latin America. After graduating from Harvard, Prescott became fascinated with the clash of Spanish and Native American worlds, as shown in *History of the Conquest of Mexico* (1843), and his three-volume *History of the Reign of Philip the Second, King of Spain* (1855–1858). The famed Scottish novelist Sir Walter Scott served as Prescott's model and he is viewed primarily as a literary artist rather than a research scholar. For Motley, the drama hinged on the saga of Holland, and he spent a decade researching his three-volume *The Rise of the Dutch Republic* (1856). Since American publishers remained leery about potential sales of such an arcane subject, he paid for the publication himself. Surprisingly, the set sold fifteen thousand copies in two years and established his reputation, especially abroad, as a literary master.

The historians George Bancroft (1800–1891) and Francis Parkman (1823–1893) remain far better known, both in their day as well as ours. Bancroft's ninety-one-year life spanned virtually the entire nineteenth century. His Harvard education and his fortunate marriage to the wealthy Sarah Dwight enabled him to pursue a career as a Democratic party politician and a scholar. Beginning in 1834 he published the first of what would become the ten-volume *History of the United States*. Bancroft argued that as the American people utilized their republican political system, they reflected the authentic voice of God. One scholar has termed Bancroft's books a "multi-volume sermon."

No armchair historian, Bancroft became deeply involved with contemporary affairs. He gave a memorial address to Congress on Abraham Lincoln, wrote speeches for Andrew Johnson, and in 1867 was selected as America's minister to Germany. While serving there, he met the famed German historian Leopold von Ranke of the University of Berlin, who praised his books as the best ever written from the democratic point of view. Although intended as a compliment, the remark stung. Rather than "the democratic point of view," Bancroft felt that he had deciphered the key to understanding the totality of the American past.

Although the last volume of Bancroft's *History* appeared in 1875, publishers repackaged the set in various formats throughout the century. The public eagerly responded, and George Bancroft is rightly designated the father of American historical writing.

Francis Parkman is the only one of the four literary historians still read. Another New England gentleman, from his Harvard days forward he was known to have had "Indians on the brain." He vowed to write a full account of the French conquest of North America. But before he did, he took a daring trip, from March to October 1846, to Wyoming territory. His account of this venture, *The California and Oregon Trail* (1849), remains his best-known book.

Fortunate that an inheritance relieved him of earning a living, Parkman battled illness all his life: severe eye problems, fierce headaches (probably migraines), insomnia and, eventually, confinement to a wheelchair. During one period he became so incapacitated that he could write only with his eyes closed, producing about six lines a day. He hired people to read to him as well. Given these multiple handicaps, his accomplishments were truly remarkable. He visited Canada at least eight times to walk over the scenes he would later describe. A lapsed Unitarian, he spent time in European monasteries to better increase his understanding of Roman Catholicism, but most of all, he became fascinated by the wilderness of North America.

Francis Parkman began his life's work with *Pioneers of France in the New World* (1865), followed by *The Jesuits in North America* (1867) and *The Discovery of the Great West* (1869). His two-volume *Montcalm and Wolfe* appeared in 1884 and he completed the series with another two-volume study, *A Half Century of Conflict* (1892), the title of which may have also referred to his own physical ailments.

Although his work was based on original research, Parkman blended history with literature. He wrote with a verve that few could duplicate, focusing on climax moments like a dramatist and painting historical characters like a novelist. His account of the deaths of the generals James Wolfe and the marquis de Montcalm at the battle of Quebec in 1759 equaled anything that Hollywood would later produce. Although often criticized for his pro-English, pro-Protestant biases, as well as for ignoring hard economic and demographic data, Parkman had few equals. He also had no successors, although some think that the famed twentieth-century historian Samuel Eliot Morison consciously modeled his own books on Parkman's literary masterpieces.

THE POPULARIZERS

The multivolume studies produced by the Romantic men of letters were not the only way by which late-nineteenth-century Americans learned about the past. This era also served as the heyday of the popular lecturer, and two larger-than-life lecturers, John Lord and John Fiske, introduced history to thousands of hearers.

John Lord is completely forgotten but during his lifetime (1810–1894) he delivered perhaps six thousand lectures on history to a wide variety of northern audiences. In 1883 Harvard president Charles Eliot Norton credited him with doing more than any other person to awaken public interest in the field. In a sense, Lord "invented" the one-hour history lecture and placed it firmly in the historian's bag of tricks.

Born into a well-connected but modest merchant family in Portsmouth, New Hampshire, Lord graduated from Dartmouth College and Andover Theological Seminary. After service as a lecturer for the American Peace Society, plus suffering the embarrassing withdrawal of a proffered appointment at Harvard, Lord devised an extensive history lecture series that he took to various locales. Terming his twenty-five history lectures a "university extension course," he began presenting them to both college audiences and the paying public by the 1870s. These classes became especially popular with upper-middle-class women, and Lord later confessed that he had to learn to speak over the steady clack of knitting needles.

Largely avoiding politics and warfare, Lord's lectures consisted of biographical sketches of such figures as Socrates, Homer, Abraham, St. Augustine, Mohammed (Muhammad), Queen Elizabeth I, and Napoleon, among others. His presentations included a good bit on art and architecture, presumably with slides. Since his audiences were largely women, he included talks on Joan of Arc, Hannah More, and George Eliot (Mary Ann Evans), among others. On the subject of American history, he profiled George Washington, Benjamin Franklin, John Adams, Thomas Jefferson, and "the American idea." Never a researcher, he confessed that he hoped to "present what is true rather than what is new." Eventually he packaged these capsule biographies into an eight-volume set, *Beacon Lights of History*. First published in 1884, the set was reprinted in 1888 and in an English edition in 1921. It sold in the millions.

Lord's approach to history was highly moralistic. He praised or condemned figures of the past according to how they measured up to his sense of virtue. Thus, Queen Elizabeth's shifty diplomatic maneuvers were reluctantly praised because he deemed the fight against Spain a worthy one; George Eliot was condemned because she was a "pagan"; and Catherine the Great was so horrible she was never even mentioned. Without the framework provided by liberal Christianity, Lord confessed, his lectures would have no meaning. During his time, however, John Lord reigned as one of the two greatest American popularizers of history.

The second popularizer, John Fiske (1842–1901), is usually remembered as a proponent of the theory of evolution rather than of history, although at the time he wore both hats with equal aplomb. Born into a middle-class New England family, Fiske was a child prodigy. At age eight he had read over two hundred books; by the time he turned twenty he could read eight languages fluently and ten others—including Sanskrit and Wallachian—partially. He graduated from

Harvard and passed the Massachusetts bar, but his vigorous advocacy of the ideas of Herbert Spencer made him religiously suspect. Like Lord, he was never offered the hoped-for teaching position at his alma mater. In 1872 Harvard president Charles W. Eliot hired him as an assistant librarian, where he stayed for seven years, after which he began a career as an independent writer and lecturer. Since he enjoyed the good life and had six children to support, Fiske spent a good deal of time on the road, traveling from Maine to Oregon, from St. Louis to Richmond. Many of his lectures were later reworked into magazine articles and books.

Fiske is usually recalled today for his two-volume defense of Herbert Spencer's evolutionary views, *Outlines of Cosmic Philosophy* (1874), but after its publication he increasingly turned to American history, which he viewed through the same evolutionary lens. He penned over fifteen historical works that touched on a variety of national themes. *The Discovery of America* (two volumes, 1892) dealt with ancient America and included much on Spanish exploration. This was followed by *Old Virginia and Her Neighbours* (two volumes, 1897), *The Dutch and Quaker Colonies in America* (two volumes, 1899), and *The Mississippi Valley in the Civil War* (1900). As the scholar Lorenzo J. Greene noted in his diary, Fiske "popularized American history by making it read like a novel" (*Working with Carter G. Woodson*, p. 259).

Fiske's *Critical Period of American History 1783–1789* (1888) is still discussed. As the title suggests, Fiske argued that the era during which the Articles of the Confederation were drafted formed a turning point in the history of the Western Hemisphere. The crucial issue was to determine whether the newly formed nation would consist of one large federal republic or fifty small warring states, as had been the model in ancient Greece and medieval Europe. In Fiske's eyes, the establishment of the Constitution showed the working out of "progress" in representative government.

These historical studies were surely sufficient to earn him his coveted position at Harvard, but by the 1880s university critics began to fault him for his lack of serious archival research. In truth, Fiske was always a better presenter than a discoverer of new material. But nothing seemed to dampen his popularity. In the preface to *The Discovery of America*, he warned readers that he had received so many unsolicited letters on his books that he could no longer read them, let alone respond. As eloquent on the lecture platform as he was in print, Fiske merged science, religion, progress, and American history. A 1920 reviewer in the *Nation* observed that philosophers thought of Fiske at his best as a historian, while historians viewed him primarily as a philosopher.

His mingling of these themes, however, helped keep him in the public eye for over a generation.

WOMEN AND MINORITIES

The chief focus of late-nineteenth-century history revolved around the political and military activities of the nation or individual states. The few mentions of women or ethnic minorities were largely subsumed under these narratives. But there were a few women or minority historians. The Kentucky geographer Ellen Churchill Semple (1863–1932) reinterpreted the U.S. past in her *American History and Its Geographic Conditions* (1903). The lone voice on Indian issues came from Annie Heloise Abel (1873–1947). During her career at Goucher and Smith, she published twelve books on Native America, including a three-volume study, *The Slaveholding Indians* (1915–1925). The most able members of this category, however, were Alice Morse Earle, George Washington Williams, W. E. B. Du Bois, and Carter G. Woodson.

Alice Morse Earle (1851–1911) was born in Worcester, Massachusetts, and from her childhood became fascinated with the New England past. Her approach, however, proved far removed from that of her contemporaries. From the publication of her first book *The Sabbath in Puritan New England* (1891) she described the social customs, daily life, and material culture of her region, concentrating, as she put it, on "the everyday life of the times." Although this approach is sometimes dismissed as antiquarianism or "pots and pans" history, her seventeen books and over thirty essays raised it virtually to the level of high art. In addition to widespread sales, Earle became recognized as an expert on early American antiques, and people contacted her from miles around.

Although not professionally trained, Earle did much research in primary documents, even traveling to England to examine materials. Her books were also among the first to address the women's sphere of life: weaving and spinning, meal preparation, attending church, what girls wore, how they managed the household. She also was the first researcher to explore the history of childhood and the family in New England. Because of their pioneering nature, many of her works have been reprinted. Representative titles include *Colonial Dames and Good Wives* (1895); *Child Life in Colonial Days* (1899); and *Home Life in Colonial Days* (1898). Her approach to the past would later be termed "social history."

Although the generation that lived through the American Civil War was well aware of the powerful role that race played in national life, the opportunities for African Americans to write their own past remained few.

The most prominent black historians were George Washington Williams (1849–1891), and, a generation later, W. E. B. Du Bois (1868–1963) and Carter G. Woodson (1875–1950).

Born in Pennsylvania, Williams ran away from home to join the Union Army, where he saw combat. After additional army service, he enrolled at the Newton Theological Institution and began a career as Baptist pastor, newspaper columnist, editor, and lawyer. Moving to Cincinnati, he became the first African American elected to the Ohio legislature, and later, thanks to funding by the railroad magnate Collis P. Huntington, he toured the Belgian Congo and wrote a scathing public report about the treatment of the natives there.

A long-term collector of African American materials, in 1882 Williams published his thousand-page, two-volume *History of the Negro Race from 1619 to 1880: Negroes as Slaves, as Soldiers, and as Citizens.* Seven years later, in 1888, he followed with *A History of the Negro Troops in the War of the Rebellion, 1861–1865.* These were the first books to assess the African American role in U.S. history.

Du Bois became one of the most recognized black scholars of his day. Born in Great Barrington, Massachusetts, Du Bois became the first black to earn a doctorate from Harvard (1895). His dissertation, *The Suppression of the African Slave-Trade to the United States of America, 1638–1870,* became the initial volume in the Harvard Historical Studies series in 1896. He later wrote a brief overview, *The Negro* (1915), but began to edge into sociology in 1899 with his study titled *The Philadelphia Negro.* His last venture into history was *Black Reconstruction* (1935). As editor of the NAACP magazine, *The Crisis,* Du Bois moved gradually into pan-Africanism and, later, an angry Marxism, eventually dying an expatriate. Although a pioneer in African American scholarship, he did not play much of a role in its development during the early twentieth century. That task fell to Carter G. Woodson.

Born in Virginia, Woodson was the second black to receive a doctorate in the field of history. Author of *The Education of the Negro Prior to 1861,* which appeared in 1915, Woodson founded the Association for the Study of Negro Life and History that same year and established the *Journal of Negro History* in 1916. In 1922 he published *The Negro in Our History,* which remained the standard overview until the appearance of John Hope Franklin's *From Slavery to Freedom* (1947, with frequent updatings). In 1928 Woodson began Negro History week—which later became Black History month. He chose February so as to commingle the birthdays of Abraham Lincoln and Frederick Douglass. As the historian Arvarh Strickland has noted, Woodson holds "the undisputed title of the father of Afro-American history" (Greene, p. xxiv).

THE REGIONALISTS

Without question, New England historians dominated the writing of the American past during the late nineteenth century. But that region's "cultural imperialism" did not extend much beyond the 1890s. New voices soon arose to argue that other sections of the nation—the Far West, the Midwest, and the South—were worthy of study as well.

The historian who first insisted that the Spanish Borderlands be included in the national saga was the Ohio-born businessman Hubert Howe Bancroft (1832–1918). After moving to San Francisco to open a bookstore, Bancroft prospered to such an extent that he retired at age thirty-seven to devote himself to collecting documents and writing the story of early California. Over the years he amassed sixty thousand volumes (plus hundreds of documents), which he eventually sold to the University of California, Berkeley.

Drawing on his background as a businessman, Bancroft anticipated both the industrialist Henry Ford and the modern historian Stephen Ambrose by developing an assembly-line technique for writing history. He hired assistants—as many as fifty at a time and perhaps six hundred overall—to research and write an enormous set of books on the history of the American Southwest that would eventually reach thirty-nine volumes. The titles ranged widely. Some examples include: *History of Arizona and New Mexico* (1889); *History of California* (seven volumes, 1884–1890); *History of Nevada, Colorado, and Wyoming* (1890), and so on. Bancroft also did yeoman work in compiling documents relating to old California and he is justly regarded as the founder of Borderlands scholarship.

Ulrich Bonnell Phillips (1877–1934) tried to do for the South what Bancroft had done for the Southwest. Born in Georgia and trained at the state university, he earned his doctorate at Columbia in 1902 with a dissertation titled "Georgia and State Rights." Later he moved to Michigan and Yale where he concentrated on the story of the Old South up to the Civil War. As few historians had explored southern history, Phillips first had to collect the appropriate documents and forge an accurate timeline. He is most famous, or infamous, for his *American Negro Slavery* (1918) and his *Life and Labor in the Old South* (1929). Borrowing from the ideas of economists, Phillips was the first historian to suggest that slavery was, indeed, unprofitable and that the system hurt the overall southern economy. Although he made no attempt to hide his views that blacks were

Frederick Jackson Turner. THE LIBRARY OF CONGRESS

the Midwest, as the cradle of the democratic ethos. But he popularized two other widely accepted concepts as well: first, that each age rewrites the past from the perspective of the crucial issues of the day; and second, that climate, ethnicity, and geography combine to produce different world views and different political responses (now termed "regionalism"). Although criticized for a number of failings—he never produced his "big book"; he ignored women, minorities, and organized religion; and he viewed Indians as "obstacles" to progress—Turner nevertheless ranks with Henry Adams as one of the few historians of his era whose ideas still resonate.

HENRY ADAMS

There is no doubt that Henry Adams (1838–1918) stands at the center of the turn-of-the-century historical world. Born into one of New England's most distinguished families, Adams attended Harvard, served as secretary to his father, Charles Francis Adams, during his term as American minister in Britain in the Civil War, and returned to find himself alienated from contemporary American society.

Although he had no specific training, Harvard invited him to teach medieval history, but he soon tired of that and moved to H Street in Washington, across from the White House, where he became an ironic, independent observer of American life. A genuine polymath, he escaped from the sordid politics of Gilded Age Washington to write a nine-volume *The History of the United States during the Administrations of Thomas Jefferson and James Madison* (1889–1891). These books emphasized the irrational nature of democracy and despaired at the Founding Fathers' inability to match their noble republican dreams with the sordid reality that eventually emerged. His classic description of American life in 1800, in volume one, has never been surpassed. His friend John Hay completed a ten-volume biography, *Abraham Lincoln: A History* (1890), around the same time, and Adams remarked that "between them they had written nearly all the American history there was to write."

Elected president of the American Historical Association, Adams also wrote two essays on the philosophy of history, "The Rule of Phase Applied to History" (1909) and "A Letter to American Teachers of History" (1910), in which he suggested that future historians should draw their analytical frameworks from the sciences, especially physics. To go from George Washington to U. S. Grant, he suggested, reflected not "progress" but a dissipation of energy. It is not clear how serious he was in these suggestions.

intellectually inferior to whites, he emphasized that each group became dependent upon the other and that, although unequals, they developed a strange rapport between them. In 1928 he called attention to the "central theme of Southern history": the political effort to retain white supremacy. Acknowledged as the founder of southern history, Phillips's historical views could be seen in the historical fiction of Thomas Dixon and other white supremacist writers. W. E. B. Du Bois and Carter G. Woodson ranked among his most severe critics.

The most famous regionalist was Frederick Jackson Turner (1861–1932), on whom more words have been written than any other American historian. Born in Portage, Wisconsin, Turner earned a doctorate at Johns Hopkins under Herbert Baxter Adams. Rejecting the then-prevalent idea that the seeds of democracy came from Europe, Turner argued in his famous 1893 speech at the World's Columbian Exposition in Chicago that the continually expanding frontier—where "savagery" and "civilization" constantly intermingled—created American democracy. The official passing of the frontier, as seen in the 1890 federal census, did not bode well for the American nation.

Although Turner's ideas have been applied to South Africa, Russia, and the Far Western frontiers, his main focus rested with the antebellum world, especially

Adams's reputation revolves less around his nine-volume *History* than his two-book attempt to reconcile the human need for order with the chaos he witnessed all around him. His classic *Mont-Saint-Michel and Chartres* (privately printed in 1904) looked back to the twelfth century, where, as he saw it, the force of Love, as represented by the Virgin Mary, united humankind. He explored the later world of chaos in his *The Education of Henry Adams* (1918; first privately printed in 1906), where the Dynamo, which he first saw at the Paris Exposition of 1900, represented the same force but without purpose or morality.

The *Education* was not really an autobiography. Adams skips over much of his life—including the 1885 suicide of his beloved wife, Marian—and hearing a privileged genius constantly whine about "failure" annoys many readers. But the book merged the fields of history, literature, and autobiography in its attempt to understand the world through the use of flexible symbols (the Virgin and the Dynamo). The critic Robert E. Spiller once depicted the *Education* as *the* book that marked the American writer's entrance into the twentieth century. Drawing on symbols rather than "facts," Adams posed cosmic questions that literature, perhaps more than history, seemed best equipped to answer.

THE NEW HISTORY

As the nineteenth century merged into the twentieth, the multivolume overviews began to fade. The businessman James Ford Rhodes's seven-volume *History of the United States from the Compromise of 1850* (1893–1906) and John Bach McMaster's eight-volume *History of the People of the United States* (1883–1913) showed that the genre had not quite expired, but they were the last of a breed. The day of the archive-based, specialized monograph had arrived.

In the introduction to his *Study of History* (1934–1961), the British historian Arnold Toynbee recalled how in the 1890s he watched the books on the shelves of a professor friend shift from general works to "the relentless advance of half a dozen specialized periodicals" (5:2). Subsequent multivolume series would all have multiple authors. The twenty-volume *Dictionary of American Biography* (begun in 1928), for example, drew on two thousand specialists.

Simultaneously with this shift, historians began to professionalize. Led by Herbert Baxter Adams, whom Woodrow Wilson once termed a "captain of industry" for scholarship, a group founded the American Historical Association (AHA) in 1884, with its flagship journal, the *American Historical Review*. Amateur historians continued to play a role until the late 1920s, but the

trend was clear. More and more historians held advanced degrees and were affiliated with colleges or universities.

Simultaneously, the professional emphasis moved away from literature to a fascination with the social sciences (especially anthropology, psychology, sociology, and economics), which, in turn, had all modeled themselves on the physical sciences, particularly biology and physics. The pre–World War I generation could concentrate on "scientific facts" because the world's value systems seemed firmly in place.

In the early years of the century, a group of "New Historians"—especially linked with Columbia and Cornell—set forth a number of agendas. The amateur historian Edward Eggleston had argued in 1900 that history as a scholarly discipline should try to recover the *whole* of a people's culture, not concern itself exclusively with war and politics. But the two foremost exponents of the "New History," James H. Robinson and Charles A. Beard, went even further. History should aid a people in *improving* their cultural life.

Born in Illinois, James H. Robinson (1863–1936) graduated from Harvard and earned a doctorate in Germany. He spent most of his career at Columbia, where his popular class in European intellectual history—nicknamed "the Downfall of Christianity"—enthralled scores of students. Robinson held great faith in the principles of the Enlightenment: He felt humankind was reasonable and that education would free people from an unhealthy reliance on church, state, and class. American citizens could be trusted to make appropriate political decisions. Robinson's *The New History* (1911) and *The Mind in the Making* (1921), which stretched from "our animal heritage" to "the sickness of an acquisitive society" (pp. 65, 71), called on historians to utilize insights from the social sciences not only to better understand the past but also to help bring in a more just social order. The proper purpose of history, he argued, was to enable people to understand themselves and help solve the social problems of the day. Carl Becker, who studied with Robinson, spread these ideas to the next generation from his position at Cornell.

Robinson's colleague at Columbia, Charles A. Beard (1874–1948), emerged as the most prominent spokesman for this group. Born in Indiana in 1874, he later received a doctorate from Columbia. His marriage to his DePauw classmate Mary Ritter (b. 1876) created the most powerful husband-wife duo in the profession. Beard achieved notoriety with his *An Economic Interpretation of the Constitution of the United States* (1913). This classic book argued that the Founding Fathers relied less on Enlightenment ideals of timeless, universal republican truths than on hard economic concerns when they forged the Constitution in 1787. Drawing on research from the Treasury archives, Beard pointed out that most proponents of the Constitution held government securities that would surely rise in value if a strong central government could be put in place. Public outrage was immediate. Critics accused him of writing a muckraking exposé of the Enlightenment generation. Beard denied he was a Marxist—he was simply a follower of James Madison's economic philosophy, he said—and supporters defended him by noting that he offered only "An" economic interpretation (not "The"). But this façade disappeared two years later with his *Economic Origins of Jeffersonian Democracy* (1915), which took a similar line of argument.

In 1917 Beard left Columbia over a dispute regarding loyalty oaths and, with Mary, devoted full time to writing. His economic critique of American life found ready audiences in the 1930s, and his 1933 AHA presidential address, "Written History as an Act of Faith," forms the classic statement that since history is relative, all historians should declare their prejudices at the onset and work for a more democratic society. His 1948 study *President Roosevelt and the Coming of the War, 1941,* where he accused Roosevelt of maneuvering Japan into attacking Pearl Harbor, marked him out as a bit of a crank. Even so, the Beards were probably the most widely read historians of the early twentieth century. As the New History showed, by the World War I era, history had shifted from a bedfellow with literature to a steady companion of the social sciences.

RETURN OF THE GRAND NARRATIVE

But something was lost in this transition. As the grand narrative became replaced by specialized monographs, few citizens grasped a sense of the whole. As scholars at the end of the twentieth century have noted, for a nation to reflect a vital collective memory, it must share an (at least partially) agreed-upon historical past. A people realizes who they are by understanding who they have been. This became especially important for a pluralistic nation, which, thanks to the extensive immigration from Europe and Asia from the Gilded Age to World War I, the United States had truly become. Moreover, in spite of various attempts at professionalization, no historical guild could ever "control" the production of history, and it was not long before others began to present their versions of the grand narrative to the public as well.

Historical themes in theater, fiction, and film began to gain in popularity. Late-nineteenth-century theater groups often seized on such themes, such as the Revolution and the Frontier. The 1831 play *The Lion of the West,* about the life of Davy Crockett, was performed often, and an 1886 stage play based on the Civil War–era classic *Uncle Tom's Cabin* (1852) proved a staple of traveling troupes until the mid-1920s. John Drinkwater's *Abraham Lincoln* (1918) and Robert Sherwood's *Abe Lincoln in Illinois* (1938) continued this emphasis in the interwar period.

Historical fiction was popular, too. Edward Eggleston had fictionalized early frontier life in Indiana with his *The Hoosier Schoolmaster* (1871). John W. De Forest did the same for the South with *Miss Ravenel's Conversion from Secession to Loyalty* (1867), as did Stephen Crane with *The Red Badge of Courage* (1895). Perhaps the classic expression of this genre—long before the advent of popular historical fiction by Kenneth Roberts in the 1930s—lay with Helen Hunt Jackson's romantic view of the Californios, *Ramona* (1884).

From 1900 forward, however, the ideal medium to re-create the grand narrative fell to film. The southern-born director D. W. Griffith's *The Birth of a Nation* (1915) showed well the power of this new medium. Based loosely on Thomas Dixon's novel *The Clansman* (1905), *The Birth of a Nation* presented the white southern view of Reconstruction with intense visual power. In the climactic scene, the Ku Klux Klan, the heroes of this particular version, dip their emblem in the blood of a slain white girl before riding off to dispatch a band of villainous blacks.

Public reaction was immediate. White southern audiences cheered, while the NAACP staged formal protests. Crowds in Boston rioted. President Woodrow Wilson, who watched a private screening in the White House, initially described the movie as "writing history with lightning," although he later deplored the film's role in increasing racial tension.

With this, and the hundreds of historical films that Hollywood would later produce, the power of the broad-sweep narrative largely slipped from the hands of professional scholars to filmmakers. At the turn of the twenty-first century, *Gone with the Wind* (1939) still ranked as the most popular American film ever made. Although *Gone with the Wind* might seem a far cry from George Bancroft's ten-volume *History of the United States* or Francis Parkman's multiple-volume saga of New France, they shared a lot in common. Each provided a fast-paced dramatic "narrative of past events, [an] account, tale, story" that Americans could relate to, positively or negatively, to better understand the complex story of their nation, and, of course, themselves.

See also The Education of Henry Adams; Frontier

BIBLIOGRAPHY

Primary Works

Abel, Annie Heloise. *The Slaveholding Indians.* 3 vols. Cleveland, Ohio: Arthur H. Clark, 1915–1925.

Adams, Henry. *The History of the United States during the Administrations of Thomas Jefferson and James Madison.* 9 vols. New York: Charles Scribner's Sons, 1889–1891.

Bancroft, George. *History of the United States, from the Discovery of the American Continent.* 10 vols. Boston: Little, Brown, 1834–1875.

Bancroft, Hubert Howe. *History of Arizona and New Mexico, 1530–1888.* San Francisco: The History Company, 1890.

Beard, Charles A. *An Economic Interpretation of the Constitution of the United States.* New York: Macmillan, 1913.

Du Bois, W. E. B. *The Suppression of the African Slave-Trade to the United States of America, 1638–1870.* New York: Longmans, Green, 1896.

Earle, Alice Morse. *The Sabbath in Puritan New England.* New York: Charles Scribner's Sons, 1891.

Fiske, John. *The Critical Period of American History, 1783–1789.* Boston and New York: Houghton Mifflin, 1888.

Lord, John. *Beacon Lights of History.* 8 vols. New York: W. H. Wise, 1921.

Parkman, Francis. *A Half-Century of Conflict.* Boston: Little, Brown, 1892.

Phillips, Ulrich B. *American Negro Slavery; A Survey of the Supply, Employment, and Control of Negro Labor as Determined by the Plantation Regime.* New York and London: D. Appleton, 1918.

Robinson, James H. *The Mind in the Making: The Relation of Intelligence to Social Reform.* New York and London: Harper & Brothers, 1921.

Semple, Ellen Churchill. *American History and Its Geographic Conditions.* Boston: Houghton Mifflin, 1903.

Toynbee, Arnold J. *A Study of History.* 12 vols. New York: Oxford University Press, 1934–1962.

Turner, Frederick Jackson. *The Frontier in American History.* New York: H. Holt, 1920.

Williams, George Washington. *History of the Negro Race from 1619 to 1880: Negroes as Slaves, as Soldiers, and as Citizens . . .* New York and London: G. P. Putnam's Sons, 1882.

Woodson, Carter G. *The Education of the Negro Prior to 1861; A History of the Education of the Colored People of the United States from the Beginning of Slavery to the Civil War.* New York and London: G. P. Putnam's Sons, 1915.

Secondary Works

Benson, Lee. *Turner and Beard: American Historical Writing Reconsidered.* Glencoe, Ill.: Free Press, 1960.

Berman, Milton. *John Fiske: The Evolution of a Popularizer.* Cambridge, Mass.: Harvard University Press, 1961.

Billington, Ray Allen. *Frederick Jackson Turner: Historian, Scholar, Teacher.* New York: Oxford University Press, 1973.

Bogue, Allan G. *Frederick Jackson Turner: Strange Roads Going Down.* Norman: University of Oklahoma Press, 1998.

Caughey, John Walton. *Hubert Howe Bancroft: Historian of the West.* New York: Russell and Russell, 1946.

Clark, Harry. *A Venture in History: The Production, Publication, and Sale of the Works of Hubert Howe Bancroft.* Berkeley: University of California Press, 1973.

Fitzpatrick, Ellen. *History's Memory: Writing America's Past, 1880–1980.* Cambridge, Mass.: Harvard University Press, 2002.

Franklin, John Hope. *George Washington Williams: A Biography.* Chicago: University of Chicago Press, 1985.

Gale, Robert L. *Francis Parkman.* New York: Twayne, 1973.

Greene, Lorenzo. *Selling Black History for Carter G. Woodson: A Diary, 1930–1933.* Edited by Arvarh E. Strickland. Columbia: University of Missouri Press, 1996.

Greene, Lorenzo. *Working with Carter G. Woodson, the Father of Black History: A Diary, 1928–1930.* Baton Rouge and London: Louisiana State University Press, 1989.

Harlan, David. *The Degradation of American History.* Chicago: University of Chicago Press, 1997.

Higham, John. *Writing American History: Essays on Modern Scholarship.* Bloomington: Indiana University Press, 1970.

Levin, David. *History as Romantic Art: Bancroft, Prescott, Mottey, and Parkman.* New York: Harcourt Brace and World, 1963.

Loewenberg, Bert James. *American History in American Thought: Christopher Columbus to Henry Adams.* New York: Simon and Schuster, 1972.

Meier, August, and Elliot Rudwick. *Black History and the Historical Profession, 1915–1980.* Urbana: University of Illinois Press, 1986.

Nore, Ellen. *Charles A. Beard: An Intellectual Biography.* Carbondale: Southern Illinois University Press, 1983.

Novick, Peter. *That Noble Dream: The "Objectivity Question" and the American Historical Profession.* Cambridge, U.K.: Cambridge University Press, 1988.

Roberts, Geoffrey, ed. *The History and Narrative Reader.* London and New York, Routledge, 2001.

Strout, Cushing. *The Pragmatic Revolt in American History: Carl Becker and Charles Beard.* New Haven, Conn.: Yale University Press, 1958.

Wish, Harvey. *The American Historian: A Social-Intellectual History of the Writing of the American Past.* New York: Oxford University Press, 1960.

Ferenc M. Szasz

HOMOSEXUALITY

See Same-Sex Love

HOUGHTON MIFFLIN

Throughout the period 1870–1920, Houghton Mifflin Company, including its preceding partnerships, was an influential Boston printing and publishing firm. During the late nineteenth century, the house established by Henry Oscar Houghton was particularly noted for its distinguished list of American writers and its publication of the *Atlantic Monthly*. Its authors, many acquired as eventual successor to Ticknor and Fields or through the *Atlantic*, included most of those associated with the New England renaissance and Indian summer: Ralph Waldo Emerson, Henry David Thoreau, Harriet Beecher Stowe, John Greenleaf Whittier, Oliver Wendell Holmes, James Russell Lowell, Henry Wadsworth Longfellow, Thomas Bailey Aldrich, Sarah Orne Jewett, and John Burroughs. But it also published the earliest works of William Dean Howells, Henry James, F. Marion Crawford, Kate Chopin, and Charles W. Chesnutt. After the turn of the twentieth century, though it did publish early works by Mary Austin, Willa Cather, Jack London, and Amy Lowell among others, its fiction became less distinguished. During this period the firm's lists emphasized somewhat old-fashioned popular novels but maintained high-quality nonfiction and educational texts. Through editorial selection and shaping of its trade publications, through the *Atlantic*'s fiction and literary criticism, and through the formation of canonical tastes by its educational texts, Houghton Mifflin exercised a considerable influence on the writing and reading of American literature during the late nineteenth century and early twentieth century.

HENRY OSCAR HOUGHTON

Henry Oscar Houghton (1823–1895), the principal force shaping the firm, was a spare, bearded Yankee who grew up in rural poverty, the eleventh child of an unsuccessful Vermont tanner. At age thirteen he began an apprenticeship as a printer for the Burlington *Free Press* and subsequently worked his way through the University of Vermont. As an ambitious young man from the provinces, he was attracted to Boston, where he worked as a reporter, compositor, and proofreader. By 1848 he had saved and borrowed from family enough small capital to meet installment payments on the first of many partnerships eventually leading to ownership of the Riverside Press in Cambridge. While Houghton successfully expanded his printing operation to nearly a hundred employees, the sharp recession of the late

Henry Oscar Houghton. Houghton as pictured in *The New England Magazine* 19, no. 2 (1895). GRADUATE LIBRARY, UNIVERSITY OF MICHIGAN

1850s and turmoil of the Civil War created instability in the supply of work. By 1864 Houghton concluded that he could better control the supply, ensure continuous operation, and take advantage of stereotype plates left him by defaulting clients by himself becoming a book publisher as well as a printer.

Many postwar conditions favored expansion of the book trade, including increases in population, public education and literacy rates; a national book distribution system; favorable postal rates; the rise of advertising; and technical advances in stereotyping, electrotyping, and later the rotary press. But there were also dangers, including lack of international copyright, piracy of texts, and a series of steep economic recessions that led to the bankruptcy of many publishers during the period. Houghton Mifflin's survival and steady, gradual expansion were partly due to its founder's character.

Houghton, one model for the title character in William Dean Howells's *The Rise of Silas Lapham* (1885), exemplified characteristic Yankee virtues and at times limitations. He practiced and expected a strong work ethic, including attention to detail and a pride in craftsmanship reflected in his firm's motto: Tout bien ou rien (Excellence or nothing). In book design he advocated simplicity, durability and clarity, counter to the prevailing Victorian taste for ornament. Unlike his competitor and onetime partner, James Osgood, he was financially conservative and deliberate rather than impulsive, avoiding excessive debt or risk as well as flamboyant liberality. But he was also farsighted, willing, for example, to sustain perennial losses on the *Atlantic* because he believed in the long run it brought prestige and authors to the house. He resisted the escalating payments to authors characteristic of the era, but authors considered him a reliable man with whom to do business, and many remained with the house for the long term. Moderately conservative in politics also, he tended to Whig and Republican views, including sound currency and high book tariffs against English imports, but he actively promoted public education as a source of upward mobility and implemented profit sharing in his business. Having himself a stubborn Yankee independence of mind, he respected his employees' right to expressions of opinion. Occasionally capable of rationalizing self-interest as principle, he was also privately generous. A respected and public-minded citizen, he was elected mayor of Cambridge, was appointed to the boards of many civic organizations, and became a leader in the international copyright movement.

Houghton was conscious of building an institution and took pride in sustaining long-term relationships with employees and partners as well as authors. He felt that both author and publisher ultimately profited from loyalty that allowed the publisher to rework and promote the list in various editions and sets. Loyal authors like Holmes, Lowell, and Burroughs were given annuities. Under first Houghton and later Mifflin, employees at all levels tended to remain at the firm for a lifetime, and senior staff were invited to become partners or directors. Long-term employees included Frank Garrison, son of William Lloyd Garrison and Houghton's confidential assistant; the brilliant early publicist Azariah Smith; his successor Roger Scaife; treasurer James Murray Kay; Susan Francis, relegated by her gender to reading manuscripts for fifty years; James Duncan Phillips, Stephen Davol, and Franklin Hoyt, later heads of the educational department; several Houghton cousins; and Ferris Greenslet, for thirty years head of the trade division. Two of Houghton's associates had longevity in the business and an influence nearly comparable to his own.

HORACE SCUDDER

Horace Elisha Scudder (1838–1902) worked with Houghton from 1864 until his death. Over this period he influenced Houghton Mifflin's publications in a range of capacities more than any other individual. Beginning in 1864 as initiator and editor of the *Riverside Magazine,* a high-quality but commercially unsuccessful children's periodical, Scudder became a literary adviser in the 1870s, then from 1886 to 1902 editor in chief of trade publications. A prodigious worker who finally drove himself to exhaustion, he was also a prolific writer who for more than three decades contributed influential reviews to the *Atlantic Monthly* and frequently edited it, serving as editor in chief from 1890 to 1898 in addition to his responsibility for the trade list.

The force that drove Scudder was an essentially religious sense of the value and influence of humanistic culture, particularly literature. Literature, he believed, without being didactic should reveal a moral pattern in human experience and can thereby be a source of spiritual and social good. This was particularly true, he felt, of American works. An admiring friend of William Dean Howells, Scudder in innumerable reviews as well as through editorial selection supported the literary realism of Howells, James, Mark Twain, Jewett, and many others. But he was ultimately not able to support the naturalism of the next generation of American writers that seemed to him reductive, despairing, or sordid.

If Scudder was an idealistic Victorian believer in the humanizing effects of literature, he was also enough of a pragmatist to operate effectively within a commercial context. As a result he had Houghton's complete confidence. He recognized that publication would ultimately have to justify itself by reaching a readership broad enough to cover costs and provide a modest margin. But he also made it his purpose to persuade Houghton and the firm to take the long view that not every book had to make an immediate profit and that quality would ultimately be recognized, respected, and rewarded. Pragmatism and idealism combined in Scudder and Houghton's initiative—progressive in the 1880s—to publish unabridged major American works, copyright mostly held by the house, as educational texts to supplant the patronizing, didactic readers of the time. This led to the establishment in 1882 of the Riverside Literature series, which by 1922 had over three hundred titles and more than $1 million in annual sales (Ballou, p. 513).

GEORGE MIFFLIN

Houghton's other most influential associate, George Harrison Mifflin (1845–1921), was a pragmatist with the principles of a nineteenth-century gentleman publisher. In their first interview in 1867, Houghton judged the wealthy, privileged Harvard graduate unsuited to business. But Mifflin's persistence led to a job at the Riverside Press, a chance to demonstrate an aptitude for sustained, demanding work, and by 1872 a 10 percent partnership. Thus began the association and the work that ended only with Mifflin's death and to which he attributed the energy and purpose of his life.

By nature Mifflin combined a conservative business sense with a somewhat boyish emotional impulsiveness, frequently giving vent to brief explosive outbursts of impatience, enthusiasm, or laughter. While confident of his business judgments, he distrusted his literary tastes, seldom intervening in book selection. He also respected editorial independence, refusing to intervene either in 1898, when Walter Hines Page, as editor of the *Atlantic*, welcomed the Spanish-American War by flying the U.S. flag on the magazine's cover and editorially praising the war as a necessary surgery for the progress of civilization, or in 1899, when the new editor, Bliss Perry, denounced the war as racism. Financially stringent, Mifflin believed that each venture should justify itself on the bottom line. But he was also capable of taking real delight in the artistry and craftsmanship of the book designer Bruce Rogers's limited editions and providing Rogers with very liberal resources.

PARTNERSHIPS AND EXPANSION

During Mifflin's fifty-three years with the firm (1868–1921), it went through a series of reorganizations initiated mainly by changes of partnership and the need for increased capital to expand. Houghton's partnership with Melancthon Hurd, initiated in 1864, was widened to include new partnership capital in 1867 and again in 1872. These additions reflected primarily the success of the Riverside Press but also provided capital for the purchase in 1873 from James Osgood and Company (successors to the old Boston firm Ticknor and Fields) of the *Atlantic Monthly,* edited by Howells, *Every Saturday,* an eclectic weekly edited by Thomas Bailey Aldrich, and the *American Naturalist.*

In 1878, when Melancthon Hurd and Houghton's cousin Albert Houghton retired, leaving their capital in the firm, Houghton again expanded the publishing side of the house by entering into a partnership with Osgood. Osgood, heavily in debt, was close to brokering an arrangement with the Harpers of New York, but Houghton convinced him that he and the list he had purchased from Ticknor and Fields, including most mid-century New England authors and many, such as Howells and James, currently writing for the *Atlantic,* should stay in Boston. The conflict between Osgood's sometimes prodigal liberality and tolerance for debt and Houghton's fiscal conservatism soon dissolved the partnership. In the acrimonious aftermath, most of the old list stayed with Houghton. This list and the *Atlantic* provided a continuing core to the firm's publications for the rest of the century. Howells, however, went to New York, taking with him something of the progressive spirit in literature.

The break with Osgood resulted in the formation in 1880 of Houghton, Mifflin and Company. The death of Houghton in 1895 and his son Harry in 1906 precipitated a need for additional capital that was substantially met by Mifflin, leading to incorporation in 1908 as Houghton Mifflin Company, George H. Mifflin, president.

During the 1880s and 1890s the firm's list expanded steadily from about twelve hundred titles to over three thousand, adding an average of about a hundred titles per year. Scudder and his assistants, including Susan Francis, Herbert Gibbs, and later Mark Howe and Walter Hines Page, were the major sources of selection. Their readers' reports were generally respected, but the firm, particularly after Mifflin's seniority beginning in 1895, tracked the sales records of each work, and the author's past and present prospects for profitability were discussed in the weekly "powwow" of department chiefs that made final decisions on acceptance.

THE *ATLANTIC*

Until 1908 the *Atlantic* continued to be a major means of attracting authors. After Howells's departure in 1881, it was edited by Aldrich (1881–1890), Scudder (1890–1898), Walter Hines Page (1898–1899), and Bliss Perry (1899–1909), all of whom also served as advisers to the trade department. The magazine lost readers and contributors to New York's illustrated magazines. But while its readership hovered frustratingly around twenty thousand and it more often made a small loss rather than a small profit, the firm maintained it because of its prestige and the contacts it afforded with authors. The old "courtesy of the trade" mandated that competitors respect the rights of a writer's first publisher to subsequent works unless the writer initiated a change. This made magazines valuable sources of new talent.

But by 1900 trade courtesy was rapidly breaking down, particularly among younger authors, under a much more freewheeling economic competition in publishing. Jack London was typical: the *Atlantic* published his first story and Houghton, Mifflin his first book in 1900, but he soon moved on to S. S. McClure, then Macmillan, drawn by increasingly large advances. Its profitability dubious and its advantages to the trade department increasingly marginal, the *Atlantic* was sold in 1908 to Ellery Sedgwick. While the magazine was supposed to continue to feed Houghton Mifflin's trade department, within a decade Sedgwick turned book publisher himself, and the long connection between Houghton Mifflin and the *Atlantic* was broken entirely.

FICTION, NONFICTION, AND EDUCATIONAL TEXTS

From 1900 to 1920 the firm's fiction list was extensive and commercially successful, but the new fiction generally lacked distinction and reflected an editorial distaste for modernism. Scudder, whose dedication to preserving nineteenth-century New England culture accounted for much of the list, died in 1902. On Scudder's death Mifflin hired Ferris Greenslet, who, like Scudder, served the firm for nearly forty years, the last thirty (1910–1940) as editor in chief of trade publications. Like Scudder, Greenslet was a gentle, self-effacing humanist who had more sympathy for the literature of the past than the bleaker, grittier literature of the present. Chilled by Boston censorship, Greenslet rejected work by many younger modernists while publishing successful historical novels, British wartime propaganda fiction, and genteel romances, including twenty-one best-sellers between 1911 and 1920. While comfortable with literary commerce, Greenslet believed in a "balanced list." He valued but lost Amy Lowell and Willa Cather and published considerable distinguished nonfiction, including major works by Henry Adams, John Muir, Havelock Ellis, Paul Elmer More, Samuel Eliot Morison, and Albert Beveridge.

While Greenslet's trade division was commercially successful, by 1920 its sales were exceeded by those of Houghton Mifflin's education division. After 1908, under the influence of Franklin Hoyt, a product of Columbia Teachers College with experience as a teacher and school administrator, Houghton Mifflin's expanding educational list was relatively progressive. Hoyt emphasized John Dewey's child-centered, age-appropriate curriculum as opposed to Scudder's classics and character. Since progressivism was newly dominant in education at the time, the texts Hoyt sponsored were both influential and successful. In the twelve years after his arrival, the education division quadrupled its sales, moving from tenth to fourth largest among educational publishers nationally.

By 1920 Houghton Mifflin's education and trade divisions together published a list of over 4,000 titles, reviewed over 10,000 submissions annually, selected 150 to 200 new titles for publication, had over $3 million in book sales, and maintained offices in Boston, New York, Chicago, and London in addition to a greatly expanded Riverside Press in Cambridge (Ballou, pp. 558, 573, 581). This reflected more than a half century of sustained growth in number and range of publications, financial success, and influence on America's reading.

See also *The Atlantic Monthly;* Book Publishing; Boston and Concord; Harper & Brothers; Literary Marketplace

BIBLIOGRAPHY

Primary Work

Houghton Mifflin. Archives. Houghton Library, Harvard University. A rich collection including letter books for the *Atlantic* and Houghton Mifflin, readers' reports, financial accounts, diaries, scrapbooks, and catalogs.

Secondary Works

Ballou, Ellen. *The Building of the House: Houghton Mifflin's Formative Years.* Boston: Houghton Mifflin, 1970. The definitive secondary source, exhaustively researched and clearly written.

Carpenter, Charles. *History of American School Books.* Philadelphia: University of Pennsylvania Press, 1963.

Greenslet, Ferris. *Under the Bridge: An Autobiography.* Boston: Houghton Mifflin, 1943.

Houghton Mifflin. *Fifty Years of Publishing.* Boston: Houghton Mifflin, 1930.

Houghton Mifflin. *The Firm of Houghton Mifflin and Company, Publishers, Boston, New York, Chicago, and London.* Cambridge, Mass.: Riverside Press, 1889.

Houghton Mifflin. *Of the Making of Books and the Part Played Therein by the Publishing House of Houghton Mifflin Company.* Boston: Houghton Mifflin, 1921.

Houghton Mifflin. *The Riverside Press.* Boston: Houghton Mifflin, 1911.

Laughlin, Henry A. *An Informal Sketch of the History of Houghton Mifflin Company.* Boston: Houghton Mifflin, 1957.

Perry, Bliss. *And Gladly Teach.* Boston: Houghton Mifflin, 1935.

Scudder, Horace. *Henry Oscar Houghton: A Biographical Sketch.* Boston: Houghton Mifflin, 1897.

Weber, Carl. *The Rise and Fall of James Ripley Osgood.* Waterville, Maine: Colby College Press, 1959.

Ellery Sedgwick

THE HOUSE OF MIRTH

Edith Wharton's *The House of Mirth* (1905) is the story of ill-fated Lily Bart, a beautiful, talented upper-class New York woman who fails at the single vocation for which society has trained her: finding a husband. The novel draws on the tradition of sentimental romance

Edith Wharton as photographed c. 1885, before the publication of her first novel. © BETTMANN/CORBIS

common to nineteenth-century American fiction but also departs from these conventions with its realistic treatment of society and marriage. Responding to a rapidly developing, post–Civil War capitalistic society and a Wall Street culture of speculation and risk, Wharton (1862–1937) offers a searing critique of a social system that debases men and women by privileging material interests over emotional ones and by treating marriage as a business contract. Wharton questions social codes that reduce men to producers of wealth and women to aesthetically pleasing, decorative objects or commodities available for male approval and consumption. A writer of naturalism as well as realism, Wharton positions Lily's quest for a husband within the context of late-nineteenth- and early-twentieth-century Social Darwinism. She depicts a heroine who, through accident of birth and training, cannot rise above circumstances that define and constrain her. Whereas many American naturalist writers of the period, such as Theodore Dreiser, Frank Norris, and Stephen Crane, constructed plots exploring the effects of natural and environmental circumstances on the poor, Wharton focuses on the upper class, demonstrating how Lily's immersion in luxury becomes detrimental to her well-being. Although ostensibly enjoying

privilege and comfort, Lily is, as Wharton writes in the novel, "so evidently the victim of the civilization which had produced her, that the links of her bracelet seemed like manacles chaining her to her fate" (p. 7).

When *The House of Mirth* opens, Lily Bart, age twenty-nine, is wearying of the search for a husband and beginning to exhaust a once-long list of eligible New York society bachelors. She repeatedly passes up chances to marry for wealth without love and gravitates instead toward Lawrence Selden, a man of modest means who returns her affection but remains emotionally detached and fails to propose. Increasingly in need of funds to support her expensive tastes, Lily accepts money from a friend's husband, Gus Trenor, who invests in the stock market on her behalf and deceptively allows her to think that the money he gives her is her own. She is also forced to rely on the beneficence of a disapproving guardian aunt and the generosity of friends, who expect repayment for their hospitality, sometimes in the form of ethically dubious social favors. The possibility for marriage recurs in the figure of a newcomer to society, Simon Rosedale, but Lily's distaste for the nouveau riche and her anti-Semitic leanings prevent her from seriously considering his proposal. By the end of the novel, Lily is reduced to poverty and forced to find employment, failing even at the mundane job of trimming hats. She dies ambiguously from an overdose of chloral and is mourned by Selden, who characteristically arrives too late to save her. Refusing to grant readers what she described in a tale, "Writing a War Story," as the desire for "a tragedy with a happy ending" (p. 360), Wharton offers instead an ironic text about the failure of love and faith in an increasingly competitive, materialistic society. She draws her title from the biblical book of Ecclesiastes, with its timeworn theme of weariness and resignation.

By using the name Lily, Wharton alludes to the flower that serves as a symbol of purity in the classical and Christian traditions, and there is a pure quality to Lily's moral superiority. The events of the novel reveal that Lily is like her namesake flower in another way as well: she is ornamental—beautiful but vulnerable to the difficult conditions she encounters. Wharton also plays off Lily Bart's last name by having her protagonist barter her beauty and integrity for financial security. With an incisive character portrayal and bleak ending, Wharton extends the novel of manners to a modernist as well as realistic critique of human significance and waste in a cultural moment of spiritual depletion.

WRITING FROM EXPERIENCE

An instant best-seller that earned critical as well popular acclaim, *The House of Mirth* marked Edith Wharton's coming-of-age as a novelist. Prior to composing the

MEETING LILY BART

The House of Mirth *opens with Selden Lawrence gazing at Lily Bart, his bemused curiosity foreshadowing the authentic but ultimately inadequate interest he will take in her throughout the novel. Poised at Grand Central Station, Lily is literally and figuratively in transit, her missed train indicative of her general homelessness and lack of direction. Writing that Lily invites "speculation," Wharton brings together dual concerns about women's precarious social position: Lily is both an object of male voyeurism and a commodity in a culture that views marriage as a market-based transaction.*

Selden paused in surprise. In the afternoon rush of the Grand Central Station his eyes had been refreshed by the sight of Miss Lily Bart.

It was a Monday in early September, and he was returning to his work from a hurried dip into the country; but what was Miss Bart doing in town at that season? If she had appeared to be catching a train, he might have inferred that he had come on her in the act of transition between one and another of the country-houses which disputed her presence after the close of the Newport season; but her desultory air perplexed him. She stood apart from the crowd, letting it drift by her to the platform or the street, and wearing an air of irresolution which might, as he surmised, be the mask of a very definite purpose. It struck him at once that she was waiting for someone, but he hardly knew why the idea arrested him. There was nothing new about Lily Bart, yet he could never see her without a faint movement of interest: it was characteristic of her that she always roused speculation, that her simplest acts seemed the result of far-reaching intentions.

Wharton, *The House of Mirth*, in *Novels*, p. 3.

novel, she had published poems; short stories; two novellas, *The Touchstone* (1900) and *Sanctuary* (1903); a two-volume historical novel set in eighteenth-century Italy, *The Valley of Decision* (1902); and nonfiction, including a coauthored guide to interior design, *The Decoration of Houses* (1897). She would go on to produce a total of twenty-five novels, including the Pulitzer Prize–winning *The Age of Innocence* (1920); volumes of short stories; books on architecture and horticulture; an autobiography; and a book about the theory of fiction. Before the publication of *The House of Mirth* at age forty-four, Wharton ventured tentatively into the world of publishing, lacking mentors and confidence. A product of the upper-class society she describes in *The House of Mirth*, with parents similar to those of her heroine, Wharton received sympathetic but ineffectual support from her literarily sensitive father and icy disapproval from her socially conscious mother, who frowned on what Wharton describes in her memoir as a childhood passion "to 'make up' stories" (p. 33). She suffered loneliness as a child but was eventually aided by a family friend who introduced her to the theories of Charles Darwin and other intellectual concepts. She later married a prominent Bostonian with whom she was fundamentally incompatible and whom she divorced after twenty-eight years. Unlike her heroine, however, who remains trapped within the narrow confines of New York society, Wharton achieved a meaningful career and escaped stifling social conventions by establishing homes of her own, first in Lenox, Massachusetts, and then in France, and by developing a circle of friends that included writers and intellectuals such as Paul Bourget, Henry James, Howard Sturgis, and Bernard Berenson.

Wharton began work on what would become *The House of Mirth* in September 1903, drawing from notes made previously. She abandoned the project during a trip to Europe and took it up again nearly a year later, accepting an invitation from *Scribner's Magazine* for serial publication of the novel beginning in January 1905. She considered various titles, including *A Moment's Ornament* and *The Year of the Rose*, but settled on *The House of Mirth*, which underlines the novel's moral as well as social import. As Wharton emphasized in a 1905 letter to Reverend Morgan Dix, who admired her achievement: "*No* novel worth anything can be anything but a novel 'with a purpose,' & if anyone who cared for the moral issue did not see in my work that *I* care for it, I should have no one to blame but myself" (*Letters*, pp. 98–99). She wrote at record speed under strict time constraints, the first installment appearing before she had devised the ending. Working under pressure proved fortuitous; as Wharton writes in *A Backward Glance*, the deadline taught her the "discipline of the daily task" and helped her develop from a "drifting amateur into a professional" (pp. 209, 208).

Sales of the novel surpassed Wharton's and Scribners' expectations. Two weeks after the book's publication, forty thousand copies of the first printing and twenty thousand copies of the second printing had sold. By the end of 1905, 140,000 copies of the book had been sold. In early 1906, *The House of Mirth* stood at the top of national best-seller lists, ahead of Upton

Illustration by A. B. Wenzell for the 1905 edition of *The House of Mirth.* SPECIAL COLLECTIONS LIBRARY, UNIVERSITY OF MICHIGAN

Sinclair's muckraking novel about the meatpacking industry, *The Jungle*. By August of that same year, earnings from *The House of Mirth* exceeded by three times the yearly income of the established realist writer William Dean Howells. A French translation of the novel was immediately issued; stage adaptations followed. Wharton clearly had struck a nerve with her detailed depictions of Lily Bart and glamorous New York society. Readers across the United States reacted emotionally to the news of Lily's death, and a lively controversy raged in the *New York Times Saturday Review of Books,* with readers who identified themselves as hailing from "Lenox" and "Newport" arguing about the accuracy of Wharton's depiction of upper-class social life.

MARRIAGE AND SOCIETY

Since its publication, *The House of Mirth* has provoked debate about the role of marriage in women's lives. Wharton offers complex, sometimes conflicting, answers to the novel's haunting question—why must Lily die?—with her portrait of a heroine who fluctuates between wanting to be "good" and liking to be "happy" (p. 7). Lily's character is fraught with contradictions. Impulsive by nature, she risks her reputation by visiting Selden's apartment alone, but she pays for these "rare indiscretions by a violent reaction of prudence" (p. 13). Described as a creature of "wild-wood grace" and "a captured dryad subdued to the conventions of the drawing-room" (p. 13), Lily has been trained for the vocation of marriage, but she is ill suited to the cutthroat New York culture in which a husband must be found. She is clearly an object of speculation in the opening scene of the novel when, having missed her train to the Trenors' country house at Bellomont, she attracts Selden's attention and idle comment, an allusion to Ecclesiastes, "there was nothing new about Lily Bart" (p. 3). But here and elsewhere, the reader sees Lily through Selden's limited vision, making it difficult to assess her character. For example, Selden views Lily as manipulative. Although Lily is capable of calculated charm, she is also dissatisfied with her lot in life and feels a need for genuine human connection. She longs for a home of her own, for a true "friend" who will not "use me or abuse me" (p. 9), and for social codes free of sexual double standards. As she tells Selden, "Your coat's a little shabby—but who cares? It doesn't keep people from asking you to dine. If I were shabby no one would have me" (p. 12). She warms to Gerty Farish's offer of friendship, but aesthetically sensitive and accustomed to luxury, she is also repelled by the "dinginess" (p. 39) of meager surroundings such as Gerty's apartment. An idealist trained for no purpose except a decorative one, Lily strains under the weight of social expectation but has no idea how to lighten her load.

Wharton demonstrates through the construction of plot and character how individual identity is formed, maintained, and regulated in the context of social relationship. Lily develops genuine rapport with Selden, who asks her to shun convention and enter with him into the lofty dominion of the "republic of the spirit" (p. 71), but such a height is attainable only with the discretionary income and freedom of movement accorded to single men, not women. Lily must operate on a more mundane level of society and work to safeguard not only her beauty but also her reputation. All too ready to judge Lily on the basis of rumor and innuendo, Selden proves to be as enslaved to society's conventions as anyone else, distancing himself when Lily attracts notoriety in New York's small circle. Others act similarly. Lily's aunt, Mrs. Peniston, hears gossip and, without "trying to ascertain its truth" (p. 133) disinherits her; her smug cousin rebuffs her request for a loan; and even her friend Judy Trenor conveniently ignores Lily once her prospects for a wealthy marriage dim. Although Lily hopes to transcend her circumstances and venture "*Beyond!*" (p. 163)—as the emblem on her stationery suggests—she is endlessly subject to the judgments and whims of others. Technically blameless of several indiscretions attributed to her, Lily is chastened by the sad realization "that a woman's dignity may cost more to keep up than her carriage; and that the maintenance of a moral attribute should be dependent on dollars and cents, made the world appear a more sordid place than she had conceived it" (pp. 178–179).

Nowhere is the line between appearance and reality more artfully drawn than in the *tableau vivant* scene at the Wellington Brys' ball, in which Lily dresses as Mrs. Lloyd, the subject of Joshua Reynolds's painting of that name. With this theatrical display, Wharton underlines the degree to which women's aesthetic and performative roles at the turn of the twentieth century could become naturalized. Lily is so accustomed to displaying herself as a beautiful object that neither she nor her transfixed admirers can tell where reality leaves off and illusion begins; although draped in artifice, she ironically appears as "the real Lily" (pp. 142, 143). She basks in the triumph of "recovered power" (p. 143) that this performance accomplishes, but victory is fleeting. The following day, lured to the Trenors' house under false pretenses, she is affronted by Gus, who expects sexual favors as repayment for the speculative investments he has made on her behalf. Wharton documents the blurred lines of sexual and economic exchange as well as a cultural shift in the terms of investment and risk that was taking place during the era. Taught to display wealth but not to produce or transact it, Lily is ignorant of new market conditions and therefore shocked by Gus's presumption. Feeling dishonored and "alone in a place of darkness" (p. 156), she finds overnight shelter in Gerty's apartment, but her social losses are irrecoverable. Selden, having witnessed her leaving Trenor's house, believes she is having an affair, and Bertha Dorset seals Lily's fate when she falsely but publicly accuses her of indiscretion with her husband, George Dorset. Ironically, Lily possesses the means to effect her own social redemption: she is holding Bertha Dorset's love letters to Selden, which she can use to blackmail her friend and rival. Instead, Lily throws the letters into the fireplace before Selden's unsuspecting gaze.

DARWINIAN TRAGEDY

Lily's decision not to use the letters for blackmail is a testament both to her moral superiority over the competitive, uncaring world in which she lives and to her unfitness for this world. Lily turns the other cheek, refusing to retaliate against those who persecute her, and is destroyed as a result. Although Lily gains stature in the reader's eyes, Wharton leaves the meaning of Lily's sacrifice unclear, letting readers decide whether such waste of beauty and possibility is tragic or merely pathetic. In *A Backward Glance,* Wharton indicates that she is disposed toward the former interpretation, asserting that the value of a literary subject depends not so much on the subject itself as "on what the author sees in it" (p. 207). As a result, Wharton believed that "a frivolous society can acquire dramatic significance only through what its frivolity destroys. Its tragic implication lies in its power of debasing people and ideals. The answer, in short, was my heroine, Lily Bart" (p. 207). Using Darwinian imagery, Wharton also locates Lily's failure in a modernist condition of rootlessness. Despite constant contact with others, Lily is conspicuously alone, abandoned by family, friends, suitors, and even enemies. By the end of the novel, this deprivation takes its toll. She feels, more than material poverty, "a sense of deeper empoverishment—of an inner destitution compared to which outward conditions dwindled into insignificance. . . . It was the clutch of solitude at her heart, the sense of being swept like a stray uprooted growth down the heedless current of the years" (p. 336). An organism without "any real relation to life" (p. 336), Lily loses the battle of the fittest for survival.

Lily's need for human connection—and for sisterly bonds, in particular—is clear in the novel's closing scene between Lily and Nettie Struther. Nettie, aided by Gerty Farish's shelter for poor working women and now a happily married mother, is living proof of Gerty's "dream" of "renovation through adversity" (p. 276). Although at the time she gave the gift no thought, Lily once made an impulsive contribution to Gerty's charity and thus had a hand in Nettie's salvation. Now, as Lily contrasts the emotional warmth of Nettie's cozy kitchen with her own inner destitution, she understands the significance of a loving husband, home, and child. The scene evokes the sentimental portraits of family life found in the domestic fiction of a generation of writers who preceded Wharton—novelists such as Susan Warner, Harriet Beecher Stowe, and Louisa May Alcott. These authors believed in the sanctity of the home and the power of feminine domesticity to counter the increasingly impersonal, competitive forces of the business world. Lily perceives Nettie to have discovered "the central truth of existence" (p. 227), and when later she takes chloral and drifts first into sleep and then into death, she is under the delusion that she holds Nettie's baby. Unlike her predecessors, however, Wharton employs sentimental conventions ironically. Although Lily feels a "penetrating thrill of warmth and pleasure" (p. 340) from imagining herself both as loving mother and as embraced child, her comfortable fantasy is just that. For Lily, trained to be an ornamental object in an aggressive, cutthroat society, spiritual comforts are more imagined than real.

A century after its publication, *The House of Mirth* remains one of Wharton's most compelling and provocative novels. A searing chronicle of the elite, turn-of-the-twentieth-century New York life that the author knew firsthand, the novel established Wharton as a consummately skilled practitioner of realism and a novelist of manners with penetrating insights into the dynamics between individuals and social groups. Wharton considers several of the major issues of her day—capitalism, Darwinism, aesthetics, and women's roles—and she demonstrates the social turmoil that ensued as the insular Anglo-Dutch neighborhoods that comprised "Old New York" confronted rapid economic and social change in the late 1800s and early 1900s. As a new generation of entrepreneurs and industrialists created wealth and Wall Street prospered, the terms of human exchange underwent revision, emphasizing individual risk and profit and threatening the communal ties on which the social fabric is woven. *The House of Mirth* also chronicles cultural uncertainty about relationships between the sexes that marked the fin de siècle transition from Victorian mores to modernist sensibilities. It examines marriage and women's social roles with brutal honesty, arguing for women to be more than beautiful objects and for marriage to be more than a business contract. Ahead of her time, Wharton voiced concern for women's lives and suggested improvements that became standard in the twentieth century. Finally, Wharton positioned her characters and their dramas against the backdrop of the major philosophical, scientific, and religious movements of her time, raising contemporary questions of fashion, money, and social inclusion as well as larger issues of ethical and moral import. She continued to probe tensions between personal desire and social expectation in the novels that constitute her major phase: *The Fruit of the Tree* (1907), *Ethan Frome* (1911), *The Reef* (1912), *The Custom of the Country* (1913), *Summer* (1917), and *The Age of Innocence* (1920). Among these achievements, *The House of Mirth* is distinguished by its incisive social commentary, brilliantly complex and detailed characterization, and sense of fatalistic determinism.

See also Courtship, Marriage, and Divorce; Naturalism; New York; Realism; Social Darwinism

BIBLIOGRAPHY
Primary Works
Wharton, Edith. *A Backward Glance.* New York: D. Appleton–Century, 1934.

Wharton, Edith. *The House of Mirth.* New York: Scribners, 1905. Reprinted in *Novels: The House of Mirth, The Reef, The Custom of the Country, The Age of Innocence,* edited by R. W. B. Lewis. New York: Library of America, 1985.

Wharton, Edith. *The House of Mirth: Complete, Authoritative Text with Biographical and Historical Contexts, Critical History, and Essays from Five Contemporary Critical Perspectives.* Edited by Shari Benstock. Boston: Bedford Books of St. Martin's Press, 1994.

Wharton, Edith. *The Letters of Edith Wharton.* Edited by R. W. B. Lewis and Nancy Lewis. New York: Scribners, 1988.

Wharton, Edith. "Writing a War Story." In *The Collected Short Stories of Edith Wharton,* vol. 2, edited by R. W. B. Lewis, pp. 359–370. New York: Scribners, 1968.

Secondary Works
Ammons, Elizabeth. *Edith Wharton's Argument with America.* Athens: University of Georgia Press, 1980.

Benstock, Shari. *No Gifts from Chance: A Biography of Edith Wharton.* New York: Scribners, 1994.

Esch, Deborah, ed. *New Essays on "The House of Mirth".* Cambridge, U.K.: Cambridge University Press, 2001.

Kaplan, Amy. *The Social Construction of American Realism.* Chicago: University of Chicago Press, 1988.

Preston, Claire. *Edith Wharton's Social Register.* New York: St. Martin's, 2000.

Singley, Carol J. *Edith Wharton: Matters of Mind and Spirit.* New York: Cambridge University Press, 1995.

Stange, Margit. *Personal Property: Wives, White Slaves, and the Market in Women.* Baltimore: Johns Hopkins University Press, 1998.

Wagner-Martin, Linda. *"The House of Mirth": A Novel of Admonition.* Boston: Twayne, 1990.

Waid, Candace. *Edith Wharton's Letters from the Underworld: Fictions of Women and Writing.* Chapel Hill: University of North Carolina Press, 1991.

Wolff, Cynthia Griffin. *A Feast of Words: The Triumph of Edith Wharton.* New York: Oxford University Press, 1977.

Carol J. Singley

HUMOR

Between 1870 and 1920 Americans produced an immeasurable traffic in humor. Some of it went beneath or beyond language through eccentricities of dress, gestures, and facial signals; as many British travelers noticed, common talk in the United States included banter, deadpanning, irony, and sarcasm. Raconteurs were imitated by scavengers of jokes, and the jokes themselves emerged as a marketable commodity. Amateurs stole from printed sources or from professional performers in minstrel shows, vaudeville acts, stage comedies, and comic "lectures." All of these outlets proved pleasing to audiences in large cities and small towns alike. They were crucial in making humor a respectable form of entertainment.

Journalism was the steadiest supplier. In 1873 contemporary historian Frederick Hudson got specific:

> Our four to five thousand daily and weekly publications have columns of "Nuts to Crack," "Sunbeams," "Sparks from the Telegraph," "Freshest Gleanings," "Odds and Ends," "News Sprinklings," "Flashes of Fun," "Random Readings," "Mere Mentions," "Humor of the Day," "Quaint Sayings," "Current Notes," "Things in General," "Brevities," "Witticisms," "Notes of the Day," "Jottings," "All Sorts," "Editor's Drawer," "Sparks," "Fun and Folly," "Fact and Fiction," "Twinklings." (*Journalism in the United States*, p. 695)

The typical newspaper had—or pretended to have—a local editor whose duties included supplying amusement, often clipped from the "exchanges," that is, the papers exchanged between different news publications so that they could share material when necessary.

Stories about eccentrics or mismatched circumstances got passed around; anecdotes and aphorisms got wider exposure; and many plays on bumbling syntax got repeated more often than they deserved. Purely comic newspapers and magazines had difficulty breaking even until *Puck* (established in 1877) attracted enough subscribers to turn a profit. Its success encouraged the startup of *Judge* (1881) and *Life* (1883). A submarket, "college humor," quickly recognized as a genre, established its viability. Gradually, the sober magazines, emboldened by the ongoing "Editor's Drawer" in *Harper's New Monthly,* added a humor department; they particularly encouraged the vogue of comic or "light verse" keyed to current customs. Newspapers, meanwhile, strained to set the pace and, as soon as the print shop could manage, expanded to cartoons and later to the comic strip.

The book trade responded to a rising demand for humorous material. At the fringes, joke books and pamphlets of ephemera circulated through hawkers and peddlers. Bottom fishers pirated hardcover collections until the laws on copyright got tighter. Humorists who built a following—such as Mark Twain and Marietta Holley—racked up totals impressive for the size of the public that could read English. Josh Billings—a pseudonym for Henry Wheeler Shaw (1818–1885)—sold over nine million copies of his *Allminax* in its best decade. Edward Noyes Westcott (1846–1898) produced *David Harum* (1898), an amateurish novel about a folksy rural banker

that sold half a million copies. Novelists with serious themes understood that light touches would help lure a following. Though genial irony came naturally for William Dean Howells, once known for his one-act farces, Henry James both consciously and perhaps disingenuously created some characters who invited smiles rather than abstract dilemmas.

The process turned into push-pull. Cumulative popularity attracted more practitioners—from the rising trade of joke-smith to almost anybody trying to make a living by writing. Humor grew self-conscious, examining itself admiringly; Henry Ward Beecher's *Beecher as a Humorist* (1887), which caused no surprise, had many loosely analytic excerpts. Ultimately, listing the authors who shunned humor is far quicker than listing those who employed it, and Theodore Dreiser stands almost alone at his level. While the name of Kate Sanborn or Charlotte Perkins Gilman can pop up in anthologies moldering away, the contents are lopsided with male freelancers. Only lately have feminists managed to exhume a gallery of humorists they judge noteworthy. Except for Jewish writers, immigrants still need a closer census. Most overlooked, the humor of the working classes—on farms and in factories—has sunk beyond reach, though joking, playful or bitter, bubbled on the job, too. Recently, the pointed jokes of the most exploited subclass, the emancipated African Americans, has come into scholarly print. Doubtless, other groups—Native Americans, Hispanics—also had comic routines and sayings.

THEORIES AND PATTERNS

Many commentators have codified this swarming of humor. Their models, however, clash when they choose their typical authors or patterns—when they choose Thomas Bailey Aldrich over Ambrose Bierce, Marietta Holley over Mark Twain because she perhaps sold more books; when they emphasize the literary comedians over the columnists who wrote drolly about horsecars instead of horses, about transcontinental travelers instead of Arkansas travelers; when they emphasize vaudeville skits over the major magazines; when they focus on personal traits over attitudes claimed as distinctively American. But the more dynamic the advocate, the more that are convinced. An eloquent, hearty critic such as Bernard DeVoto, for instance, sweeps along more believers than quieter voices.

Theorists and classifiers have tended to emphasize that exaggeration held great appeal for humorists and their audiences. British commentators, especially, pointed to overstatement of emotions, bodily shapes, quantities, and outcomes. In some cases, this can narrow to the tall tale or to a stone-faced lying that outrages common sense. Cultural analysts find the most distinctive or else the most popular attitude an untamable irreverence, painfully obvious to less approving British critics. Even Artemus Ward, always intent to entertain, twitted pieties and left biblical morality less imposing. Encouraged explicitly by the humorists themselves, analysts past and present find a hostility to humbug, hypocrisy, or pretense. That hostility also functioned to favor the idiomatic and the colloquial over school-marmish rules or a bookish vocabulary.

Theories that build from historical patterns focus on the social leveling that intensified after the Civil War. Humor about "native" types, that is, rough-hewn white males, grew more respectable to write or to enjoy and resonated more with empathy than condescension. Such types now could guide the humor rather than let it happen to themselves. A blander approach finds a conflicted mixture of nostalgia and modernizing—an affection for a rural simplicity yet amusement at outmoded standards, a resistance to the steam engine of progress yet amusement at stuck-in-the-mud bumpkins. Timeline historians, following the theorists who explain humor as the deploying of incongruity, emphasize the sensitivity to the contrasts between regions. This is not surprising given that improvements in travel infrastructure made it possible to move quickly between vastly different areas—from Chicago, for instance, to a remote mining frontier. More clearly than today, economic levels were recognized—except in campaign speeches. As the middle and upper classes coalesced in the cities, their jokes and their favored sketches and cartoons stereotyped uppity clerks and dull-witted maids. As a woman's magazine fretted over the "servant problem," its humor page chuckled over Irish cooks and handymen. Still, socioeconomic perspectives can get too ponderous. With more leisure for some, with more time and better health for boredom, empty fun sold well, too. In printed bulk, it outweighed tendentious or aggressive humor.

Whenever essayists saw salability in discussing the national distinctiveness of humor, Americans were quickest to claim it. Some British critics agreed, instancing exaggeration, informality, and brashness—further localized vaguely as Western. Still, thorough reading encounters a range that includes reworking the oldest forms such as the proverb; tall tales, likewise, turn up earlier in almost every ethnic tradition.

Much of the dominant American culture had British roots; Charles Dickens had many New World devotees. Closer to home, Canadian humorists were sometimes well received in the United States. Stephen Leacock—like "Sam Slick" (a creation of Canadian Thomas Chandler Haliburton) a century earlier—fit in so easily here that many of his readers did not know or care that he was not a U.S. citizen. American humor could itself travel far because it meshed with basic human nature. But its offhand egalitarianism and its quickness to ridicule snobbery and pomposity was stronger than that of any other country with a print culture.

Much of the humor from 1870 to 1920 does not appeal to readers in the early twenty-first century. Political barbs like those of Thomas Nast or Petroleum V. Nasby—a pseudonym for David Ross Locke (1833–1888)—rust away, but so does the topicality of needling the southern "colonel," the bloomer girl, the boardinghouse landlady, and the "masher." Racist and ethnic slurs have sunk beneath respectability, and the politically correct will merely scowl at opaque dialect. Audiences in the 2000s squeeze less glee out of misused words and none at all out of tortured spellings. Likewise, there is little demand for the light or "occasional" verse that made Oliver Wendell Holmes a celebrity until his death in 1894. Also, when later readers refer back to historic material, they are absorbing it in a way that is quite different from the way that audiences of the late 1800s and early 1900s perceived it. Contemporaries of Josh Billings, for instance, took his writing in weekly doses or skipped around in his almanacs, which made them less likely to notice the recycling of devices and even phrasing. In addition, Billings's first fans did not read his work silently, as later readers tend to do, but shared his columns in groups, much like the television sitcom is vetted around the vending machine. Above all, the modern reader no longer feels that unapologetic amusement is daring, like skipping Sunday school. The late-nineteenth-century public could enjoy themselves enjoying humor while choosing from an expanding menu rather than expecting it to be available everywhere.

ENDURING WORKS

Literary historians differ in highlighting names of important works from the hundreds of plausible candidates. They differ on weighing success at the time against appeal today or against retrospective topicality. Ellis Parker Butler's huge success with "Pigs Is Pigs" (1906) evaporated long ago, for instance. But any historian should include Washington Irving, who held his prominence in anthologies used in the schools. James Russell Lowell, more august personally each year, heard from new readers of the first series of *The Biglow Papers* (1848), which amused even after its topical point failed. For loyal if diminishing fans, B. P. Shillaber carried on the tales of Mrs. Partington. As the wall between high- and lowbrow weakened, the lusty sketches from the old Southwest edged into the parlor, nearly fit to keep company with Harriet Beecher Stowe's

Down East yarns through Sam Lawson. Though the Civil War satirists thinned away, Petroleum V. Nasby growled on for the unforgiving northerners while Bill Arp (a pseudonym for Charles H. Smith) genially reminded them that the white South still felt right-eous. Though Artemus Ward died in 1867, Josh Billings, who started out imitating Ward's style, prospered for deriding humbug and stock sentimentalism. After the first Samantha Allen collection in 1873, Marietta Holley (1836–1926) published new books until 1914, mixing Billings's old-fashioned wisdom and virtue with calls for women's rights. While the Victorian commonplace that women have no sense of humor persisted, Holley and her ongoing admirers must have laughed at that, too.

Poets working in subliterate dialect tried to turn it into humor. A mini-genre of immigrant-inflected dialect, not indicted yet as ethnocentric, was especially popular. The writer from this style who persisted the longest in anthologies was Hans Breitmann—a pseudonym for Charles Godfrey Leland (1824–1903)—but like other dialect poets of the period, he receives little attention from modern readers. The same is true of the local colorists, who once invaded every nook of the conti-nent and every magazine supplying fiction, and who usually wove some humor into their writing. The local colorists tended to profess curatorial purposes, and the writings of Joel Chandler Harris (1848–1908), in particular, have been upheld for helping preserve the folklore of African Americans. Still, the humorous content of such works is an important part of their appeal. Readers surely feel a margin of amusement over the thorny dialect, anachronistic beliefs, and stereotypical characters. They may find the reputed stiffness and practicality of New England in a Mary Eleanor Wilkins Freeman story, yet they ordinarily smile at the end.

Meanwhile, cities were naturalizing the immigrant and depopulating the farms. Chicago ambitiously sup-ported the publishing of books, magazines, and news-papers. While Eugene Field's impressive following has dwindled away because his columns were so frag-mented, the writings of George Ade (1866–1944) and Finley Peter Dunne (1867–1936) can still have a con-temporary feel—at least for those with some familiar-ity with the writing of the period. While Ade was the more versatile, competing demands on the attention of posterity have winnowed him down to the best of his "Fables in Slang" series, which were collected in nine volumes, the first appearing in 1899. Ade's ideal reader, a shrewd yet tolerant city dweller, has seen through many a mental shell game and has encoun-tered enough people to sort them into types. Dunne's Martin Dooley, who runs a saloon in an Irish enclave on the edge of Chicago, reached syndication by 1900.

HOLLEY'S INTELLIGENT HEROINE

Though Marietta Holley's "Samantha Allen" consis-tently inserted arguments for women's rights in her written monologues, she registered most effectively through her interactions with her husband Josiah. Josiah, mild, somewhat inept, holds firmly to the gender stereotypes of the small-town Northeast; yet he is fond of Samantha, his second wife, and appreciates her competence. Samantha, more senior partner than wife to him, continually demonstrates her greater practicality, keen mind, tolerant curiosity, poise, and determination—thus continually undercutting the image of the naive, near-helpless female.

In the following passage, Samantha and Josiah are going through the art gallery at the Centennial Exhibition of 1876 in Philadelphia. More particu-larly, they are looking at some classical sculptures of nude women. Samantha shows both her usual back-bone of propriety and her open-mindedness while Josiah trails along, intellectually as well as physically smaller than she.

But there was some Italian statues that instinc-tively I got between and Josiah, and put my fan up, for I felt that he hadn't ort to see 'em. Some of the time I felt that he was too good to look at 'em, and some of the time I felt that he wasn't good enough; for I well knew when I come to think it over, that human nater wasn't what it once was, in Eden, and it wasn't innocence, but lack of innocence that ailed folks. But whether he was too good, or not good enough, and I couldn't for my life tell which; either way I felt it wasn't no place for him; so I hurried him through on a pretty good jog.

Marietta Holley, *Josiah Allen's Wife as a P.A. and P.I.: Samantha at the Centennial* (Hartford, Conn.: American Publishing Company, 1877), pp. 476–79.

He commented mostly on national politics, starting with the Spanish-American War. Neither saint nor sage, he was resigned rather than outraged when deflating politicians (notably, Theodore Roosevelt) and the catch phrase of Manifest Destiny. Just as Ade's fables revive the social aura of his times and his citified coterie, so Dunne's monologues revivify the issues and the personalities as discussed by the voters rather than the pundits.

MR. DOOLEY ON THE PHILIPPINES

Finley Peter Dunne's "Mr. Dooley" reached national notice with his commentary on the Spanish-American War, especially on the behavior of Colonel Theodore Roosevelt leading the Rough Riders in Cuba. He continued his commentary, to still greater notice, when the United States occupied the Philippine Islands at the end of the war and a vigorous Filipino guerrilla movement opposed the U.S. troops.

Though a wide majority in the United States supported the policy of the Republican administration, an anti-imperialist group kept active, especially for the presidential election of 1900. Increasingly, however, it was attacked as unpatriotic, and even Mark Twain had to cope with charges of being a traitor. Finley Peter Dunne, while using humor more cross-grained than Twain's on this issue, felt that Mr. Dooley's Irish American idiom helped to deflect expansionist outrage, that readers tolerated dissent better when it was swathed in nonstandard English.

But I don't know what to do with th' Ph'lippeens anny more thin I did las' summer, befure I heerd tell iv thim. We can't give thim to anny wan without makin' th' wan that gets thim feel th' way Doherty felt to Clancy whin Clancy med a frindly call an' give Doherty's childher th' measles. We can't sell thim, we can't ate thim, and we can't throw thim into th' alley whin no wan is lookin'. And 'twud be a disgrace f'r to lave befure we've pounded these frindless and ongrateful people into insinsibility.

Finley Peter Dunne, *Mr. Dooley at His Best,* edited by Elmer Ellis (New York: Scribners, 1938), p. 65.

Spotlighting a few names can obscure, however, the hundreds of freelancers who strained for professional status and profits as the public indulged its sense of humor. Every kind of success spawned imitators. Meanwhile, the print media kept demanding more copy and the expanding live-entertainment industry always wanted fresh material. The big-city dailies felt off the pace without their byline humorist, and wordplay seeped into their headlines or stories about love triangles and petty theft. Comic verse replaced the lyric as filler for a magazine page. The joke in dialogic form hardened into an artifact, manufactured like tin cans, adaptable for every niche in the market. *Life,* started by Harvard graduates, claimed sophistication for its gags;

its more expensive format also separated it from competitors. Considering itself non-partisan, it did not need the pinpoint cartoons that were found in *Puck* (Democratic) and *Judge* (Republican). The success of all three confirmed Matthew Arnold's complaint about the "addiction 'to the funny man'" in the United States.

Whatever its quality, the greatest quantity of humor was hacked out in the 1880s. Expert journeymen who had honed their skills in previous decades continued to work during this period. One was Richard Malcolm Johnston (1822–1898), who reworked his Georgia materials that had appeared previously. Another was James Whitcomb Riley (1849–1916), who brought dialect poetry to its widest popularity, especially when he bonded sentimentality and amiable humor. Still, postbellum moods and modes would inevitably lose dominance. Changes were driven by the growth of large-scale industry, urban anonymity, and secularism. In order to cater to the metropolitan newspapers, which were increasing in number, humorists presented a middle-class frame of reference and a mainline vocabulary that was spelled conventionally. The writing of Eugene Field (1850–1895), which began to be syndicated in the 1880s, was one sign of this change. When not pandering with sentimental lyrics, Field depended on a whimsy of ideas rather than pratfalls of body or mind.

As competitors multiplied in a national market, some still used regionalism as the safest base of supply. Southerners are likeliest to remember Opie Read (1852–1939) for his Arkansas shadings; midwesterners best remember George W. Peck (1840–1916), who created the "Bad Boy" stories, or Robert J. Burdette from Iowa. Of course, the fastest road to the national market ran through Manhattan, now the center of publishing. Out of the crowd, Francis Richard ("Frank") Stockton (1834–1902), H. C. Bunner (1855–1896), and John Kendrick Bangs (1862–1922) have had the most enduring appeal. Trying every mode like the preceding generation, they excelled in the short story and the cycle of sketches. While pitched below elitism, they assumed a public that not only could read well but was well-read. Likewise, Edgar Wilson ("Bill") Nye (1850–1896), though he got to the New York *World* through the Laramie (Wyoming) *Boomerang,* learned to assume a reader too self-confident to enjoy elementary blunders in language.

MARK TWAIN

By far, the humorist of the late nineteenth century who has had the most prolonged appeal is Mark Twain, the pen name of Samuel Langhorne Clemens (1835–1910). If Twain's innate genius or the quality of his humor explain his staying power, his career nevertheless exemplified three patterns for ongoing success: a spread of forms and outlets; the manipulating of different personae, coalescing in a complex personality; and appeal to a range of attitudes, sometimes contradictory.

People with little patience for print may know only about the Tom-Huck novels and, perhaps, one or two short stories, but Twain wrote or compiled a shelf of works, including, naturally, *Mark Twain's Library of Humor* (1888). He began as one of many journalists with a byline who spun tales, sketches, hoaxes, and anecdotes. Moving up to the magazines, he predictably ground out a monthly "department," if only for a year. Meanwhile, he was refining his stagecraft as a "lecturer" so effectively as to get constant pleas for speeches at banquets and ceremonies. All along, he worked at any promising deal—a self-pasting scrapbook, low-cost pamphlets, calendars, postcards, and comic poetry, especially parody. Tenacious bibliographers still have not tracked down his every printed word or every witness to his skill as a yarn-spinner. In 1908 the incorporation of the Mark Twain Company confirmed that his pen name had prospered into a trademark, a logo. He himself marveled at his sustained popularity, which he had worried about since the early 1870s, alert to overexposure.

Twain enjoyed continuing appeal because he steadily experimented with his persona, facing up to failures and adapting to the turns in his highly visible life. Most contemporaries who made a sudden hit stuck with their original approach and so coasted toward satiating their public. While the "I" persona in Twain's first novel, *The Innocents Abroad; or, The New Pilgrims' Progress* (1869), was already complex, it changed with each of his travel books, especially as Twain became famous, wealthy, and urbane. In the short pieces from Nevada and San Francisco, the Twain persona began as politically and civically engaged; then, working toward a national appeal, he muted his partisan invective. But he could resurface as a fervent independent—close, actually, to the Republican's middle-class core—when not building around basic human predicaments, topically staged. He most often used what the literary critic Walter Blair considers the then dominant strategy of humorists: posing a persona between the fool and the sage, between comically wrong thinking and horse sense, between exuberant joking and livable principles. But Twain, flexible to the end, moved with his times and his fortunes. His uniqueness comes from the fact that he achieved more cross-grained growth than most other writers.

Cutting across the timeline, Twain always appealed to a spread of attitudes. Casual readers, going by *The Adventures of Tom Sawyer* (1876) and *Adventures of*

(Left to right) David R. Locke ("Petroleum V. Nasby"), Mark Twain, and Henry Wheeler Shaw ("Josh Billings"), photographed in the early 1870s. THE GRANGER COLLECTION, NEW YORK

Huckleberry Finn (Tom Sawyer's Comrade) (1885)—especially as illustrated later by Norman Rockwell—consider him quintessentially nostalgic. As early as the 1870s older Americans could yearn for a community nestled in the village, superior to the heartless, noisome city (a grungier place then than now). But another of Twain's publics saw him as urbanized, moving toward a modernizing future and toward an improved human nature. Already in his early days, fellow journalists had called him a moralist, just partly kidding. Showily yet sincerely, he acted out the ideal of the responsible citizen, local and national. But even as his sketches increasingly displayed him as both family man and entrepreneur, he could again droll as prodigal, lazy, irresponsible, and hostile to the thickening bureaucracy. The various publics paid their money and took their choice of Mark Twains. In spite of bursts of appreciatively quoted invective, like his most enduring competitors he laughed with people more than at them—a distinction that was becoming explicit. He was amused as well as amusing, more sympathetic than satiric. Nevertheless, skeptics could quote supportive texts from Twain, agnostics felt comfortable with him, and pessimists inferred a kindred mind.

Twain's use of language encapsulated his multiplicity. Some of his sketches came close to the literary comedians' farfetched similes and slang, but even then he showed respectful affection for colloquial rhythms. Readers of *Adventures of Huckleberry Finn* admired its flowing yet vigorous cadence more than they chuckled at the boy's fumbling grammar or Pike County dialect. Before and after that novel Twain also showed respect for the correctness set by eastern academia. Especially after 1895 he worked primarily through sanctioned English so precise and graceful as to seem beyond any markers for class. But he would still delight his lifelong admirers by downshifting into slang and regional metaphors. Invoking Americanisms much less than his admirers then or now, his demotic undertones protected him from charges of going high-hat after hobnobbing with the wealthy and the mighty. Aspiring humorists who may not have comprehended the intricacy of Twain's appeal could see the efficacy of his style. Today, novelists who clash among themselves over sociopolitical principles emulate it openly.

TWENTIETH-CENTURY ARRIVALS

Although Twain reigned as king of the humorists until his death in 1910, tastes pointed consciously toward the new century after the severe depression of the 1890s eased. Alongside the carryovers, the cartoon character Abe Martin created by Frank McKinney "Kin" Hubbard (1868–1930) rates as a throwback. A bumpkin who started shucking his kernels of a fool's wisdom in 1906, Hubbard held to a daily, syndicated readership, slowly grooming himself into an impish small-towner. But the top-paying newspapers wanted fresh talent with metropolitan themes and characters. O. Henry, a pseudonym used by William Sydney Porter (1862– 1910), moved to New York City in 1902. Don Marquis moved there in 1909, soon doing a column for the *Evening Sun*. As the low-priced, general monthlies recognized how much female subscribers counted, female humorists got more acceptances in more genres. Carolyn Wells (c. 1869–1942) set the standard for updated professionalism, displaying versatility and writing with cerebral irony on mainstream themes rather than gendered ones. But movies were already luring the less literary; after 1910 the Mack Sennett Keystone comedies leaped many cuts above primitive sight gags.

World War I quickened the self-imagings that would energize the witty clique clustering in Greenwich Village and then around *The New Yorker*, which was founded in 1925. Most of the magazine's first contributors were already well known—especially Dorothy Parker, Robert Benchley, and James Thurber. When Ring Lardner (1885–1933) gravitated to New York in 1919, he was already known as a sportswriter with a twist that hurt. His sardonic humor, close to nihilism, which now seems to belong to the 1920s, had early surpassed that of Baltimore's H. L. Mencken (1880–1956). Mencken had been charming readers since 1908 with his inventive sarcasm, whatever its real-world salience. At their kindest, Mencken and the early-twentieth-century humorists ignored the small-town's morally ribbed eccentrics, its fading cracker-box philosophers, and its fool in overalls stumbling onto a pebble of sagacity; at their meanest they ridiculed the nouveau bourgeoisie straining for a veneer of suavity. Nevertheless, the acerbic urbanite would attract a smaller audience than the developing persona of the "little man"—the apartment dweller or new homeowner trapped in a white collar, trying to cope with puzzling neighbors, servants by the day or just the hour, panhandlers, and low-level bureaucrats.

Only a fearless critic will round off humor from 1870 to 1920 neatly or, if wary of committing to a master theme, will draw a sharp contrast with antebellum modes and then with those of the 1920s. How can the career of Will Rogers (1879–1935) fit into any dovetailed survey? A cautious historian can at least assert that the most humor in the widest spread of forms was the most self-admiringly enjoyed between 1870 and 1920. With the growth of movies and then radio in the 1920s, the amount of humor printed per capita surely declined. More important, humor grew so ubiquitous that it was devaluing toward common currency, no longer a self-conscious gift from the American character to itself. In the late nineteenth century, some British and American critics decided that the flowering of humor had sprung out of democracy, out of the alleged primacy of English-speaking peoples in establishing human rights; by ignoring much, the literary historian can compile a supportive anthology. Still, the soundest perspective is to frame 1870 to 1920 as the era when the job of humorist became a profession because the idea of and the term for a sense of humor cohered to designate a talent worth having and exerting on humankind.

See also Adventures of Huckleberry Finn; Periodicals; Uncle Remus, His Songs and His Sayings

BIBLIOGRAPHY
Primary Works
Ade, George. *Ade's Fables.* Garden City, N.Y.: Doubleday, Page, 1914.

Billings, Josh. *Josh Billings: His Works, Complete*. New York: G. W. Carleton, 1876.

Dunne, Finley Peter. *Mr. Dooley at His Best*. Edited by Elmer Ellis. New York: Scribners, 1938.

Holley, Marietta. *My Opinion and Betsey Bobbet's*. Hartford, Conn.: American Publishing Co., 1872.

Lardner, Ring. *You Know Me Al*. New York: George H. Doran, 1916.

Nye, Edgar W. *Bill Nye's History of the United States*. Philadelphia: J. B. Lippincott, 1894.

Twain, Mark. *Adventures of Huckleberry Finn*. 1885. Edited by Victor Fischer and Lin Salamo. Berkeley: University of California Press, 2001.

Secondary Works

Bier, Jesse. *The Rise and Fall of American Humor*. New York: Holt, Rinehart and Winston, 1968.

Blair, Walter. *Horse Sense in American Humor, from Benjamin Franklin to Ogden Nash*. Chicago: University of Chicago Press, 1942.

Blair, Walter. *Native American Humor (1800–1900)*. New York: American Book Company, 1937.

Blair, Walter, and Hamlin Hill. *America's Humor: From Poor Richard to Doonesbury*. New York: Oxford University Press, 1978.

Blair, Walter, and Raven I. McDavid Jr., eds. *The Mirth of a Nation: America's Great Dialect Humor*. Minneapolis: University of Minnesota Press, 1983.

Gale, Steven H., ed. *Encyclopedia of American Humorists*. New York: Garland, 1988.

Hudson, Frederic. *Journalism in the United States from 1690 to 1972*. New York: Harper, 1873.

Inge, M. Thomas. "Comic Strips." In *The Greenwood Guide to American Popular Culture*, edited by M. Thomas Inge and Dennis Hall. Westport, Conn.: Greenwood Press, 2002.

Mintz, Lawrence E., ed. *Humor in America: A Research Guide to Genres and Topics*. New York: Greenwood Press, 1988. See especially David E. E. Sloane, "Humor in Periodicals," and Zita Dresner, "Women's Humor."

Nilsen, Don L. F. *Humor in American Literature: A Selected Annotated Bibiliography*. New York: Garland, 1992.

Sloane, David E. E. *The Literary Humor of the Urban Northeast, 1830–1890*. Baton Rouge: Louisiana State University Press, 1983.

Trachtenberg, Stanley, ed. *American Humorists, 1800–1950*. 2 vols. Detroit: Gale Research, 1982.

Walker, Nancy, and Zita Dresner, eds. *Redressing the Balance: American Women's Literary Humor from Colonial Times to the 1980s*. Jackson: University Press of Mississippi, 1988.

Wallace, Ronald. *God Be with the Clown: Humor in American Poetry*. Columbia: University of Missouri Press, 1984.

Watkins, Mel. *On the Real Side: Laughing, Lying, and Signifying—The Underground Tradition of African-American Humor That Transformed American Culture, from Slavery to Richard Pryor*. New York: Simon and Schuster, 1994.

Wickberg, Daniel. *The Senses of Humor: Self and Laughter in Modern America*. Ithaca, N.Y.: Cornell University Press, 1998.

Williams, Kenny J., and Bernard Duffey, eds. *Chicago's Public Wits: A Chapter in the American Comic Spirit*. Baton Rouge: Louisiana State University Press, 1983.

Yates, Norris Wilson. *The American Humorist: Conscience of the Twentieth Century*. Ames: Iowa State University Press, 1964.

Louis J. Budd

ILLUSTRATIONS AND CARTOONS

With the founding of *Harper's New Monthly Magazine* in 1850, illustration became the driving force in an exciting new era of American publishing history. The august quarterlies and monthly magazines of the previous half century, such as the *North American Review* and the *American Whig Review,* had filled their narrow columns with as many finely printed words as possible. The idea that illustration might serve a legitimate journalistic function would have been unthinkable to the editors of these somber periodicals, who understood themselves as cultural stewards rather than as publishing entrepreneurs. The old era came to an abrupt end in June 1850 with the appearance of Harper & Brothers' first magazine. The older journals had been failing already, but their fate was sealed by the astounding popularity of this new breed, which spawned an industry revolution. Within ten years, dozens of illustrated periodicals, such as *Putnam's Monthly Magazine* and *Harper's Weekly,* emerged to grab shares of the rapidly expanding market. Driven by advances in technology and by new marketing tactics, the trend toward graphic innovation continued throughout the period, prompting one alarmed commentator to opine toward the end of the century that "in point of illustration [the American magazines] have no superiors anywhere, but much of their text appears to exist only for the sake of the pictures" (Mott 4:12).

More than a few curmudgeons shared this negative view, but no one living during the latter half of the nineteenth century in America could deny that changes affecting the magazine industry were symptomatic of even more widespread developments. From roadside billboards to the pages of popular fiction, images were suddenly everywhere. Improvements in printing technology and the emergence of photography were largely responsible for the rapid spread of visual culture throughout the period, and critics of the trend frequently complained that the quantity of new mechanically reproduced images in books, magazines, newspapers, and elsewhere far outstripped their quality. Artistic taste and originality, according to members of the old guard, were irrelevant to a new generation of image peddlers and greedy publishers who joined in a frantic rush to produce endless supplies of cheap chromolithographs—or "chromos," as they were derisively called—for the decoration of middle- and working-class homes. It is true that much of the graphic material churned out by the major American publishing houses and their smaller rivals was crude and poorly executed, but the fact remains that more people were exposed to more artwork during the final decades of the nineteenth century than ever before. There may have been no Rembrandt among the illustrators who participated in this bloodless revolution, but the efforts of Thomas Nast, Frederick Opper, William Allen (W. A.) Rogers, Arthur Burdett (A. B.) Frost, and many others demonstrated the awesome and unprecedented power of visual imagery to shape public opinion on everything from politics to personal hygiene. Perhaps during no other period in American history has the work of professional artists seemed at once so trivial and so full of significance.

TECHNOLOGY AND THE LITERARY MONTHLIES

Advances in printing technology had made the Harper experiment viable in 1850, and the story of American illustration during the second half of the nineteenth century is really the story of subsequent refinements to that technology. During the 1830s and 1840s, printed images for extended pressruns were produced mainly by engraving steel or copper plates, a process that was both cumbersome and extremely expensive. The Harper art department was able to reduce overhead costs without dramatically compromising the quality of workmanship by engraving its images on wooden blocks, which were less durable but easier to produce. For all its economy this process still involved the combined efforts of an artist—who drew the illustration on wood—an engraver—who created the wooden block— and a printer—who supervised production of the final image. Even Harper & Brothers, with its relatively deep pockets, could afford to place only eight woodcuts in the inaugural issue of its new magazine.

The magazine's success proved that a stunning number of people were eager to buy illustrated magazines, but few publishers at first possessed the monetary and human resources necessary to compete in this emerging market. Thus while Harper & Brothers built an unparalleled reputation for quality woodcuts, illustration did not become widespread in American publishing until the 1860s and 1870s, when a new process known as photoengraving enabled even fledgling publishers to start printing pictures. Pioneered in 1851, the technique of photoengraving entailed developing a photographic image directly on a sensitized wooden plank that was then inscribed by an engraver before moving on to the printer. Traditionalists cried foul, noting that the new process made the artist obsolete, but of course this was the tremendous advantage of photoengraving, both financially and technically. The vast majority of illustrations in American periodicals of the era were portraits of great people, copies of European masterpieces, landscapes, and architectural sketches of significant monuments. Perhaps relishing the potential savings more than the quality of their illustrations, most publishers concluded that the camera could produce a more faithful representation of these subjects than the artist or draftsperson, who was hampered not only by his or her own subjectivity but also by the technical burden of having to invert the original image in order to create a printable mirror image. The photographic negative, by contrast, could simply be flipped to generate a more accurate and far less expensive impression on wood that would then be sent to the engraver for production. The artist had disappeared from the art of illustration, with the result that illustration became virtually standard in American magazines, books, and newspapers by 1880.

Photoengraving opened the field of illustration to a new generation of competitors, such as *Scribner's Monthly,* later renamed the *Century Illustrated Monthly Magazine,* which competed with *Harper's* for supremacy in what can still be considered the relatively traditional practice of printing on wood. Yet another innovation of the 1880s and 1890s, the halftone process, made even *Scribner's* and the *Century* appear sadly antiquated and overpriced. Originally called "the Ives process" after Frederick E. Ives, its inventor, it involved transferring a photographic image to a sensitized plate that was then treated chemically and sent directly to the printer. While the technique was developing during the 1880s, an engraver was often employed to touch up the plate, enhancing contrasts and outlines, but improvements to the process later made the engraver's contribution unnecessary, and halftone printing became the industry standard by the early 1890s. Once again traditionalists complained about the mechanical quality of the newer illustrations, but halftone printing was cheap and extremely profitable. The success of flashy new magazines, such as *Munsey's* and *Cosmopolitan*—which sold for less than half the price of *Harper's New Monthly*—demonstrated again with unmistakable clarity the ruling principle of late-nineteenth-century and early-twentieth-century publishing: consumers wanted more, not better, illustrations. Richard Watson Gilder, editor of *Century,* speculated in 1899 that readers would soon "tire of photographic reproduction," and he predicted that "original art" would eventually return to public favor. This was wishful thinking, however, and by the beginning of the twentieth century wood engraving was a disappearing art (Mott 4:154).

THE WEEKLIES

Professional artists might seem to have been the primary losers in this story of technical advancement, as publishers learned to produce illustrations without the intervention of pen and ink. Yet many artists welcomed a release from the tedious work of translating painted images from paper or canvas to wood. Indeed, as one prominent illustrator, Joseph Pennell, explained in his 1895 survey, *Modern Illustration,* technical innovation actually freed artists to think and draw for themselves, with the result that original journalistic art flourished during the latter half of the nineteenth century. Much of this activity took place not in the more cultured literary monthlies but in America's thriving weekly papers, which became venues for some of the era's most exciting visual art. This was art with a message

"THAT'S WHAT'S THE MATTER."

BOSS TWEED. "As long as I count the Votes, what are you going to do about it? say?"

A political cartoon by Thomas Nast lampooning the Tammany Society, c. 1871. Although technically a private fraternal organization, the Tammany Society controlled politics in New York City throughout much of the nineteenth and twentieth centuries. Outrage over its excesses under the leadership of William "Boss" Tweed, including vote fraud, as expressed in this cartoon, led to reforms in 1872. © CORBIS

and an attitude: biting satires of political corruption, grotesque caricatures of ethnic subjects, unabashed declarations of party or sectional loyalty, hilarious parodies of the upper class. Thomas Nast (1840–1902) became the most celebrated American artist of the period for his famous attacks on Tammany Hall and its political boss, William Tweed, who allegedly reacted to a Nast cartoon by shouting at one of his henchmen: "Stop them damned pictures," continuing, "I don't care so much what the papers say about me. My constituents can't read. But, damn it, they can see pictures!" (Fischer, p. 2). Circulation of *Harper's Weekly* tripled in 1871 as Nast's campaign against corruption in New York gained national attention, and publishers across the country

took notice of the unprecedented power and popularity of graphic caricature as an editorial tool.

Nast's success at *Harper's Weekly* inspired other talented artists to try their hands at the ephemeral but lucrative and influential craft of journalistic illustration. One of the most gifted, Joseph Keppler, founded *Puck* in 1877, a comic weekly devoted primarily to cartoons and illustrations. In addition to employing the period's leading graphic satirists, such as Frederick Opper and C. Jay Taylor, *Puck* set a new industry standard by featuring garishly colored lithographs that gave the paper an enviable newsstand appeal. *Puck*'s motto, "What fools these mortals be," expressed the paper's nonpartisan political orientation, but rivals such as Bernhard

Gillam's stridently Republican *Judge* specialized in lampooning one or another political party. John Ames Mitchell established the success of *Life,* the era's third great comic paper, by employing a new zinc etching process that allowed artists to transfer black and white line drawings directly to a printing plate. Although its copious illustrations were necessarily crude in comparison to woodcuts or steel engravings, *Life* filled its pages with original art by some of the era's finest illustrators, including Charles Dana Gibson, whose smooth-featured "Gibson girl" became a popular-culture icon.

Though the weekly papers were dominated by political humor and social satire, much of their graphic material was devoted to the ridicule of ethnic subjects. *Life* was particularly aggressive in its treatment of Jews, who were typically depicted as moneygrubbing vermin, ready to betray a friend or relative in order to turn a small profit. Other stereotypes were just as demeaning, including that of the perpetually drunken Irishman—a *Puck* favorite—and the uppity "coon." Eugene Zimmerman ("Zim") became one of the leading illustrators of the 1880s and 1890s by cultivating these ethnic clichés in *Life,* entertaining readers with the antics of such purportedly alien elements of the country's increasingly diverse population. Thomas Worth and A. B. Frost claimed to take a more sympathetic view of their ethnic subjects, but Worth's "Darktown" sketches and many of Frost's illustrations for the Uncle Remus stories confirm that racist assumptions, however well intended, were pervasive in the journalistic art of the period.

BOOK ILLUSTRATION

Art in the weekly and monthly periodicals was ephemeral by nature, but some of the same illustrators who developed their skills in *Century* or *Life* also participated in the more durable medium of book illustration. In truth Americans have produced little or no art that can be considered significant in the larger context of book and manuscript illumination, but some work from the late nineteenth century and early twentieth century deserves to be remembered for its intriguing relation to the fiction of the period. Mark Twain's (1835–1910) illustrator for *Adventures of Huckleberry Finn* (1885), to cite one famously controversial example, was Edward W. Kemble (1861–1933), who became America's premier caricaturist of African American life and the author of such racist joke books as *Kemble's Coons* (1896) and *A Coon Alphabet* (1898). Kemble was still unknown when Twain hired him to produce drawings for the novel, but critics have argued for years over his representation of Jim, the runaway slave who appears far more heroic in Mark Twain's text than in Kemble's cartoonlike illustrations. To complicate

matters, Twain expressed approval of Kemble's often demeaning images, leaving many readers unable to decide whether *Huckleberry Finn* should be understood as a celebration of human equality or as a literary version of the old-time minstrel show.

Daniel C. Beard's illustrations for another Twain novel, *A Connecticut Yankee in King Arthur's Court* (1889), provide a different example of the way visual art affected the fiction of the period. Beard (1850–1941) assumed astounding creative license in casting actual people as models for Twain's fictional characters, so that Merlin bears the likeness of the poet Alfred Lord Tennyson, Clarence is depicted as the actress Sarah Bernhardt, and the notorious "Slave Driver" is unmistakably Jay Gould, the great American robber baron of the late nineteenth century. Twain never dreamed of giving his satire such libelous specificity, but he exclaimed that Beard's illustrations were "better than the book—which is a good deal for me to say, I reckon" (David, p. 24). Beard's illustrations even imagined an alternative to the novel's ending, in which Hank Morgan dies alone, separated from his sixth-century wife and child. Explaining his deviation from the literary text, Beard declared simply: "I had not the heart to kill him as did the author" (David, p. 24).

Such aggressively independent illustrators as Kemble and Beard continue to interest readers and literary critics because they force one to reconsider the nature of meaning in a literary text. Who exactly is responsible for the satire of *A Connecticut Yankee,* and to what extent can one attribute the meaning of this or any literary text to its author alone? These questions were raised in the most immediate way during the last quarter of the nineteenth century, when virtually all novels published in America included some graphic content by artists other than the author. It may have been the compromising effects of this uncertain relationship between author and illustrator that led Henry James (1843–1916)—always a skeptic with regard to the graphic adornment of literary texts—to select a photographer, Alvin Langdon Coburn, rather than a painter or caricaturist to produce artwork for the major New York Edition of his works in 1909. Unlike Mark Twain, James was not interested in sharing the platform of his fiction with another creator.

THE COMIC STRIP

The great comic papers that presided over the golden era of American illustration did not survive long into the twentieth century: *Puck,* the industry leader, closed its doors in 1918, followed by *Life* in 1936 and *Judge* a year later. Yet their legacy endures in the form of comic strips, which began to appear in regular Sunday supplements of the major daily newspapers around the turn of the century. Drawing on the work of German caricaturist Wilhelm Busch, *Puck* had begun in the 1870s to experiment with extended image sequences, employing as many as ten or twelve frames to create a graphic narrative. Other humor magazines adopted the same technique, but it was not until 1895 that a recurring cartoon character captured the public imagination and gave birth to what is recognized as the modern comic strip. That character was the Yellow Kid, a motley ruffian who roamed the streets of New York in search of trouble. Richard Outcault had created the Kid for Joseph Pulitzer's *New York World,* a daily newspaper that managed to steal significant market share by publishing a Sunday supplement that mimicked the leading comic weeklies. Outcault's Yellow Kid was so popular that William Randolph Hearst grabbed him for the *New York Journal,* setting off a circulation war between what readers called "the Yellow Journals." The two papers competed not only for the right to publish the Kid's exploits but also for any story (fact or fiction) that would compel readers to buy a daily paper, and their sensational style of reporting the news has ever since been known as yellow journalism.

The Yellow Kid spawned a succession of popular cartoon characters, some of whom are around in the early twenty-first century. In 1897 Rudolph Dirks introduced the *Katzenjammer Kids,* followed by Frederick Opper's *Happy Hooligan* in 1900. Bud Fisher created *Mutt and Jeff* in 1907, and George Herriman's *Krazy Kat* appeared in 1910. With the popularity of these and many other recurring comic strips in the early twentieth century, American illustration took another large step away from its origins in the woodcutting studios at *Harper's New Monthly.* By the turn of the century bright colors and simple line drawings had all but eclipsed the elaborate woodcuts that still occasionally graced the pages of the older literary periodicals as yet another generation of artists, editors, and publishers adapted to shifting demographics and market conditions. Yet the legacy of the Harper revolution remains discernible to anyone who reads the funny papers, which continue to explore the possibilities of illustration as a popular art.

See also Book Publishing; *Harper's New Monthly Magazine*; Periodicals

BIBLIOGRAPHY
Primary Works
Blackbeard, Bill, and Martin Williams, eds. *The Smithsonian Collection of Newspaper Comics.* Washington, D.C.: Smithsonian and Harry N. Abrams, 1977.

Kemble, Edward Windsor. *A Coon Alphabet.* New York: R. H. Russell, 1899.

McDonell, Patrick, et al. *Krazy Kat: The Comic Art of George Herriman.* New York: Harry N. Abrams, 1986.

Twain, Mark. *Adventures of Huckleberry Finn.* 1885. New York: Oxford University Press, 1996.

Twain, Mark. *A Connecticut Yankee in King Arthur's Court.* New York: Oxford University Press, 1996.

Secondary Works
Bland, David. *A History of Book Illustration: The Illuminated Manuscript and the Printed Book.* New York: World Publishing Company, 1958.

David, Beverly R., and Ray Sapirstein. "Reading the Illustrations in *A Connecticut Yankee.*" In *A Connecticut Yankee in King Arthur's Court.* The Oxford Mark Twain series. New York: Oxford University Press, 1996.

Fischer, Roger A. *Them Damned Pictures: Explorations in American Political Cartoon Art.* North Haven, Conn.: Archon Books, 1996.

Harvey, Richard C. *Children of the Yellow Kid: The Evolution of the American Comic Strip.* Seattle, Wash.: Frye Art Museum, 1998.

Mott, Frank Luther. *A History of American Magazines.* 5 vols. Cambridge, Mass.: Harvard University Press, 1930–1968.

Payne, Harold. "Our Caricaturists and Cartoonists." *Munsey's Magazine* 10 (1894): 538–550.

Pennell, Joseph. *Modern Illustration.* London: George Bell, 1895.

Sloane, David E. E. *American Humor Magazines and Comic Periodicals.* New York: Greenwood Press, 1987.

Wonham, Henry B. *Playing the Races: Ethnic Caricature and American Literary Realism.* New York: Oxford University Press, 2004.

Henry B. Wonham

IMAGISM

Imagism was the literary movement that most deeply influenced the development of modern American poetry and the one that contributed the most to the development of modernist techniques in all genres. In reacting to the late-nineteenth-century and early-twentieth-century verse that employed images merely as decorations, it resembles the Romantic reaction against conventional eighteenth-century imagery as well as William Wordsworth's emphasis in his preface to the *Lyrical Ballads* (1802) on the poet's fidelity to personal experience. In using the term *Imagisme,* the imagists also invoked the revolution in the modern French *symbolisme* of Charles Baudelaire and Stéphane Mallarmé. In its association with *vers libre,* or "free verse," it represented a revolt against conventional

"IN A STATION OF THE METRO"

Ezra Pound's imagist poem "In a Station of the Metro" with the spacing Pound insisted upon.

The apparition   of these faces   in the crowd :
Petals   on a wet, black   bough .

Pound, "In a Station of the Metro," p. 12.

rhythm in which the sound bore little relationship to the sense.

EZRA POUND AND THE IMAGISTS

In 1914 D. H. Lawrence told Amy Lowell (1874–1925) that Ezra Pound's (1885–1972) imagism was "just an advertising scheme," and it indeed began that way (Gould, p. 137). Pound coined the term in 1912 to describe some poems of H.D. (Hilda Doolittle, 1886–1961) that he, as foreign editor, was sending to *Poetry* magazine in Chicago. In *End to Torment: A Memoir of Ezra Pound* (1979), Doolittle recalled Pound editing her poem "Hermes of the Ways" in London's British Museum tearoom and then adding "H.D. Imagiste" at the bottom of the page (p. 18). As Pound told *Poetry*'s editor Harriet Monroe in 1915, the movement was started "not very seriously," chiefly to get H.D.'s poems a hearing (Parisi and Young, p. 69). Pound described H.D.'s poems to Monroe in October 1912 as written "in the laconic speech of the Imagistes" (Parisi and Young, p. 47). He first used "Imagiste" in print in describing the five poems he appended as the "Complete Poetical Works" of T. E. Hulme (1883–1927) to his volume of poetry *Ripostes* (1912). In "A Few Don'ts by an Imagiste" (*Poetry*, March 1913), written with contributors to *Poetry* in mind, Pound defined the image as "that which presents an intellectual and emotional complex in an instant in time" and in so doing gives a "sense of freedom from time limits and space limits" (p. 200).

The March issue of *Poetry* also published an essay titled "Imagisme" written by Pound but signed (to suggest that the movement was more than a one-poet phenomenon) by F. S. Flint. Speaking of the Imagists in the past tense, the article says they were not revolutionaries but traditionalists who had only some informal rules: "1. Direct treatment of the 'thing,' whether subjective or objective. 2. To use absolutely no word that

did not contribute to the presentation. 3. As regarding rhythm: to compose in sequence of the musical phrase, not in sequence of a metronome" (p. 199). The article also referred to imagism's "Doctrine of the Image," which it said need not interest the public (p. 199). In *Poetry*'s April 1913 issue, Pound's "In a Station of the Metro" provided a brilliant example of imagist style. In the *Fortnightly Review* of 1 September 1914, Pound's essay titled "Vorticism" explained that he first tried to express his vision of beautiful faces in a Paris metro station in a thirty-line poem, six months later in half that space, and a year later in the "*hokku*-like sentence" of the final poem (p. 89). In 1914 Pound published an anthology titled *Des Imagistes* that included poems by the poets H.D., Richard Aldington, F. S. Flint, Amy Lowell, and William Carlos Williams and the two novelists Ford Madox Hueffer (Ford) and James Joyce.

Despite imagism's origin as a publicity tactic for H.D.'s poems, its tenets had been developing since 1909, soon after Pound's arrival in England from the United States. In 1912 Pound wrote of the "forgotten school of images" that formed around T. E. Hulme, who was killed in World War I (Pratt, p. 14). That early school included F. S. Flint (1885–1960), and Pound had joined the group by April 1909. Discussion included vers libre, verse forms such as the Japanese tanka and haiku, French symbolism, and the precision of French novelists such as Stendhal and Gustave Flaubert. According to Flint, Hulme insisted on accurate presentation of the object and no wasted words. Hulme's conception of language, which was influenced by the French philosopher Henri Bergson, was a crucial influence on his conception of the image. One sees what Flint must have meant by a "Doctrine of the Image" as the idea has its counterpart in Hulme's statement in his 1913 essay "Romanticism and Classicism" that "images in verse are not mere decoration, but the very essence of an intuitive language" (p. 135).

Imagism brought publicity and debate to *Poetry* magazine and soon spread to other journals connected with Pound, such as the *Egoist* (which published a special imagist issue in 1915) and the *Little Review*. But its very success led to a blurring of its program, particularly after the Boston poet Amy Lowell joined the movement. When she read H.D.'s poetry in the 1913 *Poetry*, Lowell decided that she too was an imagist. A member of a distinguished and wealthy family that included the poet James Russell Lowell and a brother who became the president of Harvard University, she became a patron as well as a contributor of imagist verse to *Poetry*. When she visited England in 1913 with the principal goal of meeting Pound and the imagists, she was at first welcomed by Pound. But Pound's interest in imagism was waning, and his anthology *Des Imagistes* was poorly received.

AMY LOWELL AND THE IMAGISTS

Lowell proposed to reinvigorate the movement through a series of anthologies titled *Some Imagist Poets*. The first anthology, in 1915, was a success thanks to Lowell's advertising and book tours, and it was followed by two more editions in 1916 and 1917. Pound claimed that Lowell ignored the tenets and lowered the standards of imagism by accepting any poem as imagist if it were in free verse, and he objected to her editorial policy of letting in too many poets who then chose their own poems. The publisher's blurb for the first anthology claimed that she was the leader of the imagist movement, and her critical book *Tendencies in Modern American Poetry* (1917) eliminated Pound from her discussion of imagism. Dismissing Lowell's movement as "*Amygisme*," Pound thought that her poets violated the imagist tenet that prohibited no word that does not contribute to the presentation. In Lowell's anthologies the poems became long and discursive (for example, John Gould Fletcher's "The Blue Symphony" in 1915) rather than concentrated and imagistic. Although Lowell's introduction to the first volume was a useful restatement of the imagist rules for good writing, she ignored imagist concentration by expanding the three original imagist rules to six, introducing elaborations such as using common speech, creating new rhythms, and asserting freedom in choosing subject matter.

To dissociate himself from Lowell and lesser poets like Lowell's close colleague Fletcher, Pound joined with Wyndham Lewis, a painter, in founding another even shorter-lived movement, vorticism. In restating imagist principles as vortices, he clarified the original imagist tenets. Vorticism believed in using the "primary pigment" of an art: in painting, color and form (often nearly abstract); in poetry, the image. As the vorticist artist juxtaposes geometric forms, the poet juxtaposes images. Pound considered "Amygisme" scenic, static, and imitative. In his 1914 "Vorticism" essay he defined the vorticist image as a "radiant node or cluster . . . from which, and through which, and into which, ideas are constantly rushing" (p. 92). His earlier description of the image as a "complex" (using the word in the psychological sense of the phrase "Oedipus complex") also implied its intellectual and emotional complexity. In the vorticist magazine *Blast* (1914), Pound quotes from H.D.'s "Oread" to exemplify the proper use of the image. In what seems a reference to "Oread" in the "Vorticism" essay, he writes that its juxtaposed images are "not an equation of mathematics . . . having something to do with form but about *sea, cliffs, night,* having something to do with mood" (p. 92). The poem does

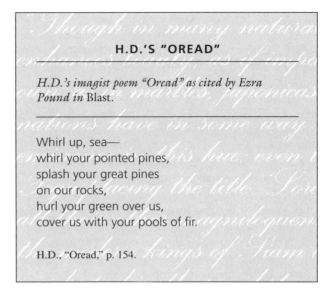

H.D.'S "OREAD"

H.D.'s imagist poem "Oread" as cited by Ezra Pound in Blast.

Whirl up, sea—
whirl your pointed pines,
splash your great pines
on our rocks,
hurl your green over us,
cover us with your pools of fir.

H.D., "Oread," p. 154.

not literally describe a seacoast or explicitly state that a crashing wave resembles a pine tree. Images are abstracted from the scene, acting as equations or formulas for the emotions the artist finds within it.

THE HERITAGE OF IMAGISM

One of poems in the second issue of *Blast* (1915) showed a further development in imagist technique. T. S. Eliot's (1888–1965) "Preludes" revealed city dwellers who reflect the "sordid images" of "grimy scraps of withered leaves," "newspapers from vacant lots," and "broken blinds and chimney-pots" (Lewis, *Blast* no. 2, pp. 4–49). Yet the poem's reflections on the "infinitely suffering thing" that the images suggest goes beyond the confines of the imagist poem. In poems like "Preludes," "The Love Song of J. Alfred Prufrock" (1915), and *The Waste Land* (1922), Eliot showed how an imagistic poem could expand beyond the confines of the short lyric poem without losing what Eliot called "first intensity." Although *The Waste Land* communicates through what it refers to as a "heap of broken images" without discursive commentary or narrative, Eliot's poem has clearly gone beyond the conciseness of imagism. Yet it has kept its intensity. *The Waste Land* may be considered one highly developed image (a "radiant node or cluster") of spiritual dryness in the way that Pound claimed in his "Vorticism" essay that Dante's *Divine Comedy* (discounting the poem's expository passages) was a single image: "The form of sphere above sphere, the varying reaches of light, the minutiae of pearls upon foreheads, all these are parts of the Image" (p. 96).

In T. S. Eliot's definition of the "objective correlative" in "Hamlet and His Problems" (1919), we see the imagist principle when he states that a work of art must communicate "a situation, a chain of events which shall be the formula of that *particular* emotion; such that when the external facts, which must terminate in sensory experience, are given, the emotion is immediately evoked" (p. 125). In Eliot's definition, one finds Hulme's praise of the image because it attempts to communicate sensations directly and Pound's description of H.D.'s poem as an "equation" for an emotion. Pound also faced the challenge of writing a long poem on imagist principles in his epic poem *The Cantos* (1925–1969). To explain a poem composed of broken images and fragmented narratives, he introduced his conception of the "ideogrammic method." According to Pound, the unit of meaning in the Chinese language, the ideogram, is composed of a cluster of details; for example, to denote "red" the ideogram combines characters for the rose, iron rust, the cherry, and the flamingo. In ideogrammic poetry, images, concepts, and quotations are juxtaposed and, theoretically, communicate their meaning as they come together in the reader's mind. As in the earlier definitions of the image, the ideogram is an intellectual and emotional "complex" or a "radiant note or cluster."

The genius of imagism was to formulate the principles of modernist writing that continued to inform twentieth-century writing long after the movement died out. In addition to the influence of the Romantics and *symbolistes,* the precision of Flaubert's prose, Henry James's emphasis on showing rather than telling, and the turn-of-the-century popularity of the haiku inspired imagism's principle of directness and concision. Eliot's "objective correlative," William Carlos Williams's slogan "no ideas but in things," and Archibald MacLeish's belief (expressed in the 1926 poem "Ars Poetica") that a poem "should not mean / But be" bear the mark of imagism. Imagism's emphasis on poetic form anticipated the formalist criticism of Eliot, Ivor Armstrong Richards, and Richard P. Blackmur. What Pound calls the imagist "freedom from time limits and space limits" anticipates the modernist conception of "spatial form," in which temporal narratives are unified through recurring motifs and scenes composed of vivid images. In prose the images that conclude Lawrence's novel *The Rainbow* (1915) or make up the interchapters of Ernest Hemingway's *In Our Time* (1925) demonstrate the importance of imagistic technique to modern prose. The technical and philosophical principles of imagism revolutionized modern literature.

See also Aestheticism; Lyric Poetry; *Poetry: A Magazine of Verse*

BIBLIOGRAPHY
Primary Works

Eliot, T. S. "Hamlet and His Problems." In *Selected Essays*. New York: Harcourt, Brace, 1964.

H. D. [Hilda Doolittle]. *End to Torment: A Memoir of Ezra Pound*. New York: New Directions, 1979.

H. D. "Oread," *Blast* no. 1 (20 June 1914): 154.

Flint, F. S. "Imagisme." *Poetry: A Magazine of Verse* 1 (March 1913): 198–200.

Hulme, T. E. "Romanticism and Classicism." In *Speculations: Essays on Humanism and the Philosophy of Art*, edited by Herbert Read. New York: Harcourt, Brace, 1961.

Lewis, Wyndham, ed. *Blast* no. 1 (20 June 1914); no. 2 (July 1915). Reprinted, Santa Barbara, Calif.: Black Sparrow Press, 1981.

Lowell, Amy. *Tendencies in Modern American Poetry*. New York: Macmillan, 1917. New York: Octagon Books, 1971.

Pound, Ezra. "A Few Don'ts by an Imagiste." *Poetry: A Magazine of Verse* 1 (March 1913): 200–206.

Pound, Ezra. "In a Station of the Metro." *Poetry* 2, no. 1 (April 1913): 12. Also available at http://www. library. yale.edu/beinecke/orient/mod2.htm.

Pound, Ezra. "Vorticism." *Fortnightly Review,* 1 September 1914. Reprinted in *Gaudier-Brzeska: A Memoir*. New York: New Directions, 1970.

Secondary Works

Coffman, Stanley K. *Imagism: A Chapter for the History of Modern Poetry*. Norman: University of Oklahoma Press, 1951.

Gould, Jean. *Amy: The World of Amy Lowell and the Imagist Movement*. New York: Dodd, Mead, 1975.

Parisi, Joseph, and Stephen Young, eds. *Dear Editor: A History of Poetry in Letters, the First Fifty Years, 1912–1962*. New York: Norton, 2002.

Pratt, William. *The Imagist Poem: Modern Poetry in Miniature*. New York: Dutton, 1963.

Timothy Materer

IMMIGRATION

Introducing her story collection *Children of Loneliness* (1923), the immigrant writer Anzia Yezierska (1885–1970) remarks, "I saw that America was a new world in the making, that anyone who has something real in him can find a way to contribute himself in this new world" ("Mostly about Myself," p. 142). She contributes through writing, declaring, "the moment I understood America enough to tell her about herself as I saw her—the moment I began to express myself—America accepted my self-expression as a gift from me, and from everywhere hands reached out to help me" ("Mostly about Myself," p. 142). Beside these optimistic reflections, Yezierska's texts also uncover the challenges immigrants confronted, as the "loneliness" in her title implies. While immigrant texts often celebrate American opportunity, they contain much greater complexity, as critics have observed. Thomas Ferraro hails immigrant writers' artistic accomplishments, citing a "self-transformation" process through writing that may engage literary currents such as modernism yet does not necessarily entail cultural assimilation. William Boelhower recognizes a "demythification" process whereby the immigrant writer exposes an "underside" to a formerly idealized America. Indeed, turn-of-the-century American immigrant writers struggled to reconcile ideals and disillusionment as they recorded the lives of America's newest citizens. Yezierska, along with many turn-of-the-century immigrant writers, addresses several common themes of immigrant challenge: experiencing racism and discrimination, seeking education, negotiating intergenerational conflicts, defining gender roles, and finding fulfilling work.

RACISM AND DISCRIMINATION

Many American hands reached out to halt rather than to help immigrants, particularly eastern European Jews like Yezierska. From the late 1870s until the early 1920s, record numbers of immigrants arrived in the United States, mainly from eastern and southern Europe, countries such as Poland, Bohemia, Slovenia, and Italy. From 1900 to 1910 alone, 9 million arrived, exceeding immigration in any previous decade by 3.5 million. They found a limited welcome. The Chinese Exclusion Act of 1882 prohibited entry of all Chinese except for merchants, scholars, diplomats, tourists, and teachers and prevented Chinese from becoming citizens. Increasingly restrictive quota laws adopted in 1921, 1924, and 1929 virtually eliminated immigration from southern and eastern Europe. Anti-immigrant agitators often cited undesirable immigrant cultures to justify restrictions, but anti-immigrant worries actually centered on race. The literary scholar Walter Benn Michaels argues that "culture" served as a cover for race, an exclusionary "way of preserving the primacy of identity while avoiding the embarrassments of blood" (p. 13). In his influential book *The Passing of the Great Race* (1916), the amateur anthropologist Madison Grant (1865–1937) describes immigrants as radically different from native-born, Anglo-Saxon Americans in physical appearance, religion, language, and customs, all factors he considered racial. As the historian John Higham explains, "nativists" such as Grant, who aimed to preserve America for those "native" to the United States, considered southern and eastern Europeans remote from

Contemporary periodicals ranging from the popular Saturday Evening Post *to the middlebrow* North American Review *to the more intellectual* Atlantic Monthly *voiced racially based, anti-immigrant fears. Writing for the* Atlantic *in 1896, Francis Walker, commissioner general of immigration, condemned recent immigrants.*

They are beaten men from beaten races; representing the worst failures in the struggle for existence. Centuries are against them, as centuries were on the side of those who formerly came to us. They have none of the ideas and aptitudes which fit men to take up readily and easily the problem of self care and self government, such as belong to those who are descended from the tribes that met under the oak-trees of old Germany to make laws and choose chieftains.

Phrases such as "struggle for existence" and "descended from the tribes . . . of old Germany" reflect scientific theories that "non-Anglo-Saxon races" progressed too slowly. Politics, the "ideas" Walker cites, become a product of racial "aptitudes," and thus he dubs new immigrants inherently incapable of democratic participation. Immigrant writers needed to disprove racialist claims such as Walker's.

Walker, "Restriction of Immigration," p. 828.

Anglo-Saxon forms of government. The sociologist Edward Ross complains in 1914, "Now we confront the melancholy spectacle of this pioneer breed being swamped and submerged by an overwhelming tide of latecomers from the old-world hive" (p. 282). He argues that immigrant races would weaken the nation, bringing inferior hereditary traits and promoting the "race suicide" of established Anglo-Saxon Americans.

However, Ross and other nativists represent only one strain in a vigorous debate. The philosopher, educator, and immigrant Horace Kallen (1882–1974) refutes Ross in his 1915 essay "Democracy versus the Melting-Pot": "What troubles Mr. Ross and so many other Anglo-Saxon Americans is not really inequality; what troubles them is difference" (p. 219). Declaring such "difference" nonhereditary, the anthropologist and immigrant Franz Boas asserts in his 1911 *The Mind of Primitive Man,* "There is no close relation between race and culture" (p. 196). Moreover, Boas also proclaims the independent value of various cultures as well

Immigrant writers often express awe over American educational opportunity. In her autobiography The Promised Land *(1912), the Russian immigrant Mary Antin conveys the magical quality education held, when she recalls the day her father brought his children to school for the first time.*

All three children carried themselves rather better than the common run of "green" pupils that were brought to Miss Nixon. But the figure that challenged attention to the group was the tall, straight father, with his earnest face and fine forehead, nervous hands eloquent in gesture, and a voice full of feeling. This foreigner, who brought his children to school as if it were an act of consecration, who regarded the teacher of the primer class with reverence, who spoke of visions, like a man inspired, in a common schoolroom, was not like other aliens, who brought their children in dull obedience to the law; was not like the native fathers, who brought their unmanageable boys, glad to be relieved of their care. I think Miss Nixon guessed what my father's best English could not convey. I think that she divined that by the simple act of delivering our school certificates to her he took possession of America.

Antin, *The Promised Land,* 1997, p. 162.

as races, rejecting a ranked order for either. The scholars Nancy Leys Stepan and Sander Gilman identify a "critical tradition" among writers from groups "stereotyped by the sciences of the day" (p. 74), and this defensive posture responding to scientific racism characterizes turn-of-the-century immigrant literature. For instance, in her 1914 book *They Who Knock at Our Gates,* the Russian immigrant writer Mary Antin (1881–1949) protests: "What have the experts and statisticians done so to pervert our minds? They have filled volumes with facts and figures, comparing the immigrants of other days, classifying them as to race, nationality, and culture. . . . Granted that Sicilians are not Scotchmen, how does that affect the right of the Sicilian to travel in pursuit of happiness?" (pp. 9–10).

Depending on class and region, the nativists that Antin and other writers faced expressed their views through print media, political agitation, and even violence. Chinese in the western United States faced harassment, expulsion from towns, and even massacres

from the 1850s into the 1880s. The Chinese immigrant writer Sui Sin Far (Edith Maud Eaton, 1865–1914) captures such incidents in her fiction, particularly the story "Her Chinese Husband" from the 1912 collection *Mrs. Spring Fragrance,* a story that details the happy married life of a white woman and Chinese man cut short by his violent murder. Sui Sin Far's work contrasts with what William Wu has termed "yellow peril" fiction by such writers as Jack London and Frank Norris, which reinforced anxiety about "uncivilized" Chinese immigrants. Such fiction stereotyped the Chinese as inscrutable, wildly excitable, and unintelligent (though sometimes unusually intelligent), with heartless husbands and women slaves. Typical plots involved Chinese invasions, revenge, lasciviousness, and opium addiction. Besides exposing anti-Asian violence, Sui Sin Far wrote to overturn race stereotypes of the Chinese by offering both fiction and journalism that provided multidimensional pictures of Chinese character. Her essay series The Chinese in America, which appeared in the 1909 *Westerner* magazine, offers a broad readership a sympathetic exploration of Chinese American family life, holidays, work, food, religion, and customs.

Besides exclusion and attack, immigrants endured other indignities, as the Italian immigrant writer Constantine Panunzio (1884–1964) recounts in his autobiography, *The Soul of an Immigrant* (1921). Though never guilty of any crime, Panunzio landed in jail three times; the third time, he was arrested for sitting on a park bench. Expecting an armed and dangerous Italian, others at his school mistook his comb for a knife. Panunzio ultimately overcame this discrimination and other "stumbling block[s] to assimilation" (p. 205) to succeed in school and in his career as a minister. In their attempts to assimilate successfully, immigrants confronted the prominent racial thinking that defined them as inferior. However, they might actually attempt to negotiate their way into its privileged levels. Matthew Frye Jacobson observes that "certain groups undergo a process of racial redefinition as shifting social and political circumstances require" and that "varying systems of 'difference' can coexist and compete with one another at a given moment" (p. 140). Immigrants could occupy what Jacobson terms a "probationary white" status on their way to fuller acceptance. Early in Yezierska's novel *Salome of the Tenements* (1923), the immigrant protagonist Sonya Vrunsky declares: "The Anglo-Saxons are a superior race to the crazy Russians. The higher life is built inch by inch on self-control. . . . They're ages ahead of us. Compared to them, we're naked savages" (p. 68). Sonya seems to have absorbed the nativist theories of Grant and Ross, but she also seems to perceive a racial/cultural mobility possible as she pursues

***The Steerage,* 1907.** Photograph by Alfred Stieglitz. One of the pioneers of photography as an art form, Stieglitz here captures the disparity between the classes of passengers sailing to the United States on the ship *Kaiser Wilhelm II.*
THE LIBRARY OF CONGRESS

marriage with the Anglo-Saxon philanthropist John Manning. Her apparently "probationary" status could solidify through her marriage; however, Yezierska has her heroine gradually reject this racial schema to instead "be what's inside of me" (p. 131). Though Sonya finally rejects a racial philosophy that demands that she remake or deny her identity, Yezierska illustrates the difficult choices immigrants faced within a racially hostile environment. In addition, her character's sudden reversal illustrates well a pattern Werner Sollors cites in ethnic writing: "Raising and thwarting initiation expectations, feeding the gullibility of readers and then pulling the rug from under their feet, or ironically undercutting the image of a presumably stable relationship between in-group and out-group are among the weapons in the rich arsenal of ethnic writers" (p. 252). In their often ambiguous and multilayered texts, immigrants challenged American conceptions of immigrant race and culture.

EDUCATION

In both fiction and nonfiction, immigrant writers chronicled efforts to gain American education, which became an elusive goal for some. The title character of Abraham Cahan's (1860–1951) novel *The Rise of David Levinsky* (1917) reaches financial success but largely by abandoning the "Temple" of his dream of higher education. Actually achieving education could also cause problems, such as alienation from family. In Yezierska's novel *Bread Givers* (1925), Sara Smolinsky chooses to pursue her studies, leading her Orthodox Jewish father to disown her. She also carries guilt over denying time away from studying to visit her mother. Despite such complications, educational achievement remained an important standard of success for many immigrants. In his autobiography *A Far Journey* (1914), the Syrian immigrant Abraham Rihbany views college education as a vital way to "relate myself to the higher life of America" (p. 253). Finding greater acceptance in preparatory school, Constantine Panunzio realizes there that he wants to become a citizen. For him, education represents the essence of America, the means for developing an "American consciousness" (p. 179). Education seemed to hold an almost mystical power. Immigrants often lacked the opportunity for sustained schooling in their native lands, but in America many school opportunities existed. Moreover, immigrants viewed education as a means to recast themselves as Americans.

The work of Mary Antin, a Russian immigrant from the Jewish Pale of Settlement, often revolves around immigrant education. Intellectual prowess and academic enthusiasm play important roles in her autobiography, as critics note. For example, William

Proefriedt argues that Antin undergoes parallel processes of education and assimilation. Antin unfolds her own educational progress as an eager learner who began publishing at an early age, but she also celebrates the intellectual accomplishments of other immigrants. Addressing the pattern of immigrant achievement also allows Antin to critique racialist thinking. In her pro-immigration treatise *They Who Knock at Our Gates,* Antin momentarily enters the mind of a native-born American: "The children of the foreigners outclass our own! They who begin handicapped, and labor against obstacles, leave our own children far behind on the road to scholarly achievement. . . . Is there a special virtue in their blood that enables them to sweep over our country and take what they want?" She explains simply, "It is a special virtue, yes: the virtue of great purpose" (pp. 129–130). Illustrating that playful quality in immigrant writing that Sollors notes, Antin responds to the predictable question of whether race or "blood" explains immigrant achievement, employing a subtle irony to shift the focus: "Purpose" is not an element of "blood," but diligence is definitely an immigrant "virtue." Race fades into the background, with only immigrant determination and effort bringing success to promising new citizens.

A prominent figure in New York's Jewish community, Abraham Cahan, who like Antin fled the Russian Pale, also emphasizes immigrant education to reduce the perceived threat from immigration. In an 1898 issue of the *Atlantic,* Cahan describes many Jews denied education in his homeland who complete studies in the United States to become doctors, dentists, and architects. Much like Mary Antin, Cahan underscores intellectual prowess to encourage goodwill toward immigrants, demonstrating that they will contribute important resources to their adopted nation. He counts the Russian Jewish immigrant "among the most ambitious and the quickest to learn both the written and spoken language of the adopted country, and among the easiest to be assimilated with the population" (p. 131). The historian Lloyd Gartner observes that public school became "the symbol and guarantee of Jewish equality and full opportunity in America" (p. 9). Cahan describes immigrant Jews flocking to public day and evening schools, which do not exclude them, and many also tutoring their fellow immigrants. Cahan, who became a longtime editor of the Yiddish daily newspaper the *Forward,* also acknowledged the role of journalism in schooling the immigrant in American customs, English language, and library use. While not all immigrants attended college or even progressed far in secondary schools, Cahan attests to significant numbers gaining formal education and an overall enthusiasm among immigrants to learn as much as possible.

The Serbian immigrant Michael Pupin (1858–1935) illustrates well this passion for education: he not only achieved high degrees but also helped to reform American education itself during his career. His autobiography, *From Immigrant to Inventor* (1923), traces his educational experiences from independent study and night courses at Cooper Union to undergraduate study at Columbia to graduate work abroad at Cambridge. Pupin merited a full scholarship to Columbia and succeeded so well in school that native-born students sought him as a tutor. Pupin consistently served others through his education, applying his own knowledge and abilities to enhance American life. While inventing the electrical resonator and developing other technologies, Pupin also helped to reinvent the American educational system. As an engineering professor at Columbia, he promoted more rigorous science courses with increased hands-on lab work to prepare the next generation of inventors. Immigrant literature established immigrant education not only as an ideal for the immigrant but also as a benefit for the entire nation.

INTERGENERATIONAL CONFLICTS

Israel Zangwill's (1864–1926) *The Melting-Pot,* the 1909 British play that established a catchphrase that many still use to imagine immigrant America, presents a quintessential conflict in the immigrant experience: alienation of one generation from another. David Quixano escapes an anti-Jewish pogrom and lands in America, where he falls in love with the Russian immigrant Vera Rivendal. His uncle rejects him for allying with a Russian, a member of the group that has persecuted David's people. David defies his uncle until he discovers that Vera's father actually started the pogrom that killed his family. Torn between his lover and their families' histories, David ultimately embraces Vera and stands by his declaration, "Each generation must live and die for its own dream" (p. 147). This idea became as much a part of American immigrant literature and thought as the concept of a melting pot of races and cultures. Negotiating histories, traditions, and expectations, newer generations of immigrants often clashed with their elders. Parental authority came into question in a new environment where rules seemed ever changing and multiple influences affected children. Priscilla Wald observes that the "strangeness of parenting one's parents is a common theme" of writing by women immigrants and those from "any culture perceived to be in need of 'Americanization'" (p. 191). Her comment suits men immigrant writers too.

Cahan's 1898 story "The Imported Bridegroom" illustrates several parent-child conflicts as two generations struggle to define their cultural identities in America. Asriel Stroon has largely abandoned his Orthodox Judaism and allowed his daughter, Flora, to have an American public school education, piano lessons, and her own library. However, later in life he determines to regain his piety and rethinks his parenting decisions, rebuking Flora for reading a "Gentile" novel while he prays. Asriel's sudden change of attitude confuses his daughter, who feels increasingly isolated from him. Hoping to reform his daughter and please God, Asriel "imports" a religious scholar from Russia as a bridegroom for Flora. The plan fails when the bridegroom chooses secular learning and socialism, rejecting both Asriel's religious program and Flora's scheme to make him a medical doctor. Cahan leaves this father alienated from both children and the young people disconnected from each other.

Sara in Yezierska's *Bread Givers* similarly chafes under the rule of a traditionally religious father. While her father arranges profoundly unhappy marriages for his other three daughters, Sara refuses this fate, leaving home to work her way through college and become a public school teacher. The dean of her college groups her among the "pioneers" (p. 232), but Sara's father sees her as a betrayer. Even with her new independent life she can never separate herself completely from her tyrannical father. Yezierska leaves an ambiguous ending to the novel, with Sara and her husband inviting her impoverished and sickly father to live with them. Sara finds that her father imposes an "old burden" that "dragged" her back (p. 295); however, she also acknowledges that she has inherited his strong will, which motivated her to establish her career. Critics are divided on the novel's resolution. Sam Girgus proposes that Sara ministers to her father out of strength, not weakness, that she has become a self-made woman. Carol Schoen similarly argues that Sara has created a working amalgam of traditions in this ending. However, Gay Wilentz asserts that the ending offers no successful synthesis of old and new traditions and that Sara has regressed into the old order. Magdalena Zaborowska concurs that traditional patriarchy ultimately reigns, with both Sara's husband and father ending her newfound independence. However one reads Yezierska's conclusion, she has captured well the intense intergenerational struggle many immigrants confronted and their difficulties in finding a satisfactory resolution.

While Cahan and Yezierska document the increased tension between domineering parents and rebellious children, other texts illustrate different approaches to intergenerational conflict. In her 1912 autobiography *The Promised Land,* Mary Antin reveals that her parents exerted far less parental control, perhaps because they themselves had abandoned many religious traditions. However, their struggles to earn a living and their perplexity over how best to Americanize their children also help determine this detached approach. Perceiving the "boundless liberty" that neighboring parents seemed to allow, the Antins followed suit (p. 213). Their children did encounter more varied cultural influences, but only as the parents relinquished the "throne of parental authority" (p. 213). This resulted in an "inversion of normal relations" that Antin retrospectively views ambivalently as her parents' "sacrifice" (p. 213). Sui Sin Far's parents (the Eatons) also distance themselves from certain conflicts, relying on their children to determine their own way. In her autobiographical essay "Leaves from the Mental Portfolio of an Eurasian" (1909), Sui Sin Far discusses how other children verbally and physically abused her and her siblings because of their mixed racial background. While the Eatons comfort their children after these incidents, they avoid interfering directly to protect them. Sui Sin Far laments that since neither parent is biracial, they cannot understand the situation fully. She notes, however, that they seem to take greater interest in each children's "battle" than they reveal (p. 219). Quite likely the Eatons hoped that this parenting approach would strengthen their children for more challenging racial battles in the future.

GENDER ROLES

As the discussion above suggests, many immigrant conflicts over issues such as education and parenting involved gender ideas. Immigrants encountered new gender behaviors, demanding that they re-envision themselves, their spouses, their interests, and their opportunities. While it might be easy to imagine that America transformed immigrant gender conceptions, perhaps offering a feminist haven for women immigrants, the reality was much more complicated. Many authors reflect a synthesis of gender ideas occurring for the typical immigrant—a combination of old and new traditions synthesized to provide personal fulfillment. In addition, men's and women's experiences of immigration often differed greatly, and they struggled to communicate with one another about their experiences. For instance, in the novel *Giants in the Earth* (1927), by the Norwegian immigrant O. E. Rölvaag (1876–1931), Per Hansa finds homesteading in the Dakota Territory stimulating, imagining that wheat grains jump with life, while his wife, Beret, experiences depression, fearing that the family will become "savages" in an untamed environment. Failing to communicate effectively about their expectations, this couple finds their relationship steadily deteriorating. Offering a "critique from the margins" model, Magdalena Zaborowska discusses immigrant writers' gender-role critiques, which extend from old to new country patriarchal practices. As immigrant writing shows, both rural and urban women faced unique challenges in America, such as negotiating unstable gender definitions, seeking greater independence, and combating sexual exploitation.

Contradictory gender expectations could lead to tragedy, as Sui Sin Far demonstrates in her story "The Wisdom of the New." Like many immigrants, the Chinese husband in this story preceded his wife to America, in this case by seven years. The husband, Wou Sankwei, has adapted to America culturally in many ways, developing platonic friendships with a woman philanthropist and her niece. However, he makes little effort to help Pau Lin, his newly arrived wife, adapt, and he spends more time with his women friends than he does with Pau Lin. Despite his open conversations with the educated American women, he denies that his wife can develop intellectually or culturally: "The time for learning with her is over" (p. 47). While he attempts to maintain a more traditional Chinese marriage, wherein his wife cannot question his motives or share open communication with him, he continues very different relationships with his women friends, conversing freely with them and treating them as peers. Isolated and upset, Pau Lin further entrenches herself against any cultural change, fearing that she has lost her husband's affection and respect and that American ways will contaminate her young son. Too late, Sankwei recognizes his inconsistent treatment of the women in his life, for his distraught wife murders their son, believing that she has "saved" him from the "Wisdom of the New" American culture (p. 47). In this story Sui Sin Far emphasizes not the woman's failure to adapt but rather her lack of opportunities to learn about new cultural possibilities and different types of relationships between men and women. Pau Lin only experiences displacement by the other women in the story, not camaraderie.

In contrast to Wou Sankwei, Abraham Rihbany (1869–1944) adjusts more successfully to new gender roles. Initially he finds American women's "prominence in domestic and social affairs. . . . a strange and unnatural phenomenon," since he is accustomed to Syrian women being silent partners (p. 259). Open affection between spouses also distresses him. As he continues to socialize outside of the Syrian community, he observes that these novel relations between spouses promote a "harmonious" family and decides that "true civilization" arises from "equal rights" (pp. 260–261). Much like Rihbany, the Japanese immigrant Etsu Sugimoto (b. 1873) at first perceives an alarming clash over gender traditions. In her autobiography, *A Daughter of the Samurai* (1925), she explains that she gradually understands the common ground between Japanese and American women; women in both countries are "volcanoes" of understated power (p. 202). She fascinates her American-born neighbor with the story of the Japanese island of Hachijo, where women perform traditionally male duties such as making laws and cultivating rice, while men handle child care and washing. While Sugimoto becomes more comfortable reevaluating long-held traditions, she discovers that immigrants and native-born American women share many gender ideals and, ultimately, that neither America nor Japan yet has achieved gender equality.

Sugimoto's "volcanoes" erupt throughout immigrant literature, as immigrant women assert new independence. Yezierska's heroine in *Bread Givers*, Sara, dramatically establishes her rights in a pivotal battle with her father. When her father tries to forbid her from moving out on her own, she declares, "In America, women don't need men to boss them" (p. 137). Pitting her will against patriarchal authority, Sara affirms her rights to make her own decisions over housing, a career, and marriage. Sui Sin Far offers a similar example of an immigrant woman who finds greater freedom in America, away from a family that constricts her. Sui Sin Far's "The Story of Iso" supports "Americanization" in marriage customs and overall gender relationships. In China, Iso's family disapproves of her, a "talking woman," who speaks her mind too freely and flouts feminine conventions (p. 117). She resents her household duties, refuses to worship ancestors, and criticizes her arranged fiancé, disgracing her family. Iso eventually finds relief in America, for "in China, 'The woman who talks too much' is called by *us* 'The new woman'" (p. 119). Along with their native-born counterparts, immigrant women tested the boundaries of gender traditions, striking out into new territory literally and figuratively, and immigrant literature celebrates these changes.

However, immigrant women and other ethnic women faced persistent obstacles to obtaining such liberation. Both Yezierska and Sui Sin Far acknowledge the sexual exploitation that hampered immigrant women's efforts to reach greater independence. In "Leaves from the Mental Portfolio of an Eurasian," Sui Sin Far reports confronting a naval officer who tries to seduce her, imagining that her Asian background makes her more receptive. Shenah Pessah, the protagonist of Yezierska's story "Wings," has a similarly demeaning experience. She becomes infatuated with the sociologist John Barnes, who kisses her passionately but then ignores her for days, while she pines away in confusion. The disillusioned Shenah Pessah realizes later that Barnes has taken liberties with her because he does not view her as "a lady alike to him" (p. 16). She sees that like many American men, Barnes follows different rules with the ethnic woman, treating her as sexual prey. While immigrant women struggled to shake off the chains of "Old World" patriarchy, they found that "New World" men threatened their progress in other ways.

Some "New World" men formed more serious relationships with immigrant women, but this type of interethnic relationship also brought challenges. In Yezierska's *Salome of the Tenements*, Manning emphasizes disturbing elements in his relationship with the immigrant Sonya, viewing their romance as a "mingling of the races. . . . The oriental mystery and the Anglo-Saxon clarity that will pioneer a new race of men" (p. 108). As Horace Kallen has noted, this racial amalgamation theory essentially reinforced Anglo-Saxon American identity to "improve" immigrants and their descendants. Sonya gradually realizes that the union, rather than evolving as a loving relationship, will degenerate into a scientific experiment. As Mary Dearborn observes, Sonya's relationship evokes Yezierska's own turbulent relationship with John Dewey, a reformer of Anglo-Saxon origin. Sonya wavers between attraction to and repulsion from her lover's ideals, wanting to be like him and wanting to retain her own unique qualities. For Manning, Sonya seems attractive as a mysterious, passionate, "primitive" woman, yet he suppresses the very expressiveness that draws him, to "raise" her into "civilization." Manning tries to limit her social life in order to reform her in his image. Zaborowska suggests that Sonya even attempts to suppress her sexuality to avoid appearing an oversexed ethnic woman. While the false distinctions between the Anglo-Saxon and the eastern European immigrant collapse in the narrative, the expectations they construct ultimately doom the marriage. Although gender became more flexible in America, immigrant writers reveal that enacting satisfactory gender roles still proved difficult, particularly for women immigrants.

WORK AND SUCCESS

If a strong work ethic involving patience, perseverance, and eventual reward characterized America's beginnings, this ideal equally characterized immigrant America at the turn into the twentieth century. By all accounts many hardworking immigrants strongly benefited the national economy. O. P. Austin, chief statistician in the Department of Commerce and Labor, reported in 1904 that immigrants contributed significantly to national wealth, particularly where they concentrated themselves, a finding that the historian Thomas Muller confirms. However, unfamiliar with American customs and language and needing work quickly, many immigrants accepted the most modest jobs in factories, manual labor, and petty retail. Racial prejudice also sharply limited opportunities, as immigrant writers emphasized. For instance, Mary Antin relates how prejudiced employers refused to hire her father due to his "Jewish appearance" and "imperfect English" (p. 229). Immigrant writers portrayed these challenges but also demonstrated inspiring career successes. While immigrants defined working success variously, definitions of achievement typically involved not only material success but also moral and creative growth as well.

One writer who found success not only as an author but also as an editor and publisher is Edward Bok (1863–1930). Embodying the Horatio Alger image of rags to riches, he worked odd jobs in youth, later networked with important mentors, and finally rose to prominence in the magazine publishing world, eventually narrating his progress in an autobiography. In *The Americanization of Edward Bok: The Autobiography of a Dutch Boy Fifty Years After* (1920), Bok suggests that immigrants may work harder than the typical native-born person, taking nothing for granted. He works his way up from window washer and delivery boy to stenographer to editor of the *Ladies' Home Journal*. Along the way this entrepreneur forms pivotal relationships that influence his progress, even keeping an autograph collection featuring such literati as Ralph Waldo Emerson, Henry Wadsworth Longfellow, and Louisa May Alcott. In Bok's definition of success, community service matters significantly. Having benefited from many mentors, he too hopes to assist others, for instance by establishing a scholarship program for his magazine employees. As Bok illustrates, immigrant writers define success as much more than monetary.

Abraham Cahan examines immigrant career success from a different angle in his well-known novel *The Rise of David Levinsky* (1917). Levinsky becomes a self-made man, rising in New York's garment industry to become extremely wealthy. However, Levinsky loses much in the process, abandoning his religious faith, giving up a college education, and avoiding meaningful personal relationships. He even chooses to exploit other immigrants for his own personal benefit, thwarting his employees' efforts to unionize. Cahan invites readers to view Levinsky's economic rise as a personal decline. Sanford Marovitz aptly describes the novel as "a moral tale that illustrates how not to live" (p. 139). Levinsky himself summarizes his life: "There are cases when success is a tragedy" (p. 529). This immigrant narrative examines closely what success entails and finds business accomplishment alone inadequate and sometimes at odds with moral and personal growth. Cahan's novel reminds readers that true career success occurs on multiple levels.

Anzia Yezierska's novels illustrate that immigrant career success need not even contain the dramatic financial gain that Bok and Levinsky enjoy. At the end of *Salome of the Tenements,* Sonya becomes a fashion designer who provides inexpensive but beautiful clothes for working-class women. This career offers a steady salary but more importantly provides a satisfying creative outlet and community contribution. Likewise, Sara of *Bread Givers* finds a rewarding career as a public schoolteacher with a modest salary. Both women achieve a professional balance that enables them to develop their talents while also helping others, an immigrant ideal that authors such as Bok, Pupin, and Panunzio also emphasize. Having transcended racism, gained a solid education, differentiated themselves from their parents, and forged professional lives, Yezierska's heroines indeed offer a compelling model for immigrant success. Turn-of-the-century immigrant writers showed that immigrants needed to overcome many obstacles, and understanding those challenges only makes their achievement more laudable.

See also Assimilation; Chinese; Jews; Labor; Migration; *The Rise of David Levinsky;* Social Darwinism; Socialism

BIBLIOGRAPHY
Primary Works
Antin, Mary. *The Promised Land*. 1912. Introduced by Werner Sollors. New York: Penguin, 1997.

Antin, Mary. *They Who Knock at Our Gates: A Complete Gospel of Immigration*. Boston: Houghton, 1914.

Austin, O. P. "Is the New Immigration Dangerous to the Country?" *North American Review* 178 (1904): 558–570.

Bok, Edward. *The Americanization of Edward Bok: The Autobiography of a Dutch Boy Fifty Years After*. New York: Scribners, 1920.

Cahan, Abraham. *The Rise of David Levinsky*. 1917. Introduced by Jules Chametsky. New York: Penguin, 1993.

Cahan, Abraham. "The Russian Jew in America." *Atlantic* (July 1898): 128–139.

Cahan, Abraham. *Yekl and the Imported Bridegroom and Other Stories of Yiddish New York*. 1896, 1898. Introduced by Bernard G. Richards. New York: Dover, 1970.

Kallen, Horace. "Democracy versus the Melting-Pot." *Nation* (18 February 1915): 190–194; (25 February 1915): 217–220.

Panunzio, Constantine. *The Soul of an Immigrant*. 1921. New York: McMillan, 1922.

Pupin, Michael. *From Immigrant to Inventor*. New York: Scribners, 1923.

Rihbany, Abraham. *A Far Journey*. Boston: Houghton, 1914.

Rölvaag, O. E. *Giants in the Earth*. 1927. New York: Harper, 1955.

Sugimoto, Etsu Inaqaki. *A Daughter of the Samurai: How a Daughter of Feudal Japan, Living Hundreds of Years in*

One Generation, Became a Modern American. Garden City, N.Y.: Doubleday, 1925.

Sui Sin Far. "Her Chinese Husband." 1912. In *Mrs. Spring Fragrance and Other Writings,* edited by Amy Ling and Annette White-Parks, pp. 78–83. Urbana: University of Illinois Press, 1995.

Sui Sin Far. "Leaves from the Mental Portfolio of an Eurasian." 1909. In *Mrs. Spring Fragrance and Other Writings,* edited by Amy Ling and Annette White-Parks, pp. 218–230. Urbana: University of Illinois Press, 1995.

Sui Sin Far. *Mrs. Spring Fragrance and Other Writings.* Edited by Amy Ling and Annette White-Parks. Urbana: University of Illinois Press, 1995.

Sui Sin Far. "The Story of Iso." *Lotus* (August 1896): 117–119.

Sui Sin Far. "The Wisdom of the New." 1912. In *Mrs. Spring Fragrance and Other Writings,* edited by Amy Ling and Annette White-Parks, pp. 42–61. Urbana: University of Illinois Press, 1995.

Walker, Francis. "Restriction of Immigration." *Atlantic* 77 (June 1896): 822–829.

Yezierska, Anzia. *Bread Givers.* 1925. Introduced by Alice Kessler-Harris. New York: Persea, 1999.

Yezierska, Anzia. *How I Found America: Collected Stories of Anzia Yezierska.* Introduced by Vivan Gornick. New York: Persea, 1991.

Yezierska, Anzia. "Mostly about Myself." 1923. In *How I Found America: Collected Stories of Anzia Yezierska,* introduced by Vivan Gornick, pp. 131–143. New York: Persea, 1991.

Yezierska, Anzia. *Salome of the Tenements.* 1923. Urbana: University of Illinois Press, 1995.

Yezierska, Anzia. "Wings." 1920. In *How I Found America: Collected Stories of Anzia Yezierska,* introduced by Vivan Gornick, pp. 3–16. New York: Persea, 1991.

Zangwill, Israel. *The Melting-Pot: Drama in Four Acts.* 1909. New York: Macmillan, 1939.

Secondary Works

Boas, Franz. *The Mind of Primitive Man.* 1911. New York: Macmillan, 1929.

Boelhower, William. "The Brave New World of Immigrant Autobiography." *MELUS* 9, no. 2 (1982): 5–32.

Dearborn, Mary. *Love in the Promised Land: The Story of Anzia Yezierska and John Dewey.* New York: Free Press, 1988.

Ferraro, Thomas. *Ethnic Passages: Literary Immigrants in Twentieth-Century America.* Chicago: University of Chicago Press, 1993.

Gartner, Lloyd. "Introduction." In *Jewish Education in the United States: A Documentary History,* edited by Lloyd Gartner. New York: Teachers College, 1969.

Girgus, Sam B. *The New Covenant: Jewish Writers and the American Idea.* Chapel Hill: University of North Carolina Press, 1984.

Grant, Madison. *The Passing of the Great Race; or, The Racial Basis of European History.* New York: Scribners, 1916.

Higham, John. *Strangers in the Land: Patterns of American Nativism, 1860–1925.* 2nd ed. New Brunswick, N.J.: Rutgers University Press, 1988.

Jacobson, Matthew Frye. *Whiteness of a Different Color: European Immigrants and the Alchemy of Race.* Cambridge, Mass.: Harvard University Press, 1998.

Marovitz, Sanford E. *Abraham Cahan.* New York: Twayne, 1996.

Michaels, Walter Benn. *Our America: Nativism, Modernism, and Pluralism.* Durham, N.C.: Duke University Press, 1995.

Muller, Thomas. *Immigrants and the American City.* New York: New York University Press, 1993.

Proefriedt, William. "The Education of Mary Antin." *Journal of Ethnic Studies* 17, no. 4 (1990): 81–100.

Ross, Edward. *The Old World in the New: The Significance of Past and Present Immigration to the American People.* New York: Century, 1914.

Schoen, Carol B. *Anzia Yezierska.* Boston: Twayne, 1982.

Sollors, Werner. *Beyond Ethnicity: Consent and Descent in American Culture.* New York: Oxford University Press, 1986.

Stepan, Nancy Leys, and Sander Gilman. "Appropriating the Idioms of Science: The Rejection of Scientific Racism." In *The Bounds of Race: Perspectives on Hegemony and Resistance,* edited by Dominick LaCapra, pp. 72–103. Ithaca, N.Y.: Cornell University Press, 1991.

Wald, Priscilla. "Immigration and Assimilation in Nineteenth-Century U.S. Women's Writing." In *The Cambridge Companion to Nineteenth-Century American Women's Writing,* edited by Dale M. Bauer and Philip Gould, pp. 176–199. Cambridge, U.K., and New York: Cambridge University Press, 2001.

Wilentz, Gay. "Cultural Mediation and the Immigrant's Daughter: Anzia Yezierska's *Bread Givers.*" *MELUS* 17, no. 3 (1991–1992): 33–41.

Wu, William. *The Yellow Peril: Chinese Americans in American Fiction, 1850–1940.* Hamden, Conn.: Archon, 1982.

Zaborowska, Magdalena J. *How We Found America: Reading Gender through East-European Immigrant Narratives.* Chapel Hill: University of North Carolina Press, 1995.

Lori Jirousek

IMPERIALISM AND ANTI-IMPERIALISM

When the Civil War drew to a close in 1865, the United States had not yet emerged as an imperialist nation, although the groundwork had long been laid. The prehistory of American imperialism lay in the European appropriation of Native Americans' lands and in post-Revolutionary demands that the United States annex Florida and Louisiana. In 1823 President James Monroe (1758–1831), hoping to prevent Spain from reclaiming former colonies in Latin America, declared the entire hemisphere off-limits for European expansion. Labeled the Monroe Doctrine in 1852, this policy provided a pretext for the threat of military intervention in 1895, when, shortly after gold was discovered in Venezuela, Great Britain, which controlled Guiana, disputed boundary lines. Throughout the twentieth century, the United States called on the Monroe Doctrine to justify its dominance over hemispheric conditions, the most notable instance being President John F. Kennedy's invocation of the doctrine during the Cuban Missile Crisis of 1962.

The United States also had a proto-imperialist history in its several moves to acquire contiguous lands. Calls for the annexation of Canada were frequent throughout the nineteenth century. The most famous—as well as the most successful—move, however, was the Mexican-American War of 1848, ending in the Treaty of Guadalupe Hidalgo, which ceded 529,200 square miles of Mexican territory to the United States—California, New Mexico, and parts of Arizona, Utah, Nevada, and Colorado. Texas, also formerly part of Mexico, had already been annexed in 1845.

This history of U.S. relations with other American states meant that by the late nineteenth century the people of the United States were already familiar with the idea of taking over neighboring lands or intervening in hemispheric disputes. They were also sharply aware of the ongoing imperialist moves by the European powers, as Great Britain, Spain, Germany, Italy, and France either acquired new colonies or centralized control over existing ones. The Boer War of 1899–1902, the Boxer Rebellion of 1900, the Belgian exploitation of the Congo, French intervention in northern Africa and the Far East all impressed Americans, some favorably, others unfavorably. What was clear to all was that the European imperial powers were reaping extraordinary economic benefits from lands far from their own geopolitical borders. For many Americans, especially those ambitious to extend American business interests, it became clear that overseas expansion was the way to harness American energies and turn

them to profitable development. Many Americans both spoke and wrote to this end; among them Alfred T. Mahan (1840–1914), whose books *The Influence of Sea Power upon History: 1660–1783* (1890) and *The Interest of America in Sea Power* (1897) advocated development of a world-class navy that could be used to protect U.S. maritime commerce. Integral to this plan was the necessity of a canal cutting through Central America and overseas colonies that could serve as military bases.

Mahan's ideas were favorably received, in large part because they fed into a general cultural investment in the idea of Manifest Destiny, the belief that the United States had a special mission to expand across the entire North American continent and beyond, especially to Central America and the Caribbean. The doctrine of Manifest Destiny, in turn, was closely allied to a set of racial ideologies that ranked the world's races according to pseudoscientific criteria of intelligence and character traits and that used Darwin's evolutionary ideas to develop, especially through the writings of the social scientist Herbert Spencer, a philosophy of "survival of the fittest" that could be used to justify military and economic conquest. In most of the charts developed to illustrate racial hierarchies, Anglo-Saxons (people who could trace their origins to the Germanic tribes—Angles, Saxons, and Jutes—who invaded Britain in the fifth and sixth centuries) were at the top and people of African origin were at the bottom, whereas "Asiastics," as they were called, occupied a variety of middle ranks, often closely related to skin color.

The promulgation of these racial ideologies throughout American society encouraged a cultural assumption that American institutions—the Constitution, the Bill of Rights, and the economic and political systems generally—were Anglo-Saxon inventions. This led to two further assumptions, deeply held even when contradictory. The first was that "inferior races," as they were known, were incapable of understanding democratic principles. The second was that it was America's duty to export U.S. economic, social, and political systems (generally coded under the rubric "civilization") to other nations. This complex was compounded by a Christian missionary tradition that had been operating since John Eliot proselytized to Native Americans in the seventeenth century, a tradition that valorized conversion to Christianity and held that no nation could be truly "civilized" unless it was fully Christianized. It is important to note here that for many Americans, especially those invested in the ideology of Anglo-Saxon superiority, the word "Christian" only referred to Protestants, and "Christianity" referred to the entire complex of Anglo-American cultural

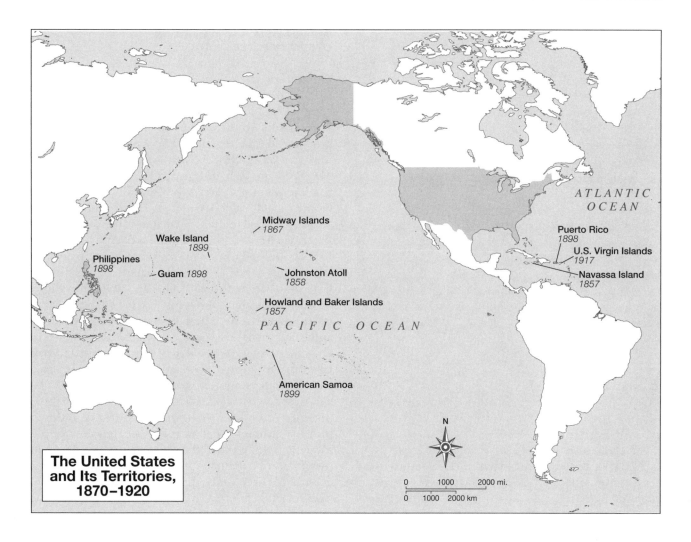

The United States
and Its Territories,
1870–1920

values. This meant that Spain's former colonies, which had been Christianized by Catholics, could usefully be regarded as fertile grounds for Protestant missionizing as well as U.S. cultural, political, and economic domination. Most important, it facilitated an American assumption that most non-European countries were militarily vulnerable compounds of inferior races and social, cultural, and religious difference. This compound of vulnerability, inferiority, and difference sanctioned American intervention overseas. Expansionists argued that nations colonized by European powers were oppressed and would welcome American aid in throwing off their oppressors and in establishing American institutions. When the erstwhile colonists resisted appropriation by the United States, the complex of American attitudes enabled the new imperialists to argue that because the insurgents were racially and culturally backward, they would require first pacification, and then a prolonged education in Western values and technologies before they could govern themselves.

Invasion of other countries also helped in the national project of post–Civil War reconstruction. Amy Kaplan has noted that one benefit of the imperial push in the late nineteenth century was to provide a means of bringing the North and the South together. Although the Civil War was officially over, sectarian hatreds still festered, and the notion that men would fight again, this time united as Americans against a foreign power, helped overcome sectional differences as the military forces looked outward, beyond U.S. borders. Here, too, emphasis on Anglo-Saxon racial superiority, U.S. political institutions, and America's Christian mission combined to convince Americans that it was, as President William McKinley (1843–1901) stated regarding the Filipinos, America's duty "to educate [them], and uplift and civilize and Christianize them, and by God's grace do the very best we could by them" (Millis, pp. 383–384). In the process of bringing Western "civilization" to other nations, Americans who had seen each other as enemies began to rediscover their commonalities, and the "work" of imperialism thus also served to facilitate the work of reunification and cultural community.

IMPERIALISM AND AMERICAN LITERATURE: 1865–1898

Imperialism rarely appears as a subject in American literature written between the end of the Civil War and the onset of the Spanish-American War, but the complex of ideas and attitudes that would facilitate imperialist activities are reflected in many of the works produced during this time. For instance, *The Squatter and the Don* (1885), the first novel by Chicana writer Maria Amparo Ruiz de Burton (1832–1895), examines the impact of the Treaty of Guadalupe Hidalgo on wealthy Californios—Mexicans living in the western territories ceded to the United States after the Mexican-American War—whose lands had suddenly come under U.S. control and who were facing dispossession through the openly biased U.S. legal system. An aristocratic Californio married to an American army officer, Ruiz de Burton illustrates the complexities of prevailing attitudes toward U.S. imperialism as she simultaneously argues for justice for Californios, affirms racial hierarchies (her protagonists are all of European ancestry and all scorn the Indians who constitute the worker class), and advocates transportation routes that will link east and west coasts and situate California as a jumping-off point for expanded trade with China. Ruiz de Burton's plea for justice for her own socioeconomic group is aimed at forcing the U.S. legal system to live up to its own ideals of impartiality, not to protest U.S. appropriation of Mexican lands, and her resentment over ethnic discrimination is limited to anger that her aristocrats are lumped together with black and brown peoples. Taking U.S. imperialism as a given, *The Squatter and the Don* recognizes the importance of technology in facilitating overseas trade and seeks only to ensure that Mexicans of European ancestry maintain their class privileges and be part of the process.

As in *The Squatter and the Don*, the compound of racial, economic, and social attitudes that facilitated American imperialism prior to the Spanish-American War constitute background assumptions rather than foreground issues in many of the well-known works of the period. For instance, many of the regionalist writers rest their assumption about the legitimacy of regional development on Manifest Destiny, the creed that justified white Americans' appropriation of native lands and that envisioned an onward march of largely northern European peoples across the continent and beyond. Thus a writer such as Hamlin Garland, who took the midwestern farmer as his subject, saw the melding of German and Scandinavian immigrants in the upper Midwest as the creation of a particularly ethnic-inflected region at the same time that he recognized that the category "region" was inseparable from the concept of nation, and that the onward push of national expansion was, paradoxically, what enabled regional development. Frank Norris would take this a step further in his "trilogy of the wheat," in which he projected an economic landscape that required foreign markets for completion. Writers who focused on white encroachments on Indian lands—such as Zitkala-Ša's sketches and stories published in 1902 and 1903 and later collected under the title *American Indian Stories* (1921); Sarah Winnemucca Hopkins's *Life Among the Piutes* (1883); and some of Mary Austin's sketches in *The Land of Little Rain* (1903) and *Lost Borders* (1909)—examined the legacies of earlier imperialist moves. Similarly, George Washington Cable, whose novel *The Grandissimes* (1880) is set in New Orleans in 1803, the year the United States took over Louisiana from France, studies the difference that rule by the white, Protestant United States made on that multiracial, multinational, and largely Catholic city.

Regionalist fiction was not the only literary mode to reflect elements of the imperialist complex. Poetry could and did embody imperialist imperatives. Walt Whitman's (1819–1892) "Passage to India" (1871, 1881), for instance, articulates the imperialist ideal in concrete detail, as the poet envisions past, present, and future joined in the imaginary space of India. Claiming this to be "God's purpose from the first," the poet sees:

> The earth . . . spanned . . .
> The oceans . . . crossed
> The lands . . . welded together . . .
> not for trade or transportation only
> But in God's name, and for thy sake o soul.
>
> *(P. 412)*

Whitman's poem may be one of the most specific literary representations of the imperialist imperative as formulated in the American grain: in a grand panoramic vision the poet projects the march of American history and technology as central to God's project, "the Pacific railroad surmounting every barrier" (p. 413), "Tying the Eastern to the Western sea / The road between Europe and Asia" (p. 414). Asking for what purpose the "rondure of the world" will be "at last accomplished," Whitman's speaker—the Poet—answers that it is at once a return to human origins and a reunion of the soul with God. In the poem, increasingly frenetic clauses build to a final call to "sail forth—steer for the deep waters only" (p. 421). In the end, Whitman's vision suggests an apocalyptic collapse of time, space, soul, and divinity.

Although it speaks much of God, Whitman's poem invokes divinity as spirituality rather than as a specific religious creed. Despite its nonsectarian gloss, however, the poem assumes that conquering the globe would fulfill America's destiny, a destiny in which technology and commerce are means to a divinely inspired end. Other literary works cast this mission in explicitly Christian, generally Protestant, terms. Embedded in most literary works of this period was the assumption that white Protestant Americans, having developed an ideal economic and religious system, had an obligation to export it to less fortunate nations. Satirically labeled the "blessings of civilization trust" by Mark Twain (1835–1910), this national pathology, especially when combined with current racial hierarchies, dictated a paternalistic approach to non-European nations and to Europeans who did not meet the criteria for "civilization." *A Connecticut Yankee in King Arthur's Court* (1884), Twain's own satiric novel about a nineteenth-century American who is transported back to sixth-century England, exhibits these attitudes in the figure of Hank Morgan. Morgan refers to the sixth-century Catholics among whom he finds himself as "savages"; he creates a variety of Protestant sects in order to encourage competition in the religious market and thus disrupt the hegemony of the Church; and he takes his understanding of the American people's constitutional right to alter their form of government as his own imperative to alter other people's form of government if it seems un-American to him. Although the young men Morgan educates to make modern inroads into the feudal system beg him not to destroy their people, when confronted he has no compunctions about using his superior technology to blow up his enemies, who by then constitute the entire populace. Between them, Whitman's "Passage to India" and Twain's *A Connecticut Yankee in King Arthur's Court* lay out the spectrum of American imperialist attitudes in the period prior to the Spanish-American War, with "Passage" seeing global economies (spiritual or material) as the fulfillment of American destinies, and *A Connecticut Yankee in King Arthur's Court* seeing the person of the imperialist as an intolerant, technological bully.

IMPERIALISM AND AMERICAN LITERATURE: 1898–1920

The Spanish-American War, a series of related military events that resulted in the U.S. acquisition of Puerto Rico, the Philippines, Guam, and the Hawaiian Islands, and in U.S. cultural dominance over Cuba, saw the U.S. entry onto the world stage as an imperial power. These events, with the various ideologies that motivated them, resonate in American writing of the period in a multitude of ways. The Anglo-Indian writer Rudyard Kipling (1865–1936), whose stories and novels about the British presence in India had long been popular reading for American audiences,

"The Art of Self-Government." Cover illustration for *Harper's Weekly* by W. A. Rogers, 27 August 1898, demonstrating the paternalism of U.S. policy. Opposing revolutionary factions in Cuba are portrayed as naughty schoolboys. Hawaii and Puerto Rico, which submitted to U.S. annexation without struggle, are shown as model students, as is Maximo Gomez, a Cuban general who retired from battle once the U.S. began fighting the Spanish. Philippine revolutionary leader Emilio Aquinaldo, who aided U.S. forces in the Spanish-American War but later resisted their control, stands in the corner in a dunce hat. THE LIBRARY OF CONGRESS

laid down the challenge in his poem "The White Man's Burden: The United States and The Philippine Islands," published in the February 1899 issue of *McClure's Magazine*. Urging Americans to

Take up the White Man's burden
Send forth the best ye breed
Go send your sons to exile
to serve your captives' need

(*P. 1*)

Kipling characterized colonized peoples as "new-caught, sullen," "half devil and half child" (p. 1). America's duty as an imperialist power was to export Western civilization, even though its reward would be "the blame of those ye better / The hate of those ye guard" (p. 1). The benefits to the United States would be a state of national "manhood" that would earn the United States entry into the community of imperialist nations.

Kipling's poem provided a magnet for American sentiments about this first venture into imperialism from all sides of the spectrum. For Theodore Roosevelt, then serving as vice president, it was "poor poetry, but good sense from the expansion point of view," whereas his friend Senator Henry Cabot Lodge, who had already advocated American intervention in China as a way to "save the teeming millions of China . . . [to] keep them free, not merely for the incoming of commerce, but for the entrance of the light of Western civilization" (Dementyev, p. 141), thought it not only good sense but also good poetry. For expansionists, the poem brilliantly combined the long-term belief in Manifest Destiny with America's Christian mission, making a fusion of the religious understanding of "foreign fields" inseparable from the capitalist understanding of "foreign markets."

Kipling's poem also served as a catalyst for the literary expression of anti-imperialist sentiment. For the journalist and writer Stephen Crane (1871–1900), military intervention in foreign lands also provided a means of examining American manhood. In sketches such as "Marine Signaling Under Fire at Guantanamo" (1899), written from the Cuban front, Crane delineates the spare, worn bravery of American soldiers under fire. In others, such as "God Rest Ye, Merry Gentlemen" (1899), Crane's own ironic strain emerges, as he portrays an embedded war correspondent who, when his company is ordered to advance, "took his mackintosh and his bottle of whiskey and invaded Cuba" (Crane, p. 1060). Similar ironic undermining of the heroic ideal appears in short stories such as "The Second Generation" (1899) in which a state senator finagles a commission for his son, a self-centered shirker who plays a sublimely incompetent role in the capture of San Juan Hill. For Crane, who was interested in any theater of action as a locus for observing men's behaviors, the Spanish-American War exposed American ideals as much as it supported them. The protagonist of "The Second Generation" is compared to his more competent colleagues, but even their courage is brought into question in passages that deliberately evoke Kipling's poem. For instance, at one point "three venerable colonels" are said to stand

behind their lines, quiet, stern, courteous old fellows, admonishing their regiments to be very pretty in the face of such a hail of magazine-rifle and machine-gun fire as has never in this world been confronted save by beardless savages when the white man has found occasion to take his burden to some new place. (Crane, p. 1115)

Stephen Crane's ironies registered his distance from the expansionists fairly quietly. Others were far noisier. Although popular writers such as Richard Harding Davis, who like Crane also reported back from the Cuban front, found Roosevelt and his Rough Riders appropriate representatives of the American ideal, many other American writers questioned the invasion of Cuba and the Philippines and the annexation of Puerto Rico, Guam, and the Hawaiian Islands. For these, the specter of American imperialism demonstrated the failure of American ideals on moral, religious, and political grounds, and they responded through a variety of genres, including essays, poems, and fiction. The philosopher William James (1842–1910), for instance, sent forth a volley of essays in protest, including a 1 March 1899 letter to the *Boston Evening Transcript* on "The Philippine Tangle" that excoriates Americans for embracing

a national destiny which must be "big" at any cost, and which for some inscrutable reason it has become infamous for us to disbelieve in or refuse. We are to be missionaries of civilization, and to bear the white man's burden, painful as it often is. We must sow our ideals, plant our order, impose our God. The individual lives are nothing. Our duty and our destiny call, and civilization must go on. Could there be a more damning indictment of the whole bloated idol termed "modern civilization" than this amounts to? (P. 2)

Mark Twain, who had originally supported the war in Cuba because he genuinely believed the United States had invaded to help the Cubans in their struggle against the Spanish, realized his mistake when the country capitalized on its Cuban victory by invading the Philippines. Twain registered his protest both orally, in interviews with the press, and literarily, in essays such as "To the Person Sitting in Darkness," published in the *North American Review* in 1901. Perhaps the most widely known of the anti-imperialist writings to emerge from this period, Twain's essay attacks Western imperialism as it was manifesting itself in South Africa, China, Cuba, and the Philippines, and berates the United States for learning to play "the European Game"—economic aggression thinly disguised as military aid and Christian benevolence. "The Blessings-of-Civilization Trust," Twain writes bitterly, "wisely and cautiously administered, is a Daisy." He continues:

There is more money in it, more territory, more sovereignty, and other kinds of emolument, than there is in any other game that is played. But Christendom has been playing it badly of late years . . . she has been so eager to get every stake that appeared on the green cloth, that the People Who Sit in Darkness have noticed it . . . [and] have become suspicious of the Blessings of Civilization. (P. 199)

With "King Leopold's Soliloquy" (1905), a fictional monologue by the Belgian King Leopold, who alternately boasts about his bloody successes in the Congo and bemoans the criticism leveled at him by other countries, and "A Defense of General Funston" (1902), which violently criticizes the lionizing of U.S. General Frederick Funston, regarded as a hero for having arrested the heroic Filipino leader Emilio Aguinaldo through devious and dishonorable means, Twain's satiric writings played a major role in the literary protest against American participation in imperialist agendas. Other satirists also answered the call, among them Finley Peter Dunne (1867–1936), whose comic character "Mr. Dooley," an Irish American saloon keeper, mocks American attitudes toward the Filipinos in particular and toward people of color in general:

We say to thim: "Naygurs," we say, "poor dissolute, uncovered wretches . . . we propose f'r to larn ye th' uses iv liberty. In ivry city in this unfair land we will erect school-houses an' packin' houses an' houses iv correction; an' we'll larn ye our language, because 'tis aisier to larn ye ours than to larn ourselves your's. . . . an', whin ye've become edycated an' have all th' blessin's iv civilization that we don't want . . . we'll threat ye th' way a father shud threat his childer if we have to break ivry bone in ye're bodies. So come to our ar-rms," says we. (P. 183)

Anti-imperialist sentiment appeared in poetry and fiction as well as in satiric essays and sketches. A common thread linking most of the protest literature is a sense that in invading countries that had manifested no enmity toward the United States, Americans had betrayed their most cherished principles, from both the Enlightenment and religious strains of American identity. Henry Blake Fuller's (1857–1929) series of poems in his collection *The New Flag* (1899) in particular inveigh against Christian hypocrisy; for example, in "Two Prayers" the second prayer, "The President went to church and joined in the singing," begins:

There amid the congregation
shaven and smooth and gravely bland
With appropriate sanctimony
See the blood-stained murderers stand

and posits an angry Deity who instructs the recording angel to

Let the deeds of hell be graven
One by one, and counted in.
Public honor prostituted
Faith betrayed and vows belied
And the sluices of corruption
Hammered up and opened wide.
Write it in the tears of Freedom
In the shambles crimson stain
Mark the thousands basely butchered
For a preaccursed gain.

(The New Flag, p. 52)

Other poets focused on the betrayal of Enlightenment ideals, as in Ernest Howard Crosby's (1856–1907) Whitmanesque "The New Freedom," which begins by evoking American freedoms and post-Revolutionary strengths and then laments that:

Times change, and freedom changes with them . . .
The political liberty of Seventy-six, the equality
before the law, of which you talk
so much, is no longer the living ideal that it was;
It is now a fossil for antiquaries to toy with.

(Plain Talk in Psalm and Parable, p. 59)

Crosby also joined numerous other poets in parodying Kipling's poem, such as his "The Real 'White Man's Burden,'" which begins:

Take up the White Man's burden
Send forth your sturdy kin
And load them down with Bibles
And cannon-balls and gin
Throw in a few diseases
To spread the tropic climes
For there the healthy niggers
Are quite behind the times.

(Swords and Plowshares, p. 73)

With the African American community, which bitterly protested the war, Crosby was one of the white anti-imperialists who recognized the racism inherent in American attitudes toward both Cubans and Filipinos.

Fictional responses to the Spanish-American War also explored the complexity of American attitudes toward war and toward the peoples they had conquered. William Dean Howells's (1837–1920) short story "Editha" (1906), rather than focusing on politics or race, instead examines the ramifications of jingoism—the persistent call to arms launched by "yellow press" journals such as the *New York World* and the *New York Journal*—on private lives. In this story, Editha, a girl steeped in romance novels, persuades her reluctant fiancé to join the army so that he can become a hero. After he is killed in combat, Editha, seeing herself as a tragic heroine, travels to Iowa to comfort his elderly mother. Instead of the romantic meeting she has envisioned, however, the older woman attacks her furiously for having persuaded her pacifist son to betray his principles. Briefly ashamed of herself, Editha's self-esteem is resurrected when a companion identifies the mother's behavior as "vulgar," that is, beneath Editha's class. With that

> a light broke upon Editha in the darkness which she felt had been without a gleam of brightness for weeks and months. The mystery that had bewildered her was solved by the word; and from that moment she rose from groveling in shame and self-pity, and began to live again in the ideal. (P. 265)

Howells's attack here is multiple: long a critic of romance novels, which he believed taught false principles—especially to young women—he also understood the class differences between those who supported the war and those who actually fought in it.

While Howells's focus is on the impact of the war internally, Ernest Howard Crosby's novel *Captain Jinks, Hero* (1902), examines American justifications for invading foreign territories. Sending his gullible protagonist, Sam (called Jinks by his companions), from West Point, to Cuba, to the Philippines, and from there to China during the Boxer Rebellion, Crosby focuses on the differences between American ideals and war's realities, with especial attention to the impact of war on Cuban, Filipino, and Chinese peasants. In Cuba, for instance, the army invades a village on a feast day, when

> the whole population had been in the streets in their best clothes. The soldiers snatched the jewels of the women and chased the men away, and then looted the houses, destroying what they could not take, and finally setting them on fire. "It's better so," said Sam to his adjutant. "Make war as bad as possible and people will keep the peace. We are the real peace-makers." He heard shouts and cries as he passed through the villages, and had reason to think that the soldiers were not contented with mere looting, but he did not inquire. (P. 328)

Later, when another officer is asked whether he thinks American Negroes make good soldiers, he replies in the affirmative, giving as reasons that "they are more submissive to discipline; they're used to being ordered about and kicked and cuffed, and they don't mind it. Besides, they're accustomed from their low social position to be subordinate to superiors, and rather expect it than not" (p. 328). Crosby also skewers the missionary movement. Sam, at a dinner in China, speaks with a missionary who exults in the invasion by the allied powers. "These are great days, Colonel Jinks," says the missionary:

> Great days, indeed, for foreign missions. What would St. John have said on the island of Patmos if he could have cabled for half-a-dozen armies and half-a-dozen fleets, and got them too? . . . As he looks down upon us to-night, how his soul must rejoice! The Master told us to go into all nations, and we are going to go if it takes a million troops to send us and keep us there. (P. 354)

The anger evinced in these works is indicative of an intense emotional engagement. Although in 1898, when the United States invaded the Philippines, many Americans did not know where the islands were located; by the end of that year, when the Treaty of Paris officially ended the first phase of the war, American consciousness of world geography had moved to a new level. Most important, American understanding of the United States' place in the world order had undergone a radical, and irrevocable, shift. The literary response overwhelmingly registers the sense of betrayal many felt when they realized that the democratic principles of freedom and tolerance, and the Christian principles of benevolence and charity, were in fact masks for economic and racial aggression, but many other Americans felt that America's destiny required exportation of American ideals and a demonstration of U.S. strength in the world order. Although a large faction would call for neutrality at the onset of World War I fifteen years later, the argument for U.S. status as a major world power had already been won.

See also Anglo-Saxonism; Annexation and Expansion; Humor; Philippine-American War; Spanish-American War; *The Squatter and the Don*

BIBLIOGRAPHY

Primary Works

Crane, Stephen. "Stories, Sketches, and Journalism, Cuba." 1899. In *Prose and Poetry: Maggie, a Girl of the Streets; The Red Badge of Courage; Stories, Sketches, and Journalism; Poetry,* edited by J. C. Levenson. New York: Literary Classics of the U.S., 1984.

Crosby, Ernest. *Captain Jinks, Hero.* 1902. In Foner, ed., *The Literary Anti-Imperialists.*

Crosby, Ernest. *Plain Talk in Psalm and Parable.* 1899. In Foner, ed., *The Literary Anti-Imperialists.*

Crosby, Ernest. *Swords and Ploughshares.* 1899. In Foner, ed., *The Literary Anti-Imperialists.*

Dunne, Finley Peter. *Mr. Dooley in the Hearts of His Countrymen.* 1899. In Foner, ed., *The Literary Anti-Imperialists.*

Foner, Philip S., ed. *The Literary Anti-Imperialists.* Vol. 2 of *The Anti-Imperialist Reader: A Documentary History* of Anti-Imperialism in the United States, edited by Philip S. Foner and Richard C. Winchester. New York: Holmes & Meier, 1986.

Fuller, Henry Blake. The New Flag. 1899. In Foner, ed., The Literary Anti-Imperialists.

Howells, William Dean. "Editha." 1906. In Foner, The Literary Anti-Imperialists.

James, William. "The Philippine Tangle." Boston Evening Transcript, 1 March 1899. Also available at www.boondocksnet.com/ai/ailtexts/tangle.html.

Kipling, Rudyard. "The White Man's Burden: The United States and The Philippine Islands." In Foner, ed., The Literary Anti-Imperialists. Also available at http://wwwnorton.com/college/history/ralph/workbook/ralprs30b.htm.

Twain, Mark. "To the Person Sitting in Darkness." 1901. In Foner, ed., The Literary Anti-Imperialists.

Whitman, Walt. "Passage to India." In Leaves of Grass, edited by Sculley Bradley and Harold W. Blodgett. New York: Norton, 1973.

Secondary Works

Dementyev, I. P. USA: Imperialists and Anti-Imperialists (The Great Foreign Policy Debate at the Turn of the Century). Translated by David Skvirsky. Moscow: Progress Publishers, 1979.

Kaplan, Amy. The Anarchy of Empire in the Making of U.S. Culture. Cambridge, Mass.: Harvard University Press, 2002.

Millis, Walter. The Martial Spirit. Cambridge, Mass.: Riverside Press, 1931.

Welch, Richard E., Jr. Response to Imperialism: The United States and the Philippine-American War, 1899–1902. Chapel Hill: University of North Carolina Press, 1979.

Susan K. Harris

IMPRESSIONISM

The impressionist movement began in the visual art world of Paris in the 1860s. The painters who were considered the first "impressionists," including Auguste Renoir (1841–1919), Camille Pissarro (1830–1903), and Claude Monet (1840–1926), among others, were influenced by contemporary advances in the science of optics that dealt with various aspects of light and color, recent philosophical ideas about the nature of time, and the relatively new study of psychology, which posited notions about perception and comprehension. Their work makes use of color, light, and shadow in ways that attempt to convey one's immediate perception of a scene on the canvas. Their primary concern was with

expressing the nature of reality through their artistic medium rather than in establishing a "school" of art. The word "impressionism" came to be associated with these ideas rather by accident, when a critic assigned the title of an 1873 Monet painting (*Impression, Sunrise*) to the group—with derogatory intent.

Impressionist painting techniques were initially a reaction against the traditional techniques of realism espoused by the art schools of Paris in the latter half of the nineteenth century, coupled with new discoveries about the nature of color and how the eye perceives it. Painters experimented with ways of depicting light and color, juxtaposing spots of color, for example, and letting the eye—or the brain—fuse them together in the mind of the perceiver, thus producing more intense hues than could be produced by mixing the colors on the palette.

Many who did not appreciate the works of the early impressionists supposed that the painters were settling for less than they were capable of—exhibiting unfinished sketches as though they were finished pieces, for example. Rather than belabor the minute details of a scene, these painters often worked quickly, frequently supplying minor brush strokes to provide suggestions rather than more fully rendered depictions of objects. The aim of such renderings, however, was not to depict a photographic reality but to capture the essence of a fleeting moment—a glimpse, rather than a long gaze—on the canvas. Such an aim demands suggestion and innuendo rather than infinitesimally exact details because by its very nature a momentary glance can provide little else. These artists believed that reality is frequently less than exact; one's perception of a scene can be blurry or obscured. In addition, they reasoned that because time is ever-moving and our perceptions are ever-changing, the same object appears differently at various times and from various vantage points. This acknowledgment of perceptive diversity prompted some painters to depict in a series of works the same object presented from different angles or at different times of the day.

Impressionism is not confined to the visual arts alone, however. It is also a significant movement in music and literature. The art world of Paris in the 1860s and 1870s was a vibrant community in which painters, musicians, and writers frequently discussed ideas and shared their experiments with each other. Thus, impressionism as a movement developed simultaneously in painting, music, and literature, and the intermingling of artists in various media established new relationships among the art forms as well.

The term "impressionism" was very controversial for the first several decades of its use. In the 1890s it was considered the antithesis of Victorianism.

***At the Seaside*, c. 1892.** Painting by William Merritt Chase. A respected teacher and practitioner of various styles of painting, Chase here demonstrates the influence of Impressionism in both his subject matter and his brushwork.
© FRANCIS G. MAYER/CORBIS

According to the critic Edwin H. Cady, "it stood for the liberation of the artist from the academy and tradition, from formalism and ideality, from narrative, and finally even from realism; for realism demanded responsibility to the common vision and impressionism responsibility only to what the unique eye of the painter saw. It was also a swearword for conservatives of every variety" (p. 132). In terms of literature, however, the word has had more varied connotations. While some have used it with derision, others have applied it much more positively. Cady comments that "it was repeatedly the highest praise of Joseph Conrad and Edward Garnett in England that [Stephen] Crane was an impressionist; it made him triumphantly avant garde" (p. 132).

LITERARY IMPRESSIONISM: AN AESTHETIC

When impressionism is manifested in literature it can be addressed both as an aesthetic and as a collection of specific techniques. As an aesthetic, impressionism assumes that the only way people live and come to any understanding of human life is through sensory experience. The primary purpose of impressionism, then, both in the visual arts and in literature, is to render the sensory

nature of life itself. In painting, this means that artists attempt to render what they actually see—the reflections of light on objects or water, the shimmer of a summer day, or the blurry surfaces of a rain-swept street. In literature, the writer's interest becomes making the reader "see" the narrative described. The effect, in the words of the literary critic James Nagel, is "to convey to the reader the basic impressions of life that a single human consciousness could receive in a given place during a restricted duration of time" (p. 21). The early-twentieth-century author and critic Ford Madox Ford (1873–1939) emphasizes the role of immediacy in impressionist description when he claims that

> any piece of Impressionism, whether it be prose, or verse, or painting, or sculpture, is the record of the impression of a moment; it is not a sort of rounded, annotated record of a set of circumstances—it is the record of the recollection in your mind of a set of circumstances that happened ten years ago—or ten minutes. It might even be the impression of the moment but it is the impression, not the corrected chronicle. (P. 41)

Thus impressions are immediate and complete; commentary or explanation is not provided. They are presented directly, as a means of producing similar impressions on the reader as they did on the writer and conveying these impressions along with the associated meaning of related sensations. Because the reader is never told how to respond to these details—the details themselves are the conveyors of meaning—meaning itself tends to operate more on an emotional than intellectual level, though both are possible.

Impressionism also involves a philosophical assumption related directly to the nature of reality: it posits that there is a distinction between reality as it is perceived and reality itself. Nagel points out,

> the logic of Realism depends on a consistent reliability of both interpretation and perception; the logic of Impressionism suggests that this correspondence is never certain and that the inscrutability and flux of life *are* its fundamental reality. Impressionistic fiction involves the constant interplay between experience and comprehension . . . qualified by the constant awareness that any description or presentation of reality is dependent upon the clarity with which it is perceived. (P. 22)

IMPRESSIONIST TECHNIQUES

The impressionist aesthetic, focusing on the sensory nature of life, the immediacy of perception, and the subjective interpretation of reality, is conveyed by writers through several techniques or combinations of techniques that involve narrative methods, characterization, figurative devices, and structure and form. The most common form of narration is limited third-person, which limits the narrator's perceptions to the level of a character in the story. Narrators may be objective or subjective, and their perceptions may blur with those of a character at times. Characters, especially protagonists, are often in flux, seeking understanding about their lives or their situations but not always achieving a clear vision of such. They are very much affected by what happens to them in the moment, and their perceptions change as their experiences influence them. Figurative devices are primarily sensory images, often focusing on color and light, whose meaning must be derived from context because the narrator's grasp of the "truth" may be in question. Meaning for the impressionists is arrived at through suggestion rather than concrete presentation. Through the use of reflections, eroded contours and blurred images, impressionists often evoke a mood or sensation rather than deliver a complete physical description. Maria Kronegger, in her study of *Literary Impressionism* (1973), aptly points out that in the work of the impressionists there is more stress on connotation than denotation (p. 47). As a result, the form or structure of an impressionist work is often fragmented or episodic.

Because the sensory images are passed along directly and in a series of fragments whose meaning is contained in the juxtaposition of these images, impressionism requires the reader to be an active participant in the process of making meaning.

The early-twentieth-century critic Harry Hartwick, in *The Foreground of American Fiction* (1934), clearly puts into perspective the roles of the writer and the reader regarding the handling of sensory imagery within the impressionistic narrative: "Impressionism is a sensory kodaking, a confused mosaic of details, a rivulet of hyphenated photographs, which the reader . . . must fuse into some eventual relationship" (p. 37). Hartwick and others have described it as a "telegraphic style" in terms of the speed and brevity of the presentation. It might also be likened to the telegraph in its form; the procession of images passes along in chunks and then is reconstructed at the other end. Reliance on this flood of images wreaks havoc on the traditional form and structure of the novel as "experience becomes a series of 'intense moments'; plot loses its importance, and from an interest in the larger aspects of [one's] product, the author turns to an interest in 'the bright, particular world'" (p. 37). For the impressionists, "experience . . . should be broken into fragments, each fragment to be respected for its own sake, each passing moment or passion to be welcomed individually and squeezed dry before it can escape us" (p. 41). It is in this way, via the passing on of sensory fragments, that the impressionists seek to convey a representation of reality to the minds of readers where it can be received and understood with directness and immediacy.

STEPHEN CRANE: *THE RED BADGE OF COURAGE*

The author Joseph Conrad (1857–1924), himself a practitioner of impressionist prose, once admiringly called Stephen Crane (1871–1900) "the foremost impressionist of his time" (p. 126). Although Crane's works have been variously described as realistic, naturalistic, imagistic, symbolistic, and impressionistic—indeed there are elements of all such styles in his canon—the lens of impressionism is perhaps most instructive, especially when considering his masterpiece, *The Red Badge of Courage* (1895). This story focuses on an especially stressful time in the life of its protagonist Henry Fleming, namely his involvement in a series of engagements during the Civil War. The changes that Henry undergoes ostensibly lead him to a comfortable conclusion at the end of the novel, but the duration of his comfort is not ensured. In fact, the constant vacillations that Henry experiences throughout the novel somewhat undermine his apparent epiphany at the end of the piece because he has had several similar instances in the course of the story in which he has felt convinced that his actions and his emotional responses were most accurate and appropriate, only to change his mind a moment later with a change of circumstances. These continual changes, highlighted by techniques such as limited narrative point of view, emotionally charged description, and irony, help Crane to underscore the instability of the world and the consequent uncertainty and fallibility of human perception, traits that are fundamental to an impressionist worldview. The people who populate this world must constantly confront change as they attempt to understand reality, a challenge that raises more doubt and apprehension than certainty.

KATE CHOPIN: *THE AWAKENING*

Crane's contemporary Kate Chopin (1851–1904) also uses an impressionistic approach to explore changes that her protagonist, Edna Pontellier, undergoes in *The Awakening* (1899). However, while Crane focuses on a singular series of events, Chopin is more interested in examining a wide spectrum of experiences and relationships in one woman's life, ultimately developing an enigmatic character who defies easy definitions and interpretations. Although Edna begins to assert herself and make her own decisions, there are always attendant complications that raise questions about how truly liberated she might be; indeed, some see her throughout the novel as a lost soul who lacks a sense of purpose or understanding of her world. The impressionistic techniques that Chopin employs (including limited third-person narration and an unclear distinction between the narrative consciousness and that of the protagonist), Edna's marginalized and solitary nature, a connection between sensory description and emotional response, and the close juxtaposition of reality and dreams all contribute to the confusion in interpreting Edna's character, and, true to an impressionist aesthetic, she remains an enigma to the end.

HENRY JAMES: *THE AMBASSADORS*

Unlike Crane and Chopin, Henry James (1843–1916) did not embrace an impressionist approach early in his career. In fact, after viewing the Second Exhibition of impressionist artists in Paris (May 1876), he wrote a decidedly negative response to the show. However, as his career progressed his opinion gradually changed, and his novel *The Ambassadors* (1903), infused with impressionism, becomes the vehicle for examining the protagonist Lambert Strether's ever-changing perception within an ever-changing world. Rather than an enigmatically soul-searching protagonist as Chopin's is, however, James's protagonist instead discovers truths about himself while focusing his concern on

In The Ambassadors, *Henry James uses the techniques of impressionism to emphasize the process of seeing through gradual perception.*

He had just made out, in the now full picture, something and somebody else: another impression had been superimposed. A young girl in a white dress and a softly plumed white hat had suddenly come into view, and what was next clear was that her course was toward them. What was clearer still was that the handsome young man at her side was Chad Newsome, and what was clearest of all was that she was therefore Mlle. de Vionnet, that she was unmistakably pretty—bright, gentle, shy, happy, wonderful—and that Chad now, with a consummate calculation of effect, was about to present her to his old friend's vision. What was clearest of all indeed was something much more than this, something at the single stroke of which—and wasn't it simply juxtaposition?—all vagueness vanished. It was the click of a spring—he saw the truth. He had by this time also met Chad's look; there was more of it in that; and the truth, accordingly, so far as Bilham's inquiry was concerned, had thrust in the answer. "Oh, Chad!"—it was that rare youth he should have enjoyed being "like." The virtuous attachment would be all there before him; the virtuous attachment would be in the very act of appeal for his blessing; Jeanne de Vionnet, this charming creature, would be—exquisitely, intensely now—the object of it.

Henry James, *The Ambassadors* (New York: Harper & Brothers, 1930), pp. 151–152.

others. As a result the novel examines the process by which Strether reverses his initial position about Chad Newsome, his life in Paris and the Woolett business concerns, and consequently his own personal relationship with Mrs. Newsome. The techniques that James uses emphasize the process of seeing through gradual perception, constant questioning, and reinterpretation of what is seen and understood. Using light and shadow, colors and shapes, he underscores the visual subjectivity of impressions, and by tying a character's emotions to a particular scene, he emphasizes the idea of subjective perception. His use of multiple perspectives highlights the relativity of reality and enables him to examine the protagonist not only in the process of changing his mind but ultimately in the process of changing his heart.

A BRIDGE TO MODERNISM

The result of employing impressionism in a work of fiction varies from writer to writer. However, there are some commonalities. By undermining the notion of a single, authoritative reality, the subjectivity and potential inaccuracies of perception are reinforced. In the absence of an authoritative reality, the notion of truth also becomes questionable. The sweep and fluctuation of life is highlighted in a number of ways, through episodically presented events and seemingly kinetic scenic description as well as through characters whose ideas and attitudes are changing constantly. The resulting works recognize that people and their situations are constantly in flux and that holding fast to some notion of reality is often nearly impossible. In contrast to some works of realism, impressionist works can be confusing, providing more questions than answers even for careful readers—and this is a reflection of the impressionist aesthetic, which sees the world and people as confusing and ever-changing, the essence of which impressionist literature seeks to capture in its pages.

These ideas, and the methods by which they are rendered in fiction, constitute a significant effort on the part of several American writers to push the notions of reality and perception beyond those of realism, pointing toward concerns that would come to characterize the twentieth century. The works of Crane, Chopin, and James solidly establish the impressionist aesthetic in American literature. Significant explorations by Harold Frederic, Hamlin Garland, Willa Cather, William Faulkner, Ernest Hemingway, and others extend its implications and move the essence of literary experimentation forward. In concert, their efforts show that as a literary movement impressionism forms a significant bridge between realism and modernism.

See also The Ambassadors; Art and Architecture; *The Awakening;* Naturalism; Realism; *The Red Badge of Courage*

BIBLIOGRAPHY
Primary Works
Chopin, Kate. *The Awakening.* 1899. Edited by Margaret Culley. New York: Norton, 1976.

Crane, Stephen. *The Red Badge of Courage.* 1895. Edited by Donald Pizer. 3rd critical ed. New York: Norton, 1994.

James, Henry. *The Ambassadors.* 1903. Edited by S. P. Rosenbaum. 2nd critical ed. New York: Norton, 1994.

Secondary Works
Cady, Edwin H. *Stephen Crane.* New York: Twayne, 1962.

Conrad, Joseph. "His War Book." In his *Last Essays.* New York: Doubleday, Page, 1926. Reprinted in *Stephen Crane: A Collection of Critical Essays,* edited by Maurice Bassan, pp. 123–127. Englewood Cliffs, N.J.: Prentice-Hall, 1967.

Ford, Ford Madox. "On Impressionism." 1914. In *Critical Writings of Ford Madox Ford,* edited by Frank MacShane, pp. 33–55. Lincoln: University of Nebraska Press, 1964.

Hartwick, Harry. *The Foreground of American Fiction.* New York: American Book Company, 1934.

Kronegger, Maria Elisabeth. *Literary Impressionism.* New Haven, Conn.: College and University Press, 1973.

Matthiessen, F. O. "The Ambassadors." In *Henry James: The Major Phase,* pp. 19–41. New York: Oxford University Press, 1971.

Nagel, James. *Stephen Crane and Literary Impressionism.* University Park: Pennsylvania State University Press, 1980.

Perosa, Sergio. "Naturalism and Impressionism in Stephen Crane's Fiction." In *Stephen Crane: A Collection of Critical Essays,* edited by Maurice Bassan, pp. 80–94. Englewood Cliffs, N.J.: Prentice-Hall, 1967.

Poole, Phoebe. *Impressionism.* New York: Praeger, 1967.

Sonja Froiland Lynch
Robert Lee Lynch Jr.

INDIANS

One of the key concepts associated with American Indians in the period 1870–1920 was "absorption." Hypothetically, once it became clear that Indians had not and probably would not actually disappear, it was the objective of philanthropists and the government alike that Indians be "absorbed" into the United States as individuals; the fact that their land would be "absorbed" into the United States went without saying. Though there are deep complexities underlying this one word, there are two significant points with which to begin a discussion. First, the hypothetical absorption of native peoples into U.S. society, no matter how well-intentioned some of the idea's advocates may have been, merely masks the systematic destruction of tribal governments, through which native land would be made U.S. land. The idea of Indians' absorption signifies the political erasure of Indian nations. Second, native people by and large did not wish to be "absorbed." Native people acquired modern things and practices, some became Christians, some farmers; they struggled with all of the problems of rapid change that U.S. imperialism and modernity brought, but they did not wish to forget who they were or where they came from. Most important, they did not wish to surrender their autonomy, their governments, and their land. Borrowing from

African American studies, historians have described this period of time as the "nadir" for native peoples in the United States, the time when they were at their weakest and when U.S. society and the U.S. government were at their most ruthless in oppressing them. While it was a low point, the period also saw the groundwork laid for the twentieth-century political and cultural resurgence of native peoples in the United States. Native people never were successfully "absorbed."

BEGINNINGS

In North America but especially in the United States, the conflict with native peoples over land was construed as a grand conflict on world-historical terms between the living embodiment of savagery (Indians) and the pinnacle of civilization (white, Protestant Americans). The United States, Americans believed, was the most morally and politically developed nation in human history. Furthermore, Providence—God Himself—had ordained the conflict between savagery and civilization, which therefore could not have any other result than the triumph of Euro-American, Protestant, and by the late nineteenth century, capitalist, civilization.

Because European nations could not claim military supremacy in North America and also competed with one another for native alliance and land, they made treaties with Indian nations for trade, alliance, and land purchase. Treaties are contracts between nations, and legitimate contracts cannot be made with inferiors or incompetents; Europeans recognized native political autonomy, control of land, and government in the treaties. It is a remarkable fact of European imperialism in North America that people who regarded themselves as the pinnacle of human civilization made so many binding legal agreements with people whom they regarded as the model of the most primitive human society, whom they held to be inherently incapable of reason and moral behavior. This did not occur because of Europeans' moral superiority or goodwill, however; circumstances required it. In the nineteenth-century United States, while treaties with Indian nations were coerced and manipulated in every conceivable way in practice, these treaties still carried with them notions of not only the U.S. government's founding principles but also, particularly in the later nineteenth century, the government's moral responsibility as the most advanced and benevolent society toward its inferiors.

At the same time that they continued to make treaties with Indian nations, Europeans also began to define property and government in such a way so as to exclude native people from ever having a legitimate claim to either. Thus at virtually the same moment that they were forced to recognize the legitimacy of Indian nations on the one hand, Europeans attempted to define

Indian nations out of existence theoretically on the other. By the late seventeenth century the English philosopher John Locke provided such a theory. Drawing on earlier justifications for colonizing distant lands, Locke argued that one had to engage in commercial agriculture on land to establish it as property and therefore lay a legitimate claim to it. Furthermore, Locke maintained, this particular kind of property was the origin of government itself, which existed to protect property so defined. The Indians of North America did not form governments; rather, they were "pre-political" because, Locke insisted, they were the earliest form of human society, savages who subsisted on the "spontaneous productions of Nature" rather than engaging in labor to produce a surplus for the market. Indians did not engage in agriculture as Europeans defined it; therefore they didn't have the capacity to form governments; therefore they had no real claim to the land.

This definition of property and government provides a structure for thinking about both native peoples' past and their possible future. Because native peoples were positioned as the origin of human society, in theory savages could be made civilized and therefore citizens if they were made Christians (the only true form of religious belief according to Europeans) and agriculturalists on the European commercial model. According to Europeans, the only civilized society, the only real government, was European government. The idea that Indians could be civilized and still be Indians and form their own separate national governments was inconceivable in this line of thought. Behind the narrative of the hypothetical civilization of Indians so prevalent in the late-nineteenth-century United States is the fact that Europeans sought to destroy native political entities in order to incorporate native land. Indians' hypothetical incorporation was not a form of democratic inclusion, no matter how well meaning its advocates sometimes professed themselves; it was, rather, a justification for their political erasure and the incorporation of their land under U.S. jurisdiction.

DETRIBALIZATION

In the post–Civil War period, contrary to the prevailing idea earlier in the century, Euro-Americans found that Indians were not dying out naturally, at least not as quickly as it had been supposed they would, and Euro-Americans felt that something had to be done about the "Indian problem" that mystifyingly persisted into the modern age. The solution was to detribalize native people and, as has been noted, to "absorb" them into civilized society. The U.S. government pursued detribalization through various means. It first sought to confine native peoples to reservations through treaty agreements whereby they would sell most of their land

INDIAN TERRITORY

Early in the nineteenth century, whites argued that Indians had to be "removed" from the eastern United States—for their own good—where they could live beyond white contact and be worked on by missionaries. In the 1820s, the area west of the newly admitted states of Arkansas and Missouri and east of Mexican territory was designated Indian territory. During and after the 1830s, many other eastern, northern, and midwestern tribes, or portions of tribes, were "removed" to the territory. This was in addition to tribes that historically lived in the territory, such as the Kiowas, and tribes that had been pushed west over a number of years, such as the Osages.

The first groups to removed to Indian territory were the Five Civilized Tribes of the southeastern United States—the Cherokees, Chickasaws, Choctaws, Creeks, and Seminoles. While small groups voluntarily moved west in the 1810s, most were forced to go to the territory in the 1830s. Though there were varying degrees of acculturation to Euro-American practices both among and within the tribes, many tribal leaders, particularly among the Cherokees, argued that their tribes had become "civilized" by converting to Christianity, seeking education, and encouraging farming. They did not desire to become citizens of the United States, however; on the contrary, the fact that they were civilized demonstrated that the sovereignty of the Indian nations should be inviolate. In light of this fundamental argument, what the U.S. government did to the Five Civilized Tribes in the nineteenth century puts the lie to the sanguine visions of Indian citizenship in the United States offered up by reformers.

After removal to Indian Territory, the Five Tribes reestablished their governments and legal systems, as well as printing presses and schools, providing a foundation for literacy not only in English but also in tribal languages. In addition to mission schools, the Cherokees, Choctaws, Chickasaws, and Creeks had all established extensive public educational systems, including, among the Cherokees, college-level institutions for men and women, by the 1840s.

After Five Tribes governments supported the Confederacy during the Civil War (the Confederacy promised to recognize their sovereignty, and some tribal people were slave-owners), the United States renegotiated its prewar treaties with the tribes as punishment. The tribes were forced to give up territory to the U.S. government, ostensibly for the resettlement of other tribes, and for the building of two railroad lines through the territory. Between 1866 and 1885, numerous reservations were created in the ceded lands of Indian territory, including those for the Cheyennes and Arapahos; Comanches, Kiowas, and Apaches; Wichitas and Caddos; Potawatomis and Shawnees; Kickapoos, Iowas, Sauks and Foxes; Pawnees, Otoes and Missouris; Poncas, Tonkawas, Kaws, Osages, Peorias, Wyandots, Eastern Shawnees, Modocs, and Ottawas.

It was not until the later nineteenth century that representatives of railroad, business, and land interests were able to secure enough political support to begin the disintegration of the Five Tribes in earnest. Because of tribal leaders' resistance, the Five Tribes and the Osages were exempted from the 1887 allotment act. In 1889, however, the United States established a federal court at Muskcogee, Indian territory, a blatant extension of U.S. authority. In April 1889 a 2 million acre tract of Cherokee land was opened up to white settlement, which began with a famous land rush. Fifty thousand settlers staked claims on one day. In 1890 the United States organized the Oklahoma territory, which consisted of the land opened to white settlement and most of the reservations. In 1893 the Dawes Commission convened to acquire Indians' "consent" for the allotment of the Osage Territory and the Five Tribes; in 1898 the Curtis Act provided for that allotment. In 1905 leaders of the Five Tribes held a convention in order to write a constitution for a native-run state called Sequoyah to be admitted to the Union; Congress rejected it. In 1907 after the divestment of land from Native Americans, the state of Oklahoma was admitted to the Union, and Native people within its boundaries were made citizens. In Oklahoma, the United States succeeded—for a time—in politically evaporating the Five Civilized Tribes.

to the United States. After establishing reservations, the government sought to distribute parcels of land to individuals, thereby undermining tribal forms of government that were based on communally held land.

Acts of fraud and corruption associated with the allotment process further eroded the tribal land base. The government sent Christian missionaries to native people; extended federal jurisdiction over "major

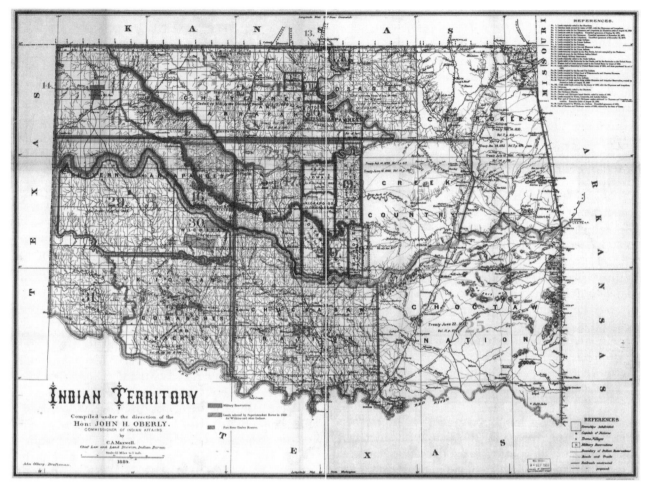

Map of Indian Territory, 1889. Compiled under the direction of the commissioner of Indian affairs and drawn by Charles A. Maxwell, this map of the territory that became Oklahoma shows the distribution of various tribes and includes details about land transfers and cessions. THE LIBRARY OF CONGRESS

crimes" (murder, manslaughter, rape, assault with intent to kill, arson, burglary, and larceny) in Indian country through the Major Crimes Act of 1885; criminalized and sought to destroy native culture; and forced native children to attend federal and mission schools, including boarding schools.

In the late 1860s and early 1870s President Ulysses S. Grant instituted a "peace policy" that officially positioned Indians as "wards" of the government who needed the federal government's help and protection. In 1869 Grant established a Board of Indian Commissioners, a group of unpaid philanthropists, to oversee the Bureau of Indian Affairs, which was infamous for its corruption. He also appointed General Ely S. Parker, a Seneca and a member of his staff during the Civil War, as the first native commissioner of Indian Affairs. Parker was later hounded out of government service on charges of malfeasance that were later

proved false. Grant invited church leaders to nominate Indian agents, school superintendents, and teachers, which effectively put reservations under the control of churches. This policy lasted until 1882. The Indian agents served to further undermine native forms of government and the authority of tribal leaders, as they distributed rations, goods, and lands at their discretion. Indian police forces, loyal to the agent, began to be established on reservations in the late 1870s; this had the same effect of undermining tribal governance.

In 1871 Congress ended the treaty system by establishing that any agreement with Indian tribes had to be accepted by both houses of Congress rather than just by the Senate, as is the case with treaties. Historians have pointed out, at that time and since, that the government continued to make agreements with Indian nations that required at least the appearance of their consent—not quite denying native autonomy even then. In the later part of the nineteenth century the Supreme Court held that Congress had unilateral authority over Indian people, first in *United States v. Kagama* (1886), which upheld the Major Crimes Act, and then in *Lone Wolf v. Hitchcock* (1903), in which the Court held that not only did Congress have unlimited plenary power over Indian nations but also that it had always had that power. This is called the "plenary power doctrine."

Federal Indian policy was to a great extent driven by the arguments and energies of white reformers. Helen Hunt Jackson's (1830–1885) *A Century of Dishonor* (1881), an extensive account of white perfidy with respect to native peoples, argued that Indians could and indeed desired to become civilized and therefore U.S. citizens. She and her supporters argued that, while the treaties should be honored, they really should not have been made in the first place, because Indians in their primitive state were not capable of forming true governments. Still, Jackson and other reformers believed that the United States should honor treaties because it was a Christian nation that should not break its promises to an inferior and defeated race, and, furthermore, that it should assiduously work to raise up that defeated race to civilization and "absorption." Like other reform groups, the highly influential Indian Rights Association was founded in 1882 by Herbert Welsh and Henry Pancoast to advocate, its members insisted, for Indian equality. Like other reformers, they argued that Indians should be completely absorbed into U.S. society as Christians, farmers, and individual property owners. Their advocacy—they even had a lobbyist in Washington, D.C.—was a principal factor in the establishment of boarding schools and the passage of the Dawes or General Allotment Act (1887), the most infamous piece of legislation directed at native people during the period.

Known as the Dawes Allotment Act for its main architect, Massachusetts Senator Henry Dawes, a longtime "friend of the Indian," the legislation provided for the distribution of plots of land to individual Indians, with the "surplus" opened up to white settlement. Indians who, after a twenty-five-year-long trust period, could prove that they had become "civilized" would then be granted fee-simple title to their land and U.S. citizenship. Between 1887 and 1917 native land holdings in the West shrank from 138 million acres to 48 million. After 1907 the secretary of the interior was given authority to bypass the twenty-five-year trust period and issue title to land to individual Indians; afterward, 60 percent of Indians given such patents lost their land.

As the Bureau of Indian Affairs extended its programs and native people grew weaker, its bureaucracy and budget grew, almost doubling in size between 1881 and 1897. The first government residential boarding school was founded by Captain Richard Henry Pratt at Carlisle, Pennsylvania, in 1879; Pratt is infamous for remarking that his objective was to "kill the Indian to save the man." The schools followed the same pattern: their purpose was to divest native children of their language, culture, and practices, turn them into Christians and farmers or laborers, and thereby make them "civilized." In the case of native people, this meant preparation for a life of lower-class labor; the boys received vocational training and the girls were trained in the "domestic arts." Intellectual achievement was deemed beyond the capacity of native children. The schools gathered children of many tribes together; by the end of the nineteenth century there were twenty-five schools in fifteen states with a total enrollment of twenty thousand students, mainly in the West.

INDIANS AND U.S. CULTURE

The symbolic absorption of Indians in U.S. culture enacts the political absorption of native land, telling over and over again the story of the triumph of civilization over savagery, the destiny of the nation that God ordained, and the participation of every American in that triumph. At bottom of every one of these manifestations is the necessity of justifying white occupation of native land, of explaining it and making it right. It is often remarked that there are savages and noble savages, and if the bad Indians are the usual conglomeration of inferiority and evil, the good Indians are at least good, even if they are all too happy to recede gracefully when their appointed time comes. The sympathy so common in representations of Indians is another manifestation of absorption. While the reformers wanted to absorb Indians and their land by making them like whites, at least on the surface, primitivists and nationalists who idealized Indians as the antidote to modernity on the one hand and the location of authentic American identity on the other absorbed Indians by idealizing them and locking them in an abstract past that never really existed. Such abstract representations reiterate the naturalness of Indians' disappearance and reestablish white Americans' benevolence.

SCIENCE AND INDIANS

John Wesley Powell, the founder in 1879 of the Bureau of American Ethnology (BAE), sought to discover the laws of social evolution by studying primitive Indians, arguing that such study provided important information for government policymakers. Early anthropologists at the BAE included Frank Hamilton Cushing, who wrote *Zuñi Fetiches* (1883), *A Study of Pueblo*

Chiricahua Apaches four months after arriving at the Carlisle Indian School. Photograph by J. N. Choate, 1886.
© CORBIS

Pottery (1886), and *Outlines of Zuñi Creation Myths* (1896). Cushing was fond of dressing himself as a Zuni Indian; he also published articles on Indian topics in popular magazines of the time. James Mooney was a young newspaperman before he joined the BAE in 1885; he published *The Sacred Formulas of the Cherokee* (1891), *The Ghost-Dance Religion and the Sioux Outbreak of 1890* (1893), *The Siouan Tribes of the East* (1894), *Calendar History of the Kiowa Indians* (1898), and *The Cheyenne Indians* (1907). One notable anthropologist not affiliated with the BAE was Daniel Garrison Brinton, who in 1884 became professor of ethnology and archeology at the Academy of Natural Sciences in Philadelphia. Brinton published many papers and books, including *American Hero Myths* (1882) and *Aboriginal American Authors and Their Productions* (1882). He also edited a series of works in what he called the Library of Aboriginal American Literature, including *The Maya Chronicles* (1882), *The*

roquois Book of Rites (1883), and *A Migration Legend of the Creek Indians* (1884). Brinton's were some of the earliest anthropological works to designate the existence of a native "literature" (and to represent it in a particular way) and then to treat it as worthy of scholarly study.

By the end of the century anthropologists moved from the government and natural history museums to new university anthropology departments. Franz Boas, a professor of anthropology at Columbia University from 1896 to 1936, led this movement. He was a practitioner of "salvage anthropology": by the late nineteenth century anthropologists believed that they were in a race against time to find and document the primitive cultures rapidly being irrevocably changed by the spread of modernity—and only primitive cultures untouched by modernity were truly authentic and therefore to be studied. In one infamous instance, anthropologists kept a native man they considered the "last of his race" in a museum as a living exhibit for several years until the man died. In 1911 Ishi, a Yaqui about fifty years old, emerged from the California wilderness, where he and his remnant tribe had been avoiding whites since the settlers' genocidal slaughter of California Indians in the 1850s. Two anthropologists, Alfred Kroeber and Thomas Waterman, brought Ishi to the University of California at Berkeley, where he lived in the university's museum while Kroeber and Waterman studied him. He died of tuberculosis in 1916.

POPULAR REPRESENTATION

One of the inescapable stock figures of Indians at this time was what has come to be called the "Vanishing American," which is essentially any representation of an Indian or Indians in which the underlying theme is their approaching, inevitable disappearance. Perhaps the best-known producer of such images, certainly today if not at the time, was the photographer and amateur ethnologist Edward S. Curtis (1868–1952). From 1907 to 1930 Curtis wrote a twenty-volume history called *The North American Indian;* each volume was accompanied by a folio of sepia-tinted plates, the most famous of which was published in 1904 and called "The Vanishing Race," showing a group of Navajos walking single-file into the distance, literally fading away. This was the first picture in the first volume of the series; observing that this picture "expresses so much of the thought that inspired" the project, Curtis wrote in the image's caption that what "this picture is meant to convey is that the Indians as a race, already shorn in their tribal strength and stripped of their primitive dress, are passing into the darkness of an unknown future" (n.p.). Joseph K. Dixon's book *The Vanishing Race* appeared in 1913, illustrated with portraits of warriors and other Indians drifting off into the sunset. The most famous representation of the Vanishing American is probably James Earl Fraser's monumental sculpture *The End of the Trail,* showing a defeated warrior slumped over his equally defeated horse, which was first exhibited in 1915 at the Panama-Pacific International Exposition in San Francisco. It was immediately popular and reproduced as bookends, ashtrays, postcards, advertisements, paperweights, trinkets, prints, and on china and silverware.

Popular writers on Indians often associated themselves with the West and outdoor life. George Bird Grinnell (1849–1938) was a prolific writer of such material, publishing Indian-themed material in leading periodicals; books of "Indian stories," including *Blackfoot Lodge Tales* (1892), *Blackfeet Indian Stories* (1913), and *By Cheyenne Campfires* (1926); and historical works such as *The Fighting Cheyennes* (1915) and *The Cheyenne Indians, Their History and Way of Life* (1923).

Frank Bird Linderman (1869–1938) published *Indian Why Stories: Sparks from War Eagle's Lodgefire* (1915) and then *Indian Old-Man Stories: More Sparks from War Eagle's Lodgefire* (1920). *Indian Why Stories* was printed for schools in 1918 as *Indian Lodge-Fire Stories.* Hamlin Garland (1860–1940) published *The Book of the American Indian* in 1923, with illustrations by Frederic Remington, but it consisted of stories that he had published in periodicals between 1890 and 1905. In addition to Remington, Charles M. Russell was another of the "cowboy artists" who made extensive use of Indian themes, vanishing and otherwise, in his work, which often appeared in the periodicals of the day.

Living native people were subject to the enactment of their own supposed primitivism and authenticity. Along with representatives of other "primitive" cultures around the world, native people were regular features of world's fairs—as at Chicago in 1893 and St. Louis in 1904—in living anthropological exhibits in which paying visitors could wander around their encampments and observe them living authentically. Wild West shows were also immensely popular. The originator of the form, William F. (Buffalo Bill) Cody (1846–1917) put together his first Wild West extravaganza in Omaha in 1883, touring the eastern United States and eventually Europe to wide popular acclaim. Performances included trick shooting, horse races, cowboy rope tricks, and set pieces like an Indian attack on a settler cabin or on the Deadwood stagecoach or a "reenactment" of Custer's Last Stand. Cody insisted that the Wild West—he never allowed the word "show" to appear—was utterly authentic. He traveled to reservations to recruit performers; given the conditions on reservations at the time, some native people were happy to go with Cody. Sitting Bull himself spent part of 1885 on tour with the Wild West. After the Wounded Knee massacre, several of the imprisoned leaders of the Ghost Dance movement toured Europe with Cody on the suggestion of the commanding general of the army, Nelson Miles. Like American military and political leaders before him, Miles argued that exposure to the grandeur of the "white race" would cause Indians to return to the reservations chastened and complacent. Wild West shows continued to tour until the 1930s.

NATIVE WRITING AND THE "NADIR"

Aside from Indian Territory, where a substantial native readership existed for native writing, most native writers wrote for white audiences. In this situation, the fantasy world to which Buffalo Bill contributed so much was the world in which native writers and political leaders had to operate. No matter what the topic of discussion, nearly every native person who stood before a white audience in any capacity was expected to appear suitably attired as whites' idea of what an "Indian" should look like. Intellectually Indians were in many respects flying in the face of their audience's expectations. Following the arguments of native writers earlier in the nineteenth century, they believed that Indians could be farmers and Christians and therefore civilized but could continue to live in autonomous and modern Indian nations. When at the end of the century there appeared to be no stopping the U.S. government in its efforts to erase native political society, many native leaders argued for U.S. citizenship. But U.S. citizenship was never the desire of the majority of native people, and for those leaders who advocated it in the period, it represented the only means left of establishing some measure of recognition. At the same time, most who argued for U.S. citizenship did not advocate the abandonment of tribal heritage. While the Society of American Indians was founded in 1911 by "progressive" native leaders—such as Charles Eastman (Santee Sioux), Carlos Montezuma (Yavapai), and Zitkala-Ša (Yankton Sioux)—to advocate for U.S. citizenship, the organization was also highly critical of white paternalism and sought to celebrate rather than denigrate the tribal past.

Anthropology was one the few areas in which native scholars could be recognized, at least to some degree, for their expertise. J. N. B. Hewitt, a Tuscarora, was a farmer, newspaper correspondent, and proprietor of a night school for men when he received funding from the Bureau of Ethnology in 1880 to study Iroquois languages and stories; in 1886 he joined the bureau to complete work on a Tuscarora-English dictionary. Hewitt transcribed Iroquois languages and ceremonies, but he left most of his work in manuscript. Francis La Flesche, an Omaha, also worked for the BAE and the Smithsonian Institution. He was trained by and collaborated with Alice Cunningham Fletcher, a philanthropist turned anthropologist, beginning in the early 1880s, working with her on *The Omaha Tribe* (1911). La Flesche also published an account of his experiences at mission school called *The Middle Five* (1900). Franz Boas encouraged Arthur C. Parker (1881–1955), a Seneca and the grandnephew of Ely S. Parker, to study anthropology at Columbia, but Parker instead concentrated on archaeology, becoming affiliated with the New York State Museum. Parker wrote over 250 articles, mainly on Indian topics, and several books for children. He was also a founder of the Society of American Indians and editor of its journal, *American Indian Magazine*. Other early native anthropologists included Jesse Cornplanter (Seneca), who published *Iroquois Indian Games and Dances* in 1913; James R. Murie (Pawnee), who published *Pawnee Indian Societies* in 1914 and, with Clark Wissler, *Ceremonies of the Pawnee* in 1921; and William

Jones (Fox), the first native university-trained anthropologist. When he could not secure funding to support his research on the Ojibwas, Jones traveled to the Philippines to study indigenous people. He was killed there by Llongot people in 1907.

Reform writers included Sarah Winnemucca (Paiute, 1844?–1891) and Susette La Flesche (Omaha, 1854–1903), the older sister of Francis La Flesche (they also had a sister, Susan, who was the first native woman physician). The daughter of a Paiute leader, Winnemucca was educated for a time in a convent and became a teacher and interpreter for the U.S. Army. Her *Life among the Paiutes* (1883) is the first history and autobiography written by a native woman. She lectured extensively on Indian affairs in San Francisco, Nevada, and then the East Coast, where she supported allotment and spoke in the homes of distinguished supporters like Ralph Waldo Emerson and John Greenleaf Whittier. She wrote her book while on tour and sold it at lectures. After counterattacks from government bureaucrats, Winnemucca returned to Nevada, where she lectured and established a school for Paiute children; she died in Idaho after the school closed in 1887.

The daughter of a chief who advocated adaptation to Euro-American ways, Susette La Flesche was educated at mission and boarding schools; she became involved in politics and writing at a significant moment in the Indian reform movement. In 1879, after the Poncas (who lived near the Omahas in Nebraska) were removed against their will to Indian Territory, Standing Bear, their chief, led a group back to their ancestral land. The U.S. Army arrested Standing Bear and others and they were put on trial. The court in Nebraska then declared them legally "persons" and set them free, after which Standing Bear lectured to wide acclaim in East Coast cities on the abuses of the government, on a tour organized by Thomas Tibbles, editor of the *Omaha Daily Herald*. La Flesche gave lectures on the tour as well and testified with Standing Bear before the U.S. Senate. She and Tibbles eventually married, and La Flesche began writing columns for the *Omaha World Herald* and *The Independent*. She also wrote short stories illustrating traditional native beliefs for the children's magazines *St. Nicholas* and *Wide Awake*.

Among northern and eastern tribes, Andrew J. Blackbird (Ottawa) published *History of the Ottawa and Chippewa Indians of Michigan: A Grammar of Their Language and Personal and Family History* in 1887 and Elias Johnson (Tuscarora) published *Legends, Traditions, and Laws of the Iroquois, or Six Nations* in 1881. Like Winnemucca's *Life among the Paiutes,* these books incorporate traditional and contemporary history, ethnographic information, and elements of the author's autobiography in narratives that are generally supportive of modernization but that celebrate tribal history and culture. In contrast to Blackbird and Johnson, Simon Pokagon (Potawatomi, 1830–1899) was a celebrity among whites as an advocate for Indian causes. He published several booklets on birchbark—*Red Man's Greeting* (1893), *The Pottawatamie Book of Genesis—Legends of the Creation of Man* (1901), and *Algonquin Legends of South Haven* (n.d.)—as well as essays on Potawatomi culture and history. His authorship of the novel *Queen of the Woods* (1899) is currently questioned. A Vanishing Indian narrative with Pokagon himself as the central figure, the story concerns an Indian who becomes civilized, rejects civilization, then becomes a drunk, after which the novel becomes a temperance tract. There is a strong argument that this novel was written by the wife of his lawyer and publicist, Cyrus Engle. The novel does, however, incorporate Potawatomi words in the story and concludes with an essay on the Algonquin language.

E. Pauline Johnson (Mohawk, 1861–1913) appeared before white audiences in a stylized Indian costume only for half of her performance; in the other half she wore an evening gown. The daughter of George Henry Martin Johnson, a Mohawk chief, and Emily Susanna Howells, a cousin of the author and editor William Dean Howells, Johnson grew up on the Six Nations Reserve in Ontario. She began performing her poetry in 1892, becoming well known in Canada, Great Britain, and the United States; she published her first book of poetry, *The White Wampum*, in 1895. A second volume, *Canadian Born*, appeared in 1903; Johnson then began contributing articles on Indian topics to a variety of periodicals. After retiring from performing she moved to Vancouver, where she published her versions of stories told her by the Squamish chief Joe Capilano in *Legends of Vancouver* (1911). Her poems were collected in *Flint and Feather* (1912), and, after her death in 1913, two collections of her short pieces were published: *The Shagganappi*, consisting of stories originally published in *Boy's World*, and *The Moccasin-Maker*, stories about both native and non-native women.

Zitkala-Ša (Gertrude Simmons Bonnin, 1876–1938) was born in South Dakota and attended mission school and Earlham College in Indiana, where she won some renown in oratory. After working at Carlisle Indian Industrial School for a year, an experience she writes about in "An Indian Teacher among the Indians," she left to attend music school (she was a violinist) in Boston but later had to leave because of ill health. Between 1900 and 1904 she published autobiographical articles and versions of traditional stories in periodicals such as *Atlantic Monthly, Harper's,* and *Everybody's Magazine.* Frederic Remington provided illustrations for some of her articles. In 1901 she published *Old Indian Legends* (1901), a collection of traditional Sioux trickster stories about Iktomi, with illustrations by Angel DeCora (Ho-Chunk), who was also a teacher at Carlisle. Her articles were collected and published as *American Indian Stories* in 1921. After 1904, Bonnin turned her attention to lecturing, teaching, and community work on behalf of native causes, although while living in Utah, she collaborated with William Hanson, a professor at Brigham Young University, on *The Sun Dance Opera,* which incorporated traditional native music. She remained involved in the Society of American Indians until its demise, serving as the editor of *American Indian Magazine* in 1918 and 1919. In 1926, together with her husband, she founded the National Congress of American Indians, an intertribal organization that remains active today.

Charles A. Eastman (Ohiyesa, 1858–1939) was brought up by his traditional relatives after his father apparently died as a result of the 1862 Dakota war in Minnesota. Years later, however, he found that his father had not only survived, he had become a Christian and advocate of modernization, and when Eastman returned to his father at age fifteen he also acquired his father's outlook on life. Educated at mission school in North Dakota, Santee Normal Training School, Beloit College, Knox College, Kimball Union Academy, Dartmouth College, and Boston University, he became the first native man to become a medical doctor—although he was never able to make a living at it. While he was a government physician at Pine Ridge Agency, Eastman witnessed the effects of the Ghost Dance and the massacre at Wounded Knee; he met his wife, the supervisor of education Elaine Goodale Eastman, and left in 1893, disgusted with the corruption of the Indian Service. He thereafter worked for the Young Men's Christian Association, spent a brief period at Carlisle Indian Industrial School, and in 1903, with the help of Hamlin Garland, got a job with the Indian Service assigning Christian names to Sioux people, which was supposed to help keep them from being swindled. He collected Ojibwa artifacts for the University of Pennsylvania museum, became involved in the Boy Scouts, and with his wife operated a summer camp for children. By the time he helped to found the Society for American Indians, Eastman had become a public figure, lecturing on Indian affairs, advocating reform of the Indian Service and civilization for native people.

Eastman is probably the most prolific native writer of the period. His earliest published works were mainly autobiographical and directed at juvenile audiences, emphasizing the closeness of Indians to nature and characterizing primitive Indian life as a model for

American children, both of them familiar primitivist themes. *Indian Boyhood* (1902), his first book, collected articles previously published in *St. Nicholas,* a children's magazine. He next published three books of traditional stories, including *Red Hunters and the Animal People* (1904) that were, like Zitkala-Ša's Iktomi stories, retellings of traditional stories in an idealized, folkloric manner. Another collection of folktales was published as *Wigwam Evenings* in 1909. His work became more explicitly addressed to adults in *The Soul of the Indian* (1911), in which he describes his own version of Sioux spirituality that incorporates many Christian elements. He next published *Indian Scout Talks* (1914), which addressed the "Indian lore" aspects of youth organizations, a topic on which he published many articles in the period. Eastman's best work is probably *From the Deep Woods to Civilization* (1916). In this book, Eastman tells the story of his experiences with the civilized world, recounting his education, the massacre at Wounded Knee, his efforts on behalf of Indian reform, and his eventual disillusionment with white society.

See also American Indian Stories; Assimilation; Battle of the Little Bighorn; Ethnology; Folklore and Oral Traditions; *Ramona;* Wounded Knee

BIBLIOGRAPHY

Primary Works

Callahan, S. Alice. *Wynema: A Child of the Forest.* 1891. Lincoln: University of Nebraska Press, 1997.

Eastman, Charles A. *From the Deep Woods to Civilization.* 1916. Lincoln: University of Nebraska Press, 1977.

Grayson, G. W. *A Creek Warrior for the Confederacy: The Autobiography of Chief G. W. Grayson.* Edited and with an introduction by W. David Baird. Norman: University of Oklahoma Press, 1988.

Hopkins, Sarah Winnemucca. *Life among the Piutes: Their Wrongs and Claims.* 1883. Reno: University of Nevada Press, 1994.

Johnson, E. Pauline. *The Moccasin Maker.* 1913. Edited and introduced by A. LaVonne Brown Ruoff. Norman: University of Oklahoma Press, 1998.

La Flesche, Francis. *The Middle Five.* 1900. Lincoln: University of Nebraska Press, 1978.

Littlefield, Daniel F., Jr., and James W. Parins, eds. *Native American Writing in the Southeast: An Anthology, 1875–1935.* Jackson: University Press of Mississippi, 1995.

Posey, Alexander. *Chinnubbie and the Owl: Muscogee (Creek) Stories, Orations, and Oral Traditions.* Edited by Matthew Wynn Sivils. Lincoln: University of Nebraska Press, 2005.

Posey, Alexander. *The Fus Fixico Letters of Alexander Posey.* Edited by Daniel F. Littlefield Jr. and Carol A. Petty Hunter. Norman: University of Oklahoma Press, 2002.

Zitkala-Ša. *American Indian Stories, Legends, and Other Writings.* Edited by Cathy N. Davidson and Ada Norris. New York: Penguin, 2003.

Secondary Works

Child, Brenda J. *Boarding School Seasons: American Indian Families, 1900–1940.* Lincoln: University of Nebraska Press, 1998.

Deloria, Philip J. *Indians in Unexpected Places.* Lawrence: University Press of Kansas, 2004.

Deloria, Philip J. *Playing Indian.* New Haven, Conn.: Yale University Press, 1998.

Deloria, Vine, Jr. *Singing for a Spirit: A Portrait of the Dakota Sioux.* Santa Fe, N.M.: Clear Light, 2000.

Dippie, Brian W. *The Vanishing American: White Attitudes and U.S. Indian Policy.* Lawrence: University Press of Kansas, 1991.

Harring, Sidney J. *Crow Dog's Case: American Indian Sovereignty, Tribal Law, and United States Law in the Nineteenth Century.* Cambridge, U.K., and New York: Cambridge University Press, 1995.

Hoxie, Frederick E. *A Final Promise: The Campaign to Assimilate the Indians, 1880–1920.* Lincoln: University of Nebraska Press, 1984.

Hoxie, Frederick E., ed. *Talking Back to Civilization: Indian Voices from the Progressive Era.* Boston: Bedford/St. Martin's, 2001.

Kilcup, Karen L. *Native American Women's Writing c. 1800–1924.* Malden, Mass.: Blackwell, 2000.

Krech, Shepard, III, and Barbara A. Hail, eds. *Collecting Native America, 1870–1960.* Washington, D.C.: Smithsonian Institution Press, 1999.

Maddox, Lucy. *Citizen Indians: Native American Intellectuals, Race, and Reform.* Ithaca, N.Y.: Cornell University Press, 2005.

Mihesuah, Devon A. *Cultivating the Rosebuds: The Education of Women at the Cherokee Female Seminary 1851–1909.* Urbana: University of Illinois Press, 1993.

Mills, Charles W. *The Racial Contract.* Ithaca, N.Y.: Cornell University Press, 1997.

Moses, L. G. *Wild West Shows and the Images of American Indians, 1883–1933.* Albuquerque: University of New Mexico Press, 1996.

Ostler, Jeffrey. *The Plains Sioux and U.S. Colonialism from Lewis and Clark to Wounded Knee.* Cambridge, U.K., and New York: Cambridge University Press, 2004.

Patterson, Michelle Wick. "'Real' Indian Songs: The Society of American Indians and the Use of Native American

Culture as a Means of Reform." *American Indian Quarterly* 26, no. 1 (winter 2002): 44–66.

Senier, Siobhan. *Voices of American Indian Assimilation and Resistance: Helen Hunt Jackson, Sarah Winnemucca, and Victoria Howard.* Norman: University of Oklahoma Press, 2001.

Tully, James. "Rediscovering America: The Two Treatises and Aboriginal Rights." In his *An Approach to Political Philosophy: Locke in Contexts,* pp. 137–176. London: Cambridge University Press, 1993.

Viola, Herman J. *Diplomats in Buckskins: A History of Indian Delegations in Washington City.* Washington, D.C.: Smithsonian Institution Press, 1981.

Welch, James. *The Heartsong of Charging Elk.* New York: Anchor Books, 2000.

Wilkins, David E. *American Indian Sovereignty and the U.S. Supreme Court: The Masking of Justice.* Austin: University of Texas Press, 1997.

Maureen Konkle

INDIAN WARS

The term "Indian wars" evokes some clichés of U.S. culture: the heroic General George Armstrong Custer and his men surrounded by whooping savages, shooting it out to the last man; a long line of dusty cavalrymen winding through western canyons, spied upon by sneaky savages about to descend; a row of beautiful savages arrayed on the crest of a hill on the plains, pausing a moment before meeting their fate. If these images, inescapable in twentieth-century film and television, did not originate in the period in question, they certainly came to their full flowering as cultural conventions at that time, in the endless reiterations of dime novels, Wild West shows, newspaper accounts, magazine stories, and popular histories. These images mask the violent political, economic, and cultural conflicts that characterized the continental expansion of the United States; indeed, these images are a means not only of justifying that violent political conflict but also of normalizing it, making it seem both necessary and inevitable. Indians must and will be defeated so that American ingenuity and commerce can secure its place on the continent; the endless references to Indian wars tell that story over and over again.

It is necessary, however, to separate the history of armed conflict between European Americans and native peoples in the late nineteenth century from the more familiar mythology of those conflicts. But even that history began in myth. U.S. intellectuals, political leaders, and ordinary people imagined the country's

expansion in remarkably abstract terms: they believed that, in the United States, civilization (white people) faced a pitched battle with savagery (Indians). Because human history progressed ever forward, savagery would be defeated and Indians would either be "exterminated" or, hypothetically, "absorbed" into U.S. society, becoming civilized Christians and farmers and no longer living as Indians. But behind this story that European Americans told themselves was a set of historical facts that contradicted it: the conflict between Europeans and Native American peoples has been principally about control of land, not misunderstandings about culture. One of the distinct peculiarities of the European colonization of North America was that, in order to form alliances and legitimate their control of Indian land, Europeans entered into treaties with Indians. Treaties are contracts between nations, and in them Europeans recognized Native American political autonomy—they did not, as is sometimes maintained, "grant" that autonomy. With the formation of the United States, treaties took on added meaning; political leaders such as Thomas Jefferson, Benjamin Franklin, and George Washington maintained that treaties with Indians established that the United States held its land legitimately and not through armed conquest, which demonstrated that it adhered to its founding principles. While in the late eighteenth century the United States did not yet have the military and technological power to subject native peoples to its will, even after it gained that material superiority, treaties remained a significant aspect of U.S. political culture. The United States was supposed to live up to its principles, to be a benevolent nation adhering to the rule of law. Political leaders maintained that the United States would buy land from Indians if they would consent to sell it.

The myth of the inevitable, foreordained conflict between savagery and civilization in the United States has obscured that political history. It has also explained and justified violence: any dead Indian in the United States could be understood as an inevitable result of this grand conflict between the abstract forces of savagery and civilization, rather than, say, the result of a specific political conflict that might have its origins in a legitimate complaint. In the face of this overwhelming insistence on the naturalness of Indians' disappearance (political or biological), native peoples continued to maintain that the treaties showed they could coexist politically with the United States—without being exterminated or absorbed or by it. The treaties gave native peoples not only a political mechanism but also their own abstract concept around which to organize their resistance to being wiped out. They insisted that, as citizens of Indian nations, they could even be Christians and farmers; they rejected the notion that to

Indian Battles, 1870–1890

be civilized was to be a citizen of the United States. When it became clear after the Civil War that Indians would not die out, contrary to what had been asserted earlier in the nineteenth century, the U.S. government actively sought to destroy Native American political authority and autonomy and confiscate Native American land, making treaties and, infamously, breaking them, and also engaging in the armed conflicts known as the Indian wars in the post–Civil War western United States.

THE U.S. ARMY IN THE POST–CIVIL WAR PERIOD

After the Civil War, the U.S. army had several responsibilities west of the Mississippi, where it was the federal government's only representative. Its principal jobs were to protect settlers, defend emigrant routes, and occupy territory. It also protected railroad and telegraph lines, which were essential to commerce and military operations. With regard to native peoples, the army's job was to subjugate them, remove them to reservations (and keep them on the reservations), and "assist" in their acculturation, which could mean anything from hunting down those who continued to practice and spread tribal cultural practices that the federal government had criminalized to preventing Native Americans from hunting buffalo to assisting in rounding up Native American children to be sent to government boarding schools. In 1869 President Ulysses S. Grant appointed William Tecumseh Sherman to be commanding general of the army (a native of Ohio, Sherman had been named for the Shawnee chief who led an alliance against the

Americans overwhelmingly understood the resistance of Indian nations to U.S. authority as further evidence that an abstract conflict between savagery and civilization was taking place in their own time. It was axiomatic to Americans that civilization would prevail and savages would die, either through their own perfidy or the simple fact that they would inevitably be eclipsed by a superior society. In this setting, military leaders commonly represented native people as less than human. General Philip Sheridan in this excerpt indicates that Indian women and children killed in their villages had only brought death on themselves, because of who they were presumably, not what they had done.

In taking the offensive, I have to select that season when I can catch the fiends; and, if a village is attacked and women and children killed, the responsibility is not with the soldiers but with the people whose crimes necessitated the attack. During the war did any one hesitate to attack a village or town occupied by the enemy because women and children were within its limits? Did we cease to throw shells into Vicksburg or Atlanta because women and children were there?

Philip Sheridan to William T. Sherman, 9 May 1873, Division of the Missouri, Letters Sent, RG 393, Records of the U.S. Army.

Americans in the early nineteenth century, then died at the battle of the Thames, Ontario, in 1813). Philip H. Sheridan served as Sherman's second in command, then succeeded Sherman as commanding general in 1882. Although military campaigns against Indians experienced a lull for several years in the late 1860s and early 1870s because of Grant's "peace policy" toward indigenous people, campaigns stepped up again by 1872. Most of the major armed conflicts were over by 1880, although the army did not know it at the time.

In the nineteenth-century United States, fears of a standing army in peacetime were deep-seated, and after the Civil War the army fell precipitously out of favor, losing the interest of politicians and the financial support of the federal government. Even public outrage over Custer's defeat did not change the general attitude of both elected officials and the bureaucracy. Cabinet-level meetings on issues related to native peoples were rare, and the planning for various campaigns against Indian nations was not done in Washington. Indeed,

according to historians, what planning existed was at best ad hoc. At the same time, the bureaucracy for administering native peoples was a subject of much contention. The Office of Indian Affairs had been transferred from the Department of War to the Department of the Interior in 1849; the reservations were run by an infamously corrupt bureaucracy, which had attracted the attention of civilian reformers such as Helen Hunt Jackson. Many officers wished to transfer the Indian office back to the War Department so that they could have clear control of Indian affairs, but a congressional bill to provide for the transfer failed to pass in 1878. Afterward, Congress showed little interest in the army until the Spanish-American War of 1898.

In the actual conduct of armed conflict, both sides had advantages and disadvantages—sometimes the same ones, such as the lack of a coherent policy. Native fighters knew the geography better than whites, had access to many horses per fighter rather than just one, as was the case with cavalrymen, and had the ability to take the initiative in planning. On the negative side, Native American leaders did not have total control over their warriors. Most of the conflicts were carried out through ambushes of one side or the other; contrary to stereotype, most attacks made by the army did not occur at dawn but rather during daylight hours, and more conflicts occurred in summer than in winter. The army tended to attack whenever meeting native people, and it often attacked from an advantageous position. Historians have also noted that it is difficult to measure the scope of armed conflict between native peoples and European Americans in the post–Civil War era because white civilians often took up arms against native people on their own, and their actions were less likely to be recorded than those of the military.

Major conflicts during the period included campaigns against the Apaches in the Southwest in the 1870s, leading to Geronimo's surrender in 1886; against the Sioux and Cheyennes throughout the 1870s, with Native American victories at the Rosebud and Little Bighorn, the death of Crazy Horse in captivity in 1877, Sitting Bull's escape across the border to Canada, and the eventual surrender of his band in 1881; the Modoc War in 1872–1873 in California; the Nez Percé War in 1877 in Montana; and the Ute rebellion in Colorado in 1879. The Geronimo campaign of 1885–1886 is usually considered the last offensive by Indian warriors, and the 1890 Wounded Knee massacre is generally taken to be the last significant military conflict.

TOTAL WAR

Historians widely acknowledge the U.S. military's use of "total war" principles in its conflicts with native

Geronimo, photographed shortly before his last surrender, 1886. Apache leader Geronimo's life and numerous confrontations with U.S. forces became a common subject for writers in the late nineteenth and early twentieth centuries. © CORBIS

peoples in this era. "Total war" designates the use of force against an enemy's resources and against noncombatants; historians disagree on whether the period of the Indian Wars was the first time this principle was consistently deployed in the United States, or whether it had been used much earlier. They agree, however, that after the Civil War, military leaders argued that the total war strategies they had used against Confederate noncombatants and resources could and should be transferred to their wars with Indians. During the Civil War, William Tecumseh Sherman posited three principles of total war: first, that the military must destroy property to shorten the war and deprive the enemy of resources; second, that the enemy must be

deprived of spirit or demoralized; and third, that the enemy must be understood—by both sides—to be collectively responsible for what is being rained down on it; that is, the enemy deserves what it gets. Sherman's 1864 March to the Sea through the southeastern states and Sheridan's campaign in the Shenandoah Valley that same year served as models for the campaigns against native peoples. Sherman gave the directives as commanding general of the army, and Sheridan carried out those directives in the West.

While the U.S. army's purpose before the Civil War had been mainly to push native peoples farther and farther west, away from the advancing borders of settlement, after the Civil War its purpose was to contain and confine native peoples, to push them onto relatively small, easily controlled reservations; those who resisted were fair game and, as far as most of the military was concerned, deserved what they got, which was often death. It is important to note here that, while Sheridan and Sherman had expressed just as much anger and mercilessness toward the civilian population of the Confederacy, far fewer noncombatants died in the Civil War than in the Indian wars. Attacks on encampments in particular often killed women, children, and old people while able-bodied men were away hunting. At the time, Sheridan was supposed to have said that as far as Indians went, "the only good one I ever saw was dead," though he always denied having made the statement. As an extension of total war principles, both Sherman and Sheridan actively supported the extermination of the great buffalo herds on the plains, though this was not official U.S. policy. Sheridan wrote the buffalo hunters "were destroying the Indians' commissary; and it is a well known fact that an army losing its base of supplies is placed at a great disadvantage. . . . For the sake of a lasting peace, let them kill, skin, and sell until the buffaloes are exterminated" (quoted in Janda, pp. 24–25). Killing the buffalo had the intended effect: with their resources cut off, the people were demoralized.

INDIAN WARS LITERATURE

Writings about the Indian Wars proliferated after the Civil War, particularly after the 1880s, and remained popular through the 1920s. What is striking about these writings is how conventionalized the political conflict with indigenous people is, to the point that the narratives all follow the same script: Indians are savages who must and will die if they do not submit to the civilization that is fast engulfing them. In this setting, famous—or infamous—tribal leaders, such as Cochise, Geronimo, Sitting Bull, Crazy Horse, Captain Jack, or Chief Joseph, become caricatures, each acting out the same story. There are roughly four types of narratives relating to the Indian wars in popular writing of the time, although they certainly overlap: frontier wars narratives, which are a development of the "border wars" narratives of the antebellum era; personal accounts, often of military men and sometimes of their wives; accounts of famous tribal leaders such as Sitting Bull and Geronimo; and late captivity narratives.

Of the first type, examples include James W. Buel's *Heroes of the Plains* (1883), Jacob Piatt Dunn's *Massacres of the Mountains* (1886), and D. M. Kelsey's *Our Pioneer Heroes and Their Daring Deeds* (1882), which covered the entire history of European settlement from Hernando De Soto and Samuel de Champlain to Generals George Crook and Nelson A. Miles. Several prominent and many not-so-prominent military men and their wives produced accounts of their lives in the West. Margaret Irvin Carrington's *Ab-sa-ra-ka, Home of the Crows* (1868) was an account of her experiences on her husband's military post in Montana. George Armstrong Custer (1839–1876) himself produced *My Life on the Plains; or, Personal Experiences with Indians* in 1874, a book that became *Wild Life on the Plains and Horrors of Indian Warfare* in 1883 and afterward, a title change that marks the shift in the 1880s to increasingly sensationalized accounts of Indians. Elizabeth Bacon Custer (1842–1933) made a career out of immortalizing her dead husband, providing an income for herself for the rest of her long life. She published *Boots and Saddles; or, Life in Dakota with General Custer* in 1885 and reprinted it six times over the next thirty years. Her second effort, *Tenting on the Plains; or, General Custer in Kansas and Texas,* was first published in 1887 and was also reprinted many times. Her *Following the Guidon* was published in 1890 and only reprinted once, in 1899. *The Boy General: Story of the Life of Major-General George A. Custer,* as told to Mary E. Burt, appeared in 1901 and was reprinted in 1909.

Two generals are notable for their contributions to the Indian wars genres. General Nelson A. Miles (1839–1925), who, like Custer, was a tireless self-promoter, published *Personal Recollections and Observations of General Nelson A. Miles* (1896). Miles led campaigns against the Cheyenne, Comanche, Kiowa, and Arapaho in Texas in the 1870s; drove Sitting Bull's band into Canada; captured Chief Joseph as well as Geronimo; and led the army in its disastrous military response to the Ghost Dance among the Lakotas in 1890. In 1911 he published *Serving the Republic* along with many magazine articles on the Indian wars, the "Indian problem," and by the turn of the century, U.S. imperial affairs around the world. Miles was one of many writers who made the connection between the U.S. mission to civilize the savages of North America and its new mission to civilize savages around the globe. General Oliver Otis

Howard (1830–1909)—an outspoken supporter of the rights of African Americans for whom Howard University in Washington, D.C., is named—published several books on his experiences: *Nez Perce Joseph* (1881), *Autobiography* (1907), *My Life and Experiences among Our Hostile Indians* (1907), and *Famous Indian Chiefs I Have Known* (1908).

The "famous Indian chiefs" narratives began to appear earlier in the nineteenth century, during the removal era. Examples include the *Life of Black Hawk* (1833), which the Sauk chief dictated to J. B. Patterson, and biographies of the Mohawk leader Joseph Brant and the Seneca leader Red Jacket by William L. Stone, published in 1838 and 1841, respectively. In the late nineteenth century S. M. Barrett published *Geronimo's Story of His Life* (1906). These biographical narratives were not nearly as popular as the "Indian massacres" stories, although such books often included rudimentary biographical narratives of Indian warriors, such as James W. Buel's account of Sitting Bull's life in *Heroes of the Plains* in 1883. Also falling off in popularity from levels earlier in the nineteenth century were captivity narratives, such as James T. DeShields's *Cynthia Ann Parker: The Story of Her Capture* (1886) and Emeline Fuller's *Left by the Indians* (1892).

See also Annexation and Expansion; Battle of the Little Big Horn; Jurisprudence; Violence; Weaponry; Wounded Knee

BIBLIOGRAPHY

Primary Works

Carrington, Margaret Irvin. *Ab-sa-ra-ka, Home of the Crows.* 1868. Lincoln: University of Nebraska Press, 1983.

Custer, Elizabeth Bacon. *Boots and Saddles; or, Life in Dakota with General Custer.* 1885. Norman: University of Oklahoma Press, 1961.

Miles, Nelson A. *Personal Recollections and Observations.* Vol. 2. Lincoln: University of Nebraska Press, 1992.

Secondary Works

Janda, Lance. "Shutting the Gates of Mercy: The American Origins of Total War, 1860–1880." *Journal of Military History* 59 (January 1995): 7–26.

Keenan, Jerry. *Encyclopedia of American Indian Wars, 1492–1890.* Santa Barbara, Calif.: ABC-CLIO, 1997.

Michno, Gregory F. *Encyclopedia of Indian Wars: Western Battles and Skirmishes, 1850–1890.* Missoula, Mont.: Mountain Press, 2003.

Ostler, Jeffrey. *The Plains Sioux and U.S. Colonialism from Lewis and Clark to Wounded Knee.* Cambridge, U.K.: Cambridge University Press, 2004.

Slotkin, Richard. *Gunfighter Nation: The Myth of the Frontier in Twentieth-Century America.* New York: Atheneum, 1992.

Utley, Robert. *The Indian Frontier of the American West, 1846–1890.* Albuquerque: University of New Mexico Press, 1984.

Welch, James. *Fools Crow.* New York: Penguin, 1986.

Welch, James, with Paul Stekler. *Killing Custer: The Battle of the Little Bighorn and the Fate of the Plains Indians.* 1833. New York: Penguin, 1994.

Williams, Walter L. "United States Indian Policy and the Debate over Philippine Annexation: Implications for the Origins of American Imperialism." *Journal of American History* 66, no. 4 (March 1980): 810–831.

Wooster, Robert. *The Military and United States Indian Policy, 1865–1903.* New Haven, Conn.: Yale University Press, 1988.

Maureen Konkle

INFLUENZA EPIDEMIC OF 1918

See Disasters; Diseases and Epidemics

IN THE TENNESSEE MOUNTAINS

In the Tennessee Mountains, a collection of eight short stories published in 1884 by Houghton, Mifflin, and Company, is the first book of Mary Noailles Murfree (1850–1922), most of whose work appeared under the pseudonym Charles Egbert Craddock. Writing in an era when women's voices in literature were barely beginning to gain credence, Murfree chose to camouflage her identity in the belief that her fiction would find a wider audience under the guise of male authorship. Whether gender mattered in her case cannot be known, but Murfree's fiction gained popularity almost from the outset. Each story in the collection was initially published in a separate issue of the *Atlantic Monthly,* starting in 1878 with "The Dancin' Party at Harrison's Cove" and continuing through March and April of 1884 with "Drifting down Lost Creek." Her editors at the *Atlantic,* first William Dean Howells and then Thomas Bailey Aldrich, were so impressed with her writing and the response it generated that Aldrich urged Houghton, Mifflin to bring out a volume of the stories. The editors' beliefs in her talent, her topic, and the tastes of the reading public were not ill founded. During Murfree's lifetime *In the Tennessee Mountains* sold out twenty-four printings. Since her death on 31 July 1922 it has gone through several more.

Despite this record, Murfree has nothing approaching the name recognition or literary acclaim of contemporaries such as Mark Twain, William Dean Howells, and Henry James. Part of the reason lies with the genre she chose to pursue: local-color fiction. A relatively short-lived movement from the end of the Civil War until around 1900, local colorism served to highlight specific regions of the country and their inhabitants. Relying heavily on descriptions of the natural environment, along with the peculiar customs and unique dialect of a region, the local colorists ignored character development and were not especially mindful of plotting. In the opinion of the critic Nathalia Wright, they leaned toward anecdote of the Washington Irving variety rather than toward Edgar Allan Poe and Nathaniel Hawthorne's kind of penetration into characters' motives and the effects of their actions. Their work can be aptly likened to the melodrama of the sentimental novel, with emphasis on a nostalgic reverence for the simple life, usually of a past time or, as in the case of Murfree, of a place where time appears to stand still—the Appalachian Mountains. Murfree's fiction is generally considered to be the first full portrayal of southern Appalachian mountaineers as a distinct type, be that for good or ill.

MURFREE'S CHOICE OF TOPIC

How did a genteel, slightly lame, southern lady from an aristocratic family in the late 1800s come to write about a remote, sometimes treacherous, allegedly violent area of the country? Primarily through the opportunities money can buy and the nurturing of her interests and talents by educated parents, especially her father who was an attorney, author, and editor of legal publications as well as a wealthy plantation owner. The opportunities included summering with her family in Beersheba Springs in the Cumberland Mountains of middle Tennessee, a refuge from the heat of the Murfree estate, "Grantland," in the lowlands near Murfreesboro, a town that derives its name from the family's.

Every year from age five until she reached her early twenties, Mary observed mountain people who came to the resort to provide services for the "summer people." As she became more accomplished in the music loved by her mother, an accomplished pianist, she would from time to time offer impromptu piano concerts in the wide hall of the fashionable and luxurious hotel situated at the brink of a spectacular mountain view. She and family members occasionally rode into the mountains to buy fresh vegetables and eggs from residents with whom they had become acquainted. Mary paid close attention to the cabin homes and their surrounds. She listened to the speech patterns and took in the dialect, syntax, grammar, and colorful expressions common among southern mountaineers. She noted the tone of

The following excerpt from the chapter "Drifting Down Lost Creek" illustrates the majestic personification of the mountains in Murfree's work and the powerful pull the mountains have on the mountaineer.

The sun had gone down, but the light yet lingered. The evening star trembled above Pine Mountain. Massive and darkling it stood against the red west. How far, ah, how far stretched that mellow crimson glow, all adown Lost Creek Valley, and over the vast mountain solitudes on either hand! Even the eastern ranges were rich with this legacy of the dead and gone day, and purple and splendid they lay beneath the rising moon. She looked at it with full and shining eyes.

"I dunno how he kin make out ter furgit the mountings," she said; and then she went on, hearing the crisp leaves rustling beneath her tread, and the sharp bark of a fox in the silence of the night-shadowed valley.

Murfree, *In the Tennessee Mountains*, p. 72.

voice, the emotion or lack of it, the physical appearances, the topics of conversation. As a young adult, encouraged by her father, she began to record her observations in story form. Thinking she had the beginnings of a novel in "The Dancin' Party at Harrison's Cove," she agreed at her father's insistence to submit it for publication to the *Atlantic Monthly*. Howells accepted and published it, and so launched a career that was to span more than forty years, eighteen novels, and seven collections of short stories.

Literary scholars generally consider *In the Tennessee Mountains* and the novel *The Prophet of the Great Smoky Mountains* (1885) to be Murfree's best works, both coming early in a long career that diminished in importance with the turning of the century and a general movement toward realism and determinism in popular fiction. Nonetheless, the historical significance of *In the Tennessee Mountains* must not be minimized. Despite literary weaknesses that mark the local color genre and this specific representation of it, Mary Murfree's picture of southern Appalachian mountaineers became fixed in the national mind and has not faded entirely. Over the years much of the effect of that portrayal has been negative, as indeed was often the case with subjects of local color writing.

RELATIONSHIPS BETWEEN OUTSIDERS AND INSIDERS

Murfree presents authentic characteristics and speech patterns but does so in such a way as to set her characters apart and mark them as alien from the mainstream of people who would be the readers of her fiction. While her intentions appear sympathetic to mountain people and she deserves credit for elevating them to literary status, she wrote patronizingly, especially in stories with interactions between outsiders and insiders. As descriptions of natural beauty soar off into hyperbolic purple prose, the mountain habitations and natives compare poorly to the sophisticated outside world of characters such as Reginald Chevis in "The Star in the Valley" and John Cleaver in "The Romance of Sunrise Rock." Cleaver in the opening scene sarcastically considers the question of a companion, described as a "hairy animal, whose jeans suit proclaimed him man," but determines that it is "not worth his while to enlighten the mountaineer" (p. 183). Later the narrator, whose consciousness is Cleaver's, muses that "it would have been impossible to demonstrate to [the mountaineers] that they stood on a lower social plane. . . . As to the artificial distinctions of money and education,—what do the ignorant mountaineers care about money and education!" (pp. 196–197). Obviously Murfree disparages the superior airs of Cleaver but at the same time points out the pitiable "innocence" of mountain people.

In "The Dancin' Party at Harrison's Cove" old Mr. Kenyon, a lay preacher in the Episcopal Church and a summer visitor to the mountain, must step in to settle an explosive conflict between two feuding mountaineers, Rick Pearson, an outlaw, and John Kossuth, a much younger man, both of whom have drawn their guns and are ready to shoot. Murfree allows authority, as represented by Kenyon and the church, to override the mountaineers' own codes of justice and social behavior. Mitigating circumstances exist between Kenyon, the "old fightin' preacher" (p. 242) and Pearson—they fought together in the Civil War—but this does not account for events in the story where the famed independence of the mountaineer is surrendered in deference to the stern outsider and the institution he represents.

PATRONAGE TOWARD MOUNTAIN PEOPLE AND THEIR HOMES

In stories where no outsider appears, the omniscient narrator takes on patronizing tones even while complimenting humble homes and humble residents. Witness the description of Mother Ware engaged in Monday's washday industry in "Drifting down Lost Creek":

She paused to prod the boiling clothes with a long stick. She was a tall woman, fifty years of age, perhaps, but seeming much older. So gaunt she was, so toothless, haggard, and disheveled, that but for the lazy step and languid interest she might have suggested one of Macbeth's witches, as she hovered about the great cauldron. (P. 3)

The family home is described thus: "The house had a very unconfiding aspect; all its belongings seemed huddled about it for safe-keeping. The beehives stood almost under the eaves; the ash-hopper was visible close in the rear; the rain-barrel affiliated with the damp wall" (p. 17). But in the eyes of daughter Cynthia's suitor, it becomes "the embowered little house, that itself turned its face upward, looking as it were to the mountain's summit. How it nestled there in the gorge!" (p. 18). A similar description of a house as refuge occurs in "Over on the T'other Mounting":

When [Mother White] turned back to the door of the little hut, the meagre comforts within seemed almost luxury, in their cordial contrast to the desolate, dreary mountain yonder and the thought of the forlorn, wandering hunter [Tony Britt]. A genial glow from the hearth diffused itself over the puncheon floor; the savory odor of broiling venison filled the room as a tall, slim girl knelt before the fire and placed the meat upon the gridiron. (P. 261)

In "The 'Harnt' That Walks Chilhowee," Murfree grudgingly compliments an impassioned response from the widower Simon Burney, a would-be suitor for Clarsie Giles's hand: "The expression of [her father's] views . . . provoked Simon Burney to wrath; there was something astir within him that in a worthier subject might have been called a chivalric thrill, and it forbade him to hold his peace" (p. 287). Later in the story she describes Burney's compassion and generosity:

There was only a sluggish current of peasant blood in Simon Burney's veins, but a prince could not have dispensed hospitality with a more royal hand. Ungrudgingly he gave of his best; valiantly he defended his thankless guest at the risk of his life; with a moral gallantry he struggled with his sloth, and worked early and late, that there might be enough to divide. (P. 321)

ILL EFFECTS OF LEAVING THE MOUNTAINS

In stories where mountaineers have left the mountains for the world beyond, the result is invariably negative, as demonstrated by Rufus Chadd, who went off to study law and become a politician in "Electioneerin' on Big Injun Mounting." Losing his sense of neighborliness and hospitality among the "town folks down thar at Ephesus" (p. 156), he is redeemed only by nearly losing his life at the hands of one of his constituents. As

if from a sudden revelation, he pleads from his sickbed that his attacker not be prosecuted. That noble impulse is enough to get him reelected in a landslide for attorney general of the state. Another backslider, Evander Price in "Drifting down Lost Creek," seemingly forgets his mountain home and homefolks, including the lovestruck Cynthia Ware, when he is sent away to prison for a crime he did not commit. There he learns iron-working skills that he plies to advantage in the outside world. Although he comes back eventually to take his family away, he never undergoes redemption nor makes amends to Cynthia, who won his pardon from prison and spent her life waiting in vain for him. In "A-Playin' of Old Sledge at the Settlemint" no one leaves the mountains permanently, but young Josiah Tait goes away to "the Cross-Roads" (p. 96), a microcosm of the world beyond, long enough to learn a card game called Old Sledge. Dubbed by disapproving old-timers as "this hyar coal o' fire from hell" (p. 95), Old Sledge proves to be the undoing of Tait. Only his opponent Budd Wray's generosity of spirit and the abolishment of the "coal o' fire from hell" save Tait and the settlement.

POSITIVE TRAITS OF MOUNTAINEERS

On the other hand, mountain people repeatedly display their "hearts of gold," a local color theme developed by Bret Harte, who initiated the genre in the late 1860s. From the first story to the last, one mountaineer after another commits acts of generosity and self-sacrifice. Cynthia Ware in "Drifting down Lost Creek" spends years of physical and emotional energy seeking a pardon from prison for Evander Price. Budd Wray in "A-Playin' of Old Sledge at the Settlemint" gives back all the material goods he won from Josiah Tait. Celia Shaw in "The Star in the Valley" walks fifteen miles in a snowstorm to the detriment of her own health to warn a family of renegades about an attack. Rufus Chadd in "Electioneerin' on Big Injun Mounting" forgives his assailant and foregoes prosecution. The outlaw Rick Pearson and young Kossuth Johns in "The Dancin' Party at Harrison's Cove" decide not to shoot each other to settle their feud. Despite attempted murder and alleged murder, Tony Britt and Caleb Hoxie in "Over on the T'other Mounting" ultimately become friends, albeit with a skittish relationship. Both Clarsie Giles and Simon Burney in "The 'Harnt' That Walks Chilhowee" show compassion for the "ghost" Reuben Crabb, and Burney ultimately takes in the ingrate to defend, feed, and clothe.

CONCLUSION

In summary Murfree's portrayal of Appalachian mountaineers—both positive and negative, exaggeration and reality—established a type that prevails into the early twenty-first century. She was a pioneer in her use of authentic dialect of the region, even though its representation through phonetic spelling often seems contrived to modern readers. Her decision to write about the Tennessee mountains led to a depiction of the mountains themselves as characters whose impact is equal to or greater than that of her human characters. Indeed a major criticism of her work is that she fails to penetrate the minds and emotions of her characters as thoroughly as she examines the qualities of the mountains. A strength, on the other hand, is her development of the concept of inseparableness of mountains and mountaineers. These are not people, she recognizes, who can easily leave their place and flourish elsewhere. Ultimately her greatest gift may be the start of a long, ongoing conversation about the identity of southern Appalachian mountaineers and the mystical attraction of the mountains in which they live.

See also Regionalism and Local Color Fiction

BIBLIOGRAPHY

Primary Work
Murfree, Mary Noailles. *In the Tennessee Mountains.* 1884. Introduction by Nathalia Wright. Knoxville: University of Tennessee Press, 1970.

Secondary Works
Cary, Richard. *Mary N. Murfree.* New York: Twayne, 1967.

Clement, Russell. "Mary Noailles Murfree." In *Tennessee Authors, Past and Present.* Tennessee Authors Project. Knoxville: University of Tennessee Libraries, 2003. Available at http://www.lib.utk.edu/refs/tnauthors/authors/murfree-m.html.

Dunn, Durwood. "Mary Noailles Murfree: A Reappraisal." *Appalachian Journal* 6, no. 3 (1979): 197–204.

Ensor, Allison R. "What Is the Place of Mary Noailles Murfree Today?" *Tennessee Historical Quarterly* 47, no. 4 (1988): 198–205.

Miller, Danny. *Wingless Flights: Appalachian Women in Fiction.* Bowling Green, Ohio: Bowling Green State University Popular Press, 1996.

Parks, Edd Winfield. *Charles Egbert Craddock (Mary Noailles Murfree).* Chapel Hill: University of North Carolina Press, 1941.

Warfel, Harry R., and George Harrison Orians, eds. *American Local-Color Stories.* New York: American Book, 1941.

Williams, Cratis D. "The Southern Mountaineer in Fact and Fiction." Ph.D. diss., New York University, 1961.

Wright, Nathalia. Introduction to *In the Tennessee Mountains.* Knoxville: University of Tennessee Press, 1970.

Grace Toney Edwards

IOLA LEROY

Frances E. W. Harper's 1892 novel, *Iola Leroy; or, Shadows Uplifted,* was in many ways the culmination of a remarkable career by an African American woman who was a poet, a novelist, and a noted speaker in the abolitionist, suffrage, and temperance movements. *Iola Leroy,* among the first novels by an African American woman, chronicles black experience during slavery, the Civil War, and Reconstruction. Harper's best-known novel provides a black perspective on a half century of American nineteenth-century history and projects an optimism for the future that, sadly, was not borne out by subsequent events in the 1890s and the first part of the twentieth century. *Iola Leroy* focuses on black identity, a concept central to this historical period and to African American literature. Her reworking and rebuttal of the "tragic mulatto" theme in African American literature was a conscious political move for her own time but also has important ramifications for the history of the African American novel.

LIFE AND CAREER
Frances Ellen Watkins was born in Maryland in 1825, the daughter of a woman who was a freed slave; her father was most likely white, although records of her early life are quite sketchy. Her mother died when she was three, and Frances was raised by her aunt and educated in her uncle's school in Baltimore. She showed promise as a writer from her early years, and she is said to have published a volume of poems, *Forest Leaves,* by 1845, although no copy now exists. Her first extant volume of poetry is *Poems on Miscellaneous Subjects* (1854), which contained protests against slavery as well as some of her earliest poems in black dialect.

The Compromise of 1850, which included the Fugitive Slave Act, brought disruption to the Watkins family. Because even freed slaves were in danger by living in a slave state, William Watkins had to close his school and move to Canada, as did many other freed blacks. Frances Watkins instead moved to Ohio, where she was briefly the first female instructor at Columbus, Ohio's Union Seminary (later Wilberforce University). In 1853 she moved to Philadelphia, where she was active in the Underground Railroad while continuing to write poetry. By 1854 she began traveling in the North and Canada as a one of the first women antislavery orators. She took direct political action, staging a sit-in to protest Philadelphia's segregated streetcars in 1858 and solicited aid for John Brown after his failed raid on Harpers Ferry (1859). Watkins's fame as a writer and speaker grew, with publication in abolitionist papers such as William Lloyd Garrison's *Liberator*

Frances E. W. Harper, 1898.

and *Douglass' Monthly.* Her antislavery poems, such as "The Slave Mother—A Tale of Olivia" and "The Slave Auction," were widely read and reprinted as well as her Aunt Chloe poems, among the first black dialect poems by an African American. *Poems on Miscellaneous Subjects* had sold ten thousand copies by 1857 and by 1871 had reached its twentieth edition. She is widely regarded as the most important African American poet of the nineteenth century before Paul Laurence Dunbar. Her 1859 short story "The Two Offers" is generally recognized as the first short story by an African American woman.

Watkins married Fenton Harper, a widower from Cincinnati, in 1860, and she spent the war years taking care of his household, his three children, and giving birth to a daughter. Fenton Harper died in 1864, leaving her in debt and with four children to raise alone. After the war, Frances E. W. Harper resumed her lecturing, this time traveling extensively in the South, continuing to write and publish and becoming active in the suffrage and temperance movements. She was one of the few African American members of the Women's Christian Temperance Union.

IOLA LEROY

The publication of *Iola Leroy; or, Shadows Uplifted* in 1892 was the culmination of what had already been a varied and accomplished career. In many ways, the novel is her crowning achievement and brings together the themes and concerns of her public and artistic life. In reaction to the popular but misguided Plantation School novelists, such as Thomas Nelson Page, who created a nostalgic and inaccurate picture of antebellum life, Harper wrote her own depiction of black life during slavery, the Civil War, and Reconstruction. Her characters, many drawn from real life, run the gamut of African American society, from slaves to freed blacks to mulattoes to the black intelligentsia and upper class.

The novel opens during the Civil War, with a scene of slaves who are intently keeping up with the war news but who transmit their knowledge to one another in code, "signifying" to one another that the news is favorable to their cause and thus hiding their knowledge from their white masters. Harper uses dialect effectively in these chapters, as she does intermittently throughout the novel, chiefly in the character of Aunt Linda, a cook and matriarch who espouses a number of Harper's political ideas in her dialect speeches. The novel includes flashbacks to the period before the war, then carries characters into the North after the war, where they encounter racism even in the supposedly enlightened states. The search for and the reunion of scattered family members drive the plot, although at several points in the novel plot is interrupted for long conversational debates between characters about pressing political issues, debates that often include bits of Harper's speeches on issues such as assimilation, emigration, education, and moral progress.

The central concern of the novel is identity, especially the choices of light-skinned blacks as they are confronted with and ultimately reject the opportunity to "pass" as white. The title character, Iola Leroy, is the daughter of a white slaveholder and a slave mother who raise their children as white within slaveholding Louisiana. She is very white-skinned, with long, straight hair and blue eyes. Iola learns her true racial identity after returning from her education in a white northern school to find her father dead of yellow fever and her mother, herself, and her siblings returned to the status of slaves. In a pattern that will be repeated by three more mixed-race characters in the novel, Iola refuses marriage to Dr. Gresham, a white northern physician who loves her and wants her to pass in white society. This central theme of the novel marks Harper's opposition to the idea of the tragic mulatto, a theme that would dominate African American fiction in the late nineteenth century and early twentieth century. Like the sentimental heroine

> *Harper makes her purpose clear in her afterword to the novel.*
>
> From threads of fact and fiction I have woven a story whose mission will not be in vain if it awaken in the hearts of our countrymen a stronger sense of justice and a more Christlike humility in behalf of those whom the fortunes of war threw, homeless, ignorant and poor, upon the threshold of a new era. Nor will it be in vain if it inspire the children upon whose brows God has poured the chrism of that new era to determine that they will embrace every opportunity, develop every faculty, and use every power God has given them to rise in the scale of character and condition, and to add their quota of good citizenship to the best welfare of the nation.
>
> Frances E. W. Harper, *Iola Leroy; or, Shadows Uplifted,* p. 282.

of much nineteenth-century fiction, the "tragic mulatto," or more accurately "tragic mulatta," since these characters were more often women, was used as a device to evoke sympathy in a white reading audience. Harper introduces a character who would fit this stereotype, but she refuses to use Iola for these purposes. Harper instead focuses on "racial uplift," an argument that blacks should sacrifice personal happiness for the betterment of their race. In this highly didactic and sentimental novel, the characters engage in dialogues on the central political concerns of racial progress, suffrage for blacks and for women, temperance, and Christian charity. In some ways, Harper's stance can be likened to the assimilationist sentiments that Booker T. Washington was to espouse in his Atlanta Exposition speech of 1895; the choice of her characters to choose their black heritage over their white appearance is much like Washington's "as separate as the fingers" accommodationist position. In an article on the mulatto and miscegenation in nineteenth-century fiction, William L. Andrews writes of the effect of Harper's mulatto characters:

> The mulatto thus represents a conservative attitude toward social and political agitation for entry into the white man's world, an attitude anticipating Booker T. Washington's position. Far from being a threat to the body politic, his particular disavowal of

passing, miscegenation, and other forms of "social equality" shows him to be racially orthodox on the central issue which so many Americans worried about. (P. 17)

Harper, however, was not writing to placate white readers; as she says in an afterword to the novel, she wrote her story to "awaken in the hearts of our countrymen a stronger sense of justice and a more Christlike humility in behalf of those whom the fortunes of war threw, homeless, ignorant and poor, upon the threshold of a new era" (p. 282).

Harper believed that the early 1890s marked an opportunity for the forces of suffrage, temperance, and racial equality to bring about lasting social change in race, class, and gender. Her note of optimism continues in her afterword:

> Nor will it be in vain if it inspire the children upon whose brows God has poured the chrism of that new era to determine that they will embrace every opportunity, develop every faculty, and use every power God has given them to rise in the scale of character and condition, and to add their quota of good citizenship to the best welfare of the nation. (P. 282)

Her hopeful didactic message flew in the face of a decade that was instead to bring the codification of Jim Crow discrimination in the Supreme Court's *Plessy v. Ferguson* decision (1896) as well as the disenfranchisement of black men and the rise of violence against blacks, culminating in widespread lynching. Instead of a hopeful new age, the last decade of the nineteenth century and the first decades of the twentieth century ushered in a bleak period for African Americans, a time that has been called the nadir of black experience. Her novel, written primarily for black audiences, sold well enough to have at least four reprintings, but of course it failed to achieve its desired political goals. Harper died in 1911, her most famous novel soon to go out of print, its author more or less lost in shifting literary trends for most of the twentieth century.

CRITICAL HERITAGE

In large part because of its didactic, sentimental, domestic thrust, *Iola Leroy* moved to the background of African American literary history, especially while it was dominated by male writers who emphasized realism and naturalism and had a harder political edge. Harper's work did not regain critical attention until the convergence of the feminist movement and the Black Arts movement of the 1970s brought about a search to recover lost or overlooked literature by African Americans, especially African American women. The republication of *Iola Leroy* in 1971 eventually brought renewed critical attention to an important early novel by an African American woman and to a pioneer in African American literature. Her work paved the way for subsequent writers such as Zora Neale Hurston, and the renewed critical attention paid to domestic, sentimental fiction as well as politically driven art has raised the novel in critical estimation. A novel that was lost for much of the twentieth century is now seen as an important step in the development of African American fiction, especially fiction by African American women.

See also Blacks; Civil Rights; Miscegenation; Race Novels

BIBLIOGRAPHY
Primary Work
Harper, Frances E. W. *Iola Leroy; or, Shadows Uplifted*. 1892. New York: AMS Press, 1971.

Secondary Works
Andrews, William L. "Miscegenation in the Late Nineteenth-Century American Novel." *Southern Humanities Review* 17 (1979): 13–24.

Boyd, Melba Joyce. *Discarded Legacy: Politics and Poetics in the Life of Frances E. W. Harper, 1825–1911*. Detroit: Wayne State University Press, 1994.

Bruce, Dickson D., Jr. *Black American Writing from the Nadir: The Evolution of a Literary Tradition, 1877–1915*. Baton Rouge: Louisiana University Press, 1989.

Foster, Frances Smith, ed. *A Brighter Coming Day: A Frances Ellen Watkins Harper Reader*. New York: Feminist Press at the City University of New York, 1990.

John Bird

IRISH

From 1845 until the 1850s, every harvest of potatoes, the sole crop for most Irish farmers, failed. The result was over a million deaths in Ireland from starvation and disease, and somewhere close to two million people emigrated, mostly to the United States. Protestant Irish had been immigrating to America since the 1700s, but the Irish Potato Famine led to the first large wave of Catholic immigrants, who for the most part were poorer, less educated, and less skilled than their Protestant counterparts. Additionally, sentiment against them was imported from England, and that, coupled with American anti-Catholicism, led to racism and prejudice.

POVERTY AND PREJUDICE
Irish immigrants in the mid-nineteenth century tended to settle in such East Coast cities as Boston, New York, and Pittsburgh. Although some went west and a few became millionaires during the California gold rush of 1848 and 1849, most Irish immigrants refused to return to farming, defeated by the potato blight. These predominantly rural Irish chose the burgeoning metropolitan areas instead, adapting to urban life just as urban life was beginning to burst. Slums and ghettos developed, and a shantytown in the Upper West Side of Central Park was established by those who were either evicted from the slums or refused to live in them.

The immigrants quickly discovered that their treatment in America was no different than it had been in Ireland by the British, although historians have noted little material evidence of the infamous No Irish Need Apply signs and the job discrimination that were said to be rampant in the mid- to late nineteenth century—what Richard Jensen calls a "myth of victimization." However, no matter the extent of prejudice against Irish Catholics, they believed themselves to be oppressed. The only comfort was the church or, for some, alcohol. The stereotype of the Irish as heavy drinkers followed them from Ireland. In Ireland people drank, but the heavy drinker was seen as natural as fairies; in America the heavy drinker became the fat, bulbous-nosed, dirty Paddy of the contemporary cartoons. The drinking patterns from rural Ireland worsened in the urban immigrant slums and led to increased crime, violence, male desertion, and insanity among the immigrant Irish.

Men often worked in the coal mines or on railroads—dangerous work that forced them to leave their families for extended periods. Irish women were often more employable than men, especially those who already had a background supporting themselves in Ireland. In the United States they were able to work as maids and to earn a decent living, room and board included; in addition they were exposed to the values of middle- and upper-class Americans, thus easing acculturation. These women encouraged their daughters to be teachers and office workers: in 1870, 20 percent of New York City schoolteachers were Irish or Irish American women (Diner, p. 97). After marriage Irish immigrant women stayed home and ran the household, often alone. Thus the stereotype of the bossy Irish matriarch exists only in the United States: in 1875, 16 percent of Irish American households were headed by women (Biddle, p. 101). The Irish American matriarch was responsible for keeping her children inside the Catholic faith and civilizing the family, keeping the men from drinking, saving the money, and pushing her children toward middle-class professions such as teachers, policemen, or priests.

ANTI-CATHOLIC SENTIMENT

Anti-Catholicism had been a feature of American society since colonial times yet became increasingly virulent as more Irish and German Catholics entered the country from the 1820s onward. The Catholic Church and Catholic immigrants were seen as bowing to a foreign power, with priests and nuns portrayed in the popular press as immoral and unsavory. In the 1850s the antiforeign and anti-Catholic American Party, commonly called the Know-Nothing Party, advocated national unity, the exclusion of foreign-born people from voting or holding public office, and anti-Catholic legislation. However, the Know-Nothing Party eventually dissolved as a result of internal conflicts, and the force of the nativist movement declined after 1856.

Although anti-Catholicism did not disappear, the issue was subsumed by the Civil War. Large-scale Irish immigration to the United States only began with the famine generation. Between 1845 and 1870, 2.5 million Irish immigrated to the Untied States; and between 1871 and 1921, 2.1 million more came (Fanning, *Irish Voice,* p. 157). Unlike the famine generation, this second wave of immigrants arrived to find an economic, political, and social network that made their acculturation easier. Their knowledge of English as well as their "whiteness" made them eligible for citizenship and thus able to enter politics more quickly than other immigrant groups. In 1880 William R. Grace, who made his money in shipping, became New York City's first Irish Catholic mayor. Such growing political power, however, led to a new wave of nativism and anti-Catholic sentiment. The Immigration Restriction League was founded in Boston in 1894, mostly against new immigrants but particularly against Catholics. As late as the 1920s, Catholics, along with Jews and African Americans, bore the brunt of attacks from the Ku Klux Klan. Yet by 1900, although Irish ghettos still existed and unskilled Irish laborers continued to take dangerous jobs on the railroads and in mines, most first- and second-generation Irish had moved from the tenements to the suburbs and thus into greater contact with Protestant Americans.

ASSIMILATION

The Catholic Church played a significant role in hastening the assimilation of Irish immigrants and their children. Church reformers tried promoting American patriotism and capitalist values among their Irish parishioners. Irish journalists and clergy denounced drunkenness and attempted to teach what were defined as the Protestant habits of "industry, thrift, sobriety, and self-

control" (Miller, p. 333). Between 1870 and 1921 the Catholics constructed thousands of churches, convents, colleges, and schools, including the Catholic University of America in Washington, D.C., which opened it doors to students in 1889. Saint Patrick's Cathedral on Fifth Avenue in New York City was completed in 1879, a powerful symbol of the success of the Irish.

However, some Irish Americans were insecure and anxious about their tenuous position within the middle class; these "lace-curtain Irish," as they were called, became the subject of much concern in the literature of the period. George McManus's popular cartoon strip "Bringing Up Father," which debuted in 1913 and became an instant hit, mocked an Irish American couple who wanted to Americanize at all costs. Their scars of poverty and social ostracism still palpable, the couple, Jiggs and Maggie, were particularly concerned with maintaining financial success and appearances. Maggie's characteristic exclamation "what will the neighbors think!" reflected a sensitivity to still perceived anti–Irish Catholic prejudice. A fear of poverty sometimes led to miserliness and identification as slumlords, as Eugene O'Neill (1888–1953) depicts in *Long Day's Journey into Night,* his autobiographical play set in 1912 and published posthumously in 1956. Irish foremen in shops, no longer subject to the oppression of their former American superiors, treated their often Slavic workers worse than they themselves had been treated decades earlier, as Upton Sinclair (1878–1968) depicts in his novel *The Jungle* (1906). This dangerous tendency to lose one's values and culture during the process of assimilation was well represented by Irish American journalists and novelists.

THE IRISH AMERICAN LITERARY RESPONSE

Fiction by Irish American writers in the late nineteenth century often focused on this conflict: the desire for middle-class respectability in the face of ongoing poverty and economic depressions versus the fear of losing one's sense of Irish identity. The Irish American press played an important role by printing an abundance of short fiction written by Irish Americans in this period. Periodicals such as the *New York Irish World* and the *Boston Pilot* sought to counteract stereotypes yet in the process often ignored reality. They published stories that rarely showed tenement life or working conditions despite the fact that many Irish were still in the ghettos in the 1870s; instead, they emphasized success stories about Irish immigrants who Americanized without losing their ethnic identity. For the most part the Irish American press printed stories that, although unrealistic, provided early positive images of Irish Americans who worked hard but stayed Catholic in the process of assimilation.

***Bringing Up Father* cartoon, 2 October 1916.** George McManus's long-running cartoon strip chronicled the efforts of an Irish family to fit into their role as newly rich American immigrants. THE LIBRARY OF CONGRESS

However, fiction by first-generation writers, often in the form of domestic novels or fallen-women novels, did depict the struggles that immigrants faced, not always successfully, in the New World: the desire for economic security; the difficulty of maintaining one's faith; the power of the Irish immigrant mother; and a nostalgia for Ireland and for the supposed innocence of the past. Some of the titles emphasize these themes: *The Lost Rosary; or, Our Irish Girls, Their Trials, Temptations, and Triumphs* (1870) by Peter McCorry (writing under the pen name Con O'Leary) and *Annie Reilly; or, The Fortunes of an Irish Girl in New York* (1873) by John McElgun. These writers used popular literary conventions to address issues of concern to Irish immigrants and their children.

The second-generation writer Katherine E. Conway's best-selling *Lalor's Maples* (1901) argues that the ruthless search for the American Dream was ultimately self-destructive and, more importantly, could destroy Irish American family life, including traditional gender roles. Mary Lalor, an immigrant from a middle-class background, marries John Lalor, another immigrant who works his way from poverty to economic success during the late 1860s. Mary is domineering, obsessed with attaining and retaining middle-class respectability and objects, including the house named in the title. Her role as mother is tarnished as she uses her daughters as a means to upward mobility and then as a way to save the family from financial ruin.

Other late-nineteenth-century and early-twentieth-century fiction, now mostly out of print but identified by the literary historian and critic Charles Fanning in his book *The Irish Voice in America: 250 Years of Irish-American Fiction* (2000), eschews sentimental plots for more realism and satire. Such works include Henry F. Keenan's *The Aliens* (1886), about the prejudices faced by famine immigrants in Rochester, New York; Maurice Francis Egan's *The Disappearance of John Longworthy* (1890), the satire of a corrupt, social-climbing Irish American politician and other lace-curtain Irish; James W. Sullivan's *Tenement Tales of New York* (1895), about a child called Slob Murphy, who lives and dies in the slums; Kate McPhelim Cleary's short story "The Stepmother" (1901), recounting the lonely experiences of an Irish immigrant woman in Nebraska; and Harvey J. O'Higgins's "The Exiles" (1906), detailing the harsh life of New York City servant girls. One of the few Irish American dramatists before Eugene O'Neill was Edward Harrigan, whose play *Squatter Sovereignty* (1881) takes place in New York's Central Park, site of the Irish shantytown created by evicted Irish immigrants. Unlike other plays of the period, which featured the so-called stage Irishman with a brogue that boomed in anger when drunk, Harrigan's play had more-realistic, less-stereotypical characters (Flynn, p. 10).

Few Irish American writers of the period reached a wide non–Irish American audience; however, one was able to bridge the ethnic reading gap. In the 1890s the Chicago journalist Finley Peter Dunne, who was American-born of Irish parents, created "the first fully realized ethnic neighborhood in American literature, Bridgeport on the South Side of Chicago" (Fanning, *Irish Voice*, p. 214), and its central character, Martin Dooley, a bachelor saloon keeper. Dunne's sketches, written in pure Irish dialect, satirize almost every aspect of Irish life in America, including drinking policemen and cheating local politicians. He sympathetically portrays the Irish American working class in Chicago yet also mocks the pretensions of the lace-curtain Irish while at the same time recognizing that assimilation is inevitable. In one sketch recounted by Charles Fanning there is a debate between a Mr. and Mrs. Hogan over the naming of their children:

> After the births of Sarsfield, Lucy, Honoria, Veronica, and Charles Stewart Parnell Hogan, the old man tries to name his tenth child "Michael" after his father. "Ye'll be namin' no more children iv mine out iv dime novels," he declares. "An' ye'll name no more iv mine out iv th' payroll iv th' bridge depar-rtmint," says his wife. In the end, Mr. Dooley is on hand to watch the new baby christened— Augustus, "th' poor, poor child." (Fanning, *Irish Voice,* p. 227)

Another sketch shows the generation gap with teenager Molly Donahue worrying her parents with her feminist viewpoints and non-Irish music on the piano. Dunne is also critical of such Irish Americans as landlords and politicians who abuse other Irish Americans. But his power lies in his depiction of the everyday Irish American at the end of the century in characters such as Father Kelly, Fireman Shay, and workingmen like Malachi Hennessy.

THE IRISH IN MAINSTREAM AMERICAN LITERATURE

The Irish are not major characters in most mainstream American fiction during the nineteenth century and early twentieth century, and often their ethnicity is never explicitly emphasized. However, anti-Irish caricatures were popular with some readers after the Civil War and into the 1890s: Thomas Nast's cartoons were published in both the popular *Harper's Weekly* (1862–1880s) and in the short-lived *America: A Journal for Americans* out of Chicago (1888–1891), a journal that was both highbrow and anti-immigrant generally, anti–Irish Catholic specifically. Nast's "Simian Irishmen—St. Patrick's Day 1867" portrays the Irish as apes attacking the law, and his "Tammany Hall" series of cartoons in 1869–1871 helped topple the rule of the corrupt political boss William Marcy Tweed of Tammany Hall.

Several American novels had stereotypical Irish characters, though their Irishness was not always relevant to their roles in the plots. Henry James, whose ancestry was Irish, had few notable Irish characters in his fiction, with the exception of Mrs. Muldoon in his short story "The Jolly Corner" (1908). In Frank Norris's novel *McTeague: A Story of San Francisco* (1899), the main character has an Irish name, but the character himself is not explicitly identified as Irish, although one could argue that the portrait of the character includes negative stereotypes associated with Irishness: an apelike body, stupidity, violence, and drunkenness. In the same way, Mark Twain's Pap Finn, the notoriously drunk and abusive father of Huck Finn, is not explicitly identified as Irish despite his Irish surname, although Twain has said that the prototype of Pap was Jimmy Finn, a Hannibal town drunk (Smith, p. 197). Twain does briefly depict lace-curtain, social-climbing Irish Americans in *The Gilded Age: A Tale of Today* (1873), with the characters of Mr. and Mrs. Patrique Oreille (O'Reilly) and their daughter Breezhay (Bridget) who pretend to be French rather than Irish; but they are relatively minor characters.

Stephen Crane's *Maggie, A Girl of the Streets: A Story of New York* (1893) depicts the dismal lives of tenement immigrants in general rather than of the Irish specifically. A journalist, Crane (1871–1900) went to the Bowery, a squalid and violent slum, in 1891–1892 to see tenement life for himself; at the time 40 percent of the population in that area was Irish (Smith, p. 200). However, although the characters listen to Irish songs, they are not identified as Irish, and Johnson, Maggie's family name, is not particularly Irish. Some critics saw Crane's purpose as illustrating the effects of tenement living, which creates the conditions for a world of its own morality and values, a world where drunkenness leads to violence and too many children: "In the street infants played or fought with other infants or sat stupidly in the way of vehicles" (p. 6). Others argued that his depiction supported the fear that these immigrants and their children would become a threat to Americans. Yet Crane's Maggie, who has the humility and chastity of the ideal nineteenth-century woman, is foiled not by her ethnicity but by her environment. Unlike her mother, who adapts to her environment by becoming the antimother—violent, drunk, a destroyer rather than a nurturer—Maggie is unable to adjust to the tenement world and is unaware of a middle-class world outside her geographical boundaries. She falls into prostitution because she has no other way to survive. For Crane, Maggie's ethnicity is less relevant than her impoverished environment.

Theodore Dreiser (1871–1945), who like Crane is identified as part of the school of naturalism, a literary realism proposing that one's environment, not free will, determines one's fate, gives a realistic portrayal of an Irish American politician and political machine in his novels *The Financier* (1912) and *The Titan* (1914), which are the first two volumes of his *Trilogy of Desire*. The first novel is set in Philadelphia in the 1870s and 1880s, when the Irish were gaining control of politics in that city. Edward Malia Butler arrives in the city an illiterate, unskilled immigrant who soon builds a successful business and becomes a politician. His stereotypical brogue and temper is modified by love for his daughter, by the Catholic faith, and by sobriety. As with Crane, however, Dreiser blames the politician's corruption on urban America rather than on his ethnicity. Similarly in *The Titan,* the politician Cowperwood's corruption, while more crude and vicious than Butler's, is also depicted as a result of the Chicago Irish political machine, an American phenomenon, rather than purely on his ethnicity. Unlike Butler, Cowperwood does not maintain family or religious ties, thus his corruption is less sympathetically portrayed.

For Upton Sinclair in *The Jungle* it is the capitalistic system that is at fault rather than ethnicity. In one of the few novels where Irish Americans interact with other immigrants—in this case Lithuanians at a Chicago meatpacking factory—the Irish foremen are the victimizers. The stereotypical Irish characters—for instance, Phil Connor is a drunk who extorts sex from the immigrant women he supervises—only reinforce Sinclair's theme of capitalism's destruction of everyone's humanity.

Two non-Irish writers in the late nineteenth century who explicitly focused on ethnicity and the interaction between Irish and non-Irish were Harold Frederic (1856–1898), particularly in his novel *The Damnation of Theron Ware* (1896), and Sarah Orne Jewett (1849–1909), in her stories from the 1880s and 1890s about Irish immigrants in coastal Maine. Frederic was a *New York Times* correspondent in London who wrote so sympathetically about Irish home rule that many readers assumed he was Irish Catholic. In his novel Theron Ware is a Methodist minister assigned to Octavius, a town with a large Irish Catholic population. At first the minister, like his wife and congregation, holds only negative opinions of the Irish. He views the priests, through his reading of anti-Catholic fiction and Thomas Nast's anti-Catholic cartoons, as "black-robed, tonsured men, with leering satanic masks, making a bonfire of the Bible in the public schools" (p. 50), though he admits to himself that "so far as personal acquaintance went, the Irish had been to him only a name" (p. 48). Yet his disillusionment with his congregation and his encounters with the Catholic sacrament of extreme unction as well as meeting the educated and cultured Celia Madden and Father Forbes eventually make him idealize the Irish as culturally and intellectually superior to the puritanical Methodists in Octavius. The ritual of extreme unction has a powerful effect on Ware, who sees it as more transformative than Protestant rituals.

Although they are relatively minor characters, Jeremiah Madden, said to be the wealthiest man in Octavius, and his son Michael Madden affirm the nobility and morality of the Irish. Jeremiah built himself up but never turned his back on his fellow Irishmen. Michael is kind and religious, recognizing that Ware's transformation is self-destructive. Frederic seems to suggest with the drunken younger brother, Theodore, that the second generation of Irish were at risk of contamination by America. Theodore (who has thus Americanized his Irish name Terence) is described as "the product of a wholly different race" (p. 87), and his alcoholism is the result of both his becoming too assimilated and his involvement in the corrupt politics of Tammany Hall. Frederic's novel echoes themes seen in Dreiser and Dunne, particularly the potentially negative effect of Americanization on Irish immigrants.

Sarah Orne Jewett's "Irish" stories also sympathetically depict the effects of assimilation on Irish immigrants and their children. In several stories Jewett describes the Irish immigrants' homesickness as well as their yearning to succeed in America, sometimes at great cost. In "Between Mass and Vespers," Dan Nolan travels west to seek his fortune but becomes instead a con man turning his back on the value system of Irish community until he is saved by Father Ryan, the village priest back in the New England mill town. Yet Jewett does not always blame Americanization specifically. In "Luck of the Bogans" the immigrants Mike and Biddy Bogan leave their farm in Ireland to immigrate to America so their son can become upwardly mobile. Instead, he is corrupted at the public school, becomes a drunk, and finally gets killed in a fight. However, the son's egoism and his parents' pushing him to succeed are identified as the causes of his death, with the narrator ironically noting that the climate in America brings out the best in the Irish, a sentiment also noted with sarcasm by Father Forbes in *The Damnation of Theron Ware.*

Eugene O'Neill, a pivotal figure in American drama, effectively brings Irish and Irish American family life into the mainstream with *Beyond the Horizon* (1920), a Cain and Abel story (influenced by the Irishman T. C. Murray's 1911 play *Birthright*) set on a small New England farm. Despite their Irish name, Mayo, the ethnicity of the characters is subsumed by their humanity, echoing the position of Irish Americans by 1920. World War I and the Easter Rising (24 April 1916) occurred at the same time that the third- and fourth-generation Irish ceased yearning for a long ago, idealized past, choosing instead to take part in America's future.

See also Assimilation; Catholics; *The Damnation of Theron Ware;* Immigration; *Maggie, A Girl of the Streets;* Poverty

BIBLIOGRAPHY

Primary Works

Conway, Katherine E. *Lalor's Maples.* Boston: Pilot, 1901.

Crane, Stephen. *Maggie, A Girl of the Streets: A Story of New York.* 1893. Boston: Bedford/St. Martin's, 1999.

Dreiser, Theodore. *Trilogy of Desire: Three Novels.* New York: World, 1972. Contains *The Financier* (1912), *The Titan* (1914), and *The Stoic* (1947).

Fanning, Charles, ed. *The Exiles of Erin: Nineteenth-Century Irish-American Fiction.* Notre Dame, Ind.: University of Notre Dame Press, 1987. This anthology contains several of the works, or excerpts from them, that are mentioned in this article.

Frederic, Harold. *The Damnation of Theron Ware.* 1896. Introduction by Scott Donaldson. New York: Penguin, 1986.

Jewett, Sarah Orne. *The Irish Stories of Sarah Orne Jewett.* Edited by Jack Morgan and Louis A. Renza. Carbondale: Southern Illinois University Press, 1996.

O'Neill, Eugene. *Beyond the Horizon: A Play in Three Acts.* New York: Boni and Liveright, 1920.

Secondary Works

Biddle, Ellen Horgan. "The American Catholic Irish Family." In *Ethnic Families in America: Patterns and Variations,* edited by Charles H. Mindel and Robert W. Habenstein, pp. 89–123. New York: Elsevier, 1976.

Bramen, Carrie Tirado. "The Americanization of Theron Ware." *Novel: A Forum on Fiction* 31, no. 1 (1997): 63–86.

Casey, Daniel J., and Robert E. Rhodes, eds. *Modern Irish-American Fiction: A Reader.* Syracuse, N.Y.: Syracuse University Press, 1989.

Daniels, Roger. *Coming to America: A History of Immigration and Ethnicity in American Life.* New York: HarperCollins, 1990.

Diner, Hasia R. *Erin's Daughters in America: Irish Immigrant Women in the Nineteenth Century.* Johns Hopkins University Studies in Historical and Political Science, 101st ser., no. 2. Baltimore: Johns Hopkins University Press, 1983.

Drewniany, Peter. "Not Marionettes: The American Irish in *The Damnation of Theron Ware.*" *Eire-Ireland: A Journal of Irish Studies* 16, no. 4 (1981): 48–58.

Fanning, Charles. *The Irish Voice in America: 250 Years of Irish-American Fiction.* 2nd ed. Lexington: University Press of Kentucky, 2000. The first edition was subtitled *Irish-American Fiction from the 1760s to the 1980s.*

Flynn, Joyce. "Sites and Sights: The Iconology of the Subterranean in Late Nineteenth-Century Irish-American Drama." *MELUS* 18, no. 1 (1993): 5–19.

Jensen, Richard. "'No Irish Need Apply': A Myth of Victimization." *Journal of Social History* 36, no. 2 (2002): 405–429.

Miller, Kerby A. *Emigrants and Exiles: Ireland and the Irish Exodus to North America.* New York: Oxford University Press, 1985.

Smith, Herbert Joseph. "From Stereotype to Acculturation: The Irish-American's Fictional Heritage from Brackenridge to Farrell." Ph.D. diss., Kent State University, 1980.

Takaki, Ronald. *A Different Mirror: A History of Multicultural America.* Boston: Little, Brown, 1993.

Stacey L. Donohue

JEWS

The half-century between 1870 and 1920 was the most dynamic period in history for the growth and development of American Jewry. By that time Sephardic and Ashkenazic Jews had already established a solid population base in the United States, the Sephardim originally from Spain and Portugal, the Ashkenazim, or "German Jews" as popularly designated, then mostly from central Europe.

In 1880, as the promise of America was being fulfilled for many Jewish entrepreneurs and professionals already in the United States, the period of mass Jewish immigration from eastern Europe was soon to commence. Since 1791 a vast number of Jews from much of this region between the Baltic Sea and the Black Sea had been confined to the Pale of Jewish Settlement under Russian control. From 1880 on for most of nearly forty-five years, almost unbearable poverty sustained by burdensome Russian restrictions and anti-Semitic pogroms drove these East European Jews from their homelands and across the Atlantic by the tens of thousands annually, seeking a better life. Not all of them found one, but many did, and of them all, few returned.

Many of these Ashkenazic East European immigrants tried to follow the scriptural laws, Talmudic rules, and ancient traditions familiar to them from birth. But adverse circumstances usually made such steadfastness difficult, and families were soon divided by generation regarding their adherence to the Hebraic laws and rituals. Generally the older immigrants were more faithful, the younger more interested in "making it" and becoming Americanized.

Similarly the older generation found it difficult to learn and use English, whereas the younger, especially children in the public schools, shifted to English from their native Yiddish much more quickly and easily, often becoming teachers of their parents, an anomalous and discomfiting reversal for the elders. Abraham Cahan's (1860–1951) most famous novel, *The Rise of David Levinsky* (1917), describes an emotional conflict between mother and daughter that develops in their home over this issue and helps drive them apart. From wherever in eastern Europe the Jews emigrated, they spoke Yiddish, a form of High German printed in Hebrew letters; it is a colloquial tongue rich in imagery and heavily mixed with Hebrew words and variants from the diverse countries and areas these Jews originally had called home. The culture they brought with them from eastern Europe, called *yidishkayt,* is based heavily on the language itself, and it evolved with the Jewish way of life in the shtetlach of the homeland, combining the religious and the secular, although with the passing of years in America it was increasingly secularized. Most Jewish men had as boys learned Hebrew to read scripture and Yiddish for daily usage; most women who could read— and many could not—understood Yiddish only. Instead of Yiddish, Jews from the Near East spoke Ladino, a Judaeo-Spanish tongue, or some form of Arabic.

Because life was so different in America, means were devised relatively early in the nineteenth century to liberalize Judaism from European rabbinical dictates yet allow Jews to remain faithful in the New World if they wished, as most did at least to some degree. Within Reform Judaism, established in the United States in the 1840s, the extent of liberalization varied. Among

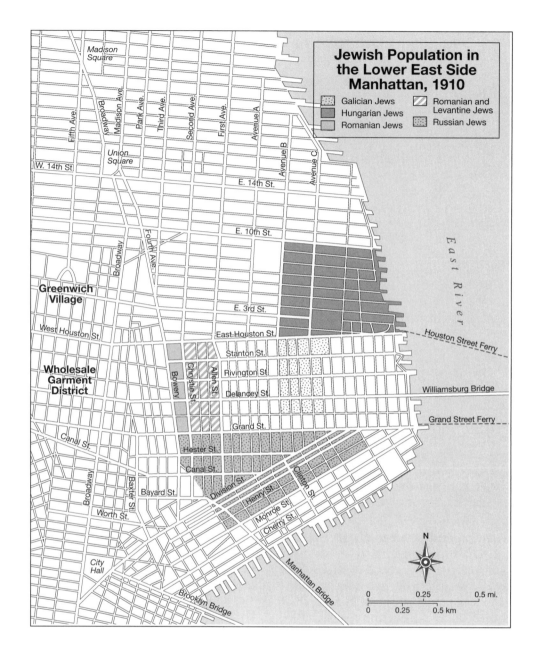

Jewish Population in the Lower East Side Manhattan, 1910

Galician Jews
Hungarian Jews
Romanian Jews
Romanian and Levantine Jews
Russian Jews

the prominent theorists behind Reform were Isaac Mayer Wise, Samuel Adler (whose son, Felix, founded the Ethical Culture movement in the 1870s), David Einhorn, and the more restrained Isaac Leeser. Late in the century, Conservative Judaism was instituted to provide a middle ground between the rigorous practice of Orthodoxy and the decidedly assimilative policies of Reform, but it did not take root until early in the twentieth century under the leadership of Solomon Schechter.

IMMIGRATION

Before 1880 relatively few Jews entered the United States annually, so the difficulties they faced were usually limited; by then about 280,000 Jews lived in the

country. The next year, however, would witness the beginning of a dramatic increase in numbers at the reception area in New York City's Castle Garden. Between the end of the Civil War and the outbreak of World War I, over two million Jews entered the United States. Moses Rischin has estimated that during this period a third of East European Jewry left home; some 90 percent of them sailed to the United States, and the vast majority of those settled at least temporarily in New York. By 1915 approximately 3.5 million Jews lived in the United States.

Part of the reason for this new influx may be found in Cahan's historical novel of 1905, *The White Terror and the Red,* in which he graphically describes a dreadful anti-Semitic pogrom in Russia. The novel is set in the early 1880s, around the time that Tsar Alexander II was assassinated, but Cahan had been motivated to begin writing it immediately on learning of the massacre that occurred in Kishinev during Easter Week 1903, leaving forty-nine Jews dead and hundreds more wounded.

Although such violent pogroms as this helped influence the Russian and Polish Jews to flee, escape from their hopeless poverty provided an even stronger motive. Aboard ships from Germany and England they sailed in steerage and after a harrowing voyage of ten days to two weeks arrived at Castle Garden through 1892 and Ellis Island afterward. Although immigrants were treated decently at the crowded processing stations, their experiences nevertheless were often distressing, even frightening because, knowing little or no English, most could not understand what was happening to them. Moreover, names were often changed in processing because they were incomprehensible as pronounced to the officials.

Most of the incoming Jews who remained in New York settled in one of the city's ghettos, mainly in the tenement district of the Lower East Side, not far from Castle Garden. In 1900 the population density of that area's tenth ward was approximately seven hundred per acre—one of the highest in the world—yet the death rate was the lowest in the city. By 1910 the population of the Lower East Side was over half a million, but by then inhabitants were moving either to ghettos elsewhere in the city or to other parts of the country.

The heavy influx of immigrants caused a dramatic increase in urban populations across the United States. In 1878 New York had a population of sixty thousand Jews, and in 1907 it was ten times that number. According to Lee Shai Weissbach, the Jewish population of other cities in the United States underwent similar or greater dynamic growth.

Not all Americans were happy with these changing Jewish demographics, including the Jews already established in the United States. Those whose businesses and professions had thrived after the Civil War eagerly sought respectability in their new homeland, that is, favorable recognition from Gentile society; not wishing to appear different as Jews, they yearned to be true Americans themselves. If these "uptown Jews" were uncomfortable with all the devout "greenhorns" (newcomers) pressing into "downtown" tenements, however, they did not turn away from their *landsleit* (landsman) in need but contributed heavily toward assisting them. From the time the first Jews arrived in the United States, they insisted that they would provide for their own and not leave their poor to be cared for by public charities.

On the other hand, most of the resentment toward the immigrants was attributable not to Jews but to Gentiles willing to accommodate the Sephardic and German Jews who sought to assimilate but not the hordes of destitute East Europeans living in squalor in Lower East Side tenements.

LIVING CONDITIONS

The tenement buildings were newly designed in 1879 to replace earlier types. The more recent structures of six or seven stories were called dumbbell tenements, with every floor holding four apartments of three or four rooms each. Shaped like dumbbells, the contiguous buildings narrowed at the center to provide for wholly inadequate airshafts between them, allowing no other space for light and ventilation. Moses Rischin describes these buildings in which every room often housed several people and served as both living and working quarters. Couples or families renting an apartment for $10 to $20 per month typically let one room to a boarder; under the worst economic circumstances, two boarders alternately used the same bed at different hours of the day and night. The excruciating summer heat drove the occupants outside to sleep on fire escapes and roofs; in winter the air inside was fetid and heavy with fumes emanating from heating units.

Outside the tenements, pushcarts and horse wagons maneuvered amid crowds of peddlers, while shoppers, hagglers, and children ferrying large bundles of piecework, among others going about their business, jammed such noisy, bustling East Side thoroughfares as Hester and Delancey Streets. Rischin's *The Promised City*, Irving Howe's *World of Our Fathers* (1976), Howe and Kenneth Libo's *How We Lived* (1979), and Stanley Feldstein's *The Land That I Show You* (1978) as well as Jacob Riis's early groundbreaking exposé *How the Other Half Lives* (1890) exhibit eye-opening photographs of the overcrowded, noisome conditions under which immigrants struggled for life in the tenement districts during these decades. Moreover, as bad as the New York tenements were, those in Chicago were allegedly worse.

Not all immigrant husbands could cope with either the constant pressure or the burdensome responsibility of keeping their families alive under such circumstances. Consequently the number of husbands deserting wives and children was high, especially in the cities. According to Arthur Hertzberg, as many as 25 percent of Jewish fathers deserted their wives during the years of mass immigration, some never sending them money in Europe for tickets to America and others abandoning them in the United States after fruitlessly attempting to earn enough to stay together. In 1911 a National Desertion Bureau was established when urban Jewish charities that could not cover the cost independently joined forces to assist deserted families.

EARNING A LIVING: THE GARMENT TRADE AND OTHERS

Not all the immigrant Jews settled in the cities. Others—although many fewer—traveled into rural New England, the South, the Midwest, and the far Northwest. Am Olam (Eternal People) groups that developed in major Russian cities promoted agricultural colonies among the emigrating Jews that led them to attempt to establish farm communities in the Dakotas, Oregon, and elsewhere in rural and wilderness areas of the United States (as well as Palestine). Few of these communities endured because not many Jews in Europe had acquired farming experience; those in the Pale could not own land at all.

Because Jews who settled in the United States after 1880 had emigrated largely from shtetlach and other restrictive communities in eastern Europe, the ways they knew of earning a living were extremely limited. Like earlier Jewish immigrants who had "made it" in business and finance by beginning as peddlers and small shop owners in different parts of the country, many East Europeans also began with backpacks and pushcarts. Countless others knew how to sew, and those who did not quickly learned. This endeavor eased when Singer sewing machines were brought into Russia in the 1870s; prospective immigrants who became accomplished on them found work soon after entering the United States.

Sewing was fundamental to the East Side Jews, who generally worked under the sweatshop system, a method already in effect when they arrived. As Ronald Sanders and Irving Howe describe the system, typically a contractor agreed to provide a set number of suits or cloaks to a merchant at a certain price. By then the merchant had purchased the requisite amount of cloth and cut it into sections for the contractor to distribute among workers he or she had hired, each of whom had a specific task to perform. Manufacturing ready-made clothes was seasonal work, and workers had little chance to earn sufficient money during the off-seasons, so when jobs were available, six-day work weeks often required seventy-two to eighty-four hours of labor.

On the Lower East Side during these years thousands of sweatshops were in existence simultaneously, but most were small operations employing but a handful of people. By 1880, even before their heyday, about half the Jewish businesses in the United States were in some aspect of the garment trade, and Arthur Hertzberg estimates that Jews already controlled as much as three-fourths of the American clothing indus-

try. Extending this point, Irving Howe states that altogether the production of the sweatshops was so great that by 1900 some 90 percent of the garment industry was under Jewish control, and by then the east Europeans were squeezing out the Germans, who had previously dominated the industry.

In addition to businesses, the professions attracted a disproportionate number of Jewish immigrants. Among the most distinguished American jurists during this period, for example, were Louis Brandeis, Benjamin Cardozo, and Louis Marshall, all three of whom contributed significantly to the nation's legal as well as Jewish history; both Brandeis and Cardozo became Supreme Court justices. Moreover, as Hertzberg indicates, by 1910 about a quarter of the students in American medical schools were Jewish (p. 200).

With the good came the bad. Arnold Rothstein (1882–1928), born of East European parents in New York, became the notorious gambler who masterminded the infamous Black Sox scandal and gained a fortune by bribing leading players on the Chicago White Sox to throw the World Series in 1919. A stylish, well-groomed wheeler-dealer among the politicians of Tammany Hall, he allegedly bribed his way to success through police stations and courtrooms alike. Although F. Scott Fitzgerald based Meyer Wolfsheim in *The Great Gatsby* (1925) on Rothstein, he transformed the dapper gambler from a brilliant gangster into a repulsive anti-Semitic Jewish stereotype.

On the Lower East Side many less-conspicuous Jewish figures were loose with the law as well, typically thwarting it by chicanery and manipulation rather than violence. Prostitution too was difficult to control in that section partly because it was on the edge of the red-light district and partly because it was supported by dance halls that abounded in the area to provide entertainment for men and women alike. In *Yekl, A Tale of the New York Ghetto* (1896), Cahan describes a dance hall but implies nothing about prostitution. Juvenile delinquency was also commonplace; parents tried to control their offspring, but peer pressure often overcame their influence. Children were no longer under the religious restrictions of the shtetlach, traditional discipline in the home had deteriorated, youngsters spoke better English than their parents, and much of their time was spent on the streets. If their fathers had deserted them, they had no place else to go.

AIMS AND ASPIRATIONS

In the miasmic atmosphere of the ghettos, advocates of socialist theory and practice—which by no means always corresponded—were prominent, especially from the 1880s until after the Bolshevik revolution in 1917. The east European Jews brought socialism from the old country, where those who expressed radical ideas toward reform were either harassed or subject to arrest and imprisonment, depending on their assumed degree of implication with the revolutionaries. Abraham Cahan, who arrived in America from Russia in 1882, became one of the strongest and most effective spokespersons for socialism on the East Side, partly by speaking to the workers in Yiddish rather than one of their native European languages but mostly through his strong voice in the Yiddish press. After editing and writing for the Socialist Labor Party's weekly, *Arbeter tsaytung*, through the mid-1890s, Cahan in 1897 founded the Jewish daily *Forverts*, popularly known as the *Forward*, which ultimately became the most widely read, distributed, and influential Yiddish newspaper in the world. One cannot overstate the importance of the *Forward* to Jewish economic and social progress during that crucial period in American Jewish history.

But the *Forward* was only one of many Yiddish newspapers published on the East Side; each of the leftist dailies and weeklies propagated its own brand of socialism, often more theoretical than practical, and each had its own coterie of adherents. The more theoretical socialists attempted to promote economic as well as social equality by ending all forms of labor exploitation, an impossibility in democratic America, where workers could vote freely and reap the benefits of their labor. In contrast, the more liberal papers recommended adapting socialist theories to suit the needs of Jews living in a different world from the tsarist autocracy.

With socialists of every stripe came others—Jewish anarchists, communists, Am Olam adherents, and Zionists among them—all with various commitments and degrees of loyalty. The Chicago Haymarket riot in 1886 began with an authorized protest by angered workers and anarchists and ended when someone unknown threw a bomb amidst a group of police, who then opened fire on the crowd. Several people were killed or wounded; eight of those at the protest were arrested and tried by a heavily biased court; four were executed and, according to Hertzberg, regarded as martyrs by Jewish socialists and radical workers.

Zionists showed little strength in the United States until the unanticipated support they gained from Louis Brandeis in 1914 rapidly increased their influence among American Jews, particularly those from eastern Europe. Hadassah, the Women's Zionist Movement, was organized two years earlier by Henrietta Szold, and it has since played a major role in American Zionism. Each group of advocates and theorists attempted to propagate its own social philosophy and practice through lectures, rallies, protests, and the Yiddish press.

Attempts to establish unions in the ghettos focused particularly on the clothing trade. In 1909 and 1910 large strikes in the clothing industry occurred in Chicago as well as New York. Of course Jews were not the only workers in that industry, which drew heavily for labor from other immigrant groups and neighborhoods in Lower Manhattan. Many young Italian and Jewish women died together, for example, in the horrifying Triangle Shirtwaist Company fire of 1911 that shocked the nation. Those on the upper floors were trapped in their workrooms behind locked doors and were among the 146 workers who burned or jumped to their deaths within only a few minutes. Such catastrophes as this exacerbated the misery of the working people and their families on the East Side in particular, and strikes became both larger and more effective. Among the most prominent labor leaders of the period were Cahan; Samuel Gompers, longtime president of the American Federation of Labor; Joseph Barondess, dubbed "King of the Cloak-Makers"; David Dubinsky, the enduring leader of the International Ladies Garment Workers Union; Morris Hillquit (né Hilkowitz), who helped establish the United Hebrew Trades with Cahan in 1888; and Meyer London, a Jewish labor lawyer elected to Congress in 1914. Their political leanings were always to the left.

Reducing anti-Semitism in the United States, always a major issue for Jewish leaders, was particularly evident during the years of mass immigration. Antipathy toward Jews gained strength with the increasing numbers of immigrants. In 1913 Leo Frank, a young Jewish plant manager in Atlanta, was framed and convicted for killing a woman in the factory; without proof that he had committed the crime, a lynch mob hanged him in 1915 as he awaited the result of his appeal in jail. Moreover, that infamous treatise *The Protocols of the Elders of Zion*, a forgery by the Russian police early in the century, was translated and published in the United States in 1919. Purporting to be a secret plan by international Jewry to take over the world, this ludicrous document, promoted by Henry Ford, gained tremendous influence soon after its publication in English. Among the organizations founded early in the twentieth century in support of Jewish civil rights are the American Jewish Committee (1906) and B'nai B'rith's Anti-Defamation League (1913).

EDUCATION AND JOURNALISM

In *The Promised City*, Moses Rischin reviews in some detail the surprising success rate of Jewish immigrant children in the East Side public schools. The average absentee rate of 8 percent was attributable almost entirely to illness, he says, and the pupils, eager to learn, were responsive and quickly Americanized. Rischin also points out that by the end of the century most children in the public schools of New York City were those of east European immigrants. Myra Kelly (1876–1910), an Irish teacher on the East Side at the end of the century, was so enthusiastic over her experiences with her Jewish pupils that she published numerous stories based on those she knew; her most popular collection was *Little Citizens: The Humours of School Life* (1904).

Several Jewish organizations assisted in the support of vocational schools, including technical training and English instruction for both girls and boys. As the numbers of incoming children increased toward the end of the century and beyond, the "uptown" Jews of the older, more established German-Jewish community contributed more heavily to the education and welfare of East Europeans in the tenement districts "downtown." The Hebrew Free School Association, the Young Men's Hebrew Association, the Baron de Hirsch Fund, and various other agencies were instrumental in helping to provide education for the immigrants, children and adults alike. In 1895 Lillian Wald established the Nurses (Henry Street) Settlement on the Lower East Side to offer nursing services and educate the immigrants about good health and hygiene. Other, more comprehensive charities such as the B'nai B'rith also helped to make education for these children possible among their broader commitments. Hebrew Union College was first established in Cincinnati in 1875 under the leadership of Isaac Mayer Wise; Gratz College, the first specifically for Jewish teachers, dates to 1897, and Dropsie College, the first postgraduate school for Jewish studies, was founded ten years later.

Education went two ways on the Lower East Side: not only were most immigrant Jews eager to learn about American manners and practices, but many Americans were equally interested in the ghetto, that "exotic" district to which the foreign Jews had immigrated. Because American journalists other than Jews did not know Yiddish, those who wished to write about the East Side sought someone there to guide them. Abraham Cahan had been hired by Lincoln Steffens, a philo-Semite (one who admires, praises, and often makes it a point to associate with Jews) (see Howe, p. 398) recently appointed city editor for the *New York Commercial Advertiser,* to report on the East Side. One outstanding result of Cahan's warm association with Hutchins Hapgood (1869–1944), also on the staff, was *The Spirit of the Ghetto* (1902), a collection of articles on East Side life by Hapgood with superb charcoal drawings by Jacob Epstein. Jacob Riis (1849–1914), widely known as the author and

photographer of *How the Other Half Lives* (1890) and *Children of the Poor* (1892), was then reporting for the *New York Sun.*

As the Gentile journalists publicized immigrant life for outsiders, the Yiddish press brought omnifarious information as well as fiction and poetry to American Jews wherever copies were available. Although the *Forward* was the most enduring of the Yiddish papers, other Yiddish dailies, weeklies, and monthlies were chiefly political, but some emphasized Jewish achievements, and still others appealed to conservative Jewish readers from a religious perspective. Apart from news and commentaries in the Jewish press, a variety of other features appeared, including tawdry, sentimental, melodramatic, and sensational fiction written quickly and strictly for commercial purposes.

THE ARTS

An outstanding novel of the period is Cahan's *The Rise of David Levinsky,* which details the life of a hypocritical Russian immigrant from his childhood in a shtetl studying to become a Hebrew scholar through his middle age in New York as a multimillionaire industrialist. As Cahan presents immigrant life in fiction from a male perspective, Anzia Yezierska (1885?–1970) reveals it from the viewpoint of a woman. Her first story, "The Fat of the Land," appeared in 1915 and her first collection, *Hungry Hearts,* in 1920; her work was so well received that it brought her to Hollywood, a dramatic change from her childhood and adolescence amid poverty as a Polish immigrant from the Pale. On arriving in America she lived on the East Side under the Old World exploitative behavior of her father, who expected women to work and serve him without question as he studied Talmud at home. So Yezierska fled and gained self-fulfillment trying to create a bridge of mutual understanding between the American people and the immigrants. Because much of Yezierska's fiction is autobiographical, it is comparable with Mary Antin's (1881–1949) popular autobiography *The Promised Land* (1912), in which she reveals the changes that occurred in her life as a Russian Jew who becomes secularized on leaving her family in Boston to gain what she believes is a new nationalistic religion as an American. Another noted female author early in the century was Fanny Hurst (1889–1968), who brought out two collections of stories before 1920, *Just around the Corner* (1914) and *Humoresque* (1919), that show the Jewish immigrants becoming assimilated into American life.

Two other Jewish fiction writers of New York from the period are Herman Bernstein (1876–1935) and James Oppenheim (1882–1932). Bernstein's stories collected in *In the Gates of Israel* (1902) are somewhat contrived and sentimental, but they expose the alienation felt by immigrants amid conflicting values of the Old World and the New; Bernstein was also founding editor of the Yiddish daily *Tog* in 1914. Oppenheim first wrote a series of realistic stories about a character named Dr. Rast, a physician on the East Side (1909), that reveals his profound sympathy with the destitute immigrants. Two years later he brought out a novel, *The Nine-Tenths,* that strongly supports the labor movement and draws on two recent historical incidents, the massive strike among garment workers in 1909 and the Triangle Shirtwaist Company fire of 1911. Sholem Aleichem (1856–1916) came to New York from Russia in 1906 but never overcame his misery over what he considered the coarseness of the eastern European immigrants.

Relatively few notable Jewish fictionists existed outside of New York. In the 1890s Emma Wolf (1865–1932) in San Francisco brought out several novels on middle-class Jewish life on the West Coast, among them *Other Things Being Equal* (1892) and *Heirs of Yesterday* (1900). After 1900 Elias Tobenkin (1882–1963) published *Witte Arrives* (1916), which portrays an enterprising, educated youth reared by Russian immigrant parents in rural Wisconsin; unhappy there with no possibility of finding a meaningful life, he leaves and gains fulfillment first in Chicago, then New York. A year after *Witte Arrives* appeared, Sidney L. Nyburg (1880–1957) brought out *The Chosen People,* set in contemporary Baltimore. This realistic fiction places many of the serious problems confronting Jewish communities in New York into a smaller arena. Liberal versus conservative, uptown Jews versus downtown Jews, owners versus workers are the crucial conflicts that confront a young rabbi trying to become a moral leader amidst a wealthy community unprepared to make essential changes.

Undoubtedly the best-known poem by a Jewish poet of the period is "The New Colossus," by Emma Lazarus (1849–1887), a Sephardic Jew living in New York. Asked to provide a manuscript to help pay for the base of the Statue of Liberty, she wrote her famed sonnet in November 1883; it is now implanted in the pedestal of the statue. Until the early 1880s Lazarus wrote traditional poetry on classical subjects, but when awakened to her Jewish commitment, she devoted herself to it.

Many other Jewish poets also were active, publishing their own collections as well as individual poems in the Yiddish press. Because nearly all their important work was in Yiddish, however, until it was translated they were virtually unknown to non-Yiddish-speaking readers. In the 1880s and 1890s a group called

Written by Emma Lazarus, a Sephardic Jew from New York, "The New Colossus" is probably the most universally recognized poem by an American poet. She drafted it in November 1883 when asked to submit a manuscript for auction to help acquire funds to provide a base for the Statue of Liberty, a recent gift to the United States from France. The poem received immediate acclaim and was eventually engraved on a plaque mounted within the pedestal.

Not like the brazen giant of Greek fame,
With conquering limbs astride from land to land;
Here at our sea-washed, sunset gates shall stand
A mighty woman with a torch, whose flame
Is the imprisoned lightning, and her name
Mother of Exiles. From her beacon-hand
Glows world-wide welcome; her mild eyes
        command
The air-bridged harbor that twin cities frame.
"Keep, ancient lands, your storied pomp!" cries
        she
With silent lips. "Give me your tired, your poor,
Your huddled masses yearning to breathe free,
The wretched refuse of your teeming shore.
Send these, the homeless, tempest-tost to me,
I lift my lamp beside the golden door!"

Lazarus, *The Poems of Emma Lazarus,* 2:202–203.

Sweatshop Poets devoted their poetry to the cause of labor on the East Side; perhaps the best known are Morris Winchevsky, David Edelstadt, and especially Morris Rosenfeld. Later more individualistic poets emerged, including such popular writers as Mani Leib, Moshe Leib Halpern, Reuben Iceland, and Zisha Landau. In *A Little Love in Big Manhattan* (1988), Ruth R. Wisse portrays Leib and Halpern, immigrants from eastern Europe, and discusses their work in the context of trends and patterns in Yiddish poetry of the period. As young poets they became part of a group called Di Yunge (Youth), which formed under the leadership of David Ignatow. Di Yunge separated art from the wretchedness they knew of East Side life by seeking to write as individuals and to emphasize internal truths over external actualities.

The Yiddish theater and the song, dance, and comic routines of early vaudeville also became popular during these years. The Yiddish theater was an art form all its own. Its first performance in New York was Abraham Goldfaden's (1840–1908) operetta *The Sorceress,* staged in August 1882 on the Lower East Side. Originally a Yiddish songwriter in Russia and Romania, Goldfaden demanded little from his audience in order to generate popular appeal. In contrast, Jacob Gordin (1853–1909) tried to educate his audience. He was the first to attempt to bring realism and serious drama to the Yiddish stage. Two of the principal early actors were Boris Thomashevsky, who achieved great popularity as a star of melodrama, and Jacob Adler, reputedly among the best actors on stage. Late in the 1910s and early 1920s, as David S. Lifson ably traces in *The Yiddish Theatre in America* (1965), a successful effort was finally made to bring art—serious drama treated seriously—into the Yiddish theater under the influence of the actor Maurice Schwartz, who founded the Yiddish Art Theater in 1918.

Stories abound of the uproarious liberties Yiddish dramatists and actors alike took with Shakespeare's plays—notably *Romeo and Juliet, Hamlet,* and *King Lear*—in the early years. Much of the pleasure, laughter, and weeping over these productions was attributable to ad-libbing by the performers and to changes made in situation and setting to accommodate the interests and limitations of Jewish audiences at the time. People familiar with a play before it began still never knew what to expect from one performance to the next, and sometimes audience members became so engaged that they shouted at the performers to encourage or instruct them. In *World of Our Fathers,* Irving Howe mentions theatergoers so overjoyed with a performance of *Hamlet* that they called for the author.

Another form of entertainment reigned over the Catskills as Jewish immigrants in New York saved enough to vacation in the mountains for a few days or a week during the summer. By 1890 East European workers began to escape temporarily from the stifling ghettos and enjoy short stays in the cooler mountain air. Aging farmhouses were purchased by entrepreneurs and converted into boardinghouses; after 1900 more lavish hotels and resorts were created. As Cahan illustrates when David Levinsky spends a weekend at the luxurious Rigi Kulm House, overeating and overdressing were the rule for evenings of dining and dancing. Although the Catskills were at their peak for Jewish summer vacationers after 1920, Cahan shows that entertainers were already appearing in the hotels earlier.

A list of names alone of the singers, dancers, and comedians with roots in Jewish neighborhoods of New York early in the last century, especially the East Side, conveys an idea of their importance in the development of American popular culture in the decades that fol-

lowed. Eddie Cantor, Al Jolson, the Ritz Brothers, Fanny Brice, Sophie Tucker ("Last of the Red-Hot Mamas"), Jack Benny, Milton Berle, the Marx Brothers, and George Burns are only a few of those named by Irving Howe who went on to become American stars in the media during the first half of the century and after. The fathers of George Gershwin, Eddie Cantor, and Harold Arlen were cantors in the synagogue, and Irving Berlin was already writing popular songs before 1910.

Prominent Jews in the visual arts also emerged from immigrant backgrounds in urban America. For example, Jacob Epstein, William Gropper, Ben Shahn, and Leonard Baskin all excelled in the graphic arts, while Moses and Raphael Soyer, Adolf Gottlieb, and later Mark Rothko achieved reputations as outstanding painters. Several of these artists either taught or studied at the Jewish Educational Alliance, which evolved when three Jewish charities of New York combined in 1893, and it continued to serve for decades after.

All told, American Jewry in the early twenty-first century cannot be understood without considering the five decades between 1870 and 1920. As well as a period of literary realism and naturalism in America, this was a dynamic age of maturation for the millions of Jewish immigrants caught between two worlds before winning the struggle to achieve their own identity as both Jews and Americans.

See also Anarchism; Assimilation; Immigration; Labor; Poverty; *The Rise of David Levinsky;* Socialism

BIBLIOGRAPHY

Primary Works
Bernheimer, Charles S., ed. *The Russian Jew in the United States: Studies of Social Conditions in New York, Philadelphia, and Chicago, with a Description of Rural Communities.* Philadelphia: John C. Winston, 1905.

Hapgood, Hutchins. *The Spirit of the Ghetto.* 1902. Edited by Moses Rischin. Cambridge, Mass.: Belknap Press of Harvard University Press, 1967.

Lazarus, Emma. *The Poems of Emma Lazarus.* 2 vols. Boston: Houghton, Mifflin, 1888.

Riis, Jacob. *How the Other Half Lives.* New York: Scribners, 1890.

Secondary Works
Birmingham, Stephen. *The Grandees: America's Sephardic Elite.* New York: Harper and Row, 1971.

Chyet, Stanley F., ed. "Forgotten Fiction: American Jewish Life, 1890–1920." *American Jewish Archives* 37, no. 1 (1985).

Feldstein, Stanley. *The Land That I Show You: Three Centuries of Jewish Life in America.* Garden City, N.Y.: Anchor Press/Doubleday, 1978.

Fishman, Priscilla, ed. *The Jews of the United States: The New York Times Library of Jewish Knowledge.* New York: Quadrangle/New York Times, 1973.

Fried, Lewis, ed. *Handbook of American-Jewish Literature: An Analytical Guide to Topics, Themes, and Sources.* New York: Greenwood, 1988.

Harap, Louis. *Creative Awakening: The Jewish Presence in Twentieth-Century American Literature, 1900–1940s.* New York: Greenwood, 1987.

Harap, Louis. *The Image of the Jew in American Literature: From Early Republic to Mass Immigration.* Philadelphia: Jewish Publication Society of America, 1974.

Hertzberg, Arthur. *The Jews in America: Four Centuries of an Uneasy Encounter.* New York: Touchstone/Simon and Schuster, 1989.

Howe, Irving. *World of Our Fathers.* New York: Harcourt Brace Jovanovich, 1976.

Howe, Irving, and Kenneth Libo. *How We Lived: A Documentary History of Immigrant Jews in America, 1880–1930.* New York: Richard Marek, 1979.

Lifson, David S. *The Yiddish Theatre in America.* New York: Thomas Yoseloff, 1965.

Marovitz, Sanford E. *Abraham Cahan.* New York: Twayne/Simon and Schuster Macmillan, 1996.

Rischin, Moses. *The Promised City: New York's Jews, 1870–1914.* Cambridge, Mass.: Harvard University Press, 1962.

Sanders, Ronald. *The Downtown Jews: Portraits of an Immigrant Generation.* New York: Harper and Row, 1969.

Sanders, Ronald. *Shores of Refuge: A Hundred Years of Jewish Emigration.* New York: Holt, 1988.

Taub, Michael. "Yiddish Newspapers in America: A Selective Overview (on the Occasion of the 105 Anniversary of the Yiddish *Forwerts*)." *Yiddish* 13, nos. 2–3 (2003): 111–119.

Weissbach, Lee Shai. "The Jewish Communities of the United States on the Eve of Mass Migration: Some Comments on Geography and Bibliography." *American Jewish History* 58, no. 1 (1988): 79–108.

Wisse, Ruth R. *A Little Love in Big Manhattan.* Cambridge, Mass.: Harvard University Press, 1988.

Sanford E. Marovitz

JIM CROW

The white minstrel show performer Thomas Dartmouth "Daddy" Rice popularized the term "Jim Crow" in the 1830s. The term originated from a song and dance that he had seen an elderly slave perform, which ended with the lyrics "Wheel about an' turn about an' do jes so, / An' eb'ry time I wheel about, I jump Jim Crow." The popularity of minstrel shows based on racist African American stereotypes transformed "Jim Crow" into a familiar word in the nation's vocabulary. Jim Crow, or racial segregation, began in northern states, where slavery was abolished in 1830, and later moved south. While northern blacks held obvious advantages over southern slaves, northerners systematically segregated free blacks and denied them the rights of citizenship, and western states such as Illinois, Indiana, and Oregon either restricted or banned blacks from entering their borders. Alexis de Tocqueville, in *Democracy in America* (1835), responded to this racial bias, commenting that "the prejudice of race appears to be stronger in the states that have abolished slavery than in those where it still exists" (p. 414). Still, by 1890 the term had become synonymous with the South's systematic segregation and disfranchisement of African Americans; by 1910 every former Confederate state had codified into law and state constitutions provisions that controlled blacks and supported white supremacy. Other measures to control blacks across the nation included acts of terror such as lynching and ritualized mob violence. Until the civil rights movement dismantled Jim Crow, its legal and social barriers hindered blacks' ability to participate fully in society.

JIM CROW RECONSTRUCTION AND ITS AFTERMATH

While Reconstruction refers to the political process of readmitting southern states to the Union after the Civil War, it also represents a period marked by the South's attempts to regain economic, political, and social power over emancipated slaves. Black Codes enacted in 1865 and 1866 laid the groundwork for Jim Crow laws that appeared in the 1890s. Like earlier slave codes, Black Codes were a series of statutes that restricted blacks' civil and political rights and included legal definitions of race, employment requirements and regulations, segregation of public facilities, and prohibitions against blacks' assembling or learning to read and write. Viewed as another effort to reintroduce slavery, Congress dismantled the codes to secure blacks the full rights of citizenship through the Civil Rights Act of 1875 and ratification of the Fourteenth (1868) and Fifteenth (1870) Amendments, after which blacks voted, participated in the political process, bought land, sought employment, built their own schools, and used public facilities. Southern Democrats elected Rutherford B. Hayes as president in 1876 with his promise to end Reconstruction with the Compromise of 1877, which cleared the way for a legally sanctioned Jim Crow. Jim Crow laws legalized segregation, and customary barriers separating the races became enforceable legal barriers.

Even the U.S. Supreme Court supported segregation. In 1883 it declared unconstitutional the Civil Rights Act of 1875 and ruled that the Fourteenth Amendment prohibited racial discrimination by state governments, not private organizations or individuals, which led railroads, businesses, and schools to practice segregation. When blacks protested an 1890 Louisiana state law that required segregated railroad cars, the Supreme Court ruled, in *Plessy v. Ferguson* (1896), that "separate but equal" accommodations were constitutional.

American literature reflected Americans' multifarious and changing attitudes toward Jim Crow. Writing during Reconstruction, Thomas Nelson Page and Joel Chandler Harris romanticized slavery. Their "plantation literature"—including *In Ole Virginia* (1887), *Uncle Remus, His Songs and His Sayings* (1880), *Nights with Uncle Remus* (1883), and *Uncle Remus and His Friends* (1892)—depicts the antebellum South as racially harmonious. In contrast, some African American writers challenged the nostalgic vision of antebellum life for slaves; consider, for example, Charles W. Chesnutt's Uncle Julius McAdoo in *The Conjure Woman* (1899) and Frances Ellen Watkins Harper's Aunt Chloe and Uncle Jacob in *Sketches of Southern Life* (1872).

In *The Grandissimes* (1880) and *Madame Delphine* (1881), George Washington Cable (1844–1925) critiqued race and class distinctions, but he would more openly advocate for blacks' full civil rights in *The Silent South* (1885) and *The Negro Question* (1890). Although the South legalized segregation, the North continued to perpetuate "de facto segregation," which Frederick Douglass challenged by advocating for political action in his "The Color Line" (1881) and "Address to the Louisville Convention" (1883) as well as by entering whites-only establishments. To survive in a racially charged climate, blacks learned how to adapt and cope through artful deception. In *Lyrics of Lowly Life* (1896), Paul Laurence Dunbar's (1872–1906) poem "We Wear the Mask" reveals the dual nature of black life. This poem attacks the need for blacks to wear a veil when in the presence of whites and anticipates W. E. B. Du Bois's (1868–1963) exploration of "double consciousness" in *The Souls of Black Folk* (1903): "It is a peculiar sensation, this double-consciousness, this sense of always looking at oneself through the eyes of others, of measuring one's soul by the tape of a world that looks on in amused contempt and pity" (p. 45). Du Bois urged blacks to step from behind the veil. Dunbar's poem also elicits another reading. The mask

as symbol provides a measure of subversive power because it can hide emotion. Dunbar validates the African American experience and the indignities suffered under white supremacy. The poem also highlights the importance of not sharing the agony with those who inflicted pain.

At the turn of the century, violent confrontation was one of the consequences of Jim Crow. Thomas Dixon's *The Clansmen* (1905) became the basis for D. W. Griffith's movie *The Birth of a Nation* (1915), which exacerbated racial tensions and led to race riots. Chesnutt based his novel *The Marrow of Tradition* (1901) on the 1898 race riot in Wilmington, North Carolina, depicting problems afflicting the New South. Race riots also occurred in northern states. The fall and summer of 1919 became known as "Red Summer," following the death of hundreds of blacks in race riots all across the United States. Claude McKay's poem "If We Must Die" (1919) urged black men to fight back and pursue their honor and dignity. Pauline Hopkins's novel *Winona* (1902), set in Kansas, affirmed organized violence against racist oppression. Seemingly rejecting Booker T. Washington's doctrine of self-help, moral virtue, industrial education, and social segregation as a means to race progress, *Winona* calls for public protests against the escalating mob violence endorsed by Jim Crow culture.

The founder and head of Tuskegee Institute, Washington (1856–1915) offered a less-confrontational solution to racial violence; he advised blacks to accept segregation and stop demanding equal rights. He also advocated a vocational rather than a college education as a way for blacks to build skills that could lead to their eventual economic prosperity. His "Atlanta Compromise" speech (1895) and autobiography, *Up from Slavery* (1901), explained his educational and political philosophies of accommodation and appeasement, which won him southern white support. A Harvard-educated historian and sociologist, Du Bois vehemently opposed Washington's tactics. In *The Souls of Black Folk*, he openly criticized Washington for asking blacks to surrender their rights and human dignity. Unlike Washington, Du Bois advocated higher education as a way to create a "talented tenth," a group of black leaders who could lead resistance efforts against Jim Crow.

Literature also explored Jim Crow's emphasis on color. In Kate Chopin's "Désirée's Baby" (1893), Désirée Aubigny's husband questions her ancestry when their newborn's physical features are clearly black. Similarly, in *Pudd'nhead Wilson* (1894), Mark Twain explored the color line that Jim Crow established when he created a story of mixed identities instigated when a slave woman exchanged her light-skinned child with her master's. The increase in education and employment opportunities among blacks led to the rise of a middle class. In certain instances, skin color played a role within black communities as this largely "mulatto elite" sought to maintain the privileged status that many had acquired during slavery. A number of mulattoes adopted the prejudices Jim Crow created by segregating themselves in communities where skin color became the key to access. In "The Wife of His Youth" (1899), Charles Chesnutt sensitively portrayed the moral dilemmas in communities such as the New Orleans or Nashville Blue Vein Societies that restricted admittance to those who were light enough to see the veins in their wrists. Many light-skinned blacks escaped Jim Crow's violence and degradation by concealing their identities and passing as white. James Weldon Johnson's *The Autobiography of an Ex-Colored Man* (1912) illustrates how Jim Crow forced many to agonize over choosing one identity over another.

THE ECONOMICS OF JIM CROW

In addition to the eradication of civil and political rights, Jim Crow also prevented blacks from bettering themselves economically. Most were forced into low-paying jobs for whites as farmhands or domestics. Jim Crow laws even insisted that blacks be employed, or they would be jailed for vagrancy. Employment laws supported sharecropping and the convict lease system, both of which resembled slavery. Former plantation owners had land but little money to pay workers for continued crop cultivation (usually cotton). In exchange for land and a portion of the crops, landowners contracted with blacks for their labor. Local stores extended them credit throughout the year to purchase seeds, food, and equipment, but high interest rates meant that blacks fell further into debt, even forcing their children to continue sharecropping. Like lynching, sharecropping became a familiar literary theme. Sharecropping also informed the lyrics of blues songs like "Cotton Field Blues" and "Boll Weevil Blues."

Many southern blacks responded to inequality, vigilante violence, and sharecropping by fleeing the South. Between 1880 and 1890 thousands made new homes in Kansas and Oklahoma. Later, in what became called the "Great Migration," hundreds of thousands moved to New York City, Chicago, Washington, D.C., and other industrial urban areas to take advantage of employment opportunities created by World War I. This large influx of blacks to New York City contributed to the rise of the Harlem Renaissance in the 1920s, a movement that refers to the blossoming of

African American literature and art. Harlem Renaissance writers celebrated African American culture.

Also blossoming was a motion picture industry with black entrepreneurs such as Oscar Micheaux (1884–1951). Inspired by Booker T. Washington's call for blacks and whites to get along with each other and Horace Greeley, who encouraged everyone to move west, Micheaux purchased land in South Dakota in 1905. His homesteading experience became the basis for his first novel, *The Conquest: The Story of a Negro Pioneer* (1913), which he later rewrote into *The Homesteader* (1917) and made into his first film. *The Homesteader* demonstrated Micheaux's understanding of segregation and desire to unite white and black communities.

Like Micheaux, many blacks discovered that their social and economic conditions in the North had remained unchanged. Restricted to menial jobs, poor housing and education, and unfamiliar with city life, blacks founded institutions to promote racial uplift and to fight Jim Crow. Two organizations formed during this time are still in existence. They include the Committee on Urban Conditions among Negroes, which eventually become the National Urban League (1910), and the National Association for the Advancement of Colored People (NAACP), founded in 1909 by Du Bois, Ida B. Wells, and others. The NAACP's numerous legal battles set a series of precedents that courts would use to strike down Jim Crow. In *Brown v. Board of Education* (1954), the Supreme Court ruled "separate but equal" in education was unconstitutional. This helped spark the civil rights movement, and with the passage of the Civil Rights Act of 1965 and the Voting Rights Act of 1966, Jim Crow was effectively dismantled.

See also Blacks; Civil Rights; Lynching; Race Novels; Racial Uplift; Reconstruction; *The Souls of Black Folk; Up from Slavery*

BIBLIOGRAPHY
Primary Works
Cable, George Washington. *The Grandissimes: A Story of Creole Life*. 1880. New York: Penguin, 1988.

Cable, George Washington. *Madame Delphine*. 1881. New York: Firebird, 2001.

Cable, George Washington. *The Negro Question: A Selection of Writings on Civil Rights in the South*. 1890. Edited by Arlin Turner. Garden City, N.Y.: Doubleday, 1958.

Cable, George Washington. *The Silent South*. 1885. Montclair, N.J.: Patterson Smith, 1969.

Chesnutt, Charles W. *The Marrow of Tradition*. 1901. New York: Penguin Books, 1993.

Chesnutt, Charles W. *Stories, Novels, Essays.* New York: Library of America, 2002.

Chopin, Kate. "The Father of Désirée's Baby." *Vogue,* 14 January 1893.

Chopin, Kate. *Kate Chopin: Complete Novels and Stories.* Edited by Sandra M. Gilbert. New York: Library of America, 2002.

Dixon, Thomas. *The Clansman: An Historical Romance of the Ku Klux Klan.* 1905. Ridgewood, N.J.: Gregg, 1967.

Douglass, Frederick. "Address to the Louisville Convention." 1883. In *Frederick Douglas: Selected Speeches and Writings,* edited by Philip S. Foner. Chicago: Lawrence Hill Books, 1999.

Douglass, Frederick. "The Color Line." 1881. In *Frederick Douglas: Selected Speeches and Writings,* edited by Philip S. Foner. Chicago: Lawrence Hill Books, 1999.

Du Bois, W. E. B. *The Souls of Black Folk.* 1903. Edited by David W. Blight and Robert Gooding-Williams. Boston: Bedford Books, 1997.

Dunbar, Paul Laurence. *The Collected Poetry of Paul Laurence Dunbar.* Edited by Joanne M. Braxton. Charlottesville: University Press of Virginia, 1993.

Harper, Frances Ellen Watkins. *Sketches of Southern Life.* Philadelphia: Ferguson Brothers, 1891. Electronic Text Center, University of Virginia Library. Available at http://etext.lib.virginia.edu.

Harris, Joel Chandler. *The Complete Tales of Uncle Remus.* Edited by Richard Chase. Boston: Houghton Mifflin, 2002.

Hopkins, Pauline. *The Magazine Novels of Pauline Hopkins.* New York: Oxford University Press, 1988.

Johnson, James Weldon. *Writings: James Weldon Johnson.* New York: Library of America, 2004.

McKay, Claude. *Complete Poems: Claude McKay.* Edited by William J. Maxwell. Urbana: University of Illinois Press, 2004.

Micheaux, Oscar. *The Conquest: The Story of a Negro Pioneer.* 1913. New York: Washington Square Press, 2003.

Page, Thomas Nelson. *In Ole Virginia; or, Marse Chan and Other Stories.* 1887. Nashville, Tenn.: J. S. Sanders, 1991.

Twain, Mark. *The Tragedy of Pudd'nhead Wilson.* 1894. Hartford, Conn.: American Publishing, 1900. Electronic Text Center, University of Virginia Library. Available at http://etext.lib.virginia.edu/toc/modeng/public/Twa2Pud.html.

Tocqueville, Alexis de. *Democracy in America.* 1835. New York: Bantam Classics, 2000.

Washington, Booker T. *Up from Slavery: An Autobiography.* 1901. Boston: Houghton Mifflin, 1901. Electronic Text Center, University of Virginia Library. Available at http://etext.lib.virginia.edu/toc/modeng/public/WasSlav.html.

Secondary Works

Dailey, Jane, Glenda Elizabeth Gilmore, and Bryant Simon, eds. *Jumpin' Jim Crow: Southern Politics from Civil War to Civil Rights.* Princeton, N.J.: Princeton University Press, 2000.

Gilmore, Glenda Elizabeth. *Gender and Jim Crow: Women and the Politics of White Supremacy in North Carolina, 1869–1920.* Chapel Hill: University of North Carolina Press, 1996.

Hale, Grace Elizabeth. *Making Whiteness: The Culture of Segregation in the South, 1890–1940.* New York: Pantheon Books, 1998.

Kaplan, Amy. "Nation, Region, and Empire." In *Columbia History of the American Novel,* edited by Emory Elliott, pp. 240–266. New York: Columbia University Press, 1991.

Packard, Jerrold M. *American Nightmare: The History of Jim Crow.* New York: St. Martin's, 2002.

Wilson, Kirt H. *The Reconstruction Desegregation Debate: The Politics of Equality and the Rhetoric of Place, 1870–1875.* East Lansing: Michigan State University Press, 2002.

Wormser, Richard. *The Rise and Fall of Jim Crow.* New York: St. Martin's, 2003.

Elizabeth Archuleta

JOURNALISM

The volatile journalism scene between 1870 and 1920 allowed American writers access to a broader, more diverse set of readers than ever before and helped to shape the content and form of American literature, particularly the novel. The objective method of reporting was not yet fully established as a journalistic ideal, nor was the sharp division between literature and journalism that many twenty-first century readers take for granted—the notion that literary writers produce art worth lingering over, while journalists produce only functional prose worth a quick read and a toss into the trash. The era's papers published poetry, fiction, and literary essays as well as news. Many celebrated literary figures—Mark Twain, Henry James, and Edith Wharton among them—published work in newspapers and magazines at the turn of the century. Willa Cather decided she wanted to be a writer in the 1890s after her college English professor got Cather's essay on Thomas Carlyle published in the *Nebraska State Journal.* Cather's career as a theater critic, editor, and sometime reporter lasted nearly two decades. Yet when she achieved success as a novelist, Cather did not hesitate to denigrate journalistic writing as commercially driven, shallow, and slipshod.

Such ambivalence was characteristic of the relationship between journalism and literature: the two realms were inevitably intertwined, but attitudes toward the press varied dramatically. Journalism was celebrated as a vibrant force that brought writers in touch with "real life." But it was also attacked as a mind-numbing phenomenon destructive to literary culture, threatening to reduce the American reading public to thoughtless consumers. Such divergent views notwithstanding, literary historians agree that the major literary movements in American fiction at the turn into the twentieth century—realism, naturalism, and modernism—all owe significant debts to journalism.

MAINSTREAM PRESSES: NEW READERS, NEW REALISM

The period after the Civil War saw a decline in the older model of partisan newspapers controlled by political parties. Instead journalism continued to evolve along the lines set by the advent of the penny press in the 1830s, which featured low prices and high accessibility. When the first mass-circulation newspapers and magazines emerged in the late nineteenth century in New York, San Francisco, Chicago, and other cities, revenue from advertising allowed them to be independent from political party support, and the press's primary motivation shifted from political to business advocacy. As a result, popular journals addressed their readers less as potential voters and more as potential consumers of mass-produced products such as soap, baking powder, medical remedies, shirtwaists, and shoes. This shift troubled some citizens, who worried that American democracy was being undermined by corporate control of public discourse. Writers, some critics complained, no longer acted as independent interpreters of the news. Hearst and Scripps emerged as the nation's biggest group owners, buying out the competition and consolidating newspapers in dozens of cities. At the same time, skyrocketing circulations indicated that more Americans, from more varied walks of life, were reading magazines and newspapers than ever before. Because so much advertising was aimed at women, attracting female readers became a priority for many papers. Newspapers and magazines also sought to expand their readerships among the working classes and immigrants, reaching out to the new urban masses, even those who were barely literate in English.

Immigrants played an influential role in the press, not only as readers but also as editors and publishers. One of the most famous was the Hungarian-born Joseph Pulitzer, who took over the New York World in 1883 and ushered in a new era of journalism, promising to entertain and inform readers with a bold mix of illustrations, human-interest stories, editorials in support of the working class, and crusades against government and corporate corruption. The average daily circulation of the World doubled during Pulitzer's first three months, from 15,000 to 30,000, and by 1887 it had reached a quarter million, an unprecedented figure. Pulitzer would soon be drawn into a legendary circulation battle with William Randolph Hearst, heir to a California mining fortune and publisher of the San Francisco Examiner. Hearst bought the New York Journal in 1895, hired away some of Pulitzer's best editors, and set out to woo the World readers. The fight led both sides to adopt increasingly aggressive strategies, such as pursuing exclusive rights to stories and trumpeting their own social-justice crusades. "While Others Talk the Journal Acts," bragged Hearst's paper while featuring eyebrow-raising headlines like "A Startling Confession of a Wholesale Murderer Who Begs to Be Hanged" and "Strange Things Women Do for Love" (Bleyer, pp. 357–364). These tactics became known as "yellow journalism" because of the World's popular "Yellow Kid" comic strip, which soon began appearing in the Journal as well. Promotions for both papers featured the goofy, vacant-looking figure, and the comic strip became a symbol of sensationalism and journalistic irresponsibility. That irresponsibility peaked in 1898, when overblown coverage of the sinking of the American battleship Maine helped to bring about an ill-advised war with Spain. Despite a chorus of critics, newspapers across the country practiced variations of the yellow journalism formula, and the number of daily newspapers continued to increase, peaking at about 2,600 between 1910 and 1914.

After the Civil War, elite "establishment" magazines such as Harper's, Century, and Scribner's continued to enjoy cultural power and prestige. The Century's popular series on Civil War battles, published in the mid-1880s, led to a four-volume book. By the 1890s, however, magazines became cheaper, and a different type of journal gained national influence. The new leaders in magazine journalism—such as Edward W. Bok, who took over as editor of Ladies' Home Journal in 1889, and S. S. McClure, who founded McClure's Magazine in 1893—printed popular fiction, general articles, and plenty of illustrations. Bok and McClure, both immigrants themselves, foresaw the future of American magazines. They helped to create syndicated journalism, and they went on to redefine the relationship between magazines and their readers. McClure's put the Progressive Era reform impulse into practice and was hailed as a muckraking journal. The term "muckraker"—first used by Teddy Roosevelt as an insult for reformers who looked only downward, wallowing in the filth of society—became a badge of honor for investigative reporters who documented government corruption, gathered evidence against business monopolies, and fought for better conditions and wages for workers. Ida Tarbell, Upton Sinclair, Lincoln Steffens, and David Graham Phillips were among the best-known muckrakers. Although Bok's *Ladies' Home Journal* did not take up reform with the fervor of *McClure's,* Bok positioned the magazine as a clearinghouse for women's domestic concerns and created a new advertising-oriented market.

This combination of reform journalism and reliance on advertising forged a new mode of "realism" that was oriented toward consumers. Even the most sensational forms of this realism could lead to beneficial reforms. The *World*'s daring Nellie Bly inspired significant improvements in conditions for the mentally ill when she pretended to be insane and had herself committed to a notorious asylum in New York City in 1887. In the heyday of the muckraking era, Samuel Hopkins Adams helped bring about new government regulations with his series on the bogus claims of patent-medicine makers, published in *Collier's* in 1905 and 1906. But some critics have argued that this new realism compromised American democracy by transforming readers from active citizens to passive consumers. According to this view, the new realism was damaging because it turned readers into mere spectators. It packaged information in a way that suggested readers did not have access to "real life" on their own. Moreover, it gave journalism a misleading aura of absolute authenticity. Although magazines and newspapers appeared to be providing readers a clear, neutral window into the real world, they were in fact manipulating information at least as carefully as political journalism had been doing for more than a century.

COUNTERPUBLICS: ALTERNATIVE VOICES

Despite the growth of advertising and the consolidation of corporate influence in journalism, Progressive Era readers could choose from among a wider variety of print sources than at any other time in the nation's history. Mainstream journals were just one part of the phenomenon; Americans also had access to alternative presses that varied widely in content, format, and even language. Although newspapers like Pulitzer's and Hearst's served as Americanizing aids for many immigrants, smaller ethnic presses in Yiddish, German, Polish, Italian, and other languages also flourished, fostering communities in the native languages of recently arrived city dwellers. Throughout America thousands of alternative presses sprang to life, providing critical outlets for voices raised in social protest, racial and ethnic pride, or artistic experimentation. These journals created counterpublics, which scholars have defined as alternative forums for groups whose members have been denied access to the dominant public

sphere. In these arenas, members of subordinated social groups circulate their own interpretations of their identities and needs. Alternative presses allowed readers relegated to society's margins to gather information, share opinions, and find entertainment.

These presses also launched and supported individual literary careers, not unlike mainstream newspapers and magazines. Zitkala–Ša, the Sioux author and Indian rights activist, served as a contributor and editor of *American Indian Magazine,* the periodical for the Society of American Indians, from 1916 to 1920. The novelist Abraham Cahan, a Russian immigrant, began writing for both English and Yiddish newspapers soon after he arrived in America in 1882. Cahan would go on to serve as editor of the *Jewish Daily Forward,* a socialist organ that became the leading Yiddish newspaper in the world in the early twentieth century. At the turn of the century radical women's publications blossomed, spurred by rising labor reform, temperance, and women's rights movements. From 1909 to 1916 the feminist activist and author Charlotte Perkins Gilman published and also wrote most of the copy for the *Forerunner,* a monthly magazine featuring fiction, poetry, editorials, and news reports. The *Masses* (1911–1917), edited by Floyd Dell and Max Eastman, and *Mother Earth* (1906–1917), edited and published by Emma Goldman, also promoted feminist goals. The so-called little magazines, such as *Poetry: A Magazine of Verse,* founded by Harriet Monroe in 1912, published experimental writing, promoting radical political views and avant-garde aesthetics. Although these magazines appeared erratically and were short-lived, they published work by important poets like Ezra Pound and Marianne Moore. Their influence went far beyond their small circulations.

Meanwhile the rising tide of racial violence against African Americans fueled an explosion of black newspapers. Between 1895 and 1915, some 1,200 African American newspapers were launched, more than in any other era of American history. At a time when almost all white-owned newspapers refused to hire African Americans, these newspapers gave writers a platform from which to condemn injustice, call for change, and celebrate the achievements of their race. Ida B. Wells, the daughter of former slaves, started writing for the black press in 1884 and went on to become an internationally recognized anti-lynching crusader. Her impassioned journalism, which exposed the hypocrisy of white society's rationale for lynchings, contrasted sharply with the approving reports that appeared in the white press. African American journals also printed poetry and fiction. The *Colored American Magazine,* founded in 1900, published the serialized fiction of Pauline E. Hopkins, now recognized as a major voice in turn-of-the-century black fiction. *The Crisis,* the official organ of the National Association for the Advancement of Colored People (NAACP), debuted in 1910. It was edited by the scholar and activist W. E. B. Du Bois, author of *The Souls of Black Folk* (1903), a groundbreaking study of African American culture.

GETTING STARTED: CHANGING PROFESSIONAL OPTIONS FOR WRITERS

When Ernest Hemingway joined the *Kansas City Star* in 1917, he launched a writing career that would make him one of the world's most famous novelists. Hemingway's spare prose style has often been linked to the brevity required of reporters, who must compress information into the limited space of newspaper columns. His first book, *In Our Time* (1925), combined journalistic reports with fiction in a complex collage of perspectives on the First World War. Although Hemingway's achievement was extraordinary, changes in journalism in the late nineteenth and early twentieth centuries set the stage for his rise from reporter to literary celebrity.

Only in the decades after the Civil War did reporting become widely recognized as a respectable profession. By the 1880s reporters had come into their own, and journalism offered new career options for Americans who wanted to write professionally. Bylines became more common as reporters achieved new prominence in news organizations. At the same time, journalists joined lawyers, librarians, social workers, chemists, economists, teachers, engineers, and doctors in carving their own specialized niche in the working world. The first professional organizations for journalists were founded in this era, as was the *Journalist,* a trade publication that appeared in 1883. Colleges and universities initiated journalism courses, and in 1908 the University of Missouri established the first college of journalism. Columbia University soon followed suit, funded by a generous grant from Joseph Pulitzer.

Although salaries remained low for all except a few top executives, writing for newspapers and magazines became known as a potentially glamorous job. Richard Harding Davis, the dashing son of the author Rebecca Harding Davis, personified that glamour for many turn-of-the-century readers. A star reporter who began in Philadelphia and moved quickly to the New York City metropolitan papers, Davis launched his career covering crime and sports and soon began writing popular fiction as well. Davis's expansive personality, good looks, and friendship with the magazine illustrator Charles Dana Gibson made him one of the best-known faces in American journalism, especially after he became the model for the male companion to Gibson's famous "Gibson girl." Davis also helped popularize the image of the journalist as a swashbuckling adventurer. He served as a correspondent in the Spanish-American War and later in World War I.

Although journalism was dominated by men, women also flocked into newsrooms in the 1880s. Most female journalists covered fashion news, domestic tips, and society events for the newly created women's pages, but some also wrote front-page news. More likely to use pseudonyms than male journalists, newswomen also were more likely to be highly visible, their names and faces promoted along with their stories. Dorothy Dix, hired in 1894 as a "girl Friday" for the New Orleans *Picayune,* became one of the most successful newspaperwomen of her day. Dix (the pen name of Elizabeth Meriwether Gilmer) began with obituaries, graduated to news events, and ended up writing a popular advice column, "Dorothy Dix Talks," for fifty years. Dix's contemporary, Nellie Bly (the pen name of Elizabeth Cochrane), made headlines with her incognito excursions into the darker parts of the city. Winifred Black, Ada Patterson, and a host of other imitators helped to make "girl stunt reporting" into a national phenomenon. This fad preceded the cross-class adventures of other late-nineteenth-century writers, the best-known of whom is Stephen Crane, whose sketches "Experiment in Misery" and "Experiment in Luxury" appeared in the New York *Press* in 1894. Two years later Crane registered as a seaman on a gunrunning ship to Cuba to seek experience as a war correspondent. He found himself reporting on a different sort of trauma when the ship sank and he spent almost thirty hours, in dangerously high seas, with three other men in a ten-foot dinghy. Soon after, Crane published a report in the New York *Press,* and a few months later his short story based on the incident, "The Open Boat," appeared in *Scribner's Magazine.*

Crane's movement between fact and fiction was not unusual. The newspaper editor and novelist Abraham Cahan's realist novel *The Rise of David Levinsky* (1917) evolved from a series *McClure's Magazine* commissioned him to write on Jewish immigrants in the garment trade. The former journalist Theodore Dreiser adapted news reports from a 1906 murder case for his important naturalist novel *An American Tragedy* (1925). Gertrude Stein and John Dos Passos were among the many writers who collected newspaper headlines to use in their own work. An unprecedented number of American authors between 1870 and 1920 began their careers as journalists, more than in any period before or since. The list includes celebrated novelists such as Crane and Hemingway as well as popular novelists whose work is less known today, such as Edna Ferber and David Graham Phillips. For many writers, journalism acted as a bracing substitute for formal education. "At a time when the respectable bourgeois youngsters of my generation were college freshmen, oppressed by simian sophomores and affronted with balderdash daily and hourly by chalky pedagogues," H. L. Mencken recalled, "I was at large in a wicked seaport of half a million people, with a front seat at every public show . . . getting earfuls and eyefuls of instruction in a hundred giddy arcana, none of them taught in schools" (p. ix).

Yet journalism's impact on American letters was too sweeping and complex for a single formula to explain. Journalism was viewed as a new form of literary apprenticeship. It offered aspiring writers steady income as well as the opportunity to immerse themselves in a broad range of American experiences. It also provided an influential venue for writers like Eugene Field, a poet whose "Sharps and Flats" column in the Chicago *Daily News* mixed urbane commentary on contemporary life with verse and whimsy. The in-house humorist became a standard feature of late-nineteenth-century newspapers, and several, such as Field, Bill Nye, George Ade, and Finley Peter Dunne, rose to prominence in this role. But commercial imperatives and deadline pressures made some journalists view their workplaces more as industrial prisons than schools. As editors exerted more control over the content and style of stories, writers resented their lack of autonomy and grew alienated from management. The press attracted some vocal critics. "The great presses of the country," the novelist Frank Norris declared, "are for the most part merely sublimated sausage machines that go dashing along in a mess of paper and printer's ink turning out meat for the monster" (pp. 104–105). The muckraker Upton Sinclair, known for his meatpacking industry exposé *The Jungle* (1906), launched a systematic, passionate attack on the commercial press in *The Brass Check: A Study of American Journalism* (1919). Comparing journalists to prostitutes, Sinclair dismantled any claims to freedom of the press and declared that corporations controlled the American news industry. "To expect justice and truth-telling of a capitalist newspaper," Sinclair concluded, "is to expect asceticism at a cannibal feast" (p. 224).

Although Sinclair's indictment was extreme, many works of fiction reflect their authors' frustration with journalism. William Dean Howells represents the newsman as a selfish, manipulative liar in *A Modern Instance* (1882). James mocks "lady-correspondents" in his characterization of Henrietta Stackpole in *The Portrait of a Lady* (1881), then goes even further with his portrayal of the villainous Boston interviewer Matthias Pardon in *The Bostonians* (1886). The conclusion of Edna Ferber's *Dawn O'Hara* (1911) rewards the hardworking reporter-heroine by affording her two avenues of escape from journalism: she gets a book contract and a husband. Journalism's influence on literature went even deeper than any individual characterizations of reporters can reveal, however. Some writers, James and Cather among them, saw newspapers as a symbol for all that was going wrong in American culture. They protested the consumerism and standardization of the new mass culture. Against a rapid-fire model of reading and writing, they fought to assert the value of contemplation and carefully crafted expression.

SHAPING FICTION: REALISM, NATURALISM, AND MODERNISM

The reporter's access to raw experience was especially prized among novelists who sought to record the brutalities of everyday life in America. The Harvard-educated Hutchins Hapgood, who complained that American novels lacked vivid realism, set out to remedy the problem by forging his own brand of participatory journalism, immersing himself in his subjects' lives as much as possible. Hapgood's series of articles on the Jewish ghetto, written for New York's *Commercial Advertiser,* were revised and published in a book, *The Spirit of the Ghetto* (1902). Although not a novel, the book was praised in literary circles. When the New York City police reporter and photojournalist Jacob Riis published a pioneering attack on tenement housing in 1890, his book's title, *How the Other Half Lives,* summed up what many writers hoped to gain from their reporting days. Riis, who spent years covering slums, took a scientific approach to fact gathering. To document the exploitation of children in tenement factories, Riis consulted a statistical table from the health department showing how to tell age by children's teeth, then went into factories and looked in little girls' mouths to see how old they were. Journalism's stress on precise observation and, more broadly, its assumption that reality was external and thus reportable, contributed to the two major movements in American fiction in the late nineteenth century, realism and naturalism.

Realism was championed by the literary critic and novelist William Dean Howells, who as a boy helped his father edit a small-town newspaper in Ohio. The movement encompassed a diverse set of approaches and authors, from the frontier humor of Mark Twain to the social-problem fiction of Howells. A reaction against the enormous popularity of sentimental fiction, realism centered on ordinary life, insisted upon verisimilitude of detail, represented vernacular speech, and attempted to present an objective view of American society. This last characteristic—the celebration of objectivity, the goal of depersonalized narration—has inspired the most skepticism from later readers because many critics rightly point out that no narrative can be value-neutral and no story exists without some particular angle of vision. Realist fiction, although less idealistic than sentimental fiction, nonetheless tended to advocate an ethical standpoint. That standpoint becomes clearer when realism is compared to its counterpart, naturalism, a pessimistic subset of realism. Naturalists, like realists, sought to document oppressive realities of turn-of-the-century lives, but their fiction featured a deterministic vision, showing individuals at the mercy of biological and social forces beyond their control. The journalists Crane, Dreiser, Norris, and Jack London all wrote major naturalist fiction.

Modernism, an elite literary movement that emerged in the 1890s in Europe and blossomed in the United States shortly after, was more directly antagonistic toward the mass culture associated with journalism. Modernist fiction, like that of the realists and naturalists, sought to create authentic portrayals of life. But modernists like Gertrude Stein and John Dos Passos challenged standard ways of reading, experimenting with unusual narrative structure and adapting the abstract methods of modernist painters to represent multiple, shifting perspectives. They rejected the idea that language could give readers access to a neutral view of reality. Their demanding, often elliptical writing forced readers to grapple with the printed word, widening the gap between how one read the newspaper and how one read literature. That so many readers take this gap for granted today reflects the power of the modernists' literary legacy.

Some scholars argue that a special category of journalism emerged at the turn of the century, an elite form that combined the creative license of fiction writers with the fact-based method of newly professionalized journalists. Authors such as Crane, Davis, Cahan, Dreiser, Hapgood, Lincoln Steffens, and the longtime New York reporter Julian Ralph have been called "literary journalists" because they sought to endow factual accounts with the grace and power of literary prose. Their writing is distinguished by the depth of its research, complexity of its topic, and subtlety of its approach. It is worth noting that almost no women from the turn of the century have been included in lists of "literary journalists." Female journalists, stereotyped as "sob sisters" who produced only emotional drivel, were rarely taken seriously as writers, even though some of them, such as the writer and editor Elizabeth Jordan, went on to have successful careers as fiction writers. Jordan's first book—a story collection titled *Tales of the City Room* (1898)—attracted attention in part because of Jordan's notoriety as one of the only female reporters to cover the murder trial of Lizzie Borden in 1893. Although women took on visible roles in newspaper and magazine journalism, newsrooms have been depicted as overwhelmingly masculine. Whether they were writing news or fiction, women were more often identified with an earlier generation's sentimentality, seen as throwbacks to a literary movement the realists and naturalists were struggling to move beyond.

By the late 1920s print culture was competing with film and radio, and a new shift in American cultural practices was occurring. But authors would continue to negotiate the multiple legacies of journalism, which inspired new forms of expression, created new reading publics, and challenged writers to invest the printed word with a newly vital sense of "the real."

See also Appeal to Reason; Century Magazine; Editors; *Harper's New Monthly Magazine;* Literary Marketplace; Little Magazines and Small Presses; *McClure's Magazine;* Newspaper Syndicates; *Scribner's Magazine*

BIBLIOGRAPHY
Primary Works

Cahan, Abraham. *The Rise of David Levinsky.* New York: Harper & Brothers, 1917.

Crane, Stephen. "The Open Boat." *Scribner's Magazine* (June 1897): 728–740.

Dreiser, Theodore. *An American Tragedy.* 1925. New York: Library of America, 2003.

Ferber, Edna. *Dawn O'Hara.* New York: Grosset and Dunlap, 1911.

Hapgood, Hutchins. *The Spirit of the Ghetto.* 1902. Edited by Moses Rischin. Cambridge, Mass.: Belknap Press of Harvard University Press, 1967.

Hemingway, Ernest. *In Our Time.* 1925. New York: Scribners, 1986.

Howells, William Dean. *A Modern Instance.* 1882. New York: Penguin Books, 1984.

James, Henry. *The Bostonians.* 1886. New York: Modern Library, 2003.

Jordan, Elizabeth G. *Tales of the City Room.* New York: Scribners, 1898.

Mencken, H. L. *Newspaper Days 1899–1906.* New York: Knopf, 1941.

Norris, Frank. *The Responsibilities of the Novelist.* New York: Doubleday, Page, 1903.

Riis, Jacob. *How the Other Half Lives.* 1890. New York: Penguin, 1997.

Sinclair, Upton. *The Brass Check: A Study of American Journalism.* 1919. Introduction by Robert McChesney and Ben Scott. Urbana: University of Illinois Press, 2003.

Secondary Works

Baldasty, Gerald J. *The Commercialization of News in the Nineteenth Century.* Madison: University of Wisconsin Press, 1992.

Batker, Carol J. *Reforming Fictions: Native, African, and Jewish American Women's Literature and Journalism in the Progressive Era.* New York: Columbia University Press, 2000.

Bleyer, Willard G. *Main Currents in the History of American Journalism.* Boston: Houghton Mifflin, 1927.

Campbell, W. Joseph. *Yellow Journalism: Puncturing the Myths, Defining the Legacies.* Westport, Conn.: Praeger, 2001.

Emery, Edwin, and Michael Emery. *The Press and America: An Interpretive History of the Mass Media.* 8th ed. New York: Pearson, Allyn & Beacon, 1995.

Fishkin, Shelley Fisher. *From Fact to Fiction: Journalism & Imaginative Writing in America.* Baltimore: Johns Hopkins University Press, 1985.

Frus, Phyllis. *The Politics and Poetics of Journalistic Narrative.* Cambridge, U.K., and New York: Cambridge University Press, 1994.

Hardt, Hanno, and Bonnie Brennen, eds. *Newsworkers: Toward a History of the Rank and File.* Minneapolis: University of Minnesota Press, 1995.

Hartsock, John C. *A History of American Literary Journalism: The Emergence of a Modern Narrative Form.* Amherst: University of Massachusetts Press, 2000.

Marzolf, Marion. *Civilizing Voices: American Press Criticism, 1880–1950.* New York: Longman, 1991.

Mindich, David T. Z. *Just the Facts: How "Objectivity" Came to Define American Journalism.* New York: New York University Press, 1998.

Mott, Frank Luther. *American Journalism.* 3rd ed. New York: Macmillan, 1962.

Pizer, Donald. *The Theory and Practice of American Literary Naturalism: Selected Essays and Reviews.* Carbondale: Southern Illinois University Press, 1993.

Robertson, Michael. *Stephen Crane, Journalism, and the Making of Modern American Literature.* New York: Columbia University Press, 1997.

Schiller, Dan. *Objectivity and the News: The Public and the Rise of Commercial Journalism.* Philadelphia: University of Pennsylvania Press, 1981.

Schudson, Michael. *Discovering the News: A Social History of American Newspapers.* New York: Basic Books, 1978.

Simmons, Charles A. *The African American Press: A History of News Coverage During National Crises, with Special Reference to Four Black Newspapers, 1827–1965.* Jefferson, N.C.: McFarland, 1998.

Sims, Norman. *Literary Journalism in the Twentieth Century.* New York: Oxford University Press, 1990.

Streitmatter, Rodger. *Raising Her Voice: African-American Women Journalists Who Changed History.* Lexington: University Press of Kentucky, 1994.

Strychacz, Thomas. *Modernism, Mass Culture, and Professionalism.* Cambridge, U.K.: Cambridge University Press, 1993.

Wilson, Christopher P. "The Rhetoric of Consumption: Mass-Market Magazines and the Demise of the Gentle Reader, 1880–1920." In *The Culture of Consumption: Critical Essays in American History, 1880–1980,* edited by Richard Wightman Fox and T. J. Jackson Lears, pp. 39–64. New York: Pantheon, 1983.

Jean Marie Lutes

THE JUNGLE

More than any work of fiction other than Harriet Beecher Stowe's *Uncle Tom's Cabin* (1852), Upton Sinclair's novel *The Jungle* (1906) had tremendous social and political impact, precipitating a widespread outcry against the meatpacking industry in particular and heightening awareness of hygienic conditions in food processing in general. President Theodore Roosevelt read the book and summoned Sinclair (1878–1968) to the White House, where the author provided detailed information gathered in Chicago's Packingtown during his research for the novel in 1904 and 1905. In his study of *The Jungle,* William A. Bloodworth Jr. reports that Sinclair "interviewed laborers, social workers, lawyers, doctors, saloonkeepers, and others who seemed to know anything about conditions in the packing plants and political corruption in Chicago" (p. 47). Sinclair also openly toured all reaches of the packinghouses, appearing to be a worker. The novel's vivid and hair-raising claims had already been validated by Doubleday, Page, and Company before it published the book, and Roosevelt conducted further investigations.

Convinced of Sinclair's veracity, the president then threw his political and rhetorical weight into persuading a reluctant Congress to pass within a few months the Meat Inspection Act and the Pure Food and Drug Act of 1906. The Food and Drug Administration was thus established to inspect animals destined for slaughter, to enforce standards of cleanliness in slaughterhouses and processing plants, to test food and drugs intended for human consumption, and to assure clear and accurate product labeling. These acts also established a vital precedent for future public health and environmental legislation. Despite the legislation's sweeping consequences, Sinclair considered his book a failure. To understand why he felt that way requires

Advertising poster for *The Jungle*, c. 1906. THE LIBRARY
OF CONGRESS

"most famous of all the free-lance socialistic periodicals" (p. 204); based in the small town of Girard,
Kansas, the *Appeal to Reason* had "a circulation of a
quarter of a million" by 1904 (p. 205). Fred D. Warren,
the managing editor of the *Appeal*, was so impressed by
Sinclair's articles as well as by his Civil War novel,
Manassas, which had been published several months
earlier by Macmillan, that he advanced five hundred
dollars to Sinclair toward the writing of a new novel
that would concern the inequities facing the working
poor, the wage slaves, of the United States and that
would be serialized in the *Appeal*. Sinclair quickly determined that the subject of his novel would be the workers of Packingtown, and he went to Chicago for a
firsthand look at the conditions they faced there.

In his introduction to the 1946 Viking Press edition of *The Jungle*, Sinclair describes arriving in
Chicago on 20 September 1904, his twenty-sixth
birthday. He spent the next seven weeks observing life
in Packingtown. He says that "wearing old clothes . . .
and carrying a workman's dinnerpail" allowed him to
pass through the meat processing plants unnoticed
during the day and that at night "he sat in the worker's
homes, asking questions and filling notebooks with
what they told him" (Introduction, p. vii). Near the
end of his stay in Packingtown, Sinclair witnessed a
Lithuanian wedding party, recognizing that this would
be the opening scene of his novel and the newly
wedded couple would provide the nucleus of his cast
of characters. He then began drafting the novel in an
eight-by-ten-foot cabin near Princeton, New Jersey,
on Christmas Day 1904.

THE JUNGLE'S PUBLICATION AND PURPOSE

After appearing serially in both the *Appeal to Reason*
and another of J. A. Wayland's socialist periodicals,
One-Hoss Philosophy, and upon completion in September
1905, Sinclair offered *The Jungle* to Macmillan Publishers, which agreed to print it if "some of the painful
details were cut out" (Introduction, p. viii). Sinclair
would not agree to this, and Macmillan declined the
book, as did four other publishers. Finally Sinclair
published it by subscription to the readers of the
Appeal, from whom he claimed to have received twelve
thousand orders (Introduction, p. ix). This so-called
Sustainer's Edition contained thirty-six chapters
instead of the thirty-one in the edition later published
by Doubleday in 1906. Of the Doubleday edition,
Gene DeGruson reports that after the five chapters
were cut, "Rearrangement of the remaining materials,
with the addition of the Mirija love story, resulted in a
novel different in concept and development than its
Girard editions" (p. xxxvii).

explanation of the author's stated intentions. Political
reform, not health-related regulations, was what
Sinclair hoped for from *The Jungle*.

THE GERMINATION OF *THE JUNGLE*

The disparity between social classes, the plight of
working-class Americans, what Sinclair perceived as a
political system ineffectual in addressing those wrongs—
these circumstances along with Sinclair's love of literature can all be said to contain the seed of *The Jungle*.
More immediately, however, an unsuccessful strike in
Chicago's meatpacking plants in the summer of 1904,
which occurred almost simultaneously with Sinclair's
officially joining the Socialist Party of America, led to
the composition of the novel. After the strike failed,
Sinclair wrote a series of articles directed toward the
dispirited workers and published in J. A. Wayland's
Appeal to Reason, which Frank Luther Mott called the

> In The Jungle *Upton Sinclair describes the inhuman treatment of the workers and the unsanitary conditions in Chicago' meatpacking plants in explicit detail.* The Jungle *outraged the American public and President Theodore Roosevelt, leading to the passage of the Pure Food and Drug Act and the Meat Inspection Act of 1906. In this passage Sinclair describes various injuries suffered by workers at Durham's, a Chicago packing plant, ending with chilling information about the composition of Durham's Pure Leaf Lard.*
>
> Of the butchers and floorsmen, the beef-boners and trimmers, and all those who used knives, you could scarcely find a person who had the use of his thumb; time and time again the base of it had been slashed, till it was a mere lump of flesh against which the man pressed the knife to hold it. The hands of these men would be criss-crossed with cuts, until you could no longer pretend to count them or to trace them. They would have no nails,—they had worn them off pulling hides; their knuckles were swollen so that their fingers spread out like a fan. There were men who worked in the cooking rooms, in the midst of steam and sickening odors, by artificial light; in these rooms the germs of tuberculosis might live for two years, but the supply was renewed every hour. . . . Worst of any, however, were the fertilizer men, and those who served in the cooking rooms. These people could not be shown to the visitor,—for the odor of a fertilizer man would scare any ordinary visitor at a hundred yards, and as for the other men, who worked in tank rooms full of steam, and in some of which there were open vats near the level of the floor, their peculiar trouble was that they fell into the vats; and when they were fished out, there was never enough of them left to be worth exhibiting,—sometimes they would be overlooked for days, till all but the bones of them had gone out to the world as Durham's Pure Leaf Lard!
>
> Sinclair, *The Jungle*, 96–97.

No doubt sales and interest in the book were heightened by Jack London's broadside of 25 November 1905 in the *Chicago Socialist*, which enthusiastically proclaims that "Comrade Sinclair's book" is "the *Uncle Tom's Cabin* of wage slavery!" (Sinclair, *Jungle*, p. 483).

London, who appears briefly along with Eugene V. Debs in *The Jungle*, although neither of them is named, goes on to say that the novel "will open countless ears that have been deaf to Socialism. . . . It will make thousands of converts to our cause" (p. 484).

London's remarks reflect what Sinclair intended to do with the novel: to expose the abuses that American industry heaped upon its workers, the "moral, spiritual, and physical degradation . . . in which humans lived barely above the level of animals" (Introduction, p. viii). The unsanitary conditions of meatpacking were not the author's primary concern. In his essay "What Life Means to Me" (1906), in what has become his most often quoted line, Sinclair says, "I aimed at the public's heart, and by accident I hit it in the stomach" (*The Jungle*, p. 594). The author was not displeased with his book's effect, but he wanted more and found it disheartening that the public was less concerned about the plight of the workers than it was about the possibility of eating tainted meat. He had failed to induce the socialist reform for which he had hoped.

There is little doubt that Sinclair's self-assessment is accurate. The novel is remembered largely for its graphic descriptions of rivers bubbling with pollutants, slaughterhouse floors flooded with blood, sick cattle being slaughtered, rat dung being canned with the meat, and, of course, workers falling into boiling vats and being cooked down with the lard. Many people, if they know the book at all, associate it with such details. Far fewer remember the saloonkeeper's serving the wedding party of Jurgis and Ona Rudkus with a half-empty keg of beer, opening a second, and then billing the newlyweds for two kegs after serving only half of the second. Others may have forgotten the Rudkus family's buying a repainted home thinking it is new and paying exorbitant hidden fees devised to drive them into insolvency so that the house can be repossessed, again repainted, and resold, all legally, with lawyers pretending to advocate for the immigrants while colluding with the realtors. Even if one were to remember the backroom political deals and corruption found in the novel, one might forget the small bribes paid to supervisors for jobs, and if one were to remember the brothel in the novel, one might forget Ona's rape by her boss.

That rape leads to Jurgis's imprisonment after he beats the rapist, resulting in his family's eviction from their home and subsequently in his sister-in-law's turning to prostitution to support them. The pregnancy caused by the rape leads to Ona's being butchered at the hands of a midwife more interested in money than in saving her patients. With this device Sinclair shows how a corrupt system affects virtuous people, and he anatomizes Chicago party politics, which further turn Jurgis from an honest workingman into a thug who robs at gunpoint and hustles to get out the vote for the machine's candidates. Sinclair thus depicts a corrupt system that corrupts the individual, thereby strengthening the system. This system, not the practices of meatpackers, was Sinclair's concern.

SOCIALISM IN *THE JUNGLE*

Sinclair provides a solution for his protagonist's problems, and that solution is socialism. At his nadir Jurgis happens across a meeting featuring a socialist orator, and what he experiences is akin to a religious conversion. His spiritual and emotional upheaval during the speech sparks his desire both to be helped and to help; he does not understand the complete implications of socialist ideology, but he instinctively realizes that he has found a solution to his problems and to those of others like him, a remedy that one of Sinclair's characters refers to as "the literal application of all the teachings of Christ" (*The Jungle*, p. 299). Sinclair does not present Jurgis's conversion as sudden and complete, however. He makes it plain that the "revolutionists were not angels." Rather, "there was only one difference between them and all the rest of the populace—that they were men with a hope, with a cause to fight for and suffer for" (p. 307). Here it should also be noted that the religious character of Jurgis's experience does not amount to an endorsement of institutional Christianity, which Sinclair distrusts.

LITERARY SIGNIFICANCE OF *THE JUNGLE*

The Jungle shows characteristics of several historical literary trends. Sinclair is often classed among the muckrakers. Ironically, it was Theodore Roosevelt who first applied this term to the socially activist writers of the early twentieth century, including Sinclair, using the term pejoratively. Sinclair can be thus grouped with writers such as Lincoln Steffens, Charles Edward Russell, David Graham Phillips, and Ida Tarbell. Given Roosevelt's application of this term to Sinclair, one might wonder if Roosevelt's concern over the Meat Trust might have been a way of downplaying the more radical political implications of *The Jungle,* which, as Michael Brewster Folsom points out, was the first novel to be described as "proletarian" (p. 503). Sinclair himself speaks of the novel in this regard, as did Jack London. In the *Chicago Socialist* broadside, London uses the words "proletarian" and "proletariat" eight times in a paragraph of seventy-five words (*The Jungle*, p. 484), and in "What Life Means to Me," Sinclair claims that *The Jungle*'s "publication marks the beginning of a proletarian literature in America," identifying the proletarian writer as "a writer with a purpose," not one who produces "art for art's sake" (pp. 351–352).

Sinclair's claim seems questionable when one considers the class consciousness and the effects of poverty treated in such earlier works as Rebecca Harding Davis's *Life in the Iron Mills* (1861) or Stephen Crane's *Maggie, A Girl of the Streets* (1893). Those works, however, differ from *The Jungle* by presenting only a problem, not a proletarian-based solution. Nevertheless the juxtaposition of Sinclair's work with Davis's and Crane's (and with London's as well) highlights the characteristics of *The Jungle* that show its relation to American naturalism, with its combination of romanticism, realism, and determinism. What Sinclair felt he was doing was trying "to put the content of Shelley into the form of Zola" and to do it in such a way that, unlike the realists he observed, his work was "written from the inside" (p. 352).

Many critics view the last four chapters of *The Jungle* as flawed, dating back to Winston Churchill, who praised the book but found its resolution unsatisfying, believing that it would take more than the hope of socialist revolution to bring comfort to Jurgis Rudkus. The last four chapters seem tacked on, moving away from the story of the novel's protagonist to a dramatized debate over socialist ideologies. Perhaps this is because, as Robert M. Crunden notes, "Sinclair planned to write a socialist tract in the form of a novel" (p. 451). Arguably the tract took over the novel, but the hopes expressed at the end of the 1906 edition for a Chicago with municipal ownership did not bear fruit. Perhaps this is why in his 1946 introduction Sinclair speaks with a much-tempered optimism, noting that the work of meat production has improved and, consequently, at least "that much comfort can be offered to present-day readers of *The Jungle*" (p. viii).

See also Appeal to Reason; Chicago; Health and Medicine; Immigration; Labor; *Maggie, A Girl of the Streets;* Muckrakers and Yellow Journalism; Naturalism; Reform; Socialism

BIBLIOGRAPHY
Primary Works
Sinclair, Upton. *The Jungle: An Authoritative Text, Contexts and Backgrounds, Criticism.* Edited by Clare Virginia Eby. New York: Norton, 2003. Quotations are taken from this edition (called Norton Critical Edition hereafter), which also includes much of the other material quoted in this essay.

Sinclair, Upton. Introduction to the *The Jungle.* New York: Viking, 1946.

Sinclair, Upton. "What Life Means to Me." *Cosmopolitan* 44 (October 1906): 591–595. Reprinted in Norton Critical Edition, pp. 348–353.

Secondary Works

Bloodworth, William A., Jr. *Upton Sinclair*. Boston: Twayne, 1977.

Crunden, Robert M. ["Muckraking, Progressivism, and the Pure Food and Drug Law"]. An excerpt from his *Ministers of Reform: The Progressives' Achievements in American Civilization 1889–1920*. New York: Basic Books, 1982. Reprinted in Norton Critical Edition, pp. 445–459.

DeGruson, Gene. Introduction to *The Lost First Edition of Upton Sinclair's "The Jungle."* Memphis, Tenn.: Peachtree, 1988.

Folsom, Michael Brewster. ["The Development of *The Jungle*"]. An excerpt from his "Upton Sinclair's Escape from *The Jungle:* The Narrative Strategy and Suppressed Conclusion of America's First Proletarian Novel." *Prospects* 4 (1979). Reprinted in Norton Critical Edition, pp. 503–512.

London, Jack. "What Jack London Says of *The Jungle*." *Chicago Socialist* 6, no. 351 (25 November 1905). Reprinted in Norton Critical Edition, pp. 483–484.

Mott, Frank Luther. *A History of American Magazines.* Vol. 4, *1885–1905.* Cambridge, Mass.: Harvard University Press, 1957.

Tim Sougstad

JURISPRUDENCE

Like every other American institution, legal theory and practice approached a gathering crisis in the late-nineteenth century. The crisis—the birth of "the modern"—was precipitated by a series of profound, interrelated transformations, both material and intellectual. The decades between 1870 and 1900 witnessed a sudden flowering of technological innovation; the "closing of the frontier" and the shrinking of the continent; the triumphant emergence of the modern industrial corporation and the concomitant creation of an increasingly well-defined laboring class; a dramatic expansion and fragmentation of the national population through immigration; and the growth of massive urban centers, densely packed with these immigrants and laborers and with emancipated slaves and their children and grandchildren. Jurisprudence negotiated this landscape of change in various ways but at first by appearing to move simultaneously in two contradictory directions.

CONSERVATIVE COURTS AND PROGRESSIVE LAWYERS

On the one hand, the courts themselves (and particularly the U.S. Supreme Court), emerging from the relative juridical confusion that followed the Civil War, tended toward detached traditionalism—as in, for example, *Plessy v. Ferguson* (1896), which established the durable racial doctrine of "separate but equal" through an assembly of arguments for states' rights, the separation of legal and social values, and the authority of "the established, usages, customs, and traditions of the people" (*Plessy v. Ferguson,* p. 550). "The argument [for racial integration] . . . assumes that social prejudices may be overcome by legislation," wrote Justice Henry Billings Brown (1836–1913) for the majority. "We cannot accept this proposition. If the two races are to meet on terms of social equality, it must be the result of natural affinities, a mutual appreciation of each other's merits, and a voluntary consent of individuals" (*Plessy v. Ferguson,* p. 551).

Increasingly, the courts reaffirmed an old idealistic view of law, appealing to the principles of absolute individual rights and their genesis in "natural law," English common law, and John Locke's political theory. Such conservative individualism could lead to rejections of states' rights arguments, as it did in the notorious case of *Lochner v. New York* (1905), which struck down state legislation limiting work hours that employers could demand of employees. Justice Rufus Wheeler Peckham (1838–1909), writing for the majority, framed the problem in purely Lockean terms as "a question of which of two powers or rights shall prevail, the power of the state to legislate or the right of the individual to liberty of person and freedom of contract" (*Lochner v. New York,* p. 57) and decided in favor of the individual. *Lochner* initiated a string of conservative Court decisions in the 1910s and 1920s in which the application of classical individual rights doctrines resulted, paradoxically, in the balance of justice tipping heavily in favor of business management and against individual employees. (An interesting exception, and one which suggests the extent to which the wounds of the Civil War still festered, is *Bailey v. Alabama* [1911], in which the Supreme Court invoked the Thirteenth Amendment, which outlawed slavery, to reject a state law allowing imprisonment for nonfulfillment of contract.)

On the other hand, and during just these years, a growing body of lawyers and law professors, sensing seismic cultural change around them and believing that a jurisprudence rooted in the seventeenth and eighteenth centuries would surely prove inadequate to the twentieth century, called for full-scale reform of the American legal system and its paradigms. The reform movement's first great spokesman was Roscoe Pound (1870–1964), the young dean of the University of Nebraska Law School. In 1906 Pound startled the American Bar Association (ABA) at its annual meeting by delivering the address "The Causes of Popular

Dissatisfaction with the Administration of Justice." His speech castigated his discipline for its deductive formalism, its cumbersome obsession with mechanical procedure, its old-fashioned individualism (out of step with the collective realities of modern society), and its lack of a productively flexible body of theory. Pound's ABA address started him on a path that led through increasingly prestigious professorial appointments to the deanship at Harvard Law School ten years later; it also introduced the great surge of legal thought that over the following thirty years self-consciously defined itself as "progressive" and later, more radically, as "realist," in sharp contradistinction to the orthodoxies that continued to dominate the post-*Lochner* Courts.

The pre–World War I legal reformers included Pound's Harvard colleague Felix Frankfurter (1882–1965), the Boston lawyer Louis Dembitz Brandeis (1856–1941), and the New York judge Benjamin N. Cardozo (1870–1938), all three of whom would become Supreme Court justices instrumental in the fading of Lochnerism and the enacting of Franklin Delano Roosevelt's New Deal. In different ways they shared and elaborated Pound's complaint: that law had become an empty shell of language and concepts, that it proceeded through mechanical deduction from unproven assumptions, and that it assumed for itself an impossible neutrality and a dubious separation from historical reality. Law had become a complex, self-serving religion. The legal realist Jerome Frank (1889–1957) later would summarize the assumptions of mainstream legal practice in his iconoclastic *Law and the Modern Mind* (1930), as a kind of Platonism:

> Law [in "the conventional view"] is a complete body of rules existing from time immemorial and unchangeable except to the limited extent that legislatures have changed the rules by enacted statutes. Legislatures are expressly empowered thus to change the law. But the judges are not to make or change the law but to apply it. The law, ready-made, pre-exists the judicial decisions. (P. 32)

In *The Transformation of American Law 1870–1960* (1992), the legal historian Morton J. Horwitz terms these assumptions "Classical Legal Thought" (p. 3). Against such sacred remoteness the reformers counterpoised their goal of an inductive jurisprudence, particularized, responsive to historical and material experience. In *The Nature of the Judicial Process* (1921), Cardozo put it in these words:

> Statutes are to be viewed, not in isolation or *in vacuo*, as pronouncements of abstract principles for the guidance of an ideal community, but in the setting and the framework of present-day conditions, as revealed by the labors of economists and stu-

dents of the social sciences in our own country and abroad. (P. 81)

Or, more memorably, "law never *is,* but is always about to be" (p. 126).

SOCIAL CRITICISM AND LITERATURE

Cardozo's fluid particularism had a legal and philosophical pedigree. It recalled Oliver Wendell Holmes's (1841–1935) famous liberal dissent in *Lochner*— "General propositions do not decide concrete cases" (*Lochner v. New York,* p. 76)—and the influential pragmatism of Holmes's contemporary William James (1842–1910), the Harvard philosopher and brother of the novelist Henry James; it also echoed a positivist tradition in British law leading back to John Austin (1790–1859) and Jeremy Bentham (1748–1832) in the early nineteenth century, which held that law existed in its operations and effects rather than in an ideal set of universal principles. Thus, progressive legal theory participated predictably enough in the general philosophical movement of Western thought toward a secular, scientific empiricism, a movement radically accelerated across the entire nineteenth century. But it also had to do, and perhaps mainly had to do, with a perception of broad social injustice—of, for instance, the paradoxical way in which *Lochner*'s reliance on an individualist logic had apparently led inevitably to the oppression of individual workers. (Unsurprisingly, one of Pound's next major articles after his 1906 address was a direct attack in 1909 on the delusive notion of a symmetrical "liberty of contract," and his career's great unfulfilled project was the full articulation of what he called a "sociological jurisprudence.") The spectacular and easily observed (in fact unavoidable) inequities of a new corporate America divided into haves and have-nots, owners and workers, underlay progressive law. These disparities also inspired the burgeoning American labor movements from 1877 forward, muckraking journalism, the explicit literature of social criticism written by the late-nineteenth-century and early-twentieth-century writers, and the new science of sociology (whose literal subject matter was provided in the academic research of scholars like George Herbert Mead and Charles Horton Cooley and in the more activist urban work of Jane Addams).

Literary history reads most well-known turn-of-the-twentieth-century American writers as naturalists who dramatized the lessons of materialist determinism, from Charles Darwin and Herbert Spencer to Karl Marx—the new scientism of the late nineteenth century. They thus produced mechanically fatalistic narratives whose protagonists are struck down by the very nature of things, the impersonal forces that drive the indifferent universe. Such a reading seems generally correct. But it is important to recognize that these writers, like the progressive legal thinkers, responded to immediate urban and economic situations: they wrote specifically about a landscape of businesses, labor, and immigrants, from Upton Sinclair's (1878–1968) graphic chamber of industrial horrors in *The Jungle* (1906) to Lily Bart's refined fall into the "unpolished and promiscuous" underworld of working women in Edith Wharton's *The House of Mirth* (1905). Similar forces played upon a host of other fictional characters from the era: Maggie's and Hurstwood's descents through the working world in Stephen Crane's *Maggie, A Girl of the Streets* (1893) and Theodore Dreiser's *Sister Carrie* (1900); Dreiser's portrait of Charles T. Yerkes in *The Financier* (1912); Jack London's underworld of the laboring classes in *The People of the Abyss* (1903); Frank Norris's depictions of working-class immigrants in *McTeague: A Story of San Francisco* (1899) or of the railroads' stranglehold on farmers in *The Octopus: A Story of California* (1901). All of these reflected quite exactly the concerns that occupied contemporary jurisprudence over how to achieve justice in a new, often brutal socioeconomic order.

American literature, like progressive jurisprudence, became "sociological" in these decades, embedding itself firmly, in Cardozo's words, in "the framework of present-day conditions." It not only took for its own the subject matter of progressive legal theory, but it did so with a similar repudiation of neutrality or detachment, manifesting an outraged energy that sometimes blurred the lines of literature, journalism, and political activism. Dreiser became a communist late in his life; London and Sinclair embraced their own brands of socialism and ran for public office. And in their works the turn-of-the-twentieth-century writers consistently echoed the central themes that energized the crisis of legal theory: the failure of abstract tradition to achieve or sustain justice and the destructive attractiveness of individualism and its singular inadequacy as a paradigm for life in a collectivist world.

MODERNIST SKEPTICISM AND LEGAL REALISM

It is conventional to see the self-conscious next generation of American writers, the high modernists of the late 1910s and 1920s, as radically different from their progressive predecessors and largely silent on the great social issues of their time. Apolitical, detached, antididactic, they concerned themselves more with formal precision than with the messy particulars of social experience. This construction of modernism bases itself on various famous aphoristic formulas that achieved the status more or less of household names, including James Joyce's injunction to artistic "silence, exile, and cunning" (p. 247), T. S. Eliot's understanding of art as a "continual extinction of personality" (p. 247), and Archibald MacLeish's "A poem should not mean / But be" (p. 107).

But a literary sea change occurring around World War I is perhaps more legend than historical truth, part of a general myth of an elite, austere "high culture" deliberately cultivated by a few writers, editors, and critics. In fact, despite their occasional pronouncements suggesting otherwise, writers of the 1920s hardly disconnected themselves from political experience, nor did reformist literature cease. Dreiser, for example, simply went on working out his chosen issues of Social Darwinism against the backdrop of modern economic realities, publishing *An American Tragedy* in 1925. Sinclair continued to expose the exploitation of the working class in *King Coal* (1917), *Oil!* (1927), and *Boston* (1928)—the last a historical novel about the trial of Nicola Sacco and Bartolomeo Vanzetti. Mainstream popular fiction also acknowledged repeatedly its particular socioeconomic context, as in Dorothy Canfield's *The Bent Twig* (1915), an occasionally Jamesian romance that manages nonetheless to glance significantly at racial injustice and whose love plot turns on a question of state versus private control of the Colorado mining industry.

Even the most committed formalists themselves, as modern scholarship increasingly demonstrates, wove social and political concerns inextricably into their work in different ways. F. Scott Fitzgerald (1896–1940) began and ended his career with works that looked explicitly at labor unrest: *This Side of Paradise* (1920) and *The Last Tycoon* (also published as *The Love of the Last Tycoon*), which was unfinished at his death in 1940. He also positioned the romantic artist of his 1920 story "May Day" against the background of the Red Scare. In his essay "Does *The Waste Land* Have a Politics?" (1999), Michael Levenson has persuasively paired Eliot's *The Waste Land* (1922) with John Maynard Keynes's *Economic Consequences of the Peace* (1919). Willa Cather in *The Professor's House* (1925) evoked exactly the issues of contract, labor, and ownership that informed progressive legal theory. William Faulkner's Quentin Compson (in *The Sound and the Fury,* 1929) is pursued by an angry, justice-seeking Italian immigrant across a Massachusetts suburban countryside made famous by Sacco and Vanzetti.

Nonetheless the major American high modernists did differ dramatically from their naturalist predecessors, both in meticulous attentiveness to form and in their bottomless ironizing, their cultivated postures of neutrality. In much of their work, observation of modern experience—"the immense panorama of futility and anarchy which is contemporary history," in Eliot's famous phrase in his 1923 *Dial* review of James Joyce's *Ulysses* (p. 483)—generates quiet gloominess rather than an impulse to action. One can perhaps best understand this passivity as arising from an anxiety over the final implications of an intellectual movement from idealist to realistic models for social organization or from a world organized around individual rights to a world organized around collective needs. The pragmatism behind progressive legal, social, and literary thought brought with it a threatened dissolution of post-Renaissance Western culture's core paradigm, the sovereign, voluntary individual: of voice itself, in fact.

Such an anxiety may have to do with modernism's well-known retreat into form, myths, and nostalgia. It certainly did have to do with Roscoe Pound's increasing conservatism in his post–World War I career at Harvard, where his early enthusiasm for administrative law (the administration of law by state agencies to serve public needs) gradually transformed itself into a reaffirmation of the unwritten English common law and a stubborn opposition to Franklin D. Roosevelt and his New Deal. But most jurisprudence in the 1920s continued to develop along the practical, neo-positivist lines set down by the progressive thinkers, and by 1930 something like the sociological jurisprudence that Pound had envisioned but never completed was being articulated as a coherent legal movement by a group of thinkers who became known as the legal realists. They were mainly based in the law schools at Columbia and Yale and included Karl Nickerson Llewellyn (1893–1962), Walter Wheeler Cook (1873–1943), William Underhill Moore

---

JUSTICE DENIED IN MASSACHUSETTS

Edna St. Vincent Millay (1892–1950), who joined the Boston protests before the Sacco and Vanzetti executions, wrote the contemporaneous poem "Justice Denied in Massachusetts" (1927). It deployed the recently familiar trope of the wasteland, suggesting an America abdicating its social responsibility.

Let us abandon then our gardens and go home
And sit in the sitting-room.
Shall the larkspur blossom or the corn grow under
   the cloud?
Sour to the fruitful seed
Is the cold earth under this cloud,
Fostering quack and weed, we have marched upon
   but cannot conquer;
We have bent the blades of our hoes against the
   stalks of them.

Let us go home, and sit in the sitting-room.
Not in our day
Shall the cloud go over and the sun rise as before,
Beneficent upon us
Out of the glittering bay,
And the warm winds be blown inward from the sea
Moving the blades of corn
With a peaceful sound.
Forlorn, forlorn,
Stands the blue hay-rack by the empty mow.
And the petals drop to the ground,

Leaving the tree unfruited.
The sun that warmed our stooping backs and
   withered the weed uprooted—
We shall not feel it again.
We shall die in darkness, and be buried in the rain.

What from the splendid dead
We have inherited—
Furrows sweet to the grain, and the weed subdued—
See now the slug and the mildew plunder.
Evil does not overwhelm
The larkspur and the corn;
We have seen them go under.

Let us sit here, sit still,
Here in the sitting-room until we die;
At the step of Death on the walk, rise and go;
Leaving to our children's children this beautiful
   doorway,
And this elm,
And a blighted earth to till
With a broken hoe.

Millay, "Justice Denied in Massachusetts," in *Collected Lyrics*, pp. 230–231.

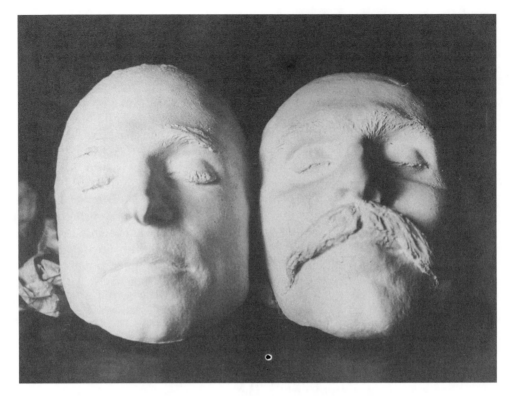

Death masks of Nicola Sacco (left) and Bartolomeo Vanzetti. Made after their execution in 1927. © BETTMANN/CORBIS

(1879–1949), William O. Douglas (1898–1980), and Herman Oliphant (1884–1939), among others. And by comparison with their predecessors they were radical skeptics, willing to let go of both legal absolutism and the autonomous subject.

The legal realists wholeheartedly embraced Holmes's particularist dissent in *Lochner,* "general propositions do not decide concrete cases," and made it the key tenet of a practical legal philosophy that located the major sources of legal decisions in facts, not in abstract principles: "no ideas but in things," as the poet William Carlos Williams (1883–1963) was to write in *Paterson* in the 1940s (p. 9). They mistrusted idealization. Jerome Frank (1889–1957), a New York attorney, produced one of the movement's most colorful early manifestoes, *Law and the Modern Mind,* using Freudian and Nietzschean terms to attack idealist jurisprudence as an expression of infantile dependency, an unacknowledged form of father worship: for law to result in justice, Frank announced, "there must be a twilight of the gods . . . law cannot function at its best if it must still also in some degree do the work of religion" (p. 199). Like the progressive legal thinkers of the century's first two decades, they insisted that lawyers needed to take cognizance of modern economics, sociology, and psychology but with a difference: for legal

realism, social science was not so much a tool for getting at justice or the legal truth as a way of thinking about law itself as a socially determined, historically fluid human activity. In short, the legal realists celebrated and theorized the quintessentially modernist epistemologies of uncertainty and indeterminacy that led many of their literary contemporaries into neoclassical formalism. Their work built flexible theoretical supports for the genuinely administrative and sociological law that articulated the New Deal, the great American triumph of collectivist thinking, in the late 1930s.

LEGAL THEATER AND THE WRITERS OF THE LEFT

Even as legal theory itself moved increasingly toward a complexly informed relativism in the twentieth century's first three decades, the American public's understanding of law grew more individualized, personalized, and simply theatrical, mainly because of increasingly efficient techniques of journalism that allowed the rapid national dissemination of news and images. Police cases and courtroom trials offered the reading public dramatic experiences like those of serialized fiction but with the additional attraction of unfolding daily—and of being "real," although such a reality, founded in the very fictive nature of law that jurisprudence sought to remedy, was paradoxical at best.

The principal performer on the legal theater's public stage was Clarence Darrow (1857–1938), the famous midwestern defense lawyer who began his career in Chicago in the 1890s representing labor organizers facing criminal prosecution. Darrow's particular skill—like that of Upton Sinclair and other reformers—lay in individualizing the oppressed, using sentimental oratory to galvanize public sympathy for the tragic figures of workers accused of striking back against injustice. An immensely attractive figure in his passionate identification with the causes that he represented, Darrow captivated journalists in the century's first decades in a series of sensational courtroom performances in the Midwest and West. But he is most remembered for two courtroom dramas of the mid-1920s far removed from issues of labor or even, to his critics, of justice: the Leopold and Loeb trial in Chicago, where he negotiated life sentences for two wealthy young men who killed a teenager in a self-aware gesture of Nietzschean will; and the celebrated Scopes "monkey trial" in Dayton, Tennessee, a showcase event for the emergent American Civil Liberties Union, in which Darrow faced the aging William Jennings Bryan over the teaching of evolution in public schools. Darrow's best legal theater (and both of these trials inspired plays and movies) turned out, unsurprisingly, to evoke the classical and timeless drama of the beleaguered individual, not the sociological analysis to which law's theory increasingly turned.

Yet the third sensational case of the 1920s, the seven-year Massachusetts murder trial of Italian immigrant anarchists Nicola Sacco and Bartolomeo Vanzetti, did in its final effects passionately revive for some writers the progressive rage for social justice. The case invoked for its audiences both the familiar plight of the powerless immigrant workingman and the court's apparent complicity, to the point of disregarding fundamental legal procedure, in carrying out the political wishes of a government enthralled by the Red Scare of 1919 and 1920. It deeply involved the Harvard legal community, leading Felix Frankfurter to an extraordinary public attack (in the *Atlantic Monthly*) in 1927 on Webster Thayer, the judge presiding over the original trial and its appeal. Frankfurter's outburst was not quite the old progressive complaint of traditional law's inadequacy to deal with collective, corporate society; it was rather that law had in the Sacco and Vanzetti trials become corrupted, an agent of the most oppressive kind of political power.

Sacco and Vanzetti became a rallying point for writers of the old Left, including Upton Sinclair and Emma Goldman. John Dos Passos (1896–1970), who had written about Sacco and Vanzetti for *New Masses* and the Sacco-Vanzetti Defense Committee (and who also took part in the pre-execution protests), wrote the trial and executions into the climax of *The Big Money* (1936), the final volume of his *U.S.A.* trilogy, as epitomizing a final division of American society between oppressors and oppressed:

> they have clubbed us off the streets they are stronger they are rich . . . their hired men sit on the judge's bench they sit back with their feet on the tables under the dome of the State House . . . they have built the electric chair and hired the executioner to throw the switch all right we are two nations. (Pp. 1156–1157)

His indictment of an entire society brutally ruled by a faceless "they," an invisible malignant alliance of business, the state, and the law, was a new kind of critique: paranoid sounding but also the product of an undistorted realism, a vision finally free of illusion. It foreshadowed the repudiation of public America that would mark protest literature through a generation of Beat writers and on into the late twentieth century, from Allen Ginsberg to Thomas Pynchon. The sustaining fiction of an orderly society founded in consistent, equitable legal principles had been stretched to the breaking point, and the deaths of Sacco and Vanzetti signaled its irreversible dissolution.

See also Capital Punishment; *The House of Mirth; The Jungle;* Law Enforcement; *Lochner v. New York; Maggie, A Girl of the Streets; McTeague; Plessy v. Ferguson;* Reform; *Sister Carrie; This Side of Paradise*

BIBLIOGRAPHY
Primary Works

Cardozo, Benjamin N. *The Nature of the Judicial Process.* New Haven, Conn.: Yale University Press, 1921.

Dos Passos, John. *The Big Money.* 1936. In *U.S.A.* 1938. New York: Library of America, 1996.

Eliot, T. S. "Memory, Order, and Myth." *The Dial* 75, no. 5 (November 1923): 480–483.

Eliot, T. S. "Tradition and the Individual Talent." 1919. In *Selected Essays of T. S. Eliot.* New York: Harcourt, Brace, and World, 1964.

Frank, Jerome. *Law and the Modern Mind.* New York: Tudor Publishing, 1935.

Frankfurter, Felix. "The Case of Sacco and Vanzetti." *Atlantic Monthly,* March 1927, pp. 409–432.

Joyce, James. *A Portrait of the Artist as a Young Man.* 1916. New York: Viking, 1964.

Lochner v. People of the State of New York, 198 U.S. 45 (1905).

MacLeish, Archibald. "Ars Poetica." In *Collected Poems, 1917–1982,* p. 107. Boston: Houghton Mifflin, 1985.

Millay, Edna St. Vincent. "Justice Denied in Massachusetts." In *Collected Lyrics,* pp. 230–231. New York: Harper & Brothers, 1943.

Plessy v. Ferguson, 163 U.S. 537 (1896).

Williams, William Carlos. *Paterson.* New York: New Directions, 1963.

Secondary Works

Fisher, William W., III, Morton J. Horwitz, and Thomas Reed, eds. *American Legal Realism.* New York: Oxford University Press, 1993.

Horwitz, Morton J. *The Transformation of American Law, 1870–1960: The Crisis of Legal Orthodoxy.* New York: Oxford University Press, 1992.

Hull, N. E. H. *Roscoe Pound and Karl Llewellyn: Searching for an American Jurisprudence.* Chicago: University of Chicago Press, 1997.

Leiter, Brian R. "American Legal Realism." In *The Blackwell Guide to Philosophy of Law and Legal Theory,* edited by W. Edmundson and M. Golding. Oxford: Blackwell, 2003. Social Science Research Network Electronic Library, http://ssrn.com/abstract=339562.

Levenson, Michael. "Does *The Waste Land* Have a Politics?" *Modernism/Modernity* 6, no. 3 (September 1999): 1–13.

Tierney, Kevin. *Darrow: A Biography.* New York: Crowell, 1979.

Wigdor, David. *Roscoe Pound: Philosopher of Law.* Westport, Conn.: Greenwood Press, 1974.

John N. Swift

KU KLUX KLAN

Ku Klux Klan (KKK) is the name given not so much to a specific organization as to a tradition of southern vigilantism that dates back to the time of African American slavery in the early to mid-nineteenth century, when "slave patrols" were used to guard against escape, uprising, and other sorts of misbehavior by slaves. The first organization to call itself "Ku Klux Klan" was founded in Pulaski, Tennessee, by six young Confederate veterans in 1866. The first two words of the name were derived from *kyklos,* the Greek word for "circle"—a designation appropriate to its mission, which revolved largely around differentiating those inside the circle (European Americans loyal to white supremacy) from those outside it. The founders regarded the Klan as a social club, a sort of fraternity, and adopted rituals, special outfits, a vow of secrecy, and an elaborate organizational structure to emphasize its exclusivity. Although the originators later claimed to have had no political intent in founding the Klan, it evolved over the course of the next year into a terrorist organization whose methods included lynchings and other tactics of intimidation.

THE KLAN AND RECONSTRUCTION

When the Civil War ended in 1865, it was immediately succeeded by a political war of comparable ferocity. The principal issues were the terms under which the rebel states would be readmitted to the Union and the status and rights of African Americans in those states. Abraham Lincoln (1809–1865), although he freed the slaves, was not a friend to the concept of African American equality, and his intention toward the southern states was to put the Civil War behind immediately and heal the Union as quickly and painlessly as possible. After Lincoln was assassinated, the new president, Andrew Johnson (1808–1875), took up Lincoln's moderate approach toward the South. However, the Radical Republicans in Congress, led by Charles Sumner of Massachusetts and Thaddeus Stevens of Pennsylvania, wanted to treat the South as a vanquished foe and immediately bring the former slaves into full citizenship with suffrage and political rights equal to those of their former masters. The Radical Republicans succeeded in passing the Civil Rights Act and the Fourteenth Amendment in 1866 (both over Johnson's opposition), giving citizenship rights with the exception of suffrage to African Americans. In 1867 they passed the Reconstruction Acts, which added suffrage for African Americans (later made permanent by the Fifteenth Amendment), disbanded the state militias of the defeated southern states, established federal military control of the governments of those states, and required approval of the Fourteenth Amendment by each state before it could be readmitted to the Union. Congress itself was divided over these measures, as reflected by the narrow defeat of the Radical Republican effort to remove Johnson from office by impeachment. Meanwhile, the Southern states were moving in the opposite direction, acting in 1865 and 1866 to establish "black codes" (based on the pre-emancipation slave codes), by which the rights of freed slaves were so radically limited as to return them to a condition not much different from slavery. The political struggle was waged largely along party lines, with Republicans advocating federal control over the Southern states and Democrats advocating "states' rights"—that is, the rights of the states to choose their own forms of government and determine their own laws.

One Vote Less. Engraving from *Harper's Weekly,* 8 August 1868, concerning the use of violence by the Ku Klux Klan and other groups to keep African Americans from voting.
© CORBIS

In this highly polarized environment it was not difficult for the Ku Klux Klan and similar groups, such as the Knights of the White Camellia in Louisiana, to attract disaffected southerners, especially former Confederate soldiers, interested in safeguarding the economic well-being and traditional values of southern society. The KKK expanded to become a statewide organization that achieved formal structure at a gathering in Nashville, Tennessee, in 1867. The former Confederate general Nathan Bedford Forrest (1821–1877) was named Grand Wizard, the top position in the Klan's hierarchy. Forrest, a vocal opponent of Republican policies toward the South, issued the "Prescript of the Order," specifying support for white control of state governments and denial of Negro equality.

By 1868 the KKK had spread to all the southern states. At first Klansmen were content to intimidate the black population by sweeping through the night in white robes, riding horses with muffled hooves, and pretending to be the ghosts of the Confederate dead returning to exact retribution. Soon, however, psychological intimidation gave way to whipping, beating, and even murder. The main targets were the former slaves, but many whites who sympathized with the Republican agenda were victims of Klan violence as well. Teachers, both black and white, at public schools established for African Americans by the Freedmen's Bureau (created by the federal government to aid the freed slaves) were among those frequently chosen for harassment.

The reign of the Klan was brief but effective. The main accomplishment was keeping African Americans from voting—an important factor enabling all the southern states within a few years to reject the Republican state governments imposed by Congress, install Democratic rule, and return the African American population to subjugation. Thus, the principal tenets of Forrest's "Prescript" were realized.

THE END OF THE KLAN
AND OF RECONSTRUCTION

The success of the Klan, however, also provided the seeds for its demise. The first great blow came from its own Grand Wizard. Declaring that he had never intended terrorist violence to be a part of the order's arsenal, Forrest in early 1869 ordered the KKK disbanded and instructed its officers to destroy all Klan regalia and Klan records. This was the end of the nineteenth-century Ku Klux Klan as a centralized organization operating throughout the South. However, many local Klan groups continued to operate independently and as violently as ever.

At about the same time, Ulysses S. Grant (1822–1885), a Republican sympathetic to Radical Reconstruction, succeeded Andrew Johnson as president. Urged on by Congress, Grant ordered an investigation of the KKK that resulted in a grand jury report which, calling the Klan the "Invisible Empire of the South," concluded:

> The operations of the Klan are executed in the night and are invariably directed against members of the Republican Party. The Klan is inflicting summary vengeance on the colored citizens by breaking into their houses at the dead of night, dragging them from their beds, torturing them in the most inhuman manner, and in many instances murdering. ("Radical Republicans")

In 1870 and 1871 Congress passed the Force Acts and the Ku Klux Klan Act, intended to curb the Klan's activities at all levels. These acts made it illegal to deprive anyone of his or her constitutional rights, including those provided by the recent amendments pertaining to freed slaves. The acts were to be enforced by the states, but if a state failed to enforce the laws, the president had the power to intervene. These federal actions successfully finished the destruction of the Klan that Forrest had begun; by the mid-1870s, when Reconstruction ended, the Klan was virtually nonexistent.

The problems of African Americans in the American South, however, were far from over. In the post-Reconstruction era their mistreatment simply became routine. Although the black codes were gone, they were replaced by Jim Crow laws that legally sanctioned racial segregation. As George Washington Cable (1844–1925) later said (in *The Negro Question*, published in 1890), "The ex-slave was not a free man; he was only a free Negro" (Trelease, p. xvi). The end of Reconstruction had occurred, curiously enough, with the election of another Republican president, Rutherford B. Hayes

(1822–1893), in 1876—an election whose outcome initially was inconclusive, hinging on disputed vote counts in three southern states. Hayes, in order to get the vote count he wanted, agreed to bring all Reconstruction activities to an end and let the southern states return to full sovereignty. The states gave Hayes the vote count that resulted in his election, and Reconstruction was over. In this climate the Ku Klux Klan was, in fact, no longer needed. Any intimidation perceived to be required could occur without interference from, and often with the active cooperation of, local and state governments. The federal government, and the North in general, apparently had lost interest in the fate of the freed slaves.

LITERARY REPRESENTATIONS
OF THE KU KLUX KLAN

Albion Tourgée's novel *A Fool's Errand*, published in 1879, recounts many Klan-related atrocities in the Reconstruction South. Tourgée (1838–1905) himself served as a federal judge in North Carolina from 1868 to 1874 and knew firsthand what it was like to experience Klan terror. In 1870 he wrote a letter to Senator Joseph Abbott (later published in the *New York Tribune*) complaining of Klan violence, including the lynching of fellow judge John Stephens. About his own situation he said: "I have very little doubt that I shall be one of the next victims. My steps have been dogged for months, and only a good opportunity has been wanting to secure to me the fate which Stephens has just met" (Tourgée, "Albion W. Tourgée"). Though *A Fool's Errand* gives primary attention to Klan crimes, it also shows sympathy for the plight of the South that provided a fertile ground for the growth of the Klan, and it criticizes the federal government's Reconstruction policy—both its omissions and its excesses.

Anger at the sort of violence perpetrated by the Klan and then institutionalized in the post-Reconstruction era led Mark Twain (1835–1910) in 1901 to write "The United States of Lyncherdom" (not published until 1923), which denounced the "moral cowardice" that prevented individuals from opposing mob violence. Twain also dealt with such violence in *Adventures of Huckleberry Finn* (1885), which includes several near-lynchings. Most notably, after Colonel Sherburn, an aristocratic resident of a small town in Arkansas, murders the town drunk (Boggs) in broad daylight in front of witnesses, a mob tries to lynch Sherburn, but he faces them down with a shotgun and a liberal dose of scorn. Sherburn's speech to the crowd refers sarcastically to Klan-style justice, though without actually mentioning the Klan (which would have been an anachronism because the novel is set in the 1840s):

The pitifulest thing out is a mob. . . . Now the thing for *you* to do, is to droop your tails and go home and crawl in a hole. If any real lynching's going to be done, it will be done in the dark, Southern fashion; and when they come they'll bring their masks. (P. 191)

The problem is that Sherburn's otherwise admirably heroic stand against mob violence is not really an attack on lynching per se. In fact, he portrays lynching, in view of the average person's cowardice, as perhaps the only viable instrument of justice: "Why don't your juries hang murderers? Because they're afraid the man's friends will shoot them in the back, in the dark—and that's just what they *would* do. So . . . then a *man* goes in the night, with a hundred masked cowards at his back, and lynches the rascal" (p. 190). In *Life on the Mississippi* (1883), Twain blames many of the South's nineteenth-century deficiencies on what he calls "the Sir Walter [Scott] disease" (p. 468)—a reliance on antiquated romantic notions "that made every gentleman in the South a Major or a Colonel, or a General or a Judge, before the war; and it was he, also, that made these gentlemen value these bogus decorations" (p. 469).

The sort of sentimentality and delusions of grandeur that Twain cites as being so harmful to the South are precisely the values promoted in novels by Thomas Nelson Page (1853–1922) and Thomas Dixon Jr. (1864–1946). The hallmark of the KKK as portrayed in Page's *Red Rock* (1898) is the preservation of purity: the purity of southern womanhood, the purity of the threatened idyllic southern lifestyle, the purity of the European American racial heritage. Dixon's much more influential *The Leopard's Spots: A Romance of the White Man's Burden, 1865–1900* (1902) and *The Clansman: An Historical Romance of the Ku Klux Klan* (1905) follow a similar trajectory but add a deep racial hatred to the mix. All three novels sold well, and their premises were for the most part not regarded as offensive. In an era in which social unrest had become a major concern for those in the North (where there were serious labor uprisings) as well as the South, an organization such as the Klan, whose mission was to stifle troublemakers and maintain an unruffled surface for society, could exert a romantic appeal.

Dixon believed that African Americans had been "idealized" and "worshipped" in accordance with their romanticized portrayal in Harriet Beecher Stowe's (1811–1896) *Uncle Tom's Cabin* (1851–1852) and that Americans had "heard only one side for forty years" (Railton). *The Leopard's Spots* straightforwardly presents itself as an antithetical rewriting of Stowe's novel. It represents blacks as subhuman, Radical Republicans as evil, and the Ku Klux Klan as heroic saviors of the wholesome traditional values of the South.

The Clansman is a heavily researched historical novel that again portrays the KKK as heroic and blacks as bestial—acceptable as domesticated animals but dangerous if allowed to roam free. The story centers on the rape of a young, white southern virgin by a black man, the girl's and her mother's suicides rather than live with their shame, and the heroic lynching of the perpetrator by the Klansmen. A subplot features Austin Stoneman, a character based on the Radical Republican senator Thaddeus Stevens. Stoneman sets the evil machinery of the Reconstruction in motion, but then, broken in health, moves to the South with his son and daughter. The daughter falls in love with a dashing ex-Confederate officer who becomes the Grand Dragon of the South Carolina KKK and, at the novel's dramatic conclusion, leads his Klan forces in rescuing Stoneman's son from an unjust execution.

THE INVISIBLE EMPIRE IN THE EARLY TWENTIETH CENTURY

The literary rehabilitation of the Ku Klux Klan was completed in 1915 when the moviemaker D. W. Griffith turned Dixon's *The Clansman* into a feature film titled *The Birth of a Nation*. The film was a cinematic masterpiece and was immensely popular. President Woodrow Wilson (1856–1924) was said to have commented after seeing the film: "It is like writing history with lightning. And my only regret is that it is all so terribly true" (Freund). Inspired by Griffith's film, William J. Simmons, a former Methodist clergyman living in Atlanta, revived the Klan tradition with a dramatic ceremony at Stone Mountain, Georgia, that included a cross burning—a ritual that had not been part of Klan ceremonies of the Reconstruction era. Simmons called his group the Knights of the Ku Klux Klan and declared himself Imperial Wizard. The new Klan grew rapidly and became a nationwide organization, though strongest in the South and the Midwest.

Simmons's Klan abstained for the most part from violence; however, it was a potent political force promoting an ultraconservative moral, religious, and social agenda. As in Page's and Dixon's novels, the emphasis was on purity—white Anglo-Saxon Protestant purity. It was opposed not only to African Americans but also to Jews, Roman Catholics, immigrants, and labor unions as well; it also supported Prohibition. At its peak in the 1920s, it had more than four million members, including about half a million members in the Women's Ku Klux Klan, and this translated into votes that were likely to be focused effectively on a narrow range of issues. The Klan successfully supported the election of sixteen U.S. senators in the 1920s, of whom five were actually members of the KKK—including Hugo Black, who later became a Supreme Court justice. President

Warren Harding also joined the Klan. The Klan gained almost total political control over the state of Indiana, but that control dissolved when Indiana's Klan boss David Stephenson was convicted of second-degree murder. When Ed Jackson, Stephenson's handpicked governor, refused to pardon him, Stephenson took revenge by releasing incriminating information showing the deep corruption of the Klan organization. These events, coming in 1925 at the height of Klan power, led to a rapid deflation of its image as defender of purity, and despite a momentary revival in 1928 to oppose the presidential candidacy of Al Smith, a Roman Catholic, membership plummeted.

In 1925 F. Scott Fitzgerald (1896–1940) published *The Great Gatsby,* in which Tom Buchanan, a rich but thoroughly boorish character, says that he has been reading a book titled *The Rise of the Colored Empires:* "The idea is if we don't look out the white race will be—will be utterly submerged. . . . It's up to us, who are the dominant race, to watch out or these other races will have control of things" (p. 17). Though Fitzgerald's treatment is satirical, Tom is articulating a concern shared by millions of his contemporaries, as exhibited by the huge, if short-lived, success of the Knights of the Ku Klux Klan.

The early twentieth century also showed a growing reaction to Klan-style violence among African American writers. Sutton Griggs's *Imperium in Imperio* (1899) chronicles a fictional attempt to establish an insurrectionist black government; characters debate what would later be called the "black power" response to racial violence and injustice (with the specific warning that a black man "beset by the Ku Klux" [p. 182] would get no help from the federal government) versus the accommodationist/integrationist approach. Charles Chesnutt's *The Marrow of Tradition* (1901), based on an actual incident of large-scale racial violence in Wilmington, North Carolina, attacks the pervasive injustice of Jim Crow laws and strongly invokes the memory of Klan violence. W. E. B. Du Bois's *The Souls of Black Folk* (1903) includes a story titled "The Coming of John," in which the title character, a promising young black man in a southern town, kills a white man who is in the act of raping a young black woman, and the story ends with the lynch mob closing in. Anti-lynching plays also constitute a notable subgenre among African American authors of the early twentieth century, especially African American women—for example, Angelina Grimké's *Rachel* (1916), Georgia Douglas Johnson's *A Sunday Morning in the South* (1925), and May Miller's *Nails and Thorns* (1933). Each of these plays is built around the lynching of a black man on the basis of a false accusation that he has raped a white woman, and each is designed to appeal to the maternal instincts of white women who might imagine such things happening to their own innocent sons. Langston Hughes's "Father and Son," published in *The Ways of White Folks* (1933), concludes with the lynching of two black men, one of whom is known by the lynchers to be innocent, and several of the stories in Richard Wright's *Uncle Tom's Children* (1938) depict incidents of Klanlike violence.

THE KLAN AND THE CIVIL RIGHTS MOVEMENT

The Klan declined through the 1930s, and in 1944 the national organization was effectively destroyed when the Internal Revenue Service hit it with a $650,000 lien for back taxes. Yet the Klan rose again when the civil rights movement began to gain momentum. This new Klan actually consisted of several separate organizations. Most notable were Robert Shelton's United Klans of America, based in Alabama, and Sam Bowers's White Knights of the Ku Klux Klan of Mississippi. Like the Reconstruction Klan, these new groups inflicted considerable violence on blacks and those supporting their right to racial equality, but unlike the Reconstruction Klan, the Klans of the 1960s were unable to halt the social forces they deplored. The federal government, under the strong leadership of President Lyndon Johnson (1908–1973), used the provisions of the Ku Klux Klan Act of 1871 to prosecute racial crimes when state courts failed to do so. Bowers received a life sentence for the murders of civil rights activists. Shelton's organization was ruined financially when the mother of a black victim of a Klan murder successfully sued the United Klans, with the help of the activist Southern Poverty Law Center, as a conspirator in the violation of her son's civil rights. Various Klan organizations have continued to exist in diminished form and, though clinging to some of the old traditions, have begun to merge with or evolve into the paramilitary and neo-Nazi organizations that have taken up the banner of white supremacy.

See also The Birth of a Nation; Blacks; Jim Crow; Lynching; *The Marrow of Tradition;* Reconstruction; Violence

BIBLIOGRAPHY
Primary Works

Cable, George Washington. *The Negro Question: A Selection of Writings on Civil Rights in the South.* 1890. Edited by Arlin Turner. Garden City, N.Y.: Doubleday, 1958.

Chesnutt, Charles W. *The Marrow of Tradition.* 1901. New York: Arno, 1969.

Dixon, Thomas, Jr. *The Clansman: An Historical Romance of the Ku Klux Klan.* 1905. Lexington: University Press of Kentucky, 1970.

Dixon, Thomas, Jr. *The Leopard's Spots: A Romance of the White Man's Burden, 1865–1900*. 1902. Gretna, La.: Pelican, 2001.

Du Bois, W. E. B. *Black Reconstruction in America, 1860–1880*. 1935. New York: Atheneum, 1992.

Fitzgerald, F. Scott. *The Great Gatsby*. 1925. New York: Scribners, 1995.

Griggs, Sutton. *Imperium in Imperio: A Study of the Negro Race Problem*. 1899. New York: Arno, 1969.

Railton, Stephen. "Dixon's *Leopard's Spots*." Stephen Railton and the University of Virginia, 2004. http://www.iath.virginia.edu/utc/proslav/dixonhp.html.

Tourgée, Albion Winegar. "Albion W. Tourgée, Letter on Ku Klux Klan Activities (1870)." *America Past and Present*. Available at http://occawlonline.pearsoned.com/bookbind/pubbooks/divine5e/medialib/timeline/docs/sources/theme_primarysources_Civil_Rights_5.html.

Tourgée, Albion Winegar. *A Fool's Errand: A Novel of the South during Reconstruction*. 1879. New York: HarperCollins, 1979.

Tourgée, Albion Winegar. *The Invisible Empire*. 1880. Baton Rouge: Louisiana State University Press, 2001.

Twain, Mark. *Adventures of Huckleberry Finn*. 1885. New York: Oxford University Press, 1996.

Twain, Mark. *Life on the Mississippi*. 1883. New York: Oxford University Press, 1996.

Secondary Works

Chalmers, David M. *Hooded Americanism: The History of the Ku Klux Klan*. New York: New Viewpoints, 1976.

Freund, Charles Paul. "Dixiecrats Triumphant: The Menacing Mr. Wilson." *Reasonline*, 18 December 2002. http://reason.com/links/links121802.shtml.

Horn, Stanley F. *Invisible Empire: The Story of the Ku Klux Klan, 1866–1871*. 2nd ed. Montclair, N.J.: Patterson Smith, 1969.

Katz, William Loren. *The Invisible Empire: The Ku Klux Klan Impact on History*. Seattle: Open Hand, 1986.

"Radical Republicans." *Teaching History Online*. 15 March 2005. http://www.spartacus.schoolnet.co.uk/USASradical.htm.

Randel, William Peirce. *The Ku Klux Klan: A Century of Infamy*. Philadelphia: Chilton, 1965.

Stampp, Kenneth M. *The Era of Reconstruction, 1865–1877*. New York: Knopf, 1965.

Trelease, Allen W. *White Terror: The Ku Klux Klan Conspiracy and Southern Reconstruction*. New York: Harper and Row, 1971.

Wade, Wyn Craig. *The Fiery Cross: The Ku Klux Klan in America*. New York: Oxford University Press, 1998.

James S. Leonard

LABOR

Between the Civil War and World War I, the United States experienced great economic changes, ultimately emerging as an industrial power. The Gilded Age and Progressive Era saw business giants achieving unparalleled wealth, while in the cities, factories, farms, and mines, Americans' worst nightmares of poverty and degradation became reality. The tumultuous and often bloody relationship between the business magnates and a burgeoning labor movement continually shocked and fascinated the American public. On the streets, in the pulpit, and in a variety of literary forms, Americans debated the rights of the worker and the social responsibilities of business, government, and the church. In short, as Alan Trachtenberg writes, these debates "took the appearance of struggles over the meaning of the term 'America'" (p. 73).

CAPITAL AND LABOR

With the mobilization of the Civil War, the United States began its shift from a small-scale agricultural and manufacturing economy to one dominated by massive industrial corporations. The emergence of the railroads played an important role in this transformation. In 1869 the first transcontinental railroad was completed. Over the next decades railroads helped increase the settlement of the West, providing transportation for settlers and the goods they produced and consumed. The rail boom also fueled the steel, iron, and coal industries. Meanwhile gold and silver mines proliferated, particularly in the West.

These large-scale industries required unprecedented amounts of capital. Corporations, used primarily in the antebellum era for financing large state-associated projects such as bridges and banks, became the major vehicles for private investment, soon emerging as a dominant force in the economic and social landscape. Although the corporation is by definition a conglomeration of people invested in a common enterprise, the great corporations the Gilded Age came to be identified with powerful individuals such as J. P. Morgan (banking), Andrew Carnegie (steel), Jay Gould (rail), and John D. Rockefeller (oil and coal). These men were known as the "robber barons," men whose notoriously ruthless competition led to virtual monopolies in their respective industries. Rockefeller (1839–1937) pioneered corporate consolidation, or "vertical integration." His Standard Oil Company took control of every step of production, transportation, and marketing, even making and selling the products that used his oil. Control of the rails enabled Rockefeller to ship his own oil at a discounted rate, and his efficient marketing system allowed him to cut prices so low that his competitors were forced to capitulate. Another corporate development was the "company town," a settlement populated by workers at the local factory, which owned all of the town's housing and businesses. By controlling wages, rents, and the price of goods, owners could keep their workers in perpetual debt to the company. Sometimes industrialists, instead of competing with each other, set up pools and trusts, sharing monopolies and cornering markets. Although the robber barons were reviled by their competitors and employees, they were

"THE MAN WITH THE HOE"

Edwin Markham's (1852–1940) famous poem "The Man with the Hoe" (1899) was inspired by Jean-François Millet's painting The Man with a Hoe, *which depicts an exhausted laborer leaning on his hoe in an empty field.*

Bowed by the weight of centuries he leans
Upon his hoe and gazes on the ground,
The emptiness of ages in his face,
And on his back the burden of the world.
Who made him dead to rapture and despair,
A thing that grieves not and that never hopes,
Stolid and stunned, a brother to the ox?
Who loosened and let down this brutal jaw?
Whose was the hand that slanted back this brow?
Whose breath blew out the light within this brain?
Is this the Thing the Lord God made and gave
To have dominion over sea and land;
To trace the stars and search the heavens for power;
To feel the passion of Eternity?
Is this the Dream He dreamed who shaped the suns
And marked their ways upon the ancient deep?
Down all the stretch of Hell to its last gulf
There is no shape more terrible than this—
More tongued with censure of the world's blind
     greed—
More filled with signs and portents for the soul—
More frought with menace to the universe.

What gulfs between him and the seraphim!
Slave of the wheel of labor, what to him
Are Plato and the swing of Pleiades?

What the long reaches of the peaks of song,
The rift of dawn, the reddening of the rose?
Through this dread shape the suffering ages look;
Time's tragedy is in that aching stoop;
Through this dread shape humanity betrayed,
Plundered, profaned and disinherited,
Cries protest to the Judges of the World,
A protest that is also prophecy.

O masters, lords and rulers in all lands,
Is this the handiwork you give to God,
This monstrous thing distorted and soul-quenched?
How will you ever straighten up this shape;
Touch it again with immortality;
Give back the upward looking and the light;
Rebuild in it the music and the dream;
Make right the immemorial infamies,
Perfidious wrongs, immedicable woes?

O masters, lords and rulers in all lands,
How will the future reckon with this Man?
How answer his brute question in that hour
When whirlwinds of rebellion shake the world?
How will it be with kingdoms and with kings—
With those who shaped him to the thing he is—
When this dumb Terror shall reply to God,
After the silence of the centuries?

The Little Book of Modern Verse, edited by Jessie B. Rittenhouse (Boston: Houghton Mifflin, 1913), pp. 116–118.

also admired by much of the American public for their business acuity, rugged individualism, and philanthropy.

With the emergence of industry came a shift in the composition of the labor force. Ten million immigrants came to the United States between 1873 and 1897. Before 1880 northern and western Europe provided the bulk of immigrants; however, after 1880 many more came from southern and eastern European countries. The Chinese Exclusion Act (1882) notwithstanding, Chinese immigration accounted for the majority of migrant farm laborers in the 1880s and 1890s. Although many immigrants came to America intending to return to Europe, most stayed, and while many immigrants were able to move up the economic ladder, many more remained in unskilled jobs.

Wage laborers often faced long hours and dangerous working conditions. The railroad industry was particularly hazardous, with two hundred on-the-job fatalities recorded yearly between 1890 and 1910. Workers were often subject to wage cuts, which were frequently used to finance ruinous price wars. Overproduction led to numerous recessions and depressions. In addition to creating massive unemployment, these economic downturns enhanced the consolidation of large industries, driving out the weaker companies and strengthening the positions of the robber barons.

EARLY LABOR ORGANIZATION

Early efforts to organize workers faced challenges from business and government as well as from class conflict and ethnic tensions among the laborers themselves. For years corporations enjoyed the support of government against the demands of labor, partially due to the notorious corruption of Gilded Age politics but mostly because of a dominant laissez-faire (hands off) philosophy of political economy. Grounded in Adam Smith's free market ideology and supported by Herbert Spencer's theory of Social Darwinism, the government and public believed that in business competition the fittest would survive, creating wealth and prosperity for the deserving and progress for the human race. Within this theoretical framework, a series of laws and court decisions entitled corporations to the same protections as citizens under the Constitution, authorized corporations to create their own police forces, and banned not only strikes but also union organization. Corporations also exploited the ethnic tensions among workers, particularly during the "new immigration." Poles, Slavs, and Italians as well as African Americans were often excluded from unions and denied access to the skilled trades. When workers went on strike, the company owners hired blacks and immigrants as strikebreakers, or "scabs," in their place. The presence of scabs, often protected by armed detectives, frequently led to violence. Jay Gould (1836–1892) once bragged, "I can hire one half of the working class to kill the other half" (Murolo and Chitty, p. 111).

The first attempt at organizing skilled and unskilled workers in a national union was the National Labor Union (NLU), formed in 1866. Cooperating with the Colored National Labor Union (founded 1869), the NLU agitated for working-class solidarity (despite its exclusion of women and the Chinese) and the eight-hour day. Although neither the NLU nor the CNLU survived the depression of 1873, local organization continued, and the 1870s saw strikes and demonstrations occurring with growing frequency. In January 1874, twenty-five thousand workers and unemployed demonstrated in New York City's Tompkins Square, resulting in a riot when mounted police attempted to disperse the protesters. A secret society known as the Molly Maguires was implicated in a variety of terrorist acts in the Pennsylvania mines, ranging from sabotage to assassination. In 1877 a series of rail strikes across the nation became known as the "Great Uprising." Beginning with a strike against the Baltimore and Ohio Railroad to protest wage cuts, the strike spread across the country. As militias were called in to quell the uprising, riots flared up in Baltimore, Pittsburgh, Chicago, and St. Louis. Ultimately the National Guard and federal troops intervened; by the end of the uprising, the death toll exceeded one hundred. Newspaper accounts of the strikes and riots sparked fears of anarchy, evoking the French Commune of 1871.

In the wake of the Great Uprising of 1877, a secret organization called the Noble and Holy Order of the Knights of Labor went public. The Knights of Labor (KOL) was founded as a garment workers union, but by the time of its emergence from secrecy, the organization included a variety of trades. After its initial leader, Uriah Stephens, stepped down, the machinist and mayor of Scranton Terence Powderly (1849–1924, mayor 1878–1884) took the reins. The KOL became the most powerful labor organization of the Gilded Age, claiming 750,000 members in 1886. Known for being the most inclusive U.S. labor organization of the nineteenth century, the KOL admitted women, immigrants, and blacks. Its political message was against monopoly and the entire wage-labor system, advocating instead the "cooperative commonwealth." Organizing producer and consumer cooperatives as well as social and educational programs, the KOL supported hundreds of strikes and sympathy strikes, its greatest victory coming against Jay Gould's southwestern rail lines in 1885.

Events in 1886 and 1887 dramatically reversed the fortunes of the KOL. After Gould, with the support of lawmen, crushed a February 1886 strike, the KOL organized a national strike for the eight-hour day. Beginning on 1 May, about 350,000 workers struck, including 65,000 in Chicago. On 3 May, Chicago police fired on workers picketing outside the McCormick Harvester Works, killing four. Chicago anarchists called for a protest at Haymarket Square for the following night. As the demonstration was winding down, police arrived to disperse the crowd; at that point, someone (it was never determined who) threw a bomb into their ranks, killing eight and wounding sixty more. The fallout from the Haymarket affair was devastating to the labor movement. Chicago activists were rounded up in massive sweeps. Eight anarchists were ultimately arrested and convicted of conspiracy to commit murder, although only two of the defendants were actually present when the explosion occurred. More so than the Great Uprising of 1877, the Haymarket episode polarized the nation. Newspapers and magazines followed the trial and subsequent execution of four of the defendants. Social activists and trade unionists denounced the proceedings and appealed for clemency, while many others denounced the labor movement. Powderly attempted to distance the KOL from the Haymarket Eight and tried to quell militancy in the organization as a whole. This led to a series of conflicts with local unions, as a series of unauthorized strikes created rifts between the national organization and individual chapters. Powderly was ousted in 1893, and by 1896 the KOL's membership had dwindled to twenty thousand.

LABOR AND CAPITAL RECONFIGURED

After the Haymarket affair, a new national labor organization supplanted the KOL, the American Federation of Labor (AFL). Led by the cigar maker Samuel Gompers (1850–1924), the AFL took a markedly different approach from the KOL, called "pure and simple craft unionism." Instead of fighting the wage-labor system, the AFL focused on tangible rewards for its members, such as shortened hours or higher pay in specific industries. Rather than attempting to be all-inclusive, the AFL was mostly made up of highly skilled workers, who had a stronger position in the workplace and tended to be white and male. By 1892 forty national unions were affiliated with the AFL, including the United Mine Workers and the United Garment Workers. In its first four years the AFL staged over seventy-five hundred strikes and utilized sympathy strikes effectively, winning the eight-hour day for the Brotherhood of Carpenters with a national strike on 1 May 1890. But a crushing defeat of the Amalgamated Association of Iron and Steel Workers, an AFL affiliate, not only showed the limitations of the AFL but also added a dark chapter to the nation's history.

When the contract between Amalgamated employees at Carnegie's steel mill in Homestead, Pennsylvania, expired in 1892, the mill manager, Henry Frick, announced that the new union contract, to go into effect that July, would cut union wages by an average of 22 percent. The Amalgamated rejected the new contract, and on 30 June, Frick locked out the union members and replaced them with scabs. The unskilled workers at Homestead and the local government rallied to the union's defense, and when armed guards from the Pinkerton Detective Agency arrived to escort the strikebreakers, fierce fighting erupted. A daylong battle on 6 July repulsed the Pinkertons, leaving three Pinkertons and seven workers dead. On 12 July the eight thousand members of the Pennsylvania militia arrived to protect the mill and the strikebreakers, and the mill reopened. By November the union was broken.

On the same day that the Pennsylvania militia intervened in Homestead, federal troops moved on Couer d'Alene, Idaho, where striking mine workers had clashed with armed scabs. In the initial battle both strikers and scabs suffered casualties, and a crusher mill was destroyed. Although this episode was overshadowed by the Homestead strike, it further served to disconcert both labor activists and the American public.

A deep depression beginning in spring 1893 provided the background for one of the more innovative labor protests, Coxey's Army. Since 1892, the Ohio businessman Jacob Coxey (1854–1951) had been lobbying Congress for a federal highway program, which would provide work for the unemployed as well as improve the nation's infrastructure. Forming a group called the Commonweal of Christ, Coxey and the itinerant lecturer Carl Browne drafted a petition supporting the project and organized a mass march of the unemployed on Washington, D.C., to deliver the petition personally. In spring 1894 news of the march reached the national press, and recruits began to gather across the country, as far west as California and Washington State. Coxey and Browne left Coxey's Ohio home with two hundred marchers on Easter Sunday and reached Washington, D.C., in five weeks. The march was a media event, with a press corps traveling alongside the marchers. Meanwhile the western contingents had a series of run-ins with the railroad and militias; some were arrested and returned home. A young Jack London traveled for a short time with a group that had originated in San Francisco. On 1 May, International Labor Day, Coxey's Army paraded through the streets of Washington, D.C., but his army clashed with police and the leaders. As the western contingents arrived, the Coxeyites moved to camps in Maryland and Virginia. Soon money and food ran out, and media attention shifted elsewhere. Congress ignored Coxey's proposal, and the camps were raided and dispersed in August by state militias.

THE PROGRESSIVE ERA

At the turn of the century the labor movement suffered both from failed strikes and new corporate strategies. A particularly violent strike by American Railway Union members at the Pullman Palace Car Company left twenty-five civilians dead and its leaders in jail. Meanwhile American industrial productivity was bolstered by a new management philosophy known as Taylorism, or "scientific management." Frederick Taylor (1856–1915), an engineer and manager at the Midvale Steel Works, analyzed his workers' tasks, timing each motion and determining the most efficient way to complete each task. Breaking down long, complicated tasks into shorter repetitive ones that unskilled workers could perform, Taylor standardized plant operations. He began publishing the results of his Midvale experiments in 1895; soon Taylorism was widely popular among employers. Taylorism's appeal lay in its effects on both plant efficiency and unions. Not only could companies replace craftsmen with lesser-paid unskilled workers, but skilled workers also lost a valuable bargaining chip—their intimate technical knowledge of their jobs—to managers and engineers. The decreased status of the skilled worker made strikes and unions harder to sustain. Meanwhile corporations organized against labor. In 1903 the National Association of Manufacturers launched the open shop drive, compiling blacklists of labor activists and distributing antiunion literature.

These setbacks created dissent in the labor movement. The Socialist Party, led by the former American Railway Union leader Eugene Debs (1855–1926), advocated a more militant and expansive approach than the AFL's "pure and simple craft unionism." The Socialists ran political campaigns in an effort to redesign the social order, and although many members of the AFL were Socialists, Gompers discouraged their activities. In 1905 a number of Socialists broke off from the AFL and formed the Industrial Workers of the World (IWW). The IWW (whose members were known as "Wobblies") reached out to the unskilled workers who were excluded by the AFL. Of the major labor organizations, the IWW was best known for prolific songwriting. The Chicago poet Carl Sandburg, whose verse celebrated the workingman, was an IWW cardholder.

The IWW gained national attention with a victory in Lawrence, Massachusetts. When the owners of the American Woolen Company cut wages, mill workers went on strike, attacking the scabs and sabotaging the factory. The AFL textile union, representing a minority of the workers, attempted to suppress the strike, so the strikers turned to the IWW. The organization helped strikers defy injunctions against picketing by creating moving picket lines and arranged for the children of strikers to be sent to safe havens in New York and Philadelphia. When police attacked mothers who were putting children on outbound trains, public opinion was indignant. Congress investigated the mills, and the strike ultimately succeeded.

Women played significant roles in several strikes in the years preceding World War I. In 1909 female workers in New York City's garment industry led a successful strike. The following year, the Chicago garment worker Hannah Shapiro led a strike against Hart, Schaffner, and Marx which spread across the city, ultimately encompassing over forty thousand workers. Mary "Mother" Jones (1830–1930) lectured and raised funds for labor activity over the course of decades. She supported Coxey's Army in the 1890s and was present at one of the bloodiest battles of the labor struggle, in Ludlow, Colorado.

Striking miners had left Rockefeller's Colorado Fuel and Iron works in September 1913 and set up a tent colony. Months of small confrontations between the strikers, the scab workers, and the state militia

Margaret Hinchley (right), head of the Laundry Workers Union of New York, marches with supporters in a Labor Day parade, 1914. © CORBIS

ensued. The standoff exploded on 20 April 1914, when the militia burned down the tent colony, killing three workers, eleven children, and two women. Armed unionists descended on Ludlow, and by the time federal troops had restored order, sixty-six miners or their family members had been killed. Although the strikers were defeated, shortly thereafter Congress passed the Clayton Act, which formally legalized unions and barred injunctions against peaceful strikes.

As the United States entered World War I the labor movement seemed to be making progress. Although the IWW refused to support the war, Samuel Gompers committed the AFL and its member unions to the war effort. Not only did the war give the AFL the opportunity to demonstrate labor's patriotism to a skeptical public, the shortage of labor and the industrial needs placed labor in an advantageous bargaining position. More strikes occurred during the war than in any two-year period before, but they were often resolved quickly and to the strikers' advantage.

After the war the situation soured very quickly for the labor movement. Antiwar groups such as the Socialist Party and IWW had already suffered repression as the government sought to root out disloyalty, particularly among recent immigrants. The fall of Russia to the communists brought a red scare to the United States, and soon the IWW was crushed. Returning veterans increased the labor pool while industrial output slowed, and the working classes divided along racial lines. In 1919 race riots flared in St. Louis and Chicago, and the Ku Klux Klan flourished in both North and South. Also that year, a general strike in Seattle and a strike by the Boston police not only failed but also aroused public opposition to unionism in general. In the 1920s government legislation and widespread racketeering further weakened unions; not until the Great Depression would the labor movement regain national significance.

LABOR IN THE LITERATURE OF THE GILDED AGE

In much of the literature and rhetoric of the Gilded Age, a republican ideology predominated, hailing the virtues of work and the importance of labor to the moral foundation of America and its citizens. Writers of success literature such as Horatio Alger (1832–1899) promoted honest labor as necessary for material and moral self-improvement. Union leaders echoed Alger's sentiments, grounding their appeals for fair treatment in rhetoric championing the dignity of labor and laborers. Furthermore, argued the KOL in its Declaration of Principles, by offering workers "sufficient leisure in which to develop their intellectual, moral,

and social faculties" (Sorge, p. 253), a shortened workday would help create a stronger citizenry.

As strikes became more prevalent, writers disagreed on the cause of labor discontent. Alger often expressed sympathy for laborers attempting to organize. Many, however, saw the labor movement as the product of criminals and con men. Such is the case in John Hay's (1838–1905) *The Bread-Winners* (1883), set in a fictional Lake Erie city during the Great Uprising. The "Bread-Winners" are a fictional labor organization headed by the "professional reformer" Andrew Jackson Offitt. Offitt corrupts the slow-witted carpenter Sam Sleeny, convincing him to join the Bread-Winners by getting him drunk and stoking his jealousy over a girl. During the strikes, Sam, Offitt, and the Bread-Winners attempt to loot the mansions of Algonquin Avenue, in particular that of Captain Farnham, Sam's supposed rival for Maud Matchin. Captain Farnham and his militia of Civil War comrades are portrayed as heroic, defending not only Farnham's home but that of the beautiful Alice Belding and her widowed mother. More important than the bravery of Farnham's militia is the contrast between Farnham's gentility and the Bread-Winners' crudeness. As Sam meets the brotherhood for the first time, he recognizes "the laziest and most incapable workmen in town—men whose weekly wages were habitually docked for drunkenness, late hours, and botchy work" (p. 118). Offitt's character is exposed after he frames Sam for robbery and assault and tries to run away with Maud himself. After being acquitted of Offitt's murder by a verdict of "justifiable homicide," Sam returns to his old position, marrying Maud. Thus *The Bread-Winners* restores Sam to an understanding of his proper station, affirming the social order and relegating labor discontent to the grumbling of the shiftless and manipulative con men. Yet Hay's description of life after the strike is ominous. "The rich and prosperous people," he writes, "gave no thought to the questions which had come so near to an issue of fire and blood" (p. 229). Instead they "kept on making money, building fine houses, and bringing up children to hate politics as they did, in fine to fatten themselves as sheep which should be mutton whenever the butcher was ready" (p. 229).

UTOPIAN RESPONSES

Increased strikes and riots throughout the 1880s, culminating in the Haymarket bombing, seemed to confirm Hay's sense of foreboding. In the wake of Haymarket, however, several influential writers took a more sympathetic view of the labor movement. Edward Bellamy, William Dean Howells, and Albion Tourgée penned utopian novels, imagining a variety of solutions to the labor crisis.

Edward Bellamy (1850–1898), a former newspaper editor with a lifelong passion for reform, set the standard for American utopian fiction with *Looking Backward* (1888). The novel was arguably the most influential American book in the last decades of the nineteenth century, sparking "Bellamy clubs" dedicated to social reform across the nation. The novel imagines America in the year 2000, when the state has taken control of the economy. Julian West, who has fallen asleep in 1887, awakens in the future, where he receives a tour and detailed description of the utopia. By taking over all industry and making employees of its citizens, the United States has applied "the principle of military service . . . to the labor question" (p. 58). In the Industrial Army, "service of the nation, patriotism, [and] passion for humanity" impel "the workers as in [the nineteenth century] they did the soldier" (p. 79). Meanwhile competition has been eliminated, not only in the domestic marketplace but also among nations, making for a peaceful and prosperous world.

Bellamy appeals to the power of science to create the perfect society. West's guide marvels that Americans of Bellamy's time could "fail to compare the scientific manner in which the nation went to war with the unscientific manner in which it went to work" (p. 212). In Bellamy's utopia the state determines the levels of production and is responsible for assigning workers the jobs for which they are best suited. While *Looking Backward* inspired the social scientists of the Progressive Era, Bellamy's rigidly structured utopia also eerily anticipates the "scientific management" developed by Frederick Taylor to promote the interests of business.

One devoted fan of *Looking Backward* was William Dean Howells (1837–1920). Already a famous author and editor by the mid-1880s, Howells had encountered harsh criticism by publicly protesting the Haymarket trial. In his 1890 novel *A Hazard of New Fortunes,* debates about the labor problem occupy major portions and precipitate the central crisis of the story, when the socialist agitator Berthold Lindau insults the owner of the periodical that employs the main characters. Engaging both Lindau and the capitalist Dryfoos are former Confederate Colonel Woodburn, who advocates a return to slavery, and Dryfoos's son Conrad, a would-be minister with labor sympathies. The arguments are mediated by Basil March, the editor of *Every Other Week,* who struggles with the labor question throughout the novel.

Critics generally agree that March functions as a stand-in for Howells, though there is debate about the extent to which the author identifies with Lindau. Some critics have argued that by presenting Lindau's arguments in German dialect, Howells marks him as a for-

eigner and his doctrines as un-American. Yet Howells markedly updates Hays's depiction of labor activists. Lindau may be a boor, but he is no crude con man. Rather, he is a Union army veteran who lost an arm in the war, translates European literature for the periodical, and moves out of his Greenwich Village apartment because he found he "was begoming a lidtle too moch of an aristograt" (pp. 164–165). March's social consciousness is shaped not only by Lindau but also by his own labor experiences. The offer of a "promotion" at his insurance firm to a position with a lower salary encourages March to take the editor's job of *Every Other Week,* where he must face the decision either to fire Lindau or be fired himself. Although these experiences do not lead March to adopt Lindau's radicalism, they demonstrate that even the middle class is subject to the dictates of the labor market.

The characters Conrad Dryfoos and Margaret Vance introduce Howells's interest in Christian socialism. This movement attempted to revise a predominant version of Christianity that linked poverty and vice, considering wealth a sign of God's election. Christian socialists drew on the image of Jesus as the friend of the poor and cited the communal lifestyle of the apostles to argue that Christ was a proto-socialist. In 1890 the novelist Albion Tourgée (1838–1905) published *Murvale Eastman, Christian Socialist,* in which Reverend Eastman risks losing his congregation and his love by preaching this new doctrine. According to Eastman, the function of the church "is to be, not the controller, but the mainspring of civilization; to see to it that in government, in business, in society, the underlying impulse is that which is enjoined for the regulation of human life, 'Bear ye another's burdens'" (p. 272). In *Hazard,* Conrad and Margaret, two members of the upper class, minister to the poor and sympathize with the railway workers who strike at the end of the novel. Conrad functions in the novel as a Christ figure; his death during the strike serves as the catalyst for his father's redemption.

The rail strike provides the most intense action of the novel. Like Hay, Howells uses the strike both as a metaphor for the class war and as a warning about the national failure to address the labor issue. However, the policeman who fatally beats Lindau does not represent order and chivalry like Captain Farnham but "irresponsible and involuntary authority" (p. 368). Ultimately Howells's solution to the labor crisis lies not in revolutionary violence but in the literary project *Every Other Week,* where the contributors share in the magazine's profits.

RAKING THE MUCK

At the turn of the century a new breed of writers developed and refined a journalistic tradition that exposed the horrors of industrial labor. Police reporter Jacob Riis (1849–1914) toured the tenements of New York, gathering the material for a series of articles that resulted in the 1890 best-seller *How the Other Half Lives*. While Riis's primary interest is the deplorable housing conditions in New York's slums, the book also details the conditions of the Ludlow Street sweatshops and describes the lives of Bohemian cigar makers working seventeen hours a day for $15.50 per week. In the 1890s *McClure's Magazine* specialized in this type of investigative journalism, later called "muckraking," providing pieces such as Stephen Crane's (1871–1900) "In the Depths of a Coal Mine" (August 1894). Crane's vivid descriptions elicit sympathy for the laborers, which include children "yet at the spanking period" (p. 157). The article seeks to spark outrage at the mine, "imperturbably cruel and insatiate, black emblem of greed," as well as at "the gods of this labor" (p. 163).

Realistic treatments of factory work, strikes, and unemployment form integral sections of *Sister Carrie* (1900) by Theodore Dreiser (1871–1945). Carrie Meeber's experiences at the Chicago shoe factory are pure drudgery. "Not the slightest provision had been made for the comfort of the employees," writes Dreiser, "the idea being that something was gained by giving them as little and making the work as hard and unremunerative as possible" (p. 41). Although Carrie is able to escape this sort of labor for a life on the New York stage, her onetime lover Hurstwood demonstrates the coldness of the capitalist system to the less fortunate. Once his bar goes out of business, Hurstwood joins the ranks of the unemployed. Desperate, he works as a scab during a trolley strike. Dreiser is sympathetic not only to the strikers but also to the strikebreakers and the police whose job it is to protect them. The policeman guarding the trolley offices is torn between his sympathy for the strikers and his duty. Even the scabs understand the strikers' plight, but they have no other options. Workers in *Sister Carrie* are tossed out because of illness and layoffs, and no job is safe. The capitalist marketplace pits the working classes against one another, making good on Gould's boast.

The apotheosis of the "muckraking" trend was *The Jungle* (1906) by Upton Sinclair (1878–1968). Sinclair, on assignment from the socialist journal *Appeal to Reason*, spent seven weeks investigating the meatpacking plants of Chicago. *The Jungle*, the story of the immigrant Jurgis Rudkus's journey from the Old World to the Chicago stockyards, exposes the meat industry as corrupt and degrading. Sinclair details the hazardous working conditions that lead to injury and death, and the harsh treatment of the managers, who cast out old and injured workers, blacklist union members, and continually demand increased production.

What Sinclair's audience found most appalling, however, was not the conditions of the worker but the unsanitary treatment of the meat. Descriptions of spoiled meat being masked with chemicals and rats being turned into sausage elicited such an uproar that Congress passed the Pure Food and Drug Act and the Meat Inspection Act within months of the book's publication. This response was somewhat disheartening to Sinclair, who saw the meat industry as emblematic of the abuses of capitalism and had hoped to convert his audience to socialism.

By the First World War many literary artists were firmly on the side of the worker against the "gods of labor." While their critiques of capitalism gained the public's attention, sympathy, and occasional indignation, the labor movement did not win the approval of the majority of Americans, nor did it enlist a majority of workers as members. The literature of labor did, however, force America to examine its values and the extent to which the nation was enabling opportunity for all.

See also Anarchism; Business and Industry Novels; City Dwellers; Haymarket Square; *A Hazard of New Fortunes; The Jungle; McClure's Magazine;* Muckrakers and Yellow Journalism; Poverty; Reform; *Sister Carrie;* Socialism; Utopias and Dystopias

BIBLIOGRAPHY
Primary Works

Bellamy, Edward. *Looking Backward*. 1888. Foreword by Erich Fromm. New York: Signet Classic, 1960.

"Carl Sandburg." In *The Norton Anthology of Modern Poetry*, 2nd ed., edited by Richard Ellmann and Robert O'Clair, pp. 268–270. New York: Norton, 1988.

Crane, Stephen. "In the Depths of a Coal Mine." 1894. In *The American 1890s: A Cultural Reader*, edited by Susan Harris Smith and Melanie Dawson, pp. 156–163. Durham, N.C.: Duke University Press, 2000.

Dreiser, Theodore. *Sister Carrie*. 1900. Afterword by Willard Thorp. New York: Signet Classic, 1980.

Hay, John. *The Bread-Winners*. 1883. Edited by Charles Vandersee. New Haven, Conn.: College and University Press, 1973.

Howells, William Dean. *A Hazard of New Fortunes*. 1890. Afterword by Benjamin DeMott. New York: Meridian, 1994.

Riis, Jacob. *How the Other Half Lives*. 1890. Edited by David Leviatin. Boston: Bedford/St. Martin's, 1996.

Sinclair, Upton. *The Jungle*. 1906. Afterword by Emory Elliot. New York: Signet Classic, 1990.

Tourgée, Albion. *Murvale Eastman, Christian Socialist*. New York: Fords, Howard, and Hulbert, 1890.

Secondary Works

Babson, Steve. *The Unfinished Struggle: Turning Points in American Labor, 1877–Present.* Lanham, Md.: Rowman and Littlefield, 1999.

Dulles, Foster Rhea. *Labor in America: A History.* Northbrook, Ill.: AHM Publishing, 1960.

Kenny, Kevin. *Making Sense of the Molly Maguires.* New York: Oxford University Press, 1998.

Le Blanc, Paul. *A Short History of the U.S. Working Class: From Colonial Times to the Twenty-first Century.* Amherst, N.Y.: Humanity Books, 1999.

Michaels, Walter Benn. *The Gold Standard and the Logic of Naturalism: American Literature at the Turn of the Century.* Berkeley: University of California Press, 1987.

Murolo, Priscilla, and A. B. Chitty. *From the Folks Who Brought You the Weekend: A Short, Illustrated History of Labor in the United States.* Illustrations by Joe Sacco. New York: New Press, 2001.

Parrish, Timothy L. "Haymarket and *Hazard:* The Lonely Politics of William Dean Howells." *Journal of American Culture* 17, no. 4 (1994): 23–32.

Phelan, Craig. *Grand Master Workman: Terence Powderly and the Knights of Labor.* Westport, Conn.: Greenwood, 2000.

Rennick, Andrew. "'A Good War Story': The Civil War, Substitution, and the Labor Crisis in Howells' A Hazard of New Fortunes." *American Literary Realism* 35, no. 3 (2003): 247–261.

Scharnhorst, Gary. *Horatio Alger, Jr.* Boston: Twayne, 1980.

Schwantes, Carlos A. *Coxey's Army: An American Odyssey.* Lincoln: University of Nebraska Press, 1985.

Sorge, Friedrich A. *Friedrich A. Sorge's Labor Movement in the United States.* Edited by Philip S. Foner and Brewster Chamberlin. Westport, Conn.: Greenwood, 1977.

Trachtenberg, Alan. *The Incorporation of America: Culture and Society in the Gilded Age.* New York: Hill and Wang, 1982.

Andrew Rennick

THE LAND OF LITTLE RAIN

Mary Austin (1868–1934) could not have hoped for a better literary market when *The Land of Little Rain,* her first book, appeared in 1903. Half of the ten best-sellers in that year—novels by Frank Norris, Thomas Nelson Page, Thomas Dixon Jr., John Fox Jr., and Owen Wister—emphasized regional settings ranging from Virginia and Kentucky to Wyoming. At a time when the West, the South, and the Midwest still appeared to retain a provincial distinctiveness, East Coast American readers craved both fictional and non-fictional glimpses of the people and customs of these regions. Such local color interest informs the fourteen sketches that make up *The Land of Little Rain,* which features the diverse people, animals, and plants found in a stretch of California terrain located between the Sierra Nevada and the Mojave Desert.

The successful reception of Austin's book was also influenced by various apprehensions defining the opening years of the Progressive Era, a period defined in part by industrial corruption, destabilizing economic speculation, and an anarchist's assassination of President William McKinley in 1901 at the Pan-American Exposition. Nature too was markedly under assault, its resources ruthlessly exploited by corporate giants antagonistic to both governmental regulation and labor unionization. The conditions of overcrowded urban laborers, generally poorly housed and underpaid despite long work hours, starkly contrasted with the unspoiled nature celebrated by President Theodore Roosevelt when he established national parks as conservational preserves. As a result *The Land of Little Rain* appealed because it, like precedent books by the naturalists John Burroughs and John Muir, also celebrated a wild environment apparently on the verge of vanishing in a country increasingly defined by technology and urbanization.

Several of the sketches included in this collection had previously appeared in the *Atlantic Monthly,* whose editor, Bliss Perry, expedited Houghton, Mifflin's publication of Austin's volume as an illustrated gift book. The book sold well, its reviewers finding more to praise than to fault. The reviewer for *The Dial* was typical in speaking positively, if not especially enthusiastically, about Austin's representation of the desert: "Because she knows and loves it she can reproduce its atmosphere of romance, of silence, and of strangeness" (1 December 1903, pp. 421–422).

AUSTIN'S DISCONTENT WITH THE BOOK
Although Austin acknowledged that her collection required more than a year of planning, she was never particularly satisfied with it, at one point even indicating to a friend that its excellent sales conflicted with her own opinion of the book. Authors often come to view their early works with such reservations, but there were good reasons for Austin to be dissatisfied with *The Land of Little Rain.* The collection had been assembled primarily to earn money, and while the sketches included in the volume all relate to a single geographic region, they read as discrete units lacking a more pleasing principle of integration.

Austin's discontent with her first book may also have been fostered by an intuitive recognition of personal feelings subtly registered below the surface of

Title page of the first edition of *The Land of Little Rain,* 1903. COURTESY OF WILLIAM J. SCHEICK

her volume. She was an unhappy person before and during the composition of *The Land of Little Rain.* A lonely childhood, awkward social interactions, a seemingly unpromising career, chronic illnesses, a mentally challenged daughter, a failing marriage, and a sense of herself as unloved and unlovable all doubtlessly contributed to the book's emotional undercurrents. Austin, who at one point in her sketches specifically mentions her "poor body," tellingly identifies with the desert terrain as a "lonely land" with "little in it to love"—an "unhappy" place of "lost rivers," "thirsty soil," "demoniac yuccas," "tormented, thin forests," and the "dolorous [coyote] whine that comes from no determinate point" (pp. 5–6, 10–11, 13, 29, 106).

A third and even more likely source for Austin's discontent with her book is its failure to convey adequately a sense of the "mystical," a sense highlighted in her autobiographical *Earth Horizon* (1932). Missing, in short, is a style capable of representing the reverential awe occasionally inspired in her by the strange beauty of the desert. In this arid region Austin witnessed the "long and imperturbable . . . purposes of God" and detected a "presence and intention," an "eternal meaning" that "trick[s] the [customary] sense of time" (pp. 16, 186, 246, 262). She had explicitly hoped to give a literary impression of the "lotus charm" of the desert's stark minimalism so that her readers' normal apprehension of the familiar would be supplanted by a new understanding of a spiritual dimension behind temporal experiences (p. 16).

Austin's prose rarely approaches such a lofty goal. The style of the book, which Austin frankly admitted had hardly concerned her during its composition, lacks rhetorical coherence, tonal consistency, and syntactic grace. It often rapidly transitions from flatly rendered factual description and enumeration to self-conscious expression inflated by romantic sentiment. Frequently her sentences are pointlessly rife with absent transitions, obscured referents, shifts in point of view, confusing circumlocutions, and jarring ellipses. The book opens awkwardly: "East away from the Sierras, south from Panamint and Amargosa, east and south many an uncounted mile, is the Country of Lost Borders" (p. 3). There are, however, later moments of crystalline phrasing: "No tree takes the snow stress with such ease as the silver fir. The star-whorled, fan-spread branches droop under the soft wreaths—droop and press flatly to the trunk" (p. 256).

THE PROBLEM OF SELF-AWARENESS

Besides her hampering emotional disposition and limitations as a writer in 1903, Austin's time-freighted self-consciousness burdens her aspirations in *The Land of Little Rain*. While the desert may hint at transcendent otherness, it also indifferently insists on "purposes not revealed" to the very observer who glimpses some mystery there (p. 184). Austin may sense something divine communicated through the desert landscape, but any such "imperturbable . . . purpose" also taxes her whenever this "land that supports no man" makes her see herself as merely a time-bound witness "of no account" (pp. 3, 21, 186). In contrast to such lotus-eaters as old desert miners oblivious to temporal realities, Austin remains all too despondently aware of time as she self-consciously celebrates nature's divinity.

To become, in Ralph Waldo Emerson's image from *Nature* (1836), a "transparent eyeball" with "the currents of the Universal Being circulat[ing] through" her, Austin would have had to merge with "the splendor of the apocalypse," as she put it (p. 248).

To yield to "the lotus charm" of the desert she would have to go "mad in time"—that is, forsake everything "but beauty and madness and death and God" (pp. 16, 69, 184). Such a state would require the total loss of her individual selfhood. This is not possible, however, because in order to appreciate the sublime otherness of nature, the perceiver must possess a temporal consciousness—the very time-bound identity that necessarily estranges the onlooker from the apocalyptic eternal. It is precisely through a sense of estrangement, as Austin's contemporary Amy Lowell often poetically observed, that one can value the beautiful otherness of nature. To some extent Austin acknowledges this unmitigated perceptual distance from the divine in nature when she refers to herself as "a mere recorder" "of no account" (pp. 21, 112). She, in other words, is not a forgetful lotus-eater blissfully at one with timeless beauty but remains instead an uncomfortably self-aware stranger in a strange land.

If certain old miners appear to have less of this sensibility of estrangement, Native Americans strike Austin as even more ideally unselfconscious in their relationship to nature's sublimity. Unwittingly participating in the early-twentieth-century romanticizing of the American Indian, Austin claims that Native Americans possess "a sort of instinct atrophied by disuse in a complexer civilization" (p. 234). The women in particular seem to enjoy the very Emersonian transparency that Austin (the reflexively theorizing and disfranchised observer) cannot experience: "Every Indian woman is an artist,—sees, feels, creates, but does not philosophize about her processes," Austin claims (p. 168–169). These women achieve an enviable "satisfaction of desire" (p. 171).

Even this imagined ideal does not finally escape the contrary impulse of Austin's self-consciousness. One comment in particular challenges such an idealization of Native American women and hints at Austin's own dilemma of unfulfilled desire: "Seyavi had somehow squeezed out of her daily round a spiritual ichor that kept the skill in her knotted fingers long after the accustomed time, but that also failed" (p. 176). This observation is intended to express an admiration of the union of universal spirit and Seyavi's basket art, in contrast to Austin's literary art registering an outsider's self-conscious separation from the divine. Yet Austin's appreciation here is compromised by her own unsatisfied desire. The qualifying word "somehow" recalls Austin's earlier point about "purposes not revealed" and hints as well at a frustration with her own occluded perception (p. 184). Likewise, the words "squeezed" and "knotted fingers" suggest Seyavi's painful rather than effortless labor—an impression less applicable to Seyavi's putative "satisfaction of desire" in her art than to Austin's own unfulfilled straining to translate the transcendent within her sketches (pp. 171, 176). And peculiar indeed is Austin's terse comment that the union of the eternal and Seyavi's artistry "failed" with the passage of time, an observation related to another passage about "strange pictures and symbols" by "an older, forgotten people" that now have "no meaning to the Indians of the present day" (p. 43). Such moments challenge Austin's privileging of Native American kinship with the eternal. It is as if time does not merely occlude higher vision (divinity) in the temporal world but possibly amounts to something far more real and intransigent.

Time's work, in fact, punctuates Austin's sketches with countless memento mori. The "ghastly sink" of the desert everywhere offers signs of the indifferent "elemental violence" of nature, including "the saw-tooth effect" of majestic mountains with "long shark-finned ridges" (pp. 8, 108–109, 186). The land of little rain is a place where the "squalid tragedy" of "the struggle of existence" easily ends badly, "takes its toll of death" (pp. 8, 49). It is a place where rabbits, for example, "appear to have no reason for existence but to furnish meals for meat-eaters" (p. 34). There, for all to see more clearly than something transcendent, are "sun-dried mummies" and "shallow graves" (p. 18). Awareness of such intimations of the decomposing work of time is symptomatic of Austin's time-bound self-awareness resisting her mystical aspirations in *The Land of Little Rain*.

ANNEXING THE LANDSCAPE

The effects of time are also evident in what might be described as Austin's acts of rhetorical annexation, acts contrary to her express literary goals. In the preface she announces her intention to avoid using official geographic names because they "originate in the poor human desire for perpetuity" (p. viii), as if such nomenclature amounted to territorial claims on a land that should not be reduced to mere human memorials or real estate. But later in the preface she speaks of her own manner of identification, which sometimes relies on Native American designations, as designed to "keep faith with the land and annex to my own state a very great territory" (p. ix). Austin perhaps means to echo "I am the monarch of all I *survey*," Henry David Thoreau's nuanced play on land ownership in *Walden* (1854). But her own time-bound metaphor of spiritual annexation of the desert implicitly highlights her inescapable estrangement from nature. The unfortunate metaphor of annexation recalls another, more obvious lapse when Austin writes of a special tract of land: "I should have no peace until I had bought ground and built me a house beside it" (p. 126). Austin's metaphor of annexation accidentally links her artistic effort to convey nature's

"eternal meaning" to the materialistic attitude of those who value landscape primarily as real estate defined by enclosing fences and names for the purpose of proprietary exploitation (p. 262).

Throughout *The Land of Little Rain*, Austin rhetorically tries to annex a landscape that always resists her desire for spiritual closure with its divine properties. Whenever she autobiographically projects her emotional disposition on the desert or anthropomorphizes its wildlife, she in effect subjectively appropriates the desert for her own emotional needs. In doing so she unwittingly enacts a version of land proprietorship that she explicitly deplores. Such language hardly indicates mystical transcendence in the desert; it instead subtly replicates the temporal "human occupancy of greed" that leads to the sort of "disfigurement" or "mark on the field" that banishes the wild (pp. 60, 128). Austin's effort to render the sublime through a rhetoric of personal appropriation effectively repeats the pattern of those who "are obsessed with [their] own importance in the scheme of things" (p. 281).

Mystical experiences, such as the rare episodes Austin knew as a child, are not encountered at will. They are, as Augustine indicates in *Confessions*, unexpected confiscations of the self. The authorial self in *The Land of Little Rain*, in contrast, remains a lonely observer, a mere recorder whose self-consciousness cannot escape a frustrating awareness of time. This narrative insistence on time's toll presses against Austin's transcendental goal and influences the textual decomposition of her book—its lack of a pleasing coherence in arrangement, style, and tone. Such memento mori narrative features are symptomatic of a time-bound self-awareness that disfranchises Austin from the divine in the desert even as, paradoxically, it enables her to treasure nature precisely because there she feels like a stranger in a strange land.

See also Ethnology; Frontier; Indians; Nature Writing

BIBLIOGRAPHY

Primary Work

Austin, Mary. *The Land of Little Rain*. Boston: Houghton Mifflin, 1903.

Secondary Works

Fink, Augusta. *I-Mary: A Biography of Mary Austin*. Tucson: University of Arizona Press, 1983.

Hoyer, Mark T. "'To Bring the World into Divine Focus': Syncretic Prophecy in *The Land of Little Rain*." *Western American Literature* 31, no. 1 (1996): 3–31.

Langlois, Karen S. "Mary Austin and Houghton Mifflin Company: A Case Study in the Marketing of a

Western Writer." *Western American Literature* 23, no. 1 (May 1988): 31–42.

Lape, Noreen G. "'There Was a Part for Her in the Indian Life': Mary Austin, Regionalism, and the Problems of Appropriation." In *Breaking Boundaries: New Perspectives on Women's Regional Writing*, edited by Sherrie A. Inness and Diana Royer, pp. 124–139. Iowa City: University of Iowa Press, 1997.

O'Grady, John P. *Pilgrims to the Wild: Everett Ruess, Henry David Thoreau, John Muir, Clarence King, Mary Austin.* Salt Lake City: University of Utah Press, 1993.

Pearce, T. M. *Mary Hunter Austin.* New York: Twayne, 1965.

Stineman, Esther Lanigan. *Mary Austin: Song of a Maverick.* New Haven, Conn.: Yale University Press, 1989.

Stout, Janis P. *Through the Window, out the Door: Women's Narratives of Departure, from Austin and Cather to Tyler, Morrison, and Didion.* Tuscaloosa: University of Alabama Press, 1998.

Young, Vernon. "Mary Austin and the Earth Performance." *Southwest Review* 35 (1959): 153–163.

William J. Scheick

LAW ENFORCEMENT

The beginning of the twentieth century saw dramatic changes to police departments, forensic techniques, and American society's relationship to law enforcement. Rapid industrialization and urbanization caused city police forces to develop from untrained, informal citizen patrols to professional, uniform, authoritative organizations. Until the 1890s the hiring of police officers was often a form of political patronage. For the most part, police mediated neighborhood disputes instead of solving serious crimes. For example, the police officer who appears in *A Modern Instance* (1882) by William Dean Howells (1837–1920) merely helps a drunken Bartley home. The officer is treated as a subordinate and not as a respected authority figure. Often, citizens criticized the police for being either inefficient annoyances or brutal, corrupt henchmen for politicians and businesspeople.

Improved technology and professionalism changed the role of the police. Officers began actively investigating and solving major crimes once they could coordinate their actions by telephone (first used by police in 1878), travel by car (1899), and fingerprint suspects (1902). Formalized criminological education and law enforcement training encouraged higher personnel standards and a new ethic of professionalism. Mark Twain (a pseudonym for Samuel Langhorne Clemens, 1835–1910) illustrates contemporary criminological advances and public sentiment for the authorities in *Pudd'nhead Wilson* (1894; also published under the title *The Tragedy of Pudd'nhead Wilson*). The townspeople ridicule Pudd'nhead, a lawyer and amateur criminologist, for his logical analyses and his interest in fingerprinting. When Judge Driscoll is robbed and murdered, Pudd'nhead's initial eyewitness testimony condemns the wrong man. Realizing his mistake, Pudd'nhead uses deductive reasoning and fingerprinting to solve the crime correctly, telling the jury: "Compare the finger-prints of the accused with the finger-prints left by the assassin—and report" (p. 111). Twain published the novel a mere two years after Sir Francis Galton (1822–1911) invented a system of using fingerprints to classify people and improve law enforcement worldwide.

URBAN POLICE FORCES

By the end of the nineteenth century, urban police forces were successfully solving major crimes, but many citizens criticized them for almost exclusively serving the interests of powerful politicians and businesspeople. The main literary genres of this era, realism and naturalism, include many works that dramatize people's concerns about unchecked corporate crime and ineffective or socially biased police enforcement. Frank Norris (1870–1902), William Dean Howells, Paul Laurence Dunbar (1872–1906), Theodore Dreiser (1871–1945), Upton Sinclair (1878–1968), and Stephen Crane (1871–1900) all present urban society as corrupting, hostile, divisive, and destructive—a force that is aided by police who enforce the law unfairly and who toady to greedy and self-serving power brokers.

In these novels, the police are, at best, ineffective. For example, a San Francisco policeman in Frank Norris's *The Octopus: A Story of California* (1901) is kind to an orphaned, homeless child, but he could not save its mother's home or life from the illegal practices of businesspeople. Also, in Theodore Dreiser's *Sister Carrie* (1900), Hurstwood runs from Chicago to Canada and later New York City after stealing a large sum of money from his employer, but official police enforcers worry him less than his own conscience and the private Pinkerton detectives his employers may send after him. The realist and naturalist authors also depict the police as corrupt. For example, in Howells's *The Rise of Silas Lapham* (1885), the police are bribed and coerced to overlook illegal business activities. In Howells's *A Hazard of New Fortunes* (1889), the oppressed working class is further limited by the police, who protect "this oligarchy of traders and tricksters, this aristocracy of railroads wreckers and stock gamblers and mine-slave drivers and mill-serf owners" (p. 193).

In some realistic and naturalistic novels the police target labor protesters, the poor, immigrants, and blacks at the same time that they are ignoring the illegal behavior of the rich and powerful. In *A Hazard of New Fortunes,* the elite trick their way to riches, while the police arrest and shoot workers during a legal strike. Howells, like other contemporary social reformers, considered the police an extension of the corrupt power structure; he writes in *A Hazard of New Fortunes* that the policeman was "as much a mere instrument as his club was" (p. 430). In Dreiser's *Sister Carrie* and Upton Sinclair's *The Jungle* (1906), the New York and Chicago police arrest and attack strikers because, as Dreiser writes, "the police will protect the companies" (p. 471). "Corrupt organizations," explains Sinclair, "were banded together, and leagued in blood brotherhood with the politician and the police; more often than not they were one and the same person—the police captain would own the brothel he pretended to raid" (p. 304).

Competition for jobs and fear of social intermixing caused the middle class to urge the police to control poor immigrants and blacks. Stephen Crane and Paul Laurence Dunbar portray the police as disrupters of the peace and participants in this vicious cycle of prejudice and crime. They deny the civil rights of poor slum dwellers in Crane's *Maggie, A Girl of the Streets* (1893), and they arrest and convict innocent blacks on mere assumptions in Dunbar's *The Sport of the Gods* (1902). Because of police harassment and social injustice, virtuous characters or potentially virtuous characters in naturalistic fiction learn to distrust authority and social rules, which sometimes causes them to become criminals. For example, in *Maggie,* an old woman begs on the street because she cannot get a job, and she is arrested for taking a purse that "a lady" had dropped. She kicks a policeman and states, "The police, damn 'em!" (p. 11). Also, Jimmie believes he has no chance to rise above "the gutter" and that "the police were always actuated by malignant impulses," so he commits petty crimes to gain money and self-respect (p. 16).

SMALL TOWN VIGILANTISM

People in rural areas often considered police ineffective and wanted to maintain a traditional sense of frontier independence, self-reliance, and justice. In Frank Norris's *McTeague: A Story of San Francisco* (1899), McTeague murders his wife, who is also Marcus's cousin, and Marcus tells the deputies who are chasing McTeague: "I'm going along, I tell you. There ain't a man of you big enough to stop me" (p. 242). When the posse refuses to chase the murderer into the desert, Marcus becomes a vigilante and catches McTeague himself. The protagonist in *The Virginian: A Horseman of the Plains* (1902) by Owen Wister (1860–1938) is not a lawman, but he believes his civic duty includes lynching cattle rustlers. Because corrupt lawmen had not arrested known cattle thieves, Judge Henry argues that the Virginian's vigilantism is a civilized act of self-policing and a proper "assertion of the law" (p. 267).

However, many vigilantes were not as independent as Marcus or as heroic as the Virginian. Small-town police forces often accepted and encouraged vigilantism against suspected and innocent blacks. Although police departments had become more professional, they were not integrated, and they acted on many of their own and society's prejudices. Charles Waddell Chesnutt (1858–1932) indicates in *The Marrow of Tradition* (1901) that southern white men would rather organize vigilante mobs, overthrow local governments, start riots, and lynch black people than obey or uphold their town's laws if those laws recognized and protected a black person's rights. Because the legality of slavery and fugitive slave laws were still fresh memories for many police officers, southern law enforcement was based on the assumption that blacks were naturally immoral criminals.

The police often supported, or were members of, white vigilante groups such as the Ku Klux Klan. Racist white police and vigilantes considered blacks guilty until proven innocent, and even if a black man was proven innocent, he could be lynched for appearing disrespectful. Chesnutt illustrates this in *The Marrow of Tradition* when the police reluctantly drop their case against a black man after his white employer proves that he was wrongly accused of raping and murdering a white woman. However, the police encourage a mob of white men to depose the local government and "police" the town themselves. The town's police prefer that innocent blacks be lynched because "it would serve notice on the niggers that we shall hold the whole race responsible for the misdeeds of each individual" (p. 182).

The gap between America's ideals of justice and the reality of racist police angered black writers. Ida B. Wells-Barnett (1862–1931) wrote editorials and pamphlets criticizing the lack of public outrage against white vigilantes and biased police. In 1892 Wells criticized the city of Memphis because it "will neither protect our lives and property, nor give us a fair trial in the courts, but takes us out and murders us in cold blood" (McMurry, p. 136). Nationally, police ignored and even participated in vigilante violence; they made few arrests as vigilantes lynched an average

Judge Roy Bean conducting a trial. The notorious Judge Roy Bean dispensed justice from this outpost in west Texas. Here seated at the table on the porch, Bean is hearing the case of an alleged horse thief. Roy Bean was one of the many morally ambiguous folk heroes created by the harsh environment of the western frontier. THE ART ARCHIVE/NATIONAL ARCHIVES, WASHINGTON, DC

of one black every three days between 1890 and 1900 (Cha-Jua, p. 52).

In response to the violence, some black authors advised readers not to fight back. James Weldon Johnson (1871–1938), in *The Autobiography of an Ex-Colored Man* (1912), recognizes the futility of fighting racist police and vigilante mobs when he sees a black man being lynched, so he passes as white to protect himself and succeed within the white society. However, some authors argued that blacks that accepted the status quo were cowards or collaborators in their own oppression. Many in the black community, including author W. E. B. Du Bois (1868–1963), criticized Booker T. Washington (1856–1915) for encouraging blacks to obey the police and be subservient but accepted members of white-dominated society, a position that Washington puts forth in *Up from Slavery* (1901). In Chesnutt's *The Marrow of Tradition,* a group of black citizens confront the mob of police and vigilantes. Overall, the 1890s marked a "national trend toward [black] militancy" (Cha-Jua, p. 60).

WESTERN LAWMEN AND PINKERTON DETECTIVES

Many Americans romanticized frontier law enforcement because dime novels mythologized outlaws and lawmen. The hero in the Deadwood Dick novels (published from 1877 through 1885) by Edward L. Wheeler (c. 1854–1885) was an archetypal lawman with unwavering masculinity and morality; he spoke directly and honestly, had certain judgment, and was courteous and chivalric. Tales of Billy the Kid, Wyatt Earp, and Jesse James were widely read in the East.

The frontier characters of Bret Harte (1836–1902) also prefer a romantic sense of justice and self-reliance to official police forces. Harte's "The Sheriff of Siskyou" (1894) presents the typical sentiment of western law and order. The lawmen must chase Overstone, after he kills a sheriff for attempting to arrest him for embezzlement, because "the lesser crime of homicide might have been overlooked by the authorities, but its repetition upon the body of their own over-zealous and misguided official could not pass unchallenged if they expected to arrest Overstone for the more serious offense against property" (p. 460). People are expendable, but property is vigorously protected by the police. Harte's short stories often make the outlaws the heroes, arguing that honorable behavior is more important than strictly obeying the law. His outlaws are exiled, hunted, jailed, and executed, but in stories like "The Luck of Roaring Camp" (1868), "The Outcasts of Poker Flat" (1869), and "Tennessee's Partner" (1869) they gain the reader's sympathy and respect because they express kindness, friendship, and selflessness.

Helen Hunt Jackson (1830–1885) offers a different interpretation of law and justice in the West. She proposes in *Ramona* (1884) that white outlaws and white lawmen rely on fraud, cruelty, prejudice, and unjust laws to forcibly take Native Americans' land and kill nonwhites with impunity. While Harte portrays the western outlaw as good-hearted and honorable for killing over an insult, Jackson posits that such an act exemplifies the corrupt, criminal nature of white society. The Native American characters in her novel learn to not trust law-enforcement officers, as they observe police supporting the "law-abiding" whites who take unfair advantage of their racial and social privileges.

One law-enforcement body common to cities, small company towns, and the western United States was the Pinkerton Detective Agency. Founded in Chicago in 1852 by Allan Pinkerton (1819–1884), the agency quickly expanded, opening branch offices in big cities and western territories. The detectives were hired by big businesses and local governments to infiltrate "suspicious" labor organizations, such as the Molly Maguires in the 1870s; to break strikes, including the 1892 Homestead strike; and to catch western bank and railroad robbers, like Jesse James and the Hole-in-the-Wall Gang.

Pinkerton wrote many books about his company's activities in which he describes how successful his detectives and his methods were. These accounts gave his operatives a legend-like status that would later be duplicated by fictional detectives. In *The Rail-Road Forger and the Detectives* (1881), Pinkerton writes that "from the beginning the capture of the outlaws was a foregone conclusion," and "the detective methods of past days and other countries, would certainly never be competent to the work which is performed by the modern Detective Agency" (p. xii). Pinkerton's agency created the first directories of files and photographs of criminal suspects, and his operatives successfully caught many criminals that the police could not or would not catch. In *Bank-Robbers and the Detectives* (1883), Pinkerton writes that his detectives' success "was accomplished by well-directed and untiring energy, and by a determination not to yield until

success was assured" (p. x). However, their methods and honesty were sometimes questioned by judges, who often required independent corroboration of their statements. Pinkerton operatives were known for their perilous undercover work, exhaustive surveillance, toughness, and thoroughness. They also had a reputation for bribing juries, fixing elections, kidnapping witnesses, and killing suspects.

Detective fiction quickly became a popular genre when former Pinkerton detectives began writing. Charles A. Siringo (1855–1928), the self-proclaimed "cowboy detective," spent twenty-two years hunting train robbers and cattle rustlers before writing detective stories and histories of famous western figures such as Billy the Kid. Pinkerton's own books directly inspired many detective novels, including Arthur Conan Doyle's Sherlock Homes stories.

See also Capital Punishment; Jurisprudence; Mystery and Detective Fiction; Reform; Prisons

BIBLIOGRAPHY
Primary Works
Chesnutt, Charles. *The Marrow of Tradition*. 1901. Ann Arbor: University of Michigan Press, 1969.

Crane, Stephen. *Maggie, A Girl of the Streets*. 1893. New York: Modern Library, 2001.

Dreiser, Theodore. *Sister Carrie*. 1900. New York: Doubleday, 1997.

Harte, Bret. "The Sheriff of Siskyou." In *A First Family of Tasajara and Other Tales*. New York: AMS Press, 1966.

Howells, William Dean. *A Hazard of New Fortunes*. 1889. Bloomington: Indiana University Press, 1976.

Howells, William Dean. *A Modern Instance*. 1882. Bloomington: Indiana University Press, 1977.

Norris, Frank. *McTeague: A Story of San Francisco*. 1899. New York: Norton, 1997.

Pinkerton, Allan. *Bank-Robbers and the Detectives*. New York: G. W. Carleton, 1883.

Pinkerton, Allan. *The Rail-Road Forger and the Detectives*. New York: G. W. Carleton, 1881.

Sinclair, Upton. *The Jungle*. 1906. New York: Penguin, 1985.

Twain, Mark. *Pudd'nhead Wilson and Those Extraordinary Twins*. 1894. New York: Norton, 1980.

Wister, Owen. *The Virginian: A Horseman of the Plains*. 1902. New York: Scribner Classics, 2002.

Secondary Works
Cha-Jua, Sundiata Keita. "'A Warlike Demonstration': Legalism, Armed Resistance, and Black Political Mobilization

in Decatur, Illinois, 1894–1898." *Journal of Negro History* 83, no. 1 (1998): 52–72.

McMurry, Linda O. *To Keep the Waters Troubled: The Life of Ida B. Wells.* New York: Oxford University Press, 1998.

Matthew Teorey

LECTURES

In nineteenth- and early-twentieth-century America, lectures were another form of publication. As Ralph Waldo Emerson once jotted in his journal, "a lecture is a new literature, which leaves aside all tradition, time, place, circumstance, & addresses an assembly as mere human beings, no more" (p. 224). By the end of the Civil War, virtually every town in the country had a local organization, often a lyceum or literary society, which sponsored a series of six to eight lectures during the late fall and winter designed to edify rural audiences between harvest and spring plowing. Particularly in the Midwest, these local organizations sometimes joined with others in nearby towns to sponsor lecturers who were otherwise too expensive. Lecture bureaus, such as the American Literary Bureau (1866), the Redpath Lyceum Bureau in Boston (1868) and Chicago (1871), and the Williams Lecture and Musical Bureau (1869), were also established.

James Redpath (1833–1891), a former journalist and editor, effectively systemized the business, managing lecture tours on commission, usually 10 percent of the "box" or box-office income. "Lecturing is becoming a distinct profession," he wrote in 1871. "The system has grown up without system; it has never been organized by competent managers or carefully studied by competent observers; but as it extends itself it will be reduced to order, its attractions multiplied, its sphere widened, its popularity increased, its influence for good augmented a hundred-fold" (Horner, p. 187). Between 1870 and 1900, the Redpath Bureau organized tours for literally hundreds of speakers, among them the minister Henry Ward Beecher, the suffragist Susan B. Anthony, the explorer Henry M. Stanley, the actor Joseph Jefferson, and such literary figures as George William Curtis, William Dean Howells, and Bret Harte. Redpath's "Star Courses" featured a headliner or two during its winter-long weekly series of lectures and filled in the other dates with second-stringers, such as the Civil War general Nathaniel Prentiss Banks and the author Edward Eggleston. Redpath required the local lecture committees or sponsors to subscribe to the entire series, and in turn the committees required auditors to purchase tickets to an entire lecture season rather than pay

Mark Twain lecturing. Caricature by Joseph Keppler from *Puck*, 16 December 1885. THE LIBRARY OF CONGRESS

to see only the headliners. As a result, both lecture fees and profits for promoters increased dramatically in the 1870s. No longer could a sponsor entice a speaker to a town with a promise of $5 and three quarts of oats for his horse, the payment Emerson once accepted.

Speakers in Redpath's stable typically received $100 to $150 per date, though a third-tier figure such as William Emerson, Ralph Waldo's brother, charged $40 plus expenses. The feminist Victoria C. Woodhull was paid $250 per lecture, and Charles Sumner, the Radical Republican senator, was paid $300 to $500. Redpath paid Beecher $1,000 for a single lecture at the Boston Music Hall in 1872 and still made a profit of nearly $2,000. Redpath offered Harte $5,000 for twelve lectures when he first arrived in Boston in 1871—when Mark Twain was earning a mere $150 per date. Some celebrities cleared thousands of dollars in a single season. By her own estimate, Kate Field, the so-called Rose of the Rostrum, earned $8,000 during her first season on the hustings (the lecture platform). Anna E. Dickinson earned an estimated $20,000 per year, John Bartholomew Gough and Artemus Ward (the penname of Charles Farrar Browne) about $30,000, and Beecher more than $40,000.

Following Redpath's lead, the burgeoning lyceum circuit after the Civil War gradually evolved from an educational or instructional medium into a form of entertainment at fifty cents a ticket or a dollar per series. The speakers who succeeded on the circuit (e.g., George Washington Cable, James Whitcomb Riley) were typically entertainers skilled at performing. J. B. (James Burton) Pond (1838–1903), who succeeded Redpath as the head of the Bureau in 1875, recalled that John Bartholomew Gough's two-hour temperance lecture "was an unbroken succession of contortions and antics that left him dripping with perspiration" (p. 5). And humorists such as Twain, Ward, Thomas Nast, Petroleum V. Nasby (a pseudonym for David Ross Locke), and Josh Billings (the penname of Henry Wheeler Shaw) enjoyed lucrative careers on the platform. In contrast, though Bret Harte (1836–1902) earned his livelihood between 1872 and 1875 by delivering his lecture "The Argonauts of '49" about 150 times across the country, his career in the field was utterly undistinguished. As he later explained, "what the people expected in me I do not know. Possibly a six-foot mountaineer, with a voice and lecture in proportion. They always seemed to have mentally confused me with one of my own characters" (Dam, p. 50). Some speakers became famous for their signature lectures, such as Twain ("An American Vandal Abroad" and "Roughing It"); Russell H. Conwell ("Acres of Diamonds"); Elihu Hubbard ("A Message to Garcia"); and Anna Eliza Young, the nineteenth wife of Brigham Young ("My Life in Bondage").

GOOD PAY AND HARD WORK

Some lecturers during the period (e.g., Gough, Anthony, Charlotte Perkins Gilman, Wendell Phillips, Frederick Douglass) advocated such causes as temperance, suffrage, spiritualism, and civil rights, to be sure. But the lure for most of them was money. As Oliver Wendell Holmes once told Herman Melville, a lecturer was a "literary strumpet who prostituted himself for an abnormally high fee" (Howard, p. 256). Kate Field admitted that she began to lecture "because it pays better than anything else, and I am tired of grubbing along" (p. 48). Mark Twain (1835–1910) put it this way: "A sensible man lectures only when butter & bread are scarce" (*Letters* 5:539). He recalled in *Roughing It* (1872) that while still in California he "launched out as a lecturer" with "great boldness. I had the field all to myself, for public lectures were almost an unknown commodity in the Pacific market" (p. 418).

Twain, of course, made several extended lecture tours during his career, including seventy-seven performances in sixteen weeks in 1871 and 1872, 103 performances in three months in company with George Washington Cable in 1884 and 1885, and 140 performances between July 1895 and July 1896. The "Twins of Genius" tour with Cable (so advertised by Pond) netted about $24,000—$16,000 for Twain, $5,000 for Cable (whom Twain paid a flat $450 a week), and $3,000 for Pond. Twain's round-the-world lecture tour in 1895 and 1896 enabled him to erase the estimated $80,000 debt he assumed in 1894 as the result of the failure of his publishing company. As he remarked while in Seattle: "Now, if I have to pay my debts by writing books as Scott had to write them, I might easily kill myself in five years as he did. But I have the advantage of this lecture bureau system, which has grown to such enormous proportions" ("Twain Brands a Fake," p. 8). Lecturing was one of the few careers open to women, moreover, much to the disdain of Twain, who never suffered rivals gladly. The "courted lady-lecturers" soar along "on a lucrative notoriety nine-tenths" the product of self-promotion, he protested in 1870 (*Letters* 4:291). Henry James (1843–1916) also satirized women lecturers in *The Bostonians* (1886) in the character of Verena Tarrant, whose lover concludes she "had queer, bad lecture-blood in her veins" (p. 253).

The occupation was not without other critics. For example, an editorial in *Scribner's Monthly* in 1872, probably penned by Josiah Gilbert (J. G.) Holland (1819–1881), the magazine's genteel editor, protested the turn from substance to entertainment. Once upon a time, the editorial complained, lecturers discussed "important topics," but now "a lecture may be any string of nonsense that any literary mountebank can find an opportunity to utter. Artemus Ward 'lectured;' and he was right royally paid for acting the literary buffoon." The editorial contended that such "triflers and buffoons" were "a constant disgrace to the lecturing guild, and a constantly degrading influence upon the public taste" ("Triflers on the Platform," p. 489). By the end of the century, lectures such as Field's "Eyes and Ears in London" had become virtual variety shows, often accompanied by popular music and illustrated with slides projected by a "magic lantern."

More to the point, professional lecturers had to cope with a variety of problems apart from their performances. First, they either hired a booking agent or bureau or booked their own lecture tours to save money. Harte repeatedly quarreled with his managers, including Redpath and D'Oyly Carte, for their failures to schedule him where he was willing to lecture, and Twain fumed in January 1873 that "there isn't pluck enough in the whole gang of lecture bureaux to run a one-horse circus" (*Letters* 5:275). Next, lecturers worried about the halls or venues where they spoke. Twain noted in 1871, for example, that he "*never* made a success of a lecture delivered in a church yet. People are afraid to laugh in a church" (*Letters* 4:434). Acoustics were also a concern. Many a lecture was ruined by the destructive echoes of a hall.

Long-distance travel by rail was not only inconvenient but potentially hazardous, especially in bad weather. On tour with Twain in 1885, George Washington Cable (1844–1925) wrote Major Pond that they "had to take cars three times yesterday & wait in and about little stove-heated way-stations, for belated trains. The whole day was taken up in going about 100 miles. The thermometer started at 24° below zero, but climbed up nearly to the zero point. We reached Oberlin at a quarter to seven and were to go upon the platform at *seven*" (Turner, p. 101). Seventeen years later, Twain remembered that the frenetic tour with Cable was "the hardest work I have ever known. It was made up of the most absurd railway jumps from one lecture point to another" ("Mark Twain Bids Missouri Farewell," p. 3). As Cable's comment suggests, moreover, winter weather was often a problem. Harte once "travelled in the dead of winter from New York to Omaha 2000 miles, with the thermometer varying from 10° to 25° below zero" (Scharnhorst, p. 106). In Kansas in 1873, Harte's train broke down and left him "at four o'clock, fifteen miles from Atchison on the edge of a bleak prairie with only one house in sight" (*Letters of Bret Harte*, p. 27). A lecturer often risked his health, particularly in the West. William Dean Howells (1837–1920) complained to Pond from Kansas in 1899 that he could not "stand the racket" in the hotels and could not "sleep without drugs" (Pond, p. 335). Similarly, Harte wrote from rural Iowa in 1873 that he had "risen at midnight—have driven directly from the lecture to the depot, have spent three nights without sleep consecutively, until I wonder at what unknown resources of vitality I am drawing upon" (*Selected Letters*, pp. 86–87).

Then there were the social obligations of the visitor, the receptions in his or her honor, and the tour of the town once he or she arrived. Howells found these duties onerous: "If I could lecture every night (which I cannot) and arrive every day too late for an afternoon reception, and get away as soon as I read my paper, it would be fine, but that is impossible" (Pond, p. 335). Twain agreed: "I had to submit to the customary & exasperating drive around town in a freezing open buggy . . . to see the wonders of the village. . . . All towns are alike— all have the same stupid trivialities to show, & all demand an impossible interest at the suffering stranger's hands" (*Letters* 3:395–396). Years after he abandoned the stage, Twain reminisced that a "country audience is the difficult audience; a passage which it will approve with a ripple will bring a crash in the city. A fair success in the country means a triumph in the city" (*Autobiography* 1:151). Field also loathed "the majority of the country audiences" (p. 88). Finally, a professional speaker feared the possibility that a quick-fingered reporter sent to cover the lecture might transcribe it verbatim and publish it in the local newspaper, ruining it for delivery in neighboring towns. Twain excoriated those "devils incarnate" who pick the lecturer's pocket "with their infernal synopses" (*Letters* 4:522).

LECTURES OUTSIDE THE LYCEUM

Other forms of lecturing also prospered during the period. Ironically, the popular Chautauqua movement, founded in 1874 in upstate New York, continued the educational function of the pre–Civil War lyceums but with a twist. The movement was almost exclusively aimed at the edification of rural audiences. At the peak of the movement early in the twentieth century, twenty-two separate "tent circuits" featuring educational lectures and other forms of practical instruction visited a total of approximately 8,000 American communities for a week at a time. "Oblivious to the sneers of the sophisticates," as Joseph Gould notes in *The Chautauqua Movement: An Episode in the Continuing American Revolution* (1961), "tent Chautauqua flourished in the United States for more than twenty years" (p. 81).

Political orators, including Theodore Roosevelt, William Jennings Bryan, Robert Marion La Follette, and Woodrow Wilson, barnstormed the country on "whistle-stop campaigns." Aimee Semple McPherson and other tent revivalists converted souls and became the target of such satires as *Elmer Gantry* (1927) by Sinclair Lewis (1885–1951). The Concord School of Philosophy, founded by Amos Bronson Alcott in 1879, hosted highbrow speakers and eager audiences on the sacred ground of Concord, Massachusetts, until 1888. Though political orators still barnstorm and evangelicals still hold revivals, the system nurtured by the lecture bureaus and the Chautauqua between 1870 and 1920 was inevitably doomed, destroyed by radio and motion pictures.

See also Education; Oratory; Reform

BIBLIOGRAPHY
Primary Works

Emerson, Ralph Waldo. *The Journals and Miscellaneous Notebooks of Ralph Waldo Emerson.* Vol. 7, *1838–1842.* Edited by A. W. Plumstead and Harrison Hayford. Cambridge, Mass.: Belknap Press of Harvard University Press, 1969.

Field, Kate. *Kate Field: Selected Letters.* Edited by Carolyn J. Moss. Carbondale: Southern Illinois University Press, 1996.

Harte, Bret. *The Letters of Bret Harte*. Edited by Geoffrey Bret Harte. Boston: Houghton Mifflin, 1926.

Harte, Bret. *Selected Letters of Bret Harte*. Edited by Gary Scharnhorst. Norman: University of Oklahoma Press, 1997.

James, Henry. *The Bostonians*. 1886. New York: Modern Library, 1956.

Twain, Mark. *Mark Twain's Autobiography*. 2 vols. New York: Harper & Brothers, 1924.

Twain, Mark. *Mark Twain's Letters*. 5 vols. Edited by Victor Fischer et al. Berkeley: University of California Press, 1988–1997.

Twain, Mark. *Roughing It*. 1872. New York: Signet, 1962.

Pond, J. B. *Eccentricities of Genius: Memories of Famous Men and Women of the Platform and Stage*. New York: Dillingham, 1900.

Secondary Works

Dam, Henry J. W. "A Morning with Bret Harte." *McClure's Magazine* 4 (December 1894): 38–50.

Fatout, Paul. *Mark Twain on the Lecture Circuit*. Bloomington: Indiana University Press, 1960.

Gould, Joseph Edward. *The Chautauqua Movement: An Episode in the Continuing American Revolution*. New York: State University of New York Press, 1961.

Horner, Charles F. *The Life of James Redpath and the Development of the Modern Lyceum*. New York: Barse & Hopkins, 1926.

Howard, Leon. *Herman Melville: A Biography*. Berkeley: University of California Press, 1951.

"The Lecture Platform." *Boston Transcript*, 19 June 1875, p. 6, col. 3.

Lorch, Frederick William. *The Trouble Begins at Eight: Mark Twain's Lecture Tours*. Ames: Iowa State University Press, 1968.

"Mark Twain Bids Missouri Farewell." *St. Louis Republic*, 9 June 1902, p. 3.

"Triflers on the Platform." *Scribner's Monthly* 3 (February 1872): 489.

Scharnhorst, Gary. *Bret Harte: Opening the American Literary West*. Norman: University of Oklahoma Press, 2000.

Turner, Arlin. *Mark Twain and G. W. Cable: The Record of a Literary Friendship*. East Lansing: Michigan State University Press, 1960.

"Twain Brands a Fake." *Seattle Post-Intelligencer*, 14 August 1895, p. 8.

Gary Scharnhorst

LIBRARIES

In the last quarter of the nineteenth century, librarians in the United States were among the many specialized groups aspiring to establish themselves as professionals. Aligning themselves with educators and attempting to establish their special expertise in the area of books and reading, librarians were necessarily sensitive to the views of the entrenched social hierarchy that held the power to grant them the status they sought.

The resulting ambiguities of purpose meant that libraries reflected changing values and social structures in the formative years of the profession to a greater degree than they influenced them, despite professional rhetoric to the contrary. The period was one of great growth for all types of libraries, but it was in public libraries that fundamental ideological struggles took place and in which the particular character and identity of American libraries was molded.

THE PUBLIC LIBRARY MOVEMENT

The year 1876 saw the publication of the U.S. Bureau of Education Report *Public Libraries in the United States: Their History, Condition, and Management*. Prepared for the nation's centennial, the report acknowledged the impressive growth in public libraries that had occurred in the two decades since the founding of the Boston Public Library and the first gathering of library enthusiasts.

Inspired by the encouraging figures in the report and facilitated by the orchestrations of Melvil Dewey (1851–1931), library leaders met at the centennial celebrations in Philadelphia in October 1876 and gave birth to the American Library Association (ALA). This, and the founding of the *American Library Journal* in the same year, signaled the beginning of the modern public library movement as well as the first stirrings toward the professionalization of librarianship.

Prominent in the early organizing efforts of the profession were three men, Justin Winsor, William Frederick Poole, and Charles Ammi Cutter, and their values, chiefly those of the prevailing social elite, were reflected in the emerging sense of the library's place in American cultural life. Winsor, director of the Boston Public Library, was elected first president of the ALA (1876–1885) and emerged as a respected spokesman for the profession. Poole, who created the standard index for access to nineteenth-century periodical literature, was librarian of the Boston Athenaeum, director of the Chicago Public Library, and later head of the prestigious Newberry Library. He succeeded Winsor as ALA president (1885–1887). Cutter, who devised a numerical system for organizing a library

Boston Public Library, c. 1900. Founded in 1848, the Boston Public Library was the first free municipal library in the United States. Originally housed in a smaller structure on Boylston Street, it was moved in 1895 to this building designed by noted architect Charles McKim. THE LIBRARY OF CONGRESS

collection that is still in use today, was assistant librarian at Harvard before becoming head of the Boston Athenaeum. He served as Poole's successor as ALA president (1887–1889) and as editor of *Library Journal* (1881–1893).

All of these men shared, in varying degree, a New England–based sense of propriety and convention that valued gentility as the distinguishing mark of the cultivated person. This genteel tradition and the egalitarian notion that gentility could be learned, led to the concept of the library as an institution most closely aligned with education. Emerging naturally from such institutions as the lyceum and the athenaeum, the public library was seen to have a clear mission to serve as a repository for culture and as an agent for the cultural elevation of those it served.

The motives behind this point of view have been variously debated, broadly divided between those who

see the library movement as a noble effort dedicated to the betterment of the common people, and those who see it as an imposition of the will of the cultural elite toward a perpetuation of shared beliefs, designed to uphold the status quo. In any case, the members of the profession saw themselves as qualified to make the value judgments necessary to assess the cultural status of users and to mold collections best suited to the goal of elevation.

Following the 1876 report, as libraries multiplied and collections grew, the necessity of having librarians dedicated to providing personal assistance to patrons became increasingly apparent. As librarians sought to define themselves, it became clear that the provision of reference service was a distinguishing feature of the profession. Reference collections were developed and reference rooms became a standard feature of library facilities, particularly in plans for new library buildings.

THE FICTION PROBLEM

In this missionary phase, one consistently troublesome issue had to do with the place of fiction in the library collection. Widely considered to be merely a low form of entertainment, it was the view of many that fiction had no place in a serious library collection at all. Yet it was clear that patrons of the library expected to find fiction there.

Furthermore, some argued, it was clear that certain forms of literature—Hawthorne was one author who met with approval—met a higher standard and could arguably be said to contribute to the library's mission to elevate. Another theory held that frequent reading of "lower" forms of literature would cultivate an appetite for something better. A library that provided such "low" literature was thus both serving the public and fulfilling its mission at the same time.

There was consensus that a work judged to be immoral was unworthy of inclusion in a library collection. The standard of morality was considered to be so commonly held as to make such works apparent, despite the fact that disagreements arose as to just which titles were immoral. The struggle to arrive at some sort of standard by which literature, particularly fiction, could justifiably be included or excluded from library collections led to an 1881 survey by the ALA, the results of which included Horatio Alger, E. D. E. N. Southworth, and G. W. M. Reynolds among the questionable authors. The survey passed judgment on the value of particular works based on assumed standards of genteel behavior. Besides works identified as immoral, writes Patrick Williams, books that were "sensational, vulgar, sentimental, and inauthentic in their portrayals of the problems and predicaments of human beings and society" (p. 13) were also deemed objectionable.

The zeal for censorship spread, causing works such as Walt Whitman's *Leaves of Grass* (1855) to be banned in 1881 by the Boston Society for the Suppression of Vice and Mark Twain's *Adventures of Huckleberry Finn* (1885) to be banned from a Concord, Massachusetts, library shortly after its publication in 1885. The assessment of *Huck Finn* neatly summed up the standards at work. The committee did not want to call it "immoral" but thought it "rough, coarse and inelegant, dealing with a series of experiences not elevating." In his response, Twain said that the ban would only increase his sales and would cause "purchasers of the book to read it, out of curiosity, instead of merely intending to do so after the usual way of the world and library committees" (Inge, pp. viii, ix).

Twain knew in 1885 what the library profession would only reluctantly admit by 1893 (when the ALA included a number of fiction and popular titles in its first book guide for libraries), that the public would read what it wanted despite the most well-intentioned attempts to guide it toward enrichment. Helped along by the advocacy of iconoclastic library thinkers such as the Denver librarian John Cotton Dana, the idea that the library could legitimately provide entertainment in the form of popular fiction as well as provide higher forms of literature gained greater acceptance. This point of view was reinforced by the fact that the forces of social change influenced by a great influx of immigrants and the growth of the working class had, by the end of the century, diminished the influence of the genteel model.

Nonetheless, remaining true to its perceived role as cultural advisor, the ALA began to publish lists of recommended books to guide libraries in developing collections that would be acceptable within what it saw as prevailing standards. New complications in evaluating literature had emerged as writers chose increasingly to write in a realistic mode, dealing with issues such as divorce, adultery, prostitution, and political matters that were thought to be unduly troublesome and provocative. Hamlin Garland's politically charged work was omitted from the ALA list in 1893, for example, and an 1896 meeting to create a supplement to the list found Stephen Crane's *The Red Badge of Courage* (1895) unacceptable for inclusion on the grounds that it was "unrealistically profane."

The trend toward overt censorship became most intense in the first decades of the twentieth century. The ALA published a list of recommended titles in 1904, and the publishing and indexing concern H. W. Wilson Company published a list of its own in 1908. The lists were strikingly in accord, and the fiction omitted from them indicates the strict standards that were being imposed.

Herman Melville, Frank Norris, William Dean Howells, and the still difficult Hamlin Garland and Stephen Crane had important works omitted. All of Henry James's most important works were omitted, and Ambrose Bierce was excluded altogether. Subsequent catalogs in 1911 and 1914 showed an increasing intolerance for anything socialist or critical of the American way of life. Jack London and Upton Sinclair were often considered troublesome, and everyone, it seemed, agreed that Theodore Dreiser was generally unacceptable.

London's case in particular pointed up the contradictions at the heart of the assessment practices. Owning a personal library of some fifteen thousand volumes, London confessed an insatiable appetite for reading and praised the Oakland Public Library from which he borrowed heavily, yet much of his work, unquestionably informed by his voracious reading, was considered too unsettling for library collections.

With the advent of the First World War and the ensuing patriotic fervor, censorship reached a peak. The Library War Service, created to supply reading materials to military camps in the United States and abroad, created lists of acceptable books that found their way into general use in libraries outside the military. A book could be omitted from these lists as seditious simply for being insufficiently critical of the Germans. There was some dissent, but many librarians willingly continued in their roles as guardians of public sensibilities through the war years, after which the profession began to shift toward its present role as defender of the right and freedom to read guaranteed by the First Amendment.

DEWEY AND FEMINIZATION

While the New England cultural aristocracy dominated the thinking of the profession in its formative years, other forces were at work from the beginning. The young and ambitious Melvil Dewey, best known for the system of classification that bears his name, was instrumental in organizing the 1876 meeting and became an inexorable force in the development of libraries as we know them. It was Dewey who in 1876 convinced his employers, Frederick Leypoldt and R. R. Bowker, to create the *American Library Journal* as a spinoff from their *Publishers Weekly*. Dewey ran the *Journal*, which still exists as the important professional publication *Library Journal*, for the first years of its existence and used it as a forum for his highly technical ideas regarding library practices.

Dewey also helped found the Library Bureau, a concern that provided business equipment and further reflected his emphasis on innovative methods and materials. His eccentric and uncharacteristically disorganized financial and bookkeeping practices caused him difficulties in his business ventures, and in 1883 he returned to library work as librarian in chief at Columbia College.

Dewey had long recognized the need for librarianship to have a standard body of knowledge as well as schools to train practitioners if it was to be taken seriously as a profession. He saw his position at Columbia as the chance to make this come about. He had openly recruited women for library work for some time and employed a number of women on his staff at Columbia with plans to employ them as faculty in the library school he envisioned. When the first library class at Columbia was about to be held in 1887, seventeen of its twenty members were women.

Hearing of this, the school denied him a room. Dewey countered by cleaning out an old storeroom for use as a classroom and went ahead as scheduled. The conflict with the trustees over coeducation that ensued led to the establishment of Barnard College annex for women and the expulsion of Dewey in 1888. He moved to Albany and became director of the New York State Library; his library school followed him in 1889, transferred officially from Columbia.

Dewey was, by all accounts, an eccentric, egotistical, and difficult man who sooner or later alienated most of those with whom he came in contact. His business practices were suspect, his lack of regard for things intellectual and his obsessive attention to the minutiae of library work earned him the disdain of the established library elite, and he was at various times accused of anti-Semitism as well as impropriety with some of his devoted women followers. An absolute force in the creation of standards for the profession, in the development of professional education, and in advocacy for women professionals, he was also probably the most influential figure in the history of American libraries.

Dewey's championing of women for the profession reflected the more general view of the times that women were, by nature, well suited to librarianship. For those women—chiefly unmarried—who chose to work, librarianship, along with the other predominantly feminine emerging professions such as social work, teaching, and nursing, provided a perfect outlet for the virtues of domesticity with which women were thought to be naturally blessed.

The catalog of these virtues for librarians varied, but invariably among them was the intimation of an altruism that traded on the traditional view of libraries as institutions with a mission to serve. In other words, women librarians could experience the fulfillment of a productive working life and could also be expected to work for very little money. Women continued to be attracted to librarianship in ever-increasing numbers, becoming dominant in the profession by the advent of the Progressive Era and serving to shape the development of library programs toward meeting the needs of previously neglected groups.

PROGRESSIVISM AND CARNEGIE

It is significant that in creating his symbolic portrait of the restless and modern woman of the Progressive Era struggling against small-mindedness and outmoded points of view, Sinclair Lewis chose to make Carol Kennicott, the protagonist of *Main Street* (1920), a librarian. Carol gives up her library position and leaves St. Paul to marry a physician and move with him to the small town of Gopher Prairie.

At a social gathering Carol talks with the town librarian, Miss Villets, who expresses her disapproval with the large city libraries that allow "tramps and all sorts of dirty persons" to use the library. Carol responds that they are "poor souls" and that the "chief task of a librarian is to get people to read." Miss Villets replies that her feeling is "that the first duty of the *conscientious* librarian is to preserve the books" (p. 112).

This exchange sums up the conflicting forces at work in the profession as well as in America at large during the first decades of the twentieth century. The view of the library as a center for community programs and service to such groups as immigrants, laborers, and children was gaining momentum at the same time that settlement houses, the social work profession, and labor movements were developing. These movements challenged the traditional social hierarchy, one symbol of which was the library as a secular temple in which the finest expressions of human progress were enshrined and preserved for the use of those culturally equipped to appreciate them.

During the period from 1886 to 1917 the traditional view was reinforced, in the view of some, by the Carnegie program. Andrew Carnegie offered to build a public library for any community willing to take on the tax burden necessary to sustain the institution. Carnegie, the members of his organization, and the trustees of local libraries were of the upper class, and the library designs that met with their approval inevitably reflected their values.

The physical placement of the library in the community, the classical and monumental elements of the exterior designs, and the floor plans all reinforced a class-based hierarchy and a clear distinction between high and low culture. After the turn of the century, individual Carnegie libraries with a progressive view managed to implement open floor plans and children's rooms, and in larger cities the foreboding and grand central library was supplemented with modest branch libraries that brought services to people in the neighborhoods.

Some communities, such as Detroit, objected to the Carnegie program on the principle that it depended on tainted money. They felt it was hypocritical of Carnegie to pretend to be the benefactor of those whom he had exploited to make his millions. Carnegie, in a version of the waning cultural elevation theory, insisted that libraries were the emphasis of his philanthropy because of his belief in making resources available—particularly to the working class—that would help the motivated and industrious to realize their full potential.

While the working class appeared to maintain an admirable immunity to the concerted efforts to elevate them and to protect them from the harmful forces at large in America, the growth in public libraries facilitated by the Carnegie program nonetheless left a lasting legacy on the cultural landscape: 1,679 public libraries came into being with Carnegie funds, and the dissemination of openly available information and community service that resulted is now widely regarded as a distinguishing feature of American democracy.

HERBERT PUTNAM AND THE LIBRARY OF CONGRESS

The Library of Congress (established in 1800) underwent changes during the visionary leadership of Herbert Putnam (librarian from 1899 to 1939) that represent another important development in American libraries. (Notably, it was once again Dewey, at a critical juncture for the profession, who placed Putnam's name in nomination for the post.) Under Putnam's guidance, the Library of Congress, unique among national libraries in the world, reinforced the democratic ideal through a radical departure from established practice. Rather than exist only as the collection of record and as a resource restricted for the use of government agencies, the Library of Congress instead became a resource for all of the libraries of the land as well as a collection for the use of all Americans. The concept of shared cataloging embodied in Putnam's Library of Congress card service (in which libraries would purchase catalog cards from the Library of Congress, rather than each individually creating their own) revolutionized the way libraries worked and brought a cooperative model and a cohesiveness to the profession in America that could not otherwise have been easily accomplished.

Putnam's vision and the subsequent central role that the Library of Congress assumed was instrumental in moving the profession more firmly toward the mission that had begun to emerge, that of creating libraries that were egalitarian and oriented toward a less judgmental provision of service. Had libraries been successful in exerting the sort of considerable cultural influence initially identified as their professional duty, America would be a different place and many of the names in American literature that we readily identify and hold in high regard might be unknown to us.

See also Boston and Concord; *Main Street;* Museums; New York

BIBLIOGRAPHY
Primary Work

Lewis, Sinclair. *Main Street*. New York: Harcourt, Brace, 1920.

Secondary Works

Carrier, Esther Jane. *Fiction in Public Libraries: 1876–1900.* New York: Scarecrow Press, 1965.

Garrison Dee. *Apostles of Culture: The Public Librarian and American Society, 1876–1920.* Madison: University of Wisconsin Press, 2003.

Geller, Evelyn. *Forbidden Books in American Public Libraries, 1876–1939: A Study in Cultural Change.* Westport, Conn.: Greenwood Press, 1984.

Hamilton, David Mike. *"The Tools of My Trade": The Annotated Books in Jack London's Library.* Seattle: University of Washington Press, 1986.

Harris, Michael H. "The Role of the Public Library in American Life: A Speculative Essay." *University of Illinois Graduate School of Library Science Occasional Papers* 117 (1975).

Heim, Kathleen M. *The Status of Women in Librarianship: Historical, Sociological, and Economic Issues.* New York: Neal-Schuman, 1983.

Inge, M. Thomas. *Huck Finn among the Critics: A Centennial Selection.* Frederick, Md.: University Publications of America, 1985.

Kaplan, Louis. "The Early History of Reference Service in the United States." In *Reference Services,* edited by Arthur Ray Rowland. Hamden, Conn.: Shoe String Press, 1964.

Rosenberg, Jane Aiken. *The Nation's Great Library: Herbert Putnam and the Library of Congress, 1899–1939.* Urbana: University of Illinois Press, 1993.

Van Slyck, Abigail A. *Free to All: Carnegie Libraries and American Culture, 1890–1920.* Chicago: University of Chicago Press, 1995.

Wiegand, Wayne A. *The Politics of an Emerging Profession: The American Library Association, 1876–1917.* New York: Greenwood Press, 1986.

Williams, Patrick. *The American Public Library and the Problem of Purpose.* New York: Greenwood Press, 1988.

Mark Woodhouse

LITERARY COLONIES

Literary colonies refer to settlements of writers who often share aesthetic and political ideals. Between 1870 and 1920, five significant literary colonies afforded American writers shelter and intellectual camaraderie.

NOOK FARM

In the 1850s a community was established on the western edge of Hartford, Connecticut. Known as Nook Farm, the colony was founded by three prominent New England activists: John Hooker, a lawyer and abolitionist; his wife Isabella Beecher Hooker, a suffragist and women's rights leader; and Francis Gillette, a senator,

abolitionist, and temperance reformer. They purchased the 140-acre farm and split it into large residential parcels in 1853. The community originally consisted of intellectuals united in their strong religious beliefs and opposition to slavery. Among them was Harriet Beecher Stowe, author of *Uncle Tom's Cabin; or, Life among the Lowly* (1852), who was Isabella Beecher Hooker's half sister.

Nook Farm's most famous resident was Mark Twain, who did not arrive until 1871. Disgusted by the grasping values of post–Civil War America—though paradoxically always tempted by get-rich-quick schemes—Clemens did not light out for the territory as did his hero Huck Finn but instead built a large, showy house—sometimes described as "Steamboat Gothic"—amid this community. Some have argued that he chose Nook Farm because it was halfway between New York and Boston, the two primary publishing centers of the time, but other considerations were undoubtedly more important. For one thing, his wife, Olivia, was a close friend of the prestigious Hooker family, particularly of their daughter Alice. Also, Hartford's honorable intellectual tradition, as well as its beautiful pastoral setting and relaxed lifestyle, appealed to him.

The community at Nook Farm was close, and the consequences of having a circle of intellectuals living in close proximity were significant. One of Twain's neighbors was the writer and newspaper publisher Charles Dudley Warner. At a dinner in February 1873, the story goes, Twain and his wife entertained Warner and his wife Susan. When the two men complained of the poor quality of popular literature, the women challenged them to do better. The two men agreed to collaborate on a work, which led to the writing of *The Gilded Age: A Tale of Today* (1873). Based on the novel's mocking portrayal of American society, the expression "the Gilded Age" soon became synonymous with the period after the Civil War, which was marked by unprecedented corruption in business and government. William Dean Howells, the senior man of American letters of the time and a frequent visitor to Nook Farm, wrote to a friend on 21 March 1874 about the collegial atmosphere at the community: "It seems to me quite an ideal life. They [Twain and Warner] live very near each other, in a sort of suburban grove, and their neighbors . . . go in and out of each other's houses without ringing" (Twain 1:16n).

Another resident of Nook Farm was the Reverend Joseph Hopkins Twichell, who was also a writer. Twichell became Twain's closest friend and accompanied him on his European tour in 1880, which led to *A Tramp Abroad* (1880); Twichell is represented by the

Mark Twain's home in Hartford, Connecticut. In this home built in Nook Farm, Twain and his wife regularly entertained many literary guests. THE GRANGER COLLECTION, NEW YORK

character Harris in the book. Twichell also suggested to Twain that he write *Life on the Mississippi* (1883), and he often read over Twain's manuscripts, offering editing and more substantial suggestions. Twichell would later write the biography *John Winthrop: First Governor of the Massachusetts Colony* (1891) and edit *Some Old Puritan Love-letters—John and Margaret Winthrop—1618–1638* (1891).

Due in part to his financial difficulties, Twain began an around-the-world tour in 1895, leaving two of his daughters, Susy and Jean, in America. Initially, the girls were expected to later join their parents in Europe, but Susy became ill and died of meningitis before her parents could return to America. Susy's unexpected death was particularly traumatic for Twain, and his writing becomes notably darker and more pessimistic afterward. Another seeming consequence of Susy's death was that Twain and his family avoided Nook Farm afterward, though they often discussed returning. However, shortly after visiting Nook Farm to attend the funeral of Charles Dudley Warner in 1900, Twain put the Connecticut home up for sale.

GREENWICH VILLAGE

Greenwich Village, a section of Lower Manhattan in New York City, is the longest-standing literary colony in America. Its history as an important retreat for writers goes back to the revolutionary period, when Thomas Paine lived and wrote there. Interestingly, Henry James and Edith Wharton were born in Greenwich Village when it was an affluent neighborhood. After 1870, however, a huge influx of German, Irish, and Italian immigrants, as well as the arrival of transplants from rural America, led to an urgent need for cheap housing in New York. As a consequence, many of the large older homes in Greenwich Village, which had escaped business development because the roads were too narrow and winding for commercial access, were subdivided into low-cost tenements. Because of its affordable rents, Greenwich Village became the intellectual center for various forms of socialism, for the feminist movement, for avant-garde literature and theater, and for various alternative lifestyles that stood in opposition to the pervasive Victorian morality of the surrounding society.

A significant literary movement beginning late in the nineteenth century was naturalism, which depicted scenes that challenged the optimism and Victorian ideals embraced by popular culture. Not surprisingly, proponents of literary naturalism initially had difficulty getting their works published and were often accused of immorality and censured. Many of these writers sought refuge in Greenwich Village. Stephen Crane, for example, stayed there in the mid-1890s while revising *The Red Badge of Courage* (1895). Another naturalist, Frank Norris, lived in the Village in 1898 while writing for *McClure's Magazine,* and he also read manuscripts for Doubleday, Page, & Company. Based on his recommendation, the company agreed to publish Theodore Dreiser's naturalistic *Sister Carrie* (1900). Dreiser stayed briefly in the Village in 1915 before moving back more permanently in 1923 to continue work on *An American Tragedy* (1925).

Greenwich Village also was home to a number of small alternative magazines that challenged the middle-class periodicals published uptown. In 1910 the *Masses,* edited by the writer and poet Max Eastman, began operation. A political magazine from a socialist perspective, it published left-wing writers such as John Reed and Floyd Dell. Of course, it was highly critical of American capitalism, and when World War I began in 1914, it argued against American involvement. Consequently, in 1917, when the United States entered the war, the U.S. government revoked the magazine's mailing privileges, making it all but impossible to get copies to subscribers. In addition, five of its editors, including Eastman, were twice tried under the Espionage Act, which made it a crime to publish any material that undermined the war effort. Both trials ended in hung juries, and since the magazine had folded in April 1918 and the war was over by the second trial in 1919, the government did not pursue the case further.

Another Greenwich Village–based magazine, the *Little Review,* founded by Margaret Anderson in 1914, was probably the most influential literary magazine of the time. It ushered in modernism, publishing writers such as Sherwood Anderson, Hart Crane, Ford Maddox Ford, Ernest Hemingway, Amy Lowell, Carl Sandburg, Gertrude Stein, Wallace Stevens, William Carlos Williams, and most significantly, James Joyce. The *Little Review* serialized Joyce's groundbreaking novel *Ulysses* beginning in 1918 (it did not appear in book form until 1922). The *Seven Arts* began in 1916 and published both literary and political works by authors such as Sherwood Anderson, Theodore Dreiser, Robert Frost, Amy Lowell, and John Dos Passos. *Bohemian* magazine, created by Dreiser in 1909, is most notable for publishing poems by Hart Crane, another Village resident. *The Dial,*

which moved to Greenwich Village from Chicago in 1918, was edited at various times by the critic Kenneth Burke and the poet Marianne Moore, both Greenwich Village residents. It was another vanguard for modernism, publishing some of the most radical poetry of the time, including *The Waste Land* by T. S. Eliot, which appeared in November 1922.

Experimental theaters also sprang up in Greenwich Village as an alternative to the lucrative but conservative productions on Broadway. Until that time, Broadway productions focused primarily on melodrama, farce, musical revues, and productions of Shakespeare. While summering in Provincetown, Massachusetts, in 1915, George Cram Cook and his new wife, Susan Glaspell, decided to produce some of the plays they had written for their own amusement. When friends and neighbors asked to see their productions, they converted an old fish house into the Wharf Theater. In 1915 the theater featured *Suppressed Desires,* a collaboration by Cook and Glaspell. Thus was born the theater group known as the Provincetown Players, a group of young, left-wing actors and writers, including Floyd Dell, John Reed, Mary Heaton Vorse, Louise Bryant, and later Eugene O'Neill and Edna St. Vincent Millay. In 1916 they staged O'Neill's play *Bound East for Cardiff* (1916), the first production anywhere of an O'Neill drama, and Glaspell's play *Trifles* (1916), both of which were popular successes. When the summer season ended in Provincetown that year, Cook, the guiding force of the company, and John Reed decided to move their base of operation to Greenwich Village and continue on through the winter. They began producing amateur plays by American playwrights in two small, uncomfortable theaters, the Playwright's Theater and the Provincetown Playhouse. Plays by Glaspell during this period include *The People* (1917) and *Inheritors* (1921). They also put on several one-act plays by O'Neill. Particularly significant was *The Emperor Jones* (1920), both because of its expressionism and because a black actor was the main character; it was another popular success.

Unfortunately, the success of the Provincetown Players eventually led to the demise of the troupe. Many of the productions were so successful they drew large crowds, and the members were divided between their desire to stay an amateur theater group to support new American playwrights and the demands for a larger theater, more professional actors, and more professional productions. After winning the Pulitzer Prize for his first full-length play, *Beyond the Horizon,* in 1920, O'Neill left the Provincetown Players to have his plays more professionally performed on Broadway. On the other hand, Glaspell and Cook, frustrated with the commercial direction the group was taking, moved to Greece in 1922. These defections led to the virtual end of the Provincetown Players. Still, their early works, often harshly realistic, nearly always tragic, and highly critical of American society, are considered the beginnings of serious American theater.

Many other journalists and novelists also lived in Greenwich Village during this period. Willa Cather was a longtime resident. She moved to New York in 1906 to write for *McClure's Magazine,* which, after 1902, focused primarily on muckraking articles. She was the magazine's editor from 1908 to 1911. Often taking short trips out west to gather material for her novels, she would then return to Greenwich Village to write. Other significant writers who lived in Greenwich Village during this period, or shortly thereafter, include Malcolm Cowley, Sinclair Lewis, John Dos Passos, Katherine Anne Porter, Allen Tate, and William Carlos Williams.

HELICON HOME COLONY

The short-lived literary community called Helicon Home Colony, in Englewood, New Jersey, was created by the socialist writer Upton Sinclair, who wanted to establish a literary colony based on communal living. Using the profits from his successful muckraking novel *The Jungle* (1906), Sinclair bought a mansion on four hundred acres complete with a tennis court, swimming pool, bowling alley, and pipe organ—not exactly the proletarian ideal. Still, the goal was to create a true cooperative, so everyone shared in the household duties, such as cooking and cleaning. Several families lived there, and the children were kept in a separate wing and watched by nurses, though their parents could visit them when they wanted (Lingeman, pp. 25–26). Among the prominent figures who stayed there briefly were William James, the philosopher and psychologist; John Dewey, the philosopher and educator; Emma Goldman, the feminist, pacifist, and anarchist; and a young Sinclair Lewis. As was often the case in Greenwich Village, charges of immorality by the mainstream press were common. Local newspapers ran articles describing Helicon House as a "free-love nest" and accusing the residents of being communists, so when it burned down mysteriously in 1907, many suspected arson. In any case, Upton Sinclair, now penniless, chose not to rebuild, and the artists dispersed. Internal problems may also have been an issue. In a humorous article that Sinclair Lewis later wrote for *Life*, he complained "that the 'workers' had become real servants and the colonists were getting tired of a simple life with institutionalized children" (Lingeman, p. 26).

CARMEL-BY-THE-SEA

On the West Coast, another literary colony formed in Carmel, California, or, as it is sometimes called, Carmel-by-the-Sea, in the first decade of the 1900s. This colony began when the San Francisco–based poet George Sterling (1869–1926) moved to Carmel with his wife in 1905 to escape the financial pressures of life in San Francisco. Soon several writers and artists followed their lead. As with Greenwich Village and Helicon Home Colony, the artists who gathered in Carmel were generally left-wing radicals, often socialists, and they expounded feminist ideas and liberal views of sexuality. Besides being beautiful, Carmel made it possible for writers to live cheaply and focus on their craft. The settlement had perhaps a dozen permanent residents living in small cabins among scattered pines along a jagged hill overlooking the bay. There was neither electricity nor paved roads.

In 1908, thanks to the efforts of the poet-dramatist Herbert Heron and the authors Mary (Hunter) Austin and Michael Williams, an outdoor theater, known as the Forest Theater, was built to stage plays. Austin, the poet Robinson Jeffers, and the journalist Lincoln Steffens, best known for his leadership in the muckraking movement, all lived in Carmel for some time. For brief periods, Upton Sinclair and Sinclair Lewis also stayed there.

Jack London, a lifelong friend of George Sterling, had been part of the Piedmont Circle of writers with Sterling in San Francisco. Sterling, in fact, was the model for the idealistic Brissenden in London's largely autobiographical novel *Martin Eden* (1909). London was also close friends with Mary Austin; they corresponded throughout London's life. Consequently, London visited Carmel often. There he met Sinclair Lewis, and after looking through his collection of story plots, eventually agreed to buy fourteen of them from him for $5 each. Later he would buy more plots from Lewis. London describes the Carmel art colony in idyllic terms in *The Valley of the Moon* (1913).

Robinson Jeffers moved to Carmel with his wife, Una, in 1914. On a barren promontory, using granite boulders he quarried himself, he built first their stone home, Tor House, which he completed in 1919, and later Hawk Tower, completed in 1924. Much of his best poetry focuses on accurate descriptions of the harshness and simultaneous beauty of nature. In particular, he often describes the rugged Carmel coastline through the lens of his philosophy, which emphasizes that humans are not at the center of the universe and contrasts the more permanent aspects of nature to the transitory values of modern society. In "Carmel Point," for example, the narrator first describes the natural beauty of Carmel before the art colony: "How beautiful it was when we first beheld it / Unbroken field of poppy and lupin walled with clean cliffs." But then he worries that they are "the spoiler" destroying the very beauty they love. Finally he realizes that nature is beyond their influence and will abide:

> does it care?
> Not faintly. It has all time. It knows people are a tide
> That swells and in time will ebb, and all
> Their works dissolve. Meanwhile the images of the pristine beauty
> Lives in the very grain of the granite,
> Safe as the endless ocean that climbs our cliff.
>
> (P. 676)

Robinson and Una Jeffers had many influential literary guests stay with them in Carmel, including Sinclair Lewis, Edna St. Vincent Millay, and Langston Hughes. Jeffers rarely left his beloved Carmel, but not surprisingly, when he did, he made several trips to another literary colony, Taos, New Mexico, beginning in 1930.

TAOS

Taos, in the high desert, was an established art community when Mabel Dodge Sterne, a wealthy East Coast socialite who had kept a salon for writers in Greenwich Village, followed her third husband, the painter Maurice Sterne, to Taos in 1917. He had come, like so many others, to paint Native American subjects. Taos's appeal to artists and writers can partly be understood by its separateness and consequential freedom from conventions both of art and society. Also, Taos's ruggedness stood in refreshing contrast to the superficiality and ease of modern society, and the local pueblo people's simpler, more communal lifestyles appealed to those fleeing the competitiveness encouraged by capitalism.

Mabel Dodge Sterne was immediately taken by the place and quickly divorced Sterne and married a Pueblo man named Tony Lujan, becoming Mabel Dodge Lujan (often spelled Luhan). Using her money and influence, she began encouraging writers she had known in Greenwich Village to come to stay at her estate in Taos. Her liberal ideas and her love of the desert landscape and of Native American cultures, as well as her attempts to defend Native American rights, created a bond between her and several writers, particularly Mary Austin and Willa Cather, who had been similarly inspired by the Southwest's landscape and people. Both Austin and Cather spent some time at Lujan's estate, and Mary Austin eventually built a permanent residence, Casa Querida (Beloved House), in nearby Santa Fe in 1924.

Cather stayed with Austin at Casa Querida while finishing *Death Comes for the Archbishop* (1927). Lujan's prize recruit, however, was the British novelist D. H. Lawrence, who arrived in 1922.

CONCLUSION

Members of these literary colonies generally shared some fundamental aesthetic or political beliefs that were at odds with mainstream culture. As a consequence, they often became close friends united by common values, and this sense of fellowship usually extended to members of other literary colonies sharing similar attitudes as well. For this reason, there was not only a great deal of camaraderie within each literary colony but also a great deal of correspondence and travel among the colonies. This interaction resulted in a rich sharing of ideas and values, which inspired the writers and became the impetus for many of their best works.

See also Aestheticism; Clubs and Salons; Literary Friendships

BIBLIOGRAPHY

Primary Works

Jeffers, Robinson. *The Selected Poetry of Robinson Jeffers.* Edited by Tim Hunt. Stanford, Calif.: Stanford University Press, 2001.

Twain, Mark. *Mark Twain–Howells Letters: The Correspondence of Samuel L. Clemens and William D. Howells, 1872–910.* Edited by Henry Nash Smith and William M. Gibson. 2 vols. Cambridge, Mass.: Belknap Press of Harvard University Press, 1960.

Secondary Works

Andrews, Kenneth R. *Nook Farm: Mark Twain's Hartford Circle.* Cambridge, Mass.: Harvard University Press, 1950.

Black, Stephen A. *Eugene O'Neill: Beyond Mourning and Tragedy.* New Haven, Conn.: Yale University Press, 1999.

Brophy, Robert J. *Robinson Jeffers.* Boise, Idaho: Boise State University, 1975.

Ellis, David. *D. H. Lawrence: Dying Game, 1922–1930.* Vol. 3 of *The Cambridge Biography of D. H. Lawrence.* Cambridge, U.K.: Cambridge University Press, 1998.

Emerson, Everett. *Mark Twain, A Literary Life.* Philadelphia: University of Pennsylvania Press, 2000.

Gerber, John C. *Mark Twain.* Boston: Twayne, 1988.

Harris, Leon. *Upton Sinclair: American Rebel.* New York: Crowell, 1975.

Lingeman, Richard. *Sinclair Lewis: Rebel from Main Street.* New York: Random House, 2002.

O'Brien, Sharon. *Willa Cather: The Emerging Voice.* New York: Oxford University Press, 1987.

Waterman, Arthur E. *Susan Glaspell.* New York: Twayne, 1966.

Richard S. Randolph

LITERARY CRITICISM

Literary criticism in the closing decades of the nineteenth century and the early decades of the twentieth century clearly reflects the growth, often tumultuous and uneven, of America's culture and sense of self-identity. Between 1870 and 1920 the way literary critics thought about the relationship between art and society began to shift dramatically. New England's "genteel tradition," derived from Calvinism and transcendentalism and represented by Oliver Wendell Holmes, Henry Wadsworth Longfellow, James Russell Lowell, and others, enjoyed wide influence upon American criticism in the nineteenth century. The "genteel" critics evaluated literature in terms of aesthetic form, good taste, and moral rectitude. Yet as America experienced unprecedented social problems—Reconstruction and its attendant strife and corruption, mass urban poverty, crime, and a shortage of sanitary living conditions—literature became a forum for discussing such problems and their potential solutions.

Criticism near the nineteenth century's close was also influenced by a growing demand for a thoroughly American literature. Prominent American Renaissance authors of the nineteenth century, such as Ralph Waldo Emerson, Herman Melville, and Walt Whitman, demonstrate the literary struggle to find a uniquely national mode of expression. Furthermore the literary landscape of America was in transition: the dominance of the romance—such as those written by Washington Irving, James Fenimore Cooper, Nathaniel Hawthorne, and Herman Melville—and the tremendous influence of transcendentalism in the writings and lecturing of Emerson, Bronson Alcott, Henry David Thoreau, and Margaret Fuller were giving way to literary realism in the novels of William Dean Howells, Henry James, Mark Twain, and others. The increasing prominence of literary naturalism as seen in the works of Stephen Crane, Frank Norris, and Theodore Dreiser, the unprecedented acceleration of urbanization and industrialization, and America's involvement in World War I produced a generation of literary critics widely varying in approach, ranging from socially and politically minded literary criticism to neoclassical humanism intent upon opposing the decline of aesthetic standards.

CRITICISM IN TRANSITION

Critics in the late 1800s were influenced by a twofold tension. They respected the genteel European standard for aesthetics, yet they were also deeply invested in the national struggle for a new and democratic American art and culture. Balancing an aesthetic, moral, and rational model of criticism with a sensitivity to cultivating American literature was the defining character of their labors. The criticism of Edwin Percy Whipple (1819–1886) is characteristic of his era's desire to achieve this balance. Considered to be one of the Boston Brahmins, Whipple, a popular lyceum lecturer, ranks with James Russell Lowell and Edgar Allan Poe as one of the most competent and widely read American critics of his day. In such works as *Recollections of Eminent Men with Other Papers* (1886) and *American Literature and Other Papers* (1887), Whipple commented favorably on American writers, particularly Emerson, while critically discussing contemporary European literature. Influenced by Samuel Taylor Coleridge's philosophy of poetry, Whipple's criticism came to be termed "critical expressionism" (Rathbun, p. 107). This ethical and humanistic method assumes that the literary work is an organic whole with an inherent and intelligible form. John W. Rathbun explains in *American Literary Criticism, 1800–1860* (1979) that for the critical expressionist "it becomes the business of the critic to sympathetically enter the [literary] work, imaginatively duplicate the artist's original experience, and come to a revelation of what the artist has done for man" (p. 108). Whipple's criticism is witty and urbane, written "in a spirited, conversational style free from the precious affectation of academics" (Pritchard, p. 141) and serves as a model of the public man of letter's contribution to culture.

William Crary Brownell (1851–1928), like Whipple, was a high-profile critic. Never associated with a university, he was recognized as exercising professional authority in the arena of literary criticism. Brownell's essays on British and American literature, *Victorian Prose Masters: Thackeray, Carlyle, George Eliot, Matthew Arnold, Ruskin, George Meredith* (1901) and *American Prose Masters: Cooper, Hawthorne, Emerson, Poe, Lowell, Henry James* (1909), comprise insightful literary analyses of prominent nineteenth-century Anglophone writers and showcase both his erudition and his critical abilities. Influenced by the British critic Matthew Arnold, Brownell insisted that authentic criticism is the work of a rational, trained mind. He rejected Impressionistic criticism, based primarily on the critic's personal response to a literary work. In *Criticism* (1914), Brownell argues that "no other than a rational criterion so well serves criticism in the most important of all its functions, that of establishing and determining the relation of art and letters to the life that is their substance and their subject as well" (Glicksberg, p. 122). For Brownell criticism is a species of writing guided primarily by human reason: it is not mere book reviewing, exposition, subjective impression, or a creative activity akin to writing fiction.

IMPRESSIONIST CRITICISM

Whipple and Brownell developed literary theories. The Impressionists did just the opposite. The Impressionist literary critics did not analyze literary form or proceed according to fixed principles; they spoke in their own voices, providing their personal responses to the literature they were criticizing. Artfully rendering subjective literary experience became an end in itself for these critics. Opponents of Impressionist criticism, including Brownell, Irving Babbitt, and Paul Elmer More, rejected it as lacking rigor, substance, and standards. Its emphasis upon subjectivity and personality made Impressionism the perfect venue for such literary personalities as James Huneker, H. L. Mencken, and George Jean Nathan.

James Gibbons Huneker (1857–1921) was an eclectic journalist and an avowed Impressionist who wrote about music, art, and theater as well as about literature. He was the most significant "importer" of European culture and ideas of his day. Huneker popularized for American readers the French Impressionist painters, the drama of George Bernard Shaw and Henrik Ibsen, and the philosophy of Friedrich Nietzsche. A cosmopolitan critic, he eschewed moralism in literature and criticism, rejecting literary puritanism and the genteel tradition. Huneker focused rather on what literature offered readers of fine sensibility, good breeding, and cultivated aesthetic taste. His reviews of art, literature, music, and drama in the New York *Sun* (1900–1917) and his book-length collections *Mezzotints in Modern Music* (1899), *Iconoclasts: A Book of Dramatists* (1905), and *Promenades of an Impressionist* (1910) exhibit little methodological consistency, yet they stand as paragons of Impressionism, showcasing Huneker's native wit and rich endowment of literary talent.

Henry Louis Mencken (1880–1956) and George Jean Nathan (1882–1958), two of the most important and well-known American critics of the 1920s, were deeply influenced by Huneker's Impressionism. From 1914 to 1923 Mencken and Nathan coedited the *Smart Set*, a witty, urban, iconoclastic magazine that scathingly critiqued contemporary American culture. In 1924 they founded the *American Mercury*, a periodical in the satiric vein of the *Smart Set*'s skeptical critique, which Mencken edited until 1933. Nathan's criticism, as found, for instance, in *Mr. George Jean Nathan Presents* (1917) and *The Critic and the Drama* (1922), primarily concerns the theater

Cover of *The Smart Set,* 1922. Edited by H. L. Mencken and George Jean Nathan, *The Smart Set* offered a scathing critique of American culture. THE GRANGER COLLECTION, NEW YORK

and champions playwrights such as Shaw, Ibsen, and Eugene O'Neill.

An immensely influential critic, particularly upon emerging novelists and poets of the early twentieth century, Mencken applauded the works of such innovative American authors as Sherwood Anderson, John Dos Passos, Theodore Dreiser, Sinclair Lewis, and Upton Sinclair because they engendered something vital, new, and necessary that American culture needed to embrace. Indeed for Mencken literary criticism is a platform whereby the critic develops his own ideas rather than executing a close study of literary works according to consistent principles. In his essay "Footnote on Criticism," originally published as "The Motive of the Critic" in the 26 October 1921 issue of the *New Republic,* Mencken asserts that the motive of the true critic "is no more and no less than the simple desire to function freely and beautifully, to give outward and objective form to ideas that bubble inwardly . . . to get rid of them dramatically and make an articulate noise in the world" (reprinted as "The Critical Process" in Van Nostrand, p. 240). Thus Mencken's Impressionistic criticism is more about his own ideas than it is a detailed analysis of particular authors or works. Much of Mencken's pungent criticism is collected in six volumes aptly titled *Prejudices* (1919–1927).

THE NEW HUMANISTS

H. L. Mencken was never reticent in expressing his opinions, but regarding contemporary literary critics, he was perhaps the most vociferous opponent of the two staunchest defenders of New Humanism, Irving Babbitt (1865–1933) and Paul Elmer More (1864–1937). Mencken's iconoclastic and Impressionistic criticism was the antithesis of Babbitt and More's neoclassical school of literary analysis. Few public literary battles between American intellectuals have been more heated and more interesting than that between Mencken and these two adversaries.

New Humanism was inspired by William C. Brownell and articulated as a school of criticism by Babbitt, More, and their literary confederate Norman Foerster (1887–1972). They called for a return to classical standards of aesthetic evaluation, emphasizing the perennial aspects of human nature as found in classical Greek and Christian culture. Rejecting Romanticism's emphasis upon subjective imagination and self-expression, naturalism's sordid realism and mechanistic suppression of free will, and radically populist or democratic models of literature, the New Humanists upheld a criticism informed by the virtues of order, decorum, and restraint. Irving Babbitt, a professor of French literature at Harvard, wrote more about the theory of literature than about particular authors or works, as exemplified in his first collection of essays, *Literature and the American College: Essays in Defense of the Humanities* (1908). He called for a return to the study of the Greek classics and roundly denounced both Romanticism, particularly Jean Jacques Rousseau and his legacy in *Rousseau and Romanticism* (1919), and the literary naturalism of such writers as Theodore Dreiser, who Babbitt thought reduced the dignity of the rational human person to the ignominy of a mere animal.

Paul Elmer More's prolific literary criticism, including essays, articles, and reviews, is collected in his eleven-volume series, the *Shelburne Essays* (1904–1921). More was involved in a journalistic countermovement to the iconoclasm of Mencken's *Smart Set* and the progressive liberalism of the *New Republic* and similar periodicals. More was the editor

of the *Nation* from 1909 to 1914, and from 1914 to 1919 he was a frequent contributor to and sometime book review editor of the *Unpopular Review*. The *Unpopular Review*, a classically liberal publication, discussed current issues of cultural significance (World War I, the League of Nations, "the woman question," labor unions) while retaining a cautious restraint in matters of public policy. Regarding literary criticism, it became an outlet for the humanism espoused by Babbitt and More. Such frequent contributors as More; the novelist, playwright, and critic Brander Matthews; and the publisher Henry Holt discussed the decline in American education, the crisis of identity and leadership within the professoriate, the nature of modern poetry, the state of the theater in America, the art of novel writing, and the malign effects of Rousseau's Romanticism upon Continental literature as well as other topics.

In general the New Humanists were not receptive to much of the contemporary literature praised by Mencken and his critical circle. In their view, literary art produced by the likes of Sherwood Anderson, John Dos Passos, Theodore Dreiser, Sinclair Lewis, Carl Sandburg, and Gertrude Stein painted a false picture of the human condition and was symptomatic of moral and cultural deterioration.

LITERARY CRITICISM AND POLITICAL RADICALISM

Socialism, including various strains of communist thought, gained unprecedented cultural support in the early twentieth century in America. Thus literature and literary criticism increasingly became a platform for radical politics and social reform. For instance, critical luminaries of the early twentieth century such as Randolph Bourne (1886–1918), Max Forrester Eastman (1883–1969), and Louis Untermeyer (1885–1977) were men of letters but were also to differing degrees partisans of radical politics. Their literary criticism reflects their political inclinations but is by no means exclusively, or in some cases even mostly, at the service of political ideology.

In his short life Randolph Bourne served in an editorial capacity at several political magazines with literary interests, including the *New Republic* and *The Dial*. Besides providing an outspoken pacifist voice opposing American involvement in World War I, Bourne influenced the literary careers of Theodore Dreiser, Sinclair Lewis, and other of his contemporaries. In his articles and reviews appearing in the *Atlantic Monthly*, *The Dial*, the *Masses*, and the *New Republic*, Bourne evaluated literature in terms of aesthetic excellence (tone, style, form, and craftsmanship) as well as social responsibility and relevance to the modern sensibility. He believed strongly in the younger generation's ability to lead the nation in a progressive direction; thus he praised literature embodying what he called "the spirit of youth." *History of a Literary Radical and Other Essays* (1920), published posthumously and edited by Van Wyck Brooks, contains much of Bourne's philosophy of criticism.

Max Eastman, influenced by socialism and the Communist experiment in Russia, was one of the most prominent radicals of the 1910s and 1920s. In 1912 he was elected by the staff to edit the socialist journal the *Masses,* a position he retained until the demise of the magazine. Under Eastman's management, the *Masses* published literary articles and poems by Sherwood Anderson, Randolph Bourne, Carl Sandburg, Upton Sinclair, and Louis Untermeyer at the same time that it "attacked bourgeois economic, social, and political institutions with a verve and abandon that involved it in libel suits, loss of mailing privileges, suspension, and eventual suppression by the government at the end of 1917" (Sutton, p. 55). Immediately afterward Eastman began to publish and edit *The Liberator,* a similar journal, which survived until 1924. Eastman's major contribution to literary criticism came with the publication of his most important and enduring book, *Enjoyment of Poetry* (1913), which, revised and republished many times during his life, exerted much wider influence than his social and political writings. His book *The Literary Mind: Its Place in an Age of Science* (1931) further articulates his theory of poetry. According to Eastman, factual truth is the domain of science, and society should look to science to guide its course. Poetry does not deal with "truths"; poetry speaks to humanity's subjective, nonpractical, and emotional experiences. Thus poetry should be enjoyed as part of human experience rather than consulted as a source of truth about humanity and society. Because Eastman distinguished between the separate functions of poetry and science, his literary criticism is much more literary than propagandistic.

Although Louis Untermeyer never finished high school, he was an autodidact who became a prominent poet, critic, and anthologist of poetry. He held politically radical views and was associated with the *Masses* and *The Liberator.* Untermeyer's literary articles and reviews of poetry were widely published in the *New Republic,* the *Independent, The Dial,* and the *New York Times.* Possessing a broad command over the formal elements of poetry and the history of poetry in English, Untermeyer's criticism favored the spirit of modernity, a populist and democratic ethos, and nonacademic poetry. In his seminal collection of essays, *The New Era in American Poetry* (1919), Untermeyer celebrates H. D. (Hilda Doolittle), Robert Frost, Amy Lowell, Edgar Lee Masters, Ezra Pound, Carl Sandburg, and others as being the needed departure from the genteel tradition and the puritan ethos. Untermeyer argues that the moderns are the first generation of truly progressive American poets, and he proclaims that modern poets have been set free "to look at the world [they live] in; to study and synthesize the startling fusion of races and ideas, the limitless miracles of science and its limitless curiosity, the growth of liberal thought, the groping and stumbling toward a genuine social democracy—the whole welter and struggle and beauty of the modern world" (Untermeyer, p. 13). Untermeyer enjoyed a lifelong influence and published an astonishing volume of poetry, criticism, and anthologies.

JOEL SPINGARN'S "NEW CRITICISM"

Joel Elias Spingarn (1875–1939) as a literary critic was unique among his contemporaries. Spingarn was, as John Paul Pritchard argues, "perhaps the best informed American on the history of literary criticism" (p. 200). He tried to blaze a new trail for criticism beyond the polemics of his day, one that surpassed mere impressionism, political radicalism, and moralistic humanism. In "The New Criticism," a lecture delivered at Columbia University in 1910, Spingarn provides a concise articulation of his critical philosophy. Maintaining that all art is expression, he rejects the subjectivity of the Impressionists, the moralizing of the humanists and the genteel critics, the urge to historically contextualize the work, and the impulse to judge the work by resurrecting classical "rules" of form and genre. Spingarn simply poses a twofold question of the literary work: What has the poet expressed, and how completely has he or she succeeded?

Spingarn rejects criteria extraneous to the work of art, believing that each work is unique and should be judged according to its own form. Thus Spingarn argues that, when the critic fully appreciates the organic unity of the work and the author's artistic intention at the moment of creation, criticism becomes a mirror to art. He argues for a common origin for criticism and art in "The New Criticism," suggesting that "in their most significant moments, the creative and the critical instincts are one and the same. . . . Criticism at last can free itself of its age-long self-contempt, now that it may realize that esthetic judgment and artistic creation are instinct with the same vital life" (Babbitt, pp. 43–44). With this essay Spingarn also provided the title that John Crowe Ransom appropriated three decades later for his book

The New Criticism (1941) and the term that came to designate the most important American critical movement in the first half of the twentieth century.

T. S. ELIOT

While T. S. Eliot (1888–1965) is not generally numbered among the New Critics—the most prominent of whom are Ransom, Cleanth Brooks, Allen Tate, and William K. Wimsatt—he provided the basic ideas and theoretical underpinnings of the New Criticism, which became the most resounding American critical trend in the first half of the twentieth century. In the early twenty-first century few students of literature would dispute John Paul Pritchard's assertion that "Eliot is undoubtedly the most commanding figure of twentieth-century criticism in the English-speaking world" (p. 233).

As a student at Harvard, Eliot studied under Irving Babbitt, whose insistence on classical standards and the virtues of reason, order, and objectivity guided Eliot's thinking. Soon after receiving his master's degree in 1910, Eliot traveled in Europe and within a few years settled in England. In 1917 his first book of poetry, the innovative and influential *Prufrock and Other Observations,* appeared, and he also began publishing important critical work in the *Egoist,* including his series of articles "Studies in Contemporary Criticism." In these essays he proposed that literary critics ignore the personality and background of the writer, withhold speculation about psychological motives and conditions underlying creative works, and forego attempting to assess the writer's intention in producing the work. Eliot eschewed both the homiletic urge of Impressionist critics and the centrality that they gave to the emotive power of the literature they were supposedly criticizing.

In 1920 Eliot published his first volume of essays, *The Sacred Wood: Essays on Poetry and Criticism,* which contains his best-known and most-influential essays, "Tradition and the Individual Talent" and "Hamlet and His Problems." In this collection of essays Eliot sweeps away the subjectivity and imprecision of past criticism and proposes objective means of evaluating literature by comparing and contrasting it with the tradition and by closely analyzing its inner workings. Former approaches yielded not criticism but varieties of biography, history, psychology, and inspirational writing. Eliot extols a distinct and scientific criticism that dissects and analyzes a literary work in the same way that a scientist would study nature. In the process he provides later criticism with such crucial concepts as the "objective correlative," the "dissociation of sensibility," and the "impersonal theory of poetry." T. S. Eliot's *The Sacred Wood* thus forms a monumental capstone to the development of American literary criticism between the end of the Civil War and 1920.

See also Aestheticism; Anti-Intellectualism; Genteel Tradition; Impressionism; "The Love Song of J. Alfred Prufrock"

BIBLIOGRAPHY
Primary Works

Babbitt, Irving, ed. *Criticism in America: Its Function and Status.* New York: Harcourt, Brace, 1924. An anthology that includes Brownell's "Criticism," Eliot's "Tradition and the Individual Talent," Mencken's "Footnote on Criticism," Spingarn's "The New Criticism," and other important essays.

Bourne, Randolph Silliman. *The World of Randolph Bourne.* Edited by Lillian Schlissel. New York: Dutton, 1965.

Glicksberg, Charles I. *American Literary Criticism, 1900–1950.* New York: Hendricks House, 1952. An anthology with critical commentary on Eliot's "Tradition and the Individual Talent," Mencken's "Footnote on Criticism," Spingarn's "The New Criticism," and essays by Babbitt, Brownell, Huneker, More, and others.

Mencken, H. L. *H. L. Mencken's "Smart Set" Criticism.* Edited by William H. Nolte. Ithaca, N.Y.: Cornell University Press, 1968.

Untermeyer, Louis. *The New Era in American Poetry.* New York: Henry Holt, 1919.

Van Nostrand, Albert D., ed. *Literary Criticism in America.* New York: Liberal Arts, 1957. An anthology that includes Eliot's "Tradition and the Individual Talent" and Mencken's "The Critical Process" ("Footnote on Criticism") as well as works by Irving Babbitt, Brander Matthews, Edwin P. Whipple, and others.

Secondary Works

Goldsmith, Arnold L. *American Literary Criticism, 1905–1965.* Boston: Twayne, 1979.

Martin, Jay. *Harvests of Change: American Literature, 1865–1914.* Englewood Cliffs, N.J.: Prentice-Hall, 1967.

Pritchard, John Paul. *Criticism in America: An Account of the Development of Critical Techniques from the Early Period of the Republic to the Middle Years of the Twentieth Century.* Norman: University of Oklahoma Press, 1956.

Rathbun, John W. *American Literary Criticism, 1800–1860.* Boston: Twayne, 1979.

Rathbun, John W., and Harry H. Clark. *American Literary Criticism, 1860–1905.* Boston: Twayne, 1979.

Sutton, Walter. *Modern American Criticism.* Englewood Cliffs, N.J.: Prentice-Hall, 1963.

Aaron Urbanczyk

LITERARY FRIENDSHIPS

By tradition, the act of writing is an isolated one. *Webster's English Dictionary* (1858) defines an author as "One who produces, creates, or brings into being; as God is the *author* of the universe." Such godlike creation implies self-sufficiency, autonomy, and apartness, a Romantic conception of the literary artist still common in the early twenty-first century despite the revisionary critical moves that followed Roland Barthes's landmark essay, "The Death of the Author" (1968). In his later years, Herman Melville wrote in solitude, lacking social contacts and largely forgotten by the reading public. Emily Dickinson also became increasingly reclusive, as evidenced in her correspondence with the critic and feminist Thomas Wentworth Higginson—a potentially sympathetic adviser but one who was unable to respond to her fully either as a person or a poet.

But the myth of the isolated artist is easily exaggerated. Male companionship was of intense importance to Melville. Evert A. Duyckinck, a close lifelong friend of Melville's, oversaw publication of his first book and introduced him to Nathaniel Hawthorne. And Dickinson had her friendships (with Helen Hunt Jackson, for instance), even in her later years. Writers undoubtedly stand reflectively apart from society, imaginatively engaged with life's essentials, critiquing commonly held assumptions and illustrating the rifts in ideological systems that others take for granted. But they are, at the same time and to lesser or greater extent, engaged and functioning members of that society. Indeed, this peculiar sense of standing both within and without social, conceptual, and ideological boundaries also defines the artist's role and identity. Henry James powerfully allegorized these two sides of the creative artist in "The Private Life" (1893), in which two (literally) different Clare Vawdreys are represented. The one "talks . . . circulates . . . [and is] awfully popular." The other lives apart from the world and dedicates himself completely to his "genius," his literary art (pp. 23–24).

Friendships are as important to the writer as they are to anyone else. The most valuable literary friendships in terms of artistic development and sustenance have often been with fellow writers. In some cases, this has involved—either on the part of one or both—revising, editing, or publishing the literary productions of the other. The whole business of authorship, however, has meant that others who are not creative writers themselves but who work professionally alongside them as secretaries, researchers, publishers, and editors must also be included within the definition of literary friends.

One form literary friendship can take is that of an unequal relationship between an established writer and an apprentice or unknown, often younger, colleague. In such a case, the former might provide support, advice, and encouragement at the start of the other's career. At this level, the term "friendship" is not inappropriate but may tend to overstate the nature of a relationship, which is not necessarily based on deep personal intimacy but rather on one party's generosity and sense of professional responsibility. The title of William Dean Howells's memoir, *Literary Friends and Acquaintance* (1900), suggests a line between such categories. It is, however, necessarily a blurred one.

WILLIAM DEAN HOWELLS AND HIS ROLE IN AMERICAN LETTERS

At its most effective, the literary support offered by an established writer can have a twofold function. First, it can consist in the giving of practical advice on matters of form, style, and content and in assisting in the publication of the work, and second, it can help develop the career trajectory of the junior partner. The more influence the senior writer has in the publishing world, the greater potentially the effect of his or her assistance. William Dean Howells (1837–1920) established himself in such a role as perhaps the most significant literary figure in late-nineteenth-century and early-twentieth-century America. Known by the early 1900s as "the Dean of American Letters," it is probably fair to say that Howells had more power in the American literary marketplace than any American author before or since. Howells was the influential editor of the *Atlantic Monthly* (1871–1881), editor and contributor for *Harper's New Monthly Magazine* from 1886, book reviewer and literary commentator, and also a respected novelist. His expertise coincided with a unique convergence of historical and cultural circumstances in which rapidly developing systems of mass consumption and communication still (just about) went hand in hand with a more traditional respect for high cultural forms and their representatives. When Howells moved from Boston to New York in 1888, he signaled a national shift in the balance of cultural power. He was also at the forefront of the move against sentimentalism and the neo-Romantic in America in favor of the more vigorous and radical literary forms of realism and naturalism.

Somewhat paradoxically, Howells's politics lay naturally on the side of caution, despite a real unease with contemporary social injustices. His recognition of the importance of European literary developments and his fostering of the talents of a diverse range of new and younger American writers illustrated both a catholicity of taste and a selfless commitment to what he saw as his wider literary obligations. A host of young writers owed him a distinct debt, as he encouraged and helped publish their work, among them Harold Frederic, Hamlin Garland, Stephen Crane, Frank Norris, Paul Lawrence Dunbar, Charles W. Chesnutt, and Sarah Orne Jewett. It was, for instance, his first enthusiastic review of Garland's *Main-Travelled Roads* (1891) that helped boost its nationwide success.

But there was a negative side to this literary philanthropy. For, as John W. Crowley pertinently notes, such cultural power also had its effect on those, such as Edith Wharton and Theodore Dreiser, whom Howells chose not to praise: "the deepest cut of all was for The Dean *not* to speak ex cathedra about a promising writer" (p. 76). Moreover, as the representative of hegemonic authority in the (white male) American publishing world, his influence could be construed—whatever his actions and motives—as working against the deepest needs and aspirations of marginalized cultural groups. Howells, however, can be defended here. The range of his literary encouragement is, to the modern critical imagination, compromised by its selective nature and the form that it sometimes took. But, from a turn-of-the-century perspective, and given the nature of his position, it is difficult to imagine how much more differently or positively he could have generally responded.

Paul Laurence Dunbar (1872–1906) later accused Howells of doing "irrevocable harm" by encouraging his work in dialect verse, a form that—in Dunbar's case—tended to foster demeaning racial stereotypes. But Howells's recognition of the value of the vernacular tradition can be read in other ways, in that it helped free American literature from a reliance on the discourse of white middle-class respectability and anticipated the Harlem Renaissance's later celebration of distinctive African American cultural difference.

Yet Howells did not do as much as he could have done to further Charlotte Perkins Gilman's (1860–1935) literary career. His recollection of the publication history of "The Yellow Wall-Paper" sounds a noticeably ambiguous, and even puzzling, note when he says that he agreed "with the editor of *The Atlantic* at the time that it was too terribly good to be printed" (Karpinski, p. 227). There is also evidence to suggest that Gilman's radical feminism and emotional intensity struck the wrong note in terms of Howells's more cautious and conventional gender politics. Although Howells conformed to conventional patriarchal models in this respect, he was influential in getting the now-famous story published in *New England Magazine* in 1892 through his influence over the editor, Edwin Mead (if his own account of the matter is to be accepted). And he did believe in gender equality to a

Mark Twain and W. D. Howells at Lakewood, 1908. The literary friendship between Howells and Twain benefited both and lasted until Twain's death. SPECIAL COLLECTIONS LIBRARY, UNIVERSITY OF MICHIGAN

degree unusual for the men of his period and offered considerable support to American women writers of his time, especially to local colorists such as Sarah Orne Jewett and Mary Wilkins Freeman.

Howells had, then, a disproportionately large influence on his period. The literary acquaintances and friendships he formed were in large part allied to his recognition that new literary forms were a necessary response to changing American social and intellectual conditions. But his work and reputation would soon be demolished (as too bourgeois, timid, and "feminine") by the modernist generation that followed.

HOWELLS AND TWAIN

Howells's role as an editor and "literary mentor" suggests that distinctions must be made between various forms of literary friendship. His position as a figure of cultural authority and the encouragement and literary patronage he gave to lesser-established and often younger writers bred respect and loyalty. Eventually, though, intergenerational rivalry and the (necessary) displacement of the symbolic literary father attenuated his influence. But there was a different quality to the friendships he made with writers of roughly his own age and background and a closer emotional connection, too. Here, other qualities of friendship supplemented relationships that could still involve editorial assistance and joint adherence to a particular set of literary principles. These included factors such as the intimacy of shared experience, including ideological values and professional interests, and the extension of friendship to the larger family group. The close friendship between Howells and Samuel Clemens (Mark Twain, 1835–1910) illustrates this point.

Howells's affection for Clemens was immensely strong and vice versa. Clemens was not always an easy man to get on with and had a reputation both for a quick temper and for fallings-out with former friends. Bret Harte (1836–1902), for instance, was close to Clemens in San Francisco in the mid-1860s and (in Clemens's words) "trimmed and trained and schooled me patiently" (p. 28) as he began his literary career. But Clemens was never entirely at ease with Harte's condescending elegance and foppish ways, and after a rupture in their friendship in early 1877, his opinion of Harte plummeted. The references Clemens made to Harte became correspondingly vitriolic: "Harte is a liar, a thief, a swindler, a snob, a sot, a sponge, a coward, a Jeremy Diddler, he is brim full of treachery" (Smith and Gibson, p. 235). In contrast, the relationship between Clemens and Howells lasted for a forty-year period and was still staunchly intact at the former's death in 1910.

Theirs was a many-faceted friendship and one that brought real pleasure to both men and much literary benefit to Clemens in particular. Howells spotted Clemens's talent early and fostered it through generous and prominent reviews of his novels and short stories and the publishing opportunities he gave him. Clemens (rightly) saw Howells as "the recognized Critical Court of Last Resort in this country" (p. 64). Howells used this authority to bolster his friend's reputation at every opportunity. Famously, it was his acceptance of "A True Story" for publication in the November 1874 *Atlantic Monthly* that first signaled Clemens's acceptance by the American literary establishment as more than just a "low" comedian. As Clemens appreciatively commented, "The *Atlantic* audience . . . is the only audience . . . that . . . don't require a 'humorist' to paint himself stripèd & stand on his head every fifteen minutes" (Smith and Gibson, p. 49). Howells also acted as editor, literary adviser, and even proofreader for Clemens. He checked the proofs of *Huckleberry Finn* at the point that the book's author had lost all patience for the task, and he did so with absolute graciousness: "If I had written half as

good a book as *Huckleberry Finn*, I shouldn't ask anything better than to read the proofs; even as it is I don't. So send them on" (Smith and Gibson, p. 499).

In turn, Howells's realist tenets influenced Clemens and to an extent not sufficiently recognized. Like Howells—but because of his role as humorist, in a different way—Clemens could never quite reconcile the need to appeal to a mass audience with a higher set of cultural aspirations. The two men also worked together on several projects. Most, such as *Colonel Sellers as a Scientist* (1887), the stage comedy based on one of Clemens's most successful created characters, brought little success. Clemens's first novel, *The Gilded Age* (1873), written in collaboration with his Hartford neighbor Charles Dudley Warner (1829–1900), proved a more successful example of how friendship could be successfully combined with literary collaboration. In his affectionate memoir *My Mark Twain* (1910), Howells recaptures something of the self-delusion that affected them both as they got caught up in whatever project was at hand. Writing of the *Sellers* play, he says, "We had a jubilant fortnight in working the particulars of the thing out. . . . I still believe the play was immensely funny. . . . But this may be my fondness" (p. 24). He then, though, confirms that this latter was indeed the likely case in admitting that no theater manager or actor would take the play. But, for whatever reason—perhaps because of certain similarities in their earlier lives, perhaps because of the patient and gentle good humor Howells brought to their relationship—this was the strongest of friendships and one that worked as well on a personal as on a professional level. Both men shared domestic sorrow, suffering the bitter blow of losing much-loved young daughters and emotionally sustaining and consoling each other as they were able. But there was also a great deal of sheer fun in the friendship too. And Howells was entirely sincere when he wrote to Clemens, "I would rather see and talk with you than any other man in the world, outside my own blood" (Smith and Gibson, p. 607).

Clemens and Howells's relationship is paradigmatic in illustrating some of the factors on which literary friendships can be based. The two men liked and trusted each other and enjoyed each other's company. They gave support to each other throughout their artistic careers (though Clemens was the primary beneficiary). They shared similarities in terms of background and experience. Both had nostalgic tendencies, which were usually held in check by a more critical and realistic habit of mind. The gulf between pre–Civil War boyhood and an adult life in a fast-modernizing postwar American world led each to construct affectionate versions of that earlier time. And each responded enthusiastically to the other's literary vision. Howells told

Clemens that *The Adventures of Tom Sawyer* (1876) was "altogether the best boy's story I ever read. . . . I wish *I* had been on that island" (Smith and Gibson, pp. 110–111). And when Howells published *A Boy's Town* (1890), Clemens answered in kind: "'A Boy's Town' is perfect—perfect as the perfectest photograph the sun ever made" (Smith and Gibson, p. 633).

JACK LONDON, SARAH ORNE JEWETT, WILLA CATHER

Literary friendships carry over from conventional models of friendship but often with an additional dimension stemming from the specific interaction of personal and professional concerns. To separate out such friendships' various orders is first to recognize—as previously shown—that different friendships fulfill different functions. Jack London's (1876–1916) friendships with three other writers show something of this. His relationship with Cloudesley Johns was based on mutual artistic appreciation. It took the form of an honest but supportive appraisal of each other's writings, the shared articulation of an aesthetic philosophy, and a joint pleasure in each other's literary successes. His friendship with the poet George Sterling (1869–1926) relied more on their close sense of personal intimacy, husbands and wives together sharing time both at London's California ranch and at the artists' colony in Carmel. Their use of nicknames—London's "Wolf" to Sterling's "Greek"— further suggests their easy companionship. London's relationship with Sinclair Lewis (1885–1951) was apparently based partly on philanthropy. For London helped the younger and struggling writer financially by buying plot ideas from him. But their relationship was not one-sided. The plotlines bought from Lewis helped London offset his own shortcomings, for as he wrote to Cloudesley Johns in 1900, "I can't construct plots worth a dam, but I can everlastingly elaborate" (London). London's use of Lewis in this way suggests that, like the title character in his *Martin Eden* (1908), he took a more pragmatic attitude to the business of writing than earlier novelists. More generally, one sees some move away from the idea of the lone artist in the growing professionalization of writing at this time.

Literary friendships can serve as the locating ground of a set of overlapping activities. Such friendships are the place where prejudices are aired and special interests fostered, where personal and artistic assumptions are confirmed or altered, where feedback on writing practices is received, and where psychological and emotional support can be given. Writers of a particular class, ethnic group, or gender whose marginal status gives them little voice in the larger social and artistic dialogue can gain confidence and sustenance from such alliances. Sarah Orne Jewett's (1849–1909) encouragement of the young Willa Cather (1873–1947) was, accordingly, a turning point in the younger writer's life. Both were unconventional in their own gender practices, and each made the gender/power nexus a central theme of her work. Cather's dissatisfaction with her early stories, "so poor that they discouraged me" (Cather), was countered by the praise and advice she received from the elder writer, who encouraged her both in the pursuit of a full-time writing career and in the representation of women's relations with other women. As Cather wrote: "Then I had the good fortune to meet Sarah Orne Jewett, who had read all my early stories and had very clear and definite opinions about them and about where my work fell short. She said, 'Write it as it is, don't try to make it like this or that. . . . Make a way of your own. If the way happens to be new, don't let that frighten you. . . . Write the truth and let them take it or leave it'" (Cather).

LONDON, PARIS, MODERNISM

Literary friends can serve as a sounding board for new artistic forms. In the early years of the twentieth century, groups of writers and artists came together—and especially in the two artistic capitals of London and Paris—to jointly engage in varieties of modernist experimentation. Gertrude Stein (1874–1946), whose rue de Fleurus apartment in Paris became one of the best-remembered artistic salons of the period, saw the expatriate urge in terms of the poverty of American cultural life: "Of course they all came to France a great many to paint pictures and naturally they could not do that at home, or write they could not do that at home either, they could be dentists at home" (Bradbury, p. 31). *The American Scene* (1907) by Henry James—whose earlier expatriation and circle of literary friends in Europe and America anticipated his modernist successors—tends to support such a reading. But perhaps a growing sense of the limitations of local and national cultural identifications and a recognition of a wider and international sense of creative artistic ferment provide an equally powerful explanation (if a less witty one than Stein's).

For Stein, who moved to Paris in 1903, "Paris was the place that suited those of us that were to create the twentieth century art and literature." For Ezra Pound (1885–1972), London—where he arrived in 1908— initially had a similar importance: "London, deah old lundon, is the place for poesy" (Witemeyer, p. 13). Although the American literary world was relatively disparate geographically following the earlier preeminence of Boston, these two capitals provided the locations for a series of close literary and artistic friendships where the shape of modernist writing was formed. But this movement was by no means contained within these settings and among these particular groups. Pound's collaboration with Harriet Monroe (1860–1936), editor of *Poetry* magazine in Chicago, was one notable example of the way new ideas of poetry were propagated on a transatlantic scale, while his correspondence with William Carlos Williams (1883–1963), whose life was mainly spent in Paterson, New Jersey, formed not just "an unparalleled documentary record of developments in modern literature and culture" but also a long-lasting if variable friendship, "an unpredictable saga of collaboration and conflict" (Witemeyer, pp. vii–viii).

Pound's friendships might have been volatile—the American poet John Gould Fletcher spoke of his "pugnacious virility"—but his publicizing, encouraging, and marshaling of fellow writers was quite extraordinary, as together they reshaped the artistic boundaries of their time. He and Hilda Doolittle (H.D., 1886–1961) were centrally involved in the founding of the imagist movement and the writing of its 1908 manifesto. Then, in 1914, with Wyndham Lewis (1882–1957), he became propagandist and prime mover behind vorticism and *Blast,* the journal that publicized it. In that same year, he met T. S. Eliot (1888–1965), beginning a friendship in which Pound took on the roles of publisher, editor, adviser, career manager, and financial sponsor. Indeed, the editing he did of *The Waste Land* (1922) is a strong reminder of the real artistic benefits that literary friendships can provide. It was Pound, too, who recognized James Joyce's (1882–1941) talents and who played a central part in putting him on the literary map, publishing *A Portrait of the Artist* in *The Egoist* (of which he was literary editor) in 1914.

Meanwhile something similar was happening in Paris, if without the factor of Pound's particular dynamic intensity. Before the war, Gertrude and Leo Stein's friendships with Picasso, Matisse, Braque, and other European artists made their apartment a forum for those working at the cutting edge of modernist art. It was here, too, that other Americans in Europe, such as Mabel Dodge and Carl Van Vechten, gathered. After the war, the household, now run by Gertrude Stein and Alice B. Toklas, became a place where writers and artists such as Pound (who moved to Paris in 1920), Paul Robeson, Virgil Thomson, Djuna Barnes, Ernest Hemingway, and others talked and worked together to encourage and widen the ongoing thrust of modernist experimentation. Stein's own relationship with Toklas was the intimate one of partner and lover. But the relationship also provided Stein with literary material (*The Autobiography of Alice B. Toklas,* 1933) and undeniably helped prompt Stein's slyly subversive critique of patriarchal language and assumptions. Artistic identity, literary style, and radical gender politics were thus directly linked to this particularly intense form of literary friendship.

FLOWERS OF FRIENDSHIP?

Richard Lingeman writes that "literary friends walk on eggshells" with "the demons of jealousy, envy, competitiveness lurking" (Donaldson, p. 272). Literary friendships have many positive benefits, but some of the comments previously made about Clemens and Harte and Pound and Williams hint at other possibilities. The artistic ego can be sensitive, even paranoid, and aggression toward present or past friends who are also literary rivals is a commonly recognized pattern as—to slightly alter part of the title of Stein's famous poem, "the flowers of friendship fade," in either a temporary or permanent way. Stein's own relationship with Ernest Hemingway (1899–1961) is a case in point. In his memoir *A Moveable Feast,* Hemingway looks back to the 1920s and "the way it ended with Gertrude Stein." He describes calling at 27 rue de Fleurus, waiting for Stein to come down and hearing "Miss Stein's voice come pleading and begging [Alice], saying, 'Don't, pussy. Don't. Don't, please don't. I'll do anything, pussy, but please don't do it. Please don't. Please don't, pussy'" (p. 118). Hemingway leaves the house, reporting, "that was the way it finished for me," and that though the relationship with Stein was later resumed, "I could never make friends again truly, neither in my heart nor in my head" (p. 119). The story is, of course, part of Hemingway's mythic narrative of artistic independence as he brings issues of writing (what Stein had taught him, "valid and valuable . . . truths about rhythms and the uses of words in repetition" [p. 17]) and sexuality together, revealing his homophobia as he confirms his own separateness and masculine self-sufficiency.

Literary friendships, then, can be of considerable importance in the encouragement, sustaining, and development of the creative impulse. But the tensions that can also exist in such relationships are integral to the very business of being a writer. Robert Sward quotes a contemporary poet "for whom the phrase 'writers' friendship' would seem an oxymoron, a contradiction in terms, like resident alien or small crowd" (Sward). Aggression and competition can be a basis for literary production as well as encouragement, intimacy, and support. If literary friendships have their great rewards, they also run such risks.

See also Literary Colonies; Literary Marketplace

BIBLIOGRAPHY
Primary Works
Cather, Willa. "Willa Cather Talks of Work." Interview by F. H. in the *Philadelphia Record,* August 10, 1913, soon after the publication of *O Pioneers!* Available at

http://www.willacather.org/InterviewsLettersetc/InterviewOPioneers!.htm.

Clemens, Samuel (Mark Twain). *Mark Twain's Letters 1867–1875.* Available at http://mark-twain.classic-literature.co.uk/mark-twains-letters-1867–1875/.

Hemingway, Ernest. *A Moveable Feast.* New York: Scribners, 1964.

Howells, William Dean. *My Mark Twain: Reminiscences and Criticisms.* New York: Harper and Brothers, 1910.

James, Henry. "The Private Life." 1893. In *Henry James: Selected Tales.* London: Dent, 1982.

London, Jack. Jack London to Cloudesley Johns, June 16, 1900. Jack London, Author and Adventurer. Literary Friendships. Huntington Library, 2002. Available at http://www.huntington.org/LibraryDiv/friends.html.

Smith, Henry Nash, and William M. Gibson, eds. *Mark Twain–Howells Letters: The Correspondence of Samuel L. Clemens and William D. Howells 1872–1910.* 2 vols. Cambridge, Mass.: Belknap Press, 1960.

Witemeyer, Hugh, ed. *Pound/Williams: Selected Letters of Ezra Pound and William Carlos Williams.* New York: New Directions, 1996.

Secondary Works

Bradbury, Malcolm. *The Expatriate Tradition in American Literature.* Durham, U.K.: British Association for American Studies, 1982.

Crowley, John W. *The Dean of American Letters: The Late Career of William Dean Howells.* Amherst: University of Massachusetts Press, 1999.

Donaldson, Scott. *Hemingway vs. Fitzgerald: The Rise and Fall of a Literary Friendship.* Woodstock, N.Y.: Overlook Press, 1999.

Karpinski, Joanne. "When the Marriage of True Minds Admits Impediments: Charlotte Perkins Gilman and William Dean Howells." In *Patrons and Protégées: Gender, Friendship, and Writing in Nineteenth-Century America,* edited by Shirley Marchalonis, pp. 212–234. New Brunswick, N.J.: Rutgers University Press, 1988.

Marchalonis, Shirley, ed. *Patrons and Protégées: Gender, Friendship, and Writing in Nineteenth-Century America.* New Brunswick, N.J.: Rutgers University Press, 1988.

Stoneley, Peter. "Rewriting the Gold Rush: Twain, Harte, and Homosociality." *Journal of American Studies* 30, no. 2 (1996): 189–209.

Sward, Robert, comp. and ed. On the Nature of Literary Friendships. Web Del Sol/Perihelion. http://www.webdelsol.com/LITARTS/Robert_Sward/Writers_Friendship/introtoc.html.

Peter Messent

LITERARY MARKETPLACE

Numerous and interrelated factors of acquisition, production, distribution, and consumption radically transformed the American literary marketplace between the close of the Civil War and the end of the First World War. A half century of demographic, social, cultural, technological, and commercial changes at once accompanied, propelled, and shaped an exploding "print ecology" in the United States. Important studies by Christopher P. Wilson, Daniel H. Borus, and Susan Coultrap-McQuin emphasize how these changes made obsolete the personal, paternalistic, leisured, and belletristic world of the "Gentleman Publisher" and of the "coterie marketplace" in antebellum and mid-century America. In its place emerged a much more robust, competitive, impersonal, professional, profit-driven, and in many ways, recognizably modern marketplace for what E. J. Phelps, in a December 1889 *Scribner's Magazine* article, disparaged as "The Age of Words." While Phelps may have looked askance at authors "more prolific than the Australian rabbit" and frontier newspapers following hard on the heels of the ubiquitous whiskey saloon, the novelist Frank Norris more charitably attributed the "sudden and stupendous demand for reading matter" to an "awakening" across classes and cultures of readers (p. 85).

NEW DEVELOPMENTS IN THE PRINT ECOLOGY

Literacy, like money, satisfied differing needs in an increasingly urban and culturally diverse nation whose population grew from 31 million in 1860 to 110 million in 1920. But no needs were more prevalent than the desires for popular entertainment, moral instruction, and cultural edification to be had from literature, whether lightsome or high-minded, ephemeral or durable. The late nineteenth century accordingly experienced an outpouring of literature in general and of fiction in particular to meet the demands of diverse and dispersed readers. Statistics provided in John Tebbel's *The History of Book Publishing in the United States* attest to the dramatic increase in new books and pamphlets published during these years: 2,076 in 1880; 4,559 in 1890; 6,356 in 1900; and 13,470 in 1910. "New" did not necessarily mean American books, however, because publishers and readers retained a sizable appetite for the staples of fiction, regardless of origin, long after copyright protection effectively ended the availability of cheap but pirated foreign titles.

Frank Luther Mott's *The History of American Magazines* documents a similar proliferation in newspapers (4,000 in 1865; 19,000 in 1899) and magazines (700 in 1865; 3,300 in 1885; 5,500 in 1900).

FRANK NORRIS ON THE BUSINESS OF WRITING

In the following excerpt from his essay "Fiction-Writing as a Business," Frank Norris describes what he calls the typical "life history" of a "properly managed" literary property.

First it is serialized either in the Sunday press or, less probably, in a weekly or monthly. Then it is made up into book form and sent over the course a second time. The original publisher sells sheets to a Toronto or Montreal house and a Canadian edition reaps a like harvest. It is not at all unlikely that a special cheap cloth edition may be bought and launched by some large retailer either of New York or Chicago. Then comes the paper edition—with small royalties, it is true, but based upon the enormous number of copies, for the usual paper edition is an affair of tens of thousands. Next the novel crosses the Atlantic and a small sale in England helps to swell the net returns, which again are added to—possibly—by the "colonial edition" which the English firm issues. Last of all comes the Tauchnitz edition, and with this (bar the improbable issuing of later special editions) the exploitation ceases. Eight separate times the same commodity has been sold, no one of the sales militating against the success of the other seven, the author getting his fair slice every time.

Norris, "Fiction-Writing as a Business," in *Complete Works* 7:125–126.

This growth helps explain Mark Twain's satire in *A Connecticut Yankee in King Arthur's Court* (1889), in which one of Hank Morgan's first official acts in Camelot is to found the *Weekly Hosannah and Literary Volcano*. Not all of the magazines and periodicals counted by Mott survived beyond infancy. The numbers nonetheless hint at the prevailing reality between the Civil War and World War I: the established publishing houses and magazines were being challenged by the competitive publishing of ever-cheaper literature for mass audiences. Also, this competition was taking place in a national marketplace rather than in the northeastern and mid-Atlantic regions that had previously been the prime markets for publishers.

Harbingers of the emerging mass market were the story papers, weekly tabloids of stories and serialized novels that had circulated in America since the 1830s. In the 1870s and 1880s, however, their numbers and their readership surpassed all of the literary magazines. For as little as five or six cents a week at the newsstands or for $1.50 to $2 a year by subscription, a reader could purchase Robert Bonner's *New York Ledger* (1855–1898), Street & Smith's *New York Weekly* (1858–1910), Norman Munro's *New York Family Story Paper* (1873–1921), his brother George Munro's *Fireside Companion* (1867–1903), or any number of similar papers. Alongside the occasional poem and back-page sermon, customers received eight to twelve densely printed pages of typically sensational, melodramatic, patriotic, sentimental, and occasionally risqué fiction. This material was frequently pirated from English periodicals, occasionally reprinted from earlier issues, and as competition demanded, commissioned from popular writers under exclusive contracts. The sentimental novelist Emma Dorothy Eliza Nevitte Southworth (1819–1899)—better known as Mrs. E. D. E. N. Southworth—for example, was a stalwart of the *New York Ledger*. Even after they were supplanted by the Sunday supplements and the literary inserts of the new daily newspapers, the story papers remained a convenient archive of material (metropolitan stories, western and military and maritime stories, science fiction stories, detective stories) for the second great wave of paperback publishing in America.

A flood of cheap paperbacks also began in the 1870s and continued into the early 1890s, until cutthroat competition, overproduction, the adoption of an international copyright law in 1891, and the financial panic of 1893 significantly stemmed the tide. In the intervening two decades paperback houses churned out disposable books with amazing rapidity, in some instances a new title daily. These uniformly priced (a quarter or less, when new clothbound books were selling for $1.50), crudely printed, and frequently pirated books were marketed in countless libraries or series of related titles targeted at specific audiences. They included George Munro's "Seaside Library," Norman Munro's "Riverside Library," Harper's more high-toned "Franklin Square Library," even a "No Name Series" of anonymous novels from Roberts Brothers. Because profit was a direct function of volume, the paperback houses inundated the market with literal and figurative bales of inexpensive reprints, frequently of popular foreign books, at the expense of new and indigenous American titles.

When publishers did not resort to pirating or reprinting, corps of staff and contract writers, more efficient than proficient, earned between $150 and $300 per original dime novel or between $75 and

$150 per half-dime novel (introduced for the less afflu-ent boys' market). The most famous of the dime novels were the pocket-size "yellow backs" of thirty-five thou-sand to forty thousand words from the New York firm of Beadle and Company, later Beadle & Adams (1851–1898). These paperback biographies and novels were affordable, and affordably disposable, throughout the ranks of the working classes. In an entry in *Publishers for Mass Entertainment in Nineteenth Century America,* Lawrence Murphy estimates that between 1860, when Dime Novel No. 1 appeared (Ann S. Stephen's *Malaeska: The Indian Wife of the White Hunter*), and 1898 Beadle & Adams distributed three titles every two weeks for almost forty-seven years. The firm's principal competi-tor, Street & Smith, eventually surpassed Beadle as the largest publisher of dime novels in more than fifty dif-ferent but always sensational dime and nickel series, including the urban uplift stories of Horatio Alger Jr. (1832–1899).

THE PROMINENCE OF THE NEW PERIODICALS

For the more serious literature of the age, though, the preeminent venue was the periodical. The novelist and editor William Dean Howells (1837–1920) observed in his 1893 essay "The Man of Letters as a Man of Business" that the prosperity and prominence of the new magazines had given "a whole class existence which, as a class, was wholly unknown among us before the war." The contemporary writer understood "perfectly well," Howells wrote, that "his reward is in the serial and not in the book" (p. 432).

Howells might have noted as well that the grow-ing dominance of the periodical press over the book trade tended to conflate literature and literary journal-ism in a manner that led a remarkable number of (mostly male) writers to serve apprenticeships and even to establish careers as journalists and "magazin-ists." The offices of the magazines and newspapers could be "cemeteries of talent" in Larzer Ziff's mem-orable phrase from *The American 1890s: Life and Times of a Lost Generation* (p. 150), but they were also the training grounds for not only Howells but also a host of other respected literary figures. These included Mark Twain (a pseudonym for Samuel Langhorne Clemens), Bret Harte, George Washington Cable, Harold Frederic, Edward Bellamy, Ida M. Tarbell, Charles Waddell Chesnutt, Hamlin Garland, Richard Harding Davis, George Ade, Lincoln Steffens, Finley Peter Dunne, Ray Stannard Baker, Frank Norris, Stephen Crane, Theodore Dreiser, Willa Cather, and Jack London. Yet the rewards of the periodical press were not without costs. Writers already accustomed to trimming their work to the presumed moral sensibilities

of the reading public had to accommodate themselves as well to the practices and policies of the mass-market periodical.

Often known as "ten-cent magazines," the mass-market periodicals typically had a circulation of a quarter million or more. They dominated the periodical trade by the mid-1890s, but they had been preceded by what were sometimes referred to as the "quality" magazines. In *Reading for Realism: The History of a U.S. Literary Institution, 1850–1910,* Nancy Glazener termed these quality periodicals the "*Atlantic* group" of magazines, and they were a veritable marketplace unto themselves through the 1880s. Such magazines were frequently owned by and used for promotional purposes by pub-lishing houses, were run by editors who thought of themselves as men of letters, were directed primarily to a genteel and conservative audience of northeastern sub-scribers, and were instrumental in fostering and shaping American literary realism by embracing in their fiction (if not in their readership) representations of the common man and woman. In addition to the *Atlantic* itself (1857–), these periodicals included the *Galaxy* (1866–1879); the *Critic* (1881–1906); the *Forum* (1886–1930); *Harper's New Monthly* (1850–1899), later to become *Harper's Monthly Magazine* (1900–1913) and *Harper's Magazine* (1913–); *Lippincott's* (1868–1916); the *Nation* (1865–); the venerable *North American Review* (1815–1939); the irregularly issued *Putnam's* (1853–1857, 1868–1870); *Scribner's Monthly* (1870–1881), which was to become *Century Magazine* (1881–1930); and *Scribner's Magazine* (1887–1939).

These literary magazines were eclipsed by their more fashionable, more popular, and more profitable mass-market competitors: the *Saturday Evening Post* (1821–), rejuvenated under the editorship of George Horace Lorimer after 1899 and boasting a million sub-scribers by 1900; *Ladies' Home Journal* (1883–), also a million-selling weekly by 1903; *Cosmopolitan* (1886–); *Collier's Weekly* (1888–1957); Frank A. Munsey's ten-cent weekly *Munsey's Magazine* (1889–1929); Samuel Sidney McClure's ten-cent monthly *McClure's Magazine* (1893–1929); and the weekly *Everybody's Magazine* (1899–1929). As a group, these magazines published popular if occasionally homogenous fiction alongside topical and "timely" articles, human-interest stories, and copious photoengravings and eventually photographs. They differed from their genteel prede-cessors in several important respects: rather than appendages to publishing houses, they were self-sus-taining and profit-driven publications with active edito-rial policies and aggressive marketing strategies; they secured mass readership through below-cost prices (ten to fifteen cents per issue and as little as a dollar a year for subscriptions) made possible by heavy advertising revenue; and they were sold on newsstands as much as through subscriptions. In an 1899 column, the editor Frank A. Munsey (1854–1925) offered his literary formula for the successful magazine: "Good easy reading for the people—no frills, no fine finishes, no hair splitting niceties, but action, action, always action" (Labor et al., p. xiv). Hamlin Garland (1860–1940) took a more jaded view of the "magazining" he witnessed while at *McClure's:* "Editing became more and more a process of purveying, and writing more and more of an appeal to shopgirls, tired business men, and others who demanded easy and exciting reading" (p. 342).

Both Christopher P. Wilson and Susan Coultrap-McQuin have emphasized the increasingly impersonal nature of the periodical market between the Civil War and World War I. The magazines relied upon advertisers for revenue, their publishers relied upon professional editors for policy, editors frequently relied upon staff writers for contributions, and everyone relied upon the marketplace rather than aesthetic standards for cues to taste. The generation of editors who came of age after the Civil War—most notably, John Brisben Walker (1847–1931) of *Cosmopolitan,* Samuel Sidney (S. S.) McClure (1857–1949) of *McClure's Magazine,* Edward W. Bok (1863–1930) of the *Ladies' Home Journal,* and George Horace Lorimer (1867–1937) of the *Saturday Evening Post*—adopted and adapted the managerial models of modern commerce while pursuing editorial policies—"magazining" (Wilson, p. 51) as McClure termed it—that emphasized the "preplanned" and "anticipatory production" of articles. Practices alien to the "quality" magazines (competing for a writer's work, commissioning articles and stories, maintaining house writers) became the norm, making the new magazines, according to Wilson, "less the province of the nonaffiliated, voluntary contributor—not laissez-faire gatherers of an independent literature but active agents in a managed market" (p. 53). One such "nonaffiliated, voluntary contributor," the popular New England writer Elizabeth Stuart Phelps (Ward) (1844–1911), no doubt spoke for many of her fellow writers in her 1910 complaint to Robert Underwood Johnson, editor of *Century Magazine:* "Sometime (if I live) I am going to make an onslaught on the whole modern magazine system of fitting an author to mechanics, instead of the mechanical spaces to the author. It was not so 'befo' the war'" (Coultrap-McQuin, p. 188).

NEW EFFICIENCIES IN THE MARKETPLACE

Meeting—and creating—the needs of diverse and dispersed readers required new efficiencies in the book, magazine, and newspaper trades that went beyond the merely mechanical, technological, or logistical. Granted,

the continuing expansion of the railroads helped to alleviate the chronic problem of book distribution, as did the emergence of large wholesalers such as Sinclair Tousey's American News Company, which kept street-corner and train-station newsstands nationwide stocked with millions of books, magazines, and newspapers. Magazine publishers benefited as well from a revision of the postal system that took place in 1879, which introduced rural free delivery and lowered rates for any printed material remotely resembling a periodical. Meanwhile, new technologies lessened the dependence of printers on time-, labor-, and cost-intensive manual skills. The Hoe and Tucker web press of 1871 was capable of enormous print runs of newspapers and periodicals. The Kraft thermochemical pulping process of 1879 produced wood-fiber paper in abundance for ever-cheaper books and magazines. Similarly, the Mergenthaler Linotype machine of 1886 finally mechanized typesetting, and the late 1880s brought the advent of less-expensive halftone rather than hand-engraved illustrations. At the same time, as Richard Ohmann argues in an essay in *Politics of Letters,* the unparalleled wealth accumulated under late-nineteenth-century industrial and finance capitalism strengthened publishing houses and periodicals, which had previously been undercapitalized and often folded after a short time in operation. Nor can one dismiss the social and cultural factors that swelled the increasingly diversified and stratified (but still predominantly female) ranks of readers: accelerating urbanization, compulsory education laws, improved access to higher education, heightened literacy rates, marginally increased leisure time, and the construction of public libraries (twenty-five hundred in 1876 and five thousand or more by 1900). Yet many of these developments, whether in transportation or in education, differ more in degree than in kind from analogous causes cited for the first great expansion of American literature in the 1830s and 1840s. More definitive of the later marketplace, though, were those developments that gave the air of efficient professionalism to the production, dissemination, and management of literary properties.

The new marketplace, whether for books or periodicals, clearly favored the steadily industrious writer. Christopher P. Wilson argues that the romanticized antebellum emphasis on authorial inspiration divorced writing from the idea of work, but the emergent standard in postbellum America was a bourgeois ideal of productivity and its associated values of timeliness, reliability, discipline, responsibility, and expertise (p. 9). In 1886 the *Atlantic Monthly,* then edited by Horace Elisha Scudder, singled out Henry James (1843–1916), F. Marion Crawford, and William Dean Howells as "the most distinctly professional novelists in America."

The magazine measured these "knights of labor" by a "year in and year out" ("James, Crawford, and Howells," p. 850) productivity that was yet to be fully reckoned: 40 novels from Crawford in a 27-year career; more than 20 volumes in the 1890s alone by Howells, a "remorselessly efficient literary machine" according to his biographer, Kenneth Lynn (p. 4); and counting only his fiction, more than 20 novels and 112 stories from James. A generation later Scudder could just as easily have cited the short-lived Jack London's record of more than fifty books—novels, short stories, essays, reportage—in a career of less than twenty years. Edith Wharton (1862–1937) won the Pulitzer Prize for *The Age of Innocence* (1920) only after she had already published nineteen volumes of novels, novellas, and poetry in the preceding two decades. Even O. Henry (a pseudonym for William Sydney Porter, 1862–1910), who started late, published nine volumes of stories between 1902 and his death and left material for an additional four posthumous volumes. And then there were the legendary dime novelists Prentiss Ingraham (1843–1904), who purportedly authored more than six hundred works for Beadle, and Gilbert Patten (1866–1945), who, writing as "Burt L. Standish," contributed hundreds of episodes for Street & Smith's "Frank Merriwell" series.

In 1891 Henry James observed that "periodical literature is a huge open mouth which has to be fed—a vessel of immense capacity which has to be filled" ("Science," p. 398). But entrepreneurs such as Ansel Nash Kellogg (1832?–1886), Irving Bacheller (1859–1950), and S. S. McClure had already recognized that even the most productive authors were unable to meet the ravenous demands of readers and editors. Their contribution in the 1880s was to form literary syndicates to distribute stories and serialized novels for simultaneous publication in newspapers and newspaper inserts. Bacheller has little to say in his memoirs about the mechanics of syndication other than to emphasize what was of no small concern to writers, "the doubling of rates all along the first rank of authorship" (p. 45). But the syndicates were responsive to shifts in popular taste, helped writers to reach wider and more dispersed audiences, and generated broad interest in a work prior to its book publication. Such was the case with Stephen Crane's *The Red Badge of Courage: An Episode of the American Civil War*, which the Bacheller-Johnson Newspaper Syndicate placed in a half-dozen American newspapers in 1894 before it was published by Appleton and Company in 1895. In his study of the syndicates, *Fiction and the American Literary Marketplace: The Role of Newspaper Syndicates, 1860–1900*, Charles Johanningsmeier emphasizes the prevalence of the practice on both sides of the Atlantic and lauds the syndicates as "the most potent catalysts for the many positive changes that came in the literary marketplace in the 1890s for both authors and readers" (p. 33).

If periodical syndication was an efficient means of reaching a widely dispersed readership, subscription publishing was an equally effective means of reaching more directly the comparatively small book-buying segment of the larger reading public. A number of subscription publishers successfully managed to bypass the bookstore, relying instead on commissioned agents to solicit individual orders for a book prior to its publication. Publishing houses already experienced with mail-order and discount sales to dry-goods and department stores such as Wanamaker's and Macy's needed little incentive to circumvent the traditional retailers. Granted, most editors and publishers tended to disparage the practice as undignified, while less-scrupulous agents exploited the system to fleece the purchaser, occasionally by outright fraud but more often by pushing on uninformed buyers oversized, overpriced, but lavishly illustrated works of dubious merit. Still, the use of subscription agents to canvass potential customers in rural areas and isolated communities that lacked bookstores was a marketing strategy well-suited to minimizing the risks of dealing in expensive reference works, deluxe editions of standard works and Bibles, sets sold on installment plans, and works of regional interest only, such as county histories. It worked as well for Mark Twain, who marketed his most popular works—*The Innocents Abroad; or, The New Pilgrims' Progress* (1869), *Roughing It* (1872), *The Gilded Age* (1873), *The Adventures of Tom Sawyer* (1876), and *Adventures of Huckleberry Finn (Tom Sawyer's Comrade)* (1885)—through the subscription agents of, first, Elisha Bliss Jr.'s American Publishing Company and then, from 1884 until its collapse in 1894, his own New York firm Charles L. Webster and Company. Success was apparently not limited to Twain or to specialty publishers. James D. Hart estimates that "outside of school books and periodicals, more than three-fourths of all the money expended in the United States for books each year passed through the hands of agents" during the 1890s and the early years of the twentieth century (Madison, pp. 119–120).

THE MANAGEMENT OF LITERARY PROPERTIES

Perhaps the defining feature of the marketplace was that it favored those writers and publishers who most successfully converted into income the multiple rights inherent in works of literature with audience appeal. These included periodical syndication, cloth and paperback editions, and international publications. These multiple outlets helped writers to recognize that their interests were not vested solely in one periodical or publishing house and that their success was not necessarily insured by personal relationships. This further moved the act of publication in the direction of business transactions founded upon contractual negotiations.

The changing relationship between those antebellum stereotypes, the grateful and deferential writer and the magnanimous if not condescending publisher, is conveyed in a series of admittedly selective vignettes. An article titled "Letter to a Young Contributor" in *Atlantic Monthly* in April 1862, likely penned by the editor Thomas Wentworth Higginson, who served as mentor to Emily Dickinson, reassured potential contributors of the essentially collaborative and congenial nature of the mid-century marketplace. The article described a mutually amicable world of letters wherein authors, editors, and publishers worked toward the common good on little more than a handshake because "the real interests of editor and writer are absolutely the same, and any antagonism is merely traditional" (p. 401). Only eight years later, however, Mary Abigail Dodge (1833–1896), the Washington essayist and journalist who used the pseudonym Gail Hamilton, signaled that the times were changing with her self-published *A Battle of the Books* (1870), a fictionalized version of her acrimonious dispute with the genteel Boston publisher James T. Fields over alleged underpayments. This contentiousness between writer and publisher became figuratively violent in Jack London's 1909 novel *Martin Eden,* wherein the self-educated, working-class Eden's struggle to have his work accepted by faceless editors is analogous to the brutal fights of his youth with his "eternal enemy" Cheese-Face. "They ain't no hand-shakin' in this," Eden warns his nemesis before their final bone-crushing clash on Oakland's Eighth Street Bridge (p. 678). Amid the avuncular Higginson, the litigious Hamilton, and the pugnacious London one can barely hear the understated Henry James, who remarked to Howells in 1880 that "there are natural limits to one's sympathy with one's publishers" (James and Howells, p. 141).

THE RISE OF LITERARY AGENTS

For many writers, there were natural limits to their willingness, much less their ability, to manage successfully the increasingly complex business of drawing a living from words. The emergence of literary agents in the last two decades of the century was another instance of entrepreneurship in the cause of efficiency, but it was also an explicit sign that the business of writing and the business of publishing were no longer synonymous. Bret Harte (1836–1902) stated the point explicitly in his May 1885 testimonial to Alexander P.

Watt (1834–1914), his English agent: "Until authors know a little more about business, and are less likely to feel that it interferes with that perfect freedom essential to literary composition, it seems better that they should employ a *business man* to represent them with those other *business men,* the publishers" (p. 323).

Watt and his colleagues—William Morris Colles, James Brand Pinker, and Albert Curtis Brown—anticipated their American counterparts by representing English authors as early as 1875, according to James Hepburn in *The Author's Empty Purse and the Rise of the Literary Agent.* The first fully professional literary agent in America was the Bostonian Paul Revere Reynolds (1864–1944), who, after first working in New York as a publisher's agent, was representing authors by the mid-1890s. Soon he was earning his standard 10 percent commission for shopping books, stories, and articles to publishers; negotiating contracts; bargaining for advances and royalty rates; arranging for English publication and translations; marketing ancillary rights, especially as film adaptations became more and more common; and a myriad of additional tasks on behalf of a clientele that included, among others, Stephen Crane, Hamlin Garland, Booth Tarkington, Willa Cather, and Ellen Glasgow.

Publishers, of course, tended to disparage agents as intrusive at best and parasitic at worst. Some, Charles Scribner and Henry Holt among them, initially shunned any writer represented by an agent. The irrepressibility of the agent, though, is clear from two editions of *Authors and Publishers: A Manual of Suggestions for Beginners in Literature,* by George Haven Putnam (1844–1930) and John Bishop Putnam (1847–1915), principals in G. P. Putnam's Sons. The first edition, in 1883, was a relatively slim volume of ninety-six pages devoted to refuting the "popular assumption that between authors and publishers little sympathy existed" (Putnam and Putnam, 1st ed., p. 1). By 1897, however, the seventh edition of the popular manual had swelled to 275 pages and included a lengthy and dismissive chapter enumerating why the practices of the literary agent—mere brokers, the Putnams called them—were rarely in the interest of an intelligent and wise writer's long, successful, and stable career with a single publishing house.

Bret Harte's defense of agents seemingly owed much to the decline of his own literary fortunes, for he emphasized the peace of mind that an agent could bring to an otherwise uncertain career. The agent "takes away half the pains of authorship," especially that of the uncertainty of placing one's work, Harte wrote. "I generally know before I trust pen to paper that my work will be disposed of and the amount it will bring"

(p. 341). A more holistic assessment of the role of the agent in the marketplace is that of James West in *American Authors and the Literary Marketplace since 1900*:

> The agent encouraged in the serious author a healthy attitude toward the business of writing, an acceptance of the idea that literary work could be artistically challenging and, at the same time, financially remunerative. The agent became a means by which commercial considerations and popular taste exerted influence on the author's work, a way in which the tension between art and commerce was communicated to the author. (P. 95)

INTERNATIONAL COPYRIGHT AND ITS CONSEQUENCES

While the rise of agents was inextricably tied to the commodification of literature, the process of commodification was itself propelled most forcefully by American passage of an international copyright bill in 1891. American writers had enjoyed domestic copyright protection since 1790, but no legislation safeguarded their financial interests in foreign markets or sheltered them and their publishers from the ruinous competition of domestic reprinters issuing foreign works in pirated editions that undercut the sales of copyrighted works. In William Dean Howells's *The World of Chance* (1893), his protagonist, a midwestern journalist who aspires to a literary career in New York, hears the same lament from publishers as he peddles his manuscript: the "demoralization of the book trade" caused primarily by the absence in America of an international copyright law. "If we can only get this international copyright measure through," one publisher claims, "and dam up the disorganizing tide of cheap publications at its source, we may hope to restore the tone of the trade" (p. 46).

Efforts on behalf of a copyright bill antedated the Civil War, were resurrected in the late-1860s and in the 1870s, and gained momentum in the 1880s with the founding of associations such as the American Copyright League (1884) and the American Publishers' Copyright League (1887), with the strong support of New York and northeastern publishers such as George Haven Putnam, Charles Scribner, Henry Holt, Henry Houghton, and William Henry Appleton. Putnam's "Pleas for Copyright," in the April 1889 *North American Review*, argued the case nobly. He appealed for adherence to international morality, encouragement of American literature, fair play for foreign authors, the provision of better and cheaper books to consumers, and the betterment of the lives of the "many American authors who have attained an honourable position in literature, and who are, nevertheless, unable to secure

from the sale of their books the annual equivalent of a book-keeper's salary" (p. 464). However, attempts to legislate copyright protection involved protracted debate between publishers, pirates, authors, free-trade advocates, protectionists, and powerful sectional (that is, rural) interests. Only with passage of the Platt-Simonds Act, effective on 1 July 1891, did American authors receive a twenty-eight year international copyright on their works, a privilege shared by foreign authors who arranged for simultaneous publication and American manufacture of their works.

The Platt-Simonds Act brought with it many things: the protection of the personal incomes of authors, a justification for higher advances and royalties, a basis for new confidence by publishers in their investments, a boost to the competitiveness of American books in their native market, a justification to publishers to bid competitively for titles, and an impetus to the kind of advertising and marketing that would help to usher in the phenomenon of the best-seller. But copyright protection was also something of an act of submission to the realities of the new marketplace. The gradual commodification of literature was all but completed with the legal recognition of property rights in the imaginative and intellectual product of a writer's labor.

THE BEST-SELLER; OR, THE "BOOMED" BOOK

Frequently cited figures suggest that while a successful novel of the 1890s sold 5,000 copies and a new novel by a well-known author might sell 10,000 copies, a "boomed" novel had astonishing immediate sales and cumulative sales typically surpassing 600,000 or 700,000 copies and oftentimes reaching into the millions. These best-sellers were written in a variety of styles, including historical romance (Charles Major's *When Knighthood Was in Flower* in 1898 and George Barr McCutcheon's *Graustark: The Story of a Love behind a Throne* in 1901), the "down-home" novels of rural New England life (Edward Noyes Westcott's *David Harum* in 1898), historical fiction (Winston Churchill's *Richard Carvel* in 1899), the western (Owen Wister's *The Virginian: A Horseman of the Plains* in 1902), exotic adventure (Jack London's *The Call of the Wild* in 1903), and the muckraking exposé (Upton Sinclair's *The Jungle* in 1906). The appendices of Frank Luther Mott's *Golden Multitudes: The Story of Best-Sellers in the United States* and Charles A. Madison's *Book Publishing in America* are invaluable for their identification of many of the best-selling books between 1870 and 1920.

Sentimental domestic novels from female authors (whom Nathaniel Hawthorne derided as the "d—d mob of scribbling women") had found sizable American audiences in the mid-century. *The Wide, Wide World* (1850) by Susan Bogart Warner, *Uncle Tom's Cabin; or, Life among the Lowly* (1852) by Harriet Beecher Stowe, *The Lamplighter* (1854) by Maria Susanna Cummins, *Ruth Hall* (1855) by Fanny Fern (the pen-name of Sara Payson Willis Parton), and *The Hidden Hand* (1859) by Mrs. E. D. E. N. Southworth are ready examples. Likewise, religious and utopian titles such as *Ben-Hur: A Tale of the Christ* (1880) by Lew Wallace, *In His Steps* (1896) by the Reverend Charles M. Sheldon, and *Looking Backward, 2000–1877* (1888) by Edward Bellamy had large and lasting sales. Because the best-seller epitomized so many of the developments in the early modern literary marketplace, though, one can plausibly wonder whether the best-seller, as distinct from the popular work, could have arisen any earlier than the mid-1890s. For the best-seller has always represented a cooperative effort, a synchronous product of the literary and the commercial, of author, agent, publisher, salesman, reader, and the times themselves. As such, the best-seller was necessarily a reflection of the marketplace.

The American best-seller emerged during what John Tebbel has called the "great fiction orgy of the nineties and the new century's first decade" (p. 653), which would continue until the onset of the First World War. Its birth had to await the confluence of a number of events traced here. The growth of a mass readership and the general cheapening of books were obvious requirements, but the best-seller rode other currents as well: the curtailing of ruinously cheap competition in the publishing world, the professionalization of authorship, the emergence of agents to place books advantageously, the developing habit among publishers of competitive bidding, the protection through copyright of a publisher's investment, the refinement of advertising and marketing strategies, and the unflinching commodification of literature as quantifiable books to be sold. Moreover, the same market that bred the best-seller commodified the maker as well as the made. Successful writers themselves became forms of public property, personages—indeed, international celebrities in the case of Mark Twain—once there was market value in a newspaper byline, in a name on a magazine or title page, and in a likeness on a frontispiece.

LOOKING FORWARD

The literary marketplace of the Gilded Age and the Progressive Era never produced the divine "literatus," that democratic authorial ideal sought by Walt Whitman (1819–1892) in 1871 in *Democratic Vistas*. Yet the years between the wars were more than just "a manufacturing, rather than creative age," as *Publishers Weekly* lamented in 1893 (Tebbel, p. 26). Changes in the manner in which literature was created, disseminated, and read encouraged writers to think of their works as marketable commodities and therefore to think of their labor as vocations if not careers.

The example of Edith Wharton is emblematic of the potential for both high seriousness and success in the new marketplace. Recalling the 1870s New York of her parents' generation, Wharton observed in *A Backward Glance* (1934) that "authorship was still regarded as something between a black art and a form of manual labour" (p. 69). But her own career would be a testament to what she called the "Atlantis-fate" of so many features of that old New York. Her achievement, according to Richard Brodhead in *Columbia Literary History of the United States,* was to transcend the prevailing literary cultures—the long-established domestic culture of women, the growing proletarian and juvenile culture of youthful males, the gentrified northeastern culture represented by the "*Atlantic* group" magazines, and the consumer culture of an advertising age—and reconcile the seemingly antithetical principles of literature and commerce. As a professional writer in the early decades of the twentieth century, Wharton accomplished what the vagaries of a mass market had so often frustrated, "serious writing made commercially successful on the basis of its quality *as* serious writing" (Brodhead, p. 478).

See also Book Publishing; Literary Criticism; New York; Periodicals

BIBLIOGRAPHY
Primary Works
Bacheller, Irving. *From Stores of Memory.* New York: Farrar & Rinehart, 1938.

Garland, Hamlin. *Roadside Meetings.* New York: Macmillan, 1930.

Hamilton, Gail [Mary Abigail Dodge]. *A Battle of the Books.* Cambridge, Mass.: Riverside Press, 1870.

Harte, Bret. *Selected Letters of Bret Harte.* Edited by Gary Scharnhorst. Norman: University of Oklahoma Press, 1997.

Howells, William Dean. "The Man of Letters as a Man of Business." *Scribner's Magazine* 14, no. 4 (October 1893): 429–445.

Howells, William Dean. *The World of Chance.* New York: Harper & Brothers, 1893.

"James, Crawford, and Howells." *Atlantic Monthly* 57 (June 1886): 850–857.

James, Henry. "The Science of Criticism." *New Review* 4, no. 24 (May 1891): 398–402.

James, Henry, and William Dean Howells. *Letters, Fictions, Lives: Henry James and William Dean Howells.* Edited by Michael Anesko. New York: Oxford University Press, 1997.

"Letter to a Young Contributor." *Atlantic Monthly* 9 (April 1862): 401–411.

London, Jack. *Martin Eden.* In *Novels and Social Writings,* by Jack London, edited by Donald Pizer. New York: Literary Classics of the United States, 1982.

Norris, Frank. *Complete Works.* 10 vols. New York: Doubleday, Doran, & Company, 1928. Contains "Child Stories for Adults," 7:85–88.

Putnam, George Haven. "Pleas for Copyright." *North American Review* 148 (April 1889): 464–475.

Putnam, George Haven, and J. Bishop Putnam. *Authors and Publishers: A Manual of Suggestions for Beginners in Literature.* 1st ed. New York: G. P. Putnam's Sons, 1883.

Putnam, George Haven, and J. Bishop Putnam. *Authors and Publishers: A Manual of Suggestions for Beginners in Literature.* 7th ed. New York: G. P. Putnam's Sons, 1897.

Wharton, Edith. *A Backward Glance.* New York: D. Appleton-Century, 1934.

Secondary Works

Anesko, Michael. *"Friction with the Market": Henry James and the Profession of Authorship.* New York: Oxford University Press, 1986.

Borus, Daniel H. *Writing Realism: Howells, James, and Norris in the Mass Market.* Chapel Hill: University of North Carolina Press, 1989.

Brodhead, Richard. "Literature and Culture." In *Columbia Literary History of the United States,* edited by Emory Elliott et al., pp. 467–481. New York: Columbia University Press, 1988.

Coultrap-McQuin, Susan. *Doing Literary Business: American Women Writers in the Nineteenth Century.* Chapel Hill: University of North Carolina Press, 1990.

Glazener, Nancy. *Reading for Realism: The History of a U.S. Literary Institution, 1850–1910.* Durham, N.C.: Duke University Press, 1997.

Hart, James David. *The Popular Book: A History of America's Literary Taste.* New York: Oxford University Press, 1950.

Hepburn, James. *The Author's Empty Purse and the Rise of the Literary Agent.* London: Oxford University Press, 1968.

Johanningsmeier, Charles. *Fiction and the American Literary Marketplace: The Role of Newspaper Syndicates, 1860–1900.* Cambridge, U.K.: Cambridge University Press, 1997.

Labor, Earle, Robert C. Leitz III, and I. Milo Shepard. Introduction to *The Letters of Jack London.* Vol. 1, *1896–1905,* by Jack London. Edited by Earle Labor, Robert C. Leitz III, and I. Milo Shepard. Stanford, Calif.: Stanford University Press, 1988.

Lynn, Kenneth S. *William Dean Howells: An American Life.* New York: Harcourt Brace Jovanovich, 1971.

Madison, Charles A. *Book Publishing in America.* New York: McGraw Hill, 1966.

Mott, Frank Luther. *Golden Multitudes: The Story of Best Sellers in the United States.* New York: Macmillan, 1947.

Mott, Frank Luther. *A History of American Magazines.* Vol. 3, *1865–1885.* Cambridge, Mass.: Belknap Press of Harvard University Press, 1938.

Mott, Frank Luther. *A History of American Magazines.* Vol. 4, *1885–1905.* Cambridge, Mass.: Belknap Press of Harvard University Press, 1957.

Murphy, Lawrence Parke. "Beadle & Co." In *Publishers for Mass Entertainment in Nineteenth Century America,* edited by Madeleine B. Stern, pp. 35–50. Boston: G. K. Hall, 1980.

Noel, Mary. *Villains Galore: The Heyday of the Popular Story Weekly.* New York: Macmillan, 1954.

Ohmann, Richard. "Where Did Mass Culture Come From? The Case of Magazines." In *Politics of Letters,* pp. 135–151. Middletown, Conn.: Wesleyan University Press, 1987.

Phelps, E. J. "The Age of Words." *Scribner's Magazine* 6, no. 6 (December 1889): 760–768.

Tebbel, John. *A History of Book Publishing in the United States.* Vol. 2, *The Expansion of an Industry, 1865–1919.* New York: R. R. Bowker, 1975.

West, James L. W. *American Authors and the Literary Marketplace since 1900.* Philadelphia: University of Pennsylvania Press, 1988.

Wilson, Harold S. *McClure's Magazine and the Muckrakers.* Princeton, N.J.: Princeton University Press, 1970.

Wilson, Christopher P. *The Labor of Words: Literary Professionalism in the Progressive Era.* Athens: University of Georgia Press, 1985.

Ziff, Larzer. *The American 1890s: Life and Times of a Lost Generation.* New York: Viking, 1966.

Steven H. Jobe

LITTLE MAGAZINES AND SMALL PRESSES

Little magazines and small presses developed simultaneously in the late nineteenth century as a reaction to large magazines and major publishers. Many short-lived little magazines—the term refers to both the physical size of these magazines and the extent of their circulation—were started by young writers unable to find outlets for their own writings. Within the covers of these little magazines their editors could publish their own work as well as the writings of their friends and, in addition, have a platform from which they could decry the literary establishment that so unfairly and ungraciously ignored them. The most memorable little magazines of the late nineteenth century, however, were those started by the day's most memorable small publishers. The founders and editors of these little magazines made creative use of graphic design, incorporating unusual typefaces and innovative illustrations. With the turn of the century, it became increasingly difficult for small publishers to compete in the marketplace let alone to devote their time to editing and publishing a magazine, too. The best little magazines of the early twentieth century, therefore, were not created by small publishers but by independent litterateurs seeking a voice the big commercial magazines ignored.

STONE & KIMBALL AND THE *CHAP-BOOK*

Herbert Stuart Stone and Hannibal Ingalls Kimball met when both were undergraduates at Harvard College, class of 1894. As sophomores, they decided to found a publishing house, and during their junior year, the firm of Stone & Kimball issued its first titles. The college experiences of the two men helped them in this venture. Stone had worked as an editor for the Harvard *Crimson,* and Kimball had served as its business manager. With their new venture, they continued these roles, Stone serving as editor and Kimball in charge of the finances. They first issued *The Terra Cotta Guide* (1893), a timely guidebook to Chicago and the World's Fair held that year. They followed this publication with Stone's bibliographic compilation, *First Editions of American Authors: A Manual for Book-Lovers* (1893), a testament to his own love of books. Their handsome, well-made publications attracted some of the most notable authors of the day. Also in 1893 Stone & Kimball published four other titles: *Main-Travelled Roads* and *Prairie Songs,* both by Hamlin Garland; *Low Tide on Grand Pré,* a collection of lyric verse by Bliss Carman; and *The Building of the City Beautiful,* by Joaquin Miller. The following year they published an authoritative ten-volume edition of the works of Edgar Allan Poe, the fullest edition of Poe's writings to appear up to that time.

In May 1894 Stone & Kimball published the first issue of the *Chap-Book.* Primarily intended as a promotional vehicle to advertise the company's imprints, the *Chap-Book* quickly became an important publication in its own right. With its attractive design and lively contents, the *Chap-Book* appealed to men and women with fine literary tastes and aesthetic sensibilities. Upon graduating from Harvard a few months after the first issue of the *Chap-Book* appeared, Stone

and Kimball shifted operations to Chicago. Throughout the magazine's existence, the quality of its contents remained high. In 1897 the *Chap-Book* published what may be its most important publication, the serialization of Henry James's *What Maisie Knew.* Stephen Crane was another of its contributors. His poem "In the Night" appeared in 1896, and his appreciation of Harold Frederic appeared two years later. Other contributors to the *Chap-Book* include Thomas Bailey Aldrich, Ellen Glasgow, Lincoln Steffens, Paul Verlaine, and H. G. Wells. Stone & Kimball also managed to solicit the work of many of the day's finest graphic artists to illustrate the text of the *Chap-Book* and to design its decorative covers. Artists who contributed to the magazine include Aubrey Beardsley, Max Beerbohm, Will Bradley, Lucien Pissarro, John Sloan, and Henri de Toulouse-Lautrec. The *Chap-Book* is often credited with inspiring the numerous little magazines that subsequently appeared that decade.

Stone & Kimball continued the *Chap-Book* and issued numerous titles under their imprint through 1895. The titles they issued that year form an appealing mix of English literary classics, such as Izaak Walton's *Lives* and William Congreve's *Comedies;* translations of modern European authors, including Maurice Maeterlinck and Henrik Ibsen; and several young American and British authors. Partway through 1896, Stone and Kimball dissolved their partnership. Kimball borrowed heavily and bought out Stone's share in the business but was unable to sustain the Stone & Kimball imprint much longer. Stone was more successful on his own. He held onto the *Chap-Book* and continued it under his new imprint, Herbert S. Stone & Company. Circulation of the *Chap-Book* reached 14,500 by the time it was merged into *The Dial* in 1898. Both Stone and Kimball continued to work in publishing until their deaths in 1915. Coincidentally, the two men happened to be returning home from Europe aboard the *Lusitania* when it was sunk by a torpedo from a German submarine.

THOMAS BIRD MOSHER AND THE *BIBELOT*

The education of Thomas Bird Mosher differed significantly from that of Herbert Stone and Ingalls Kimball. He did not attend college and never graduated from high school, but his upbringing did help him develop a love of books and literature. He was born in Biddeford, Maine, the son of a sea captain who took him to sea when he was fourteen. Stopping off in Europe, Mosher visited a secondhand shop in Hamburg, where he purchased several volumes of the pocket edition of Bell's *British Theatre* (1792). Recalling how this collection of classic English drama inspired his lifelong love of literature, Mosher wrote, "I shall never

Poster advertisement by Will H. Bradley for _The Chap-Book_, 1895. With its attractive design and lively contents, the _Chap-Book_ appealed to men and women with fine literary tastes and aesthetic sensibilities. THE LIBRARY OF CONGRESS

Mosher. The first book he issued appeared in 1891; it was a reprint of George Meredith's _Modern Love,_ which had originally been published in 1862. Mosher published many different volumes of verse in the early 1890s, including new editions of the wildly popular _Rubáiyát of Omar Khayyám_ and collections of contemplative verse by many neglected poets. Mosher's imprints were products of fine bookmanship. Well-designed and beautifully printed, the issues of Mosher's press appealed to discerning bibliophiles and continue to appeal to collectors.

Mosher saw his little magazine, the _Bibelot,_ as an extension of his book publishing activities. Its subtitle offers a good indication of its contents: _A Reprint of Poetry and Prose of Book Lovers, Chosen in Part from Scarce Editions and Sources Not Generally Known._ Editing the _Bibelot,_ Mosher saw his task as a process of selecting from previously published work that best suited his tastes. The first number, issued in January 1895, contained lyrics by William Blake. Published in small format and elegantly printed, the _Bibelot_ somewhat resembled the _Chap-Book_ and may in part have been inspired by it.

Subsequent numbers of the _Bibelot_ reveal Mosher's exquisite, if idiosyncratic, tastes. He published recent material by William Butler Yeats and John Millington Synge and older material by Sir Philip Sidney and Marcus Aurelius. With recent material, Mosher sometimes got himself into trouble because he was not always careful about clearing permissions before going to press. But his fine sensibilities mitigated his tendency toward literary piracy. Richard Le Gallienne, in an appreciation of Mosher titled "In Praise of a Literary Pirate," called the _Bibelot_ "the most fascinating miscellany of lovely thought and expression ever compiled" (p. 778).

again read books as I once read them in my early seafaring when all the world was young, when the days were of tropic splendour, and the long evenings were passed with my books in a lonely cabin dimly lighted by a primitive oil lamp, while the ship was ploughing through the boundless ocean on its weary course around Cape Horn" (quoted in Blumenthal, p. 41).

Home from the sea, Mosher settled in Portland, Maine, where he obtained a position in a law stationer's office and later became a junior partner in a law book publishing firm, McClellan, Mosher and Company. Though the reports of cases and volumes of civil procedure the firm published did not suit Mosher's tastes, the experience did give him sufficient knowledge of book design and production to enable him to establish an independent press under his own imprint, Thomas B.

ELBERT HUBBARD AND THE _PHILISTINE_

Elbert Hubbard, who was born and raised in Bloomington, Illinois, did not discover the world of letters until fairly late in life. He left school at sixteen to begin selling soap door-to-door for his cousin Justus Weller, who operated a soap business with his partner, John Larkin. Hubbard proved to be an excellent salesman, a skill he would use to his advantage once he began editing and publishing his own magazine. When the Weller-Larkin partnership broke up, Hubbard became a junior partner in the Larkin Company, which was headquartered in Buffalo, New York. Hubbard settled in East Aurora, a suburb of Buffalo known for its horse raising, a particular interest of his.

Here Hubbard became obsessed with literature, largely through the Chautauqua movement in western

New York. He became so inspired that he wrote a novel, *The Man: A Story of To-Day* (1891). His enormous success in the soap business allowed him to indulge his literary interests to their full extent. He sold his share in the soap business for $65,000 and moved to the Boston area, where he obtained conditional admission to Harvard College. However, he disliked the regimen and rigor college required, did poorly in his classes, and was denied formal admission to the college. Harvard would become an object of Hubbard's derision in the pages of his little magazine.

Despite his failure in college, Hubbard's time in Boston did prove to be a formative one. Seeking a publisher for a second novel, *One Day: A Tale of the Prairies* (1893), Hubbard came in contact with the editor and publisher Benjamin Orange Flower. Hubbard began contributing articles to Flower's magazine, the *Arena*. Much to Flower's delight, Hubbard applied his sales experience and helped add another five thousand names to the list of *Arena* subscribers. Although Hubbard's experience with the *Arena* gave him important knowledge, William Morris's Kelmscott Press provided the primary inspiration for him to become a publisher and editor. A trip to England brought Hubbard to William Morris's Kelmscott Press. Although his contact with Morris was not as great as Hubbard claimed, seeing how and why the Kelmscott Press operated inspired Hubbard to found a press and an arts-and-crafts workshop in the United States by applying Morris's ideas.

In 1895 Hubbard returned to East Aurora, where he established the Roycroft complex, which, he announced, would be dedicated to printing fine books, making handcrafted furniture, and producing copperware. It was not long before Hubbard's entrepreneurial instincts enabled Roycroft to expand operations to include workshops for cabinetmaking, leatherworking, stained glass production, and weaving. Hubbard also put up a hotel on the premises, which became a mecca for artists and craftspersons and their admirers.

Despite the influence of the Kelmscott Press, the books Hubbard issued from the Roycroft Press did not match the standards established by Morris. Neither were they as nice as the books Mosher and other small presses issued. Hubbard initially intended to produce handmade books, and his early imprints were done on a traditional handpress. Before long, however, Hubbard installed multiple steam-powered rotary presses and churned out books as fast as his mechanical presses could turn. Their limp chamois-leather bindings, more than their printing, gave the Roycroft imprints their distinct quality. As Dard Hunter, who visited the Roycroft complex as a young man, later recalled: "Just

as Hubbard had once inundated the country with soap premiums, so he now undertook to place limp-leather bindings on the golden oak tables of every sitting room in America. Books in their window-cleaner covers were turned out in mass production; the dozen or more Roycroft presses were kept humming night and day; hand-made paper was imported by thousands of reams; red and black ink was purchased by the barrel, and every goat in the world was a potential limp binding" (quoted in Blumenthal, p. 51).

The inception of Hubbard's little magazine, the *Philistine*, has been attributed to a number of his associates. Henry Parson Taber was listed as its editor for much of the magazine's first year, but Hubbard was the driving force behind the magazine from the time of its first issue in June 1895 until his death in 1915. Others may have helped him at the start, but after a few issues he took it over completely in terms of both financing and editorial decision-making. The *Philistine* became a platform for Hubbard, from which he launched tirades against the establishment. He lambasted such influential literary figures as Mark Twain and William Dean Howells or, as Hubbard called him, W. Dean Howl. He critiqued the popular magazines of the day, and he excoriated Harvard College every chance he could.

Not all contemporary authors were objects of Hubbard's scorn. The support he gave Stephen Crane may be Hubbard's greatest contribution to American literature, though not all of his comments were positive. The *Philistine* appeared shortly after Crane published his first volume of verse. In his first issue, Hubbard reprinted "I Saw a Man Pursuing the Horizon" and included a sardonic comment regarding the book's title, *The Black Riders:* "The riders might have as easily been green or yellow or baby-blue for all the book tells about them, and I think the title 'The Pink Roosters' would have been better" (quoted in Wertheim and Sorrentino, p. 135). Hubbard parodied Crane in the second issue of the *Philistine* as he included a poem beginning with the line: "I saw a man making a fool of himself." Still, Hubbard asked Crane to contribute to the *Philistine,* and Crane subsequently sent him a few poems. The publication of *The Red Badge of Courage* later that year completely won over Hubbard, who arranged a dinner in Crane's honor and published a pamphlet including some of Crane's verse and several appreciations of Crane by others.

Hubbard applied his salesmanship to his endeavors as a magazine publisher and managed to develop quite a sizable readership. By the second decade of the twentieth century, annual subscription figures for the *Philistine* went into six digits. In short, the *Philistine* was the most successful little magazine of its day. With Hubbard's death—he too was aboard the *Lusitania* in 1915—came the end of the *Philistine*.

WILL BRADLEY AND *BRADLEY, HIS BOOK*

Born in Boston, Massachusetts, and raised in Ishpeming, Michigan, Will H. Bradley worked in his early teens as a printer's devil for the *Iron Agitator,* the daily newspaper in Ishpeming. In his late teens, he left Michigan for Chicago, where he found work in the printing plant of Rand, McNally & Company. In 1887 he left Rand, McNally to become a typesetter at Knight & Leonard. Here, he went from setting type to designing page layout, an endeavor that ideally suited his artistic inclinations. By twenty-one he had established himself as an independent designer and began designing covers for *Harper's Bazar, Harper's Weekly,* and other popular magazines. He also developed a reputation for his poster designs.

In 1895 Bradley established the Wayside Press in Springfield, Massachusetts. He had become intrigued with the handmade elegance of many colonial New England imprints he had examined at the Boston Public Library. These early American books, he wrote, avoided "beauty-destroying mechanical precision." Overall, Bradley found these early imprints "the most direct, honest, vigorous and imaginative America has ever known—a sane and inspiring model that was to me a liberal education" (quoted in Blumenthal, p. 81). The issues of the Wayside Press clearly show their influence. They have an elegant simplicity that belie the extraordinary care that went into their design and production.

The primary reason Bradley established the Wayside Press was to publish a magazine, *Bradley, His Book,* which he edited and designed himself. Characterizing it on the masthead as "A Magazine of Interesting Reading Interspersed with various Bits of Art," Bradley was modest, for every issue was a model of exquisite literary tastes and fine aesthetic sensibilities. The project was far too ambitious an undertaking for any man, even one as creative and hardworking as Bradley. The magazine that bears his name folded after seven issues, and he sold the Wayside Press before the decade's end.

During the first decade of the twentieth century, Bradley established a studio in New York City and developed a reputation as one of the finest art editors in the nation. He served as art editor for many major commercial magazines, among them *Collier's, Good Housekeeping,* and *Metropolitan.* He eventually served as typographic and art supervisor for William Randolph Hearst's chain of newspapers, magazines, and motion pictures. Bradley's successful career illustrates the general fate of the small publisher and the little magazine as the nineteenth century gave way to the twentieth. The business had become so complex that it had reached a point where running a press and editing a magazine had become practically impossible. The only way Bradley could pursue his career in magazines was to enter the employ of the moneymen in the publishing world, including the biggest of them all, William Randolph Hearst.

HARRIET MONROE AND *POETRY*

Harriet Monroe entered Chicago's literary scene as a freelance journalist, writing reviews of art, music, and drama for the local papers. She became acquainted with many prominent Chicago authors. Frequent trips to New York expanded her circle of literary acquaintances. She wanted most to be a poet. Because she had experienced only modest success having her poetry published, she decided to found a magazine devoted exclusively to poetry, partly as a vehicle for her own work. Her society connections in Chicago helped her elicit enough financial support to make the magazine viable. Once she secured financial backing for its first five years, she was ready to launch her magazine.

The first issue of *Poetry: A Magazine of Verse* appeared in October 1912. Introducing it, Monroe wrote: "The present venture is a modest effort to give to poetry her own place, her own voice. The popular magazines can afford but scant courtesy—a Cinderella corner in the ashes—because they seek a large public which is not hers." Giving poetry its place: Monroe accomplished this task brilliantly. The poets represented in the first issue included Ezra Pound, who became the magazine's foreign correspondent. The first issue established the pattern for subsequent issues: in addition to poetry, the magazine also included book reviews, criticism, editorials, and poetry news.

Monroe may have initially conceived *Poetry* as a vehicle for her own verse, but it became a vehicle for the verse of many of the most memorable poets in modern American literature. H.D. (Hilda Doolittle), T. S. Eliot, Robert Frost, Vachel Lindsay, Amy Lowell, Edgar Lee Masters, Edwin Arlington Robinson, Carl Sandburg, Wallace Stevens, and William Carlos Williams—all contributed to *Poetry* in its early years. William Butler Yeats, too, contributed to the magazine and became one of its most enthusiastic supporters.

Monroe devoted the remainder of her life—the next twenty-four years—to ensuring the survival and success of *Poetry.* The magazine earned a reputation as a guiding force in the poetry renaissance of the early twentieth century and helped some of the foremost modern American poets find an audience they might not otherwise have had. Monroe's own verse may be forgettable, but her role as a facilitator and publicist for the poetry of others is unsurpassed. The magazine continues in the early twenty-first century.

MARGARET ANDERSON AND THE *LITTLE REVIEW*

Though a generation younger than Harriet Monroe, Margaret C. Anderson also found herself in Chicago around the start of the second decade of the twentieth century, that is, at the time of Chicago's great artistic renaissance. Born and raised in Indiana, Anderson had come to Chicago with a profound desire to befriend the city's brightest and most creative. She had an incessant desire for literary conversation and continually sought ways to gratify this urge. Initially, she obtained a position with the *Continent,* a religious weekly, where she reviewed scores of books. She also wrote reviews for the *Chicago Evening Post* and eventually obtained a position with *The Dial.* There she came to learn how a magazine worked from the inside, valuable knowledge that would soon help her in the most important venture of her life.

Anderson ultimately decided that the best way to gratify her need for literary conversation would be to start a magazine featuring the best contemporary authors and artists. She started her magazine on much less secure footing than had Monroe. Whereas Monroe lined up financial backing for the first five years of *Poetry* before launching her first issue, Anderson was more rash. She started the *Little Review* with barely more than a handful of promises for financial support. She trusted in her immense personal charm to get the magazine through lean times.

Anderson's personal tastes, like those of Thomas Bird Mosher before her, helped make the magazine a critical success. Whereas Mosher carefully selected works of the past, Anderson had the taste and intuition that made it possible for her to recognize and appreciate the most challenging, forward-looking works of the present, works that would shape the literature of the future. In her first issue, she identified the *Little Review* as "a magazine of the arts, making no compromise with the public taste." Disregarding public opinion, Anderson relied solely on her own critical judgment to shape the contents of the *Little Review.*

The first number of the magazine appeared in March 1914. It contained articles and reviews written by Anderson, including one titled "Paderewski and the New Gods," which celebrates her love of the piano and passion for music. The first issue also included verse by Vachel Lindsay and an article by Sherwood Anderson, who published some of his *Winesburg* sketches in later issues of the *Little Review.*

In the third issue, Anderson championed anarchism, a viewpoint that lost her the surest financial backer she had and threatened the *Little Review* with extinction. It would not be the last time. Throughout its twelve-year history, the magazine would often be in dire financial straits. But its overall high quality attracted a core readership, and Anderson's personal charm allowed her to conjure up financial support at crucial moments. Her blatant disregard of prevailing moral standards when it came to making editorial decisions sometimes got her in trouble. For the October 1917 issue of the *Little Review,* she published a Wyndham Lewis short story depicting a girl's brutal seduction. The issue was promptly confiscated by the authorities.

What is undoubtedly the most distinguished writing to be published in Anderson's magazine met a similar fate. James Joyce agreed to serialize *Ulysses* in the *Little Review.* Ezra Pound, Anderson's foreign editor, as he had been Margaret Anderson's foreign correspondent, was responsible for the coup. Although he was sometimes difficult, Pound had successfully sought contributions from many of the finest British and European authors of the time. *Ulysses* began appearing in the magazine at the start of 1918. After four issues, however, officials of the U.S. Post Office confiscated and burned all the copies of those four issues they could locate. Anderson and her companion and coeditor, Jane Heap, were convicted on obscenity charges and were fined.

Anderson's fortitude in withstanding critics and prosecutors alike paid off not in monetary terms but in terms of lasting literary value. The *Little Review,* in retrospect, was one of the most important literary journals of the twentieth century. Over its history, the magazine published works by some of the foremost writers of its day: Hart Crane, T. S. Eliot, Ernest Hemingway, Marianne Moore, Dorothy Richardson, Gertrude Stein, Wallace Stevens, and William Butler Yeats.

Whereas the most notable little magazines of the late nineteenth century were outgrowths of the small presses and the best new little magazines of the early twentieth century were independent editorial ventures, there is one key similarity between them. All these little magazines were the products of strong personalities, men and women who made their magazines reflect their profound love of literature and their most heartfelt beliefs. With each, a vigorous person with a greater-than-average combination of taste and tenacity provided the guiding force to make the magazine a reality.

See also Book Publishing; Periodicals; *Poetry: A Magazine of Verse*

BIBLIOGRAPHY
Primary Works
Anderson Margaret C. *My Thirty Years' War.* New York: Covici, Friede, 1930.

Monroe, Harriet. *A Poet's Life: Seventy Years in a Changing World.* New York: Macmillan, 1938.

Pound, Ezra. *Pound / The "Little Review": The Letters of Ezra Pound to Margaret Anderson; The "Little Review" Correspondence.* Edited by Thomas L. Scott, Melvin J. Friedman, and Jackson R. Bryer. New York: New Directions, 1988.

Secondary Works
Bambace, Anthony. *Will H. Bradley: His Work; A Bibliographical Guide.* New Castle, Del.: Oak Knoll Press, 1995.

Bishop, Philip R. *Thomas Bird Mosher: Pirate Prince of Publishers.* A Comprehensive Bibliography and Source Guide to the Mosher Books, Reflecting England's National Literature and Design. New Castle, Del.: Oak Knoll Press, 1998.

Blumenthal, Joseph. *The Printed Book in America.* Hanover, N.H.: University Press of New England, 1977.

Champney, Freeman. *Art and Glory: The Story of Elbert Hubbard.* New York: Crown, 1968.

Kramer, Sidney. *A History of Stone & Kimball and Herbert S. Stone & Co., 1893–1905.* Chicago: Norman W. Forgue, 1940.

Le Gallienne, Richard. "In Praise of a Literary Pirate." *Literary Digest International Book Review* 2 (October 1924): 778.

Lehmann-Haupt, Hellmut, Rollo G. Silver, and Lawrence C. Wroth. *The Book in America: A History of the Making and Selling of Books in the United States.* 2nd ed. New York: Bowker, 1951.

Marek, Jayne E. *Women Editing Modernism: "Little" Magazines and Literary History.* Lexington: University Press of Kentucky, 1995.

Mott, Frank Luther. *A History of American Magazines.* 5 vols. Cambridge, Mass.: Harvard University Press, 1935–1968.

Vilain, Jean-François, and Philip R. Bishop. *Thomas Bird Mosher and the Art of the Book.* Philadelphia: F. A. Davis, 1992.

Wertheim, Stanley, and Paul Sorrentino. *The Crane Log: A Documentary Life of Stephen Crane, 1871–1900.* New York: G. K. Hall, 1994.

Williams, Ellen. *Harriet Monroe and the Poetry Renaissance: The First Ten Years of Poetry, 1912–22.* Urbana: University of Illinois Press, 1977.

Kevin J. Hayes

LOCHNER V. NEW YORK

Lochner v. New York (1905) was one of several U.S. Supreme Court cases before and after the turn of the twentieth century involving state regulation of American labor conditions. Because its opinion appeared to favor the concerns of employers over those of employees, *Lochner* achieved considerable notoriety as an instance of an activist court interpreting the Constitution to support a dominant pro-business ideology, affirming legally the English philosopher Herbert Spencer's Social Darwinist doctrine of "survival of the fittest." The "Lochner era" and "Lochnerism" became conventional terms in legal scholarship, denoting a historical period (roughly 1905–1937) in which courts typically upheld laissez-faire economic principles and resisted governmental regulation; the era clearly came to an end with the depression-era court decisions that made possible President Franklin Roosevelt's (1882–1945) New Deal, with its massive regulation of the American economy. From another perspective, however, *Lochner* articulated with particular clarity the central contestations confronting American culture in its uneasy transition to the modern period: between the claims of the individual and the collective, between a traditional liberal idealism and situational pragmatism.

THE MAJORITY OPINION: LIBERTY OF CONTRACT

The case involved a baker in Utica, New York, Joseph Lochner, convicted in lower courts of violating a state statute limiting to sixty the weekly hours for bakery employees. The Supreme Court, in a 5–4 decision represented in Justice Rufus Peckham's (1838–1909) majority opinion, reversed the lower courts' rulings, invoking a fundamental "right to contract" implicit in the "due process clause" of the U.S. Constitution's Fourteenth Amendment ("nor shall any State deprive any person of life, liberty, or property, without due process of law"):

> The general right to make a contract in relation to his business is part of the liberty protected by the Fourteenth Amendment, and this includes the right to purchase and sell labor, except as controlled by the State in the legitimate exercise of its police power. (*Lochner*, p. 45)

Like the Fifth Amendment that it reinforced, and like the Declaration of Independence that it echoed, the Fourteenth Amendment's due process clause invoked the individualistic tradition of the seventeenth-century British philosopher John Locke (1632–1704), the founder of modern liberalism, who insisted on men's inalienable "perfect Freedom to order their Actions, and dispose of their Possessions, and Persons as they think fit . . . without asking leave, or depending upon the will of any other man" (p. 259). Thus, in finding for the employer Lochner, the court simply returned to the most sacred of American institutions: the natural right of the individual to freedom.

Moreover, the court argued, New York's labor law was in this case clearly *not* a "legitimate exercise" of "police power," whose proper function it defined as protecting the "safety, health, morals, and general welfare of the public" (*Lochner*, p. 53). Unlike statutes demanding compulsory vaccination or Sunday business closures, New York's law had no clear value for the public's physical or moral well-being; more important, it differed from laws regulating certain kinds of inherently hazardous labor (such as mining) because, in Peckham's words, "to the common understanding the trade of a baker has never been regarded as an unhealthy one" (*Lochner*, p. 59). Any reasonable observer would conclude that bakers needed no special protection against their own right to enter into contracts.

The criterion of "common knowledge" or "the common understanding," with its implicit appeal to reasonableness, was important to the court exactly because, as Peckham pointed out, *all* labor carried with it an element of risk or unhealthiness. To attempt general state regulation of *all* risk would open the doors to extraordinary (and paternalistic) expansions of police powers. Peckham vividly and sardonically imagined a regulatory dystopia where not only the right to contract but all fundamental rights would be jeopardized, where

> conduct . . . as well as contract, would come under the restrictive sway of the legislature. Not only the hours of employees, but the hours of employers, could be regulated, and doctors, lawyers, scientists, all professional men, as well as athletes and artisans, could be forbidden to fatigue their brains and bodies by prolonged hours of exercise, lest the fighting strength of the state be impaired. (*Lochner*, pp. 60–61)

In the majority's opinion, New York's law had passed the limits of common sense and started down the slippery slope to "meddlesome interferences with the rights of the individual" (*Lochner*, p. 61)—and to a repugnant Orwellian future.

THE DISSENTS: DATA AND "THE WILL OF THE PEOPLE"

Two dissents accompanied the *Lochner* decision. The first, written by Justice John Marshall Harlan (1833–1911) (best known for his powerful 1896 dissent to *Plessy v. Ferguson*'s justification of racial segregation) and supported by two other judges, accepted the majority argument's general premises but arrived at different conclusions concerning both "police powers" (and how to determine their legitimate use) and the courts' relation to the legislative process. To justify regulating bakers' hours, Harlan substituted professional expertise and statistical data for the "common knowledge" according to which Peckham claimed that baking as an occupation posed no particular threat to employee health. He quoted at length two scholarly researchers, cited the Eighteenth Annual Report by the New York Bureau of Statistics of Labor and other unattributed "statistics," and concluded that, despite what the "common understanding" might think, bakers indeed deserved the kind of special-case protection afforded to workers in more obviously dangerous jobs.

In addition, Harlan warned of another slippery slope: the threat of an overempowered judiciary finding in the gray areas of police powers a site upon which to make legislation counter to the people's will, rather than to judge cases under law. He ended by reminding the court of its own unanimous opinion two years previously, when it had upheld a state's labor law in *Atkin v. Kansas*:

> It is the solemn duty of the courts in cases before them to guard the constitutional rights of the citizen against merely arbitrary power. That is unquestionably true. But it is equally true—indeed, the public interests imperatively demand—that legislative enactments should be recognized and enforced by the courts as embodying the will of the people, unless they are plainly and palpably, beyond all question, in violation of the fundamental law of the Constitution. (*Lochner*, p. 74)

In other words, the collective "will of the people," expressed as legislation, had rights too—perhaps not equal to those granted individuals by the "fundamental law," but worth guarding.

The second, terser, dissent, submitted by Oliver Wendell Holmes Jr. (1841–1935), did not enter the argument over the limits of police powers. Instead, Holmes noted that the state's right to infringe individual freedoms was not itself in question, and never had been: "The liberty of the citizen to do as he likes . . . is interfered with by school laws, by the Post Office, by every state or municipal institution which takes his money for purposes thought desirable, whether he likes it or not" (*Lochner*, p. 75). Because individual liberty was thus in practice clearly not absolute, he argued, what was really at stake in *Lochner* was the endorsing of "a particular economic theory, whether of paternalism and the organic relation of the citizen to the state or of laissez faire" (*Lochner*, p. 75). In the absence of absolute principles, Holmes famously advocated a particularist, pragmatic jurisprudence—"General propositions do not decide concrete cases"—and, like Harlan, concluded by acknowledging in most cases the primacy for law of the collective "will of the people," or simply "dominant opinion":

> The word "liberty," in the Fourteenth Amendment, is perverted when it is held to prevent the natural outcome of a dominant opinion, unless it can be said that a rational and fair man necessarily would admit that the statute proposed would infringe fundamental principles as they have been understood by the traditions of our people and our law. (*Lochner*, p. 76)

LOCHNER'S AFTERMATH: LEGAL PRAGMATISM

Harlan and Holmes lost the argument, but their opinions pointed out the course of legal philosophy for the next generation and beyond. In *Lochner*'s outcome, classical liberal idealism prevailed over a nascent style of legal thinking, suggested in both dissents, that was at once scientifically empirical and flexible to the point of relativism: a jurisprudence that reflected society's real practices rather than prescribed them in accordance with a transcendent idealized "law." This legal pragmatism continued to articulate itself in a reform movement and growing body of legal theory over the following three decades.

Roscoe Pound (1870–1964), for example (the influential dean of Harvard's Law School and a leader among the "Progressive" legal theorists of the 1900s and 1910s), announced in 1914 that a "social-philosophical school" of thought could now understand law's purpose in distinctly modern, utilitarian terms that explicitly declared both *Lochner* and Locke outdated: "Instead of the maximum of individual self-assertion consistent with a like self-assertion by all others, we are now putting as the end the maximum satisfaction of human wants, of which self-assertion is only one" (pp. 367–368). By the 1930s a loosely defined movement of "Legal Realism," the inheritor of Pound's socially Progressive law, had developed at Harvard, Columbia, and other leading law schools, generally taking as its philosophical foundation an acknowledgement of the factitious or socially determined nature of law. The final assault on *Lochner*'s classical idealist/individualist principles came with the appointment of pragmatically minded judges like Benjamin Cardozo and Felix Frankfurter to Franklin D. Roosevelt's Supreme Court, where the legal foundation for a society based on the collective rather than the individual would be confirmed.

LOCHNER AND LITERATURE

The social forces that called forth *Lochner* and its dissents—urbanization, industrialization, the increasing asymmetry of employee/employer relations—also shaped American literature of the late nineteenth and early twentieth centuries in plain ways. Literary naturalism's general exposure of the failure of traditional liberal individualism, whether in the face of biology or society, repeatedly explored the question at the heart of Lochner: how can the Lockean individual negotiate with and stand against the combine, the machine, the impersonal "system" of distributed powers? And, as they articulated their indictment of the "system," naturalists typically deployed the techniques of realistic, particularized reportage advocated by Émile Zola—and by Judge Harlan in his substitution of data for "common knowledge."

Literary products more or less explicitly dramatizing *Lochner*'s dissents—narratives of labor and inequity—are ubiquitous, perhaps beginning with Hamlin Garland's "Under the Lion's Paw" (1891), which reveals precisely the power asymmetries of contract and the perils of reliance on liberal assumptions. They include the novels of Frank Norris, Upton Sinclair, and Theodore Dreiser; they continue into the Great Depression and New Deal most famously with John Steinbeck's *The Grapes of Wrath* (1939). While many of these writers and others like them were social reformers and critics, sharing the perspective of Progressive legal theorists such as Roscoe Pound, they rarely in their work envisioned a well-regulated future organized around Pound's "maximum satisfaction of human wants." Although an outmoded individualism provided no place for the naturalists to stand, collectivism offered no clear alternative. Their works returned compulsively to images of imbalances of power, of personal impotence, and of structure itself as an irresistible antagonist. Frequently, they ended narratives with the literal annihilation of the protagonist by some impersonal process.

In other words, although much literature of the Lochner era appeared to follow the leads of Harlan and Holmes in its social awareness and its particularism, its trend was tragic rather than utopian. The lure of the free individual was more powerful in literary practice than in the legal theory that followed *Lochner*. One result was literary high modernism's well-known nostalgia, a pervasive longing for a strong time of clear and equitable relations among people, uncluttered by the confusions of modern commerce and state. Another was the emergence in the century's first two decades of a popular fantasy literature that provided protagonists and readers with a landscape of empowered, "naturally" free individuals: the western, beginning with Owen Wister's *The Virginian* (1902) and including Zane Grey's immensely popular novels of the 1910s and later (as well as pseudo-westerns like Edgar Rice Burroughs's

Tarzan books or Martian romances). The western perhaps manifests the clearest literary response, a conservative one, to the conditions that generated Lochner: the imagining of a utopia, not in the present, but in an ahistorical past, something akin to Locke's "state of nature" itself, where the individual continues to take his destiny into his own free hands, where his law (sometimes explicitly an outlawed law) inevitably prevails. Nothing could be farther from *Lochner*'s vexed but necessary world of bakers, regulations, and statistics.

See also Jurisprudence

BIBLIOGRAPHY

Primary Works
Lochner v. New York, 198 U.S. 45 (1905).

Locke, John. *Two Treatises of Government.* Edited by Peter Laslett. Cambridge, U.K.: Cambridge University Press, 1988.

Pound, Roscoe. "Law and Liberty." In *Lectures on the Harvard Classics,* vol. 41, edited by William Allan Neilson et al., pp. 367–368. The Harvard Classics. New York: P. F. Collier & Son, 1914.

Secondary Works
Gillman, Howard. *The Constitution Besieged: The Rise and Demise of the Lochner Era Police Powers Jurisprudence.* Durham, N.C.: Duke University Press, 1993.

Kens, Paul. *Lochner v. New York: Economic Regulation on Trial.* Lawrence: University Press of Kansas, 1998.

Smith, Rogers M. *Liberalism and American Constitutional Law.* Cambridge, Mass.: Harvard University Press, 1985.

Tribe, Laurence H. *American Constitutional Law.* 2nd ed. Minneola, N.Y.: Foundation Press, 1988.

John N. Swift

T. S. Eliot, 1922. © BETTMANN/CORBIS

"THE LOVE SONG OF J. ALFRED PRUFROCK"

Widely acknowledged as one of the first modernist poems, T. S. Eliot's (1888–1965) "The Love Song of J. Alfred Prufrock" (1915) dramatizes the difference between a traditional love poem and its contemporary equivalent. "Love songs" used to be about seduction and sexual triumph. No longer—at least as Eliot imagines the spiritually barren landscape through which his dramatic persona, the oddly named J. Alfred Prufrock, tries to travel. Everything militates against his being able to ask the "overwhelming question," which some critics argue is "Who am I?" and others insist is a proposal of marriage to the woman with whom he had shared "tea and ices." Because the poem itself does not answer the question, meaning is no longer as stable as it once was or at least seemed to be. But the very fact that Prufrock cannot give voice to his question tells readers much about the modern condition and the ways in which an antiheroic love poem can create a portrait in neurosis such as that of Prufrock.

Along with poems such as Ezra Pound's "In a Station of the Metro," Robert Frost's "Stopping by Woods on a Snowy Evening," and Wallace Stevens's "Sunday Morning," "The Love Song of J. Alfred Prufrock" appears in nearly every anthology of poetry used by high school and college students and is prominently mentioned in studies of modern culture. Eliot's epical poem *The Waste Land* (1922) may be more ambitious and ultimately more revealing about the psychological landscape of post–World War I Europe, but "The Love Song of J. Alfred Prufrock" contains a foreshadowing of the themes and techniques Eliot would develop more fully in later poems.

In "The Love Song of J. Alfred Prufrock" (hereafter noted as "Prufrock"), theme and image are two sides of the same coin; despair, for example, dominates the deadened world that the poem invites one to "visit," whether this ubiquitous despair appears in the tawdry images of "one-night cheap hotels" and "lonely men in shirt-sleeves, leaning out of windows" or in the brittle conversation of ladies at an overly sophisticated soiree who "come and go / Talking of Michelangelo." Prufrock does not feel entirely comfortable with the latter group, partly because he is afraid that people will notice the bald spot at the back of his head and partly because he is nervous about what he will say, or not say, to the young woman "in question." No doubt a part of Prufrock would prefer to stay home altogether. At the same time, however, he cannot not go. Thus it is Prufrock's fate to stand as an emblem for the modern condition, forever caught between two equally unpleasant alternatives.

The poet-critic John Berryman argues that with the line "Like a patient etherised upon a table," "modern poetry begins." This large claim may not suit all scholars, who most certainly can find earlier lines that prefigure modern poetry (one need only look at the work of Thomas Hardy), but Berryman has a point if one appreciates the stark contrast between the conventional, even romantically lilted lines that precede the etherized patient—"Let us go, then, you and I, / When the evening is spread out against the sky"—and the stark realism of an operating theater and surgeons at the ready to probe their patient. It is but a short step from Eliot's image of the etherized patient to a wider consideration of how science had changed the landscape of modernist poetry. "Prufrock" reflects the harder edges of a world where evenings no longer spread themselves across the sky and, more important, where "love songs" are interior monologues filled with abject confession.

The etherized patient, then, is an image as the imagist poets (Eliot numbered himself among them) understood the term. Eliot's remarkable achievement was to tie discrete images into a coherent whole. He does this not by lacing his poem with hospital images but rather by transforming Prufrock's neurotic fears into something that will unconsciously remind one of the patient's essential condition. Thus when Prufrock imagines himself as a bug, a specimen "pinned and wriggling on the wall," the image reminds the reader of the evening he or she is watching unfold.

Science, then, is one part of Eliot's arsenal as he goes about tracing the bleakness of modern life. Allusions to earlier works of literature are another way that he charts the differences between a vital "then" and a more despairing, nearly hopeless "now." *The Waste Land* is filled, perhaps overfilled, with literary allusions (general readers require a road map of glosses to figure out what work is being parodied). In this sense "Prufrock" is an earlier—and easier—example of how Eliot means to use tradition to talk about contemporaneity.

Take, for example, what Eliot does when he refers to Andrew Marvell's (1621–1678) classic love poem "To His Coy Mistress." There the speaker mounts up what he imagines is a logically airtight case for seduction. After such arguments, how could his "coy mistress" refuse his favors? The stanzas go from "Had we but world enough, and time"—a condition that, alas, does not exist—to "But at my back I always hear / Time's winged chariot hurrying near," a signal that time is unfortunately running out. The poem ends, as such carpe diem poems must, with an exhortation to "seize the day" by being as sexually vibrant as possible.

Eliot has Marvell's exuberant lover in mind when he contrasts him with the bland, ineffectual Prufrock. The metaphysical images that are the building blocks of Marvell's poem ("Let us roll all our strength and all / Our sweetness up into one ball, / And tear our pleasures with rough strife / Through the iron gates of life") are ironically echoed—and diminished—in Prufrock's sadly neurotic worry that had he "bitten off the matter with a smile" and "squeezed the universe into a ball," the object of his "affection" (some have argued, the woman he is trying to propose to) would not have understood the gesture—a gesture that the self-conscious Prufrock does not in fact make. Marvell's persona acts as a lover in a metaphysical love poem should; Prufrock thinks . . . and thinks . . . and thinks about acting, but in the end he is too frightened. Women terrify him, yet another modern theme and condition.

Prufrock is a comic figure, although many of the poem's first readers were so bedazzled by its techniques—not only the reliance on relatively obscure literary allusions but also the ways in which the poem's connective tissue seemed willfully absent—that they worried themselves into missing the point. In the late twentieth century "Prufrock" attracted a good number of close, line-by-line readings, and when it appears in most anthologies, there are annotated footnotes explaining Eliot's classical allusions. These scholarly critical activities are both enormously helpful and a bit troublesome for those who now believe that the poem has been so domesticated that the thrill of making its imagistic connections inside one's head is now largely lost.

By contrast, when Eliot first began working on "Prufrock," possibly while he was still an undergraduate at Harvard but most certainly by 1911, shortly after he had graduated and was spending time in France and Germany, modernism was in its infancy, and general readers brought the same expectations to a poem that they brought to a painting: both should be representational (a girl should look like a girl, a tree like a tree), and both should be easily accessible. "Prufrock" was not, largely because its method was associative rather than chronological. Moreover, descriptions tended to slip from the real to the imagistic. Eliot's "fog" was so described that readers were encouraged to see a cat ("The yellow fog that rubs its back upon the window-panes") and then to wonder what the connection between the two might be.

In 1915 Ezra Pound, Eliot's friend and mentor, submitted "Prufrock" to Harriet Monroe, editor of the Chicago-based magazine *Poetry* and insisted that she publish it. Two years later Eliot's first book, *Prufrock and Other Observations,* appeared. Those in the avant-garde embraced what he was doing (and, more important, what Pound approved of), but Eliot's personal life began a downslide during this period, partly because his marriage to Vivian Haigh-Wood in 1915 turned out to be a disaster and partly because Eliot himself was experiencing the breakdown reflected in the general culture because of World War I.

In an essay titled "Tradition and the Individual Talent," Eliot insisted that modern poetry was not designed to be a transparent vehicle through which personal feelings were released but rather that it required the creation of a persona, a mask, entirely separate from its creator. In recent decades biographers have demonstrated that the connections between Eliot's spokespersons and himself were much stronger. Prufrock, to be sure, is meant to be an exaggeration, a comic type on the order of the "little man" that the humorist Robert Benchley would use so effectively during the 1920s and 1930s in the pages of *The New Yorker* magazine and that James Thurber would immortalize in his short story "The Secret Life of Walter Mitty." In the early twenty-first century one is likely to think of Prufrock as he is reflected in the character of George Costanza, the resident neurotic on the television sitcom *Seinfeld.*

There are, however, important differences: Prufrock knows that he is a fool, that he is "not Prince Hamlet, nor was meant to be," and this painful insight separates him from people who are foolish and do not realize it. Their ignorance, one might argue, is their bliss. By contrast, Prufrock is aware, but each instance of that awareness only brings him grief: he knows, for example, that each decision leads inevitably to a revision (just as streets follow each other "like a tedious argument"), and perhaps saddest of all, that the mermaids do not sing to him.

Hugh Kenner points out that "the name of Prufrock-Littau, furniture wholesalers, appeared in advertisements in St. Louis, Missouri, in the first decade of the present [i.e., twentieth] century" and that in 1911 "a young Missourian's whimsical feline humor prefixed the name Prufrock to what has become the best known English poem since the *Rubaiyat.*" Given the ways in which "Prufrock" is an anti-love poem, it is hardly surprising that an advertisement containing the name of "Prufrock" should have caught Eliot's eye. Add the stuffy prefix J. Alfred, and the result works in bold relief to the words "love song." Given the poem Eliot wants to write, one that would explore how barren lives have become and how love can no longer resuscitate either a patient on a table or Prufrock at a party, an ironic name is what an ironic poem demands.

Few men now dress in morning coats, with neckties set off with a "simple pin" (which a few lines later will serve to pin Prufrock on the wall, just as the bald spot at the back of his head will find its way to that of John the Baptist), but many men and women can easily relate to measuring out life in coffee spoons. As with most of us, Prufrock is a creature of routine; he makes his morning coffee every morning, and in what Eliot would later call an "objective correlative," the business of measuring out a life in coffee spoons becomes not only an objective detail but one that has a wider significance, that comments on Prufrock's entire (unhappy) life.

One knows that Prufrock will never "force the moment to its crisis" because, ironically enough, Prufrock has in effect married his pain, his sense of abiding failure. Being a loser is his identity. He cannot be an ardent lover any more than he can eat a peach (too messy, too "sexy," if you will). He might, just might, roll up his trousers and walk along the beach. He might even consider a comb-over to hide his bald spot, but one suspects that he will leave his hair line as it is. What the final lines of the poem tell is that Prufrock sees a vision of the mermaids—this despite the fact that they do not sing to him—and his descriptions of them are simultaneously sensual and sensuous: "I have seen them riding seaward on the waves / combing the white hair of the waves blown back." Not since the opening lines about the evening spread out against the sky has the reader heard so many elongated, anapestic lines, so "romantic" a rendering of the world Prufrock either actually sees or deeply imagines. Moreover, Eliot does not barge in to throw cold water on Prufrock's musings, as he did earlier with the operating table and etherized patient. Prufrock, in short, gets the final lines to himself, and they are quite lovely—until "human voices wake us and we drown." Drown, that is, back into the world where one grows old and, as Prufrock puts it, "afraid."

BIBLIOGRAPHY

Primary Works

Eliot, T. S. "The Love Song of J. Alfred Prufrock." In *The Complete Poems and Plays, 1909–1950.* New York: Harcourt, Brace, & World, 1952.

Secondary Works

Berryman, John. "Prufrock's Dilemma." In his *The Freedom of the Poet.* New York: Farrar, Straus and Giroux, 1960.

Kenner, Hugh. "Prufrock of St. Louis." *Prairie Schooner* 31, no. 1 (spring 1957): 24–30.

Locke, Frederick W. "Dante and T. S. Eliot's Prufrock." *Modern Language Notes* 78 (1963): 51–59.

Pound, Ezra. "Prufrock and Other Observations." *Poetry* 10 (1917): 264–271.

Williamson, George. *A Reader's Guide to T. S. Eliot.* London: Thames and Hudson, 1955.

Sanford Pinsker

LYNCHING

After the Civil War, with Abraham Lincoln dead and President Andrew Johnson politically ineffectual, Congress passed the Reconstruction Acts beginning in 1867, which gave northern radicals complete military control of the South. In response, extremist whites organized vigilante patrols such as the Ku Klux Klan (KKK) to intimidate black people. Thus violence, even lynching, was bred of the Civil War's turmoil and bloodshed.

Lynching is the punishment of alleged criminals by private persons (usually mobs) without due process of law. Lynch law penalizes a person without legal sanction. The vigilante mobs in the South quite frequently hung the accused person. The term "lynching" is often taken to mean death by hanging, but other forms of deadly force were also used. The term "lynch law" is associated with Charles Lynch of Bedford County, Virginia, and with William Lynch of Pittsylvania County, Virginia, both of whom meted out unofficial punishment during the American Revolution.

Statistics on lynching derive from three collections. The *Chicago Tribune* in 1882 initiated a yearly account. Ten years later, the Tuskegee Institute began collecting data about lynchings. Starting in 1912, the National Association for the Advancement of Colored People (NAACP) maintained its account of mob lynching. These sources do not entirely agree either in the definition of "lynching" or in the number of lynchings. The Tuskegee Institute generally lists the fewest killings and it cites 1892 as the year with the

Lynchings by year and race

Year	Whites	Blacks	Total
1882	64	49	113
1883	77	53	130
1884	160	51	211
1885	110	74	184
1886	64	74	138
1887	50	70	120
1888	68	69	137
1889	76	94	170
1890	11	85	96
1891	71	113	184
1892	69	161	230
1893	34	118	152
1894	58	134	192
1895	66	113	179
1896	45	78	123
1897	35	123	158
1898	19	101	120
1899	21	85	106
1900	9	106	115
1901	25	105	130
1902	7	85	92
1903	15	84	99
1904	7	76	83
1905	5	57	62
1906	3	62	65
1907	3	58	61
1908	8	89	97
1909	13	69	82
1910	9	67	76
1911	7	60	67
1912	2	62	64
1913	1	51	52
1914	4	51	55
1915	13	56	69
1916	4	50	54
1917	2	36	38
1918	4	60	64
1919	7	76	83
1920	8	53	61

SOURCE: The Archives at Tuskegee Institute.

largest number of lynchings—230 persons, of whom 161 were black and the others were white.

The Ku Klux Klan, founded in 1866 in Pulaski, Tennessee, was organized in 1867 under its first Grand Wizard, former Confederate general Nathan Bedford Forrest. Forrest resigned in 1869, angered at the actions of some local dens, but some dens continued to operate on their own. During the election of 1868, the Klan and other terror groups killed perhaps 1,000 people in Louisiana alone, most of them Republican leaders, political candidates, and others challenging white, Democratic office holders. Blacks, especially, feared these terrorist lynchings.

According to NAACP leader Walter Francis White (1893–1955) in his book *Rope and Faggot: A Biography of Judge Lynch* (1929), 4,951 people were lynched during the forty-six years between 1882 and 1927.

These lynchings occurred in forty-four states and in the territory of Alaska. Of these, 3,513 were carried out against black people, which included 76 black women. About three-quarters of all lynchings occurred in Kentucky and the nine states of the Deep South (pp. 267–268).

Ida B. Wells-Barnett (1862–1931), a black American journalist who was born a slave, offers examples of mob action that she put together in *Lynch Law in Georgia,* an 1899 pamphlet compiled from previous accounts in the *Atlanta Journal* and the *Atlanta Constitution.* Nine black men were arrested near Palmetto, Georgia, in 1899 and were accused of burning three houses. A mob of more than one hundred white men, masked and armed with Winchesters, shotguns, and pistols, broke into the town jail and shot to death five black male prisoners, wounded two, and believed that they had killed nine; in fact, two escaped without wounds. Wells-Barnett describes another incident, this time in Newnan, Georgia. Samuel Hose, a black man, was accused of murdering his employer, Albert Cranford, in a dispute about wages that were owed to him. In addition, Hose was accused of assaulting Mrs. Cranford after ruthlessly tossing her infant to the floor. A Georgia newspaper announced that Hose, when caught, would either be lynched and his body riddled with bullets or that he would be burned at the stake. On 23 April 1899, in view of 2,000 people, Hose was stripped, parts of his body hacked off, and then he was burned on a pyre as he hung. On the following day, another black man, Elijah Strickland, a colored preacher, suffered torture and lynching in the nearby town of Palmetto.

The brutality worked against seventeen-year-old Jesse Washington in 1916 was similarly gruesome. Charged with the bludgeoning of Lucy Fryer, Washington, a black, confessed to rape and murder. The trial started a week later in Waco, Texas. The all-white jury deliberated just four minutes and found him guilty. Courtroom spectators seized Washington and hustled him outside to a mob of some four hundred who threw a chain around his neck. Doused with coal oil, he was lowered onto a burning pyre. The charred body was then placed in a sack, dragged behind an auto, and eventually hung for the public to view.

Perhaps Claude McKay (full name Festus Claudius McKay, 1889–1948) had torturous burnings like these in mind when he penned the poem "The Lynching," which was published in 1922 in James Weldon Johnson's anthology, *The Book of American Negro Poetry.* McKay initiates the sonnet with these words, "His spirit in smoke ascended to high heaven." This same collection offers two other McKay poems

Ida B. Wells-Barnett in 1893. COURTESY OF THE SPECIAL COLLECTIONS RESEARCH CENTER, UNIVERSITY OF CHICAGO LIBRARY

that indirectly attack mob bigotry: "If We Must Die," and "To the White Fiends."

Bruce E. Baker in his essay "North Carolina Lynching Ballads" (1997) studies three ballads recounting the "folk culture of lynching" (p. 220). "The Death of Emma Hartsell" (1898) offers a fear-filled ballad depicting the murder of a twelve-year-old white girl and the subsequent lynching of two black men, Tom Johnson and Joe Kizer, in Concord, North Carolina. The ballad form simplifies, concentrates, and renders the incident memorable. Like folk tales, the songs skip situational factors or racial conflict and enshrine the event as timeless. The lynching victims in these songs were not always black. One North Carolina ballad recounts Alec Whitley, a white man of violence lynched for immorality. And the ballad "J. V. Johnson" refers to lynching a white man who murdered his own brother-in-law.

Women also suffered lynching. In May of 1918 in Valdosta, Georgia, Mary Turner, a black woman eight months pregnant, threatened to seek justice against the vigilantes who had previously lynched her husband. As a result, she was tied, hung upside down, doused with gasoline and burned. While she was yet alive, a man cut open her abdomen. The infant fetus had its head crushed and the mob riddled Mary's body with bullets.

LYNCHINGS OUTSIDE THE SOUTH

While the majority of lynchings took place in the South and victimized blacks, the practice was also carried out in other parts of the country and targeted other people. On 28 October 1889, Katsu Goto from Japan was a lynching victim in Honokaa, Hawaii. Goto was part of a group of eight people who were accused of setting a fire. He was hanged to death from a telephone pole before he could stand trial. Four men were found guilty of his death, and they served time in prison.

On 14 March 1891 a mob stormed a jail in New Orleans where eleven Sicilian immigrants were incarcerated after being accused of killing the city's police commissioner. A jury had found these men not guilty, yet authorities incited a mob to violence. The mob stormed the jail and shot and killed the victims. Richard Gambino graphically describes this event in *Vendetta: The True Story of the Largest Lynching in U.S. History* (1998).

In 1920 a lynching occurred in Minnesota, a northern state that had not experienced many such events. It came about after an incident at a circus in Duluth. Nineteen-year-old Irene Tusken claimed that six black circus workers threatened her and her male escort with guns and that she was raped by the black men. In the morning, the doctor found no physical indication that Tusken had been raped, nor could the police verify claims of rape. Police jailed six black circus laborers in the Duluth County Jail. The newspapers reported the affair. A large mob formed at the jail, and soon it forcibly entered, using rails, timbers, and stones to rip open doors and cells. Elias Clayton, Elmer Jackson, and Isaac McGhie were marched to a light pole, beaten, and hung. *Kingsblood Royal* (1947) by Sinclair Lewis (1885–1951) concerns racial prejudice set in a fictional city of Minnesota that resembles Duluth. This novel attacks racism and condemns lynching. Years later, Bob Dylan (1941–), who was born in Duluth, wrote and recorded the song "Desolation Row" (1965) that suggests this lynching with the mention of a circus, a spreading riot, a police commissioner wavering in his duty, and a hanging. Finally, Michael Fedo wrote a historical novel of this tragic affair, "*They Was Just Niggers*" (1979), which was later published under the title *The Lynchings in Duluth*.

POPULAR DEFENSES OF LYNCHING

The Virginian: A Horseman of the Plains (1902) by Owen Wister (1860–1938) established the western novel and became popular as exalting the individualistic hero cowboy. The Virginian presides over the mob hanging of his friend Steve, found guilty of rustling cattle. Wister sees this type of swift justice as necessary in a Wyoming territory where the law resides a long way off. In Wister's novel *Lady Baltimore* (1906), the lady says that claims of the "Republican upholding of Negro equality" are "on the wane." The white race suffers, she says, because it executes people "publicly." "What I'd never do would be to make a show, an entertainment, a circus out of it" (pp. 216–218). Wister thus accepts lynching as necessary but states that it ought not be a spectacle.

Other writers also defended the use of lynching. Thomas Dixon (1864–1946) from North Carolina became well known for his trilogy: *The Leopard's Spots: A Romance of the White Man's Burden 1865–1900* (1902), *The Clansman: An Historical Romance of the Ku Klux Klan* (1905), and *The Traitor: The Story of the Fall of the Invisible Empire* (1907). These novels offer an extremist Southern view of the Reconstruction era, vigorously promote anti-black sentiments, and forcefully support the Ku Klux Klan. In *The Clansman*, a white Klan chaplain offers a prayer, not for the accused man before him, but for the white women supposedly made fearful by the black murderers. The accused has a trial of sorts and then the Clan murders him.

The Birth of a Nation (1915), an early historical film by D. W. Griffith (1875–1948), is based on Dixon's *The Clansman*. Like the book, the film supported racist myths about black Americans, using scenes that would cause offense in that era: black legislators legalizing interracial marriage and political campaign signs calling both for marriage between the races and equal civil rights for blacks. The film masterfully employed new cinematic methods to present the Civil War, the Lincoln assassination, and the change, rise, and reuniting of Southern states with the North. But critics recognized it as "black poison," "disgraceful propaganda" (Dray, p. 202); it glorified the Ku Klux Klan and vilified black people. The anti-lynching reformer William Monroe Trotter urged that its showing be prohibited, and he declared on 17 April 1915, "if there is any lynching here in Boston, Mayor Curley will be responsible" (Dray, p. 203). Despite such protests, the film played to packed houses in Boston and across the nation.

SPEAKING OUT AGAINST LYNCHING

The NAACP strongly opposed Griffith's film and as part of its efforts produced *Rachel,* a three-act drama by Angelina Weld Grimké (1880–1958). The play appeared first in Washington, D.C., at the Myrtilla Miner Normal School in 1916 and served as a means to rally opposition against the motion picture. Griffith himself directed a sequel, *Intolerance* (1916). Black filmmakers brought forward *The Birth of a Race* (1918) by Emmett Jay Scott (1873–1957), but it failed to gather enthusiasm. Oscar Micheaux (1884–1951), another black director, offered *The Homesteader* (1919) and *Within Our Gates* (1920), which enjoyed more success.

Opposition to lynching had begun much earlier, however. Among the first opponents was Wells-Barnett. Beginning in the late 1880s Wells-Barnett helped publicize lynching incidents throughout the South, using *Free Speech,* the Memphis paper she co-owned, as the forum for most of her writings. After publishing an editorial in 1892 that attacked the myth that black men were a dangerous threat to white women, a mob ransacked the newspaper offices, destroying her printing press. Wells-Barnett relocated to the northern United States but continued her anti-lynching efforts. She published *A Red Record: Tabulated Statistics and Alleged Causes of Lynchings in the United States, 1892–1893–1894* (1895).

Albion W. Tourgée (1838–1905), a lawyer and writer, vigorously opposed the Ku Klux Klan in his several novels. His *A Fool's Errand* (1879), which sold more than 200,000 copies, concerned Reconstruction problems and evils in the South. Among other writings, he published a lengthy letter in the *New York Tribune* that was addressed to an acquaintance in the U.S. Senate. He opens his letter by accusing the Klan of murdering a judge in the grand jury room of the courthouse. He recounts the Klan's beatings and scourgings, offering specific instances in North Carolina counties. He wants federal action: "Put detectives at work to get hold of this whole organization. . . . If we have not pluck enough for this, why then let us just offer our throats to the knife, emasculate ourselves, and be a nation of self-subjugated slaves at once."

In "The United States of Lyncherdom" (1901) Mark Twain (1835–1910) quotes lynching statistics from the *Chicago Tribune.* Twain bemoans that Missouri has witnessed this terrible crime near Pierce City in the southwestern corner of the state where "the people rose, lynched three negroes—two of them very aged ones—burned out five negro households, and drove thirty negro families into the woods" (p. 140). Twain quotes a telegram from Texas in which a mob procures coal oil to fuel the flames that burn a Negro alive. Calling such events an "epidemic of bloody insanities," Twain asks for "martial personalities" who "can face mobs without flinching" (p. 145) and so end these brutalities.

The cartoonist William A. Rogers used his drawings in *Harper's Weekly* magazine to demand an end to lynching. In the 8 August 1903 issue, for example, he specifically calls for an end to mob violence against black Americans. Here, the demonic figure of "Lynch Law" wielding a bloody knife, hangman's noose, and torch, succumbs to "The Law" as applied in two northern cities, Evansville, Indiana, and Danville, Illinois.

The Autobiography of an Ex-Colored Man (1912) by James Weldon Johnson (1871–1938) is a novel about a light-skinned black man able to pass as a white. In the book, Johnson describes the narrator entering a mob scene. Rabid whites coil a chain around the victim and link it to a railroad tie sunk into the ground. The lynchers burn the victim. "He squirmed, he writhed, strained at his chains, then gave out cries and groans that I shall always hear . . . a great wave of humiliation and shame swept over me" (pp. 136, 137).

Walter Van Tilburg Clark (1909–1971) sets *The Ox-Bow Incident* (1940) in Nevada in 1883. The entire novel concerns lynching, first in the forming of a posse that seeks to hang rustlers and second in that posse's execution of the suspects. The vigilantes hang a family man, an elderly man who is witless, and a Mexican who claims to be unable to speak English. Within an hour of the hanging, the mob finds it has killed innocents and that the ranch hand whom they thought had been murdered is actually alive. The leading lyncher and his son commit suicide. The novel dramatizes turning away from the lynching evil.

POLITICAL EFFORTS TO END LYNCHING

A riot lasting three days occurred in Springfield, Illinois, in August 1908, when a white woman claimed to have been violated. The sheriff transferred the accused black man to the jail of a neighboring town, which prevented him from being victimized, but mobs lynched two other blacks in Springfield, attacked houses in the African American section of town, and dragged blacks from homes and streetcars. National Guard troops did restore order, but by then four whites and two blacks had been killed. This racial tragedy in the home city of Abraham Lincoln staggered white people. The following year in New York City, whites gathered with prominent blacks to establish the National Association for the Advancement of Colored People (NAACP).

African American William Edward Burghardt (W. E. B.) Du Bois (1868–1963) became the leader of the organization, and he campaigned for the immediate equality of black people in the NAACP's periodical *The Crisis.* Walter White (1893–1955) was one of the association's most diligent activists in regard to lynching. Although his blond hair and blue eyes indicated that he had a high percentage of white ancestry, he chose his bit of African American heritage to arrange his life. His novel *The Fire in the Flint* (1924) depicts a young black man who returns with a medical degree from Harvard to his home in the South. There, he defies racism and confronts the Klan. White's *Rope and Faggott: A Biography of Judge Lynch* became the best known of his several writings that opposed lynching. White was also active in seeking legal remedies to lynching, throwing the NAACP's support behind the Dyer Bill in 1919. Despite his efforts, a federal anti-lynching measure was never made law. Earlier congressional bills had sought to create commissions to investigate the problem. Senator John Logan of Illinois sponsored such a bill in 1884, and Representative Henry Blair from New Hampshire proposed another in 1890. A North Carolina congressperson offered an anti-lynching bill in 1900. None of these measures passed.

The NAACP's efforts to end lynching met with success. In 1911, shortly after the association began its work, there were 71 lynchings; by the time of World War II, the practice had been abolished. These efforts are detailed by Robert L. Zangrando in *The NAACP Crusade against Lynching, 1909 to 1950* (1980).

Lynching declined after World War I for several reasons. Law enforcement improved. Newspapers condemned such mob action. Organizations such as the NAACP became more effective in their efforts. Black people offered even armed resistance and some blacks left the South and its segregation that led to lynching. Black writers of the Harlem Renaissance implicitly challenged the white supremacist view that underlay lynching.

The Tuskegee Institute ended its keeping of lynching records, which had started in 1882. In 1962 the Institute found no more accounts of such violence.

See also Blacks; Jim Crow; Ku Klux Klan; Reconstruction; Violence

BIBLIOGRAPHY
Primary Works
Clark, Walter Van Tilburg. *The Ox-Bow Incident*. New York: Random House, 1940.

Dixon, Thomas. *The Clansman: An Historical Romance of the Ku Klux Klan*. New York: Doubleday, Page, 1905.

Dixon, Thomas. *The Leopard's Spots: A Romance of the White Man's Burden, 1865–1900*. New York: Doubleday, Page, 1902.

Dixon, Thomas, Jr. *The Traitor: A Story of the Fall of the Invisible Empire*. New York: Doubleday, Page, 1907.

Johnson, James Weldon. *The Autobiography of an Ex-Colored Man*. 1912. Edited by William L. Andrews. New York: Penguin, 1990.

Johnson, James Weldon, ed. *The Book of American Negro Poetry*. New York: Harcourt, Brace, 1922.

Lewis, Sinclair. *Kingsblood Royal*. New York: Random House, 1947.

Tourgée, Albion. "On the KKK." *New York Tribune*, May 1870.

Wells-Barnett, Ida B. *Lynch Law in Georgia*. Chicago: This pamphlet is circulated by Chicago Colored Citizens . . . , 1899.

Wells-Barnett, Ida B. *A Red Record: Tabulated Statistics and Alleged Causes of Lynchings in the United States, 1892–1893–1894*. Chicago: Donohue and Henneberry, 1895.

White, Walter Francis. *The Fire in the Flint*. 1924. New York: Negro Universities Press, 1969.

White, Walter Francis. *Rope and Faggot: A Biography of Judge Lynch*. 1929. New York: Arno Press, 1969.

Wister, Owen. *The Virginian: A Horseman of the Plains*. London: Macmillan, 1902.

Wister, Owen. *Lady Baltimore*. 1906. Ridgewood, N.J.: Gregg Press, 1968.

Secondary Works
Baker, Bruce E. "North Carolina Lynching Ballads." In *Under Sentence of Death: Lynching in the South*, edited by W. Fitzhugh Brundage, pp. 219–245. Chapel Hill: University of North Carolina Press, 1997.

Dray, Philip. *At the Hands of Persons Unknown: The Lynchings of Black America*. New York: Random House, 2002.

Fedo, Michael. *The Lynchings in Duluth*. Duluth: Minnesota Historical Society Press, 2000.

Gambino, Richard. *Vendetta: The True Story of the Largest Lynching in U.S. History*. Toronto: Guernica, 1998.

Hatch, James V., ed. *Black Theater U.S.A.: Forty-five Plays by Black Americans, 1847–1974*. New York: Free Press, 1974.

Oggel, L. Terry. "Speaking Out About Race: 'The United States of Lyncherdom' Clemens Really Wrote." In *Prospects: An Annual of American Cultural Studies 25*, edited by Jack Salzman, pp. 115–158. New York: Cambridge University Press, 2000.

Zangrando, Robert L. *The NAACP Crusade Against Lynching, 1909 to 1950*. Philadelphia: Temple University Press, 1980.

Emmett H. Carroll

LYRIC POETRY

In common usage, lyric poetry refers to short poems that reflect a single, focused, and highly subjective point of view. Initially associated with the ancient Greek stringed instrument the lyre, the lyric genre has its roots in songs performed by a single poet and thus characterized by metrical regularity and unitary voice. In nineteenth-century America, lyric poems customarily displayed clearly identifiable metrical patterns and predictable rhyme schemes. The rules for lyric composition became so thoroughly codified that the poet Sidney Lanier characterized mid-century American poets as captivated by a "morbid fear of doing something wrong" (Lubbers, p. 4). Despite this widespread formal conformity, however, the lyric was immensely popular in America throughout the nineteenth century and early twentieth century.

Walt Whitman's (1819–1892) 1855 publication of *Leaves of Grass* introduced a degree of flexibility touching both form and content that greatly expanded the freedom of future poets, but *Leaves* also provoked much public outcry and led to Whitman's being marginalized as a radical for much of his life. The most significant innovation in the nineteenth-century lyric came about through the posthumous publication of Emily Dickinson's (1830–1886) poetry in the 1890s. Unlike Whitman, whose poetry aspired to the scope and grandeur of the epic, Dickinson retained classic lyric brevity while transgressing the boundaries of rhyme, meter, syntax, and subject matter that had characterized the nineteenth-century American lyric.

DEFINITION AND HISTORY OF THE GENRE

Scholarly efforts to establish a clear history of the lyric genre have been exceedingly vexed. Ernest Rhys's 1913 observation that "of all the categories, the lyric is the most lawless and has the least hesitation about breaking bounds" accurately identifies the core problem (p. vi). An important consequence of broad-based scholarly agreement over the unruliness of lyric poetry has been the emergence of a generalized working definition that alludes to historical origins but leaves plenty of room for formal variation. The following definition from the *Oxford English Dictionary* fairly characterizes the sort of loose definition that has become the standard:

> Of or pertaining to the lyre; adapted to the lyre, meant to be sung; pertaining to or characteristic of song. Now used as the name for short poems (whether or not intended to be sung), usually divided into stanzas or strophes, and directly expressing the poet's own thoughts and sentiments. Hence, applied to the poet who composes such poems.

Within the scope of this working definition, the issue that bears most directly on the lyric in America during the period 1870 to 1920 is the lyric's status as a conveyance of individual subjectivity. This aspect of the lyric acquires particular importance in relationship to the rise

of individualism in nineteenth-century American culture and the influence especially of Emersonian individualism, in which the intersection of private and public experience is a primary concern.

CONTEMPORARY APPROACHES

Precisely because scholarly discussions of the lyric center on the balance of public and private content, the influence of Ralph Waldo Emerson's (1803–1882) thinking on individualism must be considered in any assessment of the American lyric from the middle of the nineteenth century to the early twenty-first century. As Harold Bloom noted in May 2003, "Emerson remains the central figure in American culture" (p. 4). This preeminence is not, however, founded on universal agreement as to the exact nature of Emerson's influence but rather on continuing controversy spawned by enigmatic utterances such as the now famous 1842 journal entry in which Emerson states, "Union is only perfect when all the Uniters are absolutely isolated" (p. 216). This language seems to justify fears Alexis de Tocqueville expressed in *Democracy in America* (1835), where he describes individualism as disposing "each individual to isolate himself from the mass of his fellows" and leave "the greater society to look after itself" (p. 506). Supporters of the Emersonian tradition point to his underlying idealism as ultimately connecting individual isolation with collective experience, while those critical of Emerson's influence see his promotion of isolated individuality as disengaging the individual from effective social action.

The history of critical responses to Emily Dickinson's poetry illustrates the way assumptions about the private or public reach of the lyric shape interpretation. As part of his preface to the 1890 first edition, coeditor Thomas Wentworth Higginson situates Dickinson at the private pole of lyric tradition, explicitly identifying Emerson as a source for Dickinson's writing and advising readers to view the text as an "expression of the writer's own mind" without "whatever advantage lies in the discipline of public criticism" (Buckingham, p. 13). William Dean Howells's (1837–1920) 1891 review of the first edition positions Dickinson at the opposing, public pole of lyric tradition when he asserts that "the interesting and important thing is that this poetry is as characteristic of our life as our business enterprise, our political turmoil, our demagoguism, our millionarism" (Buckingham, p. 78). Contemporary scholarly assessments convey similarly contrasting approaches to the public potential of Dickinson's lyric poetry. Paula Bernat Bennett represented the tendency to accentuate Dickinson's lyric isolation when she declared in 2002 that Dickinson could "afford to write in a void and write the void into her poetry, cutting its links to the social world and to the

"THE PALACE-BURNER (*A PICTURE IN A NEWSPAPER*)"

Sarah Morgan Bryan Piatt's poem exemplifies the public pole of lyric sensibility, as it is a direct response to political events in Paris that horrified Americans. Piatt was responding to an illustration that appeared in Harper's Weekly *on 8 July 1871 depicting the execution of a woman who was part of Europe's first experiment in communism, the Paris Commune. This woman was one of seventeen thousand poverty-stricken men, women, and children executed by the French government for their participation in the uprising. The speaker in the poem is a middle-class American woman who is looking at news clippings with her son in the safety of their home. Her son's zealous determination to participate in the democratic leveling so clearly symbolized by the burning of palaces provokes the mother's critical contemplation of her own protected life. After sending her son away, she wonders if domestic comforts have diminished her "soul," making her too "languid" and "dainty" to live fully through dedication to a just cause. The poem's political message is fourfold. It states that women share the desire for political action Americans considered "natural" only in men, that the domestic sphere may not provide a healthy environment for women, that women pampered by domestic ease may not be capable of instilling proper democratic virtues in their children, and that women writers—like Piatt—can forcefully engage the political issues of their day.*

She has been burning palaces. "To see
  The sparks look pretty in the wind?" Well, yes—
And something more. But women brave as she
  Leave much for cowards, such as I to guess.

But this is old, so old that everything
  Is ashes here—the woman and the rest.
Two years are oh! so long. Now you may bring
  Some newer pictures. You like this one best?

You wish that you had lived in Paris then?
  You would have loved to burn a palace, too?
But they had guns in France, and Christian men
  Shot wicked little Communists, like you.

You would have burned the palace? Just because
  You did not live in it yourself? Oh! why?
Have I not taught you to respect the laws?
  You would have burned the palace. Would not *I*?

Would I? Go to your play, Would I, indeed?
  I? Does the boy not know my soul to be

Languid and worldly, with a dainty need
  For light and music? Yet he questions me.

Can he have seen my soul more near than I?
  Ah! in the dark and distance sweet she seems,
With lips to kiss a baby's cry.
  Hands fit for flowers, and eyes for tears and dreams.

Can he have seen my soul? And could she wear
  Such utter life upon a dying face,
Such unappealing, beautiful despair,
  Such garments—soon to be a shroud—with grace?

Has she a charm so calm that it could breathe
  In damp, low places till some frightened hour;
Then start, like a fair, subtle snake, and wreathe
  A stinging poison with a shadowy power?

Would *I* burn palaces? The child has seen
  In this fierce creature of the Commune here,
So bright with bitterness and so serene,
  A being finer than my soul, I fear.

Piatt, "The Palace-Burner," pp. 246–247.

material connections she shared with others" (p. 228). Yet in the same collection of essays on Dickinson, Shira Wolosky echoes Howells's comments when she argues that "Dickinson's texts are scenes of cultural crossroads, situated within the many and profound transitions taking place around her" (p. 138).

OVERVIEW OF SIGNIFICANT LYRIC PUBLICATIONS, 1870–1920

Sarah Piatt (1836–1919) published sixteen volumes of poetry during the course of her life, but her most

significant lyrics were published in the periodical press of her day. Poetry volumes such as *A Voyage to the Fortunate Isles* (1874), *That New World* (1877), and *A Woman's Poems* (1871) show Piatt's dedication to standardized verse forms and predictable female topics, thereby confirming the widely held critical view that she aspired to the accessibility and transparency of the genteel tradition. However, the great many poems Piatt published in periodicals present her as developing a far more complicated style, one that departs from an idealized version of female experience and moves in the direction of dialogue-based lyrics that project the realist's vision of life as constituted by struggle and conflict. A clear example of her periodical poetry is "Palace-Burner," a poem published in the *Independent* in 1872. The poem comments directly on an illustration that appeared in *Harper's Weekly* depicting a woman who participated in the Paris uprising of 1871. Piatt's association with both the genteel tradition and an emergent realism that challenged genteel social conventions define her as a transitional writer whose openly political poems clearly connect with the work of twentieth-century women poets like Adrienne Rich and Sharon Olds.

The publication of *Poems by Emily Dickinson* in 1890 struck a responsive public nerve and led to the subsequent publication of two more volumes within six years: *Poems by Emily Dickinson, Second Series* (1891) and *Poems by Emily Dickinson, Third Series* (1896). Readers were ready for poetry that broke the genteel mold both in terms of content and style. Dickinson's severe compression of meaning and high level of semantic and syntactic complexity did just that. Even the highly edited lines of poems like "Much madness is divinest sense" (p. 22) demanded that readers step outside the box of convention. Complete publication of all Dickinson poems did not take place until 1955, when Thomas H. Johnson's variorum edition presented all known poems in an attempt to honor the many nuances of Dickinson's handwritten manuscripts. As a result, readers saw for the first time the extent to which Dickinson's reliance on the dash, her unusual capitalization, her startling word choices, and her experiments with rhyme characterized the entire body of nearly eighteen hundred poems. Dickinson's willingness to experiment with form, her persistent iconoclasm, and her defiant female voice have exerted a major influence on male and female poets from the nineteenth century to the present.

The 1893 publication of *Oak and Ivy* by Paul Laurence Dunbar (1872–1906) marked the emergence of America's first major black literary professional. In *Lyrics of Lowly Life* (1895) especially, Dunbar significantly contributed to the ongoing process of situating African American slave experience in a linguistic environment far removed from the racial stereotyping all too common in American culture. As a lyricist Dunbar's chief accomplishment may be his insertion of black dialect into traditional English verse forms, giving black speakers the central role in communicating lyric experience. The complex subjectivity of speakers captured in poems like his much anthologized "We Wear the Mask" announce sharp tensions within black consciousness that would later surface in the prose of W. E. B. Du Bois and the poems of

Langston Hughes. Throughout the six volumes of poetry Dunbar published during his lifetime, his careful modulation of tone and his management of rhyme, together with his mastery of metrical form and voice qualities, constitute a significant poetic achievement. His dedication to conveying the experiences of a particular community suggests parallels with writers like Emily Dickinson and Robert Frost, whose work is associated with the experience of white New Englanders.

Stephen Crane's (1871–1900) oracular lyrics immediately reminded many readers of the epigrammatic and formally innovative poems of Emily Dickinson. In the two volumes published during his lifetime, *The Black Riders, and Other Lines* (1895) and *War Is Kind* (1899), Crane consistently employs abstract language to symbolize the clash of spiritual aspiration with the absurdity of actual experience. His abandonment of metrical patterns and his departure from regular rhyme combine with his tendency to construct poems around opposing points of view to communicate a free-floating subjectivity. The resulting sense of unanchored selfhood defines Crane as a precursor of the modernists, who were similarly interested in confronting existential questions and exposing the inadequacies of cultural institutions. His persistent irony and reliance on symbols echoes Dickinson while also pointing to the future achievements of writers like T. S. Eliot.

Edwin Arlington Robinson (1869–1935) was a hugely successful poet; he published twenty volumes of poetry and was awarded three Pulitzer Prizes (1922, 1925, 1928). Four of his poetry books appeared before 1920: *The Torrent and the Night Before* (1896), *The Children of the Night* (1897), *The Town down the River* (1910), and *The Man against the Sky* (1916). Robinson even won the admiration of President Theodore Roosevelt, who published a favorable review of his poems. Despite a characteristically nineteenth-century concern with traditional poetic form and immediate accessibility, Robinson consistently describes a recognizably modern world, one filled with darkness, confusion, struggle, and loss of traditional values. Most famous for lyric portraits, like his frequently anthologized poem "Richard Cory," Robinson illuminates the troubled interior experiences of individuals, families, and communities. Like Dickinson and Robert Frost, Robinson writes about New England, though he departs from both by writing poems that deliver clear and unambiguous messages, often commenting directly on contemporary social ills.

Robert Frost (1874–1963) continues to be one of the most influential of the American lyric poets writing between 1910 and 1920. He published eleven books of poetry, including three before 1920, *A Boy's Will* (1913), *North of Boston* (1914), and *Mountain Interval* (1916). Emerson was a powerful influence on Frost, particularly through his promotion of individualism and his emphasis on colloquial style. A distinctive feature of Frost's lyrics is his ability to communicate the sounds of actual speech, or what he termed "the sound of sense," through poems that employ traditional meter, rhythm, and rhyme. Like Dickinson and Robinson, Frost writes largely about New England, and he does not hesitate to focus on the dark side of life. Unlike Dickinson, though, Frost carefully resolves the structure of his poems in an effort to achieve a single unified effect, so his poems frequently present a particular speaker and sustain a consistent tone. Unlike Robinson's poems, Frost's are often more complicated than they appear, so even the most popular of his poems, like "The Road Less Traveled" and "Stopping by Woods on a Snowy Evening," are frequently misinterpreted. Part of the reason for this difficulty is Frost's remarkable ability to make complex observations in simple language. As a consequence, first readings of Frost poems can give the illusion of carefree innocence, when in fact his subject is the inner turmoil of deeply troubled speakers.

Like Frost, Edna St. Vincent Millay (1892–1950) achieved considerable fame as a consequence of her poetic dexterity and her choice of subject matter rather than for her innovations in lyric form. Millay published eleven volumes of poetry over the course of her life but won greatest critical acclaim for her first book, *Renascence* (1917), despite the fact that in 1923 she was the first woman to win a Pulitzer Prize for her 1922 volume *Ballad of the Harp-Weaver*. Millay is widely viewed as representative of the modern woman liberated from Victorian mores. Even though her work displays the conventional formal features that also characterize Frost's lyrics, the content of Millay's poetry is altogether more liberal. Often associated with the Bohemian life of New York's Greenwich Village, Millay made no secret of her political radicalism, her feminism, and her willingness to expand the acceptable range of female experience. Though her later poems depart from the sharply cynical stance of her early work, she never ceased to delight in the mental and emotional intensity she associates with independent selfhood. The title and opening line of her most famous sonnet—"I will put chaos into fourteen lines"—effectively conveys her courageous approach to life and her dedication to traditional English verse forms.

The brief but significant emergence of imagism between 1912 and 1917 signaled a sharp departure from the patterned writing of the genteel past and the

Edna St. Vincent Millay. Photograph by Arnold Genthe, 1914. THE LIBRARY OF CONGRESS

verbal extravagance of romanticism by encouraging a rising generation of poets to imagine more concise possibilities for lyric poetry. While no absolute consensus exists concerning the precise definition of imagism, poets associated with the imagist movement generally employed free verse while seeking to anchor language in the physical world as a way of freeing the mind from preconceived concepts. Rather than writing poems with messages, imagists focused on concrete images, metaphorical juxtapositions that compel readers to construct their own meanings, and rhythms that favor the musical line rather than traditional meter. Through the energetic advocacy of prominent experimental writers, including, most prominently, Ezra Pound (1885–1972), Hilda Doolittle (H.D., 1886–1961), and Amy Lowell (1874–1925), imagism assumed an important role in advancing the modernist aesthetic that viewed poetry as timeless and removed from the world of politics and commerce. Urging instead the development of a rich interior experience, imagism gave weight to the subjective pole of lyric tradition. Perhaps the most famous imagist poem, Ezra Pound's "In a Station of the Metro," concentrates meaning in two highly compressed lines that sharply contrast natural and industrial imagery in stark, black-and-white colors to urge perception beyond binary oppositions. Pound's dedication to linguistic compression and focused symbols suggests imagist correspondences with Dickinson's brevity and concern with original expression.

Pound's early interest in poetry sprang from his study of the Middle Ages, particularly the troubadour tradition, and his desire to make poetry a vital part of modern culture. His first book of poems, *A lume spento,* appeared in Italy during Pound's first visit to Venice in 1908 and clearly shows the influence of his early studies. While in Europe, however, Pound rapidly established himself as a central figure in the imagist movement, editing the 1914 anthology *Des imagistes* and advocating the value of concise description, precise diction, and the metrical freedom central to modernist poetics. Pound's second volume of poetry, *Lustra* (1916), is wide-ranging in its experiments with technique, expanding the possibilities of English lyric poems by incorporating Chinese, Greek, and Provençal models. With the advent of the First World War, Pound decisively parted with his early aestheticism, portraying the absurdity of the aesthete in *Hugh Selwyn Mauberley* (1920). In 1919 Pound published the poem "A Pact," in which he affirms his American heritage by declaring his descent from Whitman. "We have one sap and one root," he writes, "Let there be commerce between us" (p. 269). Along with *Mauberley* and *Lume spento,* Pound published four other important volumes of poetry between 1908 and 1920: *Ripostes* (1912), *Cathay* (1915), *Quia Pauper Amavi* (1919), and *Umbra* (1920). Much of Pound's broad influence on twentieth-century poetry comes through his affiliations with other poets and his pronounced skill as an editor, especially the editorial assistance he provided Eliot with *The Waste Land.*

Hilda Doolittle, best known as H.D., was a close acquaintance of Pound's; having first met him in Philadelphia, she later entered his circle of writers when she moved to England in 1911. Pound assisted her with early publication by sending her poems to *Poetry* in 1913, attaching the signature "H.D., Imagiste," immediately linking her to the imagist movement. H.D.'s poems from this period, like "Oread" (1914), clearly represent the imagist aesthetic and rival Pound's "In a Station of the Metro" as a model of imagist technique. The lines "Whirl up, sea— / whirl your pointed pines" (p. 55) capture the tenets of clarity, precision, and provocative juxtaposition central to imagism. H.D.'s first volume of poems, *Sea Garden* (1916), is clearly in the imagist mode, displaying her skill with stark, sharply drawn images and innovative rhythms. Deeply distressed by the violence of the First World War and the loss of her brother Gilbert, who died in the conflict, H.D. became increasingly engaged with social and political concerns. In poems like "Euridice" (1917), she drew on her training in classics to reconstitute key myths, creating a distinct, female sensibility capable of redressing the failure of traditional symbol systems. In addition to "Sea Garden," her early volumes of poetry include *Hymen* (1921), *Heliodora, and Other Poems* (1924), and *Collected Poems* (1925).

Amy Lowell was a major presence in American poetry following her return from England, where she encountered imagism in 1913. Lowell introduced imagism to America and dedicated herself to experimentation with poetic form and content, drawing on her links to European poets as well as impressionist painters and musicians. She published nine volumes of poetry during the course of her life, the most important of which are *Sword Blades and Poppy Seed* (1914), *Pictures of the Floating World* (1919), and *What's O'Clock* (1925). She was awarded the Pulitzer Prize posthumously for *What's O'Clock* in 1926, though her best work probably appears in *Pictures of the Floating World.* In that volume Lowell presents a sequence of forty-three lyric poems under the heading "Two Speak Together" that chronicle her love for Ada Russell, her companion for the last decade of her life. Lowell is perhaps best known for her 1925 poem "The Sisters," in which she meditates on the challenges faced by women poets, citing Sappho, Elizabeth Barrett Browning, and Emily Dickinson as important precursors.

T. S. Eliot (1888–1965) would become the most influential poet writing in English following his publication of *The Waste Land* in 1922. Like Pound, Frost, and H.D., Eliot was nurtured by the avant-garde experimentalism he encountered in Europe. Shortly after he arrived in England in the summer of 1914, Eliot met Pound, who dedicated himself to assisting Eliot with the publication of "The Love Song of J. Alfred Prufrock." As he had done the previous year with H.D., Pound helped secure publication of Eliot's poem in *Poetry.* "Prufrock" introduces many of Eliot's central themes and stylistic devices, and it is the most important poem from this early phase of his long career. In this work Eliot sets out to dismantle the superficial gentility of the previous generation by urging disillusionment and proclaiming the impossibility of full immersion in experience. The speaker who begins by proposing "Let us go then, you and I" (p. 3) never actually goes anywhere. Instead, Eliot presents an intense lyric meditation on the impotence of individual imagination by clustering provocative images, like the often cited "eyes" and "formulated phrase" that send the speaker "Sprawling on a pin . . .

and wriggling on the wall" (p. 5). "Prufrock" also demonstrates Eliot's considerable skill at modulating emotional content appropriate to a vitiated imagination through images like the "pair of ragged claws" that scuttle "across the floors of silent seas" (ll. 73–74). Eliot's most important poetry volumes from these early years are *Prufrock and Other Observations* (1917), *Poems* (1920), *The Waste Land* (1922), and *Poems, 1909–1925* (1925).

William Carlos Williams (1883–1963) was the most important of the modernist poets to situate the lyric in a distinctly American idiom, though it took him much of the decade following his first book publication in 1909 to discover his passionate desire to do so. Like H.D., Eliot, and Lowell, Williams benefited from Pound's literary advice after he went to England in 1910. Pound sharply criticized Williams's 1909 *Poems,* condemning the work as both derivative and twenty years behind the times. Williams's next book, *The Tempers* (1913), clearly shows Pound's influence, particularly through the appearance of multiple dramatic monologues, but still fails to convey the dedication to American settings and culture that would characterize his best work. By 1915 Williams had separated himself from the European expatriate community of Pound, Eliot, and H.D., making an artistic home for himself in the avant-garde world of New York. His next book, *Al que quiere!* (1917), showed that Williams had come of age on his native turf. The short, enjambed lines, colloquial speech patterns, and shifts from almost photographic objectivity to autobiography reflect the determination to present the world as an unfolding process that would remain a central preoccupation for the rest of his life. In poems like "The Young Housewife" (1917), where his speaker salutes a "shy, uncorseted" (*Collected Earlier Poems,* p. 136) housewife, Williams invests ordinary details of American life with a sensual richness that vitalizes and elevates distinct moments in time. His aim as a poet was to scrutinize the world closely and not view life through the lens of theory or a preexisting symbol system. His phrase "no ideas but in things" (*Selected Poems,* p. 262) effectively conveys his determination to move beyond imagism to create an objective poetry concretely anchored in the immediate moment. Williams published a fourth book of poetry in 1921, *Sour Grapes,* but his 1924 *Spring and All* was the greatest achievement to emerge from this early stage of his writing career.

See also Genteel Tradition; Imagism; "The Love Song of J. Alfred Prufrock"; *Lyrics of Lowly Life; The Man against the Sky;* "The Marshes of Glynn"; *North of Boston*

BIBLIOGRAPHY

Primary Works

Dickinson, Emily. *Collected Poems.* Edited by Peter Siegenthaler. Philadelphia: Courage, 1991.

Doolittle, Hilda. *H.D. Collected Poems, 1912–1944.* Edited by Louis L. Martz. New York: New Directions, 1983.

Eliot. T. S. *The Complete Poems and Plays, 1909–1950.* New York: Harcourt Brace Jovanovich, 1962.

Emerson, Ralph Waldo. *Selections from Ralph Waldo Emerson.* Edited by Stephen E. Whicher. Boston: Houghton Mifflin, 1957.

Piatt, Sarah Morgan Bryan. "The Palace-Burner." 1872. In *Nineteenth-Century American Women Poets: An Anthology,* edited by Paula Bernat Bennett, pp. 246–247. Melden, Mass.: Blackwell, 1998.

Pound, Ezra. *Ezra Pound: Poems and Translations.* Edited by Richard Sieburth. New York: Library of America, 2003.

Tocqueville, Alexis de. *Democracy in America.* Edited by J. P. Mayer, translated by George Lawrence. New York: HarperCollins, 2000.

Williams, William Carlos. *The Collected Earlier Poems of William Carlos Williams.* New York: New Directions, 1951.

Williams, William Carlos. *Selected Poems.* Edited by Charles Tomlinson. New York: New Directions, 1985.

Secondary Works

Bennett, Paula Bernat. "Emily Dickinson and Her American Woman Poet Peers." In *The Cambridge Companion to Emily Dickinson,* edited by Wendy Martin, pp. 215–235. Cambridge, U.K.: Cambridge University Press, 2002.

Bloom, Harold. "The Sage of Concord." *Guardian,* 24 May 2003, pp. 4–6.

Buckingham, Willis J., ed. *Emily Dickinson's Reception in the 1890s: A Documentary History.* Pittsburgh: University of Pittsburgh Press, 1989.

Lubbers, Klaus. *Emily Dickinson: The Critical Revolution.* Ann Arbor: University of Michigan Press, 1968.

Rhys, Ernest. *Lyric Poetry.* New York: Dutton, 1913.

Wolosky, Shira. "Emily Dickinson: Being in the Body." In *The Cambridge Companion to Emily Dickinson,* edited by Wendy Martin, pp. 129–141. Cambridge, U.K.: Cambridge University Press, 2002.

Paul Crumbley

LYRICS OF LOWLY LIFE

Lyrics of Lowly Life (1896) is the book of poems that established Paul Laurence Dunbar (1872–1906) as the most important African American poet of his time. The volume of 105 poems is a mixture of works in

Paul Laurence Dunbar. THE LIBRARY OF CONGRESS

conventional literary English and in dialect, a split that not only defines Dunbar's poetic career but also dramatizes a central argument of the black aesthetic. Dunbar, a black poet who in a very short career reached a national audience, provided both a model and a target for subsequent African American artists, especially the poets of the Harlem Renaissance. His most productive decade, the 1890s, marks what has been called the lowest historical moment for African Americans, and his poetry reveals many of the contradictions of his times: a book of poems for both black and white readers, written in both "white" and "black" styles, intermingled seemingly randomly, not separated, and published in the same year that "separate but equal" became established as the law of the land.

The poems in *Lyrics of Lowly Life* were composed over several years, and the book is actually a successor to two earlier privately printed volumes: *Oak and Ivy* (1892) and *Majors and Minors* (1895). Dunbar's parents had been slaves in Kentucky; his father escaped slavery and, after serving in the Civil War, settled in Dayton, Ohio (an important stop on the Underground Railroad), where he met Dunbar's mother. His parents separated when Dunbar was two years old and

divorced when he was four, but his mother encouraged his burgeoning poetic talent. Dunbar composed the earliest of the poems for *Lyrics of Lowly Life* while working as an elevator operator in Dayton, where he had graduated in 1891 as the only black student at Dayton's Central High School. He established quite a presence in his otherwise white school: he wrote the class song, served as president of the school's literary society, and edited a black newspaper, the *Dayton Tattler,* aided by his boyhood friend (later the pioneering aviator) Orville Wright. After graduation, Dunbar gave poetry readings to white, black, and mixed-race audiences, and his fame as a talented young writer continued to grow regionally, boosted in 1892 by a reading at the meeting in Dayton of the Western Association of Writers, which enabled him to collect his poems in book form to sell at public readings.

At the 1893 World's Columbian Exposition in Chicago he met Frederick Douglass, who employed Dunbar as a clerk and encouraged him in his poetic career. Aided by white friends and patrons, Dunbar published his second book, *Majors and Minors* (1895), which was reviewed enthusiastically in the 27 June 1896 *Harper's Weekly* by William Dean Howells (1837–1920), the most influential writer and critic of his time. This glowing review by Howells led directly to the publication of *Lyrics of Lowly Life* later that year by Dodd, Mead of New York, who put Dunbar under contract, paid him a monthly salary of $400, and published his subsequent work. Howells wrote the introduction, a revised form of his earlier review, an important critical notice that catapulted Dunbar's work to a national audience and trumpeted him as the best poet of his race but also set critical interpretation of Dunbar's poetry in ways that hampered his wider ambitions. In reaching a national audience he became not only "the Poet Laureate of the Negro Race," as Booker T. Washington (1856–1915) called him, but also perhaps the best American poet of his time. The book had sold over twelve thousand copies by the turn of the century, and Dunbar was able to publish his poetry in such national publications as *Century Magazine,* the *Saturday Evening Post,* and the *New York Times* as well as to publish more books of poetry, novels, short stories, and essays. He managed to make his living as a writer in a time when that feat was difficult for white writers, let alone for a person of color.

HISTORICAL CONTEXT

Dunbar was born and grew up during the brief moment of optimism and opportunity of the Reconstruction period (1866 to 1877), when blacks made incredible progress in politics, business, education, and equal rights. As Reconstruction formally ended in 1877 with the withdrawal of federal troops from the South and the relaxation of political pressure on the South to reform, a backlash against black gains and freedoms ensued. By the 1890s the forces of disfranchisement, institutionalized segregation, and violence against blacks were in full swing, erasing the political, economic, and social gains of African Americans. Lynching became epidemic, with around two hundred per year reported for the decade (which does not account for unreported incidents). The gains blacks had made in integrating society were erased by segregationist Jim Crow laws, which were upheld in 1896 by the Supreme Court decision *Plessy v. Ferguson,* making "separate but equal" the law of the land. As Dunbar came of age and began his poetic career, he found himself in a society that increasingly sought to marginalize him.

Historical forces within black society also had an impact. In his famous Atlanta Exposition speech of 1895, Booker T. Washington announced a movement of assimilation and accommodation. Artistically, the black press had been calling for an African American writer who could represent the race and show white America that a "Negro artist" could contend equally with white artists. Within this context Dunbar appeared on the national scene, seeming to emerge in answer to a call and a need. His poetry reached an unprecedentedly wide audience, and the poetry itself contains a mixture that mirrors the contending forces of the time.

THE POEMS

A reader of *Lyrics of Lowly Life* in 1896 would have first encountered a frontispiece that showed an extremely young, somewhat small, neatly dressed, and decidedly dark-skinned man, announcing with no question the race of its author. Before the poetry comes an introduction by Howells, in which he praises Dunbar's achievement as a poet, especially his dialect poetry. Howells's judgments had such an impact on Dunbar's career that they bear quoting:

> The contents of this book are wholly of his own choosing, and I do not know how much or little he may have preferred the poems in literary English. Some of these I thought very good, and even more than very good, but not distinctively his contribution to the body of American poetry. What I mean is that several people might have written them; but I do not know any one else at present who could quite have written the dialect pieces. These are divinations and reports of what passes in the hearts and minds of a lowly people whose poetry had hitherto been inarticulately expressed in music, but now finds, for the first time in our tongue, literary interpretation of a very artistic completeness. (P. xix)

Dunbar recognized the double-edged nature of Howells's remarks. In his literary poems Dunbar had achieved mastery of traditional forms and themes, mastery achieved not only through natural ability but also by voracious reading in the English tradition, especially of John Keats. His attitude about his popular dialect poems is somewhat ambivalent, ranging from comments that he knew he could write such poetry better than anyone else to dismay that his more conventional works were not taken more seriously. Still, Howells's judgment remains true in the sense that, were it not for the dialect poetry, Dunbar would be remembered, if at all, as a skillful poet of a kind of traditional verse that was very soon to fall completely out of favor.

Approximately three-quarters of the 105 poems in *Lyrics of Lowly Life* are written in literary English, the remaining fourth in dialect (and not all in black dialect; Dunbar also wrote in Irish, German, and Hoosier dialects, influenced greatly by the popular James Whitcomb Riley). Taken together the poems exhibit a remarkable range, from the polished formality of the first poem, "Ere Sleep Comes down to Soothe the Weary Eyes," to the raucous hilarity of the final poem, "The Party": "Dey had a gread big pahty down to Tom's de otha night; / Was I dah? You bet! I nevah in my life see such a sight" (p. 199). The poems in literary English often focus on traditional themes of love and love lost, the nature of art and the artistic impulse, and the transitory nature of life. In several of these poems, such as "Frederick Douglass," "Ode to Ethiopia," and "The Colored Soldiers," Dunbar explicitly treats black subjects. But in the midst of these polished and serious poems sit the dialect poems, erupting from the page: "A Banjo Song," "An Ante-Bellum Sermon," and "When Malindy Sings." The interpretation of these dialect poems has shifted constantly since their publication and reveals as much about the reader and the historical moment as about the poems. "When Malindy Sings" can be read as a comic stereotype of a natural black affinity for music or as a more subversive comment: the speaker addresses the whole poem to "Miss Lucy," clearly a young white woman who is trying to sing "by the book," in contrast to Malindy's soulful, natural art. "An Ante-Bellum Sermon" can seem at first an example of more comic stereotyping, this time of semiliterate black preaching, but a closer examination of the preacher's message reveals a constant subtext of "signifying" on the slaveholder's hypocrisy.

CRITICAL REACTION

In their time, Dunbar's dialect poems were seen as a continuation of the "plantation tradition," popularized in the dialect poetry of white writers like Irwin Russell and Thomas Nelson Page. The delight white and black readers took in Dunbar's dialect poetry reflects a strong taste for dialects of all kinds around the close of the nineteenth century. But the question of how Dunbar fit into the usually racist plantation tradition has been controversial almost from the start. Poets and critics of the Harlem Renaissance looked back twenty years later and saw Dunbar as little more than a minstrel darky. The New Negroes repudiated his poetry as accommodationist and stereotypical, an embarrassing and harmful pandering to white tastes for comical and misplaced plantation nostalgia. Despite being a close friend of Dunbar and himself a prolific writer of dialect verse, James Weldon Johnson made the pronouncement in *The Book of American Negro Poetry* (1922) that dialect poetry has only "two stops—pathos and humor," thus relegating Dunbar to a much lower status in the eyes of the generation of artists that followed. Even so, Dunbar was an important influence for many African American poets, notably Langston Hughes and Countee Cullen.

Dunbar's status began to recover in 1972 with an important centennial celebration of his birth. The rise of the Black Arts movement during this period provided a new lens through which to view Dunbar's art. Poets, writers, and critics such as Nikki Giovanni, Arna Bontemps, and Darwin T. Turner called for a new look at Dunbar, and he began to be recognized as a pioneer in using authentic black speech as a medium for art. This more revolutionary aesthetic could detect in Dunbar's poems, even in the dialect poems, subtleties and undercurrents that reveal a writer who at once pleases but also subtly confronts a white audience.

One of the final poems in the book, probably Dunbar's most famous, "We Wear the Mask," has been the key for those critics who argue that the poet was conscious of subverting the plantation tradition even as he used its elements to gain an audience. This widely anthologized poem gains even more power when read amidst the dialect poetry that originally accompanied it:

> We wear the mask that grins and lies,
> It hides our cheeks and shades our eyes,—
> This debt we pay to human guile;
> With torn and bleeding hearts we smile,
> And mouth with myriad subtleties.
>
> *(P. 167)*

Dunbar was friends with both Booker T. Washington and W. E. B. Du Bois, and even though he was accused of Washington-like accommodationism, in this poem he anticipates Du Bois's influential idea in *The Souls of Black Folk* (1903) of black "double consciousness." Reading the dialect poems with the idea of masking behind them forces a reinterpretation of Dunbar's motives and strategies.

Lyrics of Lowly Life established Dunbar's reputation, a reputation that has risen and dropped and risen as political and aesthetic forces have changed. His poems, especially the dialect poems, remain controversial and subject to debate, forming a kind of literary Rorschach test that reveals as much about the reader and the times as the poems or the poet. After a long battle with tuberculosis, Dunbar died in Dayton in 1906. His career was as short as that of his literary hero John Keats, but his influence on the African American literary tradition was profound.

See also Blacks; Slang, Dialect, and Other Types of Marked Language

BIBLIOGRAPHY
Primary Works
Du Bois, W. E. B. *The Souls of Black Folk.* 1903. New York: Library of America, 1990.

Dunbar, Paul Laurence. *The Collected Poetry of Paul Laurence Dunbar.* 1895. Edited by Joanne M. Braxton. Charlottesville: University Press of Virginia, 1993.

Dunbar, Paul Laurence. *Lyrics of Lowly Life.* Introduction by William Dean Howells. New York: Dodd, Mead, 1896.

Secondary Works
Bruce, Dickson D., Jr. *Black American Writing from the Nadir: The Evolution of a Literary Tradition 1877–1915.* Baton Rouge: Louisiana State University Press, 1989.

Keeling, John. "Paul Laurence Dunbar and the Mask of Dialect." *Southern Literary Journal* 25 (spring 1993): 24–38.

Martin, Jay, ed. *A Singer in the Dawn: Reinterpretations of Paul Laurence Dunbar.* New York: Dodd, Mead, 1975.

Revell, Peter. *Paul Laurence Dunbar.* Boston: Twayne, 1979.

John Bird

McCLURE'S MAGAZINE

S. S. McClure launched his eponymous *McClure's Magazine* at the beginning of a major economic depression in 1893, hardly an auspicious time to make a debut. As the first issue hit the newsstands in May, many newspapers were already beginning to delay payments to McClure's newspaper syndicate and even discontinuing their subscriptions, drastically reducing his available operating capital; simultaneously, most major companies were cutting back drastically on their magazine advertising expenditures. McClure was further dismayed when twelve thousand of the twenty thousand copies of the inaugural issue of *McClure's* were returned from newsdealers. After such a difficult start, however, *McClure's* would go on to become one of the most popular, innovative, and influential American magazines during the period 1895–1912. Unfortunately, though, once S. S. McClure himself was deposed from the editor's chair in 1912, the magazine began a slow decline into mediocrity and ultimately suffered an ignoble end in March 1929.

EARLY HISTORY

McClure's was part of a group of magazines that in the late 1880s and early 1890s began to target the rapidly expanding middle-class audience of this period. The copiously illustrated, current events–focused *McClure's Magazine* joined such low-priced, middlebrow magazines as Edward Bok's *Ladies' Home Journal* (ten cents a month, begun in 1883), *Scribner's Magazine* (1887), *Munsey's Magazine* (1889), and *Cosmopolitan* (1886) (all at twenty-five cents per month) but at a lower price of fifteen cents a month, which prompted *Munsey's* and *Cosmopolitan* to lower their own cover prices shortly thereafter.

From the very start, the content of *McClure's* reflected the eclectic interests of S. S. McClure (1857–1959). Known as the "Chief" by his magazine staffers, McClure was constantly rushing across the country and to Europe to meet with authors, gather ideas from local periodicals, and talk to leaders in a wide variety of fields in order to learn what would be the latest subject of interest. McClure was a pioneer in the magazine field because he inaugurated a more active style of editorship, often assigning nonfiction authors their topics and even directing their approaches to particular subjects. The resulting magazine contained a broad range of articles, everything from reports on technological advances being made by Alexander Graham Bell, Thomas Edison, and Guglielmo Marconi to accounts of polar exploration and fiction by both unknown and well-known authors. The popularity of *McClure's* must in large part be attributed to the way that McClure intuited what would interest readers. Far from an intellectual himself, he later wrote, "I always felt that I judged a story with my solar plexus rather than my brain; my only measure of it was the pull it exerted on something inside of me" (p. 204).

Yet *McClure's* would never have succeeded the way it did without the extremely capable staff that McClure hired in the 1890s. John S. Phillips, McClure's college classmate, served as managing editor from the magazine's inception until he left in 1906. Highly educated with a graduate degree from Harvard, Phillips was also organized and practical—an ideal counterbalance for

In this editorial preface to one of the most famous issues of his magazine, S. S. McClure appears to be a solid progressive who believes in the power of journalistic exposure and democracy to right the wrongs of modern industrial capitalism. This one issue contained muckraking articles by the staff writers Ida Tarbell, Ray Stannard Baker, and Lincoln Steffens, all of which helped effect greater regulation of corrupt businesses, unions, and municipal governments. To what extent McClure actually believed in progressivism, however, is unclear, especially because in this same editorial he wrote about these three articles, "We did not plan it so; it is a coincidence that the January McCLURE'S is such an arraignment of American character as should make every one of us stop and think."

Capitalists, workingmen, politicians, citizens—all breaking the law, or letting it be broken. Who is left to uphold it? The lawyers? Some of the best lawyers in this country are hired, not to go into court to defend cases, but to advise corporations and business firms how they can get around the law without too great a risk of punishment. The judges? Too many of them so respect the laws that for some "error" or quibble they restore to office and liberty men convicted on evidence overwhelmingly convincing to common sense. The churches? We know of one, an ancient and wealthy establishment, which had to be compelled by a Tammany hold-over health officer to put its tenements in sanitary condition. The colleges? They do not understand. There is no one left; none but all of us.

S. S. McClure, Editorial, *McClure's Magazine,* January 1903, p. 336.

McClure's mercurial genius. Albert Brady, another college classmate, served as the extremely capable business manager until his premature death in 1900 (not coincidentally the year of greatest profitability for *McClure's*). August F. Jaccaci, the *McClure's* art director, procured and arranged the excellent, prolific illustrations that contributed greatly to the magazine's success.

THE CULT OF PERSONALITY

One thing McClure sensed instinctually was the American reading public's interest in great men and women. Beginning with the first issue, McClure sought to satisfy this desire with a regular section called "Human Documents," in each of which appeared about a half-dozen portraits of a famous person at various stages of his or her life. Subsequently the magazine launched a very popular series called "Real Conversations," which featured prominent people in a variety of fields being interviewed by other famous people.

Out of these series grew the greatest successes of the early *McClure's Magazine*. The first installment of Ida Tarbell's comprehensive, readable biographical series on Napoleon was printed in *McClure's* in November 1894, and by the final installment in April 1895 the magazine's circulation had reached 100,000. Shortly after this came Tarbell's series titled "The Early Life of Lincoln," which appeared from November 1895 to November 1896 and helped boost circulation to approximately 250,000. Notable too was Hamlin Garland's series on Ulysses S. Grant, which ran intermittently from December 1896 to May 1898. Much later, a series called "Mary Baker G. Eddy: The Story of Her Life and the History of Christian Science," which appeared from 1907 to 1908 under the byline of Georgine Milmine, was in fact substantially researched and revised by Willa Cather on her first major assignment for the magazine.

MUCKRAKING

What chiefly fueled the meteoric rise of *McClure's Magazine* to national prominence, however, was the significant role it played in the "muckraking" movement that supported progressive social and economic reforms in the late 1890s and early 1900s. Historians debate the extent to which McClure himself, exposed at Knox College in Galesburg, Illinois, to Christian progressivism, purposely used his magazine to expose the injustices of modern industrial society or whether he was simply an opportunist who believed that this kind of sensational journalism would sell more copies of the magazine and make him more money.

The debate about McClure's intentions is unlikely ever to be resolved conclusively. What is unquestionable, however, is that McClure was dedicated to producing for his readers engaging, informative, and accurate articles about life in modern America. McClure perceptively realized that to write these articles, authors needed a great deal of time to travel to the locales involved, conduct interviews, and check facts. As a result, he financed the work of such talented writers as Tarbell, Ray Stannard Baker, William Allen White, Mark Sullivan, and Lincoln Steffens, paying them liberally and reimbursing their expenses for months, sometimes even years of investigative research.

The results of such financial largesse and editorial freedom are extremely impressive. The January 1903 issue of *McClure's,* for instance, included parts of three investigative series that were being published simultaneously and that are now regarded as some of the best American journalistic writing ever. There was the third installment of Ida Tarbell's "The History of the Standard Oil Company"; an article by Ray Stannard Baker on the unfair practices of the United Mine Workers leadership; and Lincoln Steffens's "Shame of Minneapolis," the first installment of what would later be known as *The Shame of the Cities.* Steffens continued exposing corrupt local governments in a number of later issues, offering damning portrayals of the political machines operating in Minneapolis, St. Louis, Pittsburgh, and Philadelphia as well as in numerous state capitals. Baker, who had earlier written scathing accounts of lynchings and the U.S. Steel Corporation, later turned his attention to American railroads (1905–1906). Significantly, even after the departure of Tarbell, Steffens, and Baker from the magazine in 1906, *McClure's* continued to publish muckraking articles by such authors as C. P. Connolly, Burton Hendrick, Will Irwin, and George Kibbe Turner.

Muckraking certainly brought *McClure's* a great deal of attention, but it did not have an especially positive effect on circulation. In 1898 the magazine's average monthly circulation was 349,623, but in 1905 it stood at only 375,000 (Lyon, p. 251). If McClure had intended to reap huge profits from muckraking, the effort was a failure.

LITERARY SUCCESS

The catholic tastes of S. S. McClure extended to the magazine's fiction as well. No one genre was privileged more than any other, with works of historical romance printed alongside local color sketches, detective stories, and tales of domestic intrigue. British authors were well represented; these included Robert Louis Stevenson, Anthony Hope, Thomas Hardy, Arthur Conan Doyle, Walter Besant, Stanley Weyman, and Rudyard Kipling (*Captains Courageous* appeared as a serial between November 1896 and February 1897, and *Kim* ran from December 1900 through October 1901). Kipling's poem "The White Man's Burden," which drew international attention and became a widely known catchphrase used to justify—and criticize—American and British imperialism, was printed in *McClure's* in February 1899.

To save money, the magazine at first relied heavily on a stock of stories that McClure had previously purchased for his syndicate but had not yet sold to newspapers. McClure's financial straits during this time resulted in one of the magazine's greatest failures. In early 1894 Stephen Crane submitted the manuscript of *The Red Badge of Courage* to *McClure's;* however, McClure could not afford to purchase it, and Crane consequently sold it to Irving Bacheller's newspaper syndicate. McClure did recognize Crane's talent, however, publishing in the magazine a number of Crane's nonfiction and fiction works, most notably "In the Depths of a Coal Mine," "The Bride Comes to Yellow Sky," and "The Veteran."

Playing a key role in maintaining the magazine's high level of literary excellence was its literary editor from 1896 on, Viola Roseboro'. Roseboro' and her staff (including Witter Bynner, who after 1903 would serve as poetry editor) sifted through the thousands of unsolicited manuscripts sent to *McClure's.* One of her discoveries was William Sidney Porter, who wrote under the pen name of O. Henry; his first story to see print was "Whistling Dick's Christmas Story," which appeared in the December 1899 issue. Roseboro' also was the first to recognize the quality of Booth Tarkington's writing; his first novel, *The Gentleman from Indiana,* ran serially from May to October 1899.

Whether McClure or Roseboro' was most responsible, almost all the best American authors of this period published at least once in *McClure's.* The regionalists Sarah Orne Jewett, Octave Thanet (Alice French), Hamlin Garland, Joel Chandler Harris, Bret Harte, and Mary E. Wilkins (Freeman) as well as the realists Theodore Dreiser, Ernest Poole, and Jack London, whose "The Law of Life" appeared in the March 1901 issue, were contributors. The latter was, though, quite anomalous; somewhat surprisingly, given the magazine's reputation for hard-hitting, graphic journalism, it tended not to publish fictions that depicted life with unbridled, gritty realism or were too depressing.

Possibly the greatest of McClure's discoveries was a young Pittsburgh author and schoolteacher named Willa Cather. In 1903 McClure promised to print her stories in *McClure's* and to find publishers for those works he did not have room for. Cather became an editor at *McClure's* in 1906, and in 1908 she became managing editor—a position she held until she left the magazine in 1911. Her now famous story "Paul's Case" was published in the May 1905 issue, and the magazine, besides printing a good number of her early stories and poems, ran "Alexander's Masquerade" from February through April 1912; this would later be published as Cather's first novel, *Alexander's Bridge.*

In general, the quality of fiction was slightly lower after 1907. However, *McClure's* did publish a number of works by the likes of Arnold Bennett,

***McClure's Magazine* staff and contributors** From left: Samuel McClure with former staffers Willa Cather, Ida Tarbell, and Will Irwin, New York City, 1925. © BETTMANN/CORBIS

G. K. Chesterton, Kathleen Norris, P. G. Wodehouse, Rex Beach, Zane Grey, Edna Ferber, and James Branch Cabell.

A LONG, SLOW DEMISE

Always underlying the editorial successes of *McClure's Magazine,* unfortunately, was an extremely shaky financial foundation. McClure was an abysmal businessman, expending money to authors and making purchases that far outstripped revenues. Even during the period 1895–1899, when *McClure's Magazine* ran more advertising in its pages than any other monthly (often approximately half of each issue was devoted to advertisements), it usually ran in the red. Despite the fact that the magazine's highest circulation came in 1910, its last year of profitability was 1905.

In the spring of 1906 McClure hastened the demise of the magazine when he unveiled a plan to greatly expand the company by, among other things, establishing People's Bank and People's Life Insurance Company. Phillips, along with Tarbell, Baker, and Steffens, tried to talk him out of his plans but with no success. That May they all left, with McClure buying out Phillips's and Tarbell's shares in the company. The magazine's circulation was maintained and even rose somewhat in the following few years, but financing the debt on a series of ill-advised expansion plans proved unsupportable. Eventually the company was reorganized in 1911, with McClure becoming merely a salaried editor rather than the owner and publisher.

McClure continued as the magazine's editor until the spring of 1912, when he was forced to resign. After this the magazine went through a series of new owners and editors before its formal death in 1929. McClure himself came back for brief stints as editor or owner at various points in the 1920s, but the magic was gone. In 1926 Hearst Publications bought the magazine and renamed it *McClure's: The Magazine of Romance,* and from July 1928 until its final issue in March 1929 it was known as *New McClure's Magazine.*

See also Journalism; Muckrakers and Yellow Journalism; Periodicals

BIBLIOGRAPHY

Primary Work

McClure, S. S. *My Autobiography.* New York: Frederick A. Stokes, 1914. Reprinted as *The Autobiography of S. S. McClure* by Willa Cather. Lincoln: University of Nebraska Press, 1997.

Secondary Works

Lyon, Peter. *Success Story: The Life and Times of S. S. McClure.* New York: Scribners, 1963.

Mott, Frank Luther. "McClure's Magazine." In his *A History of American Magazines, 1885–1905,* vol. 4., pp. 588–607. Cambridge, Mass.: Belknap Press of Harvard University Press, 1957.

Ryan, Susan M. "Acquiring Minds: Commodified Knowledge and the Positioning of the Reader in *McClure's Magazine,* 1893–1903." *Prospects* 22 (1997): 211–238.

Stovall, James Glen. "S. S. McClure." In *Dictionary of Literary Biography: American Magazine Journalists, 1900–1960,* 1st ser., edited by Sam Riley, pp. 216–225. Detroit: Gale, 1990.

Wilson, Harold. *McClure's Magazine and the Muckrakers.* Princeton, N.J.: Princeton University Press, 1970.

Woodress, James. "The Pre-Eminent Magazine Genius: S. S. McClure." In *Essays Mostly on Periodical Publishing in America: A Collection in Honor of Clarence Gohdes,* edited by James Woodress, Townsend Ludington, and Joseph Arpad, pp. 171–192. Durham, N.C.: Duke University Press, 1973.

Charles Johanningsmeier

McTEAGUE

An acknowledged classic in the U.S. literary canon, the 1899 novel *McTeague: A Story of San Francisco* by Frank Norris (1870–1902) is also a touchstone for two important developments in American cultural history—one having to do with the impact of evolutionary theory by the late 1890s and the other with the demise of Victorian moral limitations on subject matter that could be frankly treated in fiction intended for a popular readership. Like Stephen Crane's *Maggie, A Girl of the Streets* in 1893 and James Lane Allen's *Summer in Arcady* in 1896, *McTeague* broke with long-standing precedent by addressing what in his essay "A Plea for Romantic Fiction" (1901) Norris termed "the mystery of sex." It did so, however, in a more forthright, less genteel manner than seen in Crane's and Allen's novels. Not only is the sexual arousal of the hero, McTeague, given unmistakably clear description in chapter 2; but three chapters later so is that of the woman he will marry: "Suddenly he took her in his enormous arms, crushing down her struggle with his immense strength. Then Trina gave up, all in an instant, turning her head to his. They kissed each other, grossly, full in the mouth" (p. 84). Scenes of this kind prompted the book reviewers Edward and Madeline Vaughn Abbot to protest in the *Literary World* (1 April 1899) that "grossness for the sake of grossness is unpardonable"; and when *McTeague* appeared in England, the *Spectator* reviewer echoed the sentiment, terming Norris "simply an animal painter, who, while he entirely fails to touch the heart, is often completely successful in turning the stomach" ("Novels of the Week," p. 662). There was by 1899, however, a warrant in scientific thought for rendering the great "love scene" in this novel with imagery suggesting a barnyard encounter between a rooster and hen.

Four decades earlier with the publication of *On the Origin of Species* (1859), Charles Darwin (1809–1882) opened a new chapter in Western intellectual history by sounding the death knell for thinking and speaking about male-female relationships in solely idealistic or spiritual terms. Darwinism encouraged a reconception of humanity in light of its close kinship with lower life-forms and with parent species from which it descended over vast expanses of time. As with a bull and cow in rutting season, so are McTeague and Trina's responses to each other inextricably rooted in primal instinct. That is, the *Spectator* reviewer was correct: Norris was an "animal painter," picturing and interpreting the human animal in *McTeague.*

Only once, in an 8 February 1902 article for the *Brooklyn Daily Eagle* titled "Frank Norris Writes Cleverly about Child Fiction for Old Readers," did Norris comment cogently upon one of Darwin's publications, *The Expression of the Emotions in Man and Animals* (1872). By the mid-1890s, though, Norris had come under the influence of the major literary Darwinist at work in Europe, the French novelist Émile Zola (1840–1902), known as the father of a literary school advancing the principles of naturalism in the arts. As did Darwin when excluding supernatural explanations of natural phenomena, Zola assumed that self-contained nature could be understood in terms of generalizable "laws" or conditions governing all life-forms. Thus from the late 1870s on he had set an example for Norris with his representations of the human animal. Indeed that was the very title of Zola's 1890 novel *La Bête humaine.* As a literary naturalist Norris did not deny the concept of free will, but he did dramatically qualify it by focusing upon the twin determinisms that Zola emphasized as working in everyone's life: the influences of his characters' heredity and both the shaping effects of environment upon personality and the consequences of proving either well adapted or maladapted to change when unpredictable or chance developments in the environment occur.

McTeague, however, is more than a grim survival-of-the-fittest study of how one's genes transmit particular traits that are beneficial or harmful as they become dominant because of conditions in which Norris's characters find themselves. As can be seen in several of the reviews of *McTeague* collected in *Frank Norris: The Critical Reception,* its author's broad vaudevillian sense of humor was appreciated in 1899. In fact the dominant tone in the first half of the novel is comic: in the main plot, it is not until chapter 15 (of 22 chapters) that the ill effects of "bad" heredity and unfortunate developments in their environment begin to carry the hero and heroine toward the homicidal outcome of their relationship. Along the way, two subplots further leaven the reading experience: an infusion of the silly is encountered in the geriatric love idyll featuring Old Grannis and Miss Baker; another "love story" of sorts is the bizarre tale of the delusional housekeeper Maria Miranda Macapa and her relationship with the similarly unhinged Zerkow, the archetypal miser and voyeur whose pornography is whatever figure anything made of gold assumes in his deranged imagination.

McTeague, as the 1899 reviews testify, is at once a naturalistic novel illustrating the degree to which humans, describable as normal or deviant, are governed by appetites, drives, and other forces beyond their control or even their comprehension; a realist's novel true in its local color to the urban landscape and to life among the lower middle class and the lowest socioeconomic stratum in 1890s San Francisco; a romance featuring the imaginative extravagances typical of the genre; a mock-romance satirizing the conventions of traditional love stories; and both a comic novel and a tragic one. Truly a period piece, it did not fare well through the mid-twentieth century at the hands of critics whose aesthetic values were those of modernism—as may be seen in Warren French's

Frank Norris, photographed shortly before his death in 1902 at the age of thirty-two.

Frank Norris (pp. 62–75) and William B. Dillingham's *Frank Norris: Instinct and Art* (pp. 103–119). Chided for decades as rhetorically inflated, heavy-handed in its symbolism, and intellectually simplistic in both its pre-Freudian psychology and its deterministic philosophy, *McTeague* did not come into its own as the masterpiece in the Norris canon until the 1970s. Then, in a postmodernist cultural context, historical distance sufficient for the appreciation of its period characteristics was finally achieved and was manifested in more appreciative studies such as Barbara Hochman's *The Art of Frank Norris, Storyteller* (1988, pp. 61–76) and Joseph R. McElrath Jr.'s *Frank Norris Revisited* (1992, pp. 35–53). Furthermore over the last three decades of the twentieth century the novel's reputation was not diminished by popularizations of the findings of geneticists regarding hereditary predispositions predictive of behavior. As Donald Pizer observes in "The Biological Determinism of *McTeague* in Our Time" (1997), such predispositions seen in McTeague, Trina, and other characters are no longer dismissed as a laughable pseudoscientific "bad seed" theory that enjoyed currency at the turn of the twentieth century. Rather than the oversimplification of the human condition described by John J. Conder in *Naturalism in*

American Fiction (pp. 69–85), *McTeague* is now recognized as an illumination of its sometimes bewildering complexities.

THE COMPOSITION AND PUBLICATION OF *McTEAGUE*

Norris himself never indicated that this was the case, but literary historians have inferred that the germ of *McTeague* is to be seen in 1893 San Francisco press reports concerning one Patrick Collins, an alcoholic brute who stabbed his wife to death when she refused to give him money for drink. How familiar Norris—then an undergraduate at the University of California in Berkeley—was with Zola's novels at this time also remains uncertain: his short stories seeing publication from 1890 through early 1895 do not reveal Zola's influence; and when he began to produce sketches of his Collins-like hero during 1894–1895, the year he spent as a special student at Harvard, moot is the degree to which he conceived of McTeague and Trina in Zolaesque terms. Several of these themes produced for a writing course and collected by James D. Hart in *A Novelist in the Making* (pp. 57–102) feature a violent drunkard and his battered wife. Lacking in the thematic essentials of a naturalistic work, however, the unsavory characterizations and lurid situations in the themes are reminiscent of portrayals of the victims of alcohol abuse seen in nineteenth-century temperance novels and plays. Even in one theme summarizing the novel Norris hoped to write, the plot outlined does not suggest a work like the ones for which Zola was notorious.

In 1896, when his essay "Zola as a Romantic Writer" and his review "Zola's *Rome*" were published in the San Francisco *Wave*, Norris finally made clear the depth to which he had read in the Zola canon. He wrote with intimate familiarity about no less than eight of the French writer's novels. By this time Norris had become a staff writer for that weekly magazine, and his short stories published therein increasingly displayed a naturalistic cast into the fall of 1897, when he completed the manuscript of *McTeague*.

How unconventional and "dirty" the novel then appeared is to be seen in the fact that even the publishing conglomerate in New York City by which he was employed in February 1898 declined to accept it for publication. It was not until after the S. S. McClure newspaper syndicate and the Doubleday and McClure book publishing company found Norris commercially viable as the author of an adventure romance, *Moran of the Lady Letty* (1898), that the latter decided to risk its reputation with a contract for *McTeague*. Less adventuresome was *McTeague*'s English publisher, Grant Richards. Although not offended by explicitly sexual developments, graphic descriptions of violence, and the blatantly sadomasochistic aspects of the hero's relationship with his wife, he insisted that Norris rewrite a scene in chapter 6 of the first American printing that referred to the incontinence of the heroine's young brother. It was not until 1941 that this bowdlerization was effaced by a restoration of the original text in newly printed editions of *McTeague*. Still, with or without the pants-wetting scene, it was evident in 1899 on both sides of the Atlantic Ocean that an "American Zola" had made his debut in the literary world.

THE NATURALISTIC THEMES

Viewed from the concluding paragraphs of *McTeague*, the novel provides full verification of a hypothesis common among literary works describable as naturalistic. The premise fictionally developed may be phrased formulaically as $x + y = z$: x representing genetically inherited traits in an individual; y, a typically stressful change in the individual's environment that activates or makes dominant a particular trait, resulting in modified behavior; and z, an outcome that is either a beneficial adaptation or a maladaptation to the changed environment. Clarification of the human condition is the author's intent; illustrated as cause and effect are the determinants of both McTeague and Trina's maladaptive, self-destructive behaviors rendering them unfit to survive in what Darwin termed the ceaseless struggle for existence. Thus long before it becomes pertinent in the main plot, Norris informs his readers that his Irish American hero, whose history invokes the American Dream because of his rise from "car-boy at the Big Dipper Mine" to professional status as Dr. McTeague the Polk Street dentist, is the son of a binge drinker. "For thirteen days of each fortnight his father was a steady, hard-working shift-boss of the mine. Every other Sunday he became an irresponsible animal, a beast, a brute, crazy with alcohol," who eventually dies because of his addiction, "corroded with alcohol" (p. 2). This seems an irrelevant detail here at the beginning of the novel because for many chapters McTeague does not consume spirits. He is a moderate beer drinker, never becomes intoxicated, and seems to illustrate an essential tenet of American optimism—that one's destiny is wholly in one's own hands and ultimately a matter of deliberate choice.

It is not until nearly three hundred pages later that McTeague's heredity as the son of a rage-prone alcoholic begins to loom large, after he has been barred from practicing dentistry by authorities requiring that he be a graduate of a dental college. Unemployed, depressed not only by his loss of professional identity and income but also because his increasingly penurious wife denies him carfare and he has had to walk home through the rain from an unsuccessful job interview, he accepts the offer of whiskey from a friend. Immediately it becomes apparent why he has previously avoided hard liquor: like his father he becomes vicious, and thus begins his abuse of his source of drinking money, Trina. Thus also begins the rapid downward spiral of both, Trina accelerating their descent into worse and worse conditions because she too is proving maladaptive.

The daughter of German Swiss immigrants, her hereditary predisposition is, for a while, a good one resulting in a rise in the McTeagues' standard of living: "It soon became apparent that Trina would be an extraordinarily good housekeeper. Economy was her strong point." Positive are the consequences of the fact that a "good deal of peasant blood still ran undiluted in her veins, and she had all the instinct of a hardy and penurious mountain race—the instinct which saves without any thought, without idea of consequence— saving for the sake of saving, hoarding without knowing why" (p. 134). But this "instinct" proves her undoing later in the marriage because of two wholly unexpected developments. The first is her winning $5,000 in a lottery, a happenstance that gradually produces an unfortunate psychological consequence; now she has a fortune in 1899 dollars to *lose,* and the irresistible urge to preserve and then increase her nest egg becomes a veritable mania after the second development occurs: her none too bright and emotionally volatile cousin Marcus Schouler, who once considered Trina his fiancée, comes to the conclusion that he has been cheated out of the $5,000 that might have been his had he married her. Infuriated, this German Swiss relative with an acquisitive instinct as strong as Trina's exacts his vengeance by reporting McTeague to the dental practice licensing authorities, depriving Trina too of the income to which she is accustomed and dramatically exacerbating her already well advanced hoarding compulsion.

She steadily degenerates as her mania waxes, matching the gold-mad Zerkow in her miserliness. Living in the cheapest flat she can find and denying as best she can her rapidly degenerating husband the money he needs to continue drinking, Trina discovers one day that he has absconded with the portion of her assets that she keeps on hand. By this time having sunk to the debased level of one who enjoys an erotic relationship with her coins, she retrieves the larger portion of her nest egg, which she had invested in an uncle's business, thus restoring her perverse relationship with her sole source of security. When McTeague's drinking spree ends for want of cash, he returns to beg for more. She refuses him. He beats her to death with his fists, flees with her gold coins, and is tracked down by cousin Marcus in Death Valley. He kills Marcus there, and without water or means of escaping from the desert, he is himself expiring as the novel ends.

The naturalistic formula of $x + y = z$ having been demonstrated as credibly as one finds it in Zolaesque fiction, one may still conclude that Norris has attempted to fob off a gross oversimplification, one too reductive of life's complexities. At least tempering such a criticism, however, is recognition of *how* the deterministic main theme is generated by both the plot and the kinds of characterizations fashioned by Norris. Much less sophisticated than the readers who have been aided by Norris in their understanding of what is transpiring, Trina, Marcus, and McTeague cannot discern how the formula works to effect their undoing any more than can the intellectually challenged Lenny Small in John Steinbeck's *Of Mice and Men* (1937). Like Lenny, they are buffeted by unforeseeable events, bewildered by unexpected twists of experience, and governed by appetites and drives about which they are minimally conscious. They type at their low level of intelligence the confusion and ineffectuality displayed by their more quick-witted and astute peers later featured in the fiction of one of Norris's admirers, F. Scott Fitzgerald.

While Norris as commentator and his readers enjoy the analytic perspective made possible by detachment from the scenes pictured, McTeague and the other characters are immersed in the onrushing sequence of events sweeping them uncomprehendingly into the future—as readers of *McTeague* at least sometimes find themselves in their own lives. Norris, in short, undermines a gross oversimplification popularized in the early nineteenth century by idealists such as Ralph Waldo Emerson: that the shape one's life takes is solely a result of the exercise of free will and thus the choices that one freely makes, conscious of consequences. By the close of chapter 2, Norris had begun to demonstrate his modernity by scuttling that notion, not denying that free choices are possible but limiting their significance appropriately, in light of what Darwin and his successors had disclosed about nature in general and the human condition in particular.

See also San Francisco; Naturalism

BIBLIOGRAPHY
Primary Works

Norris, Frank. "Frank Norris Writes Cleverly about Child Fiction for Old Readers." *Brooklyn Daily Eagle,* 8 February 1902, 10.

Norris, Frank. *McTeague: A Story of San Francisco.* New York: Doubleday and McClure, 1899.

Norris, Frank. *A Novelist in the Making: A Collection of Student Themes and the Novels "Blix" and "Vandover and the Brute."* Edited by James D. Hart. Cambridge, Mass.: Belknap Press of Harvard University Press, 1970.

Norris, Frank. "Zola as a Romantic Writer." *Wave* 15 (27 June 1896): 3.

Norris, Frank. "Zola's *Rome:* Modern Papacy as Seen by the Man of the Iron Pen." *Wave* 15 (6 June 1896): 8.

Secondary Works

Abbot, Edward, and Madeline Vaughn Abbot. "McTeague." *Literary World* 30 (1 April 1899): 99.

Conder, John J. *Naturalism in American Fiction: The Classic Phase.* Lexington: University Press of Kentucky, 1984.

Dillingham, William B. *Frank Norris: Instinct and Art.* Lincoln: University of Nebraska Press, 1969.

French, Warren. *Frank Norris.* New York: Twayne, 1962.

Hochman, Barbara. *The Art of Frank Norris, Storyteller.* Columbia: University of Missouri Press, 1988.

McElrath, Joseph R., Jr. *Frank Norris Revisited.* New York: Twayne, 1992.

McElrath, Joseph R., Jr., and Katherine Knight, eds. *Frank Norris: The Critical Reception.* New York: Burt Franklin, 1981.

"Novels of the Week." *Spectator* 83 (4 November 1899): 662.

Pizer, Donald. "The Biological Determinism of *McTeague* in Our Time." *American Literary Realism* 29 (Winter 1997): 27–32.

Joseph R. McElrath Jr.

MAGGIE, A GIRL OF THE STREETS

Stephen Crane's *Maggie, A Girl of the Streets (A Story of New York)* (1893, revised 1896) has long been considered a groundbreaking novel of American literary naturalism. Its depiction of a hostile, amoral universe, indifferent to the plight of its inhabitants, foreshadows the direction of much literary writing in America in the twentieth century. It is unclear, however, what influenced Stephen Crane (1871–1900) to write a brutal account of an urban slum. Before 1893 his literary output had consisted of ephemeral journalistic pieces and an assortment of satires and burlesques written in what he later called his "clever, Rudyard Kipling style" (Wertheim and Sorrentino, *The Correspondence of Stephen Crane,* p. 63). Crane could have been influenced by the fictional and nonfictional treatments of tenement life in the late nineteenth century. Émile

Zola had earlier depicted a naturalistic universe in Parisian life in *L'Assommoir* and *Nana,* and Americans were developing a growing fascination with, and fear of, slum life in urban tenements, as reflected in such sociological studies as the Reverend Thomas DeWitt Talmage's *The Night Sides of City Life* (1878) and Jacob Riis's *How the Other Half Lives* (1890) and in the popularity of sentimental, melodramatic fiction like *The Detective's Ward; or, The Fortunes of a Bowery Girl* (1871) and *Orphan Nell, the Orange Girl; or, The Lost Heiress* (1880). A dominant theme in the fiction, however, was rags to riches. In Edward W. Townsend's *A Daughter of the Tenements* (1895), for example, the heroine, despite the foils of a villain and her impoverished life selling fruit on the streets, becomes a successful ballerina, inherits a fortune, and lives happily ever after with her husband. When a slum novel lacked a happy ending—as with the seduction, betrayal, and death of the heroine in Edgar Fawcett's *The Evil That Men Do* (1889)—the ethical consequences of improper behavior were obvious.

Not only is there uncertainty concerning the influences on *Maggie,* but its dates of composition are also unclear. Whereas several college friends at Syracuse University recalled seeing a draft of *Maggie* in spring 1891, other friends thought that Crane began writing it in 1892. Given his fascination with the seamy side of urban life and his frequent trips to the Syracuse police courts to interview prostitutes, most likely he began a version of the novel while in Syracuse. The eventual subtitle of the novel reveals, though, that he ultimately thought of it as *A Story of New York.*

Crane may have first imagined the novel as a short sketch, "Where 'De Gang' Hears the Band Play," which was published in the *New York Herald* on 5 July 1891. Though the sketch was unsigned (newspapers at the time typically excluded the byline of unknown staff reporters), certain of its characteristics—the Bowery and Tompkins Square settings, the use of dialect and ethnic stereotypes, and the appearance of Jimmy (spelled "Jimmie" in *Maggie*) and his sister, Maggie, who works in a factory—strongly suggest that Crane wrote it. By the time Crane moved to New York City, in fall 1892, he had either expanded the sketch into a longer manuscript or was soon to do so. At this point he may have incorporated into the story additional geographical details that emphasize the New York setting—for example, references to the Brooklyn suburb of Williamsburg, the Central Park Menagerie, the Metropolitan Museum of Art, and Blackwell's Island, which he would have seen from his apartment overlooking the East River.

THE 1893 *MAGGIE*

Because Crane could not interest a publisher in his novel, he used his own money and possibly a loan from his brother William to print the book privately in New York sometime in late February or early March 1893 under the pseudonym "Johnston Smith." According to one of his friends, the pseudonym was meant as a joke; another thought Crane looked in the phone book for the two most common names and inserted a "t" into the first; a third thought the name "Johnson" was based on Crane's newspaper friend Willis Fletcher Johnson. The printer also chose to remain anonymous by excluding its name from the title page.

Given the subject matter, it is not surprising that Crane had trouble finding a publisher. Clearly missing from *Maggie, A Girl of the Streets* is the sentimentalizing or moralizing prevalent in other fictional treatments of tenement life in America in the late nineteenth century. Crane was not interested in analyzing the causes of, and offering solutions for, urban poverty. Although he may have been influenced by sociological tracts, sentimental fiction, or French naturalism, his *Maggie* is the first significant example of literary determinism in American literature. Crane's inscription in several copies of the novel read, in part: "It tries to show that environment is a tremendous thing in the world and frequently shapes lives regardless. If one proves that theory, one makes room in Heaven for all sorts of souls, notably an occasional street girl, who are not confidently expected to be there by many excellent people" (Wertheim and Sorrentino, *The Correspondence of Stephen Crane*, p. 52).

In *Maggie*'s environment, there is no escape from violence. As a child, Maggie's brother Jimmie, "a tiny, insane demon," defends "the honor of Rum Alley" against "howling urchins from Devil's Row" (p. 7); later, in his fight against Maggie's boyfriend Pete in a saloon, he is one of "three frothing creatures on the floor [who] buried themselves in a frenzy for blood" (p. 50). Domestic life proves to be just as violent and chaotic. When Jimmie returns home after battling the "howling urchins," his mother "tossed him to a corner where he limply lay cursing and weeping" (p. 13). Ongoing skirmishes between the parents, "as if a battle were raging," are accompanied by "the crash of splintering furniture" (p. 18). It is no wonder, then, that Maggie eats "like a small pursued tigress" (p. 14) and Jimmie comes home "with the caution of an invader of a panther den" (p. 18). Unlike sentimental fiction, Christianity, in *Maggie*, offers no haven from this war-torn jungle. At its best, it is ineffectual; at its worst, hypocritical. The poor woman who begs for money from the wealthy inhabitants of Fifth Avenue discovers that the "small sum in pennies" she receives "was

Stephen Crane. A portrait by Crane's artist friend Corwin Linson, 1894. STEPHEN CRANE COLLECTION (#5505), CLIFTON WALLER BARRETT LIBRARY OF AMERICAN LITERATURE, SPECIAL COLLECTIONS, UNIVERSITY OF VIRGINIA LIBRARY

contributed, for the most part, by persons who did not make their homes in that vicinity" (p. 16). When Jimmie visits a "mission church" (p. 20) in order to get a free bowl of soup, he is forced to listen to a preacher who condemns his listeners as sinners. It is ironic, then, that Maggie "blossomed in [this] mud puddle," grew up to be "a pretty girl," and seemed to "have [n]one of the dirt of Rum Alley . . . in her veins" (p. 24). As she watches heroes rescue entrapped heroines in melodramas, she dreams of Pete as the "knight" (p. 28) and "beau ideal of a man" (p. 26) who will take her away from her bleak existence. Her mother, however, is jealous of Maggie's newfound happiness with Pete, and when Maggie tries to impress him by decorating the family apartment, her mother wrecks it in a drunken fury.

After Mary Johnson throws her daughter out of the house because she was "gettin' teh be a reg'lar devil" (p. 29), Maggie turns to Pete for protection, but his interest in her quickly declines, as illustrated by the three music halls he takes her to in chapters 7, 12, and 14. The first one is a respectable place where

Among the more than three hundred variants between the 1893 and 1896 versions of Maggie, *the most significant revisions made by Crane occur in the ending of chapter 17. He revised wording and deleted the paragraph describing the "huge fat man in torn and greasy garments."*

Ending of Chapter 17, 1893 Edition

She went into the blackness of the final block. The shutters of the tall buildings were closed like grim lips. The structures seemed to have eyes that looked over her, beyond her, at other things. Afar off the lights of the avenues glittered as if from an impossible distance. Street car bells jingled with a sound of merriment.

When almost to the river the girl saw a great figure. On going forward she perceived it to be a huge fat man in torn and greasy garments. His grey hair straggled down over his forehead. His small, bleared eyes, sparkling from amidst great rolls of red fat, swept eagerly over the girl's upturned face. He laughed, his brown, disordered teeth gleaming under a grey, grizzled moustache from which beer-drops dripped. His whole body gently quivered and shook like that of a dead jelly fish. Chuckling and leering, he followed the girl of the crimson legions.

At their feet the river appeared a deathly black hue. Some hidden factory sent up a yellow glare, that lit for a moment the waters lapping oilily against timbers. The varied sounds of life, made joyous by distance and seeming unapproachableness, came faintly and died away to a silence.

Ending of Chapter 17, 1896 Edition

She went into the blackness of the final block. The shutters of the tall buildings were closed like grim lips. The structures seemed to have eyes that looked over them, beyond them, at other things. Afar off the lights of the avenues glittered as if from an impossible distance. Street-car bells jingled with a sound of merriment.

At the feet of the tall buildings appeared the deathly black hue of the river. Some hidden factory sent up a yellow glare, that lit for a moment the waters lapping oilily against timbers. The varied sounds of life, made joyous by distance and seeming unapproachableness, came faintly and died away to a silence.

families listen to an orchestra play "a popular waltz" (p. 30). In the second one, however, a singer "in a dress of flaming scarlet" (p. 52) performs a striptease as men pound tables with their beer glasses. In the last one, with its "twenty-eight tables and twenty-eight women and a crowd of men" (p. 52), Pete deserts Maggie for another woman. Distressed, Maggie visits Pete at the saloon where he works, in chapter 16, but her presence threatens his "respectability" (pp. 67, 68, 69). When she approaches a minister whose "eyes shone good-will," "he gave a convulsive movement and saved his respectability by a vigorous sidestep. He did not risk it to save a soul. For how was he to know that there was a soul before him that needed saving?" (p. 69). In a chapter in which the word "respectability" is used half a dozen times, Crane reiterates the importance appearance plays in the lives of his characters. When Jimmie hits Maggie in public, their father berates him to "leave yer sister alone on the street" (p. 12), implying that it is allowable to hit her at home where no one can see them; and when Maggie "goes teh deh bad, like a duck teh water," Mary Johnson laments, "Ah, who would t'ink such a bad girl could grow up in our fambly" (p. 43). As with Pete, the minister, and the father, the mother's concern with appearance and respectability is steeped in hypocrisy.

Rejected by her family, Pete, and the church's representative, Maggie turns to prostitution for survival. In the famous chapter 17, Crane compresses several months of her life as a prostitute into a single evening. As she walks from the theater district to the river, the imagery and the descriptions of her ten potential clients rehearse her deterioration and eventual death. The "blurred radiance" of the "electric lights" and the "roar of conversation" of theatergoers are replaced, by the end of the chapter, with "a deathly black hue" of the river and a final "silence," as her clients descend in respectability from the "tall young man" in "evening dress" to the "huge fat man in torn and greasy garments" (pp. 70, 71, 72).

Though Crane is not explicit about whether the fat man kills Maggie or she commits suicide, that she dies is clear. In the next chapter, Pete, the "aristocratic person" (p. 26) who had "loomed like a golden sun to Maggie" (p. 35), is reduced to a "damn fool" (p. 76); and in a bitterly ironic conclusion to the story, Maggie's mother, upon learning of the death of her daughter, screams out, "Oh, yes, I'll fergive her! I'll fergive her!" (p. 78). Although the novel emphasizes a Darwinian struggle for the survival of the fittest in a society in which family and church are meaningless institutions, Crane's use of irony throughout keeps the story from devolving into the pure naturalism of Zola or the cheap melodrama of countless stories of innocent girls seduced and ruined by villains. Repeatedly, characters shield themselves from reality by creating hypocritical moral codes that supposedly pass as middle-class values.

Given Crane's unrelenting depiction of a brutal world, it is not surprising that the book went practically unnoticed. Crane later recalled that its lack of recognition was his "first great disappointment": "I remember how I looked forward to its publication, and pictured the sensation I thought it would make. It fell flat. Nobody seemed to notice it or care for it" (Wertheim and Sorrentino, *The Correspondence of Stephen Crane*, p. 232). Although Crane sent out copies for review and inscribed others to prominent people, only two reviews are known to have been printed in 1893, one in Crane's hometown newspaper the *Port Jervis Union* and one by his mentor Hamlin Garland in the crusading reform magazine the *Arena*. Though Garland praised *Maggie* because "it voices the blind rebellion of Rum Alley and Devil's Row . . . [and] creates the atmosphere of the jungles," he criticized its lack of "rounded completeness. It is only a fragment. It is typical only of the worst elements of the alley. The author should delineate the families living on the next street, who live lives of heroic purity and hopeless hardship" (Weatherford, p. 38). Similarly, John D. Barry, editor of *Forum* magazine, privately told Crane that though he did "really believe that the lesson of your story is good . . . you have driven that lesson too hard. There must be moderation even in well-doing; excess of enthusiasm in reform is apt to be dangerous" (Wertheim and Sorrentino, *The Correspondence of Stephen Crane*, p. 50). Compounding the problem with the sale of the book would have been its high fifty-cent price at a time when cheaply produced books by unknown authors were selling on newsstands for as little as a dime. The only known copies sold were bought by a few of Crane's close friends at a party.

THE 1896 *MAGGIE*

Three years later the fate of *Maggie* was to change dramatically. Following the 1895 publication of his Civil War novel, *The Red Badge of Courage*, Crane became an international celebrity. Capitalizing on Crane's fame, Ripley Hitchcock, literary adviser to his publisher, D. Appleton and Company, wanted to republish *Maggie* and convinced Crane to revise it to eliminate objectionable passages. For several weeks in early 1896, as he wrote Hitchcock, Crane "dispensed with a goodly number of damns" and "the words which hurt" until "the book [wore] quite a new aspect from very slight omissions" (Wertheim and Sorrentino,

The Correspondence of Stephen Crane, pp. 197, 200). A collation of the 1893 and 1896 texts, however, reveals that the "very slight omissions" were actually more than three hundred variants between the two versions. For example, the cursing and blasphemy in the 1893 version are deleted or replaced with such wording as "h—l," "d—n," and "gee." In another case, Jimmie is encouraged to flee from battle with the "howling urchins from Devil's Row," and he roars back "dese micks can't make me run"; in the revised text Crane replaced "micks," the derogatory term for Irish immigrants, with "mugs" (Crane, p. 7). The numerous changes softened the language and made it less offensive. By far, however, the major revisions occur in chapter 17—the most important being the deletion of the penultimate paragraph, in which Maggie is followed by the fat, greasy man whose body "shook like that of a dead jelly fish" (p. 72).

Crane found the revision process so exhausting that he wrote to Hitchcock: "The proofs make me ill. Let somebody go over them—if you think best—and watch for bad grammatical form & bad spelling. I am too jaded with Maggie to be able to see it" (Wertheim and Sorrentino, *The Correspondence of Stephen Crane*, p. 224). The application of the Appleton house style, however, did more than just correct typographical errors and follow British orthography; in some cases it diluted meaning and tone.

Crane was eager to make *Maggie* more marketable in order to profit from the success of *The Red Badge of Courage* because he feared that whatever he subsequently wrote would constantly be compared to "the damned 'Red Badge'" (p. 127). "People may just as well discover now," he resigned himself to say, "that the high dramatic key of *The Red Badge* cannot be sustained" (p. 191). Ironically, some critics disagreed with Crane's prediction. For William Dean Howells, whereas *The Red Badge* was confusing and repetitious, *Maggie* contained "that quality of fatal necessity which dominates Greek tragedy" (Weatherford, p. 47). Similarly, a reviewer in the *Boston Beacon* praised Crane as "the first of American novelists to go into the slums of a great city with the intent of telling the truth and the whole truth, instead of seeking for humorous or romantic 'material'" (Wertheim and Sorrentino, *The Crane Log*, p. 188). Other reviewers, however, found it "an immature effort" (Weatherford, p. 45) and "not true to life" (Wertheim and Sorrentino, *The Crane Log*, p. 216). At first, the book sold because of the popularity of Crane's war novel. In August 1896 the Bookman listed *Maggie* as fifth in book sales in the East and fourth in uptown New York, but the sales were short-lived. No other later book of Crane's would make a best-seller list, and he would die in the shadow of "the accursed 'Red Badge'" (Wertheim and Sorrentino, *The Correspondence of Stephen Crane*, p. 161).

CRITICISM

Much of the criticism of the novel focuses on the establishment of the text, its sources, its structure and imagery, and its relationship to naturalism. The textual history of the two versions of *Maggie* remained unknown until the 1950s, when R. W. Stallman discovered that the 1893 and 1896 edition differed significantly. A decade later, while editing the Virginia edition of *Maggie*, Fredson Bowers made the controversial decision to conflate the two versions into what he called an "ideal" text (in terms of textual editing, what the critic W. W. Greg had earlier called an "eclectic" text). Choosing the 1893 *Maggie* as his copy-text, Bowers attempted to separate in the 1896 version Hitchcock's editorial changes from Crane's revisions and to include only the latter in the ideal text in order to represent Crane's final authorial intentions. Though scholars have discounted this version—as do Hershel Parker and Brian Higgins in their textual analysis of Maggie's "last night" in chapter 17—Bowers's comments on the chapter, though at times forced, are still worth considering.

Marcus Cunliffe published a groundbreaking examination of possible European and American sources for the novel, paying special attention to the sermons of the well-known, controversial American preacher, the Reverend Thomas DeWitt Talmage, whose newspaper articles and extensive lecture tours promulgated the temperance movement throughout the country. Joseph X. Brennan has demonstrated how the ironic and symbolic structure of the novel reveals the self-righteousness of characters and their indifference to human suffering. Donald Pizer has argued that Crane "was less concerned with dramatizing a deterministic philosophy than in assailing those who apply a middle class morality to victims of amoral, uncontrollable forces in man and society" (p. 174). Possibly the best general examination is James B. Colvert's introduction to the Virginia edition of *Maggie*, a novel that in his opinion "initiated modern American writing."

A major problem in the critical discussions of *Maggie*—indeed, one with much of Crane scholarship and criticism in the twentieth century—is that a number of the "facts" and legends about the novel have as their only source Thomas Beer's enormously influential, but apocryphal, biography *Stephen Crane: A Study in American Letters* (1923). The following assertions, for example, have no basis in fact: that Crane wrote the novel in two days before Christmas 1891; that his brother William gave the book its title and lent Crane $1,000 to print it; that Richard Watson Gilder, editor of *Century Monthly* magazine, refused to publish it because it was "too honest"; that the printer was a publisher of medical and religious books and required Crane to sign a statement that he was twenty-one; that the New York bookstore Brentano's sold only two copies and returned ten to Crane; that a maid named Jennie Creegan used copies to start a fire; that a Catholic dignitary found it "an insult to the Irish"; and that Crane called the novel "a mud-puddle" in which he "tried to make plain that the root of Bowery life is a sort of cowardice." Unfortunately, these assertions have been cited repeatedly in the criticism on *Maggie*.

See also Naturalism; New York; Poverty; Temperance

BIBLIOGRAPHY

Primary Works

Crane, Stephen. *Prose and Poetry.* Edited by J. C. Levenson. New York: Library of America, 1984.

Wertheim, Stanley, and Paul Sorrentino, eds. *The Correspondence of Stephen Crane.* 2 vols. New York: Columbia University Press, 1988.

Wertheim, Stanley, and Paul Sorrentino, eds. *The Crane Log: A Documentary Life of Stephen Crane 1871–1900.* New York: G. K. Hall, 1994.

Secondary Works

Bowers, Fredson, ed. *Bowery Tales: "Maggie" and "George's Mother."* Vol. 1 of *The University of Virginia Edition of the Works of Stephen Crane.* Charlottesville: University Press of Virginia, 1969.

Brennan, Joseph X. "Ironic and Symbolic Structure in Crane's *Maggie*." *Nineteenth-Century Fiction* 16 (1962): 303–315.

Colvert, James B. "Introduction to *Maggie: A Girl of the Streets.*" In *Bowery Tales,* edited by Fredson Bowers, pp. xxxiii–lii. Charlottesville: University Press of Virginia, 1969.

Cunliffe, Marcus. "Stephen Crane and the American Background of *Maggie*." *American Quarterly* 7 (1955): 31–44.

Katz, Joseph. "The *Maggie* Nobody Knows." *Modern Fiction Studies* 12 (1966): 200–212.

Parker, Hershel, and Brian Higgins. "Maggie's 'Last Night': Authorial Design and Editorial Patching." *Studies in the Novel* 10 (1978): 64–75.

Pizer, Donald. "Stephen Crane's *Maggie* and American Naturalism." *Criticism* 7 (1965): 168–175.

Stallman, Robert Wooster. "Stephen Crane's Revision of *Maggie: A Girl of the Streets.*" *American Literature* 26 (1955): 528–536.

Weatherford, Richard M. *Stephen Crane: The Critical Heritage.* London: Routledge and Kegan Paul, 1973.

Paul Sorrentino

MAIN STREET

Main Street, published in October 1920, was the first in a string of satiric portraits of American life authored by Sinclair Lewis (1885–1951) in the decade of the 1920s. Tapping into the prevailing mood of cynicism and the widespread feelings of betrayal of the Wilsonian ideals for which World War I had been fought, Lewis took on cherished American institutions—business, the church, medicine—and stripped them to their hollow cores. His meteoric rise to prominence culminated in 1930, when he became the first American to win the Nobel Prize in Literature. But it was in *Main Street* that Lewis probed the most sensitive spot in the public consciousness, for in that novel Lewis permanently redrew the literary landscape of the Midwest—and of much of middle-class America—by depicting the American small town, so long sanctified and idealized in Rockwellesque portraits and sentimental parlor melodies, as a place not of goodness and piety but of hypocrisy and ignorance. In short, *Main Street* demolished the most sacred of all American myths and made Lewis at once a populist hero and an enemy of the people.

THE REVOLT FROM THE VILLAGE
The popular view of the country town at that time was best represented by the essayist Meredith Nicholson's rosy assessment: "It's all pretty comfortable and cheerful and busy in Indiana," he wrote in *A Hoosier Chronicle* (1912), "with lots of old-fashioned human kindness flowing around; and it's getting better all the time. And I guess it's always got to be that way, out here in God's country" (p. 606). Lewis had grown up in a small town: Sauk Centre, Minnesota, a rural outpost in the heart of the state, some one hundred miles northwest of Minneapolis. Unlike Nicholson, however, and other cheerleaders for small-town "values," Lewis found the village to be characterized mostly by a deadening daily routine of "a savorless people, gulping tasteless food, . . . saying mechanical things . . . and viewing themselves as the greatest race in the world" (*Main Street,* p. 287). This view was the animus of *Main Street.*

Sinclair Lewis. © BETTMANN/CORBIS

The novel had a long gestation. Escaping from Sauk Centre at his earliest chance, Lewis journeyed East and then spent time in California. He returned to his hometown in the summer of 1906 and, looking around him, came up with the idea for the book. Fresh from new experiences, Lewis saw with a flash of insight how small-town life could take a curious and creative person (like himself) and break him. He played with this theme of the revolt against conformity in a series of apprentice novels he published in the 1910s, all the time shaping and reshaping in his mind what he called his "village virus" novel. On another visit in 1916, Lewis saw the village through the eyes of his new wife, a sophisticated city woman who bristled at the hick character of the scene in which she found herself, and thus was born Carol Kennicott, the central consciousness of the novel and Lewis's flawed but ultimately sympathetic heroine. Later still, in 1917 and 1918, when Lewis could no longer restrain his urgent desire to tell about "the flat hungriness of the Middle West," as he described it to his friend Joseph Hergesheimer (quoted in Lingeman, p. 100), his acute observations about village life ordered themselves into a series of rapid-fire satiric bursts, and his arguments found forceful, magnificent expression in *Main Street.*

There had already been novels aplenty in America debunking small-town life. The tradition of what the critic Carl Van Doren in 1921 identified as "the revolt from the village" had begun perhaps as early as 1871 with Edward Eggleston's *The Hoosier Schoolmaster,* continuing on with E. W. Howe's *The Story of a Country Town* in 1883, and supplemented by such works as Joseph Kirkland's *Zury: The Meanest Man in Spring County* (1887), Hamlin Garland's *Main-Travelled Roads* (1891), and Harold Frederic's *The Damnation of Theron Ware* (1896). Lewis's closest models were probably Sherwood Anderson's *Winesburg, Ohio* (1919) and Edgar Lee Masters's *Spoon River Anthology* (1915). All of these authors took greedy gulps from the endless well of criticisms about small-town life: its grubbiness, its poverty, its smug complacency and corrosive isolation. But Lewis's blast was the most devastating, for, like Harriet Beecher Stowe's 1852 novel *Uncle Tom's Cabin, Main Street* at once struck deeply and widely, covering in one broad stroke a vast expanse of the national life.

Main Street tells the story of Carol Kennicott, a free-spirited, bookish, and energetic young woman from the city who moves to Gopher Prairie as the bride of a country doctor. She is an idealist who goes to the hinterlands as much for the challenge of bringing beauty and social reform with her as for love of her husband. Having thus placed Carol's illusions squarely before her, Lewis then smashes them one by one, as Carol is rebuffed by the townspeople. For all their outward displays of friendliness, they are inwardly small-minded and hypocritical. Moreover, her husband, Will, is interested in little more than stock tips and motor cars. So Carol runs away to Washington, D.C., expecting to find there a liberal, cosmopolitan society. But all she encounters are other former Main Streeters, like her, on their own ill-defined quests for self-fulfillment. Carol therefore returns to Gopher Prairie chastened, but still feeling that she has won some battles and remained true to her ideals.

PUBLICATION AND RECEPTION

The appearance of the novel in 1920 was not so much a publishing event as it was a defining moment in American life. A legend grew that Lewis's savvy publisher, Alfred Harcourt (who had just started his own company) had some months before publication started a "whispering campaign," paying one hundred people across the country five dollars each to talk up the novel. Ernest Brace (the brother of Harcourt's partner, Donald Brace), speculated that it was simply scandal which spurred the landslide sales and that "scandal [was] always exhilarating" (quoted in Lingeman, p. 158).

Whatever the reasons, the book was a blockbuster. Harcourt's small firm could barely keep up with the incoming orders. One morning, requests came into his offices for 9,800 copies, and from that point on interest never slackened. In 1921 the book was still on a tear, burying its closest competitor, Dorothy Canfield Fisher's *The Brimming Cup* (1921)—not coincidentally, a view of small-town life that was a "response" to Lewis's novel. *Main Street* was the best-selling novel in America for the entire period from 1900 to 1925, eventually selling more than 400,000 copies in its hardcover edition alone.

Lewis's book became fodder for columnists and editorial writers in newspapers across the country, sparking a debate about whether his depiction of the American small town was distorted or accurate. Lewis and his publisher won either way, for with each new piece that appeared, sales in that region jumped. The name of the old hometown itself, Sauk Centre, became archetypal in jokes about small towns across the country. The term "Main Street" quickly entered the vernacular, with "Main Street: A Fox Trot Song," appearing, as well as several parodies of Lewis's novel, such as Carolyn Wells's *Ptomaine Street: The Tale of Warble Petticoat* (1921), in which a shallow-minded waitress from Pittsburgh moves to a small town whose residents are zealously interested in architecture, poetry, and democratic reforms.

CULTURAL CONTEXT

Main Street resonated so tellingly with the American people because Lewis was writing at a propitious historical moment. "The history of a nation is only the history of its villages written large," Woodrow Wilson had declared in 1900 (quoted in Schorer, p. 272), but by 1920 the village was no longer an important element in a capitalist economy, and the social and moral attitudes that it represented seemed outdated. The war had created an environment of restlessness and a persisting sense of dislocation. Postwar Americans left small towns in droves and moved to urban areas. In 1920 more people lived in towns and cities with a population of 2,500 or more than they did in villages of fewer than that number. These transplanted provincials were expecting, like Carol, to find fulfillment in their new worlds and a renewed sense of purpose. As Lewis says: "She fancied that her life might make a story. She knew that there was nothing heroic or obviously dramatic in it, no magic of rare hours, nor valiant challenge, but it seemed to her that she was of some significance because she was commonplaceness, the ordinary life of the age, made articulate and protesting" (p. 475). This was another appeal of Lewis's novel, the fact that most people believe there is a secret self buried beneath the day-to-day exterior that they show the world—another person who is unconventional, daring, and full of revolutionary zeal. Indeed, second only to the attack on conformity as a theme in revolt from the village novels is that of the buried life.

Yet these same people could also be defensive about where they came from. Lewis uncovered a class insecurity among the new urbanites—they retained many of their rural attitudes and loyalties, and they might even secretly have longed for the old-fashioned values of where they had been raised. They were in part influenced by the pervasive political uses of the village myth at the time. Urban America was gobsmackingly in love with its automobiles, its telephones, and its other technology as well as with the economic boom that had been created by the Republican administration. But working to limit government interference with big business, the nation's leaders invoked the myth of the small town repeatedly, promoting it as a pure, ideal world—decentralized, rural, and independent, with no need for a centralized regulatory Goliath.

Immigration, which had flooded labor and industry since the turn of the century, forms another important backdrop to the novel. Lewis was a committed progressive, and he spoke out frequently in favor of the National Nonpartisan League (NNL), a left-wing farmer-labor group. *Main Street* is a populist novel in its profarmer sentiments. In the book, the NNL is regarded by the townies as a group of cranks who want to flood the village with socialist ideas. The local patriotism, or boosterism, is embodied by "Honest" Jim Blausser, a civic promoter who wants to turn Gopher Prairie into a city and earn big bucks in doing so. He polarizes the political situation by identifying boosters as patriots and everyone else ("knocks") as pro-German subversives.

THE FEMALE AUDIENCE

But above all, the novel reached women; to many people, *Main Street* endures because it is so tellingly realistic a portrait of a marriage. The book was among the earliest in the national literature to depict women as something other than just appendages to their husbands, as seekers after autonomy and an individualized identity. Lewis was sympathetic to revolutionary causes, especially suffrage. In the 1910s Lewis was a member of the Socialist Party, and in 1914 he made several speeches on behalf of woman suffrage. He even marched in the famous Fifth Avenue parade for that cause. The Nineteenth Amendment, granting women the vote, had only been ratified in August 1920, just two months before *Main Street* appeared.

Carol forms part of an overarching social edifice that Lewis constructs in the book, the keystone of which is the liberation of women (and, by extension, all disenfranchised peoples). Carol crusades, not just on behalf of herself, but all women. She tells a friend: "I want you to help me find out what has made the darkness of the women. Gray darkness and shadowy trees. We're all in it, ten million women, young married women with good prosperous husbands, and business women in linen collars. . . . What is it we want—and need? . . . I think perhaps we want a more conscious life" (pp. 218–219). Hundreds of women wrote to Lewis after the book was published, telling him how they had seen themselves in Carol.

Like the small town she tries to reform, however, Carol does not escape critique by Lewis. She is a quixotic dreamer, foolhardy and sometimes impetuous; but she is also benevolent, well-meaning, and intelligent. Lewis's satiric method relied on a somewhat volatile mix of satire and sympathy, caricature and truth, compassion and scorn. The problem of the satirist is that he too often is remembered for the faults he lays bare and not the virtues he applauds. Nonetheless, Lewis's novel created a term that still is standard for describing an essential part of the national mythology—both what it was and what it made possible later on.

See also Satire, Burlesque, and Parody; Village Dwellers

BIBLIOGRAPHY

Primary Works

Lewis, Sinclair. *Main Street*. 1920. Reprinted in *Sinclair Lewis: "Main Street" and "Babbitt."* New York: Library of America, 1992.

Nicholson, Meredith. *A Hoosier Chronicle*. Boston and New York: Houghton Mifflin, 1912.

Secondary Works

Bucco, Martin. *Main Street: The Revolt of Carol Kennicott*. New York: Twayne, 1993.

Hilfer, Anthony Channell. *The Revolt from the Village, 1915–1930*. Chapel Hill: University of North Carolina Press, 1969.

Hutchisson, James M. *The Rise of Sinclair Lewis, 1920–1930*. University Park: Pennsylvania State University Press, 1996.

Lingeman, Richard. *Sinclair Lewis: Rebel from Main Street*. New York: Random House, 2002.

Schorer, Mark. *Sinclair Lewis: An American Life*. New York: McGraw Hill, 1961.

James M. Hutchisson

MAIN-TRAVELLED ROADS

Between his birth on a farm near West Salem, Wisconsin, on 14 September 1860 and his death in Los Angeles, California, on 4 March 1940, Hamlin Garland enjoyed a productive and varied, although sometimes controversial, literary career, during which he published nearly fifty volumes of fiction, poetry, plays, essays, and autobiographies. But his reputation rests principally on his short fiction written before 1895, particularly on his volume of short stories *Main-Travelled Roads* (1891), to which he added new stories in subsequent editions, and on his autobiographies, *A Son of the Middle Border* (1917) and his Pulitzer Prize–winning *A Daughter of the Middle Border* (1921). In these volumes Garland demonstrated that it had become possible to deal realistically with the American farmer instead of seeing him or her through the veil of literary convention. By creating new types of characters and deflating the uncomplicated romantic pictures of farm life that dominated earlier fiction, Garland not only informed readers about the painful realities of midwestern farm life but touched the deeper feelings of the nation.

As one of America's foremost local colorists, Garland graphically depicted, in *Main-Travelled Roads,* the countryside of his native Midwest, becoming in the process a principal spokesman for late-nineteenth-century agrarian society. Writing with an authentic voice and a sense of urgency and passion while remaining faithful to his innate instinct for telling the truth, he used particular settings in the Midwest (or Middle Border, to use Garland's usual term) to bring to his readers the problems that men and women in crude surroundings had to face in order to survive, reflecting at turns the severe restrictions of this life, with its loneliness and drudgery, and the waste of finer values exacted by that life. Toward that end he was one of the first novelists to view skeptically the conventional American belief in the purity, wholesomeness, and freedom of life on the farm.

Garland's reading of Henry George's *Progress and Poverty* (1879) in 1884, after moving to Boston from his prairie homestead in South Dakota, confirmed his own experiences of farm life and hastened him on the path to full-fledged reformer. Through George, Garland was converted into an advocate of the single tax, which sought to correct the injustice of the unearned increment (profits made from the increased value of land) that favored absentee property owners at the expense of the laboring farmer. George's book also filled him with enthusiasm for the populist movement, as he was convinced that the problems faced by the small farmer were not only explainable but remediable.

Prefatory statement to the 1891 edition of Hamlin Garland's Main-Travelled Roads.

The main-travelled road in the West (as elsewhere) is hot and dusty in the summer, and desolate and drear with mud in fall and spring, and in winter the winds sweep the snow across it; it does sometimes cross a rich meadow where the songs of the larks and the bobolinks and blackbirds are tangled. Follow it far enough, it may lead past a bend in the river where the water laughs eternally over its shallows.

Mainly it is long and wearyful and has a dull little town at one end, and a home of toil at the other. Like the main-travelled road of life, it is traversed by many classes of people, but the poor and the weary predominate.

Garland, *Main-Travelled Roads,* 1891, Prefatory Statement.

Garland's association with Benjamin Orange Flower, editor of the radical *Arena,* gave impetus to his publishing career, for the *Arena* became Garland's most important literary outlet. For more than two years, beginning in 1888, he had an article in nearly every issue. Early in 1891 Flower suggested that Garland collect some of his stories into a volume to be published by the Arena Publishing Company, a subsidiary of the *Arena.* In June 1891 *Main-Travelled Roads* appeared with the subtitle "Six Mississippi Valley Stories." Of these six, "The Return of the Private" had first appeared in the *Arena;* "Under the Lion's Paw," "Among the Corn-Rows," and "Mrs. Ripley's Trip" had already been published in *Harper's Weekly;* "A Branch Road" and "Up the Coolly" saw first publication in the 1891 edition. Later, in an 1899 edition, Garland added three stories, "The Creamery Man," "A Day's Pleasure," and "Uncle Ethan Ripley"; in the 1922 edition "God's Ravens" and "A Good Fellow's Wife" were incorporated; and finally, in 1930 "Martha's Fireplace" was added. However, the stories added after the first edition occasionally weaken the impact and unified vision of midwestern life that informs the first edition.

Critical reaction to *Main-Travelled Roads* was immediate. Reviews indicate both the popular reception of his books and the critical terms on which they were received; they also helped to establish Garland's reputation as a writer and called attention to his subsequent volumes.

Garland's friends in Boston and elsewhere in the East were quick to heap praise on *Main-Travelled Roads*. B. O. Flower, in the *Arena* (July 1893), called it "one of the most valuable contributions to distinctive American literature which has appeared in many years." He compared the material with the "boldness of Tolstoi, with the originality of Ibsen, and with a wealth of tenderness, love, and humanity far exceeding either." Similarly a review in the Chicago *Tribune* (13 June 1891) spoke of Garland's stories as having "attracted notice by their Tolstoian boldness, plain speaking, and accurate observation," while one in the *New York Tribune* (28 June 1891) remarked that "every one of the stories is excellent, and they are fit to be compared with the best continental work of the same kind." Enthusiastically, W. B. Harte, in the *New England Magazine* (August 1891), concluded that the stories in the volume were "as realistic as anything written by Ibsen; but at the same time, they have a more dramatic quality, and are besides relieved with an undercurrent of humor, which makes the realism, true realism." But none of the positive reviews had the critical force or influence of William Dean Howells's comments in his "Editor's Study" column for *Harper's Weekly* (September 1891). In a far-ranging review in which several of the stories came in for specific comment, Howells observed:

> These stories are full of the bitter and burning dust, the foul and trampled slush of the common avenues of life: the life of men who hopelessly and cheerlessly make the wealth that enriches the alien and the idler, and impoverishes the producer. If anyone is still at a loss to account for that uprising of the farmers in the West, which is the translation of the Peasants' War into modern and republican terms, let him read *Main-Travelled Roads* and he will begin to understand, unless, indeed, Mr. Garland is painting the exceptional rather than the average. The stories are full of those gaunt, grim, sordid, pathetic, ferocious figures whom our satirists find so easy to caricature as Hayseeds, and whose blind groping for fairer conditions is so grotesque to the newspapers and so menacing to the politicians. They feel that something is wrong, and they know that the wrong is not theirs. The type caught in Mr. Garland's book is not pretty; it is ugly and often ridiculous; but it is heart-breaking in its rude despair. (P. 639)

Not all critics were so warm in their praise of Garland's work. Many criticized the balance and tone of his stories, while others questioned their accuracy and representativeness. Still others felt that he too often emphasized the negative. Even Howells cautioned that Garland "still has to learn that though the thistle is full of an unrecognized poetry, the rose has poetry too, that even overpraise cannot spoil" (p. 639). A reviewer in *The Nation* (13 August 1891) argued: "There is no doubt that power of observation and of rendering the results with exactness is disclosed in these stories; but they lose by a successive reading. Descriptions of the same uninviting interiors, the same birds and insects, finally produce an impression of monotony and mannerism." And a reviewer for *America* (18 June 1891) protested that "though Garland's pictures are probably accurate, he seems to dwell too much on the seamy side of life." Meanwhile a critic for the *Atlantic Monthly* (February 1892) commended Garland for his earnestness but found it difficult to accept the totally grim pictures of life in the West that he paints, while a critic for the *Overland Monthly* (March 1892) felt that the harshness of the stories was only one side of the truth: "Mr. Garland would doubtless disclaim any intention of showing the whole truth in his stories, and put them forward only as dashes of shadow to modify the general picture of rural life in America."

Despite the many positive reviews of his work during this period, Garland was distressed by the negative reaction, especially from critics and reviewers in the West. He later recalled, in *A Son of the Middle Border:*

> I had the foolish notion that the literary folk of the West would take local pride in the color of my work, and to find myself execrated by nearly every critic as "a bird willing to foul his own nest" was an amazement. Editorials and criticisms poured into the office, all written to prove that my pictures of the middle border were utterly false.
>
> Statistics were employed to show that pianos and Brussels carpets adorned almost every Iowa farmhouse. Tilling the prairie was declared to be "the noblest vocation in the world, not in the least like the pictures this eastern author has drawn of it." (P. 415)

The stories in *Main-Travelled Roads* contain a number of themes, including daily lives spun out in hopeless toiling tragedy against the backdrop of natural glories, the irrelevancy of romantic love when set against the drudgery of farmwork, the ambivalence of isolation and companionship, the desire to leave the land versus the resulting guilt of leaving loved ones behind, the gap between those who have and those who have not, and loss of innocence. Garland's focus on these themes, especially the theme of lost innocence, is significant for a number of reasons. For one, it seems clear by his own admission in the foreword to his 1922 edition of the collection that his stories represented a deeply personal exploration of his own lost innocence, in his return after several years of living in the East to his parents' South Dakota home. For another, Garland increasingly saw his own loss of innocence mirrored in the passing of a more innocent time in America. His exploration of this theme consistently reflects his newly acquired beliefs after his exposure to the works of Charles Darwin and Herbert Spencer, and his conclusions therefore carry a weight that is at once literary, sociological, and political in his implied understanding that survival for his characters must include not simply a loss of innocence but acceptance of the reality that it may be necessary to leave a hostile environment rather than attempt (often in futility) to adapt to it. Interestingly, however, Garland often is as concerned with his own version of "remembrance of things past" as he is with what will happen after the loss of innocence to the characters and to the land.

While some of the stories that comprise the original edition of *Main-Travelled Roads* contain flaws, the book as a whole is a powerful and evocative treatment of western farm life. In it, Garland uses the apt metaphor of the western road as the symbolic structural center, providing a prefatory statement to the book itself that sets the dominant tone and hints at what is to come, followed by epigraphs before each story to achieve unity. In story after story, including "The Return of a Private," "A Branch Road," "Up the Coulee," and "Under the Lion's Paw," one sees characters on the move, sometimes attempting to establish a better life somewhere else, sometimes returning to the land they left. Occasionally the journey is merely one for a few days' respite from the toils of farm life, as in "Mrs. Ripley's Trip" or "A Day's Pleasure" (added in the 1899 edition). But Garland makes a central point in all of this movement: a life of numbing hardship inevitably awaits the travelers if their destination is the farm.

While several stories, particularly "Up the Coulee," "A Branch Road," and "The Return of a Private," suggest that inequities in the economic system are responsible for the farmers' plight, "Under the Lion's Paw," the best-known and most widely reprinted story in the collection, is the only one that explicitly makes use of the single-tax doctrine. The story was written as an illustration of Henry George's thesis of the harmful social effects of the unearned increment, and Garland habitually used the text when he was lecturing and campaigning for Populist candidates in 1892. In the story, the Haskins family, forced to settle in Kansas because of the high price of land in the East, is plagued by grasshoppers and forced to move again. Aided by

Hamlin Garland, 1891.

a hospitable family, they rent a farm in Iowa from Jim Butler, a villainous land speculator. After three years of hard labor, Haskins is ready to buy, but Butler doubles the price because of the improvements Haskins himself made upon the land. The banker, who has done nothing, will profit, and an enraged Haskins determines to murder Butler. However, Haskins refrains from carrying out his purpose when he sees his own child, and though crushed under the economic system, he resolves to renew his struggle for her sake.

A sense of guilt also permeates several stories in the collection, a theme that unquestionably resulted from Garland's personal guilt over leaving his family, especially his mother, and watching their plight from a distance. In "Up the Coulee," the most powerful and perhaps the most autobiographical story in *Main-Travelled Roads,* Garland depicts the return of Howard McLane, a successful actor, to Wisconsin from the East to visit his mother and his brother Grant. After first being awed by the beauty of nature upon his return, Howard is overwhelmed by the irrelevancy of this beauty in the lives of his family. When he confronts Grant and his family, he finds them living in poverty on a small, unproductive farm, for the family property has been sold to pay a mortgage. But Garland implies here, as elsewhere, that Grant's destruction is not primarily the result of Howard's neglect but rather of the overpowering evils inherent in contemporary farm conditions. Societal pressures and economic injustices have inevitably led to Grant's somber view of a life in which he feels hopelessly trapped: "A man like me is helpless. . . . Just like a fly in a pan of molasses. There ain't any escape for him. The more he tears around the more liable he is to rip his legs off" (pp. 126–127).

However, while Garland emphasizes that farm life is sometimes tragic and generally desolate and monotonous and while he constantly expresses outrage at the social injustices suffered by the farmer and the exacting toll taken on the women on the farm, his work contains exhilarating moments. Indeed, even at its most grim there is a persistent strain of romantic optimism and strength of individual will that reaffirms his compassionate view of human nature and his love of the land, which contradicts the diffused pessimism of the stories.

Ultimately *Main-Travelled Roads* remains an important cultural and historical document. In it, Garland provides a remarkably sustained fugue on the realities of late-nineteenth-century midwestern prairie life. The issues that Garland writes about and the characters that fill his pages are still relevant, and readers cannot come away from the best of his short fiction unmoved.

See also Farmers and Ranchers; Realism; Regionalism and Local Color Fiction

BIBLIOGRAPHY
Primary Works
Garland, Hamlin. *Main-Travelled Roads*. Boston: Arena, 1891.

Garland, Hamlin. *Selected Letters of Hamlin Garland*. Edited by Keith Newlin and Joseph B. McCullough. Lincoln: University of Nebraska Press, 1998.

Garland, Hamlin. *A Son of the Middle Border*. New York: Macmillan, 1921.

Howells, William Dean. "Editor's Study." *Harper's Weekly*, September 1891.

Secondary Works
Bledsoe, Thomas A. Introduction to *Main-Travelled Roads*. New York: Rinehart, 1954.

McCullough, Joseph B. *Hamlin Garland*. Boston: Twayne, 1978.

Mane, Robert. *Hamlin Garland: L'homme et l'oeuvre (1860–1940)*. Paris: Didier, 1968.

Nagel, James, ed. *Critical Essays on Hamlin Garland*. Boston: G. K. Hall, 1985.

Pizer, Donald. *Hamlin Garland's Early Work and Career*. Berkeley: University of California Press, 1960.

Pizer, Donald. Introduction to *Main-Travelled Roads*. Columbus, Ohio: Merrill, 1970.

Silet, Charles L. P., Robert Welch, and Richard Boudreau, eds. *The Critical Reception of Hamlin Garland*. Troy, N.Y.: Whitston, 1985.

Joseph B. McCullough

THE MAN AGAINST THE SKY

The course of Edwin Arlington Robinson's (1869–1935) literary career is one of the most curious and one of the saddest of any American writer. For roughly the first twenty years of his poetic life, he lived and wrote in his native Gardiner, Maine, in near-total obscurity. His residence in the Maine village (the source for his imaginary Tilbury Town) was interrupted when he attended Harvard for two years as a "special student," one who had no intention of graduating. By 1899 he had removed to New York City, where he would live for the remainder of his life. With the 1916 publication of *The Man against the Sky*, Robinson's reputation began to improve dramatically, and by 1927 he had won three Pulitzer Prizes, was awarded two honorary doctorates, and most improbably of all, published a long narrative poem, *Tristram* (1927), that became a national best-seller. Then started the slow slide into obscurity once again. When he died in 1935, Robinson was nearly as neglected as he had been at the beginning. For a time, however, he was considered the most gifted living American poet, whose nearest rival was T. S. Eliot (1888–1965).

ROBINSON'S POETIC CAREER
Robinson' s first volume of poetry, *The Torrent and the Night Before* (1896), was privately printed at his own expense, and his meager income was supplemented by an anonymous stipend donated by those who thought he showed great literary promise. His literary fortunes improved somewhat when Kermit Roosevelt showed his father a copy of *The Children of the Night* (1897). Theodore Roosevelt (1858–1919) was so taken by the poetry that he secured a position for Robinson in the New York Customs House, convinced Scribners to reissue the volume, and wrote an appreciative essay for the *Outlook*. Thus it was that one of the most public of men in the country came to the aid of one of the most demure and reclusive. The president whose favorite adjective was "bully" sponsored a poet who was widely regarded as an incurable pessimist.

E. A. Robinson's Tilbury Town belongs in the company of those other fictional villages where the outward lives and inner turmoil of its citizens are the subject of poetic or fictional treatment. Mark Twain's St. Petersburg, Missouri, Stephen Crane's Whilomville, New York, Sherwood Anderson's Winesburg, Ohio, Edgar Lee Masters's Spoon River, Illinois, and even William Faulkner's Jefferson, Mississippi, are microcosms of a larger sectional and sometimes national life. Perhaps due to his own sense of failure, Robinson often wrote poetic portraits of citizens who, for one reason or another, had not achieved in life or had fallen on hard times. Bewick Finzer is one of the latter. It is unclear how he lost his fortune; he may have been the victim of one or another of the several financial panics that occurred between 1893 and 1907. It is clear, however, that Finzer's failing could have happened to anyone in Tilbury Town. For that reason, he serves as an object lesson to the community, and its citizens are willing to grant him an annual "loan." They know he is a bad risk, but they spare him the humiliation of acting the beggar, for their sakes as well as his.

Bewick Finzer

Time was when his half million drew
   The breath of six per cent;
But soon the worm of what-was-not
   Fed hard on his content;
And something crumbled in his brain
   When his half million went.

Time passed, and filled along with his
   The place of many more;
Time came, and hardly one of us
   Had credence to restore,
From what appeared one day, the man
   Whom we had known before.

The broken voice, the withered neck,
   The coat worn out with care,

The cleanliness of indigence,
   The brilliance of despair,
The fond imponderable dreams
   Of affluence,—all were there.

Poor Finzer, with his dreams and schemes,
   Fares hard now in the race,
With heart and eye that have a task
   When he looks in the face
Of one who might so easily
   Have been in Finzer's place.

He comes unfailing for the loan
   We give and then forget;
He comes, and probably for years
   Will he be coming yet,—
Familiar as an old mistake,
   And futile as regret.

Robinson, "Bewick Finzer," in *The Man against the Sky*, pp. 119–121.

On that score Robinson had the ready answer of an unflinching realist: "There's a good deal to live for," he wrote in a letter, "but a man has to go through hell really to find it out. The process is hard but the result pays" (quoted in Anderson, p. 63).

There is no gainsaying the dark and severe outlook that saturates Robinson's poetry, but whether that derived from his individual temperament or reflected a considered philosophic judgment is an open question. His "philosophy," such as it was, he once defined in a letter as "mostly a statement of my inability to accept a mechanistic interpretation of the universe and of life" (*Selected Letters*, p. 165). While he was at Harvard, Robinson had been exposed to the antagonistic though stimulating intellectual oppositions of William James (1842–1910) and Josiah Royce (1855–1916). The first had articulated a genial pragmatic philosophy of openness and possibility, the second advanced a stoical idealism that found the human condition essentially tragic. Both James and Royce, however, set themselves against the scientific materialism of Herbert Spencer, Ernst Haeckel, and others. If for the philosopher a mechanistic worldview was an unacceptable intellectual proposition, for the average man and woman there was a felt oppressiveness to a vision that declared consciousness a mere "motor accompaniment" to the movements of the brain, God and soul pleasant and delusive fictions, and free will an impossibility. Joseph Conrad (1857–1924) was speaking dramatically but accurately when he described the current worldview in a letter in 1897:

> There is a—let us say—a machine. It evolved itself (I am severely scientific) out of a chaos of scraps of iron and behold!—it knits. I am horrified at the horrible work and stand appalled. . . . It is a tragic accident—and it has happened. . . . It knits us in and it knits us out. It has knitted time, space, pain, death, corruption, despair, and all the illusions— and nothing matters. (Watt, p. 153)

By the early years of the twentieth century, however, the authority of a mechanistic determinism was already beginning to fade. It was being challenged or displaced by a vitalist philosophy that disputed Spencerian evolutionary theory, the laboratory experiments of Marie Curie, the depth psychology of Sigmund Freud, and the mathematical calculations of Albert Einstein. Apparently none of these intellectual options was particularly appealing to Robinson, for he would not, or could not, accept a universe that was relativistic or believe the remedy to the fateful human condition was somehow contained in the anodyne slogan "Take life by storm!" Nor were the modernist techniques in poetry, cinema, and the visual arts that developed as means to disclose a new order of understanding at all satisfactory to him. As late as 1934, in *Amaranth,* he would confess:

> I lean to less rebellious innovations;
> And like them, I've an antiquated eye
> For change too savage, or for cataclysms
> That would shake out of me an old suspicion
> That art has roots.
>
> *(P. 67)*

Robinson was suspicious of free verse and imagism and, though he liked some of Eliot's poetic effects, believed that he was taking the wrong road poetically. Instead, Robinson embraced conventional poetic forms—dramatic and interior monologues, sonnets, narratives, lyrics, poetic dialogues, and others—most often with regular meter and rhyme schemes. He accepted the poetic idiom of his day, but he sought within established conventions to shape a poetry that fit his temperament. As Robert Frost (1874–1963) said of him, "Robinson stayed content with the old-fashioned way to be new" (p. 60).

And he was new. The ways that Robinson attempted to be original are several. He stripped his verse of the taint of Romantic idiom and trite symbolism in favor of poetic conversations or meter-making arguments. He avoided the self-conscious polish of so many of his contemporaries who, in the estimate of George Santayana and others, perfected a mode of expression without having anything in particular to express. On the other hand, he brought to his poetry deep erudition, but without the perplexing allusiveness of an Ezra Pound or T. S. Eliot, and he achieved a certain vividness without the support of a controlling "image" or a system of complex symbols. The building blocks of Robinson's verse were not symbols nor even words but phrases. This is appropriate because his chief interest was not in things or places or ideas but in people, in individuals who in their unique griefs and passions disclosed some mystery that could not be explained away by science, psychology, or sociology.

THE MAN AGAINST THE SKY

"The zone of individual differences," wrote William James, " . . . is the zone of formative processes, the dynamic belt of a quivering uncertainty. . . . It is the theatre of all we do not take for granted" (p. 192). By contrast, and James is speaking of Herbert Spencer here, "the sphere of the race's average, . . . no matter how large it may be, is a dead and stagnant thing, an achieved possession, from which all insecurity has vanished" (p. 192). Where there is no insecurity, there can be no tragedy and no dignity. To convey that drama of the small, individual difference, Robinson sought to use a "language that tells us, through a more or less emotional reaction, something that cannot be said." The poetic method of "Eros Turannos" (Tyrant Passion), perhaps the most disturbingly beautiful of the twenty-six poems that make up *The Man against the Sky,* is illustrative. The poem begins:

> She fears him, and will always ask
> What fated her to choose him;
> She meets in his engaging mask
> All reasons to refuse him;
> But what she meets and what she fears
> Are less than are the downward years,
> Drawn slowly to the foamless weirs
> Of age, were she to lose him.
>
> *(P. 67)*

Throughout the first four stanzas, a seemingly omniscient narrator informs one in no uncertain terms that this is a home where "passion lived and died" and yet remains for her a "place where she can hide." The woman has sacrificed her "sagacity," which once could have sounded the depths of the man behind his gestures, and has used such love as remains to her to transmute her "Judas" into something she can at least live with. Her pride is her only comforter.

Such is the woman the narrator pictures for readers, but then there is a shift in point of view:

> We tell you, tapping on our brows,
> The story as it should be,—
> As if the story of a house
> Were told, or ever could be.
>
> *(P. 69)*

As more than one critic has observed, the introduction of the "we" narrator in this poem, as in so many of Robinson's poems, functions as the chorus in a Greek tragedy—distancing the reader from the incomprehensible, or at least incommunicable, thoughts and feelings of the woman while at the same time connecting her life to the vital concerns of the community. Such speculative interest in the story of this house is not harmful, one is told, for they

That with a god have striven,
Not hearing much of what we say,
Take what the god has given.

(P. 70)

Between what the townsfolk have "guessed" and some sustaining quality within the woman herself resides the mystery of her life, James's "quivering uncertainty." This is a pervasive quality in *The Man against the Sky*. It exists in "Old King Cole," the widower with two errant sons who appears curiously merry and refuses the condescending pity of Tilbury Town: "And if I'd rather live than weep / Meanwhile, do you find that surprising?" (p. 41). It exists in the dramatic monologue "Ben Jonson Entertains a Man from Stratford." Jonson ponders the enigmatic genius of Shakespeare but is equally disturbed by Shakespeare's apparent indifference to learning, society, art, even his own gifts. It resides in the dreamy self-delusion of the once affluent "Bewick Finzer," who in punctually applying for a loan and a second chance each year has become for the town as "Familiar as an old mistake / And futile as regret" (p. 121); and in the "Veteran Sirens" who, no longer lovely, still refuse their age:

Poor flesh, to fight the calendar so long;
Poor vanity, so quaint and yet so brave;
Poor folly, so deceived and yet so strong.

(P. 86)

In "Cassandra," a latter-day prophetess whose prophecies are accurate but whom the people refuse to believe, warns an ill-fated community of its optimistic devotion to the "Dollar as your only Word":

The power is yours, but not the sight;
You see not upon what you tread;
You have the ages for your guide,
But not the wisdom to be led.

(P. 21)

Blindness, spiritual, moral, or other, is a persistent theme for Robinson. He once remarked that the world is "but a kind of spiritual kindergarten where millions of bewildered infants are trying to spell God with the wrong blocks." Cassandra asks a complacent and cheery crowd, "And are you never to have eyes / To see the world for what it is?" (p. 22). The "laughing crowd / Moved on. None heeded, and few heard" (p. 22). *The Man against the Sky* is an inventory of half-lived lives comprised of timid griefs and anxious disappointments. Robinson's characters are often wounded, but they are ennobled by their power to endure the hurt; they are blind, but they grope their way in some vague direction nevertheless. The opening and closing poems ("Flammonde" and "The Man against the Sky") bracket the others in a way that gives the volume coherence and indicate that the nightmare of a world war was much on his mind.

Flammonde, meaning literally the world on fire, is a man of obscure origins. He has fallen upon hard times and become a beggar, but he retains a courteous refinement that appeases the malcontents of the village. A certain generosity of spirit about him resolves the difficulties of others but not his own, and he himself remains a mystery:

How much of it was of him we met
We cannot ever know; nor yet
Shall all he gave us quite atone
For what was his, and his alone.

(P. 6)

The final image is of an uncommon man no longer among them who follows the path laid out for everyone:

We've each a darkening hill to climb;
And this is why, from time to time
In Tilbury Town, we look beyond
Horizons for the man Flammonde.

(P. 7)

The title poem that concludes the volume reclaims the image of a man mounting a hill at sunset in order to engage in broader meditations about enigmatic human struggles. The narrator of "The Man against the Sky" regards a hill lit by sunset as "the glory of a world on fire" (p. 130). By 1916 the conflagration of a world war forced upon untold hosts of men and women raises questions of purpose and immortality. Robinson's poem contains no answers to those questions other than the sturdy refusal to believe that "All comes to Nought" (p. 148). The narrator knows nothing of the man who climbs that hill other than that he moves alone, "As if he were the last god going home / Unto his last desire" (p. 130). By the end of the first stanza the man has crested the hill, and the remainder of the poem is a catalog of surmises.

It may be the man descended to climb yet another hill, "where more of him shall yet be given" (p. 132). Or, preserving his innocence, he may have discovered that he already possessed the "promised land" (p. 133). Or, a cynic, he may have struggled to his tomb "unreconciled" (p. 138). He may have been a materialist, who saw with his "mechanic eyes / A world without a meaning" (p. 139). Even so, the materialist in his desire for purpose may build "A living reason out of molecules / Why molecules occurred" (p. 139) and take some odd measure of pride in "being what he must have been by laws / Infrangible and for no kind of cause" (p. 139). Whatever lured the man on or made him hesitate, one is told:

His way was even as ours;
And we, with all our wounds and all our powers,
Must each await alone at his own height
Another darkness or another night.

(Pp. 141–142)

Perhaps, Robinson suggests, we are

> no greater than the noise we make
> Along one blind atomic pilgrimage
> Whereon by crass chance billeted we go
> Because our brains and bones and cartilage
> Will have it so.
>
> *(P. 143)*

But if one believes this to be true, then it is fitting to keep still and die meekly. We know nothing of the next world, and not much of this one, the poem implies, but this much we do know:

> That we may laugh and fight and sing
> And of our transience here make offering
> To an orient Word that will not be erased,
> Or, save in incommunicable gleams
> Too permanent for dreams,
> Be found or known.
>
> *(P. 144)*

What that Word may be, the narrator does not say. This is but the slightest basis for a faith in immortality, or even in some unknown purpose. Nevertheless, the poem stands as Robinson's most explicit poetic statement of what may pass for a philosophy— a rebuke to the mechanistic temper of his times. Whatever reassurances the poem offers are to be found in the steadiness of tone in the narrator, not in the painful world he describes. His is a stoic and idealist's faith founded upon the simple yet realistic observation that while men and women may "curse life" and pity their plights, so long as they continue to endure and continue to live, they willy-nilly bear witness to some imperishable absolute that outlives complaint.

See also Lyric Poetry; Philosophy; Scientific Materialism; Village Dwellers

BIBLIOGRAPHY

Primary Works

Frost, Robert. *Selected Prose of Robert Frost.* Edited by Hyde Cox and Edward Connery Lathem. New York: Colliers Books, 1968.

James, William. *The Will to Believe.* Edited by Frederick H. Burkhardt, Fredson Bowers, and Ignas K. Skrupskelis. Cambridge, Mass.: Harvard University Press, 1979.

Robinson, Edwin Arlington. *Amaranth.* New York: Macmillan, 1934.

Robinson, Edwin Arlington. *The Man against the Sky.* New York: Macmillan, 1916.

Robinson, Edwin Arlington. *Selected Letters of Edwin Arlington Robinson.* Edited by Ridgely Torrence. New York: Macmillan, 1940.

Secondary Works

Anderson, Wallace Ludwig. *Edwin Arlington Robinson: A Critical Introduction.* Cambridge, Mass.: Harvard University Press, 1968.

Barnard, Ellsworth, ed. *Edwin Arlington Robinson: Centenary Essays.* Athens: University of Georgia Press, 1969.

Coxe, Louis Osborne. *Edwin Arlington Robinson: The Life of Poetry.* New York: Pegasus, 1969.

Franchere, Hoyt C. *Edwin Arlington Robinson.* New York: Twayne, 1968.

Joyner, Nancy Carol. *Edwin Arlington Robinson: A Reference Guide.* Boston: G. K. Hall, 1978.

Kaplan, Estelle. *Philosophy in the Poetry of Edwin Arlington Robinson.* New York: Columbia University Press, 1940.

Murphy, Francis, ed. *Edwin Arlington Robinson: A Collection of Critical Essays.* Englewood Cliffs, N.J.: Prentice-Hall, 1970.

Neff, Emery Edward. *Edwin Arlington Robinson.* New York: W. Sloane Associates, 1948.

Richards, Laura Elizabeth Howe. *E. A. R.* Cambridge, Mass.: Harvard University Press, 1936.

Smith, Chard Powers. *Where the Light Falls: A Portrait of Edwin Arlington Robinson.* New York: Macmillan, 1965.

Van Doren, Mark. *Edwin Arlington Robinson.* New York: Literary Guild of America, 1927.

Watt, Ian. *Conrad in the Nineteenth Century.* Berkeley and Los Angeles: University of California Press, 1979.

Winters, Yvor. *Edwin Arlington Robinson.* New York: New Directions, 1971.

Tom Quirk

MARRIAGE

See Courtship, Marriage, and Divorce

THE MARROW OF TRADITION

The Marrow of Tradition (1901) was the magnum opus of Charles Waddell Chesnutt (1858–1932). The first African American to publish fiction in the prestigious *Atlantic Monthly*, the Cleveland, Ohio, lawyer and businessperson had launched his literary career with two short story collections, *The Conjure Woman* (1899), which capitalized on the popularity of ostensibly amusing and quaint tales told in Negro dialect, and *The Wife of His Youth and Other Stories of the Color Line* (1899), which featured comic and tragic stories

Charles W. Chesnutt. FISK UNIVERSITY LIBRARY

about black America's upwardly mobile, mixed-race elite, of which Chesnutt considered himself the first literary spokesperson. In 1900 Chesnutt's *The House Beyond the Cedars,* a novel of passing set in eastern North Carolina, where Chesnutt had grown up, came out, garnering a generally favorable reception.

Along with his Boston publisher, Houghton Mifflin, Chesnutt hoped *The Marrow of Tradition* would emulate Harriet Beecher Stowe's *Uncle Tom's Cabin; or, Life among the Lowly* (1852) and Albion W. Tourgée's *A Fool's Errand* (1879). Both were extremely popular novels about racial problems that had won their authors commercial success and sociopolitical acclaim for their literary activism. Events in the late-nineteenth-century South—violent suppression of black aspirations, the disfranchisement of black voters, and the rise of legalized, cradle-to-grave racial segregation—had reached a violent culmination in North Carolina, where Chesnutt had grown up and set much of his fiction. Although he had believed the state to be relatively progressive on the racial front, a so-called race riot of November 1898 in the port city of Wilmington, by which a cadre of white supremacists terrorized the town's black population into submitting

to white political dictation, spurred Chesnutt to pen his most outspoken protest novel. *The Marrow of Tradition* opened an unflinching broadside against racist violence while issuing a summons to racial reconciliation based on understanding, forgiveness, and respect for human rights. Since its controversial publication, *The Marrow of Tradition* has grown in critical stature, becoming the most widely read and critically appreciated novel of protest in black American fiction before the New Negro Renaissance of the 1920s.

THE NOVEL AND ITS SOURCES
The major threads of action in the novel knit the fortunes of two families: Philip and Olivia Carteret, who represent the pride and prejudices of the post-Reconstruction southern aristocracy; and Adam and Janet Miller, a mixed-race middle-class couple in whom Chesnutt invests the future of African American advancement in the so-called New South. One of the major goals of Chesnutt's second novel was to tear away the region's mask of progress and gentility to reveal the corrosive effects of its specious paternalism and moral bankruptcy on matters having to do with race. The story traces the origins and outcome of a conspiracy hatched by Philip Carteret, editor of the white newspaper in "Wellington," North Carolina, and two other former Confederate officers, the vicious and brutal George McBane, and the blandly sinister General Belmont. Their aim is to unseat the coalition of Republicans and Populists that has governed Wellington fairly and harmoniously for several years. Adam Miller, a northern-trained physician whose dedication to his people is symbolized by the hospital he has built in Wellington, is dismayed by the campaign of race baiting conducted by Carteret and his henchmen but is incapable of deterring them. Meanwhile, Olivia Carteret discovers but conceals the fact that her older half sister Janet, whom the white woman had spurned as their father's illegitimate daughter, was actually the offspring of a legally sanctioned, though socially proscribed, marriage. That Olivia is ultimately forced to acknowledge Janet as her sister, regardless of the latter's African heritage, underlines Chesnutt's commitment to the social rehabilitation of light-skinned African Americans in his fiction.

The climax of *The Marrow of Tradition* chronicles graphically the bloody Wellington coup d'état. The question of how southern blacks should respond to such violence haunts the conclusion of the novel. Offered an opportunity to lead a valiant group of armed black resisters, the pragmatic Miller declines, partly because he knows their cause is hopeless and partly because he has a moral aversion to violence. Yet

Cover drawing of *Collier's Weekly,* 26 November 1898. This inaccurate depiction of the race riot in Wilmington, North Carolina, suggested that the African American participants were calculating murderers and this inaccuracy led Chesnutt to write *The Marrow of Tradition.* COURTESY CAPE FEAR MUSEUM, WILMINGTON, N.C., 67.13.1

in conceding the defense of Wellington's blacks to the defiant but doomed working-class hero, Josh Green, Miller reveals a cleavage in his author's own thinking about the relative value of accommodation and forcible resistance in defeating racial oppression. Scholars have yet to resolve the ambivalence the novel displays towards its divergent models of black male leadership: Miller, the circumspect but compromised survivor, versus Green, the steadfast but self-destructive martyr. At the end of the novel the Millers, whose only son has been killed by an act of random white violence, prove themselves the moral superiors of the Carterets by acts of forgiveness that leave the doctor

poised to perform an operation that the Carterets' only son must have in order to survive. "There's time enough, but none to spare"(p. 329), Miller is told at the close of the novel as he enters the Carteret house, from which he had been previously barred, on his mission of mercy. This remark sums up *The Marrow of Tradition*'s urgent call for social engagement by and concomitant social respect for mixed-race figures such as Adam and Janet Miller, who exemplify the capacity for mediation, the moral clarity, and the freedom from racial prejudice necessary to effect genuine social reform along the color line in turn-of-the-twentieth-century America.

The major white characters of *The Marrow of Tradition* are based on actual historical figures. The model for Philip Carteret is Josephus Daniels (1862–1948), editor of the *Raleigh News and Observer* and a leading propagandist of the Democratic Party's takeover of the state government in 1898 on a racist campaign against supposed "Negro domination." Alfred Moore Waddell (1834–1912), an ex-congressperson who led the takeover of Wilmington, seems to have prompted Chesnutt to create General Belmont, a wily and shifty figure in Carteret's cabal. The novel also incorporates from the historical record references to a crusading black newspaper in Wilmington that published an editorial implying that interracial sexual liaisons, which whites used as an excuse to lynch black men, guilty or not, were often consensual. While Chesnutt's account of the "riot" was based on careful personal research (including a trip to Wilmington, where several of his relatives lived), his central African American characters, Adam Miller and Josh Green, seem to be the products of the author's imagination. The subplot involving the two half sisters draws on themes prevalent in Chesnutt's earlier fiction, including the deleterious effects of slavery-era miscegenation on the prospects for justice and racial reconciliation in the post–Civil War South. Characteristically, Chesnutt's position in *The Marrow of Tradition* was not to decry the interracial liaisons themselves, which he generally treated as understandable, if not always advisable, but to dramatize the personal and social cost to blacks and whites alike of treating the human products of these liaisons as racially inferior, morally suspect, and socially untouchable. The various aspects of southern "tradition" analyzed in the novel, in particular those that enforced the spurious color line, represent, for the most part, hindrances to the social and moral progress of the region. Thus, it is not accidental that at the end of the novel the mixed-race Millers are invested with the social and moral responsibility of binding up Wellington's self-inflicted wounds.

FICTIONAL DEPICTIONS OF THE "NEW" SOUTH

The triumph of white supremacy in the South by the turn of the twentieth century occasioned a literary controversy that pitted popular white Southern writers against less-well-known but equally impassioned black writers over nothing less than how to interpret Reconstruction and the so-called Redemption (that is, the reclaiming of the South by conservative Democrats) in the 1880s and 1890s. *Red Rock: A Chronicle of Reconstruction* (1898) by Thomas Nelson Page (1853–1922) and *The Leopard's Spots: A Romance of the White Man's Burden 1865–1900* (1902) and *The Clansman: An Historical Romance of the Ku Klux Klan* (1905) by Thomas Dixon (1864–1946) argued that Reconstruction had been a disaster and that the redemption of the South by white supremacy had been the only way to ensure the restoration of political order, social decency, and racial purity for the much abused white South. The rare southern white writer who challenged this official myth of the New South met with outright hostility. George Washington Cable (1844–1925) is the best example of this. Cable voiced his opinions most notably in *John March, Southerner* (1894). The negative reaction to the book in the South forced Cable to leave his native New Orleans and resettle in Massachusetts. A handful of African American novelists, who had little access to the white readership of the time, agreed with Pauline Elizabeth Hopkins (1859–1930), whose preface to her novel *Contending Forces: A Romance Illustrative of Negro Life North and South* (1900) argued that there was no significant difference between New and Old South insofar as racial atrocities and social injustice were concerned. Wilmington native David Bryant Fulton (b. 1863), who wrote under the pseudonym Jack Thorne, was the first African American to write a novel about the Wilmington outrages. He published *Hanover; or, The Persecution of the Lowly: A Story of the Wilmington Massacre* (1900) partly to warn his readers of the likelihood of the effective re-enslavement of blacks in the South under the new white supremacist regimes.

What was most important about *The Marrow of Tradition* in its own time was the indisputable fact that Chesnutt, unlike any previous African American novelist, had been able to place a hard-hitting, socially probing novel of protest with a major white commercial publisher and see it receive extensive and serious national attention. Despite its often dispiriting subject matter and its stern critique of racial orthodoxy in the South, the novel was widely noticed. Even reviewers who could not recommend its tough-minded look at social problems that many whites wanted to ignore expressed frequent appreciation of the novel's realism, honesty, and earnestness, as well as the vigor of its protest against injustice. Other reviewers, however, particularly in southern newspapers, called the book painful, vindictive, and fanatical in its condemnation of whites. William Dean Howells (1837–1920), probably the most influential critic of the era, betrayed the conflicted attitude of contemporary white liberals when he called *The Marrow of Tradition* both "bitter" and "just" in the same review. Such divergent reactions did not make *The Marrow of Tradition* the popular success Chesnutt wanted, but they guaranteed that it would become the most discussed African

American novel of its time. Nevertheless, sales of *The Marrow of Tradition* were sufficiently disappointing that its author felt obliged to return to the court-reporting business that had made him one of Cleveland's most prosperous African Americans when he launched his full-time literary career in 1899.

To those who dismissed his book as one-sided and unreliable, Chesnutt replied in a 1901 interview in the *Cleveland Press:* "I admit that 'The Marrow of Tradition' is the plea of an advocate. I can only hope that it is based upon the evidence, and that it will make out a case before an impartial jury." In the racially supercharged atmosphere of the turn of the twentieth century, Chesnutt's novelistic marshaling of the evidence against white supremacy could hardly expect an impartial hearing. By the late twentieth century, however, Chesnutt's plea for social justice and racial reconciliation in *The Marrow of Tradition* had won him permanent literary laurels and lasting recognition as a pioneering craftsman of socially conscious American fiction.

See also Blacks; Civil Rights; *The Conjure Woman;* Race Novels; Violence

BIBLIOGRAPHY

Primary Works

Chesnutt, Charles W. *Charles W. Chesnutt: Stories, Novels, and Essays.* Edited by Werner Sollors. New York: Library of America, 2002.

Chesnutt, Charles W. *An Exemplary Citizen: Letters of Charles W. Chesnutt, 1906–1932.* Edited by Jesse S. Crisler, Robert C. Leitz III, and Joseph R. McElrath Jr. Stanford, Calif.: Stanford University Press, 2002.

Chesnutt, Charles W. *The Marrow of Tradition.* Boston: Houghton Mifflin, 1901.

Chesnutt, Charles W. *"To Be an Author": Letters of Charles W. Chesnutt, 1889–1905.* Edited by Joseph R. McElrath Jr. and Robert C. Leitz III. Princeton, N.J.: Princeton University Press, 1997.

"To Shed a Light on the Race Problem." *Cleveland Press,* 1901, n.p.

Secondary Works

Andrews, William L. *The Literary Career of Charles W. Chesnutt.* Baton Rouge: Louisiana State University Press, 1980.

Duncan, Charles. *The Absent Man: The Narrative Craft of Charles W. Chesnutt.* Athens: Ohio University Press, 1998.

Elder, Arlene A. *The "Hindered Hand": Cultural Implications of Early African-American Fiction.* Westport, Conn.: Greenwood Press, 1978.

Howells, William Dean. "A Psychological Counter-Current in Recent Fiction." *North American Review* 173 (1901): 872–888.

Keller, Frances Richardson. *An American Crusade: The Life of Charles Waddell Chesnutt.* Provo, Utah: Brigham Young University Press, 1978.

McElrath, Joseph R., Jr., ed. *Critical Essays on Charles W. Chesnutt.* New York: G. K. Hall, 1999.

Pickens, Ernestine Williams. *Charles W. Chesnutt and the Progressive Movement.* New York: Pace University Press, 1994.

Sundquist, Eric. J. *To Wake the Nations: Race in the Making of American Literature.* Cambridge, Mass.: Belknap Press of Harvard University Press, 1993.

Werner, Craig. "The Framing of Charles Chesnutt: Practical Deconstruction in the Afro-American Tradition." In *Southern Literature and Literary Theory,* edited by Jefferson Humphries, pp. 339–365. Athens: University of Georgia Press, 1990.

William L. Andrews

"THE MARSHES OF GLYNN"

The fairest assessment of the life and work of Sidney Lanier (1842–1881) was written while he was dying of tuberculosis in the mountains of North Carolina. In September 1881 an editor for *Scribner's Monthly* claimed: "Sidney Lanier is a rare genius. No finer nature than his has America produced. His work is not popular, nor is it likely to become so, for his mind is of an unusual cast and his work is of exceptional character" (*CE* 1:lxxxiv, n. 171). In the time since this observation, critics have both lauded and condemned Lanier, but his achievement, despite the difficult circumstances of his life and times, remains secure. Jay B. Hubbell observes that apart from Walt Whitman and Emily Dickinson, "Lanier was beyond question the most important American poet to emerge in the later nineteenth century" (p. 771).

Of the few poems on which Lanier's renown rests—all written in the last decade of his life, beginning with the publication of "Corn" in 1875 and ending with "Sunrise," penciled out in the fever of his final illness—"The Marshes of Glynn" is the most representative. It is quintessential Lanier, "the poem of Lanier's aesthetic and spiritual maturity" (*CE* 1:lxiii), according to Charles R. Anderson, the editor of *The Centennial Edition of the Works of Sidney Lanier* (1945). The diverse forces that shaped Lanier's philosophy and style merge and find expression in this single poem, reflecting the poet's synthesis of the volatile era in which he lived.

PUBLICATION AND INITIAL RECEPTION

"The Marshes of Glynn" had an obscure beginning. In April 1878 George Parsons Lathrop, an editor for the Boston publisher Roberts Brothers, invited Lanier to contribute a poem to *A Masque of Poets*. This book is one volume in a series of works, mostly novels, that were published anonymously; according to Aubrey Harrison Starke, the publisher believed that sales would be stimulated by a reading public eager to guess the identities of the contributing authors, among them some of the best poets in America and England ("An Omnibus of Poets," p. 312). Lanier consented to become part of the endeavor, and in a letter to his father on 13 July 1878, he announced that he had just sent the poem off "hot from the mint" (*CE* 10:53).

The circumstances of its composition are sketchy. Local legend in Brunswick, Georgia, a coastal town located in the tidal marshes of Glynn County, maintains that Lanier had begun to write the poem on a visit there as early as 1875. He may, however, have composed the initial stanzas while he was in the area in 1877, on a tour he made of Florida to gather material for a guidebook (*CE* 1:358). Certainly the source of the poem lay in Lanier's intimate knowledge of the region, though most of it was written in Baltimore the summer of 1878, specifically for *A Masque of Poets*.

Although it went through three editions, the book received unfavorable reviews from critics. Lanier himself held it in contempt, calling it "an intolerable collection of mediocrity and mere cleverness" (*CE* 10:88). He claimed he could find only four poems of any merit and dismissed the rest: "This is the kind of poetry that is technically called culture-poetry: yet it is in reality the product of a *want* of culture" (*CE* 10:88).

Negativity aside, "The Marshes of Glynn" was generally acclaimed. Lanier's friend and fellow writer Richard Malcolm Johnston heralded it as "the greatest poem written in a hundred years" (*CE* 10:53). Lanier wrote his father that it had "won most of the honors of the book" (*CE* 10:97). Some critics surmised that Lanier was the rightful author; others credited the poem to Edgar Fawcett, Jean Ingelow, or Alfred, Lord Tennyson (*CE* 1:lxiii). A review in the *Atlantic* attributed to William Dean Howells, who had previously rejected Lanier's work, noted that the poem reflected the influence of Algernon Swinburne and that "the poet has almost bettered, in some passages, his master's instructions" (Starke, *Sidney Lanier*, p. 316). Within a year of the poem's publication in *A Masque of Poets*, Henry Wadsworth Longfellow republished it in his collection devoted to southern poetry, *Poems of Places* (1879).

Before his death, Lanier made several substantive revisions to the poem, but these changes were not published until 1884, when his wife, Mary Day Lanier, edited a posthumous volume titled *Poems of Sidney Lanier*, which included William Hayes Ward's "Memorial" as its introduction. The revised "Marshes of Glynn" in this edition has become the standard version (*CE* 1:xc). *Poems* went through three editions (1884, 1891, 1916) and has been reprinted more than twenty times, including an online version in 1998, part of the University of North Carolina at Chapel Hill project Documenting the American South. It is deplorable that Lanier's best poem should have had such an inauspicious start, for it gives voice to the major principles that shaped Lanier as a poet.

TRADE

Many prose writers after 1850 sharply criticized the materialistic values of the nineteenth century, but Lanier was one of the first Americans to make commercialism, with its social, economic, and moral consequences, the subject of poetry. By the time Lanier declared in "The Marshes of Glynn" that his "heart is at ease from men, and the wearisome sound of the stroke / Of the scythe of time and the trowel of trade is low" (ll. 26–27), he had already pronounced his invective against Trade. In April 1870 Lanier articulated his views on industrialism in his "Confederate Memorial Address": "The nineteenth century worships trade; and Trade is the most boisterous god of all the false gods under Heaven" (*CE* 5:266). Enumerating the ills of the factories, Lanier laments that trade has blunted human sensibility. Instead of promoting southern industries, Lanier advocated agricultural reform—the diversification of crops and a return to the stable economy of individual farms to counterbalance the sharecropping system, which fostered inefficiency and debt. Jeffersonian in outlook, Lanier condemned trade in his poem "The Symphony" and promoted his reforms in essays such as "The New South," in dialect poems such as "Thar's More in the Man than Thar Is in the Land," and in the prescriptive lyric "Corn."

Lanier's distaste for the corruptive effects of the Industrial Revolution have precedents in the sentiments of Romantic poets such as William Wordsworth, but Lanier's views also echoed the attitudes of many southerners, both before and after the Civil War, who felt that industrialization symbolized northern aggression and soullessness. Nevertheless, Lanier's aim was not to foster sectionalism. He could easily have justified feeling bitter: he had passionately fought for the Confederacy, had had his health broken in a Federal prison camp, and had walked hundreds of miles back home to Macon, Georgia, to a world where, as he wrote Bayard Taylor in August 1875, "with us of the younger generation in the South since the War, pretty much the whole of life has been merely not-dying" (*CE* 9:230). But he was among the promising writers of the New South who believed that the only hope of recovery for the region lay in reconciliation, in becoming a viable part of the Union without repudiating the cherished values of southern heritage. These ideas were embodied in Lanier's hymn "The Centennial Meditation of Columbia. A Cantata" and in "The Psalm of the West," both composed in 1876 to commemorate the nation's centennial.

More than just a protest against mercantilism, Lanier's opposition to Trade was a plea for the restoration of the human spirit through love, art, music, and nature, exemplified in "The Marshes of Glynn." Progressing like the movements of a symphony, from noon to night, this poem embodies Lanier's release from the mundane concerns of daily life. Escaping the din of trade in the "Wildwood privacies" (l. 13) of the live oaks, the poet regenerates his soul: "And my spirit is grown to a lordly great compass within" (l. 29). Lanier announces that "belief overmasters doubt" (l. 28); he has exchanged a preoccupation with temporal concerns for the certainty of faith.

NATURE

In this poem as in all his work, Lanier's wisdom and faith emanate from nature. While the melodic and intricate description offers a unique portrait of Georgia's coastal marshes and is, as Louis D. Rubin Jr. points out, "characteristically southern . . . in its strong emphasis on place" (p. 139), Lanier's view of nature clearly reflects the influence of transcendentalism, one of the most important literary movements of the nineteenth century. Lanier's empathetic relationship to the live oaks recalls a statement by Ralph Waldo Emerson (1803–1882) in *Nature:* "The greatest delight which the fields and woods minister, is the suggestion of an occult relation between man and the vegetable. I am not alone and unacknowledged. They nod to me, and I to them" (p. 24). Likewise, the trees serve as Lanier's mentors, reciprocating his affection: "Ye held me fast in your heart and I held you fast in mine" (l. 20). Nature is all-healing: the live oaks provide "Cells for the passionate pleasure of prayer to the soul that grieves" (l. 15), and the vast expanse of marsh, sea, and sky liberate the soul "From the weighing of fate and the sad discussion of sin" (l. 63). Most significant is the revelation of intuitive knowledge through nature. The poet declares, "I know that I know" (l. 28).

FAITH

For all its affinity with transcendentalism, the knowledge Lanier embraces in "The Marshes of Glynn" is derived from Christianity. Nature is not God, in Lanier's view, it is simply a manifestation of divinity: "Oh, *like* to the greatness of God is the greatness within / The range of the marshes, the liberal marshes of Glynn" (ll. 77–78; emphasis added). Furthermore, the poem introduces the contrary element of doubt: "a sense of the ultimate unknowableness of nature," says Jack De Bellis (*Sidney Lanier,* p. 117). Lanier asks, "Oh, what is abroad in the marsh and the terminal sea?" (l. 61). What Lanier discovers through his contemplation of live oak, marsh, and sea is not Emerson's cosmic Oversoul but complete acceptance of the inevitable eternity of death, symbolized by the interminable marshes, and the infinite incomprehensibility of God, made even more poignant by Lanier's impending demise. Lanier states: "Oh, now, unafraid, I am fain to face / The vast sweet visage of space" (ll. 35–36). Using the tide to represent death, the poet replaces irrational fear with unorthodox curiosity: "And I would I could know what swimmeth below when the tide comes in" (l. 101).

Philip Graham maintains that the natural images in "The Marshes of Glynn" illustrate Lanier's theory of "etherealization," or the constant progression of all matter from a state of physical sensuality to a more spiritual form of love and beauty. Graham believes the poem shows that "physical life (represented by the live oaks and the dark), through death (the marsh and the dawn), merges into spiritual existence (the sea and full light)" ("Sidney Lanier and the Pattern of Contrast," pp. 506–507). This may well be Lanier's idealized interpretation of Darwinian evolution, a concept Lanier accepted on the whole, though he rejected the theory of the genesis of species.

By grappling with evolution and the questions of faith and doubt in an age of materialism, Lanier shared the concerns of other enlightened Victorians, men such as Thomas Carlyle, John Ruskin, Matthew Arnold, Tennyson, and Robert Browning. Lanier's achievement is all the more remarkable, however, for emerging from the ruins of the post–Civil War South, where deprivation and conservative attitudes created an atmosphere of literary and intellectual stagnation.

EVALUATION AND STYLE

More recent criticism of Lanier's works is very limited and usually considers the poet in relationship to other writers or to music or medievalism. In one article of note, Jack Kerkering (2001) presents an extensive analysis of Lanier's racial identity in comparison to that of W. E. B. Du Bois, Walt Whitman, and the musician Antonín Dvořák. Starke's *Sidney Lanier: A Biographical and Critical Study* (1933) remains the definitive biography, while Anderson's *Centennial Edition,* despite the notable omission of the musical compositions, is unsurpassed in its comprehensive treatment of Lanier as man, poet, and writer.

Specific studies of "The Marshes of Glynn" include a comparison by D. M. R. Bentley of the form and content of Lanier's poem to "Tantramar Revisited" by the Canadian poet Charles G. D. Roberts. In 1965 Harry R. Warfel maintained that "The Marshes of Glynn" represents a mystic vision and that the blending of images and musical elements produces a program poem, which Warfel defines as a poem "structured in analogy with program music" (p. 34). Five years later Owen T. Reamer rejected Warfel's views, contending that the natural symbols represent Lanier's reaffirmation of God. In addition to Anderson, Roy Harvey Pearce, Edd Winfield Parks, Jack De Bellis, Louis D. Rubin Jr., and Jane S. Gabin provide insightful interpretations of the poem as part of their broader considerations of Lanier's work.

The harshest criticism of "The Marshes of Glynn" concerns its form and style. In particular, Robert Ross finds the symbolism of the woods, marsh, and sea obscure and imbalanced. Ross's argument reiterates the objections of the New Critics, notably the Fugitive-Agrarians Robert Penn Warren, Allen Tate, and John Crowe Ransom, who in the 1930s denounced Lanier for his policies on economic reform and for his poetics, which they believed lacked consistency and clarity and substituted sentimentality and didacticism for paradox, irony, and wit.

It is easy to understand these critics' quarrel with Lanier's style, for "The Marshes of Glynn" is complex, written in logaoedic dactyls, with a cacophony of alliteration, assonance, and rhyme used to create an orchestral effect. An accomplished flutist and professional musician, Lanier postulated that music and poetry are governed by identical principles of sound, a theory he developed in *The Science of English Verse* (1880). With its free-flowing syntax and word tones, "The Marshes of Glynn" is the premier demonstration of these principles. In departing from the predominant style of his contemporaries, Lanier's experiments with liberated forms parallel Whitman's free verse, though neither poet fully recognized the similarity.

Lanier was caught between two ideologies: the conservative traditions of the Old South and the progressive ideas of the New, fraught with all the unsettling doubts, conflicts, and controversies that characterized the last half of the nineteenth century. Yet he approached life with a receptive mind and optimism in the face of adversity. His work endures—in anthologies and on the Internet, as the inspiration for poetic works such as Andrew Hudgins's *After the Lost War,* and as an early proponent of the ecocritical perspective. It is this timelessness that "The Marshes of Glynn" celebrates.

See also Lyric Poetry; New South; Regionalism and Local Color Fiction

BIBLIOGRAPHY

Primary Works

Emerson, Ralph Waldo. *Nature.* In *Selections from Ralph Waldo Emerson: An Organic Anthology,* edited by Stephen E. Whicher, pp. 21–56. Riverside edition. Boston: Houghton Mifflin, 1957.

Lanier, Sidney. *The Centennial Edition of the Works of Sidney Lanier.* 10 vols. Edited by Charles R. Anderson. Baltimore: Johns Hopkins University Press, 1945. "The Marshes of Glynn" appears on pages 119–122 of the first volume. Individual volumes have introductions and notes by Anderson and other Lanier scholars. References to this work are indicated in parentheses within the text as *CE.*

Lanier, Sidney. *Poems of Sidney Lanier, Edited by His Wife: Electronic Edition.* Documenting the American South. University of North Carolina at Chapel Hill, 1998. http://docsouth.unc.edu/lanier/menu.html-6K.

Secondary Works

Allen, Gay Wilson. *American Prosody.* New York: American Book, 1935.

Bentley, D. M. R. "Roberts' 'Tantramar Revisited' and Lanier's 'The Marshes of Glynn.'" *Studies in Canadian Literature* 5 (1980): 316–319.

De Bellis, Jack. *Sidney Lanier.* New York: Twayne, 1972.

De Bellis, Jack. *Sidney Lanier, Henry Timrod, and Paul Hamilton Hayne: A Reference Guide.* Boston: G. K. Hall, 1978. A comprehensive annotated bibliography of secondary source material.

Gabin, Jane S. *A Living Minstrelsy: The Poetry and Music of Sidney Lanier.* Macon, Ga.: Mercer University Press, 1985.

Graham, Philip. "Lanier and Science." *American Literature* 4, no. 3 (November 1932): 288–292.

Graham, Philip. "Sidney Lanier and the Pattern of Contrast." *American Quarterly* 11, no. 4 (1959): 503–508.

Havens, Elmer A. "Lanier's Critical Theory." *ESQ: A Journal of the American Renaissance* 55 (1969): 83–89.

Hubbell, Jay B. *The South in American Literature, 1607–1900.* Durham, N.C.: Duke University Press, 1954.

Hudgins, Andrew. *After the Lost War: A Narrative*. Boston: Houghton Mifflin, 1988.

Kerkering, Jack. "'Of Me and of Mine': The Music of Racial Identity in Whitman and Lanier, Dvorák, and DuBois." *American Literature* 73, no. 1 (2001): 147–184.

Leary, Lewis. "The Forlorn Hope of Sidney Lanier." In his *Southern Excursions: Essays on Mark Twain and Others*, pp. 131–141. Baton Rouge: Louisiana State University Press, 1971.

Mims, Edwin. *Sidney Lanier*. 1905. Port Washington, N.Y.: Kennikat Press, 1968.

Parks, Edd Winfield. *Sidney Lanier: The Man, the Poet, the Critic*. Athens: University of Georgia Press, 1968.

Pearce, Roy Harvey. *The Continuity of American Poetry*. Princeton, N.J.: Princeton University Press, 1961.

Ransom, John Crowe. "Hearts and Heads." *American Review* 2 (March 1934): 554–571.

Reamer, Owen T. "Lanier's 'The Marshes of Glynn' Revisited." *Mississippi Quarterly* 23 (May 1970): 57–63.

Ridgely, J. V. *Nineteenth-Century Southern Literature*. Lexington: University Press of Kentucky, 1980.

Ross, Robert H. "'The Marshes of Glynn': A Study in Symbolic Obscurity." *American Literature* 32, no. 4 (1961): 403–416.

Rubin, Louis D., Jr. "The Passion of Sidney Lanier." In his *William Elliott Shoots a Bear: Essays on the Southern Literary Imagination*, pp. 107–144. Baton Rouge: Louisiana State University Press, 1975.

"Sidney Lanier (1842–1881)." *The New Georgia Encyclopedia*. The Georgia Humanities Council in partnership with the Office of the Governor, the University of Georgia Press, and the University System of Georgia. Available at http://www.galileo.usg.edu. This website provides links to the entry on Lanier in the Georgia Writers Hall of Fame Honorees, the online version of *Poems of Sidney Lanier, Edited by His Wife: Electronic Edition*, and the Carl Vinson Institute of Government: Sidney Lanier Commemorative Stamp.

Snyder, Henry Nelson. *Modern Poets and Christian Teaching, Sidney Lanier*. 1906. Foreword by Robert E. Sharp. Nashville, Tenn.: Parthenon Press, 1954.

Starke, Aubrey Harrison. "The Agrarians Deny a Leader." *American Review* 2 (March 1934): 534–553.

Starke, Aubrey Harrison. "An Omnibus of Poets." *Colophon* 4, pt. 16 (March 1934), n.p. Provides details about and reception of *A Masque of Poets*.

Starke, Aubrey Harrison. 1933. *Sidney Lanier: A Biographical and Critical Study*. New York: Russell and Russell, 1964.

Tate, Allen. "A Southern Romantic." *New Republic* 76 (30 August 1933): 67–70.

Warfel, Harry R. "Mystic Vision in 'The Marshes of Glynn.'" *Mississippi Quarterly* 19 (1965): 34–40.

Warren, Robert Penn. "The Blind Poet: Sidney Lanier." *American Review* 2 (November 1933): 27–45.

Rosemary D. Cox

MASS MARKETING

Between 1870 and 1920 many of the economic institutions and business practices central to a mass-market society began to restructure American society. These included national advertising, newspaper advertising, advertising agencies, market research, brand names, trademarks, department stores, sales and bargains, mail-order catalogs, chain stores, franchises, and the commercializing of culture.

EMERGENCE OF THE MASS MARKET

A key factor in the development of a mass-market society was the production of masses of goods that could be sold cheaply. By the second half of the nineteenth century large companies had amassed enough wealth (capital) to buy new technologically advanced machines for large-scale manufacturing, and new technology made possible the speedy, continuous factory production of goods. The period's emphasis on mechanization, systematization, and efficiency is apparent in Daniel Edward Ryan's *Human Proportions in Growth* (1880), which spurred the standardization of clothing sizes for men and boys, and in Frederick W. Taylor's *The Principles of Scientific Management* (1911), which advised managers how to regulate the time and motion of workers to increase their productivity. Mass production also involved the manufacturing of a greater variety of products. Once homemade, items such as soup, breakfast cereal, and baby food became prepackaged convenience foods. A range of new products also appeared, from Levi Strauss's denim pants and King Gillette's disposable safety razor to cameras, chewing gum, barbed wire, bicycles, telephones, electric lighting, household appliances, and the automobile.

The mass market was also fueled by a rapidly growing population and shifting demographics that supplied masses of consumers and factory workers. According to the U.S. Census Bureau, the population of the United States nearly doubled between 1870 and 1890, reaching 62.1 million by 1890. The large influx of immigrants contributed cheap labor, and many Americans left farms for the cities, furthering the transformation of Americans from producers of the goods they used into consumers who bought food, clothing, and household items.

Mass-market growth especially depended on the availability and promotion of mass-produced goods. The vast national railroad system, along with inventions such as the refrigerator train car and electrical power, spurred mass-market growth, reaching out to rural communities and creating a national market with national selling now dominating local and regional selling. Partly in response to industrial capitalism's problems of overproduction and competition, the big manufacturing corporations created national distribution networks to control the distribution and selling of their goods. Many firms became vertically integrated companies, encompassing all the stages of production and distribution of their products. For example, Sherwin-Williams Paint Company owned its own smelters and plants for making oil, chemicals, colors, and cans as well as its own retail stores.

LITERATURE'S ENGAGEMENT WITH THE MASS-MARKET SOCIETY

In the 1850s Nathaniel Hawthorne had deplored the women writers who were making a living by the sale of their popular novels. After the Civil War, the professionalization of literature and American writers' negotiations with the marketplace intensified. The novelist, critic, and editor of the *Atlantic Monthly* William Dean Howells (1837–1920), in his essay "The Man of Letters as a Man of Business" (1902), pondered literature's relationship to the powerful commercializing forces reorganizing American society. Writers contemplated the questions, Is literature a commodity like soap? Or is literature art that transcends the sordid forces of the marketplace? Similarly, literary critics today probe the relationship between late-nineteenth-century literature and the marketplace. Whereas Marxist critics such as Richard Wightman Fox and T. J. Jackson Lears assert that the literature of this period mainly critiques (stands in opposition to) the emerging mass-market society, the New Historicist critic Walter Benn Michaels argues that these realist and naturalist texts exemplify (remain thoroughly embedded in and enact the principles of) the market. Nevertheless, most literary criticism of late-nineteenth-century texts agrees that this literature was profoundly shaped by the inescapable pervasiveness of the marketplace in American life. Obliquely and overtly, these novels examine ethics, social relationships, human identity, and the idea of the self in a mass-market, consumer-capitalist society.

Many texts of the period question the way mass-market growth brought convenience and comfort to many Americans while undermining American ideals of democracy and equality through deepening class divisions. For example, some texts explored how the class of capitalists and corporate leaders amassed more wealth through their control over production (e.g., coal mines, cotton factories, railroads) and economically reorganized society, creating a class of wage-earning workers and employing and enlisting a middle class of managers and professionals. The early realist text *Life in the Iron Mills* (1861) by Rebecca Harding Davis portrays the exploitive long hours, miserable conditions, low wages, and soul-deadening mechanical work of industrial laborers. A number of novels of the post–Civil War period continue this probing of the working class's contribution to mass production. Set in the manufacturing towns of New England, Elizabeth Stuart Phelps's novel *The Silent Partner* (1871), William Dean Howells's *Annie Kilburn* (1889), and Mary Wilkins Freeman's *A Portion of Labor* (1901) depict working-class women and women's work, the problems of capitalism, and issues of class and social responsibility. Other novels portray women workers in the garment, shoe, and hat sweatshops in New York City and Chicago, among them Stephen Crane's *Maggie, A Girl of the Streets* (1893), Theodore Dreiser's *Sister Carrie* (1900), Edith Wharton's *The House of Mirth* (1905), and Abraham Cahan's *The Rise of David Levinsky* (1917). Like Abraham Cahan, Upton Sinclair focuses on immigrant laborers in his novel *The Jungle* (1906). This text's effort to expose the deadly living and working conditions of the immigrants in Chicago's stockyards and meatpacking factories was co-opted by the consumer movement's campaign for protective legislation and led to the Pure Food and Drug Act of 1906.

Some writers of the period astutely analyze the way that gender and the elite class were embroiled in production and consumption. In *Women and Economics* (1898), Charlotte Perkins Gilman protests women's economic dependence on men and marriage, emphasizes the importance of "free productive expression" (p. 117), and advocates freeing women from their roles as nonproductive consumers. In his book *The Theory of the Leisure Class* (1899), the sociologist Thorstein Veblen criticizes the leisure class for its detachment from all useful employment and for women's role as public consumers of their husbands' wealth. Originating the phrase "conspicuous consumption," Veblen describes a social hierarchy in which patterns of consumption signal social status, with the lower classes seeking to emulate the showy, extravagant consumption of the elite class. More subtly than these theoretical texts, some of Henry James's novels, featuring main characters who are the products of American entrepreneurial success, represent dramas of perception, identity, sexuality, social class, and newly made American money (*The American*, 1877; *Daisy Miller*, 1879; *The Ambassadors*, 1903). For

In this passage from his first novel, Sister Carrie (1900), Theodore Dreiser (1871–1945) captures the psychological impact of department stores on women consumers in turn-of-the-century America. Using words such as "mood," "lured by desire," "woman's heart warm with desire," "rich reverie," "greatest attraction," "delighted," and "satisfied," he makes readers identify with his character's emotional state as she feels the seductive power of the fine goods for sale in the department store. He also suggests the concrete reality and almost magical, transformative power of things in contrast to the fluidity of the self in a world dominated by materialism and market forces.

There is nothing in this world more delightful than that middle state in which we mentally balance at times, possessed of the means, lured by desire, and yet deterred by conscience or want of decision. When Carrie began wandering around the store amid the fine displays she was in this mood. Her original experience in this same place had given her a high opinion of its merits. Now she paused at each individual bit of finery, where before she had hurried on. Her woman's heart was warm with desire for them. How would she look in this, how charming that would make her! She came upon the corset counter and paused in rich reverie as she noted the dainty concoctions of colour and lace there displayed. If she would only make up her mind, she could have one of those now. She lingered in the jewelry department. She saw the earrings, the bracelets, the pins, the chains. What would she not have given if she could have had them all! She would look fine too, if only she had some of these things.

The jackets were the greatest attraction. When she entered the store, she already had her heart fixed upon the peculiar little tan jacket with large mother-of-pearl buttons which was all the rage that fall. Still she delighted to convince herself that there was nothing she would like better. She went about among the glass cases and racks where these things were displayed, and satisfied herself that the one she thought of was the proper one. All the time she wavered in mind, now persuading herself that she could buy it right away if she chose, now recalling to herself the actual condition.

Dreiser, Sister Carrie, pp. 54–55.

the genteel but financially insecure Lily Bart, Edith Wharton's main character in *The House of Mirth*, marriage itself is a market, and women's beauty, reputation, and sexuality are risky stocks, subject to rapid depreciation.

Still other texts explore questions of human agency in a world of increasing mechanization, glamorous and proliferating materialism, and rapid urbanization. William Dean Howells's novels *The Rise of Silas Lapham* (1885) and *A Hazard of New Fortunes* (1890) probe the relationship between moneymaking and self-making as well as the ethical and moral problems of conducting business in a society dominated by competition and stock market speculation. Frank Norris's novels *The Octopus* (1901) and *The Pit* (1903) portray uncontrollable market forces and corporations (the all-powerful railroads and the Chicago commodity market) destroying individuals, marriages, and small farms. Theodore Dreiser's *Sister Carrie* depicts the relationship between image, status, and personality in cities selling everything from labor to fashion to amusement. His novel *The Financier* (1912) focuses on the speculative making and selling of money itself.

Growing out of a society that considered the captains of industry its popular heroes, texts like Horatio Alger Jr.'s *Ragged Dick; or, Street Life in New York* (1867) and the Baptist minister Russell H. Conwell's famous lecture "Acre of Diamonds" (1890) celebrate the opportunity and responsibility to make the male self through making money. Other texts register their authors' deep concern over the corrupt materialism and economic and social inequities of industrial capitalism. In *The Gilded Age* (1873), Mark Twain and Charles Dudley Warner satirize democracy's compromising entanglement with buying, promoting, and getting rich. In *Looking Backward* (1888), Edward Bellamy's utopian social reform novel, he proposes an equalizing of consumer comforts. He imagines political socialism as a means to solve industrial capitalism's problems of poverty, unemployment, strikes, overproduction, and child labor. Still other writers of this period portray mass production's devitalizing of rural areas. Edith Wharton's *Summer* (1917) and Sherwood Anderson's *Winesburg, Ohio* (1919) examine identity, gender, and sexuality in communities marginalized by migration to the cities.

ADVERTISING: CONSTRUCTING CONSUMPTION AS A WAY OF LIFE

Although colonial American newspapers had been packed with advertisements, advertising achieved its real power and prominence after 1870. Was advertising a universally useful, inevitable outgrowth of mass-production expansion? Or was it a conspiratorial, manipulative scheme of the big companies and corporate leaders to brainwash the masses into a life of consumption? The most reasonable interpretations of advertising deny that advertising was a monolithic force yet identify the corporate elite as the chief beneficiaries of advertising and acknowledge that advertising functioned as a primary instrument in the transformation from industrial to consumer capitalism.

Between 1870 and 1900, in order to create and shape new markets for the proliferation of new products, advertising had to achieve multiple goals: (1) overcoming Americans' basic distrust of ads, a skepticism nurtured by years of fraudulent cure-alls and tonics; (2) finding personal appeals to dispel Americans' resistance to distant, unfamiliar, and disembodied sellers; and (3) increasing Americans' willingness to spend money by portraying shopping as pleasurable.

Trademarks and brand names created new relationships between mass-marketed products and consumers. Institutionalizing trademarks and brand names enabled companies to stabilize competition by creating market niches and dividing up the market. Most important, through trademarks and brand names, big, nebulous companies became embodied, solidified their identities and lodged them in consumers' minds, enhanced their reputations, and cultivated ongoing connections with their consumers. Trademarks and brand names promised to deliver familiar quality, the same Ivory Soap or Budweiser Beer with every purchase. The historian Daniel J. Boorstin claims that trademarks and brand names helped to unify the nation in thousands of "consumption communities" (p. 90) composed of people loosely connected by their loyalty to specific products. The hundredfold increase in trademarks registered with the U.S. patent office between 1880 and 1906 (roughly from 120 to over 10,000) testifies to the success of these strategies.

As advertising itself became a big business and a profession between the 1870s and 1900, advertising departments and the modern advertising agency emerged. Mid-nineteenth-century agents had mainly bought columns and pages in newspapers from the publishers and sold that space to companies. Eventually advertising agents began investigating who was buying particular products and which newspapers and magazines reached which consumers (early market research with attention to consumers' incomes and class). They planned campaigns and themes for ads, determined formats and designs, and wrote advertising copy. Two of the major full-service agencies of this period were J. Walter Thompson and N. W. Ayer.

One dominant trend in the advertising of this period was the increase in size and the display quality of ads. Around mid-century, the column and page space devoted to advertising was governed by a number of constraints: the cost of paper, which forced the use of tiny type (usually 5 1/2 point, called the agate rule) for ads, and the technical difficulty of spreading an item over several columns. Also, publishers believed that advertisers should appeal to customers through the content of their ads, not through competitive displays (what Boorstin calls "typographical democracy" [p. 139]). Efforts to break through these constraints pushed type itself toward visual display. The layout of type was used to form shapes and larger letters. Historians identify the year 1879 as the moment when newspapers and magazines began showing full-page ads.

In addition to the literal enlargement of ads, the number of ads in public spaces increased. Newspapers and magazines discovered that advertising could finance their production costs, thus lowering the magazines' prices for readers, and these publications began devoting increasing numbers of pages to ads. For example, by 1900 new mass circulation magazines such as *McClure's Magazine* and *Munsey's* as well as *Century Magazine, Harper's, Atlantic Monthly,* and *Cosmopolitan* featured around one hundred pages of ads. Historians of advertising point out that these mass-circulation magazines brought the marketplace right into the home, breaking down the barrier between public and private spheres. The 1870s to the 1890s also saw the increasing presence of trade cards, posters, billboards, and ads on barns, on sides of vehicles, and inside streetcars.

Ads, which began appearing everywhere, gained appeal and persuasiveness, partly by becoming increasingly visual. Advertising began to create a pictorial rhetoric with images conjuring up associations with products. For instance, to convey the gentleness of their new Ivory Soap, Proctor and Gamble commissioned artists to draw framable-quality pictures of babies and children. Other companies discovered the power of special, memorable symbols or icons such as Goodyear's winged foot and Morton Salt's girl with the umbrella. By the 1890s, engravings were replaced by half-tone reproductions of photographs.

Throughout the second half of the nineteenth century, advertising and consumer capitalism became installed in American consciousness and daily living

Miscellaneous

$85 LOVELL DIAMOND SAFETIES
FOR LADIES.
For Ladies or Gents.
SIX STYLES.
Strictly High Grade in Every Particular. No better Machines Made at Any Price.
DIAMOND FRAME. Steel Drop Forgings, Steel Tubing. Adjustable Ball Bearings. Finest material. Enamel and Nickel.
BICYCLE CATALOGUE FREE.
Send 6c. in stamps for our 100-page ILLUSTRATED CATALOGUE of Guns, Rifles, Revolvers, Bicycles, etc
JOHN P. LOVELL ARMS CO., Boston, Mass.

BARRY'S TRICOPHEROUS
FOR THE
HAIR AND SKIN.
An elegant dressing. Prevents baldness, gray hair, and dandruff. Makes the hair grow thick and soft. Cures eruptions and diseases of the skin. Heals cuts, burns, bruises and sprains. All druggists or by mail 50 cts. 44 Stone St. N. Y.

Elastic Stockings.
You can save 50 PER CENT. by purchasing direct from our factory. Send for price list and directions for self measuring.
CURTIS & SPINDELL.
ELASTIC WEAVERS,
LYNN, - - MASS.

MY WIFE SAYS SHE CANNOT SEE HOW YOU DO IT FOR THE MONEY.
$12 Buys a $65.00 Improved Oxford Singer Sewing Machine; perfect working reliable, finely finished, adapted to light and heavy work, with a complete set of the latest improved attachments free. Each machine guaranteed for 5 years. Buy direct from our factory, and save dealers and agents profit. Send for FREE CATALOGUE. OXFORD MFG. COMPANY, DEPT X 13, CHICAGO, ILL.

The Double Ve Waist

YOUNG LADIES', Style 92.
Ages, 10 to 16 years.
THIS GARMENT is made for GROWING GIRLS—the most critical period of life. It fits into the hollow of the back and CURVES OUTWARD down the line of the front, following the natural outline of the form without pressure upon any vital organ. A HYGIENIC GARMENT.—Also made for *Other Ages*—Babies, Infants, Children (Boys and Girls), Misses and Ladies.
IT IS A VERY SATISFACTORY GARMENT.
For sale by leading dealers. **Lady canvassers wanted.**
Send for Illustrated Price List.
THE FOY, HARMON & CHADWICK CO., Brooklyn, N. Y.

SEAMLESS RIBBED WAIST
FOR CHILDREN
Combines Durability with Delightful Ease and Comfort.
The only perfect low-priced Waist made. Sizes, 1 to 12 years. For sale by all first-class Dry Goods Dealers. If unable to procure in your town send to us for sample, enclosing 25 cents, or 35 cents for the better grade.
Nazareth Manufacturing Co.,
Originators and Sole Mfrs., NAZARETH, PA.

You Should Smoke
Not poisonous tobacco, but
Marshall's Prepared Cubeb Cigarettes,
The most pleasant and sure remedy ever offered.
CATARRH, HAY FEVER, COLD IN THE HEAD, ASTHMA, Etc.
The high medicinal value of these cubeb cigarettes is recognized by the highest medical authorities, and can be smoked without any fear of nicotine or other poisons. Used by ladies as well as gentlemen. Sold by druggists or sent by mail on receipt of **25c.**
JAMES B. HORNER, 44 Cedar St., New York.

25

Advertisements from *Godey's Lady's Book*, 1893. A plethora of new products were available to late-nineteenth-century consumers, especially women. THE LIBRARY OF CONGRESS through innovative appeals and new consumer-friendly merchandizing. In his book *Great American Brands: The Success Formulas That Made Them Famous* (1981), David Powers Cleary traces some of these successes and marketing firsts. Coca-Cola, registered as a trademark in 1893, succeeded in becoming a symbol of the pleasurable American life and the most recognized product in the world, in part through its classic bottle packaging and its various souvenir gifts: signs, fans, calendars, clocks, and serving trays. Anheuser-Busch cultivated a friendly relationship with consumers by inviting the public to visit its brewery. Advertisers also employed many methods: using jingles and repetition, arousing curiosity, and giving reasons to buy the product.

Advertising sought to mold behavior—to make Americans buy into the idea that the good life was, in the social historian Thomas J. Schlereth's words, the "goods life" (p. 141)—and to cultivate the belief that products would meet their psychological needs. The scholar and critic Ellen Gruby Garvey notes that by the beginning of the twentieth century advertising had fully adopted its paradoxical message: informing consumers how to cultivate their individuality and be uniquely themselves by purchasing mass-produced products used by masses of customers. T. J. Jackson Lears argues that early-twentieth-century advertising capitalized on people's sense of insulation from vital experience and loss of autonomy created by the mass market, the powerful presence of large, bureaucratic corporations, and disorienting urbanization. Playing to these psychological needs, advertising offered a "therapeutic promise of a richer, fuller life," of self-realization, "of fulfillment through consumption" (p. 18).

Besides seeking to shape a consumer consciousness, advertising adeptly engaged in constructing women consumers and white middle-class culture. Schlereth notes that by 1915, women accounted for 90 percent of all consumer spending. For example, realizing the importance of women consumers, the Bissell Carpet Sweeper Company opted to describe the beauty of the sweeper rather than explain its mechanics. Campbell's Soup pioneered trolley car advertising in 1899, believing that women especially would notice these ads. Ads also reinforced class identity by using race. Richard Ohmann and other advertising critics have pointed out how ads employed stereotypical figures of happy African American servants and children (Aunt Jemima of pancake fame and the black children in Knox's Gelatin ads) to uphold the white middle class by drawing on old social values, thus reinforcing the period's racist blindness to the real social presence of African Americans.

THE DEVELOPMENT OF DEPARTMENT STORES: GLAMORIZING AND GLORIFYING CONSUMPTION

The new institution of the department store became another way to glamorize consumption and take advantage of the opportunities created by mass productivity. Department stores, a new institution around mid-century in Paris and London as well as America, played key roles in changing people's habits from shopping locally within a few miles of their homes to going to large centers of consumption in cities, in making exposure to a huge assortment of goods available to all classes of people, and in legitimizing women's appearance in the public sphere. The quintessential novel of women's consumption and the new phenomenon of department stores is the French naturalist Émile Zola's *Au Bonheur des dames* (*The Ladies' Paradise*, 1883). Similarly, in *Sister Carrie* (1900), Theodore Dreiser portrays his main character's seduction by the material splendor of Chicago's department stores. Admiring and desiring the beautiful, fashionable corsets, earrings, and jackets on display, Carrie Meeber, who has recently moved from a small town to find work in Chicago, dreams of transforming herself through acquiring these things.

Besides the availability of mass-produced, ready-made clothes and the growth of cities, certain architectural and technological developments contributed to the burgeoning of department stores. The size, space, and splendor of these stores depended on the engineering and architectural ability to construct huge open spaces, where many different departments could display a rich array of goods, and on the manufacturing of large panes of glass for display windows to show off merchandise and attract buyers. Elevators enabled customers and merchandise to move from floor to floor within these large buildings, and electric streetcars (in the 1890s) brought consumers into the downtown districts of cities. Finally, newspaper advertising lured people to come to see and buy the marvelous goods. Although the name "department store" did not gain common currency until the 1890s, between the 1860s and 1900 department stores appeared in major cities throughout the country. In New York, R. H. Macy's opened in 1858, Lord & Taylor built its big marble store in 1860, and A. T. Stewart built his Cast Iron Palace in 1862. John Wanamaker's Grand Depot opened in Philadelphia in 1877, and Marshall Field opened in Chicago in 1882.

Department stores attracted consumers of all classes through many new retailing practices familiar to us today: buying in volume directly from manufacturers; conveniently selling in one store a huge array of items from household wares and home furnishings to all kinds of clothing; offering low, fixed prices (instead of the earlier practice of bargaining); offering money-back guarantees, credit, and installment buying (some stores demanded cash only); and having bargain basements and special sales.

Department stores transformed consumption by publicizing, popularizing, democratizing, sanctioning, and glorifying it. With their imposing structures, built around the same time as the large metropolitan museums, department stores were thought of as "Palaces of Consumption," and their magnificence endowed shopping with public value and helped make it socially acceptable (Boorstin, p. 101). Window shopping—available to all classes of people—became a favorite urban activity. The late-nineteenth-century department stores also glamorized shopping by offering extra services that particularly appealed to women, such as restrooms with maids, restaurants and tea rooms, libraries, nurseries, writing rooms with desks and paper, and organ music, post offices, and ticket agencies. Richard Ohmann notes that Macy's called itself a "shopping resort" (p. 68). Furthermore, department stores became important forces in setting women's fashions, offering seasonal clothing and staging social events like fashion shows and holiday pageants and parades. In addition, department stores created new jobs. Women salespersons were found to be more successful at dealing with the numerous women customers. The experience of department store sales representatives is portrayed in Edna Ferber's novel *Emma McChesney and Co.* (1915). Other new jobs in department stores were hired floorwalkers (supervisors of salespeople and customer interactions), merchandising managers, buyers, and advertising managers.

MASS CONSUMPTION BY MAIL: THE ADVENT OF MAIL-ORDER CATALOGS

Mass manufacturing also made possible the development of mail-order businesses. This retail institution, with its catalog pages of enticing products, brought the convenience, affordability, and abundance of mass goods to rural inhabitants and functioned as another nationalizing force. In the 1870s many Americans in the mideastern and midwestern states still lived on widely separated homesteads some distance even from towns. These farmers bartered their farm products for the household, clothing, and farming goods that they could not make and bought on long-term credit from the few available country stores. Because these goods came from wholesalers through jobbers through retailers, each of whom needed to make a profit, rural customers paid marked-up prices for the minimal selection of goods available to them. These problems

Sears, Roebuck and Company catalog, fall 1900. Mail-order catalogs such as those from Sears and Montgomery Ward offered mass consumption to those living in small towns and rural areas. © BETTMANN/CORBIS

and the needs of rural Americans became apparent to a young traveling dry goods salesman, Montgomery Ward, in the 1860s. Ward also envisioned the market potential of selling directly, and therefore more cheaply, to rural customers through a mail-order business whose stock would be bought from city manufacturers in large quantities. Rural customers would pay in cash upon delivery. In 1872 Ward started his first mail-order business by renting a shipping room in Chicago and sending a one-page list of 103 items out to the Grangers, members of the National Grange of the Patrons of Husbandry, a widespread farmers' organization.

Montgomery Ward's mail-order business and, soon after, Richard W. Sears's similar company grew rapidly. Catalog pages and items multiplied with each new volume, with woodcuts of the products, four-color illustrations, and eventually half-tone photographs of live models added to what would become a bound volume of well over five hundred pages with an index. Sears started his mail-order sales of watches in 1886 in Minneapolis and established Sears, Roebuck and Company in 1893 (with A. C. Roebuck). Most historians suggest that Sears was driven more by ingenuity and creative opportunism than Ward. Nevertheless, both of the two giant mail-order businesses catered to the needs of rural consumers, and by the mid-1890s the immensely profitable sales of both companies (in the millions) continued to increase steadily, necessitating movement to larger warehouses. Other mail-order companies also saw the market potential and began selling by mail. This mail-order retailing was aided substantially by the establishment of rural free delivery in 1896, enabling mail to be delivered directly to farmers, not to the nearest towns, and by parcel post in 1913. Both these communication services also augmented the unifying and nationalizing effects of mail-order sales, in part by enhancing the quality of roads.

Ward's and Sears's mail-order companies sold just about everything: clothing, underwear, coats, shoes, and hats; musical instruments; cutlery and jewelry; saddles and harnesses; sewing machines; farm machines (such as pumps and threshers); barbed wire; windmills and steel for the towers; and eventually telephones, electric fans, and doorbells. These mail-order companies also promoted the products of new technology and scientific advance such as electrical appliances and aluminum kitchenware. By the turn of the century Ward and Sears were even selling ready-to-assemble houses, although Sears quickly dominated this market. Between 1908 and 1940 Sears's Modern Home Department—through its special catalog Book of Modern Homes and Building Plans—sold homes in 240 designs, ranging from two-room cottages to eight- to ten-room bungalows to mansions.

The success of mail-order retailing provoked the conflict between national businesses—which could offer consumers a much bigger selection of items at much lower prices—and local businesses, exemplifying the national market's takeover of local and regional selling. Local merchants tried to fight mail-order competition by encouraging customers to bring in and burn their catalogs; in response, mail-order businesses began to send their catalogs in unmarked packages.

Ward and Sears fully grasped the multiple goals of their catalogs: displaying and promoting the merchandise; explaining how the business saved customers money (no salesmen, no costly displays, direct dealing with manufacturing); educating customers about procedures for buying items in the catalog; and most of all, winning the consumers' confidence in unseen and unknown city sellers and their merchandise. Mail-order retailers also needed to reconcile customers to standardized sizing of clothing. To implement all these social changes, Ward and Sears employed frank, direct, honest, instructive language that avoided regionalisms and that standardized words. Both Ward and Sears emphasized customer satisfaction and offered money-back guarantees and paid expenses for returned items. So powerful and important did the mail-order catalogs become in increasing the standard of living for rural Americans, especially, and in homogenizing and shaping consumer desires that they came to be known as "The Wish Book" and "The Farmer's Bible" (Schroeder, p. 74) and, as Boorstin notes, were often used in schools "to teach, writing, arithmetic, and geography" (p. 129). By the early 1900s Ward and Sears were distributing millions of catalogs each year. Edna Ferber's novel *Fanny Herself* (1917) captures some of the cultural and social importance of mail-order businesses.

MORE MASS SALES OPPORTUNITIES: CHAIN STORES AND FRANCHISES

Other new retail institutions of national marketing were the chain store and the franchise, which became popular with customers of a lower income level than most department store customers. Often appearing in smaller towns than department stores, chain stores, like the mail-order companies, operated by buying products in large quantity and selling them cheaply. Franchises gave certain stores monopolies on particular products and prices. One of the first chain stores, the Great American Tea Company, was started in New York in 1859 by George Gilman and George Hartford and sold coffee, condensed milk, spices, tea, and baking powder. By 1869 it became the Great Atlantic and Pacific Tea Company (later known as A&P), and by 1880 it had around one hundred stores and eventually manufactured its own products. Another big chain, F. W. Woolworth, a variety store, also had its beginning in the 1870s. Woolworth's based its marketing on the premise that customers would buy many items (for example, buttonhooks or tin pans) that they did not immediately need if the items were priced low enough, at five and ten cents. Thomas Schlereth notes that by 1911 Woolworth's had over three hundred nickel and dime stores worldwide. Other successful chain stores launched between 1870 and 1920 included Grand Union, Jewel Tea, and Piggly Wiggly. Like the mail-order companies with which they competed, chain stores met with opposition from local merchants, who protested that chain stores ruined the sense of community and neighborhood.

MARKETING A HOLIDAY: COMMERCIALIZING CHRISTMAS

Historians, among them Stephen Nissenbaum, have asserted that Christmas was constructed as a holiday in the early nineteenth century by the middle and upper classes in New York. In his book *The Battle for Christmas,* Nissenbaum writes that the middle and upper classes, under the leadership of a group of elite intellectuals including Washington Irving, sought to "domesticate" Christmas, to quell some of the remaining class disorder, drinking, revelry, and violence that the Puritans had objected to, and to make it a family celebration, with parents giving gifts to their children. These historians cite some of the literary texts produced by this group as instrumental in this social and cultural project of reshaping the Christmas holiday. Washington Irving's *History of New York* (1809) and *The Sketch Book of Geoffrey Crayon, Gent.* (1819–1820) mention Christmas carolers as well as St. Nicholas. Clement Moore's "A Visit from St. Nicholas," first published in 1823 in the Troy, New York, *Sentinel* and later illustrated and reprinted regularly as "'Twas the Night before Christmas," features the early American folklore version of St. Nicholas. James Fenimore Cooper's novel *The Pioneers* (1823) also includes St. Nicholas. Starting in 1863, the artist and cartoonist Thomas Nast (1840–1902) gave Santa Claus a popular physical form and fleshed out his popular identity in his Christmas illustrations and cartoons for *Harper's Weekly.* Through the 1880s Nast's cartoons visually transformed St. Nicholas, or Santa Claus, as he came to be known in America, from a holy bishop to the small "jolly old elf" of Moore's story poem to the plump, bushy-bearded magical rewarder of children. The ongoing cultural investment in this popular conception of Santa Claus can be seen in the well-known editorial in the *New York Sun* written by Francis P. Church and first published on 21 September 1897. In this piece, "Yes, Virginia, There Is a Santa Claus!" Church affirms a cultural tradition and assures a little girl that Santa is, and always will be, real. Another writer who popularized Christmas while he addressed the conflict between commercial values and humanitarian Christian values during the Victorian period was Charles Dickens with his numerous Christmas novellas, including his most famous, *The Chimes* (1840) and *A Christmas Carol* (1843).

In the latter half of the nineteenth century this rich and somewhat confused mixture of Christmas folklore, religious symbols and rituals, and cultural practices became valuable to department stores, advertisers, and mail-order businesses in their efforts to make Christmas commercially profitable. Santa Claus became a particularly useful cultural symbol. Santa Claus could be used to sell goods, indeed to legitimize buying. Nissenbaum suggests that Santa Claus minimized middle-class guilt over buying and indulgence. Some of the commercial practices that developed during this period are very familiar today. The department stores discovered the commercial potential of using Christmas themes in elaborately decorated and lighted window displays. They employed parades like Macy's Thanksgiving Day parade to launch the Christmas buying season, began using in-store Santa Clauses (by 1914 New York City had a Santa Claus Association to prepare men for this role), and stayed open late during the several weeks before Christmas. Besides Santa Claus, the Christmas tree, with its German and northern European origins, became a commercially useful Christmas symbol. Woolworth's, particularly, popularized the Christmas tree by promoting Christmas tree decorations in the 1880s, and soon there was a thriving business in both real and synthetic Christmas trees. The commercial opportunism surrounding Christmas is best epitomized by F. W. Woolworth's advice to his store managers in 1891 when he called Christmas "our harvest time" and told them to "make it pay" (Erb, p. 27).

CONSUMED BY THE MASS MARKET

Between the Civil War and World War I, the mass marketplace reconfigured American life. In his book *American Realism,* the literary critic Eric Sundquist argues that American writers tried "to master a bewildering society that seemed always, in turn, to be mastering them" (p. 7). In the decades that followed, American writers continued wrestling with authenticity, fragmentation, powerlessness, and power in the full-blown consumer culture of America's mass-market society.

See also Banking and Finance; *Sister Carrie; The Theory of the Leisure Class;* Wealth; *Women and Economics*

BIBLIOGRAPHY

Primary Works

Dreiser, Theodore. *Sister Carrie.* 1900. New York: Bantam Classic, 1972.

Gilman, Charlotte Perkins. *Women and Economics.* 1898. Edited by Carl N. Degler. New York: Harper Torchbooks, 1966.

Veblen, Thorstein. *The Theory of the Leisure Class.* 1899. New York: Penguin, 1967.

Secondary Works

Boorstin, Daniel J. *The Americans: The Democratic Experience.* New York: Random House, 1973.

Borus, Daniel H. *Writing Realism: Howells, James, and Norris in the Mass Market.* Chapel Hill: University of North Carolina Press, 1989.

Cleary, David Powers. *Great American Brands: The Success Formulas That Made Them Famous.* New York: Fairchild, 1981.

Cohn, David L. *The Good Old Days: A History of American Morals and Manners As Seen through the Sears, Roebuck Catalogs 1905 to the Present.* New York: Simon and Schuster, 1940.

Emmet, Boris, and John E. Jeuck. *Catalogues and Counters: A History of Sears, Roebuck and Company.* Chicago: University of Chicago Press, 1950.

Erb, Lyle C. "The Marketing of Christmas: A History." *Public Relations Quarterly* (fall 1985): 24–28.

Ewen, Stuart. *Captains of Consciousness: Advertising and the Social Roots of the Consumer Culture.* New York: Basic, 1976.

Garvey, Ellen Gruber. *The Adman in the Parlor: Magazines and the Gendering of Consumer Culture, 1880s to 1910s.* New York: Oxford University Press, 1996.

Glickman, Lawrence B., ed. *Consumer Society in American History: A Reader.* Ithaca, N.Y.: Cornell University Press, 1999.

Horsley, Richard, and James Tracy. *Christmas Unwrapped: Consumerism, Christ, and Culture.* Harrisburg, Pa.: Trinity Press International, 2001.

Latham, Frank B. *1872–1972: A Century of Serving Consumers. The Story of Montgomery Ward.* Chicago: Montgomery Ward & Co., 1972.

Lears, T. J. Jackson. "From Salvation to Self-Realization: Advertising and the Therapeutic Roots of the Consumer Culture, 1880–1930." In *The Culture of Consumption: Critical Essays in American History 1880–1980*, edited by Richard Wightman Fox and T. J. Jackson Lears, pp. 3–38. New York: Pantheon, 1983.

Michaels, Walter Benn. *The Gold Standard and the Logic of Naturalism.* Berkeley: University of California Press, 1987.

Nissenbaum, Stephen. *The Battle for Christmas: A Cultural History of America's Most Cherished Holiday.* New York: Vintage, 1996.

Ohmann, Richard. *Selling Culture: Magazines, Markets, and Class at the Turn of the Century.* New York: Verso, 1996.

Schlereth, Thomas J. *Victorian America: Transformations in Everyday Life, 1876–1915.* New York: HarperCollins, 1991.

Schroeder, Fred E. H. "Semi-Annual Installment on the American Dream: The Wish Book as Popular Icon." In *Icons of Popular Culture*, edited by Marshall Fishwick and Ray B. Browne, pp. 73-86. Bowling Green, Ohio: Bowling Green University Popular Press, 1970.

Stevenson, Katherine Cole, and H. Ward Jandl. *Houses by Mail: A Guide to Houses from Sears, Roebuck and Company.* Washington, D.C.: Preservation Press, 1986.

Sundquist, Eric. J., ed. *American Realism: New Essays.* Baltimore: Johns Hopkins University Press, 1982.

Trachtenberg, Alan. *The Incorporation of America: Culture and Society in the Gilded Age.* New York: Hill and Wang, 1982.

Weil, Gordon Lee. *Sears, Roebuck, U.S.A.: The Great American Catalog Store and How It Grew.* Briarcliff Manor, N.Y.: Stein and Day, 1977.

June Johnson Bube

MEXICAN REVOLUTION

In 1913 John Reed (1887–1920), who was later to gain fame in the Russian Revolution and become one of the founders of the American Communist Party, joined Pancho Villa's troops in Northern Mexico and wrote the best English language reportage on the Mexican Revolution. Jack London funneled his socialism and revolutionary idealism into the short story "The Mexican" (1911) and a year later followed Reed to Mexico to cover the revolution. The irascible and irreverent Ambrose Bierce, who was suspicious of all ideological cant and often mocked the left-wing politics of Reed, London, and other American writers, wrote letters from war-torn Mexico—including one in which he imagined ending his turbulent life "against a Mexican stone wall and shot to rags" (p. 196)—and then he simply disappeared. Lincoln Steffens, the renowned journalist and one of the first muckrakers, turned his social criticism from the "shame of the cities" to the chaos and political quagmire of the revolution; in 1914 he also went to Mexico, and he produced astute observations on the American involvement there. Richard Harding Davis, journalist, novelist, and the leading reporter of his day, personified the romantic image of the foreign correspondent. Handsome and always impeccably dressed, he had cut a dashing figure covering the Turko-Greek War of 1895 and the Sino-Japanese War of 1899. When he arrived in Mexico to report on the revolution he was bloated and dissipated; his state of being seemed to augur the corruption, disenchantment, and failed dreams of the revolution itself.

Mexican rebels. From a newspaper photograph dated 9 March 1911. THE LIBRARY OF CONGRESS

Writers from many countries, of every temperament and political stripe, flocked to this first major revolution of the twentieth century and made it the century's first media event. The drama just south of the border was a great story, in which the United States played a constant role.

THE SEEDS OF REVOLT

The U.S. involvement in the Mexican Revolution came on the heels of its imperialistic venture in the Spanish-American War of 1898 and marked the beginning of a long and often ignoble history of political and military intervention in Latin America. All along, United States foreign policy and American business interests had supported the thirty-year dictatorship of Porfirio Díaz, known as the *Porfiriato*. Díaz had opened Mexico to foreign interests, mainly American and British, and an oligarchy ruled Mexico during the Díaz regime. The great disparity between the wealth of the ruling oligarchy and the widespread poverty of the Mexican peonage system laid the seeds for revolution; the people's bitterness was aggrandized by the knowledge that Mexico's abundant natural resources

were being plundered by foreigners. The historian John Mason Hart calculates that "about 130 million acres, more than 27 percent of Mexico's land surface, came into the possession of American owners," and concludes that "the overwhelming commitment of American capital to Mexico and the subordinate origins of the Díaz regime underscore the deeper significance of the Mexican Revolution: a war of national liberation against the United States" (p. 320). With the overthrow of the Díaz regime in 1910 and the dismantling of the oligarchy that had ruled Mexico, Americans and American property were placed in jeopardy and the United States steered a protectionist course in its relations with revolutionary Mexico.

The struggle for power that ensued after the overthrow of the Díaz regime would plunge Mexico into a bloodbath and an astonishing cycle of violence that would include assassinations of leading figures of the revolution: Madero, Obregón, Zapata, and Villa. Francisco Madero was constitutionally elected president of Mexico and he tried to effect democratic reforms, but he could not control the forces that had been unleashed. General Victoriano Huerta, who had served Díaz and became one of Madero's military commanders, betrayed Madero and had him assassinated. Huerta usurped the presidency, formed a counter-revolutionary government, and plunged Mexico into civil war. It was a crucial turning point; the Mexican historian Manuel Plana has underscored the moment: "The assassination of Madero, and the illegality and trickery with which Huerta acted, sparked the immediate formation of a resistance movement that opened the next phase of the revolution, in which popular movements, in particular that led by Villa, assumed a determining role" (p. 31).

PANCHO VILLA AND THE AMERICAN EXPEDITIONARY FORCE

Francisco Villa (born Doroteo Arango) was the most famous figure to arise from the Mexican Revolution. Undoubtedly, he was the most charismatic, controversial, and paradoxical. Reed's *Insurgent Mexico* (1914), which covers the three months he spent with Villa's troops, contains some of the most breathtaking prose on the revolution; the heroic exploits recounted in Reed's sweeping narrative romanticized the revolution and mythicized Pancho Villa as the Robin Hood of Mexico. Reed wrote: "It seems incredible to those who don't know him, that this remarkable figure, who has risen from obscurity to the most prominent position in Mexico in three years, should not covet the Presidency of the Republic. But that is in entire accordance with the simplicity of his character" (p. 128). In fact, Pancho Villa was as complex and contradictory as the revolution itself: magnanimous and cruel, generous and ruthless, noble and self-serving, and a brilliant success and a catastrophic failure. He was also, at the beginning, one of the most pro-American figures of the revolution. He was from the northern border state of Chihuahua; he was familiar with the United States and American life and customs; there were Americans with his troops, supporting or fighting for the revolutionary cause. The turnabout in Villa's attitude and the negative reaction of American opinion came in 1916, culminating with Villa's raid on Columbus, New Mexico.

After the resignation of Huerta in 1914 the power struggle, mainly between Villa and Venustiano Carranza, erupted into civil war. In 1915 the United States recognized the Carranza government and Villa's eventual defeat became inevitable. The collusion between the United States and Carranza led Villa to wage guerrilla warfare in northern Mexico and along the U.S.-Mexican border. The Mexican historian Manuel Plana explains the turn of events: "Villa's response was not born of his natural instinct for rebellion, as some would have it, but rather of the political defeat of his movement, and his conviction that he was betrayed. Villa's anti-Americanism and Carranza's

inability to stop him would spawn strong conflicts between the United States and Mexico, especially during the early months of 1916" (p. 91). In early 1916 Villa sacked the Mexican headquarters of several American mining companies, and executed sixteen Americans. The most sensational episode occurred on 16 March when a five hundred–man Villa force crossed the border and attacked a military garrison in the town of Columbus, New Mexico. There were twenty-six American casualties, mostly civilian, and Villa's troops made off with a cache of arms and munitions; Villa had invaded American territory and he was now branded a renegade and outlaw. On 15 March 1916 General John Pershing, with an army of five thousand men, crossed into Mexico and went after Villa; the objective of this "punitive expedition" was to capture and punish Villa and end his guerrilla activities.

The American army that went after Villa was given a lesson that would be painfully repeated later in the twentieth century: a mobile guerrilla army, knowing and using the terrain, could hold at bay or even defeat a numerically superior invading force. The Pershing Expedition, which numbered twenty-five thousand men by the time it left Mexico in February 1917, lacked mobility or effective tactics; it chased Villa for eleven months through the deserts, mountains, and canyons of northern Mexico and never got a glimpse of him. In the end, Pershing's mission was neither punitive nor expeditious. Pershing would later command the American Expeditionary Forces with greater success in Europe during World War I. As for Villa, he was removed from power by more cunning and ruthless men. On 23 July 1932 he was ambushed and murdered near Parral, Chihuaha, his assassination plotted by Alvaro Obregón (who had once been his friend and ally) and Plutarco Calles. The death of Pancho Villa ended one chapter of the Mexican Revolution. Villa's fame, however, would outlast that of his contemporaries; he would become the stuff of legend and the subject of countless songs, stories, biographies, novels, and movies.

REFLECTIONS ON THE REVOLUTION

John Reed's *Insurgent Mexico* stands as the most extraordinary American literary product to come out of the Mexican Revolution. A melange of reportage, poetry, memoir, and political commentary, it is marked by Reed's youthful enthusiasm and revolutionary romanticism: "It was the most glorious sensation I have ever felt. . . . It was a land to love—this Mexico—a land to fight for" (p. 77). Notwithstanding his lapses into exaggeration and sentimentality, Reed had more insight into the Mexican character than any other foreign correspondent or writer. His razor-sharp prose captures the dusty sweat of troops on the march and the confused fury of battle. The most engaging aspect of Reed's book is his vivid description of rank-and-file soldiers (men and women) and his poignant depiction of the heroism and sacrifice of the peons who fought and died in revolution. Years later Reed would nostalgically recall that the happiest moments of his life were those days spent riding with Villa's troops. Reed left Mexico with his revolutionary idealism intact; his experiences in the whirlwind of the Mexican Revolution would brace him and serve him well five years later during the Russian Revolution and the writing of another memorable book: *Ten Days That Shook the World* (1919).

In contrast, Jack London's (1876–1916) experiences in Mexico were a shattering disappointment. Three years before going to Mexico as a correspondent for *Collier's Magazine*, London had enthusiastically endorsed the peasant revolt in Mexico by addressing a letter to the "brave comrades of the Mexican Revolution" and signing it "revolutionist, Jack London" (p. 352). In the same year, London further demonstrated his solidarity in one of his best short stories, "The Mexican." In this story, London romanticized the revolution and made protagonist Felipe Rivera a shinning model of revolutionary purpose. Using the story to advance his socialist ideas, London contrasts the corruption of capitalist American society with the nobility of Rivera, who becomes a prizefighter in the United States in order to raise money to buy guns for the revolution. Lacking boxing skills or the cunning of his Anglo opponents, Rivera wins on sheer fortitude and endurance and because of the spiritual righteousness of his cause. But London's dream of a socialist utopia started to disintegrate in Mexico, when faced with the brutal reality of revolution and civil war. An astonishing reversal took place. As many commentators have noted, London "shed his socialist skin" in Mexico. He took a reactionary position supporting American military intervention, and he joined the American invasion of Vera Cruz in 1916. Racked by what he called "a severe attack of rotten, bacillary, tropical dysentery" (*Letters,* p. 1334), he vented his spleen in a series of dispatches; he called the revolution a fraud, hurled racist epithets at the Mexican peon, and praised Victoriano Huerta, arguably the most vicious murderer in the long history of Mexican despotism.

Ambrose Bierce (1842–1913?), on the other hand, suffered no disappointment because he arrived in Mexico with no political baggage and a simple death wish. As he put it in one of his last letters, "To be a Gringo in Mexico—ah, that is euthanasia!" (p. 196). Inadvertently, Bierce became part of the many legends surrounding Pancho Villa. The most popular conjecture about Bierce's disappearance was that he crossed the border, joined Villa's revolutionary army and died fighting in the revolution. Bierce's biographers have discounted this romantic tale, pointing out that he had contempt for the revolution and disdain for Pancho Villa and the rabble that followed him. Most likely Bierce was robbed and killed by bandits because he was carrying fifteen hundred American dollars.

Different from both Reed and Bierce in temperament and literary vision, Lincoln Steffens (1866–1936) was perhaps the most politically astute North American witness to the revolution. Disenchanted by the corruption of Europe and the "financial imperial expansions" that he saw as the real causes of World War I, Steffens left Europe for Mexico in 1914. As he put it in his autobiography: "I looked around for a revolution, and there was Mexico in the throes of one" (p. 714). Steffens arrived in Mexico after the revolution had turned to civil war: Carranza and Villa were not only fighting the Huerta regime but each other. Using his knowledge of history and political philosophy, Steffens brought an intellectual incisiveness to the debate inside the United States. Recognizing the torturous complexity of the situation, he chided both liberals and conservatives for reducing the struggle in Mexico to cliches and using it to bolster political prejudices. His criticism of American involvement and military intervention in Mexico was withering: "The Americans who were at all interested in Mexico coveted the country, wanted to change its laws and the people, and to possess or anyhow to govern Mexico. . . . We Americans don't seem to get it, that you can't commit rape a little" (p. 716).

Richard Harding Davis (1864–1916) accompanied London and other war correspondents on the Vera Cruz campaign. Like London, he supported American intervention and he had no sympathy for the Mexican people or the goals of the revolution. Indifferent to the civil war raging between Huerta's and Villa's forces, he wrote, "It was a falling out among cattle-thieves. Between Huerta and Villa there was the choice between Lefty Louie and Gyp and Blood" (p. 82). Several times Davis was caught, almost comically, in dangerous crosscurrents. The Wheeler Syndicate arranged for him to interview Huerta in Mexico City but his trip turned into a hair-raising comedy of errors. En route to Mexico City he was arrested twice and twice threatened with death by firing squad, but he managed to secure his freedom and return to Vera Cruz. The Wheeler Syndicate arranged another meeting with Huerta. This time Davis refused the assignment and wired his employers: "I'm leaving in the morning." He also failed to find in Mexico the romantic adventures that had previously fueled his fiction and reportage. "Not that I want to catch bullets in my teeth, but I *did* expect quick action and something to write about," he wrote (p. 82). When he left Mexico on 15 June 1914, the only story he had was about revolutionist soldiers injured in a train wreck caused by a herd of cows.

Events in Europe stole the thunder of the Mexican Revolution as the attention of the American public and American writers shifted to the fighting on the other side of the Atlantic. The entry of the United States into World War I in 1917 overshadowed any other political concerns; Mexico was left to its own devices, to ten more years of bloody conflict, and to the uncertainties of the twentieth century.

See also Annexation and Expansion

BIBLIOGRAPHY

Primary Works

Bierce, Ambrose. *The Letters of Ambrose Bierce*. Edited by Bertha Clarke Pope. New York: Gordian Press, 1967.

Davis, Richard Harding. *Adventures and Letters of Richard Harding Davis*. Edited by Charles Belmont Davis. New York: Scribners, 1917.

London, Jack. *The Letters of Jack London*. Vol. 3. Edited by Earle Labor and Robert C. Leitz. Stanford, Calif.: Stanford University Press, 1988.

London, Jack. "The Mexican." 1911. In *The Night-Born*. New York: Century, 1913.

Reed, John. *Insurgent Mexico*. 1914. New York: Simon and Schuster, 1969.

Steffens, Lincoln. *The Autobiography of Lincoln Steffens*. New York: Harcourt, Brace and Company, 1931.

Secondary Works

Hart, John Mason. *Revolutionary Mexico*. Berkeley: University of California Press, 1997.

Hicks, Granville. *John Reed: The Making of a Revolutionary*. New York: The Macmillan Company Co., 1937.

O'Connor, Richard. *Ambrose Bierce: A Biography*. Boston: Little, Brown, 1967.

O'Connor, Richard. *Jack London: A Biography*. Boston: Little, Brown, 1964.

Osborn, Scott Compton, and Robert L. Phillips. *Richard Harding Davis*. Boston: Twayne Publishers, 1978.

Plana, Manuel. *Pancho Villa and the Mexican Revolution*. Translated by Arthur Figliola. New York: Interlink Books, 2002.

Tuck, Jim. *Pancho Villa and John Reed: Two Faces of Romantic Revolution*. Tucson: University of Arizona Press, 1984.

Antonio C. Márquez

MIGRATION

Americans are known as a restless people who travel and relocate, and this restlessness is part of the idea of "American exceptionalism." Euro-America was settled by immigrants who had left their homes for a better life. Many American Indian groups, especially the Plains Indians, were migratory. Some tribes were removed by the U.S. government.

African American slaves, taken by force from Africa, were frequently transferred among owners. When slaves escaped they fled north, often into Canada. After the Civil War tens of thousands of the newly freed slaves migrated to the cities of the North. Thus Americans are a people prone to "movin' on."

THE OKLAHOMA LAND RUSH

A series of events led to the rush by non-Indians for Oklahoma land, part of Indian Territory, created by the Indian Trade and Intercourse Act of 1834. In the late nineteenth century, railroad lines were rapidly covering the United States. The national rail network grew from thirty-five thousand miles in 1865 to ninety-three thousand miles in 1880. During the 1880s more than 70,000 miles of line were built, with 164,000 miles in operation by 1890. In the spring of 1887 the Santa Fe Railroad was completed from Arkansas City, Kansas, to Gainesville, Texas, creating a new passage through Oklahoma. Railroad workers and passengers sometimes settled in the area, creating tent towns, largely ignored by the authorities.

This changed with the violence of the boomers, a group of whites seeking to open the unassigned lands. Named "boomers" because they wanted a boom in real estate development, they brought national attention to the Oklahoma district. Elias Boudinot II (1854–1896), a Cherokee, declared in a *Chicago Times* article (17 February 1879) that two million acres, unassigned to any tribe, were available for settlement. The Oklahoma Territory, bordered by Kansas on the north, was known for its open, relatively uninhabited prairies of fertile soil. Boudinot's announcement added to a growing state of excitement about free land.

During the 1880s and 1890s Oklahoma's Native Americans were experiencing their own significant changes. The nations were divided concerning non-Indian settlement. At a boomer conference in Kansas City on 8 February 1888, John Earlie of the Ottawa Nation in northeastern Oklahoma supported settlement by non-Indians, believing it mutually beneficial to whites and Indians. Some other nations strongly disagreed with the boomers, protesting "invasion" by "alien forces." Finally several of the Indian nations agreed, some out of desperate financial need, to sell portions of their land to the U.S. government. In early 1889 a proclamation by President Benjamin Harrison opened the Oklahoma areas for settlement by non-Indians. Over the next few years homesteaders were able to settle the land by means of a series of "land runs," actual races by horseback or horse-drawn wagons.

Oklahoma Territory fascinated many adventurous souls, including Huckleberry Finn. At the time of the publication of Mark Twain's *Adventures of Huckleberry Finn* (1885), the Indian Territory was topical and controversial. Contemporary readers would have understood the significance of Huck's words at the end of the novel: "I reckon I got to light out for the Territory ahead of the rest" (p. 229). However, this statement is an anachronism. The action of the novel is set, according to the author, "forty or fifty years ago," with Huck lighting out long before the territory was open to white settlers.

MIGRATION OF BLACKS

Rutherford B. Hayes, who became U.S. president through the Compromise of 1877, withdrew federal troops from the South, officially ending Reconstruction. Without the support of the national government, many African Americans, former slaves, found themselves in a New South that was as physically and economically dangerous and uncertain as the Old South. They remained susceptible to the racism and hatred of whites, sometimes their former owners, who had recently been defeated in a humiliating war. In the 1880s racial bigotry was legally sanctioned by the passage of Jim Crow laws (named after a character in a minstrel song), legalizing racial discrimination and effectively segregating blacks from whites in the South.

Because African Americans were no longer valuable property, white southerners had very little to lose by terrorizing the former slaves. Blacks were tortured and publicly lynched by white supremacist groups such as the Ku Klux Klan. Leaving the South became a dream and a goal for many blacks. Consequently southern blacks escaped this oppression by moving north, especially to the large metropolitan areas of Chicago, Detroit, Philadelphia, and New York, among others. Some traveled by railroad, some by wagon, and some even walked the hundreds of miles to their new homes.

One organized effort encouraging southern blacks to migrate north was the exodus movement, the participants being called "exodusters." Benjamin "Pap" Singleton (1809–1892) of Memphis, Tennessee, was instrumental in black migration. In 1869 Singleton and Columbus M. Johnson traveled to Kansas to investigate homestead land. While in Tennessee, Singleton and W. A. Sizemore created the Edgefield Real Estate and Homestead Association for fund-raising, transportation, and Kansas homesteading. Singleton and Sizemore also collaborated to achieve the incorporation of the Singleton Colony in Dunlap, Kansas, in June 1879. Later that year migrants from Tennessee and other southern states began arriving in Singleton, Kansas. Singleton organized the Colored Links political party in an African American section of Topeka, Kansas, called "Tennessee Town" because most of its residents were from that state. For a short while he even advocated a large migration to Liberia.

A descendant of an exoduster, Oscar Micheaux (1884–1951) was a noted filmmaker who also wrote semiautobiographical novels about black settlers in the Midwest. In *The Conquest* (1913), the protagonist works at a series of jobs in northern cities until he purchases a relinquishment on the Rosebud reservation in South Dakota and attempts to homestead his thousand-acre allotment. He fails as a farmer, suffers an unhappy marriage, and is a broken man. Micheaux's *The Homesteader* (1917) is a chronicle of a black pioneer, Jean Baptiste, who also farms land in South Dakota. Unlike the protagonist of *The Conquest,* Baptiste succeeds at farming and settles into a happy marriage. In his novels and films Micheaux praises and promotes the ideals of rugged individualism, the work ethic, and moral courage in the face of adversity.

Other African American writers explored the theme of travel and migration. Paul Laurence Dunbar (1872–1906), dubbed "the Poet Laureate of the Negro Race" by Booker T. Washington, established himself as a poet writing in two distinct poetic voices, formal English and southern black dialect. The voices, varying in tone from light humor to somber elegy, are randomly combined in his volumes of poetry. In his novel *The Sport of the Gods* (titled *The Jest of Fate* when published in England in 1903), Dunbar relates the migration of the Hamilton family, former slaves, from the South to New York City. Dunbar offers an ambivalent message: the South is economically and socially disastrous for blacks, but the northern urban centers destroy their very souls.

Military enlistment was another important reason for migration and relocation of African Americans. The characters of F. Grant Gilmore's *The Problem: A Military Novel* (1915) leave their homes in Virginia to serve in Cuba during the Spanish-American War and to settle finally in Washington, D.C. This migration narrative is a treatise on the mixing of races, the "problem" of the title. It is also a polemic extolling the courage and patriotism of "Negro" troops.

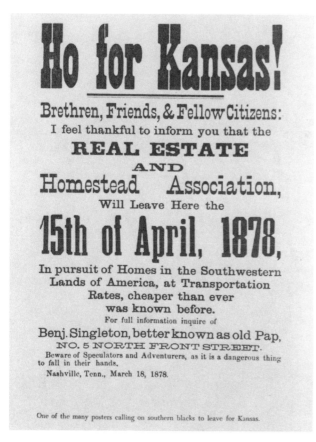

Ho for Kansas! One of Benjamin Singleton's broadsides advertising his relocation service for African Americans.
THE LIBRARY OF CONGRESS

In 1896, the year of the "separate but equal" Supreme Court ruling in *Plessy v. Ferguson,* another African-American novelist, J. McHenry Jones, published *Hearts of Gold,* a novel of black migration. However, McHenry's novel depicts black migration from the North to the South, and his northern black characters are from the middle and upper classes.

In James Weldon Johnson's (1871–1938) novel *The Autobiography of an Ex-Colored Man* (1912), the protagonist moves from the South to the North and to Europe. The protagonist lives in the South, Connecticut, New York City, Paris, and London. He finally settles into family life in New York City, feeling guilty because he has chosen to pass as white and not claim his black heritage. The protagonist of Charles Waddell Chesnutt's (1858–1932) "The Wife of His Youth" (1898) is a prominent businessman in his northern town. He is proud of his light skin and his comfortable lifestyle. On the eve of his marriage to a pale, elegant northern woman, he is confronted by an old, uneducated, and very dark woman from the South. She is his first wife, representative of his youth, for

whom, out of loyalty and honor, he jeopardizes his place in society.

Usually the first to migrate to the North were the younger men. After finding employment and settling into their new environments, these men would send money home to their families. Eventually, in the usual pattern of migration, they would move their families north. In the large city, young women, particularly if alone, faced their own difficulties. These women were vulnerable to involvement in criminal behavior, particularly prostitution. Organizations were formed to assist these young black women in adjusting to life in urban areas. Foremost among these was the National League for the Protection of Colored Women, established in New York City in 1905. Other organizations were created to unite and empower the new black citizens. The National Negro Business League was formed in 1900, the National Association for the Advancement of Colored People (NAACP) in 1909, and the National Urban League in 1911.

In addition to migration within the United States, some former slaves proposed immigration to Africa, in particular Liberia, as a solution to their problems. Liberia, "founded" by the American Colonization Society in 1817, was extolled by both blacks and whites as a panacea to race and slavery issues. Henry Adams, a freedman from Louisiana who had gained political attention through his work with the Republican Party, campaigned strongly for immigration to Liberia. During the late 1870s and early 1880s, Adams and others with similar feelings gave voice to the anguish and growing frustration of the former slaves by focusing attention on the idea of emigration. Liberia is a setting in Henry F. Downing's *The American Cavalryman: A Liberian Romance* (1917), a narrative of emotional and political relationships among white Americans, white Liberians, native black Liberians, and Americans of mixed blood.

Marcus Garvey (1887–1940) and the "Garveyites" were among proponents of sending African Americans "back" to Africa. Garvey founded the Universal Negro Improvement Association (UNIA) in Jamaica in 1914. When he migrated to New York in 1916, he moved the UNIA headquarters with him. Garvey's weekly newspaper *Negro World,* published from 1918 to 1933, was managed and staffed entirely by blacks. The UNIA proposed sending American blacks to Africa not as migrants but as missionaries and ambassadors, bringing education, independence, and Christianity to Africans.

Not all African Americans supported migration. Frederick Douglass (1818–1895) strongly opposed emigration from America to Africa. He argued that

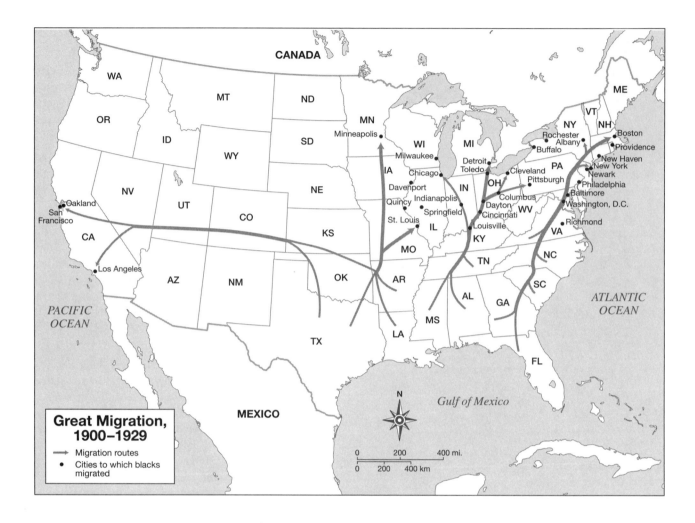

Great Migration, 1900–1929

→ Migration routes
● Cities to which blacks migrated

American Negroes were, first and foremost, Americans. For these Americans to leave their country would diminish the blacks and the country: "Drive out the negro and you drive out Christ, the Bible, and American liberty with him. The thought of setting apart a State or Territory and confining the negro within its borders is a delusion" (p. 390).

In contrast to the migration to northern cities, some southern blacks sought rural areas in the West and Midwest, where they hoped to purchase or homestead their own farmland. Due to John Brown's highly publicized abolitionist activities in Kansas during the summer of 1856, some African Americans thought of Kansas as a land of freedom. Several black Kansas towns were founded in the late 1870s and early 1880s. Of these, Nicodemus remains the most famous. Located in northwestern Kansas, Nicodemus was founded by African American settlers from Kentucky. Two white real estate developers, W. R. Hill and W. J. Niles, had recruited the settlers for the town. The Nicodemus Historical Society still promotes Nicodemus as "an all African-American pioneer town."

A Nicodemus resident and Kansas state auditor from 1883 to 1887, E. P. McCabe envisioned the settlement of Oklahoma as a black state. He helped found Langston, Oklahoma, forty miles northwest of Oklahoma City on the direct route of the Santa Fe Railroad. A college established in Langston was first named the Colored Agricultural and Normal College, then Langston College, and now Langston University; it remains a predominantly African American university. Liberty, Oklahoma, another black township, was promoted by McCabe and the African Methodist Episcopal (AME) Church but was abandoned because of the racial violence of the white residents of nearby Perry. Boley, Oklahoma, was settled on land previously owned by Creek Nation freedmen. Taft, Oklahoma, was a settlement of black freemen on land bought from D. H. Twine, a prominent black man in the area. The black Blind and Orphan Home, the State Training Institute for black girls, and the state hospital for the insane were established in Taft.

All black migrants did not travel to the North or to the Midwest. In 1900 Frank Boyer and Daniel

Keyes walked from Georgia to southeastern New Mexico. On 5 September 1903 Boyer and Keyes, among others, signed the articles of incorporation for the Blackdom Townsite Company in order to establish a "Negro colony." Blackdom was a moderately successful farming settlement even though drilling artesian wells in semiarid New Mexico was very costly. By the early 1920s, due to crop failure and lack of water, residents had abandoned Blackdom. Most relocated in nearby Roswell, Artesia, and Hobbs. These black settlements are among the dozens established between the Civil War and the Great Depression.

Due to economic difficulties, many residents left the black townships, frequently settling in established African American communities in large northern cities. In 1870 U.S. census figures indicate that over thirty-one southern-born blacks had moved from Kentucky or Tennessee to East North Central states, mostly Ohio, Indiana, and Illinois. During the same period, 13,889 Virginia-born blacks were living in Ohio.

Although some African Americans migrated to the North, most moved primarily within the South. As William Cohen states, "The pattern began to change in the 1890s, but it was not until the decade of World War I that the northward movement assumed truly significant proportions" (p. 93). According to Carter G. Woodson, among the first African American historians, the black populations of some major cities increased by several thousand in the decade between 1900 and 1910. Chicago's black population grew from thirty thousand to forty thousand, Philadelphia's from sixty thousand to eighty-five thousand, and New York's from sixty thousand to ninety thousand.

RURAL TO URBAN MIGRATION

In addition to the movement from the South to the North, Americans were moving in large numbers from rural to urban areas. In the decades after the Civil War urban population figures steadily rose, except for the 1870s. The panic of 1873 caused a decrease in manufacturing, and many industrial workers moved to rural areas. From the 1880s through the first quarter of the twentieth century, urban population steadily grew.

The literature of the period reflects this shift from rural to urban population. In the opening passage of *Sister Carrie* (1900), Theodore Dreiser (1871–1945) writes of the evil city where innocents from small towns and farms are corrupted. In the final section of Sherwood Anderson's *Winesburg, Ohio* (1919), the young protagonist, as naive as any of the era's innocents, leaves his small hometown for the big city and a career as a journalist. The protagonists of Bayard Taylor's novels *John Godfrey's Fortunes* (1864) and *Joseph and His Friend* (1871) leave rural Pennsylvania for New York City.

In *Main-Travelled Roads* (1891), Hamlin Garland (1860–1940) deals with aspects of the American migration from rural to urban communities. "Up the Coulee" is the story of a man who has moved to the city where he has become accustomed to his life as an actor in the large urban atmosphere. When he returns to his rural home, he realizes that he has very little in common with his relatives and old friends. He has moved beyond his hometown, socially and emotionally. In "God's Ravens" a Chicago man returns to the farmlands of his childhood where he recovers his failing health through the simple kindness and devotion of the farmers. He was unhappy in the city but finds peace and happiness in the village. The protagonist of "A Branch Road" also returns to his rural home and is able to save his long-time beloved from a cruel husband and the drudgery of farm labor. In dozens of novels Horatio Alger Jr. writes of the "rags to riches" stories of young men from rural areas who become successful in the big city through their determination and hard work.

THE WEST AND BEYOND

Hamlin Garland echoes Alger's sentiments in his novel *The Long Trail* (1907), in which a young man leaves Minnesota for the Klondike. Over several months of traveling north he experiences adventures with his new prospecting friends. With hard work and determination, he makes his fortune in the Yukon gold fields and returns home a local hero. Jack London (1876–1916) also wrote of travel to the Klondike and other northern regions. The characters of "To Build a Fire" (the 1908 version), "An Odyssey of the North" (1900), and *The Call of the Wild* (1903) do not have the luck of the protagonist of *The Long Trail*. Unsuited for the harsh environment, they suffer defeat and often death in their struggles against nature.

The Great Migration, homesteading, land runs, and other large-scale internal migration are indications of the vast changes occurring in the United States during the late nineteenth century and early twentieth century. Migration literature stands as a record of the growth and power of the nation between the Civil War and World War II.

See also Blacks; City Dwellers; Frontier; Immigration; *Main-Travelled Roads;* Reconstruction

BIBLIOGRAPHY
Primary Works

Anderson, Sherwood. *Winesburg, Ohio*. 1919. New York: Modern Library, 1947.

Cherokee Cavaliers: Forty Years of Cherokee History as Told in the Correspondence of the Ridge-Watie-Boudinot Family. Edited by Edward Everett Dale and Gaston Litton. Norman: University of Oklahoma Press, 1939.

Chesnutt, Charles Waddell. *Tales of Conjure and the Color Line.* Mineola, N.Y.: Dover, 1998.

Douglass, Frederick. "The Future of Blacks in the United States." In *"The Narrative" and Selected Writings.* New York: Modern Library, 1984.

Downing, Henry F. *The American Cavalryman: A Liberian Romance.* 1917. College Park, Md.: McGrath, 1969.

Dreiser, Theodore. *Sister Carrie.* 1900. New York: Penguin, 1980.

Dunbar, Paul Laurence. *The Sport of the Gods.* 1901. New York: New American Library, 1999.

Garland, Hamlin. *The Long Trail: A Story of the Northwest Wilderness.* New York: Harper & Brothers, 1907.

Garland, Hamlin. *Main-Travelled Roads.* 1891. New York: New American Library, 1962.

Gilmore, F. Grant. *The Problem: A Military Novel.* 1915. College Park, Md.: McGrath, 1969.

Johnson, James Weldon. *The Autobiography of an Ex-Colored Man.* 1912. New York: Knopf, 1927.

Jones, J. McHenry. *Hearts of Gold.* 1896. College Park, Md.: McGrath, 1969.

London, Jack. *The Call of the Wild.* 1903. New York: Dutton, 1968.

London, Jack. *Short Stories of Jack London: Authorized One-Volume Edition.* Edited by Earle Labor, Robert C. Leitz III, and I. Milo Shepard. New York: Macmillan, 1990.

Micheaux, Oscar. *The Conquest: The Story of a Negro Pioneer.* 1913. New York: Washington Square Press, 2003.

Micheaux, Oscar. *The Homesteader.* 1917. College Park, Md.: McGrath, 1969.

Taylor, Bayard. *John Godfrey's Fortunes: Related by Himself; A Story of American Life.* 1864. New York: Putnam, 1883.

Taylor, Bayard. *Joseph and His Friend: A Story of Pennsylvania.* New York: Putnam, 1871.

Twain, Mark. *Adventures of Huckleberry Finn.* 1885. New York: Norton, 1977.

Secondary Works

Chandler, Alfred D., Jr. *The Railroads: The Nation's First Big Business; Sources and Readings.* New York: Harcourt, Brace, and World, 1965.

Cohen, William. *At Freedom's Edge: Black Mobility and the Southern White Quest for Racial Control, 1861–1915.* Baton Rouge: Louisiana State University Press, 1991.

Crockett, Norman L. *The Black Towns.* Lawrence: Regents Press of Kansas, 1979.

Glaab, Charles N. *The American City: A Documentary History.* Homewood, Ill.: Dorsey Press, 1963.

Greene, J. Lee. *Blacks in Eden: The African American Novel's First Century.* Charlottesville: University Press of Virginia, 1996.

Hoig, Stan. *The Oklahoma Land Rush of 1889.* Oklahoma City: Oklahoma Historical Society, 1989.

Nicodemus, Kansas. Bogue, Kans.: Nicodemus Historical Society, 1989.

Painter, Nell Irvin. *Exodusters: Black Migration to Kansas after Reconstruction.* New York: Knopf, 1977.

Rodgers, Lawrence R. *Canaan Bound: The African-American Great Migration Novel.* Urbana: University of Illinois Press, 1997.

Vincent, Theodore G. *Black Power and the Garvey Movement.* San Francisco: Ramparts Press, 1972.

Wiseman, Regge N. *Glimpses of Late Frontier Life in New Mexico's Southern Pecos Valley: Archaeology and History at Blackdom and Seven Rivers.* Santa Fe: Museum of New Mexico, 2000.

Woodson, Carter G. *A Century of Negro Migration.* 1918. New York: AMS Press, 1970.

Kelvin Beliele

MISCEGENATION

Although the concept of miscegenation was known in Europe and England, the word was a New World neologism, first suggested by the authors of an 1863 pamphlet "Miscegenation," who coined it seemingly to advocate abolition and "the blending of the races," as stated in the work's subtitle. In fact, the tract was actually written by the anti-abolitionists David G. Croly and George Wakeman, who hoped to suggest the Republican Party and President Abraham Lincoln, who had just issued the Emancipation Proclamation, favored racial amalgamation. From its very coinage, then, the term "miscegenation" was intended to fuel racist fury. Racist attitudes toward intermarriage predated the term, of course, and the possibility that white men or women would have children with members of other races engendered hatred and fear among many people. The Puritans, for example, were outraged by the North American colonial leader Thomas Morton's suggestion that his young men, far from home and English women, should take

Native American women as wives. Likewise, cultural and legal prohibitions against "amalgamation" with African slaves and free blacks were created and, to some degree, enforced. If, as W. E. B. Du Bois (1868–1963) stated in *The Souls of Black Folk: Essays and Sketches* (1903), "the problem of the twentieth-century is the problem of the color-line" (p. xi), mixed-race characters and miscegenation in fiction pose and interrogate that problem. Literary discussions of miscegenation are, to a great degree, the history of how society tried to insist on an ineradicable line between the races, while mixed-race characters, by definition, propose a redrawing of the lines or their complete abandonment.

THE CIVIL WAR AND THE RECONSTRUCTION OF RACIAL IDENTITY

With the end of slavery, one of the legal lines between black and white was removed, but legal definitions of race were not, nor were laws against miscegenation; in fact, the term was given new legal life, with dozens of states passing antimiscegenation laws from 1867 to the 1880s. As a result, the novel of "the tragic mulatto" who is an alien in two worlds remained fashionable even after the Civil War. Such stories feature a character who may appear white but who is in fact racially mixed. Albion Tourgée (1838–1905), a northerner who served as a federal judge in the South during Reconstruction, wrote several such novels. While the best known is his autobiographical novel *A Fool's Errand* (1879), recounting his experiences as a "carpetbagger" during Reconstruction, Tourgée wrote many other novels about the race problem in the South, including some that dealt with intermarriage between blacks and whites. *Toinette* (1874), later republished as *A Royal Gentleman* (1881), features a slave owner who falls in love with his mixed-race servant only to reject her even after emancipation because she is not white. *Pactolus Prime* (1890) likewise tells the story of a mixed-blood character who hopes for equality as well as freedom after emancipation but ultimately comes to dour conclusions about the future.

George Washington Cable (1844–1925) perfected the novel of the tragic mulatto who is alienated from two societies in *The Grandissimes: A Story of Creole Life* (1880). Against the backdrop of a history that blended Native American, African American, French, Spanish, and British cultures and bloodlines, Cable's novel of postbellum Louisiana features seemingly infinite gradations of race and ethnicity. Cable's novel relates the practical difficulties facing people of mixed heritage who rise economically but who fear they will never be accepted socially. Cable's narrator

observes that even legal protections are insufficient guarantors of real freedom in a society where the law of racial purity is written in culture. The novel *Ramona* (1884) by Helen Hunt Jackson (1830–1885) is one of the most successful works of the 1880s treating the theme of miscegenation; in it Jackson challenges many mixed-race stereotypes and social strictures against intermarriage. Ramona, the daughter of a Scotsman and a Native American woman, attempts to find a social identity uniting and honoring both parents.

During the 1890s, literary depictions of mixed-race characters became, if anything, more provocative. This change was precipitated in large part by the increasing legal oppression of people of color, including those of mixed race. Legally, the "separate but equal" theory was codified in law by the Supreme Court case of *Plessy v. Ferguson* in 1896. Consequently, a person with "one drop" of so-called black blood could be legally defined as black and segregated from whites. *The Tragedy of Pudd'nhead Wilson* (1894) by Mark Twain (1835–1910) responds directly to the issues raised by the *Plessy v. Ferguson* case. This work features several mixed-race characters, among them Roxy, who appears white but has 1/16 part of "black blood" and is, therefore, a slave. She is the product of several generations of miscegenation. As the nursemaid to two children, hers and her master's, she switches the two. Her action goes undetected for decades but, ironically, her own son, trained as a white slave owner, mistreats and even sells Roxy. The master's biological son, named Chambers, might look white but is in every cultural sense black. Twain satirizes American racial attitudes, particularly the notion that such racial distinctions as the "one drop" theory have a real validity. When Roxy's switch is uncovered, her son, who has been trained as the master of the house, is sold downriver, and the illiterate Chambers inherits property, including slaves. Twain thus satirizes the very idea of such arbitrary racial distinctions, revealing race to be a cultural construct rather than a biological fact. Twain also uses race to discuss gender and vice versa by having the character Tom dress like a woman as part of the novel's mystery plot. In having a "black" pass for white and a man pass for a woman, Twain uses the novel to undermine racial and gender categories. Further, Roxy's "sermon" on free grace has her speaking on the text, "Ain't nobody kin save his own self" (p. 931). In this way, Twain describes the inevitability of the white and black bond in American society, suggesting a shared identity, fate, and community along with the shared kinship at the heart of the miscegenation plot.

The novel *Iola Leroy; or, Shadows Uplifted* (1892) by Frances Ellen Watkins Harper (1825–1911) seems in some ways to begin where *The Tragedy of Pudd'nhead Wilson* leaves off but from the perspective of a woman. At the beginning of the novel, the title character is a Scarlett O'Hara–type southern belle, at one with regional politics and mores. The daughter of a wealthy planter, Iola discovers only after her father's death that her mother was part black, a "mulatta." Sold into slavery, this flower of white, southern race training eventually escapes and becomes an advocate for black Americans. Iola ultimately embraces the identity society confers upon her, refusing to pass as white, though she certainly is capable of doing so.

An ironic twist on the theme of miscegenation is presented by Kate Chopin (1851–1904) in "Désirée's Baby," which was first published in her collection of stories *Bayou Folk* in 1894. The short story depicts the horror with which "accidental" miscegenation was held in the South, when people were uncertain of the racial heritages of those closest to them or even their own backgrounds. In this story, the formal conflict is provoked by racist prohibitions against intermarriage and by the existence of characters who can "pass" as white or who do pass as white without even being aware of their background. Having given birth to a child with a complexion suggesting he is a "quadroon" and one-quarter black, the title character is suspected of having "black blood" in her lineage. Her punctilious husband rejects her and the child and sends them away from the house, discovering later, to his horror, that he is the one with such an ancestry. In the language of their society, he is the one "guilty" of miscegenation, and his wife, from the perspective of racist laws, is the injured party.

ECONOMIES OF PASSING

Related to the novel of miscegenation is the novel of "passing," a novel featuring a character who appears white but who is, in fact, of mixed race. Such a person often "passes" as white for social or economic reasons. The incentive to do so grew as so-called Jim Crow laws proliferated in the South, as the Ku Klux Klan (KKK) became an active force of oppression and intimidation, and as large numbers of blacks were lynched. Drawing from his own observations of society, and from his own mixed-race heritage, Charles Waddell Chesnutt (1858–1932) announced in his essay "What Is a White Man?" (1889) that "the line which separates the races must in many instances have been practically obliterated" (p. 5). In his fiction, Chesnutt illustrates this idea frequently, portraying many mixed-race individuals and instances of intermarriage, most famously in *The House behind the Cedars* (1900) and *The Marrow of Tradition* (1901). In the former, Chesnutt tells the story of brother and sister, children of a woman of mixed blood. John Warwick passes as white and marries the daughter of a plantation family, while his sister is on the verge of contracting a similar marriage when her past is revealed. Chesnutt returned to the theme in *The Marrow of Tradition*.

Pauline Hopkins (1859–1930) explores similar situations in her novels *Contending Forces: A Romance Illustrative of Negro Life North and South* (1900), *Hagar's Daughter: A Story of Caste Prejudice* (1901–1902), *Winona: A Tale of Negro Life in the South and Southwest* (1902), and *Of One Blood; or, The Hidden Self* (1902–1903). In *Hagar's Daughter,* Hopkins introduces the theme of miscegenation through two young women, Jewell and Aurelia. Both are accepted in white society until the secret of Jewell's ancestry is revealed. While Aurelia is more "successful" by all contemporary social definitions, Jewell is the moral center of the novel. Hopkins's character Reuel Briggs in *Of One Blood* is one of her most interesting. The opening chapters of the book find Briggs, who believes himself white, reading a treatise called "The Unclassified Residuum," referring to a passage in William James's (1842–1910) study "The Hidden Self," which Hopkins uses as a subtitle for her novel. James had used the term "unclassified residuum" while discussing psychical phenomena, and Hopkins exploits it both for psychic and social purposes, to discuss the "residuum" of blood prejudice in American culture (p. 361). The novel charts Briggs's journey to self-discovery as he travels to Africa, finding that he is "of one blood" with Africans and, in a larger sense, that all humankind is "of one blood."

Interestingly, while "passing" undermines imposed racial definitions, it is often depicted in literature as a negative action but from different perspectives. Thomas Dixon (1864–1946) wrote the historical antimiscegenation and antiblack novels *The Leopard's Spots* (1902) and *The Clansman* (1905), which were adapted by D. W. Griffith into the controversial film *The Birth of a Nation* (1915). Both books feature mixed-race characters who pass as white as part of a covert plot to exploit the South and transform the United States into a "mulatto" society rather than one dominated by Anglo-Saxons.

However, neither is "passing" portrayed positively in James Weldon Johnson's (1871–1938) *The Autobiography of an Ex-Colored Man* (1912). Born to a mulatto mother and white father in the South, the narrator tells a story reminiscent of many other narratives featuring miscegenation as a theme. In this highly complex and delightfully ironic novel, Johnson's narrator details how passing is for him a joke. At whose expense the joke is has been a subject of much critical debate. On the one hand, the narrator plays a joke on himself, losing an integral sense of his own identity by passing as white. On the other hand, the joke is at the expense of the society that creates the context for passing through its racism and racist laws. The novel ends with the narrator passing as an anonymous white man, a racial trickster set loose within racist society. By showing that the narrator is able to pass, Johnson asserts that race definitions are artificial constructions.

Edith Maude Eaton (1865–1914), who wrote under the pen name Sui Sin Far, was born to a Chinese mother and an English father. Thus, like Charles W. Chesnutt, her own mixed-race background probably influenced her frequent choice of themes of miscegenation, passing, and crossing boundaries and borders. One is tempted to suggest that her pen name, Sui Sin Far, is itself an inversion of the usual pattern of passing, for it allows her to "pass" as Chinese. Eaton wrote in her autobiographical work "Leaves from the Mental Portfolio of an Eurasian" (1909) that she was a stranger in the world by virtue of her racial heritage, distanced even from her parents. Many of the characters in her story collection *Mrs. Spring Fragrance* (1912) are similarly estranged from two worlds, rather than belonging to both.

Indeed, the miscegenation plot itself might be defined as a literary form that foregrounds estrangement even as it imagines community. At the heart of the form is the question of the "color line" that Du Bois saw as America's preeminent challenge.

See also The Autobiography of an Ex-Colored Man; The Birth of a Nation; Blacks; Civil Rights; Iola Leroy; Ku Klux Klan; The Marrow of Tradition; Mrs. Spring Fragrance; Race Novels; Ramona

BIBLIOGRAPHY
Primary Works
Chesnutt, Charles. "What Is A White Man?" *Independent* 41 (30 May 1889): 5–6.

Croly, David G. *Miscegenation: The Theory of the Blending of the Races, Applied to the American White Man and Negro.* New York: H. Dexter, Hamilton & Company, 1864.

Dixon, Thomas. *The Clansman: An Historical Romance of the Ku Klux Klan.* New York: Doubleday & Page, 1905.

Dixon, Thomas. *The Leopard's Spots: A Romance of the White Man's Burden—1865–1900.* New York: Doubleday & Page, 1902.

Du Bois, W. E. B. *The Souls of Black Folk: Essays and Sketches.* New York: Signet, 1969.

Eaton, Edith Maude [Sui Sin Far]. "Leaves from the Mental Portfolio of an Eurasian." *Independent* 66 (1909): 125–132.

Eaton, Edith Maude [Sui Sin Far]. *Mrs. Spring Fragrance and Other Writings.* Urbana: University of Illinois Press, 1995.

Hopkins, Pauline Elizabeth. *Hagar's Daughter: A Story of Southern Caste Prejudice.* In *The Magazine Novels of Pauline Hopkins,* pp. 1–284. Cambridge, Mass.: Harvard University Press, 1988.

Hopkins, Pauline Elizabeth. *Of One Blood; or, The Hidden Self.* In *The Magazine Novels of Pauline Hopkins,* pp. 439–672. Cambridge, Mass.: Harvard University Press, 1988.

Hopkins, Pauline Elizabeth. *Winona: A Tale of Negro Life in the South and Southwest.* In *The Magazine Novels of Pauline Hopkins,* pp. 285–438. Cambridge, Mass.: Harvard University Press, 1988.

James, William. "The Hidden Self." *Scribners* 7 (1890): 361–373.

Johnson, James Weldon. *The Autobiography of an Ex-Coloured Man.* New York: Hill and Wang, 1960.

Twain, Mark. *The Tragedy of Pudd'nhead Wilson.* In *Mississippi Writings,* pp. 915–1056. New York: Library of America, 1982.

Secondary Works
Berzon, Judith R. *Neither White nor Black: The Mulatto Character in American Fiction.* New York: New York University Press, 1978.

Bost, Suzanne. *Mulattas and Mestizas: Representing Mixed Identities in the Americas, 1850–2000.* Athens: University of Georgia Press, 2003.

Cutter, Martha J. "Struggling across the Borders of Race, Gender, and Sexuality: Sui Sin Far's *Mrs. Spring Fragrance.*" In *Mixed Race Literature,* edited by Jonathan Brennan, pp. 137–164. Stanford, Calif.: Stanford University Press, 2002.

Fabi, M. Giulia. *Passing and the Rise of the African American Novel.* Urbana: University of Illinois Press, 2001.

Fredrickson, George M. *The Black Image in the White Mind: The Debate on Afro-American Character and Destiny, 1817–1914.* New York: Harper and Row, 1971.

Fulton, Joe B. "Mark Twain and the Multicultural Imagination." In *Multiculturalism: Roots and Realities,* edited by C. James Trotman, pp. 238–251. Bloomington: Indiana University Press, 2002.

Ings, Katharine Nicholson. "Blackness and the Literary Imagination: Uncovering *The Hidden Hand.*" In *Passing and the Fictions of Identity,* edited by Elaine K. Ginsberg, pp. 131–150. Durham, N.C.: Duke University Press, 1996.

Kaplan, Sidney. *American Studies in Black and White: Selected Essays, 1949–1989.* Amherst: University of Massachusetts Press, 1991.

Kinney, James. *AMALGAMATION! Race, Sex, and Rhetoric in the Nineteenth-Century American Novel.* Westport, Conn.: Greenwood Press, 1985.

Sollors, Werner. *Neither Black nor White Yet Both: Thematic Explorations of Interracial Literature.* New York: Oxford University Press, 1997.

Sollors, Werner, ed. *Interracialism: Black-White Intermarriage in American History, Literature, and Law.* New York: Oxford University Press, 2000.

Sundquist, Eric J. *To Wake the Nations: Race in the Making of American Literature.* Cambridge, Mass.: Belknap Press of Harvard University Press, 1993.

Wald, Gayle. *Crossing the Line: Racial Passing in Twentieth-Century U.S. Literature and Culture.* Durham, N.C.: Duke University Press, 2000.

Joe B. Fulton

MOON-CALF

Moon-Calf (1920), a thinly veiled autobiographical novel by Floyd Dell (1887–1969), covers the early part of the author's life to 1909. It is the story of Felix Fay, descended from a Civil War hero, born late to his parents, and from his earliest days a sickly child. It is clear to all that this boy is different—he is quiet, withdrawn, and a dreamer. Felix befriends those older than he is, many of them women who are drawn to his sensitive nature, and he engages them in talk of art, poetry, and literature. His intellectual prowess quickly outgrows his family, and he begins a series of moves that take him from the midwestern rural setting of Maple to the growing modern industrial and commercial city of Port Royal. Along the way he meets librarians and libertarians who direct his reading and thinking and who encourage his own attempts at poetry. He is openly atheistic and holds socialist views, attending meetings and becoming an activist. He is attractive to women of a certain type—women who admire him for his views and his poetry as much as for his looks. After a time of hardship and exploitation working in a candy factory, Felix gains a position at the local newspaper. He is fired after accusations of anti-Semitism by the paper's owner, but the editor who believes in his talents as a writer rehires him, and Felix becomes the regular drama critic of the publication. The final section of the novel is dedicated to Felix's affair with Joyce Tennant,

the niece of the wealthiest and most influential lawyer in Port Royal. They use an idyllic retreat known as "The Cabin," a summer cottage by the lake, to practice an alternative lifestyle that is built on love, aestheticism, and equality and that totally rejects the traditional concept of marriage.

European intellectuals like Karl Marx and Sigmund Freud were very influential in American writing of this postwar period. *Moon-Calf* is heavily influenced by Freudian symbolism and interpretation, especially in the Oedipal search that is at the core of many of Felix's relationships. In many respects the novel finds a transatlantic partner in D. H. Lawrence's *Sons and Lovers* (1913). Certainly the freedom with which Dell writes about physical relationships that shake moral conventions is one element that some readers may find surprising and extremely modern, for example, discussions between Joyce and Felix regarding the nature of marriage and the limitations of monogamy. Felix sees marriage as a social construct that serves little purpose, and at first Joyce agrees with him. In the chapter called "Ethics," Felix explains, "I don't say . . . that a free society can be created all at once, or that any two individuals should crucify themselves before the public in the name of principle. Though if any two people wanted to do that, I would think it splendid of them" (p. 293). His idea of the perfect union extends to the couple not living together, because then "they spend as much time together as they can in each other's company, precisely because they don't have to. When they have to, they want to be apart" (p. 294). In time, however, Joyce feels the need to legitimize their relationship in society, and when Felix is unable to respond to her desires—highlighted by Felix moving away from Joyce to work on his novel—Joyce announces her engagement to an alternative and traditional suitor. Felix finds himself liberated (if also confused and hurt) by her decision and decides to move to a bigger city to pursue a career in journalism. His idealism seems reasonably intact as he looks forward to a move to the "dark blotch" in the corner of the map of the Midwest: "Chicago!" (p. 346).

The genesis of *Moon-Calf* was long and painful. Dell had been attempting to write a novel for years and finally took a leave of absence from *The Liberator* in February 1920 to concentrate on it, a decision influenced by blinding headaches that he saw as "psychic." He had been frozen by the inability to sort out his experiences for retelling as fiction and by uncertainty about how to frame the work stylistically. He found the way through reading Tolstoy's "Childhood, Boyhood, and Youth" and a discussion with the British writer Arnold Bennett, who told Dell that a novelist

A discussion between Felix Fay, the central figure of Moon-Calf, *and his socialist mentor Vogelsang highlights the differences between the idealism of poetry and the reality of an industrial and capitalist America. Vogelsang tells Felix:*

"The American bourgeoisie pays millions of dollars a year to support colleges to teach young people like you to believe in ideals—and to stop looking at economic facts. You tell me that you will have to keep on working—that you cannot afford to go back to school. You are wrong. Do not think for a minute that the American bourgeoisie wants you to work in its factories. No— you might get tired of your ideals, and see what is going on in those factories. . . . You want to be a poet? Very well; lift your hand, and it is done. Say the word, and you shall spend the rest of your life writing pretty verses about yourself, like those you have shown me. No, you do not know the world you live in. . . . I have been trying to get it into your head that you are a member of what is in Europe called the intellectual proletariat. If I can get you to understand what that means, you can work out the implications of it for yourself. Perhaps I am mistaken. Perhaps you are just a romantic proletarian, and will go on working in a factory and writing bad verses; perhaps you are not a real proletarian at all, but the offspring of a broken-down, middle-class family, in which case you will go back to where you belong. That is more likely. But I have hopes for you."

"Do you mean that I should work for Socialism?"

"More romantic nonsense! No, no self-sacrifice, no martyrdom. Socialism does not need your help. On the contrary, it will help you."

Dell, *Moon-Calf,* pp. 191–193.

"learns everything he knows of people before . . . twenty-one years of age, possibly earlier" (Hart, p. 66). Psychoanalysis helped Dell choose the "emotionally important incidents and people in my youthful life, and to emphasize certain aspects of these" (p. 67). He used Felix to dramatize the ideas that were so important to him, avoiding tricks of style and constructing a true alter ego for himself through fiction. The result,

says John E. Hart, is that Felix Fay becomes "both an individual and a type" (p. 67).

Dell's novel was published two days after Sinclair Lewis's *Main Street,* and according to Dell it rode the wave of Lewis's success because of the midwestern focus and the treatment of proletarian themes. By early 1922 *Moon-Calf* had been reprinted eleven times. Critics who saw a new focus on literature from the heartland compared Lewis, Dell, Sherwood Anderson, and Zona Gale. Dell and Lewis publicly admired each other's work, although Dell deplored the fact that Lewis's idealistic heroine gives in to conventionalism and commercialism in *Main Street,* something his protagonist would never do. To explain this difference, Lewis pointed out that Felix was clearly representative of Dell—"a genius," he called him— while his heroine Carol Kennicott "distinctly is not Sinclair Lewis" (Tanselle, p. 177).

When *Moon-Calf* appeared, Dell's friends and admirers rallied to its cause, recognizing its political, social, and cultural value as well as the way it covers Dell's own political and artistic awakening. In the *Chicago Daily News,* Harry Hansen proclaimed that this single novel would earn Dell a "permanent place in the literature of America" (27 October 1920). Francis Hackett wrote in the *New Republic* that Felix Fay (and by association, Dell himself) was "the weak but ruthless literary apprentice" (8 December 1920, p. 49). The *New York Times* reviewer claimed: "So skillfully has the author drawn his poignant portrait of a sensitive idealist in conflict with a hostile, workaday world that the reader will soon cease to think of Felix as a character in a novel. Rather, he will think that he is the novelist himself dressed in the incognito of a few imaginary experiences" (12 December 1920, p. 20). Robert Benchley admired the book too, calling it "a subtle character study accomplished by narrative episodes rather than detailed analyses." He also warned, however, that "some readers will object to this on moral grounds," suggesting that the book was "not for the small library" (*Bookman,* February 1921, p. 559). Overall the novel was very favorably reviewed alongside *Main Street;* indeed, many found strengths in Dell's novel that eclipsed Lewis's work.

CAREER OF FLOYD DELL

Dell was born in Barry, Illinois, in 1887. His father was a butcher who moved the family to the old river city of Quincy and then to Davenport, Iowa (the model for Port Royal in *Moon-Calf*), in 1903. Dell was encouraged to write by his mother, who was a schoolteacher, while his father managed to find Dell a position on a local newspaper, the *Davenport Times.*

His father's connections to the Republican Party managed to protect him when he joined the local branch of the Socialist Party at age sixteen. Dell also wrote regularly for the socialist *Tri-Cities Workers' Magazine*. In 1908 he left Davenport to move to Chicago, but he returned to his roots on numerous occasions, both physically and in his fiction. Davenport provided a lot of material for his writing and was for the most part a safe venue in which to flex his political muscles: Dell could complain about local institutions and write of them critically, but Davenport was also a city that tolerated such views with reasonably good humor. As Dell grew older he was very aware of this fact, and in no way did he satirize or reject the small town, as Sinclair Lewis would do.

In 1911 Dell became the editor of the *Friday Literary Review* in Chicago, and he promoted writers he believed capable of effecting social reform through their work. He was a champion of David Graham Phillips and Charles Edward Russell as well as more established writers, such as Upton Sinclair, Theodore Dreiser, and Jack London. His knowledge of international movements and literature led him to feature work by socially aware luminaries from Europe—authors like Arnold Bennett, Susan Glaspell, G. K. Chesterton, and Hilaire Belloc. Moving to New York in 1914 to work on the *Masses,* a radical journal, Dell was instrumental in commissioning pieces from Sherwood Anderson and Carl Sandburg. In 1916 Dell became involved with the Provincetown Players, joining fellow members Eugene O'Neill, Edna St. Vincent Millay, Louise Bryant, and John Reed.

In 1917, when the United States joined the war in Europe, the *Masses* was pressured to reverse its antiwar stance. When the board refused, mailing privileges for the journal were revoked. In July 1917 Dell and Max Eastman were charged under the Espionage Act, accused of writing articles designed to undermine the war effort. The case came to court in 1918, forcing the *Masses* to close down, but after three days of deliberation, the jury could not agree upon a verdict. The case was brought again in 1919, and despite the lack of a unanimous verdict once more, the case was dropped because the war was now over. The editors of the *Masses* regrouped, and a new journal, *The Liberator,* appeared and ran until 1924. The *New Masses* began publication in 1924 and continued in print until 1939, with Dell as a frequent contributor.

The novels that followed *Moon-Calf*—*The Briary-Bush* (1921), *Janet Marsh* (1923), and *Runaway* (1925)—were less favorably received. For some, the focus on the misunderstood poet and social iconoclast restricted Dell to being somewhat one-note in his work. Robert Coates said Dell's work was focused "the same as always" on youth in revolt but that the rebels never really got anywhere, except to Chicago. Dell also wrote several nonfiction books, including *Upton Sinclair* (1927) and *Love in the Machine Age* (1930). In 1933 he published *Homecoming,* an amalgam of the autobiographical novels on which his reputation was to rest.

SOCIALISM AND THE AFTERMATH OF THE WAR

For the modern reader, *Moon-Calf* provides useful insight into social and political feelings following the apocalypse of World War I. Many Americans returned from the war disillusioned and horrified by the destruction brought by the first modern mechanized war. Approximately 120,000 enlisted Americans died in the war, and the financial cost to the United States exceeded $20 billion. For many, socialism seemed to be the ideological answer to avoiding a repeat event, and socialist movements would wax and wane in popularity and political influence over the next half century. In *Moon-Calf,* Dell cleverly captures Felix's growing awareness of real-world politics along with his growing cynicism, and yet he fondly reiterates Felix's determination to rise above such drudgery and to keep alive a positive vision for the future.

Dell's socialist stance and expression of a political ideology belongs to a tradition of socialist writing that also includes works of Upton Sinclair and Jack London. Writers more contemporaneous with Dell also saw the aftermath of the war as being a difficult, divisive, and unsettling time. This period produced novels such as Ernest Hemingway's *A Farewell to Arms* (1929), John Dos Passos's *Three Soldiers* (1921), and William Faulkner's *Soldier's Pay* (1926) as well as Maxwell Anderson and Laurence Stallings's play *What Price Glory?* (produced in 1924). Dos Passos wrote that the war, instead of being a threat to civilization, merely showed it up as a "vast edifice of sham."

Many soldiers from the United States who went to fight in Europe found the return to their homeland difficult, particularly those who were returning to rural areas reliant on agriculture. They became more aware of the changes wrought by increased mechanization and market forces that worked to keep crop prices and workers' wages low. For some American writers and thinkers, a return to Europe and an existence based on the relative strength of the dollar allowed them to take stock and reflect on how the modern world was shaping up. The Lost Generation writers gathered in Paris well into the 1920s, a "movable feast" of expatriates that included Hemingway, Dos

Passos, Gertrude Stein, Archibald MacLeish, Ezra Pound, and F. Scott Fitzgerald.

See also Free Love; Socialism; World War I

BIBLIOGRAPHY

Primary Works

Dell, Floyd. *Moon-Calf.* 1920. New York: Sagamore Press, 1957.

Hart, John E. *Floyd Dell.* New York: Twayne, 1971.

Tanselle, G. Thomas. "Sinclair Lewis and Floyd Dell: Two Views of the Midwest." *Twentieth Century Literature* 9, no. 4 (January 1964):175–184.

Secondary Works

Cooperman, Stanley. *World War I and the American Novel.* Baltimore: Johns Hopkins University Press, 1967.

Duffey, Bernard I. *The Chicago Renaissance in American Letters: A Critical History.* Westport, Conn.: Greenwood Press, 1954.

Pizer, Donald. *American Expatriate Writing and the Paris Moment: Modernism and Place.* Lafayette: University of Louisiana Press, 1997.

Roba, William H. "Floyd Dell in Iowa." *Books at Iowa* 44 (April 1986).

Shore, Elliott. *Talkin' Socialism: J. A. Wayland and the Role of the Press in American Radicalism, 1890–1912.* Lawrence: University of Kansas Press, 1988.

Smith, Carl S. *Chicago and the American Literary Imagination, 1880–1920.* Chicago: University of Chicago Press, 1984.

Stansell, Christine. *American Moderns: Bohemian New York and the Creation of a New Century.* New York: Metropolitan, 2000.

Tate, Trudi. *Modernism, History, and the First World War.* Manchester, U.K.: Manchester University Press, 1998.

Keith Gumery

MORMONS

The Church of Jesus Christ of Latter-Day Saints, founded in New York state by Joseph Smith (1805–1844) in 1830, was the most controversial religion born in the United States during the religious revival of the early nineteenth century. Although the first half of its history was troubled, it is also the most successful religion to have originated in the Americas during the modern era. The period 1870–1920 marks the turbulent transition between the demonizing and the acceptance of Mormons (a nickname derived from their new scripture the Book of Mormon, published the year the church was founded). It also includes the religious, social, economic, and political

transformation of the LDS church after 1890, when it took the first measures to give up the practice of plural marriage, or polygamy, under intense pressure from the federal government. That practice had become both its theological cornerstone and the object of the longest and most intense national campaign against any religious practice or organization in U.S. history.

THEOLOGY AND THEOCRACY

The controversy surrounding Mormons had to do in part with their claim to be the only "true and restored" church of Jesus Christ (after centuries of "apostasy" in the institutional history of Christianity) and to have a new scripture that they claimed held equal status with the Bible as the word of God. Joseph Smith said he was led by an angel to ancient inscribed gold plates and was instructed to translate them. In this "New World scripture," which charts a thousand years of history on the North American continent, Christ speaks after his resurrection to the ancient inhabitants of the Americas, descendants of lost tribes of Israel who left Jerusalem and sailed to the New World in 587 B.C., when the chronicle begins. Audacious in its theology and distinguishing itself as surely from traditional Christian sects as early Christianity had distinguished itself from ancient Judaism, Mormonism made America central to the Christian historical narrative, from the location of the Garden of Eden to that of the millennial Kingdom of God, charting a global scriptural geography that explained the origin of American Indians and that positioned Latter-Day Saints (members of the restored church) as essential to the work of human salvation. Although Mark Twain (1835–1910) called the Book of Mormon "chloroform in print," and though the books about the Mormon scripture were written predominantly by defenders and critics of its historical and religious claims and of its authorship, it is also one of the most significant and unusual texts of the nineteenth century, the most imaginative exemplar of what Harold Bloom has called "the American religion." Terryl Givens has argued that the Book of Mormon is "perhaps the most religiously influential, hotly contested, and . . . intellectually underinvestigated book in America" (*By the Hand of Mormon,* p. 6).

Even more than their beliefs and scripture, however, it was the Mormons' theocratic organization, territorial presence (first in Ohio and Missouri, and more autonomously and militarily in Illinois and finally Utah Territory), their economic communalism, and especially their practice of polygamy that elicited outrage, suspicion, and political tension. After they fled persecution in Illinois and settled the Salt Lake Valley, the Mormons established a theocratic range of settlements they called "Deseret," after a name in the Book of Mormon, that reached as far as southern California and to which converts, predominantly from Britain and Scandinavia, emigrated before the Civil War, without the benefit of the transcontinental railroad (completed in Utah in 1869). National outrage over the Mountain Meadows Massacre on 11 September 1857, during which a group led by Mormon leaders killed approximately 140 men, women, and children passing through southern Utah on their way to California, made the event a touchstone of U.S.-Mormon tensions for years to come. Adding to those tensions were stories of a secret Mormon militia of "Destroying Angels" or "Danites," which made their way into popular culture in 1881 in Joaquin Miller's very popular frontier melodrama, *The Danites in the Sierras.* As Mark Twain described them, they were "Latter-day Saints who are set apart by the Church to conduct permanent disappearances of obnoxious citizens" (p. 85). The truth in these stories lay in a Mormon belief in blood atonement, but the church organization was both less tyrannical and more communal than the popular American stories made it seem.

MARK TWAIN IN UTAH

While national attention on the Mormons diminished during the Civil War, they caught the attention of the young Mark Twain on his journey to Nevada with his brother in 1861. The literary embellishment of that experience is found in several chapters of his 1872 novel and travel narrative, *Roughing It.* Although wary of sensational journalism, Twain was an admirer of the tall tale, and the mysteries surrounding "the Mormon question," as he called it, were fertile ground for both fictional invention and journalistic skepticism. Of his short time in Salt Lake City, Twain said he and his party certainly acquired more information about the Mormons, "but we did not know what portion of it was reliable and what was not. . . . We were told, for instance, that the dreadful 'Mountain Meadows Massacre' was the work of the Indians entirely, and that the Gentiles had meanly tried to fasten it on the Mormons; we were told, likewise, that the Indians were to blame, partly, and partly the Mormons; and we were told . . . that the Mormons were almost if not wholly and completely responsible. . . . All our 'information' had three sides to it, and so I gave up the idea that I could settle the 'Mormon question' in two days. Still, I have seen newspaper correspondents do it in one" (pp. 116, 117).

Twain used hyperbole to tell a truth about the romantic fictions that shaped his own—and certainly his readers'—sense of exotic western lands. With his leveling satirical wit, he brought both Mormon religion and anti-Mormon mythologizing down to an appropriately human and outrageously humorous size. "There was fascination in surreptitiously staring at every creature we took to be a Mormon," he wrote. "This was fairyland to us . . . a land of enchantment, and goblins, and awful mystery. We felt a curiosity to ask every child how many mothers it had and if it could tell them apart." Twain wrote that because he and his party were there briefly, "we had no time to make the customary inquisition into the workings of polygamy and get up the usual statistics and deductions preparatory to calling the attention of the nation at large once more to the matter." The reform movement against polygamy would last nearly another fifty years. Polygamy was decried by Americans intent on ending a practice inimical to Christian civilization, but Twain parodied that Christian reformist impulse and turned it against itself (at Mormon women's expense): "I was feverish to plunge in headlong and achieve a great reform here—until I saw the Mormon women. Then I was touched. My heart was wiser than my head. It warmed toward these poor, ungainly, and pathetically 'homely' creatures, and as I turned to hide the generous moisture in my eyes, I said, 'No—the man that marries one of them has done an act of Christian charity which entitles him to the kindly applause of mankind, not their harsh censure—and the man that marries sixty of them has done a deed of open-handed generosity so sublime that the nations should stand uncovered in his presence and worship in silence'" (pp. 97–98). Twain's characterization of Mormon women was one of many, collectively contradictory attempts in popular fiction and periodical cartoons to portray or explain polygamy through its "victims" (see Bunker and Bitton, pp. 123–126).

ANTIPOLYGAMY SENTIMENT IN LITERATURE AND LAW

Several Mormon church leaders had been practicing polygamy since 1841; in 1852 the church announced publicly its doctrine and practice of "the plurality of wives." (Mormon leaders called upon about 10 percent of the men to marry more than one wife; some refused.) In response, the antipolygamy reform movement was born and became, after antislavery, the most successful and widespread reform movement in the United States for the next half-century, spawning a literary genre to serve its purpose, the sensationalist antipolygamy novel. Drawing on the conventions of the captivity narrative, over one hundred such books were published in the United States—most of them claiming historical authenticity. Some sold more than 100,000 copies, such as Mrs. A. G. Paddock's *The Fate of Madame La Tour: A Tale of the Great Salt Lake*

(1881). The practice was the chief reason that Utah was not admitted to the Union, despite several petitions over five decades. (A recurring counterpetition to amend the U.S. Constitution to prohibit polygamy never succeeded.) The analogy with slavery (the other "twin relic of barbarism") turned on the question of Mormon women's consent, imagined to be as nonexistent as a slave's. Hence one of the conventions of the antipolygamy novel had a Mormon man either abduct or mesmerize a soon-to-be plural wife. The comparison also had sectional resonance, given the burning antebellum questions of states' rights and of whether western territories would be slaveholding or free. In her preface to the antipolygamy novel by Mrs. Stenhouse, *Tell It All* (1874), Harriet Beecher Stowe writes that now that "the slave-pens of the South have become a nightmare of the past, the hour is come to loose the bonds of a cruel slavery whose chains have cut into the very hearts of thousands of our sisters" (p. vi).

While Mormons identified Indians as descendants of ancient Hebrews, Americans often associated Mormons with a host of nonwhite and non-Christian peoples, nations, and religions: they were called "white Indians" and "white negroes," "the Islam of America," and "Confucians," among other appellations. These affiliations drew on the sense that polygamy was a non-Western, barbaric practice; that the presumed licentiousness driving polygamy implied that Mormon men had sexual drives like those ascribed to Africans or to Arab men in their harems; and that polygamy produced offspring with physical signs of racial degeneration. This racialization or casting of Mormons as non-Western also signaled one of the ideological ambitions of Manifest Destiny: conquest was justified in the battle between civilization and savagery. Seen not just as uncivilized but as a dire threat to American and Christian civilization itself, Mormons, Indians, and Asians (at times collective subjects of Western laws denying citizens' rights) could be viewed as more than just political rivals or targets: they could serve as foils for the highest ideals that the United States claimed to serve. The trope of captivity in popular antipolygamy fiction thus had national resonance—up to the silent film era and in the westerns of Zane Grey (1875–1939)—as a morally, even cosmically inflected dramatization of America's conquest and settlement of the West.

The Latter-Day Saints defended what they saw as their constitutional right to practice polygamy as a free exercise of religion; that right was put to the test when George Reynolds, a secretary to the second president of the church, Brigham Young (1801–1877), was tried and convicted of bigamy and appealed his case, which eventually went to the U.S. Supreme Court.

Reynolds v. United States (1878) was the first Supreme Court case to determine the legal meaning of a provision in the First Amendment. In siding with the federal system and against the domestic relations of local majorities, and in delimiting the meaning of "religion" in a religiously biased manner, *Reynolds* became one of the more controversial Court decisions in American history and has never been overturned.

After Brigham Young's death, two pieces of congressional legislation, the Edmunds Act of 1882 and the Edmunds-Tucker Act of 1887, further eroded Mormon freedoms and spelled the demise of polygamy: the United States abolished the Mormon militia, disincorporated the Mormon Church (escheating most of its properties to the government), abolished female suffrage (a niece of Brigham Young's was the first American woman to vote), disenfranchised polygamists, and compelled wives to testify against their husbands. Prosecution for polygamy was permitted without a complaint by a spouse, and voters in 1887 were required to swear to uphold the Edmunds Act, which prohibited even verbal encouragement of polygamy. In its enforcement of these laws, the government jailed over a thousand polygamous men.

In 1890 the Mormon Church president Wilford Woodruff issued a manifesto instructing church members to obey U.S. law, and in 1896 Utah's request for statehood was granted. The manifesto marked the beginning of the end of the most distinctive aspects of social organization and religious practice in nineteenth-century Mormonism—and most important for American literary and political history, it marked a shift in the church's relation to the United States.

POLYGAMY AFTER THE MANIFESTO, THE EARLY WESTERN, AND ASSIMILATION

Despite the manifesto, some members of the Mormon hierarchy continued to marry polygamously, and in the first decade of the twentieth century, as governmental investigations increased in response to rumors about the continued practice of plural marriage, organized citizens, members of Congress, and the press revisited former fears and dire pronouncements about the fate of the nation should polygamy be allowed to persist. As late as 1911, for example, Theodore Roosevelt warned that the continuation of polygamy would "secure the destruction" of the Mormon Church. Following the admittance of Utah to the Union, the election of two Mormons to Congress—B. H. Roberts (a practicing polygamist before 1890) to the House in 1898 and Reed Smoot (1862–1941) to the Senate in 1904—incited petitions, congressional investigations, and a flurry of articles and cartoons raising the alarm

U.S. suspicion of Mormon political influence. This illustration, drawn by Joseph Keppler for *Puck,* 27 April 1904, was titled "The Real Objection to Smoot." COURTESY OF WILLIAM R. HANDLEY

Culturally, antipolygamy sentiment resurfaced briefly in 1911 with articles in several magazines and arguably helped produce a best-seller in 1912, when Zane Grey published *Riders of the Purple Sage,* one of the most influential westerns (because of its formula, not its Mormon antagonists). Although Grey went on to write dozens of westerns—only a handful dealing with Mormons—*Riders of the Purple Sage* was his most successful novel and the only one to depict Mormon polygamy and what the hero Lassiter calls the Mormon "empire" as a soulless evil. One sign of the assimilation of the Mormon Church into the nation was that, as a result of Mormons' objection to depictions of them in some of Grey's novels and in many silent films, a congressmen from Utah offered a legislated tax deal to Fox Pictures in 1918 if Fox would agree to omit any reference to Mormons in subsequent film versions of Zane Grey novels. That same year, Willa Cather's *My Ántonia* was published, in which Mormons are alluded to in ways previously uncharacteristic: the narrator asserts that dirt roads bordered with sunflowers—believed to have been planted by Mormon pioneers along the trail as they fled persecution—for him represent the roads to freedom. Perhaps alluding to the catastrophe of imperial collisions in World War I, the novel also depicts two bulls constantly ramming their heads together. Their names are "Gladstone"—after the nineteenth-century British prime minister who argued for Irish home rule—and "Brigham Young."

See also Annexation and Expansion; Courtship, Marriage, and Divorce; Frontier; Violence

BIBLIOGRAPHY

Primary Works

Cather, Willa. *My Ántonia.* 1918. Edited by Charles W. Mignon, with Kari Ronning. Lincoln: University of Nebraska Press, 1994.

Grey, Zane. *Riders of the Purple Sage.* 1912. Introduction and notes by William R. Handley. New York: Modern Library, 2002.

Miller, Joaquin. *The Danites in the Sierras.* Chicago: Jansen, McClurg, 1881.

Stenhouse, Mrs. T. B. H. *Tell It All: The Story of a Life's Experience in Mormonism.* Hartford, Conn.: Worthington, 1874.

Switzer, Jennie Bartlett. *Elder Northfield's Home; or, Sacrificed on the Mormon Altar.* New York: J. Howard Brown, 1882.

Twain, Mark. *Roughing It.* 1872. Vol. 2 of *The Works of Mark Twain.* Edited by Harriet Elinor Smith and Edgar Marquess Branch. Berkeley: University of California Press, 1993.

about the infiltration into the Senate of what were widely suspected to be puppets of the Mormon hierarchy. In the cartoon, "The Real Objection to Smoot," in *Puck* magazine on 27 April 1904, the Mormon hierarchy is represented by a large patriarchal figure whose coat is patched with "Resistance to Federal Authority," "Murder of Apostates," "Mountain Meadows Massacre," and other Mormon crimes, including, most prominently, "Polygamy." He dangles a puppetlike Smoot before the door to the U.S. Senate. Although antipolygamy fervor had briefly diminished in the 1890s, it returned in a virulent form: Could Mormons be trusted politically and morally? Unlike Roberts, Smoot kept his seat and the political accommodation of the Mormons began to take shape.

Secondary Works

Alexander, Thomas G. *Mormonism in Transition: A History of the Latter-Day Saints, 1890–1930.* Urbana: University of Illinois Press, 1986.

Bagley, Will. *Blood of the Prophets: Brigham Young and the Massacre at Mountain Meadows.* Norman: University of Oklahoma Press, 2002.

Bentley, Nancy. "Marriage as Treason: Polygamy, Nation, and the Novel." In *The Futures of American Studies,* edited by Donald E. Pease and Robyn Wiegman, pp. 341–370. Durham, N.C.: Duke University Press, 2002.

Brooks, Juanita. *The Mountain Meadows Massacre.* Norman: University of Oklahoma Press, 1963.

Bunker, Gary L., and Davis Bitton. *The Mormon Graphic Image, 1834–1914: Cartoons, Caricatures, and Illustrations.* Salt Lake City: University of Utah Press, 1983.

Firmage, Edwin Brown, and Richard Collin Mangrum. *Zion in the Courts: A Legal History of the Church of Jesus Christ of Latter-Day Saints, 1830–1900.* Urbana: University of Illinois Press, 1988.

Givens, Terryl. *By the Hand of Mormon: The American Scripture that Launched a New World Religion.* New York: Oxford University Press, 2002.

Givens, Terryl. *The Viper on the Hearth: Mormons, Myths, and the Construction of Heresy.* New York: Oxford University Press, 1997.

Gordon, Sarah Barringer. *The Mormon Question: Polygamy and Constitutional Conflict in Nineteenth-Century America.* Chapel Hill: University of North Carolina Press, 2002.

Handley, William R. "Distinctions without Differences: Zane Grey and the Mormon Question." *Arizona Quarterly* 57, no. 1 (2001): 1–33.

Hardy, B. Carmon. *Solemn Covenant: The Mormon Polygamous Passage.* Urbana: University of Illinois Press, 1992.

O'Dea, Thomas. *The Mormons.* Chicago: University of Chicago Press, 1957.

Quinn, D. Michael. *The Mormon Hierarchy: Origins of Power.* Salt Lake City: Signature Books, 1994.

Shipps, Jan. *Mormonism: The Story of a New Religious Tradition.* Urbana: University of Illinois Press, 1985.

William R. Handley

MOTION PICTURES

By 1920, although color and synchronized sound technology were not yet in use, filmmaking and moviegoing in the United States already closely resembled twenty-first century practices. But nothing about the early history of the medium made these practices inevitable. To paraphrase Charles Musser in his *The Emergence of Cinema* (1990), the cinema was not so much invented as it emerged, at the end of the nineteenth century, from a convergence of multiple fields of image production and spectatorship—photography, vaudeville theater, and so forth—due to the efforts of a diverse group of American and European entrepreneurs.

THE BEGINNINGS OF THE MEDIUM

Still photography was not successfully tested in France until 1839, but audiences had been viewing demonstrations of large images reflected by mirrors, under the aegis of magic or science, at least since the seventeenth century and probably for centuries prior. As the Enlightenment and the industrial age brought new technologies into general public use, shadow and projector displays like the magic lantern, a lamp that used flame and lenses to project images drawn onto glass slides, became popular entertainments. Many middle-class children owned optical toys such as flip-books and zoetropes, which produced the illusion of movement by use of incremental drawings flashed rapidly one at a time, as in a hand-drawn animated cartoon. By the end of the nineteenth century, "slip slides" (magic lantern slides with moving parts), slide series that showed scenes changing over time, and other devices to suggest movement and change entertained thousands in America's urban vaudeville houses. Though not projected, other public entertainments like panoramas and dioramas nevertheless anticipated the cinema's ability to bring faraway places closer by re-creating cities and exotic locales in meticulous detail and even simulating motion within these virtual spaces. During the same period, curious crowds were willing to pay small fees to see demonstrations of new inventions like the telegraph, the telephone, the phonograph, and even electric lighting.

Motion pictures began life as one more invention that people bought tickets to see. The principle of motion pictures was developed for more or less scientific purposes by Eadweard Muybridge in 1878 and Étienne-Jules Marey in 1879, English and French respectively, who used serial photographs and long exposures to study the motion of animals and people. In the United States, Thomas A. Edison (1847–1931) remarked, in 1888, that he was developing an invention that "does for the Eye what the phonograph"—which Edison had also invented—"does for the Ear, which is the recording and reproduction of things in motion." Edison, who owned an "invention factory" in Menlo Park, New Jersey, was practiced in marketing his inventions as amusements. After meeting both Muybridge and Marey to discuss the practical problems of capturing and representing movement and after taking notes on Muybridge's primitive Zooprax-iscope projector, Edison began work on his own moving picture camera in earnest.

The first camera concocted by Edison's lab was the Kinetograph, overseen by W. K. Laurie Dickson in 1892. After considering other storage options, Dickson recorded images on the strips of photosensitive celluloid developed by the Eastman Company for their hundred-exposure Kodak cameras, invented in 1890. The resulting films, less than a minute long and featuring both performances (women dancing) and mundane activities (a sneeze), were viewed on a Kinetoscope, a peephole viewer marketed for use in penny arcades in 1894. At the same time, Louis and Auguste Lumière were exploiting their own moving picture camera, the Cinématographe, which doubled as a projector. They screened their fifty-second films before an audience for the first time in Paris on 28 December 1895. The Kinetograph and Cinématographe cameras worked on the same principle: each exposed photographic stock to light by intermittently advancing the film through a "gate," which held it still for approximately one-eighteenth of a second (subject to wide variability, as most cameras were hand-cranked) as a shutter exposed a single frame. Other companies and individuals invented variations of cameras and viewing devices at the same time, igniting the litigious wrath of the Edison Company. A rival arcade viewer called the Mutoscope—which Dickson secretly codeveloped in 1894—avoided infringing on Edison's Kinetoscope patent by using individual flip-cards rather than a filmstrip.

While peephole viewers were popular at first, they were not very lucrative and quickly exhausted their market. Edison and his rivals soon developed projectors like the Lumières' that could display films for large audiences. On 23 April 1896, Edison's Vitascope projector (invented by C. Francis Jenkins and Thomas Armat and handled by a Kinetoscope marketing company, Raff and Gammon) premiered at Koster and Bial's vaudeville theater in New York City to rave reviews. By that time so many moving picture machines had appeared—including the Cinématographe, Robert Paul's Theatrograph in England, and numerous American rivals—that the public had trouble keeping the names straight. A famous scene from chapter 7 of Frank Norris's novel *McTeague* (1896, published 1899) inaccurately refers to the projector that entertains McTeague and his fiancée as the "Kinetograph"; whether this mistake may be attributed to the theater in the novel or to Norris himself may never be known. But Norris does give an excellent sense of what watching the first projected films was like: after brief vaudeville acts that include acrobats, comedians, and singers, Norris's

characters watch a program of short films with subjects as varied as those of the live show, and they comment loudly to one another on the astonishingly lifelike effect.

THE FIRST FILMS

What did the first spectators see? As *McTeague* attests, they did not see feature-length films. The Vitascope's sprocket system pulled the film so taut that reels much longer than fifty feet—around a minute of running time—would snap. (A system that reduced projection stress by allowing slack to the film, the Latham Loop, was developed independently in 1895 but was not immediately incorporated into the Kinetograph or the Vitascope.) Thus the earliest shows consisted of multiple short films sold in "programs." Stylistically, the films seem merely crude in the early twenty-first century. Due to the length limitation, editing was rarely considered, and even after 1897, when this limitation was overcome, filmmakers tended to minimize the number of discrete shots per film. Action was filmed from a single camera position, usually far enough from the performers to display them from head to toe, and performers were not shy about acknowledging the camera's presence. If close-ups were used, they picked out objects, people, and body parts (such as scandalously revealed female ankles) not to emphasize their significance within a story as they do in the early twenty-first century but simply to offer audiences the pleasure of looking at things and people—often performing such private activities as kissing, getting drunk, or arguing—in the strange new context of flickering images displayed before a large public. Though color cinematography was not possible, filmmakers occasionally had prints individually hand tinted, frame by frame, in multiple colors, but this practice required so much time and labor that it was limited to special subjects or particularly spectacular scenes. In 1904 Sigmund Lubin began chemically dyeing his films in solid colors that changed with each shot, and this tinting process soon caught on across the industry as a means of distinguishing daytime from nighttime scenes, establishing mood, and creating other expressive effects.

The subject matter of the first films also depended in part on the state of the technology. While the small, light Cinématographe was well suited to "documentary" films shot in the streets and homes of Paris, Edison's Kinetograph was heavy and bulky, and so the company invited performers—boxers, vaudeville players, cockfight handlers, and the like—to be filmed in a shed at Menlo Park dubbed the Black Maria. Genres developed that mirrored contemporary mass cultural forms: "actualities," which were views of places and people of interest (in keeping with the illustrated travelogues popular with social clubs); slapstick comedy scenes; bits from plays; "bad boy" films; chase films; and trick films. Though technically silent (Edison had quickly abandoned as impractical his plan to synchronize sound to the moving image), films were rarely projected without musical accompaniment or spoken commentary. The more fastidious projectionists also offered interpretive frameworks to their audiences by arranging unconnected short films into themed programs (political humor, railroad subjects, and so forth).

Crude as they may seem now, these huge projected images of diverse activities, as vibrant as life but uncannily distant and devoid of color, impressed the press and public tremendously. It is doubtful that spectators dove for cover as they watched railroad engines rush toward the camera, as Parisians supposedly did when the Lumières screened *Arrival of a Train at La Ciotat Station* in 1895. The film historian Tom Gunning has argued that, in this era of rapid and well-publicized technological change, viewers were unlikely to have been fooled into mistaking films for reality, but they did love to be astonished by the new machines that seemed to multiply daily. The first audiences consisted of a mélange of city dwellers: factory and sweatshop laborers, recent immigrants with no knowledge of English, and middle- and upper-class seekers of novel forms of amusement. The early cinema, which Gunning has called "the cinema of attractions," satisfied an increasing need for stimulus in the urban population, instilled in them by their fast-paced and often dangerous lives. As they watched these programs, viewers behaved as if they were at a fairground or a street corner. They talked loudly about the films and allowed their eyes and ears to wander from the screen to other patrons, other events taking place in the exhibition space, the lecturer, and the projector itself, which was initially the central attraction of any film show. Indeed, the brevity and diversity of the films themselves did not support the sustained attention that characterizes film spectatorship in the early twenty-first century; within a few years, the film industry would begin to see spectators' inattentive and boisterous behavior as a threat to the future of their enterprise.

STRUGGLES OVER FILMS AND THEIR EXHIBITION

During their "novelty" phase (1894–1898), moving pictures faced an uncertain future. Producers scrambled for content, trying everything from boxing matches like the Corbett-Fitzsimmons fight of 1897 to films about the Spanish-American War of 1898—a conflict that Musser speculates might have saved the film industry from running out of filmable material.

The two major producers of films in the United States during this time were Edison and the American Mutoscope and Biograph Company, which Dickson founded upon quitting Menlo Park. AM&B's Biograph projector (invented in 1896) was superior to the Vitascope and set off a furious patent war between the companies. Producers both domestic (American Vitagraph, Selig Polyscope) and foreign (Georges Méliès's Star Films, Pathé Frères) made steady headway into a market that constantly needed new films. Edison and Biograph eventually gave up competing with each other and their biggest rivals and, with Biograph's reluctant consent, formed the Motion Picture Patents Company (MPPC) on 18 December 1908 to pool patents and protect themselves against competition; the struggling producers not invited to join the MPPC referred to it as "the Trust" with good reason. The ten companies that comprised the MPPC were the best capitalized in the industry, they had the highest production values, and they controlled the distribution of their highly desirable films (as well as they could, at least, in a business overwhelmed by bootlegging and illegal exchanges of licensed for unlicensed films). All the Trust lacked was control over exhibition, and even the exhibitors were largely at the mercy of their production schedules—for the moment.

The film industry as a whole suffered during this period from public relations problems due to both film content and exhibition circumstances. The MPPC producers wanted to court a middle-class audience to expand their market, but this was not easy considering the shocking content of the films: during the medium's first decade a viewer might see trains ramming into one another, "Turks" being decapitated and their heads reattaching themselves, a respectable family blown to bits by a car crash, and burlesque dancers featured in "blue" films, all in a single film program. Religious and political leaders and social reformers worried publicly about both the content of films and the venues that screened them. At first films were shown in urban vaudeville theaters and other multiuse venues. Itinerant exhibitors made a living taking films to towns and rural areas and screening them at fairs, churches, and town halls. But by 1905 a growing number of entertainment entrepreneurs, notably Marcus Loew and Carl Laemmle, had erected highly successful nickel-and-dime theaters or "nickelodeons" dedicated to continuous film shows. These nickelodeons soon popped up in working-class hubs and middle-class neighborhoods and shopping districts all over the United States; their primary patrons included factory and sweatshop laborers, female shoppers, mothers with children to entertain, and children old enough to entertain themselves. How, asked the reformers, would the uneducated, impressionable, and immigrant viewers learn to respect American mores and laws if their favorite form of entertainment supplied little else but shocks and debauchery?

To make matters worse, the nickelodeons themselves seemed dens of iniquity—darkened, anonymous spaces regularly attended by unchaperoned working women. On Christmas Eve in 1908, the mayor of New York ordered the city's theaters closed on grounds of public indecency. The message was clear: producers and exhibitors would have to work harder and faster to make movies a respectable entertainment or cede control of their own business to city legislators and external censors.

TELLING STORIES ON FILM

The story film would prove crucial to the producers' race for respectability. Edwin S. Porter, a New York projectionist, began directing films for the Edison Company in 1901. Porter initially made single-shot slapstick films but learned, from watching the films of the French magician Georges Méliès (*A Trip to the Moon,* 1902), how to thrill audiences with cinematic tricks, such as double exposures and the "transformation" of objects accomplished by stopping and restarting the camera. Porter's films, like most story films of the time, emphasized broad physical humor and relied on the audience's knowledge of such familiar material as current events, fairy tales, and biblical tales. But Porter learned another trick from Méliès that helped change the way that American producers thought about storytelling: how to overlap discrete shots by beginning an action in one shot (for example, a character leaving a room) and completing it in the next (the same character arriving at another character's house). This trick made it possible to string together shots of different locations into a relatively lengthy story—a full twelve-minute reel or even more—without leaving the audience wondering what the shot changes meant, how much time had elapsed between shots, and so forth. By 1903, with the release of Porter's *The Great Train Robbery* following the great successes of his *Jack and the Beanstalk* and *Life of an American Fireman* (both 1902), it was becoming clear that the story film would be key to the producers' future success. Porter was proving that a well-told story could not only interest an audience but also could give it a dramatic thrill that depended on the story itself and not on the experience of seeing photographs move, which had by then lost its novelty.

The broad pantomime and slapstick plots of many early story films held little attraction for the middle class, which was more interested in literature and plays.

Hoping to cultivate this lucrative market, American Vitagraph and several foreign concerns produced "quality" films, beginning with the American release in 1909 of a film by the French producer Film d'Art called *La Mort du duc de Guise.* These films condensed Shakespeare plays, poetry, opera plots, and biblical or quasi-biblical stories down to a few reels, sported opulent sets, and used restrained acting styles at a time when comedies dominated American film. According to their marketers, these films offered "uplift," education, even the possibility of Americanization to a heterogeneous film audience. The most complex story films, however, seemed incapable of getting their narratives across. Producers had distributed their films with filmed "intertitles"—full-screen cards that provided exposition and dialogue—since 1904, but this innovation did not automatically clarify every story. Critics in the trade press speculated about the reasons for this difficulty, blaming inadequate acting, poor plots, bad camera placement, and a myriad of other infractions, but they could not agree on how producers should proceed.

More than any other individual, D. W. Griffith, a stage actor who began directing for Biograph in 1908, helped the industry to streamline its storytelling tactics. Capitalizing on the methods of Méliès, Porter, the producer-director Alice Guy Blaché, and their imitators, Griffith compiled a number of extant cinematic techniques, such as close-ups and rudimentary cause-and-effect editing, for use in his tales of domestic and ethical crisis. Rather than letting the performers pantomime all the important story information to a camera standing four yards away, Griffith varied his framings and included a much higher number of shots per film than any of his rivals. Together these stratagems implied to the viewer an omniscient narrator, akin to the narrator of a Victorian novel, commenting on the action, revealing characters' thoughts, and focusing on key story elements. Like his hero, Charles Dickens, Griffith used skillful editing to alternate between simultaneous events in different places, as in his popular race-to-the-rescue films *The Lonely Villa* (1909) and *The Lonedale Operator* (1911).

Griffith's Biograph films were so popular with the press and with audiences that other directors incorporated Griffith's techniques and focused more of their energies on story films. They also took more risks in hopes of stumbling upon a formula that would overtake the industry. The remarkable success of a few imported films—including the French film *Queen Elizabeth* (1912), starring the international stage idol Sarah Bernhardt, and two Italian historical epics, *Quo Vadis?* (1913) and *Cabiria* (1914)—proved that American audiences would sit through films running

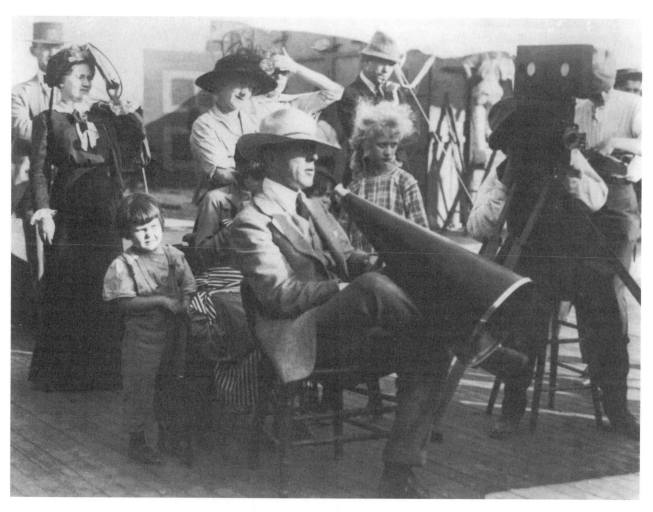

D. W. Griffith directing a film, probably *Hearts of the World,* **c. 1918.** © BETTMANN/CORBIS

one hour, two hours, or even longer. Small-time entre-preneurs like Chicago's Carl Laemmle—who began with a single nickelodeon theater and founded a small distribution company—jumped into production themselves, taking chances on longer films and new forms of publicity that the MPPC companies refused to attempt and soon overtaking the Trust producers in popularity. Perhaps these upstarts' most crucial inno-vation was to capitalize on the popularity of certain actors. By 1908 viewers tended to choose films based on their brand names. This practice served Biograph well during 1908 to 1913, when Griffith (anony-mously) directed nearly all of the more than four hun-dred films Biograph produced. As Griffith and others focused on character psychology and used close-ups to register actors' facial reactions, viewers became curi-ous about actors and began favoring a few over the rest. The "Biograph Girl," Florence Lawrence, became an attraction in her own right in 1909, and by 1910

Laemmle had lured her to his IMP company and trumpeted her arrival with a massive publicity stunt.

MOTION PICTURES BECOME BIG BUSINESS

Like the proliferation of story films, the new focus on actors was not an obvious development but a calcu-lated strategy. Initially such actors as Lawrence, Mary Pickford, Maurice Costello, Florence Turner, Francis X. Bushman, and Mabel Normand and comedian John Bunny were what Richard de Cordova calls "pic-ture personalities"—that is, figures known only for their screen personae, which tended to carry over from picture to picture. Theda Bara, one of the screen's first sex symbols (*A Fool There Was,* 1915), was also one of the first actors for whom a studio fabricated a biogra-phy specifically for public consumption. No longer simply a picture personality, she was one of the first movie stars—someone whose private life fascinated the fans as much as her on-screen presence. The

British comedian Charlie Chaplin made his star name into a franchise by 1915, proving his economic clout and his skill as a director for Mutual. By 1920 Chaplin, Pickford, Douglas Fairbanks, the western director and star William S. Hart, and the comedian-directors Roscoe "Fatty" Arbuckle and Buster Keaton were among the richest and most famous people in the world. Their tremendous successes prompted Chaplin, Pickford, Fairbanks, and Griffith to quit their studio connections and cofound United Artists, through which they would independently produce and distribute their own features.

Star actors and directors also accelerated the development of some of the most popular early feature genres: the adventure film, the western, the domestic melodrama, and the slapstick comedy. One leader in the domestic melodrama genre was Famous Players–Lasky, which later merged with its distributor Paramount. Its chief director, Cecil B. De Mille, directed many films (*The Cheat*, 1915; *Why Change Your Wife?* 1920) that irritated social reformers by glamorizing sexual innuendo and "sin." But the sophisticated immorality of De Mille's characters and his "artistic" arrangement of shadows and light—dubbed "Rembrandt" lighting by appreciative critics—appealed to a young middle-class audience that cared little about the reformist agenda; in any event, De Mille always punished iniquity in the final reel. Mack Sennett, a Biograph employee who wrote scripts for Griffith, formed the Keystone Company in 1912 and soon helped transform the least respectable of early genres, slapstick, into an art of satire and parody, free from the era's atmosphere of social repression. Chaplin and Arbuckle both began their careers at Keystone; like Chaplin, Arbuckle became so popular that he founded his own production company and gave Keaton his first film roles.

A mere seven years after the Trust was formed, the upstart companies the Trust had shut out had rebuilt the industry in their own image. Because many of them began as film exhibitors, these "unlicensed" producer-distributors controlled all three of the industry's economic centers, an arrangement known as "vertical integration." Laemmle's IMP company, for example, began with a single theater in Chicago in 1906, grew into a theater chain, joined with a multi-producer combine that was later reorganized as the Universal Film Manufacturing company (1912), and released wildly popular films—such as the sensationalist white-slavery "exposé" *Traffic in Souls* (1913)—under the Universal trademark; their combined economic strength, as producers, distributors, and exhibitors, helped place Laemmle and Universal in a dominant position in the industry. Unable to acquire theaters of their own in a market dominated by multicity

theater chains—controlled by "independents" like William Fox, Lasky, and Loew's (later to become the parent company of Metro-Goldwyn-Mayer)—the Trust companies withered. A 1912 antitrust suit leveled at the MPPC producers sounded their early death knell, and by 1918 they had all but disappeared.

Griffith contributed to the unraveling of the Trust when he left Biograph in 1913 (a move that practically killed the company on the spot) and filmed *The Birth of a Nation* (1915) independently, distributing it through Mutual. By this time multi-reel features had begun to enter the market but were still resisted, primarily because most theaters seated patrons continuously during shows and late arrivals could more easily catch up with the plot of a two-reel film than one that ran four reels or more. But *Birth* proved that big American films had a consistent market and could garner "Broadway" ticket prices of a dollar or more. Nearly three hours long, it spanned the Civil War and the Reconstruction era and treated psychological, familial, and historical crises. It did not change the industry all by itself, but it cemented the motion picture's potential for grand success (it grossed $15 million in five years of continuous bookings), social import, sophistication and subtlety of storytelling, and controversy.

The studios—which also included the Fox Film Company and Samuel Goldwyn—grew quickly thanks to their innovations in organizing and overseeing multi-film production. Thomas Ince—a director whose westerns for the Bison "101" company were so popular that he became the subject of a multi-studio bidding war—helped introduce to filmmaking what Janet Staiger calls the "central producer" system. To maximize production, Ince implemented a division of labor—full shooting scripts containing shot breakdowns; directors who managed the photography phase and executed the script's shot-by-shot instructions; and technicians subdivided into crews concerned solely with camera, costumes, staging, lighting, editing, and so on. This system rationalized and streamlined the filmmaking process. In 1910 the industry began to take another big step, this time a geographical one. Biograph and other companies slowly migrated from New York, Chicago, and other eastern cities to southern California in order to capitalize on the three hundred–plus days of sunshine per year and highly varied locales for shooting outdoors; by 1920 the word "Hollywood" was becoming synonymous with the movies and the glamour they represented.

In 1920, with the era of sound film still six years away, Hollywood was the most powerful film industry in the world, a circumstance not entirely due to sheer perseverance or marketing brilliance. World War I had decimated the Italian, French, and German industries—once powerful exporters to the American market (and still major influences on American storytelling and visual style)—and allowed Hollywood producer-distributors to get a toehold in overseas markets that desperately needed new films to distribute. By this time motion pictures were central to the lives of Americans of all classes and ages, and American films and exhibition practices dominated movie houses throughout western Europe as well. As early as 1910 some American exhibitors dressed up their theaters with opulent entryways, velvet interiors, and uniformed ushers. By the end of the decade these "picture palaces" were the norm, giving patrons the opportunity to experience the trappings of Hollywood glamour firsthand while watching its representatives enact it on the screen. But even the glamour had an American twist. Most studio "moguls" and many of the biggest stars began as poor immigrants, many of them Jewish, and their life stories held the rags-to-riches appeal of some of the country's greatest success stories in production and commerce. Many of the most popular films followed characters on a similar path from the gutter to happiness and success and were filled with luxury and decadence and humor that allowed the lion's share of patrons to ignore their own hardships for a few hours and fantasize about partaking of the abundance that eluded them in everyday life.

See also The Birth of a Nation; Photography; Science and Technology; Theater

BIBLIOGRAPHY
Primary Works
The Arrival of a Train at La Ciotat Station. Directed by Louis Lumière. Lumière Frères, 1895.

The Birth of a Nation. Directed by D. W. Griffith. 1915.

Cabiria. Directed by Giovanni Pastrone; performer Letizia Quaranta. Itala Film Company, 1914.

The Cheat. Directed by Cecil B. De Mille; performers Sessue Hayakawa, Fannie Ward, and Jack Dean. Jesse L. Lasky Feature Play Company, 1915.

A Fool There Was. Directed by Frank Powell; performer Theda Bara. William Fox Vaudeville Company, 1915.

The Great Train Robbery. Directed by Edwin S. Porter; performers Justus Barnes and Gilbert M. "Broncho Billy" Anderson. Edison, 1903.

The Lonedale Operator. Directed by D. W. Griffith; performer Blanche Sweet. Biograph, 1911.

La Mort du duc de Guise, [The death of the duc de Guise]. Directed by Charles Le Bargy and André Calmettes. Film d'Art, 1909.

Queen Elizabeth. Directed by Louis Mercanton and Henri Desfontaines; performer Sarah Bernhardt. L'Histrionic Film, 1912.

The Tramp. Directed by Charles Chaplin; performers Charlie Chaplin and Edna Purviance. Essenay, 1915.

The Trip to the Moon. Directed by Georges Méliès. Star Film, 1902.

Secondary Works
Balio, Tino, ed. *The American Film Industry.* Rev. ed. Madison: University of Wisconsin Press, 1985.

Bordwell, David, Janet Staiger, and Kristin Thompson. *The Classical Hollywood Cinema: Film Style and Mode of Production to 1960.* New York: Columbia University Press, 1985.

Bowser, Eileen. *The Transformation of Cinema 1907–1915.* Berkeley: University of California Press, 1990.

Cook, David A. *A History of Narrative Film.* 3rd ed. New York and London: Norton, 1996.

De Cordova, Richard. *Picture Personalities: The Emergence of the Star System in America.* Urbana and Chicago: University of Illinois Press, 1990.

Elsaesser, Thomas, and Adam Barker, eds. *Early Cinema: Space, Frame, Narrative.* London: British Film Institute, 1990.

Gomery, Douglas. *Shared Pleasures: A History of Movie Presentation in the United States.* Madison: University of Wisconsin Press, 1992.

Gunning, Tom. "An Aesthetic of Astonishment: Early Film and the (In)Credulous Spectator." In *Viewing Positions: Ways of Seeing Film,* edited by Linda Williams, pp. 114–133. New Brunswick, N.J.: Rutgers University Press, 1995.

Gunning, Tom. "The Cinema of Attraction[s]: Early Film, Its Spectator, and the Avant-Garde." *Wide Angle* 8, nos. 3–4 (1986): 63–70.

Keil, Charlie. *Early American Cinema in Transition: Story, Style, and Filmmaking, 1907–1913.* Madison: University of Wisconsin Press, 2001.

Koszarski, Richard. *An Evening's Entertainment: The Age of the Silent Feature Picture, 1915–1928.* New York: Scribners, 1990.

Musser, Charles. *The Emergence of Cinema: The American Screen to 1907.* Berkeley: University of California Press, 1990.

Paul Young

MRS. SPRING FRAGRANCE

Sui Sin Far (1865–1914), also known as Edith Maud Eaton, was one of the earliest Chinese American writers to publish her work in English in the United States without the help of a transcriber, translator, or editor.

Sui Sin Far (Edith Maude Eaton), photographed in December 1903. COURTESY OF THE AUTRY NATIONAL CENTER/SOUTHWEST MUSEUM, LOS ANGELES, N.35626

From 1888 to 1913 she wrote sketches, short stories, journalism, and works for children that significantly revised popular conceptions of Chinese Americans. In 1912 many of her short stories were collected in one volume, titled *Mrs. Spring Fragrance*. Published with a bright red cover embossed with dragonflies and flowering Chinese lilies and with pages lightly imprinted with Chinese characters, the graphic design of this book appears to emphasize an image of Chinese American fiction as exotic and foreign. Yet the stories within the book resolutely delineated individuals who were human, fallible, emotional, and part of the rapidly expanding social fabric of U.S. society at the turn of the century. Sui Sin Far was a "Eurasian" of mixed race (her father was British, her mother Chinese) who could have chosen to "pass" for a white. Instead she embraced an Asian American identity and used her pen to combat negative images of Chinese and Chinese Americans. It is no wonder, then, that her grave is marked with a monument thanking her for her work on behalf of the Chinese and that scholarly interest in the early twenty-first century focuses on her significant and indeed pioneering contributions to Asian American literature.

FIN DE SIÈCLE VIEWS OF ASIAN AMERICANS IN LITERATURE AND CULTURE

At the turn of the century, the Chinese in the United States were widely viewed as heathen, unassimilable, inscrutable, and cowardly individuals who spent their time smoking opium, gambling, and kidnapping white women into slavery and prostitution. Prejudice against Asians (and in particular Chinese and Chinese Americans) culminated in the 1882 Chinese Exclusion Act, which denied Chinese immigrants entry into the United States as well as citizenship on the grounds that they were an "unassimilated" race with an inferior cultural tradition (Xiao-huang, p. 2). At the turn of the century, then, "exclusion and bigotry were policy at both the state and national levels" (Foner and Rosenberg, p. 17). Furthermore, the government did little to protect Chinese immigrants present in the United States. In the 1880s Chinese Americans were violently driven out of cities such as Tacoma, Washington; Eureka, California; Rock Springs, Wyoming; Truckee, California; and many others.

Literature and journalism from this time period often reflects these attitudes toward the Chinese (known as the "yellow peril" school of writing). An 1894 piece by a San Francisco Christian newspaper editor, Ng Poon Chew, titled "The Chinese in Los Angeles," describes "between three and four thousand of these strange, little brown men residing in this city and vicinity" (pp. 102–103). An 1896 essay by Ella S. Hartnell, "Some Little Heathens," in the same newspaper purports to detail the "unsightly huts, homes of an alien people" in the "China fish-town" of Monterey (p. 153). Mainstream literature in this time period was no less derogatory. For example, Jack London's *Tales of the Fish Patrol* (1905) depicts Chinese Americans as "swarthy Mongols" (p. 1083), "dirty Chinamen" (p. 1086), and "coolies" (p. 1137) who "came swarming" (p. 1136) out of the cabins like so many rats. And Henry Harrison Lewis's *At the Mikado's Court: The Adventures of Three American Boys in Modern Japan* (1907) portrays "Chinamen, half naked and leering" (p. 99) who speak "queer broken English" (p. 99), have "slitlike eyes" (p. 158), and are "Chinks" (p. 163).

Sui Sin Far published in journals and literary magazines that contained some of these negative depictions of Chinese Americans. However, the goal of the interconnected stories that make up *Mrs. Spring Fragrance* was to present unstereotyped portrayals of Chinese and Chinese Americans. A story such as "Mrs. Spring Fragrance" describes the title character as a nosy, intelligent, sophisticated Chinese woman who, after five years in America, finds that "there are no more American words for her learning" (p. 17). In the words of one of her husband's associates, she is "just like an American woman" (p. 24). Of course, Mrs. Spring Fragrance does stay true to basic values of fidelity and wifely decorum learned in China, but Sui Sin Far's point is that Mrs. Spring Fragrance is a Chinese American—a unique fusion of ethnicities—and certainly not a "chink" or "coolie." Other stories from the collection depict the effects of pervasive anti-Chinese sentiments. The ironically titled "In the Land of the Free" describes the painful emotions a child and mother experience when immigration policies force their separation. Racism also affects relationships between men and women; in "The Story of One White Woman Who Married a Chinese" and the sequel "Her Chinese Husband," a Chinese American man who dares to marry a white woman is eventually killed by an angry mob.

The stories in *Mrs. Spring Fragrance* also address the traumas of mixed race individuals, such as Pan in "'Its Wavering Image'" and Mag-gee in "The Sing Song Woman." Mag-gee is a "half-white girl" who does not wish to be married to "a Chinaman" because "I was born in America, and I'm not Chinese in looks nor in any other way. See! My eyes are blue, and there is gold in my hair; and I love potatoes and beef, and every time I eat rice it makes me sick" (p. 126). Another recurrent theme, then, is the difficult process of Americanization, which sometimes leaves individuals cut off from their ethnic heritages, race, and family. Yet Sui Sin Far remained committed to negotiating compromises between Chinese and American cultural and ethnic heritages. She is therefore considered one of the earliest writers to depict a truly Asian American identity. As she writes in her autobiographical portrait, "Leaves from the Mental Portfolio of an Eurasian" (1909), "I give my right hand to the Occidentals and my left to the Orientals, hoping that between them they will not utterly destroy the insignificant 'connecting link'" (p. 230). Sui Sin Far's writings are certainly not "insignificant" as the connecting link between Chinese and American cultures and identities in this time period, and she did much to illustrate the humanity, spirit, and emotions of this newly developing and evolving immigrant group.

LITERARY REPUTATION AND NEW APPROACHES

Sui Sin Far was a well-received writer in her own lifetime, and she was in the process of finding a publisher for a novel at the end of her life. Yet from the time of her death in 1914 to S. E. Solberg and Amy Ling's rediscovery of her in the early 1980s, Sui Sin Far's work was almost forgotten. Since 1983 her literary reputation has grown steadily, and she is now considered an important pioneer of Asian American literature. Ling and other early critics focus on Sui Sin Far's honest and unflinching depictions of Chinese Americans and of racial prejudice. A second wave of critics, such as Annette White-Parks and Elizabeth Ammons, has delineated the contours of her literary identity, arguing for the development of a trickster persona (White-Parks) that slips subversive messages into the texts (Ammons). White-Parks's expertly researched and written literary biography *Sui Sin Far/Edith Maude Eaton* (1995) remains invaluable for studies of this author. Criticism by Carol Roh-Spaulding has focused on the mixed-race characters in Sui Sin Far's work, while critics such as Martha J. Cutter, Min Song, and Viet Thanh Nguyen have discussed her often subversive treatment of gender, sexuality, and the body; her writing for children has also been analyzed by Cutter. Another wave of criticism has discussed Sui Sin Far with her more controversial sister, Onoto Watanna (Winnifred Eaton Babcock). In part to avoid the stigma attached to being Chinese in this time period, Watanna took on the persona of a Japanese woman and wrote popular romances such as *A Japanese Nightingale* (1901). Although Watanna has been criticized by some scholars for avoiding the problems of Chinese Americans, Dominika Ferens argues for parallelism between the two sisters in terms of their use of pseudonyms and their strategies for literary success. Critics such as White-Parks remain unconvinced, however, arguing that Sui Sin Far stayed faithful to at least part of her ethnic heritage, while Watanna jettisoned all of it.

Sui Sin Far wrote at a time when Chinese Americans were vilified and caricatured. Whether "true" to her ethnic heritage or not, it is clear that Sui Sin Far sought to present a positive and redeeming portrait of Chinese Americans—one that had never been presented to the public before. As she states in a letter to a publisher about one of her stories: "I do not think anything of the sort has ever been put before the public. It is a story of Chinese American life, & I believe it will take well in Cal[ifornia]" (Letter to Charles Lummis, courtesy of the Southwest Museum Archive, Los Angeles, California). Sui Sin Far's writing did "take well" in California and in the nation. Her rediscovery illustrates that her portraits of Chinese Americans speak to us even in the early twenty-first century and that her literary artistry—which did not achieve full recognition in her lifetime—is certainly appreciated.

See also Assimilation; Chinese; Immigration; San Francisco; Short Story

BIBLIOGRAPHY

Primary Works

Hartnell, Ella. "Some Little Heathens." *Land of Sunshine* 5 (September 1896): 153–157.

Lewis, Henry Harrison. *At the Mikado's Court: The Adventures of Three American Boys in Modern Japan.* New York: D. Appleton, 1907.

London, Jack. *The Unabridged Jack London.* Edited by Lawrence Teacher and Richard E. Nicholls. Philadelphia: Running Press, 1981.

Sui Sin Far. Letter to Charles Lummis, 18 June 1896. Southwest Museum Library, Los Angeles. Quote reproduced with permission of the Southwest Museum.

Sui Sin Far. *Mrs. Spring Fragrance.* Chicago: A. C. McClurg, 1912.

Sui Sin Far. *Mrs. Spring Fragrance and Other Writings.* Edited by Amy Ling and Annette White-Parks. Urbana: University of Illinois Press, 1995. This edition, which was quoted in this essay; includes "Leaves from the Mental Portfolio of an Eurasian" (1909).

Secondary Works

Ammons, Elizabeth. *Conflicting Stories: American Women Writers at the Turn into the Twentieth Century.* New York: Oxford University Press, 1991.

Cutter, Martha J. "Empire and the Mind of the Child: Sui Sin Far's 'Tales of Chinese Children.'" *MELUS: Journal of the Society for the Study of the Multi-Ethnic Literature of the United States* 27, no. 2 (2002): 31–48.

Cutter, Martha J. "Smuggling across the Borders of Race, Gender, and Sexuality: Sui Sin Far's *Mrs. Spring Fragrance.*" In *Essays on Mixed Race Literature,* edited by Jonathan Brennan, pp. 137–164. Stanford, Calif.: Stanford University Press, 2002.

Ferens, Dominika. *Edith and Winnifred Eaton: Chinatown Missions and Japanese Romances.* Urbana: University of Illinois Press, 2002.

Foner, Philip S., and Daniel Rosenberg, eds. *Racism, Dissent, and Asian Americans from 1850 to the Present: A Documentary History.* Westport, Conn.: Greenwood Press, 1993.

Ling, Amy. "Edith Eaton: Pioneer Chinamerican Writer and Feminist." *American Literary Realism* 16 (autumn 1983): 287–298.

Nguyen, Viet Thanh. *Race and Resistance: Literature and Politics in Asian America.* New York: Oxford University Press, 2002.

Roh-Spaulding, Carol. "'Wavering' Images: Mixed Race Identity in the Stories of Edith Eaton/Sui Sin Far." In *Ethnicity and the American Short Story,* edited by Julie Brown, pp. 155–176. New York: Garland, 1997.

Solberg, S. E. "Sui Sin Far/Edith Eaton: First Chinese-American Fictionist." *MELUS: Journal of the Society for the Study of the Multi-Ethnic Literature of the United States* 8, no. 1 (1981): 27–39.

Song, Min. "The Unknowable and Sui Sin Far: The Epistemological Limits of 'Oriental' Sexuality." In *Q & A: Queer in Asian America,* edited by David L. Eng and Alice Y. Hom, pp. 304–322. Philadelphia: Temple University Press, 1998.

White-Parks, Annette. *Sui Sin Far/Edith Maude Eaton: A Literary Biography.* Urbana: University of Illinois Press, 1995.

Xiao-huang Yin. *Chinese American Literature since the 1850s.* Urbana: University of Illinois Press, 2000.

Martha J. Cutter

MUCKRAKERS AND YELLOW JOURNALISM

The years following the American Civil War were a time of industrial and technological expansion in the United States unlike any the world had seen previously. Job creation and industrial development were unequivocally considered to be social goods. The purported heroes of the age were industrial titans with names such as Carnegie, Rockefeller, and Morgan. By and large, the political leaders of the era gave way to the greed of these entrepreneurs. In such an environment, business owners resisted unions and workers were given few rights. With no regulative agency, consumers bought at their own risk. If a consumer noticed a problem with a certain item, there was no available information technology to alert others. The nineteenth century offered a frontierlike, "no safety nets" era of consumption.

Many factors altered this plight by the close of the century. Possibly most significant is that journalists began to flex their muscle by the 1890s. Referred to as "yellow journalism," this style of writing derived from dubious motives. Most notably, "yellow journalism" was magnified by the newspaper circulation battle between two publishers, William Randolph Hearst and Joseph Pulitzer. Graphic illustrations commissioned from some of the country's most talented artists and stories written by premiere authors and journalists of the day exaggerated the plight of Cubans under Spanish rule in the early 1890s and fanned the flames of war. As the public furor grew, President William McKinley (1843–1901) sent the USS *Maine* to Havana Harbor in 1898. The navy had functioned as a symbol of American expansionism. McKinley hoped that the modern ship might demonstrate American military might to the rebels. When the *Maine* exploded in Havana Harbor, the prowar press had roused national sentiment to the point that

President McKinley felt he had to act. Although the explosion could not be definitively tied to anyone, journalists pointed the finger at the Spanish occupiers and thus began the public's call to "Remember the *Maine!*" The popular will drove McKinley to initiate the Spanish-American War.

New technologies allowed publications to be distributed broadly, which also enhanced the power of the written word. During the 1890s a few writers concentrated this power for the public good. The new journalism worked in tandem with a generation of young Americans who emerged from fairly prosperous upbringing in the late 1890s with a desire for social reform. Women, particularly those of the upper class whom the Victorian era had loosed from labor and developed intellectually, fueled the call for the social reform movement. A small group of young writers chose to use their power to influence the reading public, particularly upper-class women.

The first outlets for such writing were magazines, including *Godey's Lady's Book* (1830–1898), which sold 150,000 copies monthly at its peak in the 1850s. *Godey's* writers mixed discussion of women's rights and employment with sentimental fiction and elaborate fashion plates. In addition, Amelia Bloomer's *The Lily* (1849–1856) promoted temperance and dress reform, and Elizabeth Cady Stanton and Susan B. Anthony founded *The Revolution* in 1868, a weekly magazine that branched out from women's rights to such topics as land and labor reform. Encouraged by the Postal Act of 1879, which facilitated nationwide communications with low second-class rates, the number of magazine titles grew overall from 700 in 1865 to 4,400 by 1890. The stage was set for journalists and magazines to take a more active role in educating the public.

SHAPING THE MUCKRAKING TRADITION

Magazines and serialized nonfiction would form the foundation of the "muckraking" tradition, but the subject matter continued to take shape against the culture of the late 1800s. Literary works played an important role in initiating the call for reform.

The era of big business created fortunes that allowed a younger generation to ask serious questions of the American model of progress. The expanding economy of the late nineteenth century was ripe for development by those with foresight and an aggressive approach to business. The ethics of these few successful tycoons are considered extremely dubious by twenty-first century standards. Even though they amassed some of the greatest fortunes in human history, these businessmen would become known as "robber barons." Due to the questionable way that figures acquired their wealth, the era of the robber barons is referred to as the "Gilded Age": lavish and beautiful on the outside but false on the interior. The beauty of the age was only skin-deep, and the ugly interior was dominated by human suffering. The imbalance of this situation, as described by Henry George, Edward Bellamy, Frank Norris, Lincoln Steffens, and other literary figures, fueled the political reform movement beginning in the 1890s.

These writers focused on the business practices of the barons. During the Gilded Age, many capitalists resisted considerations of workplace safety and human welfare in order to create the greatest profits. For instance, child labor became a norm in factories, mines, and other extremely dangerous environments, largely because children required the least pay. The intensity of this growth surged following the Civil War. This growth and a general faith in economic development allowed a few corporations to gain control of entire commodities and their production. Called "trusts," these conglomerates were near monopolies during an era when government and society had not yet defined such an entity as evil.

Railroads and steel were primary examples of this type of growth; however, petroleum, which had been discovered in 1859, provides the best example in the form of the Standard Oil Trust. John D. Rockefeller Sr. (1839–1937) formed a corporation that owned few oil wells but almost completely controlled the refining of crude oil into other products. He wanted to drive all of his competitors out of business. To lower his expenses, Rockefeller made a secret deal with the railroad owners. He told each that unless they gave him lower rates than anyone else, he would take his business elsewhere. By 1880 Rockefeller controlled 90 percent of the oil in the United States. Competitors were unable to match his low prices, and Rockefeller even began to receive kickbacks from the railroads he chose to use.

The ideas of Henry George (1839–1897) began the muckraking tradition. George's *Progress and Poverty,* which first appeared in 1879, functioned as a call for revision to the American political economy. Without emphasizing a single industry, George's treatise offered a philosophical approach to work and workers that was similar to what would become known as the "Social Gospel." He argued that ownership of land by private individuals was the chief cause of poverty. Although he stopped short of socialism, George argued for public ownership of railways and other monopolies such as telegraphs.

Against a culture in which Rockefeller's business ethics were the norm, reformers came to see journalism as a way of voicing discontent. Their impassioned pleas found receptive ears among the elite Americans, particularly women of the era. Activists such as Jacob Riis, who wrote *How the Other Half Lives* in 1890 to describe life in New York City slums, and Jane Addams, who started Hull-House to aid immigrant acclimation to American culture, led a movement for progressive reform. Ironically, the wealth of some robber barons would contribute to the evolution of a public consciousness on issues such as ghettoes, environmental degradation, and unfair labor practices.

BRINGING MUCK TO THE PEOPLE

A new breed of journalism became both a tool and expression of these new concerns. Writing fiction, documentaries, and serialized articles, these socially concerned writers began to critically consider the corruption and exploitation involving large companies. The term "muckrakers" was coined by President Theodore Roosevelt (1858–1919) in 1906 in reference to their ability to uncover "dirt." Roosevelt borrowed the word from John Bunyan's *Pilgrim's Progress* (1668), which spoke of a man with a "Muck-rake in his hand" who raked filth rather than look up to nobler things. Later the presidential candidate for the Progressive Party in 1912, Roosevelt recognized the muckrakers' key role in publicizing the need for progressive reform but demanded that they also know when to stop in order to avoid stirring up radical unrest.

Many fine writers made their name during the muckraking era of the 1890s and early 1900s. A crucial device in this movement was *McClure's Magazine,* which began running installments of muckraking investigations before they were released as books. Ida Tarbell (1857–1944) had been at work for years on her history of the Standard Oil Company, and it began to run in *McClure's* in November 1902.

McClure's remained at the heart of this new journalistic form. In the 1880s S. S. McClure had dropped the price of his general-interest magazine to only fifteen cents. He hoped to create a magazine that would appeal to the growing reading masses in the United States. *McClure's* circulation climbed, and it became one of many magazines constructing a new, mass culture that was not restricted to elite Americans. Muckraking articles played directly into this change in readership. From 1902 to 1912 over a thousand such articles were published in magazines specializing in the genre, including *McClure's, Everybody's,* and *Collier's.*

McClure's best-known authors of this era included Tarbell, who wrote "History of the Standard Oil Company" (November 1902–October 1904) and

McClure's Magazine, **November 1903.** Cover listing muckraking articles by Ray Stannard Baker, Lincoln Steffens, and Cleveland Moffett. THE LIBRARY OF CONGRESS

"John D. Rockefeller: A Character Sketch" (July 1905); Lincoln Steffens (1866–1936), who wrote primarily about city and state politics in "Enemies of the Republic" (March 1904), "Rhode Island: A State for Sale" (February 1905), "New Jersey: A Traitor State" (April 1905), and "Ohio: A Tale of Two Cities" (July 1905); and Ray Stannard Baker (1870–1946), who dealt with racial discrimination and other issues in articles such as "What the United States Steel Corporation Really Is?" (November 1901), "The Right to Work" (January 1903), "Reign of Lawlessness" (May 1904), "What Is Lynching?" (January 1905), "Railroads on Trial" (January 1906), and "How Railroads Make Public Opinion" (March 1906). Subsequent writers in the muckraking tradition included Thomas W. Lawson (1857–1925), who wrote about insurance and stock manipulation, David Graham Phillips (1867–1911), who wrote on political corruption, and Samuel Hopkins Adams (1871–1958), who wrote about safety issues related to medicines.

TARBELL AND SINCLAIR SET THE TONE

Muckrakers demanded action. In at least two cases, the writers inspired swift and dramatic action. Tarbell was born in the oil regions of northwestern Pennsylvania. She watched as her father's oil tank business failed due to the unfair practices of one corporation in particular, the Standard Oil Company. To Tarbell, the efforts of John D. Rockefeller to place his company in control of the nation's energy in the early 1870s created a turning point for the nation. In the episode known as "the Oil War," Rockefeller sought to dominate petroleum markets worldwide. Initially, small producers banded together and defeated his efforts. But Rockefeller built his Standard Oil from the ashes of this initial setback. By the end of the 1870s Standard controlled roughly 80 percent of the world's oil supply. By dominating transportation and refining, Rockefeller dominated the market.

An alarming picture of "Big Oil" took shape as Standard used ruthless business practices, including rollbacks and insider pricing, to squeeze out its

Upton Sinclair, photographed in 1905. © HULTON-DEUTSCH/ CORBIS

competitors. Tarbell, who had become a successful journalist and editor, wanted to expose what Rockefeller was really doing. Across the nation, readers awaited each of the nineteen installments on the story published by *McClure's* from 1902 to 1904. Though Tarbell teemed with bitterness for what Rockefeller had done to the private businessmen of Pennsylvania's oil business, she appreciated the value of allowing the details of the story to express her point of view. The articles were compiled into the *History of the Standard Oil Company* (1904). President Theodore Roosevelt, who succeeded McKinley in 1901, used the public furor created by the articles to order a federal investigation. Tarbell's work inspired new efforts to enforce antitrust laws. In 1911 the Supreme Court ordered the dissolution of Standard Oil.

Upton Sinclair (1878–1968) also achieved significant changes through his writing. Sinclair's most famous book, *The Jungle,* was published after Tarbell's work gained almost immediate action. In *The Jungle* the meatpacking industry of Chicago was the setting for the tale of a Lithuanian immigrant named Jurgis Rudkus. Although Sinclair made the difficult experience of new immigrants the primary theme of the narrative, readers were drawn to the details of squalor in which their meat and other food was prepared. In the end *The Jungle* exposed the horrors of the Chicago meatpacking plants and the immigrants who were worked to death in them to a wide audience.

In a 1906 issue of *Literary Digest,* the meatpackers themselves protested Sinclair's characterization:

> We regret that if you feel confident the report of your commissioners is true, you did not make the investigation more thorough, so that the American public and the world at large might know that there are packers and packers and that if some are unworthy of public confidence, there are others whose methods are above board and whose goods are of such high quality as to be a credit to the American nation.

However, the public reacted so strongly that Congress launched an investigation of the meatpacking plants of Chicago. Based on the commission's findings, Roosevelt pushed through the 1906 Pure Food and Drug legislation that placed regulatory authority with the federal government. It was one of the first moments in which Progressivism placed the responsibility for protecting citizens' everyday lives on the federal government.

Throughout the twentieth century, this expectation consistently increased. As president, Roosevelt held the ideal that the government should be the great arbiter of the conflicting economic forces in the nation, especially between capital and labor, guaranteeing justice to each and dispensing favors to none.

GETTING RESULTS

Spurred by the muckrakers, Roosevelt helped to create responsive federal legislation that appeared to be concerned about the welfare of "common" people. However, he remained dubious of the journalists' tendency toward sensationalism. Similar to twenty-first-century investigative journalists, muckrakers could sell more papers or copies by shocking readers. Despite such tendencies, the writing of muckrakers forever altered the role of American journalism and spurred the continued growth of a social consciousness in the United States.

In general, the writings of this era served the political movement known as Progressivism. Leaders such as Roosevelt and Gifford Pinchot argued vociferously that the government had a responsibility to its citizens. Some of this social change derived from moralism, in which Progressives instructed people on what they should decide. Some critics called this sanctimonious. Supporters of muckraking and the Progressive movement, however, argued that writers such as Sinclair were reformers who were upholding American values and the American way of life.

With the justification of reform, Roosevelt's administration entered into open confrontation with big business. Roosevelt's reputation as a Progressive grew in 1902 when Pennsylvania coal miners went on strike for higher wages and better working conditions. Roosevelt threatened to send in the army to operate mines unless the owners agreed to arbitration. Some people said that this governmental interference went against the U.S. Constitution. They argued that the government had no right to take command of public property, but Roosevelt replied that the constitution was intended to serve the people, not vice versa.

Next, Roosevelt followed the findings of the muckraking journalists and attacked a few giant business trusts. He argued that these trusts were becoming too powerful and prevented economic competition. While some business leaders were angered, many Americans cheered Roosevelt and nicknamed him the "trustbuster." Roosevelt said that he wanted to give a "square deal" to the seller, consumer, employer, and employee. He did this by utilizing the Sherman Antitrust Act, which had been enacted in 1890 but largely left unused.

Roosevelt had tapped into a spirit of the times. He perceived the impact of reformers and journalists and appropriated it as part of his progressive initiatives. Progressives argued for an activist government that foresaw problems and acted aggressively to prevent calamities before they occurred rather than reacting to damage already done. Thus Progressives in Congress demanded safety legislation, closer regulation of public health issues, and better management of things such as public utilities.

By 1906 the combined sales of the ten magazines that concentrated on investigative journalism reached a total circulation of three million. Writers and publishers associated with this investigative journalism movement between 1890 and 1914 included Riis, Norris, Tarbell, Russell, Sinclair, and Steffens, along with Henry Demarest Lloyd, Nellie Bly, David Graham Phillips, C. P. Connolly, Benjamin Hampton, Thomas Lawson, Alfred Henry Lewis, and Ray Stannard Baker. Many of these investigative journalists objected when Roosevelt described them as muckrakers. Some of the journalists felt that the president had betrayed them after they had helped improve his political standing.

The muckraking journalists can be credited with initiating a movement that created significant change between 1900 and 1915, including the dissolution of the convict and peonage systems in some states; reform of prisons; passage of a federal pure food act in 1906; adoption of child labor laws by many states; 1906 passage of a federal employers' liability act; expansion and development of the forest reserve system; the reclamation of millions of acres of land in the West after passage of the Newlands Act of 1902; construction of a policy of the conservation of natural resources; eight-hour labor laws for women were passed in some states; prohibition of racetrack gambling; twenty states passed mothers' pension acts between 1908 and 1913. Furthermore, twenty-five states had workmen's compensation laws by 1915, and an income tax amendment was also added to the Constitution. In each case, an activist federal government implemented reforms to basic portions of American life.

See also The Jungle; McClure's Magazine; Reform; Spanish-American War

BIBLIOGRAPHY
Primary Works
Addams, Jane. *Twenty Years at Hull-House.* New York: Macmillan, 1910.

Baker, Ray Stannard. *American Chronicle.* 1925. New York: Charles Scribner's Sons, 1945.

McClure, Samuel Sidney. *My Autobiography.* New York: Frederick A. Stokes Co., 1914.

"The Packers' Reply." *Literary Digest* 32 (16 June 1906).

Sinclair, Upton. *The Jungle*. New York: Doubleday, Page, and Co., 1906.

Steffens, Joseph Lincoln. *The Shame of the Cities*. New York: McClure, Phillips and Co., 1904.

Tarbell, Ida M. *All in the Day's Work*. New York: Macmillan, 1939.

Tarbell, Ida M. *The History of Standard Oil Company*. New York: McClure, Phillips and Co., 1904.

Secondary Works

Chalmers, David M. *The Social and Political Ideas of the Muckrakers*. New York: Citadel Press, 1964.

Colburn, David R., and George E. Pozzetta. *Reform and Reformers in the Progressive Era*. Westport, Conn.: Greenwood Press, 1983.

Filler, Louis. *Appointment at Armageddon: Muckraking and Progressivism in the American Tradition*. Westport, Conn.: Greenwood Press, 1976.

Filler, Louis. *Progressivism and Muckraking*. New York: R. R. Bowker, 1976.

Hofstadter, Richard. *The Age of Reform: From Bryan to F. D. R.* New York: Knopf, 1955.

Pendergast, Tom. *Creating the Modern Man: American Magazines and Consumer Culture, 1900–1950*. Columbia: University of Missouri Press, 2000.

Schneirov, Matthew. *The Dream of a New Social Order: Popular Magazines in America 1893–1914*. New York: Columbia University Press, 1994.

Shapiro, Bruce, ed. *Shaking the Foundations: 200 Years of Investigative Journalism in America*. New York: Thunder's Mouth Press/Nation Books, 2002.

Stein, Harry, ed. *Muckraking: Past, Present, and Future*. University Park: Pennsylvania State University Press, 1973.

Weinberg, Arthur and Lila. *The Muckrakers*. New York: Capricorn Books, 1964.

Wilson, Harold S. *McClure's Magazine and the Muckrakers*. Princeton, N.J.: Princeton University Press, 1970.

Brian Black

MURDER

See Violence

MUSEUMS

Most of the major museums in the United States were founded at the end of the nineteenth century. The Smithsonian Institution (1846), the American Museum of Natural History (1869), the Metropolitan Museum of Art (1870), Boston's Museum of Fine Arts (1870), the Chicago Art Institute (1879), and the Field Museum (1893) fostered original research, the results of which were more available to the public than they would have been at universities. The growth and popularity of American museums was spurred by a complex combination of sociopolitical forces at a time when rapid industrialization was transforming the American pastoral landscape into a series of major urban centers. Providing access to knowledge was the primary purpose of these institutions; the acquisition of new materials was essential for the advancement of that knowledge; and the appeal of novelty was the key to attracting the public to that knowledge housed within the museum walls.

THE CITY BEAUTIFUL MOVEMENT

American museums, as "public repositories of culture" (Steffensen-Bruce, p. 46), are connected to the City Beautiful movement and also to modern notions about the function of art and knowledge in the civic life of urban dwellers. The City Beautiful movement stemmed from the belief that a beautiful landscape would inspire a city's inhabitants to moral and civic virtue. A beautiful city would eliminate social ills, bring American cities up to the level of European ones, and attract economic investment from the wealthy classes. The museum, then, and especially the art museum, was seen as an antidote to urban moral and social decay. The belief was that the art museum, as a repository of beautiful objects to be contemplated, would bring a visitor nearer to God. These ideas were developed and institutionalized by a powerful social elite: "As an institution, [the art museum] embodied the kind of high cultural aspirations that the urban cultural elite sought to incorporate in their vision of the twentieth century American city" (Steffensen-Bruce, p. 104). Therefore, museums were founded with the goal of making knowledge accessible to as many citizens as possible for the advancement of moral values and spiritual improvement. Some would see this as a contradictory function—museums were both an "elite temple of the arts, and . . . a utilitarian instrument for democratic education"—since after all, they became the site where "bodies, constantly under surveillance, were to be rendered docile" (Bennett, p. 89).

No longer were museums solely the "treasure houses" of the wealthy elite, whose collections were designed primarily to excite the visitor's wonder at the exotic in the Renaissance tradition of the *Wunderkammern* (cabinets of wonders). Now they were also "sites of intellectual and cultural debates" where knowledge was in the hands of a few who had the power to create meaning and order for public

The opening of the American Museum of Natural History in New York City, 1869. Representing the popular conception of the city as a place of enlightenment and culture, museums were viewed variously by writers according to their opinions of the dominant cultural values. © CORBIS

consumption (Conn, p. 15). By the end of the nineteenth century, the American museum served the needs of scientists by funding expeditions and acquiring collections in the name of research. They also made themselves appealing to the general public, whose knowledge was shaped in the interest of progress and democratic civic duty. Museums, therefore, wielded enormous power over the masses; shaping public knowledge meant shaping notions of beauty, of proper behavior and morality, and of cultural dominance. Abstract concepts of beauty, morality, and culture could be displayed: "Museums have always featured displays of power: great men, great wealth, or great deeds. The emphasis could be on the spoils of war, victors in the marketplace, or man as the crown of creation. In all these instances, museums have ratified claims of superiority" (Dubin, p. 3). Stephen Greenblatt argues that there are two models for the exhibition of works of art: resonance and

wonder. Resonance is "the power of the displayed object to reach out beyond its formal boundaries to a larger world, to evoke in the viewer the complex, dynamic cultural forces from which it has emerged and for which it may be taken by a viewer to stand" (p. 42). Wonder is "the power of the displayed object to stop the viewer in his or her tracks, to convey an arresting sense of uniqueness, to evoke an exalted attention" (p. 42). Greenblatt argues, furthermore, that the museum "intensifies both access and exclusion."

Complementing the influence of the art museum was the growth of the natural history museum, closely tied to several academic disciplines. These museums were the only institutions at the time that had enough resources to fund large-scale expeditions (Conn, p. 53). Although the motivations behind the 1846 bequest from an heirless British citizen, James Smithson, to the United States remain a mystery, his desire that his money be used "to contribute to the increase and diffusion of knowledge" was taken seriously by the members of Congress. How best to carry out these wishes was not an easy question to answer. It was suggested several times that the money be invested in a college or university, but John Quincy Adams "reminded his colleagues that the purpose of a college was not to increase knowledge but to diffuse that which already existed" (Conn, p. 54). Thus, in the 1880s, the Smithsonian Institution was opened to the public.

SITES OF MEMORY

The growth of urban museums throughout the nation (more than fifty art museums were built between 1890 and 1930) at the instigation of the country's governing institutions was intricately connected to a burgeoning national identity (Steffensen-Bruce, p. 199). If museums function as sites of memory where curators "artificially organize the past, creating meanings that groups then assimilate in order to cope: with modernity" (Crane, p. 6), it appears that this fairly new nation was busy trying to prevent "the natural erosion of memory" (Crane, p. 9). These sites of memory played an important role in securing the nation's claim of natural cultural superiority. A representative for the "committee of fifty," a group of New York businessmen, financiers, and artists, made a speech to Congress in 1869 claiming that the United States needed museums and that one should be established in New York. The resulting Metropolitan Museum displayed the wealth of the new city: "A history of the Metropolitan could quite justifiably be a chronicle of dazzling acquisitions, purchases, and accumulation, beginning from the earliest days and continuing through the present. The Metropolitan, more than any other museum, stands as the elegant child produced by the union between the vast fortunes of America's robber barons and the refined good taste of its social elite" (Conn, p. 193).

This same concern for building a strong city with a glorious history and a place in the life of the growing nation can be found in Chicago. The Field Museum, which opened in 1893, served to enshrine the glorious days of the Columbian Exposition and developed hand in hand with the emerging field of anthropology. The Art Institute was built to put Chicago on the map of progressive cities, to move beyond its reputation as a meatpacking town. The Chicago Art Institute, founded in 1879, was also an effort to create a Chicago of cultural import: "They were not the Robber Barons trying to show off. They were the civic leaders trying to make culture hum in Chicago, and succeeding" (Burt, p. 181).

MUSEUMS AND LITERATURE

American literature at the turn of the century had undergone a transformation parallel to that of the museum: it secured a position both as a transmitter of "high culture" and as a form of popular culture enjoyed by the middle class. The American literary tradition of romanticism gave way to realism, which pointed out social injustices, uncovered the ills caused by out-of-control industrialization, and exposed the failures of a hypocritical elite. The threat of the urban machine that dehumanized the poor, especially in growing American cities, was demystified by some of the most important writers of the time: Henry James, William Dean Howells, Edith Wharton, Willa Cather, Stephen Crane, Theodore Dreiser, Frank Norris, and Upton Sinclair, among others. The literature of this period also responds to issues important to the museums founded at the turn of the century: the power of wonder at the possibilities of the city and the evils of acquisitiveness in American society.

The advent of publishing, the diffusion of Charles Darwin's theories, the growth of the city, and the demand for better newspapers, magazines, and museums signaled an increased interest on the public's part for objects and ideas previously reserved for the leisure class. Vocational education, universities, and the printed word were the chief instruments by which cultural knowledge was made accessible to the masses. In New York, Chicago, Boston, and Philadelphia, the book trade prospered thanks to the efforts of the gentrified class, which sought to impose its cultural values on other segments of society: "[The gentry] cared about the traditional high arts and letters—indeed, it located in the domain of the arts the sort of founding or elemental value no longer located in religion" (*Columbia Literary History,* p. 471). In these terms, the spiritual value to be derived from the museum was equally present in literature. The cultural elite, the wealthy classes in the cities, believed "that concerns for such values was the base of civilization itself, it felt entitled and even obliged to try to impose this sense of value throughout its society: to disseminate culture so conceived throughout the land" (*Columbia Literary History,* p. 471). Many cultural tensions present at the turn of the century had to do precisely with the increase and wide diffusion of a scientific knowledge that seemed to be at odds with the traditional notions of spirituality and religion. These tensions were reflected not only in how museum collections were acquired and how displays were conceived but also in the problems realist novels addressed.

William Dean Howells (1837–1920) was the most popular exponent of realism. His work was based on the belief that writers must avoid the heroic and privilege the habitual and the natural. In doing so, they would make a faithful transcription of the world. The world that Howells described in *A Modern Instance* (1882), for example, depicts all the possibilities that a city could offer—wealth, status, knowledge, as well as the inevitable corruption of a competitive society. The museum in this novel appears as a refuge from the corrupting values of the city. *A Modern Instance* chronicles the life of newlyweds from the countryside who move to the city seeking their fortune. The museum is one of the places they regularly visit as a couple. At work, the protagonist, Bartley, is mocked for spending so much time with his wife in leisure activities. Bartley's wife sadly reminisces that it was in the museum that "they found a pleasure in the worst things which the best never afterwards gave them" (p. 337). What they find instead of fortune is a life of corruption and vice, as Bartley begins to drink, gamble, and neglect his wife, eventually divorcing her. Once Bartley enters the world of business, and his wife is condemned to domesticity where she watches every penny, their marriage deteriorates. What, then, is civilization and progress? Is this what the city can offer them? What are the spiritual values that the city espouses?

Willa Cather's (1873–1947) *Song of the Lark* (1932) takes a different view, seeing the city as a place of progress, a place to look to for finer things, for freedom, for the development of youthful dreams. Yet the novel's take on the museum as a place of spiritual enlightenment is similar to Howells's. Thea Krönberg, the heroine of *Song of the Lark,* discovers the power of her voice when she moves east to New York from a small town in the Midwest. According to Cather, the novel, written in 1915, was named "for a rather second rate French Painting in the Chicago Art Institute; a picture in which a little peasant girl, on her way to work in the fields at early morning, stops and looks up to listen to a lark. The title was meant to suggest a young girl's awakening to something beautiful" (p. xxxi). When Thea stops in Chicago, she finds a booming town unlike the small town she has left behind. She visits the Chicago Art Institute, where she sees the painting that gave the book its title and is moved by it. She briefly returns to her hometown, only to find that her family does not understand her ambition. She then moves back to New York in hopes of becoming an opera singer.

Henry James (1843–1916), by contrast, sees the city as a place whose progress is stultifying to women, and the museum is symbolic of its deadening values. In the story "Julia Bride" (1907), James portrays a woman who, with the museum as the setting for her rendezvous, seems to collect marriage engagements the way museums collect works of art. In the museum she meets with her stepfather, who has recently divorced her mother, to enlist his help with a potential suitor. He has a proposition of his own, however, asking Julia to put in a good word for him with a widow he wants to marry. He tells Julia, "She loves this place—she is awfully keen on art. Like you Julia, if you haven't changed—I remember how you did love art" (p. 773). But it is not art that interests Julia. The museum is simply the place where she entertains potential suitors such as Basil French: "She saw the great shining room, with its mockery of art and 'style' and security, all the things she was vainly after" (p. 774). In this story James critiques the acquisitive power of money displayed in the museum as Julia tries to "collect" an appropriate marriage partner but fails. James is saying in part that, just as art should not be an object of trafficking, marriage as a business in the rapidly industrializing city of New York is doomed to fail (Tintner, p. 184).

Edith Wharton (1862–1937), in *The Age of Innocence* (1920), similarly critiques social norms regarding the relationship between men and women, norms that were at the time slowly falling into disuse. In that book, Archer Newland is wrestling with the plausibility of having an affair with Ellen, a married woman. He and Ellen meet at the Metropolitan Museum of Art where they look at relics. Ellen says, "It seems cruel that after a while nothing matters any more than these little things, that used to be necessary and important to forgotten people, and now have to be guessed at under a magnifying glass and labeled: Use Unknown" (p. 312). The museum has become a private space for Ellen and Archer's rendezvous, yet this reaction to the relics foreshadows how the conventions they are defying will become useless with the passing of time. Despite their recognition of how quickly these conventions are becoming obsolete, they remain prisoners to them even many years later, when they are free to resume their relationship. Archer at least is unable to act on his feelings for Ellen.

American literature at the turn of the century critiques the intellectual apparatus that give rise to institutions such as the museum. Taken together, the literature of the time reflects many of the issues that drove the evolution of the American museum, including a desire to make knowlege, albeit a carefully controlled subset of knowledge, widely available to the general public. Yet at the same time, this literature questions the morals and archaic customs to which people were subjected.

See also Art and Architecture; Chicago; Libraries; New York

BIBLIOGRAPHY

Primary Works

Cather, Willa. *Song of the Lark*. Boston: Houghton Mifflin, 1988.

Howells, William Dean. *A Modern Instance*. In *Novels, 1875–1886*. New York: Literary Classics of the United States, 1982.

James, Henry. "Julia Bride." In *American Novels and Stories of Henry James,* edited by F. O. Matthiessen. New York: Knopf, 1947.

Wharton, Edith. *The Age of Innocence*. New York: Random House, 1920.

Secondary Works

Bennett, Tony. *The Birth of the Museum: History, Theory, Politics*. London: Routledge, 1995.

Burt, Nathaniel. *Palaces for the People: A Social History of the American Art Museum*. Boston: Little, Brown, 1977.

Columbia Literary History of the United States. New York: Columbia University Press, 1988.

Conn, Steven. *Museums and American Intellectual Life, 1876–1926*. Chicago: University of Chicago Press, 1998.

Crane, Susan, ed. *Museums and Memory*. Stanford, Calif.: Stanford University Press, 2000.

Dubin, Stephen C. *Displays of Power: Memory and Amnesia in the American Museum*. New York: New York University Press, 1999.

Greenblatt, Stephen. "Resonance and Wonder." In *Exhibiting Cultures: The Poetics and Politics of Museum Display,* edited by Ivan Karp and Steven D. Lavine. Washington, D.C.: Smithsonian Institution Press, 1991.

Griffiths, Alison. "Museums and Displays of Knowledge." *Odyssey,* broadcast on Chicago Public Radio, 30 August 2004.

Steffensen-Bruce, Ingrid A. *Marble Palaces, Temples of Art: Art Museums, Architecture, and American Culture, 1890–1930*. Lewisburg, Pa.: Bucknell University Press, 1998.

Tintner, Adeline R. *The Museum World of Henry James*. Ann Arbor, Mich.: UMI Research Press, 1986.

Liza Ann Acosta

MUSIC

By 1870 practices transplanted by European colonists had taken root across the spectrum of American culture—whether it be the concert music of the elite and the aspiring middle class or the entertainment music of both urban and rural citizens. By that time, moreover, traditions identified as distinctively American in origin—ones typically percolating up from the least prestigious sectors of society—were already well seasoned. The fruits of the Industrial Revolution—notably cheap paper, mass production of instruments, and ultimately the preservation and dissemination of performances via sound recording and radio—transformed musical life in all spheres. Between 1870 and 1920 the United States experienced watershed developments in music making and music sociology that consolidated its past, gave expression to currents and crosscurrents of the time, and provided the foundation for the near future when American musicians and American musical institutions would exert great influence beyond national borders.

THE FINE ART TRADITION

With continued imitation of Continental models for composition, performance, and education, the entrenched East Coast establishment upheld European ideals—especially those of the German Romantics. The many immigrant teachers at work throughout the nation, the custom of sending young talents abroad for formal study, and a firmly held belief in the superiority of German art conditioned these practices. Symbolic of this orientation are John Knowles Paine (1839–1906), George Whitefield Chadwick (1854–1941), and Edward MacDowell (1860–1908). Each was hailed for achievements in Germany before returning home to preach the transatlantic gospel in compositions and to take leading positions as educators—Paine at Harvard University, Chadwick at the New England Conservatory, and MacDowell at Columbia University. Paine, the first full professor of music at an American university in 1875, was particularly influential as a teacher. Less than a generation later, in the 1890s, MacDowell was revered according to European standards as the most accomplished composer the country had yet produced. Chadwick displayed the highest degree of originality of the three.

Associated with this loose confederation of like-minded professionals, often identified as the Second New England School or the Boston Classicists, was Mrs. H. H. A. [Amy Marcy Cheney] Beach. Although denied the desired European pedigree because of her gender and largely self-taught, she achieved genuine fame as a composer and pianist at home and abroad. Because of success in large forms especially, Beach's pioneering example as a woman composer is historic.

Such figures, the majority holding academic positions and turning out well-crafted works in preordained forms and genres, benefited from an ingrained national inferiority complex with respect to European culture and by the propagation of professional institutions.

A CHRONOLOGY OF AMERICAN MUSIC, 1870–1920

1871: First tour of the Jubilee Singers of Fisk University (Nashville, Tenn.)

First reported written use of the term "vaudeville" in the context of American variety entertainment (Louisville, Ky.)

1873: Publication of *Sacred Songs and Solos,* first collection of gospel songs by the partners Ira David Sankey (singer/composer) and Dwight C. Moody (evangelist)

1875: Appointment of John Knowles Paine to first full professorship in music (Harvard University)

1876: First publication in Germany of a symphony written by an American composer: Symphony No. 1 in C Minor by John Knowles Paine

1877: Development by Thomas A. Edison of first commercially viable sound recording mechanism

1879: Performance in America of as many as one hundred productions of Gilbert and Sullivan's *H.M.S. Pinafore* (including one all-black, one all-children, and one Yiddish)

Affiliation of James A. Bland, composer of "Carry Me Back to Old Virginny" (1878), with Haverly's Genuine Colored Minstrels, an early all-black troupe

1881: Founding of the Boston Symphony Orchestra

The demise of the influential, Boston-based *Dwight's Journal of Music* after espousing "good music" based on German principles for twenty-nine years

Opening in New York City of the first vaudeville house conceived for men and women by Tony Pastor

Establishment in New York City of T. B. Harms, the publishing firm that revolutionized the popular song industry

1883: Opening of the Metropolitan Opera House in New York City

Most geographically extensive tour of the Theodore Thomas Orchestra, led by Theodore Thomas—from Baltimore to San Francisco and then back across the Upper Midwest

1884: First issue of the *Etude,* monthly periodical directed to piano teachers and their students (Theodore Presser, Lynchburg, Va.)

1886: Founding of the National Conservatory of Music in New York City by Jeanette Thurber

1891: Founding of the Chicago Symphony Orchestra

1892: Arrival in New York City of Antonín Dvořák to direct the National Conservatory of Music

First public concert of the Sousa Band (in Plainfield, N.J.)

1896: Composition of Symphony No. 1 in E Minor ("Gaelic") by Mrs. H. H. A. Beach, the first symphony written by an American woman and the first symphony by an American to quote folk tunes as thematic material

Composition by Edward MacDowell of the suite of character pieces for piano *Woodland Sketches,* containing "To a Wild Rose"

Formation of the American Federation of Musicians, trade union for professional musicians

1897: Publication of "On the Banks of the Wabash," best-known song of Paul Dresser

Premiere of "Stars and Stripes Forever" by John Philip Sousa (Philadelphia, Pa.)

1898: Founding of the National Federation of Musical Clubs, a network of women societies advocating the performance and study of fine-art music

1899: Publication of Scott Joplin's "Original Rags" and "Maple Leaf Rag" (John Stark, Sedalia, Mo.)

1900: Founding of the Philadelphia Orchestra

1901: Founding of the Wa-Wan Press by Arthur Farwell (Newton Center, Mass.)

1903: American debut of Italian tenor Enrico Caruso in Verdi's *Rigoletto* with the Metropolitan Opera Company

1904: Opening of *Little Johnny Jones* (with "The Yankee Doodle Boy" and "Give My Regards to Broadway") written, composed, staged, and choreographed by its star George M. Cohan

1905: Founding of the Institute of Musical Art in New York City by Walter Damrosch (after 1924 the Juilliard School of Music)

1906: First American radio broadcast of both live and recorded music—both fine-art selections (Brant Rock, Mass.)

1907: First season of the Ziegfeld Follies produced by Florenz Ziegfeld (annual productions until 1925, with four more ending in 1931)

Publication in Germany of *Early Concert-Life in America, 1731–1800* (Breitkopf and Härtel, Leipzig) by Oscar Sonneck, early landmark scholarship on the history of American music

1909: First printing of *Songs of the Workers to Fan the Flames of Discontent: The Industrial Workers of the World Songbook* ("The Little Red Songbook")

1910: Premiere of *The Pipe of Desire* (1906) by Frederick Shepherd Converse, first opera by an American composer to be mounted by the Metropolitan Opera Company

1911: Publication of the song "Alexander's Ragtime Band," which made Irving Berlin a household name

1912: First reported appearance of the blues in European notation: W. C. Handy's "The Memphis Blues"

1913: Opening of the Palace Theatre at Broadway and Forty-second Street in New York City, in its time the most prestigious booking for vaudeville performers (two shows a day until 1932)

First appearance of the word "jaz" in print (in the *San Francisco Bulletin*)

Release of the first recordings by black musicians: ragtime arrangements by James Reese Europe and His Society Orchestra (New York City)

1914: Formation of the American Society of Composers, Authors, and Publishers (ASCAP)

1915: Completion by Charles Ives of Sonata No. 2 ("Concord, Mass., 1840–60") for piano with its tributes to Emerson, Hawthorne, the Alcotts, and Thoreau

Opening of *Nobody's Home,* first of a series of so-called "Princess Theatre musicals" created by Jerome Kern and Guy Bolton, later with P. G. Wodehouse

First issue of the *Musical Quarterly* (edited by Oscar Sonneck), a periodical devoted to musicological scholarship (G. Schirmer, New York City)

Distribution of silent film *The Birth of a Nation* by D. W. Griffith with a "live" orchestral soundtrack

of original music by Joseph Carl Breil and quotations of music by Grieg and Wagner and of patriotic tunes

Premiere performance of John Alden Carpenter's orchestral suite *Adventures in a Perambulator* by the Chicago Symphony

1916: Publication of *Jubilee Songs of the United States of America,* collection of folk song and spiritual arrangements by Harry T. Burleigh

1917: First recording of jazz, "The Dixie Jazz Band One-Step"/"Livery Stable Blues" by the Original Dixieland Jazz Band

Publication of *English Folk-Songs from the Southern Appalachians* by Olive Campbell and Cecil Sharp (G. P. Putnam's Sons, New York City)

Beginning of the diaspora of jazz musicians from New Orleans because of the closing of the notorious Storyville district

1918: Ballet performance to the symphonic poem *Dance in the Place Congo* (1908) by Henry F. B. Gilbert at the Metropolitan Opera House in New York City

Premiere of Charles Wakefield Cadman's *Shanewis, or the Robin Woman,* the first opera with a contemporary American setting presented by the Metropolitan Opera Company (partly based on the life of a Creek Indian woman and including an onstage jazz band)

Composition of *Poem* for Flute and Orchestra by Charles Tomlinson Griffes

1919: Formation of the Radio Corporation of America (RCA) by General Electric

Widely heralded assessment of jazz musician Sidney Bechet as a "genius" by Swiss conductor Ernest Ansermet (published in *Revue Romande*)

First "million-selling" recording: "Japanese Sandman"/"Whispering" by Paul Whiteman and His Orchestra

1920: Emergence of earliest commercial radio stations (WWJ in Detroit, Mich., and KDKA in Pittsburgh, Pa.)

New orchestras in major cities such as Boston, Philadelphia, Chicago, St. Louis, Minneapolis, Houston, Los Angeles, and San Francisco (and many smaller cities as well) and the Metropolitan Opera Company in New York City concentrated on European masterworks; the Theodore Thomas Orchestra, founded in 1866 by the German-born conductor whose name it bore, crisscrossed the nation by rail between 1869 and 1888, showcasing a disciplined ensemble in the grand style and introducing exalted fare to neophyte concertgoers. Visiting European artists, such as the Polish pianist Ignace Paderewski and the Italian tenor Enrico Caruso, drew appreciative audiences. Unprecedented were the acceptance of the high value and serious meaning assigned to music making of this kind and its cultivation beyond East Coast centers, often with the patronage of affluent, civic-minded men and women.

The presence of Antonín Dvořák in New York City during the mid-1890s as director of the newly founded National Conservatory of Music kindled a nationalistic impulse, a powerful manifestation of the Romantic attitude in Europe and yet one that had remained largely dormant among Americans. With his example and encouragement, a number of composers attempted to create an identifiably American concert music based on indigenous idioms that the Czech master himself had identified: the music of socially marginalized Native Americans and African Americans. This gave rise to the Indianist movement, the borrowing of exotic elements from Amerindian peoples. Operas with Indian subjects and harmonized native melodies enjoyed a vogue. Taking leadership was the midwesterner Arthur Farwell, who founded the Wa-Wan Press in 1891 to promote "American" compositions by Americans and whose own appreciation of his materials enabled him to move beyond Romantic conventions. Others, like Henry Franklin Belknap Gilbert, introduced plantation melodies and slave songs into pieces in many genres and for various media. These self-conscious endeavors represent the foundation for later, better-known efforts to synthesize Old World constructs and New World details. In retrospect, these works—while many deserve to be heard—suffer from the same burden as those whose creators adopted German practices: imitation is rarely as powerful as authentic expression. The absence of Native Americans and African Americans from the ranks of educated composers reflected the greater society. The arrangements of spirituals by Harry T. Burleigh, an African American disciple of Dvořák, stand as elegant exceptions.

Ironically, the composer whose music continues to grow in critical appreciation crafted a body of work between 1898 and 1920 that remained largely unpublished and unheard and, thus, of no immediate influence. Charles Ives (1874–1954) divided his energies between an impressive career in the insurance business and his own self-indulgent need to create with little accountability to the powers of the day or their audience. With a Yale music education (from Horatio Parker and Dudley Buck), he embraced the broadest possible range of resources—European and American,

popular and fine art, sacred and secular—and conceived a challenging, pluralistic style, one that not only took advantage of his heritage but simultaneously demonstrated a progressive rethinking of its fundamental conventions. A true Yankee eccentric, Ives experimented in the same spirit as those Europeans who were rejecting the tenets of Romanticism and creating a modern musical language. Philosophically he endorsed the ideals of New England transcendentalism and paid tribute to Ralph Waldo Emerson, Henry David Thoreau, and the Alcotts. Only after World War II did Ives's music reach a larger audience and begin to inspire successors. Another businessman-composer with an eclectic style, albeit less drastic, the Chicago-born John Alden Carpenter, achieved recognition during the first two decades of the century. His music, acclaimed in its own time, has failed to hold a place in the repertoire despite merits. By the time of his death in 1920 Charles Tomlinson Griffes had also fashioned an imaginative personal style.

Women participated in greater numbers in public music making during the decades surrounding 1900. The social construction of gender and ingrained attitudes regarding the education of girls had restricted professional opportunities beyond those sanctioned by the church and Victorian notions of gentility. A debate unfolded in the press concerning women's ability to create high art and to compose in privileged forms, for example. Dedicated women persevered: the works of Margaret Ruthven Lang, Carrie Jacobs-Bond, Clara Kathleen Rogers, and Amy Marcy Cheney Beach disproved such sexist politics. Julie Rivé-King became the first American-born woman to command the stage as a concert pianist; Maud Powell joined the ranks of virtuoso violinists; sopranos such as Clara Louise Kellogg, Lillian Nordica, and Emma Eames were celebrated as divas in the opera house. Enthusiastic reception of American females abroad only added luster to hard-won reputations as musicians of the first order. Frances Densmore and Alice C. Fletcher conducted trailblazing ethnomusicological fieldwork to document the Native Indian repertoire. The women's music club movement, reportedly begun in 1871 in Portland, Maine, had dramatically improved the nature of patronage by 1900, and Isabella Stewart Gardner in Boston stands as a memorable example of the good works of an individual patron.

THE POPULAR SONG AND THE POPULAR MUSICAL THEATER

Thanks largely to urbanization, prosperity, and waves of immigration and internal migration, the popular musical theater captured the imaginations of other artists, businesspeople, and far larger audiences. Building on the immense popularity of the minstrel show, four distinct but related theatrical genres challenged the primacy of such racist fare: vaudeville, the revue, the operetta, and the musical. As the old century waned, variety entertainment of a populist nature—nonbook shows featuring music, dance, humor, novelty acts, and star personalities—came into fashion. Perversely perhaps, the last significant contributor to the fading minstrel tradition was the African American musician James A. Bland. On far-reaching vaudeville circuits, entertainers cultivated forms of broad humor based on ethnic stereotypes (lampooning the Irish, Yiddish, Germans, and Italians alongside African Americans) but at the same time made the musical idioms of these targets familiar. The revue, featuring glamorous "chorus girls" and ultimately flourishing in yearlong productions with large casts and extravagant sets, reflected the more liberal mores of the new century. Representative and, perhaps, most celebrated were the spectacular *Follies* produced almost annually by impresario Florenz Ziegfeld, the first in 1906 and the last in 1931. The operetta, a modification of Continental opera, offered a lighthearted, sentimental narrative with the interpolation of songs and lush orchestrations of loftier pretensions. Not surprisingly, the champions of operetta—Victor Herbert, Sigmund Romberg, and Rudolf Friml—were European-born and trained. The format that proved enduring was the musical play, a drama with comic elements realized by a cast of singers and dancers. Milestones before 1920 were George M. Cohan's "modern" shows, which capitalized on an energetic pacing, a man-on-the-street approach to character and language, and an unapologetic jingoism, and the so-called Princess Theatre musicals of Jerome Kern, Guy Bolton, and P. G. Wodehouse, in which the integration of plot, dialogue, and music was purposefully sought. These achievements laid the foundation for a golden age of American musical theater in subsequent decades. Their American provenance notwithstanding, these theatrical ventures shared common European influences: the British music hall, Gilbert and Sullivan operettas, Viennese operetta, the Parisian revue (such as the *Folies Bergère*), and song traditions from Germany, Italy, and the British Isles. Such a flurry of activity not only presented creative opportunity to aspiring native and immigrant musicians but also proved enormously lucrative. New York City—its now-legendary Broadway—flourished as the unrivaled center of the American theatrical universe, with companies fanning out across the country.

These developments would have been unthinkable without the coming of age during these same years of the popular song industry. Once dominated by regional publishers, the creation, publication, and merchandising of popular songs became centralized in New York City in the 1880s, giving birth to "Tin Pan Alley" (although the nickname itself only became common after 1903). The novelties and showstoppers applauded on the Broadway stage were quickly transmitted to sheet music for amateurs at home (and for ubiquitous vaudeville houses) and were ultimately distributed via phonograph recordings and radio airwaves. Composers and performers who gave life to the multifaceted musical theater were naturally intertwined with the creative and commercial world of what became known as Tin Pan Alley. Songs conceived for the fantasy realm beneath the proscenium were welcomed as general entertainment. The flowering of Tin Pan Alley witnessed a variety of song types demonstrating the richness of the culture and the enterprise: those reflecting contemporary social dances (principally the waltz), those invoking African American customs (so-called coon songs in dialect, lingering in the wake of the minstrel tradition, and eventually ragtime-inspired songs), and the sentimental ballad (a mainstay from earlier decades). Prominent as composers were Irving Berlin, George M. Cohan, Jerome Kern, Harry von Tilzer, and Paul Dresser. The four-part, straight-toned, close-harmony approach to singing popular songs known as barbershop quartet—originally associated with midwestern traveling salesmen—is particularly evocative of this period.

Mirroring the vitality of secular song was widespread interest in sacred song, notably hymn tunes and revival songs for Protestant congregations. Still experiencing aftershocks of the Great Awakening, churches embraced song imbued with exhilarating emotion and Victorian sentimentality; numerous denominations published hymnals. Closely related are many anthologies of such songs and their imitations directed to activists in the temperance, labor, and suffragist movements and the custom of modifying or parodying texts to advocate a particular social crusade and inculcate its values in the newly converted.

THE WIND BAND AND ITS INTRODUCTION IN PUBLIC EDUCATION

Another legacy enjoying a "golden age" around the turn of the century concerns the wind band. Americans had inherited the military trappings of the band from the Old World; responses to the Civil War had elevated its prominence to an unprecedented level. In addition to delivering martial music, the ensemble's suitability for disseminating music in an out-of-door setting gained broad appreciation. Most communities constituted ensembles, primarily of amateurs, as sources of local pride; all manner of compositions were rescored for the medium; and attending regular concerts alfresco became common pastimes. The centrality of professional bands to the circus experience added another dynamic dimension to its social prominence.

The respected pioneer was the Irish-born bandmaster Patrick Gilmore, who established a national reputation during the Civil War and whose "monster concerts" with thousands of instrumentalists and choristers at three World Peace Jubilees in Boston (1869, 1872, and 1873) achieved considerable notice. The Gilmore Band toured extensively and offered a model much imitated, both in terms of instrumentation and in matters of programming. Concentration on arrangements and transcriptions of well-known music, works by European masters as well as by local tunesmiths, set the standard. Riding the crest of Gilmore's triumphs was the onetime military musician John Philip Sousa, whose own band of professionals (after 1892) achieved international celebrity for virtuoso musicianship and whose compositions earned him the title "the March King." Along with marches of unquestionable quality, Sousa wrote operettas, abstract instrumental works, and genteel songs and dances. (The march is a genre of dance music, and Sousa's served that utilitarian role at public balls in the United States and Europe.) Interestingly, Sousa embraced ragtime (and is credited with its introduction to Europe) and radio broadcasts but actively resisted the rise of recorded music; he rarely led recording sessions of his own ensemble. The entertainment function of the turn-of-the-century wind ensemble and the quest for mass appeal, indicated by emphasis on accessible pieces and styles, discouraged the creation of original works of a progressive nature.

The saturation of society by wind band music spawned the most dramatic movement in music education the country has experienced. Teaching wind instruments in public schools and forming school bands resulted from the music's popularity, the aspirations of military musicians returning to civilian life, and the business acumen of instrument manufacturers who recognized an almost limitless market. Although this initiative was still in its infancy in 1920, the government documented the existence of eighty-eight high school bands in that year.

THE MAINSTREAM FOLK TRADITION

Since earliest times, those whites living in rural regions—notably the Appalachians, the South, and the Midwest—had enjoyed entertainment music of their own making, music woven into the daily lives of hardworking families and small struggling communities. At the core of their practices were folk songs (many now identified as "Anglo-American ballads") and folk dance accompaniments, both initially imported from the British Isles, transmitted orally, and later subjected to personal and local preferences. By 1920 this repertoire could boast of a hodgepodge of influences—from fiddling and Alpine yodeling to revival hymn tunes and rural blues. An unaffected, nasal sound ideal for both voices and instruments (reflecting speech), elemental formulas that served as departures in performance, a realism in terms of lyrics and subjects, and its propagation by amateurs distanced this music from its urban counterpart. By 1900 the power culture dismissed such homespun performances with the intentionally pejorative designation "hillbilly music." The honesty, ingenuity, artistry, and popularity (encompassing numerous citizens across a wide geographical area) made its commercialism after 1920 inevitable. Numerous songs in this category carried religious sentiments as well as themes of social purpose.

THE AFRICAN AMERICAN TRADITION: SPIRITUALS, BLUES, RAGTIME, AND JAZZ

Just as white settlers and their descendants had cultivated and modified the musical traditions of Europe, Africans and their descendants savored musical memories of their homelands under the burden of slavery. In hopeless servitude they synthesized a performance practice from African and European elements and created repertoires of unusual energy and emotional power passed in an oral tradition. Thus, from its beginnings the authentic music of the African American minority was generated to communicate two dynamic modes of expression: the misery of enslavement and institutionalized racism and the ecstasy of personal freedom and eternal salvation.

Because of the role of the black Protestant Church as a haven beyond the specter of mainstream dictates, sacred performances known as spirituals made up the first enduring repertoire of African American music. After emancipation, this characteristic body of song, marked by call and response patterns of African origin, qualified improvisation, encoded text, and religious fervor, was introduced into vocational schools for former slaves and was preserved in compromised European notation. Choral ensembles disseminated spirituals beyond their original matrix; the most celebrated of these, the Fisk Jubilee Singers, began touring throughout the United States and Europe in 1871.

Between the end of the Civil War and 1900, a parallel genre of secular song known as the blues was codified in the South. Evolving from work songs and field hollers and related to spirituals, the earliest blues—now designated as "rural" or "country"—were the province of a male vocalist who created the lyrics and his own accompaniment on homemade, portable stringed instruments (banjo, guitar, etc.). Melancholy lyrics addressing real experience—personal tribulations—were delivered in a realistic manner and, like spirituals, in distinctive metaphorical language. Because the performer was the creator, the early blues is a music of considerable individuality and, because of its oral context, subject to constant variation. This earthy folk expression, now recognized as the fundamental stream of African American music, has conditioned many later developments on the American landscape and ultimately music making around the world.

During the 1890s yet another music of African American derivation achieved the status of a craze. An improvised dance music for piano, originally played in black nightspots by itinerant "professors," evolved in the Midwest and the South from the cakewalk, mainstream dance music, and Romantic keyboard pieces. Its transference to European notation, with the attending compromises of melodic and rhythmic nuances, and its availability as sheet music and as player piano rolls sparked a fascination for the still exotic idiom beyond its original precincts despite social connotations. The "classic rag"—the definitive, fully notated genre emphasizing syncopated melody, reflecting march structure, and conceived for the solo pianist—became a staple of public entertainment and mainstream parlor diversion. Details of these miniatures were easily adapted for other media, the nominal ragtime band as well as the traditional wind bands, dance orchestras, and theater orchestras. Composers of popular songs followed suit. The figure who towered over his many peers, both black and white, in popularity and originality and earned accolades from historians is Scott Joplin. In rags and extended compositions (e.g., his "ragtime opera" *Treemonisha* of 1911), Joplin aspired to transcend the banality of entertainment music with artistic substance.

Even more epoch making was the emergence around the year 1900 in New Orleans of a "hot" instrumental music later called jazz. Drawing on diverse practices flourishing in the Crescent City and with the advantage of its unique political, social, and geographical legacies, a wind band music steeped in the blues and assigned a dance function found a home in the freewheeling pleasure district of the southern seaport. Momentous for its development was the passing of Jim Crow laws that forced the mingling of black musicians and those belonging to the Free People of Color, the local community of black Creoles who for generations embraced the European culture of the

***Maple Leaf Rag*, 1899.** Cover of sheet music for Scott Joplin's famous rag. GETTY IMAGES

city's educated white society, including its music. The first significant jazz musician was Buddy Bolden, a figure of mythical stature and the founder of a dynasty of trumpet players before the recorded era. From Bolden issued Joe "King" Oliver and the incomparable Louis Armstrong; among their illustrious colleagues were the clarinetist-saxophonist Sidney Bechet, the trombonist Edward "Kid" Ory, and the former one-time ragtime "professor" Jelly Roll Morton. The first jazz recording, by a quintet of white musicians from New Orleans, was released in 1917 and was followed by recordings of all-black ensembles that more faithfully communicated the original performance practice. With the availability of recordings and the diaspora of musicians caused by closing the notorious Storyville district in 1917, jazz attracted a far greater audience at home and abroad despite the lamentations of arbiters of the status quo.

MUSIC AND AMERICAN LITERATURE

Numerous intersections between musical traditions and American literature of this period can be cited. Significant authors invoked details surrounding music making of various kinds as subject, symbol, or social context, the novel revealing a rich treatment in this regard. Mark Twain took obvious pleasure in burlesquing appreciation of German opera in *A Tramp Abroad* (1880), describing the Wagnerian approach as an "insurrection": he confessed to preferring a toothache to six hours spent at Wagner's temple at Bayreuth. In Kate Chopin's once-controversial novel *The Awakening* (1899), the protagonist's emotional journey is deeply sensitized by music, specifically by the pianists in her world; Chopin herself was an accomplished pianist. Piano playing by female characters serves as a telling metaphor for society's construction of gender and contemporary attitudes vis-à-vis women and music. Willa Cather's novel *The Song of the Lark* (1915), inspired in part by the Swedish American Wagnerian soprano Olive Fremstad, testifies eloquently to the transfiguring power of art music on individual American lives; her short story "The Diamond Mine" (1916) is likewise patterned after the life of the American soprano Lillian Nordica. Edith Wharton's *The Age of Innocence* (1920) begins at the opera house, with a performance of *Faust* by the Swedish diva Christine Nilsson at New York City's Academy of Music, an apt cultural setting for the upper-class characters whose social sphere she exposed.

Popular music figures prominently in Stephen Crane's *Maggie, A Girl of the Streets* (1893), Theodore Dreiser's *Sister Carrie* (1900), and Paul Laurence Dunbar's *The Sport of the Gods* (1902), in part because of the diverse social milieu of dance halls. References to the folk tradition are found in both *Adventures of Huckleberry Finn* (1885) and *Life on the Mississippi* (1883) by Twain.

Nor is it gratuitous that W. E. B. Du Bois prefaced each chapter of *Souls of Black Folk* (1903) with a passage from the repertoire of Negro spirituals, so-called Sorrow Songs. In the final chapter of that plea for the rights of his people, he proclaimed, "And so by fateful chance, the Negro folk-song—the rhythmic cry of the slave—stands to-day not simply as the sole American music, but as the most beautiful expression of human experience born this side the seas" (p. 186). The unnamed narrator of James Weldon Johnson's novel *The Autobiography of an Ex-Coloured Man* (1912) eventually "passes" from the black world into the white and, in doing so, sacrifices his cultural inheritance. At one time known as the most compelling ragtime professor in New York, this character—recalling Scott Joplin—seeks to transcribe his music into a purer form of notation. These fictionalized aspirations might not have been too far removed from Johnson's own; he was an accomplished songwriter and among the charter members of the American Society of Composers,

Authors, and Publishers, a group that included Victor Herbert, Jerome Kern, John Philip Sousa, and Irving Berlin. It seems clear that the examples of Du Bois and Johnson represent a foundation for figures of the postwar Harlem Renaissance, who self-consciously explored relationships between literary expression and African American music in both subject and manner.

American poetry found favor with composers of solo and choral song as well as cantata. Of the Americans from this era, composers have shown the greatest interest in the poems of Henry Wadsworth Longfellow, Walt Whitman, and Emily Dickinson. Ironically perhaps, appreciation for Longfellow and Whitman was initially strongest abroad, notably in Great Britain. After 1920 an affinity for the works of Whitman and Dickinson by American "modernists" resulted in a remarkable number of compositions. In *Musical Settings of American Literature: A Bibliography* (1986), Michael Hovland documents the existence of as many as fifty-eight hundred compositions based on ninety-nine American authors by twenty-one hundred composers; this reference provides a wealth of detail for the period between 1870 and 1920.

Longfellow, a musician himself and probably the nineteenth-century American poet most frequently set to music, is represented by many songs for voice and piano; the majority of those that predate 1890 were published in London. Discussing late Victorian cantata and oratorio in *The Oxford History of British Music* (1999), John Caldwell identifies a "cult of Longfellow that seduced [Joseph] Barnett, [Arthur] Sullivan, the young [Charles Villiers] Stanford, and [Edward] Elgar" (p. 260). The frequency of performances by British singing societies of Sullivan's Longfellow cantata *The Golden Legend* (1887) was, for a time, second only to Handel's *Messiah*. Countryman Samuel Coleridge-Taylor's (1875–1912) *Hiawatha's Wedding Feast* (1898), the first of a four-part cantata cycle titled *Scenes from the Song of Hiawatha* and adapted from the enduring poem *Hiawatha* (1855), achieved distinction as the most popular secular choral work of its time in both Great Britain and the United States; the same text inspired several orchestral works, notably a symphonic poem (1888) by Frederick Delius. American choral works from the period featuring Longfellow texts—rarely performed in the early twenty-first century—include secular cantatas by Dudley Buck: *Scenes from the Golden Legend* (1880), *King Olaf's Christmas* (1881), and *Paul Revere's Ride* (1898), the last two for male choirs.

The later works of Whitman began to draw attention in the years immediately following his death. Again prominent British composers, embracing his approach as liberating, led the way. Gustav Holst is thought to have established his mature voice in *The Mystic Trumpeter* (1904, rev. 1912) for solo voice and orchestra. Delius created Whitman settings of true originality in *Sea Drift* (1904) for baritone, chorus, and orchestra and *Songs of Farewell* (1920; rev. 1930) for chorus and orchestra; and Ralph Vaughan Williams turned to Whitman texts for three early works for choral or orchestral forces: *Toward the Unknown Region* (1907), considered his first major success by both audiences and critics; *Three Nocturnes* (1908); and the innovative *A Sea Symphony* (1909). Whitman's pacifist works recalling the Civil War engaged a variety of composers during both world wars; Holst's *Dirge for Two Veterans* (1914) for male chorus, brass, and percussion and his *Ode to Death* (1919) for chorus and orchestra are representative.

The earliest songs based on Dickinson's poetry are the creations of lesser American figures, "Have you got a brook in your little heart?" (1896) by Etta Parker and *Six Songs Addressed to Mrs. Proctor Smith* (1897) by Clarence Dickinson. Well schooled in Protestant hymn tunes and sentimental songs of the day, the poet herself reportedly possessed a gift for improvisation at the keyboard. Metric patterns derived from hymnody, idiosyncratic rhyme, lyrical passion, and references to music and its terminology, nevertheless, made her a favorite of illustrious American composers for much of the twentieth century. Arthur Farwell, for example, set to music forty of her poems later in his career and considered this "collaboration" central to his mission as a composer.

Among the texts appropriated for songs by Charles Ives, a seminal figure in modern American art song and an unapologetic champion of the New England transcendentalists, are writings by a handful of mid- and late-nineteenth-century luminaries: Longfellow, James Greenleaf Whittier, Oliver Wendell Holmes, Ralph Waldo Emerson, Vachel Lindsay, Henry David Thoreau, and a young Louis Untermeyer. Ives's "General William Booth Enters Heaven" (1914) for voice and piano, a treatment of the Lindsay poem, is a landmark. Edward MacDowell set for solo voice three poems by his contemporary associate William Dean Howells.

In the first two decades of the century a number of poems by James Weldon Johnson were set in popular idioms invoking the waning minstrel show, vaudeville, and early Tin Pan Alley musicals by his brother J. Rosamond Johnson, Harry T. Burleigh, and Will Marion Cook. Still remembered is "Under the Bamboo Tree" (1902), a collaboration of the two brothers. During this same period, a notable body of

texts and melodies sustained over time through an oral tradition—both African American and rural white— were notated, arranged, and disseminated in sheet music; arrangements of "plantation melodies," for example, became commonplace.

See also Art and Architecture; Dance; Realism

BIBLIOGRAPHY
Primary Work
Du Bois, W. E. B. *The Souls of Black Folk.* 1903. Edited by David W. Blight and Robert Gooding-Williams. Boston: Bedford Books, 1997.

Secondary Works
Archer, Gleason L. *The History of Radio to 1926.* New York: American Historical Society, 1938.

Arnell, Richard A. S., and Robert L. Volz. "Longfellow and Music." *Emerson Society Quarterly: A Journal of the American Renaissance* 58, no. 2 (1970): 32–38.

Berlin, Edward A. *Ragtime: A Musical and Cultural History.* Berkeley: University of California Press, 1980.

Browner, Tara. "'Breathing the Indian Spirit': Thoughts on Musical Borrowing and the 'Indianist' Movement in American Music." *American Music* 5, no. 2 (1997): 265–284.

Burkholder, J. Peter. *Charles Ives: The Ideas behind the Music.* New Haven, Conn.: Yale University Press, 1985.

Caldwell, John. *The Oxford History of English Music: c. 1715 to the Present Day.* Vol. 2. Oxford: Oxford University Press, 1999.

Chase, Gilbert. *America's Music: From the Pilgrims to the Present.* 3rd ed. Urbana: University of Illinois Press, 1987.

Cooke, Mervyn. *The Chronicle of Jazz.* London: Thames and Hudson, 1997.

Flinn, Denny Martin. *Musical! A Grand Tour: The Rise, Glory, and Fall of an American Institution.* New York: Schirmer, 1997.

Friedberg, Ruth C. *American Art Song and American Poetry: America Comes of Age.* Vol. 1. Metuchen, N.J.: Scarecrow Press, 1981.

Garofalo, Reebee. "From Music Publishing to MP3: Music and Industry in the Twentieth Century." *American Music* 17 (fall 1999): 318–353.

Hamm, Charles. *Yesterdays: Popular Song in America.* New York: Norton, 1979.

Hazen, Margaret, and Robert Hazen. *The Music Men: An Illustrated History of the Brass Band in America, 1800–1920.* Washington, D.C.: Smithsonian Institution Press, 1987.

Hitchcock, H. Wiley. *Music in the United States: A Historical Introduction.* 4th ed. Upper Saddle River, N.J.: Prentice-Hall, 2000.

Hovland, Michael, ed. *Musical Settings of American Poetry: A Bibliography.* Westport, Conn.: Greenwood, 1986.

Johnson, H. Earle. "Longfellow and Music." Special issue. *American Music Research Center Journal* 7 (1997): 1–98.

Lowenberg, Carlton. *"Musicians Wrestle Everywhere": Emily Dickinson and Music.* Berkeley, Calif.: Fallen Leaf Press, 1992.

Nicholls, David, ed. *The Cambridge History of American Music.* Cambridge, U.K.: Cambridge University Press, 1998.

Mark, Michael L., and Charles L. Gary. *A History of American Music Education.* 2nd ed. Reston, Va.: MENC—National Association for Music Education, 1999.

Pendle, Karen, ed. *Women and Music: A History.* 2nd ed. Bloomington: Indiana University Press, 1991.

Sanjek, Russell. *American Popular Music and Its Business: The First Four Hundred Years.* 3 vols. New York: Oxford University Press, 1988.

Schuller, Gunther. *Early Jazz: Its Roots and Musical Development.* New York: Oxford University Press, 1968.

Slide, Anthony. *The Encyclopedia of Vaudeville.* Westport, Conn.: Greenwood Press, 1994.

Southern, Eileen. *The Music of Black Americans.* 3rd ed. New York: Norton, 1997.

Tawa, Nicholas E. *The Coming of Age of American Art Music: New England's Classical Romanticists.* New York: Greenwood, 1991.

Tawa, Nicholas E. *The Way to Tin Pan Alley: American Popular Song, 1866–1910.* New York: Schirmer, 1990.

Michael J. Budds

MY ÁNTONIA

When Willa Cather (1873–1947) began to write what would become her fourth published novel, *My Ántonia*, in 1916, she was a forty-three-year-old former newspaper writer, schoolteacher, and managing editor of the successful magazine *McClure's*. Of more importance—because the novel is deeply autobiographical—she was a child of Virginia whose family had moved to Nebraska when she was nine years old. At the time she was writing *My Ántonia* she resided in New York City but went back to Nebraska for long visits almost every summer. These aspects of Cather's own experience, as well as their historical context, resonate through the novel: her participation in the great migration from the settled East to the frontier West, her encounters with various immigrant groups pouring into the Midwest, the fact that as a successful journalist she was part of the great social movement known as the emergence of the "new woman," and the fact that she was writing the novel during World War I—a war that would continue to trouble her throughout her life. The evidence of how closely the novel replicates Cather's feelings about her early life is plain in her letters and interviews. Her experience of going west and becoming acquainted with people unlike those she had known in Virginia is attributed to the novel's narrator, Jim Burden. The fact of her age and that she had been reflecting on her memories of early life, sometimes in print, for many years is significant: she had arrived at a ripeness of perspective on her material.

Cather was able to draw on this maturity in a way that makes *My Ántonia* a deeply historical as well as an autobiographical novel. Not that it reads like historical fiction; she does not comment overtly on national or world issues, nor does she fictionalize actual public events. To detect the impact on her of public events such as the war one has to read between the lines to find subtle, often disguised references in the text. But the story of Jim Burden, a Virginia orphan sent to live with his grandparents in Nebraska, and his fondness for an immigrant girl named Ántonia Shimerda evokes or resonates with a number of historical strands. Not only what is in the story but also what is absent from it is of historical significance—notably the Sioux Indians who were shoved off their hereditary lands by the incursion of Anglo-Americans and immigrant Europeans in the process of westward national expansion driven by the odd idea known as Manifest Destiny.

THE WRITING OF *MY ÁNTONIA* DURING WORLD WAR I

According to James Woodress's historical essay accompanying the text of the novel in the University of Nebraska Press's authoritative Scholarly Edition, Cather began the actual writing of *My Ántonia* shortly after Thanksgiving 1916, following a three-month visit with her parents in Red Cloud, Nebraska, preceded by almost two months in New Mexico. While she was in Red Cloud she almost certainly visited her immigrant friend from childhood, Annie Sadilek Pavelka. Annie lived on a farm as the hardworking matriarch of a large family that usually spoke Czech at home. According to a letter that Cather wrote in March 1917 to the production editor at Houghton Mifflin, her publisher, she had been working on some very different material (which would become the central section of her 1925

Girl plowing. Illustration by W. T. Benda for the first edition of *My Ántonia*, 1918. THE LIBRARY OF CONGRESS

novel *The Professor's House*) but had set it aside in favor of this novel, which she thought similar to *O Pioneers!* (1913), another tale of agricultural Nebraska. The material for *My Ántonia*, then, was more compelling to her at the time than the material she had been working on about the Southwest. From her account in the letter it would seem that work on the novel was going well; she said that in three months she had written about half of the first draft.

Elizabeth Shepley Sergeant gives a somewhat different account in *Willa Cather: A Memoir* (1953). According to Sergeant, it was in the spring of 1916, rather than the late fall, that Cather began work on the novel—or at least the work of conceptualization.

Cather came to tea at Sergeant's apartment near Central Park one spring day, and while there she picked up a piece of Sicilian pottery and set it in the middle of a bare table, saying that she wanted her new heroine to stand out in just that way, to be looked at from all sides (Sergeant, pp. 138–139). It is a tantalizing anecdote, conveying the intensity of emotion that Cather felt for her fictional material and capturing to a great extent the way in which the novel is concerned with the figure of this vital woman, Ántonia, and showing how Jim Burden and other characters view her—from all sides, so to speak. But Sergeant provides another, perhaps even more poignant insight into the genesis of the novel. During that spring of 1916, she writes, Cather "had not been able to forget that, in these war days, the youth of Europe, its finest flower, was dying" (p. 138). She was haunted by the war and by fear that American youth would soon be sent to suffer and die as well.

The role of the war in *My Ántonia* is pervasive but never overt. The very fact that this is so shows what a fundamental, disruptive impact the war had on the thinking and assumptions of a generation. Readers usually recall serenity as the prevailing mood of this novel, but the peaceful ambience repeatedly proves vulnerable to sudden irruptions of senseless violence—as when a tramp waves good-bye and flings himself with no warning into a threshing machine. The Burdens' Austrian hired hand Otto Fuchs discusses some of the old national and ethnic hostilities in Europe that underlay World War I. The pertinence of Otto's words to the war then raging is, of course, tacit. The war may have played a part in Cather's decision to emphasize the presence on the Nebraska frontier of Bohemians (western Czechs), Scandinavians, and even (despite their small numbers) Russians, although Germans were by far the largest single group of immigrants in the area. By 1916, when she was beginning the novel, German immigrants were being subjected to intense suspicions and the German language was being dropped from school curricula.

Cather's letters show that she was distracted by worries about the war throughout its course, and the war would remain a preoccupation in retrospect until her death. She told friends that it seemed misery had been let loose on the whole world and there could be no happiness until the war ended. The war and a resulting paper shortage even affected production decisions relating to *My Ántonia*. It seems to have affected sales of the novel as well. The publication date was 21 September 1918, only seven weeks before the Armistice took effect on 11 November at eleven o'clock in the morning. The nation was too preoccupied with the ending of the long conflict to take as much notice of Cather's novel as it otherwise might have. Despite an adulatory critical reception early sales were not strong.

MIGRATION AND IMMIGRATION

Another war also lies in the background of *My Ántonia*: the American Civil War of 1861–1865. The area of Virginia where the Cathers and Boaks (the family of Cather's mother) lived was the far northwest corner, west of the Blue Ridge and less than five miles from what would become West Virginia when that region split off as a Union state in 1863. The entire Shenandoah Valley was a hotly contested region; both armies marched through at various times. In this corner of

what otherwise remained the Confederate state of Virginia, feelings ran high on both sides of the conflict. There is an upstairs closet in the Cather home, Willow Shade, where it is thought that soldiers may have been hidden when the enemy—whichever enemy it was—passed nearby.

After the end of the war the South was in shambles economically, and grudges between neighbors as a result of their varying loyalties remained strong. Many southerners moved west, those from the more northern Confederate states such as Virginia usually going to the Midwest and Great Plains and those from the Deep South more commonly going to Texas. The Cathers' move to Nebraska was part of this great social upheaval. First Willa's uncle George P. Cather and his wife, Frances—Aunt Franc, the author's favorite aunt—headed west to find land. They established themselves in Nebraska through a combination of homesteading and purchase of railroad lands. Then her grandparents William and Caroline Cather joined their son George and his wife; and later, after the large sheep barn at Willow Shade burned down and William decided to sell the property, Charles and Virginia Cather along with Willa and their three younger children, as well as Virginia's Confederate-sympathizing mother, Rachel Boak, went to Nebraska to make a new life. The burning of the sheep barn may in fact have been a case of arson. There was resentment against the family because of its Union sympathies and because the men of the family had taken roles in the Reconstruction government. In this way as well, the Cather family's experience of dislocation from the South reflected the conflicts of the time.

The area of Nebraska where the Cathers established their homestead had long been the customary camping and hunting ground of Sioux Indians, who were now being displaced to the Black Hills of the Dakotas despite having earlier been guaranteed permanent possession of Nebraska north of the Platte River. Five years before George Cather arrived in southern Nebraska in 1873, Chief Red Cloud of the Oglala Sioux held a war council designed to drive white settlers out of those lands. Only three years before their arrival, the town of Red Cloud had been established at the very time Chief Red Cloud was in Washington completing a new treaty. This treaty supposedly guaranteed his people possession in perpetuity of the Black Hills of the Dakotas—another guarantee that lasted only until U.S. citizens decided they wanted those lands too after gold was discovered.

The Cathers, then, came to Nebraska virtually on the heels of the Sioux—as we see from a letter written by George to a sister back in Virginia in 1876, reporting that about two hundred Omahas (another Sioux group) had passed in sight of his homestead the previous week. His description of the silent passage of this sizable band of Native Americans across the horizon is a precise invocation of the "vanishing American," a phenomenon in which Americans of the late nineteenth century very much wanted to believe. But the absence of the Sioux from the Nebraska plains is not mentioned in *My Ántonia,* despite its importance. Perhaps Cather too wanted to believe that Indians were vanishing and that her family's holdings in Nebraska were gained without harming the people who were already there.

Thus two great migrations are pertinent to *My Ántonia:* the migration from the Old South to the West and the natives' compulsory migration to reservation lands; but there is also a third: the migration of immigrant Europeans to the Great Plains. Cather may indeed have been, as Susan Rosowski writes in *The Voyage Perilous: Willa Cather's Romanticism* (1986), "the first to give immigrants heroic stature in serious American literature" (p. 45). As herself a newcomer to Nebraska, Cather took delight in visiting her family's immigrant neighbors and observing their ways, even when she could not understand their speech. But the range of immigrant groups she writes about sympathetically in *My Ántonia* is rather narrow, concentrating primarily on the Scandinavian and Bohemian settlers she had already written about in *O Pioneers!* This narrowness is another window onto history. It reflects the terms of a great public debate that had been waged over immigration since before the Civil War.

In the mid-nineteenth century hostility toward immigrants was focused on Irish and German Catholics in East Coast cities. Irish immigrants were not regarded as white (the accepted measure of ethnic worth at the time). In 1882 the Chinese Exclusion Act had suspended the immigration of Chinese laborers to the United States for ten years. During the years when Cather was the editor or managing editor of *McClure's,* roughly 1906 to 1912, the debate focused on Italians and Jews—groups that had mostly settled along the East Coast, not on the Great Plains. Articles reflecting the prejudicial terms of this debate appeared in the magazine. These debates and increasing hostility toward immigrant groups culminated in the Immigration Act of 1924, which for the first time restricted immigration from Europe and explicitly linked eligibility for citizenship to ethnic identity (Michaels, p. 30).

My Ántonia reflects this public debate over immigration, with all its ethnic hostilities, not only in its observance of the presence and contributions of certain immigrant groups on the plains but also in the discrimination toward these groups that it depicts on the part of native-born Americans in the town of Red Cloud (called Black Hawk in the novel). Jim Burden observes that although the Burdens' neighbors are fond of their Scandinavian hired girls, they do not want their sons to marry them. Despite the long-standing tendency of critics to discuss the novel in stylistic terms and to regard Cather as an apolitical writer, one can see that in this respect as in others her work resonates its real-world context.

RACE AND GENDER

In addition to questions of immigrant ethnicity, issues of race appear in *My Ántonia* in the episode of a blind African American pianist's visit to Black Hawk to give a concert. Called Blind d'Arnault in the book, this character was based on the real life Blind Tom (Thomas Greene Bethune) and Blind Boone (John William Boone), both virtuoso performers who toured the country giving piano recitals that astonished audiences with their feats of memory. Blind Tom in particular exhibited savant syndrome and seems to have been exploited by the family who, before the Civil War, had held him and his mother in slavery. Overtones of bestiality and mindlessness in Cather's depiction of Blind d'Arnault reflect the prevailing black-white racial divide of the United States in the post–Civil War years and the early decades of the twentieth century, when lynching was widespread. Her portrayal reflects the tendency of white Americans to attribute to blacks strong sexuality and an instinct for music.

Gender issues are more pervasive. Throughout the novel, Ántonia is presented as a bright, strong girl and woman and also as what is sometimes called an earth mother, a woman notable for her fertility and nurturance. This is, of course, a profoundly traditional view of women. Yet Cather herself was a "new woman," a professional woman who supported herself financially through her own efforts. Her portrayal of Ántonia in the novel exists side by side with portrayals of women characters both as temptresses and as successful career women. Lena Lingard, seen initially as a ragged Swedish immigrant girl herding her father's cattle, becomes a skilled seamstress who expands her business from Black Hawk to Lincoln to San Francisco. Her friend Tiny Soderball ventures all the way to the Yukon gold fields where she becomes wealthy as a boardinghouse operator, then invests her money in a gold mine, and finally goes into business in San Francisco with Lena. Both decline to subordinate themselves to men by marrying. The more conspicuously genteel Frances Harling manages her father's real estate business in Black Hawk and becomes an expert on farmland and farming practices in her own right. Unlike Tiny and Lena, Frances marries but remains independent and assertive. Readers who wish to see *My Ántonia* as a celebration of traditional domestic roles for women should note that Ántonia herself, last seen as a mature matriarch, has taught her children to regard Frances as "a heroine" and that she means to give her daughters a chance to do other things than domestic work (pp. 333, 339).

Ántonia may be celebrated as a "rich mine of life" (as if her generative organs define her entire being), but Cather makes it clear that her life of childbearing and housekeeping and farmwork has "battered" her (pp. 321, 342). These conflicting attitudes toward women in *My Ántonia* reflect the shifting of women's roles in American society that Cather herself experienced. She was a member of the first generation of women to attend college in significant numbers and to pursue independent careers. By 1900 the generation of which she was a member would raise women's representation in the U.S. workforce to 20 percent.

RECEPTION

Although sales of *My Ántonia* were disappointing at first, they stabilized, then climbed, and the novel remained a steady seller, producing a regular income throughout Cather's life. It was highly praised by reviewers from the first. H. L. Mencken, the influential editor of *Smart Set,* called it "intelligent" and "moving" and "one of the best [novels] that any American has ever done." Another prominent critic, Randolph Bourne, called it "something we can fairly class with modern literary art the world over." Although many reviewers emphasized its style, they also appreciated the essential truthfulness of its account of everyday life on the plains. A reviewer in *Bookman* praised it for being "true to the Nebraska soil of her own childhood, and therefore true to America and the world." (See the summary of reviews in James Woodress's historical essay in the Scholarly Edition of *My Ántonia,* pp. 392–397.) None of the reviews directly mention historical resonance, but an implied recognition of the book's submerged historical consciousness is clear in their comments on truthfulness, accuracy, and an appearance of being autobiography rather than fiction.

See also Farmers and Ranchers; Feminism; Frontier; Immigration; *McClure's Magazine;* Migration

BIBLIOGRAPHY

Primary Work
Cather, Willa. *My Ántonia*. Illustrations by W. T. Benda. Boston: Houghton Mifflin, 1918. Scholarly Edition. Edited by Charles W. Mignon, with Kari Ronning. Historical essay and explanatory notes by James Woodress, with Kari Ronning, Kathleen Danker, and Emily Levine. Lincoln: University of Nebraska Press, 1994. Quotations and some historical information in the present article are drawn from the 1994 edition.

Secondary Works
Bohlke, L. Brent, ed. *Willa Cather in Person: Interviews, Speeches, and Letters.* Lincoln: University of Nebraska Press, 1986.

Fischer, Mike. "Pastoralism and Its Discontents: Willa Cather and the Burden of Imperialism." *Mosaic* 23, no. 1 (1990): 31–44.

Lambert, Deborah G. "The Defeat of a Hero: Autonomy and Sexuality in *My Ántonia.*" *American Literature* 53, no. 4 (1982): 676–690.

Michaels, Walter Benn. *Our America: Nativism, Modernism, and Pluralism.* Durham, N.C.: Duke University Press, 1995.

Reynolds, Guy. *Willa Cather in Context: Progress, Race, Empire.* New York: St. Martin's, 1996.

Rosowski, Susan J. *The Voyage Perilous: Willa Cather's Romanticism.* Lincoln: University of Nebraska Press, 1986.

Sergeant, Elizabeth Shepley. *Willa Cather, A Memoir.* Philadelphia: Lippincott, 1953. Reprint, Athens: Ohio University Press, 1992.

Smith-Rosenberg, Carroll. *Disorderly Conduct: Visions of Gender in Victorian America.* New York: Knopf, 1985.

Stout, Janis P., ed. *A Calendar of the Letters of Willa Cather.* Lincoln: University of Nebraska Press, 2002.

Stout, Janis P. *Willa Cather: The Writer and Her World.* Charlottesville: University Press of Virginia, 2000.

Urgo, Joseph R. *Willa Cather and the Myth of American Migration.* Urbana: University of Illinois Press, 1995.

Woodress, James. *Willa Cather: A Literary Life.* Lincoln: University of Nebraska Press, 1987.

Janis P. Stout

MY FIRST SUMMER IN THE SIERRA

John Muir (1838–1914) was an ambitious geologist and botanist whose explorations took him around the world and won him admiration from the scientific community. Muir, who in 1867 and 1868 walked a thousand miles from Indianapolis, Indiana, to Cedar Keys, Florida, on the Gulf of Mexico, was an indefatigable hiker and mountaineer who completed solo ascents of peaks in the Sierra Nevada and Cascade Mountains, and whose climbing adventures are legendary. But it is as a writer and environmentalist that Muir is most celebrated. Sometimes called the "Father of the National Park System," he was largely responsible for the establishment of Yosemite National Park in 1890 and was involved in the creation of Sequoia (1890), Mount Rainier (1897), and Grand Canyon (1919) National Parks. To organize support for wilderness protection, he in 1892 helped form the Sierra Club and served as its president until his death on 24 December 1914. Muir is particularly important for helping to define the preservationist wing of the American environmental movement. In an era of environmental exploitation tempered only by the principle of conservation for long-term human use, Muir argued that wilderness should be preserved for purposes greater than utility. Combining his talents as a naturalist, outdoorsman, environmentalist, and writer, John Muir became one of America's most eloquent and persuasive literary voices on behalf of the aesthetic and spiritual value of nature.

THE DIVINE POWER OF WILDERNESS

Muir's third book, *My First Summer in the Sierra*, was published in 1911, when he was seventy-three years old. Although Muir was by this time nationally famous, the freshness and enthusiasm that make *My First Summer* a classic derive from the summer of 1869, when the thirty-one-year-old Muir encountered the high country of California's Sierra Nevada for the first time. Muir's ensuing adventure into the area within and around what is now Yosemite National Park was among the most important experiences of his life; the field journal he kept during his three-month excursion was the seed from which *My First Summer* would blossom more than forty years later. *My First Summer in the Sierra* now ranks among the best-known and most influential works of American environmental literature.

My First Summer was anticipated by Muir's earlier books—*The Mountains of California* (1894) and *Our National Parks* (1901)—but is unique in charting the transformation in perception and consciousness that can occur when an individual engages intensely with wilderness. The book follows Muir's movement from the hot, dusty lowlands of California's Central Valley up into the alpine environment of the mountains he famously called the "Range of Light." Although he was being paid to herd sheep—a problematic occupation

> When we try to pick out anything by itself, we find it hitched to everything else in the universe. One fancies a heart like our own must be beating in every crystal and cell, and we feel like stopping to speak to the plants and animals as friendly mountaineers. Nature as a poet, an enthusiastic workingman, becomes more and more visible the farther and higher we go; for the mountains are fountains—beginning places, however related to sources beyond mortal ken.
>
> Muir, *My First Summer in the Sierra*, pp. 157–158.

that inspired frequent reflections on the superiority of the wild over the domestic—Muir found time for solitude, contemplation, writing, sketching, and nature study. *My First Summer* is valuable for its precise descriptions of weather, plants, and animals and for its early insights into the glacial geology of the Sierra. The book is also important for its sharp critique of human activities that threaten the wildness, beauty, and ecological health of the natural world. Of prime importance, however, is the eloquence and energy with which Muir depicts the personal transformation inspired by his wilderness experience. In describing wild nature as a holy place where one may receive powerful spiritual, intellectual, and aesthetic insights, Muir opened the way for later nature writers who explore similar insights in other landscapes. *My First Summer* has resonated with readers who feel enriched by their own contact with nature, and it has offered an effective literary model for environmental writers who wish to convey their experiences of nature in the sort of lyrical prose for which Muir is famous.

It is useful to think of *My First Summer* as a dramatization of a wilderness experience, for the text is neither a straight field journal nor a pure product of the imagination. Instead, Muir has carefully crafted a book in which an almost mystical experience of nature is explored through the literary vehicle of a personal narrative. Like earlier American spiritual autobiographers—who used their personal experiences of trial and conversion to dramatize the role of God's grace in their lives—Muir uses his own experience in the mountains to dramatize the inspiration he receives from the wholeness and beauty of nature. *My First Summer in the Sierra* is thus Muir's self-consciously literary attempt to bear witness to what he viewed as the divine power of wilderness.

A COMPLEX TEXTUAL HISTORY

When John Muir died on Christmas Eve 1914, he left behind thousands of pages of journals and letters. It is within this context of unpublished material that *My First Summer* should be understood, for the complex textual history of the book is important to its final form. As Steven J. Holmes details in an appendix to *The Young John Muir: An Environmental Biography,* in the summer of 1869 Muir kept a journal during his excursion into the high country of Yosemite. Nearly twenty years later, in 1887, he copied that journal into three notebooks. Although the original journal has been lost, circumstantial and textual evidence suggests that the 1887 notebooks are a revised and expanded version of what Muir wrote in 1869. In 1910 and 1911, as he reworked the 1887 notebooks, he was once again editing and developing material written more than two decades earlier. The result of this prolonged textual history is a book that contains insights gleaned from several periods of Muir's life. That is, the book is both a firsthand account of an experience and a carefully elaborated retrospective on that experience. It may be helpful to think of the book as coauthored by two Muirs: the thirty-one-year-old Muir encountering the high Sierra for the first time in the summer of 1869, and the seventy-three-year-old Muir using his literary skills to convey the importance of that encounter in a book published forty-two years later.

A PHILOSOPHICAL ARGUMENT FOR PRESERVATION

Since its publication *My First Summer* has functioned as a literary record of individual enlightenment and has also contributed to an ongoing cultural debate about the need for wilderness preservation and protection. Although Muir uses little explicitly political rhetoric in *My First Summer,* the book has nevertheless contributed to American environmentalist discourse in two significant ways. First, it uses evidence of environmental damage to argue for the protection of natural areas, particularly in fragile riparian zones and high-elevation meadows. Moreover, it makes a sustained and persuasive philosophical argument for the importance of wilderness.

In his book Muir offers specific objections to the environmental degradation caused by the sheep he is charged with herding, but he also uses domestic sheep symbolically to illustrate the superiority of the wild over the domestic. Muir's philosophical argument finds special poignancy in his contrast of all things wild with the sheep—an animal he describes as unfit for the high Sierra. Whereas Muir's admiration for wilderness focuses on the elegance of its natural systems—a world "perfect in beauty and form" where "not a leaf or petal seems misplaced" (p. 95)—his denigration of sheep emphasizes the ugliness resulting from the domestication and commercialization of nature. By questioning the anthropocentric values that allow the commodification of the "hoofed locusts" (p. 86), *My First Summer* challenged the dominant environmental ethic of the day—even as it served the immediate purpose of persuading readers that wilderness required stronger protection.

John Muir's legacy is richly present not only in his published work but also in the beautiful natural places he helped to protect. Perhaps of greater import is Muir's legacy as a popular environmental philosopher who helped readers understand and articulate the sustaining value of nurturing relationships with the natural world. At the center of Muir's work is the intuition of interrelationship, the belief that nature is a harmonious whole within which each element functions with coordinated perfection and grace. Long before the birth of scientific ecology, Muir was an eloquent spokesman for the ecological principles of integrity, wholeness, complexity, and interdependency; likewise he was among the most influential voices in a rising choir of Americans concerned about the environmental and ethical implications of rending the essential fabric of nature.

The most basic and yet most radical idea expressed in *My First Summer* is the belief that humans should recognize, honor, and celebrate their embeddedness in the network of interdependencies that constitutes the natural world. Muir's visceral and emotional experience of wilderness convinced him not only that each individual is inseparable from nature but also that the human assertion of separateness from—or even superiority to—nature was nothing more than a vain and deluded presumption. Indeed Muir's expansive definition of self as inextricable from the fabric of nature directly anticipates the ecological sensibility now associated with modern environmental thought.

Muir summarizes the foundational insight of *My First Summer* in a simple sentence that is among the most quoted in American environmental literature: "When we try to pick out anything by itself, we find it hitched to everything else in the universe" (p. 157). *My First Summer* celebrates the complex, interrelated world of nature even as it expresses and inspires an ennobling feeling of familiar relationship with that world. "More and more, in a place like this," wrote John Muir from the wilderness of the high Sierra, "we feel ourselves part of wild Nature, kin to everything"

(p. 243). If *My First Summer in the Sierra* is a moving description of the loveliness of the Sierra and a powerful argument for the value of personal transformation inspired by wilderness experience, it is also a literary monument to the idea of an extended community within which humans may recognize their kinship with the wider world of nature.

See also Nature Writing; Parks and Wilderness Areas

BIBLIOGRAPHY

Primary Work

Muir, John. *My First Summer in the Sierra.* 1911. Introduction by Gretel Ehrlich. New York: Penguin Books, 1997.

Secondary Works

Cohen, Michael P. *The Pathless Way: John Muir and American Wilderness.* Madison: University of Wisconsin Press, 1984.

Holmes, Stephen J. *The Young John Muir: An Environmental Biography.* Madison: University of Wisconsin Press, 1999.

Turner, Frederick Jackson. *Rediscovering America: John Muir in His Time and Ours.* San Francisco: Sierra Club Books, 1985.

Wolfe, Linnie Marsh. *Son of the Wilderness: The Life of John Muir.* Madison: University of Wisconsin Press, 1945.

Michael P. Branch

MYSTERY AND DETECTIVE FICTION

"If I have any work to do," W. H. Auden wrote in "The Guilty Vicarage" (1948), "I must be careful not to get hold" of a detective novel. "For, once I begin one, I cannot work or sleep till I have finished it" (p. 400). Given the popularity of the genre from its earliest incarnations to the present, many readers would wholeheartedly agree. The related genres of mystery and detective fiction have captured the American reading and writing imagination as no others have. From waiting rooms to airplanes to classrooms, millions spend their reading time mesmerized by criminals who commit mundane and unthinkable crimes and by the detectives who chase them. Auden likened his love of detective stories to "an addiction, like tobacco or alcohol," and it is evident from the now more than 150-year history of the genre in the United States that other readers are likewise consumed.

Despite the countless manifestations of mysteries, criminals, and detectives that have appeared since this genre came into being, the narratives remain predictably comfortable yet still intellectually exciting. Mystery narratives require hidden secrets, which over the course of the text are revealed or discovered. Detective fiction is related in that it too narrates the investigation and solution of a crime, but with one important addition. According to John Cawelti's study of the genre, "The classical detective story requires four main roles: *(a)* the victim; *(b)* the criminal; *(c)* the detective; and *(d)* those threatened by the crime but incapable of solving it" (p. 91).

Suspense, mystery, crime, and the constant interplay between right and wrong, good and evil are popular and resilient plots. Yet these plots are still riveting for the very puzzles they present and the ways they allow their readers to participate as armchair detectives matching wits with the best fictional minds. Indeed, one crucial balance detective fiction must achieve is to temper ratiocination with mystification. As Cawelti notes, "A successful detective tale . . . must not only be solved, it must mystify" (p. 107). Writers also must temper ingenuity, often in the form of questioning suspects, with action, so as not to overwhelm the reader with interrogatory detail (pp. 107–109). Perhaps readers are drawn to finely wrought characters such as C. Auguste Dupin or Sherlock Holmes, grittier examples such as Mickey Spillane's mid-twentieth-century Mike Hammer, or Patricia D. Cornwell's medical examiner–detective Kay Scarpetta, who burst on the scene in 1990. Perhaps readers prefer their imaginative world to be populated by characters who are smarter than they are, able to piece together the most minute clues and eventually track down the criminal. Heta Pyrhönen argues that crime, particularly as articulated in fiction, "brings into play, as if automatically, moral considerations" and that it is "by definition, a breach of the boundary of what is socially and morally permitted" (pp. 50, 51). By engaging in the criminal investigation, readers and writers can safely walk on the moral wild side, knowing full well that, as Julian Symons avers, "those who [try] to disturb the established social order" will be "discovered and punished" (p. 11), social orderings will be reassured, and the armchair aficionado will take comfort in a criminal discovered and a mystery solved.

EARLY HISTORY OF THE GENRE

In the United States, the work of detection began to resemble its recognizable form of the early twenty-first century with the publication of "The Rifle" (1828) by William Leggett. However, it is Edgar Allan Poe's "The Murders in the Rue Morgue" (1841) that is often considered the first text of detection.

In homage to the influence of the French criminal turned detective François Eugène Vidocq, Poe (1809–1849) sets this and his other stories of deduction, "The Mystery of Marie Roget" (1842–1843) and "The Purloined Letter" (1844), in Paris. In "Murders in the Rue Morgue," Poe's detective, C. Auguste Dupin, sets the standard for the long line of detectives to follow with his disconnection from ordinary civil society, his quirky habits, his interest in studying the seemingly insignificant details of the crime, and his insistence that the thinking process of deduction rather than physical prowess yields success in ferreting out the criminal. Interestingly Poe did not use the term "detective"—rather his stories were tales of "ratiocination."

According to Dorothy L. Sayers, a famous English practitioner of the detective genre and creator of the suave detective Lord Peter Wimsey, "The Murders in the Rue Morgue" constitutes in itself an almost complete manual of detective theory and practice. "Poe's three detective tales proper are remarkable in many respects," Harold Haycraft concurs. "Not their least extraordinary feature is the almost uncanny fashion in which these three early attempts, totaling only a few thousands words, established once and for all the mould and pattern for the thousands upon thousands of works of police fiction which have followed" (*Art of the Mystery Story,* p. 165).

POPULARIZING THE GENRE

Creating mystery and detective fiction from real-life scenarios continued in the United States with the publication of the Pinkerton detective series, written by Allan Pinkerton (1819–1884). These stories were based on the cases of the Pinkerton National Detective Agency, which was formed in 1850 and is still recognizable with its motto, "We Never Sleep," under a large, unblinking eye; the term "private eye" is derived from this logo. Pinkerton's agency was known for compiling huge files on suspects, creating the first rogues' gallery, using photographs to identify criminals, and undertaking meticulous surveillance. Pinkerton's detective stories were known for their embellishment of those cases, as he carefully admits in his first novel, *The Expressman and the Detective* (1874): this story is "all true . . . transcribed from the records in my offices. If there be any incidental imbellishment [*sic*], it is so slight that the actors in these scenes would never detect it; and if the incidents seem to the reader at all marvelous or improbable, I can but remind him, in the words of the old adage, that 'Truth is stranger than fiction'" (n.p.). Pinkerton's influence is substantial: not only does his detective agency set

the standard for all other agencies to come, but his literary influences can be seen in Arthur Conan Doyle, Mark Twain, and later Dashiell Hammett, who had once been a private investigator for the Pinkerton Agency.

In addition to Pinkerton's stories, eager readers of mystery and detective fiction, particularly adolescents, turned in the late nineteenth century to dime novels, so called because they were inexpensive publications aimed at quick sales. Originating in the mid-nineteenth century, early dime novels tended to be intensely patriotic and featured Civil War and Wild West tales, among them stories of one of the earliest frontier "detectives," Deadwood Dick, and others that followed the exploits of the James brothers (Goulart, p. 64). Nick Carter, however, was the most famous and widely read of all characters to appear in dime novels and is considered to be one of the most published characters in all of American literature, a club that includes the detectives Dixon Hawke and Sexton Blake. He first appeared in "The Old Detective's Pupil; or, The Mysterious Crime of Madison Square" in the 18 September 1886 issue of *New York Weekly,* then he continued through 1990 in various detective magazines, radio shows, comic books, and more than 250 novels. Ormond G. Smith, the son of one of the founders of Street & Smith, outlined "The Old Detective's Pupil," and John Russell Coryell, a dime novelist, wrote it. Nick Carter stories, however, were written by more than a dozen writers in order to keep up with demand; "Chickering Carter," the pseudonym of Frederic van Rensselaer Dey (1861–1922), wrote the most Nick Carter stories.

Carter is described as an "all-American" detective with a special talent for disguise, running the gamut from a sweet old woman to ugliest ruffian. Like many detectives, Carter often was assisted by others—"Chick" Carter, a teenage ranch hand; his butler, Peter; M. Gereaux, acting chief of the Paris secret police; and Talika, a geisha girl who also was a detective, to name a few—although Carter clearly was the brains and brawn of each operation. In some remarkable plot structuring, he also was teamed with Tsar Nicholas II of Russia and Teddy Roosevelt. And like other fictional detectives, Carter faced extraordinary villains, some of whom he met with repeatedly over the course of the series, like the six Dalney brothers, who were given to vivisection and collecting people's skeletons by ripping them from their bodies.

The second half of the nineteenth century and the first decades of the twentieth century witnessed an

The Nick Carter Detective Library. Cover of the first volume, 1891.

explosion of the mystery and detective genre, providing the sleuthing world with reluctant amateur detectives, mundane criminals, and social worlds that resembled the everyday realities of many readers. Building on the same qualities that Nick Carter and other early detectives embodied but then employing a twist according to their political times, authors such as Mary Roberts Rinehart, Anna Katharine Green, Mary E. Wilkins Freeman, and Pauline Hopkins created memorable female sleuths and criminals who, as Catherine Ross Nickerson points out, had direct lineage from the women's and African Americans' rights movements and ideologies.

Mary Roberts Rinehart (1876–1958) subscribed to the American school of "scientific" detection that mixed adventure stories with mysteries in need of a solution, a combination developed even further in the hard-boiled school later in the twentieth century. Rinehart wrote her first three mystery novels and numerous short stories, most notably *The Man in Lower Ten* (1906) and *The Circular Staircase* (1908), during the pulp period of 1904–1908. In the 1906 novel Rinehart presents the reader with an unwilling detective, Lawrence Blakeley, a lawyer who is assisted along the way by a well-meaning amateur detective, Hotchkiss, described by the narrator as a "cheerful follower of Poe."

Rinehart's novels have attracted the attention of critics, who read the settings of her texts as being peppered with male symbols—the train and steel mills in *The Man in Lower Ten*—and female symbols, such as the circular staircase, which takes prominence in her 1908 novel of the same name. In this mystery the position of the unwilling detective is occupied by a "maiden aunt," Rachel Innes. In this historical prelude to the 1920 ratification of the Nineteenth Amendment, which gave women the right to vote, Innes serves as a model for women to lead active, intellectual lives instead of the dull, domestic lives they were expected to lead.

Anna Katharine Green (1846–1935) was an enormously successful author. Her stories emphasized detectives with highly developed characters—most notably Ebenezer Gryce, a low-key, middle-aged New York police officer turned detective—and detailed the deduction process in meticulous detail so that readers could watch the detectives solve the mysteries. With this emphasis on process, Green did not create plots with imaginative or surprising solutions (as in Wilkie Collins's tales, for example) but instead drew clear distinctions between the detection by amateurs and that by the police and took care to show the strengths of each. Amateurs and police worked together, each

> *In Mary E. Wilkins Freeman and Joseph E. Chamberlin's "The Long Arm," the dutiful daughter's attempts to find the murderer of her parents:*
>
> My father's murderer I will find. Tomorrow I begin my search. I shall first make an exhaustive examination of the house, such as no officer in the case has yet made, in the hopes of finding a clue. Every room I propose to divide into square yards, by line and measure, and every one of these square yards I will study as if it were a problem in algebra.
>
> I have a theory that it is impossible for any human being to enter any house, and commit in it a deed of this kind, and not leave behind traces which are the known quantities in an algebraic equation to those who can use them.
>
> Freeman and Chamberlin, "The Long Arm," p. 390.

contributing to the solution of the case, as exemplified in her best-known novel, *The Leavenworth Case*. In this novel Green's careful attention to all elements involved in detection are on display. It includes two floor maps, reproductions of handwritten letters as clues, and a timeline, not to mention long transcriptions of witness testimony during the inquest after Horatio Leavenworth is found murdered in his study. In the novel Ebenezer Gryce remains true to the form of the detective as an outsider, an aloof observer of the case whose mind puts clues together far more deftly than any who surround him.

Along with Gryce, Green also created the memorable detective Violet Strange, one in a long series of Victorian and Edwardian female detectives who appeared in the wake of Sherlock Holmes's popularity. Strange and other female detectives, such Catherine Louisa Pirkis's Loveday Brooke and George R. Sims's Dorcas Dene, work as professionals and command an extraordinary intellect. Rinehart's spinster sleuth Rachel Innes in *The Circular Staircase* and, later, the British author Agatha Christie's Miss Jane Marple are in a line that follows from Green's other well-known woman detective, Amelia Butterworth. Although Green opposed giving women the right to vote, her fiction often focuses on problems facing women. For example, *The Leavenworth Case*, like the story "The Long Arm" (1895) by Mary E. Wilkins Freeman and

Joseph E. Chamberlin, centers on the nightmarish control men exert over women's lives. The women in these stories do not seek political solutions but instead enact their rebellion in their personal lives, to the point of expressing their desires in secret lives.

Women's rights attitudes were not the only civil rights commentary delivered along with the mysteries. The African American writer Pauline Hopkins (1859–1930), in a short detective story, "Talma Gordon" (1900), addresses the nervous concerns in America about racial intermarriage, referred to by her characters as "amalgamation." Stephen F. Soitos, in his study of African American detective fiction, explores what he terms the "blues detective" who practices a method of ratiocination based on African American values, history, and cultural motifs. And Mark Twain (1835–1910), who poked fun at the detective genre in *Tom Sawyer, Detective* (1896), used the genre more seriously in *Pudd'nhead Wilson* (1894). Twain's detective, David Wilson, not only employs fingerprint analysis to solve the mystery, but since he discovers that a white and a light-skinned black boy have been switched at birth, this novel more importantly offers a polemic on the absurdities of judging people according to their skin color and the dangerous path of racial discrimination.

THE SIGNIFICANCE OF DETECTIVE FICTION

Mystery and detection fiction always has been about more than solving the puzzle. The genre is adept at capturing society's fears, and the crowning of its hero detectives is a telling marker of American values. Early tales of detection, such as Leggett's, were set on the American western frontier, a seemingly lawless land that required the steady hand of moral clarity that a detective, and the solution of a mystery or crime, embodied.

The explosive expansion of industry in the middle of the nineteenth century brought with it an increased belief in the power of science and technology to enhance daily life, a theme Ronald R. Thomas explores in his study of detective fiction and the nineteenth-century rise of forensic science. The "scientific detective" Dr. John Thorndyke, created by R. Austin Freeman (1862–1943), first appeared in 1907 in *The Red Thumb Mark* and relied on methods so carefully rendered in fiction that he has the distinction of being the only literary criminologist whose fictional methods were actually put into use by the police. Craig Kennedy, the so-called American Sherlock Holmes, created by Arthur B. Reeve (1880–1936), first appeared in the December 1910 issue of *Cosmopolitan* and predicted many advances in criminology.

It was not just the detectives and their methods that reflected the social attitudes of the country. The most popular villains of the early twentieth century were Chinese and Asian in origin. By the end of the nineteenth century the idea of the "yellow peril" was firmly fixed in the public mind, based partly on China's own increasing military power and its markedly different cultural and religious traditions and practices. Large immigrant populations of Chinese in both the United States and England made them easy material for crime and mystery, the most famous being a Sax Rohmer (1883–1959) creation: Dr. Fu Manchu. Described as one of the "slant-eyed superfiends," Fu had untold wealth and secret forces at his disposal in his quest for world domination; his exploits first appeared in the U.S. magazine *Collier's Weekly* in 1913.

The first three decades of the twentieth century became known as the "golden age" of crime fiction with the development of the "modern" detective story. Stories became more literate and believable, old-style melodrama disappeared, and detectives and criminals functioned in a more realistic world of human frailty, error, and miscalculation. But however mystery and detective fiction has evolved stylistically over the years, its basic form has remained remarkably stable. Harold Haycraft suggests that a detective story "embodies a democratic respect for law" (*Murder for Pleasure,* p. 27), while John Cawelti, along with other critics, has argued that "our fascination with mystery represents unresolved feelings about the primal scene" (p. 98). Cawelti suggests that detective fiction was not only a "pleasing artistic form" for nineteenth-century and early-twentieth-century readers but also provided a "temporary release from doubt and guilt" generated by overwhelming cultural changes (p. 104). In his "Defence of Detective Stories" (1902), G. K. Chesterton asserted that "we live in an armed camp, making war with a chaotic world, and that criminals, the children of chaos, are nothing but traitors within our gates" (p. 6). The detective serves as the "agent of social justice," he claimed, and stands alone as the guardian of social order. For whatever reasons, mystery and detective fiction became and remains popular. With its multicultural cast of detectives and villains, its exotic locales, and its crimes of violence and intellect, mystery and detective fiction continues to stem from the seminal work of Poe and his detective C. Auguste Dupin and the insistence on employing the intellect to discover secrets and deliver criminals to justice.

See also Law Enforcement; Science Fiction

BIBLIOGRAPHY

Primary Works

Auden, W. H. "The Guilty Vicarage." In *Detective Fiction/Crime and Compromise,* edited by Dick Allen and David Chako, pp. 400–410. New York: Harcourt Brace Jovanovich, 1974.

Freeman, Mary E. Wilkins, and Joseph E. Chamberlin. "The Long Arm." 1895. In *Victorian Tales of Mystery and Detection: An Oxford Anthology,* edited by Michael Cox, pp. 377–405. Oxford: Oxford University Press, 1992.

Secondary Works

Cawelti, John G. *Adventure, Mystery, and Romance: Formula Stories as Art and Popular Culture.* Chicago: University of Chicago Press, 1976.

Chesterton, G. K. "A Defence of Detective Stories." 1902. In *The Art of the Mystery Story: A Collection of Critical Essays,* edited by Howard Haycraft, pp. 3–6. New York: Simon and Schuster, 1946.

Docherty, Brian. *American Crime Fiction: Studies in the Genre.* New York: St. Martin's, 1988.

Goulart, Ron. *The Dime Detectives.* New York: Mysterious Press, 1988.

Haining, Peter, comp. *Mystery! An Illustrated History of Crime and Detective Fiction.* 1977. New York: Stein and Day, 1981.

Haycraft, Harold. *Murder for Pleasure: The Life and Times of the Detective Story.* 1941. New York: Biblo and Tanner, 1968.

Haycraft, Harold, ed. *The Art of the Mystery Story: A Collection of Critical Essays.* New York: Simon and Schuster, 1946.

Klein, Marcus. *Easterns, Westerns, and Private Eyes: American Matters, 1870–1900.* Madison: University of Wisconsin Press, 1994.

Nickerson, Catherine Ross. *The Web of Iniquity: Early Detective Fiction by American Women.* Durham, N.C.: Duke University Press, 1998.

Pyrhönen, Heta. *Murder from an Academic Angle: An Introduction to the Study of the Detective Narrative.* Columbia, S.C.: Camden House, 1994.

Smith, Erin A. *Hard-Boiled: Working Class Readers and Pulp Magazines.* Philadelphia: Temple University Press, 2000.

Soitos, Stephen F. *The Blues Detective: A Study of African American Detective Fiction.* Amherst: University of Massachusetts Press, 1996.

Symons, Julian. *Bloody Murder: From the Detective Story to the Crime Novel, a History.* New York: Viking, 1985.

Thomas, Ronald R. *Detective Fiction and the Rise of Forensic Science.* Cambridge, U.K., and New York: Cambridge University Press, 1999.

Laura L. Behling

THE NATION

The first number of *The Nation*—"A Weekly Journal Devoted to Politics, Literature, Science, and Art"—was issued on 6 July 1865. Though half of its early contributors lived in New England, its planners chose its name and based it in New York City to signal its reaching beyond regionalism. Though half of its capital likewise came from the Boston area, backers in New York and Philadelphia raised the other $50,000. Its dominant backers, former abolitionists, wanted to protect the rights and improve the welfare of the emancipated slaves. The founding editor, Edwin Lawrence Godkin (1831–1902), agreed to those goals, and the prospectus luring subscribers declared a special concern for "the laboring class at the South" (Vanden Heuvel, pp. 1–2). Godkin cared most, however, about elevating current politics and also literature, approached primarily not as belles lettres but as scholarship pertaining to the high culture of the world. Most important, *The Nation* promised to apply a "really critical spirit," an independence that would distinguish it from partisan newspapers and the religious weeklies. Its barebones format excluded illustrations, which competing weeklies kept increasing along with their circulation.

After quickly attracting 5,000 subscribers, *The Nation* grew slowly to more than 12,000, then sank below 10,000 until after World War I and a radical change of viewpoint. Godkin's inner circle discounted the low circulation against their confidence that *The Nation* spoke for the ethically elite and, as universities developed out of the colleges for training ministers, for

a professoriat aiming to raise standards of judgment. Many reminiscences confirm *The Nation*'s self-image as the base camp for leading the public toward "sweeter manners and better laws," toward finer political and aesthetic taste. As a graduate student Woodrow Wilson preserved his copies after making notes in the margins. In 1907 William Dean Howells recalled that, in the Cambridge-Harvard circle, "we looked eagerly for it every week" ("A Great New York Journalist," *North American Review* 185 [3 May 1907]: 50). Naturally *The Nation*'s writers, dropping in Latin phrases or classical allusions, aimed at the "highly cultivated classes." Academics eagerly accepted offers to review a book, to function, they hoped, as "public intellectuals" before the concept had a name. Their word-of-mouth approval brought *The Nation* far more support than its reserved self-promotion.

Fundamentally *The Nation* imported British progressivism, sometimes labeled Manchester liberalism. For its adherents its principles were as indisputable as the laws that science was announcing and technology was putting to impressive use. Both the source and the agent of those principles, "human nature" was immutably self-interested yet gradually improvable under educated leadership. The most valued principle was freedom, defined by the "science" of political economy as the right to hold private property and make contracts, thus rewarding but also safeguarding democracy. Since economic man (naturally masculine) embodied that right, government must clear the road for his enterprise; otherwise it must operate minimally, thriftily, and impartially toward any creed of person; it must enforce free trade, which brings not only prosperity but

"THE PARADISE OF MEDIOCRITIES"

This essay was well known, even notorious in its day. It irritated public opinion, sensitive about its antidemocratic undertones and its similarity to criticisms that British visitors had been making and would continue making, with Matthew Arnold soon to come. But it also appealed to the intelligentsia's sense of mission and to the self-improvement, culturally, of the rising middle class. Soon insiders knew that Charles Eliot Norton had written the essay. They worried that it might help competitors pin the label of "snobbish" or "elitist" on The Nation, *but they hoped it would strengthen* The Nation*'s reputation for fearless candor, for exacting sociocultural standards, and for learning gracefully worn (here with a Latinate vocabulary). As Norton's authorship became better known, the essay deepened the public's sense that* The Nation *had close ties with a Boston-Cambridge coterie.*

Nowhere is mediocrity more successful . . . than in America; and were it the fashion to erect temples, after the Roman manner, to personified qualities, the shrines erected by her grateful votaries to the goddess *Mediocritas* would not be less numerous than those of *Fortuna Virilis* or *Conservatrix*.

"The Paradise of Mediocrities," *The Nation,* 13 July 1865.

interdependence that outmodes expensive, bureaucratic militarism. While Christianity is God-given, fanaticism is disruptive. Privately, the Golden Rule will solve most problems; socially, the utilitarian calculus will choose the greatest good for the greatest number in an inherently moral universe. Now that the United States had exorcised the sin of slavery, it was fittest for leading democratic, entrepreneurial man to always greater progress.

E. L. GODKIN'S POLICIES

A political weekly had to apply these principles to current events, which continually shifted their perplexities. Though *The Nation* had set out to support the freed persons, their northern patrons started backing away from radical Reconstruction, and *The Nation* decided that "carpetbaggers" were undermining property holders, the base of stable society. Though Ulysses S. Grant's first term as president had drifted into corruption, no rival promoting laissez-faire business emerged in 1872. But *The Nation* proved its independence (and lost almost 3,000 subscribers) by criticizing the Republican tactics for counting electoral votes in 1876, and in 1884 it helped rally the Mugwumps, who defected to Grover Cleveland. Against the recurring schemes (such as the "silver craze") to make credit more affordable, it held up the gold standard as practically a natural law. Still more positive about free trade, it railed against the tariffs that special interests erected through the Republican Party. Because voters and their favorites so often disappointed *The Nation,* it started to doubt the working results of democracy. It supported reform of the civil service, for example, because such reform could at least claim to select for efficiency and honesty rather than WASP power, but *The Nation* explicitly indicted the wisdom of a come-all electorate. Popular criteria had already created what Godkin called a "chromo-civilization," that is, a culture prone to "mediocrity" (24 September 1874).

As the United States filled up, as workshops swelled into heavy industry, and as finance combined into trusts mightier than the federal treasury, *The Nation,* more badly even than its competitors, failed to comprehend the pace and scale of change. Though it at least tried to understand the producerist rationale of the Grangers, who pressed for political-economic reform justified by the centrality of agriculture for feeding the country, for actually creating wealth through labor, it eventually judged their demands close to "communistic." It condemned wage earners, perhaps not speaking English, who tried to put organized pressure on how an employer managed his capital. It berated labor activists and actions including the Great Strike of 1877, the Knights of Labor, the Homestead militants, and the Pullman boycotters. Shaken by the economic turmoil it branded the quasi-Populist, "free silver" campaign of William Jennings Bryan in 1896 as a threat to national stability. Its founding zeal for reform had hardened into Social Darwinism that opposed antitrust laws, regulating the railroads, income taxes (especially if graduated), and any other policy that interfered with economic man. It decided early that Theodore Roosevelt was too activist, too retro-populist, and badgered his presidency. While conceding that much, very much, had gone wrong with contemporary America, it appealed to the individual conscience. Godkin's successors, cool toward the Progressive movement while appreciating its elitist core, stayed wary of legislated programs. The liberal, visionary *Nation* did seem to have revived with its anti-imperialism centered on the Filipino-American war of 1899–1902. However, both foes and some friends argued that it was still appealing to an obsolescent ideology.

"CHROMO-CIVILIZATION"

With the title of this essay E. L. Godkin launched an epithet echoed by intellectuals and considered typical of The Nation*'s loftiness toward popular taste and ideas. It meant to encapsulate Godkin's contempt for mass journalism—especially by his competitors trying to increase their large lead over the* Nation *in circulation—and for the mass-produced chromolithographs offered to lure subscribers. Not incidentally,* The Nation *shunned any illustrations as essentially subordinating words and literacy to superficial images and helping to dull discriminating and knowledgeable taste. The passage quoted typifies* The Nation*'s attitude toward the mass of citizenry, who would be happier and more prosperous if they let themselves be governed, literally, by the opinions of educated and impartial mentors. Typical also is the use of a classical allusion.*

A society of ignoramuses who know they are ignoramuses, might lead a tolerably happy and useful existence, but a society of ignoramuses each of whom thinks he is a Solon, would be an approach to Bedlam let loose, and something analogous to this may really be seen to-day in some parts of this country.

"Chromo-Civilization," *The Nation*, 24 September 1874.

Besides the austere truth about current affairs, *The Nation* had promised in its first issue "to promote and develop a higher standard of criticism" (p. 10). Concretely, it promised to push beyond "geniality"— that is, eagerness to please authors and publishers—by using not slapdash drudges but reviewers qualified to evaluate a particular book. Though its reviews, like its other columns, went unsigned, a pattern of stern judgment soon formed. Mark Twain comforted himself that "the *Nation always* snarls. It would think it was impairing its reputation as our first critical authority if it failed to do that" (*Letters*, ed. Michael B. Frank and Harriet Elinor Smith, p. 359). He continued to subscribe, however, even when abroad. As late as the mid-1920s the book review editor of the reoriented *Nation* invoked its tradition of using demonstrable expertise. In practice it had narrowed toward having scholars sift monographs in their specialty. In 1915 an admirer claimed that "to enumerate the most noteworthy articles in *The Nation* on subjects connected

with the natural sciences, philosophy, jurisprudence, history, Biblical criticism, philology, and. . . . belles-lettres is to tell the great names of the last fifty years" (Gustav Pollak, "The *Nation* and Its Contributors, *Nation*, 8 July 1915, p. 61). Fittingly this inventory put literature last. Because *The Nation*'s reviews, with the "classics" as the touchstone, favored "healthy" poetry and morally edifying fiction, only dogged literary historians now reread them. Of course, allowed independence, reviewers occasionally sprang a surprise like the favorable commentary on Stephen Crane's avant-gardist, often cryptic display of free verse, *The Black Riders*.

Godkin himself wrote some of the reviews. Readers who took every word in *The Nation* as his were right in principle until he shifted his office to the *New York Evening Post* in 1881. Well educated and widely experienced as an Irish-English journalist, he could penetrate many subjects from fiction to war. Keenly intelligent, focused, energetic, and self-assured, he dominated any public contact that he allowed. As he aged he became more dogmatic more openly. He also became more snobbish, openly enough that complaints about his Anglophilia increased. Friends summing up his career decided he had written primarily as a moralist, even in his political columns. The elegies from the old guard also praised his humor, less evident to later tastes. His readers on campuses recalled him as conducting the "Weekly Day of Judgment."

GODKIN'S SUCCESSORS

When Wendell Phillips Garrison (1840–1907), son of the abolitionist William Lloyd Garrison, assumed management of *The Nation* in 1881—rising from (founding) literary editor—he aimed to carry on in Godkin's groove when not simply reprinting Godkin's editorials from the *Evening Post*. Still, *The Nation* grew less polemical and gave still more space to scholarly essays. Each of the three editors after 1906—all, like Garrison, with a Harvard background—followed its bookish drift, creating few enemies but losing subscribers. When Oswald Garrison Villard (1872–1949) took over as editor in January 1918, only 7,200 were paid up. In a tumultuous time he attracted 38,000 by 1920, having already reshaped a *Nation* that feels familiar to its present-day readers.

Godkin's spirit had glowered over *The Nation* into the twentieth century. Until 1908 Charles Eliot Norton exerted leverage as a founding investor, confidant of Godkin to the end and a contributor of reviews and essays. Norton exemplified the worst and the best sides of *The Nation*—its didactic elitism later vilified as the genteel tradition and its commitment to civic duty and intellectual pleasures. Among the lesser devotees who later shone elsewhere were Frederick Law Olmsted, briefly but influentially an assistant editor, and William Dean Howells, hired when just back from Venice. Later fame also picks out Henry James, a frequent reviewer and essayist until ready for his major fiction, and William James, an infrequent but loyal contributor. Godkin, intent on impact, lined up a cadre of certified personages—not just professors but presidents of Ivy League campuses, not just venerable American poets but British authorities on legal theory. Inevitably the next cohort came on slowly; in 1910 Stuart Pratt Sherman's essay on Mark Twain almost looked misplaced.

Because *The Nation* lasted in the slippery parade of magazines, it can demonstrate either continuity or change. The question of how long it stayed ideologically fixed while the economy moved from small-scale enterprise into corporate finance neglects the fact that any weekly leading off with three or four pages of topical analysis had to keep up somewhat with the ongoing realities. By 1886, nevertheless, nimbler minds conceived the monthly *Forum,* also focused on broadcloth-suited opinion while committed to policies more effective than appealing to the conscience of the rich. In 1914 the *New Republic* began building on the forthright principle that reforms would come not from enlightened laissez-faire but from planning through a centralizing government. Perhaps in rejoinder, *The Nation* advertised itself in 1916 as "the exponent of sane progress, of wise Conservatism."

In spite of its political stodginess, Garrison's successors made its format more inviting, allowed a few signatures on essays, and reviewed more American instead of foreign books. Villard, while respectful of *The Nation*'s past, moved to review more books of "wider current interest" (Carl Van Doren, "Books and the *Nation*", *The Nation* 121 [1 July 1925]: 11). Likewise he favored immediate causes rather than "deep political knowledge" or the "laws" of economics (Oswald Garrison Villard, "The *Nation* 1865–1925," *The Nation* 121 [1 July 1925]: 7–9). For the first time *The Nation* sounded pro-labor. Riskier still, it opposed U.S. troops for the First World War, pleaded against a punitive peace, and condemned violating civil liberties at home. By September 1918 the Postmaster General tried to ban it from his system. By 1919, bolder than Godkin's prospectus of 1865, it billed itself as "the foremost exponent of uncompromising liberalism in America."

While intellectuals may have overrated the influence of *The Nation*, it keeps bobbing up in biographies, personal letters (those of Theodore Roosevelt, for instance), and memoirs. At the least, its history helps to pin down one phase of that protean term "liberalism." It documents how some professed liberals reacted to specific crises in the postbellum United States and how awkwardly their abstract system fitted concrete problems, as when they had to choose between the demands of the labor unions and the owning classes. Knowing the recorded pattern of *The Nation* can orient us more generally toward the attitudes of its readers. It is more dependable still as a guide to the cultural-political values of its insiders.

See also Editors; Periodicals

BIBLIOGRAPHY

Secondary Works

Armstrong, William. M. *E. L. Godkin: A Biography.* Albany: State University of New York Press, 1978.

Cohen, Nancy. *The Reconstruction of American Liberalism, 1865–1914.* Chapel Hill: University of North Carolina Press, 2002.

Grimes, Alan P. *The Political Liberalism of the New York "Nation," 1865–1932.* Chapel Hill: University of North Carolina Press, 1953.

Mott, Frank Luther. *A History of American Magazines.* Vol. 3, 1865–1885. Cambridge, Mass.: Harvard University Press, 1938.

Sterne, Richard Clark. *Political, Social, and Literary Criticism in the New York "Nation," 1865–1881.* New York: Garland, 1987.

Tebbel, John, and May Ellen Zuckerman. *The Magazine in America, 1741–1990.* New York: Oxford University Press, 1991.

Vanden Heuvel, Katrina, ed. *The Nation 1865–1990: Selections from the Independent Magazine of Politics and Culture.* New York: Thunder's Mouth Press, 1990.

Louis J. Budd

NATIVE AMERICANS

See Indians

NATURALISM

From its late-nineteenth-century beginnings, critics of American literary naturalism have disagreed, often violently, about its nature and value. Was the movement an exotic offshoot of a decadent French culture or was it a truthful response, after a quarter-century of "lying" by an older generation of writers, to the actual conditions of late-nineteenth-century American life? Did naturalism posit a human condition in which the individual was a powerless cipher at the mercy of natural forces, including his own animal brutishness, or did it permit the individual to retain at least vestiges of both free will and human dignity? And finally, was naturalism the last gasp of a naive nineteenth-century belief that experience could be objectively represented or did it look forward, in its significant components of the impressionistic and the surreal, to the nonrepresentational aesthetic of twentieth-century literary modernism?

These issues have been in dispute for over a century. What is indisputable, however, is that a number of American writers, from approximately the early 1890s to the opening of the First World War, are conventionally identified as "naturalists." This identification began in their own time either because a writer openly expressed enthusiasm for the work of Émile Zola, the principal theoretician and exponent of French naturalism (Frank Norris, e.g., occasionally playfully signed letters "The Boy Zola") or because a writer's subject matter of alcoholism, sexual passion, and personal disintegration closely resembled that of Zola (as was true of Stephen Crane and Theodore Dreiser). The term "naturalism," whether broadly applied to the major new writing of 1890–1910 or used more pointedly to designate the nature of particular works during this period, has stuck, despite the fact that for much of its history the term has also often served as a sign of disapproval and opprobrium. To describe a novel or play as naturalistic was to indirectly accuse its writer of sensationalistic intent, shallow thinking, and inept artistry. Nevertheless, when used with sufficient care and discrimination, the term still serves the useful purpose of suggesting that a group of writers participated in similar ways in a specific cultural moment and that an attempt to describe these ways may cast light both upon their work and the moment.

AUTHORS ASSOCIATED WITH NATURALISM

The leading American naturalists are traditionally held to be Frank Norris (1870–1902), Stephen Crane (1871–1900), and Theodore Dreiser (1871–1945). Within the brief period from 1893 to 1901, these figures wrote the seminal works of American literary naturalism: Norris's *Vandover and the Brute* (1914; written 1894–1895), *McTeague* (1899), and *The Octopus* (1901); Crane's *Maggie, A Girl of the Streets* (1893) and *The Red Badge of Courage* (1895); and Dreiser's *Sister Carrie* (1900) and *Jennie Gerhardt* (1911; written principally 1901–1902). Of course, there were precursors—writers, for example, such as Rebecca Harding Davis (1831–1910), Harold Frederic (1856–1898), and Hamlin Garland (1860–1940)—whose fiction occasionally depicts the harsh

and destructive conditions of the American farm or factory. But given the sporadic nature of these efforts, the movement does appear to arise suddenly in the early 1890s as a group of young writers born shortly after the conclusion of the Civil War come of age. And it seems just as suddenly to disappear around the turn of the century. Norris and Crane died tragically young, and Dreiser, dispirited by the reception of *Sister Carrie* (its own publisher in effect suppressed it), retreated from novel writing for over a decade. The early demise of the movement, however, is more appearance than reality. Dreiser did return with a number of major novels beginning with *The Financier* in 1912. The work of Jack London (1876–1916) during the first decade of the century, though earlier often dismissed as "popular," is today receiving more and more serious attention, with his naturalism one phase of that interest. In addition, it is increasingly recognized that two of the major women writers of the period, Kate Chopin (1851–1904) and Edith Wharton (1862–1937), produced—in Chopin's *The Awakening* (1899) and Wharton's *The House of Mirth* (1905)—novels with powerfully rendered naturalistic themes despite the disparity between the upper-class worlds they portray and the conventional lower-class setting of a naturalistic novel. And finally, though the subject lies outside the range of this discussion, naturalism continued as a major thread in American fiction during the 1920s and 1930s—in the 1920s in the early work of John Dos Passos (1896–1970), Ernest Hemingway (1899–1961), and William Faulkner (1897–1962), and in the 1930s in the novels of James T. Farrell (1904–1979), John Steinbeck (1902–1968), and Richard Wright (1908–1960).

Several characteristics of specific works by Stephen Crane, one of the earliest American naturalists, can serve as a useful introduction to the late-nineteenth-century phase of the movement. Crane's sketches "An Experiment in Misery" (1894) and "In the Depths of a Coal Mine" (1894) vividly dramatize the overwhelming impact of post–Civil War industrialization and urbanization upon the nation's material and psychic existence. In the first, a young man undertakes an experiment in urban reconnaissance. In the guise of a penniless bum, he journeys to the Bowery (New York's infamous skid row) in an effort to duplicate for one night (and thus understand the nature of) the lives of the human debris inhabiting the slums and ghettos of America's greatest metropolis. In the second, Crane, in the role of reporter, descends to the depths of a Pennsylvania coal mine and encounters the backbreaking labor, darkness, and cold that characterize the dehumanizing and almost satanic industrial processes of the age. Both sketches are constructed in the form of a

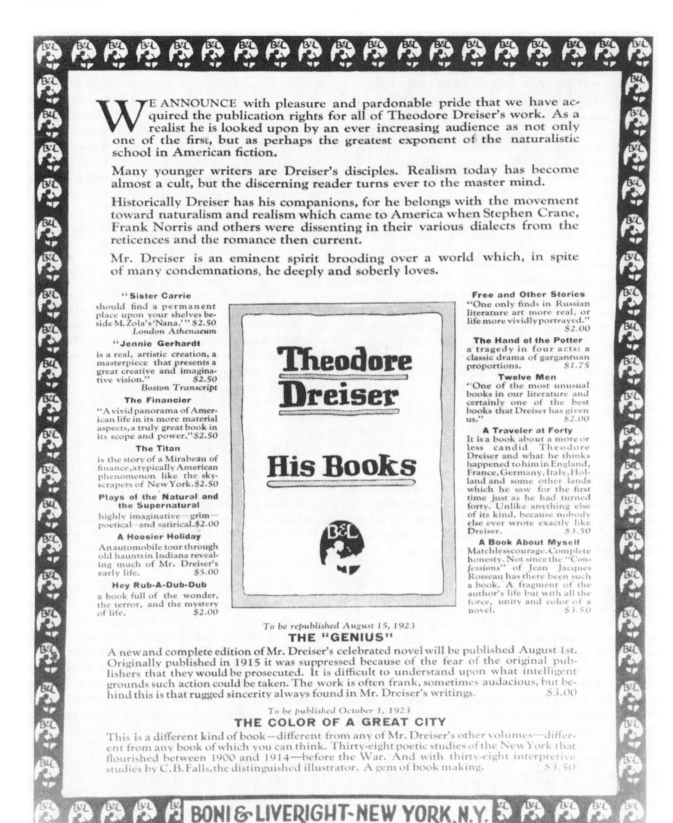

Theodore Dreiser: His Books. A 1923 advertisement in which the publisher Boni & Liveright claims that Dreiser is America's leading naturalist writer.

venture into an unknown world by a worldly young man who is nevertheless shocked by what he finds—shocked, that is, not that there are flophouses and mines but that their actual conditions, their vermin and cold, for example, bite deeply both into the body and mind of someone actually experiencing them. In these conditions, he realizes, human beings have no "higher" life—no capacity for art, religion, or love; they exist almost entirely in response to the terrible physical demands of the moment. Humans have become, as in Edwin Markham's famous poem of the period, "The Man with the Hoe" (1899), a kind of brute.

Crane's major novels also participate in this naturalistic desire to make known to an unknowing, largely middle-class audience the new and often ignored truths of life in post–Civil War America. In *Maggie* the reader is immersed in the day-to-day struggle for existence of a Lower East Side Irish American family whose drinking, physical bullying, and moral blindness accompany their downward path—a family for whom, as Crane wrote in several inscriptions to the novel, "environment shapes life regardless." And in *The Red Badge of Courage,* Crane fictionalizes an actual Civil War battle not as a specific historical event but as the permanent condition of youth encountering, and not entirely overcoming, such tests of mind and spirit as fear, anger, and self-doubt. For Henry Fleming the battle often takes the shape of an opposition of huge, almost anonymous forces in which the powerless individual combatant feels himself to be—as the powerless might feel in many late-nineteenth-century social contexts—"in a moving box" bound by "iron laws of tradition and law" (chap. 3, p.40).

The work of Frank Norris suggests another aspect of the naturalist writer as "truth teller" about contemporary American life. Whereas Crane principally uses metaphor and symbol to carry the burden of thematic expression, Norris, while he too relies on this device, wishes the reader to know more fully and openly the scientific, philosophical, and social truths underlying his specific portrayals. Émile Zola, in his essay on the scientific origins of naturalism "The Experimental Novel" (1880), maintained that the modern scientific—that is, naturalistic—novel not only depicts the actual conditions of life but does so, for the first time in history, armed with a full and truthful—that is, scientific—explanation of these conditions. And since contemporary science had proclaimed that it was the combined forces of heredity and environment that determined any human condition, it was the function of the novelist to create a kind of scientific experiment: characters would be provided with a specific heredity and environment and the novelist would observe and record their response to these forces. Norris probably

did not read "The Experimental Novel," but he did read and admire two of Zola's novels in which he adapted his stark theory into vivid fiction—*L'Assommoir* (1877) and *Germinal* (1885). In the first, members of a working-class Paris family are decimated by hereditary alcoholism; in the second, a miner and his family are destroyed while participating in a futile strike against all-powerful mine owners. Norris's *McTeague* portrays the San Francisco dentist McTeague and his wife, Trina, as they are brought low by hereditary defects—alcoholism for him, greed for her. And in *The Octopus,* the first novel in his incomplete Trilogy of the Wheat, a ruthless monopolistic railroad crushes the wheat farmers of California's San Joaquin Valley. Norris in both novels is at pains to introduce themes that complicate and mitigate the stark naturalism of a belief that humankind is completely at the mercy of biological conditions or social power. Yet the naturalism present in his explicit commentary on these conditions, as well as in such climatic scenes as the drunken McTeague murdering his wife or wheat farmers shot down by railroad agents, is nevertheless central to each work.

Inseparable in Norris's mind from his conviction, expressed in his essay "The Responsibilities of the Novelist" (1903) that "the People" must receive from a novelist "not a lie, but the Truth" (p. 8) was his belief that the truth about life included human sexual experience. Of course, literary expression had always included sexual elements, though usually as an adjunct of themes of high romantic passion, burlesque humor, or moral purity. For Norris and other naturalists, however, sexual desire or fear and the social pressures and consequences attendant on sexual expression—these and other issues arising from sex as a principal arena of biological and social experience—became major fictional strains in their own right. Maggie must sell herself on the streets to live, and Carrie learns that her sexual attractiveness can serve as a path to freedom and success. Hilma Tree (in Norris's *The Octopus*) and Dreiser's Jennie Gerhardt are feminine fecundity personified, and though McTeague desires Trina and Hurstwood desires Carrie sexually, neither man is condemned for this desire. Aided by a Darwinian climate of forthrightness (after all, Darwin had written a full book on the importance of sexual selection in evolution) and by a gradual loosening of Victorian proprieties, the naturalists now sought, as Dreiser noted in his 1903 essay "True Art Speaks Plainly," to write within the broad claim that "the extent of all reality is in the realm of the author's pen, and a true picture of life, honestly and reverentially set down, is both moral and artistic whether it offends the conventions or not" (p. 156).

Because of Dreiser's long career (his last two novels appeared in the mid-1940s) and the acknowledged greatness of *Sister Carrie* and *An American Tragedy* (1925), his work has served for almost a century as a focal point in discussions of American literary naturalism. His fiction is also especially significant because he introduces into American naturalism the theme of authenticity that was to play an important role in its twentieth-century phase. Both Crane and Norris had middle-class, Anglo-Saxon, Protestant roots. Their visits to slums, mines, and factories were in the form and spirit of "research," and their fiction occasionally reveals in its irony and condescension their distance from their subject matter. Dreiser, however, stemmed from an immigrant, German Catholic background. During his youth he and his large family were poor and struggled to survive, whether in small Indiana towns, working-class Chicago, or down-and-out New York. Carrie's and Jennie's stories derive from those of his sisters Emma and Mame, who had worked in menial jobs and had had affairs and gotten pregnant, and they also reflect his own experience of hardship, insecurity, and the fear of going under. When Dreiser wrote in "True Art Speaks Plainly" that "the sum and substance of literary as well as social morality may be expressed in three words—tell the truth" (p. 155), he was echoing Frank Norris's belief that the novelist must be a truth teller. But for Dreiser the "truth" was not only the subject and themes of literary naturalism but also a deeply felt response to these conditions.

It was this aspect of Dreiserian naturalism—his demonstration that one did not have to "travel" to become a writer, that whatever the seeming poverty of one's background one could explore it in detail and depth and find significant meaning—that made naturalism so potent a force in later twentieth-century American writing. Two social groups in particular—racial and immigrant ethnic minorities—adopted Dreiser as a model of authenticity, of the legitimacy of their efforts to represent the specific conditions of their own lives. During the 1930s this Dreiserian model is clearly reflected in two "classics" of twentieth-century American naturalism—James T. Farrell's portrayal of Chicago Irish life in his Studs Lonigan Trilogy (1932–1935) and Richard Wright's account of African American South Side Chicago in *Native Son* (1940).

Another significant aspect of Dreiserian naturalism is his confirmation of the tendency, already apparent in Norris's novels, to make the naturalistic novel openly and heavily a vehicle of ideological expression. Norris, borrowing fully from contemporary evolutionary ideas, had constructed his first two novels, *Vandover and the Brute* and *McTeague*, in relation to beliefs

about the persistence of the animal in humankind, and his last two, *The Octopus* and *The Pit* (published posthumously in 1903) on complementary beliefs about the role of natural forces in human affairs. Dreiser, deeply influenced by Herbert Spencer's concept of social evolution, depicted urban life as a complex, heterogeneous, competitive maelstrom in which the strong swim and the weak sink—as in the rise of Carrie and the fall of Hurstwood, for example. For the two novels of the Cowperwood Trilogy that he finished during his early career—*The Financier* (1912) and *The Titan* (1914)—Cowperwood, who is an amoral Nietzschean manipulator of people and money, is portrayed as an inevitable end product of Spencer's concept that all life is a struggle for existence.

American naturalism thus offered itself, as it emerged in the work of a group of brilliant young 1890s writers, as a fresh perception of a new world. Free from the restrictions of previous generations concerning both the proper subject matter of literature and the conclusions about life that could be drawn from that subject matter, they believed that they could and should depict the actualities of American experience—not only the ways that most people lived in cities and farms and shops and factories but what they thought and felt as they lived their daily lives. This belief contained not only the assumption that there was value in rendering in detail and with precision, somewhat as a scientist might, the observed characteristics of American life but that there was a causal connection between these conditions and the nature and destiny of an individual life.

Once said, however, this statement demands immediate qualification, since it appears to imply a "school" with some agreement as to method and purpose, as was indeed true to some degree of the group of French naturalists who gathered around Zola and his philosophy of literature in the 1870s. American naturalism, however, was from the first leaderless, centerless, and without a governing body of belief. In responding to a common condition and a common felt need, the first generation of naturalists often struck similar notes but seldom in any harmony.

CRITICAL RESPONSES TO NATURALISM

Despite this lack of cohesion among American naturalist writers, early critics often sought to identify a single controlling belief within the movement, one usually phrased as a form of "pessimistic determinism." Vernon Louis Parrington, for example, in the third volume (1930) of his extremely influential *Main Currents in American Thought*, wrote that "Naturalism is pessimistic realism, with a philosophy that sets man in a mechanical world and conceives of him as victimized by that world" (p. 325). This belief—whether stated flatly (as by Parrington) or metaphorically (as by Malcolm Cowley in the title of his widely read essay "'Not Men': A Natural History of American Naturalism," 1947)—was almost universally accepted until the late 1950s. Its general effect on discussions of American naturalism was to suggest that the naturalism it described was a kind of taint in writers whom it had infected and was therefore responsible for whatever was superficially sensationalistic, thinly realized, and inadequately thought out in their work.

In 1956, however, Charles C. Walcutt published *American Literary Naturalism: A Divided Stream,* a critical study that stimulated a fresh look at naturalism in America. Walcutt held that despite Zola's acknowledged role in the origin of naturalism wherever it is found, the American phase of the movement also owes much to the persistence in American belief of earlier nineteenth-century Romantic strains, especially that of transcendentalism. American writers of the 1890s and later, Walcutt argued, accepted much of Zola's premise that humankind lived in a material universe in which it was controlled, often negatively, by the material conditions of existence. But, he went on, these writers also maintained an often contradictory (or at least paradoxical) belief, epitomized by Emersonian transcendentalism, in our capacity to direct the course of our own lives and in the social progress that can flow from that capacity. Walcutt then examined the work of American naturalists from Crane through the 1930s and concluded that there were few instances of "pure" naturalism. Rather, most putative naturalistic works comprised an uneasy mix of the two "streams" of early- and late-nineteenth-century thought, in which the competing claims of each stream upon the themes and form of the work produced novels that were in effect failed efforts to write naturalistic fiction.

Walcutt's reading of American naturalism represented several advances over previous efforts to interpret the movement as a whole. Rather than starting from the premise that naturalism in America was an intellectually thin and formulaic offshoot of French naturalism, he introduced into his account of its origins a firm basis in American thought and thus provided a clearer understanding of the popularity and longevity of the movement in America. And in positing a central and unresolved conflict in American naturalism between two competing systems of value, Walcutt helped promote the premise that specific works of American naturalism were far more complex thematically than had been held and that it was necessary to accept complexity as an aspect of American

literary naturalism if works in the movement were to be properly understood.

It was no historical accident that Walcutt's study appeared when the New Criticism was at its height of popularity as a form of literary analysis; Walcutt's close reading of the interrelation of form and theme in specific naturalistic novels owes much to that method. Indeed, over the next two decades Crane's short stories and novels, because of their intricate interplay of irony and symbolism, received countless New Critical readings. *The Red Badge of Courage* became a kind of showpiece of the New Criticism applied to the novel form. Walcutt's thesis was indirectly supported by criticism of this kind in that much of it posited a novel whose author appeared to be uncertain whether he was affirming a universe in which individuals were mechanistically controlled or self-determining.

By the late 1970s a number of critics, responding to Walcutt's insights, had reexamined the basic naturalist texts for thematic strands related to earlier American beliefs and for their shaping of these into complex wholes. The criticism of Donald Pizer, from the early 1960s to the late 1990s, also played a role in this critical reorientation. Although stimulated by Walcutt's premise, Pizer, in books both on individual naturalists and on the movement as a whole, modified it in two important ways. Walcutt had argued that American naturalists were hindered from reaching their naturalistic goals by vestiges of older ideas in their beliefs; Pizer, however, held that the various impulses present in a naturalistic novel were a source of thematic density and fictional strength, and that a definition of American naturalism should therefore accommodate to the mixed nature of the movement. And unlike Walcutt, who had centered on early-nineteenth-century transcendentalism as the source of the "positive" element in American naturalism, Pizer found in specific naturalistic texts aspects of humanistic belief that varied in nature from work to work.

A third significant phase in the interpretation of American literary naturalism arose in the early 1980s, influenced by the emergence of the New Historicism and cultural studies as major critical strategies. In reaction to the ahistoricism of much of the theoretical interpretation that had dominated academic literary studies since the 1960s, both the New Historicism and cultural studies stressed that expression of any kind was inseparable from the culture that produced it. The writer, in a sense, did not write but was rather written upon, in ways usually unknown to himself, by the beliefs, values, and practices of his historical moment. This Marxist premise, which had been discredited in the 1930s by the crudity of its application, was now reinvigorated by the technique of an extremely close and sophisticated reading of the "cultural poetics" of a work—that is, its involuntary expression, through the language used to engage a cultural moment, of the underlying systems of belief of that moment.

Although this approach to the study of American naturalism has restimulated interest in the movement, it has also often had the less beneficial effect of returning its study to an emphasis on determinism. Earlier, during the first half of the twentieth century, critics had almost universally held that naturalistic writers consciously sought to impose a Darwinian-derived determinism on their material. The New Historicist or cultural critic modifies this notion to the belief that it is the culture itself that imposes its underlying values upon the naturalistic author and thus on the portrayal of characters. The weakness in this later conception as a critical strategy is that it usually has its origin in the critic's belief about conditions of race, class, gender, and similar issues during the period the critic is examining. Finding the culture flawed in these areas and assuming that the novelist is equally flawed, the critic invariably demonstrates the ways in which the novel unconsciously endorses the cultural hegemony of its day. Thus, for example, Walter Benn Michaels, a New Historicist critic, believes that Dreiser unconsciously expresses his support for a capitalistic economics of acquisition in *Sister Carrie* because Carrie desires, early in the novel, the material things that capitalism has to offer. But Carrie, later in the novel, after she has grown intellectually and emotionally, has desires beyond those for things and money, a complication in the interpretation of her character in its cultural setting that Michaels largely ignores.

AMERICAN NATURALISM AS A LITERARY MOVEMENT

These various ways of interpreting late-nineteenth-century American naturalism—from explanations that depend largely on its origins in French naturalism or on its deep roots in earlier American intellectual history or on its immersion in the culture of its own moment—suggest that the movement cannot be dealt with primarily on its own terms as a truthful representation of social reality. The naturalist, like all writers, is responsive to the literary conventions of the time—in this instance those that claim the superiority of a literature that accurately renders contemporary experience. But in functioning within these conventions, writers introduce into their effort strands of personal belief, value, and experience that have little to do with their supposed aims. Their works are not a mirror in the roadway, as Stendhal said of the French realist novel, but rather, like any other art work, a product of the complex interaction between a human intelligence and imagination and the specific world in which these function. The naturalists in this sense are no more "truthful" than any other novelist, except perhaps in expending greater attention to closely rendered social detail and to probability of motive. Other than these, their "truths" lie in the ability of their novels to convey believably the response of a distinctive mind and temperament to a distinctive condition.

Nevertheless, the major fiction by the major new writers of the 1890s, while not as easily characterized as is implied by Dreiser's and Norris's admonition that the writer should simply tell the truth, does share several significant elements of theme and effect and thus can be construed as participating in a specific literary movement. One such shared element is the one implied by the shock and outrage that greeted much of the new writing of this period, a response that arose from the writer's dramatization of the disparity between the life led by most Americans and the conventional rhetoric of the American Dream. Whether Hamlin Garland depicting an exhausted, beaten-down midwestern farmer or Dreiser detailing the mechanical, empty existence of a factory girl or Norris portraying the ruination of workers and small landholders by a huge monopoly, American naturalists openly challenged the premise that the nation was a land of opportunity, equality, and freedom. Since this premise was so deeply held as to constitute, in the words of later historians, a "civil religion," it is no wonder that those challenging it were accused of a form of heresy. Norris and Dreiser had their early novels delayed or suppressed, Crane had to publish *Maggie* privately, and cries of dismay greeted almost all their work on its appearance. ("We must destroy this race of Norrises," one reviewer cried after reading *McTeague*.) Much of this early negative criticism also stemmed, of course, from the naturalists' violation of contemporary standards of what was proper in fiction. But then as now standards of taste are often inseparable from ideals of decorum which are themselves based on deeply held social and political beliefs. Naturalistic fiction shocked much of its middle-class audience not merely because (as one critic complained) it portrayed characters one would not invite to dinner but because its depiction of a dysfunctional society was a threat to both the material and psychic well being of this audience.

Another shared characteristic of the writing of this period is related to a major difference between French and American naturalists. With the notable exception of Norris in *McTeague*, American naturalists did not adopt Zola's stress, as in his Rougon-Macquart series, on hereditary causes of individual misery and failure. In American naturalistic fiction, beleaguered farmers, beaten-down workmen, girls from slums, and immigrant families—average lower-class figures—are trapped not by their unchangeable genes but by remediable social conditions. Almost all American naturalistic fiction, in other words, is written in the spirit of William Dean Howells's ideal of critical realism, in which the novelist's depiction of social inadequacies, while it does not contain specific proposals for their resolution, does imply a pressing need for action of some kind. Occasionally, as in Upton Sinclair's sensationalistic exposé of the meat-packing industry in *The Jungle* (1906), it is possible to draw a direct line between a novel and corrective legislation. But more often, as Amy Kaplan argues in her *The Social Construction of American Realism* (1988), the novelist is opening up and participating in a kind of debate in response to a large-scale social issue in American life, a debate in which both writer and audience agree that the problem can be solved. American naturalists thus responded to the threatening social issues facing turn-of-the-century America by simultaneously outraging their audience with the implication that the American Dream was inoperative for most Americans and yet placating this audience with the implication that these inequities within American life could be corrected.

A final common element in much American naturalism is its affirmation of a major aspect of democratic idealism even while seeming to deny the principal thrust of this creed. In his classic study of the Western literary imagination, *Mimesis* (1946), Erich Auerbach traces the democratization of the tragic impulse from its inception in Greek drama to modern fiction. With only a few exceptions, Auerbach points out, tragic protagonists in the long history of the form are drawn from the upper echelons of their societies. This convention begins to ease with the onset of French realism but collapses fully only in late-nineteenth-century naturalism. Thus the central characters in most late-nineteenth-century American naturalistic fiction—McTeague and Trina, Carrie and Hurstwood, Maggie and Henry Fleming—are not important or distinguished figures in any sense. All are of common stock, and some are lower class. But all have a capacity to desire and therefore to suffer—qualities that Dreiser in particular stressed as central to the human condition whatever its social circumstance. The pain of thwarted desire in these figures, whether or not it leads to death, is the residue of the tragic impulse in modern literature. There is no doubt an unconscious irony in the naturalist's substitution of an equality of pain for one of opportunity, an irony epitomized by Clyde Griffiths, the sensitive but otherwise inadequate and unfulfilled central figure in Dreiser's *An American Tragedy.* But as Dreiser's late naturalistic classic suggests, the two themes in consort can serve as a powerful means of addressing the nature of American social life. The miseries and suffering of the average life are important, they appear to be announcing. Or, as is said in Arthur Miller's *The Death of a Salesman* (1949) of a still later tragic protagonist who is a "lowman," "Attention must be paid!"

See also Darwinism; *McTeague; Maggie, A Girl of the Streets;* Realism; *Sister Carrie*

BIBLIOGRAPHY

Primary Works

Chopin, Kate. *The Awakening.* Chicago: A. S. Stone, 1899.

Crane, Stephen. "An Experiment in Misery." *New York Press,* 22 April 1894, p. 2. Reprinted in Stephen Crane, *Tales, Sketches, and Reports,* vol. 8 of *Works of Stephen Crane,* edited by Fredson Bowers, pp. 283–293. Charlottesville: University Press of Virginia, 1973.

Crane, Stephen. "In the Depths of a Coal Mine." *McClure's Magazine* 3 (August 1894): 195–209. Reprinted in *Crane, Tales, Sketches, and Reports,* pp. 590–600.

Crane, Stephen. *Maggie, A Girl of the Streets (A Story of New York).* New York, 1893.

Crane, Stephen. *The Red Badge of Courage: An Episode of the American Civil War.* 1895. With an Introduction by Shelby Foote. New York: Modern Library, 2000.

Davis, Rebecca Harding. "Life in the Iron-Mills." *Atlantic Monthly* 7 (April 1861). Reprinted in *Life in the Iron-Mills,* edited by Cecelia Tichi. Boston: Bedford Books, 1998.

Dreiser, Theodore. *The Financier.* New York: Harper & Brothers, 1912.

Dreiser, Theodore. *Jennie Gerhardt: A Novel.* New York: Harper & Brothers, 1911.

Dreiser, Theodore. *Sister Carrie.* New York: Doubleday, Page, 1900.

Dreiser, Theodore. *The Titan.* New York: John Lane Co., 1914.

Dreiser, Theodore. "True Art Speaks Plainly." *Booklover's Magazine* 1 (February 1903): 29. Reprinted in *Theodore Dreiser: A Selection of Uncollected Prose,* edited by Donald Pizer, pp. 155–156. Detroit: Wayne State University Press, 1977.

Frederic, Harold. *The Damnation of Theron Ware.* Chicago: Stone & Kimball, 1896.

Garland, Hamlin. *Main-Travelled Roads: Six Mississippi Valley Stories.* Boston: Arena, 1891.

Markham, Edwin. *The Man with the Hoe and Other Poems.* 1899. Garden City, N.Y.: Doubleday, Doran, 1935.

Norris, Frank. *McTeague: A Story of San Francisco.* New York: Doubleday & McClure, 1899.

Norris, Frank. *The Octopus: A Story of California.* New York: Doubleday, Page, 1901.

Norris, Frank. "The Responsibilities of the Novelist." *Critic* 41 (December 1902): 537–540. Reprinted in *The Responsibilities of the Novelist and Other Literary Essays.* New York: Doubleday, 1903, and in *The Literary Criticism of Frank Norris,* edited by Donald Pizer, pp. 94–98. Austin: University of Texas Press, 1964.

Norris, Frank. *Vandover and the Brute.* New York: Doubleday, Page, 1914.

Sinclair, Upton. *The Jungle.* New York: Doubleday, Page, 1906.

Wharton, Edith. *The House of Mirth.* New York: Macmillan, 1905.

Zola, Émile. "The Experimental Novel." 1880. Reprinted in *Documents of Modern Literary Realism,* edited by George J. Becker, pp. 162–196. Princeton, N.J.: Princeton University Press, 1963.

Secondary Works

Åhnebrink, Lars. *The Beginnings of Naturalism in American Fiction.* Cambridge, Mass.: Harvard University Press, 1950.

Auerbach, Erich. *Mimesis: The Representation of Reality in Western Literature.* 1946. Translated by Willard R. Trask. Princeton, N.J.: Princeton University Press, 1953.

Conder, John J. *Naturalism in American Fiction: The Classic Phase.* Lexington: University Press of Kentucky, 1984.

Cowley, Malcolm. "'Not Men': A Natural History of American Naturalism." *Kenyon Review* 9 (1947): 414–435.

Hakutani, Yoshinobu, and Lewis Fried, eds. *American Literary Naturalism: A Reassessment.* Heidelberg: Carl Winter, 1975.

Howard, June. *Form and History in American Literary Naturalism.* Chapel Hill: University of North Carolina Press, 1985.

Kaplan, Amy. *The Social Construction of American Realism.* Chicago: University of Chicago Press, 1988.

Martin, Ronald E. *American Literature and the Universe of Force.* Durham, N.C.: Duke University Press, 1981.

Michaels, Walter Benn. *The Gold Standard and the Logic of Naturalism: American Literature at the Turn of the Century.* Berkeley: University of California Press, 1987.

Papke, Mary E., ed. *Twisted from the Ordinary: Essays on American Literary Naturalism.* Knoxville: University of Tennessee Press, 2003.

Parrington, Vernon Louis. "Naturalism in American Fiction." In *The Beginnings of Critical Realism in America, 1860–1920,* vol. 3 of his *Main Currents in American Thought.* New York: Harcourt, Brace, 1930.

Pizer, Donald. *The Theory and Practice of American Literary Naturalism.* Carbondale: Southern Illinois University Press, 1993.

Pizer, Donald, ed. *The Cambridge Companion to American Realism and Naturalism.* New York: Cambridge University Press, 1995.

Pizer, Donald, ed. *Documents of American Realism and Naturalism.* Carbondale: Southern Illinois University Press, 1998.

Seltzer, Mark. *Bodies and Machines.* New York: Routledge, 1992.

Shi, David. *Facing Facts: Realism in American Thought and Culture, 1850–1920.* New York: Oxford University Press, 1995.

Sundquist, Eric J., ed. *American Realism: New Essays.* Baltimore: Johns Hopkins University Press, 1982.

Trachtenberg, Alan. *The Incorporation of America: Culture and Society in the Gilded Age.* New York: Hill and Wang, 1982.

Walcutt, Charles C. *American Literary Naturalism: A Divided Stream.* Minneapolis: University of Minnesota Press, 1956.

Donald Pizer

NATURE WRITING

Depending upon its emphases and the period and genre in which it is written, literature concerned with the natural world is variously called natural philosophy, natural history, environmental literature, and nature writing. While "natural philosophy" generally refers to prescientific meditations on the human relationship to nature and "natural history" identifies later writing that is concerned primarily with describing flora and fauna, "environmental writing" usually indicates literature with a conservationist or preservationist agenda or sensibility. The broadest term, "nature writing," includes all forms of literature whose primary concern is nature and the human relationship to it. As Thomas Lyon explains in *This Incomparable Land: A Guide to American Nature Writing* (2001), nature writing "has three main dimensions to it: natural history information, personal responses to nature, and philosophical interpretation of nature" (p. 20).

EARLY HISTORY OF THE GENRE

American nature writing begins with the Spanish, French, Dutch, and English adventurers who explored the New World during the fifteenth and sixteenth centuries. Among the first written responses to the landscape of North America are the logbook and letters of Christopher Columbus (1451–1506), who found the new land he encountered "so enchantingly beautiful that it surpasses all others in charm and beauty as much as the light of day surpasses night" (p. 83). Another early explorer, Álvar Núñez Cabeza de Vaca (c. 1490–c. 1560), found the landscape beautiful but also intimidating. In the account of his eight-year (1528–1536), six-thousand-mile walk across the wilderness of what is now the Gulf Coast, the American Southwest, and much of northern Mexico, Cabeza de Vaca depicts a landscape in which storms, hunger, thirst, exposure, and illness constantly threaten.

During the seventeenth century, American nature writing reflected the preoccupations of colonial settlers who had begun to make their homes in the New World. One sort of place-based writing was that practiced by John Smith (c. 1580–1631), the principal founder of the first permanent British settlement in America, who wrote hyperbolic promotional tracts depicting America as a land of inexhaustible natural wealth. Another set of literary responses to the landscape was penned by Pilgrims and Puritans, such as William Bradford (1590–1657) and John Winthrop (1588–1649), who saw in the wilderness a savage, even demonic, world in need of redemption through settlement by God's servants. The transition from the colonial to the eighteenth-century worldview is marked by Cotton Mather (1663–1728), a late Puritan who studied astronomy and physics yet wondered if comets were created by God as a place to incarcerate sinners.

Eighteenth-century American nature writing begins to show the rationalist, scientific approach common to the modern form of the genre. Meriwether Lewis (1774–1809) and William Clark (1770–1838) wrote in the voluminous journals they kept during their great expedition of 1804–1806 about western American landscapes, satisfying, when published a decade or so later, readers' appetite for the sublime— a landscape aesthetic emphasizing the ennobling power of nature. Through such work the wilderness also came to be pictured as the setting for nationhood. For example, J. Hector St. John de Crèvecoeur (1735–1813), in *Letters from an American Farmer* (1782), and Thomas Jefferson (1743–1826), in *Notes on the State of Virginia* (1785), emphasize the beauty of nature while depicting the American environment as the proper setting for an agricultural Republic. The

high point of eighteenth-century American nature writing is *Travels through North and South Carolina, Georgia, East and West Florida, the Cherokee Country, the Extensive Territories of the Muscogulges, or Creek Confederacy, and the Country of the Chactaws* (1791), commonly known simply as *Travels*, by the literary botanist William Bartram (1739–1823), who combines scientific accuracy with lyrical prose and emphasizes the aesthetic and spiritual value of nature. "If we bestow but very little attention to the economy of the animal creation," writes Bartram appreciatively, "we shall find manifest examples of premeditation, perseverance, resolution, and consummate artifice" (p. 18).

The lyrical, personally engaged, observationally precise nature writing associated with modern practitioners of the form rises during the nineteenth century with such literary Romantics as William Cullen Bryant (1794–1878) and Washington Irving (1783–1859) and is sharpened by the transcendentalists, a group of New England writers who placed nature at the center of their intellectual program. Paramount among environmental literary texts from this period are *Nature* (1836) by Ralph Waldo Emerson (1803–1882) and *Walden* (1854) by Henry David Thoreau (1817–1862). *Nature* provides philosophical foundations for the American valuation of nature, whereas *Walden* takes that philosophy into the field, showing how the intellectual and spiritual values of nature may be gleaned from minute observation made in direct contact with the land.

The early history of American nature writing thus offers a trajectory of impressions of the land—a trajectory that helps measure the hopes, fears, and values of those who visited and inhabited this land in centuries past. This history also suggests that nature's cultural function is as both a window and a mirror—a lens through which one witnesses unimaginable beauty and a world in which one sees his or her own values reflected. During the half century after the Civil War, American nature writing matured and flourished, reaching a wider audience with a new, more lyrical kind of literary natural history that eloquently combined scientific observation, personal reflection, and environmental concern.

THE LITERATURE OF SCIENCE AND EXPLORATION

Although the tradition of exploring the landscapes of North America and describing them in literary dispatches dates to Columbus's voyages to the New World, the nineteenth century is the great age of the American exploration narrative. Beginning with records of Lewis and Clark's transcontinental journey in the first years of the century and continuing through the work of such popular mid-century explorers as John C. Frémont (1813–1890), American readers increasingly turned their attention to the unmapped landscapes of the West. Among those who wrote about their western adventures were a new breed of scientist-adventurers exemplified by the geologist-explorers Clarence King (1842–1901) and John Wesley Powell (1834–1902). During the 1870s each man published a book that achieved popular success while also shaping the way American literature would represent the spectacular landscapes of the West.

Travel writing, science writing, and mountaineering literature converge in King's *Mountaineering in the Sierra Nevada* (1872), a classic example of the science based heroic western exploration narrative. King was a Yale graduate and a talented young scientist when, in 1863, he joined the California Geological Survey. During this and subsequent government surveys in the West, King experienced the wilderness adventures he detailed in a series of compelling essays later published as *Mountaineering in the Sierra Nevada*. Although King reported his experiences as a geologist participating in government-sponsored scientific surveys, the thematic essence of his essays is the triumph of a courageous wilderness hero over the romantic but threatening landscapes of the West. Indeed the martial metaphors that typify Victorian mountaineering literature abound in King's book, as in the following description of his successful ascent of Mount Tyndall:

> But if Nature had intended to secure the summit from all assailants, she could not have planned her defences better; for the smooth granite wall which rose above the snow-slope continued, apparently, quite round the peak, and we looked in great anxiety to see if there was not one place where it might be climbed. (P. 93)

Unlike many later western American environmental writers, King did not place his main emphasis on the sublime beauty of the mountains or on the power of wilderness experience to transform the individual or on the need to protect wild places from the ravages of expanding commerce. The emphasis, rather, is upon the ability of the resourceful hero to conquer nature, thus proving his courage and thrilling his readers with dramatic details of perilous mountain adventures. As John Tallmadge observes in his essay "Western Geologists and Explorers: Clarence King and John Wesley Powell," King's narrative depends upon a plot structure that shows "affinities with chivalric romance, where the hero's character is repeatedly tested by encounters with the exotic" (p. 1174). King's ability to pass these epic wilderness tests, combined with his gift for lively prose animated by engaging narrative tension,

helped to define the terms of the western wilderness narrative as a subgenre of American nature writing.

Major John Wesley Powell's *Exploration of the Colorado River of the West and Its Tributaries in 1869, 1870, 1871, and 1872, Explored under the Direction of the Secretary of the Smithsonian Institution* (1875) notably differs from King's work but is also an important contribution to late-nineteenth-century western landscape writing. Unlike King, Powell was largely self-taught, and while King went west with the surveys, Powell served the Union in the Civil War, losing his lower right arm at the battle of Shiloh. Upon returning to Illinois from the war, Powell worked as a science professor, field geologist, and natural history museum curator before resolving upon the great adventure of his life: to explore and describe the unknown canyons of the Green and Colorado Rivers. Powell and his men launched their four small boats from Green River, Wyoming, on 24 May 1869. When they completed their river journey three months later, they had run some of the fiercest rapids in North America, had survived countless unforeseen hazards, had made a remarkable scientific and literary record of their adventures, and were welcomed home as national heroes.

Unlike King's *Mountaineering in the Sierra Nevada*, which is dramatically centered on the narrator's heroic accomplishments, Powell's book presents a narrator who is less egocentric—if also less colorful—and more concerned with doing his duty in the face of danger. Powell had an admirable ability to appreciate the inspiring grandeur of canyon country even as it threatened his life. During respites between deadly rapids, for example, he reflects upon the beauty of the forested valleys through which he floats:

> The little valleys above are beautiful parks; between the parks are stately pine forests, half hiding ledges of red sandstone. Mule deer and elk abound; grizzly bears, too, are abundant; and here wild cats, wolverines, and mountain lions are at home. The forest aisles are filled with the music of birds, and the parks are decked with flowers. Noisy brooks meander through them; ledges of moss-covered rocks are seen; and gleaming in the distance are the snow fields, and the mountain tops are away in the clouds. (P. 146)

Powell emphasizes neither the ferocity of the land nor his ability to conquer it; instead, he offers a contemplative, appreciative description of places that were, to his readers, simply intriguing blank spots on the map.

LITERARY NATURAL HISTORY

During the later nineteenth century and early twentieth century, interest in and production of nature writing grew more rapidly than ever before. There were a number of reasons for this renaissance in literary representations of the natural world. Emerson and Thoreau had demonstrated the richness of nature as a literary resource. Then King, Powell, and other explorers led the nation's imagination westward into dramatic new landscapes. Readers were also weary of the human violence made evident by the Civil War, and they craved nature as a green world into which they might escape the disappointments of culture and the pressures of an increasingly urbanized and mechanized life. Additionally there were more readers than ever before, as American publishing, population, income, and literacy rates all grew, combining to expand the number of people who had the ability, desire, money, and time to read books. Finally, there was an important new motivation for writing about nature: the realization that under the weight of American expansion and industry, the plants, animals, and landscapes of the United States were being transformed, damaged, and—as in the case of the once numerous passenger pigeon, which was driven to extinction by the early twentieth century—even lost forever.

Among the many nature essayists working during this period were Wilson Flagg (1805–1884), Thomas Wentworth Higginson (1823–1911), George Wharton James (1858–1923), Enos Mills (1870–1922), Dallas Lore Sharp (1870–1929), Bradford Torrey (1843–1912), and John Charles Van Dyke (1856–1932). None, however, was so widely read or so influential as the "two Johnnies," as their friends called them: John Burroughs (1837–1921) and John Muir (1838–1914). Burroughs was an eastern writer who built a national reputation by writing about the landscapes near his home, "Riverby," and his writing cabin, "Slabsides," on the Hudson River at West Park, ninety miles north of New York City. A prolific writer, he published nearly thirty books and was a premier literary essayist whose work appeared regularly in such major magazines as the *Atlantic Monthly, Century,* and *Scribner's Monthly.* Burroughs was not only widely read but also widely celebrated as the greatest nature writer of the age—a man whose work was taught to schoolchildren and whose fame led to friendships with the most powerful leaders of his day.

Although Burroughs's writing covers a variety of subjects in a number of landscapes, the hallmark of his approach was his ability to notice, describe, and meditate upon local landscapes—to explore the richness and beauty of the small-scale natural dramas being played out near people's homes and the scenes of their daily work. By focusing upon things he could study locally, Burroughs provided his readers a model for the sort of appreciative, local natural history they could also practice. Even in such early books

> *John Muir, author of* My First Summer in the Sierra *and* The Yosemite, *complains about the destruction of nature in the name of capitalism.*
>
> These temple destroyers, devotees of ravaging commercialism, seem to have a perfect contempt for Nature, and, instead of lifting their eyes to the God of the mountains, lift them to the Almighty Dollar.
>
> Dam Hetch Hetchy! As well dam for water-tanks the people's cathedrals and churches, for no holier temple has ever been consecrated by the heart of man.
>
> Muir, *The Yosemite,* pp. 196–197.

as *Wake-Robin* (1871) and *Locusts and Wild Honey* (1879), Burroughs was preoccupied with nearby nature, and he was already honing his ability to help readers observe and understand the plants and animals they noticed—or might not have noticed—in their daily walks. His focus on the nearby led Burroughs to a special interest in birds, a topic much beloved by a readership then deeply interested in amateur ornithology. Although Burroughs's later work, most notably *Accepting the Universe* (1920), covers more expansive topics and is more philosophical, his primary literary achievement remains the detailed celebration of the local. "One's own landscape comes in time to be a sort of outlying part of himself," Burroughs once wrote; "he has sowed himself broadcast upon it, and it reflects his own moods and feelings" (p. 335).

Unlike his friend John Burroughs, John Muir was a western writer whose best-known work describes extended backcountry excursions in the wilderness of California's Sierra Nevada. Muir is known for epic adventures, such as climbing a waterfall by moonlight, riding down a mountain on an avalanche, and weathering a gale in the crown of a wind-tossed tree. More so than any other writer of his generation, Muir was the champion of wilderness. While he was richly attuned to the aesthetic and intellectual pleasures of studying nature, Muir's primary concern was not with the local but rather with the wild, and he believed in wilderness as something sacred that required protection.

Unlike the prolific John Burroughs, Muir was slow to move beyond his voluminous field journals and into publishing books. Starting with his first

John Muir (right) and John Burroughs. Photographed by Edward Curtis during the Harriman Alaska Expedition, 1899. THE LIBRARY OF CONGRESS

book, *The Mountains of California* (1894), though, Muir's literary goals were clear. He wanted to combine precise descriptions of wilderness landscapes with moving personal accounts of the transformative spiritual power of those landscapes, and then he hoped to pivot from the personal to a larger argument for preservation of wilderness. Indeed Muir's literary influence and his political influence cannot be easily separated. He is rightly credited as a founder of the national park movement, as his writings helped construct the philosophical foundation upon which the parks and conservation movement was built. After helping to win national park status for Yosemite in 1890, two years later Muir became the first president of the Sierra Club, and in 1901 he published an important work of literary environmentalism called *Our National Parks*. Muir's lyrical appreciation of nature is most clear in the many ecstatic passages of *My First Summer in the Sierra* (1911), where he

writes of the infinite interconnectedness of nature: "When we try to pick out anything by itself, we find it hitched to everything else in the universe" (p. 157). Muir's explosive environmentalist rhetoric may be found in such books as *The Yosemite* (1912), which he concludes with a passionate condemnation of those who wished to dam Yosemite's Hetch Hetchy Valley:

> These temple destroyers, devotees of ravaging commercialism, seem to have a perfect contempt for Nature, and, instead of lifting their eyes to the God of the mountains, lift them to the Almighty Dollar.
>
> Dam Hetch Hetchy! As well dam for water-tanks the people's cathedrals and churches, for no holier temple has ever been consecrated by the heart of man. (Pp. 196–197)

Though their topical focus and literary style were quite different, John Burroughs and John Muir defined the new literary natural history of the late nineteenth century and early twentieth century. Both men argued that people should attend to and care for the natural world, and both wanted to inspire readers to enter the fields and forests with new enthusiasm. Both were influential writers who combined the power of lyrical language with the insights of scientific observation to make a case that the natural world should be respected as a source of insight and inspiration.

THE HEYDAY OF WOMEN NATURE WRITERS

If King and Powell popularized the environmental adventure story and Burroughs and Muir gave landscape writing a more literary turn, it was the women nature writers of the period who combined science and lyricism to articulate a new ethic of concern—a literary environmental ethic that would characterize and inform American environmental writing into the twenty-first century. Indeed the late nineteenth century and early twentieth century were an unprecedented heyday for women nature writers. Among the successful women working in the genre during this period are Elizabeth Cabot Cary Agassiz (1822–1907), Mary Austin (1868–1934), Florence Merriam Bailey (1863–1948), Liberty Hyde Bailey (1858–1954), Isabella Bird (1831–1904), Anna Botsford Comstock (1854–1930), Susan Fenimore Cooper (1813–1894), Elizabeth Fries Lummis (c. 1812–1877), Olive Thorne (Harriet Mann) Miller (1831–1918), Gene Stratton Porter (1863–1924), Celia Laighton Thaxter (1835–1894), and Mabel Osgood Wright (1859–1934).

While the diversity and richness of the works these writers produced make generalizations difficult, several common themes and approaches help to characterize their work. First, they tend to be intensely focused on developing and communicating a sense of place—a personal and local connection to the natural world that is hard-won through patient observation. Just as Muir is strongly associated with the Sierra, many of these women are associated with specific landscapes: Celia Thaxter with the New England seacoast, for example, and Gene Stratton Porter with the Limberlost Swamp. The conquering mentality of a writer like Clarence King is nowhere to be found here, and even so adventurous a woman as Isabella Bird manages to attain the summit of Long's Peak (wearing a skirt) without lapsing into the heroic mode. Instead, these writers are often characterized by profound humility and a fundamental insistence upon the primacy of the observed over the observer. This less egocentric connection to the local is a central theme of Mary Austin's *The Land of Little Rain* (1903), a book that asserts the desert's sheer indifference to human interests as the source of its power. Far from existing to serve us the arid landscape, writes Austin, is

"forsaken of most things but beauty and madness and death and God" (p. 115).

Second, there is in the writing of these women a desire to combine scientific and literary modes in order to tell the full story of humanity's relationship to the natural world. The precedent for such writing among American women was set by Susan Fenimore Cooper's *Rural Hours* (1850), an impressive work of regional natural history that continued to be published well into the 1880s. For the first time in American history, many women were receiving education in the natural sciences, and many more were turning their attention and leisure time to the increasingly popular pursuit of amateur natural history. As they did so, they sought writers who were fluent in the natural sciences—especially ornithology—but still able to convey their insights lyrically and emotionally. While male nature writers, including Theodore Roosevelt (1858–1919) and William J. Long (1867–1952), publicly argued in the famous "nature faker" controversy about the appropriate role of imagination in science writing, women writers of the period found graceful ways to convey accurate scientific information in powerful literary prose. Gene Stratton Porter, for example, is best known as a novelist, yet it was the combination of her scientific and imaginative gifts that allowed her to write *What I Have Done with Birds* (1907) and *Moths of the Limberlost* (1912). Anna Botsford Comstock studied both literature and zoology at Cornell University and went on successfully to combine her literary and scientific interests in such books as *How to Know the Butterflies* (1904) and *Handbook of Nature-Study* (1911).

Third, women nature writers of this period also made nature writing an advocacy tool by which they achieved remarkable successes in environmental protection. Because women had been the driving force behind the major social reform movements of the nineteenth century—abolition, woman suffrage, temperance—they were well positioned to make the argument on behalf of conservation. Florence Merriam Bailey, for example, not only wrote popular ornithological works such as *Birds through an Opera Glass* (1889) and *A-Birding on a Bronco* (1896) but also worked with the American Ornithologists' Union to protect birds from the fashion-driven excesses of the milliner's trade. Another successful literary advocate, Mabel Osgood Wright, was the author of *The Friendship of Nature: A New England Chronicle of Birds and Flowers* (1894) and more than twenty other books, but she also founded the Connecticut Audubon Society (1896) and did much to popularize habitat and species conservation. The scientifically informed literary natural history writing of women nature writers was thus crucial in defining an ethic of environmental concern—an ethic that would function as the engine of environmental protection throughout the twentieth century.

See also Farmers and Ranchers; *The Land of Little Rain;* Migration; *My First Summer in the Sierra;* Parks and Wilderness Areas; Resource Management

BIBLIOGRAPHY

Primary Works

Austin, Mary. *The Land of Little Rain.* 1903. Albuquerque: University of New Mexico Press, 1974.

Bartram, William. *Travels through North and South Carolina, Georgia, East and West Florida, the Cherokee Country, the Extensive Territories of the Muscogulges, or Creek Confederacy, and the Country of the Chactaws.* 1791. New York: Penguin, 1988.

Burroughs, John. *A Sharp Lookout: Selected Nature Essays of John Burroughs.* Edited by Frank Bergon. Washington, D.C.: Smithsonian Institution Press, 1987.

Columbus, Christopher. *The Four Voyages of Christopher Columbus.* Edited and translated by J. M. Cohen. Baltimore: Penguin, 1969.

King, Clarence. *Mountaineering in the Sierra Nevada.* 1872. Edited by Francis P. Farquhar. Lincoln: University of Nebraska Press, 1997.

Muir, John. *My First Summer in the Sierra.* 1911. With an introduction by Gretel Ehrlich. New York: Penguin, 1987.

Muir, John. *The Yosemite.* 1912. With a foreword by David Brower. San Francisco: Sierra Club, 1988.

Powell, John Wesley. *Exploration of the Colorado River of the West and Its Tributaries in 1869, 1870, 1871, and 1872, Explored under the Direction of the Secretary of the Smithsonian Institution.* 1875. Reprinted with an introduction by Wallace Stevens as *The Exploration of the Colorado River and Its Canyons.* New York: Penguin, 1987.

Secondary Works

Lyon, Thomas J. *This Incomparable Land: A Guide to American Nature Writing.* Minneapolis, Minn.: Milkweed, 2001. Though in a sense this is the second edition of Lyon's *This Incomparable Lande: A Book of American Nature Writing* (1989), not only is the title different, but the contents are radically altered—elimination of the three-hundred-page anthology of primary sources; more than tripling of the critical commentary, chronology, and bibliography.

Tallmadge, John. "Western Geologists and Explorers: Clarence King and John Wesley Powell." In *American Nature Writers,* vol. 2, *Peter Matthiessen to Western Geologists and Explorers,* edited by John Elder, pp. 1173–1187. New York: Scribners, 1996.

Michael P. Branch

A NEW ENGLAND NUN AND OTHER STORIES

Mary E. Wilkins Freeman (1852–1930) is best known for the short stories she published under the name Mary E. Wilkins beginning in 1883 in *Harper's Bazar,* some of the finest of which are collected in *A New England Nun and Other Stories.* By the time this collection was published in 1891, Freeman had received considerable recognition as a short story writer. She broke new ground through the creation of heroines who continually challenged gender and class boundaries. Building from a tradition of women's regionalist prose by such writers as Sarah Orne Jewett, Harriet Beecher Stowe, Alice Cary, Rose Terry Cooke, and others, Freeman wrote about the importance of place in her heroines' struggles for autonomy. She uncovered the profound effects of patriarchal strictures on women's daily lives. With her focus on the small New England villages that she knew best—Randolph, Massachusetts, and Brattleboro, Vermont—she found the freedom to step beyond the narrow expectations of her editors without seeming to do so, to explore the connection between feminine identity and place, and to subvert the domestic realm as an arena for female rebellion.

Early literary histories frequently marginalize Freeman as a local colorist, a minor writer whose primary talent was depicting the peculiarities of her region. Yet like Henry James, she was interested in inner as well as outer landscape, and like Mark Twain, she experimented with dialect and humor while probing deep questions about the nature of the human race. She shifted readers' attention to the relatively invisible realms of domesticity where large battles are fought on humble turf. With her focus almost entirely on women's struggles and concerns, Freeman's depictions of region explore the psychology of women's conflicts as she knew them.

LIFE AND WORK

Many of the stories in *A New England Nun and Other Stories* draw from the author's life experience. Mary Ella (later changed to Eleanor) Wilkins was born on 31 October 1852 in Randolph, Massachusetts, a small rural town near Boston. She moved to Brattleboro, Vermont, with her family when she was fifteen, and

Mary E. Wilkins Freeman.

the experience of pleasure was linked to sin and the means for earning love was dutiful self-sacrifice. She learned to value the subtle forms of rebellion evident in the lives of New England women, their methods of appropriating power within the domestic realm. Since many men in New England villages such as Randolph had migrated westward or to urban centers, Freeman developed in a community of women; the source of much of her fiction is the oral histories she had gathered in the kitchens of her grandmother, her mother, and her neighbors.

As she became an established writer, Freeman's literary circle grew to include her regionalist counterpart in Maine, Sarah Orne Jewett, and male writers such as Hamlin Garland, William Dean Howells, and Rudyard Kipling. She sat beside Mark Twain, whose work she admired, at his seventieth birthday banquet. Her frequent correspondence with her editors at Harper's in her richest period of publication, the late 1880s and the 1890s, reveals her effort to develop in her fiction a fresh voice, full of her unique wit and irony, and yet to win acceptance within the traditions and standards of nineteenth-century women's magazines, which required sentimentality and gentility to match their assumptions about women readers.

Caught between the longing for acceptability and the need for autonomy in her personal life, Freeman resisted the pressure to marry through her childbearing years. After nine years of hesitation, she finally married Dr. Charles Freeman in 1902; the marriage required that she part with what she called "the old me," leave Randolph, the setting for so much of her work, and move to Metuchen, New Jersey, where she found "I have not a blessed thing to write about" (letter to Harriet Randolph Mayor, 22 December 1901, *Infant Sphinx*, p. 256). The marriage dissolved in 1922 largely because of her husband's decline into severe alcoholism and drug addiction. She died on 13 March 1930 of a heart attack at the age of seventy-seven. Widely recognized for her work, in 1926 Freeman received the Howells Medal for fiction from the American Academy of Arts and Letters, and the bronze doors of the Academy still bear the inscription "Dedicated to the Memory of Mary E. Wilkins Freeman and the Women Writers of America."

THEMES AND CONTEXTS

Freeman was among the first American women authors to write openly about the complexity of female sexuality, the role of work in women's lives, the experience and stigma of nineteenth-century spinsterhood, and the unique relationships that women form outside of marriage and motherhood. Her finest

then returned after the death of her parents to Randolph in 1883 to live with her childhood and life-long friend Mary Wales for the twenty most productive years of her literary career. Much of the work she produced about women's relationships drew from the intensity of this friendship.

The first surviving child of the orthodox Congregationalists Warren and Eleanor Wilkins, Mary grew up in a repressive environment with parents who expected her to conform to traditional standards of feminine passivity. After she graduated from high school in Brattleboro, she attended Mount Holyoke Female Seminary in 1870. Like Emily Dickinson, however, she lasted for only one year. The many rules at the seminary were too restrictive for her, and she longed for the privacy she would need to write her stories. When she returned to Brattleboro, she began writing and publishing fiction.

Her family was poor, and Freeman turned to writing rather than to marriage for financial independence. Writing also became a channel for her to voice her revolt against the limitations of growing up female in New England. Much of her fiction reflects the contradictions of her roots in a culture in which

This passage depicting Louisa Ellis is a good example of Freeman's capacity for precise and detailed characterization. Here she captures the essence of unmarried life in nineteenth-century New England, both its freedom and its limitations; she also suggests the stigma attached to self-satisfied "spinsterhood."

Louisa tied a green apron round her waist, and got out a flat straw hat with a green ribbon. Then she went into the garden with a little blue crockery bowl, to pick some currants for her tea. After the currants were picked she sat on the back door-step and stemmed them, collecting the stems carefully in her apron, and afterwards throwing them into the hen-coop. She looked sharply at the grass beside the step to see if any had fallen there.

Louisa was slow and still in her movements; it took her a long time to prepare her tea; but when ready it was set forth with as much grace as if she had been a veritable guest to her own self. The little square table stood exactly in the centre of the kitchen, and was covered with a starched linen cloth whose border pattern of flowers glistened. Louisa had a damask napkin on her tea-tray, where were arranged a cut-glass tumbler full of teaspoons, a silver cream-pitcher, a china sugar-bowl, and one pink china cup and saucer. Louisa used china every day—something which none of her neighbors did. They whispered about it among themselves. Their daily tables were laid with common crockery, their sets of best china stayed in the parlor closet, and Louisa Ellis was no richer nor better bred than they. Still she would use the china. She had for her supper a glass dish full of sugared currants, a plate of little cakes, and one of the light white biscuits. Also a leaf or two of lettuce, which she cut up daintily. Louisa was very fond of lettuce, which she raised to perfection in her little garden.

Freeman, "A New England Nun," in *Selected Stories*, pp. 109–110.

work reflects her experience as an unmarried woman who struggled both within and against the ideology of nineteenth-century womanhood. Freeman's form of regionalism focuses more often on inner rather than outer landscape as she explores the effects of New England culture on the interior lives of women. The short stories in *A New England Nun and Other Stories* are her best-known, but Freeman's work includes more than a dozen novels; a similar number of short story collections, which largely reprint more than two hundred stories first published in magazines and journals; and several plays, children's works, and essays.

Since the 1970s feminist criticism has brought about a revival of interest in women regionalists such as Freeman. Although earlier critics dismissed her as a minor local colorist, she has found an increasingly enthusiastic audience among contemporary readers of American women's literature. Like Sarah Orne Jewett and Charlotte Perkins Gilman, Freeman wrote about women's strategies and responses to social conditions at the turn into the twentieth century. Yet she is neither an outspoken and committed feminist, the "new woman" who began to emerge most visibly in the 1890s, nor the passive promoter of the status quo evident in nineteenth-century women's advice books and journals. In the early 1900s she wrote amid the emergence of feminist politics and the suffrage movement. Although Freeman captured in her work the spirit of the call for economic independence and liberation from the social restrictions of her time, she did so in subtle, coded form, embedding her most rebellious material in the framework of sentimental beginnings and endings. She kept in mind at all times the need for what she called in her letter to Fred Lewis Pattee on 5 September 1919 "selling qualities" in her work (*Infant Sphinx*, p. 382.) It was her livelihood.

Freeman's voice resonates today as an odd mixture of traditions: sentimentalist, regionalist, subtle feminist, supernaturalist. She stands as one of the most significant precursors of twentieth-century psychological fiction about women. Writing within the boundaries of domesticity and region, Freeman simultaneously subverted these arenas. In *A New England Nun and Other Stories* the themes she had begun to touch upon in her earlier collection, *A Humble Romance and Other Stories* (1887), resonate still more dramatically, particularly the connection for women between identity and place, and the struggle for recognition and acceptance in the context of one's work. Her most common themes span a range of unresolved conflicts: repression and rebellion, submission and autonomy, heterosexuality and lesbianism, marriage and spinsterhood. The stories depict the struggle of rebellious though often ambivalent heroines for self-realization and empowerment. The range of voices and genres in this collection is striking, incorporating humor, satire, and drama, and drawing upon the structures of gothic, romantic, realist, regionalist, and

Hamlin Garland visited Freeman and commented on the connections he saw between Mary E. Wilkins Freeman and her character, Louisa Ellis, in "A New England Nun." He refers here to the scene in which Joe Dagget visits Louisa after their long separation, and upsets her well-ordered home.

Her home might have been used as a typical illustration for her characters. Its cakes and pies, its hot biscuits and jams were exactly right. I felt large and rude like that man in one of her tales, "A New England Nun," who came into the well-ordered sitting room of his sweetheart with such clumsy haste that he overturned her workbasket and sat down on the cat.

Hamlin Garland, *Roadside Meetings* (New York: Macmillan, 1930), p. 33.

supernatural fiction. In this sense Freeman defies categorization. Readers who enjoy these stories will find in her novel *Pembroke* (1894) a compelling extension of the themes she began to explore in *A New England Nun and Other Stories*.

THE ROLE OF DOMESTICITY

Freeman redefined domesticity in terms that suggest the possibilities of unexpected power and autonomy. Rather than viewing the choice to focus attention on the details of the home as a sign of conformity to feminine norms, she reconstructed the domestic sphere as a place of opportunity for feminine protest and often self-discovery. The title story of this collection, "A New England Nun," as well as her frequently anthologized "The Revolt of 'Mother,'" portrays her reconstruction of the domestic realm for both married and unmarried women.

Marriage for Louisa Ellis, the heroine in "A New England Nun," represents as much a threat to the world she has created for herself as it did to Freeman's, who waited until she was forty-nine to marry. Louisa has waited fourteen years for her sailor fiancé, Joe Dagget (not unlike Freeman's first love, Hanson Tyler), to return from his voyages, only to decide against marrying him when he does. She battles against the expectation that she will give up her home and shift her attention to Joe. The story raises significant critical issues for twenty-first century readers: Is Louisa the self-repressed "nun" who has rejected the possibility of

sexual fulfillment, as early critics assumed, a neurotic woman reflecting the seeds of Freeman's own neurosis? Is Louisa instead a victorious, autonomous woman, preserving the right to a home of her own and positing feminist values? Or is the story an analysis of the tension between these possibilities? Freeman's ambiguity is precisely what makes this story so brilliant. She captures the complexities of the choice Louisa ultimately makes, imparting both the cost of Louisa's form of autonomy and the victory she wins to claim and assert control over her own space. The scene at the story's beginning in which Louisa eats alone shortly before Joe's arrival provides a glimpse of the autonomy she chooses. As she prepares her tea, she serves herself on her best china with a setting for one, for she is "a veritable guest to her own self" (p. 110). Although the story does suggest through images of repressed sexuality the cost of Louisa's choices, it also honors her defense of her world from intrusion, her determination to continue the work she loves, storing the essences of rose petals, threading and unthreading a stitch for the pure delight she takes in the act of sewing, and enjoying the art of living alone. The story makes clear Louisa's understanding that she would have to part with all of this if she were to marry Joe. "All alone by herself," Louisa weeps a little after her rejection of Joe; "but the next morning, on waking, she felt like a queen who, after fearing lest her domain be wrested away from her, sees it firmly insured in her possession" (p. 124).

In "The Revolt of 'Mother'" the issues of domain and possession within the domestic realm intensify as Freeman shifts her focus from unmarried to married life. In this story Sarah Penn transforms the new barn her husband has built to house his cows; while he is out of town, she creatively redesigns it into the home of her dreams, with a fine kitchen as a tribute to her only arena of power, her form of work. Here once again a heroine defies patriarchal assumptions. Freeman creates a woman capable of reframing marital discourse so that her domesticity is honored, becoming a place of meaning. The spirit of the story conveys the pleasure that Freeman took in transforming her own mother Eleanor's experience into revolt and in creating imaginatively the new home Eleanor never had. Facing financial decline Freeman's father gave up his plan to build a new house with a fine kitchen for Eleanor. Instead the family moved in 1877 into the home in which Eleanor was to serve as the housekeeper. Suddenly Eleanor was placed in a position of domestic servitude. In Freeman's story Sarah Penn's domesticity defies the concept of servitude, for it is a space she claims as her own, a place where she can simultaneously care for her family and "think my own thoughts an' go my own ways" (p. 310).

GENDER, CLASS, AND AGE

Much of Freeman's fiction focuses on the conditions and experience of poverty and aging for women. Her interest in the culture and economy of rural New England mixes in her work with her focus on gender. She was familiar with financial struggle. When she sold her first piece of writing, a lengthy children's ballad entitled "The Beggar King," she began to help her family pull out of years of economic difficulty.

Many of her stories describe the struggle and victory of aging women to support themselves, and their call to be accepted and supported by their communities across gender and class assumptions. In "A Church Mouse," Hetty Fifield, the heroine, must fight for the right to choose her form of work independently rather than being placed in a home as a poor and aging woman. Hetty rejects her community's assertion that the job of sexton, cleaning and tending the local church, should be held only by a man. Her poor circumstances drive the need to support herself, but she also takes pride in the work she has chosen. Male authorities in the village object: How can she ring the bell, clearly a man's job? But Hetty creates a room for herself in the church gallery. She cooks cabbage, creates a stench, makes her presence known to financially comfortable churchgoers. When a boy comes to ring the bell, she sends him away with pride: "I'm goin' to ring the bell; I'm saxton" (p. 280). Finally she barricades herself inside the church, physically barring men from intruding, and looks out at the crowd below with the "magnitude of her last act of defiance" (p. 290). Soon after, Hetty pleads far more submissively for the right to continue as sexton, and all of the middle-class women in the village now demand that the men submit to Hetty's will. In this way Freeman shows that Hetty's war is every woman's war. The story crosses class boundaries, moving from an individual plea to a collective demand. Moreover Freeman herself achieves what Hetty does, rebelling but safely and with a receptive audience: her story was first published in a woman's magazine that would reach an audience composed largely of women.

Most striking in this story is Hetty's position in the church. It suggests a context for Freeman's feelings about the role of work in her life. Hetty's room in a corner of the church gallery is behind a brilliant sunflower quilt she has made. In this way Freeman places her character in the nineteenth-century woman writer's predicament: Hetty is both trapped within the boundaries of the narrow congregation, ultimately answerable to its rules, and she is set apart by the quilt she hangs—her art—to announce the significance of her separateness, her individuality, her ability to assert.

SPINSTERHOOD AND MARRIAGE

In 1877 Susan B. Anthony described the single woman as a model for all women to emulate. Freeman, like many of her contemporaries, was not prepared to assert openly a position that so opposed the general public opinion and her own mother's choices. Freeman was far too conflicted to become active in the feminist movement; yet even at its most ambiguous, her work and her life fully support Anthony's manifesto and continually defy the negative cultural stereotyping of the spinster or "old maid." Based on the advice books readily available in Freeman's time, a spinster could look forward to a shortened life span and possible insanity. In response to these assumptions Freeman offers a sharp critique in several of the stories in *A New England Nun and Other Stories,* most especially "Christmas Jenny." Here Jenny Wrayne defines herself against, rather than within, the context of male values. As are so many of Freeman's singular heroines, Jenny is set apart from the rest of the community, viewed as "love-cracked" (p. 207), having been in love with a man who married someone else. Yet she redefines love in matriarchal terms and chooses an alternative to what her friend calls the "reg'lar road of lovin'" by loving creatures of nature, "starvin' chippies an' lame rabbits" instead of a husband. As her married friend Mrs. Carey explains, "She ain't love-cracked no more'n other folks" (p. 213). Jenny comes down from her mountain abode to sell evergreen trees and wreaths in the winter and vegetables in the summer. Her influence on the married couple down the road suggests Freeman's analysis of both the institution of marriage and the stigma of spinsterhood. By the end of the story Jenny has taught Mrs. Carey how to enjoy a feast for her own pleasure and how to appreciate the sacred refuge that Jenny has created for herself.

REFLECTIONS ON HER CRAFT

Much of Freeman's work comments on itself. Stories such as "A Village Singer" and "A Poetess" describe the painful process involved in pursuing a craft that may not reach the level of one's aspirations. In her response in the *New York Times* to winning the American Academy Medal, Freeman described her sense of victory upon acceptance of her first major story in *Harper's Bazar* and receipt of a check for twenty-five dollars: "I felt my wings spring from my shoulders capable of flight and I flew home" (24 April 1926, sec. 1.7). Acutely self-critical, however, she knew that home was a place where she was grounded in realities that often interfered with her craft— the need to earn money and the consequent goal of satisfying her editors. She worked in feverish ten-hour blocks of time. She acknowledged to her editor, Elizabeth Garver Jordan, on 12 July 1904 that "sentiments and uplifting ones are in demand" (*Infant Sphinx,* p. 301). Yet in a letter to Hamlin Garland on 23 November 1887 she asserted, "the idea of being true is always with me. . . . Yes, I do think more of making my characters *true* and having them say and do just the things they would say and do, than anything else, and that is the only aim in literature of which I have been really conscious myself" (*Infant Sphinx,* p. 83). Representing the finest of her work, the extraordinary heroines in *A New England Nun and Other Stories* meet this high expectation. The collection makes a rich and important contribution to the field of American literary realism.

See also Courtship, Marriage, and Divorce; Domestic and Sentimental Fiction; Feminism; Regionalism and Local Color Fiction; Realism; Short Story; Slang, Dialect, and Other Types of Marked Language

BIBLIOGRAPHY
Primary Works
Freeman, Mary E. Wilkins. *A New England Nun and Other Stories.* New York: Harper & Brothers, 1891. First published under the name Mary E. Wilkins.

Freeman, Mary E. Wilkins. *Selected Stories of Mary E. Wilkins Freeman.* Edited by Marjorie Pryse. New York: Norton, 1983. The quotations from Freeman's stories that are used in the present article come from this volume.

Freeman, Mary E. Wilkins. *The Infant Sphinx: Collected Letters of Mary E. Wilkins Freeman.* Edited by Brent L. Kendrick. Metuchen, N.J.: Scarecrow, 1985.

Secondary Works
Dwyer, Patricia M. "Diffusing Boundaries: A Study of Narrative Strategies in Mary Wilkins Freeman's 'The Revolt of Mother.'" In *Legacy: A Journal of American Women Writers* 10, no. 2 (1993): 120–127.

Glasser, Leah Blatt. *In a Closet Hidden: The Life and Work of Mary E. Wilkins Freeman.* Amherst: University of Massachusetts Press, 1996.

Fetterley, Judith, and Marjorie Pryse. *Writing Out of Place: Regionalism, Women, and American Literary Culture.* Urbana: University of Illinois Press, 2003.

Hirsch, David H. "Subdued Meaning in 'A New England Nun.'" *Studies in Short Fiction* 2 (winter 1965): 124–136.

Leah Blatt Glasser

NEW ORLEANS

In the spring of 1862, only a year after Louisiana had seceded, the Union commodore David Farragut pushed his fleet up the Mississippi to New Orleans. As he approached, bonfires set by retreating Confederates blazed along the levee. In short order, the Union major general Benjamin Butler landed troops on the wharves and occupied New Orleans. That moment captured in tableau three nascent writers: George Washington Cable stood at a shop door watching in dismay as Union troops spilled into the city. Captain John William De Forest marched his Union company toward Lafayette Square amid the jeers of townsfolk. Ten-year-old Grace King, peering down from her room high above Camp Street, saw the approaching troops and feared they would massacre her family.

These writers would later respond in very different ways to the Civil War and its aftermath in New Orleans, a period in which the fortunes and politics of the city were dramatically altered. Once the wealthiest city in the South, New Orleans forfeited access to its markets in the upper Mississippi Valley, in the Northeast, and in other nations. It was occupied for almost a year by "Beast" Butler, so called because he treated New Orleanians like a subjugated people and because he issued the infamous "woman order" stating that any woman who reviled federal troops would be dealt with like a prostitute.

As federal troops moved through outlying plantation country, many thousands of former slaves left their former owners and fled to "contraband camps," one of them in New Orleans. African American soldiers, who were recruited—and sometimes impressed—by the Union army, fought in many major Louisiana battles.

Federal military Reconstruction officially began in 1867, in part as a Northern reaction to "Black Codes" adopted by Southern legislatures to effectively return freedmen to slavery and in part as a response to the New Orleans riot of 30 July 1866, in which dozens of black Unionists were killed by police. The Reconstruction Acts disenfranchised any man who had voluntarily aided the Confederacy; the acts thus nominally and briefly increased African American political power in Louisiana. White racists seethed under a Republican state administration propped up by the federal government. This tension reached a pitch in 1874, when armed insurgents calling themselves the White League defeated metropolitan police and black militiamen in the streets of New Orleans. President Ulysses S. Grant sent federal troops into the city to restore the Republican government.

In 1876 a bizarre political compromise with the federal government allowed Louisiana Democrats to elect a Confederate war hero governor. The next year, federal troops left New Orleans, and Reconstruction, an abysmal failure in Louisiana, came to an end. In the wake of Reconstruction, African Americans quickly

Birds-eye view of New Orleans. Currier & Ives lithograph, c. 1885. THE LIBRARY OF CONGRESS

lost what little ground they had gained and under Bourbon reactionaries and their successors suffered degrading political and social conditions as racism silenced even the old paternalist voices.

Though still a major port, New Orleans remained a poor city. Its cultural makeup had been changing rapidly after the initial waves of "Americans" following the Louisiana Purchase in the early nineteenth century had begun to threaten Creole dominance. In the 1850s and 1860s, the city was flooded with Irish and German immigrants; by 1910, Italians made up about 30 percent of the population. White Creole wealth and influence gradually declined.

LITERATURE

George Washington Cable (1844–1925) was born in New Orleans to parents from the Northeast. In a Catholic city, he was reared a Presbyterian. When his widowed mother refused to sign an oath of allegiance to the Union and fled the city during Butler's occupation, Cable joined the Confederate army and was twice wounded. After the war, he adopted liberal views

on race, which he expressed in both fiction and nonfiction and which made him, by one account, "the most hated little man in New Orleans." In the 1880s, Cable moved to New England.

Cable's major fiction includes a story collection, *Old Creole Days* (1879), and his masterpiece, *The Grandissimes* (1880). Set in 1803–1804, when the Americans assumed power in New Orleans, *The Grandissimes* imports an American outsider, Joseph Frowenfeld, as a liberal commentator on white Creole pride and prejudice. Drawn into the alien world of Creole caste, Frowenfeld discovers a friend in the white Creole protagonist, Honoré Grandissime, whose wealthy and educated brother of the same name bears the ignominious suffix "f.m.c."—free man of color. The novel is both a traditional romance, in which the white Honoré courts and wins the white Creole Aurore Nancanou, and a realist indictment of the Creole caste system, in which the patriarch Agricole Fusilier reigns as the ignorant and proud embodiment of white Creole aristocracy—dueling, scheming, and oppressing the "niggahs"—while

African slaves and mixed-race Creoles are shunned, mutilated, or murdered. Honoré f.m.c., the white Honoré's doppelgänger, gives his fortune to rescue his brother's finances and takes his own life. William Dean Howells (1837–1920) remarked that the novel's "blend of romance and reality . . . does no wrong to either component" (Turner, p. 99). Contemporary southern readers could not have missed parallels between the 1803 American takeover of Creole New Orleans and the recent Union occupation of the city. Cable's denunciation of racial prejudice, though temporally displaced, struck a Bourbon nerve. His depiction of white Creoles likewise offended a litterateur of their number, Adrien Rouquette, who lambasted Cable's critique in *A Critical Dialogue between Aboo and Caboo* (1880).

In 1885 Grace King (1852–1932), a New Orleans native but a Protestant of Alsatian descent, launched her literary career the night after a northern editor, Richard Watson Gilder, asked her why New Orleanians who, like herself, hated George Washington Cable so much, did not "write better." She took up the gauntlet, wrote the first of her stories, "Monsieur Motte," sold it to *Princeton Review* for good money, and became a writer. King was well read in nineteenth-century thinkers—Charles Darwin, Thomas Huxley, Herbert Spencer, John Ruskin, and Thomas Carlyle, among others. She moved in literary circles and was a close friend of Sam and Livy Clemens. King considered herself part of the larger realist movement, once avowing, "I am not a romanticist, I am a realist" (p. 398).

In her collection *Balcony Stories* (1893) and in her novel *The Pleasant Ways of St. Médard* (1916), King worked out her Confederate apologetics with a foot in both camps. For the most part, she rejected the romantic love interest as a plot device and wrote instead of frustration, loss, aging, and death. In nuanced and restrained prose, she captured the speech, dress, habits, political opinions, and economic circumstances of her characters. Her manner is analytical, sometimes sententious, and rhetorically unsentimental. Her plots, often involving refugees, are typically driven by historical circumstance. And her insights into contemporary gender issues are often frank and progressive.

However, King's professed realism was tainted by her own tempered nostalgia for a slaveholding culture. Her Confederate sympathies, which arose from her family's painful experiences during the Civil War, blinded her to the economic circumstances that had led to the war and shut off sympathy for African Americans who did not submit to gracious servitude.

In her fiction, meddling Yankees sundered the warm bond between master and slave and blighted the virtues of Louisiana's white Creole and American aristocracy. For example, in "A Crippled Hope," when Butler's Union forces invade New Orleans and free its slaves, a lame slave woman who nurses other slaves in a slave auction house finds that the soldiers, like her slave-trading master, deny her "some master whom she could have loved, some mistress whom she could have adored" (p. 117). In "La Grande Demoiselle," African American Union troops occupy the resplendent plantation home of Idalie Sainte Foy Mortemart des Islets; when the house burns, the troops carry her out in her *chemise de nuit*. King renders this tableau, which adumbrates Idalie's descent into poverty as a teacher of black children, with the objective restraint of a patrician who would not stoop to sensational Negrophobia. But the message is plain. "The Little Convent Girl," one of King's best stories, follows a young woman who has just lost her father as she journeys from a Cincinnati convent to New Orleans, "the terminus of the never" (p. 156), to meet her mother for the first time. The crew of the steamboat is astonished when the mother, a "colored" woman, comes to claim her daughter. When the young woman returns to the wharf a month later seeking comfort from the crew she had befriended, she is rebuffed and either jumps or falls into the Mississippi and drowns. Without censure or sentiment, King's treatment of the tragic mulatta figure creates a resonant sympathy for the young woman who lives in three worlds and belongs to none.

John William De Forest (1826–1906), a Connecticut Yankee by birth, temperament, and military allegiance, gave no quarter to the city he helped to occupy in 1862. In *Miss Ravenel's Conversion from Secession to Loyalty* (1867), he juxtaposed liberal New England ideals and reactionary southern ideals. De Forest draws his ideological lines broadly, depicting New Orleans as a Sodom and the South as a land of barbarians, root diggers, Hottentots, and jackasses, but he has been justly praised for the nervous, grisly realism of his battle scenes, unmatched by his contemporaries.

A New Orleans native of black, white, and possibly Native American ancestry, Alice Dunbar-Nelson (1875–1935), born Alice Moore, published *Violets and Other Tales* (1895) when she was twenty. Its most striking piece is an essay called "The Woman," which champions the independent working woman who escapes "a serfdom . . . which too often becomes galling and unendurable" (1:25). The writer recast some stories from *Violets* and added new ones in *The Goodness of St. Rocque* (1899). In this collection of spare and formally assured tales, she wrote primarily about multi-ethnic characters in and around New Orleans—usually small, lonely figures in melancholy circumstances. Dunbar-Nelson's tonal and stylistic restraint deflects the sentimental trajectory of her plots. She attends social detail and dialect with painterly exactitude and thrift but forfeits subjective complexity in the bargain. The racial composition of her Creole characters is often coded, so that local readers recognize mixed-race characters whom outsiders may read as unraced. Her social criticism is objective and subdued. A deadly labor melee between Irish longshoremen and black stevedores (based on labor riots in 1892) rages offstage in "Mr. Baptiste" as the title character, a Creole, is murdered by an Irish laborer for siding with the "negroes." But the motives of Mr. Baptiste, who may be a mixed-race character, are apparently selfish, and the pathos of his death obscures the racial tension behind it. In "Tony's Wife," the title character, who is not Tony's wife, suffers regular beatings from her brutal Italian "husband." On his deathbed, he refuses to marry her and gives his business and all his money to his brother. Blunting the sentimental potential of this tale, Dunbar-Nelson makes the protagonist "meek, pale, little, ugly, and German," a woman whose eyes flicker to life only when she learns that Tony will die. Though in the end she has clearly been cheated by Tony and by convention, the feminist strain voiced earlier in "The Woman" is here subdued by the author's aversion to sentimentality.

The best story of this collection is "Sister Josepha," in which an orphaned New Orleans girl of mixed race who has been left on the doorstep of a white convent takes orders after refusing the guardianship of a white couple because the husband leers at her. She finds her regimen at the convent bleak and intolerable. The cool narrator understands Sister Josepha's romantic yearnings for "the ethereal airiness of earthly joys" and her distaste for "the ugly garb, the coarse meats," yet grudges her an escape: "Sister Josepha did not know that the rainbow is elusive, and its colours but the illumination of tears; she had never been told that earthly ethereality is necessarily ephemeral, nor that bonbons and glacés, whether of the palate or of the soul, nauseate and pall upon the taste" (1:164). Alternatives to the convent may indeed have been bleak for a young female orphan of mixed race. In the end the young nun weeps as the heavy door of her convent closes upon "narrow, squalid Chartres Street." Dunbar-Nelson's stoical vision of New Orleans holds romantic carnality, uncertain racial identity, and cloistral austerity in grim suspension.

Born in Greece to a British citizen and a Greek mother, Lafcadio Hearn (1850–1904) spent ten years in New Orleans, beginning in 1878. He was an editor at both the *Item* and the *Times-Democrat*. He published *"Gombo Zhèbes": A Little Dictionary of Creole Proverbs* (1885), a cookbook, and *Chita: A Memory of Last Island* (1889). The last is a lyrical, impressionistic novella about a girl who survives the 1856 hurricane that destroyed the resort of Ile Derniére. Though dramatically flawed, the book is a stylistic tour de force by the polyglot Hearn, who wrote lovely, if occasionally cloying, English and captured both the dialects and native languages of Louisiana's marsh cultures.

Kate Chopin (1851–1904) may have married into Louisiana at nineteen, when she moved with her husband to New Orleans in 1870, but her maternal rearing was St. Louis French Creole. Even her Irish father spoke French. The decade she spent in New Orleans and seven subsequent years in Clotierville before she returned to St. Louis provided urban Creole and rural Acadian material for an early novel, *At Fault* (1890); two collections of stories, *Bayou Folk* (1894) and *A Night in Acadie* (1897); and her classic novella, *The Awakening* (1899). The novella, in which Chopin brought her considerable literary and scientific learning to bear upon the life of young Edna Pontellier, was received with a mixture of praise for its formal accomplishment and censure for its moral latitude. The protagonist, a Kentucky Protestant by birth, marries a bourgeois New Orleans Creole, grows dissatisfied in her marriage, and awakens to her position in society as a mother and as a possession of her husband. With regard to sex, Creole society is, paradoxically, both verbally frank and conventionally rigid. This tension, coinciding with Edna's social and sexual awakening, abrades her romantic personality, and she drowns herself at the beach resort of Grand Isle.

Other New Orleans writers of the period included the local colorist Ruth McEnery Stuart, the historians Charles Gayarré and Rodolphe Desdunes, and the Bourbon journalist and fiction writer Sallie Rhett Roman.

CULTURE

Serial publications in New Orleans waned during the Civil War. The *Picayune* was the only English-language newspaper to endure it. Other English-language postbellum newspapers included the *Item*, the *States*, the *Times*, the *Democrat*, and the *Times-Democrat*, which became the *Times-Picayune* in 1914. For almost ten years, beginning in 1889, the *New Orleans Crusader*, an African American newspaper, fought Bourbon oppression. The German-language *New Orleans Deutsche Zeitung*, founded in 1848, was succeeded fifty-nine years later by the *Neue Deutsche Zeitung*, which was published until 1917. New Orleans newspapers often printed serialized novels, such as Sally Rhett Roman's *Tonie* (*Times-Democrat,* 1900) and Baron Ludwig von Reizenstein's *The Mysteries of New Orleans* (*Zeitung,* 1854–1855). Influential magazines of the period included *De Bow's Review,* published from 1846 until 1880, and the literary *Comptes-Rendus de L'Athéné Louisianais.*

From 1880 until a massive failed strike in 1892, New Orleans witnessed a large growth of labor organizations and a number of small strikes. Black and white unions often competed against one another, a tension Dunbar-Nelson dramatized in "Mr. Baptiste."

Just after the turn of the century, yellow fever outbreaks that had plagued New Orleans throughout the last decades of the nineteenth century were ended when the city's open gutters were salted and its tens of thousands of open drinking water cisterns were screened and oiled.

A number of universities were established in or near New Orleans between 1860 and 1920: the Louisiana State Agricultural and Mechanical College (1874), later known as Louisiana State University at Baton Rouge; Tulane University (1884) and its adjunct H. Sophie Newcomb Memorial College for Women (1886); Loyola College and Academy (1904); St. Mary's Dominican Academy (1861); three African American institutions, Dillard University (1869), Xavier University (1915), and Southern University (1880, later Southern University at Baton Rouge); and New Orleans Baptist Theological Seminary (1917).

The theater, always vigorous in New Orleans, also revived after the war. Major venues after 1880 included the Grand Opera House, the Crescent, and the Tulane, and after 1900 the Elysium, Lyric, Schubert, and Baldwin theaters and Welch's Hippodrome. Plays by black actors and writers appeared at the Orleans, Pythian Hall, Lyric, and Palace theaters.

Storyville, the notorious lower Basin Street district of legalized prostitution, thrived from 1897 until 1917, when the Navy Department effectively shut it down. For a quarter, patrons could purchase the Blue Book, which listed all working prostitutes, black and white. At the district's pitch about two thousand prostitutes worked in over two hundred houses.

Ferdinand "Jelly Roll" Morton, one of the first great jazz pianists, played at least one of the Storyville houses. Other legendary figures of jazz (or "jass") music—Louis Armstrong, Buddy Bolden, King Oliver—built on an improvisational syncopated style that had evolved earlier in the nineteenth century from (among other sources) martial music played by roving brass bands. Remarkably, the diverse ethnic voices of antebellum New Orleans and the liberal voices of its postwar era survived Bourbon rule—in the fiction of Dunbar-Nelson, in Hearn's polyglot narratives, in Morton's jazz, and elsewhere—only slightly the worse for wear.

See also The Awakening; New South; Regionalism and Local Color Fiction

BIBLIOGRAPHY
Primary Works
Dunbar-Nelson, Alice Moore. *The Works of Alice Dunbar-Nelson.* Edited by Gloria T. Hull. 3 vols. New York: Oxford University Press, 1988.

Howells, William Dean. *Heroines of Fiction.* 2 vols. New York: Harper & Brothers, 1901.

King, Grace. *Balcony Stories.* 1893. Ridgewood, N.J.: Gregg, 1968.

King, Grace. "To Fred Lewis Pattee." 19 January 1915. In *Grace King of New Orleans,* edited by Robert Bush. Baton Rouge: Louisiana State University Press, 1973.

Turner, Arlin. *George W. Cable: A Biography.* Durham, N.C.: Duke University Press, 1956.

Secondary Works
Bush, Robert. *Grace King: A Southern Destiny.* Baton Rouge: Louisiana State University Press, 1983.

Davis, Edwin Adams. *Louisiana: A Narrative History.* 3rd ed. Baton Rouge, La.: Claitor's, 1971.

Gargano, James W., ed. *Critical Essays on John William De Forest.* Boston: G. K. Hall, 1981.

Kirby, David. *Grace King.* Boston: Twayne, 1980.

Larson, Susan. *The Booklover's Guide to New Orleans.* Baton Rouge: Louisiana State University Press, 1999.

Leavitt, Mel. *A Short History of New Orleans.* San Francisco: Lexikos, 1982.

Light, James F. *John William De Forest.* New York: Twayne, 1965.

Martin, Wendy, ed. *New Essays on "The Awakening."* New York: Cambridge University Press, 1988.

Perry, Carolyn, and Mary Louise Weaks. *The History of Southern Women's Literature.* Baton Rouge: Louisiana State University Press, 2002.

Richardson, Thomas J., ed. *"The Grandissimes": Centennial Essays.* Jackson: University Press of Mississippi, 1981.

Rubin, Louis D. *George W. Cable: The Life and Times of a Southern Heretic.* New York: Pegasus, 1969.

Taylor, Helen. *Gender, Race, and Region in the Writings of Grace King, Ruth McEnery Stuart, and Kate Chopin.* Baton Rouge: Louisiana State University Press, 1989.

Taylor, Joe Gray. *Louisiana: A History.* New York: Norton, 1984.

Toth, Emily. *Kate Chopin.* New York: Morrow, 1990.

Kris Lackey

NEW SOUTH

The term "New South" entered public discourse in the United States after 1877, the year Reconstruction ended and the last federal occupation troops were withdrawn from the former Confederacy. State governments (often called the "redeemer" governments) across the South could finally reassert the power of the white majority, but the whole region faced systemic problems deriving from the Civil War, Reconstruction, and an outdated agrarian economy that had lost its chief labor unit, the slaves. Intentionally a politically neutral slogan behind which a wide range of individuals and groups could line up, the New South suggested a future-oriented, pragmatic, and conciliatory vision that could move the region beyond the trauma of the defeat of the Confederacy and into alignment with the rest of the nation. Its governing ideas were free-enterprise economics, a meritocratic social hierarchy, and harmonious (but not equal) relations between whites and African Americans.

The modernizers of the New South—those businessmen, political leaders, and journalists who wanted to direct the region toward the industrial model of the North—had to be cautious when it came to the sensitivities of many of their fellow southerners. During the last decades of the nineteenth century and continuing into the twentieth, a significant number of people throughout the South saw their feelings and attitudes reflected in a more powerful term, the "Lost Cause." The name designated a particular Southern motif launched in 1866 by the Richmond newspaperman Edward A. Pollard (1831–1872). The meaning of the Lost Cause was abundantly clear: in the Civil War the South had fought a legitimate battle for the cause of states' rights, one that had not been compromised by the surrender at Appomattox, but had, if anything, been glorified in defeat. The Lost Cause drew upon the memory of the blood sacrifice of the war and an inflexible belief in the superiority of Southern agrarian civilization. The New South idea was, in their view, an attempt "to "corrupt Southern principles by bringing material prosperity to the South" (Wilson, *Baptized,* p. 84). The partisans of the Lost Cause took an uncompromising position on any transformation that involved jettisoning a social order based on the concept of

The Queen of Industry, or, The New South. Cartoon by Thomas Nast for the cover of *Harper's Weekly,* 1882. Nast comments on the transition in the economy of the South from one of slavery to one of mechanized industry. Although the figure of Liberty at the loom seems to represent a more benign system, the cotton-pickers outside the factory door provide a reminder that the southern economy continues to rest on the hard labor of blacks. © BETTMANN/CORBIS

honor, an evangelical moral code, and the maintenance of a clear racial hierarchy. Whether or not these ideals were useful or appropriate for postwar southern society, they were articles of faith for many people, and those who proposed an alternative path for Dixie had to proceed with caution.

A GEORGIAN IN NEW YORK

When Henry Woodfin Grady (1850–1889), the managing editor of the *Atlanta Constitution,* stepped off the train in New York in December 1886 to deliver a speech to the annual banquet of the New England Club, he faced a major opportunity. As a young newspaper owner in the southern metropolis, itself only recently arisen from the ashes of General Sherman's punitive campaign twenty-two years earlier, he arrived in the North uncertain of his status. On his side Grady had relative youth (born in 1850, he had not served in the war), commercial and journalistic achievement, and the sense that he would have a curious, if not sympathetic, audience. Working against him, however, was a subsoil layer of Northern beliefs about the South that still carried some of the animosity of the war years and the early Reconstruction period. Grady knew also that his words would find their way back to Atlanta and the wider South, where sensitivities could be offended by even a mild note of criticism of the Confederate past, particularly from the editor of the *Constitution*.

Grady's speech, "The New South," is in many ways a masterpiece of tightrope walking. In its course he plays with motifs of New England moral rigor, Virginia liberality, the efforts of Confederate veterans to revitalize their devastated farms, amicable race relations, and most importantly the idea of a region committed to a commercially and industrially progressive future. He paints a picture of a defeated South conscious of the honorable struggle in which it had engaged, but prepared to face the future without rancor. Grady also cleverly turns the direction of his speech toward the one region of the country that had contributed the most to the decades-long battle against slavery, when he asks

> Now, what answer has New England to this message? Will she permit the prejudice of war to remain in the hearts of the conquerors, when it has died in the hearts of the conquered? Will she transmit this prejudice to the next generation, that in their hearts which never felt the generous ardor of conflict it may perpetuate itself? Will she withhold, save in strained courtesy, the hand which straight from his soldier's heart Grant offered to Lee at Appomattox? (Pp. 40–41)

This was, to an extent, humbug. In no sense could the "prejudice of war" be said to have "died in the hearts of the conquered." If anything it was sharper in 1886 than it had been in 1866. Neither did the gesture toward Grant echo a southern consensus; rather, more southerners were concerned (and would continue to be for many decades) with reducing the status of Grant in every way in order to elevate the historical reputation of Robert E. Lee.

Nevertheless Grady was successfully articulating an important strand in postwar southern thinking. Behind the sentimental invocations of plantation life in popular fiction and the obsessional nurturing of pieties regarding the military prowess of the Confederacy was a recognition that the economic, commercial, and infrastructural lag visible across much of the South had been the principal reason for defeat, and that a livable future would come only through

increased—and increasingly harmonized—connections with the rest of the country. That meant finding some way of improving agricultural efficiency, expanding the rail network, and exploring new industrial relations in a region largely dominated for generations by a mentality that despised the economic and social model represented by the North.

"BAWN IN A BRIER-PATCH!"

The most memorable cultural manifestation of the theory of the New South involved the popularization of the rich assets of southern black folklore through the work of Joel Chandler Harris (1848–1908), a white journalist who had grown up as the child of an unmarried mother in the poverty of rural Georgia. Originating in a series of sketches Harris began writing for the *Atlanta Constitution* in the late 1870s, *Uncle Remus, His Songs and His Sayings* (1880) is one of the best-loved literary works in American history. The collection is centered around allegorical stories written in Harris's rendition of the speech of plantation slaves and recounted by the fictional Uncle Remus, a former African American slave, now a trusted servant and farmworker in the postbellum South. In Harris's framing narrative the audience for Uncle Remus's tales of Brer Fox and Brer Rabbit is the young son of the southern lady and the former Union soldier who are now Remus's employers. One of the more substantial pieces in the book is a short narrative called "A Story of the War," in which Uncle Remus saves the life of his master, a Confederate soldier about to be shot by a Union soldier. Though in the newspaper version of the tale Remus kills the Union soldier, in the book's revised version the Union soldier is only injured by Remus's bullet, losing an arm as a consequence. After the war the Union soldier marries the woman who nursed him through his injury—the sister of the Confederate he almost killed (Sundquist, p. 325). The couple's son is the boy enthralled by Remus's folktales and songs.

The implications of the Uncle Remus stories are manifold, touching on issues of culture, folklore, anthropology, and the range of national attitudes regarding the status of African Americans in the decades after the Civil War. The dynamic of the tales reflects Harris's dual role as conscientious folklorist and creative writer, and the implications of the work—both Uncle Remus's natural intelligence and the moral architecture of the Brer Rabbit narratives—could be construed both to support and to attack efforts at black self-improvement and the exercise of political rights. The ambiguity of the New South is unmistakably present in Harris's writing. The narrative atmosphere is a heady mix of genuine affection for faithful black servants, belief in an established social hierarchy, commitment to economic improvement, paternalistic respect for folkloric authenticity, and a sense that the South had something particular—a warmth and feeling for local human experience—to offer an increasingly depersonalized and standardized American nation.

It was a winning combination. The character of Remus and his stories brought Harris wealth and fame, propelling him from his niche as a shy and inarticulate amateur folklorist working in an obscure corner of feature journalism into the exposed position of a nationally known writer. After the success of *Uncle Remus, His Songs and His Sayings,* nine more volumes of Uncle Remus stories were published up to and past Harris's death in 1908. Their popularity with several generations of both children and adults, both in the United States and abroad, seemed to defy changing social history and the invention of twentieth-century entertainment technology: the stories reemerged, for example, in sentimental and nostalgic triumph in the 1946 Walt Disney movie *Song of the South.* Despite the strand of cultural resistance in *Uncle Remus,* the stories embody what almost all white Americans wanted to believe about the consequences of the Civil War: that reconciliation between North and South was achieved; that a constructive relationship between former slaves and their masters was possible; and that the racial hierarchy was stable. With its dramatic allegories and emotional clarity, the black folklore newly packaged by Harris became for many years an important part of American children's literature.

WASHINGTON AT ATLANTA

The New South was not, however, an exclusively white southern vision. Booker T. Washington (1856–1915), the Tuskegee educator and one of the most influential black Americans in the latter part of the nineteenth century, was the most tenacious promoter of the ideal of the New South among African Americans. Himself philosophically and politically conservative in important ways, he recognized nevertheless that an expanding and technologically innovative southern economy could protect the emancipated slaves, as increasing prosperity would mitigate racial tensions and the South would become a place where the African American worker could prove himself and gain a command of useful skills.

Washington was suspicious of the kind of rhetoric that pushed black professional and political ambitions in a way that failed to recognize either the debilitating legacy of slavery or the potential for a racist backlash from southern whites. Washington looked to a stable environment in which basic economic security could be achieved by a large number of individuals. The most dramatic platform from which he expounded his ideas was at the opening of the Cotton States and International Exposition in Atlanta in September 1895, when he offered himself as a spokesman on behalf of the African Americans of the South. The Exposition was itself one of the achievements of the New South, as it sought to reopen connections between the region and the wider nation and the world. Washington's speech and its motif of fingers and hand became famous: "In all things that are purely social we can be as separate as the fingers," he declared, "yet one as the hand in all things essential to mutual progress" (p. 148).

Washington expressed in those few words the idea of the New South, this time from a black leader's perspective. His vision was, however, broadly the same vision as that of the white southerners who wanted an exit from the hatreds and resentments of the postwar era and to steer the economy and political structure of the South toward that of the rest of the United States. The idea of an economic and social harmony between blacks and whites that would benefit all, without any revolutionary disruptions from angry parties on either side, was at the heart of the New South paradigm. Like many of the key elements of the New South vision, it was presented well but foundered ultimately on the rocks of southern history and a defensive racial order.

The New South was never as popular a slogan as the more poetic evocations of Confederate memory, but a wide spectrum of people—including not only entrepreneurs but also a folklorist from rural, working-class origins like Joel Chandler Harris, a moderate opinion maker like Henry Grady, and a conservative African American leader such as Booker T. Washington—worked toward manifesting this vision of the New South. The New South project was a courageous attempt to get past the legacy of frustration and intransigence that had dogged southern life after the humiliating defeat of 1865. It also represented the unavoidable arrival of modern American capitalism in an agrarian society. It had its own internal contradictions, but it embodied at its best a spirited ideal and signaled, if not a reality, then at least a viable hope for a different future.

See also Jim Crow; Reconstruction; Regionalism and Local Color Fiction; *Uncle Remus, His Songs and His Sayings; Up from Slavery; The Voice of the People*

BIBLIOGRAPHY

Primary Works

Grady, Henry Woodfin. *The New South and Other Addresses.* New York: Maynard, Merrill, and Co., 1904.

Harris, Joel Chandler. *Uncle Remus, His Songs and His Sayings.* 1880. Edited by Robert E. Hemenway. New York: Penguin, 1986.

Washington, Booker T. *Up from Slavery.* 1900. In *Three Negro Classics.* Introduction by John Hope Franklin. New York: Avon Books, 1965.

Secondary Works

Aaron, Daniel. *The Unwritten War: American Writers and the Civil War.* New York: Knopf, 1973.

Ayers, Edward L. *The Promise of the New South: Life after Reconstruction.* New York: Oxford University Press, 1992.

Blight, David W. *Race and Reunion: The Civil War in American Memory.* Cambridge, Mass.: Harvard University Press, 2001.

Gaston, Paul M. *The New South Creed: A Study in Southern Mythmaking.* New York: Knopf, 1970.

Genovese, Eugene D. *A Consuming Fire: The Fall of the Confederacy in the Mind of the White Christian South.* Athens: University of Georgia Press, 1998.

Sundquist, Eric J. *To Wake the Nations: Race in the Making of American Literature.* Cambridge, Mass.: Harvard University Press, 1993.

Wilson, Charles Reagan. *Baptized in Blood: The Religion of the Lost Cause, 1865–1920.* Athens: University of Georgia Press, 1980.

Wilson, Edmund. *Patriotic Gore: Studies in the Literature of the American Civil War.* New York: Oxford University Press, 1962.

Woodward, C. Vann. *Origins of the New South, 1877–1913.* Baton Rouge: Louisiana State University Press, 1951.

Martin Griffin

NEWSPAPER SYNDICATES

The syndication of news and other features to American newspapers began in 1861, and literary materials were first syndicated shortly after this. It was only in the 1880s, though, that syndicates began significantly to affect literary authors, readers, and the American publishing world in general. For the following two decades syndicates played a major role in the literary marketplace. After approximately 1905, however, even though syndicates continued to distribute

> *Some readers were dismayed to learn that the contents of their local newspapers were not all written specifically for those papers, and they frequently complained about how syndicates faked "originality." As seen in this quotation, however, not everyone felt this way.*
>
> ---
>
> I may find it provoking when seven out of ten of my weekly papers have the same serial, or short story . . . , but perhaps the family next door has only one weekly and no daily paper; surely the well-written articles bought by a good syndicate are better for my neighbor's instruction and amusement than would be the trash possibly served to him otherwise.
>
> Adelaide Cilley Waldron, "Business Relations between Publishers and Writers," *Writer* 1 (1887): 57.

numerous short stories and serial novels to newspapers, their importance declined dramatically.

THE EARLY HISTORY OF NEWSPAPER SYNDICATES

Technically newspaper syndicates are defined as firms that sell and distribute the same materials—be it advice columns, cartoons, or political columns—to multiple newspapers for nearly simultaneous publication. Although primitive forms of syndication known as "readyprint" or "patent insides" were introduced by Ansel Nash Kellogg in the United States as early as 1861, the first syndicate to have any major impact on the literary marketplace was the American Press Association. Founded in Chicago in 1882, the APA by 1890 was supplying over six thousand daily and weekly newspapers in twenty-eight states with stereotype-plate blocks of news, features, and fiction, which local editors could simply insert into the printing forms for the newspaper. Unlike the readyprint companies that typically used previously published magazine fiction, the APA was the first to purchase fiction directly from authors for first-time serial use, thereby providing an entry to the publishing world for hundreds of authors in small towns and cities across the United States who had literary aspirations but little hope of placing their work in major magazines. Some of the better-known authors who had contact with the APA early in their careers were Jack London, Maurice Thompson, Charlotte Perkins Stetson (later Gilman), Kate Chopin, and Kate Field.

> *Having grown up in rural Indiana, the early syndicator S. S. McClure knew what it felt like to go without good reading materials. Always concerned with financial success, McClure nonetheless was motivated by a strong desire to provide cultural uplift for Americans who felt similarly limited in their choices of reading materials.*

[Syndication] is an attempt to give to the great mass of people through the newspapers reading equal to that which appears in the best magazines.

S. S. McClure, 1891 circular, Lilly Library, Indiana University, Bloomington.

THE HEYDAY OF LITERARY SYNDICATION

The year 1884 would prove to be the most important turning point for American newspaper literary syndication. In the spring of that year the British newspaperman William Frederic Tillotson (1844–1889) visited the East Coast to view the American operations of his company, Tillotson's Newspaper Fiction Bureau. Founded in Bolton, England, in 1873, this firm copied the French method of the feuilleton, whereby one company purchased an original work from an author and then sold galley proofs (printed slips of paper) of that fiction to multiple, widely dispersed newspapers that would publish them simultaneously on a fixed date; each paper was guaranteed exclusive rights within its circulation area. The local newspaper editor, after receiving the galley proofs of fictions in the mail, would edit the work to fit the space available or to suit his or her audience, have it typeset, and print it. Tillotson's advanced only minimally in the American market in the late 1870s and early 1880s, though, and it confined itself chiefly to syndicating British and Irish serial novels, almost exclusively romances by the likes of Mary Elizabeth Braddon, The Duchess (Margaret Hungerford), Ouida (Marie Louise de la Ramée), and Florence Marryat.

Even after the mid-1880s, because American newspaper editors generally declined to purchase harshly realistic works by French and British authors, the few dozen American papers that purchased Tillotson's materials tended to get a continued steady dose of British historical romances. The Authors' Syndicate too, founded in London in 1890 by the British Society of Authors, offered similar fare to American newspapers.

Possibly Tillotson's greatest claim to literary fame has to do with one work it turned down: after Thomas Hardy had, under contract, finished half the manuscript of what would become *Tess of the d'Urbervilles* (1891), the editors rejected it for its supposed immorality. One of Tillotson's most popular writers, ironically, was the American western romance writer Bret Harte, who was living in England in the 1890s; he ended up selling the English-language serial rights of fourteen short stories and novels to Tillotson's at very high prices for worldwide distribution. After the opening of a New York City office in 1888, Tillotson's Newspaper Fiction Bureau began to purchase a small number of American short stories, but the only noteworthy American author whose works were purchased and distributed by this office was Jack London, whose tales "The Unmasking of a Cad" and "The Grilling of Loren Ellery" were syndicated to American newspapers in 1899.

Possibly in consequence of William Frederic Tillotson's visit to the United States in early 1884, the *New York Sun* editor Charles A. Dana that spring contacted four major American authors to see if they would like to be paid large sums of money in return for the right to syndicate their original works to multiple newspapers across the country. Mark Twain expressed interest initially but then dropped out in June; William Dean Howells, after writing a long narrative play with which he was displeased, also opted out. Bret Harte, however, contributed "A Blue Grass Penelope," and Henry James sold his short stories "Pandora" and "Georgina's Reasons" to Dana; all were published in June or July of 1884.

Dana did not continue in the syndicate business, but late in 1884 two young American entrepreneurs with little capital founded two separate syndicates that began taking on the risky business of promising authors large amounts of money for first serial rights with no guarantee of recouping their outlays as well as assuming the laborious task of selling the fictions to multiple newspapers across the country. These men were Irving Bacheller (1859–1950), whose syndicates went by many names, including the Bacheller Syndicate, the New York Press Syndicate, and Bacheller, Johnson, and Bacheller; and Samuel Sidney (S. S.) McClure (1857–1949), whose firm was known as the Associated Literary Press and, after 1900, the McClure Newspaper Syndicate.

On the whole authors welcomed Bacheller and McClure (and, to a lesser extent, the Authors' Alliance and the United Press syndicates) because in the days before the Chace Act of 1891 neither British nor American authors had been reaping the full financial

> *Syndicators were in large part salespeople, and much of their time was spent traveling across the country to sell their literary wares face-to-face with newspaper editors.*
>
> ---
>
> Then came the first of many journeys up and down the continent. I slept on Pullman cars; I climbed innumerable flights of stairs, often late at night, to ratty editorial rooms in all the big cities. . . . There was a steep grade in the way of the syndicate man [in] those days.
>
> Irving Bacheller, *From Stores of Memory* (New York: Farrar and Rinehart, 1938), p. 44.

benefits of their work. In the state of copyright law existing prior to the Chace Act, British authors' works could be pirated by American periodical editors for free, and consequently such editors had naturally shied away from purchasing copyrighted works by American authors.

Many newspaper editors were interested in syndicated fiction because they hoped it would boost their newspapers' circulations and thus their advertising revenues. However, not surprisingly, numerous members of the book and magazine publishing establishment, reacting to the success of the syndicates, lashed out at these competitors. Edward W. Bok (1863–1930), who was the editor of the *Ladies' Home Journal* from 1889 until 1919, railed in 1895 against what he saw as the syndicates' injection of "commercialism" into the relationship between publishers and authors, arguing that the high prices the syndicates paid were turning authors into mere workers writing to order rather than true artists. He concluded, "For the most part the newspaper syndicate is the sewer of the author" (Bok, p. 340).

What truly angered magazine and book editors and publishers, however, was that the syndicates—with Bacheller and McClure in the lead—were driving up prices generally and luring authors away with offers of much higher payments. Bacheller and McClure paid large sums to British authors such as Robert Louis Stevenson, Thomas Hardy, and Wilkie Collins for first serial rights to their works, even though legally such payment was not required. Rudyard Kipling and Sir Arthur Conan Doyle received their first major exposure to American audiences via newspaper syndication; most of Doyle's Sherlock Holmes stories, in

fact, were syndicated by McClure in the early 1890s. In 1894 Bacheller offered to pay Doyle £30 per thousand words for the first serial rights to a new series of Holmes stories, double what Sir George Newnes of the *Strand Magazine* had been paying him, which resulted in Doyle breaking his exclusive arrangement with Newnes.

American authors, though, were the ones who benefited most from Bacheller's and McClure's syndicates. To solicit the works of American authors, they posted announcements in magazines, ran prize contests, sent out flyers, wrote directly to authors, and occasionally even called on them at their homes. Some American authors, like the British ones before them, initially balked at the idea of having their works first appear in newspapers, a print venue that some felt was rather déclassé, but when they heard of the extremely high amounts these syndicates were paying, this reluctance appeared to evaporate. Sarah Orne Jewett first sold a story to McClure in 1884 ("Stolen Pleasures") and would later sell nine more stories to Bacheller and him. Mary E. Wilkins (later Freeman) sold "The Emmets" and "A Wayfaring Couple" to McClure in 1884 and 1885, respectively, and subsequently contributed eleven more stories to these syndicates. Mark Twain, desperate to raise as much money as he could to pay off his own debts, in 1891 had already accepted an offer of $6,000 from the *Ladies' Home Journal* for the American serial rights to *The American Claimant* (1892), but he changed course rapidly when McClure visited him and offered twice that amount for American and British serial rights. Henry James returned to syndication only once after 1884; in 1892, at a time when he needed money to finance his experiments in writing drama, James sold "The Real Thing" to McClure. Even William Dean Howells sold one serial novel, *The Quality of Mercy,* to McClure in 1891 (for $10,000), and at least one children's story, "The Flight of Pony Baker," to the syndicate in 1895. Many better-known authors also appreciated the syndicates for their willingness to purchase their "secondary" works at generous prices. Both syndicates, for example, liberally paid Mary E. Wilkins Freeman for her children's and holiday fictions that she could not always place in major magazines; Bacheller paid her $50 per thousand words and arranged for her to win a $2,000 prize for "The Long Arm," an experimental detective story she coauthored with Joseph Chamberlin in 1895.

As a result of their efforts, Bacheller and McClure were able to offer their newspaper customers a wide array of fictions, including historical romances, local color sketches, domestic dramas, and traditional love stories. Bacheller's and McClure's only general stipulation

Irving Bacheller, c. 1917. THE LIBRARY OF CONGRESS

his contests, bought and syndicated approximately ten of his earliest stories between 1885 and 1888. Frank Norris was brought east by McClure in 1898 and given a half-time sinecure at the syndicate office from early 1898 to December 1899; this afforded him a great deal of time to write, much of which he used to draft *McTeague* (1899).

Stephen Crane (1871–1900) skewered McClure in some letters to his friends, at one point calling him a "Scotch ass," chiefly because he had held on to the manuscript of *The Red Badge of Courage* for many months in 1894 while considering it for publication, yet Crane neglected to mention how frequently McClure advanced him money and paid him generously for his work at critical times in the mid-1890s. Irving Bacheller also played a key role in Crane's career. He purchased and syndicated *The Red Badge of Courage* (in truncated form) in December 1894, which allowed Crane to approach the book publisher D. Appleton in 1895 as a nationally well-known author, no doubt greatly contributing to this publisher's decision to bring out *Red Badge* in book form later that year. It was also Bacheller who financed Crane's trip throughout the western United States and Mexico in 1895, an experience that would eventually result in such stories as "The Blue Hotel" (1898) and "The Bride Comes to Yellow Sky" (1898). Crane was also on assignment to Cuba for the Bacheller Syndicate in 1897 when his ship, the *Commodore*, was sunk off the Florida coast, an experience Crane turned not only into a newspaper report but also into his classic story "The Open Boat" (1897), which he sold to *Scribner's Monthly.*

For various reasons, however, syndicates declined in importance as players in the American literary world around 1900. One major reason was that the Chace Act leveled the playing field for American and British authors, who were now both receiving their just rewards from American magazines for literary work. Another reason was that the many cheap, mass-market magazines that appeared on the scene in the mid-1890s were able—because they reached a national audience and could thus carry national, name-brand advertising—to pay authors higher amounts than did the limited-circulation magazines with which the syndicates had competed in the late 1880s. Syndicates found too that transportation advances hurt their ability to pay high fees to authors. Swift and reliable railroads expanded the circulation of each metropolitan newspaper that bought a particular syndicated fiction, and because each newspaper wanted exclusive publication rights within its circulation area, the number of newspapers to which a syndicate could sell an individual work declined, thereby reducing the amount the

was that fictions could not be morbid or immoral or offend southern readers, for these qualities would make them unappealing to newspaper editors and, it was assumed, their readers. Because Bacheller and McClure both greatly enjoyed regionalist fiction and stories written in dialect, though, their customers received an extremely heavy dose of this type of fiction. Charles W. Chesnutt, Mary Noailles Murfree, Hamlin Garland, Joel Chandler Harris, Sarah Orne Jewett, Mary E. Wilkins Freeman, Octave Thanet, Rose Terry Cooke, and Ruth McEnery Stuart were only a few of the regionalists whose works they syndicated.

These syndicates did not, however, publish only the works of the most famous authors; they also discovered and fostered numerous up-and-coming writers who are now recognized as major voices of the era. Jack London, for instance, might have disparaged syndicates in his later novel *Martin Eden* (1908) as requiring only formulaic fiction, but McClure encouraged him as a young author, bought many of his stories, and at a critical time of his life paid him a stipend to write a novel. Charles W. Chesnutt's first major encouragement as a writer came from S. S. McClure, who, after reading Chesnutt's submissions to one of

> *Syndicates represented a great financial boon for numerous British and American authors. Some, however, such as the British novelist Ouida, criticized what they saw as the syndicates' strict regulations as to the subject matter, length, and treatment of acceptable fictions. These guidelines, however, were imposed more by the customers—the newspaper editors—than by the syndicators themselves.*
>
> ---
>
> [A syndicate] is an "immense organization" which treats authors precisely as the Chicago killing and salting establishments treat the pig; the author, like the pig, is purchased, shot through a tube, and delivered in the shape of a wet sheet (as the pig is in the shape of a ham), north, south, east, and west, wherever there is a demand for him.
>
> Ouida (Marie Louise de la Ramée), Letter to the Editor, *London Times,* 22 May 1891, p. 3.

syndicate could pay its authors. In addition, after S. S. McClure founded *McClure's Magazine* in 1893, he had little to do with the syndicate, leaving it in less capable hands until it ceased operations in 1912. Bacheller sold his syndicate in 1898 not only because it was not sufficiently profitable but also because he wanted to spend more time with his wife and become a full-time novelist himself.

In the wake of these pioneers, other syndicates continued for many decades to distribute fiction. These included the American Short Story Company, the American Press Company, Frank Carpenter's Newspaper Syndicate, the International Syndicate of Baltimore, the Albert Bigelow Paine Syndicate, the Editors' Literary Syndicate, the Pacific Press Syndicate, the Lorraine Literary Press Association, the Bell Syndicate, the Authors' Co-Operative Company, and the Wilson Press Syndicate. Many individual major metropolitan dailies also operated their own syndicates: the *Chicago Daily News,* the *New York Journal,* and the *New York World,* for instance, in the late 1890s started selling to other newspapers various materials that had originally appeared in their own pages. With rare exceptions, however, these syndicates purchased either second serial rights or first serial rights to fictions by less-talented authors. For all intents and purposes the heyday of literary newspaper syndicates had passed by 1905.

SIGNIFICANCE

Despite the relatively brief time during which they played a key role in literary publishing, newspaper syndicates affected the American publishing world in many long-term ways. First, they greatly encouraged the distinctively American genre of the short story. In his 1893 article "The Man of Letters as a Man of Business," William Dean Howells gave the syndicates much of the credit for increasing the demand for short stories and the prices paid for them. Concomitantly, syndicates played a major part in transforming American fiction authors into true professionals. Because the syndicates required vast numbers of fictions and helped increase the pay for such work, authorship—especially for Americans—became a viable profession for a much larger number of people than had previously been possible. Further, many authors used the syndicates as bargaining chips in negotiations with magazine and book editors and publishers for higher pay; in this way syndicates broke open the genteel publishing world and helped authors to be free agents in control of their labor rather than writers working under exclusive contracts to specific firms.

Possibly most important, syndicates reached hitherto unrecognized and underserved audiences outside of the urban, northeastern United States. Each fiction syndicated by Bacheller and McClure, for instance, was typically published in 20 to 140 newspapers across the country, from the *Portland Oregonian,* to the *Nebraska State Journal,* to the *Boston Globe* and the *Atlanta Constitution.* Given the quite large circulations of many of these papers, the combined audience for each syndicated fiction was approximately one to two million readers, a much greater circulation than any of the major monthly magazines of the time enjoyed. Moreover, the low price of these newspapers (two cents on weekdays and five cents on Sundays) meant that even though newspaper editors might have intended to use syndicated fiction to attract middle-class readers to their newspapers, millions of working-class readers were now able to enjoy the type of first-run fiction that previously only wealthier people could purchase. Some East and West Coast magazines did circulate nationally in the 1880s, but it was the syndicates who helped make their editors and publishers more fully aware of the importance of the large, socioeconomically diverse market for quality fiction that existed throughout the country. Because editors, authors, and publishers had to take these readers more into account, the syndicates thus in some ways helped determine the content of and paved the way for the success of the many low-priced, mass-market magazines founded in the late 1880s and early 1890s. Fiction, in large part because of the syndicates, became a part of Americans' everyday lives, something to be read on horse-drawn trolleys and subway cars, during a break at work, on the farmstead, at a park, or in one's parlor. Syndicates affected hundreds if not thousands of authors and exposed millions of readers to generally good short stories and novels; in so doing they truly helped transform the conditions under which the American literary marketplace operated.

See also Journalism; Literary Marketplace; Presidential Elections; Spanish-American War

BIBLIOGRAPHY

Primary Works

Bacheller, Irving. *Coming up the Road: Memories of a North Country Boyhood.* Indianapolis, Ind.: Bobbs-Merrill, 1928.

Bok, Edward W. "The Modern Literary King." *Forum* 20 (1895): 334–343.

McClure, S. S. *My Autobiography.* New York: Frederick A. Stokes Company, 1914. Reprinted as *The Autobiography of S. S. McClure* by Willa Cather. Lincoln: University of Nebraska Press, 1997.

Secondary Works

Colby, Robert A. "'What Fools Authors Be!': The Authors' Syndicate, 1890–1920." *Library Chronicle of the University of Texas* 35 (1986): 60–87.

Harter, Eugene. *Boilerplating America: The Hidden Newspaper.* Edited by Dorothy Harter. Lanham, Md.: University Press of America, 1991.

Johanningsmeier, Charles. *Fiction and the American Literary Marketplace: The Role of Newspaper Syndicates in America, 1860–1900.* Cambridge, U.K.: Cambridge University Press, 1997.

Johanningsmeier, Charles. "Henry James's Dalliance with the Newspaper World." *Henry James Review* 19, no.1 (1998): 36–52.

Johanningsmeier, Charles. "Sarah Orne Jewett and Mary E. Wilkins (Freeman): Two Shrewd Businesswomen in Search of New Markets." *New England Quarterly* 70 (1997): 57–82.

Katz, Joseph. "Bibliography and the Rise of American Literary Realism." *Studies in American Fiction* 2 (1974): 75–88.

Mrja, Ellen M. "Ansel Nash Kellogg." In *American Newspaper Journalists, 1873–1900,* vol. 23 of *Dictionary of Literary Biography,* edited by Perry J. Ashley, pp. 180–183. Detroit: Gale Research, 1983.

Watson, Elmo Scott. *A History of Newspaper Syndicates in the United States, 1865–1935.* Chicago: N.p., 1936.

Charles Johanningsmeier

NEW YORK

Commentators on New York City tend to insist that it has always been a commercial center rather than an intellectual one, and that "the literary" has had a very minor place among its residents' concerns. Literary critics writing about the period between 1870 and 1920 repeat this truism even while recognizing that those years also saw major publishers moving into New York from their original locations in Philadelphia and Boston and that the twentieth century would see this city become the nation's major publishing center. In fact the claim that New York had no intellectual or literary life is altogether misleading; what critics really mean is that it never boasted one ongoing, identifiable intellectual tradition, as did Boston. There, the predominance of white Anglo-Saxon Protestants with a common history going back to the Puritan hegemony created a literary tradition of shared experiences and values that are reflected in the works they produced. In New York, by contrast, the constant shifting of the population from one ethnic or national group to the next (from the Dutch to the English in the seventeenth and eighteenth centuries and then on to the "invasions" of Irish, Jews, African Americans, and Asians in the nineteenth and twentieth) meant not that literary traditions did not exist but rather that more than one intellectual tradition jostled and competed. The "problem" with New York City (as always) is its complexity.

This is especially evident in the ways that writers have reflected the city in their work. In the 1870–1920 period in particular one sees two major ways of imagining New York. On the one hand, there is a small but powerful group of writers who, by reason of wealth, family, social standing, or business connections, believed that they "possessed" New York City, that it was theirs by virtue of their birth and status. For these writers, the image of the city was enshrined in memories of their childhood, almost as a prelapsarian idyll existing prior to the influx of immigrants and other disruptive forces; consequently they saw the post–Civil War city as chaotic and threatening. The other contingent—consisting of a much larger group of people—were the newcomers themselves, writers whose origins ranged from other states to other countries. These writers too found the city frightening, but beyond the immediate threat of poverty, loneliness, and crime, they were gripped by its possibilities. New York City offered opportunities: for wealth, for learning, for individual growth, for transformations of all kinds. The ways these writers portrayed the city, and each other, demonstrate how the complexity of New York's intellectual traditions manifested the diversity of its peoples.

The Great East River Suspension Bridge. Chromolithograph by Currier & Ives, c. 1886. The 1883 completion of John Roebling's Brooklyn Bridge, connecting Manhattan with Brooklyn, in itself an engineering triumph, was also a major step in the development of New York City as the cultural heart of the United States. THE LIBRARY OF CONGRESS

NATIVE-BORN NEW YORK WRITERS

Henry James (1843–1916) and Edith Wharton (1862–1937) are generally seen as New York's major "native" writers in the period between the Civil War and World War I. Both were born there to wealthy families, and both left, spending most of their adult lives elsewhere. Hence both imagined New York as the city of their childhoods. For James, writing in *The American Scene* (1907), that meant "the precious stretch of space between Washington Square [where his family lived] and Fourteenth Street" (p. 84)—in those days an area of large houses surrounded by pleasant gardens. *Washington Square* (1881) revisits the scene of that boyhood in the story of a woman who comes to realize that her suitor only wants her for her money and that her most honorable course is to remain single. In *The American Scene*, James's reflections on his return to the United States after many years abroad, he keeps the memory of a "pleasanter,

easier, hazier past" (p. 85) as a contrast to the New York City of the new century, where not only rampant capitalism but "the alien" was "truly in possession" (p. 114). "The Jolly Corner" (1909), written during the same period, features a native New Yorker returning to his family residence on Washington Square after decades devoted to the arts in Europe, chasing the "ghost" of the commercial man he would have become had he stayed home. In these later works one sees James's uneasiness both with the capitalist explosion of the late nineteenth century and the immigrant invasions that followed in its wake.

Edith Wharton's sense of post–Civil War New York was similar to James's, but her childhood memories were not so pleasant. As a woman, and especially as a woman of her very exclusive social class, she could not wander freely as James had; rather, her childhood experience was of a restrictive, oppressive social scene.

In her memoir *A Backward Glance* (1934) she evokes the rigidity of a New World aristocracy, where "the man who 'kept a shop' was . . . rigorously shut out of polite society" (p. 784). Despite her rebellion against the overbearing society of her youth, however, she never warmed to the commercial class that replaced it. In *The House of Mirth* (1905) she shows her repugnance for the newly rich and recently arrived through her story of the descent of a society belle through the social layers. *The Age of Innocence* (1920) revisits the rigid rules of her childhood but opts for the securities of the social order over the potential chaos of alternatives. Like James, Wharton had difficulty imagining a viable moral order in this commercial, increasingly "alien" urban landscape.

TRANSPLANTED NEW YORK WRITERS

If James and Wharton are in many ways writers about a city that seems to have gone beyond their class control, other native-born (but not New York City–born) writers came to the city for the new opportunities it offered. William Dean Howells (1837–1920), the Ohio native whose editorial career had perhaps more influence on the shape of American letters than any other man of his time, moved to New York after having established a career in Boston, where he edited the *Atlantic Monthly*. Although he came to take up the editorship of the New York–based *Harper's New Monthly Magazine*, Howells entered the city slowly and hesitantly, doing much of the job in absentia until he finally settled into his new environment in 1888. Perhaps because he had removed himself from New England's narrow definitions of the literary, Howells developed his theories about realism in fiction during his time in New York, calling for a literary mode that portrayed people and their motives as they actually were rather than as, in an ideal world, they should be. Howells also featured New York in his fiction, most notably *A Hazard of New Fortunes* (1890), a semiautobiographical novel that traces the history of an editor as he and his family shop for housing and adjust to a new environment. The New York imagined in this novel is turbulent and pluralistic; its central plot involves a labor strike and a German socialist, and its protagonist wanders through streets filled with immigrants. Far more open to ethnic pluralism than James, Howells was curious about the city's new residents and encouraging of their own literary efforts. For him the city was both intimidating and exhilarating.

Perhaps because they shared the experience of growing up in deeply religious households, Stephen Crane (1871–1900) and Theodore Dreiser (1871–1945) saw a darker side to the city. Crane, a preacher's son from New Jersey, and Dreiser, an Indiana native whose father was a devout Catholic, came to New York with long-standing interests in the sensibilities of poverty and failure. Both gravitated to the branch of realism known as naturalism, which saw human beings less as individuals with energy and volition and more as creatures molded by their environment. For Crane this was manifested in fiction that portrayed the hopelessness of poverty, especially in short sketches like "Men in the Storm" (1894), where men stand in line in a driving snowstorm as they wait to be admitted to a homeless shelter, or in the novella *Maggie, A Girl of the Streets* (1893), which chronicles the short, desperate life—seduction, abandonment, prostitution, suicide—of a pretty girl from the slums. In Dreiser's New York fiction the city is more layered; as with Howells, there is an interest in real estate—apartments—manifested as protagonists search for housing, and *Sister Carrie* (1900) especially shows the pleasures that the city can offer to those who can afford it. For those who cannot, however, New York is the same city as it is for Crane; Hurstwood, Dreiser's male protagonist, dies in a flophouse in a scene much like those in Crane's work. For these writers, especially Dreiser, New York's lure depends on the money one has to exploit it.

Horatio Alger (1832–1899) and O. Henry (1862–1910), two writers immensely popular in their time, point to two other mainstream traditions fostered by the city on writers' imaginations. The "rags to riches" story had been an institution in American letters at least since Benjamin Franklin published his *Autobiography* (1818), but Alger made it the stuff of American myth in his compelling, if formulaic, stories of poor but honest country boys who come to the city and, after trials and tribulations, get rich. Like Dreiser and Crane, Alger uses the city's geography to demonstrate class divisions and, not incidentally, to teach newcomers how to navigate both its streets and its mores. Once codified in Alger's books, the "rags to riches" story became probably the dominant narrative of the late nineteenth century, appearing in titles such as Abraham Cahan's *The Rise of David Levinsky* (1917) and Booker T. Washington's *Up from Slavery* (1901). In a different vein, the New York imaged in the short stories of O. Henry (William Sydney Porter) is the world of ordinary people doing ordinary jobs. Although the stories themselves tend to hinge on a turn of the plot, they portray a city in which little people struggle to make and keep a living, an urban landscape in which human interactions make all the difference.

"OTHER" NEW YORK WRITERS

Like the New England writers and despite differences in class among them, James, Wharton, Howells,

Crane, Dreiser, Alger, and O. Henry were all native-born white writers mainly from Protestant backgrounds. In the late nineteenth century and early twentieth century this gave them an advantage over all other residents—they were by birth what most people considered "American," and even though they had very different values and interests, they shared a worldview premised on the assumption that even if they were not particularly powerful as individuals, they were racially superior to most of the rest of the world. In part because of this worldview, most of these writers only feature white Americans in their fiction, and when they feature "others," they manage to convey their intrinsic dislike for these "interlopers." In fact the incursion of the interlopers was one of the main reasons that the white writers feared New York; between 1815 and 1860 the city's population jumped from 100,000 to 800,000, largely because of immigrants from Europe. Many of these newcomers were desperately poor: Irish peasants escaping the potato famine or Italian peasants escaping the isolated farms of rural Italy. Between 1880 and 1919 another seventeen million European immigrants landed; in 1910, one-quarter of the population was composed of Jews, most from the shtetls (villages) of eastern Europe. Members of the old white establishment felt overwhelmed, and a major reason that New York City appears in so much of their fiction as a chaotic place full of pushy, uneducated foreigners is that they were unable to surmount the cultural distance between themselves and the new arrivals.

African Americans did not exactly "arrive" during this period; they had lived in New York for two centuries. The state abolished slavery in 1799, and the first black congregation was formed by the Methodist Episcopal Church during Mayor DeWitt Clinton's administration in the first decades of the nineteenth century. Still, New York was often a dangerous place for black people. In 1741, in an incident known as the "Negro Plot," more than a hundred African Americans were arrested and charged with setting fires; twenty-nine were burned at the stake and eighty-eight deported. During the Civil War, African Americans were lynched by Irish Americans protesting conscription into the Union army. Throughout the city's history, residential patterns dictated ethnic enclaves that forced African Americans (as well as other ethnic groups) into virtual ghettos.

Despite this history, African Americans came to New York, as they did to other northern cities, for opportunity. They came especially in the early twentieth century during a period known as the Great Migration, when the families of thousands of former slaves left the increasing segregation and oppression of the South for the supposedly better conditions of the North. Many found themselves trapped in cold, urban spaces where racism was as bad or worse as that they had encountered at home, but others determined to make the North a new world. This would explode into the literary period of the 1920s and 1930s commonly known as the Harlem Renaissance, but in New York City two earlier writers helped prepare the way. Setting a tradition among African American writers of seeing New York as a moral trap for innocent black youths, Paul Laurence Dunbar's (1872–1906) *The Sport of the Gods* (1902) shows his protagonists (who had come here seeking the anonymity of the city to escape false accusations in their southern home) destroyed by the false sophistication of the New York underworld. James Weldon Johnson (1871–1938), on the other hand, saw the city in a more positive light. Born in Florida, Johnson, a lawyer, teacher, editor, songwriter, poet, and fiction writer who also served as U.S. consul to Venezuela and Nicaragua, arrived in New York in 1901. His novel *The Autobiography of an Ex-Colored Man,* published anonymously in 1912, at first uses New York City as Dunbar does, as a place where his still-innocent mulatto protagonist is introduced to the underworld of gambling, alcohol, racial mixing, and the "new" American music, ragtime. Later in the novel, however, Johnson uses the city as a place where the narrator can shed his "colored" identity, becoming a successful businessman and raising a family. Although the conclusion suggests that the protagonist was wrong to have cut himself off from his ethnic roots, the fact that New York City facilitated his "success" in the white world signals the kind of transformation this particular urban space became for writers seeking to develop their own American voice. As Ralph Ellison would vividly demonstrate many years later, New York was transformative precisely because it was so chaotic; the character Reinhart, in *Invisible Man* (1952), takes on successive personalities as he passes from neighborhood to neighborhood, street to street. He can do this precisely because the city's size and pluralism facilitated anonymity.

For immigrants from abroad, this possibility made for both the appeal and the terror of New York. For many immigrants, especially those from eastern Europe, New York was all they knew of the United States. One of the reasons the city developed ethnic-centered neighborhoods was that immigrants tended to bunch together for psychological (and sometimes physical) security. Hence the rise of Little Italy, the Lower East Side Jewish ghetto, and Chinatown. In these areas common languages, experiences, religion, and culture helped to buffer the transition to the New World. While Jacob Riis's book of photographic essays *How*

> *In this passage from Abraham Cahan's* The Rise of David Levinsky *(1917), David, the novel's first-person narrator and protagonist, has just arrived in New York from his native Russia, where he grew up in a small, pious town. He has been processed through immigration in Castle Garden and has been directed to the Jewish quarter, then located in the Lower East Side.*
>
> Ten minutes' walk brought me to the heart of the Jewish East Side. The streets swarmed with Yiddish-speaking immigrants. The sign-boards were in English and Yiddish, some of them in Russian. The scurry and hustle of the people were not merely overwhelmingly greater, both in volume and intensity, than in my native town. It was of another sort. The swing and step of the pedestrians, the voices and manner of the street peddlers, and a hundred and one other things seemed to testify to far more self-confidence and energy, to larger ambitions and wider scopes, than did the appearance of the crowds in my birthplace.
>
> Abraham Cahan, *The Rise of David Levinsky* (New York: Harper and Row, 1960), p. 93.

the Other Half Lives, first published in 1890, confirmed white Americans' suspicion that immigrants lived in appalling squalor, it also identified the ethnic topography of immigrant New York. In their literary portrayals of the urban experience, immigrant writers alternately celebrate the ethnic communities such enclaves provide, demonstrate how badly many immigrants wanted to leave those neighborhoods, and lament the loss of native cultures that transpires when they succeed. The works of Abraham Cahan (1860–1951), for instance, feature New York as the vivid backdrop against which his protagonists evolve from eastern European peasants to American Jews. Like Dreiser's, Cahan's New York is specific, palpable; he names streets, parks, buildings, fabrics, furnishings, and foods, placing his characters among these cultural markers as they grapple with both the material and psychological conundrums of culture-switching. Like Johnson's protagonist, Cahan's characters can disappear into the city, not in order to "pass" but rather to escape from the surveillance of their neighbors as they try out new identities. In "The Imported Bridegroom"

(1898), for instance, a young rabbinical scholar brought to the United States to be a successful immigrant's pious son-in-law "escapes" his role as religious genius by befriending a group of socialists and applying his debating skills to their meetings. *The Rise of David Levinsky* (1917) explores the social geography of New York City as the Jewish community moves out of the downtown ghetto and begins populating enclaves in Harlem and Brooklyn. Again like Dreiser, Cahan uses the cityscape as an ongoing, dynamic environment in his fiction.

Anzia Yezierska (1885–1970), also a Jewish immigrant, focuses more narrowly on the Jewish ghetto in her writing, although some of the settings in her novels take her protagonists out of strictly Jewish enclaves into the world of her "other"—white Protestant Americans. For Yezierska, Hester Street, in the heart of the Lower East Side ghetto (a two-mile-square area of Lower Manhattan that contained at its height two million Jews from all over Europe), was also the locus of emerging Jewish American identity. In works such as *Hungry Hearts* (1920), her characters, mostly female, yearn to develop themselves "into a person," as they constantly reiterate; for Yezierska that means obtaining an education (most Jewish women coming from eastern Europe had little or no education), learning to dress and walk like Americans, meeting "real" (i.e., white Protestant) Americans and conversing with them as equals, and having control over their own destinies. For Yezierska, as for Cahan, success is imaged geographically in the move out of the ghetto into "good" apartments uptown; also like Cahan, material success is often countered by protagonists' realization that in moving uptown they have also lost their community and in many ways their culture. If New York City is imaged as squalid in Yezierska's downtown scenes, it is imaged as cold, often contemptuous, and friendless in her uptown ones.

Such loss is also registered by other immigrant groups of the 1870–1920 period. Irish American writers in particular approached the city as the locus of cultural and especially spiritual loss. Most Irish American writers of this period chose political and social commentary rather than fiction; for instance, the Chicago-born Finley Peter Dunne created the character "Mr. Dooley," an Irish saloon keeper who humorously critiques contemporary politics through humor and dialect. Those Irish writers who chose fiction over political commentary voiced the ambivalence of a community in transition between worlds, where immigrants who fled the hunger and oppression of the Old World find themselves manipulated economically and politically and threatened socially and religiously in the new. Like the first-generation

Jews of the ghetto, first-generation Irish were appalled at the loss of faith and religious practice that their American-born children demonstrated. The immigrant Mary Anne Sadlier, whose didactic novels were published just prior to this period, presented New York as a place where Irish immigrants faced particular sets of problems, many resulting from the threat to their Catholic faith posed by the Protestant mainstream. James W. Sullivan (1848–1938), on the other hand, was a Pennsylvania-born Irish descendant whose writings focused on labor and the urban poor. His *Tenement Tales of New York* (1895) fictionalized the situations he observed, especially as they existed among ethnic enclaves. In "Slob Murphy," his story of the death of an eight-year-old slum boy, the Irish community is depicted as morally undermined by ignorance, alcohol, and indifferent priests.

These two contradictory views—that New York is a city of great opportunity and that New York is a city that destroys families and communities—do not terminate with the First World War; subsequent writers, immigrant and native, would continue telling the story of individuals struggling to achieve success among an ever-larger metropolis whose populace alternates between heartlessness and sentimentality. Although the physical presence of the city tends to dominate, the intellectual engagement in determining what the city means to specific groups and individuals— what the city offers, and what it takes away—is evident in nearly all of the fiction. While New York had been prominently featured in the works of earlier writers, most notably Washington Irving, James Fenimore Cooper, Catharine Maria Sedgwick, Herman Melville, and Walt Whitman, writers' fascination with the city came to maturity in the period between the Civil War and World War I, when distinct intellectual communities, often rooted in ethnic identifications, began to form. As James Weldon Johnson wrote in *The Autobiography of an Ex-Colored Man:* "New York City is the most fatally fascinating thing in America. She sits like a great witch at the gate of the country, showing her alluring white face and hiding the crooked hands and feet . . . constantly enticing thousands from far within and tempting those who come from across the seas. . . . Some she crushes . . . others she condemns to a fate like that of galley-slaves, a few she favours and fondles, riding them high on the bubbles of fortune" (p. 442). For writers tracking the transition from traditional communities to modernity, New York City was the ideal location for attempting Émile Zola's "experimental novel"—a city of multiple forces and communities, where any mixture of good and evil, fortune and disaster, could plausibly explain the course of individual lives.

See also Assimilation; *The Autobiography of an Ex-Colored Man;* Blacks; Book Publishing; Catholics; City Dwellers; Immigration; Irish; Jews; *The Rise of David Levinsky; Sister Carrie*

BIBLIOGRAPHY
Primary Works
Dunbar, Paul Laurence. *The Sport of the Gods.* 1902. London: Collier-Macmillan, 1970.

James, Henry. *The American Scene.* 1907. New York: Harper & Brothers, 1907.

Johnson, James Weldon. *The Autobiography of an Ex-Colored Man.* 1912. In *Three Negro Classics,* edited by John Hope Franklin. New York: Avon, 1965.

Wharton, Edith. *A Backward Glance.* 1934. In *Edith Wharton: Novellas and Other Writings,* edited by Cynthia Griffin Wolff. New York: Library of America, 1990.

Secondary Works
Fanning, Charles, ed. *The Exiles of Erin: Nineteenth-Century Irish-American Fiction.* Notre Dame, Ind.: University of Notre Dame Press, 1987.

Fanning, Charles. *The Irish Voice in America: 250 Years of Irish-American Fiction.* Lexington: University Press of Kentucky, 1999.

Maurice, Arthur Bartlett. *New York in Fiction.* 1901. Port Washington, N.Y.: Ira J. Friedman, 1969.

O'Connell, Shaun. *Remarkable, Unspeakable New York: A Literary History.* Boston: Beacon Press, 1995.

Susan K. Harris

NORTH OF BOSTON

North of Boston (1914) was Robert Frost's (1874–1963) second book of poetry and it established him as the American poet of New England. The collection is considered the major achievement of a career that included writing, farming, teaching, journalism, and lecturing. Frost's poems, stripped of Victorian artifice, were regarded by some as a program for a new poetry, something Frost denied. Oddly enough, the book was first published in England, where he was living at the time. But American publishers were slow to accept any poetry that did not satisfy a late-nineteenth-century taste for rhyme and ornamentation or respect certain poetic conventions. (The debate over poetic style— ornamental versus easily accessible language—began in about 1905.)

The outbreak of World War I, about which he later wrote protest poems, brought Frost and his

Robert Frost. © BETTMANN/CORBIS

with the British Georgian poets. Georgian poetry, however, reacted against industrialism by retreating to an idealized pastoral world with abundant charm, but was so low on imagination that it amounted to mere escapism. Frost himself pointed to the influence on his verse of the ten eclogues of Virgil.

North of Boston is regional poetry and its subject is the region's people. In it, the poet withdraws artistically from the urban world to New England. But industrialism encroaches in any case, as in the poem "The Self-Seeker," in which a workman's coat becomes caught in a mill and his legs and feet are badly injured. He is forced to sell the land on which he cultivates flowers in order to buy new feet. The man and his artistry are both victims of industrialization.

RECEPTION

Reviews were generally positive. The well-known modernist poet Ezra Pound (1885–1972) praised Robert Frost's "artistic vigor" and the tone of honesty and irony in the poems, whose pervasive humor contains a touch of the sinister. Frost depicted real people who converse in the natural speech of New England and he wrote of their reticence, stubbornness, and tragedies. Because Frost's blank verse was so similar to prose, his work was also noted for its proximity to good short story writing. Amy Lowell (1874–1925), a poet of the imagist school, writes in her review of *North of Boston* that Frost's characters are "the remainder of a once fine stock" (p. 49). Ironically, she laments that, unlike Europe, New England had lost the "sturdy peasantry" of the soil, who, she speculates, may have gone west fleeing "violent and ugly" religious beliefs (p. 49). Others find the characters hardy and reflective. In either case, readers consider the people and places comfortably familiar. Because of *North of Boston*, Frost became known as a kindly "poet-philosopher" who could express complex ideas and strong feelings in simple colloquial language very different from the Victorian forms of expression and, as Pound wrote, with no "tricks." For a time the critics debated whether Frost was a traditional poet because he sometimes used regular stanzas and rhymes or an early modern poet because he experimented with blank verse and free forms. Frost's theory of "the sound of sense," which he considered a choice rather than an imperative, entailed using prose dialogue to establish a rhythm. The apparently simple surface of Frost's poems contrasts pleasantly with the difficult modernism of poems by Pound and T. S. Eliot (1888–1965). Frost said that he refused to use footnotes as these poets did because he wrote for people who did not need them.

family back to the United States. Frost's colloquial style and the technique he called "the sound of sense" was greatly admired by his readers in England and *North of Boston*'s success there prompted the American publishing company Henry Holt to bring it out in the United States. The book sold only moderately well at first but gradually gained momentum until it was a commercial success.

INFLUENCES

The volume contained several of what have become Robert Frost's most famous poems: "Mending Wall," "The Death of the Hired Man," "Home Burial," and "After Apple-Picking." Critics found the influence of many poets in his work, most prominent among them the American poets Walt Whitman and Ralph Waldo Emerson and the British poets William Wordsworth, Thomas Hardy, and Robert Browning, though Frost rarely wrote in the confessional mode Browning sometimes adopted. Because Frost so often set his poetry in rural New England, his work has been called "pastoral," and "bucolic" and has often been associated

Although a less-familiar poem to most readers, Frost's "A Servant to Servants" captures the slow discovery of horrors that can contrast with the aura of an apparently peaceful scene. This same tone and realistic exposition can be found in some of the work of Elizabeth Gaskell and in Edith Wharton's novel, Ethan Frome, also set in New England.

My father's brother, he went mad quite young.
Some thought he had been bitten by a dog,
Because his violence took on the form
Of carrying his pillow in his teeth;
But it's more likely he was crossed in love,
Or so the story goes. It was some girl.
Anyway all he talked about was love.
They soon saw he would do someone a mischief
If he wa'n't kept strict watch of, and it ended
In father's building him a sort of cage,
Or room within a room, of hickory poles,
Like stanchions in the barn, from floor to ceiling—
A narrow passage all the way around.
Anything they put in for furniture
He'd tear to pieces, even a bed to lie on.
So they made the place comfortable with straw,
Like a beast's stall, to ease their consciences.
Of course they had to feed him without dishes.
They tried to keep him clothed, but he paraded
With his clothes on his arm—all of his clothes.
Cruel—it sounds. I s'pose they did the best
They knew. And just when he was at the height,
Father and mother married, and mother came,
A bride, to help take care of such a creature,
And accommodate her young life to his.
That was what marrying father meant to her.
She had to lie and hear love things made dreadful
By his shouts in the night. . . .
. . . I've heard them say, though,
They found a way to put a stop to it. . . .

Frost, "A Servant to Servants," in *North of Boston*, ll. 104–130, 138–139.

Frost's poetry sheds the influence of cities and science. As a result, some think, they slough off the traditional European consciousness, so that an openness to new ideas produces fresh poetry that reflects modern life. Frost's rural New England is not Eden but a worn world, a mature realistic world in which forests have been cut and soil depleted, where houses are crumbling and proud families have disintegrated. In "The Black Cottage" and "The Housekeeper," this is a world where old beliefs are affirmed but reconsidered. People there are wounded physically or psychologically. A woman is subject to hereditary insanity in "A Servant to Servants." A mother goes nearly insane after losing her child in "Home Burial." But Frost presents his characters tenderly, without condescension, and measures them against normal, helpful neighbors.

THEMES AND MOTIFS

The theme of loneliness is never absent from Frost's poetry, but in "A Servant to Servants" the horror of its consequences is acute. The narrator is a builder's wife who cooks for her husband's hired help. She talks with a fern collector, presumably a woman, who is camped on the couple's lakefront property, having chosen temporary solitude as a mode of recreation. We know the wife has previously been acquainted with this camper because she mentions "that day I showed you [where] we used to live" (ll. 62–63). The wife begins discussing how happy the move had made her, how it had lifted her spirits to leave the family home, where the cage in the ell was filled with "attic clutter" (l. 143). She enjoys the new view of Lake Willoughby from her kitchen window while she does the dishes, but the pleasure has worn off "like a prescription" (l. 154). Her depression returns and the lake comes to symbolize the woman's feelings: deep and narrow and like a river cut off at both ends.

The wife reveals her worries indirectly. Some are financial: sometimes they rent the "cottages Len built / Sometimes we don't" (ll. 41–42). The move caused financial losses and Len worked to overcome "sacrifices" but probably with "small profit" (ll. 64, 68). Len works hard, says his wife, "when he works" (l. 66), but he is taking too much time in town, involving himself in everything. "This year / It's highways" (ll. 71–72).

When Len is in town, his wife suffers from loneliness. Meanwhile she fries bacon for itinerant hired men, her husband's "servants," making her a "servant to servants." These four crude boarders brag about taking advantage of Len, of wasting things, then laugh at him behind his back. The men talk around the wife as if she were invisible. "It would be different if more people came" (l. 39). Because of her depression, Len's wife, who has no name in the poem, feels cut off from her emotions: "It seems to me / I can't express my feelings" (ll. 6–7). But beneath the lake of her subconscious, she represses anger: "And all our storms come up toward the house"; "(oh, I can lift [my hand] when I want to)" (ll. 24, 9). The wife reveals her fatigue and her frustration at the maddening repetition of cooking, of "doing / Things over and over that just won't stay done" (ll. 51–52). She reveals fears about theft and rape by men whose names and characters she doesn't know in a house where the doors are never locked.

At the exact middle of the poem, the monologue turns more troubling. The woman confesses that she has been in the state asylum once already, but even so, the optimistic Len "thinks [she'll] be all right / With doctoring" (ll. 46–47). The narrator feels she needs rest, not doctors, and her physician has dared to agree with her. Len insists, however, that the "best way out is always through" (l. 56). So her husband either takes the situation too lightly or refuses to understand it, further increasing her loneliness and frustration and trapping her. Then the wife says she thinks this mental disorder runs in families and tells the story of an uncle who went mad and was kept in a cage in the ell of the farmhouse. She tells how he ran naked in this jail, incessantly shouting obscenities in the night after the woman's father brought home his bride. Eventually, "They found a way to put a stop to it" (l. 139), and her insane uncle, secretly dispatched, is never mentioned again. The implication is that the same thing could happen to her.

At this point, the camper begins to back away from this woman who so desperately needs company. The wife tells her: "Bless you, of course you're keeping me from work / But . . . I'd *rather* you'd not go unless you must" (ll. 172–173, 177). The listener may fear she is dealing with a madwoman, since a fern collector can hardly be in a hurry. Or does she stay? The word "rather" renders the line ambiguous. Either way, it seems likely that a short reprieve is all that can be expected for the wife. The woman's anger, fears, loneliness, and family history are symptomatic of clinical depression as doctors understand it today. No wonder Frost is considered not only a great observer of humanity but a great poet and psychologist.

The loneliness of many of Frost's characters is due only partly to physical isolation, though there is rarely any sense of community in the poetry. In "The Mountain," the ox driver tells the traveler there is no village near the mountain, merely a township and "a few houses sprinkled around the foot" (l. 97). A husband and wife may be psychologically isolated by a disagreement. In "Home Burial," the wife, tortured by the sorrow of losing a child, misunderstands her husband's way of dealing with grief. The isolation may be only temporary, however, caused by a difference of opinion, as in "The Death of the Hired Man." In this poem, a sense of companionship binds Mary and Warren, the speakers; but Silas has come home alone to die. Sometimes neighbors are isolated because they protect their privacy, as in "Mending Wall." Nature destroys the wall, but in spite of the speaker's reluctance the neighbors cooperate in rebuilding it every spring, ironically the season of renewal, since "good fences make good neighbors" (l. 27). When Frost presents a platitude such as this, however, he always examines its irony and sometimes presents an alternative: "Something there is that doesn't love a wall" (l. 1). In "Blueberries" the isolation is selfish. The father of the large Loren family refuses to tell the speaker that he knows the location of a patch of wild blueberries because he wants them for himself, even though the land belongs to Mr. Patterson and the Loren family members have already gathered more than they can eat. The individualism fostered by American democracy, combined with the cultural reticence of New Englanders, also plays a part in the loneliness and isolation.

Another theme in Frost's poetry is the need to work to the point of exhaustion, an expression of the Puritan work ethic. In "After Apple-Picking" the speaker stands on the ladder picking apples for so long that he can feel the impression of its rungs in the soles of his feet. The speaker looks forward to a well-deserved rest, since after harvest comes the symbolic winter of peaceful sleep. In "The Code" two farm workers are insulted when their boss goads them to work hard, since they take pride in doing so already. After thinking it over for hours, one simply stops and walks away without a word. The other calmly tries to smother the boss under a load of hay. "The hand that knows his business won't be told / To do work better or faster—" (ll. 22–23).

A third theme is the creation and destruction of physical, moral, and emotional barriers, captured in the central image of "Mending Wall." In "The Death of the Hired Man," Mary "put out her hand / Among the harplike morning glory strings / Taut with the dew from garden bed to eaves / As if she played unheard some tenderness / That wrought on him beside her in the night" (ll. 106–110). Mary is compared to an angel playing a harp and leading Silas to the glory of heaven. Immediately afterward, Mary tells Warren that Silas has come home to die. Frost believed that such metaphors and analogies are at the heart of poetry, but his use of them is never obvious.

Departures alternate with images of home in "The Mountain," "The Wood-Pile," and "The Death of the Hired Man," from which comes the famous definition: "Home is the place where when you have to go there / They have to take you in" (ll. 118–119). Frost's dramatic dialogue, following in the path of Browning, realistically portrays a region peopled by reserved and neurotic characters, some in rural poverty.

Constantly absent from the narrative is any cheap sentimentality or moral judgment of the characters' hopes, sorrows, and fears. For example, Frost raises the sensitive subject of women living with men in common-law marriages. In "The Housekeeper," Estelle has given everything—work, love, and money— to John, who has assumed the role of affectionate husband but neglects to marry her or even notice the strain she feels in her humiliating circumstances. Her unspoken anger and mortification erupt, and she runs away to marry a less desirable man. In "The Fear" he depicts a woman constantly afraid that her husband will come after her violently, and the implication may be that she fears that he will not value her enough to come after her at all. Also absent in most of the poems are strong sensations used for effect, such as the element of surprise. In "The Death of the Hired Man," readers know from the title that the hired man is dead or dying. What we observe is Warren's gradual change from anger at Silas's repeated desertions to pity and mercy as Mary gradually and confidently coaxes him into his final forgiving mood.

Departures and journeys bring with them fears, such as violence in a strange place, as in the humorous "A Hundred Collars." Another fear, less easily conveyed, is that of losing one's identity. In "The Wood-Pile," a poem largely about absences, the speaker ventures forth on a winter's walk in a white world where most observable details are obliterated by snow. Even the trees are "too much alike to mark or name a place by" (l. 7). With few physical or psychological reference points, the speaker risks losing his sense of himself, his identity, a sure path toward madness or death. In the blank, white world, the speaker defines himself by projecting his characteristics onto a bird. His fear first takes the shape of paranoia, when he imagines that the bird is afraid he is after its tail feather. When he stops at a woodpile, the bird flies on. Although the woodpile seems solid, it is held together by only delicate clematis vines, a still-growing tree, and a stake that is about to fall over. Hence the solidity of the woodpile is ephemeral, rendered more so because the woodcutter has forgotten it. When a person wanders so far physically or psychologically from people and places that provide accurate points of reference, the self may be lost or erased. The vacant landscape nearly destroys the speaker's personality. Frost seems to believe it imperative that, however much their voices are rooted in the vernacular of the region, people should not disappear into the landscape.

In another poem, "Good Hours," the narrator goes alone on a winter evening's walk. Vicariously he enjoys the activities in the cheerfully lit cottages he passes. He hears the music of a violin and watches young people through the lace curtains of a window, assuming that the "eyes" of the cottages also see him. When he reaches the edge of town where the cottages end, he suddenly "repents."

As so often in Frost's poems, a moment of mystery has arrived. Of what has he repented? At the edge of the winter of death has he realized that he should be connected to the people in his community? He turns back only to find the cottage windows now dark. His feet disturb the sleeping street "like profanation" (ll. 14–15). But how could his feet disturb anything in the quiet snow? Why should the disturbance be profane unless his passage disturbs the sleep of the dead, symbolized by black windows? But it is only ten o'clock, not yet the midnight of death. Perhaps he still has a day or two left to take a walk in the company of another. And unless he himself represents Death, come two hours early, his apology, "by your leave" (l. 15) seems, like Emily Dickinson's personification of death in "The Chariot," enigmatically understated.

One of Frost's motifs is thresholds. In "The Generations of Men" a man at a family reunion jokes to a girl that their great-grandmother nine times removed is telling him to take charred wood from the foundation of a destroyed house and build a doorsill and a new house around it on the old spot. In "The Black Cottage," the minister and his companion sit at the threshold of a house as he talks about the owner. She was an old woman who lost her husband and two sons in the Civil War. Innocently, she believed "that all men are created free and equal" (l. 60). The minister says reflectively and paradoxically, "Why abandon a belief / Merely because it ceases to be true. / Cling to it long enough, and not a doubt / It will turn true again" (ll. 105–108). Truths seem to cross back and forth over an imaginary threshold.

Some critics call these narrative poems "stark," "harsh," or "grim." They seem so only because their meanings are not hidden, which is not to say they are simple or devoid of aesthetic value. For instance, inspiration and alliteration produce beautiful lines such as "the blue's but a mist from the breath of the wind" ("Blueberries," l. 25). *North of Boston* is a record of the New England landscape—a landscape to return to—filtered through a philosophical mind. By virtue of his accessibility, his warmth, and his insight, Robert Frost may be the most beloved American poet of the twentieth century.

See also Imagism; Lyric Poetry; Realism

BIBLIOGRAPHY

Primary Work

Frost, Robert. *The Poetry of Robert Frost: The Collected Poems, Complete and Unabridged*. New York: Henry Holt, 1979.

Secondary Works

Cox, James M., ed. *Robert Frost: A Collection of Critical Essays*. Englewood Cliffs, N.J.: Prentice-Hall, 1962.

Faggan, Robert, ed. *The Cambridge Companion to Robert Frost*. New York: Cambridge University Press, 2001.

Gerber, Philip L. *Robert Frost*. New York: Twayne, 1966.

Greenberg, Robert A., and James G. Hepburn, eds. *Robert Frost: An Introduction*. New York: Holt, Rinehart and Winston, 1961.

Greiner, Donald J. *Robert Frost: The Poet and His Critics*. Chicago: American Library Association, 1974.

Lowell, Amy. Review of *North of Boston*. *New Republic*, 20 February 1915, pp. 81–82. Quoted in Greenberg and Hepburn, eds., *Robert Frost*, pp. 48–49.

Poirier, Richard. *Robert Frost: The Work of Knowing*. New York: Oxford University Press, 1977.

Sharma, T. R. S. *Robert Frost's Poetic Style*. Atlantic Highlands, N.J.: Humanities Press, 1981.

Thompson, Lawrence. *Fire and Ice: The Art and Thought of Robert Frost*. New York: Russell and Russell, 1961.

Wagner, Linda W., ed. *Robert Frost: The Critical Reception*. New York: B. Franklin, 1977.

Helen Killoran

ORAL TRADITION

See Folklore and Oral Tradition

ORATORY

Oratory in the United States died out, some have said, in the second half of the nineteenth century. Millions of people, eager to rise during Reconstruction and in reform movements between the Civil War and World War I, however, were learning to read and write. They were founding, buying, and poring over affordable and widely available journals, newspapers, and books. They were honing elements of elocution and speech-making in common schools and public universities. How could oratory be dead if so many new speakers performed it and audiences yearned for it? The literature at the turn of the twentieth century represents this American struggle over the public podium.

Emblematic of that struggle was a young Yankton Sioux woman who beat out all white students, both men and women, in the 1899 student oratory contest at Earlham College. Zitkala-Ša (also known as Gertrude Simmons Bonnin, 1876–1938) was surprised at receiving friendly overtures from her usually distant white classmates after the speech. A few weeks later, she won an intercollegiate meet, this time under a banner that mocked her Quaker school for allowing a "squaw" to represent it. Zitkala-Ša's autobiographical narrative, "School Days of an Indian Girl," was published by the *Atlantic Monthly* in 1900, a few months after these

oratorical contests. These events suggest several aspects of what was at stake for oratory in U.S. literary culture of the time. At the end of the nineteenth century, exemplary performance of public oratory continued to signal academic success. In Zitkala-Ša's case, the prize honored mastery of speech conventions by a person until then considered an outsider to mainstream culture. Success at the Earlham and intercollegiate podium, moreover, was every bit as significant to Zitkala-Ša as the later print appearance of her autobiographical essay in a prestigious periodical. One marked her earliest public mastery of a powerful medium of dominant culture; the other signaled her literary success with an even broader public. Fine students of higher learning won prizes for oratory. Fine writers were published in the *Atlantic Monthly.*

That a young American Indian woman managed both, however, suggests that issues of oratory had shifted away from questions asked before and during the Civil War: Plain or elaborate language? Logic of sensationalist epistemology and the mental faculties, or flat assertions of fact? Instead, in the last quarter of the nineteenth century and into the twentieth, the questions concerned who got to speak to the American public: Men only, or women too? Just whites, or also blacks, Indians, and other people of color? Oratory in literature and as an art in its own right foregrounded questions of ethos, the speaker, the rhetor.

SENSATIONAL OR PLAIN SPEECH?

Earlier questions about oratory were most famously articulated in two vastly different orations delivered 19 November 1863 by Abraham Lincoln and Edward

Everett, dedicating the Soldiers' National Cemetery at Gettysburg. The difference was not just that one speech was two minutes and the other two hours. Following Lincoln's brief remarks, what has become the preferred rhetorical—and literary—style includes a self-deprecating humility, echoes of a rural American lifestyle, and at the same time an appeal to lofty, universal values. In "The American Scholar" (1837), Ralph Waldo Emerson (1803–1882) had famously avowed, "I embrace the common, I explore and sit at the feet of the familiar, the low" (p. 113). But not too low.

Like Lincoln, Walt Whitman (1819–1892) used biblical cadences and plain diction in his poems. The 1891 final, deathbed version of *Leaves of Grass* includes even more parataxis than earlier texts; for example, part 33 of "Song of Myself" embraces all with these lines:

> Pleas'd with the native and pleas'd with the foreign, pleas'd with the new and the old,
> Pleas'd with the homely woman as well as the handsome,
> Pleas'd with the quakeress as she puts off her bonnet and talks melodiously,
> Pleas'd with the tune of the choir of the white-wash'd church,
> Pleas'd with the earnest words of the sweating Methodist preacher, impress'd seriously at the camp meeting, . . .
>
> *(Pp. 54–55)*

Piling up pleasures in parallel sentence structure, Whitman fully enjoys "the familiar, the low," as Emerson directed. While Whitman is "pleas'd with the quakeress" who speaks up for herself and others in public, and he is impressed with the Methodist minister, it may be this preacher's sweat more than his oratory that moves the great "mother-man" of the American people, for the poet claims in section 30 of the same 1891 edition,

> Logic and sermons never convince,
> The damp of the night drives deeper into my soul.
>
> *(P. 50)*

The preacher's passionate life of the body conveyed with "earnest words" invokes his hearers' own experiences, their damp and dark nights of the soul. Whitman's accordion-like psalmic catalogs of human experience announced a new egalitarian American eloquence, both oratorical and literary, that has affected speakers and writers into the twentieth century.

SHAPING PUBLIC SENTIMENT

Not that the rhetoric of sentiment was done for—far from it. When Frances Ellen Watkins Harper (1825–1911) publicly exhorted a mixed-race, mixed-gender crowd honoring the 1875 centennial of the Pennsylvania Society for Promoting the Abolition of Slavery, she aimed to shape a new social sentiment of justice by use of appeals directed simultaneously at her audience's passions, intellect, imagination, and will. A far from perfect Reconstruction, she asserted, was in fact reproducing the horrors of slavery:

> I do not believe there is another civilized nation under Heaven where there are half so many people who have been brutally and shamefully murdered, with or without impunity, as in this republic within the last ten years. And who cares? Where is the public opinion that has scorched with red-hot indignation the cowardly murderers of Vicksburg and Louisiana? . . . What we need today in the onward march of humanity is a public sentiment in favor of common justice, and simple mercy, . . . a sense of humanity, which shall crystallize into the life a nation the sentiment that justice, simple justice, is the right, not simply of the strong and powerful, but of the weakest and feeblest of all God's children; a deeper and broader humanity, which will teach men to look upon their feeble breth[r]en not as vermin to be crushed out, or beasts of burden to be bridled and bitted, but as the children of the living God. (Harper, p. 220)

Born a free black in Baltimore, Harper had traveled the abolitionist circuit since 1854 when the Maine Anti-Slavery Society commissioned her to present speeches she often crowned with her own poems. It was still rare for a woman to speak in public, but Harper's oratory resounded in countless public meetings all over the North arousing sentiments of "red-hot indignation" in order to end chattel slavery. After the war, as an itinerant teacher of newly freed slaves in the South, she saw firsthand ongoing racial oppression that enslaved her people all over again, terrorizing them into submission with mob violence and lynching. Discourse punctuated with sentence fragments, question marks, and parallel adjectives describing both the oppressors and the oppressed among "God's children," as well as alliteration in the metaphor "beasts of burden to be bridled and bitted"—these rhetorical strategies of sentimentalism still effectively touched audience passions in much public oratory during and after Reconstruction. Harper was herself upset, her agitated text indicates, and she undoubtedly meant to upset any complacent souls in her audience, moving them to change their ways and American culture. Along with other reformers who had designs on public sentiment, she kept using sentimental strategies on the podium and in print right into the twentieth century. These strategies mark her most famous work, *Iola Leroy; or, Shadows Uplifted* (1892), a staple of nineteenth century American novel studies, which

Frances Ellen Watkins Harper (1825–1911) became the best known and most prolific black woman speaker, poet, novelist, and essayist of her day. In "The Greater Problem to Be Solved," she addresses the 1875 centennial conference of the Pennsylvania Society for Promoting the Abolition of Slavery. Chattel slavery ended with the Civil War, but she urges abolitionists to take up the next great cause: not only to find compassion for all but to assert the rights of all.

What we need to-day in the onward march of humanity is a public sentiment in favor of common justice and simple mercy. We have a civilization which has produced grand and magnificent results, diffused knowledge, overthrown slavery, made constant conquests over nature, and built up a wonderful material prosperity. But two things are wanting in American civilization— a keener and deeper, broader and tenderer sense of justice [and] a sense of humanity, which shall crystallize into the life of a nation the sentiment that justice, simple justice, is the right not simply of the strong and powerful, but of the weakest and feeblest of all God's children.

Harper, "The Greater Problem to Be Solved," p. 220.

sense" or universal faculty psychology. A sensationalist rhetoric was then devised to appeal to an audience's mental faculties in order to shape public moral sentiment.

The rhetoric of sentiment was elaborated into a comprehensive system most famously by the Scottish professors George Campbell (1719–1796) and Hugh Blair (1718–1800) in the late eighteenth century. Their texts—including chapbook abridgements, revisions, and knock-offs of them—appeared in colleges, on bookshelves, and in the hip pockets of newly literate U.S. citizens throughout the nineteenth century. As Campbell and Blair taught up-and-coming offspring of British merchants to parley with nobility, seminary students to preach with taste, and lawyers to win in courts and legislatures, the rhetoric of sentiment spread even more widely among all strata of U.S. citizenry. Sentimentalism was a web of shared lore about how to appeal to the public mind and so to pressure the powers that be. Discovery of just such a chapbook, *The Columbian Orator* (1797), inspired Frederick Douglass (c. 1818–1895) to flee slavery, and the persistent strength of oratory may be measured by his ease with the medium at century's end; in *Life and Times of Frederick Douglass* (1881; revised 1892), Douglass claims "that writing for the public eye never came quite as easily to me as speaking to the public ear" (p. 397). Another well-known orator, Julia Ward Howe (1819–1910), penned the "Battle Hymn of the Republic" lyrics in 1861, but only in the last decades of the nineteenth century, after her husband's death, did she become a stump speaker for women's rights and pacifism. In her 1899 *Reminiscences, 1819–1899,* Howe confesses a continued fondness for Blair's 1783 *Lectures on Rhetoric and Belles Lettres,* "with its many quotations from the poets" (p. 57) to rate persuasive strategies that could move the heart and mind.

Relative status and economic issues arose also in the mixed reviews accorded the standard Enlightenment rhetorics by writers who are now thought of as literary giants, such as Herman Melville (1819–1891). In *Billy Budd, Foretopman* (1924), Melville does admit that public address by Captain Vere is sometimes delivered "in clear terms and concise," yet the writer expresses his doubts about Vere's rhetoric when the captain's cloud of courtroom verbiage seals the fate of his young sailor Billy Budd, accused of murder. Vere's declamation on the incident deploys "a certain pedantry socially alleged," which obscures the liability of either sailor charged with the crime (p. 2341). In effect, the captain's foggy oratory dooms the boy to execution.

Another anti-pedant, Emily Dickinson (1830–1886) notoriously did not stand with first-year Mt. Holyoke classmates when a preacher urged them to

among other issues includes class tensions in the racial uplift movement.

Oratory and rhetorical tactics have had to do with issues of economics and class since before 400 B.C.E. when Sophists trained Greek litigants trying to recover Athenian property from victors of ancient wars. Although rhetorical theory that informed prevailing nineteenth-century U.S. discourse turned away from classical topics and deductive thinking to induction and experience, questions about material context— something like the cases in antiquity—were also asked. Eighteenth-century Enlightenment thinkers had asserted the rights and worth of individuals over monarchy and privilege, and studies of rhetoric (both for oratory and writing) were afterward available to students from a rising middle class. It is no accident that Enlightenment theories of knowledge grew not from the logic of hierarchical authority but from sensory impressions recorded in each person's mind. This epistemology was premised on everyone's perceptions—up and down the social strata—being the same, a "common show their souls had been saved. In her poems, unpublished except for a handful until after her death in 1886, Dickinson finds oratory still feeding her doubts. Politicians (such as perhaps her father, a U.S. Congressman from Massachusetts) receive even harsher criticism than preachers: "How dreary – to be – Somebody! / How public – like a Frog –." Dickinson's critique of political stump speeches makes the politician a low amphibian. His message consists of one thing, his name. The orator's audience ("an admiring Bog"), with its affinity for muck, is granted no sentience at all. This reclusive poet was no fan of sensational political oratory.

Sensational political orations—political stump speeches—came in for similar criticism by another nineteenth-century writer. Samuel Clemens (better known as Mark Twain) panned the genre unmercifully in his text of comic oratory "Cannibalism in the Cars" (1875). In it Clemens exposes aggressions latent in tricky speechifying. His oral tale within a tale cloaks behind mock legislative deliberations that snowbound, hungry railway passengers are choosing which of their fellow travelers will be the main course. These train-wrecked strangers, all men, are adrift in an amoral "world of eddying flakes shutting out the firmament above" (p. 41). Harrumphing at "proceedings . . . in every way, irregular and unbecoming," Reverend James Sawyer of Tennessee objects not to eating or being eaten, but to lack of a chairman and subordinates to run the meeting; he insists all previous actions (nominating him) are invalid until officers have been elected. Mr. Belknap of Iowa argues, "This is no time to stand upon forms and ceremonious observances," declaring himself and "every gentleman present" to be "satisfied with the nominations" and ready to elect Sawyer for breakfast (p. 42). The representative from Tennessee must either put up a fight, a sign he is no gentleman, or shut up and be eaten. He does employ a diversionary tactic that takes him off the menu, but it does not prevent him and seven survivors from consuming sixteen others. Darwin's description of dog-eat-dog competition necessary for earthly survival of the fittest (in *On the Origin of Species,* 1859) becomes in Clemens's imagination a nightmare of human cannibalism, horrific with orderly government machinations that chew up humanity with gear teeth. From legislature or pulpit, the speechifying said to crown civilization Clemens's reveals instead as a means to bestial ends.

The height of Clemens's admiration for successful mocking oratory turned up in his own "flyting," a centuries-old traditional speech competition of bragging and foolery, often performed by men as after-dinner entertainment. Clemens famously delivered such pieces at Oxford when he was awarded an honorary doctorate

there in 1907. The depth of his abhorrence for manipulative "blattering" also appears in his "War Prayer" (1904). A kind of fable, this short narrative focuses on political war oratory in "packed mass meetings" called to whip up "devotion to flag and country" (p. 3). Every night the crowds "listened, panting, to patriot oratory which stirred the deepest depths of their hearts, and which they interrupted at briefest intervals with cyclones of applause, the tears running down their cheeks the while" (p. 3). Clemens's contemporary, William Jennings Bryan, aroused crowds with just such populist oratory in 1896, winning the first of three Democratic Party presidential nominations with his "Cross of Gold" speech, in which he championed silver to back common currency versus the gold standard favored by big banks and big business. The panting, the open hearts, cyclones of applause, and tears in Clemens's crowd are the bodily affect looked for by sensationalist rhetoric as evidence that a speaker has moved an audience to accept his or her message.

A few local dissenters in Clemens's story, warned not to "cast a doubt" on the war's "righteousness," have absented themselves from the patriotic gatherings (p. 5). But a robed Merlin-like stranger steps to the pulpit, motioning the minister to step side after a long militaristic prayer for the troops. It seems the second speaker brings an answer from God to the pastor's prayer for victory, that is, if the people still endorse the prayer after the messenger unfolds its implications. The stranger observes that their prayer really asks the Almighty to make "bloody shreds" (p. 33) of the other side's men. God should scatter the foe's bodies over "smiling fields" (p. 35), burn their homes with "a hurricane of fire" (p. 39), and turn out their widows and children who will then bitterly also pray to God "for the refuge of the grave and [be] denied it— for our sakes who adore Thee, Lord" (p. 51). One side wins, but winning begets terrible tragedy for the vanquished, Clemens's messenger reminds the congregation. Reflecting on the carnage of war in his long lifetime, the author asks patriots what kind of perverse pulpit oratory and prayer tells believers that the Source of Love takes only "our" side? One might conclude that Clemens, like many of his day, excoriated all oratory. His mysterious stranger's message, however, may simply underscore a challenge raised at the turn of the twentieth century specifically against overwrought rhetoric and an unreflective public.

NOT HOW—BUT WHO—CAN SPEAK?

At the end of the nineteenth century, the cause of peace called to the podium a host of other unexpected earnest messengers, women among them. Outspoken advocates of reform in education, prisons, temperance, women's suffrage, and especially the abolition of slavery, a handful of women of color such as Frances Harper and some very few white Quaker women had been speaking in public since the late 1820s. The women's club movement in the 1870s gave semipublic audiences to many middle- and upper-class white women, and they soon stepped into the public eye. With larger numbers of women and other newly confident speakers at the podium, the style of a speech became less important than its underlying ethos or who delivered it. At the end of the century, Julia Ward Howe recalled her 1872 Peace Crusade, a series of speeches she delivered from British pulpits and podiums. She wrote of that campaign, "My dominant thought was that women, as the mothers of men, alone knew the cost of human life, and that this fact gave them a sacred and indisputable right to become the guardians of the world's peace" ("Change in the Position of Women," p. 148). A widely held belief that mothers held the moral high ground influenced Howe's "dominant thought." This premise evoked for her the vision of "a mighty and august Congress of Mothers, which should constitute a new point of departure for the regeneration of society by the elimination of the selfish and brutal elements which lead to war and bloodshed" ("Change in the Position of Women," pp. 148–149). Howe's Latinate diction and long, balanced periodic sentences show off a privileged education gained in large part from her older brothers' tutors. Yet, the venerable pacifist matron urging peace and women's rights upon turn-of-the-twentieth-century Boston clashes with the writer of erotic poems in *Passion-Flowers* (1854) and of lyrics for "Battle Hymn of the Republic" (1862).

Rhetorical theory, with implications for women's education and their participation in public oratory, was advanced at the turn of the twentieth century by Gertrude Buck (1871–1922), a self-described "hopeless radical" who held one of the first doctorates awarded a woman and who taught and wrote for many years at Vassar (Ritchie and Ronald, p. 211). An ethics of cooperation, collaboration, and social responsibility grounded her view of rhetoric. Mary August Jordan (1855–1941), likewise, encouraged supporters of women's rights and her women students at Smith College to be socially responsible "restless disturbers" of the status quo in rhetorical practice (Ritchie and Ronald, p. 218). Reforms in rhetorical theory advocated by these middle-class white women had broad application. But their ranks were thin, and their audiences among the most privileged in the country. As early as 1866, speaking to the Eleventh National Women's Rights Convention, Frances Harper pulled the rug out from under any myth of white motherhood

as a foundation for participation in public practices such as oratory and voting: "I do not believe that white women are dewdrops just exhaled from the skies. I think that like men they may be divided into three classes, the good, the bad, and the indifferent" (Harper, p. 218). Because she stood with her people for black men's right to vote, recognized by the Fourteenth Amendment in 1868, Harper broke with the convention's call for women's (meaning white women's) suffrage first. Among its racial uplift themes, Harper's novel *Iola Leroy* is believed to celebrate the astonishing courage of another African American woman, Ida B. Wells (1862–1931), a columnist with the pen name Iola who was editor and part owner at age twenty-seven of the *Memphis Free Speech and Headlight* newspaper and a tireless public speaker on behalf of anti-lynching laws.

A high point of resistance to women's oratory, and in retrospect perhaps a sign of women's increasing numbers as public speakers, was Henry James's (1843–1916) 1886 novel, *The Bostonians*. While protagonist Basil Ransom is at first pejoratively described as a "lean, pale, sallow, shabby" figure from conquered Mississippi when he arrives at his wealthy female cousin's doorstep expecting a job (p. 4), Ransom's "provincial" view of female activism and of oratory drives the novel's plot (p. 11). Olive Chancellor is keeper of the family wealth, benefactor of women's rights, and Ransom's chief rival for the affections of Verena Tarrant, a rising prodigy on the women's rights scene. Driven by her causes, Olive is "morbid," the visiting cousin tells himself. James repeats the adjective five times in five lines to underscore his point about this female activist and perhaps to suggest his own fascinated aversion to same-sex living arrangements springing up among Boston women. From his perspective, Miss Olive "hated men, as a class" (p. 22). When Verena at last speaks to a parlor gathering of women activists, she charms the crowd and Ransom, too. Verena casts her spell with "those charming notes of her voice," Ransom believes, and not with "the argument, the doctrine" (p. 61). Not incidentally, James would later deliver a long graduation speech on women's vocal tone to the Smith College class of 1905. Ransom asserts of Verena's topic, "She didn't mean it, she didn't know what she meant, she had been stuffed with this trash by her father" (p. 62). She is manipulated, Ransom thinks, as a "preposterous puppet" mouthing others' thoughts (p. 336). So he sets out to prove the young star orator's lack of conviction and "hollowness of character" (p. 62) by persuading her to the exact opposite position, his own: females are made for men's private pleasure and not to address the public good. He insinuates himself into

Verena's affections and carries her off to marry him moments before she would have spoken for the first time in a public hall. The book's sensational ending reads like a fantasy that, though thwarted by later feminist movements, articulates a powerful challenge to women's participation in U.S. oratory and public life.

SPEAKING ON THE COLOR LINE

Two famous exchanges of the late nineteenth century underscore the shift from rhetorical style and theory to an emphasis on who gets to speak. Both exchanges occurred at first in speeches, and both mark the breadth of the expanded public podium. Booker T. Washington (1856–1915) and W. E. B. Du Bois (1868–1963) spoke both from the podium and in print about what approach African American people should take to mainstream American cultural power. Chief Joseph (In-mut-too-yah-lat-lkekht in his tribal language, 1840–1904) appealed to dignitaries in Washington, D.C., for his people's return from exile in Kansas and Oklahoma to traditional lands in the Pacific Northwest.

Booker T. Washington famously advocated at the Cotton States and International Exposition in 1895 that by self-help and solidarity his people could gain pride and yet accommodate southern white supremacy and separation of the races. From the speech as it appears in his autobiography *Up from Slavery* (1901), blacks should seek only training for industrial and agricultural work and so, according to Washington, "put brains and skill into the common occupations of life." In 1881 he had founded Tuskegee Institute in Alabama, a school for vocational education and teacher training. He likened his people to a ship lost at sea that arrives at the mouth of the Amazon River and yet can find no fresh water; "cast down your bucket where you are," he said (p. 514). Washington also likened that ship to whites, who should continue to support institutions like Tuskegee and hire its graduates, rather than immigrants, so that "in the future, as in the past, . . . you and your families will be surrounded by the most patient, faithful, law-abiding, and unresentful people that the world has seen." And blacks, as potential employees, should cultivate "friendly relations with the Southern white man" (p. 515). Not racial equality, but a measure of economic opportunity, Washington argued, would eventually allow blacks to earn respect from white leaders.

In the last years of the century, W. E. B. Du Bois could not endorse Washington's quietism at African Americans' continued exclusion from political power, civil rights, and higher education. For "it practically accepts the alleged inferiority" (p. 639) of blacks, he wrote in The *Souls of Black Folk* (1903), a collection of

Du Bois's speeches and published writings. Raised by the extended family of a single mother in Massachusetts, trained in public school and then at Fisk University and Harvard as an undergraduate, Du Bois studied in Berlin and earned a doctorate in history from Harvard in 1895. Giving credit to the complex context and real accomplishments of Washington's agenda, Du Bois nevertheless maintained that neither flattery nor jobs could adequately help black people, but "straightforward honesty" and "firm adherence to their higher ideals and aspirations will ever keep those ideals within the realm of possibility" (p. 640). Du Bois articulated a "double-consciousness" in blacks' self-perception as one effect of "the color-line" that he prophesied would dominate the American twentieth century. And he urged a return to Frederick Douglass's ideal of "ultimate assimilation *through* self-assertion" of black identity as a means to equality in all spheres of cultural life (p. 637). At issue for these two leaders was not "Who can speak?" from a public platform, but "Who are we as African Americans?" in American politics.

Harper's Weekly and the *North American Review* made popular the oratorical mastery of Chief Joseph and the plight of his Nez Percé people displaced from tribal lands by the Oregon gold rush and later settlers. After a seven-hundred-mile dash for the Canadian border marked by one Indian victory after another over astonishing odds, Joseph's fellow chiefs were dead. Believing he had negotiated safe passage to a reservation for his tribal remnant, Joseph gave up the fight, and the surrender speech he delivered was published in the 17 November 1877 issue of *Harper's Weekly*:

> I want to have time to look for my children and see how many of them I can find. Maybe I shall find them among the dead. Hear me, my chiefs, my heart is sick and sad. From where the sun now stands I will fight no more against the white man. (P. 906)

In violation of the treaty, the U.S. government divided his tribal unit, with Joseph and his followers herded into boxcars bound for Kansas and then Oklahoma. Two years later, an honest officer present at the surrender arranged passage for Joseph to the nation's capitol where at Lincoln Hall the chief recounted his people's history to President Rutherford B. Hayes and congressional leaders. This speech (published in the *North American Review* in April 1879) was perhaps more famous in its day than even his surrender because it details an Indian's perspective of settlers coming to eastern Oregon. "Some of you think an Indian is like a wild animal. This is a great mistake. I will tell you all about our people, and then you can judge whether an Indian is a man or not," Joseph began. Echoing principles of Christian morality, but in the name of the Great Spirit who "is looking at me, and will hear me" (p. 260). Joseph described the encroachment of outsiders into the Wallowa Valley:

> I learned then that we were but few, while the white men were many, and that we could not hold our own with them. We were like deer. They were like grizzly bears. We had a small country. Their country was large. We were contented to let things remain as the Great Spirit Chief made them. They were not; and would change the rivers and mountains if they did not suit them. (P. 267)

In the kind of twist that the new century's literary modernism would enjoy, Enlightenment ideals played a dual role surrounding Joseph's speech, revealing the limitations of those ideals. Enlightenment notions were urging individual settlers to go west and rise in the world, while these ideals were also endorsing free speech and the mass marketing of Joseph's public address criticizing white settlement. Joseph maintained,

> If the white man wants to live in peace with the Indian he can live in peace. There need be no trouble. Treat all men alike. Give them all the same law. Give them all an even chance to live and grow. All men were made by the same Great Spirit Chief. They are all brothers. The earth is the mother of all people, and all people should have equal rights upon it. (P. 282)

In response to this appeal, public sentiment finally shifted, pressing for return of the Nez Percé in 1885 to a reservation near their homeland. Still, before his death, Joseph was permitted only one visit to his father's grave in the Wallowa Valley.

If oratory died toward the end of the nineteenth century, it is good riddance to a formulaic, deductive version of public rhetoric that displayed classical tropes and figures familiar only to those who could learn Latin and Greek. Engaging first an elaborate new inductive rhetoric of sentiment and then rustic appeal and a plain tone, a more diverse American public would read, write, and claim space upon the podium of the coming twentieth century.

See also Lectures; Presidential Elections; Reform; Women's Suffrage

BIBLIOGRAPHY

Primary Works

Bonnin, Gertrude Simmons (Zitkala-Ša). "School Days of an Indian Girl." *Atlantic Monthly* 85 (1900): 185–194.

Chief Joseph (In-mut-too-yah-lat-lkekht). "I Will Fight No More." *Harper's Weekly* 21 (17 November 1877): 906.

Chief Joseph (In-mut-too-yah-lat-lkekht). "An Indian's View of Indian Affairs." *North American Review* (April 1879): 412–434. In *Indian Oratory: Famous Speeches by Noted Indian Chieftains,* edited by W.C. Vanderwerth,

pp. 259–284. Norman: University of Oklahoma Press, 1971.

Clemens, Samuel (Mark Twain). "Cannibalism in the Cars." 1875. *New Literary History* 29, no. 1 (1998): 39–45.

Clemens, Samuel (Mark Twain). "War Prayer." In *Europe and Elsewhere.* New York: Harper & Brothers, 1923. Reprinted as *The War Prayer.* Edited by John Groth. New York: Harper and Row, 1984. Page citations are from the latter edition.

Douglass, Frederick. *Life and Times of Frederick Douglass.* 1881; revised 1892. In *Norton Anthology of African American Literature,* edited by Henry Louis Gates Jr. and Nellie McKay, pp. 391–401. New York: Norton, 1997.

Du Bois, W. E. B. *The Souls of Black Folk.* 1903. In *Norton Anthology of African American Literature,* edited by Henry Louis Gates Jr. and Nellie McKay, pp. 613–740. New York: Norton, 1997.

Emerson, Ralph Waldo. "The American Scholar." In *The Selected Writings of Ralph Waldo Emerson,* edited by Brooks Atkinson. New York: Modern Library, 1950. Quoted in Kenneth Cmiel, *Democratic Eloquence,* p. 113.

Harper, Frances Ellen Watkins. "The Greater Problem to Be Solved." In *A Brighter Coming Day: A Frances Ellen Watkins Harper Reader,* edited by Frances Smith Foster, pp. 219–222. New York: Feminist Press, 1990.

Harper, Frances Ellen Watkins. "We Are All Bound Up Together." In *A Brighter Coming Day: A Frances Ellen Watkins Harper Reader,* edited by Frances Smith Foster, pp. 217–219. New York: Feminist Press, 1990.

Howe, Julia Ward. "The Change in the Position of Women." In *The Woman Suffrage Movement,* edited by Florence Howe Hall, pp. 136–151. Boston: Dana Estes and Company, 1913. Essay on Howe's earlier Peace Crusade speeches.

Howe, Julia Ward. *Reminiscences: 1819–1899.* Boston: Houghton, Mifflin, 1899.

James, Henry. *The Bostonians.* New York and London: Macmillan and Co., 1886.

Melville, Herman. "Billy Budd, Foretopman." 1924. Reprinted as "Billy Budd, Sailor" in *Norton Anthology of American Literature,* vol. 1, 3rd ed., edited by Nina Baym, Ronald Gottesman, Laurence B. Holland, David Kalstone, Francis Murphy, Hershel Parker, William H. Pritchard, Patricia B. Wallace, pp. 2300–2355. New York: Norton, 1989.

Washington, Booker T. "Up from Slavery." In *Norton Anthology of African American Literature,* edited by Henry Louis Gates Jr. and Nellie McKay, pp. 490–521. New York: Norton, 1997.

Whitman, Walt. "Song of Myself." 1891. In his *Leaves of Grass,* pp. 25–76. Garden City, N.Y.: Doubleday and Company, 1926.

Secondary Works

Berlin, James. *Writing Instruction in Nineteenth-Century American Colleges.* Carbondale: Southern Illinois University Press, 1984.

Clark, Gregory, and S. Michael Halloran, eds. *Oratorical Culture in Nineteenth-Century America: Transformations in the Theory and Practice of Rhetoric.* Carbondale: Southern Illinois University Press, 1993.

Cmiel, Kenneth. *Democratic Eloquence: The Fight over Popular Speech in Nineteenth-Century America.* New York: William Morrow, 1990.

Herzberg, Bruce, and Patricia Bizzell, eds. *The Rhetorical Tradition: Readings from Classical Times to the Present.* 2nd ed. New York: Bedford/St. Martin's, 2000.

Johnson, Nan. *Gender and Rhetorical Space in American Life, 1886–1910.* Carbondale: Southern Illinois University Press, 2002.

Logan, Shirley Wilson. *"We Are Coming": The Persuasive Discourse of Nineteenth-Century Black Women.* Carbondale: Southern Illinois University Press, 1999.

Mattingly, Carol. *Well-Tempered Women: Nineteenth-Century Temperance Rhetoric.* Carbondale: Southern Illinois University Press, 2000.

Ritchie, Joy, and Kate Ronald, eds. *Available Means: An Anthology of Women's Rhetoric(s).* Pittsburgh: Pittsburgh University Press, 2001.

Royster, Jacqueline Jones. *Traces of a Stream: Literacy and Social Change among African American Women.* Pittsburgh: Pittsburgh University Press, 2000.

Wendy Dasler Johnson

ORIENTALISM

Orientalism is a concept whose meaning has evolved from its first uses in British and French cultures in the age of European imperialism, when it referred specifically to political governance and visual art. Now, in its contemporary postcolonial valence, Orientalism is understood as the powerful discourse embodying Western attitudes toward Asia. Orientalism first defined a particular attitude to British imperial policy in India in the late eighteenth century, which valued the languages, laws, and culture of the subjugated colony. This response fostered academic disciplines founded on intellectual inquiry into all aspects of Islamic and Hindu India and, later, other Near and Far Eastern colonies occupied by the British. In France, early in the nineteenth century, Orientalism, in a more limited way, described a particular genre of painting and the popular vogue for Middle Eastern and North African subject matter in art.

In these contexts, Orientalism had positive, or neutral, meanings. But since the publication of Edward Said's *Orientalism* in 1978, along with the work of Said's contemporaries Anouar Abdel-Malek, A. L. Tibawi, and Bryan Turner, the limits of the term have expanded, with more negative connotations, to encompass cultural production in all forms. Most important, Orientalism has been refigured in terms of the discourses that have produced a controlling Western master narrative to comprehend the East—which is seen as mysterious, inscrutable, threatening, despotic, childlike, erotic, savage, mystical, perverse, and uncivilized. Said's epochal work has itself spawned much debate about the degree to which Asia has been imagined, represented, and governed in purely Orientalist terms, with many scholars revising Said's theory of Orientalism to allow for a more complex and nuanced rendition of the West's relations to the East. While Said initially posited Orientalism as the expression of a monolithic European domination over the colonized Other, further explorations of the concept have revealed that the full scope of the West's cultural engagement with Asia has been marked by both mutual influence and resistance, respect and opprobrium, fascination and fear, attraction and repulsion. Indeed, revisionist scholarship has uncovered the degree to which the East was able to undermine and challenge cultural appropriation by the West as well as irrevocably alter the cultural landscape of the West.

AMERICAN ORIENTALISM

The influence of Orientalism has been much less apparent in the United States than in Europe because America has, despite the actuality of history, denied being an imperial power. America has habitually clung to a myth of itself as unsullied by the desire for overseas empire, and yet it is easy to trace a fascination with the East in American culture, given the nation's occasional forays into Asia in the late nineteenth century and early twentieth century and the very presence of immigrants from Asia on American soil. If nothing else, Orientalist impulses in America manifested themselves as surface decoration in a vast range of cultural production, both elite and popular. Orientalizing urges to ornament ran the gamut, in 1903 alone, from Henry James's (1843–1916) fanciful description of *The Golden Bowl*'s (1904) Fanny Assingham as "a daughter . . . of the East, a creature formed by hammocks and divans" (p. 34) to the illuminated minarets of Coney Island's Luna Park. And a full engagement with Asia by such eminent figures as the artists Mary Cassatt and James McNeill Whistler, the poets Ezra Pound and Amy Lowell, the travel writer Lafcadio Hearn, the playwright David Belasco, the novelist

Stephen Crane, the satirist Mark Twain, and the film directors D. W. Griffith and Cecil B. DeMille comprises a significant body of work that reflects America's awareness of the Orient as an inspirational, alluring, and terrifying space upon which to project American national desires and anxieties—as well as America's sense of itself as a uniquely forward- and outward-looking culture of assimilation (however uneasy) and modernity (however socially retrograde).

There was no single originating moment in American Orientalism, because Asian motifs and themes in the visual and applied arts were omnipresent in the European culture imported to America well before the mid-nineteenth century (such as Spode's Willow Ware). But a signal event in American fascination with the Orient came in 1854, when an American naval officer, Matthew C. Perry, forced Japan to open trade with the West. Gradually Japan, after the Meiji restoration (1868), was willing to engage with the West, and by 1882 the Japanese had replaced the Chinese as the largest Asian group to immigrate to America. So by the end of the nineteenth century the American mainland had become a contact zone between Asians and other Americans, however much Asians were despised and disenfranchised (as they were in the 1879 California state constitution, which denied suffrage to all "natives of China, idiots, and insane persons").

ORIENTALISM AND RACISM

Indeed, the very worst tendencies of American nativism and racism frequently emerged in American cultural production that attempted to engage with the Orient. Bret Harte's (1836–1902) hugely popular 1870 poem "The Heathen Chinee" articulated the full range of attitudes to which Asians were subjected: bemused condescension for their charming childlike ways, hatred for their manipulative duplicity, and a mixture of fascination and terror at their exotic Otherness. Even the lofty patrician Henry Adams (1838–1918), in his account of an 1886 visit to Japan, considered it a "child's country . . . a nursery" (p. 17). Later, in a letter to John Hay, Adams found Japan to be "primitive," and he described the people in overtly simian terms. More well-meaning works still infantilized the Asian. A prime example would be David Belasco and John Luther Long's cross-racial stage romance *Madame Butterfly* (1900), which emphasized the long-suffering, masochistic passivity and childlike nature of the female protagonist, however much it cast her American lover Pinkerton in an unsympathetic light.

Racist fears of a "Yellow Peril" were reinforced during the American occupation of the Philippines after 1898 and American involvement in suppressing the Chinese Boxer uprising (1900). Stephen Crane's potboiler *Active Service* (1898), set in the Greco-Turkish War, posits the Turks as a dark, amorphous horde threatening the protagonists Rufus and Nora, sparring war correspondents seeking adventure and fame. The couple's love-hate relationship becomes the novel's focus, and Nora is defined in Orientalist terms as an alluring figure of Otherness because she represents the destabilizing threat of the American New Woman. Orientalizing characters became a stock method writers used to make their characters seem "different," dangerously seductive, decadent. Kate Chopin, for example, did this in *The Awakening* (1899), in the scene at Edna's party when Mrs. Highcamp's garland of roses transforms Victor into "a vision of Oriental beauty" (p. 110). So, too, Edith Wharton's *The House of Mirth* (1905), in which the arriviste Jew Simon Rosedale's physical appearance is associated with conventionally represented Asian characteristics, especially his "small sidelong eyes" (p. 249). Mrs. Hatch, one of Lily Bart's way stations along her sordid road down and down the social hierarchy, is criticized for her "Oriental indolence and disorder" (p. 267). These negative connotations of the East were inextricably linked to America's occasional interventions in Asia during the nineteenth century. But such one-dimensional manifestations of Orientalism, however ethnocentric and demeaning to the Other, were merely one aspect of a more complex cultural dynamic of attraction and repulsion that ultimately served to further familiarize Americans with the presence of Asia in the economic, political, and—most importantly for cultural production—imaginary realms. The Orient, in the American mind, was less the product of mimetic or realistic representation than a diametrically opposed Other against which a sense of essential American identity, however illusory, could take form.

THE ORIENT IN THE AMERICAN IMAGINATION

As a sort of manifesto for Orientalism, Walt Whitman's (1819–1892) poem "Passage to India" (1870) celebrated the closeness of the West and East made increasingly real by advances in technology. Just as the American continent was connected by the joining of the Union and Central Pacific railroads, so was Asia becoming easier to reach and traverse thanks to the completion of the Suez Canal. Whitman's poem conceives geographical connectedness between the two hemispheres; more than that, it is a self-reflexive meditation on the power of the Orient to incite a kind of ecstatic artistic inspiration, for the poet catalogs the epic histories of the entire Eastern Hemisphere as a means of lauding the idea of visionary mastery in all forms. The poet is especially inspired by Marco Polo,

Kate Chopin's short story "An Egyptian Cigarette" was written in April 1897 and published in Vogue in April 1900. In the story, "Madam," the otherwise unnamed narrator, retires to a friend's "smoking-den" to savor a cigarette he brought back from Cairo. Here Chopin describes the first sensations of inhaling the mysterious pale-yellow cigarette and the beginning of the fevered, masochistic reverie it induces.

I took one long inspiration of the Egyptian cigarette. The gray-green smoke arose in a small puffy column that spread and broadened, that seemed to fill the room. I could see the maple leaves dimly, as if they were veiled in a shimmer of moonlight. A subtle, disturbing current passed through my whole body and went to my head like the fumes of disturbing wine. I took another deep inhalation of the cigarette.

"Ah! the sand has blistered my cheek! I have lain here all day with my face in the sand. Tonight, when the everlasting stars are burning, I shall drag myself back to the river."

He will never come back.

Thus far have I followed him; with flying feet; with stumbling feet; with hands and knees, crawling; and outstretched arms, and here have I fallen in the sand.

The sand has blistered my cheek; it has blistered all my body, and the sun is crushing me with hot torture. There is shade beyond the cluster of palms.

Kate Chopin, A Vocation and a Voice: Stories (New York: Penguin, 1991), pp. 68–69.

Batouta the Moor, and other adventurers and explorers, linking himself to their quests: "Doubts to be solv'd, the map incognita, blanks to be fill'd" (p. 536). American Orientalism could be said to act on that same questing desire to fulfill curiosity and exert agency in the world: "The foot of man unstay'd, the hands never at rest. Thyself, O soul, that will not brook a challenge" (p. 536), he apostrophizes.

Whitman's Orientalism enunciated itself in typically huge, expansive gestures. By contrast, Herman Melville's (1819–1891) Clarel (1876) takes its title character on a contemporary journey to the Holy Land, and at the end of it Clarel finds the experience a meaningless and solitary one. Amid a collective of

"strangers and exiles" (p. 497), he finds his encounter with the Orient dispiriting; unlike Whitman, with his effusive delight in global unification through technology, Clarel notes the irony of humankind's ability to "wire the world" via cables "far under the sea" while unable to hear any "message from beneath the stone" of biblical history (pp. 497–498).

ORIENTALISM AND TASTE

So, as Melville's long narrative poem articulates, the reality of cultural producers' appropriation of Asia was, of course, frequently less magnificent in execution and borne of far less-idealistic grandiosity than Whitman's. Indeed, much American Orientalism had the intended and unintended effect of embracing and embodying kitsch. The intentional appropriation and parody of Orientalist stereotypes and aesthetic conventions was merely one way of acknowledging the complexities inherent in viewing the East. Kate Chopin's (1851–1904) short story, "The Egyptian Cigarette" seems at first to represent the Orient in a degrading manner, as a space for the West's exotic fantasies to run amok. Chopin's narrator expresses a hallucinatory vision of the Arab world that is, on the surface, stereotypically hyperbolic in its exoticism and Technicolor eroticism. Yet in the story's very excess, Chopin makes gentle fun of popular urges to represent the East in purely fantastic terms, most apparently in cigarette advertising.

Some of that same parodic or satiric spirit is omnipresent in Mark Twain's (1835–1910) writings about Asia. Following the Equator: A Journey Around the World (1897), for example, mocks the very processes of Orientalizing Asia. The chapter "In Ceylon" complains that Cairo was insufficiently Oriental, that it was "a tempered Orient—an Orient with an indefinite something wanting" (p. 339). Ceylon, according to the narrative voice, "was Oriental in the last measure of completeness—utterly Oriental" (p. 339). Ceylon perfectly meets the traveler's preconceptions of what the Orient should be, a riot of lush tropical foliage and colorful, exotic dress. Twain piles on the descriptive narrative to an excessive degree. Further in the chapter, however, "this dream of fairyland and paradise" is rudely interrupted by "grating dissonance" (p. 343) as a small group of young girls dressed in missionary school uniform enters the scene. Twain's complex satiric voice layers a yearning for cultural purity with an implicit recognition that such a longing exoticizes the Other to its disadvantage.

More often than not, however, "fake" Orientalism was the product of aesthetic failings born of serious, rather than satiric, intent. This kind of Orientalism was consecrated in public spectacle, like the World's Columbian Exposition held in Chicago in 1893. The masses wandered through a mock Turkish village, visited the Moorish Palace, watched belly dancers in the Egyptian theater, and lost their nickels and dimes at midway carnival attractions on the "Streets of Cairo." Celebrating the rise of American power in the world, the exposition enabled more than two million people to capture glimpses of an exotic world seemingly open to enlightened conquest.

In the cinema, audiences of 1916 were awestruck at the Babylonian sequences in D. W. Griffith's (1875–1948) "colossal spectacle" *Intolerance*. Kitsch is often defined as artistic ambition that exceeds conventions of "good taste," and the massive plaster sets and thousands of extras in "Middle Eastern" dress produced a monumentally kitschy rendition of Babylon. The vast processional pageantry of *Intolerance* was offset by the titillating spectacle of scantily clad women in the "Love Temple," writhing seductively in the rituals of the "sacred fires of life." Still, Griffith insisted that the vulgar splendor of his "vision" was authentic. One of the many dogmatic intertitles earnestly assured cinemagoers: "Note: Replica of Babylon's encircling walls, broad enough for the passing of chariots."

Similarly kitschy was the persona of one of the greatest early film divas, Theda Bara, who enacted such characters as Cleopatra in *Cleopatra* (1917), Salome in *Salome* (1918), and the priestess in *The Soul of Buddha* (1918). Her trademark kohl-rimmed eyes and "vamp" personality were hugely popular, and many fans suspended their disbelief about the Cincinnati-born star who was, as studio publicity maintained, born "in the shadow of the pyramids" and whose name was an anagram of "Arab Death." Such versions of the East, however seriously intentioned, are so inauthentic as to constitute camp, a strain in American Orientalism that mirrored much of the visual excess of such academic realist painters as Jean-Léon Gérome and Henri Regnault. French Orientalism's visual iconography provided much of the inspiration for more popular spectacle in American culture that pushed renditions of the East even further into fanciful excess.

ORIENTALISM, AUTHENTICITY, AND MODERNISM

By contrast, a more serious effort at representing the Orient, and more dutifully borrowing Asian aesthetic practices in art and literature, developed alongside more demotic renditions of the East as a place of sensual pleasure and erotic fantasy. There was a distinctive strain of American Orientalism, emerging from more elite artistic and literary circles, that was marked by understatement

and even "delicacy," which attempted to render the Orient in terms of tranquility, mystery, and remoteness from the debased Western values inhering in industrialism and urban life. This dichotomy is enacted in Griffith's 1919 film *Broken Blossoms,* which dignified the "Yellow Man," Cheng Huan (played by the Caucasian actor Richard Barthelmess) as a fragile, sensitive rescuer of an abused street urchin in the filthy hovels and opium dens of London's Limehouse. A male variation on Madame Butterfly, Cheng Huan renames the urchin White Blossom and, in a magical moment, places "a ray from the lyric moon" in her hair as she sleeps peacefully in his bed. He stands in direct opposition to the girl's drunken, violent, and abusive father and is therefore seen as a self-sacrificing and asexual aesthete who inhabits a world of pretty objets d'art. Thus Asia embodied, for American artists and poets, the aesthetic appeal of gentle understatement and handcrafted refinement in opposition to the coarseness of mass-produced consumer goods churned out of factories by alienated pieceworkers.

Chief among American visual artists in the period who relied on Asian forms and themes were James McNeill Whistler (1834–1903) and Mary Cassatt (1844–1926). Whistler popularized Japanese artistic motifs and methods in his domestic interiors (such as the splendid Peacock Room of 1876–1877) and misty oil paintings. In such works as *Nocturne: Blue and Silver—Chelsea* (1871) Whistler superimposed on portrayals of industrial London an escapist, mysterious, and idyllic "mood" derived from Japanese landscapes. Whistler was also instrumental in popularizing the use of Asian objets d'art and dress in his society portraiture, influencing later generations of portraitists such as William McGregor Paxton. Paxton's *The New Necklace* (1910) at the Museum of Fine Arts, Boston, depicts a young American woman languorously seated at her writing desk (upon which is set a geisha doll), set against a silk screen, wearing a pink silk tunic, the very picture of resplendent Orientalist consumption. Even more directly influenced by Japanese aesthetics and techniques was Mary Cassatt, whose drypoint and aquatint works of the early 1890s depicting women and children in domestic interiors were among the high points of her career. Entranced by the Japanese woodblock prints she collected, Cassatt emulated their compositions and soft, pale chromatics. Spare, elegant, formal: these characteristics of Asian art and literature energized modernism in all its forms, perhaps most significantly for literature in a movement known as imagism.

Before Ezra Pound (1885–1972) and Amy Lowell (1874–1925), among others, transmuted Asian aesthetics into poetry to "make it new," as Pound enjoined

The New Necklace, **1910.** Painting by William McGregor Paxton. Paxton depicts a young American woman languorously seated at her writing desk (upon which is set a geisha doll), set against a silk screen, wearing a pink silk tunic, the very picture of resplendent Orientalist consumption. © MUSEUM OF FINE ARTS, BOSTON, MASSACHUSETTS, USA, ZOE OLIVER SHERMAN COLLECTION/THE BRIDGEMAN ART LIBRARY

others to do, the journalist Lafcadio Hearn popularized the charm of Japan and Japanese art forms in America in a dozen books, beginning in 1894 with *Glimpses of Unfamiliar Japan.* His essays respectfully enlightened American readers on the frequent superiority of Japanese culture and, in particular, praised the visual beauty of the ideograph over the West's "dull, inanimate symbols of vocal sounds." Similarly, Ernest Fenollosa, after twelve years of teaching in Japan, returned to America to popularize Asian literature and art, inspiring Ezra Pound to adopt Asian poetic models and theories of the ideograph in his own poetry of the mid-1910s. Ostensibly, *Cathay* (1915) consists of Pound's reworkings of Fenollosa's notes, but the effect of the work is strikingly modern and original: simple, elegant, refined poetry stripped of all Victorian moralizing and bombast. "In a Station of the Metro" is only the best-known and most anthologized of Pound's prolific, Asian-inspired works of the period; these, in turn, inspired a short-lived vogue in the late 1910s for accessible, concentrated, image-oriented poetry modeled on the Chinese and Japanese. Amy Lowell's *Pictures of the Floating World* (1919) and John Gould Fletcher's *Japanese Prints* (1918) were two of the most prominent imagist efforts, however individually personalized and even Americanized, at responding to Asian verse forms and thematics. The titles of some of Lowell's poems in her collection suggest the Orientalist effect she wanted to achieve: "Passing the Bamboo Fence," "Temple Ceremony," "The Camellia Tree of Matsue," and "Ombre Chinoise."

If imagism was the most refined and respectful manifestation of Orientalism in American modernism, more populist modernism in the cinema displayed the racism inherent in the concept of the "Yellow Peril." Cecil B. DeMille's (1881–1959) 1915 film *The Cheat* endures as an astonishingly modern examination of the limits of female agency within upper-class marriage in a consumer society, and its formal aspects, such as cinematography and narrative pace, were miles ahead of Griffith's ponderous Victorian pageantry. Yet DeMille was as unenlightened as Griffith. The Japanese actor Sessue Hayakawa, playing the role of a wicked "Burmese ivory king," is portrayed as a monster of possessiveness, infiltrating and contaminating the world of the "Long Island smart set," corrupting the female protagonist, and ultimately burning his mark on her body with an ivory brand. This shocking act is obviously a displacement for an otherwise unrepresentable sexual assault. *The Cheat* was merely the most technically sophisticated rendition of much cultural production that used the conventions of Orientalism to express a terror of miscegenation and cross-racial sexual relations—and the ensuing collapse of a social order predicated on a racial hierarchy.

Tracing the ways America has engaged with its own imaginary representation of Asia suggests that America has looked eastward for cultural inspiration out of alienation from the West and has established its own identity as a Western nation in opposition to the East. Perhaps even more significantly, America could better express itself as a "modern" nation by looking away from Europe and toward the Orient, a new, fresh source of inspiration in the arts and literature. This complex cultural dynamic of attraction and repulsion has been a feature of the American cultural landscape at all levels, from elite culture to the carnival sideshow and nickelodeon, making American culture all the more rich for its appropriations, however much they might be lacking in true respect and integrity.

See also Aestheticism; Art and Architecture; Chinese; Imagism

BIBLIOGRAPHY
Primary Works

Adams, Henry. *The Letters of Henry Adams.* Vol. 3, *1886–1892.* Edited by J. C. Levenson et al. 6 vols. Cambridge, Mass.: Harvard University Press, 1982–1988.

Chopin, Kate. *The Awakening.* 1899. Edited by Nancy A. Walker. Boston: Bedford Books of St. Martin's Press, 1993.

Hearn, Lafcadio. *Writings from Japan: An Anthology.* Edited by Francis King. New York: Penguin Books, 1984.

James, Henry. *The Golden Bowl.* 1904. New York Edition, vol. 23. New York: Scribners, 1937.

Lowell, Amy. *Complete Poetical Works.* Boston: Houghton Mifflin, 1955.

Melville, Herman. *Clarel: A Poem and Pilgrimage in the Holy Land.* 1876. Northwestern-Newberry edition, vol. 12. Evanston: Northwestern University Press, 1991.

Twain, Mark. *Following the Equator.* 1897. New York: Oxford University Press, 1996.

Wharton, Edith. *The House of Mirth.* 1905. Edited by Martha Banta. New York: Oxford University Press, 1994.

Whitman, Walt. "Passage to India." 1870. In *Poetry and Prose.* Library of America. New York: Literary Classics of the United States, 1996.

Secondary Works

Bernstein, Matthew, and Gaylyn Studlar, eds. *Visions of the East: Orientalism in Film.* New Brunswick, N.J.: Rutgers University Press, 1997.

Edwards, Holly. *Noble Dreams, Wicked Pleasures: Orientalism in America 1870–1930.* Princeton, N.J.: Princeton University Press, 2000.

Lewis, Reina. *Gendering Orientalism: Race, Femininity, and Respresentation.* London: Routledge, 1996.

MacKenzie, John M. *Orientalism: History, Theory, and the Arts.* Manchester, U.K.: Manchester University Press, 1995.

Qian, Zhaoming. *Orientalism and Modernism: The Legacy of China in Pound and Williams.* Durham, N.C.: Duke University Press, 1995.

Said, Edward. *Culture and Imperialism.* New York: Knopf, 1993.

Said, Edward. *Orientalism.* New York: Pantheon Books, 1978.

David A. Boxwell

OTHER PEOPLE'S MONEY

Other People's Money and How the Bankers Use It (1914) by Louis Dembitz Brandeis (1856–1941) is a key document of the Progressive Era and that particular genre of literature that Theodore Roosevelt characterized as

muckraking. Few other works depict the sense of moral outrage and political anger at what the industrialization of America, and the concentration of great wealth in a few hands, had done to traditional social and political values. Brandeis, however, was not a Don Quixote tilting at imaginary windmills. The Industrial Revolution following the Civil War had indeed transformed the United States. Whatever one might argue about the material benefits that factories and mills had brought to the nation, one could not deny that this "progress" had come at a high cost. The price that the country paid for this progress, and what it meant to the United States, is central both to *Other People's Money* and to the Progressive movement itself.

EARLY REFORM EFFORTS

Louis Brandeis had been a successful attorney in Boston when, like many other Progressives, he became interested in reform. In a pattern similar to that of other activists at the turn of the twentieth century, he first engaged in local reforms in Boston, in particular the fight against traction interests that attempted to bilk the city and its citizens through high commuter transportation costs. He then moved to the state and regional level, fighting John Pierpont (J. P.) Morgan's efforts to monopolize New England transportation. He also got involved in the great insurance scandals of 1906 and helped focus criticism on industrial insurance plans that allowed large companies to charge outrageous prices to workers for minimal coverage. Brandeis always considered his greatest accomplishment to be the creation of savings bank life insurance that gave workers decent coverage at a fair price.

Brandeis burst onto the national scene in 1908, when he defended a state maximum-hours law before the Supreme Court in *Muller v. Oregon.* His creative use of data to instruct the Court on the facts of industrial life won praise from fellow Progressives, and the "Brandeis brief" became a major tool in the arsenal of reformers defending protective labor legislation before courts that were often hostile to business reform.

In 1912 Brandeis met Woodrow Wilson and after Wilson's election as president in November 1912 played a key role in fashioning the New Freedom reforms, especially the Federal Reserve Act, the Federal Trade Commission Act, and the Clayton Antitrust Act. In crafting this last law, Wilson relied heavily on a series of articles Brandeis had written.

BANKING IN THE SPOTLIGHT

Representative Arsène Paulin Pujo, a Democratic congressperson from Louisiana and head of the House Banking and Currency Committee, had held hearings in 1912 to discover whether a money trust actually existed as many reformers claimed and, if it did, the extent of its powers. The committee had called leading bankers such as J. P. Morgan to the stand and uncovered a tangled web of connections among the banks, the major industries on whose boards banker representatives sat, and the stock exchange, where the banks placed and sold the securities of these companies. At the end of the hearings, the *Philadelphia North American* echoed the sentiments of many reformers when it editorialized that "the Money Trust is the Wall Street system. But it is clearer to say that the Stock Exchange is the machinery through which the Money Trust operates—in unloading upon the public its manufactured securities and in maintaining its control of prices, of cash, and of credit" (*Literary Digest,* p. 388).

Although Brandeis did not himself participate in the hearings, he followed them closely. As soon as the committee released its report in March 1913, he wrote to Samuel Untermyer, the committee's counsel, praising its work and noting that while he "heartily approved" of most of the recommendations for reform, "in some respects it seems to me that the recommendations do not go far enough" (Mason, p. 412). He began to gather additional information, writing to people all over the country to garner further examples of banker influence in the economy. In the midst of his research, Wilson called him to Washington, where Brandeis played a key role in convincing the president and his advisers that the nation's central bank, to be called the Federal Reserve System, should be controlled by the government and not placed in private hands. With the president now determined to wrest control away from private bankers, he mobilized his followers in Congress and secured passage of the Federal Reserve Act in December 1913.

THE BOOK AND ITS RECEPTION

Even as Wilson oversaw the final stages of that fight, *Harper's Weekly,* edited by Brandeis's close friend Norman Hapgood, in November 1913 published "Breaking the Money Trust, Part I: Our Financial Oligarchy," the first of nine articles that Brandeis would assemble (along with one additional article) as *Other People's Money and How the Bankers Use It.* In the book Brandeis built on the Pujo Committee findings and added his own research to show how a small group of bankers, through their control of money and credit, dominated the American industrial world. He described, for example, how J. P. Morgan's representatives manipulated all the different companies involved in an industry, with one Morgan-controlled company selling raw materials to another that then manufac-

tured a product, a third distributing the product, and a fourth handling the financial arrangements—all working not to promote efficiency and competition but to enhance the power and profits of the Morgan firm.

The response to the articles and to the book was predictable, with reformers hailing Brandeis's exposé and members of the business and banking communities condemning it. One enthusiastic reader told Brandeis that "no man ever did so much to enlighten the people." Senator Robert Marion La Follette, a Republican from Wisconsin, called the book "epoch-making," while the *Washington Star* termed it "concrete and amazingly circumstantial, clear and forceful." B. H. Meyer of the Interstate Commerce Commission told Brandeis, "I had never before seen these matters focused so intensively and brought within the range of understanding of the average intelligent citizen" (Mason, pp. 418–419).

Bankers, understandably, viewed the work far less charitably. Frank Arthur Vanderlip, president of the National City Bank of New York, called the whole notion of a money trust "moonshine" and denounced the findings of both the Pujo Committee and the Brandeis articles as a "bureau of misinformation" (Mason, pp. 418–419). Other business leaders had similar comments.

In the articles and ensuing book Brandeis engaged in serious muckraking, exposing the evils of finance capitalism in a responsible manner, using sensational facts not for the sake of sensationalism but to make important points. Muckraking was central to Progressive reform, since it served an important tenet of the reformers. Brandeis and others believed that for a democracy to work, the citizens had to take an active, engaged, and above all, informed part in government. People could not be expected to solve difficult social problems if they did not understand the issues involved; they could not be expected to act against evils if they did not know that the evils existed. "Publicity is justly recommended as a remedy for social and industrial diseases," Brandeis wrote. "Sunlight is said to be the best of disinfectants; electric light the most efficient policeman" (p. 92).

In addition to exposing what he considered betrayal of the people's trust, Brandeis informed *Other People's Money* with an important underlying philosophy, namely that excellence and achievement derive from the struggle of life or, in the economic sphere, from competition. Brandeis never questioned the rightness of the free enterprise system; that it had its defects he freely admitted, and he did a great deal to formulate proposals on how these should be corrected. But he believed that the struggle made people better. He objected to monopoly and to what he termed the "curse of bigness" because they foreclosed competition and therefore denied people the opportunity to test themselves and, if they had the necessary talents and determination, to succeed.

At least one of the many people who read the articles took them quite seriously. Woodrow Wilson not only read them carefully and made notes in the margin, he also utilized Brandeis's suggestions in a special message to Congress in January 1914 calling for reform of the antitrust law. Congress responded with the Clayton Antitrust Act of 1914, a statute that Brandeis played a major role in crafting.

The first book version of *Other People's Money and How the Bankers Use It* came out in 1914, with an introduction by Norman Hapgood. Its argument lost favor during the heyday of business triumphalism in the 1920s, but all of Brandeis's prophecies about the curse of bigness appeared to come true in the 1929 stock market crash and the Great Depression that followed. "The present depression," he wrote, "the debunking of the great financial kings . . . have made men realize that *Other People's Money* should have been heeded" (Urofsky and Levy 5:494). Brandeis personally arranged for an inexpensive edition of the book to be republished in 1933, and he noted with great satisfaction that a Washington department store had sold over eleven hundred copies in one week.

Although many economists have dismissed the theory that underlay Brandeis's economic ideas, his warnings against the dangers of great concentrations of economic power have time and again been proven true. As the historian Richard M. Abrams wrote in his introduction to a 1967 edition to *Other People's Money*, "Only a willful reluctance to test fundamentals can obscure its refreshing pertinence" (p. xliii).

See also Banking and Finance; Muckrakers and Yellow Journalism

BIBLIOGRAPHY

Primary Work

Brandeis, Louis D. *Other People's Money and How the Bankers Use It.* 1914. Edited by Melvin I. Urofsky. Boston: Bedford Books of St. Martin's Press, 1995.

Secondary Works

Abrams, Richard M. Introduction to *Other People's Money and How the Bankers Use It,* by Louis Dembitz Brandeis. New York: Harper and Row, 1967.

Literary Digest, 4 January 1913, p. 388.

Mason, Alpheus Thomas. *Brandeis: A Free Man's Life.* New York: Viking, 1946.

Strum, Philippa. *Louis D. Brandeis: Justice for the People.* Cambridge, Mass.: Harvard University Press, 1984.

Urofsky, Melvin I. *Louis D. Brandeis and the Progressive Tradition.* Boston: Little, Brown, 1981.

Urofsky, Melvin I., and David W. Levy. *Letters of Louis D. Brandeis.* 5 vols. Albany: State University of New York Press, 1971–1978. See Brandeis to Louis B. Wehle, 19 January 1932.

West, Robert Craig. *Banking Reform and the Federal Reserve, 1863–1923.* Ithaca, N.Y.: Cornell University Press, 1977.

Wiebe, Robert H. *The Search for Order, 1877–1920.* New York: Hill and Wang, 1967.

Melvin I. Urofsky

OVERLAND MONTHLY

Published from 1868 until 1935, San Francisco's *Overland Monthly* has been remembered chiefly as the journal that launched the writer Bret Harte (1836–1902), its first editor, to national and international fame. Reciprocally, Harte may be credited with launching the *Overland* toward what fame it has enjoyed: after his departure at the end of 1870 successive proprietors inherited immediate distinction and authority with the journal's name and its emblem of a grizzly bear snarling down a railroad track. Although the later files usually attract less attention than the five semiannual volumes edited by Harte, the *Overland* maintained its status as a leading regional magazine into the early twentieth century and as such remains valuable for a literary history of the American West. Furthermore, questions about the way literature articulates ideas of class, region, and nation have generated renewed interest in the *Overland,* a periodical that for most of its history affirmed the manifest destiny of its readers and its region.

HARTE'S *OVERLAND*

Bret Harte's *Overland* would not have existed without Anton Roman (1826–1903), the San Francisco bookseller and publisher who in 1868 felt he could support a new monthly magazine and who persuaded Harte to edit it. A few other local magazines had attempted a high literary standard, and the most recent of these, the *Californian,* had folded in February. Roman's status as a long-standing local businessman and his extensive contacts with area readers and writers enabled him to secure advertising contracts that would bring in $900 per month for the first year and to guarantee a circulation of 3,000 copies. To lure the skeptical Harte, the leading man of letters on the West

HOW THE JOURNAL GOT ITS NAME

According to Harte, a name referring only to California would not be sufficient for a magazine with the ambitions of the Overland Monthly. *He explained the title in the July 1868 issue, the magazine's first.*

Turn your eyes to this map made but a few years ago. Do you see this vast interior basin of the Continent, on which the boundaries of States and Territories are less distinct than the names of wandering Indian tribes; do you see this broad zone reaching from Virginia City to St. Louis, as yet only dotted by telegraph stations, whose names are familiar, but of whose locality we are profoundly ignorant? Here creeps the railroad, each day drawing the West and East closer together. . . . Shall not the route be represented [in a magazine] as well as the *termini*? And where our people travel, that is the highway of our thought.

Bret Harte, "Etc.," *Overland Monthly,* July 1868, p. 99.

Coast in 1868, Roman agreed to provide half the editorial content for the first volume from material submitted to him as a publisher, and he engaged two local journalists to assist in editorial duties.

Although Roman wanted the magazine to promote the commercial interests of California, Harte steered it—as Roman had feared—on a more literary and intellectual course. In one oft-cited incident, for example, Harte mocked the skittish journalists who underreported an 1868 earthquake because they thought news of damage would frighten away capital. Not that Harte set out to be contrarian with the magazine. In the "Etc." column of the first number he warmly anticipated the civilizing effects of the approaching transcontinental railroad, but he also published Henry George's cautionary essay "What the Railroad Will Bring Us" in the October issue a few months later. Working out some theories of political economy that would inform his classic *Progress and Poverty* (1879), Henry George (1839–1897) posed questions about the California of the "new era":

> She [California] will have more wealth; but will it be so evenly distributed? She will have more luxury and refinement and culture; but will she have . . . so little of the grinding, hopeless poverty that chills

and cramps the souls of men, and converts them into brutes? . . . And so the California of the future . . . will be a better country for some classes than the California of the present; and so too, it must be a worse country for others. Which of these classes will be the largest? (1 *Overland* 1 [1868], p. 301)

Setting the tone for the magazine for decades to come, Harte's *Overland* devoted itself to the free discussion of ideas and original material rather than one-sided attention to either commerce or criticism.

Harte earned the authority to work so independently by increasing the circulation of the magazine (meeting Roman's goal of three thousand copies within six months) on the merits of his own remarkably popular stories and poems. After "The Luck of Roaring Camp" appeared anonymously in the second number (August 1868), the prestigious *Atlantic Monthly* invited Harte to contribute something in the same style. Samuel Bowles of the *Springfield Republican*, to which Harte had been a regular and recent contributor, also praised "The Luck" as "a genuine California story" before he knew the identity of its author (Scharnhorst, p. 40). As Harte often repeated later in his career, the first success of the *Overland* depended on favorable notices from the East. More to the point, Harte seems to have brokered more local authority for himself as editor by earning the critical praise and the subscriptions of outsiders.

Following the lead of those contemporary easterners, twentieth-century critics have usually agreed that Harte's *Overland* stories offered something new and worthwhile in the national literature, although they have long differed about the reasons for the stories' value. Harte's first champions appreciated what they considered his realism—his ability to convey the language, costumes, customs, and scenery of California's mid-nineteenth-century mining districts; but for every Californian with supposed evidence of Harte's fictional verisimilitude, another asserted that his sketches actually distorted the life of miners and mining. A second set of champions, arguing against opponents who accused Harte of bad craftsmanship, claimed that he helped to pioneer the short story genre. More lasting claims for the significance of Harte's *Overland* tales and poems include his skill as a humorist, his defense of Indians and Chinese immigrants against Anglo prejudice and violence, his satire of social and literary conventions, his creation of a market for the genre western, and his transformation of local gold rush folklore into an international mythos. The ongoing interest in Harte's fiction—to which these debates and rereadings bear testimony—has ensured the first five volumes of the *Overland Monthly,* published from July 1868 through December 1870, a place in literary history.

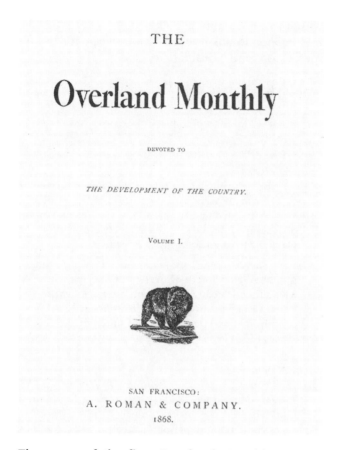

THE

Overland Monthly

DEVOTED TO

THE DEVELOPMENT OF THE COUNTRY.

VOLUME I.

SAN FRANCISCO:
A. ROMAN & COMPANY.
1868.

The cover of the first *Overland Monthly*. GRADUATE LIBRARY, UNIVERSITY OF MICHIGAN

THE NEXT HALF-CENTURY

The reputation and legacy of the later *Overland* are less secure, in part because no other single personality placed such a stamp on the magazine or caught the attention of distinguished outsiders. After Harte's departure, the magazine lost money for its second publisher, John H. Carmany, and ceased publication in the midst of an economic depression in 1875. Revived under new management in 1883, it was handed from one publisher or editor to the next for another fifty-two years. Latter-day owners merged it with *Out West Magazine* in 1923 and moved it to Los Angeles five years later, where it finally ceased publication in 1935 with more of a promotional than literary character. In sum, the magazine had two and a half years under Bret Harte and fifty-seven years without him, about which scholars have had much less to say.

Critics tend to accept the verdict of the literary historian who referred to the *Overland* in its second series (1883–1935) as "still the most important magazine of the Pacific Coast" (Mott 4:105). The number of later contributors who achieved a lasting fame—including Frank Norris, Jack London, Gertrude Atherton, and Mary Austin—helps to ensure some respect for the journal's second series. However, Ambrose Bierce's reference to the "Warmed-Overland" (Scharnhorst, p. 52) represents a pervasive view that the journal was never as good or as influential after Harte's departure.

Nonetheless the *Overland* continued to cast itself and its region in grand terms and at times to enjoy a strong circulation. Several months after its price was reduced to ten cents per issue to remain competitive with other national magazines, James Howard Bridge (1856?–1939), then the editor of the *Overland*, crowed that

> at its present rate of progress it is only a matter of a few months before [the *Overland*] establishes itself as the leader of all the magazines outside of the metropolis [New York]. . . . It is the most characteristically American of all illustrated periodicals. It represents in literature the most virile of American traits. (2 *Overland* 31 [1898], p. 179)

Although sales fluctuated during the 1880s and 1890s, the magazine boasted a circulation of thirty thousand when the publisher Frederick Marriott bought it in 1900, and that number rose to seventy-five thousand twelve years later (Mott 3:408). Whether such staying power is explained by the magazine's ability to attract writers such as Atherton and London or whether there are other explanations the thin critical record does not make plain.

The *Overland* owed part of its grand sensibility to a vision of San Francisco and the West that the journal had always fostered. In his 1868 essay "What the Railroad Will Bring Us," George anticipated that San Francisco would become the leading commercial city in the world, with the ocean to the west and the railroad to the east connecting it with all the world's markets. Echoing him thirty years later in a jubilee issue of the journal, Bridge remained convinced that the city's geographic position destined it for greatness. According to Bridge, "In thirty years [California] will be the center of American mercantile life. The doors of the Orient are being flung open; a colonial domain is unrolling itself like a map at our threshold" (2 *Overland* 32 [1898], p. 90). As editor during and after the imperial year of 1898, in which the United States annexed Hawaii and took control of Spain's former colonies in the Caribbean and the Pacific, Bridge predicted greatness for the magazine commensurate with the national, even global, rank he envisioned for San Francisco and the Anglo-American West.

According to the critic Nancy Glazener, the *Overland*'s promotion of itself and its region were not at all unusual for the era of American realism. Magazines of

---

HARTE'S *OVERLAND* STORIES

"The Luck of Roaring Camp" (August 1868)

"The Outcasts of Poker Flat" (January 1869)

"Miggles" (June 1869)

"Tennessee's Partner" (October 1869)

"The Idyl of Red Gulch" (December 1869)

"Brown of Calaveras" (March 1870)

"Mr. Thompson's Prodigal" (July 1870)

"The Iliad of Sandy Bar" (November 1870)

"The Christmas Gift That Came to Rupert"
(January 1871)

Glazener's "*Atlantic* group"—those that resembled the *Atlantic Monthly* in their editorial content, book reviews, and sense of cultural authority—were actually in the business of creating a high-ranking class identity for themselves. In this context the *Overland* is both a lower-ranking regional magazine in the eyes of such self-proclaimed national magazines as the *Atlantic* (as evidenced by the recurring pattern of young writers graduating from the *Overland* to the more prestigious and lucrative Boston monthly) and a self-proclaimed elite magazine itself with imperial aspirations. Featuring contributions from professors at the University of California, among other authoritative sources, the *Overland* through most of its history assumed an audience of "high civilization" and "genuine education," to borrow phrases from an 1883 book review (2 *Overland* 1 [1883], p. 100). Among those who wrote for the *Overland* were Louis Agassiz, Gertrude Atherton, Mary Austin, Ambrose Bierce, Noah Brooks, J. Ross Browne, Alice Cary, Phoebe Cary, Samuel Clemens, Josephine Clifford (McCracken), Ina Coolbrith, Rollin Daggett, Dan De Quille, Henry George, Bret Harte, Helen Hunt Jackson, Georgiana Bruce Kirby, Jack London, Joaquin Miller, Prentice Mulford, John Muir, John G. Neihardt, Frank Norris, Josiah Royce, Charles Warren Stoddard, Frances Fuller Victor, and Woodrow Wilson.

Setting aside the Hartean gallery of chivalric miners and gamblers and tender prostitutes for which the magazine has long been remembered, the legacy of the founding editor most relevant to the purposes of half a century of subsequent writers and proprietors may have been the air of authority that allowed the name *Overland Monthly* to elevate those associated with it to a high cultural rank commensurate with the high economic rank reached in the same period by railroad barons and industrial tycoons.

See also The Atlantic Monthly; Realism; Spanish-American War

BIBLIOGRAPHY

Primary Works

Mighels, Ella Sterling. *The Story of the Files: A Review of California Writers and Literature.* San Francisco: World's Fair Commission, 1893. Contains quotations, photographs, profiles, and a subjective history of the *Overland* from an admiring perspective.

Overland Monthly, July 1868–December 1900. Making of America digital library. University of Michigan. http://www.hti.umich.edu/m/moajrnl/browse.journals/over.html. Contains the complete first series (1868–1875), cited in text as 1 *Overland,* and much of the second series (1883–1935), cited in text as 2 *Overland.*

Secondary Works

Glazener, Nancy. *Reading for Realism: The History of a U.S. Literary Institution, 1850–1910.* Durham, N.C.: Duke University Press, 1997. Compares the *Overland* to other contemporary periodicals that promoted literary realism and their own high-cultural status.

Marovitz, Sanford E. "Romance or Realism? Western Periodical Literature: 1893–1902." *Western American Literature* 10 (1975): 45–58. Provides a brief analysis of western fiction in some middle volumes of the *Overland* and a comparison of similar material published in other U.S. magazines.

Mott, Frank Luther. *A History of American Magazines.* Vols. 3–4. Cambridge, Mass.: Harvard University Press, 1957. Includes the best profile to date of the entire run of the *Overland* as well as invaluable material about American magazines during the *Overland*'s era.

Scharnhorst, Gary. *Bret Harte: Opening the American Literary West.* Norman: University of Oklahoma Press, 2000. Provides an authoritative, updated history of Harte's relationship to the *Overland* based on primary sources, including some material not available in Stewart.

Stewart, George R. *Bret Harte, Argonaut and Exile.* Boston: Houghton Mifflin, 1931. The definitive biography of Harte until 2000, this remains a useful source of information about Harte's relationship to the *Overland.*

Walker, Franklin Dickerson. *San Francisco's Literary Frontier.* New York: Knopf, 1939. This study ends at 1875, so it only covers the first series of the *Overland.* Excellent source of biographical and historical information to that point.

Tara Penry

PARKS AND WILDERNESS AREAS

The national park is an American invention that has served as a model for the preservation of natural sites throughout the world. Its origin lies in the European garden park, but the American national park is an attempt to preserve wildness, not to manicure nature. Similarly the origin of the wilderness area lies in the European forest reserve, but the latter was reserved for the private use of nobility, whereas the American wilderness area is part of the public domain.

URBAN PARKS

Proposals for public parks first emerged during the 1830s both in Europe and in the United States. These parks were to serve the common welfare, and, in America, were also to serve as nature museums. By the 1840s and 1850s, literary men such as Henry David Thoreau (1817–1862) were encouraging Americans to set aside plots of city land for preservation. William Cullen Bryant (1794–1878), writing as editor of the *New York Evening Post,* called in 1844 for the creation of a park in New York City. He wanted to preserve part of the rocky shore of Manhattan before it was all converted into "muddy docks" ("A New Public Park"). Horace Greeley (1811–1872), the editor of the *New York Tribune,* concurred, and the poet James Russell Lowell (1819–1891) added his voice to the call. Largely due to Bryant's efforts, work on Central Park began in 1857, although the project was moved to the swampy, polluted interior of the island instead of being placed on the shore. Landscape architects Frederick Law Olmsted (1822–1903) and Calvert

Vaux (1824–1895) designed the 843-acre park, incorporating natural features into its design and setting standards for future park planners. Indeed the design for Central Park made Olmsted famous; after the project was finished, he was commissioned to design similar parks in other cities, including Fairmont Park in Philadelphia, Prospect Park in Brooklyn, South Park in Chicago, and Mount Royal Park in Montreal. Thus began a wave of park construction in the United States that set aside parcels of land for preservation in the urban environment.

WILDERNESS PRESERVATION AND CONSERVATION

Conceptually the movement to preserve wilderness in the United States began in the 1820s, when American statesman DeWitt Clinton (1769–1828) proposed that large expanses of wilderness be maintained in a wild state. Washington Irving (1783–1859) made a similar suggestion in the 1830s while editing the exploration journals of Captain Benjamin Bonneville for publication, remarking that the uninhabited, undeveloped land comprising the Rocky Mountains should remain "irreclaimable wilderness" (p. 372). At about the same time, the idea of the national park came to George Catlin (1796–1872), the well-known painter of Native American subjects. During a trip to the South Dakota territory in May of 1832, he realized that the bison and the American Indian were in danger of extinction. While he contemplated the loss, it suddenly occurred to him that the inhabitants of this wilderness, both human and animal, could be preserved in "a magnificent park," "a nation's Park" (p. 263).

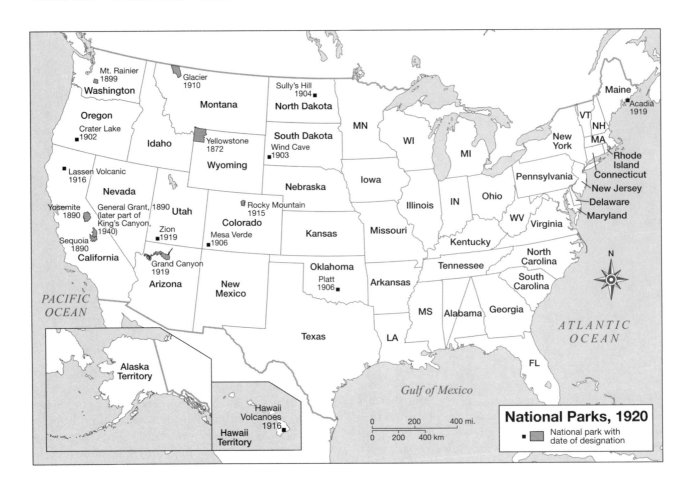

National Parks, 1920

As Catlin explains in *Letters and Notes on the Manners, Customs, and Conditions of the North American Indians* (1841), he envisioned this park as a place to display the primitive to the rest of the world for all time. It was to be an American contribution to humanity, and it would be managed by the federal government for the benefit of all citizens.

Catlin's idea had little chance of being taken seriously until Americans developed an appreciation for what was being lost as the wilderness dwindled. This process began with eastern literary figures and artists lamenting the disappearance of primeval forests. For instance the painter and naturalist John James Audubon (1785–1851) complained in *Ornithological Biography; or, An Account of the Habits of the Birds of the United States of America* (1831–1839) that settlers were rapidly destroying forests in the Ohio Valley. A similar complaint shows up in *The Pioneers* (1823), a novel by James Fenimore Cooper (1789–1851) in which Natty Bumppo expresses a desire to leave the clearings and reenter the woods that have not yet been decimated by settlers. Similarly, after the poet William Cullen Bryant toured the Great Lakes region in 1846, he mentioned in personal letters looking ahead sadly to a future in

which the woods would be filled with settlements. Adopting a much more dire tone, the landscape painter Thomas Cole (1801–1848) declared in his 1836 "Essay on American Scenery" that the wilderness was already showing the "ravages of the axe" (p. 17), and in 1841 he wrote a poem called "The Lament of the Forest" in which the forest grieves for its losses at the hands of man, the destroyer. Henry David Thoreau comments wryly on man's destructive powers in his journal from 1852, writing that "this winter they are cutting down our woods more seriously than ever" (p. 273), and observing that "it is a thorough process— this war with the wilderness" (p. 320). Just who would win this war seemed all too clear to these defenders of the forest, whose writings helped Americans to see something other than utilitarian value in the disappearing trees of the wilderness.

Other streams of thought and feeling contributed to the new attitude toward wilderness that was emerging by the time of the Civil War. One such trend involved a Romantic enthusiasm for wild nature. Another involved a new landscape aesthetic, one that focused on the sublime and picturesque. Yet another involved deism and transcendentalism investing the

> The tendency nowadays to wander in wilderness is delightful to see. Thousands of tired, nerve-shaken, over-civilized people are beginning to find out that going to the mountains is going home; that wildness is a necessity; and that mountain parks and reservations are useful not only as fountains of timber and irrigating rivers, but as fountains of life. . . . This is fine and natural and full of promise. So also is the growing interest in the care and preservation of forests and wild places in general, and in the half-wild parks and gardens of town.
>
> Muir, "The Wild Parks and Forest Reservations of the West," in *Nature Writings*, p. 721.

natural world with spirit, thereby counteracting the traditional Judeo-Christian antipathy toward wilderness. Moreover many Americans came to understand that the wilderness was an essential part of the American scene, and the realization that it was vanishing led naturally to the idea of preservation.

A parallel movement to conserve wilderness was stimulated by the work of George Perkins Marsh (1801–1882), whose career as a conservationist began in the 1840s when as a congressman from Vermont he lobbied for a national museum to preserve artifacts of natural history. In 1847 Marsh made a speech calling for a limitation on the clearing of forests for agricultural purposes. Then, in 1864, he published *Man and Nature*, a seminal study of humankind's relationship with the natural world. Marsh begins his investigation with an indictment of human wastefulness and destructiveness and moves into a discussion of the wanton unbalancing of ecological systems. Using the effects of uncontrolled logging as his main illustration, Marsh argues that clear-cutting forests results in drought, floods, and erosion, and that the spongelike qualities of the primeval forest make it the best possible regulator of water flow. He also asserts that "the earth is fast becoming an unfit home for its noblest inhabitant" (p. 43) and calls for the preservation of remaining forests as well as the careful use of resources in the future. Because Marsh's arguments supported the preservation of wilderness on economic grounds, his views had a major influence on preservationist rhetoric. A year after *Man and Nature* first appeared, William Cullen Bryant wrote an essay called "The Utility of Trees" in

which he echoes Marsh's views: "Thus it is that forests protect a country against drought, and keep its streams constantly flowing and its wells constantly full" (p. 404). In fact, *Man and Nature* became an incredibly influential and popular book; its first edition sold out in a few months, and subsequent editions had a large impact on the thinking of men such as Frederick Law Olmsted and John Muir (1838–1914), who converted Marsh's thoughts into legislative action. Lewis Mumford, writing in *The Brown Decades: A Study of the Arts in America, 1865–1895* (1931), justifiably refers to Marsh's book as "the fountainhead of the conservation movement" (p. 78).

THE NATIONAL PARK SYSTEM

Despite the calls to preserve and conserve wilderness, early proposals to protect undeveloped land focused more on natural wonders or curiosities than on virgin forests. Among the sites mentioned for preservation were the redwood groves of California, the Shoshone Falls on the Snake River in Idaho, and the geothermal phenomena at Yellowstone. A pivotal figure in the movement to protect spectacular sites was Olmsted, who believed that the government had a responsibility to protect features such as Niagara Falls from exploitation or development. After moving to California in 1863, he joined the fight to preserve Yosemite Valley and the Mariposa Big Tree Grove. Congress had granted these lands to the state of California, which created the Yosemite Commission and made Olmsted chairman. In his 1865 "Preliminary Report upon the Yosemite Valley and Big Tree Grove," he asserted that the government was obligated to protect the citizen's right to enjoy scenic areas that were part of the public domain. He also supported the national park concept by arguing that the government had a "duty of preservation" (p. 508) to protect such places as Yosemite Valley from private exploitation. Olmsted's argument was anticipated by the thought of earlier Americans such as Thomas Jefferson (1743–1826), who in 1815 had refused to sell land surrounding the Natural Bridge in Virginia because he viewed the bridge as a public trust and wanted it to be open to public view as long as it was protected from defacement. Olmsted recommended that Yosemite and the Mariposa Grove be protected as scenic parks, but, unfortunately, his report was suppressed by other members of the commission who feared that funding for Yosemite would divert funds away from the Geological Survey, and another twenty-five years would pass before John Muir convinced Congress to adopt Olmsted's recommendations.

In the meantime, the geothermal wonderland of Yellowstone became more widely known after several groups explored the region in 1869 and 1870. In

1871 the scientist Ferdinand V. Hayden (1829–1887) led an expedition that included the photographer William Henry Jackson (1843–1942) and the landscape painter Thomas Moran (1837–1926). Both artists created compelling graphic images of the area's magnificent features, and soon every member of Congress knew of Yellowstone. After a brief lobbying campaign, the Yellowstone Park Act became law on 1 March 1872, creating the world's first national park. In part the law states that the region was "reserved and withdrawn from settlement, and dedicated and set apart as a public park or pleasuring-ground for the benefit and enjoyment of the people" (Tolson, pp. 26–27). This statement echoes some of the language Olmsted used in his 1865 report concerning the use of the public domain. To understand just how radical this point of view was at the time, one needs to keep in mind that the Yellowstone Park Act took effect when the federal government was enthusiastically parceling out the public domain through railroad land grants as well as homestead, mining, and timber acts. As a park, Yellowstone encompasses over 3,000 square miles of wilderness, but this land was set aside mainly because it might contain undiscovered geothermal features. It was not until the 1880s or 1890s, after several surveys, that Americans took note of the rivers, meadows, forest land, and wildlife that had been pre-

served in Yellowstone Park in addition to the geysers, waterfalls, and hot springs.

The next phase of park creation revolved around John Muir, the wanderer, writer, and wilderness sage. Four years after Olmsted issued his report on Yosemite, Muir began exploring the region while working as a sheepherder. Before long he was taking such notable persons as Ralph Waldo Emerson (1803–1882) on guided tours of the area. Muir also became entangled in a scientific dispute over the geological history of Yosemite when his theory that glaciers shaped the valley was attacked by the geologist Josiah D. Whitney (1819–1896). After writing letters on the subject and finding a living glacier in the mountains, Muir published his first essay, "Yosemite Glaciers," in the *New York Tribune* in 1871. He then became a regular contributor to the *Overland Monthly*, publishing numerous articles on places of interest in the Sierra Nevada mountain range. In 1876 Muir published an article in the *Sacramento Record-Union*, "God's First Temples: How Shall We Preserve Our Forests?" in which he argues that the government should take responsibility for protecting forests.

Continuing his travels throughout the American West and Alaska, Muir left the Yosemite area for several years. When he returned in 1889, he met Robert

The Grand Canyon of the Yellowstone, 1872. Painting by Thomas Moran. NATIONAL MUSEUM OF AMERICAN ART, SMITHSONIAN INSTITUTION/BRIDGEMAN ART LIBRARY

Underwood Johnson (1853–1937), an editor of *Century Magazine,* and showed Johnson around the valley. The two were appalled to see the damage done in the area by timber cutting, visitors, and grazing sheep, and Johnson suggested that a national park be created to protect the valley and its environs. The editor then lobbied for the park in Washington, D.C., while Muir wrote two articles for *Century Magazine* entitled "The Treasures of Yosemite" and "Features of the Proposed Yosemite National Park," which appeared in 1890. The purpose of these articles was to describe Yosemite as a "delightful summer pleasure park" (p. 687) that could be reserved "for the use and recreation of the people" (p. 699), and a close look at the text of "Features" reveals that Muir knew how to reach his audience. He writes the article in the style of a travelogue, describing the landmarks, scenery, plant life, and seasonal weather in language that appeals to the senses. He also focuses on the experiences to be had by the reader in Yosemite, stating that "perhaps none of [these experiences] will be remembered with keener delight than the days spent in sauntering in the broad velvet lawns by the river, sharing the pure air and light with the trees and mountains" (p. 689). To make the descriptions more immediate, Muir shifts to the second person early in the article and addresses the reader directly, as when he states, "Now your attention is turned to the moraines, sweeping in beautiful curves from the hollows and cañons of the mountains, regular in form as railroad embankments" (p. 690). After enticing the reader with word-pictures of the "marvelous grandeur" (p. 693) of the scenery and the sensory experiences to be had in Yosemite, Muir ends the article with a warning: "Unless reserved or protected the whole region will soon or late be devastated by lumbermen and sheepmen, and so of course be made unfit for use as a pleasure ground" (pp. 699–700). The message here is plain enough, and the effectiveness of Muir's rhetoric may be gauged in part by the fact that Yosemite became a national park on 1 October 1890.

Muir continued to play a major role in the creation of new parks. Within a week after Yosemite became a national park, General Grant National Park and Sequoia National Park were established to protect groves of giant redwood trees. Muir's efforts were also responsible to a large degree for the establishment of Mount Rainier, Petrified Forest, and Grand Canyon national parks. In 1903 he took President Theodore Roosevelt (1858–1919) on a three-night camping trip in Yosemite; the experience made such an impression on the president that he came away convinced of the need for quick federal action to preserve the great scenic places of America. During Roosevelt's time in

office, the boundaries of Yosemite were expanded, and Crater Lake, Mesa Verde, and Wind Cave became national parks. Roosevelt also created the United States Forest Service in 1905 and preserved other tracts of land, including the Grand Canyon, Lassen Peak, and Petrified Forest, which later became national parks. Because of his influence on policy and public figures such as Roosevelt, Muir has often been called the father of our national park system.

However, other men of letters and artists contributed to the expansion of the park system as well. It was Thomas Moran who illustrated Muir's articles on Yosemite for *Century Magazine,* and one of his paintings of Yellowstone hung in the lobby of the U.S. Senate for decades. Another of his paintings, one depicting the Grand Canyon, hung in the office of George Horace Lorimer (1867–1937), an editor of the *Saturday Evening Post* who fought to preserve the canyon. In Colorado, writer Enos Mills (1890–1922) championed the Rocky Mountains. William Gladstone Steel (1854–1934) of Oregon was the advocate of Crater Lake. George Bird Grinnell (1849–1938), an editor of *Forest and Stream* who had helped to survey Yellowstone Park in 1875, argued that national parks should serve as wildlife sanctuaries. After much effort by Grinnell, an area in northern Montana populated by grizzly bears and mountain goats became Glacier National Park in 1910. Grinnell also had an influence on the national park system by intellectually preparing Theodore Roosevelt for Gifford Pinchot (1865–1946), the president's environmental administrator.

A parallel system of forest reserves was established in 1891 at the urging of Carl Schurz (1829–1906), who was the secretary of the interior from 1877 to 1881. The Forest Service administered the reserves, which in 1907 were renamed national forests. In 1916 the National Park Service was created to administer the park system. At about the same time, the Forest Service began creating public recreation programs, and the two agencies became bureaucratic rivals. In 1924 the Forest Service encroached on responsibilities claimed by the Park Service by designating part of the Gila National Forest in New Mexico as the first wilderness area. Stephen T. Mather (1867–1930), the first director of the Park Service, wrote a paper in 1925 in which he disputed claims made by advocates of the Forest Service that it could manage the park system "at little extra cost beyond that of managing the forests" (Sellars, p. 58), and he argued that placing the parks under the Forest Service would result in the "commercial exploitation of natural resources" (Sellars, p. 58), thereby destroying the parks. Mather also believed that the parks were "more truly national playgrounds than are the forests" (Sellars, p. 58), and so he argued that the parks should be developed for recreational tourism. Since then, the two agencies have sorted out their respective areas of responsibility; in the early twenty-first century, the Forest Service manages more than 192 million acres of land according to the principle of multiple use, meaning that the resources of the land can be exploited for commercial purposes, while the Park Service manages about 80 million acres of national parks, preserves, monuments, recreation areas, seashores, lake shores, historic parks, scenic trails, parkways, and battlefields, for recreational and educational purposes.

See also My First Summer in the Sierra; Nature Writing; Resource Management

BIBLIOGRAPHY

Primary Works

Bryant, William Cullen. "A New Public Park." *New York Evening Post,* 3 July 1844.

Bryant, William Cullen. "The Utility of Trees." 1865. In *The Prose Writings of William Cullen Bryant,* vol. 2, edited by Parke Godwin, pp. 402–405. New York: Russell and Russell, 1964.

Catlin, George. *Letters and Notes on the Manners, Customs, and Conditions of the North American Indians.* 1841. Republished as *North American Indians,* edited by Peter Matthiessen. New York: Viking, 1989.

Cole, Thomas. "Essay on American Scenery." 1836. In *Thomas Cole: The Collected Essays and Prose Sketches,* edited by Marshall Tymm, pp. 3–19. St. Paul, Minn.: John Colet Press, 1980.

Grinnell, George Bird. *The Passing of the Great West: Selected Papers of George Bird Grinnell.* Edited, with introduction and commentary, by John F. Reiger. New York: Winchester Press, 1972.

Irving, Washington. *The Adventures of Captain Bonneville.* 1837. Edited by Edgeley W. Todd. Norman: University of Oklahoma Press, 1961.

Marsh, George Perkins. *Man and Nature.* 1864. Edited by David Lowenthal. Cambridge, Mass.: Harvard University Press, 1965.

Muir, John. *Nature Writings.* 1871–1920. Edited by William Cronon. New York: Library of America, 1997.

Olmsted, Frederick Law. "Preliminary Report upon the Yosemite Valley and Big Tree Grove." 1865. In *The California Frontier, 1863–1865,* edited by Victoria Post Ranney et al., pp. 488–516. Vol. 5 of *The Papers of Frederick Law Olmsted.* Baltimore: Johns Hopkins University Press, 1990.

Thoreau, Henry David. "Chesuncook." In his *The Maine Woods.* 1864. Edited by Robert F. Sayre, pp. 656–712. New York: Library of America, 1985.

Thoreau, Henry David. *Journal.* 1851–1852. Vol. 4 of *The Writings of Henry D. Thoreau,* edited by Robert Sattelmeyer, Leonard N. Neufeldt, and Nancy Craig Simmons. Princeton, N.J.: Princeton University Press, 1992.

Secondary Works

Lyon, Thomas J. *John Muir.* Boise, Idaho: Boise State College, 1972.

Mitchell, Lee Clark. *Witnesses to a Vanishing America: The Nineteenth-Century Response.* Princeton, N.J.: Princeton University Press, 1981.

Mumford, Lewis. *The Brown Decades: A Study of the Arts in America, 1865–1895.* New York: Harcourt, Brace and Company, 1931.

Nash, Roderick. "The American Invention of National Parks." *American Quarterly* 22, no. 3 (1970): 727–735.

Nash, Roderick. *Wilderness and the American Mind.* Rev. ed. New Haven, Conn.: Yale University Press, 1973.

Sellars, Richard West. *Preserving Nature in the National Parks: A History.* New Haven, Conn.: Yale University Press, 1997.

Todd, John Emerson. *Frederick Law Olmsted.* Boston: Twayne, 1982.

Tolson, Hillory Alfred. *Laws Relating to the National Park Service, the National Parks and Monuments.* Washington, D.C.: United States Department of the Interior, National Park Service, 1933.

Wernert, Susan J., ed. *Our National Parks: America's Spectacular Wilderness Heritage.* Pleasantville, N.Y.: Reader's Digest Association, 1985.

Wolfe, Linnie Marsh. *Son of the Wilderness: The Life of John Muir.* New York: Knopf, 1945.

Seth Bovey

PENITENTIARIES AND PRISONS

Historically the term "penitentiary" referred to institutions that accepted prostitutes who vowed to reform themselves and to relinquish their sinful ways. These goals of repentance and correction are apparent in the very name "penitentiary," which arises from the word "penitent." Prisons, however, typically have had no such pretensions; confinement in these places is meant simply to prevent escape and to protect people outside of the prison. Despite these semantic differences, however, in contemporary use "penitentiary" and "prison" have come to hold much the same meaning: they are sites of confinement that both protect the free public and offer an opportunity for reform. Isolation from the larger population, at least, and at times from the prison population itself, was to provide time for reflection and meditation. According to Quakers who originally established many of the prisons in the United States and their spiritual descendants who sought to reform the prison system in the mid-nineteenth century, because humans are essentially moral creations of God, reflection upon the acts that brought them to their imprisoned state would cause incarcerated persons to understand and amend their unlawful behavior. Certainly there was no shortage of incarcerated persons on whom reformers might apply their theories.

Though reliable statistics on incarceration are not available prior to 1925, prison populations do appear to rise in response to economic stagnation; in 1939 incarceration rates peaked at 137 persons per 100,000 before declining in the pre–World War II economy. A much earlier report by Gustave de Beaumont and Alexis de Tocqueville reveals that from its inception the prison system served as a form of racial control as well as crime control. The French researchers, who came to America in 1831 to investigate the U.S. prison system and report back to the French government, wrote in *On the Penitentiary System in the United States and Its Application in France* (1833) that in states where the whites-to-blacks ratio was thirty to one, in those states' prisons the ratio was four to one. More disturbing is the rate in the South; from the late nineteenth to early twentieth centuries, in southern states blacks accounted for 75 percent of people imprisoned.

Unfortunately few of these men and women could expect to emerge reformed from their time in prison. The Quakers' theory of reform is supported by only a few documented cases, but the penal system did inspire many prisoners to write. The experience of incarceration is also found in works by writers "on the outside" because the same experiences of isolation, meditation, and reformation that enliven convicts' writing also invigorate fiction. Often the prisoner and the writer on the outside converged when professional writers were jailed or when the experience of imprisonment offered the convict an opportunity to become a published writer. Though the prisoner created by the fiction writer may appear in many guises—the kidnap victim, the imprisoned man, and the slave—writings by prisoners largely fall into one of two categories: the confessional or the protest. These forms are hardly accidental; prison writing is an autobiographical form that tends to mirror contemporary social conditions. The confessional as an expression of repentance dominated the genre early in its development, from the 1700s through the early 1800s. But with the industrialization of the young United States, and the Industrial Revolution's concomitant demand for labor, which was often filled by imprisoned men and women, by

1835 protest became the primary theme in prison writings.

THE U.S. PRISON AND ITS WRITERS

The earliest example of American prison writing dates from 1738 when the "Dying Lamentation and Advice of Philip Kennison" was published in Boston. In Kennison's confessional tone and desire for God's forgiveness this tract is typical of prisoners' writing published in the eighteenth and early nineteenth centuries. By the mid-nineteenth century, however, prison narratives began responding to a desire in the reading public for adventure and a picaresque hero. Often semiautobiographical, these novels presented heroes who superficially confessed and sought redemption but in practice reveled in their daring and wit. This style of adventure novel is well represented by the *Sketches of the Life of William Stuart, The First and Most Celebrated Counterfeiter of Connecticut, Comprising Startling Details of Daring Feats Performed by Himself—Perils by Sea and Land—Frequent Arrests and Imprisonments. . . . As Given by Himself* (1854). A later subset of prison writing, the political/protest text, overlapped with the adventure tale and gradually came to dominate the genre. Prior to the American Civil War these writings largely came from people imprisoned for abolitionist activities. However, after the Civil War social and economic changes, especially in the emancipated South, created new challenges and a new sort of political prisoner, the convict laborer.

Prisoners had, from the earliest incarnations of the penitentiary, worked at various piecework labor and gardening. The protagonist of Theodore Dreiser's (1871–1945) *The Financier* (1912), Frank Cowperwood, is promised the simple and undemanding task of chair caning when he is imprisoned. But the most pernicious among the labor practices in post–Civil War prisons was the convict lease program. Found primarily in the South, under this system men and a few women convicted of petty and serious crimes were leased to men who purchased their labor for the price of offenders' fines. Indeed, demand for leased convicts became great enough to warrant entrapment of the poor and homeless, who were arrested on charges of vagrancy and of adultery with bribed prostitutes. In an indictment of the convict lease system Charles W. Chesnutt (1858–1932) incorporates the practice of arresting unemployed black men into his novel *The Colonel's Dream* (1905). Peter, a slave who cared for the colonel when both were children, is arrested for vagrancy. In a slave-sale inspired scene, the colonel purchases Peter's labor for the rest of the man's life from the local justice of the peace. Peter benefits from the colonel's kindness, but his capture and sale clearly condemn the widespread practice. Still, in terms of cost and economic benefit, convict labor was more advantageous than chattel slavery for the purchaser because the practice enforced social hierarchies and filled an economic need, and if the laborer died the plantation owner did not lose any property; he simply leased another convict from the county to replace the lost worker. And certainly many of the leased criminals did die. In his decisive study *The Victim as Criminal,* H. Bruce Franklin cites a statistic uncovered by R. W. Dawson, president of the Board of Inspectors of Convicts for the State of Alabama. Dawson learned that in 1869 the death rate for leased black prisoners was 41 percent (p. 102). Dawson's study focused on black males because these men were the targets of the entrapment schemes and comprised by far the largest demographic in southern prisons. Mirroring the South in a fashion, by the 1870s in the North another marginalized group, new immigrants, constituted up to half of the people sent to prison (Rothman, p. 126). U.S. prisons housed an excessive number of people belonging to minorities and had replaced a mission of reform with one of supplying inexpensive labor; in its capitalistic endeavors the penal system abused prisoners no less than did the sweatshops of the same period.

PRISON REFORM AND THE REFORMERS

The organization and goals of these correctional institutions as they existed at the turn of the century reflected the changing belief systems of the late nineteenth century. The mid- to late nineteenth century in U.S. history is characterized by extremes; both laissez-faire capitalists and liberal social reformers practiced their callings. Social reformers and activists called for the abolition of slavery, for improved living and working conditions for the poor, for women's suffrage, and for the humane treatment of the insane and the convicted. Protesting for reform was not always a safe or pleasant calling, and many agitators were verbally and physically abused. Many too were jailed for their activities. Alice Paul (1885–1977), who, along with dozens of women, marched in front of the White House in 1917 for the right to vote, was arrested and imprisoned for seven months. Paul carried her protest to prison where she went on a hunger strike and was force-fed, a painful and humiliating procedure. Despite her treatment Paul maintained her commitment to women's rights, and after the ratification of the Nineteenth Amendment she worked for the passage of the Equal Rights Amendment.

Another well-known activist is Dorothea Lynde Dix (1802–1887), who advocated prison reform, though her primary work was with insane asylums and hospitals. It was in fact her work on behalf of the insane that brought her to the cause of prison reform. From 1841 through 1846, as Dix traveled throughout the United States locating people labeled insane, she discovered that many of her interviewees had been committed to local jails. Dix toured hundreds of jails, asylums, and poorhouses in states along the Mississippi River and throughout the southern United States. She was the only New England reformer to tour extensively in the South and was therefore one of the few activists to gain credibility with southerners. After gathering information from both patients and their caregivers, who were as often family members as professionals, Dix wrote "memorials," accounts of what she saw and learned, to state senates and assemblies. Dix convinced several legislatures to approve and fund asylums for the insane and also wrote to urge changes in the prison system. Despite Dix's efforts, however, the U.S. prison system continued to rely upon corporal punishment to maintain order and to house prisoners in cramped, four-by-seven-foot cells. After the Civil War, when the Reconstruction period again infused people with a spirit of reform and hope, another study of the prison system was commissioned.

Enoch Cobb Wines (1806–1879), a professional penologist, and Theodore Dwight (1822–1892), a lawyer and educator, toured penal institutions in eighteen states and Canada collecting seventy volumes of notes and documents. Their *Report on Prisons and Reformatories of the United States and Canada* (1867) noted that no institution sought reformation as its primary goal, and the report listed many failures on the part of the U.S. prison system including the physical condition of facilities, lack of trained staff, and an absence of systematic centralized supervision of the institutions. Wines and Dwight further recommended that the judiciary employ indeterminate sentencing for setting incarceration terms, a system that provided an incentive for reformation. Prisoners would not be sentenced immediately upon conviction but would learn the length of their incarceration once they had shown, or failed to show, a willingness to participate in reformative activities. The first institution to practice many of the recommendations in the Wines and Dwight report was the Elmira Reformatory, opened by Zebulon Brockway in New York in 1876. Elmira failed to fulfill its promise, however, likely because the majority of prisoners sent there were already hardened criminals, a population largely immune to Brockway's efforts. Given the conditions of their conviction and imprisonment, certainly these prisoners had stories to tell.

THE CONFESSIONAL AND THE PROTEST

Inspired, sometimes haunted, by the experience of incarceration and often with a desire to reform the conditions that put them there, many prisoners wrote. Jack London (1876–1916); O. Henry (William Sydney Porter, 1862–1910); and Julian Hawthorne (1846–1934), son of Nathaniel Hawthorne, all spent time in U.S. prisons. And though fewer in number, women also wrote of their experiences while behind bars. Agnes Smedley (1892–1950), a young journalist working with the birth-control advocate Margaret Sanger, spent six months in the Tombs, a New York City jail used primarily for detention. Other writers took up the pen only after they had experienced the U.S. prison system. Typically these writers composed autobiographical sketches that answered public demand for adventure tales. These autobiographies provided vivid details to a voyeuristic audience, but they also delved into the conditions that made the prison system necessary. Thus the genre of prison writing moved from the confessional to a form of protest and call for social justice.

The most famous of the prison-inspired writers is Jack London. His classic novel *The Call of the Wild* (1903) and the widely anthologized short story "To Build a Fire" (1908) have introduced his work to millions of high school and college students, but London was also a fiery socialist whose writing incorporated his political views. His brief incarceration in 1894 for vagrancy only solidified London's devotion to the socialist cause, and many of his works directly or covertly indict the capitalism of the early twentieth century. London describes his conversion from an unquestioning individualist to an advocate of socialism in "How I Became a Socialist," first published in *The Comrade* in March 1903. Other London texts that fall into the genre of prison writing include a series of articles published in *Cosmopolitan Magazine* between June 1907 and March 1908 entitled "My Life in the Underworld" and the novels *The Iron Heel* (1907) and *The Star Rover* (1915). And while these works unmistakably reveal his political sympathies, none of London's work is unconnected to his time spent working as a convict and his later experiences as an outspoken socialist.

O. Henry was more fortunate than London in his jailhouse employment. After fleeing charges of embezzling while employed as a bank teller, William Sydney Porter returned to Texas when he learned of his wife's illness. Upon his return, Porter was captured, tried, and found guilty. While serving his time in an Ohio penitentiary, Porter worked as the prison's druggist and completed a thirty-nine month course in short-story writing. Porter adopted the pseudonym

O. Henry while incarcerated and integrated details from his adventures as a fugitive into his narratives, writing a dozen short stories, including "Whistling Dick's Christmas Stocking," which appeared in *McClure's Magazine* in 1899, while he was still in prison. After serving three years of a five-year sentence, Porter was released. He continued to use his newly developed skill to support his daughter, Margaret, and was one of the most popular short-story writers of the early twentieth century, writing a story a week for two years for the *New York World*.

Another popular writer of the period was Julian Hawthorne. Convicted of mail fraud, Hawthorne spent almost a year in the Atlanta State Penitentiary. Days after his release, Hawthorne began drafting *The Subterranean Brotherhood* (1914), an account of his experience while incarcerated. In this report Hawthorne confesses that though he was familiar with prison writing prior to his confinement, only after he had spent time in prison did he understand prison life and its effect upon a person. In this narrative Hawthorne concludes that imprisonment for crime does not lead to reform, serves only to enslave the inmates, and must be abolished.

Like Julian Hawthorne, Agnes Smedley was a professional writer prior to her period of incarceration. After a brief marriage that ended in divorce, Smedley was working as a journalist in New York City when she became involved in Margaret Sanger's work in birth control and socialist politics. She was arrested in March 1918 and held for six months on the charges of violating anti–birth control laws and the Federal Espionage Act. The details of her time in the Tombs of New York City appear directly in "Cell Mates" (descriptions of Smedley's fellow inmates), which appeared in the *New York Call,* and less directly in the autobiographical novel *Daughter of Earth* (1929). Smedley's "Cell Mates" provides rare descriptions simply because these descriptions come from a woman, but they are also well written, sympathetic portrayals of the hardened, diseased women who cannot tell their own stories.

Like all trauma, imprisonment compels the person at the center of the experience to verbalize his or her trauma. This telling also satisfies a need in the listener, likely a mingling of voyeuristic and empathetic impulses. Occasionally this need to tell is recorded and can therefore satisfy a need both in readers contemporaneous with the writer and in readers of later generations. Prison writing from the turn of the twentieth century records the experiences of people who struggled to survive prior to social safety nets such as Social Security. But these men and women also inhabited a country in the throes of impending modernity, and science and humanitarian goals guided many reformers as they sought to ameliorate the worst excesses of industrialization and individualism. Recording their experiences permitted reformers such as Dorothea Dix and Jack London to report on and occasionally convince affluent people that the U.S. prison system did not reform and often needlessly punished people committed to penitentiaries. But these reports did not often find a wide audience. The fictionalized accounts of U.S. incarceration history have fared better and are still anthologized and read.

See also Capital Punishment; Jurisprudence; Reform

BIBLIOGRAPHY
Primary Works
Dreiser, Theodore. *The Financier.* New York: Harper & Brothers, 1912.

Dwight, Theodore, and Enoch Cobb Wines. *Report on Prisons and Reformatories of the United States and Canada.* Albany, N.Y.: Van Benthuysen and Sons, 1867.

Secondary Works
Abramowitz, Isidore, ed. *Great Prisoners: The First Anthology of Literature Written in Prison.* Freeport, N.Y.: Books for Libraries, 1946.

Brown, Thomas J. *Dorothea Dix: New England Reformer.* Cambridge, Mass.: Harvard University Press, 1998.

Davis, David Brion. *Homicide in American Fiction, 1798–1860: A Study in Social Values.* Ithaca, N.Y.: Cornell University Press, 1957.

Franklin, H. Bruce. *Prison Writing in Twentieth-Century America.* New York: Penguin, 1998.

Franklin, H. Bruce. *The Victim as Criminal and Artist: Literature from the American Prison.* New York: Oxford University Press, 1978.

Lightner, David L., ed. *Asylum, Prison, and Poorhouse: The Writings and Reform Work of Dorothea Dix in Illinois.* Carbondale and Edwardsville: Southern Illinois University Press, 1999.

Morris, Norval, and David J. Rothman, eds. *The Oxford History of the Prison: The Practice of Punishment in Western Society.* New York: Oxford University Press, 1995.

New York Correction History Society. Available at http://www.correctionhistory.org/index.html.

"Paul, Alice." In *The Reader's Companion to Literature.* Houghton Mifflin. Available at http://college.hmco.com/history/readerscomp/rcah/html/ah_067600_paulalice.htm.

"Prisons and Executions—The U.S. Model: A Historical Introduction." *Monthly Review* 53, no. 3 (July–August 2001). Available at http://www.monthlyreview.org/0701editr.htm.

Rothman, David J. "Perfecting the Prison." In *The Oxford History of the Prison: The Practice of Punishment in Western Society,* edited by Norval Morris and David J. Rothman, pp. 111–129. New York: Oxford University Press, 1995.

Scheffler, Judith, ed. *Wall Tappings: An International Anthology of Women's Prison Writings, 200 to the Present.* 2nd ed. New York: Feminist Press at City University of New York, 2002.

Mary P. Anderson

PERIODICALS

Sometime in the 1880s a visionary entrepreneur, flush from a successful venture in syndicating literature to newspapers, decides to found a new magazine in New York, one that he thinks will be the greatest thing since the "creation of man." Securing the financial backing of a newly wealthy natural gas baron, he approaches an acquaintance, a Boston insurance man with a literary bent whom he met on a Great Lakes cruise, to become the editor. Despite reservations, the insurance man agrees to the offer, moves to New York City, and *Every Other Week* is launched. With its founder's commercial sense and knack for publicity and the editor's "taste," the new venture succeeds, although not without a cool reception from the New York literary world and a share of internal struggles.

Every Other Week is fictional—the backbone of William Dean Howells's novel *A Hazard of New Fortunes* (1889), one of the few literary works of the post–Civil War period to deal at all with what was perhaps one of its most salient cultural features: the exponential growth of magazine publishing. Between the end of the war and the turn of the twentieth century, according to Frank Luther Mott's estimates, the number of magazines grew from some seven hundred to over five thousand; between 1885 and 1905, Mott estimates, some seventy-five hundred magazines were founded, and about half that number failed or merged. Not only were more magazines being published, they were reaching more readers. In 1900 aggregate circulation of all magazines, according to Theodore Peterson, was 65 million; Richard Altick estimates that in 1905 there were at least 20 magazines with circulations over 100,000 selling an aggregate 5.5 million copies, a 900 percent increase over 1885. Earlier in the period, in the 1870s, according to an estimate by Kenneth Price and Susan Belasco

Smith, the aggregate circulation of cheap weekly story papers was over ten million, at a time when the population of the country was about thirty million. These periodicals spanned a range of tastes and styles, from the high-toned *Atlantic Monthly* to the raffish *Police Gazette*, from the uplifting *Century Magazine* to the self-styled "magazine of cleverness," the *Smart Set*. After 1900 new periodicals came and old ones faded, and circulation figures for the industry leaders continued to rise. In 1903 the *Ladies' Home Journal* became the first magazine to reach over a million in circulation; by 1912 its companion publication, the *Saturday Evening Post*, reached two million weekly. John Drewry, writing in 1924 of the magazine scene of the last half of the nineteenth century and the early decades of the twentieth, claimed that magazines were the single most important institution in the America of that era. While this is perhaps hyperbolic, it nonetheless captures the important role that magazines played in the cultural and intellectual life of the age.

THE POST–CIVIL WAR PERIOD
Following the Civil War, the expansiveness of the nation was accompanied by an equal expansiveness in periodical production, spurred by a combination of improved transportation, improved printing technology, cheaper postal rates, and the rise of national advertising. The boom, of course, was not immediate, and these factors were not all present at once (the typewriter was introduced in 1865 and the linotype machine in 1885; the transcontinental railroad was completed in 1869; cheap postal rates date from 1879). But by the early 1890s the modern magazine had taken form, becoming, as Richard Ohmann has argued, the first instance of a truly mass culture.

The period 1870 to 1920 can be divided roughly into several phases as far as magazines are concerned. In his monumental history of American magazines, Mott discusses the late-nineteenth-century periodicals in two volumes (volume 3, *1865–1885;* volume 4, *1885–1905*). While 1865 and the end of the War between the States is a conventionally convenient date for periodization, the twenty-year intervals seem overly schematic and arbitrary; it is not clear what criteria Mott used for the division at 1885 or the terminus of 1905. The year 1893, when several leading monthlies cut their prices and experienced substantial growth in circulation, seems a more significant date in the history of magazines, although, as Ohmann and Matthew Schneirov have each argued, the seeds for the transformation of the American magazine were already in place by that date. A decade later, when *Ladies' Home Journal* (founded in 1885) reached a million in circulation and *McClure's Magazine* published

in the same issue of January 1903 the early installments of Ida Tarbell's *History of the Standard Oil Company*, Lincoln Steffens's *Shame of the Cities*, and Ray Stannard Baker's *The Right to Work* (all published in book form in 1904), the new inexpensive monthlies (and weeklies like *Collier's* and *Saturday Evening Post*) reached maturity and another milestone. The muckraking phase inaugurated by *McClure's* lasted until around 1910, when most of the major magazines cut back or abandoned crusading articles in favor of lighter fiction and less-consequential articles. The next decade saw little in the way of significant innovation in the field as a whole, although newer periodicals like *Smart Set* (founded 1900), *Vanity Fair* (1914), the *New Republic* (1914), and the reconstituted *Dial* (founded in 1880; reorganized in 1918) made their mark on the literary culture of the age, while what were by now old warhorses (*Collier's, Saturday Evening Post, Century, Cosmopolitan*) continued to flourish in varying degrees.

TYPES OF PERIODICALS
Many types of journals were produced in this period and aimed at different audiences, although categorization into more definitive groups is often difficult. At one end of the spectrum (and excluding trade and professional journals) were cheaply priced weekly and monthly papers emphasizing popular fictional genres. Often produced in newspaper format on cheap stock, these papers were, as Mott comments, "sub-literary" (3:42). Many were, nonetheless, successful, especially those that came to be known as mail-order magazines because of their extensive advertisements for products available by mail order. *People's Literary Companion*, the original mail-order monthly, founded in 1869 by a manufacturer of washing soap and produced in Augusta, Maine, reached a circulation of half a million in a relatively brief time. In the wake of its success, Augusta became the mail-order magazine capital. The major cities also had their weeklies, which often appeared in time for weekend reading. The *Saturday Evening Post*, before Cyrus Curtis purchased it in the 1890s, was a Philadelphia story paper that had had several incarnations since the early nineteenth century (its owners suggested a longer continuity back to Ben Franklin). The Beadles of dime-novel fame produced several periodicals of this type. Frank Munsey and Frank Leslie, who both went on to found significant publications in the 1880s and 1890s, started with story papers. The cheap periodical class had several subgenres: papers directed at women (the early *Woman's Home Companion*), at young boys (*Boy's New York*), and at working men. The latter, which included the *Police Gazette* and a host of imitators,

Magazine covers. A sample of the thousands of magazines in circulation in 1900. © BETTMANN/CORBIS

were often vilified as "veritable Bibles of damnation" (Mott 3:43) for their combination of salaciousness and sensation. Sharing some aspects of the cheap weeklies, but aimed at a more middle-class audience, were the weekly humor papers (*Life, Puck, Judge*), which combined light verse, facetious anecdotes, cartoons, and satire in a gentle mocking of contemporary morals and values.

At the other end of the spectrum were the "quality" monthlies associated with the major book publishers, often referred to by historians as the "genteel magazines." Continuing a trend already apparent in the antebellum period, the book publishers Lippincott, Scribners, and Putnam, among others, produced eponymous house journals, joining Harper & Brothers. The *Atlantic,* although launched as an independent periodical, became associated first with Ticknor and Fields and then with Henry Houghton's various enterprises. These house magazines often featured the work of

authors associated with the specific publishing firm, but they were open to other contributors. To various degrees, they filled their pages with a variety of material including reprints of English authors (a specialty of *Harper's New Monthly Magazine,* particularly before the adoption of international copyright), short stories and serial novels, articles on travel, general literary comment, accounts of scientific developments, and some attention to social issues. Their circulation remained somewhat modest in comparison to that of *Harper's,* which, as Ellery Sedgwick notes in his history of the *Atlantic,* was more popular in appeal and more lavishly illustrated than the other quality magazines. One of the more successful examples of the house-type of periodical was *Scribner's Monthly*—but only when it broke away from the publishing house and was renamed the *Century Illustrated Monthly* (under the Century Company, which also became a book publisher). Some magazines of this type were independent of major publishing houses, but they often were not long lived because they may have lacked the financial backing of the established publishers. The *Galaxy* (1866–1878), founded as a New York alternative to the *Atlantic,* is notable for its criticism and fiction by Henry James and a regular humor column by Mark Twain.

In between the cheap papers and the quality house magazines are the general interest periodicals that began in the late 1880s and burgeoned in the 1890s and the early decades of the twentieth century. Although it might be simplifying the genesis of this type of magazine, they could be described as combining elements of the popular and quality periodicals in a style and formula that appealed to a middle-class audience. Several of the more successful founders of these periodicals—Frank Leslie, Frank Munsey, S. S. McClure, Cyrus H. K. Curtis—began their careers working for or starting up inexpensive papers; others were entrepreneurs, like the department store founder John Wanamaker (*Everybody's*) or the publishing giant William Randolph Hearst. Despite their antecedents, many of these entrepreneurial types saw the quality magazines as their model, even as they tailored their contents to a less elite audience. The formula they created positioned their magazines to become the first medium for national advertising.

Another type of magazine, although for the most part not as widely circulated as the popular middle-class general interest weeklies and monthlies, was nonetheless important in the intellectual climate of the period: the current affairs review. *The Nation*, a weekly founded four months after the end of the Civil War and edited by E. L. Godkin, is the leading example of this type, joined by the end of the century by the *Review of Reviews* (1890), the *Outlook* (founded as the *Christian Union* in 1869 by Henry Ward Beecher; title and orientation changed in 1893) and the *Literary Digest* (which despite its name was not a literary magazine but a digest of news and opinion published by Funk and Wagnalls and one of the most successful weeklies until the publication of *Time* in the 1920s). Early in the twentieth century new reviews included *World's Work* (1900) and *New Republic* (1914).

Another class of periodicals with limited distribution, the "little" magazines, were influential on literary developments beyond their circulations. Descendants of coterie and movement periodicals like the transcendentalist *Dial* and founded in reaction perhaps to the commercialization of literature in the major magazines, these journals, many often produced on a shoestring and erratically distributed, were the major outlets for avant-garde writers. Margaret Anderson's

Little Review (1914–1929) and Harriet Monroe's *Poetry: A Magazine of Verse* (founded in 1912 and still publishing in the twenty-first century) are only two examples of the scores if not hundreds of such journals that came on the scene. The London-based *Blast,* which published only two issues between 1914 and 1915, was significant in publishing the work of Ezra Pound and T. S. Eliot; Pound also contributed to and acted as European agent for both the *Little Review* and *Poetry*. Somewhere between the commercial magazines and the "littles" were such publications as the *Smart Set,* especially after 1914, when H. L. Mencken and George Jean Nathan became coeditors, and *The Dial,* especially under the editorial aegis of Scofield Thayer after 1918; they were founded as commercial enterprises but had limited circulations. *Smart Set* was for most of its run cheaply produced with no illustrations or artwork, yet it published a number of new writers (including Eugene O'Neill and F. Scott Fitzgerald) and established itself as a trendsetter in the literary culture of the time (although much of its content was pedestrian). More elegantly produced than *Smart Set, The Dial* became a significant voice in the modernist movement.

INSIDE THE EDITORIAL OFFICE

The editorial domain, at least in the early years of the period, was often leisurely despite the pressures of editorial activity. Basil March, Howells's semiautobiographical hero in *A Hazard of New Fortunes,* feels that *Every Other Week* virtually puts itself together, and he seems to have plenty of time to wander the New York streets absorbing material for a series of sketches on city life and to attend social functions. Magazine staffs were generally small in the early years of the period and at the "genteel" magazines very club-like. L. Frank Tooker, a longtime editor at *Century,* recalled the atmosphere of the magazine in 1870s and 1880s as "restful and homelike" (p. 89); its editor, Richard Watson Gilder, was famous for his Friday nights at home, where he entertained artists, writers, and political figures. As magazines became more commercially driven, the atmosphere changed; as circulations increased, staff expanded, and editors became more aggressive in shaping their products with an eye to sales, as Christopher Wilson has argued.

Willa Cather depicts such a change in her short story "Ardessa," published in the *Century* in 1918. Based on Cather's experience working on *McClure's,* the story depicts the offices of the *Outcry,* a "red-hot magazine of protest" (p. 105) that was once a genteel journal until the arrival of its new owner, Marcus O'Mally (based on Cather's boss, S. S. McClure). O'Mally is a self-made millionaire and a restless sort who "went in for everything and got tired of everything; that was why he made a good editor" (p. 107). O'Mally's secretary, Ardessa Devine, is a holdover from the days of the magazine's former editor, "a conservative scholarly gentleman of the old school" (p. 107). Ardessa keeps "banker's hours" (p. 105), sitting in her office, "cool and cloistered, daintily plying her needle" (p. 107); she treats would-be authors who frequent the reception rooms with deference and dignity despite O'Mally's wish that they be dismissed. She is also a master at passing her real work off to the lower echelons of typists, whom she treats with condescension. Eventually, O'Mally succeeds in displacing Ardessa in favor of a more skilled young woman (the daughter of Jewish immigrants), symbolizing the passing of the old order.

Some magazines developed a madcap house culture—as was the case with Mencken and Nathan's *Smart Set* and the humor weeklies. Mencken and Nathan even found time to create other periodicals and to contribute to the daily press while they edited *Smart Set*. While most editors and publishers were largely invisible to their audiences (especially earlier in the period when anonymity was a dominant feature of most magazines), some of the more successful popular magazine founders—for example, Frank Brisbane Walker (the founder of *Cosmopolitan*) and S. S. McClure—saw themselves as agents of national uplift and improvement and floated plans for, among other things, a correspondence university, a bank, an insurance company, and an ideal settlement with cheap homes for the masses. Walter Hines Page, the editor of the *Atlantic* (from 1898 to 1899) and founder of *World's Work*, ended his career as Woodrow Wilson's ambassador to Great Britain.

The world of late-nineteenth-century and early-twentieth-century magazines was predominantly a white male preserve, but women made some limited inroads into the editorial precincts in roles other than secretary. Sarah J. Hale, longtime editor of *Godey's Lady's Book*, was a pioneer in the field; Louisa Knapp Curtis was the first editor of *Ladies' Home Journal* (under her maiden name), and Mary Mapes Dodge was the longtime editor of the successful children's publication *St. Nicholas*. Many women writers found the magazines, and not just those aimed at women, open to their fiction and poetry. African Americans found themselves less welcome in the mainstream magazines. Charles Chesnutt, George Washington Cable, Paul Laurence Dunbar, and Booker T. Washington were published, but most magazines were as segregated as the society at large. When African Americans appeared in the magazines, it was most often as characters in dialect stories written by white writers. A small number of African American publications struggled for an audience—many, according to John Tebbell, supported by Booker T. Washington as vehicles for spreading his accommodationist philosophy.

THE AUTHOR'S GRIND

While life for the editors might have been leisurely and genteel or madcap, many authors scraped a precarious living together writing for the magazines. Pay rates were often modest—or nonexistent—although some authors made out very well. After his success on the San Francisco–based *Overland Monthly*, Bret Harte received the princely sum of $10,000 in 1870–1871 for a series of contributions to the *Atlantic*, at a time when, as Richard Grant White wrote, "a man who undertakes to live by occasional contributions to weekly or daily papers, for which he receives five to fifteen dollars, or to the magazines, for which he gets five dollars a page . . . will soon find himself a fit subject for the poor-house" (Mott 3:14–15).

At the turn of the twentieth century, things had not improved much for many would-be writers. Martin Eden, the title character of a 1909 novel by Jack London, based partially on London's own experiences as a young man, imagines that he can earn $1,000 a month by his contributions to all sorts of periodicals, but he is shocked to find that many journals pay considerably less than the rates he has seen mentioned in newspapers and some do not pay at all. Nonetheless, a phalanx of professional "magazinists" and occasional contributors developed, estimated to number around twenty thousand at the turn of the century. In addition to the forgotten names like Octave Thanet, H. H. Boyesen, John Kendrick Bangs, Frank Stockton, and Sarah N. Cleghorn—just to mention several who appeared regularly in many different magazines—the professional magazinists included Henry James, Mark Twain, William Dean Howells, Edith Wharton, Stephen Crane, Hamlin Garland, Jack London, and Willa Cather. The *Saturday Evening Post* under its longtime editor George Horace Lorimer developed a stellar reputation for paying on acceptance. Mencken and Nathan did the same on the *Smart Set* but less generously than Lorimer. Mencken and Nathan, although shareholders in *Smart Set*, were paid modest salaries for their editorial work and received the same rates as other authors for their monthly columns of criticism. They made out well financially, however, by starting several salacious and sensational story magazines (*Parisienne* and *Black Mask*) and selling their interests back to *Smart Set*'s owner.

One form of publication was lucrative for some authors: the serial novel. Most of the major commercial-quality and popular magazines, as well as the cheap story papers, ran serials, often several at the

A STRUGGLING AUTHOR RECEIVES AN ACCEPTANCE AND IS DISAPPOINTED, C. 1900

After a period of working as a seaman and as a gold prospector, Jack London's hero Martin Eden returns to California and falls in with a cultured and literary set. Impelled by his desire for Ruth Morse, a wealthy young society woman, Martin pursues a career as a writer. Working sixteen-hour days, he turns out a stream of essays, stories, and serials in his garret room on a rented typewriter. Having read of handsome sums being paid to successful writers for their work, Martin exhausts his credit and pawns his belongings as he waits for his efforts to sell.

It was at this time, at the lowest ebb, that . . . the postman brought him one morning a short, thin envelope. Martin glanced at the upper left-hand corner and read the name and address of the *Transcontinental Monthly*. His heart gave a great leap, and he suddenly felt faint, the sinking feeling accompanied by a strange trembling of the knees. . . .

Of course this was good news. There was no manuscript in that thin envelope, therefore it was an acceptance. . . . And, since first-class magazines always paid on acceptance, there was a check inside. Two cents a word—twenty dollars a thousand; the check must be a hundred dollars. One hundred dollars! As he tore the envelope open, every item of all his debts surged in his brain—$3.85 to the grocer; butcher, $4.00 flat; baker, $2.00; fruit store, $5.00; total $14.85. Then there was room rent, $2.50; another month in advance, $2.50; two months' type-writer, $8.00; a month in advance, $4.00; total, $31.85 And finally to be added, his pledges, plus interest, with the pawnbroker—watch, $5.50; overcoat, $5.50; wheel, $7.75; suit of clothes, $5.50 (60% interest, but what did it matter?)—grand total, $56.10. He saw, as if visible in the air before him, in illuminated figures, the whole sum, and the subtraction that followed and that gave a remainder of $43.90. . . .

By this time he had drawn the single sheet of type-written letter out and spread it open. There was no check. . . . He read the letter, skimming it line by line, dashing through the editor's praise of his story to the meat of the letter, the statement why the check had not been sent. He found no such statement, but he did find that which made him suddenly wilt. . . .

Five dollars . . . for five thousand words! Instead of two cents a word, ten words for a cent! And the editor had praised it, too. And he would receive the check when the story was published. Then it was all poppycock, two cents a word for minimum rate and payment upon acceptance. It was a lie, and it had led him astray. He would never have attempted to write had he known that. He would have gone to work—to work for Ruth. He went back to the day he first attempted to write, and was appalled at the enormous waste of time—and all for ten words for a cent. . . .

The *Transcontinental* . . . was a staid, respectable magazine, and it had been published continuously since long before he was born. Why, on the outside cover were printed every month the words of one of the world's great writers, . . . words proclaiming the inspired mission of the *Transcontinental* by a star of literature whose first coruscations had appeared inside those self-same covers. The great writer had recently died in a foreign land—in dire poverty, Martin remembered, which was not to be wondered at, considering the magnificent pay authors receive. . . . The disappointment of it, the lie of it, the infamy of it, were uppermost in his thoughts; and under his closed eyelids, in fiery figures, burned the "$3.85" he owed the grocer.

London, *Martin Eden*, pp. 262–265.

same time. As Michael Lund has argued, serialization was the key to survival for a number of authors, including Henry James. In the 1870s and 1880s most of James's major novels appeared in serial form in the magazines, as did Howells's and later Edith Wharton's and Willa Cather's. The 1885 *Century* ran serial versions of James's *The Bostonians* and Howells's *The Rise of Silas Lapham* at the same time it was also publishing excerpts from Twain's *Adventures of Huckleberry Finn* and its famous series of accounts of Civil War battles. In the same year James's *Princess Casamassima* ran in the *Atlantic*, while Howells's *Indian Summer* began its serialization in *Harper's*. Later in the period and into the 1920s, the quality of the serial fiction did not often reach these Olympian heights, but there were still major works to be found among the romantic, sentimental, and gimmick-laden genre contributions of a host of now-forgotten authors.

REPRESENTATIVE CONTENTS

Looking over the first issue of *Every Other Week*, Howells's editor hero is pleased with the result.

> There had to be, of course, a story, and then a sketch of travel. There was a literary essay and a social essay; there was a dramatic trifle, very gay, very light; there was a dashing criticism on the new pictures, the new plays, the new books, the new fashions; and then there was the translation of a bit of vivid Russian realism [Dostoyevsky, supplied by March's socialist mentor, Lindau]. . . . The poem was a bit of society verse with a backward look into simpler and wholesomer experiences. (Pt. 2, chap. 13, 1:260)

Fulkerson, the magazine's entrepreneurial founder (who bears some resemblance to McClure in his being a successful syndicator), finds the contents "too good" (1:260) and implores March that "it should never happen again" (1:261) if the magazine were to succeed. (Life does imitate art: Christopher Wilson tells the story of how Lorimer, upon being told that the *Saturday Evening Post* was attracting "thoughtful" readers, quipped that he would try to "correct the error" [p. 42].) With his long experience as editor of the *Atlantic* (and later his associations with *Century*, *Cosmopolitan*, and *Harper's*), Howells certainly understood the nature of the magazines of the time, and in this portrait he captures the miscellany and range of their contents and their often rarified air, which had recognizable similarities among the various quality journals setting the pattern for the more popular monthlies like *Munsey's*, *Cosmopolitan*, and *McClure's*.

In *Selling Culture*, Richard Ohmann describes the experience of a hypothetically reconstructed Cleveland middle-class family reading an issue of *Munsey's* magazine in 1895. *Munsey's* (founded as a weekly in 1889, changed to a monthly in 1891) was not as high-toned as the fictional *Every Other Week* or the real *Century;* its founder was also the founder and editor of *Golden Argosy*, a periodical aimed at young boys and specializing in Horatio Alger–type fare. *Munsey's* provided, as Frank Luther Mott put it, illustrations that put "no little emphasis on the female form divine in the semi-nude" (4:611) alongside features on leading celebrities (Ohmann compares it to the modern-day *People* magazine), culture, and sports; genre serials and stand-alone stories; and some informative articles on national and world affairs. It published fewer of the leading writers of the day than the other popular magazines, however. Frank Brisbane Walker's *Cosmopolitan* (founded in 1886, purchased by Hearst in 1905), the first of the popular monthlies of the last two decades of the century to emphasize articles of a more timely nature than the genteel periodicals, featured travel articles, art reproductions, biographies of leading business executives, "the progress of science," and the Chicago World's Fair of 1893 (a popular topic in the other magazines of the time) as well as fiction by British and American authors; Edith Wharton and Jack London contributed to its pages, as did Mark Twain.

The January 1903 issue of *McClure's* began a trend toward even more topical articles and investigative reports that eventually gained the name of "muckraking," initially as a pejorative characterization by President Theodore Roosevelt and then a term of praise. *McClure's* was joined by *Munsey's* and *Collier's* in uncovering social evils and later by *Cosmopolitan* (after Hearst acquired it), *Everybody's*, and the *American Magazine*, which was purchased in 1906 by disaffected members of *McClure's* staff (Tarbell, Baker, and Steffens). Stephen Crane and Hamlin Garland, among others, joined the journalists in contributing articles that focused upon poor working conditions and other social ills calling out for reform. The fiction of Jack London and Upton Sinclair struck similar notes. As Cather's narrator comments in "Ardessa," this kind of reporting was born "in that good time when people were eager to read about their own wickedness" (p. 106). That this trend remained strong for nearly a decade seems a remarkable accomplishment in the world of popular publishing; that it ended almost abruptly after 1910 led some at the time to suspect a conspiracy of the business interests to suppress reform. While the mainstream journals published fewer such crusading pieces into the second decade of the twentieth century, magazines like the *Masses* and some of the opinion magazines like the *New Republic* and *The Nation* continued these reform efforts.

By the time of America's entry into World War I, many of the industry leaders, like the *Saturday Evening Post, Cosmopolitan,* and *Literary Digest*—their covers and pages lavishly illustrated with photographs and illustrations by leading graphic artists like Norman Rockwell, Charles Dana Gibson, James Montgomery Flagg, and Maxfield Parrish—were fat with advertising and would remain so for many years despite (or perhaps because of) their complacent and conventional contents. A new generation of periodicals like *Vanity Fair* (under the editorship of Frank Crowninshield), however, were beginning to respond to new cultural trends, joined a few years later by some upstarts (*Readers' Digest, American Mercury, Time, True Confessions, The New Yorker*) that would define the spectrum of a new postwar world.

See also Appeal to Reason; The Atlantic Monthly,; Century Magazine; Editors; *Harper's New Monthly Magazine;* Literary Marketplace; Little Magazines and Small Presses; *McClure's Magazine;* Muckrakers and Yellow Journalism; *Overland Monthly; Poetry: A Magazine of Verse; Scribner's Magazine;* Short Story

BIBLIOGRAPHY
Primary Works
Cather, Willa. "Ardessa." *Century* 96, no. 1 (1918): 105–116.

Drewry, John. *Some Magazines and Magazine Makers.* Boston: Stratford, 1924.

Howells, William Dean. *A Hazard of New Fortunes.* New York: Harper & Brothers, 1889.

London, Jack. *Martin Eden.* 1909. New York and London: Penguin, 1984.

Tooker, L. Frank. *The Joys and Tribulations of an Editor.* New York and London: Century Company, 1924.

Secondary Works
Altick, Richard D. *Writers, Readers, and Occasions.* Columbus: Ohio State University Press, 1989.

Cohn, Jan. *Creating America: George Horace Lorimer and the "Saturday Evening Post."* Pittsburgh: University of Pittsburgh Press, 1989.

Damon-Moore, Helen. *Magazines for the Millions: Gender and Commerce in the "Ladies' Home Journal" and the "Saturday Evening Post, 1880–1910."* Albany: State University of New York Press, 1994.

Douglas, George H. *The Smart Magazines: Fifty Years of Literary Revelry and High Jinks at "Vanity Fair," "The New Yorker," "Life," "Esquire," and the "Smart Set."* Hamden, Conn.: Archon, 1991.

Hoffman, Frederick J., Charles Allen, and Carolyn Ulrich. *The Little Magazine: A History and a Bibliography.* Princeton, N.J.: Princeton University Press, 1947.

Johanningsmeier, Charles. *Fiction and the American Literary Marketplace: The Role of Newspaper Syndicates, 1860–1900.* Cambridge, U.K.: Cambridge University Press, 1997.

John, Arthur. *The Best Years of the Century: Richard Watson Gilder, "Scribner's Monthly," and the "Century Magazine" 1870–1909.* Urbana: University of Illinois Press, 1981.

Lund, Michael. *America's Continuing Story: An Introduction to Serial Fiction, 1850–1900.* Detroit: Wayne State University Press, 1993.

Mott, Frank Luther. *A History of American Magazines.* 5 vols. Cambridge, Mass.: Harvard University Press, 1930–1968.

Ohmann, Richard. *Selling Culture: Magazines, Markets, and Class at the Turn of the Century.* London: Verso, 1996.

Peterson, Theodore. *Magazines in the Twentieth Century.* 2nd ed. Urbana: University of Illinois Press, 1964.

Price, Kenneth M., and Susan Belasco Smith, eds. *Periodical Literature in Nineteenth-Century America.* Charlottesville: University Press of Virginia, 1995.

Reed, David. *The Popular Magazine in Britain and the United States 1880–1960.* Toronto: University of Toronto Press, 1997.

Schneirov, Matthew. *The Dream of a New Social Order: Popular Magazines in America, 1893–1914.* New York: Columbia University Press, 1994.

Sedgwick, Ellery. *The "Atlantic Monthly" 1857–1909: Yankee Humanism at High Tide and Ebb.* Amherst: University of Massachusetts Press, 1994.

Tebbel, John, and Mary Ellen Zuckerman. *The Magazine in America, 1741–1990.* New York: Oxford University Press, 1991.

Wilson, Christopher P. *The Labor of Words: Literary Professionalism in the Progressive Era.* Athens: University of Georgia Press, 1985.

Wilson, Harold. *"McClure's Magazine" and the Muckrakers.* Princeton, N.J.: Princeton University Press, 1970.

Martin Green

PERSONAL MEMOIRS OF U. S. GRANT

It is both fitting and surprising that Ulysses S. Grant (1822–1885) wrote a Civil War memoir. By the end of the war, Grant was the highest-ranking general of the victorious Union army; and he rode his immense popularity to two terms as president of the United States (1868–1876). In America during the late nineteenth century, many celebrated figures wrote autobiographies, and many Civil War heroes less prominent than Grant published memoirs to great acclaim. Yet for all his fame, Grant was a private man not given to literary pursuits. More known for his reticence than for his eloquence, he was often depicted as a cigar-chewing stoic rather than a leader who expressed himself publicly. What caused Grant to become not simply a memoirist but one of the most successful memoirists of his day? As with so many of his achievements, necessity and circumstance figured heavily.

THE CONTEXT
After stepping down as president, traveling the world, and seemingly settling toward retirement, Grant fell victim to bad investments run by his son and a fraudulent business partner. Suddenly bankrupt, the

Ulysses S. Grant. The ailing former president writes his memoirs on the porch of his home in Mount McGregor, New York, 27 June 1885. He died of throat cancer less than one month later. © BETTMANN/CORBIS

sixty-two-year-old Grant was also diagnosed with fatal throat cancer, leaving him little time to clear his debts and return his family to financial security. For years Grant had declined to write his memoirs despite interest from publishers and the public; but as his health declined, he took up the task, initially writing four articles for the *Century* magazine series, *Battles and Leaders of the Civil War*, and later agreeing to write a book that became *Personal Memoirs of U. S. Grant* (1885). Working feverishly from his home in Mount McGregor, New York, Grant found support on a number of fronts. His friend Mark Twain (1835–1910) published

the book and offered him a favorable book contract; his sons served as research assistants; stenographers took down his dictation until speaking became too painful; and cocaine (used medicinally at the time) brought temporary energy and relief. Grant spent less than a year composing his lengthy memoirs; and with the public tracking his decline, he died just a few weeks after completing the manuscript. Indeed, as Elizabeth Samet has emphasized, the strain of finishing the project may have hastened Grant's demise, for he called the work of writing his life "adding to my book and to my coffin" (Samet, p. 1117).

As with many of his Civil War battles, Grant's sacrifice was a hard-won success. In economic terms, the book was a triumph, selling 300,000 copies in the first two years and earning $450,000, more than enough to cover Grant's debts and guarantee his family's well-being. Yet *Personal Memoirs of U. S. Grant* did much more than secure Grant's financial legacy. Twain, Gertrude Stein, and a grudging Matthew Arnold appreciated the literary qualities of the book. As opposed to his presidential farewell address, which tried to explain in apologetic tones the scandals that plagued his administration, Grant's memoirs focus on the war experiences that made him a hero of American history. In doing so, Grant participated in a broader cultural effort to heal (or perhaps more accurately to repress) sectional differences that, as David Blight shows, survived beyond the Civil War. *Personal Memoirs* is critical of slavery, secession, and romantic Southern accounts of the war, but it also makes a strong case for national unity, calling for forgiveness and either de-emphasizing or vindicating some of the most divisive aspects of the war. As Nina Silber has argued, post–Civil War literature advanced the cause of sectional reconciliation. No less than novels, poems, and speeches—or for that matter memorials, paintings, and pageants—*Personal Memoirs of U. S. Grant* tells a story of recovered nationalism.

THE TEXT

Grant's style is plain, his background modest, his stories often self-deprecating, and he largely focuses on what he knows best: the details and decisions of the Civil War battles in which he participated. Yet as much as Grant presents himself as a soldier struggling with the exigencies of his time, the ambitious claims of *Personal Memoirs* should not go unnoticed. By tracing his family history from the great Puritan migration of 1630 to Bunker Hill and through a series of westward movements, Grant offers himself as a representative man rooted in a (Yankee) narrative of U.S. history and bolstered by the fact that Grant and his family were artisans, farmers, and above all "American" (p. 5). Even the opening line of the book—"Man proposes and God disposes"—suggests a humble but deepseated confidence, for while Grant acknowledges the power of God he also implies that his personal success is part of God's design (p. 3). Grant's opening line also indicates another element of *Personal Memoirs.* Though Grant's prose is forthright and simple and though he remarks on his indifferent educational achievements, he also addresses profound topics—from the nature of humans to the principles of justice, to questions of perception and agency. In the tradition of Benjamin Franklin, Frederick Douglass, and

---

ULYSSES S. GRANT ON THE SURRENDER OF LEE

What General Lee's feelings were I do not know. As he was a man of much dignity, with an impassable face, it was impossible to say whether he felt inwardly glad that the end had finally come, or felt sad over the result. . . . I felt like anything rather than rejoicing at the downfall of a foe who had fought so long and valiantly, and had suffered so much for a cause, though that cause was, I believe, one of the worst for which a people ever fought, and one for which there was the least excuse. I do not question, however, the sincerity of the great mass of those who were opposed to us.

Grant, *Personal Memoirs of U. S. Grant,* pp. 601–603.

Abraham Lincoln, Grant presents himself as a self-made man who learns mainly by experience and rises to both wisdom and prominence through a combination of character, labor, and luck.

One formative experience is particularly revealing. As a child, Grant wanted to buy a horse, and so his father gave him money and bargaining instructions. But when Grant went to the owner of the horse, he said, "Papa says I may offer you twenty dollars for the colt, but if you won't take that, I am to offer twenty-two and a half, and if you won't take that, to give you twenty-five" (p. 13). Grant relates other humorous anecdotes (causing some readers to suspect Twain's influence). For Grant, however, the story of his horse trading was not simply funny, for it circulated through his boyhood home of Georgetown, Ohio, embarrassing the young man who would come to face more pressing negotiations. Grant's first major victory at Fort Donelson was marred by complaints that his terms of surrender were too lenient; and so in his subsequent capture of Vicksburg, Grant initially offered only "unconditional surrender," offending his opponent and Mexican-American War acquaintance J. C. Pemberton (p. 307). Grant's staff eventually convinced him to offer lighter terms, but in *Personal Memoirs* the challenge is clear: Grant must find a way to defend the interests of the Union without humiliating an enemy that must eventually be reintegrated into the nation.

For Grant and the newly reunited states of America, the problem of reconciliation remained in 1885; for

ULYSSES S. GRANT ON THE CIVIL WAR

It is probably well that we had the war when we did. We are better off now than we would have been without it, and have made more rapid progress than we otherwise should have made. . . . monarchical Europe generally believed that our republic was a rope of sand that would part the moment the slightest strain was brought upon it. Now it has shown itself capable of dealing with one of the greatest wars that was ever made, and our people have proven themselves to be the most formidable in war of any nationality.

But this war was a fearful lesson, and should teach us the necessity of avoiding wars in the future.

Grant, *Personal Memoirs of U. S. Grant*, pp. 634–635.

the main cause of the war, a position that became increasingly unpopular with the rise of the "Lost Cause" myth. As might be expected from his battlefield tactics, Grant does not shy away from controversy. He explicitly criticizes fellow generals and politicians for bad judgment and character flaws. He provides statistics and descriptions that chronicle the unprecedented carnage of the war. Despite some efforts to defend his own decisions, Grant even admits some mistakes of his own (for instance, during the unfortunate battles of Spotsylvania and Cold Harbor). Rather than deny the failures and tragedies of the Civil War and rather than exonerate the South under the aegis of romance, Grant offers the balanced but subjective perspective of an antislavery Union man who neither forgets nor dwells upon the animosities of the past.

Instead, Grant moves toward national unity. Like many northerners and southerners alike, he looks to Lincoln as a figure for reconciliation, praising the president's wisdom, benevolence, and ability to forge consensus: "He always showed a generous and kindly spirit toward the Southern people. . . . never in my presence did he evince a revengeful disposition" (p. 563). As with his Appomattox meeting with Lee, Grant finds in Lincoln a model for peace; for while Grant describes the Civil War as ultimately advantageous for both sections, he believes that the war "should teach us the necessity of avoiding wars in the future" (p. 635). It is something of a tense position. On the one hand, Grant bemoans the waste and horrors of the war, not unlike the way he criticizes the war with Mexico. On the other hand, *Personal Memoirs* sees the Civil War leading to justice, praises both Union and Confederate soldiers, and suggests that war forms strong characters for both individuals and nations. Grant's view of the Civil War and of war in general is complicated and personal. He spends much time recounting battles, strategies, and geography while also describing the conflicts and affinities between important leaders of the time. Grant's perspective and accuracy can be measured against memoirs by his colleagues Horace Porter and Adam Badeau as well as against historical studies by William McFeely, Brooks Simpson, and others. But for readers less committed to military and political history, *Personal Memoirs of U. S. Grant* also speaks to broader concerns: the morality of war, the burdens of leadership, the literary form of autobiography, the ongoing construction of national identity for both communities and individuals. No one predicted that Grant—a middling student, failed businessman, failed farmer, and low-ranking officer—would rise to become a preeminent general and president of the United States. Neither would one suspect that the most important Civil War memoir would come from a dying man with limited literary experience. Nonetheless, in

despite the end of the Civil War and the Compromise of 1876, differences between the South and North continued to generate conflict. In *Personal Memoirs*, Robert E. Lee's surrender to Grant at Appomattox stands as a model solution. Grant debunks romantic myths of the meeting (for instance, Lee never offered Grant his sword). More importantly, the negotiations do not feel like negotiations at all. Without formality or bargaining strategy, the two men agree on terms of surrender as colleagues or even friends might, looking forward not to future battles or historical reputations but rather to the coming winter and the need for soldiers to return to their farms. In the scene, which is the closest thing to a climax of the book, Grant finally overcomes his struggle with negotiation just as the Union finally overcomes the threat of Confederate victory. In the grand tradition of American autobiography, the personal and the national become one, so much so that Grant's initials ("U. S.") equate him with the country as a whole.

None of which should imply that *Personal Memoirs* underestimates the trauma of the Civil War or the challenge of reconciliation. Grant does ignore some of the war's worst moments, such as the horrors of Andersonville Prison and the massacre of black troops at Fort Pillow. However, Grant does defend at length William T. Sherman's March to the Sea, an incendiary topic in the South in 1885 and beyond. Grant also supports, if somewhat tersely, African American political rights, an abiding source of conflict between the North and South. Grant explicitly names the sin of slavery as his letters as in his public life Grant won unexpected success.

See also Autobiography; Civil War Memoirs

BIBLIOGRAPHY

Primary Work

Grant, Ulysses S. *Personal Memoirs of U. S. Grant*. 1885. New York: Penguin, 1999.

Secondary Works

Blight, David, W. *Race and Reunion: The Civil War in American Memory*. Cambridge, Mass.: Belknap Press of Harvard University Press, 2001.

Keegan, John. *The Mask of Command*. New York: Penguin, 1987.

McFeely, William. *Grant: A Biography*. New York: Norton, 1981.

McPherson, James. Introduction to *Personal Memoirs of U. S. Grant*. New York: Penguin, 1999.

Samet, Elizabeth. "'Adding to My Book and to My Coffin': The Unconditional Memoirs of Ulysses S. Grant." *PMLA* 115, no. 5 (2000): 1117–1124.

Silber, Nina. *The Romance of Reunion: Northerners and the South, 1865–1900*. Chapel Hill: University of North Carolina Press, 1993.

Simpson, Brooks. *Ulysses S. Grant: Triumph over Adversity, 1822–1865*. Boston: Houghton Mifflin, 2000.

Wilson, Edmund. *Patriotic Gore: Studies in the Literature of the Civil War*. New York: Oxford University Press, 1962.

Maurice S. Lee

PHILIPPINE-AMERICAN WAR

Surely the Philippine-American War (1899–1902) is America's least-known war. If it is referred to at all, it is only as an afterthought of the Spanish-American War (1898). Yet that conflict lasted only three months, and the war in the Philippines—often called the "Bolo War" by Americans for the "bolo" knives or machetes used with great effect by the Filipino fighters—officially lasted three years and in reality lasted fifteen years.

Moreover, that conflict was America's first global war, and occurring as it did at the turn of the twentieth century, it heralded a new era both in America's view of itself and in the world's view of America. Rudyard Kipling (1865–1936), a British writer with strong ties to America, expressed a view that was welcome among American policy makers. In his poem "The White Man's Burden," published in *McClure's Magazine* in

February 1899 and later subtitled "The United States and the Philippine Islands," he called upon America to follow Europe's lead and assume the "burden" of empire. Though the "harness" be "heavy," he wrote, though the task be "thankless," the white man's duty is to carry civilization to the "new-caught, sullen peoples / Half-devil and half-child" (ll. 7–8).

That same month, on 6 February, the United States Senate formally agreed with the call to imperialism by ratifying the December 1898 Treaty of Paris ending the war between Spain and the United States. Yet the patronizing racialism that infused Kipling's poem also produced strong opposition, and the Senate decision met the requirement of a two-thirds majority by only one vote. Discussions of the parts of the treaty that officially recognized the American occupation of Cuba and that ceded Puerto Rico and Guam to the United States were not especially contentious, but the argument was heated about the far-distant Philippines, thought by many not to be of vital importance to the United States. Adding to the intensity of the debate was Spain's argument at the peace talks that because it had signed a peace agreement with the United States before America seized Manila, the future of its colony in the archipelago should not even be a part of the negotiations. The United States insisted, however, and, compensating Spain with $20 million for the loss, it annexed the islands. The Spanish colony thereby became an American colony. Neither side had allowed the representative of the newly formed Filipino government a seat at the treaty table.

THE NATION POLARIZED

With this treaty, especially the part about the Philippines, America designed and implemented its foreign policy almost overnight. Just as the topic had polarized the Senate, it also divided the nation. Imperialists like the Republican senator from Massachusetts Henry Cabot Lodge (1850–1924) agreed with Kipling's chauvinism by maintaining that not approving the treaty would "brand" the United States as being incapable of taking a place alongside the other great world powers. In agreeing, another Republican, Minnesota senator Knute Nelson (1843–1923), recalled the nation's zest for Manifest Destiny and appealed to missionary zeal by declaring that "Providence has given the United States the duty of extending Christian civilization. We come as ministering angels, not despots" ("Timeline: January 1899").

Anti-imperialists sided with the other Massachusetts senator, George Frisbie Hoar (1826–1954), also a Republican and the most outspoken "anti" in the Senate. Hoar might as well have had Kipling's poem

---

"ON A SOLDIER FALLEN IN THE PHILIPPINES"

This poem by the poet and playwright William Vaughn Moody (1869–1910) gained widespread recognition when it was published in 1901 and is still anthologized. The poem praises national ideals and the soldier who has died in battle believing he is advancing those ideals, but it laments the wound that the war is inflicting in the nation's soul.

Streets of the roaring town,
Hush for him, hush, be still!
He comes, who was stricken down
Doing the word of our will.
Hush! Let him have his state,
Give him his soldier's crown.
The grists of trade can wait
Their grinding at the mill,
But he cannot wait for his honor, now the trumpet
    has been blown.
Wreathe pride now for his granite brow, lay love on
    his breast of stone.

Toll! Let the great bells toll
Till the clashing air is dim.
Did we wrong this parted soul?
We will make it up to him.
Toll! Let him never guess
What work we set him to.

Laurel, laurel, yes;
He did what we bade him do.
Praise, and never a whispered hint but the fight he
    fought was good;
Never a word that the blood on his sword was his
    country's own heart's blood.

A flag for the soldier's bier
Who dies that his land may live;
O, banners, banners here,
That he doubt not nor misgive!
That he heed not from the tomb
The evil days draw near
When the nation, robed in gloom,
With its faithless past shall strive.
Let him never dream that his bullet's scream went
    wide of its island mark,
Home to the heart of his darling land where she
    stumbled and sinned in the dark.

Moody, *The Poems and Plays,* 1:29–30.

---

in mind when he pointed directly at race and classism in exclaiming, "This Treaty will make us a vulgar, commonplace empire, controlling subject races and vassal states, in which one class must forever rule and other classes must forever obey" ("Timeline: January 1899").

Joining the minority in the Senate were several vocal and distinguished national figures—the industrialist and philanthropist Andrew Carnegie, the former U.S. presidents Grover Cleveland and Benjamin Harrison, the political leader Carl Schurz, as well as members of the intelligentsia, such as the Harvard professors Charles Eliot Norton and William James and *The Nation's* editor E. L. Godkin. Literary figures were highly visible, and their outspokenness betokens the riveting importance of this national issue. The prominence of these writers was so great that it has become a regular feature of the histories and scholarly studies of the period. Stuart Creighton Miller, for example, in his *"Benevolent Assimilation": The American Conquest of the Philippines, 1899–1903,* highlights the views of a broad array of "novelists, poets, playwrights,

and humorists" (p. 117). A few of them, such as Brooks Adams, Julian Hawthorne, Gertrude Atherton, Walter Hines Page, and Julia Ward Howe, supported imperialism (p. 117), but they were not distinctive and according to Richard E. Welch Jr., what little they wrote was "justifiably soon forgotten" (p. 124). The overwhelming majority of writers were opposed to expansion. Miller lists Thomas Bailey Aldrich, George W. Cable, Henry Blake Fuller, Edgar Lee Masters, William Dean Howells, Charles Dudley Warner, Ambrose Bierce, Joaquin Miller, Hamlin Garland, Edwin Arlington Robinson, Bliss Perry, William Vaughn Moody, John Jay Chapman, Lincoln Steffens, Finley Peter Dunne, and George Ade as making "clear their opposition to imperialism and the war" (p. 117). Welch adds Gamaliel Bradford and Thomas Wentworth Higginson (p. 124). Still others were Katharine Lee Bates, Henry Van Dyke, and William Lloyd Garrison Jr. Novels satirized the war—Ernest Crosby's *Captain Jinks, Hero* (1902), Raymond L. Bridgman's *Loyal Traitors* (1903), and a Broadway musical by George Ade,

The Sultan of Sulu (1903), laughed at the imperialists. A vast number of poems against the war were published in newspapers and magazines, and many were collected in *Liberty Poems: Inspired by the Crisis of 1898–1900* (1900).

The best known of all the antiwar writers, and the one whom historians of the war have accorded most importance, was Mark Twain (1835–1910). David Haward Bain's *Sitting in Darkness: America in the Philippines,* taking its title and its inspiration from Twain's especially vitriolic essay, begins with "It was Mark Twain who sent me to the Philippines" (p. 1). Although "To the Person Sitting in Darkness" was and still is the best and best-known of Twain's expressions of opposition against imperialism and the war, it was by no means the only one. Jim Zwick has identified more than twenty public expressions by Twain opposing imperialism in the Philippines. The Anti-Imperialist League, formed in 1898, was a ready outlet for Twain. He became a vice president of the New York chapter in 1901 and of the national organization in 1905.

Despite this impressive display of distinguished opposition, Republican president William McKinley (1843–1901) remained unswayed. In December of 1898, following the signing of the Treaty of Paris, he issued a proclamation declaring that the intention of the United States was to stay in the Philippines permanently but with a policy of "benevolent assimilation" that substituted "the mild sway of justice and right for arbitrary rule" (McKinley). His orders to General Elwell Otis, commander of ground forces in the Philippines, indicated a more "manly" attitude, though: to "extend by force American sovereignty over this country" (Bautista). The age was caught up in just this ethos of manliness, an athletic figure with strong moral backbone best typified by Theodore Roosevelt (1858–1919) who won fame as a Rough Rider in Cuba during the Spanish-American War and then lectured and wrote about "the strenuous life." The next year the American people seemed to approve the Senate's ratification of the treaty as well as of McKinley's proclamation when they rejected the Democratic presidential candidate William Jennings Bryan (1860–1925), an outspoken anti-imperialist, and by a wide majority reelected McKinley for another term in the White House. His running mate was Roosevelt. A year later, when Roosevelt became president after McKinley was assassinated, the manly image gained added strength. Apropos, Filipinos were "insurrectos," the conflict itself was officially named the "Philippine Insurrection," and it was America's manly duty to put it down. The "Philippine-American War" has been used only since the 1960s.

THE COURSE OF THE WAR

Most of the Philippine archipelago had been ruled by Spain since 1521 when Ferdinand Magellan (c. 1480–1521) stopped there on his attempt to circumnavigate the world and spread Christianity. He was killed on the island of Mactan by Muslims who refused the choice of conversion or death. More than three and a half centuries later, in 1896, an organized effort by the Filipinos to gain independence began under the leadership of twenty-seven-year-old Emilio Aguinaldo (1869–1964). With the defeat of the Spanish navy in Manila Bay by American forces under the command of Commodore George Dewey (1837–1917) in May 1898—the first battle of the Spanish-American War—Aguinaldo, as the country's first president, declared his nation free at last, and by the end of the following January, two weeks before the ratification vote in the United States Senate, the country had a constitution modeled on America's and had proclaimed itself the Philippine Republic. The Filipino people would have had every reason to think they had America's support in their move to independence had it not been for the Treaty of Paris and President McKinley's proclamation. But these caused such serious doubts that Aguinaldo had already moved his capital to a more defensible position.

The war broke out almost by accident. Two American soldiers on nighttime sentry duty on the outskirts of Manila encountered three armed Filipinos. After some uncertainty about the intentions of the Filipinos, problems made worse by language differences, the Americans killed them. Soon Filipino troops fired on American lines, and before daybreak open warfare had broken out. That was 4 February 1899. Two days later, in ratifying the Treaty of Paris, the United States colonized a country it putatively was fighting *for* in the cause of independence. Aguinaldo tried to stop the war, but General Otis replied, that the "fighting, having begun, must go on to the grim end" (*The Filipino Americans*). The end did not come soon, and when it did the cost was $400 million, twenty times the "compensation." More than 126,000 American soldiers had seen action; with only partial numbers, more than 4,200 of them were killed. It was much worse for the Filipinos: upwards of 17,500 soldiers were killed, and estimates put the civilian toll at more than half a million.

The symbolic conclusion to the war came on 23 March 1901, when Aguinaldo was captured. In a plot that combined duplicity and courage, General Frederick Funston (1865–1917) and four other American officers pretending to be prisoners gained access to Aguinaldo's mountain hideout. Seeing the futility of further resistance, Aguinaldo swore allegiance to the United States and called upon Filipinos to lay down their arms. Strong resistance continued, however. The surrender in April 1902 of General Miguel Malvar, the leader of a well-organized guerrilla force, caused Congress to pass the Philippine Government Act on 1 July 1902 and prompted President Roosevelt to declare on 4 July that the "insurrection" was ended. But that was more politics than fact for skirmishes continued until 1907, and in the Moro province Muslims were again so strongly resistant that American forces remained until 1914.

PROVOCATIVE LITERARY OPPOSITION TO THE WAR

Before the fighting had started, when Americans' awareness of the Philippines was simply that Dewey had ended the Spanish-American War there by destroying the Spanish fleet, prominent writers had begun to express doubts about a war with a country so far away. One of the most popular was Finley Peter Dunne (1867–1936), whose probing humor, expressed in the thick Irish American dialect of his persona Martin T. Dooley, a Chicago saloon keeper, was published regularly in the *Chicago Evening Post* and the *Chicago Journal* and later collected in the popular *Mr. Dooley in Peace and in War* (1898) and several later books. In one column, "On the Philippines," Mr. Dooley and his friends discussed the best course of action for "Mack" (President McKinley) and "George" (Admiral George Dewey). Mr. Hennessey had no doubts: "I KNOW what I'd do if I was Mack," he said. "I'd hist a flag over th' Ph'lippeens, an' I'd take in th' whole lot iv thim." Mr. Dooley, though, troubled and uncertain, admitted "And yet, Hinnissy, I dinnaw what to do about th' Ph'lippeens. An' I'm all alone in th' wurruld. Ivrybody else has made up his mind. . . . But I don't know'" (Dunne, pp. 43, 47).

Mr. Dooley's doubts, like the nation's, were specifically about the war in the Philippines. The country had strongly supported the just war with Spain for Cuban independence, but the stipulations about the Philippines in the Treaty of Paris were a different matter altogether and many felt the change was a betrayal.

It is true that such views were in the minority, but when Mark Twain added his voice the dissent was by no means unnoticed or unfelt. Alone and in concert with organizations, in newspaper interviews and in scorching journal essays, he repeatedly mocked the government's hypocrisy and brutality in the Philippines. "I have read carefully the treaty of Paris," he said in an interview in the *New York Herald* in October 1900, "and I have seen that we do not intend to free, but to subjugate the people of the Philippines. . . . And so I am an anti-imperialist. I am opposed to having the eagle put its talons on any other land" (Twain, p. 5). Late the following winter, in the *North American Review,* he published his most famous condemnation of American policy in the islands, "To the Person Sitting in Darkness," an essay infused with ironic use of the self-righteous rhetoric of those like Senator Nelson. Historians honoring Twain's role in public discourse about the war have praised this essay in particular. Welch, for example, noting the effect when the essay's irony "flashes into angry eloquence," explains that the "person" is

> the benighted heathen who is being whipped into the march of progress by the "Blessings-of-Civilization Trust." While ostensibly seeking to reconcile the victim, Twain reviews the tangle of broken promises and acts of deceit that had characterized the relations of the American government with the people of the Philippines:
>
> > "True, we have crushed a deceived and confiding people; . . . we have stabbed an ally in the back . . . ; we have invited our clean young men to shoulder a discredited musket and do a bandit's work . . . ; we have debauched America's honor and blackened her face before the world; but each detail was for the best." (P. 125)

Twain followed this essay the next year with a blistering attack aimed at General Funston, now a national hero for capturing Aguinaldo. Sarcastic throughout, "A Defence of General Funston" concludes in humiliation at America's behavior: "He [Aguinaldo] is entitled to his freedom. If he were a king of a Great Power, or an ex-president of our republic, . . . Civilization (with a large C) would criticize and complain until he got it" (Twain, p. 132).

In early 1901 Twain devised a kind of verbal cartoon exposing authoritarian political and religious regimes. Titled "The Stupendous Procession," it imagines a grotesque parade of human misery perpetrated by America and other imperialist nations. A banner recalls Kipling's poem of two years earlier. On it is inscribed "The White Man's Burden has been sung. Who will sing the Brown Man's?" (Twain, p. 53).

Despite Roosevelt's declaration in 1902, three years later this war was not over. For some writers it had grown to represent the folly of all wars. In 1905 Twain and his close friend William Dean Howells (1837–1920), the best-known novelist and literary critic of the age, wrote antiwar pieces that continue to resonate. Howells's "Editha," first published in *Harper's Monthly* and doubtless his best-known short story, pits romanticized patriotism against unblinking truthfulness. Editha thinks of war as an opportunity for heroism, but her fiancé, George, whose own father had

The Best Joke Yet. Cartoon from the *Minneapolis Tribune,* 20 March 1901. The cartoonist suggests that despite his prominence as a humorist, Twain is powerless in the face of Republican determination to pursue the war in the Philippines. COURTESY OF LOUIS J. BUDD

lost an arm in war and who died before his time, is not so sure. George says "It's war." When Editha replies, "How glorious!" George repeats, "It's war." After George is killed in war, the shallowness of Editha's religious idealism stands pitiably exposed (p. 156).

Twain's "The War Prayer" is an unrelenting exposé of religious justification for war. An aged stranger confronts a minister and his congregation as they pray to God, "the Source of Love," for a bloody victory that devastates the enemy. The conclusion shows that the people remain unenlightened: "It was believed afterwards, that the man was a lunatic, because there was no sense in what he said" (p. 160). Like Twain's "The Stupendous Procession," which he did not even attempt to make public, "The War Prayer" was not published in its time. Although he offered it to *Harper's Bazar*, the editor, Elizabeth Jordan, rejected it, saying that it was "not quite suited to a woman's magazine" (Twain, p. 156).

See also Imperialism and Anti-Imperialism; Spanish-American War

BIBLIOGRAPHY

Primary Works

Dunne, Finley Peter. *Mr. Dooley in Peace and in War*. Boston: Small, Maynard, 1899.

Howells, William Dean. *Selected Short Stories of William Dean Howells*. Edited by Ruth Bardon. Athens: Ohio University Press, 1997.

Kipling, Rudyard. *Rudyard Kipling's Verse*. New York: Doubleday, Doran, 1940.

McKinley, William. "Benevolent Assimilation" Proclamation. Available at http://www.msc.edu.ph/centennial/mc981221.html.

Moody, William Vaughn. *The Poems and Plays of William Vaughn Moody*. 2 vols. New York: AMS, 1969.

Roosevelt, Theodore. *The Strenuous Life: Essays and Addresses*. New York: Century, 1901.

Twain, Mark. *Mark Twain's Weapons of Satire: Anti-Imperialist Writings on the Philippine-American War*. Edited by Jim Zwick. Syracuse, N.Y.: Syracuse University Press, 1992.

Secondary Works

Bain, David Haward. *Sitting in Darkness: Americans in the Philippines*. Boston: Houghton Mifflin, 1984.

Bautista, Veltisezar. "The Philippine-American War." In *The Filipino Americans (From 1763 to the Present): Their History, Culture, and Traditions*. Available at http://www.filipino-americans.com/filamwar.html and http://www.msc.edu.ph/centennial/filam0.html.

Foner, Philip S., ed. *The Anti-Imperialist Reader: A Documentary History of Anti-Imperialism in the United States*. Vol. 2, *The Literary Anti-Imperialists*. New York: Holmes and Meier, 1986.

Hoganson, Kristin L. *Fighting for American Manhood: How Gender Politics Provoked the Spanish-American and Philippine-American Wars*. New Haven, Conn.: Yale University Press, 1998.

Linn, Brian McAllister. *The Philippine War, 1899–1902*. Lawrence: University Press of Kansas, 2000.

Miller, Stuart Creighton. *"Benevolent Assimilation": The American Conquest of the Philippines, 1899–1903*. New Haven, Conn.: Yale University Press, 1982.

Ochosa, Orlino A. *Bandoleros, Outlawed Guerrillas of the Philippine-American War, 1903–1907*. Quezon City, The Philippines: New Day, 1995.

"The Philippine Revolution." Available at http://www.msc.edu.ph/centennial/independence.html.

"Philippines." Available at http://www.globalsecurity.org/military/ops/philippines.htm.

"Rudyard Kipling." Available at http://www.dailycelebrations.com/123099.htm.

Shaw, Angel Velasco, and Luis H. Francia, eds. *Vestiges of War: The Philippine American War and the Aftermath of an Imperial Dream, 1899–1999*. New York: New York University Press, 2003.

"The Spanish-American War: The War of Philippine Independence, 1898–1901." Available at http://www.ualberta.ca/∼vmitchel/fw4.html.

"Timeline: January 1899: Senate Debate over Ratification of the Treaty of Paris." Available at http://www.pbs.org/crucible/tl17.html.

"Treaty of Paris." Available at http://www.u-s-history.com/pages/h828.html.

Walker, Robert H. *The Poet and the Gilded Age: Social Themes in Late 19th Century American Verse*. Philadelphia: University of Pennsylvania Press, 1963.

Welch, Richard E., Jr. *Response to Imperialism: The United States and the Philippine-American War, 1899–1902*. Chapel Hill: University of North Carolina Press, 1979.

Zwick, Jim. "Mark Twain on War and Imperialism." Available at http://www.boondocksnet.com//ai/twain/

Terry Oggel

PHILOSOPHY

Philosophy in the latter part of the nineteenth century was multifarious, being found not only in the colleges and emerging universities but also in lecture halls and journals published outside of academia. Its practitioners included clergymen, college presidents, public lecturers, journalists, scientists, and a small number of university specialists. And if Jack London's account in *Martin Eden* (1909) is at all reflective of life at the turn of the century, nonprofessionals engaged in knowledgeable discussion of philosophical issues as those issues had been defined by prominent philosophers. Most usually the philosophy taught in the colleges was

PHILOSOPHY IN A WORKING-CLASS GHETTO

Jack London's Martin Eden, in the 1909 novel of the same name, finds himself—in chapter 36—in San Francisco's "working-class ghetto, south of Market Street," participating in an animated philosophical discussion.

The books were alive in these men. They talked with fire and enthusiasm, the intellectual stimulant stirring them as he [Martin] had seen drink and anger stir other men. What he heard was no longer the philosophy of the dry, printed word, written by half-mythical demigods like Kant and Spencer. It was living philosophy, with warm, red blood, incarnated in these two men [Kreis and Norton] till its very features worked with excitement. Now and again other men joined in, and all followed the discussion with cigarettes going out in their hands and with alert, intent faces.

Idealism had never attracted Martin, but the exposition it now received at the hands of Norton was a revelation. The logical plausibility of it, that made an appeal to his intellect, seemed missed by Kreis and Hamilton, who sneered at Norton as a metaphysician, and who, in turn, sneered back at them as metaphysicians. *Phenomenon* and *noumenon* were bandied back and forth. They charged him with attempting to explain consciousness by itself. He charged them with word jugglery, with reasoning from words to theory instead of from facts to theory. At this they were aghast. It was the cardinal tenet of their mode of reasoning to start with facts and to give names to the facts. . . .

"You have given me a glimpse of fairyland," Martin said [to Brissenden] on the ferry-boat [to Oakland]. "It makes life worth while to meet people like that. My mind is all worked up. I never appreciated idealism before. Yet I can't accept it. I know that I shall always be a realist. I am so made, I guess."

London, *Martin Eden*, in *Novels and Social Writings*, pp. 840–842.

science of psychology. (The two disciplines began to separate in 1892 with the formation of the American Psychological Association.) By the 1920s, however, philosophy was primarily a professionalized, academic specialty that religion could no longer count on for support and from which psychology had separated itself. To be sure, there continued to be colleges teaching philosophy in the nineteenth-century tradition, but they were not the leading ones.

COLLEGIATE PHILOSOPHY

Throughout the nineteenth century various denominational colleges were the main locus of higher education. Typically, the college president would be a Protestant clergyman and would teach the senior course in philosophy. Every senior would study—in a single yearlong course—a wide range of fields, including logic, epistemology, metaphysics, and moral philosophy. The latter would encompass not only ethics but also what were to become the social sciences. The philosophy being taught found its origins in European thought, notably an amalgam of Christianity and empiricism, often referred to as "Scottish common sense realism." The realism is to be understood as the expectation that reality was independent of the mind and could be known empirically or through sense experience. (Philosophical realism is not to be confused with literary realism or the faithful representation of reality. The philosophical usage, while varied, focuses on the nature of this reality. Often, the point for realist philosophers is to identify a reality outside of the mind; reality is not a projection of the mind but something that exists whether there were any minds or not.) This realism was Scottish in that it had been mediated through several prominent philosophers who taught in Scottish universities—Thomas Reid (1710–1776), Dugald Stewart (1753–1828), and Thomas Brown (1778–1820)—and the graduates of these universities who immigrated to the United States, notably John Witherspoon (1722–1794), a signer of the Declaration of Independence, and James McCosh (1811–1894), both of whom were presidents of Princeton, albeit a century apart. McCosh, in particular, came to represent this collegiate philosophy. But the important claim for these realists was that they thought that what was real was knowable by ordinary human understanding; what humans took to be real was in fact what was real. Hence "common sense realism." It was "commonsensical" in two senses: it was knowable by the ordinary understanding of everyone, and it constituted the generally accepted beliefs of everyone. As such it countered the skeptical conclusions of the scientifically oriented David Hume (1711–1776) and the metaphysical idealism of George

understood to be supportive of Christianity or at least not in open conflict with it. It was also just beginning to be distinguished from what was to become the social

Berkeley (1685–1753), who regarded all of reality as either a mind or dependent on a mind for its existence.

In general, according to the contemporary account of G. Stanley Hall (1844–1924), collegiate instruction was uninspired and controlled by the theological commitments of the college (*Mind* [1879]). Hall was a knowledgeable but hardly dispassionate observer. Recipient of the first PhD in psychology awarded in the United States (Harvard, 1878, under the direction of William James [1842–1910]), Hall studied in Germany, taught at the newly established Johns Hopkins University, and was later president of Clark University. He clearly reflected the view of the newly emerging scientific and professional orientation of philosophy in the United States. The aim of the instruction in the collegiate philosophy course was not to develop independent and original thinking, as Hall desired, but to complete the student's introduction to the existing body of knowledge. According to Hall and other sources, the total faculty in many colleges would have numbered ten or less and would have covered mathematics, science, languages ancient and modern, history, literature, and oratory. The conditions, as Hall pointed out, were hardly conducive to originality.

Hall acknowledged that there were a small number of educational institutions that embodied the values he prized—Williams, Yale, and Harvard Colleges. And he had hope for the newly formed University of Baltimore (as Johns Hopkins was initially known), whose faculty he would join two years later. But on the whole his view of academic philosophy in the United States was that it was "backward." Other observers, such as Elizabeth Flower and Murray G. Murphey (1:203–204), acknowledge many of Hall's criticisms and record that many more recent historians share his judgment. But Flower and Murphey attempt to counter this "jaundiced appraisal," emphasizing that Scottish common sense realism inherited from the Scottish Enlightenment an empirical and scientific orientation that served to liberalize and humanize a Christian and philosophic synthesis that admittedly was neither fresh nor exciting in approach and presentation yet was open to new developments in geology, biology, and psychology.

But, significantly, philosophy in the nineteenth century was carried on only in part in educational institutions. Keep in mind that the transcendentalists lived, wrote, and lectured largely outside of such institutions. Also, as Hall reported, there was much original and stimulating thought being done in journals and elsewhere by practicing scientists, such as Charles Sanders Peirce (1839–1914), one of the originators of

pragmatism, and professional men of "partial leisure," in which category he apparently placed the St. Louis Hegelian William Torrey Harris (1835–1909). It would be unusual in the twenty-first century for "amateurs," such as Ralph Waldo Emerson (1803–1882), the elder Henry James (1811–1882), Peirce, and Harris, to be considered as serious contributors to philosophical reflection. But it was not unusual in their day, for there was no expectation that philosophy was a narrow, academic, technical field. Thus to call them "amateurs" is to import a twentieth-century, professionalized understanding into the more diverse and fluid nineteenth-century situation.

THE ST. LOUIS HEGELIANS

This broad nineteenth-century understanding of philosophy is clearly seen in the movement that developed in St. Louis that has become known as the St. Louis Hegelians. The movement played a prominent and significant role in the latter part of the nineteenth century primarily because of the work of several individuals who came together in 1866 to form the St. Louis Philosophical Society and then became prominent in Missouri and elsewhere politically, educationally, and philosophically.

Harris, who was superintendent of the St. Louis public schools from 1868 to 1880, founded and edited the *Journal of Speculative Philosophy* (1867–1893) and served as the first U.S. commissioner of education from 1889 to 1906. Prior to the American Civil War the New Englander Harris had met a German immigrant, Henry Conrad Brokmeyer (1828–1906), following a talk that Harris had given at the St. Louis Mercantile Library. Brokmeyer, who was to become a lieutenant governor (and, for a time, acting governor) of Missouri (1876–1881), challenged Harris's defense of Victor Cousin (1792–1867) and urged him to study Georg Wilhelm Friedrich Hegel (1770–1831). This they did over the decades that followed, providing a Hegelian orientation to the group they formed after the war. An early participant in the group, but oriented toward Greek philosophy and culture rather than Hegel, was Thomas Davidson (1840–1900), a graduate of St. Andrews University (Scotland), who joined the St. Louis Philosophical Society in 1868. Later, with financial assistance from Joseph Pulitzer (1847–1911), Davidson would organize the Glenmore Summer School of the Culture Sciences in New York. Many prominent philosophers, including William James (1842–1910), Josiah Royce (1855–1916), and John Dewey (1859–1952) lectured at the school.

All three—Harris, Brockmeyer, and Davidson—exemplified a commitment to public service, education, and scholarship that formed a distinctive understanding of philosophy, one that had commonalities in differing ways with the transcendentalists, pragmatists, and ethical culture movement. But this edifying, publicly engaged orientation has largely been lost in the professionalized philosophy of the twentieth and twenty-first centuries.

Yet during the latter third of the nineteenth century this distinctive approach played a major role in the development of American philosophy, for it informed the only American philosophical journal for much of the period, the *Journal of Speculative Philosophy.* The first English-language philosophical periodical, it provided a publishing outlet not only for the St. Louis group but also for many other American philosophers and had an international readership.

THE CONCORD SCHOOL OF PHILOSOPHY
In the late 1870s the long-held dream of many of the transcendentalists, notably Ralph Waldo Emerson and Amos Bronson Alcott (1799–1888), to establish a school of philosophy was realized in the establishment of the Concord School of Philosophy. It began with a six-week session in the summer of 1879 and held sessions every summer through 1887. It has been estimated that some two thousand people participated in the sessions over the nine years of its existence.

Intended to provide an institutional base for the various idealisms—Platonic, Hegelian, and transcendental—current at the time, the school's main lecturers that first summer included not only Emerson and Alcott but also Harris and the Platonist Hiram Jones of Illinois College. Davidson also lectured that summer. The next year, further strengthening the ties between West and East, Harris moved to Concord, and according to Flower and Murphey, "quickly emerged as the strongest lecturer on the faculty" (2:506). In succeeding years Noah Porter (1811– 1892), the president of Yale, and McCosh, Princeton's president, also lectured at the Concord School of Philosophy, as did William James in 1883. The school survived Emerson's death in April 1882 and Alcott's stroke later that year, but less emphasis was given to philosophy in the remaining years and more to literature. With Alcott's death in the spring of 1888, the school failed to resume. With its passing, philosophic idealism increasingly found its home in the emerging universities.

JOSIAH ROYCE AND ACADEMIC IDEALISM
The Harvard philosopher Josiah Royce (1855–1916) most successfully articulated the idealist, or mind-constituted reality, orientation in the United States at the turn of the century. A Californian, Royce was a prominent member of the brilliant philosophy department that included William James and their student, George Santayana (1863–1952). James, one of the originators of pragmatism, along with Peirce, can only be considered briefly in this general article, but his significance is too great, then and now, to be passed over completely.

Royce and James were not only colleagues but also neighbors who carried on an extensive conversation in letters, in walks to and from their offices, over the fence, and in their published writings. James, who was more empirical in his approach, was critical of the idealist position, for it too neatly accounted for the diverse phenomena of everyday existence. Failing to develop a systematic alternative to the idealisms and often materialist empiricisms of his day, James had to settle for a probing, restless, questioning result. Royce was a constant adversary against which he contended. Yet one should not think that their sharp intellectual differences created animosity between them, for they were dear friends.

Royce, unlike James, sought to comprehend reality in a single vision and articulate it systematically. This, of course, was not unusual for a philosopher in the nineteenth century, but Royce attempted the grand synthesis with considerable knowledge of the scientific and intellectual developments of his day and the history of philosophy. The "strong impression" of the essayist John Jay Chapman (1862–1933), during his freshman year at Harvard, was that Royce "was very extraordinary and knew everything and was a bumblebee—a benevolent monster of pure intelligence, zigzagging, ranging, and uncatchable. I always had this feeling about Royce—that he was a celestial insect" (Clendenning, p. 118). Moreover, he pursued his project in the face of James's continuing challenges. His way into the project was also distinctive. He would show that the opening to absolute truth begins with an understanding of the "logical conditions of error" (Clendenning, pp. 119–120). Or as Edward Everett Hale (1822–1909), author of *The Man without a Country,* put it to the pluralistic idealist philosopher George H. Howison (1834–1916) upon hearing Royce lecture, Royce attempted to show that "our human ignorance is the positive proof that there is a God—a Supreme Omniscient Being" (Howison p. 234).

Royce's formidable project was developed in several books, and he enjoyed considerable prominence within the profession and increasingly in the public at large, but his project did not meet the concerns of the new generation. They were impressed with his learning, vision, intellectual passion, and dialectical skill, but rather than being persuaded, they became his critics.

William James (left) with Josiah Royce, 1903. BY PERMISSION OF THE HOUGHTON LIBRARY, HARVARD UNIVERSITY

Idealism, and its most forceful American academic advocate, would give way to the new realists.

SANTAYANA AND INCLUSIVE NATURALISM

George Santayana entered Harvard as a freshman in 1882, the same year that Royce began as an instructor. Although born in Spain, Santayana was reared in Boston, educated there and in Cambridge, and then taught at Harvard for twenty-three years before retiring to Europe, where he spent most of his time in France and Italy. Nevertheless his influence on philosophy in America was considerable.

In 1912 Santayana went to Europe. The Harvard philosophy department hoped that he would recruit new faculty on his visit. Instead, he resigned, blasting the "unintelligible sanctimonious and often disingenuous Protestantism" that he associated with Royce.

Detesting "the Absolutes and the dragooned myths by which people try to cancel the passing ideal, or to denaturalize it," Santayana signaled the significant philosophic change that was occurring at the beginning of the twentieth century (Clendenning, p. 344). The coming years would clearly reveal the backward orientation of Royce's overall approach despite his immense learning and attention to new developments in science and logic.

In 1896 Santayana published an early book, *The Sense of Beauty,* which employed an empirical and psychological approach with regard to aesthetic experience, similar to what his teacher James was to do in *The Varieties of Religious Experience* (1902). Nine years later Santayana published the five-volume *Life of Reason,* in which, with much learning and considerable literary grace, he proposed an inclusive naturalism. Philosophic naturalism understands reality to be fundamentally material rather than mental or spiritual. Thus it opposes metaphysical idealism. Naturalists differ over the nature of matter, with some naturalists regarded as reductionistic, reducing reality to matter, whereas others, such as Santayana, attempt to be inclusive, or nonreductionist. Santayana not only paid considerable attention to the arts, imagination, and religion, he also argued that material nature could have "spiritual functions" and "spirit a natural cause" (1:282).

Various materialisms (reality is composed of matter) and positivisms (reality is what science says it is; it is what there are positive facts of) had come to the fore in the nineteenth century, primarily in Europe. And the possibility of a naturalistic—that is nonsupernaturalistic—account of the origins of life had clearly been opened with Charles Darwin's (1809–1882) evolutionary theory. The English thinker Herbert Spencer (1820–1903) attempted a synthesis of science and religion that appealed to many in Europe and the United States. He was widely read; his ideas on the necessity of progress toward a society of cooperative, free individuals was welcomed by a public whose traditional beliefs had been challenged by the publication of Darwin's *On the Origin of Species* (1859). He was also influential. John Fiske (1842–1901), lawyer, historian, philosopher, and lecturer, was one of several writers and thinkers to popularize Spencer's views. But Spencer's approach lacked rigor and was unacceptable in many ways to a variety of sophisticated readers. Although it appeared to be a form of mechanistic, positivistic, and behavioristic materialism, it can be regarded, according to Flower and Murphey, as "a form of Berkeleyan idealism, for matter is defined in terms of force, and force is regarded as the direct action of God upon us" (2:531).

James, although an empiricist, did not find the materialisms of his day acceptable. His pragmatism was, he thought, a way beyond the standoff between intellectualist idealism and crude materialism. Santayana did not follow James in his pragmatism, but he did openly embrace materialism. Yet his materialism accommodated his aesthetic sensibility. This was something new, and it opened the way for those who would embrace both religion and science and yet reject idealism. The philosophical naturalists associated with Columbia University in the early to middle part of the twentieth century regarded *Life of Reason* as a "classic" (Eldridge, p. 54).

CRITICAL REALISM AND THE TRIUMPH OF PROFESSIONALISM

Santayana also played a role in the critical realism movement that would eventually supplant idealism.

This realism, unlike the nineteenth-century realism that idealism had vied against, was much reduced in scope and focus. The earlier one had been a part of a total view of reality and a way of life. The new realism was a movement within academic philosophy, limiting itself to the concerns of philosophers as philosophers.

One can trace this realism to the work of James; reviews of Royce's books by two recent Harvard PhDs (and students of both James and Royce), William Pepperell Montague (1873–1953) and Ralph Barton Perry (1876–1957); and the origins of British analytic philosophy in the work of Bertrand Russell (1872–1970) and George Edward Moore (1873–1958). But the triggering event for realism was the 1910 manifesto "The Program and First Platform of Six Realists," that is, Montague, Perry, Edwin Bissell Holt, Walter T. Marvin, Walter B. Pitkin, and Edward Gleason Spaulding. Philosophical disagreement, these six contended, was due to the use of imprecise language and the failure of philosophers, unlike scientists, to cooperate in research. Accordingly, they proposed a collaborative program of research that would set the language and guiding principles of investigation and apply these agreed-upon ideas and careful language to "a program of constructive work" (Campbell, p. 124). This manifesto and a subsequent book soon became the focus of discussion among academic philosophers, and thus a three-way debate was joined of idealists, pragmatists, and realists.

This new realism was unable to sustain itself in the ensuing debate, due in part to disagreements among its proponents and their inability to answer their external critics on the problem of error and illusion. The new realists asked how one could know if what was regarded as knowledge was actual knowledge rather than an illusion. But the nascent movement quickly developed a response. In 1916 Roy Wood Sellars (1880–1973) published *Critical Realism,* which led to a new cooperative volume, *Essays in Critical Realism: A Co-operative Study of the Problem of Knowledge* (1920). Among the authors were Sellars, Santayana, and Arthur O. Lovejoy (1873–1962).

Sellars, like Santayana, was willing to declare himself a materialist and, also like Santayana, was not antireligious. But where Santayana was quick to withdraw from teaching and society, spending his later, but very active, years as a wandering solitary figure in Europe, Sellars participated in public life and taught at the University of Michigan for forty-five years. That he was able to enjoy a successful career at a state university as a philosophical materialist is telling. When George Sylvester Morris (1840–1889) and Dewey taught at Michigan in the 1880s, the philosophy department, according to a colleague in the Latin department, was "pervaded with a spirit of religious belief" (Dykhuizen, p. 47). By the time Sellars was declaring himself a materialist, Dewey had come to share roughly similar views about reality and religion. Both, for instance, signed the Humanist Manifesto in 1933, the initial draft of which had been prepared by Sellars.

Lovejoy, a feared and respected critic, taught at Johns Hopkins from 1910 to 1938. In 1908 he published "Thirteen Pragmatisms," in which he distinguished thirteen distinct meanings of "pragmatism," thus establishing himself both as critic of pragmatism and a careful, precise thinker. A cofounder of the American Association of University Professors in 1915, Lovejoy also developed the "history of ideas" approach in his *Great Chain of Being* (1936). But what is worthy of some notice here is his presidential address, titled "Some Conditions of Progress in Philosophy," at the sixteenth annual meeting of the American Philosophical Association in 1916. Lovejoy thought it scandalous that philosophers so readily accepted disagreement among themselves. Instead, he felt philosophers, like scientists, should aspire to overcome disagreement by a much more careful, collaborative effort than was the case at the time. Problems should be isolated and attacked piecemeal by many investigators who have developed a common terminology. What was most important was that philosophers attempt to avoid the "overlooked consideration." Only by adopting this attitude, Lovejoy believed, could they leave behind the "good, old fashioned, casual, disconnected, individualistic, disorganized, and essentially amateurish way" that then prevailed (p. 139).

Lovejoy's proposal was neither universally accepted nor implemented precisely as he wished. The attitude he recommended became the ideal not only of realists such as himself but also of the analytic philosophers who practiced a rigorous examination of philosophical problems by a careful examination of language. Philosophy became not just academic but highly specialized and technical. That which was considered to be within the grasp of every college senior in the nineteenth century would become remote from the concerns and abilities of most educated persons in the last half of the twentieth century.

Pragmatism's second generation, led by Dewey most prominently but also by George Herbert Mead (1863–1931) and James Hayden Tufts (1862–1942), came of age during the period after the Civil War. These "social pragmatists," as James Campbell in *The Community Reconstructs* has rightly termed them, taught together at the University of Chicago before Dewey—who became America's best-known philosopher in the first half of the twentieth century—moved to Columbia University in 1904. Mead, Tufts, and Dewey remained friends and collaborators and sought to develop pragmatism as an inclusive naturalism that would enhance human practices. Their efforts met with considerable success in a variety of ways, both within academia and with the public at large, yet they were regarded as not sufficiently rigorous by the emerging realist-analytic movement, which came to dominate the profession of philosophy.

Not included among Campbell's "social pragmatists" but someone who should have been, according to Charlene Haddock Seigfried (pp. 43–45), is Jane Addams (1882–1935). The founder of Hull-House, the author of several books, and the 1931 Nobel Peace Prize laureate, Addams was not regarded as either a philosopher or a pragmatist, despite her close association with her academic colleagues at the University of Chicago (Seigfried, p. 44) and her public lectures and books; she was marginalized as a social worker and activist. Seigfried also makes the case that Charlotte Perkins Gilman (1860–1935), author of *Women and Economics* (1898) and "The Yellow Wall-Paper" (1899), should be regarded as both a pragmatist and a philosopher. But like Addams, with whom she cofounded the Women's Peace Party in 1915, Gilman did not fit the masculine academic model of what a philosopher should be (Seigfried, pp. 40–41).

In addition to the plurality of approaches already cited—idealism, realism, and pragmatism—there was some attention to European philosophers who are not easily characterized, such as Arthur Schopenhauer (1788–1860), Friedrich Nietzsche (1844–1900), and Henri Bergson (1859–1941). Although they were read within academic philosophy, they had perhaps greater appeal in the wider reading public. Bergson, in particular, with his embrace of both spirituality and evolution, was attractive to novelists such as Willa Cather (1873–1947), whose *O Pioneers!* observes Tom Quirk, "may be fairly characterized as a vitalistic novel, and the author clearly took much of her inspiration from Henri Bergson" (p. 122). Bergson's thought also appealed to William James, who summarized and commented on Bergsonism in his sixth Hibbert lecture, "Bergson and His Critique of Intellectualism," and in *A Pluralistic Universe* in 1909 (pp. 52–53).

James, more than most academic philosophers, was open to a variety of approaches and ideas. But this inclusiveness was to give way to the more narrowly professional path championed by Lovejoy and the realists, who initiated, as this article has shown, what was to become by the middle of the twentieth century the preferred orientation of academic philosophers. Philosophy, which had been a diverse affair practiced by many sorts of people, was well on its way to being primarily concerned with the problem of knowledge and the possibilities of close attention to language and logic.

See also Pragmatism; *Pragmatism;* Scientific Materialism

BIBLIOGRAPHY

Primary Works

Hall, G. Stanley. "Philosophy in the United States." *Mind* 4 (January 1879): 89–105.

London, Jack. *Novels and Social Writings.* 1909. New York: Library of America, 1982.

Lovejoy, Arthur. "On Some Conditions of Progress in Philosophical Inquiry." *Philosophical Review* 26 (March 1917): 123–163.

Santayana, George. *The Life of Reason; or, The Phases of Human Progress.* 5 vols. New York: Scribners, 1905–1906.

Secondary Works

Campbell, James. *The Community Reconstructs: The Meaning of Pragmatic Social Thought.* Urbana: University of Illinois Press, 1992.

Campbell, James. "The Early Years of the American Philosophical Association." Unpublished manuscript, 2003. This manuscript originated in six talks presented at several meetings of the American Philosophical Association (APA) during 1998–2000 and were sponsored by the APA's History Committee.

Clendenning, John. *The Life and Thought of Josiah Royce.* Rev. and expanded ed. Nashville, Tenn.: Vanderbilt University Press, 1999.

Dykhuizen, George. *The Life and Mind of John Dewey.* Edited by Jo Ann Boydston. Carbondale: Southern Illinois University Press, 1973.

Eldridge, Michael. "Naturalism." In *The Blackwell Guide to American Philosophy,* edited by Armen T. Marsoobian and John Ryder, pp. 52–71. Malden, Mass.: Blackwell, 2004.

Flower, Elizabeth, and Murray G. Murphey. *History of Philosophy in America.* 2 vols. New York: Capricorn Books, 1977. A full, authoritative treatment of the major figures and movements.

Good, James A. "The Development of Thomas Davidson's Religious and Social Thought." The Autodidact Project. http://www.autodidactproject.org/other/TD.html.

Good, James A. "The Journal of Speculative Philosophy, 1867–1893." Thoemmes Continuum. http://www.thoemmes.com/american/journal_intro.htm.

Howison, George H. "Josiah Royce: The Significance of His Work in Philosophy." *Philosophical Review* 25 (May 1916): 231–244.

Kuklick, Bruce. *A History of Philosophy in America, 1720–2000.* New York: Oxford University Press, 2001. A readable survey of the entire sweep of philosophy in America, but some of his expositions must be supplemented with a reading of the text that he is explicating to be understandable.

Quirk, Tom. *Bergson and American Culture: The Worlds of Willa Cather and Wallace Stevens.* Chapel Hill: University of North Carolina Press, 1990.

Seigfried, Charlene Haddock. *Pragmatism and Feminism: Reweaving the Social Fabric.* Chicago: University of Chicago Press, 1996.

Michael Eldridge

PHOTOGRAPHY

Between the end of the U.S. Civil War and the end of World War I, photography was transformed from a slow, static process of image making by specialists into a mobile, distinct, democratic art form. Although sometimes suspicious of its perceived artistic weaknesses, American writers, taking note of photography's unparalleled realistic qualities and its broad popularity, were influenced by its documentary strengths and often incorporated them into their own literary projects.

TECHNOLOGICAL TRANSFORMATIONS

Two of the most iconic images in 1870s America were Andrew Russell's 1869 photograph of the joining of the rails at Promontory Point, Utah, and Eadweard Muybridge's 1872 image of a horse's four hooves suspended above the ground, which appeared in *Scientific American* in 1878. The first was commemorative proof that the immense continent had been spanned; the second, achieving for the dimension of time what the first had done for space, isolated and froze a fraction of a second's motion. With a bank of cameras and a rapid shutter, Muybridge (1830–1904) captured what the human eye could not see and prepared the way for moving pictures. In his 1871 poem "Passage to India," Walt Whitman (1819–1892) ecstatically describes the Pacific Railroad overcoming all barriers, a description dependent on the camera's production of images because the poet had not witnessed the events himself. New technologies were shrinking the world and its visual mysteries were increasingly laid bare by evolving photographic practices and the practitioners who took their cameras into the unknown.

The western American landscape was photographically cataloged throughout the 1870s via the government surveys of Ferdinand Hayden, George Wheeler, and John Wesley Powell, with the work of

Walt Whitman. Seated by a window in his house in Camden, New Jersey. Photograph by Thomas Eakins, 1887. THE LIBRARY OF CONGRESS

the photographers William Henry Jackson, Timothy O'Sullivan, and others, detailing for easterners the country's varied geography, elegizing the passing wilderness, and setting the stage for its development. Innovations moved the chemical process of photography from a bulky, wet-plate ordeal in which the latent image had to be developed in the field, to dry-plate image making where the developing could be done elsewhere. The 1880s saw the beginning of a democratic revolution when George Eastman (1854–1932) introduced the first Kodak box camera and flexible roll film, placing picture-taking power in the hands of amateurs and altering forever what would be recorded with the camera. By the 1890s, the halftone process of photographic newspaper reproduction was perfected; in the early 1900s photographs largely replaced drawings in newspapers; and by 1920 the content of tabloid newspapers began to be driven by photographs. Successive formats and technologies moved photography into the modern age, increasing its speed, versatility, applications, and popularity.

As amateur "snapshot" photography was exploding with the introduction of the first inexpensive Kodak Brownie in 1900 and the company's promise "You press the button, we do the rest," serious photographers of the time were representing the American

experience with astonishing diversity and power. The New York City newspaper reporter Jacob Riis (1849–1914), combining newly developed flash technology and moral anger at the complex web of forces creating the squalor in the city's Lower East Side tenements, agitated for housing reform, ultimately producing *How the Other Half Lives* (1890), a book that drew considerable attention and even moved the young Theodore Roosevelt. Like Muybridge, the painter Thomas Eakins (1844–1916) experimented with motion photography but also employed the camera as a tool and model for his detail-laden paintings. In 1887 he took one of the last photographs of Whitman, portraying him as the "good, gray poet." In 1902 the photographer Alfred Stieglitz (1864–1946) initiated the Photo-Secession, breaking away from the Camera Club of New York and championing photography as a complex art form practiced by serious artists, in opposition to the amateur Kodak images flooding the scene. By 1906 Lewis Hine (1874–1940), following Riis, was using the camera as a lever for social reform, working for the National Child Labor Committee to educate Americans about the need for legislation to protect child workers. Hine made use of slide shows to disseminate his message, as did Edward Curtis (1868–1952), who in 1907 embarked on what would prove to be a nearly thirty-year project to document a "vanishing race." Curtis's opulent twenty-volume *North American Indian* (1907–1930) was sold by subscription mainly to a wealthy eastern audience, and his elegiac images were similar to the painterly pictorialist project of Stieglitz and his followers but owed a great deal as well to conventions of portraiture and ethnography. In the late 1890s and in the first years of the twentieth century, the German émigré Arnold Genthe and the obscure E. J. Bellocq chronicled relatively unknown subcultures, the community of San Francisco's Chinatown and the world of prostitutes in New Orleans, respectively. The year 1905 saw the first extensive use of photographs in *National Geographic* magazine, bringing global exoticism and an implicit approval of colonialism to increasing numbers of American homes. Photo postcards, including horrific images of lynchings, traveled widely through the U.S. mail, while World War I brought the U.S. government a sharpened sense of the power of the art form as propaganda. Strict government control kept images of trench warfare and dead American soldiers from the public's sight. The artistic project of the pictorialists gradually gave way by 1920 to the aesthetic of "straight photography," which embraced sharp, "objective" images, and the investigation of abstract form, initiated by Paul Strand (1890–1976) and championed by Stieglitz in a break with his earlier pictorialist leanings.

In addition to the published works of Riis and Curtis, notable photographic books published in the late nineteenth and early twentieth centuries include Muybridge's *Animal Locomotion* (1887) and *Human Figure in Motion* (1901), and the ten-volume *Photographic History of the War of the Rebellion* (1912), which extended the popular market for Civil War imagery and which had first been successfully presented in Alexander Gardner's *Photographic Sketch Book of the War* (1865). Several photographers were also writers or diarists, including the Hayden geological survey photographer Jackson and Seneca Ray Stoddard, who paired his photography with his own writing to promote the tourist trade in the Adirondacks and to later agitate for the creation of an Adirondack Park. Photography had its own exhibit hall at the 1876 Philadelphia Centennial Exhibition, complete with works by Marcus Aurelius Root, author of *The Camera and the Pencil* (1864), the first published history of the medium by an American. Photographs played an important role as well at the 1893 Columbian Exposition in Chicago, although it was more commercial and even corporate in nature—there was no separate photographic hall, but patrons could choose from hundreds of approved souvenir photo albums of the event. With the publication of how-to books such as Charles Taylor's *Why My Photographs Are Bad*

(1902), it was evident that the era of the amateur photographer had arrived. Popular camera clubs and photographic societies formed, including salon-like gatherings where serious "art" photographers could find sustenance and purpose in a shared pursuit. In 1902 Stieglitz's Photo-Secession linked the project of serious photography with the broader insurrection of artists in Europe. The same year, Stieglitz opened the 291 Gallery in New York, whose first major exhibition of a hundred photographs met with critical approval when it debuted on 24 November 1905. From 1903 to 1917 Stieglitz published the journal *Camera Work,* an eclectic celebration and promotion of the avant-garde, photography included. In the journal, Stieglitz championed the work of the photographers Paul Strand, Gertrude Käsebier, and Edward Steichen and in a 1912 issue publicly introduced the work of the writer Gertrude Stein.

LITERARY AFFINITIES

The art and science of photography significantly influenced the style, content, and reception of American literature of the period. The perceived affinities between literary and photographic art became increasingly obvious in the context of a search for authentic artistic representations of life. Many writers embraced photography's verisimilitude, its seeming ability to objectively catalog the details of culture and external character heretofore unrepresented. Whitman, who had reported on the heady days of daguerreotypy, not only lived to be one of the most photographed American authors of the nineteenth century but also incorporated the art form's aesthetic into his oft-revised *Leaves of Grass* (1855–1892). The poet claimed everything in *Leaves* was "literally photographed" and pronounced his final version of the book "my definitive *carte visite*" (photo calling card). Whitman was also adept at using his own photo iconography to promote his celebrity and writing; he projected so many identities of himself that he confessed confusion over which was the "real" poet. Mark Twain (1835–1910), the only nineteenth-century author to be photographed more than Whitman, both damned and praised photography. He called it an eternal lie (1866) but complimented his fellow writer William Dean Howells (1837–1920) in an 1879 letter, saying that whatever Howells writes "leaves a photograph." Twain incorporated photographic situations and references into some of his writings, such as *A Tramp Abroad* (1880) and *King Leopold's Soliloquy* (1905), exploring the gulf between appearance and reality and deploying photographic metaphors in the service of his satire. Like Whitman, Twain also extensively managed his own public imagery. Although ultimately ambivalent about the art form's usefulness for literature,

Howells worked photographic subjects into his fiction. Photography serves notable functions in *A Modern Instance* (1882), in *The Rise of Silas Lapham* (1884), and in *London Films* (1905), in which a writer carries and employs a "mental Kodak." Kate Field published *Pen Photographs of Charles Dickens's Readings: Taken from Life* (1871), whose title is an attempt to capitalize on the reportorial cachet of photography. *The Red Badge of Courage* (1895) by Stephen Crane (1871–1900) is indebted to the Civil War imagery of Mathew Brady and others. In a review of the novel, the writer Harold Frederic (1856–1898) compared Crane to Muybridge, and Crane, reviewing Frederic's work in turn, compared the author to a sensitive photographic plate. Howells alluded to photograph-like impartiality in his praise of Frank Norris's *McTeague* (1899). Theodore Dreiser's *Sister Carrie* (1900) was hailed for its photo-realism in depicting urban life, and his 1915 novel *The "Genius"* explores a young artist immersed in a cityscape indebted to Stieglitz's pictorialist images. Dreiser (1871–1945) had taken an interest in the handmade painterly photographs of the Photo-Secession, only to reject that aesthetic in favor of the sharper photojournalistic documentation of Riis and Hine.

Yet there were objections and ambivalence as well as enthusiasm. While literary realism and naturalism were often favorably labeled "photographic" for their attention to detail, the label began to be attached to supposedly mechanical or unimaginative writing. Authors such as Howells and Henry James (1811–1882) were sometimes cast as little more than indiscriminate operators or mechanical recorders lacking artistic ability. For some, literature that appeared to be using the camera's power to record suffered when compared to true art, which was decidedly nonmechanical and could transport the soul. Émile Zola (1840–1902) in "The Experimental Novel" (1880) was compelled to defend the literary naturalists against derisive dismissals that they were "merely photographers." James, who regularly employed the metaphors of lens and point of view in his fiction, in *The Aspern Papers* (1888) linked photography to other modern conveniences that have "annihilated surprise." Authenticity and the role of the artist as either objective recorder or imaginative creator were core concerns for artists in both visual and literary arts of the time. James explored this problem in the story "The Real Thing" (1893), which concerns the inapplicability of the notion of authenticity where artistic representation and marketability are concerned. Where Zola had advocated that writers practice a photographic attentiveness, James resisted the camera's supposed objectivity and its use as a revolutionary model for writers.

CONFLUENCES OF LITERATURE AND PHOTOGRAPHY

Despite his early ambivalence about photography, James came to value it enough to select Alvin Langdon Coburn (1882–1936) to illustrate photographically the twenty-four-volume New York edition of his collected works (1907–1909). James extensively advised Coburn on the images that were to begin each volume and even participated enthusiastically in photographic expeditions to London with the photographer to secure appropriate "optical symbols." James undoubtedly saw Coburn's soft images as an evocative art form that complemented but did not compete with his literary works. The author included a tribute to Coburn's work in the preface to *The Golden Bowl* (1909). Bernhard Tauchnitz had previously used photography as an appropriate illustration and salable feature for literary works, notably in the Leipzig edition of Nathaniel Hawthorne's *Marble Faun* (1860), which remained popular for decades among Americans touring Europe. Each book came with several blank pages, inviting tourist readers to select their own images to include in the book, thus participating in its ongoing construction. In 1890 Houghton Mifflin published a new two-volume edition of *The Marble Faun,* complete with fifty photogravures.

Most American writers of the period found themselves frequent subjects of the camera, and some practiced photography as well. Bret Harte (1836–1902), who wrote "A Niece of Snapshot Harry's" (1900) and claimed that photography was his "only recreation," was an avid if less than adept amateur who had his own darkroom. Henry Adams learned to take photographs, "dabbling" in the medium because he was unable to draw. Jack London (1876–1916) took and developed his own pictures, illustrating *The People of the Abyss* (1903) and *The Road* (1907) with his own images. In 1904 Hearst newspapers published some of his photographs from the Russo-Japanese War.

Stieglitz's advocacy of photography as a serious art form existed within a context where, strategically, photography was practiced and photographs exhibited within the sphere of influence of other artistic forms. Stieglitz sought to encourage a steady confluence of artistic thought and expression, ultimately encouraging many modernist writers, including Stein, Sherwood Anderson, Waldo Frank, William Carlos Williams, and Hart Crane. The poet Ezra Pound (1885–1972) embraced the avant-garde theory of vorticism, the belief that at the core of all artistic creations lay a geometric concentration of energy, and he collaborated with Coburn on a series of "vortographs," prismatic photographs that fragmented the subject. Pound and

Vortograph, 1917. Ezra Pound photographed by Alvin Langdon Coburn. © MUSEUM OF FINE ARTS, HOUSTON, TEXAS, USA/THE BRIDGEMAN ART LIBRARY

BIBLIOGRAPHY

Secondary Works

Davenport, Alma. *The History of Photography: An Overview.* Albuquerque: University of New Mexico Press, 1999.

Folsom, Ed. *Walt Whitman's Native Representations.* Cambridge, U.K.: Cambridge University Press, 1994.

Marien, Mary Warner. *Photography: A Cultural History.* Upper Saddle River, N.J.: Prentice Hall, 2002.

Orvell, Miles. *The Real Thing: Imitation and Authenticity in American Culture, 1880–1940.* Chapel Hill: University of North Carolina Press, 1989.

Rabb, Jane M., ed. *Literature and Photography Interactions, 1840–1990: A Critical Anthology.* Albuquerque: University of New Mexico Press, 1995.

Sandweiss, Martha A., ed. *Photography in Nineteenth-Century America.* New York: Harry N. Abrams, 1991.

Shloss, Carol. *In Visible Light: Photography and the American Writer, 1840–1940.* New York: Oxford University Press, 1987.

Szarkowski, John. *Photography until Now.* New York: Museum of Modern Art, 1989.

Trachtenberg, Alan. *Reading American Photographs: Images as History, Mathew Brady to Walker Evans.* New York: Hill and Wang, 1989.

West, Nancy Martha. *Kodak and the Lens of Nostalgia.* Charlottesville: University Press of Virginia, 2000.

Andrew Smith

Coburn had a vexed relationship with each other over the vortographs, exhibited in 1917, but the kaleidoscopic images suggested the themes of alienation and fragmentation so central to the modernist literary project. In the same year, the final issue of *Camera Work* reproduced eleven of Strand's new "straight" photography images, along with an essay, written by the photographer himself, that trumpeted the medium as a pathway to "intense self-realization." Influenced by the modernist painters he had seen at Stieglitz's 291, Strand initiated an investigation of abstract form that would touch many artists across multiple media. Strand saw corollaries to his aspiration to offer honest portrayals of ordinary subjects in Edgar Lee Masters's *Spoon River Anthology* (1915) and Sherwood Anderson's *Winesburg, Ohio* (1919). Strand wrote Anderson (1876–1941) in 1920, saying that *Winesburg* had enlarged his spirit and given him renewed hope in the artistic fight against the craven materialism of America.

See also Periodicals; Motion Pictures; Science and Technology

"PLAIN LANGUAGE FROM TRUTHFUL JAMES"

By any objective measure—the frequency with which it was reprinted, the number of parodies it inspired, the times it was quoted or set to music—Bret Harte's (1836–1902) "Plain Language from Truthful James," more commonly known as "The Heathen Chinee," was one of the most popular poems ever published. It was as nearly an overnight sensation as was possible in the days when San Francisco was four or five days distant from New York via transcontinental railroad. Within days of its original appearance in the September 1870 issue of the *Overland Monthly*, the poem had been reprinted in dozens of newspapers and magazines across the country, including the *New York Evening Post*, *New York Tribune*, *Louisville Courier-Journal*, *Washington Star*, *Albany Journal*, *Boston Transcript*, *Providence Journal*, *Hartford Courant*, and *Saturday Evening Post* (twice). More than his celebrated stories "The Luck of Roaring Camp" or "The Outcasts of Poker Flat," which had appeared earlier in the *Overland Monthly* without signature, "Plain Language

Bret Harte. © CORBIS

from Truthful James" made Bret Harte a household name in the East.

At first glance, the meaning of the dramatic monologue seems transparent. For "ways that are dark" and "tricks that are vain, / The heathen Chinee is peculiar" (ll. 3–5), the speaker Truthful James avers. The "pensive" (l. 11) Chinese laundryman Ah Sin seems an easy mark to James and his friend Bill Nye, Irish cardsharps who stack a deck of cards against him, especially when the laundryman protests he "did not understand" the rules of euchre: "But he smiled as he sat by the table, / With the smile that was childlike and bland" (ll. 22–24). Ah Sin turns the tables on the Irishmen and beats them at their own game, however, by concealing cards in his sleeves and marking them with wax. When Nye realizes the deception,

> . . . he rose with a sigh,
> And said, "Can this be?
> We are ruined by Chinese cheap labor,"
> And he went for that heathen Chinee.
>
> (Ll. 39–42)

While Bill Nye metes out punishment to Ah Sin for trumping him, the poem omits any description of overt violence.

To judge from all extant evidence, Harte clearly intended the poem to satirize anti-Chinese prejudices pervasive in northern California among Irish day laborers, with whom Chinese immigrants were competing

for jobs. As early as April 1863, Harte wrote in a San Francisco literary paper, the *Golden Era*, that the Chinese are "generally honest, faithful, simple, and painstaking," and he blamed the campaign to restrict Chinese immigration on "the conscious hate and fear with which inferiority always regards the possibility of even-handed justice" (p. 4). In a piece for the *Springfield Republican* published in March 1867, Harte noted that the "quick-witted, patient, obedient and faithful" Chinese were "gradually deposing the Irish from their old, recognized positions in the ranks of labor," and he predicted that the Chinese would "eventually supplant" the Irish in menial occupations (p. 1). "Plain Language from Truthful James" satirizes class resentment at precisely this point: the economic threat the Chinese posed to the Irish underclass in California. To the end of his life, Harte insisted that he had written the poem "with a satirical political purpose" (Dam, p. 43).

Harte's intent, of course, has no necessary correlation to the cultural work the poem actually performed. In fact, "Plain Language from Truthful James" was read by many a xenophobic reader as satire not of the Irish cardsharps but of Ah Sin and the so-called Yellow Peril. Whether or not Truthful James spoke plainly, Harte's language was easy to misconstrue. On the surface, the poem represents Ah Sin in stereotypical terms; only when read ironically does the poem resist or subvert the stereotype of the "inscrutable Oriental." The predominantly white middle-class readers of the *Overland*, the *Saturday Evening Post,* and the papers that reprinted the poem identified not with the "heathen" Ah Sin but with his presumed racial superior, Bill Nye, the ostensible victim of his trickery.

(MIS)APPROPRIATIONS OF THE POEM

Put another way, "Plain Language from Truthful James" was transformed into a culture text that was appropriated for a variety of purposes, few of them intended by the poet. During its first months in print, the poem was parodied dozens of times—for example, to satirize flirtatious women ("Plain Language from Truthful Jane"), the presidential ambitions of Horace Greeley ("The Heathen Greelee"), the Treaty of Washington ("Plain Language from Truthful Bull" and "Plain Language to Untruthful Bull"), and cheating at British colleges ("The Heathen Passee"). A number of contemporary reprintings included illustrations that pandered to racist sentiment. Before the end of 1870 the Western News Company of Chicago issued a pirated edition illustrated by Joseph Hull that sold thousands of copies. Though for the most part unremarkable, at least two of Hull's drawings depicted

And he went for that heathen Chinee

"And he went for that heathen Chinee." Illustration by Joseph Hull from the 1870 edition of *The Heathen Chinee* published in Chicago by the Western News Company. COURTESY OF GARY SCHARNHORST

explicit violence against Ah Sin. The reading of the poem they represent is not only literal—without any sense of irony or ambiguity—but it also revises Harte's text, filling its gaps and silences with scenes of overt brutality. Bill Nye targets Ah Sin's queue, an ornament of honor and male pride; that is, Nye not only pummels Ah Sin, he figuratively emasculates him. The implications were plain. Before long the phrase "Ah Sin" had become a racial slur for Asians. The poem was even recited on the floor of the U.S. Congress in January 1871 by a foe of Chinese immigration.

All of which may begin to explain Harte's repudiation of the poem. As early as April 1871, in a letter enclosing a manuscript copy of the poem transcribed at the request of his friend and publisher James T. Fields, Harte lamented "all this 'damnable iteration' and inordinate quotation" which "have divested it of all meaning to me, and make me loathe it so that I can not even copy it legibly" (*Selected Letters,* p. 52). Harte used to conclude his lecture, "The Argonauts of '49," which he delivered over a hundred and fifty times between 1872 and 1875, by protesting the caricature of "what you [in the audience] call the heathen Chinee" and enumerating what he considered to be some outstanding characteristics of the Chinese: "Quiet, calm, almost philosophic, but never obtrusive or aggressive, he never flaunts his three thousand years [of civilization] in the face of the men of today. . . . He accepted a menial position with dignity and self-respect. He washed for the whole community, and made cleanliness a virtue" ("Bret Harte at Steinway Hall," p. 5). His friend and biographer T. Edgar Pemberton recalled after Harte's death in 1902 how "in quite recent years" Harte, "while reading his morning papers," made "half humorous, half earnest protest against" the way the poem was cited in the press (p. 110).

Despite repeated disavowals, however, Harte was willing and even eager to capitalize on the poem's popularity. Soon after he agreed to write exclusively for the Boston firm of Fields, Osgood, and Company, his new publishers prepared their own illustrated edition of the poem. In March 1871, in the same letter in which he agreed to contract terms, Harte wrote James R. Osgood that he had given the artist Sol Eytinge "several ideas about the 'Heathen Chinee' and his Pagan brother—the California miner" (*Selected Letters,* p. 53). Eytinge's eight drawings, which first accompanied a reprinting of the poem in *Every Saturday* on 29 April, proved so popular that the number soon sold out. Fields, Osgood, and Company issued a chapbook of the poem later that year priced at a quarter and featuring Eytinge's sketches with a note that they had been approved by Harte, making it "the only illustrated edition of the poem published with the author's sanction" (Harte, *Heathen Chinee,* p. 6). While Eytinge's drawings are aesthetically superior to Hull's, they interpret the poem in much the same way: Bill Nye and Truthful James are more vulgar figures, and the violence against Ah Sin is less blatant, but the sketches do not dispute the anti-Chinese reading the poem had been given in the press and by all other illustrators.

LATER (MIS)READINGS OF THE POEM

However much Harte criticized the poem privately, he willingly accommodated the demands of the literary market in hopes of turning a profit. In the mid-1870s, with his career in decline, he scripted a play entitled *Two Men of Sandy Bar* that featured a Chinese laundryman reminiscent of Ah Sin. Played by a white actor, the character amused both audiences and critics during the four-week run of the play in New York in the summer of 1876. Mark Twain (1835–1910) later reminisced that Harte once "wrote a play with a perfectly delightful Chinaman in it—a play which would have succeeded if anyone else had written it" (p. 275). To capitalize on the popularity of the character, Harte proposed in the fall of 1876 that the two of them write a play together under the working title "The Heathen Chinee" and "divide the swag." The result was the most disastrous collaboration in the history of American letters. *Ah Sin* ran on Broadway and in the provinces for several months, but the production was a financial and critical flop, and in the end the collaboration effectively ended Harte and Twain's friendship.

In the end, too, the foes of Chinese immigration carried the day. As the result of congressional ratification of a treaty with China, the number of new immigrants

Illustration by Sol Eytinge from the 1871 edition of *The Heathen Chinee* published in Boston by James Osgood. COURTESY OF GARY SCHARNHORST

declined from a high of nearly forty thousand in 1882 to ten—not ten thousand, but ten—only five years later. This policy was formally enacted into law by the Chinese Exclusion Act of 1892, four years before the U.S. Supreme Court sanctioned the "separate but equal" doctrine of racial apartheid in *Plessy v. Ferguson.* Not surprisingly, given its earlier history of appropriation by race-baiters, Harte's poem enjoyed a burst of new popularity around the turn of the century. Allen Thurman, the Democratic candidate for vice president in 1888, recited it during the campaign to prove his opposition to Chinese immigration; and the artist E. W. Kemble, best known for illustrating the first edition of *Adventures of Huckleberry Finn* (1885), pandered to anti-Chinese prejudices in illustrating "Plain Language" for *Mark Twain's Library of Humor,* issued the same year. More than the illustrations printed in the 1870s, Kemble's most memorable sketch depicts exaggerated and graphic violence against the Chinese as Bill Nye—holding an unholstered pistol nowhere mentioned in the poem—flings Ah Sin into the air by his queue. The poem was reprinted in at least eight other anthologies between 1887 and Harte's death in 1902. The frequency with which Harte's poem was appropriated by other writers also spiked around the turn of the twentieth century. Frank Norris planned to publish a volume of short stories in 1897 under the title *Ways That Are Dark,* for example, and the California journalist Adeline Knapp endorsed the racist reading of "Plain Language" in a crude "Yellow Peril" tale, also titled "The Ways That Are Dark," printed in the *San Francisco Sunday Call* in August 1895.

The anti-Chinese reading of Harte's poem has remained essentially fixed in American culture since its first publication. While it may seem at first glance little more than a quaint relic to bad taste, the poem was construed throughout the final decades of the nineteenth century to favor limits on Chinese immigration. However well intentioned the poem may have been, the comic stereotype appropriated from "Plain Language from Truthful James" has historically— and most unfortunately—been invoked to justify racial discrimination.

See also Chinese; Popular Poetry

BIBLIOGRAPHY
Primary Works
Harte, Bret. "Bohemian Papers/John Chinaman." *Golden Era,* 5 April 1863, p. 4.

Harte, Bret. "From California." *Springfield Republican,* 30 March 1867, p. 1.

Hart, Bret. *The Heathen Chinee.* Boston: Osgood, 1871.

Harte, Bret. "Plain Language from Truthful James." *Overland Monthly,* September 1870, pp. 287–288. Reprinted in *The Heathen Chinee.*

Harte, Bret. *Selected Letters of Bret Harte.* Edited by Gary Scharnhorst. Norman: University of Oklahoma Press, 1997.

Secondary Works
"Bret Harte at Steinway Hall." *New York World,* 17 December 1872, p. 5.

Dam, Henry J. W. "A Morning with Bret Harte." *McClure's,* December 1894, pp. 38–50.

Duckett, Margaret. *Mark Twain and Bret Harte.* Norman: University of Oklahoma Press, 1964.

Duckett, Margaret. "Plain Language from Bret Harte." *Nineteenth-Century Fiction* 11 (March 1957): 241–260.

Gardner, Joseph H. "Bret Harte and the Dickensian Mode in America." *Canadian Review of American Studies* 2 (fall 1971): 89–101.

Kolb, Harold H., Jr. "The Outcasts of Literary Flat: Bret Harte as Humorist." *American Literary Realism* 23 (winter 1991): 52–63.

May, Ernest R. "Bret Harte and the *Overland Monthly.*" *American Literature* 22 (November 1950): 260–271.

Oliver, Egbert S. "The Pig-Tailed China Boys out West." *Western Humanities Review* 12 (spring 1958): 175–177.

Pemberton, T. Edgar. *The Life of Bret Harte.* London: Pearson, 1903.

Scharnhorst, Gary. *Bret Harte: Opening the American Literary West.* Norman: University of Oklahoma Press, 2000.

Twain, Mark. *Mark Twain in Eruption.* Edited by Bernard De Voto. New York: Harper, 1940.

Gary Scharnhorst

PLESSY V. FERGUSON

In a seven-to-one decision, with one justice not participating, the United States Supreme Court on 18 May 1896 ruled that an 1890 Louisiana law mandating "equal but separate" accommodations for "whites" and "coloreds" on intrastate railroads did not violate the constitutional rights of Homer Plessy (1863–1925), who, because he had one-eighth African ancestry, was considered a "colored" person under state law. The Court's decision allowed states to impose a legal system of racial segregation, until the 1954 ruling of *Brown v. Board of Education.* The majority decision was written by Justice Henry Billings Brown (1836–1913), born in Massachusetts. The lone dissenter was Justice John Marshall Harlan (1833–1911), a former slave owner and one of two southerners on the Court. Plessy's attorney was Albion W. Tourgée (1838–1905), a novelist and lawyer who was one of the period's most vocal advocates of civil rights for African Americans.

CIVIL RIGHTS AND THE THIRTEENTH AND FOURTEENTH AMENDMENTS
Plessy v. Ferguson tested the limits of the Thirteenth and Fourteenth Amendments, which were added to the Constitution after the Civil War. The Thirteenth Amendment forbids slavery and involuntary servitude, except as punishment for the commission of a crime. Soon after its 1865 ratification, the Court ruled that it also forbids "badges and incidents" of slavery. Ratified in 1868, the Fourteenth Amendment states, "All persons born or naturalized in the United States, and subject to the jurisdiction thereof, are citizens of the United States and of the State wherein they reside. No State shall make or enforce any law which shall abridge the privileges or immunities of citizens of the United

States; nor shall any State deprive any person of life, liberty, or property, without due process of law; nor deny to any person within its jurisdiction the equal protection of the laws."

These two amendments prompted Congress to pass important civil rights acts in 1866 and 1875. The 1866 Civil Rights Act extended U.S. citizenship to African Americans and others by declaring, "All persons born in the United States and not subject to any foreign power, excluding Indians not taxed, are hereby declared to be citizens of the United States." It also guaranteed "citizens of every race and color" various rights, especially economic ones, such as the right "to make and enforce contracts, to sue, . . . to inherit, purchase, lease, sell, hold, and convey real and personal property" (Thomas, ed., *Plessy v. Ferguson*, p. 13). The 1875 Civil Rights Act made it illegal to discriminate on the basis of color in theaters, amusement parks, places of public accommodation, public transportation, and so on. The more comprehensive Act of 1875 marked the high point for the legal protection of civil rights in the postbellum period, but it also sparked heated controversy. The Supreme Court resolved the controversy in the *Civil Rights Cases* of 1883 when an eight-to-one majority, with Justice Harlan again dissenting, declared the Act of 1875 unconstitutional.

In the *Civil Rights Cases* the U.S. government argued that the Act of 1875 was supported by both the Thirteenth and the Fourteenth Amendments. Racial discrimination, it argued, was a product of the institution of slavery and thus constituted a "badge of servitude." It also claimed that discrimination violated both the due process and the equal protection clauses of the Fourteenth Amendment. Finally, it asserted that freedom from discrimination was one of the privileges and immunities of citizenship protected by the Fourteenth Amendment. The majority of the Court, however, disagreed. It countered the Thirteenth Amendment justification by pointing to laws in the North prior to the Civil War that denied equal rights to free blacks. Racial discrimination, it concluded, was not inextricably linked to the institution of slavery. In denying the government's Fourteenth Amendment justification, the majority looked at the amendment's exact language. The privileges and immunities clause, the due process clause, and the equal protection clause, it noted, place restrictions on states, not individuals. Whereas the Act of 1875 had forbidden private parties from discriminating on the basis of race, the Fourteenth Amendment forbids only state action. Thus the Act of 1875 was not supported by the Constitution.

The *Civil Rights Cases* set the stage for *Plessy*. Emboldened by the Court's decision, various states passed laws like the one in Louisiana, mandating separate but equal facilities. Since these laws were clearly the actions of states, not individuals, the question before the Court in *Plessy* was: How far could a state go in forcing people to be assorted by race?

A COURT CHALLENGE AND A DECISION

Albion W. Tourgée, contacted in September 1891 by New Orleans blacks who wanted to protest the 1890 law, proposed challenging the Jim Crow law with someone of mixed blood, hoping that doing so would point out the arbitrariness of creating mutually exclusive categories of "whites" and "coloreds." Plessy volunteered to test the law. Because he was able to pass as white, he could have ridden in the white car undetected, but Tourgée needed a legal challenge. That challenge received some silent support from railroad companies, which did not like the added expense of providing separate cars. By prearrangement the railroad conductor and a private detective detained Plessy on 7 June 1892 when he sat in the forbidden coach. He was convicted and his case wound through a series of appeals until it reached the Supreme Court four years later.

Tourgée argued that the Louisiana law violated both the Thirteenth and the Fourteenth Amendments. Again the Court disagreed. Relying on the *Civil Rights Cases,* it dismissed the Thirteenth Amendment appeal with little comment. The Fourteenth Amendment appeal, it admitted, was more complicated. In his decision Brown first addressed intention. "The object of the [Fourteenth] amendment was undoubtedly to enforce the absolute equality of the two races before the law, but in the nature of things, it could not have been intended to abolish distinctions based upon color, or to enforce social as distinguished from political equality, or a commingling of the two races upon terms unsatisfactory to either" (Thomas, ed., *Plessy v. Ferguson,* p. 44). He then established that every state has certain police powers that can be used for the public good. The question facing the Court in *Plessy,* therefore, was whether the Louisiana law was reasonable. "In determining the question of reasonableness," Brown argued, "[a legislature] is at liberty to act with reference to the established usages, customs and traditions of the people, and with a view to the promotion of their comfort, and the preservation of the public peace and good order" (Thomas, ed., *Plessy v. Ferguson,* p. 50). According to this standard, the Louisiana law was deemed constitutional. Indeed, to stress its reasonableness, Brown cited the antebellum Massachusetts case of *Roberts v. City of Boston* (1849). Speaking for the Court, Lemuel Shaw, Herman Melville's famous father-in-law, declared that segregated schools did not violate the Massachusetts constitution's guarantee of equality before the law.

It is important to remember that, without the guarantee of equal facilities, the Louisiana law would not have passed constitutional scrutiny. Because a white was forbidden to sit in a black car just as a black was in a white car and because facilities in both were supposed to be equal, whites and blacks were, Brown reasoned, treated equally under the law. Indeed, the "underlying fallacy" of Plessy's argument, he asserted, was the "assumption that the enforced separation of the two races stamps the colored race with a badge of inferiority. If this be so, it is not by reason of anything found in the act, but solely because the colored race chooses to put that construction upon it" (Thomas, ed., *Plessy v. Ferguson,* p. 50).

A second fallacy of Plessy's argument, according to Brown, was the assumption "that social prejudices may be overcome by legislation, and that equal rights cannot be secured to the negro except by an enforced commingling of the two races." The Constitution, he asserted, guarantees equal civil and political rights, but it cannot create social equality. As to Tourgée's effort to have someone of mixed blood challenge legal assortments by color, Brown concluded that in the federal system states have the right to determine racial classifications.

A DISSENTING OPINION

The majority opinion did not go unchallenged. Comparing the decision to that of *Dred Scott* (1856–1857) on the status of slavery in the Federal territories, Justice Harlan delivered a powerful dissent. The Louisiana law, he declared, "is inconsistent not only with that equality of rights which pertains to citizenship, National and State, but with the personal liberty enjoyed by every one within the United States" (Thomas, ed., *Plessy v. Ferguson,* p. 53). Despite its guarantee of equal conditions, "every one knows that the statute in question had its origin in the purpose, not so much to exclude white persons from railroad cars occupied by blacks, as to exclude colored people from coaches occupied or assigned to white persons" (Thomas, ed., *Plessy v. Ferguson,* p. 55). Countering the majority's claim that the crucial issue was whether the law was a reasonable use of a state's police powers, he asserted that the question facing the Court was not reasonableness but constitutionality. According to him, it was unconstitutional because "our Constitution is color-blind, and neither knows nor tolerates classes among citizens" (Thomas, ed., *Plessy v. Ferguson,* p. 57). He went on to add a warning that, far from promoting the public good, such laws would "arouse race hate" and "perpetuate a feeling of distrust" between the two races. "The thin disguise of 'equal' accommodations for passengers in railroad coaches," he concluded, "will not mislead any one, nor atone for the wrong this day done" (Thomas, ed., *Plessy v. Ferguson,* p. 59).

As powerful as his dissent was, Harlan was a product of his time. He continued to subscribe to the belief that the white race was the "dominant race" in the country "in prestige, in achievements, in education, in wealth and in power" (Thomas, ed., *Plessy v. Ferguson,* pp. 56–57). Also, to bolster his argument for blacks, he made statements at the expense of the Chinese, whom he called a "race so different from our own that we do not permit those belonging to it to become citizens of the United States" (Thomas, ed., *Plessy v. Ferguson,* p. 58).

PLESSY AND LITERATURE

Indirectly, *Plessy* is related to numerous works of literature written in the era of Jim Crow. It is most directly connected, however, to the works of Tourgée and Charles W. Chesnutt (1858–1932), who was also trained as a lawyer. In an unpublished speech entitled "The Courts and the Negro" (c. 1911), Chesnutt declared:

> The opinion in *Plessy v. Ferguson* is, to my mind, as epoch-making as the Dred Scott decision. Unfortunately, it applies to a class of rights which do not make to the heart and conscience of the nation the same direct appeal as was made by slavery, and has not been nor is it likely to produce any such revulsion of feeling. (Thomas, ed., *Plessy v. Ferguson,* p. 157)

All three novels that Chesnutt published in his lifetime undertake the difficult task of producing such a feeling. There are a number of allusions to the case in all three works. The most obvious is a scene in *The Marrow of Tradition* (1901). Forced to ride in a colored car, the book's protagonist, Dr. Miller, watches as "a Chinaman, of the ordinary laundry type, boarded the train, and took his seat in the white car without objection. At another point a colored nurse found a place with her mistress" (p. 59). The detail of the Chinaman shows the care with which Chesnutt read Harlan's dissent. The detail of the nurse alludes to a provision in the 1890 Louisiana law that exempted nurses of children from separate car restrictions. Dr. Miller's response to this exemption is almost exactly the same as Tourgée's response in his brief to the Court: "White people . . . do not object to the negro as a servant. As the traditional negro,—the servant,—he is welcomed; as an equal, he is repudiated" (p. 59). Indeed, since few blacks had white nurses for their children, this provision betrayed the true intent of the law.

Tourgée's literary works are related to the case in different ways. Some were not a response but rather a rehearsal of arguments Tourgée would later make before the Court. For instance, one of his most ingenious claims in *Plessy* was that the Louisiana law allowed the conductor, without due process, to impair Plessy's reputation as a white man. Since reputation affects earning power, the law deprived Plessy, or at least seven-eighths of him, of the Fourteenth Amendment's protection of property. Tourgée worked out the logic of this argument in his 1890 novel *Pactolus Prime,* in which the black protagonist advises a young mulatto training for the law to pass as white to increase his earnings. In other works Tourgée did not so much rehearse arguments as complicate them. For instance, Harlan borrowed his famous metaphor of color blindness from Tourgée's brief to the Court, which proclaimed, "Justice is pictured as blind and her daughter, the Law, ought at least be color-blind" (Thomas, ed., *Plessy v. Ferguson,* p. 29). Tourgée first used the metaphor in his 1880 novel, *Bricks without Straw.* But in this novel he did not use color blindness as a positive quality that keeps people from discriminating. Instead, he considered it a defect that does not allow people to see the actual condition of freedmen. Describing how the freedman had been granted legal rights, the narrator complains, "Right he had, in the abstract; in the concrete, none. Justice would not hear his voice. The law was still color-blinded by the past" (p. 35).

See also Civil Rights; Jim Crow; Jurisprudence

BIBLIOGRAPHY
Primary Works
Chesnutt, Charles. *The Marrow of Tradition.* Boston: Houghton Mifflin, 1901.

Thomas, Brook, ed. *Plessy v. Ferguson: A Brief History with Documents.* Boston: Bedford Books, 1997. Includes the *Plessy v. Ferguson* decision; the dissent of Justice Brown; Charles W. Chesnutt's "The Courts and the Negro"; writings by W. E. B. Du Bois, Booker T. Washington, and others; and press reactions to the decision.

Tourgée, Albion W. *Bricks without Straw.* New York: Fords, Howard, and Hulbert, 1880.

Tourgée, Albion W. *Pactolus Prime.* New York: Cassell, 1890.

Secondary Works
Crane, Gregg. *Race, Citizenship, and Law in American Literature.* New York: Cambridge University Press, 2002.

Fiss, Owen M. *Troubled Beginnings of the Modern State, 1888–1910.* New York: Macmillan, 1993.

Garraty, John A., ed. *Quarrels That Have Shaped the Constitution.* Rev. ed. New York: Perennial Library, 1987.

Lofgren, Charles A. *The "Plessy" Case: A Legal-Historical Interpretation.* New York: Oxford University Press, 1987.

Olsen, Otto H. *Carpetbagger's Crusade: The Life of Albion Winegar Tourgée.* Baltimore: Johns Hopkins University Press, 1965.

Olsen, Otto H., ed. *The Thin Disguise: Turning Point in Negro History, "Plessy v. Ferguson."* New York: Humanities Press, 1967.

Sundquist, Eric J. *To Wake the Nations: Race and the Making of American Literature.* Cambridge, Mass.: Harvard University Press, 1993.

Thomas, Brook. *American Literary Realism and the Failed Promise of Contract.* Berkeley: University of California Press, 1997.

Thomas, Brook. "*Plessy v. Ferguson* and the Literary Imagination." *Cardozo Studies in Law and Literature* 9 (1997): 45–65.

Weiner, Mark S. *Black Trials: Citizenship from the Beginnings of Slavery to the End of Caste.* New York: Alfred A. Knopf, 2004.

Brook Thomas

POETRY: A MAGAZINE OF VERSE

Poetry: A Magazine of Verse published most of the poets who revolutionized modern American poetry. From the time Harriet Monroe (1860–1936) brought out the first issue in October 1912, her goal was not only to publish the innovative poets who were not receiving a hearing in contemporary literary magazines but also to find the poet who, like Walt Whitman in the nineteenth century, would be the twentieth century's great poet. Monroe's ambition was more than fulfilled when early contributors to her magazine included W. B. Yeats, Edwin Arlington Robinson, Edgar Lee Masters, Hilda Doolittle (H.D.), Ezra Pound, D. H. Lawrence, T. S. Eliot, William Carlos Williams, Robert Frost, Wallace Stevens, and Marianne Moore. Her pages were open to all styles of poetry, from the experimental free verse of H.D. to the traditional blank verse of Wallace Stevens, from the expansiveness of Vachel Lindsay to the spare notations of William Carlos Williams. Romantic authors such as Rupert Brooke and Joyce Kilmer (whose "Trees," in August 1913, was the most popular poem the magazine ever published) appeared along with modernists such as Eliot and Pound. The celebration of life, however crude its manifestations, in poets like Lindsay and Carl Sandburg, was balanced with laments about its oppressive power in poets like Eliot and Frost.

Unlike other important modern journals, such as *The Egoist* and *The Dial, Poetry* was devoted exclusively to verse. Unlike the *Little Review* and *Others,* it placed no premium on experimental work even though some of the most innovative poems of Pound, Eliot, and Hart Crane appeared in its pages. It took no direct stands on social issues except to assert the right of poets to be heard, however controversial their subject matter or style. In an era of embattled, short-lived literary journals, *Poetry* distinguished itself through regular monthly publication from 1912 into the early twenty-first century.

BEGINNINGS IN CHICAGO

Although New York was a greater cultural and publishing center, Chicago also had a claim to high culture, established by institutions such as the Chicago Symphony Orchestra, the Little Theatre, and the Art Institute. Harriet Monroe came from a pioneer Chicago family, which gave her entrée to art patrons such as Cyrus McCormick, Mrs. George M. Pullman, Charles H. Swift, and Clarence Darrow.

In her own career as a poet (she was fifty-one when she founded her magazine), she had found few places in America that published poetry. Little was published in popular magazines such as the *Atlantic Monthly, Scribner's,* and *Harper's,* and that was of a conventional and inspirational type. Monroe's single commercial success was her "Columbian Ode," for which she was paid $1,000 and which was performed at the World's Columbian Exposition in 1892. Monroe believed that the poet should enjoy the same kind of commissions, prizes, and institutional support as the artist, playwright, and musician. With this argument, she began implementing in June 1911 her plan to convince one hundred people to underwrite the magazine.

By June 1912 she had over a hundred "guarantors" (a number she later learned would not be adequate) to underwrite the magazine at $50 a year for five years and printed up a "poet's circular," sporting *Poetry*'s Pegasus logo and a quotation from Whitman, "To have great poets, there must be great audiences too," that she sent out to potential contributors. The flyer announced that contributors would be paid, all types of poetry would be considered, and a prize would be awarded for the best poem published each year. In *Poetry*'s second issue, in November 1912, she stated the "Open Door" policy of the magazine: to

avoid any "entangling alliances" with schools of poetry or editorial policies. The Chicago poet Alice Corbin Henderson joined her as associate editor for the salary of $40 per month.

Poetry survived a series of financial crises. Because it paid about $10 a page for contributions, its publishing costs in its first years were high—between $9,000 and $10,000 annually. A third of this sum came from the patrons, and the rest from subscriptions of $1.50 per year, gifts, and some advertising. Monroe was counting on libraries and lovers of the arts to support *Poetry,* but paid subscriptions for 1912–1913 totaled only 1,030 subscriptions. With a subscription list that never went above three thousand, Monroe kept the magazine going year to year through tireless solicitation of gifts and grants.

EARLY ARTISTIC SUCCESS AND EZRA POUND

From the start the magazine was an artistic success. Monroe sent out letters to those she considered the best of the established poets, such as W. B. Yeats and Edwin Arlington Robinson, and to newer poets, such as Vachel Lindsay, Amy Lowell, and Ezra Pound. Pound (1885–1972) not only sent two poems of his own that were used in the first issue but served as an unpaid foreign correspondent, sending contributions from such poets as Rabindranath Tagore, Hilda Doolittle, James Joyce, and T. S. Eliot. Tagore's poems in the December 1912 issue appeared before the Bengali poet won the Nobel Prize in 1913. Pound immediately brought controversy and welcome publicity to *Poetry* when it published in January 1913 a group of poems that he submitted by Hilda Doolittle signed, "H.D., Imagiste." Both the readers who wished to ridicule the gnomic utterances of the highly compressed, haiku-like imagist poems and poets who, like Amy Lowell, discovered that they too were imagists wanted to know more about the movement. Pound provided the information in an essay "A Few Don'ts by an Imagiste" (March 1913), which stated the principles of good writing that *Poetry* was proud to be associated (but not identified) with: the image as expression rather than ornament, no wasted words, and rhythms that would express rather than override the meaning. Pound's own two-line poem, "In a Station at the Metro" (April 1915), was one of the celebrated imagist pieces that appeared in the journal. Poems by D. H. Lawrence, William Carlos Williams, Amy Lowell, and Wallace Stevens as well as H. D. seemed to develop out of the imagist program. Although it was not an imagist poem, one of Yeats's poems that Pound sent Monroe was among his most compressed lyrics, "The Magi" (May 1914).

Pound's greatest find for *Poetry* was T. S. Eliot's (1888–1965) "The Love Song of J. Alfred Prufrock." Monroe at first hesitated to print Eliot's poem because she disliked what she took to be its morbid tone; she also regretted that it did not come to a resounding finish like a poem by Lindsay or Sandburg. Pound later claimed that he had to prod Monroe to publish it; it appeared after some delay as the last poem in the June 1915 issue. Yet Monroe soon published more of Eliot's poetry: "Conversation Galante," "La Figlia che Piange," "Mr. Apollinax," and "Morning at the Window" appeared in the September 1916 issue. However, she annoyed Pound further when she decided on her own to eliminate the word "foetus" from "Mr. Apollinax" and, in the same issue, "bloody" from Pound's poem "Phyllidula." In that literary era editors had more control over their texts, and the U.S. post office represented a constant threat of prosecution of "obscene" material in the mail. Pound and Monroe also clashed when Pound insisted that the *Poetry*'s first Guarantors' Prize go to an established Irish poet rather than Monroe's choice, the young American poet Vachel Lindsay (1879–1931). Pound was right as far as rewarding the better poet, and Monroe graciously deferred to Pound's judgment in awarding the prize to Yeats for "The Grey Rock" rather than to Lindsay for "General William Booth Enters into Heaven." Monroe then managed to scrape up $100 for a special Guarantors' Prize for Lindsay.

HARRIET MONROE AND POETIC TALENT

Monroe felt that Lindsay was the first major talent she had helped to find. The flashy imagery and sound effects of his poetry pleased her and her readers better than imagist compression. When Monroe arranged a banquet on 1 March 1914 to honor W. B. Yeats during his visit to Chicago, she invited Lindsay to speak. In Yeats's speech, the Irish poet generously praised *Poetry* and Lindsay's "General Booth" poem. Instead of a speech, Lindsay read his dramatic poem "The Congo," which surpassed the sound effects of his Booth poem with refrains like "Boomlay, boomlay, boomlay, BOOM" and "Mumbo-Jumbo will hoo-doo you." The poem launched a career of public performances that included one for President Woodrow Wilson's cabinet in 1915. *Poetry* awarded him a Levinson Prize for "The Chinese Nightingale" (February 1915), and Monroe's interest in Lindsay extended to an unsuccessful attempt at matchmaking between Lindsay and the St. Louis poet Sara Teasdale.

A poet nearly as flamboyant as Lindsay, Carl Sandburg (1878–1967), received the first of the Levinson Prizes, which were specifically for an American poet, for his "Chicago Poems." Monroe's associate

Harriet Monroe. Photograph from a *Vanity Fair* article, August 1920, in which Monroe is credited with "the revival of interest in contemporary American poetry." THE YALE COLLECTION OF AMERICAN LITERATURE, THE BEINECKE RARE BOOK AND MANUSCRIPT LIBRARY. COURTESY OF THE ESTATE OF HARRIET MONROE

editor Alice Henderson chose Sandburg's work from the unsolicited submissions, and it opened the March 1914 issue. When *The Dial* magazine attacked Sandburg's supposed formlessness, Monroe answered in an editorial in the May 1914 issue that was one of her finest statements of principle: "We have taken chances, made room for the young and the new, tried to break the chains which enslave Chicago to New York, America to Europe, and the present to the past." A more established but still relatively unknown poet, Robert Frost (1874–1963), appeared in the February 1914 issue with "The Code-Heroics." Pound had met Frost in England and sent his poems to Monroe. Frost was a poet whom both Monroe and Pound were proud to publish. Frost's impressive narrative poem, "The Witch of Coös," appeared in January 1922 and won the Levinson Prize. Frost wrote to Monroe, "I don't care what people think of my poetry so long as they award it prizes."

One of Monroe's most satisfying experiences was discovering and encouraging the work of Wallace Stevens (1879–1955). Monroe was so excited when she read Stevens's "Phases" among the unsolicited manuscripts that she telegraphed him immediately, accepting the poems, and then reorganized the November 1914 issue to make space for them. In Stevens's "Sunday Morning" (November 1915), Monroe published a poem to rival Eliot's "Love Song" in its centrality to modern American poetry. *Poetry* published two of the most famous modernist lyrics in Stevens's "Anecdote of the Jar" (part of his "Pecksniffiana" sequence, October 1919) and "The Snow Man" (October 1921). Monroe's relationship with Stevens was so cordial that Stevens agreed when she stipulated that three of the eight stanzas of "Sunday Morning" be dropped. He restored his own stronger version of the poem in his volume *Harmonium* (1923). Stevens won the Levinson Prize in 1920 for "Pecksniffiana," and Monroe published his verse dramas *Three Travelers Watch a Sunrise* (which won a one-act play prize of $100, July 1916) and *Carlos among the Candles* (December 1917). Stevens in turn became Monroe's loyal supporter, returning his contributor's payments and later becoming one of the magazine's guarantors (anonymously). As she did with Lindsay and many other poets, Monroe became a close personal friend of Stevens. They visited each other in Chicago and Stevens's home in Hartford, and Monroe became "Aunt Harriet" to Stevens's daughter Holly.

Harriet Monroe began publishing a series of anthologies in 1917 entitled *The New Poetry* that became a sourcebook for a new generation of poets. By then *Poetry* was no longer introducing so many major poets, and the experimental impact of new poems by Pound, Eliot, and H. D. could no longer be matched. But original voices such as Edna St. Vincent Millay, Yvor Winters, Langston Hughes, Louise Bogan, Allen Tate, and Hart Crane were published throughout the 1920s. T. S. Eliot wrote in 1954: "There is nothing quite like it anywhere: *Poetry* has had its imitators, but has so far survived them all. It is an American Institution." *Poetry* not only survives in the early twenty-first century but also is flourishing with the bequest of $100 million that it announced in 2002 from the heir to the Eli Lilly pharmaceutical fortune, Ruth Lilly, whose verse was rejected in the 1970s

courteously and personally (in the tradition of Harriet Monroe) by the editor of *Poetry*.

See also Chicago; Little Magazines and Small Presses; "The Love Song of J. Alfred Prufrock"; Lyric Poetry

BIBLIOGRAPHY
Primary Works
Monroe, Harriet. *A Poet's Life: Seventy Years in a Changing World*. New York: Macmillan, 1938.

Parisi, Joseph, and Stephen Young, eds. *Dear Editor: A History of* Poetry *in Letters: The First Fifty Years, 1912–1962*. New York: Norton, 2002.

Parisi, Joseph, and Stephen Young, eds. *The "Poetry" Anthology, 1912–2002: Ninety Years of America's Most Distinguished Verse Magazine*. Chicago: Ivan R. Dee, 2002.

Secondary Works
Hoffman, Frederick J., et al. *The Little Magazine: A History and a Bibliography*. 2nd ed. Princeton, N.J.: Princeton University Press, 1947.

Williams, Ellen. *Harriet Monroe and the "Poetry" Renaissance: The First Ten Years of "Poetry," 1912–22*. Urbana: University of Illinois Press, 1977.

Timothy Materer

POLITICAL PARTIES

The so-called Gilded Age, which extended from roughly 1876 to 1896, saw two major parties, the Republicans and the Democrats, dominate the political landscape. Also, during this era big businesses increased their wealth, social power, and political influence, which encouraged the two major parties to become more professional, conservative, and corrupt. As a result, some liberal reformers attempted to institute idealistic programs from within the major parties, while other citizens formed third parties to make their needs known. Many authors of realistic and naturalistic fiction wrote about political issues and were themselves politically active. In fact, this era was named after the 1873 novel *The Gilded Age: A Tale of Today* by Mark Twain (a pseudonym for Samuel Langhorne Clemens, 1835–1910) and Charles Dudley Warner (1829–1900). It satirically contrasts America's political ideals with its political realities and presents political corruption as so common that every spring Congress must arraign dozens of its members "for taking bribes to vote for this and that and the other bill [the previous] winter" (p. 465).

MAJOR PARTIES: THE REPUBLICANS AND DEMOCRATS

Immediately following the Civil War, the Republican Party dominated the national political landscape. The young party's symbol was Abraham Lincoln; its legacy was preserving the Union and liberating the South's black slaves. The Republicans considered themselves the guardians of America's morality and social responsibility. The Democratic Party had lost national prominence because it had initiated secession in the South and continued to advocate political authority from the state and local level even after the war. Many northerners disliked the reform-minded Republicans and supported the Democrats' policies during and after the war, but in national elections they voted Republican to avoid being labeled unpatriotic "Copperheads"—a term used to refer to persons from the North who opposed the Civil War.

In the 1870s, a group known as the Radical Republicans determined the party's policies. They, and the authors who supported them, often "waved the bloody shirt," which meant they used the legacy of the war to promote their policies and proclaim the North to be financially, intellectually, and morally superior to the South. They used patriotic rhetoric to maintain political power and pass liberal social reforms in southern states. The war had devastated the South, and the Republicans' Reconstruction programs allowed northern businesspeople and politicians to exploit their advantage for profit and power. This caused deep resentment in the former Confederate states, and many people directed their anger toward Republicans, northerners, and freed blacks.

Writers of this time were interested in politics and active in political parties. William Dean Howells (1837–1920), a Republican before he became a Christian Socialist in the 1880s, supported President Ulysses S. Grant and his Reconstruction policies. Howells promoted the Republicans' war legacy while he was editor of the *Atlantic Monthly* in the 1870s, and in 1876 he wrote a favorable biography of the Republican presidential candidate Rutherford B. Hayes, who was his wife's cousin. Furthermore, in Howells's *A Modern Instance* (1882), the amoral antihero, Bartley Hubbard, supports the 1876 Democratic candidate, Samuel Jones Tilden, while his honest, honorable foil, Ben Halleck, supports Hayes.

Mark Twain also supported the Radical Republicans' militant Reconstruction policies, which meant modernizing and industrializing the South as well as attempting to change the attitudes of racist and sectionalist whites. Twain equates Republican values with human values in *Adventures of Huckleberry Finn (Tom Sawyer's Comrade)* (1885). Huck ultimately rejects the Democrats' attitude that blacks are naturally inferior and that whites have a responsibility to return fugitive slaves. Huck, ignoring Democratic political propaganda, bases his convictions on his innate sense of morality and his experiences with Jim, whom Huck saw as a human being and a friend.

While some writers used their talents to influence politics, others used their political contacts for personal favors. For example, Twain asked Howells to instruct President Hayes to block the consular appointment of fellow author Bret Harte (1836–1902). Twain felt that Harte had insulted him by not repaying a loan. "To send this nasty creature to puke upon the American name in a foreign land is too much," Twain wrote (*Letters*, p. 114), and he also called Harte a liar and a thief. In *Mark Twain in Eruption*, Twain criticizes Harte for refusing to vote in the 1876 election after securing promises for a consularship from both candidates. Twain remarks that Harte's maneuvering "was a curious satire upon our political system" (p. 288). However, Howells ignored Twain's protests and secretly advised Hayes to appoint Harte, who gained a consulship to Prussia in 1878.

At a time when blacks were asserting their citizenship and humanity, many southern whites used the political system to deny black men their newly acquired right to vote. Southern Democrats, with the aid of the Ku Klux Klan, limited blacks' civil and political rights. They intimidated or killed those who supported Republican candidates or black suffrage. Poll taxes and citizenship exams, from which whites often were exempt, also limited black voting and political change. W. E. B Du Bois (1868–1963) writes in *The Souls of Black Folk: Essays and Sketches* (1903) that "not a single Southern legislature stood ready to admit a Negro, under any conditions, to the polls" (p. 23). Although a few blacks were elected to state and national offices, Du Bois writes that many whites told blacks to "be content to be servants, and nothing more; what need of higher culture for half-men? Away with the black man's ballot, by force or fraud" (p. 6). The white voters of the "Solid South" continued to elect Democrats to local and federal positions, which put social pressure on southern blacks to remain second-class citizens and political pressure on Republicans to abandon Reconstruction.

Black writers supported the Radical Republicans' reforms by describing the hardships slaves endured and emphasizing the humanity, intelligence, and value of black people. These writers appealed to white citizens and white politicians for protection of their rights and their lives. Frederick Douglass (1817–1895) addressed Congress directly, asking that black suffrage be protected. The Equal Rights Party nominated Douglass for vice president in 1872, but he refused the nomination and campaigned for Grant's reelection instead. Douglass was criticized by some black writers for accepting several presidential appointments after the Republicans abandoned their protection of blacks' rights in the South to appease southern white voters. Douglass was U.S. marshal for the District of Columbia (1877–1881), recorder of deeds for Washington, D.C. (1881–1886), and consul general to Haiti (1889–1891).

The Marrow of Tradition (1901) by Charles Waddell Chesnutt (1858–1932) directly critiques the racism in American politics. The novel is based on the 1898 Wilmington, North Carolina, race riot in which white citizens, enraged that a suspected black rapist was found innocent, took over the city government and lynched black citizens at random. This came about after a committee of Democrats, the "Secret Nine," removed the Republican government and urged local whites to attack blacks on the city's streets (Roe, p. 233). In the novel, it is the "Big Three" who spark a racial massacre after deposing the Republican city government that had passed unpopular social-reform laws (Chesnutt, p. 242). In the novel, the Republicans could not stop the coup or the violence. In America at that time, the Republicans could not or would not stop intimidation at the polls, Jim Crow legislation, and lynch mobs.

In addition to their political control of the Solid South, the Democratic Party controlled many northern cities with their political "machines." These corrupt local organizations bribed, coerced, and intimidated voters so that party candidates were elected, graft continued unchecked, and civil service jobs were given to party supporters. The Democratic machine in New York City was known as Tammany Hall. William Marcy "Boss" Tweed, who represented the first generation of professional politicians, took control of Tammany and, in the words of John G. Sproat in *"The Best Men": Liberal Reformers in the Gilded Age,* "plundered and ruled the first city of the land from 1866 to 1871" (p. 46). A few decades later, George Washington Plunkitt held tremendous power as a state senator in New York and a Tammany man. In interviews with William Riordon, which were published in 1905 as *Plunkitt of Tammany Hall: A Series of Very Plain Talks on Very Practical Politics,* Plunkitt

defends himself and his party. He differentiates dishonest and honest graft, explaining that buying cheap land that the city intends to use for a new park and selling it to the city at a large profit is successfully playing the game of politics. He brags, "I seen my opportunities and I took 'em" (Riordon, p. 3). Plunkitt argues that "politics is as much a regular business as the grocery" (p. 19) and that intellectuals, orators, and reformers ultimately fail because they are not trained to play the political game.

Several authors criticize Tammany politicians in their work, including Theodore Dreiser (1871–1945) in his novel *Sister Carrie* (1900) and Frances Ellen Watkins Harper (1825–1911) in "Aunt Chloe's Politics" (1872). Harper's poem objects to the corrupt politicians' "mighty ugly tricks," naming "Boss" Tweed as one of the worst culprits. Harper writes that everyone must stand up to them, arguing,

this buying up each other
Is something worse than mean,
Though I thinks a heap of voting,
I go for voting clean.

(P. 1980)

In the 1870s the Radical Republicans resisted the Republicans who wanted more economically and socially conservative policies, but the party was beginning to fracture. A group known as the Liberal Republicans was formed, which served as a precursor to the Mugwumps of the 1880s. The Liberal Republicans defected from the party in 1872 and created a short-lived movement that criticized the Grant administration's political corruption and inefficiency, its Reconstruction policies, its practice of giving civil service jobs to party patrons, and its institution of unfairly high tariff rates. Politicians could no longer build coalitions among voters and within the party by "waving the bloody shirt." Realistic conceptions of American life and politics replaced the romantic image of the North's moral superiority. This change is evident in works by Howells, Frank Norris (1870–1902), Theodore Dreiser, and Stephen Crane (1871–1900).

As voters shifted their focus from the nation's past to their own present and future, the Republican Party abandoned its Reconstruction and civil rights programs to gain support during the 1876 elections. Hayes won the White House, in part, because the party's more conservative policies attracted more voters. However, many Americans felt unhappy with the party's new priorities, and they sought new representation. New political movements gathered supporters from these disenfranchised citizens and put pressure on both the Republicans and Democrats.

FRONTIER PARTIES: THE GREENBACKS AND POPULISTS

In the 1870s and 1880s almost half of the nation's voters lived on farms, and many of them felt they had no political representation. Liberal reformers within the two major parties stood for many of the same policies that were supported by farmers and laborers, in particular, the elimination of political corruption, protective tariffs, and paper currency. However, the reformers defended the rights of property owners and called discontented farmers and laborers the "dangerous classes" (Sproat, p. 205). Therefore, many western farmers united to form the Granger movement and successfully lobbied to pass "Granger Laws," which limited railroad freight and grain elevator rates. Several state supreme courts declared these laws unconstitutional, but the reforms were soon federalized with the passage of the Interstate Commerce Act of 1887. Eager to join political parties that directly represented them, many farmers turned to the Greenback Party in the 1880s and the Populist Party in the 1890s.

After the Civil War, the two major parties allowed the dollar ("greenbacks") to lose value and supported big business during the financial crisis known as the panic of 1873, which destroyed desperate farmers. The Greenback Party (1874–1884) was formed to institute currency expansion, and after uniting farmers with urban labor and winning fourteen seats in Congress in 1878, the Greenbacks broadened their platform to endorse woman suffrage and a graduated income tax. By 1884 farmers in the western United States were more prosperous, causing the party to lose support and dissolve.

Third party interest revived in the 1890s. Again, economically desperate farmers and laborers criticized Republicans and Democrats for supporting urban, corporate interests and ignoring their needs. Some of the leaders of the Greenback Party reorganized in 1892, and the Populist, or "People's," Party was born. Hamlin Garland (1860–1940), whose stories dramatize the bitterly hard life farmers had, advocated political reform that would protect farmers from greedy bankers and unfair railroad prices. Garland made political speeches, advising farmers to unite. In his novel *A Spoil of Office* (1892), young Grangers idealize the Populist Party. They claim that if they elect a Populist congressman, he will "fight [for] the interests of the farmer" (p. 10). Their prediction comes true because Garland's fictional Populist, unlike the typical politician, is selfless, altruistic, and responsive to his constituents.

URBAN PARTIES: THE MUGWUMPS, POPULISTS, AND SOCIALISTS

Following the Civil War, the two major parties suppressed third party development in eastern cities. Their political control was challenged when the Mugwumps, a group of Republicans who left their party in 1884 to become independents, threw their support behind the Democratic presidential candidate Grover Cleveland in that year's election. The Mugwumps rejected the patronage system and refused to compromise their beliefs in order to belong to one party. In 1898 Twain criticized the Republicans' imperialism, but he refused to vote for the Democratic candidate William Jennings Bryan. He called himself a Mugwump because instead of blindly voting for a party, he analyzed every candidate and issue individually.

Because fewer people were blindly accepting the policies and activities of the two major parties, Populist Party membership increased in eastern cities, especially among the working class. Howells publicly asserted that Edward Bellamy (1850–1898) founded and legitimized the populist movement with his book *Looking Backward 2000–1888* (1888) and his speeches in the 1890s. In his novel, Bellamy advocates economic and social reforms in order to change America's social and economic ideology from competition and prejudice to cooperation, equality, and reciprocity. In his speeches, Bellamy praised the Populist Party's nationalist agenda and its interest in the rights of poor farmers, poor workers, and women. He stated that it was the only American organization that could justify calling itself a national party.

The Democratic Party appropriated populist themes and nominated populist leader William Jennings Bryan as their candidate in 1896, 1900, and 1908. These elections undermined the agrarian insurgency, and the Populist Party dissolved, but popular interest in a third party did not die. Many writers joined the Socialist Party and criticized the government for allowing businesses to exploit their workers. Unlike European Socialists, American Socialists were more populist than Marxist, but the Socialist Party survived longer than other third parties because the Republicans and Democrats resisted appropriating its ideology to boost their memberships.

The Socialist Party's fight against worker exploitation is depicted in *The Jungle* (1906) by Upton Sinclair (1878–1968). Jurgis, a poor immigrant, becomes cynical after working for both of the major parties and seeing the corruption that occurred. Jurgis states that "at the last election the Republicans had paid four dollars a vote to the Democrats' three" (p. 308), which encourages him to vote "half a dozen times himself" (p. 315). Jurgis is disillusioned by politics and the politicians' unwillingness to help those truly in need. However, he regains his self-respect, his hope, and his faith in humanity after hearing a Socialist

The Mugwump Mabille. Cartoon by George Yost Coffin, c. 1884. Dancers representing factions within the Mugwump Party are shown with James Gillespie Blair, the Republican candidate for president in 1884. Blair lost the election when the Mugwumps supported Democrat Grover Cleveland. Coffin compares the election to the popular entertainment presented at the Jardin Mabille in Paris. THE LIBRARY OF CONGRESS

speech and joining the Socialist Party. Sinclair's novel directly influenced politics by encouraging voters to question the practices of the meatpacking industry and support the Pure Food and Drug Act, which was passed in 1906.

Frustrated that American society was based on self-interest, injustice, and the accumulation of personal wealth, Howells became a Christian Socialist in the 1880s and advocated a society based on brotherhood, equality, and freedom. His politics changed because of events like the unjust trial and execution of four anarchists associated with the 1886 Haymarket riot. Although Howells "disliked the anti-individualist implications of unionism" (Sproat, p. 218), he decided

that his novels must encourage workers to organize and fight for their rights. In *The Rise of Silas Lapham* (1885), the protagonist succeeds financially by being selfish, greedy, and competitive, but when he recognizes America's corrupt socioeconomic foundation, he acts morally and accepts financial and social ruin. In Howells's *A Hazard of New Fortunes* (1889), a businessman's son rejects his father's competitive commercialism and joins a group of striking workers. The son agrees with a worker who argues that the Socialists should run the country because they guarantee that every man "haf voark, and that he haf foodt. All the roadts and mills and mines and landts shall be the beople's and be ron *by* the beople *for* the beople. There shall be no rich and no boor; and there shall not

The 1916 presidential election. Woodrow Wilson (left) and Charles Evans Hughes are depicted attempting to capture the attention of a moose, symbol of the Progressive Party. After the decision of their leader, Theodore Roosevelt, not to run in the election, the votes of the Progressives were eagerly sought by both parties. © BETTMANN/CORBIS

be war any more" (p. 310). In an 1890 book review, Hamlin Garland praises *A Hazard of New Fortunes* for dealing "with the most vital of all questions . . . the persistence of poverty, vice and crime," and for being "a magnificent study of the reform spirit of today" (Pizer, p. 409).

Jack London (1876–1916), concerned with economic and social injustices committed against the poor, converted to socialism in 1896. He wrote two pro-socialist books: the nonfiction title *People of the Abyss* (1903) and the novel *The Iron Heel* (1908). Also, he gave impromptu speeches to large Oakland, California, crowds in 1896, he campaigned as a Socialist mayoral candidate in 1901 and 1905, and he formed the Intercollegiate Socialist Society with Upton Sinclair in 1905. After years of frustration over the Socialists' lack of "fire and fight," London quit the party and

supported Theodore Roosevelt's Progressive Party candidacy in 1916.

POWERFUL NEW PARTY: THE PROGRESSIVES

At the beginning of the twentieth century, many Americans were calling for direct democracy to replace the political machines. In 1912 a group of Republicans rejected William Howard Taft's conservative administration and asked former president Theodore Roosevelt to run against Taft as a candidate of the Progressive, or "Bull Moose," Party. The Progressives wanted to end political corruption and fought for liberal reforms, such as increased political rights for blacks and women. By splitting the Republican vote, Roosevelt's candidacy enabled the Democrat Woodrow Wilson to defeat Taft. Wilson subsequently adopted several of the Progressive Party's policies, and the third party dissolved.

Although the two major parties tried to maintain their power by excluding third party participation, reformism did have an effect on local and national policy. For example, the prohibitionists and the women's movement forced Congress to pass significant legislation between 1900 and 1920. Although temperance organizations existed throughout the nineteenth century and the Prohibition Party was founded in 1869, it was not until the first decade of the 1900s that the antialcohol crusade became a powerful political force. Twain, in *Adventures of Huckleberry Finn*, humorously shows Huck negotiating between an escape to the western frontier and obeying his aunt's small town temperance and becoming civilized. *The Bostonians* (1886) by Henry James (1843–1916) satirizes the busybody, meddlesome nature of reformism, including temperance preaching, in the character of Miss Birdseye. The Prohibition Party also supported woman suffrage, free public education, and prison reform. In 1919 the party found success when the Eighteenth Amendment passed and alcohol was prohibited by law.

Although the Nineteenth Amendment, giving women the vote, was not passed until 1920, American female writers and activists demanded their political rights during the Gilded Age and into the twentieth century. Charlotte Perkins Gilman (1860–1935), a suffragist and a Socialist, argued that women should be educated about politics and be allowed to vote for those whose laws directly affect women. In a 1910 essay in the *Forerunner,* a journal she wrote and published, she asserts that many women are, and more can be, knowledgeable and passionate about politics. Gilman sees a new political consciousness emerging in America and feels that everyone should be allowed to participate. "The day of the masculine monarchy is passing," she writes, "and the day of the human democracy is coming in" (p. 18).

See also The Education of Henry Adams; Oratory; Reform; Temperance; Women's Suffrage

BIBLIOGRAPHY

Primary Works

Chesnutt, Charles Waddell. *The Marrow of Tradition*. 1901. Ann Arbor: University of Michigan Press, 1969.

Du Bois, W. E. B. *The Souls of Black Folk*. 1903. New York: Dover, 1994.

Garland, Hamlin. *A Spoil of Office*. 1892. New York: Johnson Reprint Corporation, 1969.

Gilman, Charlotte Perkins. "Our Androcentric Culture; or, The Man-Made World." *Forerunner* 1, no. 10 (1910): 17–20.

Harper, Frances Ellen Watkins. "Aunt Chloe's Politics." In *The Heath Anthology of American Literature,* 2nd ed., edited by Paul Lauter et al. Lexington, Mass.: D. C. Heath, 1994.

Howells, William Dean. *A Hazard of New Fortunes*. 1890. London: Oxford University Press, 1965.

Riordon, William. *Plunkitt of Tammany Hall*. 1905. New York: Dutton, 1963.

Sinclair, Upton. *The Jungle*. 1906. New York: Penguin, 1985.

Twain, Mark. *Mark Twain in Eruption: Hitherto Unpublished Pages about Men and Events*. New York: Harper, 1940.

Twain, Mark. *Selected Mark Twain-Howells Letters, 1872–1910*. Edited by Fredrick Anderson, William M. Gibson, and Henry Nash Smith. Cambridge, Mass.: Belknap Press of Harvard University Press, 1967.

Twain, Mark, and Charles Dudley Warner. *The Gilded Age*. 1873. New York: Oxford University Press, 1996.

Secondary Works

Gibson, William M. "Mark Twain and Howells: Anti-Imperialists." *New England Quarterly* 20, no. 4 (1947): 435–468.

Murphy, Francis. "The End of a Friendship: Two Unpublished Letters from Twain to Howells about Bret Harte." *New England Quarterly* 58, no. 1 (1985): 87–91.

Pizer, Donald. "Hamlin Garland in the *Standard*." *American Literature* 26, no. 3 (November 1954): 401–415.

Roe, Jae H. "Keeping an 'Old Wound' Alive: *The Marrow of Tradition* and the Legacy of Wilmington." *African American Review* 33, no. 2 (1999): 231–243.

Sadler, Elizabeth. "One Book's Influence: Edward Bellamy's *Looking Backward*." *New England Quarterly* 17, no. 4 (1944): 530–555.

Sproat, John G. *"The Best Men": Liberal Reformers in the Gilded Age*. New York: Oxford University Press, 1968.

Matthew Teorey

POPULAR POETRY

In 1907 Sam Walter Foss (1858–1911), a country boy from New Hampshire who had become a prolific poet and, in his other life, library director in Somerville, Massachusetts, published what turned out to be his last volume of poetry, *Songs of the Average Man*. Bound in a sturdy green cloth cover sprinkled with pretty little violets, the book also contained nine pen-and-ink illustrations by Merle Johnson. A particularly reveal-ing one shows an elderly couple in their parlor. The wife, her hair neatly tied in a bun, is leaning forward in her big armchair, mesmerized by the book she is hold-ing in her hand. More books are stacked on the coffee table by her side. Her husband, white-bearded and shirt-sleeved, sits stiffly on a dining-room chair he has pulled up to be closer to her. His wife is reading to him, and he seems to be all ears. Smiling broadly, he informs the reader (and the caption for Johnson's pic-ture is a direct quotation from the poem that precedes it): "For I jest soak in Literacher sence Mary jined the club." Reading the works of "Tennerson" (the "potery man, you know") and "James Rustle Lynn" has actually made the lives of Mary and her husband if not better then at least bearable. Or so the husband claims: "Yis, life 'ith us hez allus bin a pooty serious rub; / But somehow things is pleasanter sence Mary jined the club" (*Songs*, p. 61).

Johnson's drawing and Foss's poem, titled simply "Sence Mary Jined the Club," handily epitomize some of the radical transformations the literary marketplace underwent in the decades between the end of the Civil War and the end of World War II. The lives of average Americans changed drastically during those years. Between 1870 and 1900, the total number of wage earners increased from twelve to twenty-nine million, a development that was also reflected in the number of labor strikes that rocked American cities. Notions of what it meant to be American were challenged by the steady influx of immigrants. Everything was changing. As local companies went out of business, giant new corporations or trusts took over or controlled the pro-duction of many of the items the average American used every day. And books suddenly seemed to be everywhere. Between 1880 and 1900, American pub-lishers tripled their output, and the price of books—once regarded as "the great refiner" of literature, according to James Russell Lowell ("James Rustle Lynn")—dropped, too. All over the country, book clubs and reading circles mushroomed. Sam Walter Foss, during his tenure at the Somerville public library, was able to increase the circulation of books from 193,000 in 1897 to 353,000 in 1904.

Foss's "Sence Mary Jined the Club" seems writ-ten as if to illustrate the fastidious Lowell's worst fears, warning readers what may happen when affordable books reach the untweedy masses, people like the Yankee and his "Tennersen"-declaiming wife who say "rennysarnce" instead of Renaissance and pronounce "homogeneity" like "Homer G. Nierty." By the same token, Foss's poem also sends a comforting message to the middle-class reader who just happens to know how to spell these two words but is not too sure about

"Sence Mary Jined the Club." Merle Johnson's illustra-tion in Sam Walter Foss's *Song of the Average Man*, 1907. THE COLLECTION OF CHRISTOPH IRMSCHER, BALTIMORE

many others. Under the guise of satire, "Sence Mary Jined the Club"—as a place where high and low cul-ture meet—ultimately legitimizes the enjoyment of those who have traditionally not had easy access to the pleasures of "Literacher."

The paradoxes behind Foss's "Sence Mary Jined the Club" are the contradictions of American popular poetry in general. The poems discussed here happily inhabit the space Virginia Woolf, in her famous essay on the middlebrow, ridiculed as "the betwixt and between" (p. 155). Their authors, many of whom were avid readers and performers of their poetry, were widely recognized and admired. By 1897 schools in Missouri, at the recommendation of the State Superin-tendent of Public Schools, observed the date of Eugene Field's death each year with "suitable programs made up from the dead poet's writings and articles eulogistic of him and his works" (Conrow, p. 101). The "Hoosier" poet James Whitcomb Riley, after his death in July 1916, lay in state under the dome of the Indiana state capitol, where more than thirty-five thousand people filed past it. The Michigan legislature designated 21 October as Will Carleton Day (Public Act 51 of 1919), in honor of Michigan's "Pioneer Poet." And Ella Wheeler Wilcox, who, according to the newspapers, had "out-Swinburned Swinburne and out-Whitmaned Whitman" (Ballou, p. 82), toured army camps during World War I, capitalizing on her fame and reciting poems to American troops, whom she encouraged to "come back clean" (Ballou, p. 256).

Today the popular poems written in the decades between the two wars are considered as "beneath and beyond the intellectual life of the country" (Ballou, p. 8). Their makers are familiar to us perhaps from a few highway rest stops that have been named after them or from a handful of tattered copies in second-hand bookstores. And yet, in their own day, these writers' achievements were considerable. They helped increase and solidify an audience for poetry in America. And, following the model of America's first "pop" poet, Henry Wadsworth Longfellow, yet adopting their own distinctive approaches, they opened up the language of literature to the joys and concerns of ordinary people. Thus, they indeed created, as Pound's Hugh Selwyn Mauberley would demand later, "something for the modern stage" (p. 98).

HOMESPUN BROWN

In 1873 Longfellow published the last installment of his American answer to Boccaccio, *Tales of a Wayside Inn,* which contained, among other things, a heated debate about the proper course of American poetry. One of Longfellow's storytellers, a student, ridicules those writers who believe that the literary sun rises and sets in their own backyards only. But another member of the group, a theologian, snaps back: "I maintain / That what is native still is best" (p. 284). He prefers "bards of simple ways," whose "singing robes were homespun brown / From looms of their own native town" (p. 284). These words (which do not reflect the cosmopolitan Longfellow's own views) might serve as the mantra of the new generation of popular poets that emerged after the Civil War. It is no coincidence that its most prominent representatives came not from Boston or New York but from states in the Middle West: James Whitcomb Riley (1849–1916), a former sign painter and peddler in "miracle cures," was born in rural Greenfield, Indiana; Eugene Field (1850–1895) hailed from St. Louis, Missouri, and worked as a journalist in Detroit and Chicago; Will Carleton (1845–1912) boasted of his origins on a pioneer farm in Michigan; Ella

Wheeler Wilcox (1850–1919) came from a farmhouse in Johnstown Centre, Wisconsin. Riley once said that, as far as he was concerned, the phrase "home-folks" sounded "jis the same as *poetry*"—that is, he added disingenuously, "ef poetry is jis / As sweet as I've hearn tell it is" ("Home-Folks," p. 384). Over and over again, Riley's poems repeat the same message: home is where it is best ("We Must Get Home"; "Home Ag'in"; "Writin' Back to the Home-Folks"; "The Old Home by the Mill"; "The Poems Here at Home"). "We hear the World's lots grander," concedes the speaker in "Right Here at Home," but that is no good reason to run off: "We'll take the World's word fer it and not go" (p. 209). What could be better than "old Hoosierdom"?

Eugene Field's singing robes were decidedly homespun, too—but the hard-hitting columnist for the *Chicago Daily News* who collected rare books and translated Horace wore them rather self-consciously. Consider "In Amsterdam," in which Field both makes fun of his own passion for antiques and uses it as an occasion to celebrate the superiority of American craftsmanship. Field's speaker reminisces about a visit to Hans Von der Bloom's antiques store in Kalverstraat, where he casts a desirous eye on a bed with ornate carvings, "whose curious size and mould bespoke, / Prodigious age." The dealer, an "honest Dutchman," wants a thousand guilders for this rare piece of furniture, once slept on by "King Fritz der Foorst, of blessed fame." This is more than the speaker can pay, of course. He deplores the fact that he is from America, a country that is "full of stuff / That's good, but is not old enough." But then he notices a sticker on the frame featuring a rampant wolverine ("a strange device"), as Field says, no doubt remembering the "banner with the strange device" from Longfellow's "Excelsior"). And with relish he shares with the readers what the label says: "Patent Antique. Birkey [*sic*] & Gay, Grand Rapids, Michigan, U.S.A." The Dutch antique turns out to be the product of modern American industry. Concludes Field's speaker:

> . . . when I want a bed
> In which has slept a royal head
> I'll patronize no middleman,
> But deal direct with Michigan.
>
> (*Poems, p. 115*)

Berkey and Gay quickly picked up on the free advertising Field had given them here, and they promoted Field's poem in an ad they ran in *The Century.* The circle closes: a popular American poet endorses a popular American manufacturer who in turn endorses the poet's popular poem ("if you want the Field poem—on a pretty card ready for framing or mounting—tell us, please").

THE POET.

Who is this Creature with Long Hair and a Wild Eye? He is a Poet. He writes Poems on Spring and Women's Eyes and Strange, unreal Things of that Kind. He is always Wishing he was Dead, but he wouldn't Let anybody Kill him if he could Get away. A mighty good Sausage Stuffer was Spoiled when the Man became a Poet. He would Look well Standing under a Desending Piledriver.

"The Poet." From Eugene Field's series of satirical vignettes published in the *Denver Tribune.* THE COLLECTION OF CHRISTOPH IRMSCHER, BALTIMORE

Michael R. Turner has mocked the lurid subjects of much of what he calls "Victorian parlor" poetry, with its moribund babies, dead toddlers, starving paupers, suspected criminals facing the gallows, and artists who have fallen on hard times. Of course, death was an everyday reality for contemporary readers (out of the eight Field siblings, only Eugene and his brother survived infancy; his mother died of cholera when he was six; and Field lost three of his own children). Yet, for each popular poem about someone's untimely or well-deserved demise there are at least two or three others addressing more mundane issues, such as—to quote a few examples from the poetry of Sam Walter Foss—whether or not a man should shave his whiskers off ("The Shaving of Jacob"); what the proper posture is for prayer, down upon one's knees or standing up straight with outstretched arms ("The Prayer of Cyrus Brown"); how you can still love your wife even after she has knocked you out with a sink pipe for breaking a lamp ("Matilda's New Year Resolutions"); how losing your job makes you realize "the whole blund'rin' mistake" of your birth ("W'en a Feller Is Out of a Job," *Dreams,* p. 179); and how the worst loss you incur after a house fire, one for which no insurance can compensate you, might be that old bib and baby shoe ("Mother Putney's 'Things'").

"The city's heat and dust" (Riley, "Herr Weiser," p. 231) is present in these poems, but mostly as the memory of people who have just escaped from there:

W'y, of all the good things yit
I ain't shet of, is to quit
Business, and git back to sheer
These old comforts waitin' here—.
(Riley, "Back from Town," p. 248)

Not that the countryside makes no demands on you. Take the poems of Will Carleton, who made a name for himself as the author of sentimental ballads about the hardscrabble lives of rural people: "I'd have died for my daughters, I'd have died for my sons" ("Over the Hill to the Poor-House," p. 38) exclaims the old woman dragging herself to the local poorhouse, realizing that, at least in her case, what goes around does not come around: "when we're old and gray / I've noticed it sometimes somehow fails to work the other way" (*Farm Ballads,* p. 34). But in the country things often have a way of working out. In *Farm Ballads* (1873), "Over the Hill to the Poor-House" is followed by a poem in which a despondent son takes responsibility for his destitute mother ("Over the Hill *from* the Poor-House"), just as Carleton's ballad about divorce, "Betsey and I are Out," is immediately followed by "How Betsey and I Made Up." But life in the city is a different matter altogether. Here, disasters are irreversible: "This city *wastes* what any one would call / Nine hundred times enough to feed us all" (*City Ballads,* p. 62). No wonder that Carleton's Farmer Harrington breathes a sigh of relief when he is back on his farm in the country ("the old, old homestead"), where he and his wife now feed hungry children from the city, "with features pinched an' spare" (*City Ballads,* p. 172). After spending several years in Boston and New York, Carleton was given a hero's welcome when he returned to his native Michigan in 1907.

"It takes a heap o' livin' in a house to make it home" ("Home," p. 28) the Detroit newspaper man Edgar Guest rhapsodized in 1916. Sometimes even that was not enough. The poetry of Lizette Woodworth Reese (1856–1935), founder of the Women's Literary Club of Baltimore, is full of houses that are nobody's home anymore. Less optimistic than Carleton, Reese writes about the vanishing countryside around Baltimore,

with its gnarled willows baring their teeth to the wind, meadows rich with the scent of herbs and wildflowers, and collapsing old buildings haunted by the ghosts of the past. At its most effective, Reese's clipped lines acquire an incantatory, spell-like quality, in which the boundaries between life and death blur and emotions are just barely contained:

Topple the house down, wind;
Break it and tear it, rain;
She is not within,
Nor will come again.
That not even her ghost
Will know it for her own;—
Topple it into dust;
Tear it bone from bone.
("Nocturne," p. 161)

But Reese is no Dickinson. In her most famous poem, the sonnet "Tears," first published in *Scribner's Magazine* in 1899, Reese assures her readers that while life, "a wisp of fog betwixt us and the sun" (l. 2) might seem hard and short and is over before we know it, our real home is somewhere else anyway. "Make me see aright," the poet-speaker addresses the souls of her dead poetic precursors. "How each hath back what once he stayed to weep" (p. 82).

"HUSHABYE, SLUSHABYE"

The limits of poetic ambition, for the poets discussed here, were always defined by the realities of everyday life because they knew that this is how things were for their readers. "Who cares for thrones his thoughts to rouse," intoned Sam Walter Foss in *Dreams of Homespun:* "Who has a baby in the house?" ("A Good Domestic Man," p. 82). Eugene Field, widely recognized as the "Children's Laureate" even in his lifetime, made the pleasures and pains of children one of the focal themes of his poetry (in a less upbeat moment, he referred to his poems for children as "mother rot"). Remembered chiefly for the sentimental "Little Boy Blue" and the playful "Dutch" lullaby "Wynken, Blynken, and Nod" (and not at all for the pornography he also wrote), Field produced reams of verse in which boys will be boys and girls are, well, girls, and Mother's biggest problem is how to get the baby to sleep through the night, in the "garden where dreamikins grow" ("So So Rockabye So," *Poems,* p. 280) and the "Dinkey-Bird goes singing / In the amfalula tree" ("The Dinkey-Bird," *Poems,* p. 275). Like Riley, whose Hired Man believes that "all childern's good" ("The Hired Man's Faith in Children"), even the bad ones, Field evokes a world ruled not by bona fide adults but by the mysterious "Rock-a-By Lady from Hushaby Street" ("The Rock-A-By Lady").

There is no indication anywhere in these sweet-sounding ditties that child labor had, by 1900, become one the most pressing problems in American society, with one and three-quarter million children between the ages of ten and fifteen working in cotton mills, mines, factories, cranberry bogs, and so forth. That said, the sardonic vignettes Field penned for the *Denver Tribune* earlier in his career show that he nevertheless had a fairly realistic view of the realities of childhood. Field used the model of *The New England Primer,* capitalization and all, and turned the religious doctrines behind it upside down by literalizing the emblems: "The Apple is in a Basket. A Worm is in the Apple. It is a juicy little white Worm. Suppose you Eat the Apple, where will the Worm be?" (p. 60). Field knew how prone to violence the youngsters were about whom he wrote, and he did not shrink back from exploring the nether regions of a typical child's imagination: "The Cat is Asleep on the Rug. Step on Her Tail and See if she Will Wake up. Oh, no; She will not wake. She is a heavy Sleeper. Perhaps if you Were to saw her Tail off with the Carving knife you might Attract her attention. Suppose you try" (p. 26).

These early comic vignettes and the later sentimental lullabies evoking the magic of childhood share with each other the notion that children are not "proto-adults" but that, for better or worse, they live in a world of their own, barred to most adults except the readers of Field's poetry, who can at least vicariously express their longing to be young again: "I'd wish to be a boy again, / Back with the friends I used to know" ("Long Ago," *Poems,* p. 242).

LOVE IS (NOT) ENOUGH

Unlike her male colleagues, Ella Wheeler Wilcox, the ex-farmgirl from Wisconsin, was much more committed to living her life in the present. Although she was, like Field, quite attuned to the pleasures of the "Land of Nod," she felt no nostalgia for her lost childhood. Wilcox spent her life reinventing herself as the "Poetess of Passion," and she was so successful in that endeavor that even her milk baths became a matter of public discussion. Wilcox's own and, to date, only biographer unmercifully called her a "lowbrow," but her skill with words is undeniable. Take her clever handling of the form of the Italian sonnet in "Friendship after Love," which later earned a prominent place in the chapter on "Badness in Poetry" in I. A. Richards's *Principles of Literary Criticism.* Wilcox takes a truism—that ex-lovers cannot be friends—and turns it into memorable if not particularly original poetic conceit, likening the passing of love to the changing of the seasons:

> After the fierce midsummer all ablaze
> Has burned itself to ashes, and expires
> In the intensity of its own fires,

> There come the yellow, mild, St. Martin days
> Crowned with the calm of peace, but sad with
>   haze.

> (Poems of Passion, *p. 21)*

St. Martin's Day, in the European tradition, marks the beginning of the winter season. Worse, it is named after a man whose selflessness led him to share his coat with a beggar who was freezing by the side of the road. As passion yields to charity, the relationship described in the poem begins to falter: "We do not wish the pain back, or the heat; / And yet, and yet, these days are incomplete" (p. 21). Notice the insistent repetition of "yet" here—contrary to what I. A. Richards says, the speaker does not seem to be "appeased." Wilcox's sestet, a bit unusually, rhymes *cddcee.* In a true Italian sonnet, the rhymed couplet closure would be considered taboo, and that is exactly what the message of Wilcox's lines is, too: erotic desire, though impossible, is also irrepressible. Thomas Wyatt and John Donne used the same variation of the Italian norm with great success, though one hesitates to invoke such illustrious names in a context where "heat" indicates not a sudden rise in the outdoor temperature.

Writing poems of passion for "millions of passionless readers" (Kreymborg, p. 255), Wilcox was fascinated by sex and the war it wages on our socially sanctioned "yearning / For spiritual perfection" ("As by Fire," *Poems of Passion,* p. 104). "Love Is Enough," she once declared in a poem with that title, but her fans were not fooled. As in a modern photo-novel, they preferred to read about the erotic complications of Wilcox's protagonists, mouthing along to their "sweet words of passion" and relating them to their own lives.

Wilcox's obsession with what she termed "the Soul's calisthenics" (p. 15) found its most remarkable expression in her book-length narrative poem called *Three Women* (1897). Thoroughly contemporary in its language (the characters eat corn muffins and sit down to enjoy fricasseed chicken and strawberry cake, pp. 26, 36), the poem nevertheless sends an old-fashioned message that is not much different from the values espoused by Riley and Carleton. Wilcox's story revolves around the parallel lives of two close friends, the dreamy poet Maurice Somerville and the cynical Roger Montrose. The action takes place on Short Beach in Connecticut, where Maurice and his sister Ruth own a house (as did Wilcox). When Roger comes for a visit, Ruth falls in love with him. Avoiding Ruth's "soft mother-eye" (l. 363), Roger makes the fatal mistake of courting the one local girl his friend Maurice likes, too, Mabel Lee, a devotee of charitable causes, whom he seduces and then weds. Unsurprisingly, Mabel turns out to be completely unsuited for marriage as well as motherhood. Their only child dies, quietly passing on to better, "mother-filled" pastures (l. 1127), while the self-involved Mabel is attending a conference in Boston. Heartbroken, Mr. Montrose throws himself into the soft, pliable arms of a woman he meets at the beach, Zoe Travers. In a striking mimicry of the male gaze, Wilcox, her imagery dripping with innuendo, dwells on Zoe's "clinging" silk bathing suit (l. 1588), her "ardent skin" (l. 1600), her sensuous mouth ("a rose Love had dropped in the snow / of her face," p. 115), and her eyes, which are "the color the sunlight reveals / When it pierces the soft, furry coat of young seals" (p. 103). Nothing good can come from so much sex appeal.

Wilcox's provocatively direct representation of erotic desire is embedded in—or made safe by—a rather conventional idea of a woman's place in the home. On the one hand, she appears to be sympathetic to women who break out of the "mold / Of a man's wishes and passions" and live "as our century bids us" (p. 135). Why shouldn't Ruth Somerville be allowed to go to Medical School? After all, "true modesty dwells / In the same breast with knowledge." On the other hand, it soon becomes obvious that Wilcox is talking out of both sides of her mouth. Ruth's "warm woman face," she reveals, is really "made for fireside nooks," not for bending over textbooks, and she fondly imagines "the cheeks of fair children" resting on Ruth's motherly chest, "love's sweet downy cushion of rest" (p. 175).

Coincidentally, Roger Montrose, after being shot by a desperate Zoe Travers, ends up at the very hospital where Ruth is a medical student. Her diagnosis is clear: "'Tis the world's over-virtuous women, ofttimes, / Who drive men of weak will into sexual crimes" (p. 191). A true woman is neither a saint like Mabel nor a slut like Zoe:

> The world needs wise mothers, the world needs
>   good wives,
> The world needs good homes, and yet woman
>   strives
> To be everything else but domestic
>
> *(P. 195)*

Ruth, who at the end of the book returns to Short Beach to keep house for her brother, knows where she belongs. Out of the three women featured in the book, she, the homeliest, is the one the reader is supposed to emulate:

> Once a wife, I will drop from my name the M.D.
> I hold it the truth that no woman can be
> An excellent wife and an excellent mother,
> And leave enough purpose and time for another
> Profession outside
>
> *(P. 195)*

SOMEPIN' YOURS AND MINE

In *Three Women*, Ella Wheeler Wilcox combined a frank representation of erotic desire with an intentionally conservative notion of the poet's task: "The souls whom the gods bless at birth / With the great gift of song, have been sent to the earth / To better and to brighten it" (p. 66). The truly popular poet never forgets that he or she is writing for an audience. He or she also knows that his or her poetry, considered strictly as poetry, might not amount to very much. Generations of New Jersey schoolchildren memorized a poem by their homegrown poet Joyce Kilmer, in which they were told that no poem could ever be as "lovely as a tree" ("Trees," p. 19). Form, in the poetry of Kilmer and others, serves as an *aide de mémoire,* as Guy Davenport put it, never as an end in itself: no fancy rhyme schemes here, no perfumed metaphors. The earthier the better: "What we want, as I sense it, in the line / O' poetry is somepin' Yours and Mine," rhapsodized James Whitcomb Riley, "Somepin' with live stock in it, and out-doors" ("The Poems Here At Home," p. 195).

And yet, while many popular poems were intended to be just "songs for the average man," their makers still firmly believed that they were, all things considered, less-than-average poets. They were not like the guy in Sam Walter Foss's poem who thought that he would only have to purchase an inkwell to get going on his masterpiece: "what avails a sea of ink / To him who has no thoughts to think?" ("A Bottle of Ink," *Dreams,* p. 190). A strong belief in the superiority of poetry was part of the "homespun" message delivered in these poems—as was the message that poetry is not for sissies. "Take up your needles, drop your pen, / And leave the poet's craft to men" ("To Certain Poets," (ll. 25–26) is Joyce Kilmer's less-than-friendly advice to all those "little poets" (l. 7) with "tiny voices" (l. 15), those "wet, amorphous things" (l. 18) despised by everyone. "Who is this Creature with Long Hair and a Wild Eye?" asks Field in his *Tribune Primer.* Answer: "He is a Poet," God forbid, someone who writes poems about spring and such. And Field immediately envisions the poet's destruction: "A mighty good Sausage Stuffer was Spoiled when the Man became a Poet. He would Look well under a Desending [*sic*] Piledriver" (p. 83). In a similar vein, Will Carleton writes of a farmer's son who wanted to be "one of these long-haired fellers a feller hates to see; / One of these chaps forever fixin' things cute and clever" ("Tom Was Goin' for a Poet," ll. 2–3). When Tom went "a-sowin'" (l. 16) he was dropping metaphors instead of seed; when he went "a-ploughin'" (l. 31), he "sat down on the handles, an' went to spinnin' verse" (l. 32). Clearly an intolerable situation. But Tom's wife quickly cured him of such highfalutin notions, disseminating his poems the only way she knew how: "she shoved up the window and slung his poetry out" ("Tom Was Goin' for a Poet," *Farm Ballads,* pp. 48–51). No Will Carleton he.

The authors discussed here all believed, rather traditionally, in the dignity and importance of poetry. None of them was innovative formally, unless one counts their preference for dialect verse as a major step forward. The subjects that they wrote about were familiar to everyone. Yet within those narrow parameters they, for a few decades, made American poetry the most inclusive it has ever been, envisioning ways in which the pleasures of ordinary readers—like that of Foss's "literecher"-besotted Yankee—could find a place in the sacred sphere of culture. And they were not without any influence on writers better remembered today: the African American poet Paul Laurence Dunbar, for example, admired Riley's dialect verse, and Louise Bogan, in her poem "Woman," responded directly to Lizette Woodworth Reese. Officially, though, the modernists reestablished and celebrated the division between appetite and taste, between the common reader and the connoisseur. "I beg you my friendly critics," declared Ezra Pound, Longfellow's distant relative, in "Tenzone" (1913), "Do not set about to procure me an audience" (p. 40). And, later still, John Ashbery, in "Variations, Calypso, and Fugue on a Theme of Ella Wheeler Wilcox," made fun not only of the banality of Wilcox's rhymes but also of the basic idea apparently championed by all popular poets: "But of all the sights that were seen by me / In the East or West, on land or sea, / The best was the place that is spelled H-O-M-E" (p. 240).

See also Lyric Poetry

BIBLIOGRAPHY
Primary Works
Ashbery, John. *The Mooring of Starting Out: The First Five Books of Poetry.* Hopewell, N.J.: Ecco, 1997.

Carleton, Will. *City Ballads.* New York: Harper & Brothers, 1886.

Carleton, Will. *Farm Ballads.* New York: Harper & Brothers, 1873.

Carleton, Will. *Farm Festivals.* New York: Harper & Brothers, 1882.

Field, Eugene. *The Poems of Eugene Field.* New York: Scribners, 1915.

Field, Eugene. *Sharps and Flats.* Collated by Slason Thompson. 2 vols. New York: Scribners, 1900.

Field, Eugene. *The Tribune Primer.* 1882. Boston: Henry A. Dickerman, 1900.

Foss, Sam Walter. *Dreams in Homespun.* Boston: Lee and Shepard, 1898.

Foss, Sam Walter. *Songs of the Average Man.* Boston: Lothrop, Lee and Shepard, 1907.

Guest, Edgar. *A Heap o' Living.* Chicago: Reilly & Lee, 1916.

Kilmer, Joyce. *Trees & Other Poems.* 1914. New York: Doubleday, 1942.

Longfellow, Henry Wadsworth. *The Complete Poetical Works of Henry Wadsworth Longfellow.* Cambridge edition. Boston: Houghton Mifflin, 1895.

Lowell, James Russell. "The Five Indispensable Authors." *The Century* 47 (November 1893–April 1894): 223–224.

Pound, Ezra. *Selected Poems.* Rev. ed. London: Faber & Faber, 1977.

Reese, Lizette Woodworth. *The Selected Poems of Lizette Woodworth Reese.* New York: George H. Doran, 1927.

Riley, James Whitcomb. *The Best Loved Poems and Ballads of James Whitcomb Riley.* New York: Blue Ribbon, 1934.

Wilcox, Ella Wheeler. *Maurine and Other Poems.* Chicago: Conkey, 1888.

Wilcox, Ella Wheeler. *Maurine, Illustrated with Photographic Life Studies by Jans Matzens and Views by Eugene J. Hall.* Chicago: Conkey, 1901.

Wilcox, Ella Wheeler. *Poems of Passion.* 1883. Chicago: Conkey, 1894.

Wilcox, Ella Wheeler. *Three Women.* Chicago: Conkey, 1897.

Secondary Works
Ballou, Jenny. *Period Piece: Ella Wheeler Wilcox and Her Times.* Boston: Houghton Mifflin, 1940.

Bourdieu, Pierre. *Distinction: A Social Critique of the Judgement of Taste.* Translated by Richard Nice. Cambridge, Mass.: Harvard University Press, 1984.

Conrow, Robert. *Field Days: The Life, Times, and Reputation of Eugene Field.* New York: Scribners, 1974.

Davenport, Guy. *The Geography of the Imagination: Forty Essays.* San Francisco: North Point Press, 1981.

Hollander, John, ed. *American Poetry: The Nineteenth Century.* 2 vols. New York: Library of America, 1993.

Kreymborg, Alfred. *A History of American Poetry: Our Singing Strength.* New York: Tudor, 1934.

Richards, I. A. *Principles of Literary Criticism.* London: Kegan Paul, Trench, Trubner, 1924.

Rubin, Joan Shelley. *The Making of Middlebrow Culture.* Chapel Hill: University of North Carolina Press, 1992.

Saum, Lewis O. *Eugene Field and His Age.* Lincoln: University of Nebraska Press, 2001.

Turner, Michael R., ed. *Victorian Parlour Poetry: An Annotated Anthology.* 1969. New York: Dover, 1992.

Walker, Cheryl, ed. *American Women Poets of the Nineteenth Century: An Anthology.* New Brunswick, N.J.: Rutgers University Press, 1992.

Van Allen, Elizabeth J. *James Whitcomb Riley: A Life.* Bloomington: Indiana University Press, 1999.

Woolf, Virginia. "Middlebrow." 1912 In *The Death of the Moth and Other Essays,* 152–160. Harmondsworth, U.K.: Penguin, 1961. First published 1942 by Harcourt, Brace.

Christoph Irmscher

POPULISM

"What's the matter with Kansas?" the journalist William Allen White (1868–1944) asked in 1896 as he surveyed the political landscape of his native state, wondering at the preponderance of politicians "who can bellow about the crime of '73, who hate prosperity, and who think, because a man believes in national honor, he is a tool of Wall Street" (p. 86). The frenzy of the state's ruling Populists had not been slaked, in White's view, by their having created a climate hostile to investment and become the laughingstock of the rest of the country: "Then, for fear some hint that the state had become respectable might percolate through the civilized portions of the nation, we have decided to send three or four harpies out lecturing, telling the people that Kansas is raising hell and letting the corn go to weed" (p. 86). In his essay, widely reprinted in the Republican press, White dripped sarcasm as he sought to convey how his state had lost touch with reality: "Whoop it up for the ragged trousers; put the lazy, greasy fizzle, who can't pay his debts, on the altar, and bow down and worship him. Let the state ideal be high. What we need is not the respect of our fellow men, but the chance to get something for nothing" (p. 86).

The bewilderment of White and other Republicans notwithstanding, Populism resonated among southern, midwestern, and western farmers because it bespoke their situation and articulated their often inchoate sense that America had betrayed its democratic principles. Seagraves, the small town editor in Hamlin Garland's 1890 story "Among the Corn-Rows," thinks, after speaking with a midwestern farmer, "This working farmer had voiced the modern idea. It was an absolute overturn of all the ideas of nobility and special privilege born of the feudal past. . . . It was a wild, grand upstirring of the modern democrat against the aristocrat,

against the idea of caste and the privilege of living on the labor of others. This atom of humanity (how infinitesimal this drop in the ocean of humanity!) was feeling the nameless longing of expanding personality. He had declared rebellion against laws that were survivals of hate and prejudice. He had exposed also the native spring of the emigrant by uttering the feeling that it is better to be an equal among peasants than a servant before nobles" (pp. 92–93). Seagraves tells the farmer he would like to use his ideas in an editorial, prompting the farmer to comment: "My ideas! Why I didn't know I had any" (p. 93).

THE FARMER FEEDS US ALL

In the post–Civil War era, farmers found themselves victimized by the growing incursion of market forces into formerly remote areas, which ensnared them in a web of national and even international commercial relations. With the goal of contracting currency, Congress had demonetized silver in 1873—an act Populists would later decry as "the crime of '73," though it was little noticed at the time—and moved the country onto the gold standard by the end of the 1870s. For many farmers, the result was the cycle of ever-increasing debt characteristic of sharecropping, tenancy, peonage, or the crop-lien system. As Hamlin Garland (1860–1940) termed it in the title of another story, they were "under the lion's paw." In the South, the lien system came to be viewed by farmers as a new form of slavery: they were forced to sign over to the furnishing merchant first their crop and eventually their land. "In fact," the historian C. Vann Woodward has concluded, the crop-lien system "came to be more widespread than slavery had been, for it was no respecter of race or class; and if it be judged objectively, by its economic results alone, the new evil may have worked more permanent injury to the South than the ancient evil" (*Origins of the New South,* p. 180). The dominant economic and social theories, with their emphasis on laissez-faire capitalism and Social Darwinism, expressed no sympathy for debt-ridden farmers or for the growing number of unemployed wandering the country in the many depression years of the late nineteenth century. As an editorial in the Lincoln, Nebraska, *Farmers' Alliance* described the situation, "The actual state of society to-day is a state of war, active irreconcilable war on every side, and in all things. . . . Competition is only another name for war. It means slavery to millions—it means the sale of virtue for bread—it means for thousands upon thousands starvation, misery and death. After four thousand years of life is this the best that we can achieve? If so, who cares how soon the end may come?" (Pollack, *Populist Mind,* p. 4).

Farmers frequently joined together to sing Knowles Shaw's ballad "The Farmer Feeds Us All" (ca. 1870) with its chorus:

> Then take him by the hand,
> All ye people of the land,
> Stand by him whatever troubles befall;
> We may say whate'er we can,
> Yet the farmer is the man,
> Yes, the farmer is the man that feeds us all.

But integration into larger market networks drove crop prices down while increased reliance on monopolies such as the railroads, over whose rates the farmers had no control, made it more difficult for them to feed their own families. In an era of spectacular economic growth, the irony that their desperate straits existed in the midst of economic abundance was not lost on farmers. In the words of the Alabama Populist Milford Howard (1862–1937), "The granaries are bursting with wheat; the bins are filled with corn; the stock-yards are overflowing with cattle, hogs and sheep; the fields of the South have been white with cotton—an abundance everywhere throughout the entire country. Of it we can say, as was said of the Promised Land of Canaan, 'It flows with milk and honey.' Notwithstanding all this, the people are starving" (p. 244).

Throughout the 1870s and 1880s, farmers in all regions had responded to the situation by forming a variety of cooperative organizations, including the Granger and the Northern Alliance in the Midwest, the Agricultural Wheel in the South, and the Texas Alliance in the Southwest. These cooperative organizations had been crucial in the development of what Lawrence Goodwyn has termed the "movement culture," which allowed farmers to understand the commonality of their interests and the nature of those who opposed them, whether furnishing merchants, land companies, banks, railroads, or grain elevator companies. Out of this movement culture there developed the collective self-confidence necessary to allow the farmers en masse to formulate an alternative to the dominant cultural understanding of the American economy and their role in it. Economists told the farmers they were responsible for their own troubles, having overproduced and thus driven prices down. But farmers found a different culprit: the monopolies and trusts that wielded extensive control over Gilded Age society. "Between [the] plenty ripening on the boughs of our civilization and the people hungering for it," wrote the Populist muckraker Henry Demarest Lloyd (1847–1903) in his 1894 classic, *Wealth against Commonwealth,* "step the . . . syndicates, trusts, combinations, with the cry of 'overproduction'—too much of everything. Holding back the riches of the earth, sea and sky from their fellows who famish and

freeze in the dark, they declare to them that there is too much light and warmth and food. They assert the right, for their private profit, to regulate the consumption by the people of the necessaries of life, and to control production, not by the needs of humanity, but by the desires of a few for dividends" (Pollack, *Populist Mind,* p. 9).

THE PEOPLE'S PARTY

With the failure of attempts at economic mutual aid, farmers began to realize that a turn to politics had become necessary, and so in the early 1890s the People's Party was born. In its major statement of purpose, the 1892 Omaha Platform, the party called for a flexible paper currency to be distributed through the subtreasury plan, a system of government-owned warehouses in which farmers could store their crops while borrowing against them; the public ownership of the railroad, telegraph, and telephone companies; a graduated income tax; and the direct election of U.S. senators. With precious few allies in the universities, the mainstream press, and other traditional seats of cultural power, the populist movement developed its own methods for spreading its message, including the National Reform Press Association, with its hundreds of newspapers across the nation. "For a fact," Nebraska's *Platte County Argus* commented, "this ought to be a campaign of education" (Pollack, *Populist Mind,* p. 447). The Populist leaders took seriously their role as educators, as can be seen in the extensive use of statistics in the writings of the Populist senator from Kansas William Peffer; in Lloyd's densely detailed descriptions of corporate malfeasance; in the many case studies discussed in the 1892 presidential candidate James Weaver's campaign book *A Call to Action;* and in the learned disquisitions on such subjects as the Indian caste system and English labor history that peppered the speeches of the South's most famous Populist, Tom Watson. Such material provided fodder for the extensive network of stump speakers who campaigned throughout the country. The message spread rapidly, as the Populists won elections in several southern, midwestern, and western states, and their presidential ticket in 1892 earned more than one million popular and twenty-two electoral votes.

In his dystopian novel *Caesar's Column* (1890), the Minnesota Populist Ignatius Donnelly (1831–1901) described American republicanism as a sham: "We are a Republic only in name; free only in forms. Mohammedanism . . . never knew, in its worst estate, a more complete and abominable despotism than that under which we live. And as it would be worse to starve to death in sight of the most delicious viands than in the midst of a foodless desert, so the very assertions, greed as the dominating nexus of social relations. As the Texas Populist intellectual Thomas Nugent (1841–1895) described it, "The spirit of plutocratic capitalism is the dominating force in our organized social and industrial life. . . . It robs genius of its glory, makes of intellect a drudge and a slave, and utilizes the achievements of science to raid the stock markets and enlarge the margin of profits. Thus it wipes out as with a sponge the distinction between right and wrong, makes merchandise of the noblest ideals, sets gain before the world as the highest end of life, and converts men into predatory human animals" (Pollack, *Populist Mind*, pp. 305–306).

At its base, the Populist argument rested on the labor theory of value, namely, that labor created wealth, which then became capital. But as capital became concentrated in fewer and fewer hands, it began to dominate political channels, and the combination of concentrated capital and state power served to impoverish the working classes, both rural and industrial. In Nugent's words, "Capital could never have attained such ascendancy, but for the legislation which has given it unjust advantages and enabled it to monopolize both natural resources and public functions and utilities" (Pollack, *Populist Mind*, p. 306). Or, as Weaver claimed, "Labor can create wealth but it cannot create money. It requires a statute to speak money into existence. It is the creature of law, not the product of nature" (Pollack, *Populist Mind*, p. 132). Watson pondered, "What is the labor question? In a nutshell it is this: Labor asks of capital, 'Why is it you have so much and do so little work, while I have so little and do so much?'" (Pollack, *Populist Mind*, p. 424).

Ironically, the Populists' wide-ranging and penetrating critique of Gilded Age capitalism rested on a belief in the sanctity of competition and private property. Populists sought some degree of individual economic independence and believed private property was essential for achieving it. In their view, as the historian Norman Pollack has said, "Property was only a threat when it became integrated with mechanisms of domination" (*The Just Polity*, p. 6) and thus worked contrary to the interests of the community, and the Populist goal was to use the power of the state to prevent the growth of monopolies where practicable and assume ownership of natural monopolies to serve the public interest. Existing monopolies thwarted genuine competition and the philosophy of laissez-faire resulted only in brutal competition among surplus laborers that drove wages downward and among farmers who were working to pay off their debts in a deflated economy.

Self-consciously standing against the dominant ideology, Populists challenged justifications of excessive

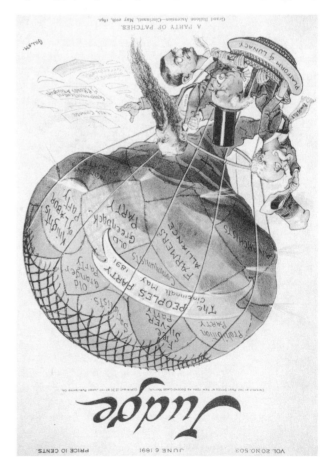

Populist Party cartoon. Drawn by Bernhard Gillam for *Judge* magazine, 6 June 1891. Gillam satirizes the party as a patchwork of radical groups. THE GRANGER COLLECTION, NEW YORK

constantly dinned into our ears by the hireling newspapers, that we are the freest people on earth, serve only to make our slavery more bitter and unbearable" (p. 37). Seeing themselves as inheritors of the republican ideology of "producerism" dating back to the American Revolution, Populists believed they were completing the unfinished democratic project of the Civil War. As Weaver said, "We shall proceed to show that in the very midst of the struggle for the overthrow of the slave oligarchy, our institutions were assailed by another foe mightier than the former, equally cruel, wider in its field of operation, infinitely greater in wealth, and immeasurably more difficult to control. It will be readily understood that we allude to the sudden growth of corporate power and its attendant consequences" (Pollack, *Populist Mind*, p. 121).

Corporate powers had come to dominate government, the courts, and the press, but their fundamental impact was even more pernicious in that they ensconced wealth and poverty such as Social Darwinism, arguing instead that government had a responsibility to protect the weak. In the words of Lorenzo D. Lewelling (1846–1900), the Populist governor of Kansas, "The survival of the fittest is the government of brutes and reptiles, and such philosophy must give place to a government which recognizes human brotherhood. It is the province of government to protect the weak, but the government to-day is resolved into a struggle of the masses with the classes for supremacy and bread, until business, home and personal integrity are trembling in the face of possible want in the family . . . If it be true that the poor have no right to the property of the rich let it also be declared that the rich have no right to the property of the poor" (Pollack, Populist Mind, pp. 51–52). Populists also delighted in subverting the dominant discourse and using the language of the business classes for their own ends. In an age when the specter of anarchism haunted capitalists, the Decatur, Texas, Times argued that the monopolists were the true anarchists." "Red-handed anarchy is fast developing in the soldiery of our beloved Republic, in the courts, the elections, in the

legislatures and congress" (Pollack, Populist Mind, p. 56). Similarly, Henry Demarest Lloyd used the language of self-interest and Social Darwinism for populist ends: "The whole problem can be argued out from the point of view of self-interest, putting the self-interest of the community against the self-interest of the individual; the self-interest of the better against the self-interest of the worse; and reading the survival of the strongest to mean the survival of the stronger virtues, not the stronger greed" (Pollack, Populist Mind, p. 69).

Populists saw their movement as very much in the American grain and presented themselves as the true defenders of the Constitution and the law. In their view, the corporate hijacking of the courts and law-making bodies represented a betrayal of the American constitutional system. This commitment to established constitutional means also set the parameters of acceptable Populist activity, largely defined by party organizing and participation in elections, and a rejection of violence as a political tool. As Nugent cautioned, "In combating monopoly, let us never forget

---

Adopted in July 1892, the Omaha Platform represents a comprehensive statement of the Populist worldview, with its apocalyptic vision of Gilded Age America. The preamble was written by Ignatius Donnelly, a Minnesota novelist, journalist, stump speaker and tireless party activist. The platform's resolutions included demands for a policy of economic inflation, limitations on the power of monopolies to dominate the economy, greater democratization of political life, and support for the rights of industrial workers.

The conditions which surround us best justify our cooperation: we meet in the midst of a nation brought to the verge of moral, political, and material ruin. Corruption dominates the ballot-box, the legislatures, the Congress, and touches even the ermine of the bench. The people are demoralized; most of the States have been compelled to isolate the voters at the polling-places to prevent universal intimidation or bribery. The newspapers are largely subsidized or muzzled; public opinion silenced; business prostrated; our homes covered with mortgages; labor impoverished and the land concentrating in the hands of the capitalists. The urban workmen are denied the right of organization for self-protection; imported pauperized labor beats down their wages; a hireling standing army, unrecognized by our laws, is established to shoot them down, and they are rapidly degenerating

into European conditions. The fruits of the toil of millions are boldly stolen to build up colossal fortunes for a few, unprecedented in the history of mankind; and the possessors of these, in turn, despise the republic and endanger liberty. From the same prolific womb of governmental injustice we bred the two great classes—tramps and millionaires. . . .

Our country finds itself confronted by conditions for which there is no precedent in the history of the world; our annual agricultural productions amount to billions of dollars in value, which must, within a few weeks or months, be exchanged for billions of dollars of commodities consumed in their production; the existing currency supply is wholly inadequate to make this exchange; the results are falling prices, the formation of combines and rings, the impoverishment of the producing class.

Ignatius Donnelly, "The Omaha Platform" (1892), in Pollack, Populist Mind, pp. 60, 62.

---

that neither force nor infringement of individual liberty is justifiable or safe. Let us remember that we ought above all others to set ourselves against anarchy in every form, against every measure calculated to break down the security which the laws afford to private property, and in favor only of those lawful and orderly methods which can always be successfully defended, and the observance of which will never fail to enlist for the workingman the sympathies of the good and worthy people of every class. . . . A good cause committed to violent methods inevitably finds in them its grave. An intelligent ballot is the only refuge of justice and liberty" (Pollack, *Populist Mind*, pp. 311–312). Similarly, Donnelly's cautionary tale, *Caesar's Column*, warned of a coming apocalypse when the workers would turn to violence, culminating in "a hell of injustice, ending in a holocaust of slaughter"(Donnelly, p. 57).

BREAKING DOWN BARRIERS

In order to build a mass movement, the Populists attempted to form alliances across several of the deepest rifts in Gilded Age America. From their agrarian origins, farmers reached out to industrial workers and the unemployed, fellow victims, in their view, of the war between the ruling classes and the masses. The Omaha Platform championed the cause of industrial labor with its call to limit immigration to reduce competition for jobs, to enforce the eight-hour workday, to abolish the strikebreaking Pinkerton Agency, and to support the Knights of Labor. The party stood with labor in all the major conflicts of the era. In the 1892 strike against Andrew Carnegie's Homestead Steel Plant, Mary E. Lease (1853–1933), one of the most famous Populist stump speakers, specifically called on Kansas farmers to send the striking workers a trainload of supplies: "'We have been told by those who deal in misrepresentations that the farmers were not in sympathy with the wants and demands of laborers in town and city. Let us hurl this falsehood back, and show to the world that the farmers of Kansas are imbued with the spirit of 1776, and in sympathy with the toilers and oppressed humanity everywhere" (Pollack, *Populist Mind*, p. 449). In *A Strike of Millionaires against Miners* (1890), Henry Demarest Lloyd described miners caught in a circle of debt similar to the that of the crop-lien system. "Sometimes it was one thing, sometimes another; but the upshot of it was that, mostly, when the miner came to settle with the company for the preceding month's work, he found that, after paying for his oil, and the sharpening of his tools, his rent or his monthly installment on the lot he had bought, his monthly contribution to the doctor, and his bill at the company's store, there was nothing left.

He had just made ends meet; perhaps he was a little behind"(Pollack, *Populist Mind*, pp. 411–412).

The Populists also supported the cause of the unemployed. Llewelling and others viewed the growing number of unemployed as resulting directly from the combination of monopolies and increasing mechanization. "In this country, the monopoly of labor-saving machinery and its devotion to selfish instead of social use, have rendered more and more human beings superfluous until we have a standing army of the unemployed numbering even in the most prosperous times not less than one million able-bodied men"(Pollack, *Populist Mind*, p. 331). In his 1891 novel, *Congressman Swanson*, Charles C. Post (1854–1914) described the response of the business classes to the growing number of unemployed: "And as the machinery of legislation was in their hands, or the hands of their dupes and tools, the politicians, 'Tramp laws' were passed, and it became a crime for a man out of employment and out of money to ask for bread" (Pollack, *Populist Mind*, p. 353). Standing as staunch supporters of demonstrations by the unemployed like that led by Jacob Coxey in 1894, the Populists called for the federal government to create a program of public works to provide jobs for the unemployed.

In trying to build a national movement, the Populists found themselves confronting the sectionalism and the regional hold the two main political parties had on American politics. In an era in which the Civil War was a recent memory and parties were closely tied to sectional divisions, the Populists called on farmers and workers to break with their traditional political loyalties and support a third party. And in the South especially, this split involved even more basic social issues, as the politics of the existing parties became entangled in the region's racial divisions. Populists in the South, in challenging the dominant Democratic Party, confronted directly that party's ideology of white supremacy. Not all Populists were willing to make this break with the past, but many in the South proved ready to stand in economic and political solidarity across racial lines. Speaking of black and white farmers, Watson said, "Now the People's Party says to these two men, 'You are kept apart that you may be separately fleeced of your earnings. You are made to hate each other because upon that hatred is rested the keystone of the arch of financial despotism which enslaves you both. You are deceived and blinded that you may not see how this race antagonism perpetuates a monetary system which beggars both'" (Pollack, *Populist Mind*, pp. 371–372). Similarly, the Louisiana People's Party adopted a resolution proclaiming, "We declare emphatically that the interests of the white and colored races in the South are identical. . . . Legislation beneficial to the white man must, at the same time, be beneficial to the colored man." Black Populists too realized that joining the movement involved a wrenching break with traditional loyalties; as a black Georgia farmer wrote, "It seems to be a hard thing for us colored men to give up the republican party, but let us stop and consider: We are living in another man's house, working another man's land, and our smoke house and meal-tub are in town. Let us quit the old party and vote for wife and children and a chance for a home" (Pollack, *Populist Mind*, pp. 395–396). And yet, as white southern Populists stressed, this willingness to break with the region's racial heritage and withstand the Democrats' fearmongering cries of "Negro Rule" had its limits. As one white Alabama Populist wrote, "This has nothing whatever to do with social equality. It is a question of the material interests of both races" (Pollack, *Populist Mind*, p. 389).

FUSION

Populism, by allowing itself to be contained largely within existing political processes, saw its protest "largely, if not exclusively, confined to the channels that the society had established to neutralize dissent" (Pollack, *The Just Polity*, pp. 64–65). These self-imposed ideological parameters created a profound dilemma for the party in 1896 when the question of fusion with the Democrats seemed to offer the best chance for electoral victory. As the historian Robert McMath comments, "Here the logic and history of Populism as a *movement* collided with the ultimate *political* question: how to get more votes than the other guy" (p. 175). Within the Democratic Party, a faction emerged in the mid-1890s calling for the free and unlimited coinage of silver. Fueled by such popular works as W. H. Harvey's *Coin's Financial School* (1894), bimetallists called for a policy of inflation that, in the Populist view, still left the fundamental issues unresolved: it did nothing to counter the trend toward monopoly nor did it create a flexible monetary system that could keep up with industrial growth. When the free silver faction took control of the Democratic Party and nominated William Jennings Bryan, Populists faced the choice of fusing with the Democrats and thus jettisoning most of their platform, or running their own candidate and guaranteeing the election of the gold standard Republican William McKinley. Led by such fusionists as Watson and Weaver, the party chose to ally itself with the Democrats, though many Populists never accepted the decision. As an outraged Donnelly said, "The Democracy raped our convention while our leaders held the struggling victim" (Ridge, p. 357). The

Populist Party, having channeled its militancy into electoral politics, was devastated by the 1896 defeat and never recovered. In Pollack's words, "Populism did not decline gradually. It fell over a precipice, to some extent a situation of its own making" (*The Just Polity*, p. 21).

See also Political Parties

BIBLIOGRAPHY

Primary Works

Donnelly, Ignatius. *Caesar's Column: A Story of the Twentieth Century.* 1890. Edited with an introduction by Nicholas Ruddick. Middletown, Conn.: Wesleyan University Press, 2003.

Garland, Hamlin. *Main-Travelled Roads.* Lincoln: University of Nebraska Press, 1995.

Lloyd, Henry Demarest. *Wealth against Commonwealth.* 1894. Englewood Cliffs, N.J.: Prentice Hall, 1963.

Pollack, Norman, ed. *The Populist Mind.* Indianapolis: Bobbs-Merrill, 1967.

White, William Allen. "What's the Matter with Kansas?" 1896. In *American Issues, Volume 2: Since 1865,* edited by Irwin Unger and Robert Tomes. Upper Saddle River, N.J.: Prentice Hall, 1999.

Secondary Works

Goodwyn, Lawrence. *The Populist Moment: A Short History of the Agrarian Revolt in America.* New York: Oxford University Press, 1978.

Kazin, Michael. *The Populist Persuasion: An American History.* Rev. ed. Ithaca, N.Y.: Cornell University Press, 1998.

McMath, Robert C., Jr. *American Populism: A Social History, 1877–1898.* New York: Hill and Wang, 1993.

Pollack, Norman. *The Just Polity: Populism, Law, and Human Welfare.* Urbana: University of Illinois Press, 1987.

Ridge, Martin. *Ignatius Donnelly: The Portrait of a Politician.* Chicago: University of Chicago Press, 1962.

Woodward, C. Vann. *Origins of the New South, 1877–1913.* Baton Rouge: Louisiana State University Press, 1971.

Woodward, C. Vann. *Tom Watson, Agrarian Rebel.* New York: Macmillan, 1938.

David Cochran

PORNOGRAPHY

Because war stimulates sexual expression, pornography flourished during the Civil War and again during the First World War, the conflicts that bracket this literary period. Civil War soldiers of both the North and the South purchased erotic pictures, appliances, magazines, and fiction from camp followers and mail-order distributors, much to the alarm of Congress, which in 1865 passed a statute prohibiting the mailing of obscene materials across state lines. The innocence that Congress sought to preserve had already ended; veterans continued to seek the kinds of books they had enjoyed in the trenches near Antietam and Chancellorsville. Improved cylindrical rotary presses (1865) made it possible for publishers in Boston, Cincinnati, New Orleans, and New York to mass produce erotic books and pamphlets for a steadily widening audience.

According to the erotica bibliographer Henry Spencer Ashbee, publisher William Haynes of New York assembled a backlist of 320 erotic titles by 1871; by 1885 one hundred thousand such books were sold in New York City alone. Most were imports: translations of Boccaccio's *Decameron* and other bawdy European classics; stronger fare such as John Cleland's *Memoirs of a Woman of Pleasure* (a.k.a. *Fanny Hill*, 1748), which had been pirated continuously by American publishers since 1815, or Alfred de Musset's *Gamiani, or Two Nights of Excess* (1833), a roman à clef of the author's liaison with George Sand; and milder stuff, such as collections of ribald verse or sensational novels by the French Paul de Kock (*Confessions of a Lady's Waiting Maid* [1860]). Publishers also commissioned fiction from among the growing ranks of professional American writers. Their anonymous titles included *The Libertine Enchantress, or The Adventures of Lucinda Hartley* (New Orleans, 1863), *Beautiful Creole of Havana* (New Orleans, 1863), *Sodom in Union Square, or Revelations of the Doings in Fourteenth Street, By an Ex-Police Captain of New York* (New York, 1885?), and *John, the Darling of the Philadelphia Ladies* (Boston?, 1890?). Favorite themes were female abduction, loss of virginity, voyeurism, secret marriages, incest, and miscegenation, often accompanied by satire of public figures or institutions, as in *The Secret Life of Linda Brent, a Curious History of Slave Life* (London, 1882), a pornographic parody of Harriet Jacobs's anti-slavery narrative, *Incidents in the Life of a Slave Girl* (1861). Ashbee referred to most American examples as "semi-erotica": stories of urban street life, treatises on sexology, or "gallantia"—"jestbooks, ballads, reflections on love, or novels of romantic bombast. While the orientation was masculine, evasion was also the rule: if a "snowy orb" escaped from a bodice, for instance, it would not sport a nipple. To be sure, the reticence of the period's discourse kept the threshold of arousal low—and sales high.

REACTION TO PORNOGRAPHY

Increased traffic in erotica roused opposition, not only from the prudish but also from progressives worried about corruption, crime, and prostitution (which at the time had only recently been linked to venereal disease), all of which they feared indecent books somehow promoted. As Walter Kendrick has pointed out, industrialization and growing affluence helped consolidate a still-insecure American middle class that defined itself in part by distinguishing its morals and tastes from those of lower classes whose allegedly insatiable sexuality threatened social stability. While the upright middle-class male might savor a risqué story, denying such pleasures to inferiors seemed only prudent, and for their own good as well—a pattern of hypocrisy that has come to seem particularly American. Legal strategies for combating indecency came quickly to hand.

Obscenity as a concept was still evolving from its origins in laws governing blasphemy, and "pornography" was as yet an unfamiliar term, but American prosecutors trained in English common law seized upon the *Regina v. Hicklin* decision of 1868, a legal precedent established by an English judge's dislike of Alexandre Dumas's *The Lady of the Camellias*. The London court ruled that the Crown could condemn a book if *any* passages were judged likely to "deprave and corrupt" certain citizens—that is, women, children, and immigrants, all of whom were assumed to be of weak mind and therefore at risk from exposure to sexual candor. American courts soon routinely applied "the *Hicklin* test" to books charged with transgressions against morality.

In 1873 New York State authorized the New York Society for the Suppression of Vice, the invention of a grocery clerk named Anthony Comstock (1844–1915), to prosecute a wide range of perceived evils: blasphemy, gambling, violent sporting events, birth control advocacy, indecent theatrical performance, and lewd writing and pictures. The politically well-connected Comstock immediately lobbied Congress to revise Title 18 of the U.S. Code. The new sections (1461, 1462, and 1463), collectively called the Comstock Act (1873), prohibited the publication, manufacture, importation, interstate transportation, and advertising of materials for "indecent or immoral use," a category that included both contraceptive information and sexual expression. To enforce these restrictions, Comstock was also appointed Special Agent for the Post Office. Comstock's success led to similar organizations in other states: Boston's New England Watch and Ward Society, Chicago's Illinois Vigilance League, Washington's International Reform Federation, and Cincinnati's Western Society for the Suppression of Vice were the most vigorous.

At first, such groups prosecuted trashy novels and pulp magazines that they insisted promoted promiscu-ity and degeneracy. Wielding *Hicklin* as his weapon, Comstock attacked marginal lower-Manhattan pub-lishers such as William Haynes, George Ackerman (a.k.a. George Akarman and James Ramerio), Jeremiah H. Farrell, and John Uln, all of whom issued both sensational and "fancy" (i.e., sexually explicit) pam-phlets and books. Comstock used ruthless tactics: entrapment, docket-fixing, and persecution; he boasted of having driven Haynes to suicide. As John Burnham has noted, these tactics pushed "real" pornography underground and made it "economically unimpor-tant" by limiting its circulation to wealthy collectors such as J. P. Morgan and Henry Huntington (p. 180). By the end of the century, few American publishers dared release works such as *The Bar Maid of Old Point House, Being the Secret History of the Amours and Intrigues of a Bar Maid Whose Amorous Disposition and Voluptuous Achievements on the Couch of Cupid Made Her the Envy of Her Own Sex and the Admiration of the New World* (1889!). However, men's clubs occa-sionally printed bawdy monologues and erotic verse in limited subscription editions such as *The Stag Party* (Boston or Chicago, 1888 or 1889), which contains erotic works by Eugene Field (e.g., *Only a Boy* [1886]); *The Lady and the Flea* (1910?), a volume of erotic sto-ries; and James C. Harvey's *The Point of View* (1905), a gathering of erotic poems. Mark Twain's surrepti-tiously printed burlesques (*1601: Conversation as It Was by the Social Fireside in the Time of the Tudors* [1876], *Some Thoughts on the Science of Onanism* [1879], and *The Mammoth Cod* [1890s!]) also fall into this category.

By century's end, vigilant suppression forced dis-tributors again to import erotica from publishers in Paris, London, Amsterdam, or Brussels. The most important of these was Charles Carrington (Paul Ferdinando [1877–1922]), who shipped his wares to the United States through Cuba. Though published abroad, some highly explicit Carrington books, espe-cially those capitalizing on alleged American proclivi-ties for free love, miscegenation, and oral sex, were probably written by Americans. In this group are *A Town Bull or the Elysian Fields: How Priapus blessed a poor man, made a living for him, and how, finally, a paradise for free-lovers was established, where fathers and daughters, mothers and grandsons, brothers and sis-ters, white, brown and black cohabited indiscriminately* (1893); *Sue Suckit, Maid and Wife: How Her Virgin Lips Made Her Fortune Banqueting on Spermatic Sweets; How Her Tongue Tickled Touchy Tit-Bits of Testicular Treasures, Until as Wanton Wife and Maid We Leave Her Ready to Receive in All Parts of Her Pretty*

Person A Man's Hot Tongue or Red and Rigid Rod, and Give Him Back, with Coral Lips or Slit, A Rapturous Roland for His Oily Oliver (1893); *Maidenhead Stories Told By a Set of Joyous Students* (1894); and *Erototre-meron; or, How four of us lost our maidenheads. Four highly licentious stories of Love-Adventure and frantic deviltries related by Mollie, Lizzie, Maude & Kate, 4 frisky women left alone to pass the summer days in the Catskill-Mountains N. America* (1892). Perhaps the most famous "American" erotic novel of the period, however, was *The Memoirs of Dolly Morton* (1900), a tale of flagellation and interracial sex in the Deep South, probably written for Carrington by the French symbolist Georges Grassal (1867–1905) under the name Hugues Rebell.

Anti-vice organizations had also begun to pres-sure American carriage trade publishers. When the Watch and Ward Society in Boston condemned *Leaves of Grass* in 1882, publisher James Osgood tore up his contract with Walt Whitman. Censorship actual or threatened delayed publication of Stephen Crane's *Maggie, A Girl of the Streets* (1893), Elinor Glyn's *Three Weeks* (1907), Theodore Dreiser's *Sister Carrie* (1900) and *The "Genius"* (1915), and James Branch Cabell's *Jurgen* (1919), or caused the expurgation of David Graham Phillips's *Susan Lenox; Her Fall and Rise* (1915) and numerous other works. Fortunately, attorneys such as Theodore Schroeder had begun cod-ifying constitutional challenges to *Hicklin*. In 1913 federal judge Learned Hand, though declining to overturn the conviction of Daniel Goodman's socio-logical novel, *Hagar Revelly*, predicted that such pros-ecutions would become increasingly untenable (*United States v. Kennerly* [209 F. 119, 1913]). Seven years later a New York court accepted arguments that a book should be evaluated as a whole by literary critics, not by private citizens offended by selected portions in *Halsey v. New York Society for the Suppression of Vice* (180 N.Y. S. 836, 1920). Those decisions enraged censors, who launched the Clean Books crusade of the 1920s, a campaign against literary candor whose indis-criminately chosen targets would eventually marginal-ize their organizations. In New York, police closed Sholem Asch's *God of Vengeance* (1923) and Eugene O'Neill's *Desire Under the Elms* (1925). By 1927 Boston's Watch and Ward Society had banned nearly one hundred books, including Dreiser's *An American Tragedy* (1925), John Dos Passos's *Manhattan Transfer* (1925), Ernest Hemingway's *The Sun Also Rises* (1926), Sinclair Lewis's *Elmer Gantry* (1927), Carl Van Vechten's *Nigger Heaven* (1926), Babette Deutsch's *In Such a Night* (1927), and William Faulkner's *Mosquitoes* (1927).

THE LEGACY

In retrospect, it seems clear that censors were resisting urbanization, industrialization, science (especially Freudian psychoanalysis), and immigration, factors that also fostered American literary realism. World War I ended the country's isolationism, weakened rigid social protocols, and exposed Americans to art and ideas from Europe. Just as important, according to Jay Gertzman, motion pictures, jazz, and theatrical spectacle "eroticized leisure time" (p. 50). To help fill that leisure, a new generation of sub-rosa publishers made available erotica in genres enumerated by Gertzman as "curiosa" (mild erotic fiction), "sex pulps" (titillating romances and mysteries), "erotology" and sexology" (scientific and pseudoscientific texts), "sleaze" (explicit stories), and "classic" forbidden works (p. 61ff). Their activities emboldened mainstream publishers such as Horace Liveright, Albert Boni, and Pascal Covici.

That influence aside, it is difficult to calculate the impact of erotica on mainstream writers. By the twentieth century, industrialization had blunted the revolutionary and democratic force of a vulgar pornography that Lynn Hunt and other historians have credited with helping to undermine authoritarian social and political structures of earlier centuries. Even so, sexual candor—as a tool for revealing psychological states and illuminating relationships—figured prominently in efforts to make literature more realistic. James Gibbons Huneker's *Painted Veils* (1920), whose explicit innovations anticipated James Joyce's erotic interior monologues in *Ulysses*, circulated clandestinely. Edith Wharton hid her "Beatrice Palmato Fragment" (c. 1917?), a pornographic exploration of oral-genital incest, among her unpublished papers. Margaret Anderson, arrested in 1920 for printing an episode from *Ulysses* in *The Little Review*, forty years later could not publish her own lesbian novel, *Forbidden Fires* (1958). Talented realists with far less reason for such self-censorship found their fiction described as "filth" anyway. For Clean Books zealots, realism was synonymous with pornography, an association that colored literary experimentation for years. As Gershon Legman has observed, by the 1920s "erotica" had become a code word for avant-garde literature.

See also Sex Reform; Sex Education; "Some Thoughts on the Science of Onanism"

BIBLIOGRAPHY

Primary Works

Ashbee, Henry Spencer [Pisanus Fraxi, pseud.]. *Bibliography of Forbidden Books*, 1877, 1879, 1885. New York: Jack Brussel, 1962.

New England Watch and Ward Society. *Annual Reports.* Boston: New England Watch and Ward Society, 1905–1939.

Secondary Works

Boyer, Paul S. *Purity in Print: The Vice-Society Movement and Book Censorship in America.* New York: Scribners, 1968.

Broun, Heywood, and Margaret Leech. *Anthony Comstock: Roundsman of the Lord.* New York: Boni, 1927.

Comstock, Anthony. *Frauds Exposed; or, How the People Are Deceived and Robbed, and Youth Corrupted.* 1880.

Comstock, Anthony. *Traps for the Young.* Edited by Robert Bremner. 1883. Cambridge, Mass.: Belknap Press, 1967.

Schroeder, Theodore. *Freedom of the Press and "Obscene" Literature.* New York: Free Speech League, 1906.

Burnham, John C. *Bad Habits: Drinking, Smoking, Taking Drugs, Gambling, Sexual Misbehavior, and Swearing in American History.* New York: New York University Press, 1993.

Gertzman, Jay. *Bookleggers and Smuthounds: The Trade in Erotica, 1920–1940.* Philadelphia: University of Pennsylvania Press, 1999.

Gilfoyle, Timothy J. *City of Eros: New York City, Prostitution, and the Commercialization of Sex, 1790–1920.* New York: Norton, 1992.

Gilmer, Walker. *Horace Liveright: Publisher of the Twenties.* New York: David Lewis, 1970.

Haight, Anne Lyon. *Banned Books: Informal Notes on Some Books Banned for Various Reasons at Various Times and in Various Places.* 3rd ed. New York: Bowker, 1970.

Horowitz, Helen Lefkowitz. *Rereading Sex: Battles Over Sexual Knowledge and Suppression in Nineteenth-Century America.* New York: Knopf, 2002.

Hunt, Lynn, ed. *The Invention of Pornography: Obscenity and the Origins of Modernity, 1500–1800.* Cambridge, Mass.: MIT Press, 1993.

Kendrick, Walter. *The Secret Museum: Pornography in Modern Culture.* New York: Viking, 1987.

Legman, Gershon. "Bawdy Monologues and Rhymed Recitations." *Southern Folklore Quarterly* 40 (1976): 59–123.

Legman, Gershon. "The Lure of the Forbidden." In *Libraries, Erotica, and Pornography*, edited by Martha Cornog, pp. 36–68. Phoenix, Ariz.: Oryx Press, 1991.

Lowry, Thomas P. *The Story the Soldiers Wouldn't Tell: Sex in the Civil War.* Mechanicsburg, Pa.: Stackpole Books, 1994.

Mendes, Peter. *Clandestine Erotic Fiction in English, 1800–1930: A Bibliographical Study.* Aldershot, U.K.: Scolar Press, 1993.

New York Society for the Suppression of Vice. *Annual Reports.* New York: New York Society for the Suppression of Vice, 1874–1940.

Reynolds, David. *Beneath The American Renaissance: The Subversive Imagination in the Age of Emerson and Melville.* New York: Knopf, 1988.

Roebuck, John. *The Wicked and the Banned.* New York: MacFadden Books, 1963.

Slade, Joseph W. *Pornography and Sexual Representation: A Reference Guide.* 3 vols. Westport, Conn.: Greenwood Press, 2001.

Joseph W. Slade

THE PORTRAIT OF A LADY

The Portrait of a Lady (1881) is Henry James's (1843–1916) most accessible major novel, rich in social detail and psychological insight, written with elegance and wit. As such, it is a brilliant example of the prime imaginative form of his youth, the nineteenth-century realist novel. But *Portrait* also anticipated the genre that was to follow it: the modern novel, that form which questions the very possibilities of realistic representation. James does both by putting front and center the matter of gender. Like the novels of Jane Austen, *Portrait* centers on the courtship of young women; like those of George Eliot, it tracks their disillusionment once the wedding knot has been tied. But James complicates the marriage plot by yoking it to the question of how the novel, the society, and the self all try to define female identity, how they paint a *portrait* of a lady. In the novel's most audacious moments, he suggests that these efforts fail—and that, in a world without stable codes of gender, men and women alike must struggle to shape their own identities through the choices they make, however blindly.

ISABEL ARCHER: THE SHAPING OF A HEROINE

These concerns are announced on the first pages of the book. The setting is Mr. Touchett's beloved country house in England, Gardencourt, and the time is "the hour dedicated to the ceremony known as afternoon tea" (p. 17). Gardencourt is not merely an "old English country house"; it is its most perfect expression, harmoniously uniting the pastoral and the social. And although it is the "perfect middle of a splendid summer afternoon" (p. 17), the moment is haunted by impending nightfall. When we meet them, Ralph Touchett, Daniel Touchett, and Lord Warburton are described by "straight and angular" shadows cast by the late-afternoon sun on the "perfect lawn" (p. 17). And these shadows literally foreshadow what we soon learn, that all of these characters are shadowy presences in life as well. Daniel sits in a wicker chair, "taking the rest that precedes the great rest" (p. 19). The other two men pacing in front of him are suffering either from a mortal illness (Ralph) or a more historical one: for all of his vitality, Lord Warburton is an anachronism, the representative of a dying aristocratic order. These men are also shadowy in the sense that they are defined as less than full-blooded males, at least in the ways masculinity has traditionally been defined. Thus before the plot of the novel even begins, the narrative has sketched a social situation marked by a pervasive sense of decline, if not impotence.

At least until they glance up to see, framed in a doorway, "a tall girl in a black dress" (p. 25): Ralph's cousin Isabel. At that moment, things change utterly. Isabel is everything these men are not. She is young; she is lively; she is independent. Throughout the first pages of the novel she shows a spirited freedom of thought and expression that places her in stark contrast to these overcivilized men. To be sure, she is profoundly sensitive to the artistic riches of Gardencourt and the old-world culture it represents. She is also deeply and proudly American, however, and hence both a breath of fresh air and a potential vexation: "Isabel Archer was a young person of many theories," we are told later; "her imagination was remarkably active" (p. 52). For now, we are asked to see her in the kindest possible light, as a beautiful if naive counter to the attenuated, dying world in which she finds herself—a new Eve, one who might potentially regenerate the Garden(court) she has entered.

It is certainly in this light that all of the characters of the novel treat her. The first to do so is Mrs. Touchett, who has invited her to England. Mrs. Touchett had encountered her niece Isabel in America, following the death of her brother. Out of sorts with England but in love with Italy, Lydia Touchett sees in Isabel a vessel to be filled with knowledge—as well as an impecunious relative to be taught the ways of the world. However, the very qualities that draw Mrs. Touchett to Isabel cause Isabel to struggle against her aunt's authority. In a significant moment in the novel, Lydia Touchett warns her niece about the impropriety of staying up late with Ralph and Lord Warburton. Isabel rejects the advice but asks always to be told "the things one shouldn't do." "So as to do them?" asks Lydia. "So as to choose," Isabel replies (p. 67). Isabel's desire to test conventional ideas by her own standards is articulated in the classic American terms of liberty. But such choices will prove dangerously ill-informed: seeking to escape from Mrs. Touchett's notions of propriety, Isabel will fall back on her power to make choices without possessing the experience to make them wisely.

Mrs. Touchett is not the only one to experience Isabel's resistance. Isabel encounters—and refuses—a stunning variety of men. Lord Warburton is the first to succumb to her charms, and much of the first phase of the novel is devoted to his courtship. Were this a different book—for example, Jane Austen's *Pride and Prejudice*—this would comprise its major action. And indeed James seems to be setting us up for a replay of Austen's novel. Like Elizabeth Bennett, Isabel is a dazzlingly self-possessed woman with perhaps too many opinions; like Darcy, Lord Warburton is a somewhat overweening aristocrat who seems perfect for her but whom she rejects. James invokes this plot, however, to show its inadequacy. For Warburton is if anything not proud enough: wealthy beyond measure, he is ashamed of his own class. As Daniel Touchett shrewdly observes, he is torn between his understanding that things must change and his affection for his own privileges, and he looks to Isabel to save him from his bad faith. What might in another novel be viewed as prejudice is here instead a sign of discernment.

A similar dynamic is at work in Isabel's relationship with Caspar Goodwood. If Lord Warburton represents a declining English power, Caspar embodies an ascending American one. Like Warburton he has inherited wealth, but Goodwood is no idler, having invented and manufactured an "improvement in the cotton-spinning process" (p. 106). Physically Goodwood is described in terms that make him Warburton's antithesis: he is "square and set . . . his figure straight and stiff" (p. 106). Resolutely he pursues Isabel to England, with the encouragement of *another* American who joins the cavalcade, the reporter Henrietta Stackpole. Isabel resists his attentions as much as she does Warburton's and for many of the same reasons: to exercise her own powers of judgment. Along with the rejection of Caspar, Isabel seems to be rejecting another narrative for herself, one like Emily Brontë's *Wuthering Heights*, in which a woman experiences a blind, romantic passion for a manly man. Isabel wants to write the narrative of her own destiny, not have it determined for her by this passionate if single-minded lover.

Isabel's desire to construct a new narrative for herself continues in her relation with a third man, Ralph. To be sure, Ralph disavows any amorous intent, to his father, to his mother, and to himself. Yet it is evident from the first that his feelings for Isabel are powerful, if complicated. "I had never been more blue, more bored, than for a week before she came . . ." he says. "Suddenly, I received a Titan, by the post, to hang on my wall—a

Greek bas-relief to stick over my chimney-piece" (p. 63). Ralph's response is troubling. It is clear from his interior monologue that he is rechanneling his affections for his cousin into distanced appreciation. To a certain extent, this appreciation is admirable; not only does he compare Isabel to great works of art but he also understands that her generous, expansive character is finer than anything art can offer. But Ralph's response to Isabel is also touched with a detached connoisseurship that verges on voyeurism. Moreover, he does not stop with mere spectatorship; rather, Ralph actively intervenes in Isabel's life. He prevails upon his father to leave her half of the money he had intended for Ralph. Ralph's motives in doing so are undeniably generous, but this plan also chimes with his vicarious desires. He asks his father to "put money in her purse" so that she may "meet the requirements" of *his* "imagination" (pp. 160, 163). Moreover, far from freeing Isabel from culturally scripted narratives, the plan merely places her in a different one. The plot device of an inheritance mysteriously passing to an unsuspecting orphan is a staple of literary romance. By unwittingly constructing *this* narrative for Isabel, Ralph also unwittingly plots a tragedy. For as both learn painfully, neither of their imaginations exerts itself in a vacuum; rather, they have entered a world of power, desire, and chicanery that is all too real.

These lessons are taught to Isabel in another of the relationships that shapes her life, with a new housequest, Serena Merle. Ralph calls her "the cleverest woman I know, not excepting yourself" (p. 154). As Isabel intuits, this is not intended as a compliment. But Ralph's warning falls on deaf ears: Isabel, so resistant to her aunt's, Lord Warburton's, Caspar's, and Henrietta's attempts to place her in their narrative frames, falls easily into Madame Merle's, although—so great is her cleverness—Isabel never suspects her until it is too late.

Through Madame Merle, James sets up a debate that resonates throughout the novel. At one point she tells Isabel:

When you've lived as long as I you'll see that every human being has his shell and that you must take the shell into account. . . . There's no such thing as an isolated man or woman; we're each of us made up of some cluster of appurtenances. What shall we call our "self"? Where does it begin? where does it end? It overflows into everything that belongs to us—and then it flows back again. . . . I've a great respect for *things*. (P. 175)

Isabel answers her friend in terms that take precisely the opposite view: "I know that nothing else expresses me. Nothing that belongs to me is any measure of me; everything's on the contrary a limit, a barrier, and a perfectly arbitrary one. Certainly, the clothes which as you say, I choose to wear, don't express me, and heaven forbid that they should" (p. 175). The conflict between these two visions has been brewing for much of the novel. If "clothes" metaphorically signify social convention, then this is a version of the quarrel between Isabel and Mrs. Touchett. If "things" imply objectification—the treating of human beings as if they were objects—then it is congruent with Ralph's own split image of Isabel as transcending and being equivalent to a work of art. And if the "cluster of appurtenances" represents the objects with which culture surrounds the self, then the debate here is between a European and an American understanding of the relation between history and identity. Madame Merle puts one side of that debate with lucidity, just as Isabel argues powerfully for the other. Each side in the debate ultimately loses, however. The novel enforces the tragic recognition that neither an objectified vision, no matter how realistic, nor a transcendental one, no matter how idealistic, is adequate to a world of human choices and their consequences.

The teacher of this harsh lesson is the one figure who approaches the status of villain, Gilbert Osmond. Yet another expatriate—a widower raising a young daughter in Rome, a connoisseur of Renaissance art, and a former lover of Madame Merle's in the distant past—Osmond seems the most unlikely possible partner for Isabel. Yet he is the linchpin of Madame Merle's plan. She begins talking him up early in her acquaintance with Isabel, puts her in contact with him when they visit Rome, and entices Osmond to drop his habitual indolence to woo Isabel. It is not until he learns of her fortune, however, that he decides that she is qualified "to figure in his collection of choice objects" (p. 258).

It is Gilbert's seeming uniqueness that captivates Isabel. "He resembled no one she had ever seen," the narrator tells us. "Her mind contained no class offering a natural place to Mr. Osmond—he was a specimen apart" (p. 224). She cannot see that her failure to place Osmond is utterly appropriate: having no positive characteristics of his own, he can be defined only in terms of negation. Isabel commits the error of mistaking Gilbert's passivity for mystery, his fastidiousness for subtlety, his indifference for reserve. She responds to the mystery of his poverty in the same way as Ralph does to that of her plenitude, by transforming Gilbert, mentally, into a work of art: "the image of a quiet, sensitive, distinguished man, strolling on a moss-grown terrace above the sweet Val d'Arno and holding by the hand a little girl whose bell-like clarity gave a new grace to childhood" (p. 237). This genre painting is a complete misperception of Osmond and a sentimental evasion of the truth of his relationship to Pansy: Gilbert seeks the same spirit-crushing obedi-

ence from his daughter that he is going to ask from Isabel. But far more troubling is the way that Isabel, like Ralph, misuses her aesthetic idealism. She cannot see that despite his artistic cultivation and sensitive demeanor, Osmond is nothing more than an arrogant fortune hunter. The irony here is manifest: it is usually aesthetes like Osmond who are accused of confusing

Madame X. Painting by John Singer Sargent, 1884. Henry James's Isabel Archer is described as a young, lovely, and independent "tall girl in a black dress," not unlike Sargent's famous, and scandalous, Madame X.
© BETTMAN/CORBIS

the line between art and life. Sadly it turns out to be the kindest and most generous-spirited characters in this book who make that mistake—and who must face its consequences.

ISABEL AND THE "MELODRAMA OF CONSCIOUSNESS"

It is at this moment in the novel that James begins to experiment most audaciously with literary form. After detailing Osmond's courtship, the novel leaves the reader suspended in midair. It defers our vision of Isabel for many pages, focusing on a hitherto minor character, a young collector named Ned Rosier, who has fallen in love with Pansy Osmond. We follow Rosier when, after Isabel's marriage and honeymoon, he enters the door into the Osmonds' grand home in Rome, the Palazzo Roccanera. We witness his encounter with a cold Osmond, who warns Rosier to stay away from Pansy, and we look through his eyes as he encounters a changed Isabel: "Framed in the gilded doorway, she struck our young man as the picture of a gracious lady" (p. 310). Here, as in her first appearance in the novel, Isabel is placed in a doorframe; here too she is wearing black. But both of these images have taken on a new significance. The black velvet seems to be a form of mourning—perhaps for her previous life of possibility, perhaps for the daughter whom, we learn, she lost in childbirth. And her "framing" of this "picture of a gracious lady" by a doorway suggests not only that she is a subject in a portrait but also that she has been imprisoned in a gilded cage. The novel, then, raises questions not only about Isabel's marriage but also about itself. Insofar as the novel claims to be a "portrait of a lady"—a detached, realistic, objective account of Isabel's experience—it aligns itself with possibilities that it criticizes.

In this way James's fiction turns from the realistic register in which it has been written and becomes more self-critical. It does so, paradoxically, by moving simultaneously in two distinctly different representational directions. On the one hand, the novel dives inward and starts to investigate, at great length, the thought processes of its characters. At the same time, it gives us scenes that are hyperbolic, even at times out-and-out melodramatic. James thereby creates the form that Peter Brooks has called "the melodrama of consciousness"—a form that brings to the inner life of the novel's characters the same dramatic force that melodrama lends to those in the theater.

Thus the narrative begins on the inside, showing us Isabel undergoing a long, painfully slow process of introspection in which she struggles to make sense of how she could have entered such an unhappy marriage. James performs the remarkably delicate act of showing us a character not so much thinking as rethinking, puzzling out the choices that led to a disastrous set of consequences. Even as Isabel mulls over her own motives, she faces radically new complications. Many of them center on Pansy. Isabel has come increasingly to favor Ned's suit—largely because his feelings are reciprocated by the girl'—while Osmond, predictably, favors Lord Warburton's, for the meanest of reasons and with the vilest of implications. Osmond believes, correctly, that Warburton still fancies Isabel, and wants Isabel to use her influence with Lord Warburton to encourage his suit for Pansy. Most important, Isabel muses on Madame Merle's relation to her marriage. The novel traces her growing suspicion of her former friend, who goes to great lengths to press Warburton's case while disavowing any connection to Osmond. The latter leads Isabel, moreover, to a new alertness. Returning home one day, she encounters a scene that makes her suspicious: Madame Merle and Osmond together in a position of social intimacy, silently gazing, with his glance dominating her.

Even as Isabel prepares her entrance on the social stage, the novel moves deeper into her consciousness. In its most audacious formal experiment, James gives us a chapter-long account of Isabel's own thoughts as she sits by the fire and muses over her marriage. Through it we finally learn why she has chosen Osmond: as an act of generosity designed to match Mr. Touchett's and a way of dealing with her sense of guilt at having been given her fairy-tale-like gift. But Isabel's language suggests that her motives may not have been quite as pure as she intended: "The finest—in the sense of being the subtlest—manly organism she had ever known had become her property, and the recognition of her having but to put out her hands and take it had been originally a sort of act of devotion" (p. 358). However generous-spirited she might have been, Isabel is starting to reckon with the possibility that her own motives may have been touched by a version of the acquisitiveness she is forced to discover in Gilbert.

In addition to exhibiting this psychological complexity, the chapter demonstrates an artistic one. As Isabel revisits the course of her marriage, trying to figure out how it went so disastrously wrong, she employs some of the image patterns the novel has used to define her, most notably the house imagery: "It was not her fault," Isabel assures herself, "she had taken all the first steps in the purest confidence, and then she had suddenly found the infinite vista of a multiplied life to be a dark, narrow alley with a dead wall at the end" (p. 356). Until now, we may remember, Isabel has been pictured in doorways. But now she images herself in the reverse, a cul-de-sac leading to a blank wall, a windowless prison not unlike the Palazzo Roccanera—literally Blackrock. And, indeed, this palazzo, so much the opposite of the open, airy Gardencourt, comes to serve as Isabel's image for the prison house that is her marriage: If Gardencourt has been established by James as an Edenic spot and Osmond is identified with the tempting serpent ("his egotism lay hidden like a serpent in a bank of flowers," p. 360), Isabel images her new life as a demonic parody of that in the innocent Garden: "Her mind was to be his—attached to his own like a small garden-plot to a deer-park" (p. 362).

Here the novel might best be thought of not as a realistic fiction but rather as self-reflexive and modernist. James's aim in creating this effect, it needs to be stressed, is not to raise questions about representation per se. Rather, it is to advance his account of the relationship between narrative and gender, between the stories a culture tells about women and a woman's desire to tell new stories about herself. But Isabel's task is no longer that of Emersonian self-reliance; instead it is one of refashioning the terms that she has been given. But before Isabel can even get to this point, she must deal with all the people who have attempted to control her: Madame Merle and Osmond, to be sure, but also Lord Warburton, Caspar Goodwood, and Ralph. Most important, she must come to terms with herself—with who she has become and what she is to do with that self-knowledge.

The first negotiations occur with Osmond. Isabel is forbidden by her husband to go to the long-dying Ralph's deathbed, to which she is summoned by Mrs. Touchett. She is thereby forced to choose between her loyalty to her most loyal and loving friend and her commitment to a troubled marriage. The stakes for Isabel—and in the novel—are high, and to raise them even higher James, in the very same chapter, turns the dramatic screw one more notch. Osmond's sister, the Countess Gemini, reveals to Isabel that Pansy is not, as everyone has hitherto believed, the daughter of his dead wife. Rather, Pansy is the product of his affair with Madame Merle, and she and Osmond have been engaged in a complicated deception ever since. Isabel may have imagined Osmond as a kind of a second Satan, but only now does she actually encounter what evil looks like, out and open in the social world.

In order to capture that sense of pure evil, this most supple of novels has increasingly explicit recourse to the mode it has been exploring: to melodrama— that dramatic form in which good and evil come into definitive and ferocious conflict with each other. But James has, as usual, a complex relationship to genre.

While Isabel may respond to Osmond by constructing metaphors that partake of melodrama, her encounters with Madame Merle move explicitly into its terrain. Their first quarrel, over Lord Warburton's suit, ends as follows: "'What have you to do with me?' Isabel went on. Madame Merle slowly got up, stroking her muff, but not removing her eyes from Isabel's face. 'Everything!' she answered." (p. 430).

We have come a long way indeed from the realistic register and genteel authorial commentary that marked the opening chapters of the book. Here gestures are dramatic to the point of unnatural intensity, the language heightened to the point of hyperbole. Melodramatic as it seems, however, this encounter between two women complicates the gender dynamics of melodrama. For the scene reproduces the power play we have seen in the equally dramatic scene between Osmond and Madame Merle—the one Isabel comes in at the end of—in which his "evil eye" seems to possess the power to transfix her, except that in this scene, it is a woman who uses this power to dominate another woman. James later asks us to keep this reversal in mind in the next confrontation between the two, one fraught with even greater intensity, when Isabel meets Madame Merle, whom she now knows to be Pansy's mother, in the convent school in which the girl is more or less incarcerated. Even though Isabel's first response on learning of her relationship to Pansy was to sympathize, in this confrontation scene she remains "silent still," denying Madame Merle not only sympathy but identity itself. Isabel's silence is tantamount to negating Madame Merle's motives, her very subjectivity—the same move that Osmond has made in her marriage. And, like Osmond, Isabel signifies her own triumph by silently staring—signifying both her own superior knowledge and the superiority of her refusal to use it. Isabel and Osmond may be on the verge of severing their marriage bond, but ironically they are at one in their common rejection of the woman who links them.

The novel's invocation of melodrama, then, suggests that Isabel has learned her lesson well: in a world of dramatic performances where sincerity is suspect and naïveté a species of victimization, she must act a part whether she likes it or not. But she must learn to act in another sense as well: perform in such a way as to affirm her own values. She already has made the first fateful decision—to defy Osmond and visit Ralph at his deathbed. Once she is there, the novel gives another great dramatic scene. When Isabel tells Ralph of the abomination that her marriage has become he responds with a characteristic warmth purged of any irony or reserve. "Remember this," Ralph tells her, "that if you've been hated you've also been loved. Ah but,

Isabel—*adored?* "Oh, my brother," Isabel cries, "with a movement of still deeper prostration" (p. 479).

If the scenes between Madame Merle, Osmond, and Isabel have been shaped by the conventions of melodrama, this one resembles a different, if linked genre: that of the sentimental novel, in which deathbed scenes, complete with tears, gestures of emotional prostration, and emotion-laden final words are a staple. Then, after Ralph dies, the novel takes another step beyond realism and turns into something of a ghost story. Awakening from sleep as Ralph passes away, Isabel is led to his bedside by the spectral image of Ralph himself: "a vague, hovering figure in the vagueness of the room" (p. 479). In both these scenes, James finds one more use for generic experimentation: he shifts into the representational registers of sentimental fiction and ghost story in order to reproduce human emotions at their highest pitch of intensity.

NARRATIVE CLOSURE AND THE THEME OF CHOICE

The novel has one more formal trick up its sleeve, one that enacts the theme of choice. Soon after Ralph's burial, she encounters the indefatigable Caspar Goodwood, who has heard from Henrietta of Isabel's breach with Osmond. Although she has not yet decided to divorce, he proposes again. All the cues in the text direct us to believe that she will fall—as a romantic heroine should—into Caspar's strong arms. His arguments are persuasive indeed, and the text's language as he embraces her—an embrace compared, among other things, to a lightning bolt—reminds us that she is sexually attracted to him as she has not been to any of the other men who engage her. But this is precisely what does *not* happen. Rather than launch herself into a life with Caspar, Isabel flees his presence and, we learn, decisively returns to Rome. Poor Caspar is bereft but encouraged by Henrietta Stackpole to follow Isabel as the novel closes.

In so doing, James creates one of the most famous cruxes in American literature. Is Isabel's precipitous retreat from Caspar, as many readers have thought, a retreat as well from her own passions? Does Caspar offer her, as he claims, a form of freedom? Or, as other readers have argued, is his offer just another mode of enthrallment? For these latter readers, her decision to renounce Goodwood and return to Italy is not to be read as an exercise in masochism but rather as a fulfillment of her promise to Pansy—and a sign that Isabel has fully accepted the price of her own freedom.

But, still other readers wonder, how long will she stay married to Osmond and on what terms? Here too possibilities proliferate. In its 1881 version the novel ends with Henrietta's encouraging words to Caspar, adding simply: "On which he looked up at her" (*Novels*, p. 800). In the later New York edition, James adds a paragraph that makes the quest seem futile:

On which he looked up at her—but only to guess, from her face, with a revulsion, that she simply meant he was young. She stood shining at him with that cheap comfort, and it added, on the spot, thirty years to his life. She walked him away with her, however, as if she had given him now the key to patience. (P. 490)

As downbeat as this ending may be, the inveterate optimist might remember the door imagery with which Isabel's career in the novel begins and ends. The words with which James chooses to close, "the key to patience," might suggest to such a reader that Caspar may yet unlock the door behind which Isabel has immured herself. Or "it may be," as F. O. Matthiessen suggests and as Isabel herself conjectures, Osmond may finally "'take her money and let her go.' [Or] it may be that once she has found a husband for Pansy, she will feel that she no longer has to remain in Rome" (pp. 185–186). The best we can conclude is that by ending Caspar learning of Isabel's fate rather than with an account of that fate itself, James leaves these matters thoroughly up to our imaginations.

In so doing, he suggests one possible solution to the representational problems that the novel has posed. If reading Isabel in such a way as to fix her identity and fate one way or another puts the reader in the same difficult position as virtually all the characters of the novel, then the ambiguity of its end frees us from interpretive error. More important, especially in terms of James's concern with gender and representation, this open conclusion suggests the difficulty of the choices available to Isabel. It reminds us that all of the available models of closure offered by the representational forms of the nineteenth century—the realistic novel, which usually ends, however unrealistically, in marriage; the sentimental melodrama, which usually ends in death; or the social problem novel, which usually ends in social degradation—lock women into an all-too-familiar set of no-win positions. By leaving his own ending open, James asks us to question all of these socially powerful forms of narrative closure, even while, with the utmost of authorial generosity, granting Isabel her fondest wish: to choose—and to go on choosing, in the reader's imagination, even after the novel is over.

See also The Ambassadors; Americans Abroad; Daisy Miller; Realism

BIBLIOGRAPHY

Primary Works

James, Henry. *The Golden Bowl.* 1905. Vols. 23 and 24 of *The Novels and Tales of Henry James.* New York: Scribners, 1907–1917.

James, Henry. *Novels, 1881–1886.* New York: Library of America, 1985. Includes *Washington Square, The Portrait of a Lady,* and *The Bostonians.*

James, Henry. *The Portrait of a Lady.* 1881. Vols. 3 and 4 of *The Novels and Tales of Henry James.* New York: Scribners, 1907–1917. Quotations in the essay are to this edition.

James, Henry. *The Novels and Tales of Henry James.* New York: Scribners, 1907-1917.

Secondary Works

Agnew, Jean-Christophe. "The Consuming Vision of Henry James." In *The Culture of Consumption: Critical Essays in American History 1880–1980,* edited by Richard Wightman Fox and T. J. Jackson Lears. New York: Pantheon, 1983.

Anderson, Charles Roberts. *Person, Place, and Thing in Henry James's Novels.* Durham, N.C.: Duke University Press, 1977.

Brodhead, Richard H. *The School of Hawthorne.* New York: Oxford University Press, 1986.

Brooks, Peter. *The Melodramatic Imagination: Balzac, Henry James, Melodrama, and the Mode of Excess.* New Haven, Conn.: Yale University Press, 1995.

Buitenhuis, Peter, ed. *Twentieth-Century Interpretations of The Portrait of a Lady: A Collection of Critical Essays.* Englewood Cliffs, N.J.: Prentice-Hall, 1968.

Feidelson, Charles. "The Moment of The Portrait of a Lady." In *"The Portrait of a Lady": An Authoritative Text, Henry James and the Novel, Reviews and Criticism,* 2nd ed., edited by Robert Bamberg. New York: Norton, 1995.

Freedman, Jonathan. *The Cambridge Companion to Henry James.* New York: Cambridge University Press, 1998.

Freedman, Jonathan. *Professions of Taste: Henry James, British Aestheticism and Commodity Culture.* Stanford, Calif.: Stanford University Press, 1990.

Holland, Laurence Bedwell. *The Expense of Vision: Essays on the Craft of Henry James.* Baltimore: Johns Hopkins University Press, 1982.

Matthiessen, F. O. *Henry James: The Major Phase.* New York: Oxford University Press, 1944.

Pippin, Robert B. *Henry James and Modern Moral Life.* Cambridge, U.K.: Cambridge University Press, 2000.

Porte, Joel, ed. *New Essays on "The Portrait of a Lady."* Cambridge, U.K.: Cambridge University Press, 1990.

Porter, Carolyn. *Seeing and Being: The Plight of the Participant-Observer in Emerson, James, Adams, and Faulkner.* Middletown, Conn.: Wesleyan University Press, 1981.

Stafford, William T., ed. *Perspectives on James's "The Portrait of a Lady": A Collection of Critical Essays.* New York: New York University Press, 1967.

Van Ghent, Dorothy Bendon. "On *The Portrait of a Lady.*" In her *The English Novel: Form and Function,* pp. 221-228. New York: Holt, Rinehart and Winston, 1953.

Jonathan Freedman

POVERTY

For nearly two centuries Americans have struggled to understand and assist the poor. Unfortunately, the ongoing discussion of poverty has done relatively little to solve the problem. In the nineteenth century one did not have to look far into America's major cities to see evidence of rampant poverty and its negative effects. Both in the public square and in varied publications, questions were posed and debated: Were the poor a degenerate breed beyond help? Was poverty a moral or social crisis? Should the poor be helped or taught to help themselves? Who was to blame for the poor? What types of aid and poverty reform should be instituted? Could poverty be reduced or eliminated? Competing attitudes about the fate of America's poor both contributed to and complicated reform efforts of the time. While many agreed that aid and reform were needed, there was less agreement about what those aid and reform measures should be.

ENDURING QUESTIONS

The nineteenth century debate over the poor was generally divided into two main camps: those who perceived the poor as lazy, feckless, genetically inferior impediments to social progress and those who perceived the poor as materially disadvantaged victims. Members of the former group included Social Darwinists, immigrant restrictionists and exclusionists, natives, and others, including many apathetic members of the upper class who believed that social reform and assimilation of the lower classes were not only dangerous endeavors but also futile. Of those who noticed the poor at all, some found it easier to dehumanize, objectify, and demean them with various epithets: "Brutes," "Savages," "the Underclass," "the Lower Orders," "Wretches," "Waifs," "the Lumpen Proletariat," and "the Dangerous Classes." Others more benevolent toward the poor believed what history would show— that the poor were particularly subject to and victimized by their environment, hard luck, discrimination, and systematic economic hardships, evidenced most dramatically by a series of depressions experienced in

America in the latter parts of the nineteenth century. Those seeking help for America's poor included members of various reform groups, including settlement and Christian charity organizations, that believed reform and social assimilation were possible and crucial if America's poor were to survive.

Unfortunately, American reform efforts in the nineteenth century were hindered by divisiveness, a lack of resources, apathy, and a lack of imagination. For many, poverty and welfare were perceived as moral problems for which the cures were the mission or the asylum, particularly if the sufferers were male. From 1810 to 1850, America saw its public aid for the poor reduced and hostility toward them increased. By the middle of the century many were leery of assisting the poor at all. Taking a cue from the English political economist Thomas Malthus and his *Essay on Population* (1798), some Americans advocated abstinence and welfare reduction for the poor, believing that welfare equaled dependence. In Philadelphia the Union Benevolent Association (UBA) was formed, and necessities such as food and fuel were given to the poor in the place of monetary assistance. By mid-century charity aid was expanded, and Protestant and Catholic charity organizations vigorously competed for the poor in order to evangelize them. Bible societies, tract societies, moral-control societies (such as those supported by the temperance preacher Lyman Beecher), and single-issue crusades (such as prostitution reform) proliferated, as did Sunday schools and paternalistic societies (such as the new industrial city of Lowell, Massachusetts, conceived as a controlled Utopia for workers). New reform organizations appeared: the Association for Improving the Condition of the Poor, the Children's Aid Society of New York (founded and supported by Charles Loring Brace), and the Young Men's Christian Association (YMCA). Harriet Beecher Stowe published *We and Our Neighbors* in 1873 to show how the church could positively influence behavior and help regulate American society and its moral awareness. But in the

wake of the Civil War, Social Darwinist theories flourished, placing the blame on the poor themselves and furthering the idea that welfare only hindered the process of natural selection. Among those reluctant to help the mostly immigrant poor were people like Josiah Strong (1847–1916), author of the 1885 best-seller *Our Country* and a leading figure in the Evangelical Alliance of Protestant Ministers. Strong adamantly believed that immigration caused criminality and pauperism and that the mixing of cultures via assimilation would debase the culture and the bloodlines of all true "Americans." Speaking in an 1883 Senate hearing, the iron foundry proprietor and wealthy capitalist John Roach (1813–1887) argued that the poor were responsible for their own poverty.

Toward the end of the century, society's understanding of the poor began to change, and for the first time in America, poverty was perceived as complex, systematic, and profoundly economic. In Chicago in 1889 Jane Addams opened Hull-House, which quickly became one of America's most prominent and effective settlement houses. In her *Twenty Years at Hull-House* (1910), Addams would directly challenge Strong and Roach, as well as the most-fit philosophy of other America's capitalists like Andrew Carnegie (1835–1919), author of *The Gospel of Wealth* (1900). Addams's response to Strong, Carnegie, and others was that environment, not heredity, was the leading cause of social problems; that the classes were dependent on each other; that open dialogue among all citizens was necessary; and that every citizen had the right and the capacity to join in this dialogue. In chapter 6 of *Hull-House*, in which she discusses a speech she delivered in 1892 at the School of Applied Ethics Conference, "The Subjective Necessity for Social Settlements," Addams writes: "The Settlement, then, is an experimental effort to aid in the solution of the social and industrial problems which are engendered by modern conditions of life in a great city . . . . It must be grounded in a philosophy whose foundation is on

Deaths and death rates in 1888 in Baxter and Mulberry Streets, between Park and Bayard Streets

	Population			Deaths			Death rate		
	Under 5 years	5 years old and over	Total	Under 5 years	5 years old and over	Total	Under 5 years old	5 years old and over	General
Baxter Street	1,198	315	2,233	26	46	72	13.56	146.03	32.24
Mulberry Street	2,788	629	3,417	44	86	130	15.78	136.72	38.05
Total	4,706	944	5,650	70	132	202	14.87	139.83	37.75

Note: Death rates are expressed as deaths per thousand live persons.

SOURCE: Riis, *How the Other Half Lives*, pp. 100–101.

could and must be managed and that America's poor, those he came to call "the other half" in his most famous work, *How the Other Half Lives* (1890), needed to be seen and heard. An immigrant who arrived in America from Denmark in 1870, Riis embodied the American success story. His Horatio Alger–like rise from immigrant carpenter, to middle-class reporter, to author of note was remarkable yet not unique. Moreover, Riis arrived in New York at a time of great growth and opportunity. Within a decade of his arrival, Americans would see remarkable advances during its so-called Gilded Age, including the completion of the Brooklyn Bridge (1883) and the Statue of Liberty (1886) and the founding of the American Federation of Labor (1886).

By the end of the nineteenth century, America would also experience growing pains and face sobering realities: the Chinese Exclusion Act (1882) and the hanging of the Chicago Haymarket anarchists (1886) coincided with the perfection of the machine gun and the first use of the electric chair (1890). Immigration trends were shifting, as a largely Protestant influx from northwestern Europe was replaced by a dominantly Catholic and Jewish presence originating from southeastern Europe. On the West Coast the Chinese American population was growing yet still feeling the dehumanizing effects of the Chinese Exclusion Act—reverberations that would last well into the twentieth century. Edith Maud Eaton (pen name Sui Sin Far, 1865–1914), was among the first to write in defense of Chinese immigrants victimized in a so-called land of opportunity. In "The Land of the Free," for example, a story from her 1912 collection, *Mrs. Spring Fragrance,* customs agents take Lae Choo's son away for lack of proper paperwork. Eaton writes, "Thus was the law of the land complied with" (p. 1673). This tremendous growth resulting from immigration would not be stemmed until the 1924 War and Immigration Act.

During this dramatic growth of the urban poor and on the heels of ineffective tenement laws (initiated in 1867, revised in 1879 and 1887), Riis, who was influenced by the builder and reformer Alfred T. White, began to investigate the connections between urban poverty in New York City and its tenement housing. Innovatively using the latest technology, flash photography and the stereopticon or "magic lantern," Riis would radically alter the way Americans viewed the poor. In his 25 January 1888 lecture, titled "The Other Half: How It Lives and Dies in New York," Riis graphically (and, some critics argue, sensationally) showed Americans the squalor and sordidness of the urban tenement. Riis believed that in the tenement houses "all the influences

THE OTHER HALF

For many during the latter half of the nineteenth century the question was: Could America's major cities handle unprecedented growth and still meet the needs of all its citizens, regardless of economic status or skin color? If America was going to meet the needs of its citizens, it had to recognize them first, for better or worse. Jacob Riis (1849–1914), journalist, writer, and social reformer, believed that poverty

Rich and Poor. Illustration from *Harper's Weekly,* 11 January 1873, by Sol Eytinge. America's rapid growth in the latter half of the nineteenth century provided great opportunity and wealth for some but meant extreme hardship for many. THE LIBRARY OF CONGRESS

the solidarity of the human race" (p. 95). The efforts of Addams and other reformers in the late nineteenth and early twentieth centuries would help usher in the Progressive Era.

make for evil" (*How the Other Half Lives*, p. 60). With the publication of *How the Other Half Lives* (which went through eleven editions in five years) and *The Battle with the Slum* (1902), Riis not only solidified his reputation as social reformer and significant nineteenth-century author, but he also revealed to Americans a new frontier, the urban slum. Fifty years earlier, E. Z. C. Judson's (Ned Buntline) dime novel *The Mysteries and Miseries of New York* (1848) had sensationally shown America's inner-city squalor in notoriously poor places like New York's Five Points district and the Bend, described by Riis as "the home of the tramp as well as the rag-picker" (*How the Other Half Lives*, p. 96). Other writers in the late nineteenth century, such as Helen Campbell, author of *Darkness and Daylight; or, Lights and Shadows of New York Life* (1892), would continue to creatively and graphically depict what Riis's photographs showed. Riis's point in *How the Other Half Lives* is simple and direct: "What are you going to do about it? is the question of to-day" (*How the Other Half Lives*, p. 61).

Stephen Crane (1871–1900), in his short story "Experiment in Misery" (1894), follows Riis's suggestion about tenements: "Suppose we look into one" (*How the Other Half Lives*, p. 88). In this journalistic piece turned short story, Crane follows a youth who finds his way by bad luck and fate into New York's Bowery. "Experiment" begins with Crane's description of the youth wandering alone at night, "clothed in an aged and tattered suit . . . going forth to eat as a wanderer may eat, and sleep as the homeless sleep" (p. 83). Soon, the youth finds his place in Chatham Square among the other bums and hobos; he is among "aimless men strewn in front of saloons and lodging houses, standing sadly, patiently, reminding one vaguely of the attitudes of chickens in a storm" (p. 84). Along with these miserable sights, Crane provides the horrid smells. The youth is led into a dark tenement and is overtaken by "strange and unspeakable odors that assailed him like malignant diseases with wings" (p. 88). He sees for himself the building's innards, human contents depicted in the waning evening light as a graveyard of the living, "statuesque, carven, dead" (p. 89). Crane's point in "Experiment" is profound: to contrast the poor (men, in this case) as they are perceived—full of "bumps and deficiencies of all kinds" (p. 91)—with the poor as they are, human beings, "standing massively like chiefs" (p. 91) in the morning light. Crane's "Experiment" demonstrates how little society knows of the poor. "It did not know because it did not care" (Riis, *How the Other Half Lives*, p. 59).

THE AMERICAN DREAM AND ITS REALITY

As Riis, Campbell, Crane, and others showed America its darker underside, its unseen other half, more Americans were beginning slowly to understand themselves in relation to the poor. Specifically, by the turn of the century, Americans could see that widespread poverty, with its urban slums, and later urban ghettos, was the tangible result not only of apathy, ignorance, and misperception but also of more readily visible economic and social factors as well, such as widespread industrialization, rampant capitalism, technological advances, and destructive social attitudes that were leading to blatant discrimination and systematic segregation of the lower classes. Americans had already had an opportunity to see the truth of the country's unequal conditions in the work of a French-born visitor, Alexis de Tocqueville, who came to America in the 1830s to study its prison system. Tocqueville's *Democracy in America* (1835) remains a profound and penetrating critique of American democracy and American society in general. In his chapter titled "Equality Suggests to the American the Idea of Indefinite Perfectibility in Man," Tocqueville challenges the idea of equality in America, warning that it, like perfectibility, is a falsehood, an "always fugitive perception that presents itself to the human mind" (p. 157), yet is never fully realized. Near the end of the century, following the failed Reconstruction and failed promises for equality and opportunity, many of America's disenfranchised classes were all too willing to concede Tocqueville's point. Despite Americans' idealistic belief in democracy, equality, and the American Dream, Riis and others had a less-optimistic story to tell.

America's rapid growth in the latter half of the nineteenth century came with a heavy price, as many Americans found themselves lost in a society that provided great opportunity and wealth for some and extreme hardship for many. In his short story "A Deal in Wheat" (1902), Frank Norris shows through his central character, the Kansas farmer Sam Lewiston, the unfortunate fate of many who left farming for the cities as a result of necessity, only to find few prospects awaiting them. Norris's story is an overwhelmingly pessimistic tale in which Lewiston's situation is portrayed as particularly sinister because he fails to realize that his fate is in the hands of two corrupt Chicago capitalists, indifferent and powerful financiers—Truslow, the commodities bear, and Hornung, the bull—who control the price of grain going in and out of Chicago and thereby control Sam. "It's the Chicago price that does it, Lewiston. Truslow is bearing the stuff for all he's worth. It's Truslow and the bear clique that stick the knife to us" (p. 875), states the apologetic Kansas grain buyer, Bridges, to the flabbergasted Sam, who finds that his wheat is worth only sixty-two cents a bushel.

Dismayed and without prospects, Sam moves to the city, where his downward movement is vividly described by Norris: "Thrown out of work, Lewiston drifted aimlessly . . . till at last the ooze of the lowest bottom dragged at his feet and the rush of the great ebb went over him and engulfed him and shut him out from the light, and the park bench became his home and the 'bread line' his chief makeshift of existence" (pp. 880–881). The final cruel irony for Sam is that his spiral into poverty leads him to a breadline that can no longer afford to give out its day-old remains because the price of wheat (now selling for an unheard-of two dollars a bushel) is too high. Sam survives, remarkably, but Norris makes it clear that among the poor and des-titute in the latter half of the nineteenth century, mere cogs in a society that neither knows nor cares about them, Sam is one of the lucky few.

ENVIRONMENT AND THE POOR: PARADOX AND PROSPECTUS

For some, the correlation between environment and social condition was key in determining why the poor were poor: Did a deficient environment lead to degra-dation and potentially destructive behavior? Did inde-cent homes produce indecent lives? Did the poor create their environment, or did their environment create the poor? For many, the situation of the poor presented a paradox, and the best way to help them was anything but clear. As the critic David Ward adeptly puts it, "On the one hand, the limitations of the slums obstructed the self-improvement of their residents, but on the other hand, the hereditarian and cultural disabilities of residents inhibited their capacity for self-improve-ment" (p. 146). In Maggie, A Girl of the Streets (1893), Crane explores the underworld of the Bowery, exam-ines questions of cause and effect, and undermines the belief that the poor can improve themselves. Maggie's world of the Bowery is cruel and indifferent, a world in which death and life are parceled out in matter-of-fact sentences: "The babe, Tommie, died. He went away in an insignificant coffin, his small waxen hand clutching a flower that the girl, Maggie, had stolen from an Italian. She and Jimmie lived" (p. 15). Although one is later told that "The girl, Maggie, blossomed in a mud puddle. She grew to be the most rare and wonderful production of a tenement district, a pretty girl" (p. 20), Crane's praise is cynical and ironic. There is little to believe in regarding Maggie's prospects as one of America's many poor and disen-franchised souls. Maggie is shown to be a product of her environment, but by the end of the nineteenth century, it was generally agreed upon that America's slums and their inhabitants were a consequence rather than a cause of poverty.

For others, the poor were simply not human and therefore not worthy of consideration, time, or money; they were simply brutes, incapable of reform despite a democratic America inclined toward a belief in human and societal perfectibility. In his Vandover and the Brute (an experimental novel, writ-ten early in his career but published posthumously, in 1914), Norris shows mankind as a complex animal, often controlled by its baser nature. Vandover, son of a wealthy owner of slum proper-ties, is portrayed as all too vulnerable to his own desires and to all the negative influences of San Francisco in the 1890s. As a result, he regresses, actually moving backward on the evolutionary scale. Moreover, Norris seems directly to challenge Tocqueville, who writes in Democracy in America, "Although man has many points of resemblance with the brutes, one trait is peculiar to himself—he improves: they are incapable of improvement" (p. 156). Vandover tells a different story, one in which his transformation works in reverse; his "improvement" results in his utter decline, and his degeneration is a strong corrective to the American ideal of self-improvement and moral and social progress.

Paul Laurence Dunbar (1872–1906) would also use literature to investigate the effects of society on mankind, particularly on people of color, those labeled the lowly. In his novel The Sport of the Gods (1902), Dunbar introduces us to the Hamiltons, a black family caught in the middle between black and white society, the North and the South, social and racial discrimina-tion. In chapter 14, "Frankenstein," Joe Hamilton succumbs to the pressures of his situation, his cruel fate, and the decadence of New York City, where the Hamiltons have relocated after the head of the family, Berry, has been imprisoned for allegedly stealing from his former employer in the South. A victim of social, racial, and economic circumstances, Joe degenerates into something less than human. Dunbar writes: "Five years is but a short time in the life of a man, and yet many things may happen therein. For instance, the whole way of a family's life may be changed. Good natures may be made into bad ones and out of a soul of faith grow a spirit of unbelief" (p. 113). Later in chapter 14 the incredulous and powerless Joe searches for answers, and he seeks to lay blame for his decline, desperately telling Hattie Sterling that he has been victimized: "'You put me out—you—you, and made me what I am.' The realisation of what he was, of his foulness and degradation, seemed just to have come to him fully. 'You made me what I am, and you sent me away'" (p. 119). Dunbar's work anticipates what modern critics more fully understand, that "poverty abides no line drawn by color or culture" (Jones, p. 1).

Historically unrecognized, the plight of America's poor was given visibility in the literature of the nineteenth and early twentieth centuries. The questions posed then are enduring, as they speak to modern society's need to pay attention to the poor lest it drown in their misery. As America continues to seek ways to meet the needs of its poor and disenfranchised citizens, poverty remains an issue full of questions and controversies—and divergent perspectives, attitudes, and responses.

See also City Dwellers; Health and Medicine; Reform; Socialism; Tramps and Hobos; Wealth

BIBLIOGRAPHY

Primary Works

Addams, Jane. *Twenty Years at Hull-House.* 1910. Edited by Victoria Bissell Brown. Boston: Bedford/St. Martin's, 1999.

Crane, Stephen. *Maggie, A Girl of the Streets and Other Stories.* 1893. Edited by Alfred Kazin. New York: Signet, 1991. Includes "Experiment."

Dunbar, Paul Laurence. *The Sport of the Gods.* 1902. New York: Signet, 1999.

Eaton, Edith Maud. "In the Land of the Free." 1912. In *The Heath Anthology of American Literature,* concise ed., edited by Paul Lauter. New York: Houghton Mifflin, 2004.

Norris, Frank. "A Deal in Wheat." 1902. In *Anthology of American Literature,* vol. 2, *Realism to the Present,* 4th ed., edited by George McMichael. New York: Macmillan, 1989.

Riis, Jacob A. *The Battle with the Slum.* New York: Macmillan, 1902.

Riis, Jacob A. *How the Other Half Lives.* 1890. Edited by David Leviatin. New York: Bedford/St. Martin's, 1996.

Tocqueville, Alexis de. *Democracy in America.* 1835. Edited by Richard D. Heffner. New York: Mentor/Penguin, 1956, 1984.

Secondary Works

Boyer, Paul. *Urban Masses and Moral Order in America, 1820–1920.* Cambridge, Mass.: Harvard University Press, 1978.

Jones, Jacqueline. *The Dispossessed: America's Underclass from the Civil War to the Present.* New York: Basic, 1992.

Ward, David. *Poverty, Ethnicity, and the American City, 1840–1925: Changing Conceptions of the Slum and the Ghetto.* New York: Cambridge University Press, 1989.

Chad Rohman